Practical Insights for Financial Managers

Practical Insights is a unique feature of this text (found at the end of each part) that contains guidelines to help you identify the important issues faced by financial managers. The following table shows the tasks of financial managers (e.g., Allocating Capital for Real Investment, Financing the Firm, Knowing Whether and How to Hedge Risk, and Allocating Funds for Financial Investments) and the key Practical Insights relevant to each of these tasks. For example, to locate Practical Insights on Allocating Capital for Real Investments, you would look under that task, determine which Practical Insight applies to the issue you wish to know more about, and then reference the far left-hand column to determine which Part it is located under. The Practical Insights feature enables the book to serve as a reference as well as a primer on finance. We hope you find it useful.

	Allocating Capital for Real Investment	Financing the Firm	Knowing Whether and How to Hedge Risk	Allocating Funds for Financial Investments
Part I Financial Markets and Financial Instruments		Be familiar with the various sources of financing Understand the legal and institutional environment for financing	Understand the financial instruments available for hedging Be familiar with the market environment in which hedging takes place	Understand the financial instruments available for investment and the markets they trade in
Part II Valuing Financial Assets	Know how projects affect the risk of the firm: • Individual projects • Acquisitions Compute discount rate or risk associated with portfolio of financial assets that tracks the real asset cash flows	Know how to value the financial instruments considered for financing	Know how to value a hedging instrument	Determine the proper mix of asset classes Derive a proper mix of individual assets Determine whether investments are fairly valued Understand risk and return of financial investments and mixtures of various financial investments
Part III Valuing Real Assets	Know what forecasts of cash flows should do: • Estimate mean • Sometimes adjust for risk Estimate a portfolio of financial assets that track real asset cash flows Understand pitfalls in various methods of obtaining present value Analyze how financing and taxes affect valuation Identify where value in projects comes from: • Estimated cash flows • Growth opportunities	Understand how taxes affect the costs of various financial instruments (see also Part IV)		
Part IV Capital Structure	Analyze how financing and taxes affect capital allocation decisions	Determine an optimal debt/equity ratio Know how financing affects real investment decisions Know how financing affects operating decisions		
Part V Incentives, Information and Corporate Control	Consider effects of delegated decisions: • Incentives • Asymmetric information	Understand the relation between financing and managerial incentives Understand the information communicated by financing decisions		
Part VI Risk Management	Determine whether to focus capital on a few projects or diversify		Understand how value is created by hedging Design and implement a hedging strategy	

Excellence makes its mark...

"Integrating capital structure and corporate financial decisions with corporate strategy has been a central area of research in finance and economics for more than a decade and it has clearly changed the way we think about these matters. What is remarkable about this book is that it can take this relatively new material and so comfortably and seamlessly knit it together with more traditional approaches to give the reader such a clear understanding of corporate finance. Anyone who wants to probe more deeply into financial decision making and understand its relation to corporate strategy should read this text. Nor is this a book that will gather dust when the course is over; it will become part of every reader's tool kit and they will turn back to it often. I know that I will."

Stephen A. Ross, *Yale University*

"I have always welcomed the arrival of a new book or treatise on finance if it is conceptually sound and has intellectual integrity. The Grinblatt & Titman text is outstanding by all criteria. It is a fresh, innovative approach rooted in the modern theory of finance, providing a bridge to effective applications. This book will be among the leaders for decades to come and will be widely imitated—a clear demonstration of its value. Grinblatt & Titman have arrived and the finance field has been enriched thereby."

J. Fred Weston, *UCLA*

"Other texts have lagged behind current financial techniques and practices. This book [by Grinblatt & Titman] provides a modern, cutting-edge treatment of all topics. This text has set an impressive new standard by thoroughly examining important topics such as the role of financial decisions on corporate strategy."

Jeffrey Pontiff, *University of Washington*

"The content of this book [Grinblatt & Titman] brings to the classroom current research issues that academics have been interested in for the past decade and more. As such, it is a welcome addition and is needed by the field. I have been waiting for such a book to appear."

Gordon Phillips, *University of Maryland*

"[Grinblatt & Titman's] most important asset is its ability to synthesize the various strands of financial theory and simultaneously allow the reader to see the forest through the trees."

Ivan Brick, *Rutgers University*

Financial Markets and Corporate Strategy

THE IRWIN/MCGRAW-HILL SERIES IN FINANCE, INSURANCE AND REAL ESTATE

Stephen A. Ross
Sterling Professor of Economics and Finance
Yale University
Consulting Editor

FINANCIAL MANAGEMENT

Benninga and Sarig
Corporate Finance: A Valuation Approach

Block and Hirt
Foundations of Financial Management
Eighth Edition

Brealey and Myers
Principles of Corporate Finance
Fifth Edition

Brealey, Myers and Marcus
Fundamentals of Corporate Finance

Brooks
PC FinGame: The Financial Management Decision Game
Version 2.0—DOS and Windows

Bruner
Case Studies in Finance: Managing for Corporate Value Creation
Second Edition

Chew
The New Corporate Finance: Where Theory Meets Practice

Grinblatt and Titman
Financial Markets and Corporate Strategy

Helfert
Techniques of Financial Analysis: A Modern Approach
Ninth Edition

Higgins
Analysis for Financial Management
Fifth Edition

Hite
A Programmed Learning Guide to Finance

Kester, Fruhan, Piper and Ruback
Case Problems in Finance
Eleventh Edition

Nunnally and Plath
Cases in Finance
Second Edition

Parker and Beaver
Risk Management: Challenges and Solutions

Ross, Westerfield and Jaffe
Corporate Finance
Fourth Edition

Ross, Westerfield and Jordan
Essentials of Corporate Finance

Ross, Westerfield and Jordan
Fundamentals of Corporate Finance
Fourth Edition

Schall and Haley
Introduction to Financial Management
Sixth Edition

Smith
The Modern Theory of Corporate Finance
Second Edition

White
Financial Analysis with an Electronic Calculator
Third Edition

INVESTMENTS

Ball and Kothari
Financial Statement Analysis

Bodie, Kane and Marcus
Essentials of Investments
Third Edition

Bodie, Kane and Marcus
Investments
Third Edition

Cohen, Zinbarg and Zeikel
Investment Analysis and Portfolio Management
Fifth Edition

Farrell
Portfolio Management: Theory and Applications
Second Edition

Gibson
Option Valuation

Hirt and Block
Fundamentals of Investment Management
Fifth Edition

Jarrow
Modelling Fixed Income Securities and Interest Rate Options

Lorie, Dodd and Kimpton
The Stock Market: Theories and Evidence
Second Edition

Morningstar, Inc. and Remaley
U.S. Equities OnFloppy Educational Version
Annual Edition

Shimko
The Innovative Investor
Version 2.0—Lotus and Excel

FINANCIAL INSTITUTIONS AND MARKETS

Flannery and Flood
Flannery and Flood's ProBanker: A Financial Services Simulation

James and Smith
Studies in Financial Institutions: Non-Bank Intermediaries

Johnson
Financial Institutions and Markets: A Global Perspective

Kohn
Financial Institutions and Markets

Rose
Commercial Bank Management: Producing and Selling Financial Services
Third Edition

Rose
Money and Capital Markets: Financial Institutions and Instruments in a Global Marketplace
Sixth Edition

Rose and Kolari
Financial Institutions: Understanding and Managing Financial Services
Fifth Edition

Santomero and Babbel
Financial Markets, Instruments, and Institutions

Saunders
Financial Institutions Management: A Modern Perspective
Second Edition

INTERNATIONAL FINANCE

Eun and Resnick
International Financial Management

Kester and Luehrman
Case Problems in International Finance

Levi
International Finance
Third Edition

Levich
International Financial Markets

Stonehill and Eiteman
Finance: An International Perspective

REAL ESTATE

Berston
California Real Estate Principles
Seventh Edition

Berston
California Real Estate Practice
Sixth Edition

Brueggeman and Fisher
Real Estate Finance and Investments
Tenth Edition

Corgel, Smith and Ling
Real Estate Perspectives: An Introduction to Real Estate
Third Edition

Lusht
Real Estate Valuation: Principles and Applications

McLoughlin
Principles of Real Estate Law

Sirmans
Real Estate Finance
Second Edition

FINANCIAL PLANNING AND INSURANCE

Allen, Melone, Rosenbloom and VanDerhei
Pension Planning: Pension, Profit-Sharing, and Other Deferred Compensation Plans
Eighth Edition

Crawford
Life and Health Insurance Law
Eighth Edition (LOMA)

Hirsch
Casualty Claim Practice
Sixth Edition

Kapoor, Dlabay and Hughes
Personal Finance
Fourth Edition

Kellison
Theory of Interest
Second Edition

Lang
Strategy for Personal Finance
Fifth Edition

Skipper
International Risk and Insurance

Williams, Smith and Young
Risk Management and Insurance
Eighth Edition

Financial Markets and Corporate Strategy

Mark Grinblatt
University of California at Los Angeles

Sheridan Titman
University of Texas—Austin

Irwin/McGraw-Hill

Boston, Massachusetts • Burr Ridge, Illinois • Dubuque, Iowa
Madison, Wisconsin • New York, New York • San Francisco, California
St. Louis, Missouri

To my dear brother Arnie, for his courage, perseverence, and inspiration.
M.G.

To my family, for their enduring love and support.
S.T.

Irwin/McGraw-Hill

*A Division of The **McGraw-Hill** Companies*

FINANCIAL MARKETS AND CORPORATE STRATEGY
International Editions 1998

Exclusive rights by McGraw-Hill Book Co – Singapore, for manufacture and export. This book cannot be re-exported from the country to which it is consigned by McGraw-Hill.

3 4 5 6 7 8 9 0 KKP PMP 20 9

Library of Congress Cataloging-in-Publication Data

Grinblatt, Mark.
   Financial markets and corporate strategy / Mark Grinblatt,
Sheridan Titman.
      p.   cm. – (The Irwin/McGraw-Hill series in finance, insurance,
and real estate)
   Includes index.
   ISBN 0-256-09939-1
   1. Financial institutions–United States.   2. Corporations–United
States–Finance.   3. Strategic planning–United States.   I. Titman,
Sheridan.   II. Title.   III. Series: Irwin/McGraw-Hill series in
finance.
   HG181.G75   1998
   658.15–dc21   97-25720

www.mhhe.com

When ordering this title, use ISBN 0-07-115761-1

Printed in Singapore

About the Authors

Mark Grinblatt, University of California at Los Angeles

Mark Grinblatt is Professor of Finance at UCLA's Anderson School, where he currently serves as chair of the Finance area, and where he began his career in 1981 after graduate work at Yale University. He is also a director on the board of Salomon Swapco, Inc., a consultant to numerous firms, and serves as an associate editor of the *Journal of Financial and Quantitative Analysis* and the *Review of Financial Studies*.

From 1987 to 1989, Professor Grinblatt was a visiting professor at the Wharton School and, while on leave from UCLA in 1989 and 1990, he was a vice-president for Salomon Brothers, Inc., valuing complex derivatives for the fixed income arbitrage trading group in the firm.

Professor Grinblatt is a noted teacher at UCLA, having been awarded teacher of the year in 1993 for UCLA's Fully Employed MBA Program by a vote of the students. This award was based on his teaching of a course designed around early drafts of this textbook.

Professor Grinblatt's areas of expertise include investments, performance evaluation of fund managers, fixed income markets, corporate finance, and derivatives.

Sheridan Titman, University of Texas—Austin

Sheridan Titman holds the Walter W. McAllister Centennial Chair in Financial Services at the University of Texas. He is also a research associate of the National Bureau of Economic Research and a consultant to a number of firms.

Professor Titman began his academic career in 1980 at UCLA, where he served as the department chair for the finance group and as the vice chairman of the UCLA management school faculty. He designed executive education programs in corporate financial strategy at UCLA and the Hong Kong University of Science and Technology, based on material developed for this textbook.

In the 1988-89 academic year Professor Titman worked in Washington, D.C., as the special assistant to the Assistant Secretary of the Treasury for Economic Policy, where he analyzed proposed legislation related to the stock and futures markets, leveraged buyouts and takeovers. Between 1992 and 1994, he served as a founding professor of the School of Business and Management at the Hong Kong University of Science and Technology, where his duties included the vice chairmanship of the faculty and chairmanship of the faculty appointments committee. From 1994 to 1997 he was the John J. Collins, S.J. Chair in International Finance at Boston College.

Professor Titman's areas of expertise include investments, performance evaluation of portfolio managers, corporate finance, and real estate. He is an editor of the *Review of Financial Studies* and serves on the board of a number of other finance and real estate journals. He has served as a director for the American Finance Association, the Asia Pacific Finance Association, and the Western Finance Association.

Foreword

After an introduction to corporate finance, students generally experience the subject as fragmenting into a variety of specialized areas, such as investments, derivatives markets, and fixed income, to name a few. What is often overlooked is the opportunity to introduce these topics as integral components of corporate finance and corporate decision making. Before now, it was difficult to convey this important connection between corporate finance and financial markets. By doing just that, this book simultaneously serves as a basis and a practical reference for all further study and experience in financial management.

The central corporate financial questions address which projects to accept and how to finance them. This text recognizes that to provide a framework to answer these questions, along with the associated issues of corporate finance and corporate strategy that they raise, requires a deep understanding of the financial markets. The book begins by describing the financing instruments available to the firm and how they are priced. It then develops the logic, the models, and the intuitions of modern financial decision making from portfolio theory through options and on to tax effects. The treatment focuses on project evaluation and the uses of capital and financial

structure, and it is enriched with a wealth of real world examples. The questions raised by managerial incentives and differences in the information held by management and the financial markets are also taken up in detail, supplementing the familiar treatment of the tradeoffs between taxes and bankruptcy costs. Lastly, and wholly appropriately, financial decision making is shown to be an essential part of the overall challenge of risk management.

Integrating capital structure and corporate financial decisions with corporate strategy has been a central area of research in finance and economics for more than a decade, and it has clearly changed the way we think about these matters. What is remarkable about this book is that it can take this relatively new material and so comfortably and seamlessly knit it together with more traditional approaches to give the reader such a clear understanding of corporate finance. Anyone who wants to probe more deeply into financial decision making and understand its relation to corporate strategy should read this text. Nor is this a book that will gather dust when the course is over; it will become part of every reader's tool kit and they will turn back to it often. I know that I will.

Stephen A. Ross

Preface

Textbooks can influence the lives of people. We know this first hand. As high school students, each of us read a textbook that ignited our interests in the field of economics. This text, *Economics* by Paul Samuelson, resulted in our separate decisions to study economics in college, which, in turn, led to graduate school in this field. There, each of us had the great fortune to study under some exceptional teachers (including the author of the foreword to this text) who stimulated our interest in finance. Satisfying, rewarding careers have blessed us ever since. To Paul Samuelson and his textbook, we owe a debt of gratitude.

As young assistant professors at UCLA in the early 1980s, we discovered that teaching a comprehensive course in finance could be a valuable way to learn about the field of finance. Our course preparations invariably sparked discussion and debates about points made in the textbooks used to teach our classes, which helped to jump-start our scholarly writing and professional careers. These discussions and debates eventually evolved into a long-term research collaboration in many areas of finance, reflected in our coauthorship on 15 published research papers over 15 years, and culminating in our ultimate collaboration—this textbook.

We began writing this textbook in early 1988, after several years of being hounded by a hungry sponsoring editor named Mike Junior. Mike was still hounding us, almost ten years later, to finish this, with substantial additional clout as the editorial director for Irwin/McGraw-Hill.

It took almost 10 years to complete this effort because we did not want to write an ordinary textbook. Our goal was to write a book that would break new ground in both the understanding and explanation of finance and its practice. We wanted to write a book that would influence the way people think about, teach, and practice finance. A book that would elevate the level of discussion and analysis in the classroom, in the corporate boardroom, and in the conference rooms of Wall Street firms. We wanted a book that would sit on the shelves of financial executives as a useful reference manual, long after the executives had studied the text and received a degree.

Time will determine whether the lofty goals set for this book will be realized. We can assure the reader, however, that every effort has been made to produce the best book we can, not only in terms of knowledge, but in terms of pedagogy, clarity, and novelty.

The Need for This Text

The changes witnessed since the early 1980s in both the theory of finance and its practice make the pedagogy of finance never more challenging than it is today. Since the early 1980s, the level of sophistication needed by financial managers has increased substantially. Managers now have access to a myriad of financing alternatives as well as futures and other derivative securities that, if used correctly, can increase value and decrease the risk exposure of their firms. Markets have also become more competitive and less forgiving of bad judgment. Although the amount of wealth created in financial markets in these past years has been unprecedented, the wealth lost by finance professionals in a number of serious mishaps has received even more attention.

Today, there is a unique opportunity for the financial manager. Clearly, the returns to having even a slight edge in the ability to evaluate and structure corporate investments and financial securities have never been so high. Yet, while the possibilities seem so great, the world of finance has never seemed so complex.

As our understanding of financial markets has grown more sophisticated, so has the practice of trading and valuing financial securities in these markets. At the same time, our understanding of how corporations can create value through their financial decisions has also advanced, suggesting that financial management is on the verge of a similar transformation to that seen in the financial markets. We believe that successful corporate managers will be those who can take advantage of the growing sophistication of the financial markets. The key to this will be the ability to take the lessons learned from the financial markets and apply them to the world of corporate financial management and strategy. The knowledge and tools that will enable the financial manager to transfer this knowledge from the markets arena to the corporate arena are found within this text.

Intended Audience

This book provides an in-depth analysis of financial theory, empirical work, and practice. It is primarily designed as a text for a second course in corporate finance for MBAs and advanced undergraduates. The text can stand alone or in tandem with cases. Because the book is self-contained, we also envision this as a textbook for a first course in finance for highly motivated students with some previous finance background.

The book's applications are intuitive, largely nontechnical, and geared toward helping the corporate manager formulate policies and financial strategies that maximize firm value. However, the formulation of corporate strategy requires an understanding of corporate securities and how they are valued. The depth with which we explore how to value financial securities also makes about half of this book appropriate for the Wall Street professional, including those on the sales and trading side.

The Underlying Philosophy

We believe that finance is not a set of topics or a set of formulas. Rather it is the consistent application of a few sensible rules and themes. We have searched long and hard for the threads that weave finance theory together, on both the corporate and investment side, and have tried to integrate the approach to finance used here by repeating these common rules and themes whenever possible.

A common theme that appears throughout the book is that capital assets must be valued in a way that rules out the possibility of riskless arbitrage. We illustrate how this powerful assumption can be used both to price financial securities like bonds and options and to evaluate investment projects. To identify whether the pricing of an investment allows one to create wealth, it is generally necessary to construct a portfolio of financial assets that tracks the investment. To understand how to construct such tracking portfolios, a part of the text is devoted to developing the mathematics of portfolios.

A second theme is that financial decisions are interconnected and, therefore, must be incorporated into the overall corporate strategy of the firm. For example, a firm's ability to generate positive net present value projects today depends on its past investment choices as well as the financing choices that it made in the past.

For the most part, the book takes a prescriptive perspective; in other words, it examines how financial decisions should be made to improve firm value. However, the book also takes the descriptive perspective, developing theories that shed light on which financial decisions are made and why, and analyzing the impact of these decisions in financial markets. At times, the book's perspective combines aspects of the descriptive and prescriptive. For example, the text analyzes why top management incentives may differ from value maximization and describes how these incentive problems can bias financial decisions as well as how to use financial contracts to alleviate incentive problems.

This is an up-to-date book, both in terms of theoretical developments, empirical results, and practical applications. Our detailed analysis of the debate about the applicability of the CAPM, for example (Chapters 5 and 6), cannot be found in any existing corporate finance text. The same is true of the book's treatment of value management (Chapters 9 and 17), practiced by consulting firms like Stern Stewart and Co., BCG/Holt, and McKinsey and Co.; the text's treatment of hedging with futures contracts and its impact on companies like Metallgesellschaft (Chapter 21); and of its treatment of interest rate risk and its impact on Orange County's bankruptcy (Chapter 22).

Pedagogical Features

Our goal was to provide a text that is as simple and accessible as possible without superficially glossing over important details. We also wanted a text that would be eminently practical. Practicality is embedded from the start of each chapter, which begins with a **real-world vignette** to motivate the issues in the respective chapter.

As a pedagogical aid to help the reader understand what should be gleaned from each chapter, the vignettes are immediately preceded by a set of **learning objectives,** which itemize the chapter's major lessons that the student should strive to master.

> **Learning Objectives**
>
> After reading this chapter you should be able to:
> 1. Describe the types of equity securities a firm can issue.
> 2. Provide an overview of the operation of secondary markets for equity.
> 3. Describe the role of institutions in secondary equity markets and in corporate governance.
> 4. Understand the process of going public.
> 5. Discuss the concept of informational efficiency.
>
> *On August 9, 1995, after just two years in business, Netscape Communications Corporation issued five million shares in an initial public offering (IPO). The underwriters originally anticipated an offering at around $14 a share, but because of strong demand at that price, the offering price was raised to $28.*
>
> *The price of the shares skyrocketed from their $28.00 per share issue price to over $70.00 in the initial trading before closing at $58.25 per share, implying a total value of over $2 billion. However, within months of the original offering the price had again doubled. At these prices, the shares retained by the company's cofounders—Marc*

The text can provide depth and yet be relatively simple by presenting financial concepts with a series of examples, rather than with algebraic proofs or "black-box" recipes. Virtually every chapter includes numerous **examples** and **case studies,** some hypothetical and some real, that help the student gain insight into some of the most sophisticated realms of financial theory and practice. Our experience is that practice by doing, first while reading and then reinforced by numerous end-of-chapter problems, is the best way to learn new material. We feel it is important for the student to work through the examples and case studies. They are key ingredients of the pedagogy of this text.

What if No Pure Comparison Firm Exists?

Many firms are large diversified entities that have many lines of business. In this instance, the equity returns of potential comparison firms are distorted by other lines of business that are inappropriate as comparisons. A financial manager in this situation still may be able to obtain an appropriate comparison by forming portfolios of firms that generate a "pure" line of business. The mathematics behind the approach taken in Example 10.3, which illustrates how to create comparison investments in a pure line of business when none initially exists, is similar in spirit to the formation of pure factor portfolios in Chapter 6.

Example 10.3:   Finding a Comparison Firm from a Portfolio of Firms

Assume that Time-Warner is interested in acquiring the ABC television network from Disney. It has estimated the expected incremental future cash flows from acquiring ABC and desires an appropriate beta in order to compute a discount rate to value those cash flows. However, the two major networks that are most comparable, NBC and CBS, are owned by General Electric and Westinghouse—respectively—which have substantial cash flows from other sources. For these comparison firms, the table below presents hypothetical equity betas, debt to asset ratios, and the ratios of the market values of the network assets to all assets:

	β_E	$\dfrac{D}{D+E}$	$\dfrac{\text{Network Assets}}{\text{All Assets}} = \dfrac{N}{A}$
General Electric	1.1	.1	.25
Westinghouse	1.3	.4	.50

Estimate the appropriate beta for the ABC acquisition. Assume that the debt of each of the two comparison firms is risk free. Also assume that the non-network assets of General Electric and Westinghouse are substantially similar and thus have the same beta.

Answer: Using equation (10.2a), $\beta_A = [E/(D + E)] \beta_E$, first find the asset betas of the two comparison firms. For the two firms, these are, respectively,

---

Salomon Swapco, Inc.: The Importance of an AAA Credit Rating

In the early 1990s, after a couple of tough years, a number of Wall Street firms observed that their interest rate swap business was "drying up." After the dissolution of Drexel, Burnham, Lambert in 1990, many healthy companies and financial institutions were afraid to enter into contracts with Wall Street firms with less than AA or AAA credit ratings. When corporations enter into interest rate swaps with an investment bank, they are primarily concerned with hedging interest rate risk, and they do not want to monitor the credit-worthiness of their investment bank counterparty. As a result, AAA-rated corporations like American International Group, an insurance company, were making great inroads into the interest rate swap business.

In addition to the numerous examples and cases interwoven throughout the text, we highlight **major results** and define **key words and concepts** throughout each chapter. The **functional use of color** is deliberately and carefully done in order to call out what is important.

Result 11.4   Most projects can be viewed as a set of mutually exclusive projects. For example, taking the project today is one project, waiting to take the project next year is another project, and waiting three years is yet another project. Firms may pass up the first project, that is, initiate the capital investment immediately, even if doing so has a positive net present value. They will do so if the mutually exclusive alternative, waiting to invest, has a higher *NPV*.

At the end of each of the six parts of the book are two unique features. The first is **Practical Insights,** a feature that contains unique guidelines to help the reader identify the important practical issues faced by the financial manager and where to look in that part of the text to help analyze those issues. The feature enables the book to serve as a reference as well as a primer on finance.

Practical Insights is organized around what we consider the four basic tasks of financial managers: allocating capital for real investment, financing the firm, knowing whether and how to hedge risk, and allocating funds for financial investments. For each of these functional tasks, *Practical Insights* provides a list of important practical lessons, each bulleted, with section number references to which the reader can refer to for further detail on the insight.

PRACTICAL INSIGHTS FOR PART II

Allocating Capital for Real Investment

- Mean-variance analysis can help determine the risk implications of product mixes, mergers and acquisitions, and carve-outs. This requires thinking about the mix of real assets as a portfolio. (Section 4.6)
- Theories to value real assets identify the types of risk that determine discount rates. Most valuation problems will use either the CAPM or APT, which identify market risk and factor risk, respectively, as the relevant risk attributes. (Sections 5.8, 6.10)
- An investment's covariance with other investments is a more important determinant of its discount rate than is the variance of the investment's return. (Section 5.2)

- Portfolio mathematics can enable the investor to understand the risk attributes of any mix of real assets, financial assets, and liabilities. (Section 4.6)

Allocating Funds for Financial Investments

- Portfolios generally dominate individual securities as desirable investment positions. (Section 5.2)
- Per dollar invested, leveraged positions are riskier than unleveraged positions. (Section 4.7)
- There is a unique optimal risky portfolio when a risk-free asset exists. The task of an investor is to identify this portfolio. (Section 5.4)

The second feature, **Executive Perspective,** provides the reader with testimonials from important financial executives, who have looked over respective parts of the book and highlight what issues and topics are especially important from the practicing executive's perspective.

EXECUTIVE PERSPECTIVE

Myron S. Scholes

At Long-Term Capital Management, financial models are critical to our success. Since we are a liability manager in addition to an asset manager, models are crucial, not only in selecting alternative investments and position sizes, but also in managing the risk of our positions. Indeed, financial models, similar to those developed in Part II of this text, are in everyday use in the firm.

The mean-variance model, developed in Chapters 4 and 5, is one example of this. We, as well as other portfolio managers, must optimize the return-to-risk profile of the portfolio. The mean-variance approach has influenced our optimal capital size and assists us in determining the scale of our positions.

The risk-expected return models presented in Part II, such as the CAPM and the APT, represent another set of useful tools for money management and portfolio optimization. These models have profoundly affected the way investment funds are managed and the way individuals invest and assess performance. For example, passively managed funds, which generally buy and hold a proxy for the market portfolio, have grown dramatically, accounting for more than 20 percent of institutional investment. This has occurred, in part, because of academic writings on the CAPM and, in part, because performance evaluation using these models has shown that professional money managers as a group do not systematically outperform these alternative investment strategies. Investment banks use both debt and equity factor models—extremely important

tools—to determine appropriate hedges to mitigate factor risks. For example, my former employer, Salomon Brothers, uses factor models to determine the appropriate hedges for its equity and debt positions.

All this pales, of course, with the impact of derivatives valuation models, starting with the Black-Scholes option-pricing model that I developed with Fischer Black in the early 1970s. Using the option-pricing technology, investment banks have been able to produce products that customers want. An entire field called financing engineering has emerged in recent years to support these developments. Investment banks use option pricing technology to price sophisticated contracts and to determine the appropriate hedges to mitigate the underlying risks of producing these contracts. Without the option-pricing technology, presented in Chapters 7 and 8, the global financial picture would be far different. In the old world, banks were underwriters, matching those who wanted to buy with those who wanted to offer coarse contracts such as loans, bonds, and stocks. Derivatives have reduced the costs to provide financial services and products that are more finely tuned to the needs of investors and corporations around the world.

Mr. Scholes is currently a principal, co-founder, and limited partner at Long-Term Capital Management, L.P., located in Greenwich, Connecticut. He is also the Frank E. Buck Professor of Finance Emeritus, Stanford University Graduate School of Business.

Organization of the Text

Part I opens the text with a description of the capital markets: the various financial instruments and the markets in which they trade. Part II develops the major financial theories that explain how to value these financial instruments, while Part III examines how these same theories can be used by corporations to evaluate their real investments in property, plant, and equipment, as well as investments in nonphysical capital like research and human capital. Parts IV, V, and VI look at how the modern corporation interacts with the capital markets. The chapters in these parts explore how firms choose between the various instruments available to them for financing their operations and how these same instruments help firms manage their risks. These corporate financial decisions are not viewed in isolation, but rather, are viewed as part of the overall corporate strategy of firms, affecting their real investment and operating strategies, their product market strategies, and the ways in which their executives are compensated.

Acknowledgments

This book could not have been produced without the help of many people. First, we are grateful to our wives for their support of what must have seemed like an additional child in the family. They also provided great advice and comments on critical issues and parts of the book over the years. And of course, we are grateful for the five children that have blessed our two families. They are the inspiration for everything we do.

A number of people wrote exceptional material for this book. Stephen Ross wrote a terrific foreword and provided comments on many key chapters. Rob Brokaw, Thomas Copeland, Lisa Price, Myron Scholes, David Shimko, and Bruce Tuckman were extremely gracious in taking the time to read chapters of the book, provide comments, and write insightful Executive Perspectives. Finally, Dennis Sheehan prepared material on financial institutions, much of which was worked into Chapters 1 through 3.

We received exceptional detailed comments on earlier drafts of all 22 chapters from a number of scholars that were selected by the editors at McGraw-Hill/Irwin. They went far beyond the call of duty in shaping this book into a high-quality product. We owe gratitude to the following reviewers:

Sanjai Bhagat, University of Colorado, Boulder
Ivan Brick, Rutgers University
David Denis, Purdue University
Diane Denis, Purdue University
Bill Francis, University of North Carolina, Charlotte
Larry Glosten, Columbia University
Ron Giammarino, University of British Columbia
Kenneth Lehn, University of Pittsburgh
Michael Mazzeo, Michigan State University
Chris Muscarella, Pennsylvania State University
Gordon Phillips, University of Maryland
Annette Poulson, University of Georgia
James Seward, Dartmouth College
Dennis Sheehan, Penn State University
Katherine Speiss, Notre Dame University
Neal Stoughton, University of California, Irvine
Michael Vetsuypens, Southern Methodist University

Leslye Givarz, developmental editor, helped us make sense of all the reviewer comments and gave us wonderful style comments of her own. To Leslye, whose help had a huge impact on the style and writing quality of this book, we owe a heartfelt thanks.

The professional staff at Irwin/McGraw-Hill was first rate. First, to Mike Junior, who envisioned the potential of this book before we ever did and saw it through to the end, thank you for always pushing us so hard and for accommodating us with whatever we needed to produce a quality book. Our senior sponsoring editor, Gina Huck, can only be described as a jewel in the final six months. Jean Lou Hess, senior project manager, was not only as professional a person as we have ever met in publishing, but she played the invaluable role of politician, calming psychologist, and stern schoolmaster at the same time. The tireless quest for quality of Gina and Jean Lou, and their ability to work as hard as we were working in the winter and spring of 1997 were the motivating forces that pushed us across the finish line. We are grateful and proud of the rest of the Irwin/McGraw-Hill/, including Charles Olson, copyeditor; Paula Krauza, editorial assistant, and Matthew Baldwin, designer.

Two Ph.D. students at UCLA, Toby Moskowitz and Yihong Xia, deserve special mention for volunteering extraordinary amounts of time to check the book for accuracy and assist with homework problems. Two superb administrative assistants at UCLA, Sabrina Kaplan and Susanna Szaiff, also deserve mention for service beyond the call of duty under time pressure that would cause most normal human beings to collapse from exhaustion. Also, Michael Schill at the University of Washington offered a valuable, critical eye as an accuracy checker for what he now knows to be less than minimum wage.

We are so fortunate to have received what must surely be an unprecedented amount of help from former MBA students, Ph.D. students, colleagues at UCLA, Wharton, the Hong Kong University of Science and Technology, and Boston College, and from numerous colleagues at universities on four different continents: Australia, Asia, Europe, and North America. (We hope to add South America and Africa for the next edition. Antarctica may take a while.) The text has also benefited from discussions and comments from a number of practitioners on Wall Street, in corporations, and in consulting firms. From the bottom of our hearts, thank you to those listed below:

Timor Abasov, *UC Irvine*
Doug Abbott, *Cornerstone Research*
Dawn Anaiscourt, *UCLA*
George Aragon, *Boston College*
Paul Asquith, *UCLA*
Trung Bach, *UCLA*
Lisa Barron, *UCLA*
Harvey Becker, *UCLA*
Antonio Bernardo, *UCLA*
Rosario Benevides, *Salomon Brothers, Inc.*
David Booth, *Dimensional Fund Advisors*
Jim Brandon, *UCLA*
Michael Brennan *UCLA*
Bhagwan Chowdhry, *UCLA*
Bill Cockrum, *UCLA*
Michael Corbat, *Salomon Brothers, Inc.*
Nick Crew, *The Analysis Group*

Kent Daniel, *Northwestern University*
Gordon Delianedes, *UCLA*
Giorgio DeSantis, *University of Southern California*
Laura Field, *Penn State University*
Murray Frank, *University of British Columbia*
Julian Franks, *London Business School*
Bruno Gerard, *University of Southern California*
Rajna Gibson, *University of Lausanne*
Prem Goyal, *UCLA*
Matt Hardy, *UCLA*
Kevin Hashizume, *UCLA*
David Hirshleifer, *University of Michigan*
Edith Hotchkiss, *Boston College*
Sandra Howe, *Boston College*
Dena Iura, *UCLA*

Brad Jordan, *University of Missouri*
Philippe Jorion, *University of California at Irvine*
Ed Kane, *Boston College*
David Krider, *UCLA*
Jason Kwan, *UCLA*
Marvin Lieberman, *UCLA*
Olivier Ledoit, *UCLA*
Virgil Lee, *UCLA*
Francis Longstaff, *Salomon Brothers, Inc.*
Douglas Lucas, *Salomon Swapco, Inc.*
Ananth Madhavan, *University of Southern California*
Susan McCall-Bowen, *Salomon Brothers, Inc.*
Julian Nguyen, *UCLA*
Sunny Ngyuen, *UCLA*
Tim Opler, *Ohio State*
Jay Patel, *Boston University*
Michelle Pham, *UCLA*
Jeff Pontiff, *University of Washington*

Michael Randall, *UCLA*
Traci Ray, *Boston College*
Jay Ritter, *University of Florida*
Richard Roll, *UCLA*
Pedro Santa-Clara, *UCLA*
Matthias Schaefer, *UCLA*
Eduardo Schwartz, *UCLA*
Linley Sides, *UCLA*
Peter Swank, *First Quadrant*
Hassan Tehranian, *Boston College*
Siew-Hong Teoh, *University of Michigan*
Rawley Thomas, *BCG/Holt*
Nick Travlos, *ALBA*
Garry Twite, *Australian Graduate School of Management*
Ivo Welch, *UCLA*
Russell Wermers, *University of Colorado*
David Wessels, *UCLA*
Fred Weston, *UCLA*
Bill Wilhelm, *Boston College*
Scott Wo, *UCLA*

Over a 10-year period, it is very difficult to remember everyone who had a hand in helping out on this textbook. To those we inadvertently omitted, our apologies and our thanks; please let us know so we can properly show you our gratitude.

Concluding Remarks

Although we have taken great care to discover and eliminate errors and inconsistencies in this text, we understand that, like most first editions, this text is far from perfect. Our goal is to substantially improve the text prior to the second edition and to continually improve the text thereafter. Please let us know if you discover any errors in the book, or if you have any good examples, problems, or just better ways to present some of the existing material. We welcome your comments (c/o Irwin/McGraw-Hill Editorial, 1333 Burr Ridge Parkway, Burr Ridge, IL 60521).

Mark Grinblatt
Sheridan Titman

Brief Contents

Contents

PART I

Financial Markets and Financial Instruments

The title of this finance text is *Financial Markets and Corporate Strategy*. The title reflects our belief that to apply financial theory to formulate corporate strategy, it is necessary to have a thorough understanding of financial markets. There are two aspects to this understanding. The first aspect, to be studied in Part I, is that a corporate strategist needs to understand financial institutions. The second, studied in Part II, is that the strategist needs to know how to value securities in the financial markets.

Financial markets, from an institutional perspective, are covered in three chapters. Chapter 1, a general overview of the process of raising capital, walks the reader through the decision-making process of how to raise funds, from whom, in what form, and with whose help. It also focuses on the legal and institutional environment in which securities are issued and compares the procedure for raising capital in the United States with the procedures used in other major countries, specifically, Germany, Japan, and the United Kingdom.

Chapter 2, devoted to understanding debt securities and debt markets, emphasizes the wide variety of debt instruments available to finance a firm's investments. However, the chapter is also designed to help the reader understand the nomenclature, pricing conventions, and return computations found in debt markets. It also tries to familiarize the reader with the secondary markets in which debt trades.

Chapter 3 covers equity securities, which are much less diverse than debt securities. The focus is on the secondary markets in which equity trades and the process by which firms "go public," issuing publicly traded equity for the first time. The chapter examines the pricing of equity securities at the time of initial public offerings and introduces the concept of market efficiency, which provides insights into how prices are determined in the secondary markets.

Raising Capital

The Process and the Players

Learning Objectives

After reading this chapter you should be able to:

1. Describe the ways in which firms can raise funds for new investment.
2. Understand the process of issuing new securities.
3. Comprehend the role played by investment banks in raising capital.
4. Discuss how capital is raised in countries outside the United States.
5. Analyze trends in raising capital.

On June 6, 1991, Time Warner, the multimedia giant, announced a novel approach to raising capital. It would issue a variable-price right to existing shareholders, giving them the option to buy Time Warner shares. In contrast to typical rights offerings, which give shareholders the option to buy additional shares at a specified price, the option to buy shares provided by these rights did not specify a fixed price, but depended on how many of the rights the shareholders exercised. With 100 percent participation, shareholders would pay $105 per share; with 60 percent participation, they would pay only $63 per share. When Time Warner announced this variable-price rights offering, the company's stock price immediately fell by $11.25 to $99.50 and continued to decline in the ensuing weeks to less than $90. The decline presented shareholders with a quandary: if all of them participated in the offering, they would pay $105 for stock that was worth $90. However, if many shareholders did not participate, those who did would be able to buy shares for less than their market value.

Under pressure from shareholders and institutional investors, Time Warner altered the structure of the deal, converting it into a typical fixed-price rights offering that gave existing shareholders the right to buy new shares for $80 a share. In August 1991, this $2.5 billion offer was completed.

Finance is the study of trade-offs between the present and the future. For an individual investor, an investment in the debt or equity markets means giving up something today to gain something in the future. For a corporate investment in a factory, machinery, or an advertising campaign, there is a similar sense of giving up something today to gain something in the future.

The decisions of individual investors and corporations are intimately linked. In order to grow and prosper by virtue of wise investments in factories, machinery, advertising campaigns, and so forth, most firms require access to capital markets. **Capital markets** are an arena in which firms and other institutions that require funds to finance their operations come together with individuals and institutions that have money to invest. To invest wisely, both individuals and firms must have a thorough understanding of these capital markets.

Capital markets have grown in complexity and importance over the past 25 years. As a result, the level of sophistication required by corporate financial managers has also grown. The amount of capital raised in external markets has increased dramatically, with an ever-increasing variety of available financial instruments. Moreover, the financial markets have become truly global, with thousands of securities trading around the clock throughout the world.

To be a player in modern business requires a sophisticated understanding of the new, yet ever-changing institutional framework in which financing takes place. As a beginning, this chapter describes the workings of the capital markets and the general decisions that firms face when they raise funds. Specifically, this chapter focuses on the classes of securities that firms issue, the role played by investment banks in raising capital, the environment in which capital is raised, and the differences between the U.S. financial systems and the financial systems in other countries. It concludes with a discussion of current trends in the raising of capital.

1.1 Financing the Firm

The financial system in every developed economy is composed of households, firms, financial intermediaries, and governments. **Financial intermediaries** are institutions such as banks that collect the savings of individuals and corporations, and funnel them to firms that use the money to finance their investments in plant, equipment, research and development, and so forth. Some of the most important financial intermediaries are described in Exhibit 1.1.

In addition to financing firms indirectly through financial intermediaries, households finance firms directly by individually buying and holding stocks and bonds. The government also plays a key role in this process by regulating the capital markets and taxing various financing alternatives.

Decisions Facing the Firm

Firms can raise investment capital from many sources with a variety of financial instruments. The firm's financial policy describes the mix of financial instruments used to finance the firm.

Internal Capital.   Firms raise capital internally by retaining the earnings they generate and by obtaining external funds from the capital markets. Exhibit 1.2 shows that in the aggregate, the percentage of total investment funds that U. S. firms generate internally— essentially retained earnings plus depreciation—is generally in the 50–80 percent range. Thus, internal cash flows are typically insufficient to meet the total capital needs of most firms.

EXHIBIT 1.1   Description of Financial Intermediaries

Financial Intermediary	Description
Commercial bank	Takes deposits from individuals and corporations and lends these funds to borrowers.
Investment bank	Raises money for corporations by issuing securities.
Insurance company	Invests money set aside to pay future claims in securities, real estate, and other assets.
Pension fund	Invests money set aside to pay future pensions in securities, real estate, and other assets.
Charitable foundation	Invests the endowment of a nonprofit organization such as a university.
Mutual fund	Pools savings from individual investors to purchase securities.
Venture capital firm	Pools money from individual investors and other financial intermediaries to fund relatively small, new businesses, generally with private equity financing.

EXHIBIT 1.2   Aggregate Percent of Investment Funds Raised Internally

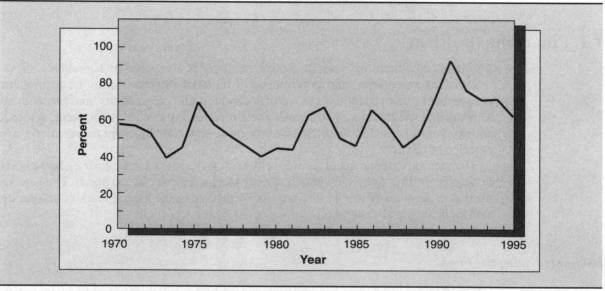

Source: Federal Reserve Flow of Funds.

External Capital: Debt vs. Equity.   When a firm determines that it needs external funds, it must gain access to capital markets and make a decision about the type of funds to raise. Exhibit 1.3 illustrates the two basic sources of outside financing: debt and equity, as well as the major forms of debt and equity financing.[1]

---

[1]The different sources of debt financing will be explored in detail in Chapter 2; the various sources of equity capital are examined in Chapter 3.

EXHIBIT 1.3   Sources of Capital

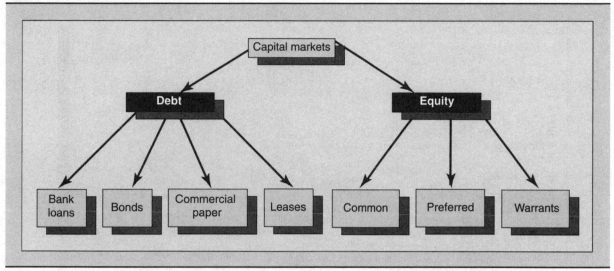

The main difference between **debt** and **equity** is that the debt holders have a contract specifying that their claims must be paid in full before the firm can make payments to its equity holders. In other words, debt claims are **senior**, or have priority, over equity claims. A second important distinction between debt and equity is that payments to debt holders are generally viewed as a tax-deductible expense of the firm. In contrast, the dividends on an equity instrument are viewed as a payout of profits and therefore are not a tax-deductible expense.

Major corporations frequently raise outside capital by accessing the debt markets. Equity, however, is an extremely important but much less frequently used source of outside capital.

Result 1.1 summarizes the discussion in this subsection.

Result 1.1   Debt is the most frequently used source of outside capital. The important distinctions between debt and equity are:

- Debt claims are senior to equity claims.
- Interest payments on debt claims are tax deductible, but dividends on equity claims are not.

How Big Is the U.S. Capital Market?

Exhibit 1.4 shows the value of the outstanding debt and equity capital of U.S. firms since 1970.[2] The relative proportions of debt and equity have not changed dramatically over time. Since 1970, firms have been financed with about 60 percent equity and 40 percent debt, with the percentage of equity financing increasing somewhat in the 1990s.

In the 1980s, the aggregate amount of debt financing relative to equity financing, with debt and equity measured in book value terms, increased substantially. Countless

---

[2]Unfortunately, the data are not strictly comparable because the equity is expressed in market value terms, the price at which the security can be obtained in the market, and the debt is expressed in book value terms, which is generally close to the price at which the debt originally sold.

EXHIBIT 1.4   Value of Debt and Equity Outstanding in the U.S., Billions of Dollars

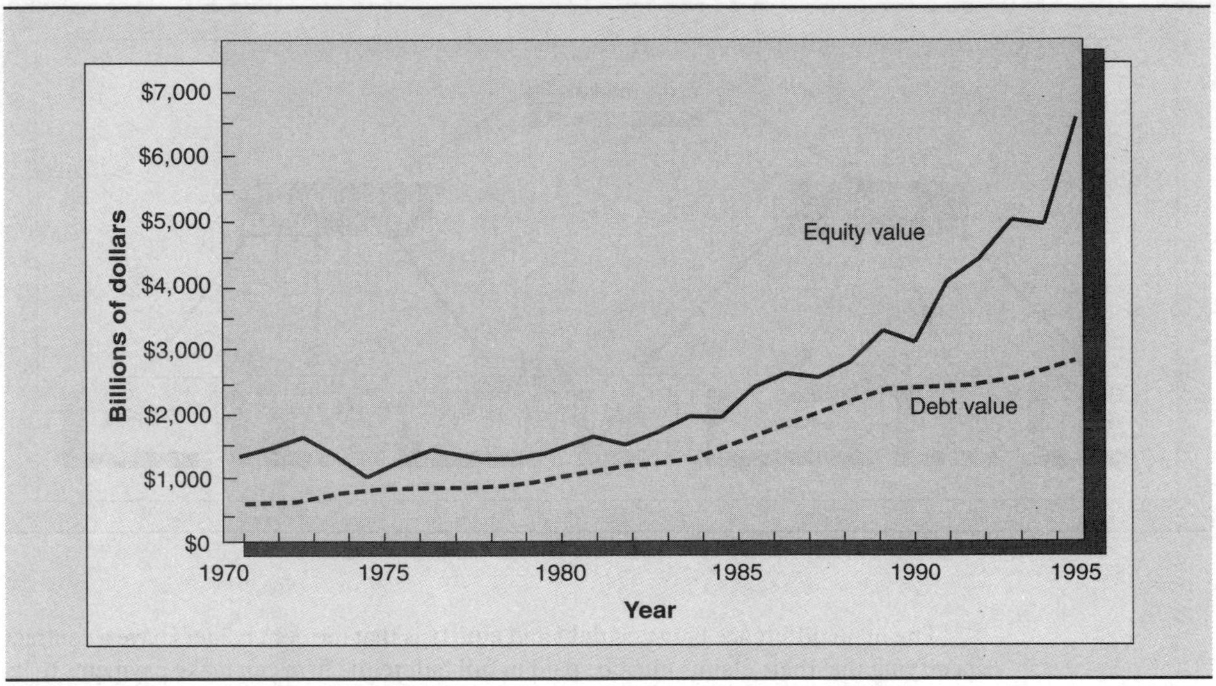

Source: Federal Reserve Flow of Funds

writers in the business press, as well as countless politicians, have interpreted this to mean that firms were replacing equity financing with debt financing in the 1980s. This interpretation is somewhat misleading. Firms retired a substantial number of shares in the 1980s, through either repurchases of their own shares or the purchases of other firms' shares in takeovers. Far more shares were retired than were issued. However, offsetting these share repurchases was an unprecedented boom in the stock market that substantially increased the market value of existing shares. As a result, firms were able to retire shares and issue debt without increasing their debt/equity ratios, expressed in market value, above their pre-1980 levels. As Exhibit 1.4 illustrates, using market values, the ratio of debt to equity remained relatively constant in the 1980s.

1.2 Public and Private Sources of Capital

Firms raise debt and equity capital from both public and private sources. Capital raised from public sources must be in the form of registered securities. In the United States, **securities** are financial instruments registered with the **Securities and Exchange Commission (SEC)**, the government agency established in 1934 to regulate the securities markets.

Public securities differ from private financial instruments because they can be traded on public **secondary markets** like the New York Stock Exchange or the American Stock Exchange, which are two institutions that facilitate the trading of public securities. Examples of publicly traded securities include common stock, preferred stock, and corporate bonds.

Private capital comes either in the form of bank loans or as what are known as **private placements**, which are financial claims exempted from registration requirements that apply to the securities. To qualify for this private placement exemption, the issue must be restricted to a small group of sophisticated investors—fewer than 35 in number—with minimum income or wealth requirements. Typically, these sophisticated investors include insurance companies and pension funds as well as wealthy individuals. They also include venture capital firms, as noted in Exhibit 1.1.

Financial instruments that have been privately placed cannot be sold on public markets unless they are registered with the SEC, in which case they become securities. However, **Rule 144A**, adopted in 1990, allows institutions with assets exceeding $100 million to trade privately placed financial claims among themselves without first registering them as securities.

Public markets are anonymous; that is, buyers and sellers can complete their transactions without knowing each others' identities. Because of the anonymous nature of trades on this market, uninformed investors run the risk of trading with other investors who are vastly more informed because they have "inside" information about a particular company and can make a profit from it. However, insider trading is illegal and uninformed investors are at least partially protected by laws that prevent investors from buying or selling public securities based on **inside information**, which is internal company information that has not been made public. In contrast, investors of privately placed debt and equity are allowed to base their decisions on information that is not publicly known. Since traders in private markets are assumed to be sophisticated investors who are aware of each others' identities, inside information about privately placed securities is not as problematic. For example, if a potential buyer of a debt instrument has reason to believe that the seller possesses material information that he or she is not disclosing, the buyer can choose not to buy. If the seller misrepresents this information, the buyer can later sue. Because private markets are not anonymous, they generally are less liquid; that is, the transaction costs associated with buying and selling private debt and equity is generally much higher than the costs of buying and selling public securities.

Result 1.2 summarizes the key points of this subsection.

Result 1.2   U.S. corporations raise capital from both private and public sources. The advantages associated with private sources include:

- The terms of private bonds and stock can be customized for individual investors.
- No costly registration with the SEC.
- No need to reveal confidential information.
- Easier to renegotiate.

Privately placed financial instruments also can have disadvantages.

- Limited investor base.
- Less liquid.

Depending on the state of the market, about 70 percent of debt offerings are made to the public and about 30 percent are private placements. In some years, private debt offerings can top 40 percent of the market. In contrast, private equity placements have averaged about 20 percent of the new capital raised in the equity market.

Corporations can raise funds directly from banks, insurance companies, and other sources of private capital without going through investment banks. However, corporations generally need the services of investment banks when they issue public securities. This will be discussed in the next section.

1.3 The Environment for Raising Capital in the United States

The Legal Environment

A myriad of regulations govern public debt and equity issues. These regulations certainly increase the costs of issuing public securities, but they also provide protection for investors which enhances the value of the securities. The value of these regulations can be illustrated by contrasting the situation in Western Europe and the United States, where markets are highly regulated, to the situation in some of the emerging markets, which are much less regulated. A major risk in the emerging markets is that shareholder rights will not be respected and, as a result, many stocks traded in these markets sell for substantially less than the value of their assets. For example, in 1995 Lukoil, Russia's biggest oil company with proven reserves of 16 billion barrels, was valued at $850 million, which implies that its oil was worth about five cents a barrel.[3] At about the same time, Royal Dutch/Shell, with about 17 billion barrels of reserves, had a market value of $94 billion in 1995, making its oil worth more than $5 a barrel. Lukoil is worth substantially less because of uncertainty about shareholders' rights in Russia. Although economists and policymakers may argue about the optimal level of regulation, most prefer the more highly regulated U.S. environment to that in the emerging markets where shareholder rights are usually not as well defined.

Although government regulations play an important role for securities issued in the United States, this was not always so. Regulation in the United States expanded substantially in the 1930s because of charges of stock price manipulation that came in the wake of the 1929 stock market crash. Congress enacted several pieces of legislation that radically altered the landscape for firms issuing securities. The three most important pieces of legislation were the Securities Act of 1933, the Securities Exchange Act of 1934, and the Banking Act of 1934 (commonly called the Glass-Steagall Act after the two congressmen who sponsored it).

The Securities Acts of 1933 and 1934.   The **Securities Act of 1933** and the **Securities and Exchange Act of 1934** require registration of all public offerings by firms except short-term instruments (less than 270 days) and intrastate offerings. Specifically, the acts require that companies file a **registration statement** with the SEC. The required registration statement contains:

- General information about the firm and detailed financial data.
- A description of the security being issued.
- The agreement between the investment bank that acts as the **underwriter**, who originates and distributes the issue, and the issuing firm.
- The composition of the **underwriting syndicate**, a group of banks that sell the issue.

Most of the information in the registration statement must be made available to investors in the form of a **prospectus**, a printed document that includes information about the security and the firm. The prospectus is widely distributed before the sale of the securities and bears the dire warning, printed in red ink, that the securities have not yet been approved for sale.[4]

---

[3]*The Economist,* Jan. 21, 1995.
[4]Because of the red ink, the prospectus prior to approval is often called the "red herring."

Once filed with the SEC, registration statements do not become effective for 20 days, the so-called cooling off period during which selling the stock is prohibited. If the SEC determines that the registration statement is complete, they approve it or "make it effective." If, however, the registration exhibits egregious flaws, the SEC requires that the firm fix it. Once the SEC approves the registration statement, the underwriter is free to start selling the securities in what is known as the *primary offering*. The SEC's approval of the registration statement is not an endorsement of the security, but simply an affirmation that the firm has met the disclosure requirements of the 1933 act.

Because all signatories to the registration statement are liable for any misstatements it might contain, the underwriters must investigate the issuing company with due diligence. **Due diligence** means investigating and disclosing any information that is relevant to investors and providing an audit of the accounting numbers by a certified public accounting firm. If material information is not disclosed and the security performs poorly, the underwriters can be sued by investors.

The Glass-Steagall Act.   In the wake of the Depression, Congress enacted the **Banking Act of 1933**, commonly called the **Glass-Steagall Act**. This legislation changed the landscape of investment banking by requiring banks to divorce their commercial banking activities from their investment banking activities.

Glass-Steagall gave rise to many of the modern investment banks, both living and defunct, that most finance professionals are familiar with today. For instance, the firms of J. P. Morgan, Drexel, and Brown Brothers Harriman opted to abandon underwriting and instead concentrate on private banking for wealthy individuals. Several partners from J. P. Morgan and Drexel decided to form Morgan Stanley, an investment banking firm. Similarly, the First Boston Corporation is derived from the securities affiliate of the First National Bank of Boston.

After Glass-Steagall, firms that stayed in the underwriting business were forced to build "Chinese walls" to separate their underwriting activities from other financial functions. **Chinese walls** involve structuring a company's procedures to prevent certain types of communication between the corporate side of the bank and the bank's sales and trading sectors. The underwriting part of these businesses must have no connection with other activities, such as stock recommendations, market making, and institutional sales.

A Trend toward Deregulation.   Roe (1994) advanced the provocative argument that these three pieces of legislation and others, such as the **Investment Company Act of 1940**, which regulates mutual funds, and the **Bank Holding Company Act of 1956**, which allows limited banking mergers, fundamentally altered the role of financial institutions in corporate governance. Roe argued that the legislation caused the fragmentation of financial institutions and institutional portfolios, thereby preventing the emergence of powerful large-block shareholders who might exert pressure on management. In contrast, countries such as Japan and Germany, which do not operate under the same constraints, developed systems in which banks played a much larger role in firms' affairs.

Congress and the regulatory agencies, recognizing that U.S. financial institutions are heavily constrained, have started relaxing these constraints. Glass-Steagall restrictions are being steadily weakened. Commercial and investment banks have been drawing closer to **universal banking**; that is, they are beginning to offer a whole range of services from taking deposits to selling securities. In addition, interstate banking was legalized in 1994 and full interstate branch banking is expected in 1997. Because of the fierce competition that these trends will generate, there will almost certainly be fewer commercial and investment banks in the United States in the future. Surviving banks will tend to be bigger, better capitalized, and better prepared to serve business firms in creative ways.

Investment Banks

Just as the government is ubiquitous in the process of issuing securities, so too are investment banks. Modern investment banks are made up of two parts: the corporate business and the sales and trading business.

The Corporate Business.   The corporate side of investment banking is a fee-for-service business; that is, the firm sells its expertise. The main expertise banks have is in underwriting securities, but they also sell other services. They provide merger and acquisition advice in the form of prospecting for takeover targets, advising clients about the price to be offered for these targets, finding financing for the takeover, and planning takeover tactics or, on the other side, takeover defenses. The major investment banking houses are also actively engaged in the design of new financial instruments.

The Sales and Trading Business.   Investment banks that underwrite securities sell them on the sales and trading end of their business to the bank's institutional investors. These investors include mutual funds, pension funds, and insurance companies. Sales and trading also consists of public market making, trading for clients, and trading on the investment banking firm's own account.

Market making requires that the investment bank act as a **dealer** in securities, standing ready to buy and sell, respectively, at wholesale (**bid**) and retail (**ask**) prices. The bank makes money on the difference between the bid and ask price, or the **bid-ask spread**. Banks do this not only for corporate debt and equity securities, but also as dealers in a variety of government securities. In addition, investment banks trade securities using their own funds, which is known as **proprietary trading**. Proprietary trading is riskier for an investment bank than being a dealer and earning the bid-ask spread, but the rewards can be commensurably larger.

The Largest Investment Banks.   Although there were more than 400 investment banks in the United States alone in 1996, the largest banks account for most of the activity in all lines of business. Exhibit 1.5 lists the top 15 global underwriters for 1994 and the amounts they underwrote. These underwriters accounted for 80–90 percent of all underwritten offers. Although U.S. underwriters hold a dominant position in their business, foreign underwriters, such as Nomura Securities and Swiss Bank, are strong competitors in global issues. In addition to those listed in Exhibit 1.5, other significant foreign underwriters include Deutsche Bank, Daiwa Securities, ABN-AMRO, Nikko Securities, Barclays, and National Westminster.

Result 1.3 summarizes the key points of this discussion.

Result 1.3   In the wake of the Great Depression, U.S. financial markets became more regulated. These regulations forced commercial banks, the most important provider of private capital, out of the investment banking business. These regulatory constraints were relaxed in the 1980s and 1990s, making the banking industry more competitive and providing corporations with greater variety in their sources of capital.

EXHIBIT 1.5   Top Global Underwriters of Debt and Equity, 1996

Underwriter	Amount of Debt and Equity Underwritten (billions of dollars)	Number of Issues Underwritten
Merrill Lynch	$187.7	1,329
Goldman Sachs	124.7	938
Lehman Brothers	112.2	875
Salomon Brothers	110.3	715
Morgan Stanley	105.5	675
J. P. Morgan	87.2	601
CS First Boston/Credit Suisse	83.5	602
Bear Stearns	45.9	399
Donaldson Lufkin Jenrette	35.6	264
Deutsche Morgan Grenfell	33.5	222
SBC Warburg	32.5	169
Union Bank of Switzerland (UBS)	30.7	263
Smith Barney	30.4	386
ABN AMRO Hoare Govett	22.3	148
Chase Manhattan	21.2	159

Source: Reprinted by permission of IDD Enterprises LP, © 1997 by *Investment Dealers' Digest*.

The Underwriting Process

The essential outline of investment banking in the United States has been in place for almost a century. The players have changed, of course, but the way they do business now is roughly the same as it was a century ago.

The underwriter of a security issue performs four functions: (1) origination, (2) distribution, (3) risk bearing, and (4) certification.

Origination.   **Origination** involves giving advice to the issuing firm about the type of security to issue, the timing of the issue, and the pricing of the issue. Origination also means working with the firm to develop the registration statement and forming a syndicate of investment bankers to market the issue. The managing or lead underwriter performs all these tasks.

Distribution.   The second function an underwriter performs is the **distribution**, or the selling, of the issue. Distribution is generally carried out by a syndicate of banks formed by the lead underwriter. The banks in the syndicate are listed in the prospectus along with how much of the issue each has agreed to sell. Once the registration is made effective, their names also appear on the **tombstone ad** in a newspaper which announces the issue and lists the underwriters participating in the syndicate.

Risk Bearing.   The third function the underwriter performs is **risk bearing**. In most cases, the underwriter has agreed to buy the securities the firm is selling and to resell them to its clients. The **Rules of Fair Practice** (promulgated by the National Association of Security Dealers) prevents the underwriter from selling the securities at a price higher than that agreed upon at the pricing meeting, so the underwriter's upside is limited. If the issue does poorly, the underwriter may be stuck with securities that must be sold at bargain prices. However, the actual risk that underwriters take when marketing securities is generally limited since most issues are not priced until the day, or even hours, before they go on sale. Until that final pricing meeting, the investment bank is not committed to selling the issue.

Certification.   An additional role of an investment bank is to certify the quality of an issue, which requires that the bank maintain a sound reputation in capital markets. An investment banker's reputation will quickly decline if the certification task is not performed correctly. If an underwriter substantially misprices an issue, its future business is likely to be damaged and it might even be sued. A study by Booth and Smith (1986) suggested that underwriters, aware of the costs associated with mispricing an issue, charge higher fees on issues that are harder to value.

The Underwriting Agreement

The **underwriting agreement** between the firm and the investment bank is the document that specifies what is being sold, the amount being sold, and the selling price. The agreement also specifies the **underwriting spread**, which is the difference between the total proceeds of the offering and the net proceeds that accrue to the issuing firm, and the existence and extent of the **overallotment option**. This option, sometimes called the **"Green-Shoe option"** after the firm that first used it, permits the investment banker to request that more shares be issued on the same terms as those already sold.[5] Exhibit 1.6, which contains parts of a stock prospectus, illustrates many of the features of the agreement.

The underwriting agreement also shows the amount of fixed fees the firm must pay, including listing fees, taxes, SEC fees, transfer agent's fees, legal and accounting costs, and printing expenses. In addition to these fixed fees, firms may have to pay several other forms of compensation to the underwriters. For example, underwriters often receive warrants as part of their compensation.[6]

Classifying Offerings

If a firm is issuing equity to the public for the first time, it is making an **initial public offering (IPO)**. If a firm is already publicly traded and is simply selling more common stock, it is making a **seasoned offering**. Both IPO's and seasoned offerings can include both primary and secondary issues. In a **primary issue**, the firm raises capital for itself by selling stock to the public; a **secondary issue** is undertaken by existing large shareholders who want to sell a substantial number of shares they currently own.[7]

---

[5]Since August 1983, the overallotment shares can be, at most, 15 percent of the amount issued, which means that if the agreement specifies that the underwriter will issue 1.0 million shares, the underwriter has the option to issue 1.15 million shares. Nearly all industrial offerings have overallotment options, which are generally set at 15 percent. In practice, investment bankers typically offer 115 percent of an offering for a firm going public and then stand ready to buy back 15 percent of the shares to support the price if demand in the secondary market is weak.

[6]See Barry, Muscarella, and Vetsuypens (1991). Also, Chapter 3 discusses warrants in more detail.

[7]Sometimes the term *secondary* means any non-IPO, even if the shares are primary. To avoid confusion, some investment bankers use the term *add-on*, meaning primary shares for an already public company.

EXHIBIT 1.6   A Stock Prospectus: Cover Page

PROSPECTUS

2,500,000 Shares

Common Stock

All of the 2,500,000 shares of common stock, $0.01 par value (the "Common Stock"), offered hereby are being sold by QuadraMed Corporation, a Delaware corporation ("QuadraMed" or the "Company"). Prior to this offering, there has been no public market for the Common Stock. See "Underwriting" for a discussion of the factors considered in determining the initial public offering price. The Common Stock has been approved for quotation on the Nasdaq National Market under the symbol "QMDC."

The shares offered hereby involve a high degree of risk.

See "Risk Factors" beginning on page 6 herein for a discussion of certain matters that should be considered by potential investors.

THESE SECURITIES HAVE NOT BEEN APPROVED OR DISAPPROVED BY THE SECURITIES AND EXCHANGE COMMISSION OR ANY STATE SECURITIES COMMISSION NOR HAS THE SECURITIES AND EXCHANGE COMMISSION OR ANY STATE SECURITIES COMMISSION PASSED UPON THE ACCURACY OR ADEQUACY OF THIS PROSPECTUS. ANY REPRESENTATION TO THE CONTRARY IS A CRIMINAL OFFENSE.

	Price to Public	Underwriting Discount(1)	Proceeds to Company(2)
Per Share	$12.00	$.84	$11.16
Total(3)	$30,000,000	$2,100,000	$27,900,000

---

(1) The Company has agreed to indemnify the several underwriters identified elsewhere herein (the "Underwriters") against certain liabilities under the Securities Act of 1933, as amended (the "Securities Act"). See "Underwriting."

(2) Before deducting expenses payable by the Company estimated at $900,000.

(3) The Company has granted the Underwriters a 30-day option to purchase up to 375,000 additional shares of Common Stock on the same terms and conditions as set forth above, solely to cover over-allotments, if any. If the Underwriters exercise this option in full, the total Price to Public, Underwriting Discount and Proceeds to Company will be $34,500,000, $2,415,000 and $32,085,000, respectively. See "Underwriting."

The shares of Common Stock are offered by the Underwriters, subject to prior sale, when, as and if issued to and accepted by the Underwriters and subject to approval of certain legal matters by counsel for the Underwriters. It is expected that delivery of the Common Stock will be made against payment therefor on or about October 15, 1996, in New York, New York.

Jefferies & Company, Inc.   Pacific Growth Equities, Inc.

October 10, 1996

(continued)

EXHIBIT 1.6   (*continued*)   A Stock Prospectus: An Underwriting

UNDERWRITING

Subject to the terms and conditions of the Underwriting Agreement, the Company has agreed to sell an aggregate of 2,500,000 shares of Common Stock to the Underwriters named below (the "Underwriters"), for whom Jefferies & Company, Inc. and Pacific Growth Equities, Inc. are acting as representatives ("Representatives"), and the underwriters have severally agreed to purchase from the Company the number of shares of Common Stock set forth opposite their respective names in the table below at the price set forth on the cover page of this Prospectus.

Underwriter	Number of Shares
Jefferies & Company, Inc.	930,000
Pacific Growth Equities, Inc.	930,000
Bear, Stearns & Co. Inc.	40,000
Alex. Brown & Sons Incorporated	40,000
Donaldson, Lufkin & Jenrette Securities Corporation	40,000
Lehman Brothers Inc.	40,000
Montgomery Securities	40,000
Morgan Stanley & Co. Incorporated	40,000
Prudential Securities Incorporated	40,000
Smith Barney Inc.	40,000
Brean Murray, Foster Securities, Inc.	20,000
Cowen & Company	20,000
Fahnestock & Co. Inc.	20,000
First of Michigan Corporation	20,000
Hampshire Securities Corporation	20,000
M.H. Meyerson & Co. Inc.	20,000
Morgan Keegan & Company, Inc.	20,000
Needham & Company, Inc.	20,000
Piper Jaffray Inc.	20,000
Punk, Ziegel & Knoell	20,000
The Robinson-Humphrey Company, Inc.	20,000
Unterberg Harris	20,000
Vector Securities International, Inc.	20,000
Wessels, Arnold & Henderson, L.L.C.	20,000
Wheat First Butcher Singer	20,000
The Williams Capital Group, L.P.	20,000
Total	2,500,000

The Underwriting Agreement provides that the obligation of the Underwriters to purchase shares of Common Stock is subject to certain conditions. The Underwriters are committed to purchase all of the shares of Common Stock (other than those covered by the over-allotment option described below), if any are purchased.

The Underwriters propose to offer the Common Stock to the public initially at the public offering price set forth on the cover page of this Prospectus, and to certain dealers at such price less a concession not in excess of $0.52 per share. The Underwriters may allow, and such dealers may reallow, a discount not in excess of $0.10 per share to certain other dealers. After this offering, the public offering price, the concession to selected dealers and the reallowance to other dealers may be changed by the Representatives. The Representatives have informed the Company that the Underwriters do not intend to confirm sales to any accounts over which they exercise discretionary authority.

The Company has also granted to the Underwriters an option, exercisable for 30 days from the date of this Prospectus, to purchase up to 375,000 additional shares of Common Stock at the public offering price, less the underwriting discount. To the extent such option is exercised, each Underwriter will become obligated, subject to certain conditions, to purchase additional shares of Common Stock proportionate to such Underwriter's initial commitment as indicated above in the preceding table. The Underwriters may exercise such right of purchase only for the purpose of covering over-allotments, if any, made in connection with the sale of the shares of Common Stock.

The Costs of Debt and Equity Issues

Exhibit 1.7 shows the direct costs of both seasoned and unseasoned equity offerings as well as the direct costs of bond offerings. Three things stand out: First, debt fees are lower than equity fees. This is not surprising in view of equity's larger exposure to risk and the fact that bonds are much easier to price than stock. Second, there are economies of scale in issuing. As a percentage of the proceeds, fixed fees decline as issue size rises. Again, this is not surprising given that the expenses classified under fixed fees simply do not vary much. Whether a firm sells $1 million or $100 million, the auditors, for example, have the same basic job to do. Finally, initial public offerings are much more expensive than seasoned offerings because the initial public offerings are far riskier and much more difficult to price.[8]

Result 1.4 summarizes the main points of this subsection.

Result 1.4   Issuing public debt and equity can be a lengthy and expensive process. For large corporations, the issuance of public debt is relatively routine and the costs are relatively low. However, equity is much more costly to issue for large as well as small firms, and it is especially costly for firms issuing equity for the first time.

Types of Underwriting Arrangements

Firm Commitment vs. Best-Efforts Offering.   A public offering can be executed on either a firm commitment or a best-efforts basis. In a **firm commitment offering**, the underwriter agrees to buy the whole offering from the firm at a set price and to offer it to the public at a slightly higher price. In this case, the underwriter bears the risk of not selling the issue, and the firm's proceeds are guaranteed. In a **best-efforts offering**, the underwriter and the firm fix a price and the minimum and maximum number of shares to be sold. The underwriter then makes the "best effort" to sell the issue. Investors express their interest by depositing payments into the underwriter's escrow account. If the underwriter has not sold the minimum number of shares after a specified period, usually 90 days, the offer is withdrawn, the money refunded, and the issuing firm can try again later. Nearly all seasoned offerings are made with firm commitment offerings. The more well-known firms that do IPOs tend to use firm commitment offerings for their IPOs, but the less established firms tend to go public with best-efforts offerings.

Negotiated vs. Competitive Offering.   The issuing firm also can choose between a negotiated offering and a competitive offering. In a **negotiated offering**, the firm negotiates the underwriting agreement with the underwriter. In a **competitive offering**, the firm specifies the underwriting agreement and puts it out to bid. In practice, except for a few utilities that are required to use them, firms almost never use competitive offerings. This is somewhat puzzling since competitive offerings generally have lower issue costs.[9]

Shelf Offerings.   Another way to offer securities is through a **shelf offering**. In 1982, the SEC adopted **Rule 415** which permits a firm to register all the securities it plans to issue within two years. The firm can file one registration statement and make offerings in any amount and at any time without further notice to the SEC. When the need for financing arises, the firm simply asks an investment bank for a bid to take the securities

---

[8]The costs associated with initial public offerings of equity will be discussed in detail in Chapter 3.

[9]For a discussion of this matter, see Bhagat and Frost (1986).

EXHIBIT 1.7   **Direct Costs as a Percentage of Gross Proceeds for Equity (IPOs and SEOs) and Straight and Convertible Bonds Offered by Domestic Operating Companies, 1990–1994**

Proceeds (millions of dollars)	Equity						Bonds					
	IPOs			SEOs			Convertible Bonds			Straight Bonds		
	GS[a]	E[b]	TDC[c]	GS	E	TDC	GS	E	TDC	GS	E	TDC
$ 2–9.99	9.05%	7.91%	16.96%	7.72%	5.56%	13.28%	6.07%	2.68%	8.75%	2.07%	2.32%	4.39%
10–19.99	7.24	4.39	11.63	6.23	2.49	8.72	5.48	3.18	8.66	1.36	1.40	2.76
20–39.99	7.01	2.69	9.70	5.60	1.33	6.93	4.16	1.95	6.11	1.54	0.88	2.42
40–59.99	6.96	1.76	8.72	5.05	0.82	5.87	3.26	1.04	4.30	0.72	0.60	1.32
60–79.99	6.74	1.46	8.20	4.57	0.61	5.18	2.64	0.59	3.23	1.76	0.58	2.34
80–99.99	6.47	1.44	7.91	4.25	0.48	4.73	2.43	0.61	3.04	1.55	0.61	2.16
100–199.99	6.03	1.03	7.06	3.85	0.37	4.22	2.34	0.42	2.76	1.77	0.54	2.31
200–499.99	5.67	0.86	6.53	3.26	0.21	3.47	1.99	0.19	2.18	1.79	0.40	2.19
500 and up	5.21	0.51	5.72	3.03	0.12	3.15	2.00	0.09	2.09	1.39	0.25	1.64
Average	7.31%	3.69%	11.00%	5.44%	1.67%	7.11%	2.92%	0.87%	3.79%	1.62%	0.62%	2.24%

Note:
[a]GS—gross spreads as a percentage of total proceeds, including management fee, underwriting fee, and selling concession.
[b]E—other direct expenses as a percentage of total proceeds, including management fee, underwriting fee, and selling concession.
[c]TDC—total direct costs as a percentage of total proceeds (total direct costs are the sum of gross spreads and other direct expenses).
Source: Reprinted with permission from the *Journal of Financial Research,* Vol. 19, No. 1 (Spring 1996), pp. 59–74, "The Costs of Raising Capital," by Inmoo Lee, Scott Lochhead, Jay Ritter, and Quanshui Zhao.

"off the shelf" and sell them. If the issuing firm is not satisfied with this bid, it can shop among other investment banks for better bids.

Rights Offerings.   Finally, for firms selling common stock, there is a possibility of a **rights offering**. Rights entitle existing shareholders to buy new shares in the firm at what is generally a discounted price. Rights offerings can be made without investment bankers or with them on a standby basis. A rights offering on a **standby basis** includes an agreement by the investment bank to take up any unexercised rights and exercise them, paying the subscription price to the firm in exchange for the new shares.

In some cases, rights are actively traded after they are distributed by the firm. The opening vignette to this chapter describes how Time Warner used a rights offering to raise additional equity capital in 1991. As the case study below illustrates with respect to this offering, the value of a right is usually close to the value of the stock less the **subscription price**, which is the price that the rights holders must pay for the stock.

The Time Warner Rights Offer
The Time Warner rights offer became a fixed-price rights offering after the controversy about the variable subscription price. The right gave shareholders the option to purchase one share at $80 per share for each right owned. Time Warner issued three rights for each five shares owned. If you purchased the stock on the July 16, 1991, or later, you did not receive the right. The rights expired on August 5, 1991.

Exhibit 1.8 shows Time Warner's stock price [column (*a*)], the price at which the rights traded [column (*b*)], the exercise value of a right [column (*c*)], and the difference, which

EXHIBIT 1.8   Daily Prices for the 1991 Time Warner Rights Offer

Date	Stock Price (a)	Rights Price (b)	Exercise Value (c)	Difference (c) − (b)
July 15	$88.750	$5.500	$8.750	$3.250
July 16	86.750	7.250	6.750	−0.500
July 17	87.625	8.250	7.625	−0.625
July 18	88.125	8.875	8.125	−0.750
July 19	87.250	8.250	7.250	−1.000
July 22	86.500	7.000	6.500	−0.500
July 23	85.375	6.375	5.375	−1.000
July 24	83.750	4.625	3.750	−0.875
July 25	84.875	5.500	4.875	−0.625
July 26	83.750	4.250	3.750	−0.500
July 29	82.500	2.500	2.500	$0.000
July 30	82.750	3.125	2.750	−0.375
July 31	84.750	4.750	4.750	$0.000
Aug. 1	85.750	5.625	5.750	$0.125
Aug. 2	85.000	5.000	5.000	$0.000
Aug. 5	85.000	4.500	5.000	$0.500

is calculated as the exercise value, estimated as the stock price minus the exercise price of a right, minus the market price of a right. After July 15, the last date at which the stock price is worth both the value of the stock and the value of the right, the stock price drops, reflecting the loss of the right. From July 16 on, the market price of a right is close to its exercise value.

The Time Warner rights offer was unusual in many respects. First, it was one of the largest equity offerings. Second, the original structure of the deal was unique. Finally, only rarely do U.S. firms choose to use rights offerings to issue new equity.

Some financial economists are puzzled that so few firms use rights offerings since the direct cost of a rights issue is substantially less than the direct cost of an underwritten offering. A plausible explanation for this is that rights offerings, when used, are less expensive because firms using them have a large-block shareholder who has agreed to take up the offer. This is true in Europe, where large-block shareholders, who are likely to agree to exercise the rights, are more prevalent.[10] Where rights are not used, there may be no large-block shareholders, which would make the rights offering more expensive. In addition, studies of the costs of rights offers examine only the costs to the firm and ignore the costs to the shareholders, which could conceivably be quite large.

---

[10]Eckbo and Masulis (1992), Hansen (1988), and Hansen and Pinkerton (1982) discuss the various trade-offs between underwritten and rights offerings. Rights offerings may also be more popular in Europe because of regulatory reasons.

1.4 Raising Capital in International Markets

Capital markets have truly become global. U.S. firms raise funds from almost all parts of the world. Similarly, U.S. investors provide capital for foreign as well as domestic firms. A firm can raise money internationally in two general ways: in what are known as the Euromarkets or in the domestic markets of various countries.

Euromarkets

The term Euromarkets is something of a misnomer because the markets have no true physical location. Instead, **Euromarkets** are simply a collection of large international banks that help firms issue bonds and make loans outside the country in which the firm is located. Firms domiciled in the United States could, for instance, issue dollar-denominated bonds known as **Eurodollar bonds** outside the United States or yen-denominated bonds known as **Euroyen bonds** outside Japan. Or a German multinational could borrow through the Euromarkets in either British pounds or Swiss francs.

Direct Issuance

The second way to raise money internationally is to sell directly in the foreign markets, or what is called **direct issuance**. For example, a U.S. corporation could issue a yen-denominated bond in the Japanese bond market. Or a German firm might sell stock to U.S. investors and list its stock on one of the U.S. exchanges. Being a foreign issuer in a domestic market means satisfying all the regulations that apply to domestic firms as well as special regulations that might apply only to foreign issuers.

1.5 Major Financial Markets outside the United States

We now focus on three important countries—Germany, the United Kingdom, and Japan—to analyze how their financial systems differ from the U.S. financial system. These three countries have the largest capital markets outside the United States.

Germany

Germany has the third largest economy in the world, behind the United States and Japan. However, its financial system is quite different from those of the other major economies. In particular, German firms rely much more on commercial banks to obtain their capital.

Universal Banking.   One of the most important differences between the U.S. and German financial systems is that Germany has universal banking—its banks can engage in both commercial and investment banking—which is precluded in the United States under the Glass Steagall Act (although, as noted earlier, the situation in the United States is about to change). The three largest banks, Deutsche Bank, Dresdner Bank, and Commerzbank, are universal banks. German firms generally do business with one main bank, a *Hausbank,* which handles stock and bond placements, extends short- and long-term credit, and possibly has an ownership position in the firm. For German multinationals, the main bank is usually one of the Big Three. There are, however, several large regional banks (Bayerische Vereinsbank, DG Bank, and Bayerische Hypotheken und Wechsel-Bank) that are nearly the equivalent of the Big Three in terms of financing German firms.

Public vs. Private Capital Markets.   A second difference between the German and the U.S. capital markets is that in Germany publicly traded equity has not been an important source of funds for firms. A large portion of German firms are privately financed. The German stock market capitalization is about 25 percent of the German gross domestic product (GDP) as opposed to being roughly 70 percent of GDP for the United States or Japan. The Frankfurt Stock Exchange, which trades both stocks and bonds and is the largest exchange in Germany, had more than DM 300 billion worth of issues in 1994, of which only DM 15 billion represented equity. These figures are echoed by the level of initial public offerings in Germany. In the 1980s, roughly 200 firms went public in Germany; more than 20 times that number went public in the United States.

Corporate Governance.   The third difference between the German and the U.S. capital markets lies in the area of corporate governance, which is in turn affected by the first two differences. By law, listed German firms have two-tiered boards of directors. The *Vorstand,* or management board, is composed of company executives who manage the firm on a day-to-day basis. The *Aufsichtsrat,* or supervisory board, consists of 10 to 20 members, half of which must be worker representatives. The other half of this board is elected by shareholders; these directors are similar to outside directors in the United States. It is common for these directors to be substantial shareholders in the firm either directly or indirectly as representatives of the banks, insurance companies, or families that have financed the firm. Kester (1992) estimated that banks and insurance firms own about 20 percent of the stock in German firms; the comparable figure in the United States is about 5 percent. Large-block shareholdings probably account for roughly 60 percent of the total stockholdings in Germany; that figure is about 10 percent in the United States.

Banks can vote the shares they own, as well as the shares they hold in "street name"; that is, those shares owned by customers but held in bank brokerage accounts and mutual funds. These additional shares give banks more voting power and thus greater influence than their own shareholdings would command per se.

Other Differences between the United States and Germany.   The German financial system has several other, less salient, differences from the U.S. system. In Germany, a number of specialized banks restrict their activities to specific industries such as shipbuilding, agriculture, and brewing. The *Landesbanken,* owned by state governments and regional savings bank associations, are active in financing German firms. Several of them (e.g., Bayerische Landesbank and Westdeutsche Landesbank) are among the 10 largest banks in Germany. Finally, foreign commercial banks in Germany have approximately 5 percent of the market share of total assets, but they conduct much more than 5 percent of the transactions in, for example, Eurobond issues, foreign currency trading, and derivatives.

Deregulation.   Deregulation in Germany, as in the United States, is changing the markets and the way firms raise capital. Until the early 1990s, the commercial paper market was nonexistent in Germany.[11] In 1991, the government abolished a tax that discouraged transactions in commercial paper and the Ministry of Finance no longer required the approval of domestic debt issues. This deregulation led to the emergence of a growing commercial paper market, making it the fourth largest in Europe, and a growing bond

---

[11]Commercial paper is described in Chapter 2.

market. Although the domestic bond market is small (DM 500 million in 1994), German Eurobond placements in recent years have been in the DM 60–90 billion range.

Japan

At first glance, the Japanese financial system appears similar to that of the United States. Commercial and investment banking are separate and firms must file registration statements to issue securities. The Tokyo Stock Exchange is the second largest in the world, after the New York Stock Exchange, and the Japanese also have active markets in bonds, commercial paper, and Euromarket offerings. However, this superficial similarity masks a financial system that is markedly different from that in the United States. In particular, banks are much more influential in Japan than in the United States, and cross-ownership with interlocking directorships is much more common. We now touch briefly on these two important aspects of Japanese finance.

The Role of Japanese Banks.   Exhibit 1.9 shows that 8 of the 10 largest banks in the world are located in Japan. Measured by assets, the 10 largest Japanese banks have more than three times the assets of the 10 largest U.S. banks—in an economy that is two-thirds the size of the U.S. economy. Japan's largest banks are called "city banks," something of a misnomer because they are nationwide banks. These 10 city banks are the primary suppliers of funds to Japanese firms. A city bank serves as the so-called "main bank" for each large industrial corporation in Japan.

Historically, banks have been the major source of funds for Japanese firms, furnishing more than half of the financing needs of Japanese firms in the 1970s and 1980s. In recent years, however, as Japanese bond markets have developed, this proportion has fallen to approximately one-third of the funds needed.[12]

As in Germany, many Japanese firms are affiliated with a "main bank" which takes an active role in monitoring the decisions of the borrowing firm's management. Furthermore, additional lenders, such as other banks and insurance companies, look to the main bank for approval when loaning a firm money. Finally, the banks have significant powers to seize collateral, both as a direct lender and as a trustee for secured bond issues.[13]

The influence of Japanese banks is further enhanced by their stock ownership. In contrast with the United States, Japanese banks can hold common stock, although the holdings of any single bank in a firm are limited to 5 percent of a company's shares. Even though 5 percent is not a large block, banks collectively own more than 20 percent of the total shares outstanding. When combined with insurance companies, the ownership percentage of financial institutions rises to 40 percent. A study by Kester (1992) estimated that the top five shareholders in major Japanese firms own about 20 percent of the shares, forming a voting block that cannot be ignored. The large-block shareholders frequently meet to exchange information about the financial condition of the firm, and representatives of the main bank do not hesitate to step in when the firm experiences difficulties.

Cross-Holdings and *Keiretsus*.   The large cross-holdings of Japanese firms are a significant feature of the Japanese financial system. Japanese corporations typically own stock in other Japanese corporations which in turn also own stock in the corporations that partly own them. A *keiretsu* is a group of firms in different industries bound together

---

[12]See Hodder and Tschoegl (1993).
[13]Ibid.

EXHIBIT 1.9   Assets of the 10 Largest Banks in the World

Bank Name	Headquarters Location	Total Assets as of Dec. 31, 1995 (in billions of dollars)
Deutsche Bank	Frankfurt, Germany	$502
Sanwa Bank	Osaka, Japan	500
Sumitomo Bank	Osaka, Japan	498
Dai-Ichi Kangyo Bank	Tokyo, Japan	497
Fuji Bank	Tokyo, Japan	486
Sakura Bank	Tokyo, Japan	477
Mitsubishi Bank	Tokyo, Japan	474
Norinchukin Bank	Tokyo, Japan	428
Credit Agricole Mutuel	Paris, France	384
Industrial Bank of Japan	Tokyo, Japan	360

Source: © 1996 American Bankers Association. Reprinted with permission. All rights reserved.

by cross-ownership of their common stock and by customer-supplier relationships. Kester provides an example of Mitsubishi *keiretsu* members, which as a group, hold 25 percent of the shares of the group members' companies. The substantial cross-holdings of customers and suppliers means that firms are less subject to contractual problems. For example, an automobile manufacturer may be less likely to sue the company supplying its steel if the steel company owns a significant percentage of the automobile company's stock and the automobile company owns a significant percentage of the steel company's stock. For similar reasons, group members tend to help each other when a member of the group experiences financial difficulties.

Deregulation.   Until the 1980s, Japan's bond and stock markets were highly regulated, effectively preventing Japanese firms from raising money in the public markets. For instance, most firms could not issue unsecured bonds until 1988. Moreover, firms could not issue foreign currency bonds (e.g., Eurobonds) and swap the proceeds into yen until 1984, and the Ministry of Finance did not allow a commercial paper market until 1988.

The main bank system and the influence of the main bank appear to be waning as a result of the 1980s deregulation of Japanese financial markets. One piece of evidence that bank debt has become a less important source of funds is that debt and equity issues more than doubled, from about 5 percent in the 1970s to more than 10 percent in the 1980s. It seems likely that further deregulation—abolishing the separation of commercial and industrial banking and removing limits on debt issues—will occur, leading to even more public capital and a concomitant reduction in the influence of the main bank.[14]

United Kingdom

Along with New York and Tokyo, London is one of the great financial centers of the world. Among those three financial centers, it has the distinction of being the oldest and

---

[14]See Hoshi, Kashyap, and Scharfstein (1990).

the most international. Just as "Wall Street" connotes both a physical location and the set of capital markets and associated firms in the United States, "the City" refers to both a physical location in London and the set of markets and firms that do business there.

Though the activities of the City started in the 1600s, it assumed its dominant position in the 18th century and remained in that position until World War I. Following the economic disruptions of two world wars and the Great Depression, London's place as the leading financial center of the world gradually gave way to New York and, more recently, Tokyo. Nonetheless, London remains the leading market for international transactions in stocks, bonds, and foreign exchange.

Deregulation: The Big Bang.   Like many financial markets, London benefited from deregulation in the 1980s. As international capital flows increased in the 1970s, London was in danger of losing business to other markets. In particular, fixed brokerage commissions were causing large institutional investors to take their trade elsewhere. In response to competitive pressures, the London Stock Exchange instituted a wide ranging series of changes in October 1986 that have come to be known as the **"Big Bang."** The Big Bang produced four major changes:

1. The elimination of fixed commissions.
2. The granting of permission to foreign banks and securities firms to enter the British market on their own or to buy domestic firms, thus exposing British domestic firms to intense competition.
3. The elimination of the system of wholesale traders (jobbers) and retail traders (brokers) in favor of a system where members were free to act as both brokers and dealers.[15]
4. The introduction of a computerized trading system, much like the NASDAQ system in the United States.[16]

The results of these reforms were dramatic. Average transaction costs fell by 50 percent or more. Prior to the Big Bang, five jobbers (brokers) handled essentially all the transactions. After the Big Bang, more than 30 securities firms became market makers. With increased competition, lower costs, and the increase in stock prices, trading in London quadrupled in the two years following the Big Bang.

Just as stock exchange members were exposed to more competition in the 1980s, so too were other financial firms. The Big Bang induced many more international banks to do business in London. Of the more than 500 banks in London in 1996, nearly two-thirds were foreign banks or subsidiaries of foreign parents. These foreign banks hold more than 80 percent of nonsterling deposits and about 20 percent of sterling deposits.[17] Thus, in both numbers and funds, foreign banks are a major force in London. Because London is the center of the Euromarkets, all the major U.S. and Japanese banks have subsidiaries there. The extensive interbank buying and selling of deposits explains the dominance of LIBOR, the London interbank offered rate, which is the interest rate at which banks in London borrow and lend to each other. It also is the benchmark rate used to set the rate on loans all over the world.

---

[15]See Chapter 3 for a discussion of brokers and dealers.

[16]See Chapter 3 for a discussion of exchanges, including the National Association of Security Dealers Automated Quotation System (NASDAQ).

[17]The pound sterling, often shortened to sterling, is the currency of the U.K. Hence, nonsterling deposits refer to U.S. dollars, yen, Swiss franc, and deutsche mark deposits in London banks.

The Banking Sector.   Although the British banking system has a much more international flavor than the American system, in other respects it is surprisingly similar. In the past, a British firm's commercial banking and investment banking needs were serviced by separate banks, even though this is not mandated by law as it is in the United States. This appears to be changing. The Bank of England, which regulates banks in the United Kingdom, has not discouraged universal banking, but historically there have been two main types of banks: clearing banks, which are similar to commercial banks in the United States, and merchant banks, which are similar to U.S. investment banks. The four largest clearing banks—National Westminster, Barclays, Midland, and Lloyds—perform the same services as U.S. commercial banks. The merchant banks, the largest of which are SBC Warburg, Morgan Grenfell (now owned by Deutsche Bank), and Kleinwort Benson, perform the same functions as investment banks in the United States.

Because the United Kingdom has no law similar to the Glass-Steagall Act, banks are free to engage in whatever businesses they wish. As a result, clearing banks have established subsidiaries to undertake the full range of investment banking activities, and merchant banks have moved from solely financial advising (e.g., underwriting, syndication, and portfolio management) to become securities dealers and brokers in stocks and bonds. Given the increased competition in both commercial and investment banking, a consolidation of banks seems likely in the United Kingdom, similar to that taking place in the United States in the 1990s.

The similarity between the banking structures in the United States and the United Kingdom also extends to the influence of banks on the management of domestic firms. In contrast to the power of the banks in Germany and Japan, U.K. banks, like U.S. banks, are not strongly involved in the firms with which they do business. Stock ownership by banks is not prohibited, but banks have seemingly been reluctant to assume the risks entailed in equity ownership. Despite the banks' reluctance to hold major stakes, the U.K. equity market is almost completely dominated by institutional investors. About 85 percent of the common stock of U.K. firms is held by institutions such as insurance companies, pension funds, and mutual funds. Trading by these institutions accounts for more than 90 percent of the volume on the London Stock Exchange.

Although U.K. banks have not been major equity holders, they have traditionally been an important source of funds for firms. While the most important source of funds for U.K. firms is internal, accounting for roughly 50–70 percent of total sources, banks supply about 75 percent of the external capital raised by U.K. firms.

Public Security Markets.   In terms of raising new debt and equity, the U.K. public markets occupy a middle position. They are relatively more important than public markets in Germany and Japan but less important than those in the United States. For instance, from 1970–1992 more than 340 firms a year went public in the United States. Comparable figures for Germany are 8–10 firms a year; for Japan, 35–45 firms a year; and for the United Kingdom, which has a much smaller economy than either Germany or Japan, 50–60 firms a year.

The process of going public in the United Kingdom is similar to the process in the United States. The firm hires an underwriter who advises the firm about timing and pricing and helps in the preparation of a prospectus. In the United Kingdom, however, shares are sold in several different ways that are not observed in the United States. For example, when a firm uses an **offer for sale by tender**, the shares are auctioned off, with the price set at the minimum bid that leads to the sale of the number of shares desired. When *placing* securities, which combines aspects of a private placement and a public sale, up to 75 percent of the issue may be privately placed with institutions, but at least

25 percent must be offered to the public market. In contrast with the United States, seasoned equity issues are nearly all accomplished through rights offerings. By law, U.K. firms must offer shareholders the rights unless shareholders have granted a temporary waiver.

Like the capital markets in other financial centers, the London market is experiencing the difficulties of adjusting to a global capital market. The London Stock Exchange, like the U.S. exchanges, is struggling with how best to organize trading across many different kinds of financial instruments. The clearing banks and merchant banks are attempting to figure out which combinations make sense and which lines of business are profitable. British firms, like their counterparts elsewhere, are bypassing traditional financial intermediaries and are going directly to the capital markets to obtain financing. It is hard to predict when and how these forces will work themselves out, but we can be reasonably certain that the outcome will make London an even more international market than it is today.

1.6 Trends in Raising Capital

This chapter has so far provided a general overview of the process of how the modern firm raises capital. Much of what you have learned—the sources of external financing, the process of issuing securities, parts of the regulatory environment—has remained the same for decades and, in some cases, as long as a century. In many respects, however, the capital markets throughout the world have changed dramatically over the past 10 to 20 years and should continue to change in the future. Although no one can predict the future, we should note a number of trends in the capital markets.

Globalization

Capital markets are now global. Large multinational firms routinely issue debt and equity outside their home country. By taking advantage of the differences in taxes and regulations across countries, corporations can sometimes lower their cost of funds. As firms are better able to shop globally for capital, we can expect regulations around the world to become similar and the taxes associated with raising capital to decline. As a result, the costs of raising capital in different parts of the world are likely to equalize.

Deregulation

Deregulation and globalization go hand in hand. Capital will tend to go to countries where returns are large and restrictions on inflows and outflows are small. As countries have opened up their domestic markets to foreign issues and foreign buyers, firms and investors have responded with massive capital movements. In turn, countries now find it difficult to maintain highly regulated capital markets because capital flows to other countries escape this regulation so easily.

Innovative Instruments

Globalization has also spurred financial innovation. Wall Street firms have cleverly designed new instruments that (1) allow firms to avoid the constraints and costs imposed by governments, (2) tailor securities to appeal to new sets of investors, and (3) allow firms to diminish the effects of fluctuating interest and exchange rates. The result is an astonishing range of financial instruments available in the global marketplace.

Technology

Technology allows many of these recent trends to take place. The ability to simultaneously issue billions of dollars of securities in a score of countries across the globe, to trade trillions of dollars in the secondary markets, and to price new instruments requires the latest information technology. Technology is likely to lead to continuous, 24-hour trading around the world, thus producing a true world market in some securities.

Securitization

Securitization is the process of bundling, that is, combining, financial instruments that are not securities, registering the bundles as securities, and selling them directly to the public. For example, securitization has produced a revolution in the mortgage market through the creation of collateralized mortgage obligations (CMOs), which consist of bundles of publicly traded mortgages. It has also launched a whole new market in asset-backed securities. Firms can now sell assets, like their accounts receivable, that were previously costly or impossible to sell.

Result 1.5   Current trends are likely to have an important influence on how corporations raise capital in the future. These include the globalization and deregulation of capital markets, an abundance of new financial instruments, more efficient trading technology, and securitization.

1.7 Summary and Conclusions

Because of the changes taking place in financial markets, financial managers face vastly more complex choices now than they did 20 years ago. Because of this increase in complexity, corporate finance professionals are required to have an advanced knowledge of how these financial markets operate, how financial instruments are priced, and how they can be used to add value to their corporations.

This text is devoted to making its readers adept at dealing with the new world of finance around them and the new challenges they face in this world. The first step in developing the necessary skills is to become familiar with what the new world looks like, who the players are, and what the choices are. In this vein, this chapter has attempted to broadly describe the securities available for external financing, current trends in financing the firm, the institutional and regulatory environment in which securities are issued, the process of issuing securities, and global differences and recent trends in raising capital. A more detailed discussion of the debt and equity markets will be provided in the following two chapters.

Key Concepts

Result 1.1: Debt is the most frequently used source of outside capital. The important distinctions between debt and equity are:

- Debt claims are senior to equity claims.
- Interest payments on debt claims are tax deductible, but dividends on equity claims are not.

Result 1.2: U.S. corporations raise capital from both private and public sources. The advantages associated with private sources include:

- The terms of private bonds and stock can be customized for individual investors.
- No costly registration with the SEC.

- No need to reveal confidential information.
- Easier to renegotiate.

Privately placed financial instruments also can have disadvantages.

- Limited investor base.
- Less liquid.

Result 1.3: In the wake of the Great Depression, U.S. financial markets became more regulated. These regulations forced commercial banks, the most important provider of private capital, out of the investment banking business. These regulatory constraints were relaxed in the 1980s and 1990s, making the banking industry more competitive and providing

corporations with greater variety in their sources of capital

Result 1.4: Issuing public debt and equity can be a lengthy and expensive process. For large corporations, the issuance of public debt is relatively routine and the costs are relatively low. However, equity is much more costly to issue for large as well as small firms, and it is especially costly for firms issuing equity for the first time.

Result 1.5: Current trends are likely to have an important influence on how corporations raise capital in the future. These include the globalization and deregulation of capital markets, an abundance of new financial instruments, more efficient trading technology, and securitization.

Key Terms

Exercises

1.1 In many European countries such as the United Kingdom and Switzerland, rights issues are much more common than the public, underwritten offers that firms in the United States chiefly use. Can you think of some reasons for this?

1.2 In a rights offering with a fixed price for exercising the right, does it matter what the exercise price is? Do shareholders care? Explain.

1.3 Competitive underwritings are cheaper than negotiated ones, but almost no firms use the former. Can you give some reasons for this?

1.4 The Securities Exchange Act of 1934 made insider trading illegal. What are the costs and benefits of prohibiting insider trading?

1.5 Smaller firms tend to raise most of their outside capital from private sources, mainly banks. As firms become larger, they obtain greater proportions of their outside capital needs from the public markets. Explain why.

1.6 Why do you think the largest banks in the world are in Japan and Germany, not the United States? Do you expect this to change in the future?

References and Additional Readings

Ang, James, and Terry Richardson. "The Underwriting Experience of Commercial Bank Affiliates Prior to the Glass-Steagall Act: A Re-examination of Evidence for Passage of the Act." *Journal of Banking and Finance* 18 (1994), pp. 351–95.

Barry, Christopher; Chris Muscarella; and Michael Vetsuypens. "Underwriter Warrants, Underwriter Compensation, and the Costs of Going Public. *Journal of Financial Economics* 29 (1991), pp. 113–35.

Bhagat, Sanjai. "The Effect of Management's Choice between Negotiated and Competitive Equity Offerings on Shareholder Wealth." *Journal of Financial and Quantitative Analysis* 21 (1985), pp. 181–96.

———. "The Effect of Pre-emptive Right Amendments on Shareholder Wealth. *Journal of Financial Economics* 12 (1983), pp. 289–310.

Bhagat, Sanjai, and Peter Frost. "Issuing Costs to Existing Shareholders in Competitive and Negotiated Underwritten Public Utility Equity Offerings." *Journal of Financial Economics* 15 (1986), pp. 233–60.

Bhagat, Sanjai; M. Wayne Marr; and G. Rodney Thompson. "The Rule 415 Experiment: Equity Markets." *Journal of Finance* 40 (1985), pp. 1385–1401.

Booth, James R., and Richard L. Smith II. "Capital Raising Underwriting and the Certification Hypothesis." *Journal of Financial Economics* 15 (1/2) (1986), pp. 261–81.

Carosso, Vincent. *Investment Banking in America.* Boston: Harvard University Press, 1970.

Creating World Class Financial Management. New York: Business International Corp., 1992.

Denis, David. "Shelf Registration and the Market for Seasoned Equity Offerings." *Journal of Business* 64 (1991), pp. 189–212.

Dyl, Edward, and Michael Joehnk. "Competitive versus Negotiated underwriting of Public Utility Debt." *Bell Journal of Economics* 7 (1976), pp. 680–89.

Eckbo, B. Espen, and Ronald Masulis. "Adverse Selection and the Rights Offer Paradox." *Journal of Financial Economics* 32 (1992), pp. 293–332.

Economist Intelligence Unit. *Financing Foreign Operations.* London: Business International Group, 1992–1994.

Global Treasury Management. Bill Millar, ed. New York: Harper Business, 1991.

Hansen, Robert. "The Demise of the Rights Issue." *Review of Financial Studies* 1 (1988), pp. 289–309.

Hansen, Robert, and John Pinkerton. "Direct Equity Financing: A Resolution of a Paradox." *Journal of Finance* 37 (1982), pp. 651–65.

Hansen, Robert, and Paul Torregrosa. "Underwriter Compensation and Corporate Monitoring. *Journal of Finance* 47 (1992), pp. 1537–55.

Hodder, James, and Adrian Tschoegl. "Corporate Finance in Japan." In *Japanese Capital Markets.* Shinji Takagi, ed. Cambridge, MA: Blackwell, 1993.

Holderness, Clifford, and Dennis Sheehan. "Monitoring an Owner: The Case of Turner Broadcasting." *Journal of Financial Economics* 30 (1991), pp. 325–46.

Hoshi, Takeo; Anil Kashyap; and David Scharfstein. "Bank Monitoring and Investment: Evidence from the Changing Structure of Japanese Corporate Banking Relationships. In *Asymmetric Information, Corporate Finance, and Investment*. R. Glenn Hubbard, ed. Chicago: University of Chicago Press, 1990.

Kester, W. Carl. "Governance, Contracting, and Investment Horizons: A Look at Japan and Germany." *Journal of Applied Corporate Finance* (1992), pp. 83–98.

Kidwell, David; M. Wayne Marr; and G. Rodney Thompson. "SEC Rule 415: The Ultimate Competitive Bid." *Journal of Financial and Quantitative Analysis* 19 (1984), pp. 183–95.

Kroszner, Randall, and Raghuram Rajan. "Is the Glass-Steagall Act Justified? A Study of the United States Experience with Universal Banking before 1933." *American Economic Review* 84 (1994), pp. 810–32.

Lee, Inmoo; Scott Lochhead; Jay Ritter; and Quanshui Zhao. "The Costs of Raising Capital." *Journal of Financial Research* 19 (1996), pp. 59–74.

Logue, Dennis, and Robert Jarrow. "Negotiation vs. Competitive Bidding in the Sale of Securities by Public Utilities." *Financial Management* 7 (1978), pp. 31–39.

Roe, Mark. *Strong Managers, Weak Owners*. Princeton, NJ: Princeton University Press, 1994.

Sahlman, William. "The Structure and Governance of Venture Capital Organizations." *Journal of Financial Economics* 27 (1990), pp. 473–524.

Sherman, Ann. "The Pricing of Best Efforts New Issues." *Journal of Finance* 47 (1992), pp. 781–90.

Smith, Clifford. "Alternative Methods of Raising Capital: Rights versus Underwritten Offerings." *Journal of Financial Economics* 5 (1977), pp. 273–307.

Debt Financing

Learning Objectives

After reading this chapter you should be able to:

1. Describe the main sources of debt financing: bank loans, leases, commercial paper and debt securities.
2. Describe the various characteristics of the debt securities that a firm can issue.
3. Understand the principle of amortization for some types of debt securities and its effect on the cash flows of those securities.
4. Describe the global environment in which firms issue debt securities.
5. Discuss the operation of secondary markets for debt securities.
6. Understand what a yield to maturity is and how it relates to a coupon yield.

In February 1993, the largest U.K. mortgage lender, Halifax Building Society, issued £100 million of collared floating-rate notes due February 2003.

Chapter 1 noted that the most frequently used source of external financing is debt.[1] Corporate managers, whose firms finance their operations by issuing debt, and the investors who buy corporate debt need to have a thorough understanding of debt instruments and the institutional features of debt markets.

Debt instruments, also called **fixed-income investments**, are contracts containing a promise to pay a cash flow stream to the investors who hold the contracts. The debt contract can be **negotiable**, a feature specified in the contract that permits its sale to another investor, or **nonnegotiable**, which prohibits sale to another party. Generally, the promised cash flows of a debt instrument are periodic payments, but the parties involved can negotiate almost any sort of cash flow arrangement. Thus, a debt contract may specify the size and timing of interest payments and a schedule for repayment of

---

[1]It is a huge market. Public debt outstanding at year-end 1995 was about $20 trillion. In addition, there is privately placed debt and bank debt.

principal, the amount owed on the loan. In addition to promises of future cash, a debt contract also establishes:

- The financial requirements and restrictions that the borrower must meet.
- The rights of the holder of the debt instrument if the borrower **defaults**, that is, violates any of the key terms of the contract, particularly the promise to pay.

The sheer variety of debt contracts generates a huge nomenclature and classification system for debt. A thorough education in this nomenclature and classification system is needed to implement many of the theoretical concepts developed in this text. For example, the simplest calculation of the returns of a financial instrument requires knowledge of the precise timing and magnitude of cash flows. Debt is full of conventions and shorthand language that reveal this cash flow information to knowledgeable participants in the debt market. To participate in the debt markets, either as a corporate issuer or as an investor, it is important to be grounded in the culture of the debt markets.

Punctuating this message is the Halifax note. The description of this note in the opening vignette may seem like an incomprehensible sentence to the novice. To knowledgeable debt-market players, however, a **collar**, which restricts the floating rate of interest, means that the interest charged on the issue has a cap and a floor. A **cap** specifies a maximum interest rate and a **floor** specifies a minimum interest rate. The players would know by convention that the coupon rate was reset every six months, and they could look up features on a screen or bond sheet that would indicate that the floating interest rate for the Halifax issue is LIBOR less 6.25 basis points.[2] They would know from similar sources that the cap prevents the floating interest rate from rising above 10.75 percent and that the floor keeps it from falling below 7 percent.

The sophisticated investor also knows the conventions that determine the cash flows for LIBOR and the **credit spread**, which is a markup, that is, an amount added to LIBOR. This person would have access to information about the credit risk of the bond and how to interpret the nomenclature and shortcut symbols in the credit risk arena. In short, the sophisticated investor can construct the exact cash flows of a debt instrument from what initially seems like a limited set of information.

This chapter can be thought of as a reference manual for the novice who wants to participate in the debt markets, but on a more level playing field. We begin this chapter by focusing on the four most common forms of debt contracts that corporations employ to finance their operations: bank loans, leases, commercial paper, and bonds (sometimes called notes). We then analyze the relationship between the price of a debt instrument and a commonly used measure of its promised return, the *yield* (defined later; see yield-to-maturity.) This relationship between price and yield requires an understanding of a number of concepts that are peculiar to debt: accrued interest, settlement conventions, yield quotation conventions, and coupon payment conventions.[3]

2.1 Bank Loans

Although bank loans remain a major part of the total amount of debt that firms take on, the volume of bank financing has shrunk drastically since the 1960s when loans, along

---

[2]One hundred **basis points** equal 1 percent.

[3]Some details about these concepts appear in the appendix to this chapter.

EXHIBIT 2.1   Types of Bank Loans

Line of credit	An arrangement between a bank and a firm that requires the bank to quote an interest rate, typically for a short-term loan, when the firm requests the loan. The bank authorizes the maximum loan amount when setting up the line of credit.
Loan commitment	An arrangement that requires a bank to lend up to a maximum prespecified loan amount at a prespecified interest rate at the firm's request as long as the firm meets the requirements established when the commitment was drawn up. There are two types of loan commitments:

- A **revolver**, in which funds flow back and forth between the bank and the firm without any predetermined schedule. Funds are drawn from the revolver whenever the firm wants them, up to the maximum amount specified. They may be subject to an annual cleanup in which the firm must retire all borrowings.
- A **nonrevolving loan commitment** in which the firm may not pay down the loan and then subsequently increase the amount of borrowing.

---

with bonds, made up about half of the corporate debt outstanding.[4] Today, bank loans account for only about 25–30 percent of the debt outstanding. Major corporations with good credit ratings have found that commercial paper, a short-term debt security, and nonbank loans from syndicates of wealthy private investors and institutions, such as insurance companies, are less expensive than bank debt as a way to raise funds.

Types of Bank Loans

Exhibit 2.1 shows the two general types of bank loans: lines of credit and loan commitments.

Lines of credit do not in a practical sense commit the bank to lend money because the bank is free to quote any interest rate it wishes at the time the borrowing firm requests funds. If the interest rate is too high, the firm will decline the available line of credit. The more formal contract, the loan commitment, specifies a preset interest rate.

Harman International: A Preference for a Revolving Loan
In September 1994, Harman International, a U.S.-based manufacturer of audio products, set up its first revolving credit facility. Previously, the firm had relied on lines of credit to finance working capital requirements.

The new facility is a $200 million, five-year, multicurrency revolving loan commitment, priced at LIBOR + 50 (i.e., the interest rate is the floating rate known as LIBOR plus an extra 50 basis points or 0.5 percent per year). The arrangement took 60 days to set up. As compensation for setting up the deal, Harman paid a required one-time up-front fee of 10 basis points ($200,000) to the lead bank and another 9.5 basis points to participating banks. For ongoing servicing of the credit facility, the lead bank is paid an annual fee of $25,000.

The chief operating officer of Harman noted several advantages of the revolver over earlier lines of credit: The facility is committed, that is, the bank must lend when Harman

---

[4]Many features of bank loans—for example, the description of floating rates and debt covenants—also apply to corporate debt securities such as bonds that are held by the investing public.

EXHIBIT 2.2   Benchmark Rates for Floating-Rate Loans

Treasury rate	The yields on U.S. Treasury securities for various maturities ranging from 1 month to 30 years. These yields are computed from the **on-the-run Treasuries**, that is, from the most recently auctioned Treasury issues which have the greatest liquidity.
	• **Treasury bills** are the zero-coupon Treasury issues with maturities that range from one month to one year at issue. The bill rates for one-month, three-month, and six-month maturities are the most popular Treasury-based benchmark rates. • **Treasury notes** are the coupon-paying issues with maturities from 1 year to 10 years at their initial issue date. • **Treasury bonds** are the coupon-paying issues with maturities greater than 10 years at their issue date. Their maximum maturity is 30 years.
Fed funds rate	Federal funds are overnight loans between two financial institutions. For example, one commercial bank may be short of reserves, requiring it to borrow excess reserves from another bank or a federal agency that has a surplus. The Fed funds rate, which is strongly affected by the actions of the Federal Reserve, is the rate at which banks can borrow and lend these excess reserves.
LIBOR	As noted in Chapter 1, the London interbank offered rate is a set of rates for different time deposits offered to major international banks by major banks in the Eurodollar market. One-month, three-month, or six-month LIBOR are the most common maturities for benchmark rates. There also is **LIBID**, the bid rate for interbank deposits.
Commercial paper rate	The yields on short-term, zero-coupon notes issued by major corporations.
Prime rate	Traditionally, the rate charged by banks to their most credit-worthy customers. The prime rate means less now than it did in previous years because banks have linked the prime rate either to the Treasury rate or a commercial paper rate and because large borrowers typically prefer LIBOR as a benchmark rate.

---

asks; Harman does not have to provide an explanation every time there is a **takedown** (i.e., a borrowing of additional funds from the credit facility); and the fees are lower than they were for earlier lines of credit.

Source: *Corporate Cashflow*, Feb. 1995.

To understand the terms of a revolving loan like the one described for Harman, you need to have a thorough understanding of the floating interest rates that are used for loans. We turn to this topic next.

Floating Rates

Floating rates are interest rates that change over time. Both lines of credit and loan commitments (revolver and nonrevolver) are floating-rate loans, priced as a fixed spread over a prevailing **benchmark rate**, which is the floating interest rate specified in the

EXHIBIT 2.3   Benchmark Rates, August 1996

Benchmark Instrument	Maturity	Rate
Treasury bills	3 months	5.07%
Treasury bills	6 months	5.16
Fed funds rate	1 day	5.24
AA commercial paper	3 months	5.39
AA commercial paper	6 months	5.42
LIBOR	3 months	5.53
LIBOR	6 months	5.72
Constant-maturity Treasury note	10 years	6.74
AAA corporate bond rate	Long term	7.62
Bank prime rate	Short-term floating	8.25

Source: Federal Reserve and *The Wall Street Journal*, Aug. 1996.

contr..ct. The spread usually depends on the default risk of the borrower. We will discuss default risk in detail after describing some commonly used benchmark rates below.

Benchmark Rates.   Exhibit 2.2 describes commonly used benchmark rates. Exhibit 2.3 displays the benchmark rates that prevailed at the end of August 1996 in order of increasing interest rates.

Creditworthiness and Spreads.   Spreads to these benchmark rates are quoted in terms of basis points, where 100 basis points equals 1 percent. For example, the spread of a borrower with almost no default risk might be LIBOR plus 20 basis points, which means that if LIBOR is at 8 percent per year, the borrower pays 8.2 percent per year. The creditworthiness of the borrower determines the spread over the benchmark rate. For example, a firm with outstanding credit risk such as the Halifax Building Society described in the opening vignette was able to borrow at 6.25 basis points *below* LIBOR. By contrast, highly leveraged companies with substantial default risk may end up borrowing at a rate between 150 basis points and 300 basis points *above* LIBOR.

Caps, Floors, and Collars.   As the Halifax issue demonstrated, floating-rate lending agreements often have caps (maximum interest rates) or floors (minimum interest rates). If a loan has a spread of 50 basis points to LIBOR, and LIBOR is at 7 percent, but the cap is set at 7.25 percent, the interest rate charged on the loan over the period will be the cap interest rate, 7.25 percent, instead of the benchmark rate plus the spread, which would be 7.5 percent. A **collared floating rate loan** has both a cap and a floor on the interest rate.

Loan Covenants

Lending agreements contain **loan covenants**, which are contractual restrictions imposed on the behavior of the borrowing firm.[5] For instance, managers of the borrowing company may be required to meet minimum net worth constraints on a quarterly basis.[6] They

---

[5]Covenants will be studied in greater depth later in this chapter when we focus on bonds.
[6]A net worth constraint requires book assets to exceed book liabilities by a threshold amount.

may face restrictions on dividend payouts or restrictions on the extent to which they can borrow from other sources. Alternatively, they may be asked to pledge certain assets such as accounts receivable or inventory as collateral. If the firm defaults on the loan, the bank can claim the accounts receivable or the inventory in lieu of the forgone loan repayment.

2.2 Leases

A **lease** can be viewed as a debt instrument in which the owner of an asset, the **lessor**, gives the right to use the asset to another party, the **lessee**, in return for a set of contractually fixed payments. The contract between the lessor and the lessee defines:

- The length of time for which the lessee can or must use the asset.
- The party responsible for maintenance of the asset.
- Whether the lessee has the right to buy the asset at the end of the leasing period and, if so, at what purchase price.

Driven by innovative providers and the demands of buyers, the volume of leasing has grown sharply since the mid-1970s, when lease payments were less than $20 billion a year, to over $150 billion a year in 1995.[7]

The list of assets available for lease is almost endless. For example, it is possible to lease copiers from Xerox, computers from IBM, and bulldozers from Caterpillar. A number of firms also specialize in leasing. For example, GE Capital leases airplanes, automobiles, trucks, trailers, tank cars, medical devices, office equipment, and even whole office buildings which they will erect for you in short order.

Exhibit 2.4 describes the two basic types of leases—operating leases and financial leases. Operating leases are more complicated to value than financial leases because of the uncertainty about the length of the lease. To understand whether the payments required on such leases are fair, it is important to understand derivative securities valuation.[8]

EXHIBIT 2.4   Types of Leases

Operating lease	An agreement, usually short term, allowing the lessee to retain the right to cancel the lease and return the asset to the lessor.
Financial lease (or capital lease)	An agreement that generally extends over the life of the asset and indicates that the lessee cannot return the asset except with substantial penalties. Financial leases include the **leveraged lease** (asset purchase financed by a third party), **direct lease** (asset purchase financed by the manufacturer of the asset), and **sale and leaseback** (asset purchased from the lessee by the lessor).

---

[7]Equipment Leasing Association and Department of Commerce.
[8]Derivatives are covered in Chapter 7. Taxes and leasing are covered in Chapter 13.

2.3 Commercial Paper

The most actively traded short-term source of financing for corporations is commercial paper. As first defined in Chapter 1, *commercial paper* is a contract by which a borrower promises to pay a prespecified amount to the lender of the commercial paper at some date in the future, usually one to six months. This prespecified amount is generally paid off by issuing new commercial paper. On rare occasions, the borrower will not choose this rollover, perhaps because short-term interest rates are too high. In this case, the company pays off the note with a line of credit (announced in the note) from a bank. This bank backing, along with the high quality of the issuer and the short-term nature of the instrument, makes commercial paper virtually risk free.[9] However, defaults have occurred, the most famous of which was the Penn Central default of June 1970 on $82 million of commercial paper.

Who Sells Commercial Paper?

Firms that lend money, such as bank holding companies, insurance companies, and private consumer lenders like Household Finance, Beneficial Finance, and General Motors Acceptance Corporation, issue about two-thirds of all U.S. commercial paper. The highest-quality nonfinancial corporations issue the remaining portion. While large financial firms issue their own commercial paper directly, much of it to money-market funds, nonfinancial firms issue their commercial paper through dealers.

Buyback Provisions

Most commercial paper can be sold to other investors, although this rarely occurs because the costs of such transactions are high. A consequence of this lack of secondary market activity is that virtually all issuers of commercial paper stand ready to buy back their commercial paper prior to maturity, often with little or no penalty. However, less than 1 percent of commercial paper is redeemed prematurely.

2.4 Corporate Bonds

Bonds are tradable fixed-income securities. Exhibit 2.5 on page 36 describes the most important features that bond issuers can set: covenants, option features, cash flow pattern (via coupon and principal schedule), maturity, price, and rating. Much of the nomenclature used in referring to bonds derives from these features.

Bond Covenants

As later chapters of this text point out, equity holders who control the firm can expropriate wealth from bondholders by making assets more risky, reducing assets through the payment of dividends, and adding liabilities. Virtually all debt contracts contain covenants to restrict these kinds of activities. In the absence of such covenants, the incentives of equity holders to expropriate bondholder wealth would be captured in the bond's coupon or price, resulting in higher borrowing rates.

---

[9]In a few cases, lower-quality issuers offer collateral as a guarantee of payment.

EXHIBIT 2.5   Bond Features

Bond covenants (also called **bond indentures**)	The rules that specify the rights of the lender and the restrictions on the borrower. Smith and Warner (1979) identified four major kinds of bond covenants: asset covenants, dividend covenants, financing covenants, and bonding covenants. Not all of these types are included in every bond.
Options	Bond features that allow both buyers and sellers to terminate the bond agreement, often requiring the party exercising the option to make certain payments or take on different risks. The most important embedded options are callability, convertibility, and putability (see Exhibit 2.10).
Cash flow pattern	Specified by the annual interest payments, or **coupon,** per $100 of principal, schedule for payment of principal, known as **amortization,** and **face value,** a number which denominates the size of the bond.[10]
	• Fixed-rate bonds typically pay half the stated coupon every six months. The **coupon rate,** which is the coupon stated as a percentage of the bond's face value, determines the coupon. Hence, an 8 percent coupon typically means two $4 payments per $100 of face value per year.
	• Floating-rate bonds are more complicated because of the many ways in which they can float. The interest rates on such bonds are typically some benchmark rate plus a fixed or a variable spread.[a]
Maturity	The maximum length of time the borrower has to pay off the bond principal in full. Maturities on corporate bonds are generally less than 30 years, but it is possible to sell bonds with longer maturities.[b]
Price	The amount at which a bond sells, particularly in relation to principal owed.
Bond rating	A sequence of letters and numbers that specifies the creditworthiness of a bond.

---

[a]More exotic floaters exist. Some are tied to a commodity price. During the Persian Gulf War in 1990, Salomon Brothers designed an issue that paid as principal the minimum of four times the price of oil or $100. Others, such as inverse floaters, that were bought by Orange County and were partly responsible for its bankruptcy in December 1994, have coupons that rise as the benchmark rate falls. (See Chapter 22 for a discussion of inverse floaters.)

[b]Conrail and TVA issued 50-year bonds in the early 1990s. IBM issued 100-year bonds in 1996. News Corp., Wisconsin Electric Power, Bell South Telecommunications, and Columbia/HCA Healthcare sold 100-year bonds in 1995. Walt Disney, ABN-AMRO (a Dutch bank), and Coca-Cola sold 100-year bonds in 1993. In spite of these unusual cases, the average maturity of bonds has been falling in the last 25 years and is now less than 10 years. The decline in average maturity is probably due to the increasing volatility of interest rates.

Exhibit 2.6 classifies covenants by type. Exhibit 2.7 on page 38 contains a portion of the bond covenants from Philip Morris's sinking fund bond, due in the year 2017.[11] The covenants shown are largely financing covenants. In plain language, the paragraph states

---

[10]Face value is usually either the principal at the maturity date of the bond or the amount borrowed at the issue date of the bond. For mortgages and other annuity bonds (defined later in this chapter), face values are the amount borrowed at the issue date of the bond.

[11]Sinking funds are defined shortly.

EXHIBIT 2.6   Types of Bond Covenants

Asset covenant	Governs the firm's acquisition, use, and disposition of assets.
Dividend covenant	An asset covenant that restricts the payment of dividends.
Financing covenant	Description of the amount of additional debt the firm can issue and the claims to assets that this additional debt might have in the event of default.
Bonding covenant	Description of the mechanism for enforcement of the covenants. It includes an independent audit of the company's financial statements, the appointment of a trustee to represent the bondholders and monitor the firm's compliance with bond covenants, periodic signatures by company officers that certify compliance with bond covenants, and "lock-box mechanisms."[a]

[a]A **lock-box** is a bank account whose beneficial owner is the debt holder. Hence, the cash in the account is a form of collateral for the bondholder. For example, when debt is collateralized by accounts receivable, the checks of the firm's "accounts receivable" clients are written to the bank and directed to the account held in the name of the debt holders.

that in the event of default the sinking fund bonds have equal claims to the firm's existing assets as other unsecured and unsubordinated debt (defined subsequently), and that new financing shall not take precedence over this debt issue in making claims on any materially important manufacturing facility in the event of default.

Asset Covenants.   Among other things, asset covenants specify what rights the bondholder has to the firm's assets in case of default. Some bonds are **senior bonds**, which give its investors the rights to liquidate or manage the assets to satisfy their claims before any of the holders of **junior bonds**, which have **subordinated claims** on a company's assets receive payment. Other bonds are **secured bonds**, which means the firm has pledged specific assets to the bondholders in case of default. Some asset covenants may prevent acquisitions of other companies.

Bonds are often named for their asset covenants. In addition to "senior" and "junior," the names used to refer to a bond depend on whether a bond is backed by collateral and, if so, what that collateral is. Exhibit 2.8 on page 39 illustrates this point.

Dividend Covenants.   Dividend covenants are beneficial in preventing a manager from leaving bondholders penniless by simply liquidating the firm and paying out the liquidation proceeds as a dividend to shareholders. Bondholders view even a partial payment of dividends as a liquidation of a portion of the firm's assets; thus, dividends per se are detrimental to bondholders. Simply prohibiting dividends, however, is not likely to be a good policy because it might cause the firm to waste cash by investing in worthless projects instead of using the cash to pay dividends. Kalay (1982) described the typical form of a dividend covenant: a formula that defines an inventory of funds available for dividend payments. The inventory will depend on the size of earnings, new funds derived from equity sales, and the amount of dividends paid out so far.

Financing Covenants.   Financing covenants prevent the firm from promiscuously issuing new debt, which would dilute the claims of existing bondholders to the firm's assets. Such covenants generally specify that any new debt has to have a subordinated claim to the assets. If the firm is allowed to issue new bonds having the same priority to the firm's assets in the event of bankruptcy as existing debt, the issuing amount is generally limited and often contingent on the financial health of the firm.

Exhibit 2.7   Bond Covenants

MOODY'S INDUSTRIAL MANUAL   4089

FINANCIAL & OPERATING DATA (Cont'd):	1994	1993	1992	1991	1990	1989	☐1988
Capitalization:							
% long term debt	48.06	50.88	48.55	48.68	53.47	56.21	64.56
% deferred income taxes	10.90	10.25	9.62	8.47	6.91	7.59	6.48
% common stock & surplus	41.04	38.87	41.83	42.85	39.63	36.20	28.96
②Revs.+inventory	6.73	6.88	6.43	6.46	6.20	6.67	4.71
②Revs.+receivables	12.27	12.71	12.08	11.66	10.81	12.97	11.43
②% revs. to net property	481.39	483.81	475.74	483.25	461.51	453.26	293.61
②% revs. to total assets	102.14	98.86	100.16	101.44	95.18	99.49	68.70
% net income to total assets	8.97	6.04	9.88	6.34	7.60	7.65	6.32
% net income to net worth	36.95	26.58	39.31	24.02	29.63	30.78	30.43
Analysis of Operations	%	%	%	%	%	%	%
Operating revenues	100.00	100.00	100.00	100.00	100.00	100.00	100.00
Cost of sales	43.53	43.96	44.11	45.36	47.74	49.61	43.38
Excise taxes on products	17.43	16.88	15.28	14.87	13.38	13.04	18.81
Gross profit	39.04	39.16	40.61	39.77	38.88	37.35	37.82
Marketing, admin. & research costs	23.60	25.77	22.72	23.61	22.47	21.08	23.36
Amortization of goodwill	0.93	0.93	0.88	0.88	0.88	0.87	0.40
Operating income	14.51	12.46	17.01	15.27	15.53	15.40	14.06
Interest & other debt exp., net	1.89	2.28	2.45	2.92	3.20	3.93	2.14
Earnings before income taxes & acctg. changes	12.62	10.17	14.56	12.35	12.33	11.47	11.92
Provision for income taxes	5.36	4.32	6.20	5.39	5.42	4.79	5.32
Earnings bef. cum. effect of acctg. changes	7.26	5.86	8.35	6.96	6.92	6.68	6.60
Cumulative effect of changes in method of accounting	......	(0.78)	......	(1.63)	......	......	0.87
Net earnings	7.26	5.08	8.35	5.32	6.92	6.68	7.47

☐Certain amounts were reclassified to conform with 1989 presentation. ②Operating revenues after deducting excise taxes. ③As reported by Company. ④Adjusted for 4-for-1 split 9/89.

LONG TERM DEBT

1. Philip Morris Companies Inc. 8¼% notes, due 2003:

Rating - A2
AUTH - $350,000,000.
OUTSTG - Dec. 31, 1994, $350,000,000.
DATED - Oct. 28, 1991.
DUE - Oct. 15, 2003.
INTEREST - A&O 15 to holders registered Mar. 31 & Sept. 30.
TRUSTEE - Chemical Bank.
DENOMINATION - Fully registered, $1,000 integral multiple thereof. The ~~~
form of one or mo~~~
will b~~~

SECURITY - Not secured. Ranks on a parity with Co.'s other unsecured and unsubordinated. Co. or any subsidiary will not create, assume, incur or suffer to be created, assumed or incurred any mortgage, lien, charge or encumbrance of any kind upon any shares of stock, indebtedness or other obligation of a subsidiary owned by Co. or another subsidiary and Co. will not create, assume, incur or suffer to be created, assumed or incurred any lien on any materially important manufacturing facility directly owned and operated by Co., as determined by its board of directors without, in each case, making effective provision whereby all the securities shall be directly secured equally and ratably with the indebtedness or other obligations secured by such lien.

such issuance, or (iv) any extension, renewal or replacement in whole or in part, thereof. Morover, the foregoing restriction does not apply to liens securing an aggregate amount of indebtedness, which together with the aggregate "value" of sale and leaseback transactions referred to below, does not exceed 5% of consolidated net tangible assets.
SALE AND LEASEBACK - Sales and leasebacks by Co. of any materially important manufacturing facility are prohibited unless an amount equal to the greater of the proceeds of sale or the fair value of the property is applied to the retirement of long-term non-subordinated indebtedness for money borrowed of Co., except that such sales and leasebacks are permitted to the extent that the "value" thereof plus the other secured debt referred to in the last sentence of the previous paragraph does not exceed the amount stated therein.
INDENTURE MODIFICATION - Indenture may be modified, except as provided, with consent of 50% of notes outstg.
RIGHTS ON DEFAULT - Trustee, or 25% of notes outstg., may declare principal due and payable (30 day's grace for payment of interest).
PURPOSE - Proceeds will be used to reduce short-term borrowings incurred to finance the acquisition of Kraft and Jacobs Suchard and for general corporate purposes.
OFFERED - ($350,000,000) at 99.582 plus accrued interest (proceeds to Co., 98.957) on Oct. 21, 1991 thru Merrill Lynch & Co.; Donaldson, Lufkin & Jenrette Securities Corp.; Nomura Securities International, Inc.; Bear, Stearns & Co. Inc.; Kidder, Peabody & Co. Inc, and Paine Webber Inc. and associates.

PRICE RANGE -	1994
High	114½
Low	96½

2. Philip Morris Companies Inc. 7½% notes, due 1996:

Rating - A2
AUTH - $100,000,000.
OUTSTG - Dec. 31, 1994, $7,205,000.
DATED - Aug.1, 1986.
DUE - Aug. 1, 1996.
INTEREST - F&A 1 to holders registered J&J 15.

TRUSTEE - Chemical Bank.
DENOMINATION - Fully registered, $1,000 and integral multiples thereof. Transferable and exchangeable without service charge.
CALLABLE - Not callable prior to maturity.
SECURITY - Unsecured. Ranks on a parity with Co.'s other unsecured and unsubordinated indebtedness. Co. will not and will not permit any subsidiary ~~~
assume, incur or suffer to be ~~~
incurred any mortgage ~~~
any kind ~~~

such sales and leasebacks are permitted to the extent that the "value" thereof plus the other secured debt referred to in the last sentence of the previous paragraph does not exceed the amount stated therein.
INDENTURE MODIFICATION - Indenture may be modified, except as provided, with consent of 50% of notes outstg.
RIGHTS ON DEFAULT - Trustee, or 25% of notes outstg., may declare principal due and payable (30 day's grace for payment of interest).
PURPOSE - Proceeds will be used to reduce outstg. short-term borrowings incurred to finance the acquisition of General Foods Corp.
OFFERED - ($100,000,000) at 99.645 plus accrued interest (proceeds to Co., 99.02) on July 31, 1986 thru First Boston Corp. and associates.

PRICE RANGE -	1994
High	106¼
Low	98⅞

3. Philip Morris Companies Inc. sinking fund debenture 8⅜s, due 2017:

Rating - A2
AUTH - $200,000,000.
OUTSTG - Dec. 31, 1994, $200,000,000.
DATED - Jan. 15, 1987.
DUE - Jan. 15, 2017.
INTEREST - J&J 15 to holders registered J30 & D31.
TRUSTEE - Chemical Bank.
DENOMINATION - Fully registered, $1,000 and integral multiples thereof. Transferable and exchangeable without service charge.
CALLABLE - As a whole or in part at any time, at the option of Co., on at least 30 but not more than 60 days' notice to each Jan. 14 as follows:

1993	106.281	1994	105.863	1995	105.444
1996	105.025	1997	104.606	1998	104.188
1999	103.769	2000	103.350	2001	102.931
2002	102.513	2003	102.094	2004	101.675
2005	101.256	2006	100.838	2007	100.419

and thereafter at 100 plus accrued interest. Not callable, however, prior to Jan. 15, 1997, redeem any debs., or anticipation of, any refunding operation by the application, directly or indirectly, of moneys borrowed at an

interest cost of less than 8.55% per annum. Also callable for sinking fund (which see) at 100.
SINKING FUND - Annually, Jan. 15, 1998-2016, sufficient to redeem $10,000,000 principal amount of debs., plus similar optional payments. Sinking fund is designed to retire 95% of debs. prior to maturity.
SECURITY - Not secured. Ranks on a parity with Co.'s unsecured and unsubordinated. Co. or any subsidi~~~ will not create, assume, incur or suffer to be created, ~~~med or incurred any mortgage, lien, charge or ~~~mbrance of any kind upon any shares of stock, indebtedness or other obligation of a subsidiary owned ~~~o. or another subsidiary and Co. will not create, ~~~me, incur or suffer to be created, assumed or ~~~red any lien on any materially important manufac~~~g facility directly owned and operated by Co., as ~~~mined by its board of directors without, in each ~~~ making effective provision whereby all the securi~~~hall be directly secured equally and ratably with the ~~~edness or other obligations secured by such lien.
~~~ENTURE MODIFICATION - Indenture may be ~~~fied, except as provided, with consent of a majority ~~~ebs. outstg.
~~~HTS ON DEFAULT - Trustee, or 25% of debs. out~~~ may declare principal due and payable (30 days' ~~~e for payment of interest).
~~~RPOSE - Proceeds will be used to reduce outstg. ~~~rt-term borrowings incurred to finance the acquisi~~~n of General Foods Corp.
~~~FERED - ($200,000,000) at 98.125 plus accrued ~~~terest (proceeds to Co., 97.250) on Jan. 8, 1987 thru ~~~rst Boston Corp.; Goldman, Sachs & Co.; Morgan ~~~tanley & Co., Inc. and associates.

~~RICE RANGE -	1994
High	105⅜
Low	92⅜

4. Philip Morris Companies Inc. eurodeutschemark bonds 6s, due 1996:

Rating - A2
AUTH - DM $225,000,000.
OUTSTG - Dec. 31, 1994, $225,000,000.
DATED - Mar. 20, 1986.
DUE - May, 1996.
DUE - 1996
INTEREST - March 20.
OTHER DETAILS - Not reported.

5. Philip Morris Companies Inc. Swiss Franc eurobond 6⅞s, due 1998:

Rating - A2
AUTH - SFr 250,000,000; outstg. Dec. 31, 1993, $250,000,000.
OUTSTG - Dec. 31, 1994, $250,000,000.
DATED - May 22, 1991.
DUE - May 22, 1998.
INTEREST - Payable annually in arrears on May 22. For this purpose the bonds are furnished with coupons, the first of which will become due and payable on May 22, 1992.
DENOMINATION - In bearer form, in the denomination of SFr5,000 and SFr100,000. Transferable and exchangeable without service charge.
CALLABLE - Not callable prior to maturity except, for tax reasons, in whole but not in part, at any time, at the option of Co. at 100.
SECURITY - Not secured. Ranks pari passu among themselves and all other present or future direct, unsecured and unsubordinated obligations of Co. for money borrowed, issued or guaranteed. Co. or any subsidiary will not, directly or indirectly, create, assume, incur or suffer to be created, assumed or incurred, any mortgage, lien, charge or encumbrance on, or conditional sale or other title retention agreement with respect to any shares of stock, indebtedness or other obligation of a subsidiary owned by Co. or another subsidiary and (i) Co. will not, directly or indirectly, create, assume, incur or suffer to be created, assumed or incurred any lien on any manufacturing plant or facility owned and operated by Co. which is determined to be a materially important manufacturing plant or facility by the Board of Directors in its discretion, without making effective provision whereby all the bonds shall be directly secured equally and ratably with the indebtedness or other obligations secured by such lien, so long as such indebtedness or other obligations shall be so secured.
SALE AND LEASEBACK - Sale and leasebacks by Co. of any materially important manufacturing facility

---

EXHIBIT 2.8   Bond Type Based on Asset Claims in Default

Secured bond	A bond for which the firm has pledged title to specific assets.
Mortgage bond	A type of secured bond giving lenders a first-mortgage lien on certain assets, such as land, a building, or machinery. If the firm defaults, the lien allows the lender to foreclose and sell the assets.
Collateral trust bond	A type of secured bond involving assets placed in a trust. the trustee gives the assets to the bondholder in the event of default.
Equipment trust certificate	A type of secured bond with indentures that give lenders the right to specific pieces of equipment in the event of default.
Debenture	A type of unsecured bond. In the event of default, debenture holders are **unsecured creditors,** meaning that they have a claim on all of the firm's assets not already pledged.

The debt contracts of companies with exceptional credit ratings generally do not contain subordination clauses. For these companies, "straight" subordinated debt issues almost never exist. In contrast, convertible debt (discussed in the next section; see Exhibit 2.10) generally is subordinated to straight debt, even for high-quality issuers.

Financial Ratio Covenants.   Both asset covenants and financing covenants are embedded in covenants that require the firm to maintain certain financial ratios. For instance, a covenant may specify a minimum value for **net working capital**—that is, current assets less current liabilities—or for net worth, as noted earlier. Similarly, such covenants may prescribe a minimum **interest coverage ratio**—that is, the ratio of earnings to interest— or a minimum ratio of tangible assets to total debt. When the firm cannot meet the financial ratio conditions, it is technically in default even when it has made the promised payments to bondholders.

Sinking Fund Covenants.   A common covenant related to financing is a **sinking fund provision**, which requires that a certain portion of the bonds be retired before maturity. A typical sinking fund on a 30-year bond might ensure that 25 percent of the bonds are retired between years 10 and 20. The firm makes payments to the trustee, who then repurchases randomly chosen bonds. The trustee may do this in the open market or, more typically may retire the bonds by exercising the call provision in the bond (see the subsection on bond options for details).

Exhibit 2.9a on page 40 describes the sinking fund in the Philip Morris bond due in 2017. It specifies that 95 percent of the bond issue will be retired early, with at least $10 million in principal redeemed annually.

Bonding Mechanism.   Covenants generally specify some sort of **bonding mechanism**, or provision to ensure that the borrower is upholding the bond indentures. Large bond issues require the appointment of a trustee to ensure that no violation of the bond indentures takes place.

EXHIBIT 2.9a Sinking Fund Example

MOODY'S INDUSTRIAL MANUAL 4089

FINANCIAL & OPERATING DATA (Cont'd):	1994	1993	1992	1991	1990	1989	[1]1988
Capitalization:							
% long term debt	48.06	50.88	48.55	48.68	53.47	56.21	64.56
% deferred income taxes	10.90	10.25	9.62	8.47	6.91	7.59	6.48
% common stock & surplus	41.04	38.87	41.83	42.85	39.63	36.20	28.96
[2]Revs.+inventory	6.73	6.88	6.43	6.46	6.20	6.67	4.71
[2]Revs.+receivables	12.27	12.71	12.08	11.66	10.81	12.97	11.43
[2]% revs. to net property	481.39	483.81	475.74	483.25	461.51	453.26	293.61
[2]% revs. to total assets	102.14	98.86	100.16	101.44	95.18	99.49	68.70
% net income to total assets	8.97	6.04	9.88	6.34	7.60	7.65	6.32
% net income to net worth	36.95	26.58	39.31	24.02	29.63	30.78	30.43
Analysis of Operations	%	%	%	%	%	%	%
Operating revenues	100.00	100.00	100.00	100.00	100.00	100.00	100.00
Cost of sales	43.53	43.96	44.11	45.36	47.74	49.61	43.38
Excise taxes on products	17.43	16.88	15.28	14.87	13.38	13.04	18.81
Gross profit	39.04	39.16	40.61	39.77	38.88	37.35	37.82
Marketing, admin. & research costs	23.60	25.77	22.72	23.61	22.47	21.08	23.36
Amortization of goodwill	0.93	0.93	0.88	0.88	0.88	0.87	0.40
Operating income	14.51	12.46	17.01	15.27	15.53	15.40	14.06
Interest & other debt exp., net	1.89	2.28	2.45	2.92	3.20	3.93	2.14
Earnings before income taxes & acctg. changes	12.62	10.17	14.56	12.35	12.33	11.47	11.92
Provision for income taxes	5.36	4.32	6.20	5.39	5.42	4.79	5.32
Earnings bef. cum. effect of acctg. changes	7.26	5.86	8.35	6.96	6.92	6.68	6.60
Cumulative effect of changes in method of accounting	......	(0.78)	......	(1.63)	......	......	0.87
Net earnings	7.26	5.08	8.35	5.32	6.92	6.68	7.47

[1]Certain amounts were reclassified to conform with 1989 presentation. [2]Operating revenues after deducting excise taxes. [3]As reported by Company. [4]Adjusted for 4-for-1 split 9/89.

LONG TERM DEBT

1. Philip Morris Companies Inc. 8¼% notes, due 2003:

Rating - A2

AUTH - $350,000,000.
OUTSTG - Dec. 31, 1994, $350,000,000.
DATED - Oct. 28, 1991.
DUE - Oct. 15, 2003.
INTEREST - A&O 15 to hold
Sept. 30.

SINKING FUND - Annually, Jan. 15, 1998-2016, sufficient to redeem $10,000,000 principal amount of debs., plus similar optional payments. Sinking fund is designed to retire 95% of debs. prior to maturity.

permit any subsidiary to create, assume, incur or suffer to be created, assumed or incurred any mortgage, lien, charge or encumbrance of any kind upon any shares of stock, indebtedness or other obligation of subsidiary owned by Co. or another subsidiary and (ii) Co. will not create, assume, incur or suffer to be created, assumed or incurred any lien on any materially important manufacturing facility directly owned and operated by Co., as determined by its board of directors, without, in each case, making effective provision whereby all the debt securities shall be directly secured equally and ratably with the indebtedness or other obligations secured by the lien. This covenant does not apply to (i) certain statutory or judgment liens or other liens incurred in the ordinary course of business, (ii) liens securing indebtedness owed by a subsidiary to the Co. or another subsidiary, (iii) in the case of liens upon any materially important manufacturing facility, liens incurred in connection with the issuance by a state or a political subdivision thereof of any securities the interest on which is exempt from federal income taxes by virtue of section 103 of the Code, or any other laws and regulations in effect at the time of such issuance, or (iv) any extension, renewal or replacement in whole or in part, thereof. Morover, the foregoing restriction does not apply to liens securing an aggregate amount of indebtedness, which together with the aggregate "value" of sale and leaseback transactions referred to below, does not exceed 5% of consolidated net tangible assets.
SALE AND LEASEBACK - Sales and leasebacks by Co. of any materially important manufacturing facility are prohibited unless an amount equal to the greater of the proceeds of sale or the fair value of the property is applied to the retirement of long-term non-subordinated indebtedness for money borrowed of Co., except that such sales and leasebacks are permitted to the extent that the "value" thereof plus the other secured debt referred to in the last sentence of the previous paragraph does not exceed the amount stated therein.
INDENTURE MODIFICATION - Indenture may be modified, except as provided, with consent of 50% of notes outstg.
RIGHTS ON DEFAULT - Trustee, or 25% of notes outstg., may declare principal due and payable (30 day's grace for payment of interest).
PURPOSE - Proceeds will be used to reduce short-term borrowings incurred to finance the acquisition of Kraft and Jacobs Suchard and for general corporate purposes.
OFFERED - ($350,000,000) at 99.582 plus accrued interest (proceeds to Co., 98.957) on Oct. 21, 1991 thru Merrill Lynch & Co., Donaldson, Lufkin & Jenrette Securities Corp., Nomura Securities International, Inc., Bear, Stearns & Co. Inc., Kidder, Peabody & Co. Inc. and Paine Webber Inc. and associates.

PRICE RANGE -	1994
High	114½
Low	96½

2. Philip Morris Companies Inc. 7½% notes, due 1996:

Rating - A2

AUTH - $100,000,000.
OUTSTG - Dec. 31, 1994, $7,205,000.
DATED - Aug.1, 1986.
DUE - Aug. 1, 1996.
INTEREST - F&A 1 to holders registered J&J 15.
TRUSTEE - Chemical Bank.
DENOMINATION - Fully registered, $1,000 and integral multiples thereof. Transferable and exchangeable without service charge.
CALLABLE - Not callable prior to
SECURITY - Unsec
other un

business, (ii) liens securing indebtedness owed by a subsidiary to the Co. or another subsidiary, (iii) in the case of liens upon any materially important manufacturing facility, liens incurred in connection with the issuance by a state or a political subdivision thereof of any securities the interest on which is exempt from federal income taxes by virtue of section 103 of the Code, or any other laws and regulations in effect at the time of such issuance, or (iv) any extension, renewal or replacement in whole or in part, thereof. Morover, the foregoing restriction does not apply to liens securing an aggregate amount of indebtedness, which together with the aggregate "value" of sale and leaseback transactions referred to below, does not exceed 5% of consolidated net tangible assets.
SALE AND LEASEBACK - Sales and leasebacks by Co. of any materially important manufacturing facility are prohibited unless an amount equal to the greater of the proceeds of sale or the fair value of the property is applied to the retirement of long-term non-subordinated indebtedness for money borrowed of Co., except that such sales and leasebacks are permitted to the extent that the "value" thereof plus the other secured debt referred to in the last sentence of the previous paragraph does not exceed the amount stated therein.
INDENTURE MODIFICATION - Indenture may be modified, except as provided, with consent of 50% of notes outstg.
RIGHTS ON DEFAULT - Trustee, or 25% of notes outstg., may declare principal due and payable (30 day's grace for payment of interest).
PURPOSE - Proceeds will be used to reduce outstg. short-term borrowings incurred to finance the acquisition of General Foods Corp.
OFFERED - ($100,000,000) at 99.645 plus accrued interest (proceeds to Co., 99.02) on July 31, 1986 thru First Boston Corp. and associates.

PRICE RANGE -	1994
High	106¼
Low	98⅞

3. Philip Morris Companies Inc. sinking fund debenture 8⅜s, due 2017:

Rating - A2

AUTH - $200,000,000.
OUTSTG - Dec. 31, 1994, $200,000,000.
DATED - Jan. 15, 1987.
DUE - Jan. 15, 2017.
INTEREST - J&J 15 to holders registered J30 & D31.
TRUSTEE - Chemical Bank.
DENOMINATION - Fully registered, $1,000 and integral multiples thereof. Transferable and exchangeable without service charge.
CALLABLE - As a whole or in part at any time, at the option of Co., on at least 30 but not more than 60 days' notice to each Jan. 14 as follows:

1993	106.281	1994	105.863	1995	105.444
1996	105.025	1997	104.606	1998	104.188
1999	103.769	2000	103.350	2001	102.931
2002	102.513	2003	102.094	2004	101.675
2005	101.256	2006	100.838	2007	100.419

and thereafter at 100 plus accrued interest. Not callable, however, prior to Jan. 15, 1997, redeem any debs., or anticipation of, any refunding operation by the application, directly or indirectly, of moneys borrowed at an interest cost of less than 8.55% per annum. Also callable for sinking fund (which see) at 100.
SINKING FUND - Annually, Jan. 15, 1998-2016, suffi-
nt to redeem $10,000,000 principal amount of debs.,
s similar optional payments. Sinking fund is designed
etire 95% of debs. prior to maturity.
CURITY - Not secured. Ranks on a parity with Co.'s
er unsecured and unsubordinated. Co. or any subsidi-
will not create, assume, incur or suffer to be created,
umed or incurred any mortgage, lien, charge or
cumbrance of any kind upon any shares of stock,
debtedness or other obligation of a subsidiary owned
Co. or another subsidiary and Co. will not create,
ssume, incur or suffer to be created, assumed or
ncurred any lien on any materially important manufac-
turing facility directly owned and operated by Co., as determined by its board of directors without, in each case, making effective provision whereby all the securities shall be directly secured equally and ratably with the indebtedness or other obligations secured by such lien.
INDENTURE MODIFICATION - Indenture may be modified, except as provided, with consent of a majority of debs. outstg.
RIGHTS ON DEFAULT - Trustee, or 25% of debs. outstg., may declare principal due and payable (30 days' grace for payment of interest).
PURPOSE - Proceeds will be used to reduce outstg. short-term borrowings incurred to finance the acquisition of General Foods Corp.
OFFERED - ($200,000,000) at 98.125 plus accrued interest (proceeds to Co., 97.250) on Jan. 8, 1987 thru First Boston Corp.; Goldman, Sachs & Co.; Morgan Stanley & Co., Inc. and associates.

PRICE RANGE -	1994
High	105⅝
Low	92⅜

4. Philip Morris Companies Inc. eurodeutschemark bonds 6s, due 1996:

Rating - A2

AUTH - DM $225,000,000.
OUTSTG - Dec. 31, 1994, $225,000,000.
DATED - Mar. 20, 1986.
DUE - May, 1996.
DUE - 1996
INTEREST - March 20.
OTHER DETAILS - Not reported.

5. Philip Morris Companies Inc. Swiss Franc eurobond 6⅞s, due 1998:

Rating - A2

AUTH - SFr 250,000,000; outstg. Dec. 31, 1993, $250,000,000.
OUTSTG - Dec. 31, 1994, $250,000,000.
DATED - May 22, 1991.
DUE - May 22, 1998.
INTEREST - Payable annually in arrears on May 22. For this purpose the bonds are furnished with coupons, the first of which will become due and payable on May 22, 1992.
DENOMINATION - In bearer form, in the denomination of SFr5,000 and SFr100,000. Transferable and exchangeable without service charge.
CALLABLE - Not callable prior to maturity except, for tax reasons, in whole but not in part, at any time, at the option of Co. at 100.
SECURITY - Not secured. Ranks pari passu among themselves and all other present or future direct, unsecured and unsubordinated obligations of Co. for money borrowed, issued or guaranteed. Co. or any subsidiary will not, directly or indirectly, create, assume, incur or suffer to be created, assumed or incurred, any mortgage, lien, charge or encumbrance on, or conditional sale or other title retention agreement with respect to any shares of stock, indebtedness or other obligation of a subsidiary owned by Co. or another subsidiary and (i) Co. will not, directly or indirectly, create, assume, incur or suffer to be created, assumed or incurred any lien on any manufacturing plant or facility owned and operated by Co. which is determined to be a materially important manufacturing plant or facility by the Board of Directors in its discretion, without making effective provision whereby all the bonds shall be directly secured equally and ratably with the indebtedness or other obligations secured by such lien, so long as such indebtedness or other obligations shall be so secured.
SALE AND LEASEBACK - Sale and leasebacks by Co. of any materially important manufacturing facility

Source: Reprinted with permission from Moody's Investment Service of 1996.

Bond Options

Exhibit 2.9b contains a description of an option embedded in the 2017 bond from *Moody's Industrial Manual*. This option gives Philip Morris the right to call (i.e., redeem) the bond at a price per $100 of face value that is given in the exhibit. The price varies according to the date the bond is called. Virtually all bonds with sinking fund provisions have this call feature, so that the firm has the ability to implement the sinking fund in the event that it is unable to find a sufficient number of bonds to repurchase on the open market.

Exhibit 2.10 on page 43 describes the various types of options embedded in bonds.

How Abundant Are These Options?   At one time, nearly all long-term corporate bonds were callable. Since the mid-1980s, however, call provision are rarely found except in the bonds issued by the least creditworthy firms.[12] Of course, exceptions exist to every observed pattern. For example, in November 1993, Canon, a Japanese firm with a superb credit rating, issued ¥100 billion of yen-denominated bonds in the United States with maturities at time of issue ranging from 10 to 15 years. The 15-year bonds are callable at any time after January 2002 at a price of ¥106 per ¥100 face value, with the call price declining by ¥1 annually to ¥100 on January 2008.

Convertible bonds, which possess desirable properties for resolving certain bond-holder-stockholder conflicts,[13] are frequently issued by small firms, although some large firms do use them. For example, the Canon issue described above is convertible into Canon's common stock.

In another example, Carnival Cruise Lines issued $100 million of 4.5 percent convertible subordinated notes in July 1992, due in five years. The notes were convertible at any time at a conversion price of $34.75 per share, which would be about 28.78 shares per bond (the $1,000 face value divided by the conversion price). At the time Carnival issued the notes, its stock was trading at $28.375 per share, implying that the conversion premium was slightly more than 20 percent.

The Conversion Price of a Convertible Bond.   If we invert the formula used for Carnival, we learn that the conversion price of a convertible bond is its face value divided by the number of shares into which each bond can be converted.

Example 2.1 illustrates the calculation.

Example 2.1:   Computing a Conversion Price

Lowe's Companies, a hardware store chain, issued $250 million of convertible subordinated notes in July 1993 which mature in 2003. The notes had a 3 percent coupon rate, but sold at an offer price (per $100 face value) of $88.027 with the firm getting $86.927 and the rest going for fees. The notes were convertible into 19.136 shares of common stock for each $1,000 of principal. Lowe's common stock was selling for $38.875 per share. What was the conversion price and the conversion premium? Express the premium as a percentage of the stock price.

Answer: The conversion price was $52.258 ($1000/19.136). With Lowe's selling at $38.875, the conversion premium was about 34 percent ($52.258 − $38.875)/$38.875.

---

[12]We believe that the decline in the issuance of callable bonds is due to the substitution by many firms of a derivative security known as an *interest rate swap option* for the call features in bonds. See Chapter 7 for a discussion of both swaps and options.

[13]See Chapter 15.

EXHIBIT 2.9b Call Feature Example

MOODY'S INDUSTRIAL MANUAL 4089

FINANCIAL & OPERATING DATA (Cont'd):	1994	1993	1992	1991	1990	1989	[1]1988
Capitalization:							
% long term debt	48.06	50.88	48.55	48.68	53.47	56.21	64.56
% deferred income taxes	10.90	10.25	9.62	8.47	6.91	7.59	6.48
% common stock & surplus	41.04	38.87	41.83	42.85	39.63	36.20	28.96
[2]Revs.+inventory	6.73	6.88	6.43	6.46	6.20	6.67	4.71
[2]Revs.+receivables	12.27	12.71	12.08	11.66	10.81	12.97	11.43
[2]% revs. to net property	481.39	483.81	475.74	483.25	461.51	453.26	293.61
[2]% revs. to total assets	102.14	98.86	100.16	101.44	95.18	99.49	68.70
% net income to total assets	8.97	6.04	9.88	6.34	7.60	7.65	6.32
% net income to net worth	36.95	26.58	39.31	24.02	29.63	30.78	30.43
Analysis of Operations	%	%	%	%	%	%	%
Operating revenues	100.00	100.00	100.00	100.00	100.00	100.00	100.00
Cost of sales	43.53	43.96	44.11	45.36	47.74	49.61	43.38
Excise taxes on products	17.43	16.88	15.28	14.87	13.38	13.04	18.81
Gross profit	39.04	39.16	40.61	39.77	38.88	37.35	37.82
Marketing, admin. & research costs	23.60	25.77	22.72	23.61	22.47	21.08	23.36
Amortization of goodwill	0.93	0.93	0.88	0.88	0.88	0.87	0.40
Operating income	14.51	12.46	17.01	15.27	15.53	15.40	14.06
Interest & other debt exp., net	1.89	2.28	2.45	2.92	3.20	3.93	2.14
Earnings before income taxes & acctg. changes	12.62	10.17	14.56	12.35	12.33	11.47	11.92
Provision for income taxes	5.36	4.32	6.20	5.39	5.42	4.79	5.32
Earnings bef. cum. effect of acctg. changes	7.26	5.86	8.35	6.96	6.92	6.68	6.60
Cumulative effect of changes in method of accounting	......	(0.78)	......	(1.63)	......	......	0.87
Net earnings	7.26	5.08	8.35	5.32	6.92	6.68	7.47

[1]Certain amounts were reclassified to conform with 1989 presentation. [2]Operating revenues after deducting excise taxes. [3]As reported by Company. [4]Adjusted for 4-for-1 split 9/89.

LONG TERM DEBT

1. Philip Morris Companies Inc. 8¼% notes, due 2003:

Rating - A2

AUTH - $350,000,000.
OUTSTG - Dec. 31, 1994, $350,000,000.
DATED - Oct. 28, 1991.
DUE - Oct. 15, 2003.
INTEREST - A&O 15 to holders registered Mar. 31 & Sept. 30.
TRUSTEE - Chemical Bank.
DENOMINATION - Fully registered, $1,000 and any integral multiple thereof. The notes will be issued in the form of one or more fully registered Global Notes which will be deposited with, or on behalf of, The Depository Trust Company, New York, New York and registered in the name of the Depository's nominee. Transferable and exchangeable without service charge.
CALLABLE - Not callable prior to maturity.
SECURITY - Not secured. Ranks equally with all other unsecured senior indebtedness. Co. will not and will not permit any subsidiary to create, assume, incur or suffer to be created, assumed or incurred any mortgage, lien, charge or encumbrance of any kind upon any shares of stock, indebtedness or other obligation of subsidiary owned by Co. or another subsidiary and (ii) Co. will not create, assume, incur or suffer to be created, assumed or incurred any lien on any materially important manufacturing facility directly owned and operated by Co., as determined by its board of directors, without, in each case, making effective provision whereby all the debt securities shall be directly secured equally and ratably with the indebtedness or other obligations secured by the lien. This covenant does not apply to (i) certain statutory or judgment liens or other liens incurred in the ordinary course of business, (ii) liens securing indebtedness owed by a subsidiary to the Co. or another subsidiary, (iii) in the case of liens upon any materially important manufacturing facility, liens incurred in connection with the issuance by a state or a political subdivision thereof of any securities the interest on which is exempt from federal income taxes by virtue of section 103 of the Code,

CALLABLE - As a whole or in part at any time, at the option of Co., on at least 30 but not more than 60 days' notice to each Jan. 14 as follows:

1993	106.281	1994	105.863	1995	105.444
1996	105.025	1997	104.606	1998	104.188
1999	103.769	2000	103.350	2001	102.931
2002	102.513	2003	102.094	2004	101.675
2005	101.256	2006	100.838	2007	100.419

and thereafter at 100 plus accrued interest. Not callable, however, prior to Jan. 15, 1997, redeem any debs., or anticipation of, any refunding operation by the application, directly or indirectly, of moneys borrowed at an

OFFERED - ($350,...
interest (proceeds to Co., 98.95...
Merrill Lynch & Co., Donaldson, Lufkin &...
Securities Corp., Nomura Securities International, Inc., Bear, Stearns & Co. Inc., Kidder, Peabody & Co. Inc. and Paine Webber Inc. and associates.

PRICE RANGE -	1994
High	114½
Low	96½

2. Philip Morris Companies Inc. 7½% notes, due 1996:

Rating - A2

AUTH - $100,000,000.
OUTSTG - Dec. 31, 1994, $7,205,000.
DATED - Aug.1, 1986.
DUE - Aug. 1, 1996.
INTEREST - F&A 1 to holders registered J&J 15.

TRUSTEE - Chemical Bank.
DENOMINATION - Fully registered, $1,000 and integral multiples thereof. Transferable and exchangeable without service charge.
CALLABLE - Not callable prior to maturity.
SECURITY - Unsecured. Ranks on a parity with Co.'s other unsecured and unsubordinated indebtedness. Co. will not and will not permit any subsidiary to create, assume, incur or suffer to be created, assumed or incurred any mortgage, lien, charge or encumbrance of any kind upon any shares of stock, indebtedness or other obligation of subsidiary owned by Co. or another subsidiary and (ii) Co. will not create, assume, incur or suffer to be created, assumed or incurred any lien on any materially important manufacturing facility directly owned and operated by Co., as determined by its board of directors, without, in each case, making effective provision whereby all the debt securities shall be directly secured equally and ratably with the indebtedness or other obligations secured by the lien. This covenant does not apply to (i) certain statutory or judgment liens or other liens incurred in the ordinary course of business, (ii) liens securing indebtedness owed by a subsidiary to the Co. or another subsidiary, (iii) in the case of liens upon any materially important manufacturing facility, liens incurred in connection with the issuance by a state or a political subdivision thereof of any securities the interest on which is exempt from federal income taxes by virtue of section 103 of the Code, or any other laws and regulations in effect at the time of such issuance, or (iv) any extension, renewal or replacement in whole or in part, thereof. Morover, the foregoing restriction does not apply to liens securing an aggregate amount of indebtedness, which together with the aggregate "value" of sale and leaseback transactions referred to below, does not exceed 5% of consolidated net tangible assets.
SALE AND LEASEBACK - Sales and leasebacks by Co. of any materially important manufacturing facility are prohibited unless an amount equal to the greater of the proceeds of sale or the fair value of the property is applied to the retirement of long-term non-subordinated indebtedness for money borrowed of Co., except that ...ed to the extent that ...cured debt referred ...paragraph does not

...denture may be ...nsent of 50% of

...5% of notes out ...yable (30 day's

...reduce outstg. ...e the acquisi-

...plus accrued ...31, 1986 thru

	1994
	106¼
	98⅞

...nking fund

...30 & D31.

...00 and integral multip... ...xchangeable without service charge.
CALLABLE - As a whole or in part at any time, at the option of Co., on at least 30 but not more than 60 days' notice to each Jan. 14 as follows:

1993	106.281	1994	105.863	1995	105.444
1996	105.025	1997	104.606	1998	104.188
1999	103.769	2000	103.350	2001	102.931
2002	102.513	2003	102.094	2004	101.675
2005	101.256	2006	100.838	2007	100.419

and thereafter at 100 plus accrued interest. Not callable, however, prior to Jan. 15, 1997, redeem any debs., or anticipation of, any refunding operation by the application, directly or indirectly, of moneys borrowed at an interest cost of less than 8.55% per annum. Also callable for sinking fund (which see) at 100.
SINKING FUND - Annually, Jan. 15, 1998-2016, sufficient to redeem $10,000,000 principal amount of debs., plus similar optional payments. Sinking fund is designed to retire 95% of debs. prior to maturity.
SECURITY - Not secured. Ranks on a parity with Co.'s other unsecured and unsubordinated. Co. or any subsidiary will not create, assume, incur or suffer to be created, assumed or incurred any mortgage, lien, charge or encumbrance of any kind upon any shares of stock, indebtedness or other obligation of a subsidiary owned by Co. or another subsidiary and Co. will not create, assume, incur or suffer to be created, assumed or incurred any lien on any materially important manufacturing facility directly owned and operated by Co., as determined by its board of directors without, in each case, making effective provision whereby all the securities shall be directly secured equally and ratably with the indebtedness or other obligations secured by such lien.
INDENTURE MODIFICATION - Indenture may be modified, except as provided, with consent of a majority of debs. outstg.
RIGHTS ON DEFAULT - Trustee, or 25% of debs. outstg., may declare principal due and payable (30 days' grace for payment of interest).
PURPOSE - Proceeds will be used to reduce outstg. short-term borrowings incurred to finance the acquisition of General Foods Corp.
OFFERED - ($200,000,000) at 98.125 plus accrued interest (proceeds to Co., 97.250) on Jan. 8, 1987 thru First Boston Corp.; Goldman, Sachs & Co.; Morgan Stanley & Co., Inc. and associates.

PRICE RANGE -	1994
High	105⅝
Low	92⅜

4. Philip Morris Companies Inc. eurodeutschemark bonds 6s, due 1996:

Rating - A2

AUTH - DM $225,000,000.
OUTSTG - Dec. 31, 1994, $225,000,000.
DATED - Mar. 20, 1986.
DUE - May, 1996.
DUE - 1996
INTEREST - March 20.
OTHER DETAILS - Not reported.

5. Philip Morris Companies Inc. Swiss Franc eurobond 6⅞s, due 1998:

Rating - A2

AUTH - SFr 250,000,000; outstg. Dec. 31, 1993, $250,000,000.
OUTSTG - Dec. 31, 1994, $250,000,000.
DATED - May 22, 1991.
DUE - May 22, 1998.
INTEREST - Payable annually in arrears on May 22. For this purpose the bonds are furnished with coupons, the first of which will become due and payable on May 22, 1992.
DENOMINATION - In bearer form, in the denomination of SFr5,000 and SFr100,000. Transferable and exchangeable without service charge.
CALLABLE - Not callable prior to maturity except, for tax reasons, in whole but not in part, at any time, at the option of Co. at 100.
SECURITY - Not secured. Ranks pari passu among themselves and all other present or future direct, unsecured and unsubordinated obligations of Co. for money borrowed, issued or guaranteed. Co. or any subsidiary will not, directly or indirectly, create, assume, incur or suffer to be created, assumed or incurred, any mortgage, lien, charge or encumbrance on, or conditional sale or other title retention agreement with respect to any shares of stock, indebtedness or other obligation of a subsidiary owned by Co. or another subsidiary and (i) Co. will not, directly or indirectly, create, assume, incur or suffer to be created, assumed or incurred any lien on any manufacturing plant or facility owned and operated by Co. which is determined to be a materially important manufacturing plant or facility by the Board of Directors in its discretion, without making effective provision whereby all the bonds shall be directly secured equally and ratably with the indebtedness or other obligations secured by such lien, so long as such indebtedness or other obligations shall be so secured.
SALE AND LEASEBACK - Sale and leasebacks by Co. of any materially important manufacturing facility

---

EXHIBIT 2.10   Types of Bond Options

Callability	Allows the *issuing firm* to retire the bonds before maturity by paying a prespecified price. Typically, the bond indenture contains a schedule of dates and the prices on those dates at which the firm can call the bonds. These call provisions:
	• Give firms protection from bondholders who refuse to renegotiate bond covenants that the firm believes, after the fact, are too restrictive.
	• Allow firms to retire high-coupon bonds when interest rates have fallen or when the firm's creditworthiness has improved.
	• Enable firms to implement sinking fund provisions.
	• Result in bonds that sell for lower prices than noncallable bonds.
	If covenants do not prevent the call from being financed by issuing new lower interest rate debt, the bonds are called **refundable bonds**.
Convertibility	Gives the *bondholder* the option to convert the bond into another security, typically the common stock of the firm issuing the convertible bond. The terms of the conversion option are specified in the bond covenants by indicating the conversion price or the number of shares that the bondholder can exchange for the bond.
	• The **conversion premium** is the difference between the market price of the security for which one exchanges the bond and the conversion price.
Exchangeability	Gives the *issuing firm* the right to exchange the bond for a bond of a different type. For example, the firm might be able to exchange a bond with floating-rate payments for one with fixed-rate payments.
Putability	Gives the *bondholder* the right, under certain circumstances, to sell the bond back to the firm. If the value of the outstanding bonds falls (perhaps owing to a proposal to leverage the firm much more highly), bondholders could force the firm to buy back the outstanding bonds at an exorbitant price. Putable bonds sell for higher prices than nonputable bonds.

Poison Puts.   Putable bonds became popular after the merger and acquisition boom in the mid-1980s. A popular type of putable bond, known as a **poison put bond**, is designed to protect bondholders in the event of a corporate takeover.[14] The **leveraged buyout**—that is, a purchase of a firm with large amounts of debt—of RJR-Nabisco by Kohlberg, Kravis, and Roberts (KKR) in 1988 provided the major impetus for poison put provisions. When KKR finally won the $25 billion bidding battle, RJR-Nabisco bonds had dropped by 16 points or $160 for each $1,000 bond. With long-term debt of roughly $5 billion, bondholders had losses of $800 million, which meant plenty of work for lawyers suing RJR-Nabisco. New issuers responded to bondholder concerns by including put options in their bonds.

In July 1993, for example, after recently going through a **leveraged recapitalization**—a procedure in which debt is issued to buy back equity—the Kroger Company

---

[14]Lehn and Poulsen (1991) reported that 32 percent of the corporate bonds issued in 1989 contained poison put provisions. This percentage has declined substantially since that time.

EXHIBIT 2.11   Bond Types Based on Coupon or Cash Flow Pattern

Straight-coupon bond (also called a **bullet bond**[a])	Fixed-rate instrument in which the coupon is typically paid in two equal semiannual installments with only the last installment including the principal repayment. Straight-coupon bonds are usually priced at **par**, meaning that the coupon rate is set so that the bond sells for roughly its face value.
Zero-coupon bond (Also called **pure discount bond**)	Bonds that pay no periodic interest but have a single payment at maturity. These bonds are sold at a discount from their face value. The size of the discount depends on prevailing interest rates and the creditworthiness of the borrower.
Deferred-coupon bond	Bonds that permit the issuer to avoid interest payment obligations for a certain period (e.g., five years). This allows cash-constrained firms some breathing space in the hope that their cash flows will grow. • In one variation, the coupon deferral causes the bondholder to be paid in kind with additional bonds; hence the name **PIK (payment-in-kind) bonds**. • In another variation, the coupon is at a fixed rate, hence the name **Zerfix bond**.
Perpetuity bond (also called a **consol**)	Bonds that last forever and only pay interest.[b]
Annuity bond	Bonds that pay a mix of interest and principal for a finite amount of time. In contrast to a straight coupon bond, there is no balloon payment of principal at the bond's maturity date.

[a]In some circles, zero-coupon bonds, which do not pay interest periodically, are also considered bullets. We will consider as bullets only those bonds that pay interest.

[b]Perpetuities, while useful for understanding bond pricing because of their mathematical properties, are extremely rare in practice. They are found mostly in the United Kingdom where they are generally referred to as consols.

---

issued $200 million of senior secured debentures with a 10-year maturity and a poison put provision. The put option allowed bondholders to sell bonds back to the firm at a price of $101 should any person or group obtain more than 50 percent ownership of the voting stock of Kroger or a majority on the board of directors.

Cash Flow Pattern

Bond types are often categorized by their cash flow pattern, as Exhibit 2.11 describes. Exhibit 2.12 contrasts the cash flows patterns for the five types of bonds described in Exhibit 2.11. Note the pattern of cash flows for a straight-coupon bond. This pattern is composed of a set of small, equal cash flows every period until the maturity date of the bond, at which time there is a much larger cash flow. The stream of small, level periodic cash flows are typically semiannual coupons until the bond's maturity date. At maturity, the large **balloon payment**[15] of straight-coupon bonds reflects the payment of all of the principal due in addition to the semiannual coupon. The coupon is usually set so that the bond initially trades close to *par value* ($100 per $100 of face value).

---

[15]A balloon payment refers to a bond payment that is much larger than its other payments.

EXHIBIT 2.12 **Cash Flows of Various Bond Types**

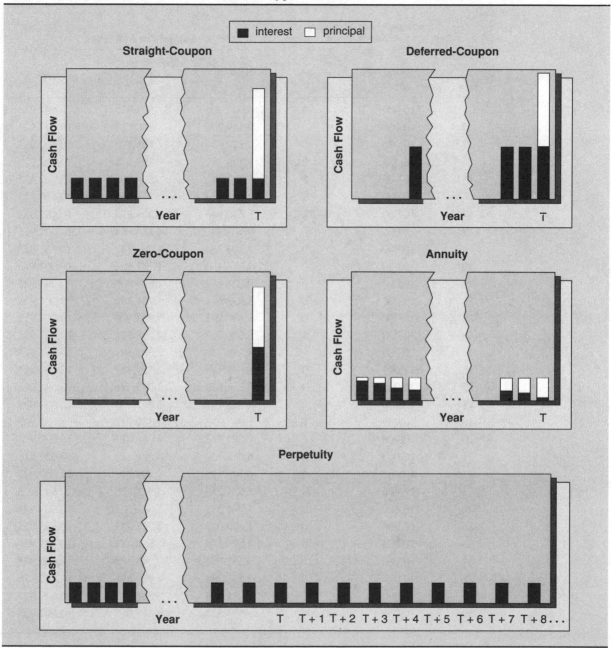

Amortization of Annual Pay Annuity Bonds. The promised cash flows of some bonds resemble an annuity rather than a straight-coupon bond. For instance, residential mortgages and many commercial mortgages pay a level monthly payment, a portion of which is interest and another portion principal.

The right-hand side of Exhibit 2.13 on page 46 illustrates the pattern of principal paydown for a 30-year annual pay mortgage over time (i.e., its amortization). It shows

EXHIBIT 2.13   Amortization of Straight-Coupon Bonds and Mortgages

Year	Annual Pay Straight-Coupon Bond Interest (a)	Principal (b)	Annual Pay Mortgage Interest (c)	Principal Paid (d)	Total (c) & (d)
1	$10,000	$ 0	$10,000.000	$ 607.925	$10.607.925
2	10,000	0	9,939.208	668.717	10,607.925
3	10,000	0	9,872.336	735.589	10,607.925
4	10,000	0	9,798.777	809.148	10,607.925
5	10,000	0	9,717.862	890.063	10,607.925
6	10,000	0	9,628.856	979.069	10,607.925
7	10,000	0	9,530.948	1,076.976	10,607.925
8	10,000	0	9,423.251	1,184.674	10,607.925
9	10,000	0	9,304.784	1,303,141	10,607.925
10	10,000	0	9,174.470	1,433.455	10,607.925
11	10,000	0	9,031.124	1,576.800	10,607.925
12	10,000	0	8,873.444	1,734.480	10,607.925
13	10,000	0	8,699.996	1,907.929	10,607.925
14	10,000	0	8,509.203	2,098.721	10,607.925
15	10,000	0	8,299.331	2,308.594	10,607.925
16	10,000	0	8,608.472	2,539.453	10,607.925
17	10,000	0	4,814.527	2,793.398	10,607.925
18	10,000	0	7,535.187	3,072.739	10,607.925
19	10,000	0	7,227.913	3,380.012	10,607.925
20	10,000	0	6,889.912	3,718.013	10,607.925
21	10,000	0	6,518.111	4,089.814	10,607.925
22	10,000	0	6,109.129	4,498.796	10,607.925
23	10,000	0	5,659.250	4,948.675	10,607.925
24	10,000	0	5,164.382	5,443.543	10,607.925
25	10,000	0	4,620.028	5,987.897	10,607.925
26	10,000	0	4,021.238	6,586.687	10,607.925
27	10,000	0	3,362.569	7,245.355	10,607.925
28	10,000	0	2,638.034	7,969.891	10,607.925
29	10,000	0	1,841.045	8,766.880	10,607.925
30	10,000	100,000	964.357	9,643.568	10,607.925

that early in the life of this annuity bond the largest portion of the payment is interest. With each subsequent payment, a greater portion of the payment applies to principal.

Over the life of the 30-year mortgage, there are 30 identical annual payments of $10,607.925. The present value of these 30 payments at a 10 percent discount rate is $100,000. The interest on $100,000 at 10 percent per year is $10,000. Hence, of the $10,607.925 first payment, $10,000 is interest (column (c)) and the remaining $607.925 is principal (column (d)), which serves to pay down the principal balance (i.e., amount due) on the mortgage. Ten percent interest on the outstanding loan balance of

$99,392.075 in year 2 ($100,000 less the principal payment of $607.925 in year 1), is $9,939.208 (column (*c*)). Subtracting this interest from the $10,607.925 payment made that year yields the principal paid on the loan in year 2, which is $668.717 (column (*d*)). The outstanding loan balance for year 3 is the loan balance of $99,392.072 in year 2 less the principal paydown of $668.717, or $98,723.36, 10 percent of which is the interest in year 3, and so forth.[16]

The Amortization of an Annual-Pay Straight Coupon Bond.   The left-hand side of Exhibit 2.13 illustrates the amortization of a straight-coupon bond. In contrast with the annuity on the right-hand side, the $10,000 first-year payment on the straight-coupon bond, the sum of columns (a) and (b) on the left-hand side is sufficient only to cover the bond's 10 percent interest on the $100,000 principal. Hence, there is no reduction in the principal balance due on the loan, and the borrower still owes $100,000 principal on the bond in year 2. In subsequent years, only interest is covered by each $10,000 annual payment. Thus, not until the final year of the bond is any principal paid. In this case, both the $10,000 in interest due and the entire $100,000 principal make up the final payment.

Amortization of Perpetuities and Zero-Coupon Bonds.   The amortization of a perpetuity is identical to that of a straight-coupon bond except that, lacking a maturity date, there is never any payment of principal in one final balloon payment. In contrast, a zero-coupon bond has **negative amortization**. No payment is made, so the principal on which interest is owed grows over time. The principal of a zero-coupon bond at year *t*, denoted P_t, satisfies the equation:

$$P_t = P_{t-1}(1 + r)$$

where *r* is the stated rate (sometimes called the yield) of the zero-coupon bond. Since the initial principal of a zero-coupon bond, P_0, is the price paid for the *T*-year zero-coupon bond, the tax authorities in most countries will impute an interest rate and charge tax on interest earned but not paid. The interest imputed by the tax authorities is at a rate *r* that satisfies the equation:

$$r = \left(\frac{P_T}{P_0}\right)^{\frac{1}{T}} - 1$$

Tax is then paid each year on the imputed interest. For year $t, t \leq T$, the imputed interest is

$$P_{t-1}r$$

Amortization of Monthly Mortgages.   The right-hand side of Exhibit 2.13 oversimplifies the cash flows of most mortgages by assuming annual payments and compounding. In reality, the interest rate on virtually every residential mortgage is an annualized interest rate, compounded monthly.[17] Hence, the monthly payment per $100,000 of a Y-year mortgage with interest rate *r* is the number *x* that satisfies

---

[16]Note that at each stage along the way, the beginning-of-year principal balance on which the year's interest is owed, 10 times the year-end interest in Exhibit 2.13, is the present value of the remaining annual payments, each in the amount of $10,607.925. Hence, the $99,392.08 principal balance for the beginning of the second year, 10 times the 9,939.208 interest at year 2, is also the discounted value (at 10 percent) of the 29 remaining payments at the end of years 2–30.

[17]See the appendix at the end of this textbook for a discussion of compounding frequencies.

$$\$100{,}000 = \sum_{t=1}^{12Y} \frac{x}{\left(1 + \dfrac{r}{12}\right)^t}$$

Example 2.2 illustrates how to compute a monthly mortgage payment.

Example 2.2:   Computing Monthly Mortgage Payments

Compute the monthly mortgage payment of a 30-year fixed-rate mortgage of $150,000 at 9 percent.

Answer: The monthly unannualized interest rate is .09/12 or .0075. Hence, the monthly payment x solves:

$$\$150{,}000 = \sum_{t=1}^{360} \frac{x}{1.0075^t}$$

Using a financial calculator, trial and error, or the annuity formula,[18] the monthly mortgage payment is:

$$x = \$1206.93$$

In general, to compute the amount of interest on a monthly mortgage, take the principal balance on the mortgage and multiply it by $r/12$, where r is the annualized interest rate. The remainder of the payment reduces the principal balance on the mortgage, which is the amount used to compute the next month's interest payment. With a fixed-rate mortgage, the new principal balance equals the present value of the remaining level payments using the mortgage interest rate to discount the payments.

Example 2.3 illustrates the amortization of the monthly mortgage from Example 2.2.

Example 2.3:   Amortizing a Monthly Mortgage

Compute the interest paid, principal paid, and principal balances after the first and second mortgage payments are made for the mortgage in Example 2.2. Verify that the principal balance for the second and third payments is the present value of the remaining level payments.

Answer:

1st payment: Interest = $1,125 = $150,000 (.0075)
Principal payment = $81.93 = $1206.93 − $1125.00
Principal balance = $149,918.07 = $150,000 − $81.93

Using the annuity formula:

$$\$149{,}918.07 = \$1{,}206.93\left(\frac{1}{.0075}\right)\left(1 - \frac{1}{1.0075^{359}}\right)$$

2nd payment: Interest = $1,124.39 = $149,918.07(.0075)
Principal payment = $82.54 = $1,206.93 − $1,124.39
Principal balance = $149,835.53 = $149,918.07 − $82.54

$$\$149{,}835.53 = \$1{,}206.93\left(\frac{1}{.0075}\right)\left(1 - \frac{1}{1.0075^{358}}\right)$$

---

[18]The annuity formula is in the appendix at the end of the textbook.

EXHIBIT 2.14   Bond Type Based on Market Price

Premium bond	Bond with a quoted price that exceeds the face value of the bond.
Par bond	Bond with a quoted price that equals the face value of the bond.
Discount bond	Bond with a face value that exceeds the quoted price of the bond.

Amortizing an Adjustable-Rate Mortgage.   The computation of the amortization of an adjustable-rate mortgage is similar to that used for a fixed-rate mortgage. Each month, compute last month's principal balance and the current monthly payment, the interest and principal breakdown, and the principal balance that applies to the subsequent month. In contrast to the fixed rate mortgage, however, the interest rate used in an adjustable-rate mortgage changes each month. The payment for a given month is equal to the level payment for the remaining life of the mortgage that has a present value at that new interest rate equal to the principal balance on the mortgage.[19]

Bond Prices: Par, Discount, and Premium Bonds

Bonds are also categorized by their market price in relation to the amount of principal due, as Exhibit 2.14 illustrates.

As time elapses, a straight-coupon bond that traded at par when it was issued can become a discount bond or a premium bond. This occurs if either riskless bonds of the same maturity experience price changes, which implies a change in the level of interest rates, or if the credit risk of the bond changes.

Bonds that are issued at a discount are known as **original issue discount (OID)** bonds. This occurs when the coupon rate is set lower than the coupon rate of par bonds of the same maturity and credit risk. There may be no coupon as in the case of zero-coupon bonds. Alternatively, the bond may pay a dual coupon; a **dual-coupon bond** has a low coupon initially and a higher coupon in later years. Dual coupons are typically found in a number of high-yield bonds or bonds that have large amounts of default risk (to be discussed later in this chapter).

Maturity

It is also possible to classify debt instruments based on their maturity. Generally, a bill or paper issue consists of a zero-coupon debt security with one year or less to maturity at the issue date. A note generally refers to a medium-term debt security with maturity at issue of 1 to 10 years. A bond generally refers to a debt security with more than 10 years to maturity. However, these distinctions are not always so sharp. For example, the terms medium-term note, structured bond, and structured note can refer to a particular type of debt security of almost any maturity. The term *bond* also can be a generic term referring to any debt security, as we have used it here.

---

[19]See Exercise 2.5.

Bond Ratings

A *bond rating* is a quality ranking of a specific debt issue. There are four major bond-rating agencies: Moody's, Standard & Poor's (S&P), Duff & Phelps (D&P), and Fitch.

The Process of Obtaining a Rating.   For a fee ranging from $5,000 to $20,000, each agency will rate the credit quality of a debt issue and follow that issue over its lifetime with annual or more frequent reviews. Debt may be upgraded or downgraded depending on the financial condition of the firm. In 1995, more than 2,000 U.S. firms had their debt rated by rating agencies.[20]

A rating agency is hired to rate a bond before the firm offers it to the public. To produce a rating, the agency must first scrutinize the financial statements of the firm and talk to senior management. After the agency notifies the firm of its initial rating, the firm's management generally provides additional information if it believes the rating is too low. Once the final rating is determined, the rating agency will continue to monitor the firm for any changes in its financial status.

The Ratings Designations and Their Meaning.   Exhibit 2.15 shows the rating designations used by the four leading rating agencies and their meaning.

The Relation between a Bond's Rating and its Yield.   Bond ratings can have an important influence on the promised rates of return of corporate bonds, known as bond yields. For instance, during 1983 the spread between AAA-rated bonds and BBB-rated bonds varied between 180 and 246 basis points, which was unusually large. In contrast, that spread varied between 75 and 90 basis points during 1993.

When Ederington, Yawitz, and Roberts (1987) investigated the relation between bond yields and both ratings and accounting measures of creditworthiness, they found that both types of information influenced bond yields. Thus, according to their study, the bond of a firm with a high rating would sell at a higher price than the bond of a firm with a lower rating if the two firms have similar financial ratios and their bonds have the same features (e.g., similar seniority, coupon, collateralization, and options).

The High-Yield Debt Market

An **investment-grade rating** on a bond is a rating of Baa and above by Moody's and BBB and above for the other three agencies. Because many large investors are prohibited from owning below-investment-grade bonds, also known as **high-yield** or **junk bonds**, most firms strive to maintain an investment-grade rating.[21] Despite these negative consequences, the growth of the high-yield bond market has been spectacular.

Growth of the High-Yield Debt Market.   The volume of outstanding noninvestment-grade bonds rose from about $25 billion in 1980 (about 10 percent of the total corporate bond market) to roughly $200 billion in 1992. Experts have estimated that since 1992, 25 percent of the outstanding debt securities have been below investment grade,

---

[20]The 1995 edition of *Moody's Industrial Manual* has this number of firms.

[21]Government workers' pension funds and teachers' pension funds in most states are prohibited by law from investing in junk bonds. The charters of numerous corporate pension funds have similar prohibitions.

EXHIBIT 2.15   Summary of Rating Symbols and Definitions

Moody's	S&P	Fitch	D&P	Brief Definition
Investment Grade–High Creditworthiness				
Aaa	AAA	AAA	AAA	Gilt edge, prime, maximum safety
Aa1	AA+	AA+	AA+	
Aa2	AA	AA	AA	Very high grade, high quality
Aa3	AA−	AA−	AA−	
A1	A+	A+	A+	
A2	A	A	A	Upper medium grade
A3	A−	A−	A−	
Baa1	BBB+	BBB+	BBB+	
Baa2	BBB	BBB	BBB	Lower medium grade
Baa3	BBB−	BBB−	BBB−	
Distinctly Speculative–Low Creditworthiness				
Ba1	BB+	BB+	BB+	
Ba2	BB	BB	BB	Low grade, speculative
Ba3	BB−	BB−	BB−	
B1	B+	B+	B+	
B2	B	B	B	Highly speculative
B3	B−	B−	B−	
Predominantly Speculative–Substantial Risk or in Default				
	CCC+			
Caa	CCC	CCC	CCC	Substantial risk, in poor standing
	CCC−			
Ca	CC	CC		May be in default, extremely speculative
C	C	C		Even more speculative than those above
	CI			Income bonds—no interest being paid
		DDD		
		DD	DD	Default
	D	D		

Source: Reprinted with permission of The McGraw-Hill Companies, Inc., from *The New Corporate Bond Market*, by Richard Wilson and Frank Fabozzi, © 1990 Probus Publishing Company.

which would bring the 1995 estimate of outstanding noninvestment grade debt to about $400 billion.

Exhibit 2.16 on page 52 shows the dollar volume of junk bonds issued for each year from 1980 to 1993. Two features of the line graph are worth noting:

· The number of issues plunged in 1990 and 1991.
· A striking rebound occurred in the market beginning in 1992 and 1993.

Causes of the Increase in High-Yield Debt Issuance.   Much of the 1980–1987 increase in high-yield debt issuance was linked to the increase in corporate takeovers that was taking place simultaneously. There were two reasons for the subsequent 1990–1991 "bust." First, Drexel, Burnham, Lambert, underwriter of more than 50 percent of high-yield issues and the center of the over-the-counter market in junk bonds at the time (and the employer of junk-bond *wunderkind* Michael Milken), went bankrupt in February 1990. Drexel experienced a great deal of financial distress prior to the bankruptcy and many other Wall Street firms shunned dealings with the firm to avoid exposure to Drexel's credit risk. Second, Congress passed the Financial Institutions Reform,

EXHIBIT 2.16 Volume of High-Yield Debt Issues

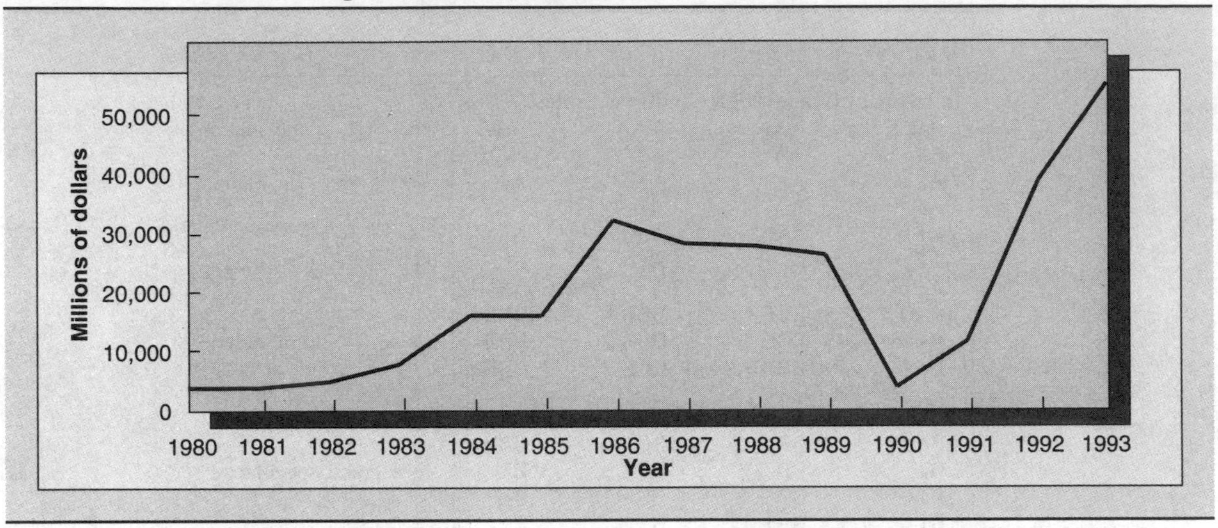

Source: *Information Please Business Almanac and Sourcebook*, 1995. Reprinted with permission of Inso Corporation.

Recovery, and Enforcement Act (FIRREA) in 1989, forcing insurance companies and thrifts to divest their holdings of noninvestment-grade debt.

The rebound of the early 1990s demonstrated, however, that high-yield debt was an innovative product with staying power. Prior to this innovation, bank loans were the only available sources of debt capital for small firms and for leveraged buyouts. With the advent of the junk bond market, firms in need of debt financing found a public market willing to provide financing at lower cost than the banks and often with more flexible covenants.

To its supporters, the evolution of the junk bond market illustrates how the financial markets respond to a demand and create enormous value in doing so. There had always been high-yield debt. Prior to 1980, however, nearly all of it was comprised of so-called **"fallen angels,"** that is, investment-grade debt that had been downgraded because the issuing firm had experienced financial distress. Milken and Drexel had the genius to realize that there could be a primary market for noninvestment grade debt.

Drexel was fortunate to be in the right place at the right time. The late 1970s and the early 1980s were characterized by high interest rates, high interest rate volatility, and an economic environment in which short-term interest rates were as much as 400 basis points (4 percent) above long-term rates.[22] This situation made banks wary of lending long-term, thereby drying up the most important source of funds for unrated firms. Drexel, aware of the funding gap, created the market for high-yield securities. When the banks began to make long-term loans again in the mid-1980s, it was too late. The securitized financing issued with the help of Drexel was popular with investors and cheaper than the financing the banks were providing. The rest is history.

The Default Experience and the Returns of High-Yield Debt. The junk bond market continues to be controversial. Early studies by Altman and Nammacher (1985), Altman (1987), and Weinstein (1986–1987) claimed that the probability of default on a typical

---

[22]Risk-free, short-term interest rates hit a peak of about 16 percent in 1981.

junk bond was quite low while its return relative to a typical investment-grade bond was high, implying that junk bonds were a great buy. However, such studies underestimated default probabilities because they measured the default rate as the percentage of bonds defaulting in a year divided by the total amount of bonds outstanding.

More recent studies by Altman (1989) and Asquith, Mullins, and Wolff (1989) pointed out that the huge growth in the high-yield market meant that old issues with relatively high default rates were masked by the large volume of new issues, which had much lower default rates. In the first year after issue, bonds did have low default rates, in the range of 2–3 percent, but once they had aged by 6–10 years, the proportion that ultimately defaulted rose to 20–30 percent. As expected, this compares unfavorably to investment-grade debt whose cumulative default rate is roughly 1–2 percent after 10 years.[23]

Evidence on the value of investing in junk bonds is less clear-cut. Although the present consensus is that about 20–30 percent of the junk bonds issued in any given year are likely to eventually default, the returns from holding junk bonds continue to be disputed. Altman (1989) showed that default-adjusted spreads over Treasuries on high-yield bonds were large and positive, indicating that investors did well. Because Altman adjusted only for default risk, however, his results must be viewed with skepticism.

Cornell and Green (1991) and Blume, Keim, and Patel (1991) reached different conclusions. Cornell and Green analyzed returns from mutual funds that invested in junk bonds, thus circumventing the data problems associated with individual bonds. Blume, Keim, and Patel used bond price data from Drexel and Salomon, which are more reliable than a random sample of bonds. Both studies found that, on average, the returns from holding junk bonds lie between the returns from holding high-grade bonds and from holding common stock. Both studies concluded that the average returns experienced by investors in junk bonds compensated them fairly for the risk they bore.

2.5 More Exotic Securities

One of the chief characteristics of financial markets is their ability to develop innovative financial instruments. This section explores a few examples of these innovations and the forces that drive them.

Tax and Regulatory Frictions as Motivators for Innovation

Firms issue innovative securities for many reasons, but two of the most important are to escape the bite of taxes and regulation. The following is an example of a dual-currency bond, an exotic innovative security driven by regulation.

RJR's Dual-Currency Bonds

As part of the financing of RJR's acquisition of Nabisco in 1985, Morgan Guaranty Trust suggested a dual-currency Eurobond (defined shortly). The bond would pay the annual coupons in yen, but the principal would be repaid in dollars.

There was a peculiar regulatory reason for issuing the dual-currency bond. Japanese insurance funds could pay dividends to policyholders only out of the cash yield of investments. Thus, their need for high-coupon bonds was great. The bond suggested by Morgan

---

[23]Moody's (1994) estimates recovery rates—that is, what fraction of principal is recovered after a default has occurred—as varying from about 40 percent to 60 percent for corporate bonds. Bank debt recovery rates tend to be about 20–30 percent higher.

had a coupon of roughly 150 basis points higher than a competing straight Euroyen bond. The larger coupon was compensated for by a favorable implicit forward currency exchange rate that translated the yen principal into dollars.

The Japanese insurance companies were willing to take a loss at maturity in return for higher coupons along the way. The dual-currency Eurobonds were much like private placements because they were presold to the insurance companies and there was no secondary market trading for them. Regulations also prohibited Japanese firms from holding more than 10 percent of assets in foreign securities. Despite the dollar payment at the end, the dual-currency bond was not counted as a foreign security. RJR was able to issue the bond at just 30 basis points above Treasury yields at a time when other recent issues were priced to yield 50 to 100 basis points above Treasuries.

Source: Kester and Allen (1991).

Collateralization as a Force for Innovation

Other recent innovations include the creation of **asset-backed securities**, which are securities that are collateralized by cash flows from assets, like mortgages and accounts receivable. The mortgage-backed securities market is perhaps the pioneer in this vein, but other interesting examples abound. Asset-backed securities have become one of the cheapest ways of turning an asset like receivables into ready cash.

In March 1994, for example, Northwest Airlines brought the first airline industry asset-backed certificates to the market. They were backed by Northwest's accounts receivable—their ticket payments. The receivable certificates were sold in a private placement, priced at LIBOR plus 87.5 basis points with a cap at 12 percent. Even though Northwest was not in good financial shape, since the certificates were backed by receivables, they obtained a AA rating.[24] Similar asset-backed securities have been issued by credit card companies and automobile financing units.

Financial Innovation in Emerging Capital Markets

Other frictions in the financial markets of some countries may drive financial innovation. Firms located in countries with emerging capital markets can be just as inventive as U.S. firms. In 1994, Avtovaz, a Russian automobile manufacturer, issued 300,000 bonds convertible into Ladas, the car it makes. If held to maturity, an Avtovaz bond is redeemable for one Lada. For people who want an automobile, buying the Avtovaz bond is an easy choice; at the time, the only other way to get a car in Russia is to pay a bribe to be put at the top of the waiting list.

Another Russian example is Komineft, an oil company, which issued zero-coupon bonds whose principal is tied to the *dollar* price of oil. Investors are thus protected against the decline in the value of the ruble caused by Russian inflation.[25]

The Junk Bond Market and Financial Innovation

The junk bond market also seems to be a driving force for innovative security design. Once the junk bond market took off, many innovations followed. Instead of straight bonds with high coupons, firms began to issue bonds with special features and embedded options. Thus, they created Zerfix bonds, (short for *zero* and *fixed* coupons), a deferred

---

[24]Financing Foreign Operations, Economist Intelligence Unit, March 1995.
[25]*The Economist,* June 18, 1994.

coupon bond which consisted of an initial zero coupon followed by a *fixed* coupon after three to seven years. Zerfix bonds were intended to help the issuing firm conserve cash. Similarly, firms issued PIK bonds, which gave them the option to pay either in cash or in additional bonds. As an implicit promise to retire or refinance debt, firms sold **increasing-rate notes (IRNs)**, which required the firm to increase the coupon quarterly at a predetermined rate in the range of 20–50 basis points.

A Perspective on the Pace of Financial Innovation

The pace of financial innovation has been remarkable given that new security designs cannot be patented, are easily copied, and, once copied, their profitability to the inventor drops dramatically.[26] To encourage such a rapid pace of innovation, successful security designs have to be phenomenally profitable to the inventor for that brief period of time before competitors introduce imitations.

Will the pace of financial innovation ever slow down? As long as governments continue to tax, regulate, and restrain trade, firms will devise ways to minimize taxes, reduce the effectiveness of regulations, and overcome trading frictions in the economy. Therefore, we expect financial innovation to continue.

2.6 Raising Debt Capital in the Euromarkets

As Chapter 1 suggested, there are two general ways that a firm can raise money internationally: in the Euromarkets or in the domestic markets of other countries. Firms using the Euromarkets can either sell bonds or take out loans. Firms also can sell debt directly to foreign investors or borrow directly from a foreign bank in a variety of currencies.

Features of Eurobonds

A **Eurobond** typically has the following features:

- It is sold outside the country in whose currency it is denominated.
- It is a **bearer bond**, which means it is unregistered and payable to the person who carries it; losing a Eurobond is like losing a wallet filled with currency.[27]
- It is offered to investors in many different countries, usually by an international syndicate of investment banks.
- It is generally sold only by large and well-known multinational firms.
- Its coupons are typically paid annually.

Because the Eurobond market is not located in any one country, it is mostly self-regulated by the Association of International Bond Dealers. A typical issuer, such as a U.S. multinational company, does not have to meet SEC requirements to sell a Eurobond security. This allows deals to be completed in just a few days.

---

[26]See Tufano (1992).

[27]While having a bearer bond means that you must physically clip a coupon on the bond to obtain an interest payment, this is viewed by some governments as inconveniencing tax collectors more than bondholders.

RJR made heavy use of the Eurobond market after it bought Nabisco in 1985. As part of the financing, the company went to the Euromarkets with eight separate issues between August 1985 and May 1986, raising more than $850 million from both straight- and dual-currency bonds in five different countries—the dollar, yen; ECU (the currency of the European Union), Swiss franc, and deutsche mark (DM)—using four different lead underwriters.

Size and Growth of the Eurobond Market and the Forces behind the Growth

The growth in the Eurobond market has been spectacular. By 1995, the amount of Eurobond debt issues outstanding, between $1.5 trillion and $2 trillion, was more than 15 times larger than the amount outstanding in 1980.[28] This growth has been driven in part by the growth in the currency swap market. A **currency swap** is simply an agreement between parties to periodically exchange the future cash flows of bonds with pay-offs in two different currencies.[29] For example, in 1991 Daimler-Benz issued more than DM 3 billion in Eurobonds denominated in Canadian dollars, Swiss francs, ECUs, Italian lire, British pounds, and U.S. dollars. These were swapped into deutsche marks, U.S. dollars, lire, Spanish pesetas, and French francs.

Swaps enable firms to issue bonds in whatever currency they choose and to swap the proceeds into whatever currency they need. They allow multinational firms like Daimler-Benz to take full advantage of global capital markets to obtain the lowest borrowing rate, and then to hedge the currency risk of their global operations and their financing with a series of swap agreements.

Eurocurrency Loans

Firms can also raise funds in the Euromarkets through a **Eurocurrency loan**. A Eurocurrency is a major currency on deposit in a bank outside of the country of origin for the currency. Thus, when AT&T deposits dollars into the London branches of Citibank or Barclays, their deposits become **Eurodollar deposits**. Similarly, when Daimler-Benz deposits deutsche marks in the London branches of Deutsche Bank or Fuji Bank, the marks become Euromark deposits. The banks loan the funds out short-term as LIBOR loans to other major banks. Alternatively, banks may lend the funds as long-term Eurocurrency loans to a firm.

Features of Eurocurrency Loans.   The following features characterize long-term Eurocurrency loans:

• They are issued on a floating-rate basis, usually at a fixed spread above LIBOR.

• The margin varies between about 50 and 300 basis points, depending on the credit risk of the borrowing firm or bank, with the benchmark LIBOR rate generally reset every six months.

• They have a maturity of 3 to 10 years.

• They are issued by a syndicate of banks which charge fixed fees of 0.25–1 percent of loan value. The syndicate allows great flexibility in the timing of takedowns of the loan commitment.

---

[28]See Benevides (1996).
[29]See Chapter 7 for additional discussion of currency swaps.

The case below illustrates a Eurocurrency loan.

Comdisco's Use of Eurocurrency Loans

Comdisco, a U.S.-based firm that leases computers, peripherals, and other high-tech equipment to customers worldwide, has subsidiaries in more than 60 countries. Naturally, customers prefer to transact in the local currency. To fund working capital needs in the early 1990s, Comdisco set up a credit facility with a syndicate of banks that included LaSalle National in Chicago, Westpac in Australia, the Union Bank of Switzerland, and three Japanese banks: Yasuda Trust, Toyo Trust, and Mitsui Taiyo Kobe. The credit function is centralized in Comdisco's Chicago headquarters; all the local subsidiaries have to do to borrow is make one phone call to headquarters, thus avoiding the time-consuming process of credit approval from a foreign bank. Centralization also means that the spread paid on all loans is a small margin over LIBOR plus a flat fee to arrange the facility. The local units enjoy the advantages of cheaper borrowing, low transaction costs, and the ability to borrow in almost any currency from the branch offices of syndicate members.

Source: *Creating World-Class Financial Management*

Why the Rates of Eurocurrency Loans are Relatively Low.　For a number of reasons, lending rates in the Eurocurrency market are often cheaper than those in domestic markets. First, banks have no reserve requirements for Eurodeposits. Second, borrowers are large, well-known companies with good credit ratings, which diminishes the degree of investigation required by the lender firm. Finally, the lack of regulation means that banks can price loans more aggressively in the Eurocurrency market than they can in the domestic market. For all of these reasons, the market has grown substantially since the mid-1980s. Medium-term Eurocurrency loans have grown from $50 billion a year in 1984 to more than $250 billion in the mid-1990s.

2.7 Primary and Secondary Markets for Debt

One of the biggest financial markets in the world is the bond market, but corporate bonds are not the big draw. Instead, U.S. government bonds and the government bonds of a few other key nations such as Japan are the major focus of bond trading activity.

The Primary and Secondary Market for U.S. Treasury Securities

The prices of U.S. Treasury securities are set initially in Treasury auctions. The secondary market functions because a few hundred dealers actively trade these securities through a telephone-linked network and telephone-linked brokers who exist primarily to provide anonymity when these dealers trade with one another. Because this secondary market is not an organized exchange, it is described as **over the counter (OTC)**. The Federal Reserve designated more than 40 OTC dealers[30]—many of which are commercial banks and investment banks—as primary dealers because of their participation in Treasury auctions, financial strength, and customer base. These primary dealers make markets in Treasury securities by quoting bid-ask spreads. They finance many of their purchases with **repurchase agreements** (or repos or simply RPs)—loans that use Treasury securities as collateral and thus need cash for only a small fraction of the purchase price, typically about 2 percent.

---

[30]This number changes from time to time.

Short sales,[31] which involve selling bonds that the seller does not own, make use of reverse RPs, the opposite side of a repurchase agreement. Dealers use these short sales in complicated trading strategies to offset interest rate risk from the purchases of other debt securities. The dealers borrow the Treasury securities, usually overnight, and provide loans to the security lender. The loan proceeds come out of the short sale.

The Primary and Secondary Market for Corporate Bonds

In contrast to the initial pricing of Treasury securities, the initial prices of U.S. corporate bonds, including notes, are typically set by the syndicate desk of the investment bank, which issues the bonds to its largely institutional clients. The **syndicate desk** is the meeting place of the sales and trading and corporate sides of the investment bank. The members of this desk price securities, talking simultaneously to the corporate issuer and the investment bank's salespeople, who are obtaining from institutional clients the prices at which they are likely to buy a particular issue. Up until the moment of issue, the likely pricing of these bonds is quoted to the borrowing firm and investors as a spread to the on-the-run Treasury security of closest maturity because the interest rate level, which is set in the Treasury market, is volatile. In contrast, the spread to Treasuries is more stable and thus a better indicator of how hard the investment bank has worked to keep the firm's borrowing costs low.[32]

The secondary market for corporate debt is largely an over-the-counter market consisting of many of the secondary market dealers in Treasuries. The dealers also are linked by phone and computerized quotation systems. Corporate bonds also are traded on exchanges, but the number of exchange-listed bonds has been dropping over time. In the mid-1980s, more than 1,000 firms listed bonds on the New York Stock Exchange (NYSE); ten years later, about half that number did so.

Exhibits 2.17 (opposite) and 2.18 (on page 60) provide secondary market pricing for corporate debt on the NYSE and for Treasury securities on the over-the-counter market, respectively. Note that the corporate bonds, like stocks, trade in eighths, while Treasuries trade in 32nds.[33]

Most corporate bonds are not actively traded. The illiquidity of these bonds stands in marked contrast to recently issued Treasury notes and bonds and the common stock of large corporations, which are all actively traded.

2.8 Bond Prices, Yields to Maturity, and Bond Market Conventions

Now that you are familiar with the varieties of bonds and the nature of the bond market, it is important to understand how bond prices are quoted. There are two languages for talking about bonds: the *language of prices* and the *language of yields*. It is important to know how to speak both of these languages and how to translate one language easily into the other. While people refer to a number of yields when discussing bonds, our focus is primarily on the yield to maturity. The **yield to maturity** is the discount rate that makes

---

[31]For more information on short sales, see the appendix at the end of this textbook, and also see Chapter 4.

[32]The issuance process, described in more detail in Chapters 1 and 3, is similar to that for U.S. equities.

[33]The numbers after the colon for the bonds and notes in the Treasury Bonds, Notes, and Bills section of the *Wall Street Journal,* Exhibit 2.18, represent 32nds. Hence, a price quote of 117:04 means $117 plus 4/32nds of a dollar per $100 of face value.

EXHIBIT 2.17 Secondary Market Pricing for Corporate Debt

NEW YORK EXCHANGE BONDS

Quotations as of 4 p.m. Eastern Time
Monday, October 14, 1996

Volume $10,407,000

	Domestic Mon.	Domestic Fri.	All Issues Mon.	All Issues Fri.
Issues traded	236	285	244	294
Advances	97	141	97	144
Declines	80	101	83	105
Unchanged	59	43	62	45
New highs	4	9	5	9
New lows	3	4	3	4

SALES SINCE JANUARY 1
(000 omitted)

1996	1995	1994
$4,456,115	$5,796,521	$5,877,110

Dow Jones Bond Averages

–1995– High	–1995– Low	–1996– High	–1996– Low		–1996– Close	–1996– Chg.	–1996– %Yld	–1995– Close	–1995– Chg.
105.34	93.63	106.09	100.99	20 Bonds	102.48	+0.17	7.23	104.04	+ 0.07
102.30	89.08	102.43	97.46	10 Utilities	99.46	+0.26	7.27	100.58	+ 0.12
108.96	98.08	109.94	104.06	10 Industrials	105.49	+0.07	7.19	107.51	+ 0.03

CORPORATION BONDS
Volume, $10,043,000

Bonds	Cur Yld	Vol	Close	Net Chg.
AMR 8.10s98	7.9	4	102¾	...
AMR 9s16	8.3	45	108½	– ¼
ATT 4⅜99	4.6	5	95½	...
ATT 6s00	6.1	25	98¼	+ ⅛
ATT 7⅛02	7.0	30	101⅞	+ ¼
ATT 8⅝31	8.2	30	105⅜	– ⅛
AcmeM 12½02	11.8	25	106⅜	+ ⅝
AirbF 6¾01	cv	33	97½	– 1
AlaPw 9¼21	8.8	11	105	...
AlskAr 6½05	cv	10	115	+ 1¼
AlskAr 6⅞14	cv	50	92¾	...
AlldC zr2000	...	20	77¾	– ¼
AlldC zr09	...	20	38⅜	– ¾
Alza 5s06	cv	49	98½	...
AMedia 11⅝04	11.2	10	104¼	– ⅛
Amoco 8⅝16	8.2	4	105½	+ 1½
Apache 9¼02	8.6	20	108	...
Argosy 12s01	cv	89	90½	...
Arvin 7½14	cv	26	104¼	– ¼
Ashlnd 6¾14	cv	22	104	+ 1
BBN 6s12	cv	15	88	+ ½
Barnet 9⅞01	8.8	10	112½	+ 2½
BellsoT 7⅞32	7.8	10	101⅛	...
BstBuy 8⅝00	8.6	40	99⅞	+ ⅞
BethSt 6⅞99	7.1	29	96½	– ⅛
BethSt 8⅜01	8.5	50	98½	...
Bevrly 7⅝03	cv	17	94	...
Bevrly 9s06	9.1	60	98⅜	+ 1
Bluegrn 8¼12	cv	11	85¼	+ ¼
BorgWS 9⅛03	9.4	25	97½	+ ⅜
BrnhP 8½02	cv	15	98¾	– ½
ChsCp 7⅞04	7.7	30	101⅞	+ ¼
ChsCp 8s05	7.8	10	102½	...
ChespkE 9⅛06	9.0	20	101½	+ 2⅜
Chryslr 10.4s99	10.0	50	104⅜	...
Chryslr 10.95s17	10.0	35	109	...
ChryF 13¼99	11.2	16	118⅛	+ 1¼
ChryF 12¾99	10.9	18	116½	+ 1⅜
Clardge 11¾02	15.2	267	77⅜	– ¼
ClrkOil 9½04	9.3	67	102⅛	+ ⅜
ClevEl 8¾05	8.6	57	101⅝	+ 1⅜
ClevEl 9¼09	9.1	7	102	– 1⅞
ClevEl 8⅜11	8.8	70	95⅛	+ ½
ClevEl 8⅜12	8.8	24	95	– ¼
Coeur 6⅜04	cv	5	90½	+ ½
ColeWld zr13	...	44	29¾	+ ¼
CmwE 7⅝03F	7.7	1	99⅜	+ 1¼
CmwE 8⅛07J	8.1	10	100	– ½
CompUSA 9½00	9.2	63	103	...
ConrPer 6¾01	cv	123	114	– ½
ConrPer 6½02	cv	87	126	– 1
Consec 8⅛03	7.8	48	103⅝	– ¼
CnNG 5⅞98	6.0	5	98⅝	– ⅝
ConNG 7¼15	cv	10	109	+ 1¾
CoopIn 7.05s15	cv	37	107	– ½
DatGen 8⅜02	8.6	5	97½	– 2
Datpnt 8⅞06f	cv	8	58	+ ⅜
Dole 7s03	7.0	10	100	– ½
duPnt dc6s01	6.2	5	96⅝	– ⅝
DukePw 8s99	7.7	15	104	...
DukePw 6¼04	6.5	15	96⅝	+ 2½
DukePw 7⅜23	7.7	19	95½	– ½
Eckerd 9¼04	8.8	20	104⅝	...
ElPaso 8⅝12	8.4	1	103	– 2
EquilCos 6⅛24	cv	6	119	– ¾
EthAln 8¾01	8.5	10	102⅞	– ⅞
FabrCtr 6¼02	cv	3	87⅝	+ ⅛
FairCp 12s01	11.8	10	102	+ 1¾
FairCp 13⅛06	13.0	42	101⅜	+ ⅜
Fedders 8½12	cv	13	94	+ 1
FedDS 10s01	9.2	10	108⅝	+ ⅜
FedDS 5s03	cv	51	112	– 1¼
FldNtl zr09	...	1	46	...
Fldcst 6s12	cv	8	73	...
FUnRE 8⅞03	9.5	160	93⅞	– ⅛
Florsh 12¾02	12.5	168	102¼	+ ¾
FMRP 8¾04	8.6	20	101⅞	– ⅛
FremntGn zr13	...	27	57¼	+ ¼
GPA Del 8¾98	8.7	11	100⅜	...
GnCorp 8s02	7.2	38	111½	+ 3
GHost 11½02	11.8	83	97⅝	+ ⅝
GHost 8s02	cv	2	78½	...
GMA 8⅜97	8.3	7	100⅞	– ⅝
GMA 9⅜00	8.8	20	106	+ 1¼
GMA zr12	...	13	299¼	– ¾
GMA zr15	...	10	248	– 2
Genesc 10⅜03	10.3	85	100½	– 1
GrandCas 10⅛08	10.0	139	101	...
Gulfrd 6s12	cv	5	97½	+ ½
Hallwd 7s00	7.9	15	88⅜	– ⅝
HltRet 7½03	cv	221	99	...
Hlthso 9½01	9.0	10	105⅛	...
Hills 12½03	13.4	25	93¼	+ ⅝
HomeDpt 3¼01	cv	15	103½	+ ¾
ICN Ph 8½99	cv	40	107	– 1
IBM 6⅜97	6.4	65	100⅜	...
IBM 6⅜00	6.4	10	99⅞	+ ⅜
IBM 7½13	7.3	10	102⅞	+ 1⅝
IBM 8⅜19	7.9	2	106⅝	– 2¾
InterSec 7¾11	cv	85	95½	– ¼
JPS Aut 11⅛01	10.8	10	103	+ 1
KaufB 9⅜03	9.2	26	101⅝	...
Kolmrg 8¾09	cv	100	100	+ 1
LaFrg 7s13	cv	24	104½	...
Leucadia 10⅜02	9.6	21	107⅞	...
LgIsLt 7.05s03	7.5	35	94½	+ ⅜
LgIsLt 8⅝04	8.5	7	101⅜	– ⅛
LgIsLt 8.9s19	9.3	47	95¾	– ⅛
LgIsLt 9¾21	9.7	15	100¼	– ⅜
LgIsLt 9s22	9.2	30	98	+ ⅝
LgIsLt 8.2s23	8.8	20	92¾	+ ½
Magntx 8s01	cv	11	98½	...
Malan 9½04	cv	25	93	...
MarO 7s02	7.0	35	100¼	+ ½
Masco 5¼12	cv	16	94	– 1
Mascotch 03	cv	11	78	+ ¼
McDnlDg 9¼02	8.3	6	111	+ 1
MerLyGlbl 98	...	20	101	...
MerLyCo 98	...	12	100	...
Metrom 9½98	9.5	20	99½	...
MichB 7¾11	7.6	10	101⅜	+ ⅛
MichB 7s12	7.3	15	95⅞	+ ½
MKT 5½33fr	...	5	63	+ ⅛
MPac 4¾20f	...	6	62¼	– 1¼
MPac 5s45f	...	5	58	– ½
Motrla zr13	...	86	70½	– ¼
NETelTel 4⅝99	4.8	19	95½	+ ⅛
NETelTel 4½02	5.1	10	88¾	– 1⅜
NETelTel 7⅜07	7.4	7	100	...
NJBTl 7⅜12	7.5	15	98⅞	+ ⅞
NYTel 7¾06	7.7	5	100⅞	...
NYTel 7½09	7.5	10	100	+ 1⅛
NYTel 7⅜11	7.6	8	97⅜	– ⅜
NYTel 7⅞17	7.9	13	99⅝	...
Noram 6s12	cv	27	85	+ ⅜
NoPac 3s47r	3.7	5	82	+ 7
Novacr 5½2000	cv	76	89⅛	– ⅞
OffDep zr07	...	5	68	...
OreStl 11s03	10.4	180	105⅞	...
Oryx 7½14	cv	100	93¼	...
OutbM 7s02	cv	14	97½	+ ¾
OwnIll 10¼99	10.1	198	101¾	...
OwnIll 10½02	10.0	10	105	...
OwIll 11s03	10.0	40	109⅞	– ⅛
OwnIll 9¾04	9.4	15	104¼	+ ¾
PacBell 7¼02	7.1	43	102	– ¼
PacBell 7½33	7.8	6	96⅜	+ ⅞
Pathmk zr03	...	8	67⅝	– 1⅜
PaylCsh 9⅛03	13.6	215	67⅜	+ ⅛
PennTr 9⅝05	16.1	586	59¾	+ ⅛
PepBoys zr11	...	75	57	– ¼
Pepsic 7⅝98	7.4	10	103⅝	+ 1¼
PhilEl 6⅛97	6.2	1	99¼	+ ⅛
PhilEl 7⅜01	7.3	10	101¾	+ 1
PhilEl 7¾23	7.9	30	97⅝	+ ⅛
4	7.9	16	92	+ 1¼
PSEG 8¾22	8.2	2	106⅞	+ ⅛
Quanx 6.88s07	cv	43	101¾	+ 1
RJR Nb 8s01	8.0	55	100½	...
RJR Nb 7⅝03	7.9	5	96	+ ½
RJR Nb 8¾05	8.7	30	100¼	+ ¼
RJR Nb 8¾07	8.8	35	98⅞	...
RJR Nb 9¼13	9.3	48	99⅜	– ⅝
RJR Nb 8¾04	8.7	59	100⅜	+ ⅜
Rallys 9⅞00	11.5	115	86⅛	– ⅜
RelGrp 9s00	8.8	69	102⅛	– ⅝
RelGrp 9¾03	9.5	18	102⅛	– 1
Revl 9½99	9.2	60	103	– ⅜
Revl 10⅞10	10.5	78	104	– 1⅛
Roadmst 8s03	cv	98	87	– ¼
Rohr 7s12	cv	22	88¼	+ ½
Rowan 11⅞01	11.2	27	106⅜	+ ⅛
Royce 5¾04	cv	20	100	...
Safwy 9.35s99	8.9	5	105¼	– ⅛
Safwy 10s01	9.0	73	111½	+ 1⅜
Safwy 9⅞07	8.9	10	111	– ⅞
Sequa 9⅜03	9.4	10	99⅞	– 1⅛
SvcMer 8⅜01	8.6	20	97½	...
SvcMer 9s04	10.4	555	86½	– ¼
Showboat 9¼08	9.2	102	100⅝	+ ½
Showboat 13s09	11.1	10	116¾	+ 1¾
Snyder 7s01	cv	10	94	...
SoCnBel 7⅜12	7.6	5	97½	+ ⅜
SouBell 4⅜98	4.5	5	97⅜	– ⅛
SouBell 7⅜10	7.5	5	98⅞	+ ⅜
StdCmcl 07	cv	4	76	+ 1¾
StdPac 10½00	10.2	85	102⅞	+ ⅛
StoneC 10¾97	10.5	52	101 21/32	...
StoneCn 11⅞98	11.1	5	106⅝	...
StoneCn 11s99	10.5	25	104⅜	...
StoneC 9⅞01	9.8	142	100¾	+ ¼
StoneC 10¾02A	10.5	123	102¾	– ¼
StoneC 10¾02O	10.2	55	105½	+ ⅛
StoneC 11½04	10.0	48	106¾	+ ½
StoneCn 6¾07	cv	10	88½	...
StrTch 8s15	cv	95	123½	+ 1
SumtBc 7¾97	7.8	15	99⅝	– 1⅜
TJX 9½16	9.3	2	102	...
TVA 7.45s01	7.4	20	101⅛	– ⅛
TVA 7⅞01	7.8	5	101	– ¾
TVA 6⅞02	6.9	8	99⅞	– ⅛
TVA 6⅞02	6.9	10	99½	– ½
TVA 6⅛03	6.4	14	96½	...
TVA 7⅝22	7.6	13	100⅛	...
TVA 7¾22	7.7	5	101¼	– ¼
TVA 8⅝29	8.1	25	106⅛	– ¼
TVA 8¼34	8.2	4	101	– 1
TennGas dc6s11	7.0	12	85¾	– ⅞
Tesor 13s00cld	...	36	100½	+ 15/32
Texco 9s99D	8.5	5	106½	– 1¾
TmeWar 7.45s98	7.4	130	101¼	– ⅛
TmeWar zr13	...	42	42¾	...
TolEd 7½02	7.8	10	96⅜	– ⅝
Toll 9½03	9.1	67	104½	...
Trimas 5s03	cv	4	110½	– ¾
TucEP 7.65s03	7.7	35	99⅝	+ ⅜
Tyco 10⅛02	10.0	123	101⅜	+ ⅝
USX 5¾01	cv	28	93	+ ¼
USX 7s17	cv	52	96½	...
Unisys 8¼00	cv	89	99½	+ 1¼
Unisys 8¼06	cv	27	127	+ 2
Viacm 7s03A	7.6	15	91⅝	+ 1¾

Source: Reprinted by permission of *The Wall Street Journal*, © 1996 by Dow Jones & Company. All Rights Reserved Worldwide.

EXHIBIT 2.18 Secondary Market Pricing for Treasury Securities

TREASURY BONDS, NOTES & BILLS

Tuesday, February 18, 1997

Representative and Indicative Over-the-Counter quotations based on $1 million or more.

Treasury bond, note and bill quotes are as of mid-afternoon. Colons in bond and note bid-and-asked quotes represent 32nds; 101:01 means 101 1/32. Net changes in 32nds. Treasury bill quotes in hundredths, quoted in terms of a rate discount. Days to maturity calculated from settlement date. All yields are based on a one-day settlement and calculated on the offer quote. Current 13-week and 26-week bills are boldfaced. For bonds callable prior to maturity, yields are computed to the earliest call date for issues quoted above par and to the maturity date for issues quoted below par. n-Treasury note. i-Inflation-Indexed. wi-When issued. iw-Inflation-Indexed when issued; daily change is expressed in basis points.

Source: Dow Jones Telerate/Cantor Fitzgerald.

U.S. Treasury strips as of 3 p.m. Eastern time, also based on transactions of $1 million or more. Colons in bid-and-asked quotes represent 32nds; 99:01 means 99 1/32. Net changes in 32nds. Yields calculated on the asked quotation. ci-stripped coupon interest. bp-Treasury bond, stripped principal. np-Treasury note, stripped principal. For bonds callable prior to maturity, yields are computed to the earliest call date for issues quoted above par and to the maturity date for issues below par.

Source: Bear, Stearns & Co. via Street Software Technology Inc.

GOVT. BONDS & NOTES

Rate	Maturity Mo/Yr	Bid	Asked	Chg.	Ask Yld.
6 3/4	Feb 97n	100:00	100:02	....	4.10
6 7/8	Feb 97n	100:00	100:02	....	4.22
6 5/8	Mar 97n	100:04	100:06	....	4.79
6 7/8	Mar 97n	100:05	100:07	....	4.75
8 1/2	Apr 97n	100:14	100:16	– 1	5.02
6 1/2	Apr 97n	100:07	100:09	....	4.93
6 7/8	Apr 97n	100:09	100:11	....	4.98
6 1/2	May 97n	100:08	100:10	....	5.07
8 1/2	May 97n	100:23	100:25	....	5.02
6 1/8	May 97n	100:05	100:07	....	5.25
6 3/4	May 97n	100:11	100:13	....	5.19
5 5/8	Jun 97n	100:03	100:05	....	5.15
6 3/8	Jun 97n	100:12	100:14	....	5.10
8 1/2	Jul 97n	101:08	101:10	....	5.14
5 1/2	Jul 97n	100:02	100:04	....	5.20
5 7/8	Jul 97n	100:07	100:09	....	5.22
6 1/2	Aug 97n	100:17	100:19	– 1	5.25
8 5/8	Aug 97n	101:18	101:20	....	5.21
5 5/8	Aug 97n	100:02	100:04	– 1	5.38
6	Aug 97n	100:08	100:10	– 1	5.38
5 1/2	Sep 97n	100:01	100:03	....	5.33
5 3/4	Sep 97n	100:06	100:08	....	5.32
8 3/4	Oct 97n	102:02	102:04	....	5.37
5 5/8	Oct 97n	100:03	100:05	....	5.38
5 3/4	Oct 97n	100:06	100:08	....	5.36
7 3/8	Nov 97n	101:09	101:11	– 1	5.47
8 7/8	Nov 97n	102:12	102:14	....	5.43
5 3/8	Nov 97n	99:28	99:30	– 1	5.45
6	Nov 97n	100:11	100:13	– 1	5.45
5 1/4	Dec 97n	99:25	99:27	– 1	5.43
6	Dec 97n	100:13	100:15	– 1	5.43
7 7/8	Jan 98n	102:01	102:03	....	5.46
5	Jan 98n	99:15	99:17	....	5.51
5 5/8	Jan 98n	100:01	100:03	– 1	5.52
7 1/4	Feb 98n	101:18	101:20	....	5.54
8 1/8	Feb 98n	102:13	102:15	....	5.52
5 1/8	Feb 98n	99:17	99:19	....	5.54
5 1/8	Mar 98n	99:16	99:18	– 1	5.53
6 1/8	Mar 98n	100:18	100:20	....	5.53
7 7/8	Apr 98n	102:15	102:17	– 1	5.56
5 1/8	Apr 98n	99:14	99:16	....	5.56
5 7/8	Apr 98n	100:09	100:11	....	5.56
6 1/8	May 98n	100:18	100:20	– 1	5.59
9	May 98n	103:31	104:01	....	5.56
5 3/8	May 98n	99:21	99:23	– 1	5.60
6	May 98n	100:13	100:15	– 1	5.61
5 1/8	Jun 98n	99:11	99:13	....	5.58
6 1/4	Jun 98n	100:25	100:27	....	5.59
8 1/4	Jul 98n	103:14	103:16	– 1	5.61
5 1/4	Jul 98n	99:13	99:15	– 1	5.63
6 1/4	Jul 98n	100:25	100:27	....	5.63
5 7/8	Aug 98n	100:07	100:09	– 1	5.67
9 1/4	Aug 98n	105:00	105:02	....	5.66
4 3/4	Aug 98n	98:20	98:22	....	5.66
6 1/8	Aug 98n	100:19	100:21	– 1	5.67
4 3/4	Sep 98n	98:17	98:19	– 1	5.67
6	Sep 98n	100:13	100:15	– 1	5.69
7 1/8	Oct 98n	102:05	102:07	– 1	5.69
4 3/4	Oct 98n	98:13	98:15	....	5.71
5 7/8	Oct 98n	100:05	100:07	– 1	5.73
3 1/2	Nov 98	98:30	99:30	....	3.54
5 1/2	Nov 98n	99:18	99:20	– 1	5.72
8 7/8	Nov 98n	105:02	105:04	– 1	5.72
5 1/8	Nov 98n	98:30	99:00	....	5.72
5 5/8	Nov 98n	99:24	99:26	– 1	5.73
5 1/8	Dec 98n	98:28	98:30	– 1	5.73
5 3/4	Dec 98n	99:30	100:00	– 1	5.75
6 3/8	Jan 99n	101:02	101:04	– 1	5.74
5	Jan 99n	98:18	98:20	....	5.75
5 7/8	Jan 99n	100:05	100:06	– 1	5.77
5	Feb 99n	98:16	98:18	– 1	5.77
8 7/8	Feb 99n	105:22	105:24	– 1	5.77
5 1/2	Feb 99n	99:13	99:15	– 1	5.78
5 7/8	Mar 99n	100:04	100:06	– 1	5.78
7	Apr 99n	102:11	102:13	– 1	5.79
6 1/2	Apr 99n	101:12	101:14	– 1	5.79
6 3/8	May 99n	101:03	101:05	– 1	5.81
9 1/8	May 99n	106:25	106:27	– 1	5.81
6 3/4	May 99n	101:28	101:30	– 1	5.82
6 3/4	Jun 99n	101:31	102:01	– 1	5.81
6 3/8	Jul 99n	101:05	101:07	– 2	5.82
6 7/8	Jul 99n	102:08	102:10	– 2	5.85
6	Aug 99n	100:09	100:11	– 1	5.85
8	Aug 99n	104:28	104:30	– 1	5.84
6 7/8	Aug 99n	102:10	102:12	....	5.85
7 1/8	Sep 99n	102:31	103:01	– 1	5.85
6	Oct 99n	100:12	100:14	– 1	5.82
7 1/2	Oct 99n	103:29	103:31	– 1	5.88
5 7/8	Nov 99n	99:29	99:31	– 1	5.88
7 7/8	Nov 99n	104:30	105:00	– 1	5.86
7 3/4	Nov 99n	104:20	104:22	– 1	5.89
7 3/4	Dec 99n	104:24	104:26	– 1	5.89
6 3/8	Jan 00n	101:10	101:12	....	5.85
7 3/4	Jan 00n	104:27	104:29	– 1	5.91
5 7/8	Feb 00n	99:28	99:29	– 1	5.91
8 1/2	Feb 00n	106:29	106:31	– 2	5.92
7 1/8	Feb 00n	103:07	103:09	– 1	5.92
6 7/8	Mar 00n	102:19	102:21	– 1	5.92
5 1/2	Apr 00n	98:25	98:27	– 1	5.90
6 3/4	Apr 00n	102:08	102:10	– 1	5.94
8 7/8	May 00n	108:18	108:20	– 1	5.90
6 1/4	May 00n	100:26	100:28	– 1	5.95
5 7/8	Jun 00n	99:22	99:24	– 1	5.96
6 1/8	Jul 00n	100:14	100:16	– 1	5.96
8 3/4	Aug 00n	108:18	108:20	– 2	5.98
6 1/4	Aug 00n	100:26	100:28	– 1	5.97
6 1/8	Sep 00n	100:12	100:14	– 2	5.99
5 3/4	Oct 00n	99:05	99:07	– 1	5.99
8 1/2	Nov 00n	108:08	108:10	– 1	5.98
5 5/8	Nov 00n	98:22	98:24	– .1	6.00
5 1/2	Dec 00n	98:06	98:08	– 1	6.01
5 1/4	Jan 01n	97:14	97:16	– 2	5.97
7 3/4	Feb 01n	106:01	106:03	– 2	6.01
11 3/4	Feb 01	120:01	120:07	– 2	5.98
5 5/8	Feb 01n	98:18	98:20	– 1	6.01
6 3/8	Mar 01n	101:05	101:07	– 2	6.03
6 1/4	Apr 01n	100:23	100:25	– 1	6.03
8	May 01n	107:07	107:09	– 2	6.02
13 1/8	May 01	126:04	126:10	– 1	5.99
6 1/2	May 01n	101:20	101:22	– 2	6.04
6 5/8	Jun 01n	102:04	102:06	– 2	6.04
6 5/8	Jul 01n	102:04	102:06	– 2	6.06
7 7/8	Aug 01n	107:00	107:02	– 2	6.06
13 3/8	Aug 01	128:12	128:18	– 2	6.02
6 1/2	Aug 01n	101:21	101:23	– 2	6.06
6 3/8	Sep 01n	101:05	101:07	– 2	6.07
6 1/4	Oct 01n	100:21	100:23	– 2	6.07
7 1/2	Nov 01n	105:23	105:25	– 2	6.07
15 3/4	Nov 01	139:10	139:16	– 3	6.03
5 7/8	Nov 01n	99:04	99:06	– 2	6.07
6 1/8	Dec 01n	100:04	100:06	– 2	6.08
6 1/4	Jan 02n	100:23	100:24	– 2	6.07
14 1/4	Feb 02	134:23	134:29	– 3	6.04
7 1/2	May 02n	106:08	106:10	– 2	6.07
6 3/8	Aug 02n	101:09	101:11	– 2	6.08
11 5/8	Nov 02	126:09	126:15	– 3	6.08
6 1/4	Feb 03n	100:18	100:20	– 4	6.12
10 3/4	Feb 03	122:23	122:29	– 3	6.12
10 3/4	May 03	123:11	123:17	– 4	6.15
5 3/4	Aug 03n	97:26	97:28	– 3	6.15
11 1/8	Aug 03	126:01	126:07	– 5	6.16
11 7/8	Nov 03	130:26	131:00	– 5	6.17
5 7/8	Feb 04n	98:07	98:09	– 5	6.18
7 1/4	May 04n	106:00	106:02	– 5	6.20
12 3/8	May 04	135:10	135:16	– 6	6.21
7 1/4	Aug 04n	106:03	106:05	– 5	6.21
13 3/4	Aug 04	144:12	144:18	– 7	6.22
7 7/8	Nov 04n	109:29	109:31	– 5	6.23
11 5/8	Nov 04	132:15	132:21	– 8	6.24
7 1/2	Feb 05n	107:23	107:25	– 7	6.25
6 1/2	May 05n	101:16	101:18	– 7	6.25
8 1/4	May 00-05	105:28	105:30	– 3	6.19
12	May 05	136:08	136:14	– 9	6.26
6 1/2	Aug 05n	101:15	101:17	– 8	6.26
10 3/4	Aug 05	128:29	129:03	– 9	6.28
5 7/8	Nov 05n	97:09	97:11	– 8	6.27
5 5/8	Feb 06n	95:16	95:18	– 9	6.28
9 3/8	Feb 06	121:02	121:08	–10	6.25
6 7/8	May 06n	103:30	104:00	– 9	6.30
7	Jul 06n	104:26	104:28	– 9	6.30
6 1/2	Oct 06n	101:11	101:13	–10	6.30
3 3/8	Jan 07i	101:01	101:02	– 2	3.25
6 1/4	Feb 07	99:26	99:27	– 1	6.27
6 1/4	Feb 07n	99:26	99:27	– 1	6.27
7 5/8	Feb 02-07	105:14	105:16	–23	6.32
7 7/8	Nov 02-07	108:10	108:12	– 4	6.12
8 3/8	Aug 03-08	111:12	111:16	– 7	6.20
8 3/4	Nov 03-08	112:29	113:01	– 7	6.34
9 1/8	May 04-09	115:25	115:29	– 7	6.35
10 3/8	Nov 04-09	124:04	124:10	– 8	6.35
11 3/4	Feb 05-10	133:12	133:18	–10	6.33
10	May 05-10	122:27	123:01	– 9	6.36
12 3/4	Nov 05-10	142:04	142:10	–10	6.36
13 7/8	May 06-11	151:18	151:24	–11	6.37
14	Nov 06-11	154:15	154:21	–10	6.37
10 3/8	Nov 07-12	129:19	129:25	–13	6.48
12	Aug 08-13	143:30	144:04	–13	6.49
13 1/4	May 09-14	156:01	156:07	–15	6.51
12 1/2	Aug 09-14	150:13	150:19	–14	6.52
11 3/4	Nov 09-14	144:29	145:03	–15	6.49
11 1/4	Feb 15	148:28	149:02	–19	6.56
10 5/8	Aug 15	142:17	142:23	–19	6.59
9 7/8	Nov 15	134:20	134:26	–19	6.61
9 1/4	Feb 16	128:01	128:07	–18	6.62
7 1/4	May 16	106:19	106:21	–17	6.63
7 1/2	Nov 16	109:08	109:10	–17	6.64
8 3/4	May 17	123:01	123:07	–20	6.65
8 7/8	Aug 17	124:17	124:23	–21	6.65
9 1/8	May 18	127:21	127:27	–22	6.66
9	Nov 18	126:15	126:21	–22	6.66
8 7/8	Feb 19	125:03	125:09	–22	6.67
8 1/8	Aug 19	116:19	116:23	–22	6.68
8 1/2	Feb 20	121:03	121:09	–22	6.68
8 3/4	May 20	124:03	124:09	–23	6.68
8 3/4	Aug 20	124:07	124:13	–23	6.68
7 7/8	Feb 21	113:31	114:03	–23	6.69
8 1/8	May 21	117:00	117:04	–24	6.69
8 1/8	Aug 21	117:03	117:07	–24	6.69
8	Nov 21	115:21	115:25	–24	6.69
7 1/4	Aug 22	106:24	106:26	–23	6.69
7 5/8	Nov 22	111:11	111:15	–24	6.68

the discounted value of the promised future bond payments equal to the market price of the bond.

Exhibit 2.19 graphs the relation between the yield to maturity and the price of the bond. Since the promised cash flows of a bond are fixed, and the price of the bond is the discounted value of the promised cash flows using the yield to maturity as a discount rate, increasing the yield to maturity decreases the present value (or current market price) of the bond's cash flows. Hence, there is an inverse relationship between bond price and yield.

EXHIBIT 2.19   Bond Price/Yield Relationship

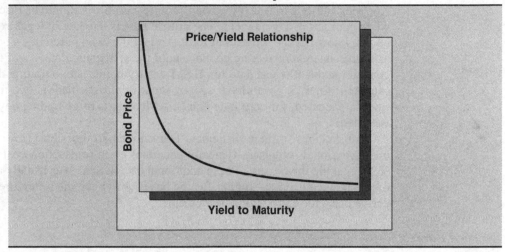

The price-yield curve also has a particular type of curvature. The curvature in Exhibit 2.19, known as **convex curvature**, occurs because the curve must always decline but always at a slower rate as the yield increases.[34]

The results of this subsection can be summarized as follows:

Result 2.1   For straight-coupon, deferred-coupon, zero-coupon, perpetuity, and annuity bonds, the bond price is a downward sloping convex function of the bond's yield to maturity.

Compounding Conventions for Yields to Maturity

Any interest rate, including a yield to maturity, is an ambiguous concept without knowing the compounding convention.[35] The convention in debt markets is to use the yield to maturity that has a compounding frequency equal to the number of times per year a coupon is paid. For instance, the yield quotes for residential mortgages, which have monthly payments, represent monthly compounded interest. Most U.S. government and corporate bond coupons are paid twice a year, so the yield to maturity is a rate compounded semiannually. For debt instruments with one year or more to maturity, the **bond-equivalent yield** is the yield to maturity stated as a semiannually compounded rate.

There are a few exceptions to this convention. U.S. Treasury bills and short-term agency securities have a type of quoted yield related to simple interest.[36] **Treasury strips**, zero-coupon bonds that are obligations of the U.S. Treasury, are closely tied to the coupon-paying Treasury market and thus have yield quotes compounded semiannually. In addition, bids for Treasury bonds and notes at Treasury auctions are based on Treasury yields, which combine semiannually compounded interest and simple interest if the first coupon is not due exactly one-half year from the issue date.[37] Finally, Eurobonds, with annual coupons, have a coupon rate compounded annually.

---

[34]We will have more to say about convexity in Chapter 22.

[35]See the appendix to Chapter 2 for a discussion of compounding frequencies for interest rate quotes.

[36]Short-term agency securities, like Federal Deposit Insurance Corporation bonds, are issued by an agency of the U.S. government other than the Treasury.

[37]See the appendix to Chapter 2.

Settlement Dates

Knowing the date to which the bond's future cash flows should be discounted is essential when computing a bond yield. The critical date is the date of legal exchange of cash for bonds, known as the **settlement date**. An investor who purchases a bond does not begin to accrue interest or receive coupons until the settlement date. As of the mid-1990s, the conventional settlement date for U.S. Treasury bonds is one trading day after a trade is executed; for U.S. government agency securities, settlement is two trading days after a trade is executed; for corporate bonds, settlement is three trading days after an order is executed.

Alternatives to these settlement conventions are possible. However, requesting an unconventional settlement typically generates extra transaction costs for the buyer or seller making the request. These additional transaction costs usually are manifested in a disadvantageous price—higher for the buyer, lower for the seller—relative to the transaction price for conventional settlement.

Accrued Interest

Yield computations also require knowledge of which price to use. This would seem to be a simple matter except that, for bonds not in default, the price paid for a bond is not the same as its quoted price. The price actually paid for an interest-paying bond is understood by all bond market participants to be its quoted price plus accrued interest.

Accrued interest is the amount of interest owed on the bond when the bond is purchased between coupon payment dates. For example, halfway between payment dates accrued interest is half the bond coupon. We will discuss this computation in more depth in the appendix to this chapter. Here, it is sufficient to know that the sum of the bond's quoted price and the accrued interest is the amount of cash required to obtain the bond. This sum is the appropriate price to use when computing the bond's yield to maturity.

The quoted price of a bond is called its **flat price**. The price actually paid for a bond is its **full price**. For a bond not in default, the full price is the flat price plus accrued interest. A price quote for a bond represents a quote per $100 of face value.

When the issuer of the bond is not paying interest—that is, when the bond is in default—buyers are not expected to make partial payments of interest to sellers. In this case, the quoted price is the same as the flat price one has to pay for the bond, which is indicated by an "f" next to the bond price on a quote sheet.

2.9 Yields to Maturity and Coupon Yields

The **coupon yield** of a bond is its annual interest payment divided by its current flat price.[38] For example, a bond with a flat price (i.e., net of accrued interest) of $92, which pays coupons amounting to $10 each year, has a coupon yield of 10/92 = 10.87 percent.

It is easy to show that a straight-coupon bond with a yield to maturity of 10 percent and a price of 100 has a coupon yield of 10 percent on a coupon payment date and vice versa. Try it on a financial calculator. More generally, we have:

Result 2.2   Straight coupon bonds that (1) have flat prices of par (i.e., $100 per $100 of face value) and (2) settle on a coupon date, have yields to maturity that equal their coupon yields.

Result 2.2 at first seems rather striking. The yield to maturity is a compound interest rate while the coupon yield is a simple quotient. It appears to be a remarkable coinci-

---

[38]Whenever the term *yield* is used alone, it refers to the yield to maturity, not the coupon yield.

dence that these two should be the same when the bond trades for $100 per $100 of face value, or par.

To see what is behind this coincidence, recall that the discounted value of all the cash flows of a perpetuity simplifies to a simple quotient, the periodic payment divided by the per period interest rate. Thus, a perpetuity bond with semiannual coupons of $100r/2$ has a present value of 100 when r is the semiannually compounded discount rate (implying that $r/2$ is the per period discount rate). Thus, if the bond is trading for $100, r is both the coupon yield and the semiannually compounded yield to maturity.

A straight-coupon bond with semiannual payments of $r/2$ differs from this perpetuity by having a principal payment of $100 at maturity in lieu of future coupon payments. However, this $100 cash flow at maturity is equivalent to subsequent semiannual coupons of $100r/2$ in perpetuity if r is the semiannually compounded discount rate.

When a bond is trading at par on a coupon date, discounting at the coupon yield is the same as discounting at the yield to maturity. However, coupon yields can give only approximate yields to maturity when a bond is trading at a premium or a discount.

When a bond is between coupon dates or if its first coupon differs in size from other coupons because of its irregular timing—what is known as an *odd first coupon*—the coupon yield of a bond trading at par is not the same as its yield to maturity.

Result 2.3 A bond between coupon dates has a flat price that is less than par when its yield to maturity is the same as its coupon rate.

The phenomenon described in Result 2.3, known as the **scallop effect**, is shown in Exhibit 2.20. The scallop effect occurs because yields to maturity are geometric; that is,

EXHIBIT 2.20   Price of a Bond: Coupon Rate Equals Yield to Maturity over Time

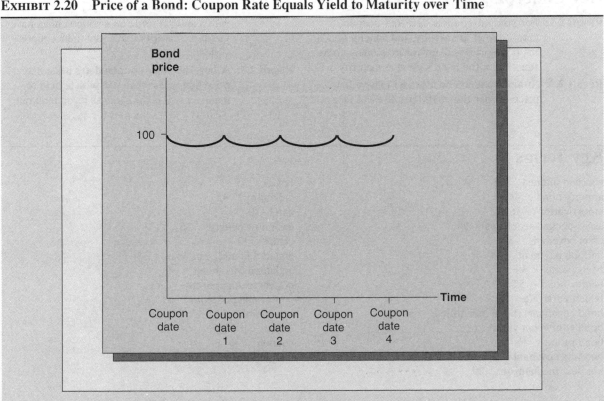

they reflect compound interest. The prices at which bonds are quoted—the flat prices—partly reflect compound interest and partly simple interest. The simple interest part is due to accrued interest, which is generally subtracted from the bond's traded price to obtain the bond's quoted price.

2.10 Summary and Conclusions

This chapter has provided an introduction to the various sources of debt financing: bank loans, leases, commercial paper, and debt securities. A large variety of debt financing is available. In addition, there are many ways to categorize debt instruments: by their covenants, options, cash flow pattern, pricing, maturity, and rating.

One of the goals of this text is to bring the reader from having merely an intuitive feel for the time value of money—as exemplified by the discussion in the appendix at the end of this textbook—to being able to pick up a business newspaper or examine a computer screen and usefully employ the data displayed to value financial and real assets. Accomplishing this goal requires a substantial amount of knowledge about debt securities, some of which is found in this chapter.

In addition to learning how debt prices and yields are quoted, a variety of skills are acquired in this chapter. Among them is how to value and amortize mortgages and other annuities, where to trade debt, where to issue debt, and what role debt plays in global capital markets. These skills are useful to the corporate manager who needs to determine whether to finance an investment with debt securities or equity securities.

To complete the institutional education of the financial manager, it is important to explore in similar detail the main competitor to debt financing: equity financing. For this, we turn to Chapter 3.

Key Concepts

Result 2.1: For straight-coupon, deferred-coupon, zero-coupon, perpetuity, and annuity bonds, the bond price is a downward sloping convex function of the bond's yield to maturity.

Result 2.2: Straight-coupon bonds that (1) have flat prices of par (i.e., $100 per $100 of face

value) and (2) settle on a coupon date, have yields to maturity that equal their coupon yields.

Result 2.3: A bond between coupon dates has a flat price that is less than par with a yield to maturity that is the same as its coupon rate.

Key Terms

accrued interest   62
annuity bond   44
amortization   36
asset-backed securities   54
asset covenant   37
balloon payment   44
basis points   30
bearer bond   55
benchmark rate   32
bond covenants (bond indentures)   36
bond equivalent yield   61
bond rating   36
bonding covenant   37
bonding mechanism   39

bonds   35
callability   43
cap   30
cash flow pattern   36
collar   30
collared floating rate loan   33
collateral trust bond   39
commercial paper rate   32
conversion premium   43
convertibility   43
convex curvature   61
coupon   36
coupon rate   36

Exercises

2.1. Critics of ratings agencies argue that because the firm pays rating agencies to rate the firm's debt, the rating agencies have the wrong incentives. What do you think of this argument? Can you think of ways to assess its validity?

2.2. On October 31, 1994, the *Wall Street Journal* wrote:

> Once one of the raciest and most profitable areas of investment banking, the Eurobond market has become boring and, even worse, not very profitable. Though the volume of new issues this year in the market which comprises bonds underwritten outside a borrower's home country is likely to exceed $900 billion, up from $337 billion in 1980, profit margins have plummeted.

What do you think is happening in the Eurobond market?

2.3. An article in *The Economist* (Sept. 25, 1993, p. 93) said, in part:

> Neither fish nor fowl, convertible bonds, which give investors an option to convert into equities, have been gaining popularity in America. There were $103 billion of them outstanding at the end of August, up from $52 billion in 1990. Why the enthusiasm? For an issuing company, convertibles have several good features. A firm can borrow at about three percentage points below the cost of straight debt. It does not give up as much equity as with an ordinary share issue. That is why convertibles are particularly popular with small companies that hope to grow rapidly.

Do you think that convertible debt represents a cheap way to finance the firm? Can you think of any reasons why small, growing firms might favor convertibles?

2.4. The diagram in the next column shows default rates of rated bonds.

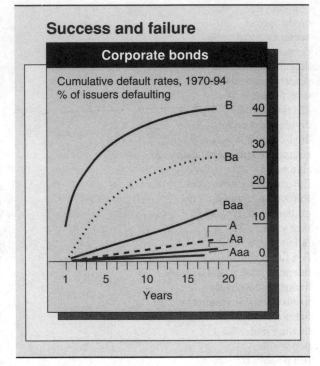

What conclusions can you draw from the diagram?

2.5. Assume that a homeowner takes on a 30-year, $100,000 floating-rate mortgage with monthly payments. Assume that the floating rate is 7.0 percent at the initiation of the mortgage, 7.125 percent is the reset rate at the end of the first month, and 7.25 percent is the reset rate at the end of the second month. What are the first, second, and third mortgage payments, respectively, made at the end of the first, second, and third months? What is the breakdown between principal and interest for each of the first three payments? What is the principal balance at the end of the first, second, and third months?

References and Additional Readings

Altman, Edward. "The Anatomy of the High-Yield Bond Market." *Financial Analysts Journal* 43 (1987), pp. 12–25.

———. "Measuring Corporate Bond Mortality and Performance." *Journal of Finance* 44 (1989), pp. 909–22.

Altman, Edward, and Scott Nammacher. "The Default Rate Experience on High-Yield Corporate Debt, *Financial Analysts Journal* 41 (1985), pp. 25–41.

Asquith, Paul; David Mullins; and Eric Wolff. "Original Issue High-Yield Bonds: Aging Analyses of Defaults, Exchanges, and Calls." *Journal of Finance* 44 (1989), pp. 923–52.

Bencivenga, Joseph. "The High-Yield Corporate Bond Market." In *The Handbook of Fixed Income Securities.* Frank Fabozzi, ed. Burr Ridge, IL: Irwin Professional Publishing, 1995.

Benevides, Rosario. "How Big Is the World Bond Market?" *Economic and Market Analysis: International Bond Market Analysis.* New York: Salomon Brothers, August 1996 update.

Blume, Marshall; Donald Keim; and Sandeep Patel. "Returns and Volatility of Low-Grade Bonds,

1977–1989." *Journal of Finance* 46 (1991), pp. 49–74.

Cornell, Bradford, and Kevin Green. "The Investment Performance of Low-Grade Bond Funds. *Journal of Finance* 46 (1991), pp. 29–48.

Duffie, Darrell. "Special Repo Rates." *Journal of Finance* 51 (1996), pp. 493–526.

Ederington, Louis, and Jess Yawitz. "The Bond Rating Process." In *Handbook of Financial Markets and Institutions.* Edward Altman, ed. New York: John Wiley, 1986.

Ederington, Louis; Jess Yawitz; and Brian Roberts. "The Informational Content of Bond Ratings." *Journal of Financial Research* 10 (1987), pp. 211–26.

Fabozzi, Frank. *Bond Markets, Analysis, and Strategies.* 3rd ed. Upper Saddle River, NJ: Prentice Hall 1996.

Fabozzi, Frank, and Dessa Fabozzi. *The Handbook of Fixed Income Securities.* 4th ed. Burr Ridge, IL: Irwin Professional Publishing, 1995.

Franks, Julian, and Walt Torous. "An Empirical Investigation of U.S. Firms in Chapter 11 Reorganization." *Journal of Finance* 44 (1989), pp. 747–67.

Goh, Jeremy, and Louis Ederington. "Is a Bond Rating Downgrade Bad News, Good News, or No News for Stockholders?" *Journal of Finance* 48 (1993), pp. 2001–8.

Grinblatt, Mark. "An Analytic Solution for Interest Rate Swap Spreads." Working paper, University of California at Los Angeles, 1996.

Hand, John; Robert Holthausen; and Richard Leftwich. "The Effect of Bond Rating Agency Announcements on Bond and Stock Prices." *Journal of Finance* 47 (1992), pp. 29–39.

Holthausen, Robert, and Richard Leftwich. "The Effect of Bond Rating Changes on Common Stock Prices." *Journal of Financial Economics* 17 (1986), pp. 57–89.

Jefferis, Richard. "The High-Yield Debt Market, 1980–1990." Federal Reserve Bank of Cleveland *Economic Commentary* 26 (1990), pp. 1–6.

Jones, Christopher. "Evidence on the Importance of Market Making: Drexel's Failure and the Junk Bond Market." Working paper, Stanford University, Stanford, CA.

Kalay, Avner. "Stockholder-Bondholder Conflict and Dividend Constraints." *Journal of Financial Economics* 10 (1982), pp. 211–33.

Kester, W. C., and W. B. Allen. "R.J. Reynolds International Financing." Harvard Case 9-287-057, November 1991.

Lehn, Kenneth, and Annette Poulsen. "Contractual Resolution of Bondholder Stockholder Conflicts." *Journal of Law and Economics* 34, 2, part 2 (October 1991), pp. 645–73.

McDaniel, Morey. "Bondholder sand Corporate Governance." *Business Lawyer* 41 (1986), pp. 413–60.

Moody's Investors Service. *Corporate Bond Defaults and Default Rates 1970–93.* Global Credit Research Division. 1994.

Rosengren, Eric. "The Case for Junk Bonds." *New England Economic Review* (May/June), Federal Reserve Bank of Boston, 40–49.

Ruback, Richard. "RJR Nabisco." Harvard Case 9-289-056, 1989.

Salomon Brothers Bond Portfolio Analysis Group. "Odd Coupon Treasury Bonds: Price-Yield Calculations." July 1985.

Schallheim, James. *Lease or Buy.* Boston: Harvard University Press, 1995.

Smith, Clifford, and Jerry Warner. "On Financial Contracting: An Analysis of Bond Covenants." *Journal of Financial Economics* 7 (1979), pp. 117–61.

Smith, Clifford, and Lee Wakeman. "Determinants of Corporate Leasing Policy. *Journal of Finance* 540 (1985), pp. 896–908.

Stigum, Marcia. *The Money Market.* Burr Ridge, IL: Irwin Professional Publishing, 1990.

Tufano, Peter. "Financial Innovation and First Mover Advantages." *Journal of Applied Corporate Finance* 5 (1992), pp. 83–87.

Weinstein, Mark. "A Curmudgeon's View of Junk Bonds." *Journal of Portfolio Management* 13, no. 3 (1986–87), pp. 76–80.

Wilson, Richard, and Frank Fabozzi. *The New Corporate Bond Market.* Chicago: Probus Publishing, 1990.

APPENDIX 2A
ACCRUED INTEREST AND YIELD TO MATURITY CONVENTIONS

For bonds that are not in default, bond prices are quoted net of accrued interest. Hence, it is necessary to compute accrued interest if one wants to know how much the bond actually costs. Moreover, the full price of the bond, which requires an accrued interest calculation, is the price used to compute the bond's yield to maturity.

Exhibit 2A.1   Methods for Calculating Accrued Interest

Securities	Accrual Method	=	Days of Accrued Interest	Divided by	Times
U.S. Treasury bonds and notes	Actual/actual		Number of days since last coupon date	Number of days in current coupon period	Semiannual coupon
Eurobonds, and Euro-floating rate notes (FRNs), many foreign (non-U.S.) govt. bonds	Actual/365		Number of days since last coupon date	365	Annual coupon
Eurodollar deposits, commercial paper, banker's acceptances, repo transactions, many FRNs and LIBOR-based transactions	Actual/360		Number of days since last coupon date	360	Annual coupon
Corporate bonds, U.S. agency securities, municipal bonds, mortgages	30/360		Number of days since last coupon date, assuming 30-day months	360	Annual coupon

The accrued interest quotation convention prevents a quoted bond price from falling by the amount of the coupon on the ex-coupon date. The ex-coupon date (**ex-date**) is the date on which the bondholder becomes entitled to the coupon. If the bondholder sells the bond the day before the ex-date, the coupon goes to the new bondholder. If the bond is sold on or after the ex-date, the coupon goes to the old bondholder. In contrast, stocks do not follow this convention when a dividend is paid. Therefore, stock prices drop abruptly at the ex-date of a dividend, also called the *ex-dividend date*.

2A.1 Day-Count Conventions for Computing Accrued Interest

Accrued interest calculations are based on simple interest. Accrued interest is zero immediately on the ex-date. The coupon payment to the bondholder as of the ex-date reflects the payment in full of the bond interest owed. Just before the ex-date, accrued interest is the amount of the coupon to be paid. On days between ex-dates, accrued interest is the full coupon for the current coupon period times the number of "days" elapsed between the last coupon date and the settlement date of the transaction divided by the number of "days" in the current coupon period, that is:

$$\text{Accrued interest} = \left[\frac{\text{"Days" elapsed}}{\text{"Days" in current coupon period}} \right] \times \left[\begin{array}{c} \text{Coupon per} \\ \text{coupon period} \end{array} \right]$$

"Days" appears in quotes because several day-count conventions for computing accrued interest exist in the bond market. These vary from bond to bond. Among these are actual/actual, actual/365, actual/360, and 30/360. Exhibit 2A.1 outlines the various interest rate computations. The two most difficult accrued calculations are actual/actual and 30/360.

Accrued Interest and Coupons for U.S. Treasury Notes and Bonds: Actual/Actual.   As noted earlier, many corporate securities, particularly those about to be issued, have prices quoted as a spread to Treasury securities of comparable maturity. The most popular interest rate derivative security is the **interest rate swap**, a contract to exchange fixed for floating interest rate payments.[1] Traders quote the terms of this contract as a spread to the yield of the on-the-run U.S. Treasuries with the same maturity as the swap. It is important to understand the pricing and cash

---

[1] See Chapter 7 for a detailed description of interest rate swaps.

flow conventions of U.S. Treasuries because of their role as benchmark securities, in which they often set the trend for the yields on other securities.

Coupons for U.S. Treasuries.   With the possible exception of the first coupon, U.S. Treasury notes and bonds pay coupons every six months. The maturity date of the bond determines the semiannual cycle for coupon payments. For example, the bond with the 8⅛ coupon that matures on May 15, 2021 (highlighted on Exhibit 2.18) pays interest every May 15 and November 15. The amount of interest that accrues over a full six-month period is half of the 8⅛ coupon, or $4.0625 per $100 of face value. The number of days between May 15 and November 15 or between November 15 and May 15 is never half of 365, or 182.5. For example, in 1999 there are 184 days between May 15 and November 15, and 182 days between November 1, 1999 and May 15, 2000. This means that the accrued interest accumulating per day depends on the year and the relevant six-month period.

Accrued Interest Computation for a Typical U.S. Treasury Security.   Example 2A.1 shows an accrued interest calculation for this bond.

Example 2A.1:   Computing Accrued Interest for a Government Bond

Compute the accrued interest for the 8⅛'s maturing May 15, 2021, for a trade settling on Monday, August 16, 1999. This generally means the trade was agreed to the previous business day, or Friday the 13th of August 1999.

Answer: Use the formula from the U.S. Treasury bonds and notes row in Exhibit 2A.1. The number of days between May 15, 1999, and August 16, 1999 (days-of-accrued interest column), is 93. Dividing 93 by 184 (days in current coupon period) yields the fraction of one semiannual coupon due. Multiplying this fraction, 93/184, by the full semiannual coupon, 4.0625 (half of 8⅛) yields $2.05333. Thus, $2.05333 is the amount of accrued interest per $100 face value that must be added to the flat price agreed upon to buy the bond.

Settlement Dates.   In Example 2A.1, May 15, 1999, is a Saturday. Although all settlement dates are business days, it is possible that one or both coupon dates may fall on a nonbusiness day—a weekend or holiday. This does not alter the accrued interest calculation, but does affect the day a coupon is received because the U.S. Treasury is closed on nonbusiness days. In this case, the May 15, 1999 coupon will be received on Monday, May 17, 1999. Based on convention in the bond trading industry, both the yield to maturity and accrued interest calculations should assume that the coupon is received on Saturday. Example 2A.2 gives a sample illustration.

Example 2A.2:   How Settlement Dates Affect Accrued Interest Calculations

Compute the accrued interest on a (hypothetical) 10 percent Treasury note maturing March 15, 2001, with a $100,000 face value if it is purchased on Wednesday, May 19, 1999. What is the actual purchase price if the quoted price is $100.1875? (*Note:* U.S. Treasury notes and bonds are quoted in 32nds. Hence, 100.1875 would appear as 100:6, meaning 100 plus 6/32nds.)

Answer: Since there is no legal holiday on May 20 (a weekday), the settlement date is May 21, one trading day later. The prior coupon date is March 15. The subsequent coupon date is September 15. Thus, the number of days since the last coupon is:

$$16(\text{March}) + 30(\text{April}) + 20(\text{May}) = 66 \text{ days}$$

The number of days between coupons is 184 days. The accrued interest is $5 × (66/184) per $100 of face value, or approximately $1793.48. Thus, the true purchase price is the sum of $100,187.50 and $1793.48, or $101,980.98.

Accrued Interest, Coupons, and Yields of U.S. Treasuries with Long and Short First Coupons.   Accrued interest calculations are slightly more complicated when a coupon is paid over a period greater or less than six months. Such coupons are known as **odd coupons**. If they occur,

EXHIBIT 2A.2   Pseudo-Coupon Dates for Short and Long First Coupons

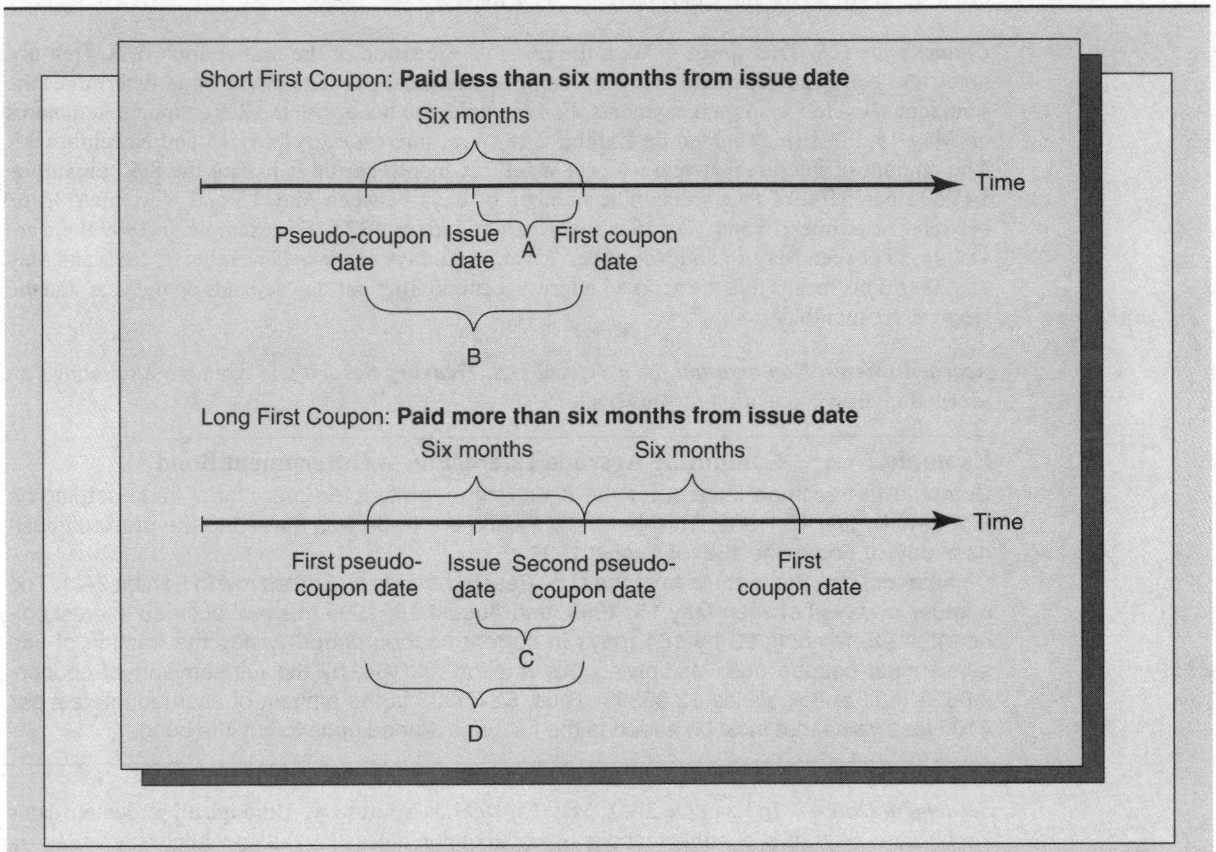

Short First Coupon: **Paid less than six months from issue date**

Six months

Time →

Pseudo-coupon date   Issue date   A   First coupon date

B

Long First Coupon: **Paid more than six months from issue date**

Six months   Six months

Time →

First pseudo-coupon date   Issue date   Second pseudo-coupon date   First coupon date

C

D

they are usually the first coupon after the Treasury security is issued. (Rarely, and not in recent memory, is this the last coupon.)

A **short first coupon** is paid for a period less than six months from the issue date of the Treasury security. The Treasury *coupon* will be the usual six-month coupon times the number of days between the issue date and the first coupon date ("A" in Exhibit 2A.2), divided by the number of days in the six-month period prior to the first coupon date ("B" in Exhibit 2A.2). The date six months before the first coupon date is known as the **pseudo-coupon date** because a coupon is not actually paid on this date (see Exhibit 2A.2). With a short first coupon, *accrued interest* is the full six-month coupon times the number of days between the issue date and the first coupon date divided by the number of days between the pseudo-coupon date and the first coupon date.

A **long first coupon**, which is paid more than six months from the date of issue, has two pseudo-coupon dates. The first is 12 months prior to the first coupon date, while the second is 6 months prior to the first coupon date; thus, the second pseudo-coupon date occurs after the issue date (see Exhibit 2A.2). The accrued interest for the first pseudo-coupon period is the full six-month coupon times the ratio of the number of days between the issue date and the second pseudo-coupon date ("C" on Exhibit 2A.2), to the number of days in the six months between the two pseudo-coupon dates ("D" on Exhibit 2A.2). The coupon paid by the Treasury is the sum of this accrued interest plus one full six-month coupon (see Exhibit 2A.3).

Prior to the second pseudo-coupon date, accrued interest is computed as if there were a short first coupon, with the second pseudo-coupon date serving as the first coupon date. After the second pseudo-coupon date, accrued interest is the sum of the full short coupon accrued

EXHIBIT 2A.3   Accrued Interest: Long First Coupon for a Treasury Issue with a Coupon Rate of *r*

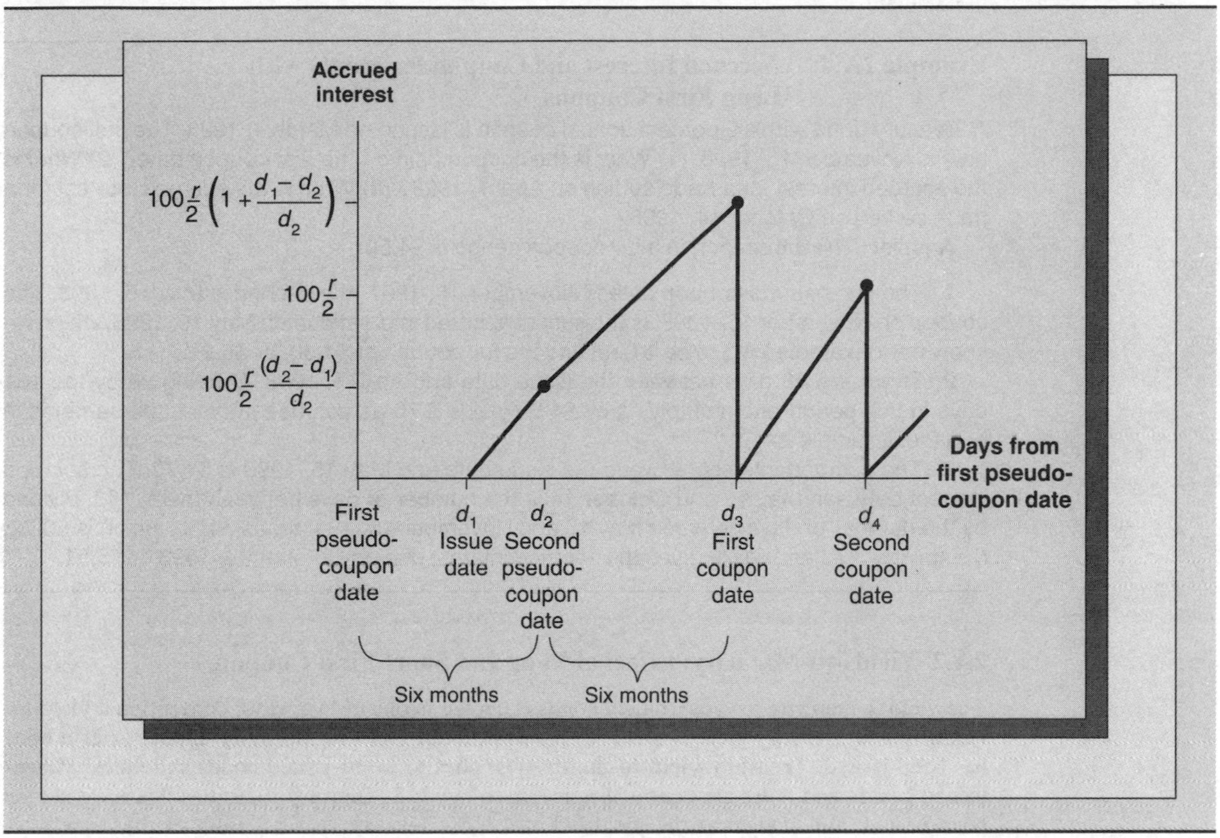

interest and the accrued interest as if a coupon were actually paid on the second pseudo-coupon date.

Example of How to Calculate Accrued Interest and Coupons with Odd First Coupons.   Example 2A.3 illustrates the calculation of coupon payments and accrued interest with a short first coupon.

Example 2A.3:   Accrued Interest and Coupon Payments with a Short First Coupon

A Treasury bond with a 9 percent annual coupon is issued on March 4, 1998. The first coupon date is May 15, 1998. (1) What is the coupon paid on the first coupon date? (2) What is the accrued interest for a trade settled on April 1, 1998? (3) What is the accrued interest for a trade settled on October 14, 1998?

Answer: The full coupon in a full coupon period is $4.50.

1. There are 72 days between March 4, 1998 and May 15, 1998. The pseudo-coupon date is November 15, 1997. There are 181 days between the pseudo-coupon date and the first coupon date. Hence, the coupon on May 15 per $100 face value will be the product of $4.50 and 72/181, or about $1.79.

2. There are 28 days between the issue date and April 1. Dividing 28 by the 181 days in the period and multiplying by $4.50 yields $.70 as accrued interest.

3. The accrued interest between May 15 and October 14 is the number of days between them, 152, divided by the number of days between May 15 and November 15, 184, times $4.50, which is $3.72.

Example 2A.4 illustrates the calculation of coupon payments and accrued interest with a long first coupon.

Example 2A.4:   Accrued Interest and Coupon Payments with Long First Coupons

A Treasury bond with a 9 percent annual coupon is issued on March 4, 1998. The first coupon date is November 15, 1998. (1) What is the coupon paid on the first coupon date? (2) What is the accrued interest for a trade settled on April 1, 1998? (3) What is the accrued interest for a trade settled on October 14, 1998?

Answer: The full coupon in a full coupon period is $4.50.

1. The first pseudo-coupon date is November 15, 1997, the second is May 15, 1998. The coupon on November 15, 1998, is the sum of accrued interest due on May 15, 1998, which we know from Example 2A.3 to be $1.79, and the full coupon of $4.50, or $6.29.

2. There are 28 days between the issue date and April 1, 1998. Dividing 28 by the 181 days in this period and multiplying by $4.50 yields $.70 as accrued interest, the same as in part 2 of Example 2A.3.

3. The accrued interest between the issue date and May 15, 1998 is $1.79. The accrued interest between May 15 and October 14 is the number of days between them, 152, divided by the number of days between May 15 and November 15, 184, times $4.50, which is $3.72. Summing $3.72 and $1.79 gives the accrued interest due on October 14, 1998 or $5.51.

2A.2 Yields-to-Maturity: Effect of Long and Short First Coupon

The yield to maturity for government bonds is quoted in one of two ways: conventional yield-to-maturity and Treasury yield-to-maturity. **Conventional yield-to-maturity** applies after a bond has been issued. **Treasury yield-to-maturity** applies to when-issued bonds and notes. **When-issued bonds** and notes are contracts agreeing to buy U.S. Treasury securities that have not yet been issued, and bought at the yield bid at a U.S. Treasury auction. Both of these yield-to-maturities have rates that are compounded semiannually. Except for the first coupon, both also assume that coupons are paid at six-month intervals, ignoring the possibility that six-month intervals might be slightly greater or less than one-half a year. The conventional yield uses compound interest to discount back to the settlement date, while the Treasury yield uses compound interest to discount back to the first coupon date and simple interest to discount back to the settlement date, which is always the issue date for Treasury yields.

We now provide the formulas for conventional and Treasury yield to maturity. Let P denote the full price per $100 face amount of a bond due on the settlement date. The bond has T coupons remaining. The first coupon is C_0 and the other coupons are $C/2$. Note that $C_0 = C/2$ unless the first coupon is the first coupon after issuance and represents a long or short first coupon in which case $C_0/(C/2)$ is less than 1 for a short first coupon or greater than 1 for a long first coupon. The conventional yield is the discount rate r that makes:

$$P = \frac{1}{(1 + r/2)^{\frac{C_0}{C/2}}} \left(C_0 + \sum_{t=2}^{T} \frac{C/2}{(1 + r/2)^{t-1}} + \frac{100}{(1 + r/2)^{T-1}} \right)$$

Example 2A.5 illustrates how to compute a bond's price from its conventional yield.

Example 2A.5:   Computing a Bond's Price from Its Conventional Yield

Assume the bond in Example 2A.4 is about to be settled on its issue date. If it has a coupon of 9 percent, what is its price at issue if the yield to maturity is a 9 percent conventional yield?

Answer: A 9 percent conventional yield bond with a 9 percent coupon has a discounted value of 100 on November 15, 1998. Discounting the November 15 coupon of $6.29 and the ex-coupon date bond value of 100 back to March 4, 1998, the issue date, results in a discounted value on May 15 of:

$$\$99.95 = \frac{\$100 + \$6.29}{1.045^{6.29/4.5}}$$

Using the same notation, if the first coupon is a short first coupon, the Treasury yield is the discount rate r that makes:

$$P = \frac{1}{\left(1 + \frac{r}{2}\frac{C_0}{C/2}\right)}\left(C_0 + \sum_{t=2}^{T}\frac{C/2}{(1 + r/2)^{t-1}} + \frac{100}{(1 + r/2)^{T-1}}\right)$$

If the first coupon is a long first coupon, the Treasury yield is the discount r that makes:

$$P = \frac{1}{\left(1 + \frac{r}{2}\right)\left[1 + \frac{r}{2}\left(\frac{C_0}{C/2} - 1\right)\right]}\left(C_0 + \sum_{t=2}^{T}\frac{C/2}{(1 + r/2)^{t-1}} + \frac{100}{(1 + r/2)^{T-1}}\right)$$

Example 2A.6 illustrates how to calculate a bond's price from its Treasury yield, using the long coupon formula.

Example 2A.6:   Computing a Bond's Price from its Treasury Yield

Assume the bond in Example 2A.4 is about to be settled on its issue date. If it has a coupon of 9 percent and its Treasury yield is 9 percent, what is its price at issue?

Answer: A 9 percent bond with a 9 percent coupon has a Treasury (and a conventional) discounted value of 100 on November 15, 1998. Discount the November 15 coupon of $6.29 and the ex-coupon bond value of 100 back to March 4, 1998, the issue date. Both conventional and Treasury discounting gives the discounted value on May 15, that is:

$$\$101.71 = \frac{\$100 + \$6.29}{1.045}$$

Discount this value back to March 4. $C_0/(C/2) - 1$ in this example is .39779, the 72 days between March 4 and May 15 (the second pseudo-coupon date) divided by the 181 days between November 15, 1997, and May 15, 1998. Hence, the full and flat price (there is no accrued interest at issue) computed with Treasury discounting is:

$$\$99.92 = \frac{\$101.71}{1 + .045(.39779)}$$

Thus, Treasury yields discount in the same fashion as a conventional yield until we get to the first coupon if it is a short first coupon, or the second pseudo-coupon date if it is a long first coupon. However, in discounting back to the settlement date, r is interpreted as a simple interest rate, whereas the r is a compound interest rate when discounting with the conventional method.

Why does the U.S. Treasury Department maintain this archaic mix of simple interest and compound interest discounting? One reason is that bonds with short first coupons, issued at the same Treasury yield as their coupon yield, will be issued at par (see Example 2A.7).

Example 2A.7:   Treasury Yields and Par Bond Issuance

Assume the bond in Example 2A.3 is about to be settled on its issue date. If it has a coupon of 9 percent and a yield of 9 percent, what is its price at issue if the yield to maturity is (*a*) a conventional yield or (*b*) a Treasury yield?

Answer: A 9 percent bond with a 9 percent yield has a Treasury and a conventional discounted value of 100 on May 15, 1998. Discount the May 15 coupon of 1.790055 plus the ex-coupon value of 100 back to March 4, 1998, the issue date.

For this example, $C_0/(C/2) = .39779 =$ the 72 days between March 4 and May 15 divided by the 181 days between November 15, 1997, and May 15, 1998.

(*a*) The conventional discounting full and flat price (there is no accrued interest at issue) is:

$$101.790055/1.045^{.39779} = 100.0233$$

(*b*) With Treasury discounting, it is:

$$101.790055/(1 + .045(.39779)) = 100$$

2A.3 Accrued Interest for Corporate Securities: 30/360

As Exhibit 2A.1 illustrates, U.S. agency notes and bonds, municipal notes and bonds, and most corporate notes and bonds pay interest on a 30/360 basis. Thus, to compute the number of days of accrued interest on the basis of a 30-day month requires dividing by 360 and multiplying by the annualized coupon.

Here is the tricky part: To calculate the numbers of days that have elapsed since the last coupon calculated on the basis of a 30-day month, assume that each month has 30 days. Begin by counting the last coupon date as day 1 and continue until reaching the 30th day of the month. (Do not forget to assume that February has 30 days.) The count continues for the following month until reaching the 30th day of the month. Then it continues for the following month, and so on, until reaching the settlement date. The settlement date is not counted for accrued interest because interest is assumed to be paid at the beginning of the coupon date, that is, midnight, and only full days are counted.[2]

For example, there are 33 days of accrued interest if January 31 is the last coupon date and March 3 is the settlement date in the same year, whether or not it is a leap year. January 31 is day 1 even though the month exceeds 30 days, there are 30 days in February, and 2 days in March before settlement. February 29 to March 2 in a leap year contains three days of accrued interest—two days in February and one in March. February 28 to March 1 also has three days of accrued interest, all in February, regardless of whether it is a leap year.

Example 2A.8 provides a typical calculation.

Example 2A.8:   Computing Accrued Interest with 30/360 Day Counts

Compute the accrued interest on an 8 percent corporate bond that settles on June 30. The last coupon date was February 25.

Answer: There are 25 days of accrued interest: 6 days in February; 30 in March, April, and May; and 29 in June. 125/360 = .3472222. The product of .3472222 and $8 is $2.77778. Thus, the bond has $2.77778 of accrued interest per $100 of face value.

Key Terms

conventional yield-to-maturity 72	pseudo-coupon date 70
ex-date 68	short first coupon 70
interest rate swap 68	Treasury yield-to-maturity 72
long first coupon 70	when-issued bonds 72
odd coupons 69	

---

[2]It is comforting to know that most financial calculators have internal date programs to compute the number of days between two dates using the 30/360 day/count method.

Exercises

2A.1. Consider a straight-coupon bond (or bank loan) with semiannual interest payments at an 8 percent annualized rate. Per $100 of face value, what is the semiannual interest payment if the day count is based on the following methods?

  a. Actual/actual

  b. 30/360

  c. Actual/365 if the coupon payment date is August 15, 1998

  d. Actual/360 if the coupon payment date is August 15, 1998.

2A.2. Refer to the bond in Exercise 2A.2. What is the accrued interest for settlement of a trade on August 1, 1998, with each of the four day-count methods. For parts *a* and *b,* assume that the coupon payment date is August 15, 1998.

2A.3. What is the conventional yield to maturity compounded semiannually for the bond in Exercise 2A.1 if it is trading for $100, matures on August 15, 2010, and settles on August 15, 1998? Provide an answer for both the actual/actual and the 30/360 day-count methods.

2A.4. How does your answer to Exercise 2A.3 change if the yield to maturity is computed on August 1, 1998?

2A.5. XYZ Corporation takes out a $1 million loan that semiannually pays six-month LIBOR + 50 bp on March 4, 1999. Assume that LIBOR is at 9 percent on March 4, 1999, 8.75 percent on September 4, 1999, and 9.125 percent on March 4, 2000. What are the first three interest payments on the loan? When are they paid?

2A.6. On August 16, 2000, the Treasury issues a 10 percent bond maturing on May 15, 2031. Assume that the first bond coupon is paid on May 15, 2001. Prior to issue on August 1, 2000, a Treasury yield to maturity of 8.2 percent was quoted for this bond. What price was being contracted on August 1, 2000? Note that the payment for the bond is settled on August 16, 2000.

2A.7. A 5 percent corporate bond maturing November 14, 2020 (originally a 25-year bond at issue), has a yield to maturity of 6 percent on June 9, 2001. What are the flat, full, and accrued prices of the bond on June 9, 2001?

2A.8. A deferred coupon bond of Centaurcor pays its first coupon 5.5 years from today. The annual coupon of 16 percent is paid semiannually on a 30/360 basis. The bond is currently trading for par. This straight-coupon bond matures in 10 years. What is its yield to maturity? *Hint:* Guess a yield and determine whether the discounted value of the bond is above or below $100 per $100 of face value. If lower, update your guess by increasing the yield and vice versa. Proceed until you achieve accuracy to $0.10 per $100 of face value.

Equity Financing

Learning Objectives

After reading this chapter you should be able to:

1. Describe the types of equity securities a firm can issue.
2. Provide an overview of the operation of secondary markets for equity.
3. Describe the role of institutions in secondary equity markets and in corporate governance.
4. Understand the process of going public.
5. Discuss the concept of informational efficiency.

On August 9, 1995, after just two years in business, Netscape Communications Corporation issued five million shares in an initial public offering (IPO). The underwriters originally anticipated an offering at around $14 a share, but because of strong demand at that price, the offering price was raised to $28.

The price of the shares skyrocketed from their $28.00 per share issue price to over $70.00 in the initial trading before closing at $58.25 per share, implying a total value of over $2 billion. However, within months of the original offering the price had again doubled. At these prices, the shares retained by the company's cofounders—Marc Andreesen, a 24-year-old programming whiz; Jim Clark, a former Stanford University professor; and the company's CEO, James Barksdale—were worth hundreds of millions of dollars. (Clark, with over nine million shares, was an instant billionaire at Netscape's high in the months following the offering.)

Netscape has been quite successful. Its revenues are growing rapidly and it is showing modest profits. However, it remains to be seen whether Netscape can live up to the expectations generated by the reception of its initial public offering.

Chapter 2 discussed debt financing, a major source of external capital for firms. We turn now to equity, the second major source of external capital. Although debt and equity are alike in that both provide resources for investment in capital equipment, research and development, and training that allow firms to prosper, they differ in several important respects.

- Debt holder claims must be paid in full before the claims of equity holders can be paid.
- Equity holders elect the board of directors of the corporation and thus ultimately control the firm.[1]
- Equity holders receive cash in the form of dividends, which are not tax deductible to the corporation, while the interest payments of debt instruments are tax deductible.[2]

This chapter describes various equity instruments, how they are traded, and the individuals and institutions that own them. It also briefly discusses the efficient markets hypothesis which provides some insights into how equity is priced in the capital markets. In addition, it examines the distinction between firms that are privately owned and hence have no publicly traded stock, and firms that are publicly owned with publicly traded stock. Finally, the chapter covers why a firm might want to have its stock publicly traded and the process by which a firm goes public.

3.1 Types of Equity Securities

Firms obtain equity capital either internally by earning money and retaining it within the firm or externally by issuing new equity securities. There are three different kinds of equity that a firm can issue: (1) common stock, (2) preferred stock, and (3) warrants.

Common Stock

Common stock is a share of ownership in a corporation that usually entitles its holders to vote on the corporation's affairs. The common stockholders of a firm are generally viewed as the firm's owners. They are entitled to the firm's profits after other contractual claims on the firm are satisfied and have the ultimate control over how the firm is operated.[3]

Some firms have two classes of common stock (dual-class shares), usually called class A and class B, which differ in terms of their votes per share. **Dual-class common stock** is largely confined to firms that are majority controlled by some person or group. Such firms include Ford Motor, Reader's Digest, Smucker's, the Washington Post Group, and Adolph Coors. These firms were family-owned firms until they grew too large to be financed by the family alone. Because the families did not want to give up control, they created two classes of common stock, with one class having more votes per share than the other class. In these situations, family members will usually own the majority of the shares with the greater voting power. Although only a limited number of U.S. firms have more than one class of common stock, multiple classes of stock with different voting rights are popular outside the United States. The stocks in a number of countries outside the United States are divided into A and B classes, with foreigners restricted to holding the B shares, which often have no voting rights. In some cases, the B shares have voting rights, but not enough to permit foreigners to control the firm.

---

[1]In reality, however, managers may be more influenced by bankers and other debt holders with whom they must deal on a day-to-day basis than by shareholders with whom they have much less contact. Issues relating to who controls corporations will be discussed in more detail in Chapter 17.

[2]In this way, the U.S. tax code favors debt over equity financing. The tax advantages of debt versus equity financing will be discussed in great detail in Chapters 12, 13, and 14.

[3]As Chapter 17 discusses, it is often difficult for stockholders to exercise their control.

Preferred Stock

Preferred stock is a financial instrument that gives its holders a claim on a firm's earnings that must be paid before dividends on its common stock can be paid and a senior claim in the event of reorganization or **liquidation**, which is the sale of the assets of the company. However, the claims of preferred stockholders are always junior to the claims of the firm's debt holders. Preferred stock is used much less than common stock as a source of capital. The biggest issuers of preferred stock have historically been electric utilities which have been allowed to claim the dividends as an expense when setting electricity rates. Because of tax advantages, financial institutions more recently have become big issuers of new kinds of preferred stock that are described below.

Preferred stock is like debt in that its dividend is fixed at the time of sale. In some cases, preferred stock has a maturity date much like a bond. In other cases, preferred stock is more like common stock in that it never matures. Preferred shares are almost always **cumulative**: If the corporation stops paying dividends, the unpaid dividends accumulate and must be paid in full before any dividends can be paid to common shareholders. At the same time, a firm generally cannot be forced into bankruptcy for not paying its preferred dividends.[4] The voting rights of preferred stock differ from instrument to instrument. Preferred stockholders do not always have voting rights, but they often obtain voting rights when the preferred dividends are suspended.

Convertible Preferred.   **Convertible preferred stock** is similar to the convertible debt instruments described in Chapter 2. These instruments have the properties of preferred stock prior to being converted, but can be converted into the common stock of the issuer at the shareholder's discretion. In addition to the standard features of preferred stock, convertible preferred stock specifies the number of common shares into which each preferred share can be converted.

Adjustable-Rate Preferred.   About half of the preferred stock issued in the 1990s is some variant of **adjustable-rate preferred stock**, an instrument that was invented in the 1980s. This kind of preferred stock goes by various acronyms, including ARPS (adjustable-rate preferred stock), DARTS (Dutch auction rate stock), APS (auction preferred stock), and RP (remarketed preferred). In each form of adjustable-rate preferred stock, the dividend is adjusted quarterly by an amount determined by the change in some short-term interest rate. Most of the adjustable-rate preferred stock is sold by financial institutions seeking deposits and is bought by corporate financial managers seeking a tax-advantaged investment for short-term funds. The tax advantage arises because, as of 1997, U.S. corporations may exclude from taxable income 70 percent of the dividends received from the preferred or common shares of another domestic corporation.[5]

MIPS.   One of the biggest advantages of preferred stock is that it allows corporations to issue a debtlike security without lowering the ratings on their existing debt. However, in contrast to a debt security with its tax-deductible interest, preferred stock has the disadvantage that its dividends are not tax deductible. In response to the desire for a security that provides the best of debt and preferred equity, investment bankers have developed a security they call either MIPS (monthly income preferred securities) or trust preferred securities.

---

[4]For the newer kinds of preferred stock, discussed below, preferred shareholders can sometimes force the firm into bankruptcy.

[5]We will discuss this in greater detail in Chapter 14.

Texaco's Monthly Income Preferred Securities (MIPS)

In October 1993 Goldman Sachs and Texaco brought the first MIPS issue to market. **Monthly income preferred securities (MIPS)** combine features of debt and equity. Like equity, they pay dividends, they can be perpetual, the dividends can be deferred if there are cash flow problems, and they aren't counted as debt on the firm's balance sheet. Like debt, however, they carry a fixed payment, they are rated by the rating agencies, and the payments to investors are classified as tax-deductible interest. The cash flows can be dividends to investors and interest to the firm through a special tax trick in which a wholly owned financing subsidiary is created that issues the preferred stock and then loans the proceeds to the parent company. The interest payments are passed back to the subsidiary, which records these payments as dividends to investors who are classified as partners of the subsidiary. This convoluted arrangement allowed Texaco to issue MIPS at their A-rated dividend yield of 6.875 percent but to have an after-tax financing rate of approximately 4.6 percent per year.

Source: Reprinted by permission of *The Wall Street Journal*, © 1995 Dow Jones & Company, Inc. All Rights Reserved Worldwide.

A key distinction between a MIPS and a typical preferred security is that the MIPS can defer the dividends for only five years while standard preferred stock can defer the dividends indefinitely. Unlike standard preferred stock, MIPS can force the firm into bankruptcy for failure to pay the dividend on this instrument. The Internal Revenue Service (IRS) has ruled that this distinction is sufficient to make the dividends on MIPS tax deductible, which in turn implies that corporate holders of these instruments are taxed on the entire dividend.[6] However, some Washington policymakers have tried unsuccessfully to get the IRS to treat MIPS as an equity instrument and to deny the tax deduction. Indeed, the Treasury Department proposed a series of tax law changes that would, among other things, deny the deductibility of the interest on instruments that do not show up as debt on the firm's balance sheet. However, these proposals were still under consideration in early 1997.

Warrants

There are several other equity-related securities that firms issue to finance their operations. Firms sometimes issue **warrants**, which are long-term call options on the issuing firm's stock. **Call options**[7] give their holders the right to buy shares of the firm at a prespecified price for a given period of time. These options are often included as part of a **unit offering**, which includes two or more securities offered as a package. For example, firms might try to sell one common share and one warrant as a unit. Schultz (1993) suggested that this kind of unit offering serves as a form of staged financing in which investors have an option to either invest more in the firm if it is successful or to shut it down by refusing to invest at the option's prespecified price. Warrants also are often bundled with a firm's bond and preferred stock offerings.

Volume of Financing with Different Equity Instruments

Exhibit 3.1 on page 80 shows the annual amounts of common and preferred stock that firms have issued since 1970. As you can see, common stock dominates preferred stock by a wide margin; almost 80 percent of equity financing is in common stock. In 1986, for example, U.S. corporations issued about $50 billion in common stock and only about $10 billion in preferred stock. And the total amount raised through warrants is even less than the amount raised with preferred.

---

[6]MIPS are sold almost exclusively to individual investors.

[7]Call options will be discussed in more detail in Chapters 7 and 8.

EXHIBIT 3.1   Annual Volume of Common and Preferred Stock Issues

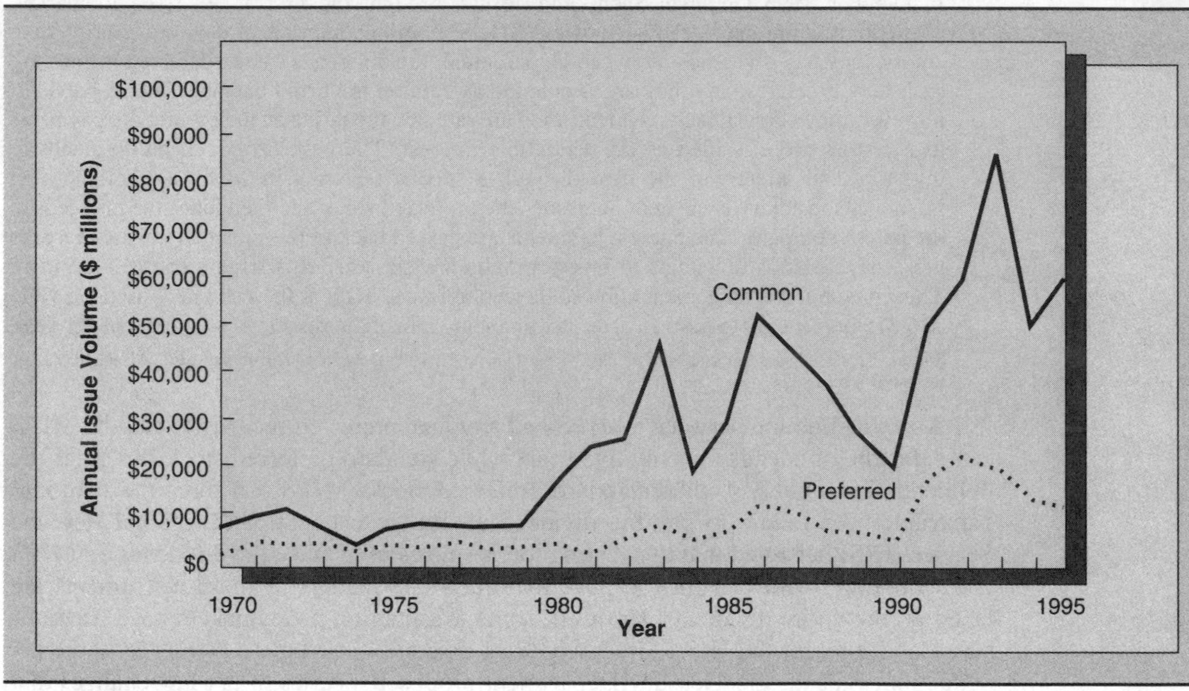

Source: *Federal Reserve Flow of Funds.*

3.2 Who Owns U.S. Equities?

The ownership of U.S. equities can be roughly divided into two groups: individuals and institutions. As Exhibit 3.2 demonstrates, there has been a dramatic increase since 1950 in the percent of equity held by U.S. institutions such as pension funds, insurance companies, university endowments, and mutual funds. A large part of the increase in institutional equity holdings, from 6 percent in 1950 to 44 percent in 1995, comes from the increased importance of pension funds, whose holdings rose from 1 percent in 1950 to 22 percent in 1995. Pension funds hold about half of their portfolios in debt instruments and proportionately are an even bigger player in the corporate bond market than in the equity markets. A large part of the increase in the institutional ownership of U.S. equities during the 1990s is the result of the increased popularity of mutual funds, which provide better diversification than investors can achieve on their own. Mutual funds held over $1 trillion in equity in 1995 compared with only $233 billion in 1990.[8]

3.3 The Globalization of Equity Markets

U.S. corporations sometimes raise equity capital from foreign investors by listing common equity on foreign stock exchanges. For instance, Bell Atlantic has equity listed not only on U.S. stock exchanges, but also on exchanges in the United Kingdom, Switzerland, and Japan. Listing securities in each of these countries means complying with all

---

[8]*New York Stock Exchange Fact Book*, 1995.

EXHIBIT 3.2   Percentage of U.S. Equity Held by Institutions

	1950	*1970*	*1990*	*1995*
Equities held by U.S. pensions	1%	9%	25%	22%
Equities held by all U.S. institutions	6	27	43	44

Source: *NYSE Fact Book,* 1995.

local regulations and possibly with some that apply specifically to foreign issuers. Foreign investors also buy U.S. stocks directly on U.S. exchanges or, indirectly, through financial institutions such as mutual funds.

Foreign firms also raise capital in the United States. Because the United States has one of the world's largest capital markets, it is natural for many foreign firms to list their equities there. A firm must meet certain requirements, however, to be listed on a U.S. exchange. For example, U.S. financial disclosure requirements are among the strictest in the world, and many foreign firms face significant costs in producing U.S.-style financial statements. **American Depository Receipts (ADRs)** provide a way to get around these listing problems. With an ADR, a foreign firm deposits a number of its own shares with a money-center bank in New York. The bank then issues an ADR, which is a security that has a legal claim on the cash flows from the deposited shares. In other words, the bank holding the shares receives the stock's dividends which it pays to the holder of the ADR after deducting a small fee. In 1995, more than 350 firms were listed on the U.S. exchanges, either directly, or indirectly (through ADRs). Other major exchanges also trade large numbers of foreign issues: More than 800 are listed in London, 250 in Zurich, and 125 in Tokyo.

3.4 Secondary Markets for Equity

As Chapter 1 discussed, the advantage of publicly traded securities is that they can be sold later in public secondary markets. This section discusses the types of secondary equity markets that exist and how each type operates.

Types of Secondary Markets for Equity

Secondary equity markets can be organized either as an exchange or as an over-the-counter (OTC) market. An exchange is a physical location where buyers and sellers come together to buy and sell securities. The New York Stock Exchange (NYSE) is probably the best example, though there are many more, both in the United States and abroad. An over-the-counter (OTC) market, in contrast, allows buyers and sellers to transact without meeting at one physical place. For example, OTC transactions, such as the debt-based Euromarkets described in the last chapter, often take place over computer networks. The National Association of Security Dealers Automated Quotation System (NASDAQ) market in the United States is a noteworthy example of a computer-linked OTC equity market.

Two alternatives to the traditional exchange-based and OTC-based markets, known as the third market and the fourth market, include elements of both OTC and exchange markets. The **third market** is composed of exchange-listed stocks that can be bought and sold over the counter by a broker. The **fourth market** consists of large investors who trade exchange-listed stocks among themselves, bypassing the exchange. Although it is difficult to obtain data on transaction costs in alternative markets, an estimate of the cost of trading on the exchange floor is $0.05 to $0.10 per share.[9] In contrast, costs of trading in the off-exchange markets can be as low as $0.01 per share.

In all markets, trading is done by brokers, dealers, or both. A **broker** facilitates a trade between a buyer and a seller by bringing the two parties together. Brokers profit by charging a brokerage commission for this service. Alternatively, *dealers* buy and sell securities directly; that is, they maintain an inventory in the security and stand willing to take the opposite side of a buy or sell. Dealers make their money on the bid-ask spread, buying at the bid price and selling at the ask.

Exchanges

Numerous exchanges in the United States trade everything from stocks and bonds to options and futures contracts. The major stock exchanges are the NYSE and the American Stock Exchange (AMEX). There are also a number of regional exchanges such as the Midwest Exchange in Chicago, the Pacific Exchange in San Francisco, and the Boston and Philadelphia exchanges, which often trade stocks that are also listed on the major exchanges. By far the most important exchange in terms of capitalization and trading volume is the NYSE, where, in terms of capitalization, 80 to 90 percent of all U.S. equities trade.

Like all exchanges, the NYSE has certain listing requirements. One requirement, which can change over time, specifies the minimum size of the firm to ensure that the firm is large enough to be of interest to many investors. As of 1995, the NYSE required the firm to have at least $20.0 million in assets, a pretax income of $2.5 million, a market value of $20.0 million, and 2,000 shareholders. The AMEX and the regional exchanges have less stringent minimums: The AMEX requires a pretax income of only $750,000 and a market value of $3 million; NASDAQ requires that a firm have a market value exceeding $1 million, 400 shareholders, and assets of $4 million.

Once a firm has applied for and been accepted to list on the NYSE, it is assigned a **specialist** to "make a market" in the security. The specialist acts as both broker and dealer. As a broker, the specialist brings together a buyer and a seller, either physically in front of the specialist's booth or electronically by matching buy and sell orders. The specialist also functions as a dealer, ready to buy and sell from his or her own inventory. In this role, the specialist is supposed to make a "fair and orderly market" in the security, which means ensuring that prices do not move up or down precipitously.

Specialists take both market orders and limit orders. A **market order** is an order to buy or sell at whatever the prevailing market price may be. For small-sized orders, this usually means purchasing at the specialist's quoted ask price and selling at the specialist's quoted bid price. A **limit order** is an offer to buy or sell at a prespecified share price.

Dealer Markets for Equity

Despite the enormous capitalization of the NYSE, only about 2,500 of more than 12,000 U.S. public firms are traded there. The majority of firms not listed on the NYSE trade over the counter through a network of dealers. Dealer networks can be telephone- or computer-based, although there has been a clear movement toward more computer-based

---

[9]See Story (1988).

trading. Computers make it easier to gather price quotes and to see what the prices were in recent transactions. In any dealer network, a customer who wants to buy or sell a security calls a broker. The broker in turn contacts dealers to get price quotes, selecting the dealer with the best quote to make the trade.

The most sophisticated dealer network is NASDAQ, which originated in the early 1970s to automate the old over-the-counter system, in which dealers would record quotes and trades manually. NASDAQ links brokers and dealers by a computer system that allows them to see all the quotes on a particular stock. The typical firm listed on NASDAQ has approximately 10 dealers or market makers who are active in trading the stock. Each market maker is required to give a bid-ask quote and a **"depth,"** that is how many shares the market maker is willing to buy at the bid price and sell at the ask price. NASDAQ regulations insist that the quote and depth be good for at least one trade. Of course, there is no requirement that the quote be competitive and, indeed, there is some evidence suggesting that most stocks have just a few active market makers.[10]

At present, there is a great deal of ferment in the secondary markets. The governing bodies of the exchanges and the regulatory authorities confront issues such as the demand for 24-hour trading; the advantages of moving from quoting in eighths, the current practice, to quoting in cents; the desire of firms to list internationally, and the attendant problem of accounting standards; the efficiency and fairness of dealer markets compared with exchanges; and the movement toward a fully computerized worldwide trading system.

International Secondary Markets for Equity

So far, we have concentrated on U.S. markets. However, since large corporations now raise capital from all over the world, financial managers need to have a basic understanding of the markets outside the United States.

Exhibit 3.3 on page 84 lists the top 20 equity markets by capitalization and trading volume. The list of countries holds few surprises: Large economies generally have large equity markets. The United States, Japan, and the United Kingdom have been and continue to be the three largest stock markets in the world. One surprise is that the German stock market is quite small relative to the size of its economy (see Chapter 1). Economies about one-tenth the size of Germany's, such as those in Switzerland, Hong Kong, and the Netherlands, have stock markets that are about 50 to 60 percent of Germany's market capitalization.

The exact rankings of countries probably should be treated with some skepticism because different countries measure activity in different ways, making direct comparisons difficult. However, the rankings are indicative of the relative sizes of the various stock markets and are fairly stable over time.

3.5 The Decision to Issue Shares Publicly

Many economists believe that the relatively liquid equity markets and the active new issues market provide a competitive advantage to young firms in the United States. Without access to good capital markets, many entrepreneurs and venture capitalists would find it difficult or impossible to cash out or diversify their holdings. That in turn would make starting a firm more expensive and reduce the rate at which firms are created.

---

[10]See Christie and Schultz (1994).

EXHIBIT 3.3 **Market Value of Shares Outstanding and Value of Shares Traded, 1992**

Value of Shares Outstanding		*Value of Shares Traded*	
Country	*Market Capitalization (millions of dollars)*	*Country*	*Volume (millions of dollars)*
United States	$4,757,879	United States	$2,678,523
Japan	2,399,004	Germany	892,037
United Kingdom	838,579	Japan	635,261
France	350,858	United Kingdom	382,998
Germany	348,138	Taiwan	240,667
Canada	243,018	France	125,052
Switzerland	195,285	South Korea	116,101
Hong Kong	172,106	Hong Kong	90,611
Netherlands	171,435	Netherlands	89,849
Mexico	139,061	Canada	83,448
Australia	135,451	Switzerland	76,407
Italy	115,258	Thailand	72,060
South Korea	107,448	Australia	45,771
Taiwan	101,124	Mexico	44,582
Spain	98,969	Spain	39,987
Malaysia	94,004	Sweden	28,411
Sweden	76,622	Italy	28,129

Source: International Finance Corporation, *Emerging Stock Markets Factbook* (1993).

As an example, investors plowed $10 billion into U.S. start-up firms in 1993 as opposed to about $4 billion in Europe, even though the economies of Europe and the United States are about the same size.[11] This means that about 3 percent of European investments went into start-ups as opposed to 14 percent in the United States. Part of the reason for the much larger share of U.S. investment in start-up companies is the ease with which U.S. firms can go public and initial investors can take their money out of the firm.

The initial public offering (IPO) market for common stock in the United States is both large and active. Between 1970 and 1995 more than 8,000 firms went public, raising more than $130 billion in the process. Exhibit 3.4 shows the annual number of firms going public and the total annual proceeds raised by those firms. The IPO market is extremely cyclical; in 1974, only 9 firms went public, compared with more than 900 in 1986. Proceeds have ranged from $50 million to almost $25 billion. Some of the reasons for this cyclical behavior are discussed below.

Demand- and Supply-Side Explanations for IPO Cycles

There are both demand-side and supply-side explanations for the cyclical nature of the IPO market. On the demand side, there are periods when an especially large number of

---

[11]*The Economist,* Nov. 12, 1994.

EXHIBIT 3.4   Number of IPO Issues and Proceeds, 1970–1992

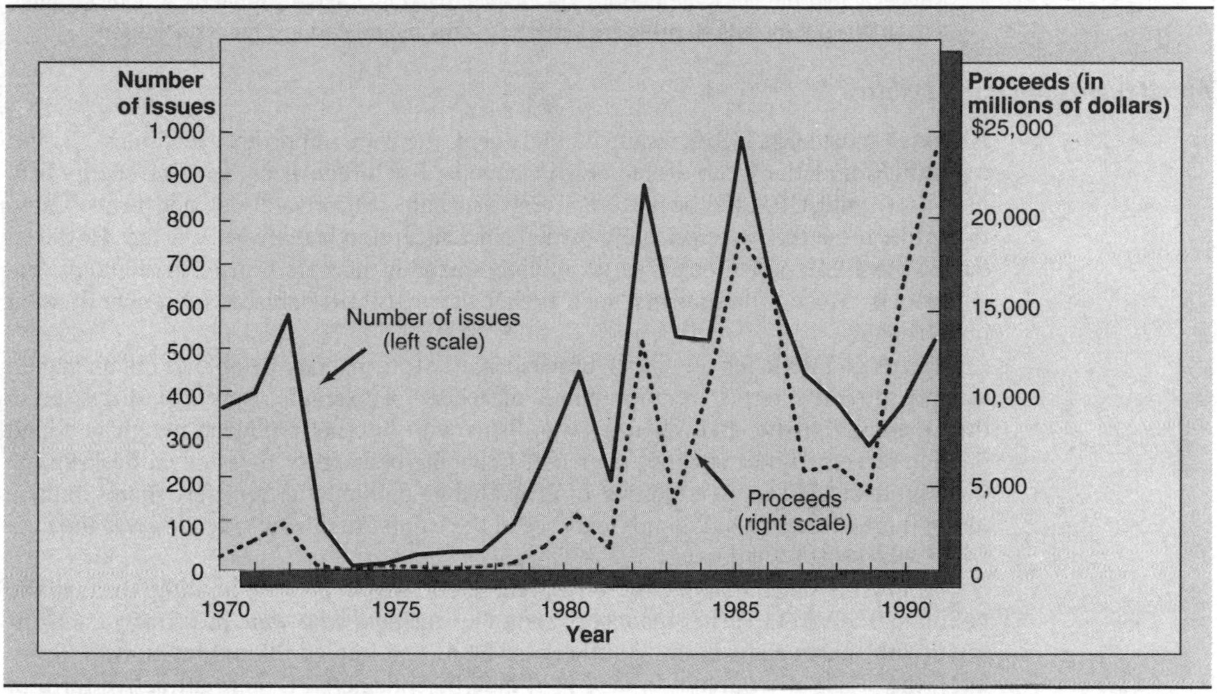

Source: Reprinted with permission from *The Journal of Applied Corporate Finance,* No. 6, "The Market's Problems with the Pricing of Initial Public Offerings," by Ibbotson, Sindelar, and Ritter (1993).

new firms, which are unlikely to obtain private funding at attractive terms, have investment projects that need to be funded. The Internet start-ups in 1995 and 1996 are good examples. On the supply side, there might be periods when investors and institutions that traditionally invest in IPOs have a lot of money to invest. This could happen for example, if a large inflow of money went into mutual funds that invest in small stocks.[12]

A firm considering going public would be interested in knowing whether **hot issue periods**—periods during which large numbers of firms are going public—are driven by a large demand for public funds by firms that need financing or, alternatively, by a large supply of public funds that need to be invested. If the hot issue periods are demand driven, entrepreneurs may wish to avoid going public during that time because the competition for funds would suggest that the firm might get a better price by waiting. However, the supply-side explanation would suggest the opposite: IPOs are observed frequently in some years and not in others because entrepreneurs are able to time their initial public offerings to correspond with the greater supply of available funding and thereby get better deals in the hot issue periods. Loughran and Ritter's empirical study (1995) suggested that the post-issue stock returns of firms that go public in hot issue periods are quite low, which supports the supply-side explanation. What this means is that entrepreneurs may benefit by timing their IPOs so that they come out in hot issue periods. From an investor's perspective, however, this would not be a good time to buy IPOs.

---

[12]See Choe, Masulis, and Nanda (1993) for a discussion and evidence on demand-side effects. Loughran and Ritter (1995) discuss and provide evidence of supply-side explanations of the hot issue market.

Result 3.1   IPOs are observed frequently in some years and not in other years. The available evidence suggests that the hot issue periods are characterized by a large supply of available capital. Given this interpretation, firms are better off going public during a hot issue period.

The Benefits of Going Public

Although most large U.S. firms are publicly held, there are important exceptions. Cargill, a multibillion dollar grain dealer in Minneapolis, Koch Industries, a major energy firm in Kansas, and UPS, the package delivery firm, are still privately owned firms. Large firms like these that were privately owned since inception had always existed. However, during the 1980s, a number of large publicly traded firms were transformed into private companies. Most of these firms, such as Safeway and RJR Nabisco, subsequently went public again.

Firms go public for a number of reasons. First, firms may be able to obtain capital at more attractive terms from the public markets. For example, Netscape, discussed in the opening vignette, and other start-up firms with Internet products, may have found public markets to be a cheaper source of financing because of investor enthusiasm for their products. However, a number of firms that go public issue very few shares in their initial public offering and do not really need the capital that is raised. This was the case when Microsoft went public.[13]

Microsoft stated that one reason it went public was to provide liquidity through the public markets to the firm's managers and other insiders who were previously compensated with shares and who might otherwise be locked into an illiquid investment. Similarly, the stock of a publicly traded firm may be considered a more attractive form of compensation than the stock of a private firm, making it easier for the public firm to attract the best employees. Being public means that the original owners, investors, and old and new managers can cash out of the firm and diversify their portfolios.

An additional advantage to being public is that stock prices in the public markets provide a valuable source of information for managers of the firm. Every day, investors buy and sell shares, thereby rendering their judgments about the firm's prospects. Although the market isn't infallible, it can be a useful reality check. For example, a manager would probably think twice about expanding the firm's core business after its stock price fell. A falling stock price indicates that a number of investors and analysts have unfavorable information about a firm's prospects, which would tend to imply that an expansion would not be warranted.

Finally, some managers believe that going public is good publicity. Listing the firm's stock on a national exchange may bring name recognition and increase the firm's credibility with its customers, employees, and suppliers. In some businesses, this kind of credibility matters very little. However, for a firm such as Netscape, a buoyant stock price may help convince consumers that they have succeeded in setting the standard for Web browsers.

The Costs of Going Public

It costs a lot of money to go public. An obvious cost is hiring an investment banker, attorneys, and accountants, but by far the largest expense is the underwriting fee. As Exhibit 1.7 in Chapter 1 shows, the total direct costs associated with taking a firm public are about 11 percent of the amount of money raised.

While direct costs may be large, there exists an additional and equally important cost of going public. The price at which the investment banker sells the issue to the

---

[13]For a discussion of Microsoft's IPO, see Utal (1986).

original investors is generally 10 to 15 percent below the price at which the stock trades in the secondary market shortly thereafter. Regardless of the reason for the observed underpricing of new issues, firms should add the typical 10 to 15 percent underpricing to their cost of going public. Taking all of these costs into account, the total cost of going public could exceed 25 percent of the amount raised in the initial public offering. However, firms often raise very little in the initial public offering, so the cost as a fraction of the firm's total value is generally considerably smaller.

Once a firm is public, it faces other costs that private firms do not bear. Public firms are required to provide proxy statements and quarterly and annual reports. They also must hold shareholder meetings and communicate with institutional shareholders and financial analysts. Because a public firm's communication with its shareholders must be relatively open, any information provided to shareholders also will be available to competitors, which may put the firm at a competitive disadvantage.

Because a public corporation is more visible than a private company, it may be pressured to do things in ways that it would not otherwise do. For example, Jensen and Murphy (1990) advanced the idea that the required revelation of managerial compensation by public companies constrains them from paying their executives too much. In addition, shareholders may put pressure on managers to make "socially responsible" investment choices they might not otherwise consider. Examples include shareholder pressure to pull investments out of South Africa prior to the abandonment of apartheid or pressure to avoid using nuclear energy.

Result 3.2 summarizes the discussion in the last two subsections.

Result 3.2   The advantages and disadvantages of going public are described below:

Advantages
- Better access to capital markets.
- Shareholders gain liquidity.
- Original owners can diversify.
- Monitoring and information are provided by external capital markets.
- Enhances the firm's credibility with customers, employees, and suppliers.

Disadvantages
- Expensive.
- Costs of dealing with shareholders.
- Information revealed to competitors.
- Public pressure.

In general, a firm should go public when the benefits of doing so exceed the costs.

The Process of Going Public

Taking a company public is a lengthy process that usually requires several months.

The Registration Statement.   Once the firm chooses an underwriter, it begins assembling the data required for the registration statement. This includes the audited financial statements and a complete description of the firm's business: products, prospects, and possible risks (e.g., reliance on major customers or contracts and dependence on key personnel). The underwriters are legally responsible for ensuring that the registration statement discloses all material information about the firm. **Material information** is information that, if omitted, would significantly alter the value of the firm.

Marketing the Issue.   The underwriter is also responsible for forming the underwriting syndicate, marketing the stock, and allocating shares among syndicate members.

Marketing the stock may involve "road shows" in which the firm's management and the underwriter explain and try to sell the IPO to institutional investors. These presentations not only enable investors to get a feel for management, but also, and equally important, they enable the underwriter to form an estimate of the demand for an issue. Although "expressions of interest" from potential buyers are nonbinding, they influence the offer price, number of shares, and allocations to particular investors.

Pricing the Issue.   Once the SEC approves the registration statement, the process of going public can move into its final stage of pricing the issue, determining the number of shares to be sold, and distributing the shares to investors. In many cases, the IPO is oversubscribed. An **oversubscribed offering** means that investors want to buy more shares than the underwriter plans to sell. For example, when Netscape went public, the underwriters had five million shares to sell. However, the issue was substantially over-subscribed and the underwriters probably could have sold many times that number of shares at the offering price. In oversubscribed offerings, U.S. underwriters have discretion to allocate the shares as they see fit. Individual investors who are not regular buyers of IPOs are unlikely to be allocated shares in oversubscribed offers. As we will discuss below, in many countries outside the United States, the underwriter is required to allocate some shares to all investors who request them.

Book Building vs. Fixed-Price Method.   The description of the way in which investment bankers price and market a new issue is called a **book-building process**. The important thing to note about a book-building process is that it allows the investment banker to gauge the demand for the issue and, as a result, to price the issue more accurately. This book-building process is used for all but the smallest U.S. IPOs and has become increasingly popular for foreign IPOs that are marketed internationally.

Although the book-building process is becoming more popular outside the United States, most non-U.S. IPOs are sold with the **fixed-price method**. For example, fixed-price offerings in the United Kingdom advertise the number of shares and the offer price by prospectus 14 days prior to accepting applications from interested investors. The important distinction between the fixed-price and book-building methods is that with the former method the investment bank is less able to gauge investor demand. In addition, investors in fixed-price offerings are generally allocated shares in oversubscribed offerings on a pro rata basis. In other words, if a company offers one million shares to investors, and investors, in aggregate, request two million shares, then each investor will receive only half of what he or she requested. Some deviations from these pro rata allocations exist. For example, in some cases underwriters can discriminate in favor of small investors, giving them a larger proportion of the shares they request. In contrast to the book-building method used mainly in the United States, where the underwriter has considerable discretion, in fixed-price offerings, in countries like the U.K., investment banks generally have little leeway in how to allocate the shares of new issues.

3.6 Stock Returns Associated with IPOs of Common Equity

We noted previously that, on average, IPOs are underpriced. For example, the opening vignette indicates that Netscape's stock was issued at $28 a share and closed the first day at $58.25, which suggests that the underwriter underpriced the shares by 108 percent [($58.25 − $28.00)/$28.00], which is an extreme example of underpricing.

Exhibit 3.5   Summary of IPO Pricing Studies

Study	Initial Return (percent)	Data for Return Interval	Period Studied	Sample Size
McDonald & Fisher (1972)	29%	Weekly	1969–1970	142
Logue (1973)	42	Monthly	1965–1969	250
Reilly (1973)	10	Weekly	1966	62
Neuberger & Hammond (1974)	17	Weekly	1965–1969	816
Ibbotson (1975)	11	Monthly	1960–1971	128
Ibbotson & Jaffe (1975)	17	Weekly	1960–1970	2,650
Reilly (1978)	11	Weekly	1972–1975	486
Block & Stanley (1977)	6	Weekly	1974–1978	102
Neuberger & LaChapelle (1983)	28	Weekly	1975–1980	118
Ritter (1984)	19	Daily	1960–1982	5,162
Miller & Reilly (1987)	10	Daily	1982–1983	510
Ibbotson, Sindelar, & Ritter (1988)	15	Daily	1960–1992	10,626
Ritter (1987), sample of firm commitment offers	15	Daily	1977–1982	664
Ritter (1987), sample of best efforts offers	48	Daily	1977–1982	364

Source: *Emerging Stock Fact Book*, International Finance Corporation.

IPO Underpricing of U.S. Stocks

Because the cost associated with the underpricing is a major cost associated with going public, researchers have conducted a number of studies to learn more about this phenomena. Exhibit 3.5 summarizes some of these studies, which are listed in roughly chronological order. The exhibit shows initial returns, calculated from the offer price, P_0, to the price, P_1, at the end of the first day, the first week, or the first month. Average returns, $(P_1 - P_0)/P_0$, are roughly 15 percent, a number sufficient to arouse the interest of both investors and academic researchers.

Estimates of International IPO Underpricing

Exhibit 3.6 on page 90 reveals that IPOs are underpriced all over the world. The magnitude of the underpricing is especially large in some of the less developed capital markets in countries such as Malaysia, Brazil, and South Korea. Although large differences appear in the amount of underpricing in developed capital markets relative to the less developed ones, the difference between the amount of underpricing in the United Kingdom, where fixed-price offers dominate, and the United States, where book-building dominates, is not particularly large.

3.7 What Explains Underpricing?

The tendency of IPOs to be underpriced is of interest for a variety of reasons. For example, the underpricing of IPOs increases the cost of going public and may thus deter some firms from going public. To investors, however, underpriced IPOs appear to

EXHIBIT 3.6   Average Initial Returns of IPOs in 25 Countries

Country	Average Initial Return (percent)	Period Studied	Sample Size
Malaysia	80%	1980–1991	132
Brazil	79	1979–1990	62
Korea	78	1980–1990	347
Thailand	58	1988–1989	32
Portugal	54	1986–1987	62
Taiwan	45	1971–1990	168
Sweden	39	1970–1991	213
Switzerland	36	1983–1989	42
Spain	35	1985–1990	71
Mexico	33	1987–1990	37
Japan	33	1970–1991	472
New Zealand	29	1979–1991	149
Italy	27	1985–1991	75
Singapore	27	1973–1987	66
Hong Kong	18	1980–1990	80
Chile	16	1982–1990	19
United States	15	1960–1992	10,626
United Kingdom	12	1959–1990	2,133
Australia	12	1976–1989	266
Germany	11	1978–1992	170
Belgium	10	1984–1990	28
Finland	10	1984–1992	85
Netherlands	7	1982–1991	72
Canada	5	1971–1992	258
France	4	1983–1992	187

Source: Reprinted from *Pacific Basin Finance Journal*, 1994, No. 2, Loughran, Ritter, and Rydqvist, Table 1, pp. 165–199. © 1994 with kind permission of Elsevier Science-NL, Sara Burgerhartstreet 25, 1055 KV Amsterdam, The Netherlands.

provide "the free lunch," or the sure thing, that most investors dream about. Before Netscape went public, it was well known that its shares were going to be substantially oversubscribed at the initial offering price and most analysts predicted that the stock would trade well above this initial price in the secondary market. Indeed, as the opening vignette indicates, investors who bought at the offering price, and then sold their shares immediately in the secondary market, more than doubled their money.

How Do I Get These Underpriced Shares?

As with most free lunches, there are hidden costs to the allocation of underpriced new issues. It is not possible to simply open a brokerage account and expect to be able to buy many new issues at the offering price. Investors should consider why underwriters under-price new issues before they attempt to realize the apparent profit opportunity in this market.

The Incentives of Underwriters

In setting an offering price, underwriters will weigh the costs and benefits of raising or lowering the issue's price. Pricing an issue too low adds to the cost of going public. Therefore, to attract clients, underwriters try to price their issues as high as possible. This tendency, however, is offset by the possibility that the issue may not sell if it is priced too high, leaving the underwriter saddled with unsold shares. Because the cost of having unsold shares is borne directly (firm commitment) or indirectly, as a loss of reputation (best efforts), by the underwriter, it may have a substantial influence on the pricing choice and even lead the underwriter to underprice the issue.

Baron (1982) analyzed a potential conflict of interest between underwriters and issuing firms that arises because of their differing incentives and the underwriter's better information about market conditions. Given superior information, the underwriter has a major say on the price of the issue. This will not be a problem if the underwriter has exactly the same incentives as the issuing firm, but that is unlikely. The underwriter's incentive is to set the offering price low enough to ensure that all the shares will sell without much effort and without subjecting the underwriter to excessive risk. Underpricing the issue makes the underwriter's job easier and less risky.

Although this explanation seems plausible and probably applies in some cases, a study by Muscarella and Vetsuypens (1989) suggested that Baron's explanation is probably incomplete. They examined a sample of 38 investment bankers who took themselves public and, hence, did not suffer from the information and incentive problems suggested by Baron. These investment bankers underpriced their own stock an average of 7 percent; the underpricing rose to 13 percent for the issuing firm that also was the lead manager of the underwriting syndicate.

An underwriter might also want to underprice an issue because of the costs that could arise from investor lawsuits brought on by a subsequently poor performance of the issue. Tinic (1988) examined this possibility, arguing that concerns about being sued increased following the Securities Act of 1933. Comparing a pre-1933 sample of issues to a post-1933 sample, Tinic found that the initial return, or the degree of underpricing, was much higher after the 1933 act, which lends support to this theory.

Drake and Vetsuypens (1993), however, provided more recent evidence that makes us somewhat skeptical about any large effect on pricing caused by concern over legal liability. They examined 93 firms that were sued after their IPOs. The sued firms were as underpriced as other IPOs, suggesting that underpricing an issue does not effectively prevent lawsuits. Furthermore, the average settlement was only 15 percent of the proceeds, or roughly the same as the average amount of the underpricing. From the issuing firm's point of view, one cannot justify underpricing an issue by 15 percent simply to lower the *chance* of a lawsuit that will cost 15 percent on average (assuming it takes place). Nevertheless, since the underwriting firm may be the object of the lawsuit, it may still have an incentive to underprice the issue.

The Case Where the Managers of the Issuing Firm Have Better Information Than Investors

Often firms go public as a precursor to a larger seasoned issue in the near future. This allows managers to first test the waters with a small issue and, if that issue is successful, to subsequently raise additional equity capital. Investment bankers have frequently suggested that it is a good idea to underprice the initial offering in these circumstances to make investors feel better about the secondary issue. The belief is that investors will be more likely to subscribe to a firm's secondary offering after making money in the IPO.

A number of academic papers have noted that entrepreneurs who expect their firms to do well, and who have opportunities for further investment, will have the greatest incentive to underprice their shares.[14] These papers argue that investors understand that only the best-quality firms have the incentive to underprice their issues; therefore, these investors take a more favorable view of the subsequent issues of firms that underpriced their IPOs. The incentive to underprice an issue is therefore determined by a firm's intention to seek outside financing in the near future. Although this argument seems plausible, empirical research on the pricing of new issues provides no support for this hypothesis.[15]

The Case Where Some Investors Have Better Information Than Other Investors

An innovative paper by Rock (1986) explained the hazards of using one's knowledge that IPOs tend to be underpriced to place orders for all available IPOs. To understand these hazards, recall the famous line by Groucho Marx, who said, "I would never join a club that would have me for a member."

To have an IPO allocated to you is a bit like being invited to join an exclusive club. Since the hot issues are underpriced, on average, there is usually excess demand that makes the shares difficult to obtain. While it might be nice to be asked to join a club, you have to ask whether the club is really so exclusive if you were asked to join. Likewise, it is important to ask whether the IPO is really so hot if your broker is able to get you the shares.

To understand Rock's argument, suppose that there are two kinds of investors: the informed and the uninformed. Informed investors know the true value of the shares, perhaps through costly research. Hence, they will put in an order for the IPO only when the shares are underpriced. Uninformed investors do not know what shares are worth and put in orders for a cross-section of IPOs. Unfortunately, they get allocated 100 percent of the overpriced "dogs" and only a fraction of the underpriced "stars."

If new issues are not underpriced, uninformed investors will, on average, systematically lose money. The allocation of the dogs to investors is an example of what economists refer to as the **winner's curse**, a term derived from an analysis of auctions, in which the bidder who wins the auction ultimately realizes that he or she was willing to pay more for the object than everyone else in the room—and thus overpaid. Similarly, an investor who is allocated shares in an IPO could be subject to the winner's curse if he or she is allocated shares because more informed investors have chosen not to purchase them. Because of this winner's curse, individuals who are aware of their lack of knowledge avoid auctions, and uninformed investors generally avoid buying IPOs.

Rock's article suggested that investment bankers, wanting to broaden the appeal of the issues, may underprice the issues to induce uninformed investors to buy them. One implication of this line of reasoning, supported by Beatty and Ritter's study (1986), is that riskier IPOs that are more subject to the winner's curse must be underpriced more, on average, than the less risky IPOs.

Koh and Walter's (1989) study of IPOs in Singapore and Keloharju's (1993) study of IPOs in Finland provide more direct tests of Rock's model. These countries use the U.K. fixed-price method to distribute and allocate shares, and the degree of rationing is public knowledge. The results of both studies show that (1) buyers receive more shares with

---

[14]This explanation for underpricing new issues is developed in papers by Allen and Faulhaber (1989), Welch (1989), Grinblatt and Hwang (1989), and Chemmanur (1993).

[15]Garfinkel (1993), Jegadeesh, Weinstein, and Welch (1993), and Michaely and Shaw (1994) look at the relation between the amount an issue is underpriced and whether the issuer subsequently follows with a secondary offering. All conclude that there is no such relation.

overpriced issues and fewer shares with underpriced issues, and (2) since investors receive a greater allocation of the bad issues, on average, they realize zero profits from buying IPO shares even though the shares are underpriced.

The Case Where Investors Have Information That the Underwriter Does Not Have

The Rock model provides a good explanation for underpricing in countries that use the U.K. fixed-price method. In addition, the model provides an important lesson for uninformed investors in the United States who learn about the average underpricing of IPOs and see it as a profit opportunity. However, Rock's model may not explain why issues tend to be underpriced in the United States where a book-building procedure is generally used.

Recall that with the book-building procedure, underwriters rely on information learned from potential investors when they price the IPO. If investors express enthusiasm for the issue, the underwriter raises the price. If investors are less enthusiastic, the underwriter lowers the price.

Because their information affects the price, investors have an incentive to distort their true opinions of an IPO. In particular, investors might want to appear pessimistic about the issuing firm's prospects in hopes of getting allocated shares of the issue at a more favorable price. Obtaining truthful information may be especially difficult when there are one or two market leaders, such as Fidelity Investments, whose decisions are likely to influence the decisions of other investors.[16] Welch (1992) suggested that influential investors can play a very important role in determining the success or failure of an offer because smaller investors may ignore their own information and decide whether to subscribe to an issue based on the stated opinions of market leaders. For example, if Fidelity expresses no interest in an issue, small investors may choose to ignore their own information and decide not to participate in the offering, causing the IPO to fail.

Benveniste and Spindt (1989) and Benveniste and Wilhelm (1990) suggested that the way investment banks price and allocate the shares of new issues when they use a book-building process may make it easier for them to elicit credible information from their large investors. In particular, the authors suggested that IPOs are priced and the shares are allocated in the following way:

- Investment banks underreact to information provided by investors when they price the IPOs.
- Investors who provide more favorable information are allocated more shares.

The underreaction of investment banks to investor-provided information implies that when investors do provide extremely favorable information, the banks are likely to underprice the issue the most. Informed investors, therefore, would like to be allocated a large share of these issues. Hence, to receive a greater allocation, investors truthfully reveal their favorable opinion of the issue.

Hanley (1993) provided empirical evidence that investment banks price IPOs in the manner suggested above. She classified IPOs according to whether the offering prices were above or below the initial price range set by the investment banker in the prospectus:

- When investors express strong demand for an issue, the investment banker tends to price the issue above the expected price range listed in the prospectus. This occurred when Netscape went public. If investment bankers tend to underreact to

---

[16]Benveniste and Wilhelm (1996) report that Fidelity, one such market leader, buys about 10 percent of all newly issued shares.

information that strong investor demand for the IPO is likely, then these IPOs will be underpriced. Hanley found that IPOs priced above the initial range were underpriced by about 20.7 percent, on average.

· When the opinions expressed by investors corresponded with the investment banker's initial expectations, the price of the issue generally fell within the expected price range stated in the prospectus. Hanley found that these IPOs were underpriced 10 percent, on average.

· When the demand expressed by investors was relatively low, the issue is generally priced below the expected price range and might be withdrawn. These issues are expected to exhibit the least amount of underpricing. Hanley found that IPOs were underpriced only 0.6 percent, on average, when the offerings were priced below the expected range listed in the prospectus.

Individual investors hoping to gain from the underpriced new issues should be aware that not all IPOs are underpriced, and that they may not be in a position to obtain those IPOs that are.

3.8 Long-Term Performance of IPOs

A series of papers—Ritter (1991), Loughran, Ritter, and Rydqvist (1994), and Aggarwal and Rivoli (1990)—have shown that the long-term return to investing in IPOs is surprisingly low. Examining the shareholder return to owning a portfolio of IPOs for up to 5 years after the companies went public, these studies find annual returns to be in the range of 3 percent to 5 percent, far below other benchmark returns. Given these returns, the terminal value of an IPO portfolio after 5 years is only 70 percent to 80 percent of the value of a portfolio that invested in all NYSE and AMEX stocks or a portfolio that invested in the S&P 500 Index. The evidence reviewed in Loughran, Ritter, and Rydqvist (1994) shows that investors in Brazil, Finland, Germany, and the United Kingdom would have been just as disappointed with their investments in IPOs as investors in the United States.

More recent evidence suggests that the low returns in the years following U.S. IPOs are found mainly for smaller firms taken public by less reputable underwriters (see Field (1996)). This research suggests that larger firms, like Netscape, whose shares are held mainly by large institutions, do not seem to have unusually low returns following their initial public offerings.[17]

Implications for Market Efficiency

Some financial economists have suggested that the poor long-term performance of small firm IPOs suggests that the market is not informational efficient. Stock markets are **informationally efficient** if the prices of publicly traded stock *rationally reflect* all publicly available information. The key phrase in the preceding sentence is "rationally reflect" which is a somewhat vague concept meaning that a firm's stock market price fully reflects the fundamental or intrinsic value of the firm. Financial theories, discussed in Part II of the text, determine what we mean by the fundamental or intrinsic value of the firm.

---

[17]Another recent paper, Teoh, Welch, and Wong (1997), advances the idea that the smaller IPOs are overpriced because investors fail to understand the incentives of entrepreneurs to "dress up" their accounting numbers prior to going public. This study finds that the firms that artificially inflate their earnings the most prior to their IPO have the greatest negative excess returns in the years following the IPO.

How Market Prices Allocate Capital

Economists are concerned about the efficiency of stock prices because stock prices affect how capital is allocated throughout the economy. Consider again Netscape's IPO, which generated so much attention because of its high price relative to its near-term profit potential. Some people believed that Netscape's stock was substantially overpriced, perhaps because investors overreacted to the media hype.[18] Their argument was that a company with very little revenue and almost no profits could not rationally be valued at over $6 billion, which was approximately its market capitalization at its 1995 high.

Whether Netscape was overpriced is something that can never be verified. Although we will eventually know whether the company did as well as its investors anticipated, it can never be known whether those expectations were rational at the time when Netscape's stock was bid up to what some considered an irrational level. Perhaps, different investors rationally developed very different opinions about Netscape's prospects.

However, it is clear that the market's enthusiastic acceptance of the Netscape IPO had a major effect on the Internet industry. After Netscape's IPO, it was widely acknowledged that public markets were providing equity financing at very favorable terms for Internet firms. As a result, a substantial amount of capital flowed into newly formed Internet firms and a major new industry was born.

The important point to remember from this example is that stock market prices provide valuable signals that indirectly allocate capital to various sectors of the economy. Some economists and policymakers have argued that the U.S. economy is more vibrant than, for example, the German economy, because of its active stock market that allocates capital to new industries. These new industries would be less likely to get funding in an economy like Germany's, where new issues are very rare. However, if the stock market is inefficient, then the market will provide too much capital to some industries and not enough to others. For example, if Netscape's critics are correct in their assertions about irrational pricing, then the U.S. economy may be providing too much capital to the Internet industry.

Although it is not clear how informationally efficient markets are, stock prices convey valuable information, at least for the larger more established firms. Indeed, the framework developed in this text for analyzing the capital expenditure decisions made within firms is based on the idea that firms should use signals from the financial markets as key inputs in their capital investment decisions.[19] However, stock prices may be a less reliable indicator of fundamental values for smaller, newer companies. Because the stocks of smaller companies provide institutional investors with lesser profit opportunities when they are mispriced, they are generally followed less by stock market analysts. The result is that investors may be less informed about smaller stocks, suggesting that their market prices can have a greater tendency to deviate from fundamental values.

The Decision to Go Public Revisited

A number of corporate decisions are influenced by the deviations between market prices and managers' beliefs about the fundamental values of their firms.[20] The decision to go public is only the first of many decisions faced by financial managers that are subject to this influence. If entrepreneurs believe that the market would underprice the firm if it were to go public, they may choose to keep their firms private in the hopes that the

---

[18]Some of our colleagues at places like UCLA, the University of Chicago, and MIT not only argued that the stock was substantially overpriced, but actually backed up their claims by short-selling the stock.

[19]This topic will be discussed in Part III.

[20]Chapter 18 provides a detailed discussion of this issue.

market will view the firm more favorably in the future. On the other hand, other entrepreneurs may choose to take their firms public earlier than they would otherwise have done because they believe the market overprices their stock.

In an efficient market, investors recognize the incentives of those entrepreneurs who are taking their firms public and price the shares accordingly. However, some financial economists believe that investors are not always as savvy as the efficient markets hypothesis would suggest. These economists argue that entrepreneurs are often successful at selling their stock when market prices are too high relative to fundamentals and that, because of this, investors would be smart to avoid buying IPOs shortly after they go public, especially when the market seems especially hot.

3.9 Summary and Conclusions

This chapter reviews some of the institutional features of U.S. and overseas equity markets. It describes the various equity instruments, the types of investors who hold these equity investments, and the markets on which they are traded. It points out there are many fewer types of equity securities than there are debt securities. Although the equity markets are less dominated by institutions than are the debt markets, it is still the case that in the United States, almost half of all equities are held by institutions.

The chapter also discussed the process by which firms go public. When firms go public, they transform their private equity, which cannot be traded, into common stock that can be traded in the public markets. Our discussion of the incentives of firms to go public raised a number of questions that will be addressed in more detail in later chapters. For example, since firms generally raise substantial amounts of new equity when they go public, the decision to go public must be considered along with the firm's capital structure choice, which is examined in Part IV of this text. Going public also affects the amount of influence shareholders have on a corporation's management, which is examined in Part V of this text. Finally, the decision to go public is strongly influenced by the difference between the fundamental value of the firm, as perceived by the firm's management, and the price for the shares that can be obtained in the public markets. However, this type of comparison requires additional knowledge of what determines both fundamental values and market prices. The determination of these values are considered in Parts II and III of this text.

Key Concepts

Result 3.1: IPOs are observed frequently in some years and not in other years. The available evidence suggests that the hot issue periods are characterized by a large supply of available capital. Given this interpretation, firms are better off going public during a hot issue period.

Result 3.2: The advantages and disadvantages of going public are described below:

Advantages
- Better access to capital markets.
- Shareholders gain liquidity.
- Original owners can diversify.
- Monitoring and information are provided by external capital markets.
- Enhances the firm's credibility with customers, employees, and suppliers.

Disadvantages
- Expensive.
- Costs of dealing with shareholders.
- Information revealed to competitors.
- Public pressure.

In general, a firm should go public when the benefits of doing so exceed the costs.

Key Terms

adjustable-rate preferred stock   78
American Depositary Receipts (ADRs)   81

book-building process   88
broker   82

Exercises

3.1. The William Wrigley Jr. Company is the world's largest maker of chewing gum. The CEO is William Wrigley, Jr., the son of the founder. Wrigley has two classes of shares: common and class B stock. In 1995, there were 91.2 million shares of common stock outstanding, entitled to one vote per share; there were also 25.1 million shares of class B stock outstanding with 10 votes per share. The Wrigley family owns directly or through trusts about 22.1 million shares of common stock and about 12.9 million shares of class B stock. What percentage of the total votes do the Wrigleys control?

3.2. In many European countries such as the United Kingdom and Switzerland, rights issues are much more common than the public, underwritten offers that firms in the United States chiefly use. Can you think of some reasons why this might be true?

3.3. Suppose a firm wants to make a $75 million initial public offering of stock. Estimate the transaction costs associated with the issue.

3.4. Suppose your firm wants to issue a security with a guaranteed fixed payment, but which receives an additional benefit when the firm's stock price increases. Describe how such a security can be designed, and name existing securities that have this characteristic.

3.5. When investment bankers bring a new firm to market, do you think they have conflicting incentives? What might these be and what are their causes?

References and Additional Readings

Amihud, Yakov, and Haim Mendelson. "Liquidity and Asset Prices." *Financial Management* 17 (1988), pp. 5–15.

Aggarwal, Reena, and Pietra Rivoli. "Fads in the Initial Public Offering Market." *Financial Management* 19 (1990), pp.45–57.

Allen, Franklin, and Gerald Faulhaber. "Signaling by Underpricing in the IPO market." *Journal of Financial Economics* 23 (1989), pp. 303–23.

Baron, David. "A Model of the Demand for Investment Banking Advice and Distribution Services for New Issues." *Journal of Finance* 37 (1982), pp. 955–76.

Barry, Christopher; Chris Muscarella; and Michael Vetsuypens. "Underwriter Warrants, Underwriter Compensation, and the Costs of Going Public." *Journal of Financial Economics* 29 (1991), 113–15.

Beatty, Randolph, and Jay Ritter. "Investment Banking, Reputation, and the Underpricing of Initial Public Offerings." *Journal of Financial Economics* 15 (1986), pp. 213–29.

Benveniste, Lawrence, and Paul Spindt. "How Investment Bankers Determine the Offer Price and Allocation of New Issues." *Journal of Financial Economics* 24 (1989), pp. 343–61.

Benveniste, Lawrence, and William Wilhelm. "A Comparative Analysis of IPO Proceeds Under Alternative Regulatory Environments." *Journal of Financial Economics* 28 (1990), pp. 173–207.

―――. "Initial Public Offering: Going by the Book" *Journal of Applied Corporate Finance* 10 (1997), pp. 000–000.

Chemmanur, Thomas. "The Pricing of IPOs: A Dynamic Model with Information Production." *Journal of Finance* 48 (1993), pp. 285–304.

Christie, William, and Paul Schultz. "Why Do Market Makers Avoid Odd-Eighth Quotes?" *Journal of Finance* 49 (1994), pp. 1813–40.

Choe, Hyuk; Ronald Masulis; and Vikram Nanda. "Common Stock Offerings across the Business Cycle: Theory and Evidence," *Journal of Empirical Finance* (1993), pp. 3–31.

Drake, Philip, and Michael Vetsuypens. "IPO Underpricing and Insurance against Legal Liability." *Financial Management* 22 (1993), pp. 64–73.

Field, Laura. "Is Institutional Investment in Initial Public Offerings Related to Long-Run Performance of those Firms." UCLA Working Paper, University of California at Los Angeles, 1996.

Garfinkel, John. "IPO Underpricing, Insider Selling, and Subsequent Equity Offerings: Is Underpricing a Signal of Quality?" *Financial Management* 22, pp. 74–83.

Grinblatt, Mark, and Chuan-Yang Hwang. "Signaling and the Pricing of New Issues." *Journal of Finance* 44 (1989), pp. 393–420.

Hanley, Kathleen. "The Underpricing of Initial Public Offerings and the Partial Adjustment Phenomenon." *Journal of Financial Economics* 34 (1993), pp. 231–50.

Hanley, Kathleen, and William Wilhelm. "Evidence on the Strategic Allocation of Initial Public Offerings. *Journal of Financial Economics* 37 (1995), pp. 239–57.

Ibbotson, Roger. "Price Performance of Common Stock New Issues." *Journal of Financial Economics* 2 (1975), pp. 235–272.

Ibbotson, Roger, and Jeffrey Jaffe. "Hot Issue Markets." *Journal of Financial Economics* 2 (1975), pp. 1027–42.

Ibbotson, Roger; Jody Sindelar; and Jay Ritter. "Initial Public Offerings." *Journal of Applied Corporate Finance* 1 (1988), pp. 37–45.

―――. "The Market's Problems with the Pricing of Initial Public Offerings." *Journal of Applied Corporate Finance* 6 (1994), pp. 66–74.

Jegadeesh, Narasimhan; Mark Weinstein; and Ivo Welch. "An Empirical Investigation of IPO Returns and Subsequent Equity Offerings." *Journal of Financial Economics* 34 (1990), pp. 153–76.

Jensen, Michael, and Kevin Murphy. "CEO Incentives—It's not How Much You Pay but How." *Journal of Applied Corporate Finance* 3 (3), pp. 36–49.

Keloharju, Matti. "The Winner's Curse, Legal Liability, and the Long-Run Price Performance of Initial Public Offering in Finland." *Journal of Financial Economics* 34, pp. 251–77.

Koh, Francis, and Terry Walter. "A Direct Test of Rock's Model of the Pricing of Unseasoned Issues." *Journal of Financial Economics* 23 (1989), pp. 251–72.

Logue, Dennis. "On the Pricing of Unseasoned Equity Issues: 1965–1969." *Journal of Financial and Quantitative Analysis* 8 (1973), pp. 91–103.

Loughran, Tim, and Jay Ritter. "The New Issues Puzzle." *Journal of Finance* 50 (1995), pp. 23–52.

Loughran, Tim; Jay Ritter; and Kristian Rydqvist. "Initial Public Offerings: International Insights." *Pacific-Basin Finance Journal* 2 (1994), pp. 165–99.

McConnell, John, and Gary Sanger. "A Trading Strategy for Listing on the NYSE." *Financial Analysts Journal* 40 (1984), pp. 34–48.

McDonald, J., and A. Fisher. "New-Issue Stock Price Behavior." *Journal of Finance* 27 (1972), pp. 97–102.

Michaely, Roni, and Wayne Shaw. "The Pricing of Initial Public Offerings: Tests of Adverse Selection and Signaling Theories." *Review of Financial Studies* 7 (1994), pp. 279–313.

Miller, Robert, and Frank Reilly. "An Examination of Mispricing, Returns, and Uncertainty of Initial Public Offerings." *Financial Management* 16 (1987), pp. 33–38.

Muscarella, Chris, and Michael Vetsuypens. "A Simple Test of Baron's Model of IPO Underpricing." *Journal of Financial Economics* 24 (1989), pp. 125–35.

Neuberger, Brian, and Carl Hammond. "A Study of Underwriters' Experience with Unseasoned New Issues." *Journal of Financial and Quantitative Analysis* 9 (1974), pp. 165–77.

Neuberger, Brian, and Chris LaChapelle. "Unseasoned New Issue Price Performance on Three Tiers: 1975–1980." *Financial Management* 12 (1983), pp. 23–28.

NYSE, New York Stock Exchange, Inc., Fact Book 1995.

Reilly, Frank. "Further Evidence on Short-Run Results for New-Issue Investors." *Journal of Financial and Quantitative Analysis* 8 (1973), pp. 83–90.

―――. "New Issues Revisited." *Financial Management* 6 (1977), pp. 28–42.

Ritter, Jay. "The Costs of Going Public." *Journal of Financial Economics* 19 (1987), pp. 269–82.

―――. "The 'Hot' Issue Market of 1980." *Journal of Business* 57 (1984), pp. 215–40.

―――. "The Long-Run Performance of Initial Public Offerings." *Journal of Finance* 46 (1991), pp. 3–27.

Rock, Kevin. "Why New Issues Are Underpriced."
Journal of Financial Economics 15 (1986),
pp. 187–212.

Sanger, Gary, and John McConnell. "Stock Exchange
Listings, Firm Value, and Security Market
Efficiency: The Impact of NASDAQ." *Journal of
Financial and Quantitative Analysis* 21 (1986),
pp. 1–25.

Schultz, Paul. "Unit Initial Public Offerings: A Form of
Staged Financing." *Journal of Financial Economics*
34 (1990), pp. 199–230.

Stickel, Scott. "The Effect of Preferred Stock Rating
Changes on Preferred and Common Stock Prices."
Journal of Accounting and Economics 8 (1986),
pp. 197–216.

Story, Edward. "Alternative Trading Systems:
INSTINET." In *Trading Strategies and Execution*

Costs. Charlottesville, VA: Institute of Chartered
Financial Analysts, 1988.

Teah, Siew Hong; Ivo Welch; and T. J. Wong. "Earnings
Management and the Long-Term Performance of
IPOs," UCLA Working Paper, 1997.

Tinic, Seha. "Anatomy of Initial Public Offerings of
Common Stock." *Journal of Finance* 43 (1988),
pp. 789–822.

Uttal, Bro. "Inside the Deal That Made Bill Gates
$350,000,000." *Fortune,* July 21, 1986.

Welch, Ivo. "Seasoned Offerings, Imitation Costs and
the Underwriting of IPOs." *Journal of Finance*
44 (1989), pp. 421–49.

PRACTICAL INSIGHTS FOR PART I

Financing the Firm

- Debt is a more commonly used source of outside capital and has lower transaction costs than equity financing. (Sections 1.1–1.3)
- Advantageous financing terms are generally achieved by understanding the frictions faced by investors and trying to overcome them with clever security designs. (Section 2.5)
- Euromarkets and foreign issues are attractive sources of financing. It pays to be familiar with them. (Sections 1.4, 1.5, 2.6, 3.3)
- Debt instruments are complex, diverse, and filled with conventions that make comparisons between financing rates difficult. Get a full translation of all features and rate conventions. (Sections 2.1–2.4, 2.8, 2A)
- Equity capital obtained during hot issue periods may be cheaper than equity capital obtained at other times. (Sections 3.5, 3.8)
- Include underpricing, which averages about 15 percent, when figuring out the total cost of IPO equity financing. (Section 3.5)
- Public capital is generally cheaper but comes with a host of hidden costs that make it unattractive to some firms. In particular, one should factor in the costs of regulations imposed by government agencies and exchanges on capital costs obtained from public sources. Because of these costs, most small firms obtain outside capital from private sources. (Sections 1.2, 1.3, 3.5)

Knowing Whether and How to Hedge Risk

- Before hedging, it is essential to be familiar with the securities and derivatives used for hedging, and the arenas in which these financial instruments trade. (Sections 2.4, 2.7, 3.4)
- Issuing securities or entering into contractual agreements often requires the aid of a trusted investment banker and thus knowledcge of how such bankers operate. (Section 1.3)

Allocating Funds for Financial Investments

- Most debt instruments are not traded very actively. Such illiquidity needs to be accounted for when making investment decisions. (Section 2.7)
- When there are restrictions on investment for tax, regulatory, or contractual reasons, the wide variety of financial instruments available allows one to skirt these restrictions. (Sections 2.4, 2.5, 2.6, 3.1)
- Historically, IPOs have been good short-term investments, especially for investors who can obtain hot issues. (Sections 3.6, 3.7)
- Historically, the typical IPO has been a bad long-term investment. (Section 3.8)
- When investing in debt instruments, one must have full mastery of all of the debt quotation conventions. (Sections 2.8, 2A)
- Preferred stock investment is generally motivated by tax considerations. (Sections 3.1)
- Commercial paper, while generally not traded, will generally be redeemed early by the issuing corporation if the investor requests it. It is about as safe as Treasury bills, yet offers more attractive rates, especially to tax-advantaged institutions, like pension funds. (Section 2.3)

EXECUTIVE PERSPECTIVE

Bruce Tuckman

Part I of this book introduces you to the process of raising capital, the diversity of traded securities, the complex features of debt securities, and the international nature of today's markets. I received a preliminary version of this book just a week or two after the U.S. Treasury sold its first issue of TIPS (i.e., "Treasury Inflation Protected Securities") in 1997. Immediately after the U.S. TIPS issue, the Federal Home Loan Bank, J. P. Morgan, Salomon Brothers, and Toyota also sold inflation-linked bonds. It struck me that, as a reader of Part I, you would have been well prepared to analyze this new development in financial markets because the basics required are included there.

The most important feature of TIPS is that their payments increase with the inflation rate, thus "protecting" investors from declines in the purchasing power of fixed cash flows. Several countries issued similar securities years ago, including the United Kingdom, Canada, and Sweden. Why had these countries issued inflation-protected securities before the United States? Furthermore, newspapers at the time of the U.S. issue reported that foreign investors showed great interest in the U.S. issue. Why would that be the case? So, you see, what at first seemed to involve only a domestic market cannot be understood except in its international context.

It was also interesting to speculate on why other U.S. issuers sold inflation-protected bonds so soon after the U.S. Treasury did so. Or, put another way, if there was a market for these securities, why did the issuers wait so long? Rumors began that some of the issuers had swapped their inflation-indexed liabilities for other floating rate cash flows. This led to a question: who took the other side of these swaps? Here we have a phenomenon in the corporate bond market depending on something happening in the swap market.

The TIPS issue also involved a myriad of details one had to understand. Here are some examples. First, the Treasury decided to delay the issue from January 15 to January 29, 1997. But, to keep the bond cash flows in line with those of other bonds, the Treasury kept coupon dates on July 15 and January 15 and kept the maturity date on January 15, 2007. Hence, this bond has a short first coupon, a topic discussed in Chapter 2 of this text. Second, the cash flows of all the indexed bonds depend on the inflation levels two and three months before the cash flow date. As a result, for some time after issue and after each cash flow date, the subsequent cash flow is not known in advance. So how do we compute accrued interest? Third, since the cash flows of this bond are not known in advance, how do we compute a yield measure? Fourth, the Treasury bonds were strippable, we so may some day have inflation indexed zeros.

I'm sure you see that you can follow this discussion because of the material you've read in this part. Good luck in figuring out the whole story!

Mr. Tuckman currently is a vice president at Salomon Brothers, Inc. Previously, he taught at New York University's Stern School of Business, where he was an Assistant Professor of Finance. He is the author of *Fixed Income Securities: Tools for Today's Markets.*

PART II

Valuing Financial Assets

The modeling of how prices are determined in financial markets (e.g., stocks, bonds, and derivatives) is very different from the way prices are modeled in economics. In economics, the prices of guns and butter are determined by specifying how consumer preferences for guns and butter interact with the technology of producing them. By contrast, finance is focused on asset valuation *in relation to the values of other assets*.

This difference in focus often allows the field of finance to dispense with the language of preferences (e.g., utility functions, indifference curves) and the language of production technology (e.g., marginal cost) which is so often used in economics. Instead, financial valuation has its own language. It uses terms like *arbitrage, diversification, portfolios, tracking,* and *hedging*.

The next five chapters illustrate this point nicely. Chapter 4 introduces the mathematics of portfolios. It is the ability to form portfolios, which are simply combinations of financial assets, that makes it possible to compare a financial asset and value it in relation to other financial assets. In particular, most of the valuation of financial assets in Chapters 5–8 is based on a comparison of the financial asset to be valued with a portfolio whose value or rate of expected appreciation is known. The latter portfolio, known as the *tracking portfolio,* is designed to have risk attributes identical to the stock, bond, option, or other financial asset that one is trying to value.

The ability to form portfolios also leads to another major insight: diversification. Diversification means that investors might be able to eliminate some types of risk by holding many different financial assets. The implications of diversification are profound. In particular, it implies that the tracking portfolio to which one compares a financial asset need not match the asset being valued in *all* risk dimensions—only in those risk dimensions that cannot be diversified away.

We use the theme of the tracking portfolio throughout much of this text. It is first developed in Chapter 5, where the portfolio tools from Chapter 4 are applied to determine how to invest optimally and the first major valuation model, known as the Capital Asset Pricing Model, is developed. This model suggests that the expected returns of all investments are determined by their market risk. In this model each financial asset is tracked by a combination of a risk-free security and a special investment known as the market portfolio. The precise weighting of the combination varies from asset to asset. Knowing the expected return of this tracking portfolio thus determines the expected return of the tracked asset.

The theme of the tracking portfolio is carried further in Chapter 6, where we develop a statistical tool known as a factor model and show how combining factor models with the clever formation of portfolios leads to a valuation insight known as the arbitrage pricing theory. According to this theory, the expected returns of assets are determined by their factor risk. In this model, each financial asset is tracked by a combination of a risk-free security and special investments known as factor portfolios. Knowing the expected return of this factor-based tracking portfolio thus determines the expected return of the tracked asset.

If the valuation relationship between the tracked asset and its tracking portfolio did not hold, an arbitrage opportunity would arise. This concept leads to powerful insights into valuation. An *arbitrage opportunity,* which essentially is a money tree, is a set of trades that make money without risk. Specifically, an arbitrage opportunity requires no up-front cash and results in riskless profits in the future.[1]

The arbitrage opportunity that arises when the valuation relationship between an asset and its tracking portfolio is violated involves buying the misvalued investment and hedging its risk by taking an opposite position in its tracking portfolio, or vice versa. This arbitrage opportunity exists not only because of the ability to form tracking portfolios that match the factor risk of the investment being valued, but also because of the ability to form diversified portfolios, first discussed in Chapter 4.

Diversification plays no role in the valuation of the derivatives, discussed in Chapters 8 and 9. This is because the tracking portfolio in this case, a combination of the underlying financial asset to which the derivative is related, and a risk-free asset, tracks the derivative perfectly. Once again, arbitrage opportunities are available unless the derivative security has the same price as its tracking portfolio.

The perfect tracking of derivatives comes at the cost of additional complexity. A dynamic strategy in which the weighting of this combination is constantly changing is typically required to form the tracking portfolio of a derivative. This can make the valuation formulas for derivatives appear to be fairly complex in relation to the valuation formulas developed in Chapters 5 and 6.

All of the tools developed in Part II are essential not only for investment in financial assets, but for the ongoing valuation of real assets (e.g., machines and factories) that takes place in corporations. The analysis of real asset valuation, developed in Part III of the text, generally involves some forecast of the future cash flow of the real asset before using these tools to develop fair values. In some cases, the tools developed in Part II, like those used in the valuation of derivatives, directly give a fair value for the financial asset. In other cases, e.g., when using the Capital Asset Pricing Model and Arbitrage Pricing Theory for financial asset valuation, the tools are equations that relate risk to the expected appreciation of a financial asset. In these cases, one must make the same sort of forecast of the financial asset's future cash flows undertaken with real assets in order to determine the fair value of the asset.[2]

The tools developed in Part II also are useful for understanding some aspects of financial structure developed in Part IV of the text, and the theory of risk management, developed in Part VI of the text. In particular, we use the mathematics of portfolios repeatedly and make liberal used of tree diagrams, which are seen in great detail in Chapters 7 and 8, in much of our later analysis. As such, Part II is central to what follows. Even students with a background in investment theory should review these chapters before proceeding to the remainder of the text, which is devoted almost entirely to corporate applications.

---

[1]Chapters 7–9 provide a variation of this definition: riskless cash today and no future cash paid out.

[2]The interested reader is referred to Chapter 10.

The Mathematics and Statistics of Portfolios

Learning Objectives

After reading this chapter, you should be able to:

1. Compute both the covariance and the correlation between two returns given historical data.
2. Identify a mean-standard deviation diagram and be familiar with its basic elements.
3. Use means and covariances for individual asset returns to calculate the mean and variance of the return of a portfolio of N assets.
4. Use covariances between stock returns to compute the covariance between the return of a stock and the return of a portfolio.
5. Understand the implications of the statement that "the covariance is a marginal variance" for small changes in the composition of a portfolio.
6. Compute the minimum variance portfolio of a set of risky assets and interpret the equations that need to be solved in this computation.

After several decades of robust growth, international stock funds turned in a dismal performance in the first three years of the 1990s. This was peculiar given that most international stock markets appeared to have performed reasonably well. The reason for the turnabout? The remarkable decline of the Japanese stock market. The Nikkei 225 average, the "Dow-Jones Industrial Average" of Japan, dropped over 55 percent, from 38877 at the end of 1989 to 16925 at the end of 1992. Most international stock funds had a large proportion of their wealth in Japanese stocks; many were in proportion to the size of the Japanese stock market in the international arena. As Japanese stocks sunk, so did the funds. The Fidelity Overseas Fund, for example, which had about half of its funds invested in Japanese stocks, lost over 10 percent during this period. Disappointing returns were also seen by Fidelity's International Growth and Income Fund and its Diversified International Fund, which was so "diversified," it lost almost 14 percent of its value in 1992.

The modern theory of how to invest, originally developed by Nobel laureate in economics, Harry Markowitz, plays a role in almost every area of financial practice and can be a useful tool for many important managerial decisions. This theory was developed to help investors form a **portfolio**—a combination of investments—that achieves the highest possible expected return[1] for a given level of risk. The theory assumes that investors are **mean-variance optimizers**; that is, seekers of portfolios with the lowest possible return variance for any given level of mean (or expected) return. This suggests that the *variance* of an investment return, a measure of how dispersed its return outcomes are, is the appropriate measure of risk.[2]

The term coined by Markowitz for this theory, **mean-variance analysis**, describes mathematically how the risk of individual securities contribute to the risk and return of portfolios. This is of great benefit to portfolio managers making **asset allocation** decisions, which determine how much of their portfolio should be earmarked for each of the many broad classes of investments (e.g., stocks, bonds, real estate, Japanese equities). Mean-variance analysis also is useful to corporate managers. Most large corporations contain a number of different investment projects; thus, a corporation can be thought of as a portfolio of real assets. Although the objectives of a corporate manager differ from those of a portfolio manager, the corporate manager is interested in how the risk of individual investments affects the overall risk of the entire corporation. Mean-variance analysis provides the necessary tools to evaluate the contribution of an investment project to the expected return and variance of a corporation's earnings. In addition, corporate managers use mean-variance analysis to manage the overall risk of the firm.[3] Finally, mean-variance analysis is the foundation of the most commonly used tool for project and securities valuation, the *Capital Asset Pricing Model (CAPM)*, a theory that relates risk to return.[4]

Diversification, the holding of many securities to lessen risk, is the most important concept introduced in this chapter. It means that portfolio managers or individual investors balance their investments among several securities to lessen risk. As a portfolio manager or individual investor adds more stocks to his portfolio, the additional stocks *diversify* the portfolio if they do not covary (i.e., move together) too much in concordance with other stocks in the portfolio. Because stocks from similar geographic regions and industries tend to move together, a portfolio is diversified if it contains stocks from a variety of regions and industries. Similarly, firms often prefer to diversify, selecting investment projects in different industries to lower the overall risk of the firm. Diversification is one factor that corporate managers consider when deciding how much of a

---

[1]A **return** is profit divided by amount invested. Formally, the return, R, is given by the formula:

$$R = \frac{P_1 + D_1 - P_0}{P_0}$$

where

P_1 = End-of-period value of the investment
P_0 = Beginning-of-period value of the investment
D_1 = Cash distributed over the period

The three variables for determining a return are thus: beginning value, ending value, and cash distributed. Beginning value is the amount paid for the investment. Similarly, end-of-period value is the price that one would receive for the investment at the end of the period. One need not sell the investment to determine its end-of-period value. Finally, the cash distributions are determined by the type of investment: cash dividends for stocks, coupon payments for bonds.

[2]Other measures of risk exist, but variance is still the predominant measure used by portfolio managers.
[3]See Chapter 21.
[4]Chapter 5 discusses the CAPM in depth.

corporation's capital to allocate to operations in Japan, Europe, and the United States or, for example, when deciding how much to invest in various product lines. Diversification is also relevant to the management of a firm's pension fund and the management of risk.

The international stock funds in the opening example did not take complete advantage of the diversification potential in international stocks. They overweighted Japanese stocks without consideration for the effect that this might have on the variance of the overall portfolio. Chapters 4 and 5 discuss how to avoid this type of mistake, and how to make full use of historical information to form portfolios that minimize risk.[5]

While the principle of diversification is well known, even by students new to finance, implementing mean-variance analysis—for example, coming up with the weights of portfolios with desirable properties, such as a portfolio with the lowest variance—requires some work. This chapter will examine some of the preliminaries needed to understand the mathematics of mean-variance analysis. It shows how to compute summary statistics for securities returns, specifically, *means, variances, standard deviations, covariances,* and *correlations,* all of which are discussed later in the chapter. These are the raw inputs for mean-variance analysis. It is impossible to implement the insights of Markowitz without first knowing how to compute these raw inputs.

This chapter also shows how the means, variances, and covariances of the securities in the portfolio determine the means and variances of portfolios. Perhaps the key insight a portfolio manager could learn from this analysis is that the desirability of a particular stock is determined less by the variance of its return and more by how it covaries with other stocks in the portfolio.

4.1 Portfolio Weights

To develop the skills to implement mean-variance analysis, we need to develop mathematical ways of representing portfolios.

> The **portfolio weight** for stock j, denoted x_j, is the fraction of a portfolio's wealth held in stock j, that is:
>
> $$x_j = \frac{\text{Dollars held in stock j}}{\text{Dollar value of the portfolio}}$$

By definition, portfolio weights must sum to 1.

The Two-Stock Portfolio

Example 4.1 illustrates how to compute portfolio weights for a two-stock portfolio.

Example 4.1:   Computing Portfolio Weights for a Two-Stock Portfolio

A portfolio consists of $1 million in IBM stock and $3 million in AT&T stock. What are the portfolio weights of the two stocks?

Answer: The portfolio has a total value of $4 million. The weight on IBM stock is $\frac{\$1,000,000}{\$4,000,000} = .25$ or 25 percent, and the weight on AT&T stock is $\frac{\$3,000,000}{\$4,000,000} = .75$ or 75 percent.

---

[5]Should portfolio managers diversify? Most financial economists and financial practitioners would argue that they should. Should firms diversify? That issue is much more controversial and will be discussed in detail in Parts V and VI of this text, which analyze mergers and acquisitions and corporate risk management practices. The focus here is on the mechanics of diversification, not its economic justification.

Short Sales and Portfolio Weights.   In Example 4.1, both portfolio weights are positive. However, investors can **sell short** certain securities, which means that they can sell investments that they do not currently own. To sell short common stocks or bonds, the investor must borrow the securities from someone who owns them. This is known as taking a **short position** in a security. To close out the short position, the investor buys the investment back and returns it to the original owner.

The Mechanics of Short Sales of Common Stock: An Illustration

Consider three investors, Mike, Leslye, and Junior, all three of whom have accounts at Charles Schwab, the brokerage firm. Mike decides to sell short Times Mirror stock, selling 100 shares that he does not own to Junior. Legally, Mike has to deliver 100 shares, a physical piece of paper to Junior, within three working days. Schwab personnel enter the vault where shares are kept (in what is known as "street name") and remove 100 shares of Times Mirror that are owned by Leslye. They don't even tell Leslye about it. The 100 shares are deposited in Junior's Schwab account. Everyone is happy. Mike has sold short Times Mirror and delivered the physical shares to Junior. Junior has shares of Times Mirror that he bought. And Leslye still thinks she owns Times Mirror. Because no one is going to tell her that the shares are gone—she doesn't care either. From an accounting perspective, even Schwab is happy. They started out with 100 shares among their customers. They credited Junior's and Leslye's accounts with 100 shares (even though Leslye's are missing) and gave Mike a negative 100 share allocation.

A minor problem arises when a dividend needs to be paid. Times Mirror pays dividends only to holders of the physical shares. Hence, Leslye thinks Times Mirror will pay her a dividend, but her dividend is going to Junior. Schwab solves the problem by taking the dividend out of the cash in Mike's account and depositing it in Leslye's account. Again, the accounting adds up. Junior gets a dividend from Times Mirror, Mike gets a negative dividend, and Leslye gets a dividend (through Mike).

Has Leslye given up any rights by allowing her shares to be borrowed? The answer is she has, because when it comes time to vote as a shareholder, only Junior, the holder of the physical shares, can vote. Hence, Leslye has to give Schwab permission to borrow her shares by signing up for a margin account and allowing the shares to be held in Schwab's "street name."

What if Leslye wants to sell her shares? She doesn't have them any more. No problem for Schwab. They'll simply borrow them from some other customer. However, if there are too many short sales and not enough customers from whom to borrow shares, Schwab may fail to execute Leslye's trade by physically delivering the shares in three days to the person who bought her shares. This is called a **short squeeze**. In a short squeeze, Schwab has the right to force Mike to close out his short position by buying physical shares of Times Mirror and delivering them on Leslye's sale.

To sell short certain other investments, one takes a position in a contract where money is received up front and paid back at a later date. For example, borrowing from a bank can be thought of as selling short, or equivalently, taking a negative position in an investment held by the bank—namely, your loan. For the same reason, a corporation that issues a security (e.g., a bond) can be thought of as having a short position in the security.

Regardless of the mechanics of selling short, it is only relevant for our purposes to know that *selling short an investment is equivalent to placing a negative portfolio weight on it*. In contrast, a **long position**, achieved by buying an investment, has a positive portfolio weight. To compute portfolio weights when some investments are sold short, sum the dollar amount invested in each asset of the portfolio, treating shorted (or borrowed) dollars as negative numbers. Then divide each dollar investment by the sum. For example, a position with $500,000 in a stock and $100,000 borrowed from a bank has a total dollar investment of $400,000 (= $500,000 − $100,000). Dividing $500,0000 and −$100,000 by the total dollar investment of $400,000 yields the portfolio weights of 1.25 and −.25 on the stock and the bank investment, respectively. Note that these sum to 1.

Feasible Portfolios.   To decide which portfolio is best, it is important to mathematically characterize the universe of **feasible portfolios**, which is the set of portfolios that one can invest in. For example, if you are able to invest in only two stocks and cannot sell short either stock, then the feasible portfolios are characterized by all pairs of positive weights that sum to 1. If short sales are allowed, then any pair of weights that sums to 1 characterizes a feasible portfolio.

Example 4.2 illustrates the concept of feasible portfolio weights.

Example 4.2:   Feasible Portfolio Weights

Suppose the world's financial markets contain only two stocks, IBM and AT&T. Describe the feasible portfolios.

Answer: In this two-stock world, the feasible portfolios consist of any two numbers, x_{IBM} and x_{ATT}, for which $x_{ATT} = 1 − x_{IBM}$. Examples of feasible portfolios include:

1. $x_{IBM} = .5$ $x_{ATT} = .5$
2. $x_{IBM} = 1$ $x_{ATT} = 0$
3. $x_{IBM} = 2.5$ $x_{ATT} = −1.5$
4. $x_{IBM} = \sqrt{2}$ $x_{ATT} = 1 − \sqrt{2}$
5. $x_{IBM} = −1/3$ $x_{ATT} = 4/3$

An infinite number of such feasible portfolios exist because an infinite number of pairs of portfolio weights solve $x_{ATT} + x_{IBM} = 1$.

The Many-Stock Portfolio

The universe of securities available to most investors is large. Thus, it is more realistic to consider portfolios of more than two stocks, as in Example 4.3.

Example 4.3:   Computing Portfolio Weights for a Portfolio of Many Stocks

Describe the weights of a $40,000 portfolio invested in four stocks. The dollar amounts invested in each stock are as follows:

Stock:	1	2	3	4
Amount:	$20,000	−$5,000	$0	$25,000

Answer: Dividing each of these investment amounts by the total investment amount, $40,000, gives the weights:

$$x_1 = .5 \quad x_2 = −.125 \quad x_3 = 0 \quad x_4 = .625$$

For an arbitrary number of assets, we represent securities with algebraic notation (see Exhibit 4.1). To simplify the language of this discussion, we refer to the risky assets selected by an investor as stocks. However, the discussion is equally valid for all classes of assets, including securities like bonds and options or real assets like machines, factories, and real estate. It is also possible to generalize the "risky assets" to include mutual funds in which case the analysis applies to portfolios of portfolios!

EXHIBIT 4.1   Notation for the Mathematics and Statistics of Portfolios

Term	Notation
Portfolio return	$\tilde{R}_p$
Expected portfolio return (mean portfolio return)	$\overline{R}_p$ or $E(\tilde{R}_p)$
Portfolio return variance	σ_p^2 or $\sigma^2(\tilde{R}_p)$
Portfolio weight on stock i	x_i
Stock i's return	$\tilde{r}_i$
Stock i's expected return	$\bar{r}_i$ or $E(\tilde{r}_i)$
Stock i's return variance	σ_i^2 or $\mathrm{var}(\tilde{r}_i)$
Covariance of stock i and stock j's returns	σ_{ij} or $\mathrm{cov}(\tilde{r}_i, \tilde{r}_j)$
Correlation between stock i and stock j's returns	ρ_{ij} or $\rho(\tilde{r}_i, \tilde{r}_j)$

The next few sections elaborate on each of the items in Exhibit 4.1.

4.2   Portfolio Returns

There are two equivalent methods to compute portfolio returns. The **ratio method** divides the dollar value of the portfolio at the end of the period (plus distributed cash, such as dividends) by the portfolio value at the beginning of the period and then subtracts 1 from the ratio. The **portfolio-weighted average method** weights the returns of the investments in the portfolio by their respective portfolio weights and then sums the weighted returns.

Example 4.4 illustrates both methods.

Example 4.4:   Computing Portfolio Returns for a Two-Stock Portfolio
A $4,000,000 portfolio is composed of $1,000,000 of IBM stock and $3,000,000 of AT&T stock. If IBM stock has a return of 10 percent and AT&T stock has a return of 5 percent, determine the portfolio return using both (1) the ratio method and (2) the portfolio-weighted average method.

Answer: (1) For $1,000,000 of IBM stock to have a 10 percent return, the end-of-period value plus dividends for the stock must amount to $1,100,000. Similarly the end-of-period value of the AT&T stock plus dividends must amount to $3,150,000 to yield a 5% return. Hence, the portfolio's end-of-period value is $4,250,000, the sum of $1,100,000 and $3,150,000, implying that the return of the portfolio is:

$$\left(\frac{\$4,250,000}{\$4,000,000}\right) - 1 = .0625 \text{ or } 6.25\%$$

(2) The portfolio weight is .25 for IBM and .75 for AT&T. Thus, the portfolio-weighted average return is .25(.1) + .75(.05) = .0625.

For N stocks, indexed 1 through N, the portfolio return formula becomes:

$$\tilde{R}_p = x_1\tilde{r}_1 + x_2\tilde{r}_2 + \ldots + x_N\tilde{r}_N \tag{4.1}$$

$$= \sum_{i=1}^{N} x_i\tilde{r}_i.$$

4.3 Expected Portfolio Returns

So far, we have looked at actual investment returns. However, no one has the luck to invest with perfect foresight. Consequently, finance theory and mean-variance analysis focus on the anticipated future returns of investments. A variety of future return outcomes are likely to exist for a given risky investment, each occurring with a specific probability. To compute the **expected return** (also called the **mean return**), weight each of the return outcomes by the probability of the outcome and sum the probability-weighted returns over all outcomes.

In practice, one often estimates the expected return by computing the historical average return. A typical period for such a computation can be anywhere from 5 to 50 years in the past.

Example 4.5 shows how to estimate expected returns.

**Example 4.5:   Estimating an Expected Return for a Portfolio of
                 Large Company Stocks**

The S&P 500 stock index portfolio had returns of 30.55 percent in 1991, 7.67 percent in 1992, 9.99 percent in 1993, 1.31 percent in 1994, and 37.43 percent in 1995. What is the estimate of the expected return of the S&P 500?

   Answer: The average of the five returns is 17.39 percent per year, which is an estimate of the expected annual return of the S&P 500 portfolio.

Source: Roger Ibbotson and Rex Sinquefeld, *Stocks, Bonds, Bills, and Inflation,* Ibbotson Associates, Chicago, IL, 1996.

The 17.39 percent average return for the S&P 500 is only an estimate of the true mean return that governs the probability distribution of future return outcomes. Most researchers would say that this estimate is high because 1991–1995 was an exceptionally good five-year period for owning stocks. By contrast, the average annual return of the same S&P 500 index portfolio from 1926 to 1995 was 12.5 percent per year. This is still quite impressive compared with the average annual return over the same 70-year period of only 6.0 percent for the Ibbotson-Sinquefeld portfolio of corporate bonds, 5.5 percent on government bonds, and 3.8 percent on Treasury bills.

Portfolios of Two Stocks

Expected returns have some useful properties:

1. The expected value of a constant times a return is the constant times the expected return, that is:

$$E(x\tilde{r}) = xE(\tilde{r}) \tag{4.2}$$

2. The expected value of the sum or difference of two returns is the sum or difference between the expected returns themselves, that is:

$$E(\tilde{r}_1 + \tilde{r}_2) = E(\tilde{r}_1) + E(\tilde{r}_2) \text{ and } E(\tilde{r}_1 - \tilde{r}_2) = E(\tilde{r}_1) - E(\tilde{r}_2) \tag{4.3}$$

Combining these two equations implies:

3. The expected return of a portfolio is the portfolio-weighted average of the expected returns; that is, for a portfolio of two stocks:

$$E(\tilde{R}_p) = E(x_1\tilde{r}_1 + x_2\tilde{r}_2) = x_1E(\tilde{r}_1) + x_2E(\tilde{r}_2) \tag{4.4a}$$

As Example 4.6 shows, using algebraic symbols for weights leads to formulas that often contain valuable insights.

Example 4.6:   Expected Portfolio Returns with Arbitrary Weights

The Quant Fund has a portfolio weight of *x* in the S&P 500, which has an expected return of 11 percent. The fund's investment in Treasury bills, with a portfolio weight of $1 - x$, earns 5 percent. What is the expected return of the portfolio?

Answer: Using equation (4.4a), the expected return is:

$$E(\tilde{R}_p) = .11x + .05(1 - x) = .05 + .06x$$

Selling short an investment with a low expected return (i.e., borrowing at a low rate and using the proceeds to increase a position in an investment with a higher expected return) results in an expected return larger than can be achieved by investing only in the investment with the high expected return. This is known as **leveraging an investment**.

Example 4.6, for instance, illustrates that the larger *x* is, the larger is the expected return of the portfolio. If *x* is greater than 1, implying that $1 - x$ is negative (i.e, risk-free borrowing), the expected return per dollar invested of one's own money exceeds 11 percent. In theory, an investor can achieve arbitrarily high expected returns by taking a large positive position in the asset with the higher expected return and taking a large negative position in the asset with the lower expected return (i.e, by making *x* arbitrarily large). For example, if the investor in Example 4.6 is using $200,000 of his own money for investment, he could achieve an expected return exceeding 100 percent by borrowing an additional $5 million at 5 percent and investing the proceeds in the stock portfolio. (In the real world, a bank would be unwilling to make such a loan because the investor would be likely to default if the stock portfolio declines in value too much.)

Portfolios of Many Stocks

The formula for the mean return of a portfolio consisting of many stocks is a direct extension of the two-stock formula shown in equation (4.4a). As with two stocks, it is necessary to know only the expected returns of individual stocks and the portfolio weights. Taking the expectation of both sides of equation (4.1) and applying equations (4.2) and (4.3) tells us:

Result 4.1   The expected portfolio return is the portfolio-weighted average of the expected returns of the individual stocks in the portfolio[6]:

$$\overline{R}_p = \sum_{i=1}^{N} x_i \bar{r}_i \tag{4.4b}$$

4.4 Variances and Standard Deviations

Example 4.6 illustrates that it is possible to generate arbitrarily large expected returns by buying the investment with the largest expected return and selling short the investment

---

[6]The only difference between the portfolio expected return formula, equation (4.4b), and the portfolio return formula, equation (4.1), is that the return formula has tildes (˜) above the *r*'s (or *R*'s), representing the uncertain return outcomes, and the expected return formula equation has bars (‾) above them, representing the expected returns. Otherwise, the equations appear the same.

with the lowest expected return. Thus, if investors are **risk neutral**, which means they select portfolios solely on the basis of expected return, supply could not possibly equal demand; every investor would be buying the same investment, but no one would be selling it![7] The force that prevents this from happening is risk. When leveraging a portfolio to achieve higher expected returns, the investor also increases the risk of the portfolio.

Return Variances

Most investors are concerned with risk as well as expected returns. In general, they must increase the risk of their portfolios in order to increase their expected returns. The concern investors have for large losses is known as **risk aversion**. A fundamental research area of finance theory is how to define and quantify risk. Mean-variance analysis defines the risk of a portfolio as the variance of its return.

To compute return variances, the examples below assume that there is a finite number of possible future return outcomes. Given these possible return outcomes:

1. Compute demeaned returns. (**Demeaned returns** simply subtract the mean return from each of the possible return outcomes.)
2. Square the demeaned returns.
3. Take the probability-weighted average of these squared numbers.

The **variance** of a return is the expected value of the squared demeaned return outcomes, that is:

$$var(\tilde{r}) = E[(\tilde{r} - \bar{r})^2]$$

where $\tilde{r}$, the return of the investment, is a random variable, and $\bar{r}$, the expected return of the investment, is a statistic that helps summarize the distribution of the random variable.

Example 4.7:   Computing Variances

Compute the variance of the return of a $400,000 investment in SINTEL, which over the next period earns 20 percent 80 percent of the time, loses 10 percent 10 percent of the time, and loses 40 percent 10 percent of time.

   Answer: The mean return is:

$$11\% = .8(20\%) + .1(-10\%) + .1(-40\%)$$

Subtract the mean return from each of the return outcomes to obtain the demeaned returns.

$$20\% - 11\% = \quad 9\% = \quad .09$$
$$-10\% - 11\% = -21\% = -.21$$
$$-40\% - 11\% = -51\% = \quad .51$$

The variance is the probability-weighted average of the square of these three numbers

$$var = .8(.09)^2 + .1(-.21)^2 + .1(-.51)^2 = .0369$$

A useful property of variances is that the variance of a constant times a return is the square of that constant times the variance of the return, that is:

$$var(x\tilde{r}) = x^2 var(\tilde{r}) \tag{4.5}$$

---

[7]Even if all short sales were prohibited, investors would want to hold only the asset with the highest expected return.

Estimating Variances: Statistical Issues

The variances in Example 4.7 are based on return distributions computed with a "forward-looking approach." With this approach, the analyst estimates the variances and covariances by specifying the returns in different scenarios or states of the economy that are likely to occur in the future. More commonly, the variance is computed by averaging squared historical demeaned returns, as outlined in Example 4.8.

Example 4.8:   Estimating Variances with Historical Data

Estimate the variance of the return of the S&P 500. Recall from Example 4.5 that the annual returns of the S&P 500 from 1991 to 1995 were 30.55 percent, 7.67 percent, 9.99 percent, 1.31 percent, and 37.43 percent, respectively, and that the average of these five numbers was 17.39 percent.

Answer: Subtracting the average return of 17.39 percent from each of these five returns results in demeaned returns of 13.16 percent for 1991, −9.72 percent for 1992, −7.4 percent for 1993, −16.08 percent for 1994, and 20.04 percent for 1995. Thus, the average squared demeaned return is:

$$\frac{.1316^2 + (-.0972)^2 + (-.074)^2 + (-.1608)^2 + .2004^2}{5} = .01965$$

It is important to stress that the number computed in Example 4.8 is only an estimate of the true variance. For instance, a different variance estimate for the return of the S&P 500, specifically .0416, would result from the use of data between 1926 and 1995. Recent years have been good for holding stocks, given their exceptionally high average return and low variance.

Several fine points are worth mentioning when estimating variances with historical data on returns. First, in contrast with means, one often obtains a more precise estimate of the variance with more frequent data. Hence, when computing variance estimates, weekly returns would be preferred to monthly returns, monthly returns to annual returns, and so forth.[8] Daily data often present problems, however, because of how trading affects observed prices.[9] If the data are sufficiently frequent, a year of weekly data can provide a fairly accurate estimate of the true variance. By contrast, the mean return of a stock is generally estimated imprecisely, even with years of data.

Some statisticians recommend computing estimated variances by dividing the summed squared demeaned returns by one less than the number of observations instead of by the number of observations.[10] In Example 4.8, this would result in a variance estimate equal to 5/4 times the existing estimate, or .02456.

It is also important to stress that in some instances—for example, valuing real estate in Eastern Europe—historical data may not be available for a variance estimation. In this case, the forward-looking approach is the only alternative for variance computation.

Standard Deviation

Squaring returns (or demeaned returns) to compute the variance often leads to confusion when returns are expressed as percentages. It would be convenient to have a measure of

---

[8]To obtain an annualized variance estimate from weekly data, multiply the weekly variance estimate by 52; to obtain it from monthly data, multiply the monthly estimate by 12, and so on.

[9]This stems from dealers buying at the bid and selling at the ask, as described in Chapter 3, which tends to exacerbate variance estimates.

[10]This altered variance estimate is unbiased, that is, tending to be neither higher nor lower than the true variance.

average dispersion from the mean that is expressed in the same units as the variable itself. One such measure is the standard deviation. The **standard deviation** (denoted σ or $\sigma(\tilde{r})$), is the square root of the variance. One typically reports the standard deviation of a return in percent per year whenever returns are reported in units of percent per year. This makes it easier to think about how dispersed a distribution of returns really is. For example, a stock return with an expected annual return of 12 percent and an annualized standard deviation of 10 percent has a typical deviation from the mean of about 10 percent. Thus, observing annual returns as low as 2 percent or as high as 22 percent would not be unusual.

The standard deviation possesses the following useful property: The standard deviation of a constant times a return is the constant times the standard deviation of the return, that is:

$$\sigma(x\tilde{r}) = x\sigma(\tilde{r}) \tag{4.6}$$

This result follows from equation (4.5) and the fact that the square root of the product of two numbers is the product of the square root of each of the numbers.

4.5 Covariances and Correlations

To compute the variance of a portfolio return, it is important to understand covariances and correlations, which measure the degree to which a pair of returns tend to move together. A positive covariance or correlation between two returns means that the two returns tend to move together: When one return is above its mean, the other tends to be above its mean. A negative covariance or correlation means that the returns tend to move in opposite directions.

Covariance

The **covariance** is a measure of relatedness that depends on the unit of measurement. For example, the height of parents covaries positively with the height of their children. However, the size of the covariance will differ, depending on whether the height is measured in inches, feet, meters, or centimeters. For example, the covariance measured in inches will be 144 times (12×12) the covariance measured in feet. For this reason, it is often convenient to employ a measure of relatedness that does not depend on the unit of measure. A correlation, discussed shortly, is such a measure.

The covariance between two returns (often denoted as σ_{12} for stocks 1 and 2) is the expected product of their demeaned outcomes, that is:

$$\sigma_{12} = E[(\tilde{r}_1 - \bar{r})(\tilde{r}_2 - \bar{r}_2)]$$

Covariances and Joint Distributions.   To compute a covariance between two returns, it is necessary to pair each outcome for one return with a corresponding outcome for the other return. The set of probabilities attached to each pair is known as the **joint distribution** of the two returns. Example 4.9 calculates variances using the forward-looking approach, but it shows that it is impossible to calculate a covariance from the information typically used to compute return variances and means.

Example 4.9:   Distributions Where Covariance Information Is Unavailable

Is it possible to compute the means, variances, and covariances of the two stock returns described below? If so, compute them.

Stock A (Appul)		Stock B (Bull Atlantic)	
Probability	Return Outcome	Probability	Return Outcome
1/3	.1	3/4	0
1/2	.2	1/4	.5
1/6	.3		

Answer: The covariance between the returns of stocks A and B cannot be computed because there is no information about how the various outcomes pair up; that is, the joint distribution of the returns is not reported. The mean returns are $E(\tilde{r}_A) = 11/60 = .183333$ and $E(\tilde{r}_B) = 1/8 = .125$, implying that the variances are:

$$var(\tilde{r}_A) = .00472 = \frac{1}{3}\left(.1 - \frac{11}{60}\right)^2 + \frac{1}{2}\left(.2 - \frac{11}{60}\right)^2 + \frac{1}{6}\left(.3 - \frac{11}{60}\right)^2 = \frac{17}{3600}$$

$$var(\tilde{r}_B) = .04688 = \frac{3}{4}\left(0 - \frac{1}{8}\right)^2 + \frac{1}{4}\left(.5 - \frac{1}{8}\right)^2 = \frac{3}{64}$$

To compute a covariance with the forward-looking approach, determine the probability-weighted average of the product of the two demeaned returns associated with each of the paired outcomes using the joint distribution (see Example 4.10).

Example 4.10:   Computing the Covariance from a Joint Distribution
Determine the covariance between the returns of Appul (A) and Bull Atlantic (B) given the following joint distribution.

Event	Probability	Return A	Return B
1	1/6	.1	0
2	1/6	.1	.5
3	1/2	.2	0
4	0	.2	.5
5	1/12	.3	0
6	1/12	.3	.5

Answer: The covariance calculation sums the probability-weighted product of the demeaned outcomes. The mean return for Appul is 11/60 and the mean return for Bull Atlantic is 1/8, implying:

$$cov = \frac{1}{6}\left(.1 - \frac{11}{60}\right)\left(0 - \frac{1}{8}\right) + \frac{1}{6}\left(.1 - \frac{11}{60}\right)\left(.5 - \frac{1}{8}\right) + \frac{1}{2}\left(.2 - \frac{11}{60}\right)\left(0 - \frac{1}{8}\right) + 0$$

$$+ \frac{1}{12}\left(.3 - \frac{11}{60}\right)\left(0 - \frac{1}{8}\right) + \frac{1}{12}\left(.3 - \frac{11}{60}\right)\left(.5 - \frac{1}{8}\right)$$

$$= -.00208333 \text{ (approximately)}$$

Estimating Covariances with Historical Data.   As with means and variances, covariances are estimated by looking at the average demeaned product of historical returns (see Example 4.11).

Example 4.11:   Computing the Covariance from Historical Returns

Determine the covariance between the returns of the S&P 500 and a portfolio of corporate bonds given the following annual returns.

Year	S&P 500 Return (Percent)	Corporate Bond Return (Percent)
1991	30.55%	19.30%
1992	7.67	8.05
1993	9.99	18.24
1994	1.31	−7.77
1995	37.43	31.67

Answer: Recall from Example 4.8 that the demeaned S&P returns from 1991 to 1995 were, respectively, .1316, −.0972, −.074, −.1608, and .2004. Hence, the covariance estimate is

$$.01601 = \frac{.1316(.1930) - .0972(.0805) - .074(.1824) - .1608(-.0777) + .2004(.3167)}{5}$$

Note that this covariance computation does not demean the corporate bond return. One obtains the same answer regardless of whether one demeans the corporate bond return as long as one demeans the S&P return.

Source: Roger Ibbotson and Rex Sinquefeld, *Stocks, Bonds, Bills, and Inflation*, Ibbotson Associates, Chicago, IL, 1996.

Variance Is a Special Case of the Covariance.   It is useful to remember that the variance of a return is merely a special case of a covariance. The variance measures the covariance of a return with itself, that is:

$$cov(\tilde{r}, \tilde{r}) = var(\tilde{r})$$

This identity follows directly from a comparison of the formulas for the variance and the covariance.

Translating Covariances into Correlations.   The correlation between two returns, denoted ρ, is the covariance between the two returns divided by the product of their standard deviations, that is:

$$\rho(\tilde{r}_1, \tilde{r}_2) = \frac{cov(\tilde{r}_1, \tilde{r}_2)}{\sigma_1 \sigma_2} \tag{4.7}$$

Applying equation (4.7) to Example 4.11 yields a correlation between the returns of the S&P 500 and corporate bond portfolio of .69.

The correlation can be thought of as a covariance where all random variables have been rescaled to have a variance of 1, that is:

$$\rho(\tilde{r}_1, \tilde{r}_2) = cov\left(\frac{\tilde{r}_1}{\sigma_1}, \frac{\tilde{r}_2}{\sigma_2}\right)$$

Because of this rescaling, all correlations are between −1 and +1. A coefficient of +1 is defined as perfect positive correlation; the returns *always* move together. A coefficient of −1 is defined as perfect negative correlation; the returns *always* move in opposite directions. Perfectly positively or negatively correlated random variables have paired outcomes that plot as a straight line in an *X-Y* graph.

Translating Correlations into Covariances.   A formula for translating correlations into covariances can be obtained by rearranging equation (4.7) as follows:

$$cov(\tilde{r}_1, \tilde{r}_2) = \rho(\tilde{r}_1, \tilde{r}_2)\sigma_1\sigma_2$$

More generally, given stocks i and j:

$$\sigma_{ij} = \rho_{ij}\sigma_i\sigma_j \tag{4.8}$$

The next section uses this equation to compute portfolio variances from correlations.

4.6 Variances of Portfolios and Covariances between Portfolios

Covariances of stock returns are critical inputs for computing the variance of a portfolio of stocks.

Variances for Two-Stock Portfolios

Consider an investor who holds an airline stock and is considering adding a second stock to his or her portfolio. You would expect the new portfolio to have more variability if the second stock were another airline stock as opposed to, say, a pharmaceutical stock. After all, the prices of two airline stocks are more likely to move together than the prices of an airline stock and a pharmaceutical stock. In other words, if the returns of two stocks covary positively, a portfolio that has positive weights on both stocks will have a higher return variance than if they covary negatively.

Computing Portfolio Variances with Given Inputs.   To verify this relation between portfolio variance and the covariance between a pair of stocks, expand the formula for the variance of a portfolio:

$$var(x_1\tilde{r}_1 + x_2\tilde{r}_2) = E\{[x_1\tilde{r}_1 + x_2\tilde{r}_2 - E(x_1\tilde{r}_1 + x_2\tilde{r}_2)]^2\}$$

It is possible to rewrite this equation as:

$$var(x_1\tilde{r}_1 + x_2\tilde{r}_2) = E\{[x_1\tilde{r}_1 + x_2\tilde{r}_2 - (x_1\bar{r}_1 + x_2\bar{r}_2)]^2\} = E\{[x_1(\tilde{r}_1 - \bar{r}_1) + x_2(\tilde{r}_2 - \bar{r}_2)]^2\}$$

Squaring the bracketed term and expanding yields:

$$var(x_1\tilde{r}_1 + x_2\tilde{r}_2) = E[x_1^2(\tilde{r}_1 - \bar{r}_1)^2 + x_2^2(\tilde{r}_2 - \bar{r}_2)^2 + 2x_1x_2(\tilde{r}_1 - \bar{r}_1)(\tilde{r}_2 - \bar{r}_2)]$$

$$= x_1^2 E[(\tilde{r}_1 - \bar{r}_1)^2] + x_2^2 E[(\tilde{r}_2 - \bar{r}_2)^2] + 2x_1x_2 E[(\tilde{r}_1 - \bar{r}_1)(\tilde{r}_2 - \bar{r}_2)]$$

$$= x_1^2 var(\tilde{r}_1) + x_2^2 var(\tilde{r}_2) + 2x_1x_2 cov(\tilde{r}_1, \tilde{r}_2)$$

$$= x_1^2\sigma_1^2 + x_2^2\sigma_2^2 + 2x_1x_2\sigma_{12} \tag{4.9a}$$

Equation (4.9a) indicates that the variance of a portfolio of two investments is the sum of the product of the squared portfolio weights and the variances of the investment returns, plus a third term, which is twice the product of the two portfolio weights and the covariance between the investment returns. Thus, consistent with the intuition provided above, when the portfolio has positive weight on both stocks, the larger the covariance, the larger is the portfolio variance.

Example 4.12 illustrates how to apply equation (4.9a).

Example 4.12:   Computing the Standard Deviation of Portfolios of Two Stocks

Stock A (Appul) has a standard deviation (σ_A) of 30 percent per year. Stock B (Bull Atlantic) has a standard deviation (σ_B) of 10 percent per year. The annualized covariance between the returns of the two stocks (σ_{AB}) is .0002. Compute the standard deviation of portfolios with the following sets of portfolio weights:

1. $x_A = .75$ $x_B = .25$ 3. $x_A = 1.5$ $x_B = -.5$
2. $x_A = .25$ $x_R = .75$ 4. $x_A = x$ $x_B = 1 - x$

Answer: The stocks' variances are the squares of their standard deviations. The variance of Appul's return is therefore .09, Bull Atlantic's is .01. Applying equation (4.9a) gives the variances for the four cases.

1. $.75^2(.09) + .25^2(.01) + 2(.75)(.25)(.0002) = .051325$
2. $.25^2(.09) + .75^2(.01) + 2(.75)(.25)(.0002) = .011325$
3. $1.5^2(.09) + (-.5)^2(.01) + 2(1.5)(-.5)(.0002) = .2047$
4. $.09x^2 + .01(1 - x)^2 + 2(.0002)(1 - x)$

Because these are variances, the standard deviations are the square roots of these results. They are approximately:

1. 22.65%   3. 45.24%
2. 10.64%   4. $\sqrt{(.09x^2 + .01(1 - x)^2 + 2(.0002)(1 - x)}$

Using Historical Data to Derive the Inputs: The Backward Looking Approach. Example 4.12 calculates the standard deviations of portfolios of two stocks, assuming that the variances (or standard deviations) and covariances of the stocks are given to us. As noted earlier, these variances and covariances must be estimated. A common approach is to look backward, using variances and covariances computed from historical returns as estimates of future variances and covariances. Example 4.13 shows how to use this approach to predict the variances of a major bank and entertainment company following two major mergers.

**Example 4.13:   Predicting the Return Variance of Chase and Westinghouse
                          Following Major Mergers**

At the beginning of 1996, two major mergers were consummated. Chemical Bank merged with Chase Manhattan and Westinghouse Electric acquired CBS. The 12 monthly returns for the four firms during 1994 and their market values are given in Exhibit 4.2.[11] Predict the variances of Chase and Westinghouse after their mergers are consummated.

---

[11]The returns for 1995 are excluded because of their contamination by the merger negotiations.

EXHIBIT 4.2   Monthly Returns and Market Values for Four Firms in 1994

		Monthly Returns		
	CBS	*Chase Manhattan*	*Chemical Bank*	*Westinghouse Electric*
Jan.	.0607	.0767	−.0156	−.0053
Feb.	.0057	−.0969	−.0570	.0268
Mar.	−.0041	−0115	−.0130	−.1652
Apr.	−.0098	.0646	−.0447	−.0313
May	−.1372	.1103	.1043	.1228
June	.1992	.0132	.0132	−.1058
July	.0000	−.0255	−.0032	.0430
Aug.	.0284	.0237	.0098	.1698
Sept.	−.0019	−.0828	−.0854	−.0796
Oct.	−.0666	.0516	.0857	.0904
Nov.	−.0714	−.0104	−.0428	−.0973
Dec.	−.0045	−.0351	−.0016	−.0392

Year-end 1994 Market Values

Merging Firm	*Market Value of Equity ($ millions)*
Westinghouse Electric	$4,370.7
CBS	$3,387.2
Chase Manhattan	$6,090.4
Chemical Bank	$8,771.9

Answer: First, calculate the variances of the four stocks and the covariances between Chase and Chemical, CBS and Westinghouse. The historical data implies the following estimates for variances, covariances, and portfolio weights:

	Return Variance	*Covariance with Merging Firm*	*Portfolio Weight in Merged Firm*
Westinghouse Electric	.0092558	−.0025873	$.5634 = \dfrac{4370.7}{4370.7 + 3387.2}$
CBS	.0060597	−.0025873	$.4366 = \dfrac{3387.2}{4370.7 + 3387.2}$
Chase Manhattan	.0036241	.0021590	$.4098 = \dfrac{6090.4}{6090.4 + 8771.9}$
Chemical Bank	.0027566	.0021590	$.5902 = \dfrac{8771.9}{6090.4 + 8771.9}$

The variances of the merged firms are calculated using equation (4.9a). Thus, the variance of the merged Westinghouse/CBS is:

$$var(\text{West/CBS}) = .5634^2(.0092558) + .4366^2(.0060597) + 2(.5634)(.4366)(-.0025873)$$

$$= .00282$$

The variance of the merged Chase Manhattan/Chemical Bank is:

$$var(\text{Chase/Chem}) = .4098^2(.0036241) + .5902^2(.0027566) + 2(.4098)(.5902)(.002159)$$

$$= .00261$$

The relatively high covariance between Chase Manhattan and Chemical Bank enables only a modest reduction in variance from the merger relative to the stock return variances of each of the premerged firms. However, CBS and Westinghouse have a negative covariance and this provides for a significant merger-related variance reduction.[12]

Correlations, Diversification, and Portfolio Variances

Substituting equation (4.8)—the formula for computing covariances from correlations and standard deviations—into equation (4.9a), the portfolio variance formula, generates a formula for the variance of a portfolio given the correlation instead of the covariance.

$$var(x_1\tilde{r}_1 + x_2\tilde{r}_2) = x_1^2\sigma_1^2 + x_2^2\sigma_2^2 + 2x_1x_2\rho_{12}\sigma_1\sigma_2 \qquad (4.9b)$$

Equation (4.9b) illustrates the principle of diversification. For example, if both stock variances are .04, a portfolio that is half invested in each stock has a variance of:

$$.02 + .02\rho = .25(.04) + .25(.04) + 2(.5)(.5)\rho_{12}(.2)(.2)$$

This variance is lower than the .04 variance of each of the two stocks as long as ρ is less than 1. Since ρ is generally less than 1, more stocks almost always imply lower variance. Equation (4.9b) also yields the following result:

Result 4.2   Given positive portfolio weights on two stocks, the lower the correlation, the lower the variance of the portfolio.

Portfolio Variances When One of the Two Investments in the Portfolio Is Riskless. A special case of equation (4.9b) occurs when one of the investments in the portfolio is riskless. For example, if investment 1 is riskless, σ_1 and ρ_{12} are both zero. In this case, the portfolio variance is:

$$x_2^2\sigma_2^2$$

The standard deviation is either:

$$x_2\sigma_2, \text{ if } x_2 \text{ is positive}$$

or

$$-x_2\sigma_2, \text{ if } x_2 \text{ is negative}$$

Hence, when σ_1 is zero, the formula for the standard deviation of a portfolio of two investments is the absolute value of the portfolio-weighted average of the two standard deviations, 0 and σ_2. Notice also that since $x_2 = (1 - x_1)$, which necessarily implies a positive weight on a risk-free asset and risky asset return, that both weights are less than 1—reduces variance relative to a 100 percent investment in the risky asset. Moreover, a negative weight on a risk-free asset (implying $x_2 > 1$), results in a larger variance than a 100 percent investment in the risky asset. Hence, leverage increases risk (see part B of exercise 4.18).

---

[12]All of the returns variances and covariances are based on monthly returns. To obtain annualized variances and covariances, multiply by 12.

Portfolio Variances When the Two Investments in the Portfolio Have Perfectly Correlated Returns.   Equation (4.9b) also implies that when two securities are perfectly positively or negatively correlated, it is possible to create a riskless portfolio from them; that is, one with a variance and standard deviation of zero, as Example 4.14 illustrates. Perfect correlations often arise with derivative securities. A **derivative security** is a security whose value depends on the value of another security.[13]

Example 4.14:   Forming a Riskless Portfolio from Two Perfectly Correlated Securities

The return of merged Westinghouse/CBS stock from Example 4.13 (referred to with the combined, albeit incorrect, name to avoid ambiguity) has an annualized standard deviation of about 18 percent per year. Over extremely short investment horizons, the stock is perfectly positively correlated with the return of a call option on the stock, which has an annualized standard deviation of approximately 72 percent per year. What portfolio weights on Westinghouse/CBS stock and its call option create a riskless investment over a short investment horizon?

Answer: Using a portfolio weight on Westinghouse/CBS stock of x, the variance of the portfolio, using equation (4.9b) to compute the covariance, is:

$$.18^2 x^2 + .72^2(1 - x)^2 + 2x(1 - x)(.18)(.72) = [(.18x + .72(1 - x)]^2$$

which equals zero when $x = \dfrac{4}{3}$. Thus, the weight on Westinghouse/CBS is $\dfrac{4}{3}$, the option weight is $-\dfrac{1}{3}$.

For the portfolio in Example 4.14, the standard deviation, the square root of the variance, is the absolute value of $.18x + .72(1 - x)$. This is the portfolio-weighted average of the standard deviations. In sum, we have:

Result 4.3   The standard deviation of either (1) a portfolio of two investments where one of the investments is riskless or (2) a portfolio of two investments that are perfectly positively correlated, is the absolute value of the portfolio-weighted average of the standard deviations of the two investments.

For special cases (1) and (2), Result 4.3 suggests that when the weight on the riskier of the two assets is positive, the equations for the standard deviation and of the mean of the portfolio are, respectively, the portfolio-weighted averages of the individual asset return standard deviations and the individual asset return means.

Portfolios of Many Stocks

To compute the variance of a portfolio of stocks, one needs to know the following:

- The variances of the returns of each stock in the portfolio.
- The covariances between the returns of each pair of stocks in the portfolio.
- The portfolio weights.

---

[13]For example, the value of a call option written on a stock—the right to buy the stock for a given amount—described in Chapter 3, or a put option—the right to sell the stock for a given amount—described in Chapter 2, depend entirely on the value of the stock. Derivative securities are discussed further in Chapters 7 and 8.

A Portfolio Variance Formula Based on Covariances. Given the information described above, it is possible to compute the variance of the return of a portfolio of an arbitrary number of stocks with the formula given in the result below:

Result 4.4   The formula for the variance of a portfolio return is given by:

$$\sigma_p^2 = \sum_{i=1}^{N} \sum_{j=1}^{N} x_i x_j \sigma_{ij} \tag{4.9c}$$

where σ_{ij} = covariance between the returns of stocks i and j.

Example 4.15 illustrates how to apply equation (4.9c).

Example 4.15:   Computing the Variance of a Portfolio of Three Stocks

Consider three stocks, AT&T, GTE, and ITT, denoted respectively as stocks 1, 2, 3. Assume that the covariance between the returns of AT&T and GTE (stocks 1 and 2) is .002; between GTE and ITT (2 and 3), .005; and between AT&T and ITT (1 and 3), .001. The variances of the three stocks are respectively, weight on ATT, GTE, and ITT are respectively $x_1 = 1/3$; $x_2 = 1/6$; and $x_3 = 1/2$. Calculate the variance of the portfolio.

Answer: From equation (4.9c), the variance of the portfolio is:

$$x_1 x_1 \sigma_{11} + x_1 x_2 \sigma_{12} + x_1 x_3 \sigma_{13} + x_2 x_1 \sigma_{21} + x_2 x_2 \sigma_{22} + x_2 x_3 \sigma_{23} + x_3 x_1 \sigma_{31} + x_3 x_2 \sigma_{32} + x_3 x_3 \sigma_{33}$$

$$= \frac{.04}{9} + \frac{.002}{18} + \frac{.001}{6} + \frac{.002}{18} + \frac{.06}{36} + \frac{.005}{12} + \frac{.001}{6} + \frac{.005}{12} + \frac{.09}{4} = .03$$

In equation (4.9c), note that σ_{ij} is the variance of the ith stock return when j = i and that N^2 terms are summed. Therefore, the expression for the variance of a portfolio contains N variance terms—one for each stock— but $N^2 - N$ covariance terms. For a portfolio of 100 stocks, the expression would thus have 100 variance terms and 9,900 covariance terms. Clearly, the covariance terms are more important determinants of the portfolio variance for large portfolios than the individual variances.

Note also that a number of the terms in the expression for a portfolio's variance repeat; for example, see equation (4.9c) and the answer to Example 4.15. Therefore, you sometimes will see equation (4.9c) written as:

$$\sigma_p^2 = \sum_j x_j^2 \sigma_j^2 + 2\sum_{i<j} x_i x_j \sigma_{ij}$$

For two stocks, this reads as:

$$\sigma_p^2 = x_1^2 \sigma_2^1 + x_2^2 \sigma_2^2 + 2x_1 x_2 \sigma_{12}$$

A Portfolio Variance Formula Based on Correlations. Covariances also can be computed from the corresponding correlations and either the variances or standard deviations of the stock returns. Substituting equation (4.8) $\sigma_{ij} = \rho_{ij}\sigma_i\sigma_j$, into equation (4.9c) yields an equation for the variance of a portfolio of many stocks in terms of correlations and standard deviations:

$$\sigma_p^2 = \sum_{i=1}^{N} \sum_{j=1}^{N} x_i x_j \rho_{ij} \sigma_i \sigma_j$$

A Simple Procedure for Computing Variances of Portfolios of Many Stocks

It is not necessary to memorize variance formulas. This subsection introduces a simple procedure to figure out the covariance of any combination of returns with any other combination. This procedure allows you to figure out either the covariance between any two combinations of returns or, as a special case, the variance of any combination of returns. To apply it, you need to be able to multiply expressions together and substitute covariances for products, as Example 4.16 illustrates.[14]

Example 4.16:   Steps to Compute Covariances between Combinations of Returns
Compute the $cov(2\tilde{r}_1 + 3\tilde{r}_2 + 1, \tilde{r}_1 + 2\tilde{r}_2 + 2\tilde{r}_3 + 4)$, where $cov(\ ,\ )$ represents the covariance between the expressions on the left and right sides of the comma.
Answer:

Step 1. Throw out constants that do not multiply returns (because these have no effect on variance or covariance computations). This leaves:

$$cov(2\tilde{r}_1 + 3\tilde{r}_2, \tilde{r}_1 + 2\tilde{r}_2 + 2\tilde{r}_3)$$

Step 2. Group the remaining terms on each side of the comma into parentheses and multiply the two expressions in parentheses together, which yields:

$$(2\tilde{r}_1 + 3\tilde{r}_2)(\tilde{r}_1 + 2\tilde{r}_2 + 2\tilde{r}_3) = 2\tilde{r}_1^2 + 6\tilde{r}_2^2 + 7\tilde{r}_1\tilde{r}_2 + 4\tilde{r}_1\tilde{r}_3 + 6\tilde{r}_2\tilde{r}_3$$

Step 3. Replace the products of returns by their covariances. This leaves as the covariance:

$$2\sigma_{11} + 6\sigma_{22} + 7\sigma_{12} + 4\sigma_{13} + 6\sigma_{23}$$

Step 4. Replace the covariance of a return with itself by its variance. This leaves as the covariance:

$$2\sigma_1^2 + 6\sigma_2^2 + 7\sigma_{12} + 4\sigma_{13} + 6\sigma_{23}$$

Using the Simple Procedure to Derive the Portfolio Variance Formula.   You can use the technique shown in Example 4.16 to derive equation (4.9c), which is the formula for the variance of a portfolio of securities. In the case of two stocks, for example, it is possible to derive $var(x_1\tilde{r}_1 + x_2\tilde{r}_2)$ by recognizing that the variance of the return of a portfolio is the covariance of the return with itself:

$$var(x_1\tilde{r}_1 + x_2\tilde{r}_2) = cov(x_1\tilde{r}_1 + x_2\tilde{r}_2, x_1\tilde{r}_1 + x_2\tilde{r}_2)$$

To evaluate this expression, apply the four step process of Example 4.16, as follows:

Step 1. Unnecessary. There are no constants to eliminate.
Step 2. $(x_1\tilde{r}_1 + x_2\tilde{r}_2)(x_1\tilde{r}_1 + x_2\tilde{r}_2) = x_1^2\tilde{r}_1^2 + x_2^2\tilde{r}_2^2 + 2x_1x_2\tilde{r}_1\tilde{r}_2$
Step 3. Variance $= x_1^2\sigma_{11} + x_2^2\sigma_{22} + 2x_1x_2\sigma_{12}$
Step 4. Variance $= x_1^2\sigma_1^2 + x_2^2\sigma_2^2 + 2x_1x_2\sigma_{12}$

Numerical Examples of the Four-Step Procedure.   We now illustrate the application of the four-step procedure in two examples. Example 4.17 computes the variance of a portfolio of three stocks. This is the same variance that Example 4.15 computed with a brute-force application of the formula.

---

[14]The reason the simple procedure works is that all variance and covariance computations first subtract the means of random variables. As a result, means do not affect these calculations, allowing us to compute variances and covariances by pretending that the returns in the formulas have means of zero. Expectations of the products of mean zero random variables are, by definition, covariances. Similarly, the expectation of squared mean zero random variables are, by definition, variances.

Example 4.17:   The Variance of a Portfolio of Three Stocks Using the Four-Step Method

Compute the variance of the return of the portfolio of the three communications stocks in Example 4.15, using the four-step process described above. Recall that AT&T, GTE, and ITT, denoted as stocks 1, 2, 3, respectively, had σ_{12} = .002, σ_{23} = .005, and σ_{13} = .001. The variances of the three stocks were .04, .06, and .09, respectively. The portfolio weights were x_1 = 1/3, x_2 = 1/6, and x_3 = 1/2, respectively.

Answer: To use the four-step method to compute

$$cov\left(\frac{1}{3}\tilde{r}_1 + \frac{1}{6}\tilde{r}_2 + \frac{1}{2}\tilde{r}_3, \frac{1}{3}\tilde{r}_1 + \frac{1}{6}\tilde{r}_2 + \frac{1}{2}\tilde{r}_3\right)$$

do the following:

Step 1. There are no constants in this expression.

Step 2. Multiplying $\frac{1}{3}\tilde{r}_1 + \frac{1}{6}\tilde{r}_2 + \frac{1}{2}\tilde{r}_3$ by itself yields:

$$\frac{1}{9}\tilde{r}_1^2 + \frac{1}{36}\tilde{r}_2^2 + \frac{1}{4}\tilde{r}_3^2 + \frac{1}{9}\tilde{r}_1\tilde{r}_2 + \frac{1}{3}\tilde{r}_1\tilde{r}_3 + \frac{1}{6}\tilde{r}_2\tilde{r}_3$$

Steps 3 and 4.

$$var = \frac{1}{9}\sigma_1^2 + \frac{1}{36}\sigma_2^2 + \frac{1}{4}\sigma_3^2 + \frac{1}{9}\sigma_{12} + \frac{1}{3}\sigma_{13} + \frac{1}{6}\sigma_{23}$$

$$= \frac{1}{9}(.04) + \frac{1}{36}(.06) + \frac{1}{4}(.09) + \frac{1}{9}(.002) + \frac{1}{3}(.001) + \frac{1}{6}(.005)$$

$$= .03$$

The second of the two examples, Example 4.18, uses real-world data to determine the risk of a particular mix of international investments.

Example 4.18:   Computing the Variance of an Asset Allocation Plan

In July 1995, First Quadrant, a fund management firm in Pasadena, California, estimated the covariances between the returns of four portfolios: a popular portfolio of U.S. stocks (asset 1), of Japanese stocks (asset 2), of U.K. stocks (asset 3), and of Canadian stocks (asset 4). The covariances were respectively σ_{11} = .0220, σ_{12} = .0093, σ_{13} = .0191, σ_{14} = .0181, σ_{22} = .0517, σ_{23} = .0120, σ_{24} = .0096, σ_{33} = .0342, σ_{34} = .0204, and σ_{44} = .0290. Calculate the variance of the portfolio (of the four national portfolios) with weights, x_1 = 1/6, x_2 = 1/3, x_3 = 1/4, and x_4 = 1/4, using the four-step method.

Answer: To apply the four-step procedure to compute

$$cov\left(\frac{1}{6}\tilde{r}_1 + \frac{1}{3}\tilde{r}_2 + \frac{1}{4}\tilde{r}_3 + \frac{1}{4}\tilde{r}_4, \frac{1}{6}\tilde{r}_1 + \frac{1}{3}\tilde{r}_2 + \frac{1}{4}\tilde{r}_3 + \frac{1}{4}\tilde{r}_4\right)$$

Step 1. There are no constants in this expression.

Step 2. Multiplying $\frac{1}{6}\tilde{r}_1 + \frac{1}{3}\tilde{r}_2 + \frac{1}{4}\tilde{r}_3 + \frac{1}{4}\tilde{r}_4$ by itself yields:

$$\frac{1}{36}\tilde{r}_2^2 + \frac{1}{9}\tilde{r}_2^2 + \frac{1}{16}\tilde{r}_3^2 + \frac{1}{16}\tilde{r}_4^2 + \frac{1}{9}\tilde{r}_1\tilde{r}_2 + \frac{1}{12}\tilde{r}_1\tilde{r}_3 + \frac{1}{12}\tilde{r}_1\tilde{r}_4 + \frac{1}{6}\tilde{r}_2\tilde{r}_3 + \frac{1}{6}\tilde{r}_2\tilde{r}_4 + \frac{1}{8}\tilde{r}_3\tilde{r}_4$$

Steps 3 and 4.

$$var = \frac{1}{36}\sigma_1^2 + \frac{1}{9}\sigma_2^2 + \frac{1}{16}\sigma_3^2 + \frac{1}{16}\sigma_4^2 + \frac{1}{9}\sigma_{12} + \frac{1}{12}\sigma_{13} + \frac{1}{12}\sigma_{14} + \frac{1}{6}\sigma_{23} + \frac{1}{6}\sigma_{24} + \frac{1}{8}\sigma_{34}$$

$$= \frac{1}{36}(.0220) + \frac{1}{9}(.0517) + \frac{1}{16}(.0342) + \frac{1}{16}(.0290) + \frac{1}{9}(.0093)$$

$$+ \frac{1}{12}(.0191) + \frac{1}{12}(.0181) + \frac{1}{6}(.0120) + \frac{1}{6}(.0096) + \frac{1}{8}(.0204)$$

$$= .0206$$

Covariances between Portfolio Returns and Stock Returns

Some of the portfolios that we will be interested in (e.g., the minimum variance portfolio), can be found by solving for the weights that generate portfolios that have prespecified covariances with individual stocks. Here, the following result is often used:

Result 4.5   For any stock, indexed by k, the covariance of the return of a portfolio with the return of stock k is the portfolio-weighted average of the covariances of the returns of the investments in the portfolio with stock k's return, that is:

$$\sigma_{pk} = \sum_{i=1}^{N} x_i\sigma_{ik}$$

As an illustration of why this result holds, consider the case where the portfolio is composed of two stocks.

$$cov(x_1\tilde{r}_1 + x_2\tilde{r}_2, \tilde{r}_1) = E\{[x_1\tilde{r}_1 + x_2\tilde{r}_2 - E(x_1\tilde{r}_1 + x_2\tilde{r}_2)][\tilde{r}_1 - E(\tilde{r}_1)]\}$$

This equation can be expanded to obtain the two-stock version of Result 4.5 with the algebra used to obtain a portfolio variance formula for two stocks in equation (4.9a). However, one can also derive Result 4.5, perhaps more easily, with the four-step procedure, as illustrated below for the portfolio's covariance with stock 1.

Step 1. Unnecessary. There are no constants to eliminate.
Step 2. $(x_1\tilde{r}_1 + x_2\tilde{r}_2)\tilde{r}_1 = x_1\tilde{r}_1^2 + x_2\tilde{r}_1\tilde{r}_2$
Step 3. Covariance $= x_1\sigma_{11} + x_2\sigma_{12}$
Step 4. Covariance $= x_1\sigma_1^2 + x_2\sigma_{12}$

A portfolio comprised of N stocks has more terms in the expansion of the above formula, but the principle is the same.

Finding the Covariance of the Returns of Two Portfolios

This subsection uses the four-step procedure to derive a formula for the covariance between the returns of two portfolios. For example, consider two portfolios of two stocks, where the first portfolio has weights x_1 and x_2, and the second portfolio has weights y_1 and y_2. It is possible to derive the covariance between the returns of the two portfolios with this procedure as follows:

Problem: Compute $cov(x_1\tilde{r}_1 + x_2\tilde{r}_2, y_1\tilde{r}_1 + y_2\tilde{r}_2)$.

Step 1. None, because there are no constants.

Step 2. $(x_1\tilde{r}_1 + x_2\tilde{r}_2)(y_1\tilde{r}_1 + y_2\tilde{r}_2) = x_1y_1\tilde{r}_1^2 + x_2y_2\tilde{r}_2^2 + (x_1y_2 + x_2y_1)\tilde{r}_1\tilde{r}_2$

Steps 3 and 4. $x_1y_1\sigma_1^2 + x_2y_2\sigma_2^2 + (x_1y_2 + x_2y_1)\sigma_{12}$

This equation can be generalized to portfolios of N stocks, as shown in Result 4.6.

Result 4.6   The covariance between the returns of two different portfolios of N stocks each, where the weights of the first portfolio are $(x_1, x_2, \ldots, x_N)$ and those of the second portfolio are $(y_1, y_2, \ldots, y_N)$, is given by the formula:

$$\sigma_{xy} = \sum_{i=1}^{N} \sum_{j=1}^{N} x_i y_j \sigma_{ij}$$

Example 4.19 provides a numerical illustration of how to compute covariances between portfolios.

Example 4.19:   Computing Covariances between Portfolios

Compute the covariance between the return of the portfolio in Example 4.15 and a portfolio that equally weights the three stocks in Example 4.15. Recall from Example 4.15 that AT&T, GTE, and ITT, denoted as stocks 1, 2, and 3, respectively, had $\sigma_{12} = .002$, $\sigma_{23} = .005$, and $\sigma_{13} = .001$. The variances of the three stocks were respectively .04, .06, and .09. The portfolio weights were respectively $x_1 = 1/3$, $x_2 = 1/6$, and $x_3 = 1/2$.

Answer: $cov\left(\dfrac{1}{3}\tilde{r}_1 + \dfrac{1}{6}\tilde{r}_2 + \dfrac{1}{2}\tilde{r}_3, \dfrac{1}{3}\tilde{r}_1 + \dfrac{1}{3}\tilde{r}_2 + \dfrac{1}{3}\tilde{r}_3\right)$

Step 1. There are no constants in this expression.

Step 2. $\left[\dfrac{1}{3}\tilde{r}_1 + \dfrac{1}{6}\tilde{r}_2 + \dfrac{1}{2}\tilde{r}_3\right] \times \left[\dfrac{1}{3}\tilde{r}_1 + \dfrac{1}{3}\tilde{r}_2 + \dfrac{1}{3}\tilde{r}_3\right]$

$$= \frac{1}{9}\tilde{r}_1^2 + \frac{1}{18}\tilde{r}_2^2 + \frac{1}{6}\tilde{r}_3^2 + \frac{3}{18}\tilde{r}_1\tilde{r}_2 + \frac{5}{18}\tilde{r}_1\tilde{r}_3 + \frac{4}{18}\tilde{r}_2\tilde{r}_3$$

Steps 3 and 4.

$$cov = \frac{1}{9}\sigma_1^2 + \frac{1}{18}\sigma_2^2 + \frac{1}{6}\sigma_3^2 + \frac{3}{18}\sigma_{12} + \frac{5}{18}\sigma_{13} + \frac{4}{18}\sigma_{23}$$

$$= \frac{1}{9}(.04) + \frac{1}{18}(.06) + \frac{1}{6}(.09) + \frac{3}{18}(.002) + \frac{5}{18}(.001) + \frac{4}{18}(.005)$$

$$= .0245$$

4.7 The Mean-Standard Deviation Diagram

Having learned how to compute, not only the means, variances, and standard deviations of portfolios, but also covariances between the returns of portfolios, it is time to put all of this information together. This section focuses on a graph that will help in understanding how investors should view the trade-offs between means and variances when selecting portfolio weights for their investment decisions. This graph, known as the **mean-standard deviation diagram**, plots the means (Y-axis) and the standard deviations

(*X*-axis) of all feasible portfolios in order to develop an understanding of the feasible means and standard deviations that portfolios generate. The mastery of what you have just learned—namely, how the construction of portfolios generates alternative mean and standard deviation possibilities—is critical to understanding this graph and its implications for investment and corporate financial management.

Combining a Risk-Free Asset with a Risky Asset in the Mean-Standard Deviation Diagram

When Both Portfolio Weights Are Positive.   Results 4.1 and 4.3 imply that both the mean and the standard deviation of a portfolio of a riskless investment and a risky investment are, respectively, the portfolio-weighted averages of the means and standard deviations of the riskless and risky investment when the portfolio weight on the risky investment is positive. This implies that the positively weighted portfolios of the riskless and risky investment lie on a line segment connecting the two investments in the mean-standard deviation diagram. This is a special case of the following more general mathematical property:

Result 4.7   Whenever the portfolio mean and standard deviations are portfolio-weighted averages of the means and standard deviations of two investments, the portfolio mean-standard deviation outcomes are graphed as a straight line connecting the two investments in the mean-standard deviation diagram.

As suggested above, the portfolios that combine a position in a risk-free asset (investment 1 with return r_f) with a long position in a risky investment (investment 2 with return $\tilde{r}_2$) have the property needed for Result 4.7 to apply and thus plot as the topmost straight line (line *AB*) in Exhibit 4.3.

To demonstrate this, combine the equation for the mean and standard deviation of such a portfolio,

$$\bar{R}_p = x_1 r_f + x_2 \bar{r}_2 \tag{4.10}$$

$$\sigma_p = x_2 \sigma_2$$

to express the mean of the return of a portfolio of a riskless and a risky investment as a function of its standard deviation. When the position is long in investment 2, the risky investment, we can rearrange the standard deviation equation to read:

$$x_2 = \frac{\sigma_p}{\sigma_2}$$

implying that:

$$x_1 = 1 - \frac{\sigma_p}{\sigma_2}$$

Substituting these expressions for x_1 and x_2 into the expected return equation, equation (4.10), yields:

$$\bar{R}_p = r_f + \frac{\bar{r}_2 - r_f}{\sigma_2} \sigma_p$$

This equation is a straight line going from point *A*, representing the risk-free investment (at $\sigma_p = 0$), through the point representing the risky investment (at $\sigma_p = \sigma_2$). The line thus has an intercept of r_f and a slope of $(\bar{r}_2 - r_f)/\sigma_2$.

EXHIBIT 4.3   Mean-Standard Deviation Diagram: Portfolios of a Risky Asset and a Riskless Asset

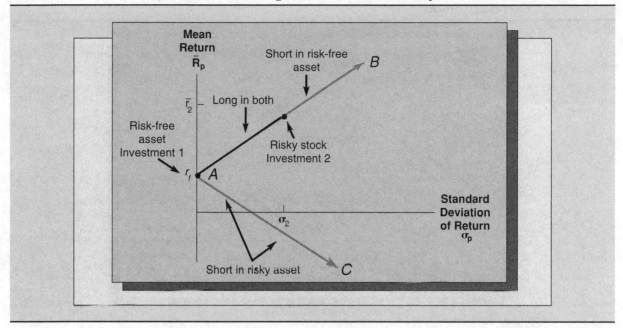

When the Risky Investment Has a Negative Portfolio Weight.   When the new portfolio is short in the risky investment, the formula for the standard deviation is:

$$\sigma_p = -x_2\sigma_2$$

implying:

$$x_2 = -\frac{\sigma_p}{\sigma_2}$$

To make the weights sum to 1:

$$x_1 = 1 + \frac{\sigma_p}{\sigma_2}$$

When these two portfolio weight expressions are substituted into the formula for the expected return, equation (4.10), they yield:

$$\overline{R}_p = r_f - \frac{\bar{r}_2 - r_f}{\sigma_2}\sigma_p$$

This also is the equation of a straight line. This line is graphed as the bottom line (*AC*) in Exhibit 4.3. Since the risky investment has a negative weight and the graph has a mean return for the risky investment that is larger than the return of the risk-free asset, the slope of this line is negative.

When the Risk-Free Investment has a Negative Portfolio Weight.   Consistent with our earlier discussions, Exhibit 4.3 shows that when the risk-free security is sold short, the portfolio will be riskier than a position that is 100 percent invested in $\tilde{r}_2$. In other words:

Result 4.8   When investors employ risk-free borrowing (i.e., leverage) to increase their holdings in a risky investment, the risk of the portfolio increases.

EXHIBIT 4.4   Mean-Standard Deviation Diagram: Portfolios of Two Perfectly Positively Correlated Stocks

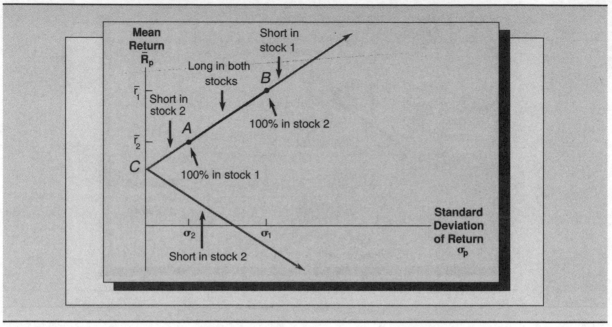

Depending on the portfolio weights, risk also may increase when the holdings of a risky investment are increased by selling short a different risky security.

Portfolios of Two Perfectly Positively Correlated or Perfectly Negatively Correlated Assets

Perfect Positive Correlation.   Exhibit 4.4 shows the plotted means and standard deviations obtainable from portfolios of two perfectly positively correlated stocks. Points *A* and *B* on the line, designated, respectively, as "100% in stock 1" and "100% in stock 2," correspond to the mean and standard deviation pairings achieved when 100 percent of an investor's wealth is held in one of the two investments. Bold segment *AB* graphs the means and standard deviations achieved from portfolios with positive weights on the two perfectly correlated stocks. Moving up the line from point *A* towards point *B* places more weight on the investment with the higher expected return (stock 2). Above point *B*, the portfolio is selling short stock 1 and going "extra long" (weight exceeds 1) in stock 2. Below point *A*, the portfolio is selling short stock 2.

Exhibit 4.4 demonstrates that it is possible to eliminate risk, i.e., to achieve zero variance, with a portfolio of two perfectly positively correlated stocks.[15] To do this, it is necessary to be long in one investment and short in the other in proportions that place the portfolio at point *C*.

The graph of portfolios of two perfectly positively correlated, but risky, investments has the same shape (a pair of straight lines) as the graph for a portfolio of a riskless and a risky investment. This should not be surprising because a portfolio of the two perfectly correlated investments is itself a riskless asset. The feasible means and standard deviations generated from portfolios of, say, the riskless combination of stocks 1 and 2 on the

---

[15]This also was shown in Example 4.13.

one hand, and stock 2 on the other, should be identical to those generated by portfolios of stocks 1 and 2 themselves. Also, when the portfolio weights on both investments are positive, the mean and the standard deviation of a portfolio of two perfectly correlated investments are portfolio-weighted averages of the means and standard deviations of the individual assets. Consistent with Result 4.7, such portfolios are on a line connecting the two investments whenever the weighted average of the standard deviations is positive.

Perfect Negative Correlation.   For similar reasons, a pair of perfectly negatively correlated risky assets graphs as a pair of straight lines. In contrast to a pair of perfectly positively correlated investments, when two investments are perfectly negatively correlated, the investor eliminates variance by being long in both investments.

Example 4.20:   Forming a Riskless Portfolio from Two Perfectly Negatively Correlated Securities

Over extremely short time intervals, the return of Westinghouse/CBS is perfectly negatively correlated with the return of a put option on the company. The standard deviation of the return on Westinghouse/CBS stock is 18 percent per year, while the standard deviation of the return on the option is 54 percent per year. What portfolio weights on Westinghouse/CBS stock and its put option create a riskless investment over short time intervals?

Answer: The variance of the portfolio, using equation (4.9b), is:

$$.18^2 x^2 + .54^2(1 - x)^2 - 2x(1 - x)(.18)(.54) = [.18x - .54(1 - x)]^2$$

This expression is 0 when $x = .75$. Thus, the weight on Westinghouse/CBS stock is 3/4 and the weight on the put option is 1/4.

The Feasible Means and Standard Deviations from Portfolios of Other Pairs of Assets

We noted in the last subsection that with perfect positive correlation, the standard deviation of a portfolio with positive weights on both stocks equals the portfolio-weighted average of the two standard deviations. Now, consider the case where risky investments have less than perfect correlation ($\rho < 1$). Result 4.2 states that the lower the correlation, the lower the portfolio variance. Therefore, the standard deviation of a portfolio with positive weights on both stocks is less than the portfolio-weighted average of the two standard deviations, which gives the curvature to the left shown in Exhibit 4.5 on page 132. The degree to which this curvature occurs depends on the correlation between the returns. Consistent with Result 4.2, the smaller the correlation, ρ, the more distended the curvature. The ultimate in curvature is the pair of lines generated with perfect negative correlation, $\rho = -1$, which is the smallest correlation possible.[16]

The combination of the two stocks that has minimum variance is a portfolio with positive weights on both stocks only if the correlation is not too large. If the covariance is smaller than the lesser of the two stock return variances, or if the correlation is smaller than the lesser of the two ratios of the standard deviations, forming the **minimum variance portfolio**, the portfolio of risky investments with the lowest variance, requires positively weighting both investments. Otherwise, a long position in one investment and a short position in the other is required.[17]

---

[16]Although not pictured in Exhibit 4.5, smaller correlations increase the standard deviation when short sales of one of the investments occurs.

[17]While short positions are not displayed in Exhibit 4.5, they can easily be added to an analogous diagram. See exercise 4.20.

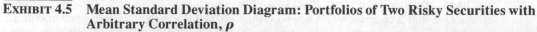

EXHIBIT 4.5 **Mean Standard Deviation Diagram: Portfolios of Two Risky Securities with Arbitrary Correlation, ρ**

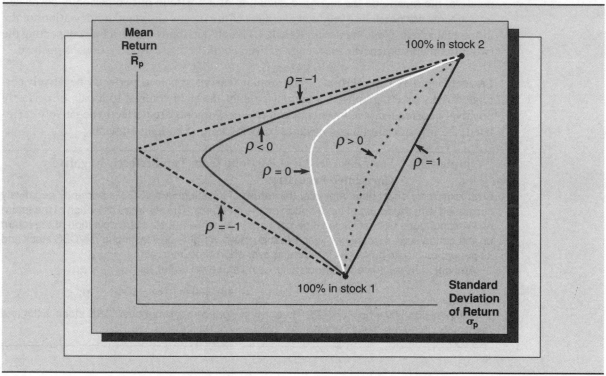

4.8 Interpreting the Covariance as a Marginal Variance

It is useful to interpret the covariance between the return of a stock and the return of a portfolio as the stock's **marginal variance**, which is the change in the variance of a portfolio for a small increase in the portfolio weight on the stock.

Result 4.9   The covariance of a stock return with the return of a portfolio is proportional to the variance added to the portfolio return when the stock's portfolio weight is increased by a small amount, keeping the weighting of other stocks fixed by financing the additional holdings of the stock with another investment that has zero covariance with the portfolio.

A Proof Using Derivatives from Calculus

To prove that the covariance is a marginal variance, add \$m, per dollar invested in the portfolio, of stock k to the portfolio and finance this purchase by borrowing \$m of a risk-free security with return r_f which, being risk free, has zero variance and a zero covariance with the portfolio. If, prior to the addition of stock k, the portfolio had return $\tilde{R}_p$, the new portfolio return, $\tilde{R}$, is:

$$\tilde{R} = \tilde{R}_p + m(\tilde{r}_k - r_f)$$

where r_f is the risk-free return. Because the risk-free return is constant and has no effect on the variance, the variance of this portfolio, σ^2, is:

$$\sigma^2 = var[\tilde{R}_p + m(\tilde{r}_k - r_f)] = \sigma_p^2 + m^2\sigma_k^2 + 2m\sigma_{pk} \tag{4.11}$$

where

$$\sigma_p^2 = var(\tilde{R}_p), \qquad \sigma_k^2 = var(\tilde{r}_k), \qquad \text{and} \qquad \sigma_{kp} = cov(\tilde{r}_k, \tilde{R}_p)$$

by applying the portfolio variance formula, equation (4.9a). The derivative of the variance in equation (4.11) with respect to m is:

$$\frac{d\sigma^2}{dm} = 2(m\sigma_k^2 + \sigma_{pk})$$

Evaluate this derivative at $m = 0$ to determine how the portfolio variance is affected by a marginal addition of stock k. At $m = 0$, the derivative has the value:

$$\frac{d\sigma^2}{dm} = 2\sigma_{pk} \tag{4.12}$$

Equation (4.12) implies that adding stock k to the portfolio increases the portfolio variance if the return on the stock covaries positively with the portfolio return. The addition of stock k decreases the portfolio variance if its return covaries negatively with the portfolio return. This result applies only for small m (i.e., for a sufficiently small amount of stock k added to the portfolio), and it assumes that this amount is appropriately financed with an opposite, and similarly small, short position in the risk-free asset, so that the new portfolio weights still sum to 1 after the stock is added to the portfolio.

Numerical Interpretations of the Marginal Variance Result

Increasing a Stock Position Financed by Reducing or Selling Short the Position in the Risk-Free Asset.   The marginal variance result of the last subsection generates predictions about the impact of marginal changes in the weights of a portfolio. For example, consider a $100,000 portfolio that has $60,000 invested in IBM, $30,000 invested in Compaq, and $10,000 invested in risk-free Treasury bills. If IBM's return positively covaries with the return of this $100,000 portfolio and Compaq's return negatively covaries with it, then the marginal variance result implies that:

1. A portfolio with $60,001 invested in IBM, $30,000 in Compaq, and $9,999 invested in Treasury bills will have a higher return variance than the original portfolio—$60,000 in IBM, $30,000 in Compaq, and $10,000 in T-bills—because, at the margin, it has an additional dollar invested in the positively covarying stock, financed with an additional *negative* dollar in the risk-free asset.

2. A portfolio with $60,000 invested in IBM, $30,001 in Compaq, and $9,999 invested in Treasury bills will have a lower return variance than the original portfolio because, at the margin, it has an additional dollar invested in the negatively covarying stock, financed with an additional *negative* dollar in the risk-free asset.

3. A portfolio with $59,999 invested in IBM, $30,000 in Compaq, and $10,001 invested in Treasury bills will have a lower return variance than the original portfolio because at the margin, it has one less dollar invested in the positively covarying stock and an additional dollar in the risk-free asset.[18]

Increasing a Stock Position Financed by Reducing or Shorting a Position in a Risky Asset.   To generalize the interpretation of the covariance as a marginal variance, substitute the returns of some stock for the risk-free asset in equation (4.11). In this case, the

---

[18]We have confidence in these results because the change in the portfolio is small. Specifically, $m = .00001$ in cases (1) and (2) and $m = -.00001$ in case 3.

marginal variance is proportional to the difference in the covariances of the returns of the two stocks with the portfolio. Adding a bit of the difference between two stock returns is equivalent to slightly increasing the portfolio's position in the first stock and slightly decreasing its position by an offsetting amount in the second stock.

In the IBM, Compaq, Treasury bill example, suppose that IBM's return has a covariance of .03 with the return of the $100,000 portfolio, while Compaq's return has a covariance of −.01. In this case:

1. A portfolio with $60,001 invested in IBM, $29,999 in Compaq, and $10,000 invested in Treasury bills will have a higher return variance than the original portfolio because, at the margin, it has an additional dollar invested in positively covarying stock, financed with an additional *negative* dollar in a stock with a lower covariance.

2. A portfolio with $59,999 invested in IBM, $30,001 in Compaq, and $10,000 invested in Treasury bills will have a lower return variance than the original portfolio because, at the margin, it has an additional dollar invested in the negatively covarying stock, financed with an additional negative dollar in a stock with a higher covariance.

Example 4.21:   How to Use Covariances Alone to Reduce Portfolio Variance
IBM and AT&T stock have respective covariances of .001 and .002 with a portfolio. IBM and AT&T are already in the portfolio. Now, change the portfolio's composition slightly by holding a few more shares of IBM and reducing the holding of AT&T by an equivalent dollar amount. Does this change increase or decrease the variance of the overall portfolio?

Answer: This problem takes an existing portfolio and adds some IBM stock to it, financed by selling short an equal amount of AT&T (which is equivalent to reducing an existing AT&T position). The new return is:

$$\tilde{R}_p + m(\tilde{r}_{IBM} - \tilde{r}_{ATT})$$

The covariance of $\tilde{r}_{IBM} - \tilde{r}_{ATT}$ with the portfolio is .001 − .002, which is negative. If m is small enough, the new portfolio will have a smaller variance than the old portfolio. More formally, taking the derivative of the variance of this expression with respect to m, and evaluating the derivative at $m = 0$ yields;

$$2[cov(\tilde{r}_{IBM}, \tilde{R}_p) - cov(\tilde{r}_{ATT}, \tilde{R}_p)]$$

which is negative.

Result 4.10 summarizes the conclusions of this section:

Result 4.10   If the difference between the covariances of the returns of stocks A and B with the return of a portfolio is positive, slightly increasing the portfolio's holding in stock A and reducing the position in stock B by the same amount increases the portfolio return variance. If the difference is negative, the change will decrease the portfolio return variance.

Why Stock Variances Have No Effect on the Marginal Variance.   It is somewhat surprising that the variances of individual stocks play no role in the computation of what has been termed the *marginal variance*. However, bear in mind that computations involving infinitesimal changes in a portfolio require the use of calculus. In the IBM and Compaq examples, the portfolio changes, while extremely small, are not infinitesimal, and the variance of IBM and Compaq affects the variance of the new portfolio return. However, the portfolio changes are so small that any effect from the variances of IBM and Compaq are minuscule enough to be swamped by the covariance effect.

The lesson about covariance as a marginal variance is important because it allows us to understand the necessary conditions for identifying the precise portfolio weights of portfolios that investors and corporate financial managers find useful. The first of these portfolios is introduced in the next section.

4.9 Finding the Minimum Variance Portfolio

This section illustrates how to compute the weights of the minimum variance portfolio, a portfolio that is of interest for a variety of reasons. Investors who are extremely risk averse will select this portfolio if no risk-free investment is available. In addition, this portfolio is useful for understanding many risk management problems.[19] This section discusses insights about covariance as a marginal variance presented in the last section to develop a set of equations that, when solved, identify the weights of this portfolio.

Properties of a Minimum Variance Portfolio.   The previous section discussed how to adjust the portfolio weights of stocks in a portfolio to lower the portfolio's variance by following these steps:

1. Take two stock returns that have different covariances with the portfolio's return.
2. Take on a small additional positive investment (i.e., a slightly larger portfolio weight) in the low covariance stock financed with an additional negative offsetting position (i.e., a slightly lower portfolio weight) in the high covariance stock.

With this process, the portfolio's variance can be lowered until all stocks in the portfolio have identical covariances with the portfolio's return. When all stocks have the same covariance with the portfolio's return, more tinkering with the portfolio weights at the margin will not reduce variance, implying that a minimum variance portfolio has been obtained.

Result 4.11   The portfolio of a group of stocks that minimizes return variance is the portfolio with a return that has an equal covariance with every stock return.

Identifying the Minimum Variance Portfolio of Two Stocks.   The procedure for finding this type of portfolio is illustrated in a two-stock problem (see Example 4.22).

Example 4.22:   Forming a Minimum Variance Portfolio for Asset Allocation
Historically, the return of the S&P 500 Index (S&P) has had a correlation of .8 with the return of the Dimensional Fund Advisors small cap index, which is a portfolio of small stocks that trade mostly on NASDAQ. S&P has a standard deviation of 20 percent per year; that is, $\sigma_{S\&P} = .2$. The DFA small cap stock return has a standard deviation of 39 percent per year; that is, $\sigma_{DFA} = .39$. What portfolio allocation between these two investments minimizes variance?

Answer: Treat the two stock indexes as if they were two individual stocks. If x is the weight on the S&P, the covariance of the portfolio with the S&P index (using Result 4.5) is:

$$cov(x\tilde{r}_{S\&P} + (1 - x)\tilde{r}_{DFA}, \tilde{r}_{S\&P}) = x\,cov(\tilde{r}_{S\&P}, \tilde{r}_{S\&P}) + (1 - x)cov(\tilde{r}_{DFA}, \tilde{r}_{S\&P})$$

$$= .2^2x + (.2)(.39)(.8)(1 - x)$$

$$= -.022x + .062$$

---

[19]See Chapter 21 for a discussion of risk management.

The covariance of the portfolio with the return of the DFA index is:

$$cov(x\tilde{r}_{S\&P} + (1 - x)\tilde{r}_{DFA}, \tilde{r}_{DFA}) = x\,cov(\tilde{r}_{S\&P}, \tilde{r}_{DFA}) + (1 - x)cov(\tilde{r}_{DFA}, \tilde{r}_{DFA})$$

$$= (.2)(.39)(.8)x + (1 - x)(.39^2)$$

$$= -.090x + .152$$

Setting the two covariances equal to each other and solving for x gives:

$$-.022x + .062 = -.090x + .152$$

$$x = 1.32 \text{ (approximately)}$$

Thus, placing weights of approximately 132 percent on the S&P index and −32 percent on the DFA index minimizes the variance of the portfolio of the two stock indexes.

Example 4.22 implies that a short position in the DFA small cap index reduces variance relative to a portfolio with a 100 percent position in the S&P. Indeed, until we reach the 132 percent investment position in the S&P index, additional shorting of the DFA index to finance the more than 100 percent position in the S&P index reduces variance.

For example, consider what happens to the variance of a portfolio that is 100 percent invested in the S&P 500 when its weights are changed slightly. Increase the position to 101 percent invested in the S&P, the increase financed by selling short 1 percent in the DFA small cap index. The covariance of the DFA small cap index with the initial position of 100 percent invested in S&P is $.06 = (.8)(.39)(.2)$, while the covariance of the S&P with itself is a lower number $.04 = (.2)(.2)$. Moreover, variances do not matter for such small changes, only covariances. Hence, increasing the S&P position from 100 percent and reducing the DFA position from 0 percent reduces variance.

Identifying the Minimum Variance Portfolio of Many Stocks.   With N stocks, we recommend a two-step process, based on Result 4.11, to find the portfolio that has the same covariance with every stock. First, solve N equations with N unknowns. Then, rescale the portfolio weights. Example 4.23, using a portfolio of three stocks, illustrates the technique:

Example 4.23:   Finding the Minimum Variance Portfolio

Amalgamate Bottlers, a U.S. soft-drink bottler, wants to branch out internationally. Recognizing that the markets in Japan and Europe are difficult to break into, it is contemplating capital investments to open franchises in India (investment 1), Russia (investment 2), and China (investment 3). Given that Amalgamate has a fixed amount of capital to invest in foreign franchising, and recognizing that such investment is risky, Amalgamate wants to find the minimum variance investment proportions for these three countries. Solve Amalgamate's portfolio problem. Assume that the returns of the franchise investments in the three countries have covariances as follows:

	Covariance with		
	India	*Russia*	*China*
India	.002	.001	0
Russia	.001	.002	.001
China	0	.001	.002

Answer: Treat franchise investment in each country as a portfolio investment problem.

Step 1. Solve for the "weights" that make the covariance of each of the three country returns a constant. These "weights" are not true weights because they do not necessarily sum to 1. (Some constant will result in weights that sum to 1. However, it is easier to first pick any constant and later rescale the weights.) Let us use "1" as that constant. The first step is to simultaneously solve three equations:

$$.002x_1 + .001x_2 + \quad 0x_3 = 1$$

$$.001x_1 + .002x_2 + .001x_3 = 1$$

$$0x_1 + .001x_2 + .002x_3 = 1$$

The left-hand side of the first equation is the covariance of the return of a portfolio with weights x_1, x_2, x_3 with the return of stock 1 (using Result 4.5). The first equation shows that this covariance must equal 1. The other two equations make identical statements about covariances with stocks 2 and 3.

Now, solve these equations with the substitution method. Rewrite the first and third equations as:

$$x_1 = 500 - \frac{x_2}{2}$$

$$x_3 = 500 - \frac{x_2}{2}$$

Substituting these values of x_1 and x_2 into the second equation yields:

$$.001x_2 = 0$$

or

$$x_2 = 0$$

Substitution of this value into the remaining two equations implies that:

$$x_1 = 500$$

$$x_3 = 500$$

Step 2. Rescale the portfolio weights so they add to 1. After rescaling, the computed solution is:

$$x_1 = .5 \quad x_2 = 0 \quad x_3 = .5$$

Solving for the minimum variance portfolio of a large number of stocks usually requires a computer.[20]

---

[20]Many software packages, including spreadsheets, can be used to obtain a numerical solution to this type of problem. The solution usually requires setting up a matrix (or array) of covariances, where the row i and column j of the matrix is the covariance between the returns of stocks i and j, denoted σ_{ij}. Then instruct the software to first *invert the matrix,* which is an important step that the computer uses to solve systems of linear equations, then to sum the columns of the inverted covariance matrix, which is the same as summing the elements in each row. The sum of the columns is then rescaled so that the entries sum to 1. The matrix inversion method is partly analogous to the substitution method in Example 4.23. In Microsoft Excel, matrix inversion uses the function MINVERSE.

4.10 Summary and Conclusions

This chapter reviewed basic concepts in probability and statistics that are fundamental to most of investment theory. In particular, to prepare you in the use of the mean-variance model, this chapter examined means, variances, standard deviations, covariances, and correlations. It also computed the means, variances, and covariances of portfolios of securities given the means, variances, and covariances of the individual securities.

The variance formulas presented for both the two-stock or many-stock cases can easily be derived with a simple four-step procedure. This chapter also interpreted the covariance as a marginal variance, using this insight to derive a formula for the minimum variance portfolio. The return of such a portfolio has the same covariance with the return of every security in the portfolio.

Chapter 5 takes the analysis one step further: analyzing the mean-standard deviation diagram in greater depth, identifying other interesting portfolios, developing a theory of the optimal investment mix of assets, and deriving a theory of the relation between risk and mean return. All of this is predicated on the basic mathematics and intuition developed in this chapter.

Key Concepts

Result 4.1: The expected portfolio return is the portfolio-weighted average of the expected returns of the individual stocks in the portfolio:

$$\overline{R}_p = \sum_{i=1}^{N} x_i \overline{r}_i.$$

Result 4.2: Given positive portfolio weights on two stocks, the lower the correlation, the lower the variance of the portfolio.

Result 4.3: The standard deviation of either (1) a portfolio of two investments where one of the investments is riskless or (2) a portfolio of two investments that are perfectly positively correlated, is the absolute value of the portfolio-weighted average of the standard deviations of the two investments.

Result 4.4: The formula for the variance of a portfolio return is given by:

$$\sigma_p^2 = \sum_{i=1}^{N} \sum_{j=1}^{N} x_i x_j \sigma_{ij}$$

where σ_{ij} = covariance between the returns of stocks i and j.

Result 4.5: For any stock, indexed by k, the covariance of the return of a portfolio with the return of stock k is the portfolio-weighted average of the covariances of the returns of the investments in the portfolio with stock k's return, that is:

$$\sigma_{pk} = \sum_{i=1}^{N} x_i \sigma_{ik}$$

Result 4.6: The covariance between the returns of two different portfolios of N stocks each, where the weights of the first portfolio are $(x_1, x_2, \ldots, x_N)$ and those of the second portfolio are $(y_1, y_2, \ldots, y_N)$, is given by the formula:

$$\sigma_{xy} = \sum_{i=1}^{N} \sum_{j=1}^{N} x_i y_j \sigma_{ij}$$

Result 4.7: Whenever the portfolio mean and standard deviations are portfolio-weighted averages of the means and standard deviations of two investments, the portfolio mean-standard deviation outcomes are graphed as a straight line connecting the two investments in the mean-standard deviation diagram.

Result 4.8: When investors employ risk-free borrowing (i.e, leverage) to increase their holdings in risky investment, the risk of the portfolio increases.

Result 4.9: The covariance of a stock return with the return of a portfolio is proportional to the additional variance added to the portfolio return when a small amount of the stock is added to it, keeping the positions in other stocks fixed by financing the position with another investment that has zero covariance with the portfolio.

Result 4.10: If the difference between the covariances of the returns of stocks A and B with the return of a portfolio is positive, slightly increasing the portfolio's holding in stock A and reducing its position in stock B by the same amount increases the portfolio return variance. If the difference is negative, the change will decrease the portfolio return variance.

Result 4.11: The portfolio of a group of stocks that minimizes return variance is the portfolio with a return that has an equal covariance with every stock return.

Key Terms

Exercises

4.1. Prove that $E[(\tilde{r} - \bar{r})^2] = E(\tilde{r}^2) - \bar{r}^2$ using the following steps:

a. Show the $E[(\tilde{r} - \bar{r})^2] = E(\tilde{r}^2 - 2\bar{r}\tilde{r} + \bar{r}^2)$

b. Show that the expression in part *a* is equal to:

$$E(\tilde{r}^2) - 2E(\bar{r}\tilde{r}) + \bar{r}^2$$

c. Show that the expression in part *b* is equal to:

$$E(\tilde{r}^2) - 2\bar{r}^2 + \bar{r}^2.$$

Then add.

4.2. Derive a formula for the weights of the minimum variance portfolio of two stocks using the following steps:

a. Compute the variance of a portfolio with weights x and $1 - x$ on stocks 1 and 2, respectively. Show that you get:

$$var(\tilde{R}_p) = x^2\sigma_1^2 + (1 - x)^2\sigma_2^2 + 2x(1 - x)\rho\sigma_1\sigma_2$$

b. Take the derivative with respect to x of the expression in part *a*. Show that the value of x that makes the derivative 0 is:

$$x = \frac{\sigma_2^2 - \rho\sigma_1\sigma_2}{\sigma_1^2 + \sigma_2^2 - 2\rho\sigma_1\sigma_2}.$$

c. Compute the covariance of the return of this minimum variance portfolio with stocks 1 and 2.

4.3. Compute the expected return and the variance of the return of the stock of Gamma Corporation. Gamma stock has a return of:

24 percent with probability 1/4

8 percent with probability 1/8

4 percent with probability 1/2

−16 percent with probability 1/8.

4.4. If the ratio of the return variances of stock A to stock B is denoted by k, find the portfolio weights for the two stocks that generate a riskless portfolio if the returns of the two stocks are (*a*) perfectly negatively correlated or (*b*) perfectly positively correlated.

4.5. John invests $10,000 in IBM stock with a $3 annual dividend selling at $100 per share, and $15,000 in real estate partnership shares with $6 annual rental income at $25 per share. The following year, IBM stock is trading at $104 per share while the real estate shares trade at $23.50. Calculate John's portfolio weights and returns.

4.6. Sara decides to buy a 6 percent, 10-year straight-coupon bond for $100, which pays annual coupons of $6 at the end of each year. At the end of the first year, the bond is trading at $115. At the end of the second year, the bond trades at $100.

a. What is Sara's return over the first year?

b. What is Sara's return over the second year?

c. What is the return per year for the two-year period?

4.7. Sara's portfolio consists of $10,000 in face value of the bonds described in exercise 4.6 and an $8,000 bank CD that earns 3.5 percent per year for the first year and 3.0 percent the second year. Calculate *a*, *b*, and *c* as in exercise 4.6.

4.8. Show that the return of the minimum variance portfolio in Example 4.20—75 percent Westinghouse/CBS and 25 percent Westinghouse/CBS's put option—has the same covariance with Westinghouse/CBS's stock return as it does with the put option. Show that no other portfolio of the two stocks has this property.

Exercises 4.9 through 4.17 make use of the following data:

ABCO is a conglomerate that has $4 billion in common stock. Its capital is invested in four subsidiaries: entertainment (NET), consumer products (CON), pharmaceuticals (PHA), and insurance (INS). The four subsidiaries are expected to perform differently, depending on the economic environment.

	Investment in $millions	Poor Economy	Average Economy	Good Economy
ENT	$1,200	+20%	−5%	−8%
CON	800	+15	+10	−20
PHA	1,400	−10	−5	+27
INS	600	−10	+10	+10

4.9. Assuming that the three economic outcomes (1) have an equal likelihood of occurring and (2) that the good economy is twice as likely to take place as the other two:

a. Calculate individual expected returns for each subsidiary.

b. Calculate implicit portfolio weights for each subsidiary and an expected return and variance for the equity in the ABCO conglomerate.

4.10. Assume in exercise 4.9 that ABCO also has a pension fund, which has a net asset value of $5 billion, implying that ABCO's stock is really worth $9 billion instead of $4 billion. The $5 billion in pension funds is invested in short-term government risk-free securities yielding 5 percent per year. Recalculate parts *a* and *b* of exercise 4.9 to reflect this.

4.11. Assume in exercise 4.9 that ABCO decides to borrow $8 billion at 5 percent interest to triple its current investment in each of its four lines of businesses. Assume this new investment has the same per dollar return outcomes as the old investment.

a. Answer parts *a* and *b* of exercise 4.9 given the new investment.

b. How does this result compare with the results from exercise 4.9? Why?

c. To whom does this return belong? Why?

4.12. ABCO's head of risk management now warns of focusing on expected returns to the exclusion of risk measures such as variance. ABCO decides to measure return variance.

a. For each ABCO subsidiary, compute the return variance with the standard formula $var(\tilde{r}) = E[(\tilde{r} - \bar{r})^2]$.

  (i) The three economic scenarios are equally likely.

  (ii) The good economic scenario is twice as likely as the other two.

b. Show that the alternative variance formula, $E(\tilde{r}^2) - [E(\tilde{r})]^2$, from exercise 4.1, yields the same results.

4.13. Assuming that the three economic scenarios are equally likely, compute the covariances and the correlation matrix for the four ABCO subsidiaries. Show that an alternative covariance formula, $cov(\tilde{r}_1, \tilde{r}_2) = E(\tilde{r}_1\tilde{r}_2) - E(\tilde{r}_1)E(\tilde{r}_2)$, generates the same covariances.

4.14. ABCO is considering selling off two of its four subsidiaries and reinvesting the proceeds in the remaining two subsidiaries, keeping the same relative investment proportions in the surviving two. Assuming that the three economic scenarios are equally likely, compute the return variance of the $4 billion in ABCO stock for each of the six possible pairs of subsidiaries remaining.

4.15. For each of the six cases in exercise 4.14, ABCO wants to consider what would happen to the return variance of ABCO's $4 billion in stock if it revised the relative investment proportions in the two remaining subsidiaries. In particular, for each of the six possible sell-off scenarios, what proportion of the $4 billion should be invested in the two remaining subsidiaries if ABCO were to minimize its variance?

Short sales are not permitted. Can you figure out how to solve the problem given this constraint?

4.16. Draw six mean-standard deviation diagrams, one for each of the six remaining pairs of subsidiaries in exercise 4.15. Mark the individual subsidiaries, the minimum variance combination, and ABCO's return variance for a 50/50 percent combination.

4.17. Assume that ABCO can effectively sell short some of its lines of business by entering into derivative contracts. Find the minimum variance investment proportions for the four subsidiaries, assuming that the three economic scenarios—poor, average, good—are equally likely.

4.18. The three-stock portfolio in Example 4.15 (portfolio variance: .03) is combined with a risk-free investment.

   a. What is the variance and standard deviation of the return of the new portfolio if the percentage of wealth in the risk-free asset is 25% What are the portfolio weights of the four assets in the new portfolio?

   b. Repeat the problem with −50% as the weight on the risk-free asset.

4.19. Assume that the covariances between the returns of Nike, Netscape, and GE are given in the matrix below:

	Nike	*Netscape*	*GE*
Nike	.001	0	.001
Netscape	0	.001	.003
GE	.001	.003	.002

Compute the minimum variance portfolio of these three stocks.

4.20. Graph a generalization of Exhibit 4.5 that includes portfolios with short positions in one of the two investments.

References and Additional Readings

Bodie, Zvi; Alex Kane; and Alan Marcus. *Investments.* 3d ed. Burr Ridge, IL: Irwin Publishing, 1996.

Constantinides,George and A. G. Malliaris, "Portfolio Theory," *Handbooks in Operations Research and Management Science: Volume 9, Finance.* Robert Jarrow, V. Maksimovic, and W. Ziemba, eds., Amsterdam, The Netherlands: Elsevier Science, B.V., 1995.

Markowitz, Harry. *Portfolio Selection: Efficient Diversification of Investments.* New York: John Wiley, 1959.

———. "Portfolio Selection." *Journal of Finance* 7 (1952), pp. 77–91.

Merton, Robert. "An Analytic Derivation of the Efficient Portfolio Frontier." *Journal of Financial and Quantitative Analysis* 7 (1972), pp. 1851–72.

Sharpe, William. *Portfolio Theory and Capital Markets.* New York: McGraw-Hill, 1970.

Sharpe, William; Gordon Alexander; and Jeffrey Bailey. *Investments.* 5th ed. Englewood Cliffs, N.J.: Prentice-Hall, 1995.

Tobin, James. "Liquidity Preference as Behavior Towards Risk." *Review of Economic Studies* (Feb. 1958), pp. 65–86.

Mean-Variance Analysis and the Capital Asset Pricing Model

Learning Objectives

After reading this chapter, you should be able to:

1. Understand the importance of the mean-standard deviation diagram and know how to locate within it the efficient frontier of all assets (the capital market line), the efficient frontier of risky assets, the minimum variance portfolio, and the tangency portfolio, as well as how to use the diagram in a variety of investment and corporate finance applications.

2. Compute and use both the tangency portfolio and the efficient frontier of risky assets.

3. Understand the linkage between mean-variance efficiency and risk-expected return equations.

4. Describe how to compute the beta of a portfolio given the betas of individual assets in the portfolio and their respective portfolio weights.

5. Comprehend what the market portfolio is, what assumptions are needed for the market portfolio to be the tangency portfolio—that is, for the Capital Asset Pricing Model (CAPM) to hold—and the empirical evidence on the CAPM.

First Quadrant, a portfolio management firm, has found a niche in its industry by advising clients on international portfolio strategies. One of its products employs a model, obtained from BARRA, the investment advisory firm, that provides estimates of the covariances between stock indexes in the United States, Japan, the United Kingdom, and Canada. The model also estimates the mean returns of the four stock indexes. In July 1995, the model suggested that the covariances between the stock index futures for the four countries were as follows:

	Covariance with		
	Japan	United Kingdom	Canada
United States	.0093	.0191	.0181
Japan		.0120	.0342
United Kingdom			.0204

The annualized means and standard deviations for the stock index returns associated with the four countries were estimated as follows:

	U.S.	Japan	United Kingdom	Canada
Mean	*15.4%*	*11.3%*	*23.2%*	*13.2%*
Standard deviation	*14.8*	*9.6*	*13.8*	*13.5*

Based on this model and these data, First Quadrant manages portfolios.

When most investors think about quantifying the risk of their portfolios, they think about the variance or standard deviation of their portfolio's return. While variance is not the only way to quantify risk, it is the most widely used measure of it. This chapter analyzes the portfolio selection problem of an investor who uses variance as the sole measure of a portfolio's risk. In other words, the investor wishes to select a portfolio that has the maximum expected return given the variance of its future returns. To do this, he or she must understand the trade-off between mean and variance.

Chapter 4 introduced the analysis of this trade-off, known as "mean-variance analysis." To analyze problems like those in the opening vignette, however, one needs to develop mean-variance analysis in more depth. For example, based on the data in the vignette, one can show that a portfolio 54 percent invested in U.S. stocks, 25 percent in Japanese stocks, 15 percent in U.K. stocks, and 6 percent in Canadian stocks could earn the same mean return as a portfolio 100 percent invested in the U.S. stocks. At the same time, this multinational stock portfolio would have a standard deviation of about 13.5 percent per year compared with the U.S. stock portfolio's standard deviation of 14.8 percent per year. Mastery of certain portions of this chapter is a requirement for understanding how to come up with superior portfolio weights in situations like this.

As one of the cornerstones of financial theory, mean-variance analysis is significant enough to have been mentioned in the award of two Nobel Prizes in economics: to James Tobin in 1981 and Harry Markowitz in 1990. While an important tool in its own right, mean-variance analysis also indirectly generated a third Nobel Prize for William Sharpe in 1990 for his development of the **Capital Asset Pricing Model (CAPM)**, a model of the relation of risk to expected return.[1] This chapter will examine this model, which follows directly from mean-variance analysis.

The chapter is organized into three major parts. After a brief introduction to applications of mean-variance analysis and the CAPM in use today, the first part focuses on the trade-off between mean and variance and uses the tools developed in this chapter to design optimal portfolios. The second part looks at the risk-expected return relation derived from mean-variance analysis, focusing on the CAPM as a special case. The last part examines how to implement the CAPM and analyzes the empirical evidence about the CAPM.

---

[1]Sharpe (1964) shares credit for the CAPM with Lintner (1965).

5.1 Applications of Mean-Variance Analysis and the CAPM in Use Today

Mean-variance analysis and the Capital Asset Pricing Model have practical applications for both professional investors and individuals working in corporate finance.

Investment Applications of Mean-Variance Analysis and the CAPM

As tools for illustrating how to achieve higher average returns with lower risk, mean-variance analysis and the CAPM are routinely applied by brokers, pension fund managers, and consultants when formulating investment strategies and giving financial advice. For example, mean-variance analysis is widely used in making decisions about the allocation of assets internationally. Also, when investment bankers suggest real estate investments to pension fund managers, their presentations are often based on the mean-standard deviation diagram.

Corporate Applications of Mean-Variance Analysis and the CAPM

A firm grasp of mean-variance analysis and the CAPM also is becoming increasingly important for the corporate manager. In a world where managers of firms with declining stock prices are likely to lose their jobs in a takeover or restructuring, the need to understand the determinants of share value, and what actions to take to increase this value in response to the pressures of stockholders and directors, has never been greater.

For example, corporations can use mean-variance analysis to hedge their risks optimally and diversify their portfolios of real investment projects. However, one of the lessons of the CAPM is that while diversifying investments can reduce the variance of a firm's stock price, it does not reduce the firm's **cost of financing**, which is a weighted average of the expected rates of return required by the financial markets for a firm's debt and equity financing. As a result, a corporate diversification strategy can create value for a corporation only if the diversification increases the expected returns of the real asset investments of the corporation.[2]

Corporations also use the CAPM and mean-variance analysis to evaluate their capital expenditure decisions. Financial managers use the insights of mean-variance analysis and the CAPM not only to derive important conclusions about how to value real assets, but also to understand how debt financing affects the risk and the required return of a share of stock.[3]

5.2 The Essentials of Mean-Variance Analysis

To illustrate how to use the mean-standard deviation diagram for investment decisions, it is necessary to first understand where all possible investments lie in the diagram. The first subsection discusses what the diagram implies about the feasible mean-standard deviation outcomes that can be achieved with portfolios. The second subsection analyzes the assumptions of mean-variance analysis and discusses which feasible mean-standard deviation outcomes are desirable.

---

[2] Chapters 20–21 provide further discussion of this application.
[3] Chapters 10–12 provide further discussion of this application.

EXHIBIT 5.1   The Feasible Set

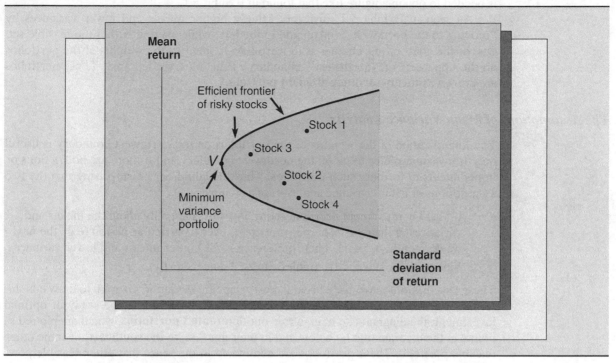

The Feasible Set

The **feasible set** of the mean-standard deviation diagram is the set of mean and standard deviation outcomes, plotted with mean return on the vertical axis and standard deviation on the horizontal axis,[4] that are achieved from all feasible portfolios.

To simplify exposition, Exhibit 5.1 assumes that the feasible set is formed from portfolios of only four stocks, the four points inside the hyperbolic-shaped boundary of the blue shaded area. This hyperbolic shape occurs whenever a risk-free security or portfolio is not available. This and the next few sections analyze the problem of optimal investment when a risk-free investment both is and is not available.

Chapter 4 noted that the mean and variance of the return of a portfolio are completely determined by three characteristics of each security in the portfolio:

- The mean return of each security, also known as the expected return.
- The variance of the return of each security.
- The covariances between the return of each security and the returns of other securities in the portfolio.

---

[4]At one time, mean-variance analysis was conducted by studying a diagram where the axes were the mean and variance of the portfolio return. However, certain important portfolio combinations lie on a straight line in the mean-standard deviation diagram but on a curved line in the mean-variance diagram. Although the focus today is on the simpler mean-standard deviation analysis, the name "mean-variance analysis" has stuck with us.

Hence, knowing means, variances, and covariances for a group of investments is all that is needed to obtain a figure like that found in Exhibit 5.1.

As seen in Exhibit 5.1, investors achieve higher means and lower variances by "moving to the northwest," or up and to the left, while staying within the feasible set. One of the goals of this chapter is to learn how to identify the weights of the portfolios on the upper-left or "northwest" boundary of this blue shaded area. These portfolios are known as **mean-variance efficient portfolios.**[5]

The Assumptions of Mean-Variance Analysis

The identification of the weights of the portfolios on the northwest boundary is useful only if investors prefer to be on the northwest boundary and if there are no frictions or impediments to forming such portfolios. Thus, it should not be surprising that the two assumptions of mean-variance analysis are as follows:

- In making investment decisions today, investors care only about the means and variances of the returns of their portfolios over a particular period (e.g., the next week, month, or year). Their preference is for higher means and lower variances.
- Financial markets are frictionless (to be defined shortly).

These assumptions allow us to use the mean-standard deviation diagram to draw conclusions about which portfolios are better than others. As a tool in the study of optimal investment, the diagram can help to rule out **dominated portfolios**, which are plotted as points in the diagram that lie below and to the right (i.e., to the southeast) of some other feasible portfolio. These portfolios are dominated in the sense that other feasible portfolios have higher mean returns and lower return variances and thus are better.

The Assumption that Investors Care Only about the Means and Variances of Returns.   The first assumption of mean-variance analysis—that investors care only about the mean and variance[6] of their portfolio return, and prefer higher means and lower variances—is based on the notion that investors prefer portfolios that generate the greatest amount of wealth with the lowest risk. Mean-variance analysis assumes that the return risk, or uncertainty, that concerns investors can be summarized entirely by the return variance. Investors prefer a higher mean return because it implies that, on average, they will be wealthier. A lower variance is preferred because it implies that there will be less dispersion in the possible wealth outcomes. Investors are generally thought to be *risk averse;* that is, they dislike dispersion in their possible wealth outcomes.

Statisticians have shown that the variance fully summarizes the dispersion of any normally distributed return. The motivation behind the use of variance as the proper measure of dispersion for analyzing investment risk is the close relation between the observed distribution of many portfolio returns and the normal distribution.

The Assumption that Financial Markets are Frictionless.   The second assumption behind mean-variance analysis—frictionless markets—is actually a collection of assumptions designed to simplify the computation of the feasible set. In **frictionless mar-**

---

[5]Because of the popularity of mean-variance analysis, a number of commercially available software packages include an option to find mean-variance efficient portfolios. An example is the domestic and international risk management and optimization system developed by Berkeley CA-based Quantal International Inc. Details and examples of how such systems are used can be found at: *http://www.quantal.com*.

[6]The standard deviation, the square root of the variance, can be substituted for "variance" in this discussion and vice versa.

kets, all investments are tradable at any price, not just in eighths or thirty-seconds, and in any quantity, both positive or negative (i.e., there are no short sales restrictions). In addition, there are no transaction costs, regulations, or tax consequences of asset purchases or sales.

How Restrictive Are the Assumptions of Mean-Variance Analysis?   Because both of these assumptions are stringent, the simplicity gained from making them comes at some cost. For example, Fama (1976) noted that most stock returns are not distributed normally. Moreover, investors can generate returns that are distinctly nonnormal, for example, by buying index options or by using option-based portfolio insurance strategies.[7] Given two portfolio insurance strategies with the same mean and variance, an investor who cares primarily about large losses might prefer the investment with the smallest maximum loss. The variance does not capture precisely the risk that these investors wish to avoid.

An additional objection to mean-variance analysis, which applies even if returns are distributed normally, is that investors do not view their portfolio's return in isolation, as the theory suggests. Most investors are concerned about how the pattern of their portfolio returns relates to the overall economy as well as to other factors affecting their well-being. Some investors, for example, might prefer a portfolio that tends to have a high return in the middle of a recession, when the added wealth may be needed, to an otherwise equivalent portfolio that tends to do well at the peak of a business cycle. The former investment would act as insurance against being laid off from work. Similarly, retirees living off the interest on their savings accounts might prefer an investment that does well when short-term interest rates decline.

Because it is a collection of assumptions, the frictionless markets assumption may or may not be critical, depending on which assumption one focuses on. Relaxing portions of this collection of assumptions often leads to basically the same results, but at the cost of much greater complexity. In other cases, relaxing some of these assumptions leads to different results. In most instances, however, the basic intuitive lessons from this chapter's relatively simple treatment remain the same: Portfolios dominate individual assets; covariances are more important than variances for risk-return equations; and optimal portfolios, in a mean-variance sense, can generally be found if one knows the inputs.

5.3 The Efficient Frontier and Two-Fund Separation

The top half of the boundary in Exhibit 5.1 is sometimes referred to as the efficient frontier of risky stocks. The **efficient frontier** represents the means and standard deviations of the mean-variance efficient portfolios. The efficient frontier is the most efficient trade-off between mean and variance. By contrast, an inefficient portfolio, such as a 100 percent investment in the U.S. stock market, wastes risk by not maximizing the mean return for the risk it contains. A more efficient portfolio weighting scheme can earn a higher mean return and have the same variance (or, alternatively, the same mean and a lower variance).

The Quest for the Holy Grail: Optimal Portfolios

Based on the assumptions of the last section, the efficient frontier is the "holy grail"— that is, the efficient frontier is where an investor wants to be. Of course, the efficient frontier contains many portfolios; which of these portfolios investors select depends

---

[7]Options and portfolio insurance strategies are discussed in Chapter 8.

on their personal trade-off between mean and variance. For example, the endpoint of this frontier is point *V,* which characterizes the mean and standard deviation of the minimum variance portfolio.[8] This portfolio will attract only those investors who dislike variance so much that they are willing to forgo substantial mean return to minimize variance. Other investors, who are willing to experience higher variance in exchange for higher mean returns, will select portfolios on the efficient frontier that are above point *V* in Exhibit 5.1.

Chapter 4 noted that point *V,* the minimum variance portfolio, is a unique portfolio weighting that can be identified by solving a set of equations. In most instances, each mean standard-deviation point on the boundary is achieved with a *unique* portfolio of stocks. On the interior of the feasible set, however, many combinations of stocks can achieve a given mean-standard deviation outcome.

Because investors who treat variance as the sole measure of risk want to select mean-variance efficient portfolios, it is useful to learn how to construct them. The task of identifying these special portfolios is greatly simplified by learning about an important property known as "two-fund separation."

Two-Fund Separation

Two-fund separation means that it is possible to divide the returns of all mean-variance efficient portfolios into weighted averages of the returns of two portfolios. As one moves along the efficient frontier, the weights may change, but the two separating portfolios remain the same.

This insight follows from a slightly more general result:

Result 5.1   All portfolios on the mean-variance efficient frontier can be formed as a weighted average of any two portfolios (or funds) on the efficient frontier.

Result 5.1 can be generalized even further. Two funds generate not only the northwest boundary of efficient portfolios, but all of the portfolios on the boundary of the feasible set: northwest plus southwest (or lower left boundary). This implies that once any two funds on the boundary are identified, it is possible to create *all* other mean-variance efficient portfolios from these two funds!

Exhibit 5.2 highlights four boundary portfolios, denoted A, B, C, and D, and the minimum variance portfolio, *V.* All of the portfolios on the western (or left-hand) boundary of the feasible set are weighted averages of portfolios A and B, as well as averages of C and D, B and D, or B and V, and so on. Moreover, *any* weighted average of two boundary portfolios is itself on the boundary.

Example 5.1 provides an illustration of two-fund separation.

Example 5.1:   Two-Fund Separation and Portfolio Weights on the Boundary
Consider a mean-standard deviation diagram constructed from five stocks. One of its boundary portfolios has the weights

$$x_1 = .2, x_2 = .3, x_3 = .1, x_4 = .1, \text{ and } x_5 = .3$$

The other portfolio has equal weights of .2 on each of the five stocks. Determine the weights of the five stocks for all other boundary portfolios.

Answer: The remaining boundary portfolios are described by the weighted averages of the two portfolios (or funds). Portfolio weights (.2, .3, .1, .1, .3) describe the first fund. Weights

---

[8]This is described at the end of Chapter 4.

(.2, .2, .2, .2, .2) describe the second fund. Thus, letting w denote the weight on the first fund, it is possible to define all boundary portfolios by portfolio weights x_1, x_2, x_3, x_4, and x_5 that satisfy the equations

$$x_1 = .2w + .2(1 - w)$$
$$x_2 = .3w + .2(1 - w)$$
$$x_3 = .1w + .2(1 - w)$$
$$x_4 = .1w + .2(1 - w)$$
$$x_5 = .3w + .2(1 - w)$$

For example, if the new boundary portfolio is equally weighted between the two funds ($w = .5$), its portfolio weights on stocks 1–5 are, respectively, .2, .25, .15, .15, and .25. For $w = -1.5$, the boundary portfolio weights on stocks 1–5 are, respectively, .2, .05, .35, .35, and .05.

Example 5.2 finds a specific portfolio on the boundary generated in the last example.

Example 5.2:   Identifying a Specific Boundary Portfolio

If the portfolio weight on stock 3 in Example 5.1 is $-.1$, what is the portfolio weight on stocks 1, 2, 4, and 5?

   Answer: Solve for the w that makes $.1w + .2(1 - w) = -.1$. The answer is $w = 3$. Substituting this value into the other four portfolio weight equations in Example 5.1 yields a boundary portfolio with respective weights of .2, .5, $-.1$, $-.1$, and .5.

One insight gained from Examples 5.1 and 5.2 is that whenever a stock has the same weight in two portfolios on the boundary, as stock 1 does in the last two examples, it

---

EXHIBIT 5.2   Two-Fund Separation and the Boundary of the Feasible Set

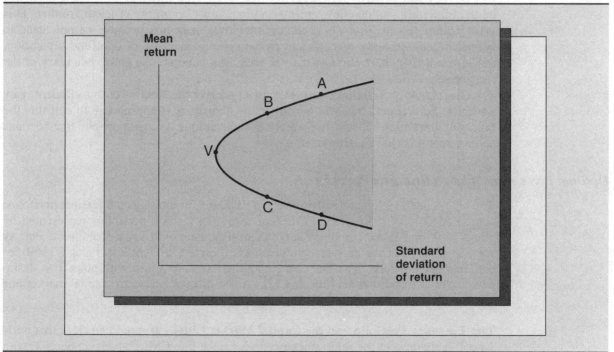

must have the same weight in all portfolios on the boundary. More typically, as with other stocks in these examples, observe that:

- Some stocks have a portfolio weight that continually increases as w increases.
- Other stocks have a portfolio weight that continually decreases as w increases.

Although these insights help to characterize the boundary, they do not identify precisely the weights of two portfolios on the boundary. This chapter will address this topic after describing how a risk-free asset affects the analysis.

5.4 The Tangency Portfolio and Optimal Investment

So far, this chapter has studied how to invest optimally by looking at the portfolios formed only from risky stocks. Generally, whenever an additional asset is added to the set of investments that can be held in a portfolio, the feasible set of the mean-standard deviation diagram expands. The risk-free asset is no exception, but it is notable for the manner in which it changes the shape of the feasible set and the efficient frontier.

Chapter 4 indicated that portfolios of a risk-free investment and a risky investment lie on a straight line in the mean-standard deviation diagram. Because of this, the addition of a risk-free asset to the analysis of risky stocks not only greatly expands the feasible set, but also it changes the shape of the efficient frontier from a hyperbola to a straight line. This greatly reduces our search for the optimal portfolio.

Indeed, as this chapter will show, when there is risk-free investment, only one "key" portfolio needs to be found because of the principle of two-fund separation (i.e., the efficient frontier can be generated by only two portfolios). This was illustrated in the last section where, because the analysis precluded the existence of a risk-free investment, the two portfolios that generated the efficient frontier were necessarily risky portfolios; that is, they had positive variance. However, a risk-free investment, if one exists, will be the minimum variance investment, and thus must be on the efficient frontier. This greatly simplifies the problem of the optimal investment mix because we now need to be concerned with only one efficient risky portfolio. Because of two-fund separation, this efficient risky portfolio and the risk-free asset generate the entire boundary of the feasible set.

The analysis that follows illustrates how to derive the weights of this efficient risky portfolio. For reasons that will become clear shortly, it is appropriate to call this the **tangency portfolio**. This portfolio represents the unique optimal portfolio that contains no investment in the risk-free asset.

Optimal Investment When a Risk-Free Asset Exists

The blue shaded region and its boundary in Exhibit 5.3 represents the feasible portfolios composed only of risky stocks. Consider three risky stock portfolios represented by points A, B, and T, and combine each of them separately with a risk-free investment. As we saw in the last chapter, such combinations generate a straight line. Point T identifies the tangency portfolio. The line connecting the risk-free return with point T is designated as the **capital market line**, or CML. As we discuss below, the capital market line represents the portfolios that optimally combine all investments.

The Tangency Portfolio and the Capital Market Line.   It should be clear that portfolio T is the best of the three stock portfolios since line CML, which connects T with the risk-free investment (at point r_f), lies above the other two lines. More generally, the

EXHIBIT 5.3   Combining Risky Portfolios with a Risk-Free Portfolio

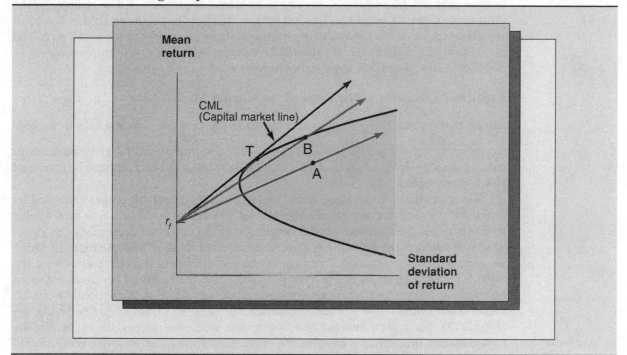

line going through portfolio T is tangent to the efficient frontier of *risky* investments; as a result, no feasible portfolio lies northwest of this line. Investors want to invest in portfolios that have the best trade-off between mean and variance and such portfolios all lie on this line. Result 5.2 summarizes this important point.

Result 5.2   Under the assumptions of mean-variance analysis, and assuming the existence of a risk-free asset, all investors will select portfolios on the capital market line.

Result 5.2 states that the capital market line is the key to optimal investment for every investor interested in maximizing expected return for a given amount of variance risk. Investors who are extremely risk averse will select a portfolio close to the risk-free asset, achieving a low expected return but also a low variance for their future wealth. Investors who are only slightly risk averse will select a portfolio high up on the CML, possibly above T if they choose to sell short the risk-free asset. They would achieve a higher expected return than more risk-averse investors, but the larger variance also makes the *possibility* of realizing large losses quite high.

The Equation of the Capital Market Line.   Line CML is represented by the equation:

$$\overline{R}_p = r_f + \frac{\overline{R}_T - r_f}{\sigma_T} \sigma_p \tag{5.1}$$

where $\overline{R}_T$ and σ_T are, respectively, the mean and standard deviation of the tangency portfolio's return and r_f is the return of the risk-free asset. As the steepest sloped line available from combining a risk-free investment with any risky investment, the CML plots the set of mean-variance efficient portfolios that can be achieved by combining the risky stocks with a risk-free investment. All of the portfolios above r_f on line CML—as weighted averages of the weights of portfolio T and the risk-free asset—have the same relative proportions invested in any two risky stocks as portfolio T. For example, if the ratio of portfolio T's weight on Hewlett Packard (HP) to its weight on IBM is 1 to 6, all portfolios on line CML have relative weights on these two stocks in ratios of 1 to 6. The actual portfolio weights on HP and IBM, however, will scale down proportionately as one moves down line CML toward the risk-free asset.

Empirical Estimates of the Slope of the Capital Market Line.   The slope of the capital market line, $\dfrac{\bar{R}_T - r_f}{\sigma_T}$, measures the trade-off between risk and return. Steeper slopes imply that the market provides greater return improvements for given increases in risk. Less steep slopes imply that the marginal increase in return generated by increased risk is more modest.

The magnitude of this slope has to be larger than comparable slopes estimated by looking at the historical returns of some popular investment portfolios. Exhibit 5.4 helps to characterize the numerator and denominator of the ratio that determines this slope. The numerator of the ratio, $\bar{R}_T - r_f$, is often referred to as a "risk premium."[9] Using an average T-bill return of 3.8 percent as the risk-free rate, the risk premium of the S&P 500 has been about 8.7 percent per year while the standard deviation has been about 20.4 percent per year, generating a slope of .42. For a portfolio of small-capitalization stocks, that is, small companies, the slope is .41; for corporate bonds, the slope is .25. Some portfolios of these investments have even steeper slopes. Hence, the capital market line, which is based on the optimal combination of all investments, should have a slope greater than .42. In other words, for investments on the capital market line, an increase in standard deviation from 10 percent to 20 percent per year will generate more than a 4.2 percent per year increase in expected return.

An interesting feature of Exhibit 5.4 is that the investment portfolios with the larger mean returns generally have the larger standard deviations. This is not true, however, for all investment portfolios. For example, the portfolio of government bonds has a lower mean return and a higher standard deviation than the portfolio of corporate bonds. In general, one learns from the mean-standard deviation diagram that there is no necessary relation between mean and standard deviation. Portfolios with the same standard deviation in the diagram can have very different means. As a result, it pays to identify efficient portfolios, which maximize mean return for a given standard deviation.

If standard deviations have no relation to mean returns, what then determines mean returns? Here, our study of the tangency portfolio serves double duty because not only is this portfolio useful from the perspective of identifying proper investment weights, but also it is useful for addressing what determines mean returns, as will be emphasized later in this chapter.

Identification of the Tangency Portfolio

Because the tangency portfolio is generally a unique combination of individual stocks and is the key to identifying the other portfolios on the capital market line, determining the weights of the tangency portfolio is an important and useful exercise.

The Algebraic Formula for Finding the Tangency Portfolio.   For all investments—efficient ones, such as the portfolios on the capital market line, and the dominated investments—the following result applies:

---

[9]The **risk premium** of a stock or portfolio is its expected return less the risk-free return.

EXHIBIT 5.4   Means, Standard Deviations, Risk Premiums, and Mean-Standard Deviation Slopes

Portfolio	Mean Return	Risk Premium	Standard Deviation	Slope
S&P 500	12.5%	8.7%	20.4%	.42
Small cap stocks	17.7	13.9	34.4	.41
Long-term corporate bonds	6.0	2.2	8.7	.25
Long term government bonds	5.5	1.7	9.2	.18

Source: © Computed using data from STOCKS, BONDS, BILLS & INFLATION 1997 YEARBOOK™, Ibbotson Associates, Chicago (annually updates work by Roger G. Ibbotson and Rex Sinquefield). Used with permission. All rights reserved. Data are from 1926 to 1995. Risk premiums are based on the average T-bill return of 3.8 percent. Means are averages of annual returns. Standard deviations are sample standard deviations of annual returns.

Result 5.3   The ratio of the risk premium of every stock and portfolio to its covariance with the tangency portfolio is constant; that is, denoting the return of the tangency portfolio as $\tilde{R}_T$,

$$\frac{\bar{r}_i - r_f}{cov(\tilde{r}_i, \tilde{R}_T)}$$

is identical for all stocks.

Result 5.3 suggests an algebraic procedure for finding the tangency portfolio which is similar to the technique used to find the minimum variance portfolio. Recall that to find the minimum variance portfolio, it is necessary to find the portfolio that has equal covariances with every stock. To identify the tangency portfolio, find the portfolio that has a covariance with each stock that is a constant proportion of the stock's risk premium. This proportion, while unknown in advance, is the same across stocks and is whatever proportion makes the portfolio weights sum to 1. This suggests that to derive the portfolio weights of the tangency portfolio:

1. Find "weights" (they do not need to sum to 1) that make the covariance between the return of each stock and the return of the portfolio constructed from these weights equal to the stock's risk premium.
2. Then rescale the weights to sum to 1 to obtain the tangency portfolio.

A Numerical Example Illustrating How to Apply the Algebraic Formula.   Example 5.3 illustrates how to use Result 5.3 to compute the tangency portfolio's weights.

Example 5.3:   Identifying the Tangency Portfolio

Amalgamate Bottlers, from Example 4.23, wants to find the tangency portfolio of capital investments from franchising in three less developed countries (LDCs). Recall that covariances between franchising operations in India (investment 1), Russia (investment 2), and China (investment 3) were:

	Covariance with		
	India	Russia	China
India	.002	.001	0
Russia	.001	.002	.001
China	0	.001	.002,

Find the tangency portfolio for the three investments when they have expected returns of 15 percent, 17 percent, and 17 percent, respectively, and the risk-free return is 6 percent per year.

Answer:

Step 1: Solve for the portfolio "weights" that make the portfolio's covariance with each stock equal to their risk premiums. These weights are not true weights because they do not necessarily sum to 1. The first step is the simultaneous solution of the three equations:

$$.002x_1 + .001x_2 + \quad 0x_3 = .15 - .06$$

$$.001x_1 + .002x_2 + .001x_3 = .17 - .06$$

$$0x_1 + .001x_2 + .002x_3 = .17 - .06$$

The left-hand side of the first equation is the covariance of a portfolio with weights x_1, x_2, and x_3 with stock 1. Thus, the first equation states that this covariance must equal .09. The other two equations make analogous statements about covariances with stocks 2 and 3.

Using the substitution method, the first and third equations can be rewritten to read:

$$x_1 = 45 - \frac{x_2}{2}$$

$$x_3 = 55 - \frac{x_2}{2}$$

Upon substitution into the second equation, they yield:

$$.001x_2 = .01, \text{ or } x_2 = 10$$

Substituting this value for x_2 into the remaining two equations implies:

$$x_1 = 40 \quad x_3 = 50$$

Step 2: Rescale the portfolio weights so that they add to 1. After rescaling, the solution for the weights of the tangency portfolio is:

$$x_1 = .4 \quad x_2 = .1 \quad x_3 = .5$$

The Intuition for the Algebraic Formula.   Why is the ratio of the risk premium to the covariance so relevant? Consider the case where the ratio of a stock's risk premium to its covariance with the candidate tangency portfolio differs from stock to stock. In this case, it is possible to alter the weights of the portfolio slightly to increase its mean return while lowering its variance. This can be done by slightly increasing the weight on a stock that has a high ratio of risk premium to marginal variance, while slightly lowering the weight on a stock with a low ratio and altering the weight on the risk-free asset so that the weights add up to 1. This action implies that the candidate tangency portfolio was not on the capital market line to begin with.

A Numerical Illustration of How to Generate a Mean-Variance Improvement.   Example 5.4 demonstrates how to achieve this mean-variance improvement by taking a portfolio for which the ratio condition in Result 5.3 is violated and constructing a new portfolio that is mean-variance superior to it.

Example 5.4:   Developing a Superior Portfolio When Condition 5.1 Is Violated

The return of ACME Corporation stock has a covariance with Henry's portfolio of .001 per year and a mean return of 20 percent per year, while ACYOU Corporation stock has a return covariance of .002 with the same portfolio and a mean return of 40 percent per year. The risk-free rate is 10 percent per year. Prove that Henry has not chosen the tangency portfolio.

Answer: To prove this, construct a **self-financing** (i.e., zero-cost) investment of ACME, ACYOU, and the risk-free asset that has a negative marginal variance and a positive marginal mean. Adding this self-financing investment to Henry's portfolio generates a new portfolio with a higher expected return and lower variance. Letting the variable m represent a small number per dollar invested in Henry's portfolio, this self-financing investment is long $\$.99m$ in the ACYOU Corporation, short $\$1.99m$ in the ACME corporation and long $\$m$ in the risk-free asset. When added to Henry's portfolio, this self-financing investment increases the expected return by:

$$.99m(40\%) - 1.99m(20\%) + m(10\%) = 9.8m\% \text{ per year}$$

However, if m is sufficiently small, the addition of this portfolio to the existing portfolio reduces return variance because the covariance of the self-financing portfolio of the three assets with Henry's portfolio is:

$$.99m(.002) - 1.99m(.001) = -.00001m$$

A negative covariance means a negative marginal variance when the added portfolio is sufficiently small.

The risk premium-to-covariance ratio from Result 5.3 should be the same whether the ratio is measured for individual stocks, projects that involve investment in real assets, or portfolios. For example, using the tangency portfolio in place of stock i, the ratio of the tangency portfolio's risk premium to its covariance with itself should equal the ratio in Result 5.3, or[10]:

$$\frac{\bar{r}_i - r_f}{cov(\tilde{r}_i, \tilde{R}_T)} = \frac{\overline{R}_T - r_f}{var(\tilde{R}_T)} \tag{5.2}$$

5.5 Finding the Efficient Frontier of Risky Assets

One can reasonably argue that no risk-free asset exists. While many default-free securities such as U.S. Treasury bills are available to investors, even a one month U.S. T-bill fluctuates in value unpredictably from day to day. Thus, when the investment horizon is shorter than a month, this asset is definitely not "risk-free." In addition, foreign investors would not consider the U.S. Treasury bill a risk-free asset. An Italian investor, for example, views the certain dollar payoff at the maturity of the T-bill as risky because it must be translated into Italian lire at an uncertain exchange rate. Even to a U.S. investor with a one-month horizon, the purchasing power of an asset, not just its nominal value, is critical. Thus, the inflation-adjusted returns of Treasury bills are risky, even when calculated to maturity. Also, in many settings there may be no risk-free assets. For example, a variety of investment and corporate finance problems preclude investment in a risk-free asset. For these reasons, it is useful to learn how to compute all of the portfolios on the (hyperbolic-shaped) boundary of the feasible set of risky investments, detailed in Exhibit 5.1. This section uses the insights from Section 5.4 to find this boundary.

Because of two-fund separation, the identification of any two portfolios on the boundary is enough to construct the entire set of risky portfolios that minimize variance for a given mean return. Use the minimum variance portfolio of the risky assets as one

---

[10]Section 5.7 develops more intuition for equation 5.2 and (the equivalent) Result 5.3.

of the two portfolios since computing its weights is so easy. For the other portfolio, note that (with one exception)[11] it is possible to draw a tangent line from every point on the vertical axis of the mean-standard deviation diagram to the hyperbolic boundary. We will refer to the point of tangency as the "hypothetical tangency portfolio." Hence:

1. Select any return that is less than the expected return of the minimum-variance portfolio.
2. Compute the hypothetical tangency portfolio by pretending that the return in step 1 is the risk-free return, even if a risk-free asset does not exist.
3. Take weighted averages of the minimum variance portfolio and the hypothetical tangency portfolio found in step 2 to generate the entire set of mean-variance efficient portfolios. The weight on the minimum variance portfolio must be less than 1 to be on the top half of the hyperbolic boundary.

Example 5.5 illustrates this three-step technique.

Example 5.5:   Finding the Efficient Frontier When No Risk-Free Asset Exists

Find the portfolios on the efficient frontier constructed from investment in the three franchising projects in Examples 5.3 and 4.23.

Answer: Solve for the portfolio "weights" that make the covariance with each stock equal to their risk premium. (In this example, "risk premium" refers to the expected return less some hypothetical return that you select.) If the hypothetical return is 6 percent, the weights (unscaled) are given by the simultaneous solution of the three equations:

$$.002x_1 + .001x_2 + \quad 0x_3 = .15 - .06$$

$$.001x_1 + .002x_2 + .001x_3 = .17 - .06$$

$$0x_1 + .001x_2 + .002x_3 = .17 - .06$$

The solution to these equations (after rescaling) from Example 5.3 is:

$$x_1 = .4 \quad x_2 = .1 \quad x_3 = .5$$

(Not surprisingly, with a hypothetical risk-free return in this example that is identical to the risk-free return in Example 5.3, the weights in the two examples, .4, .1, and .5, match. Alternatively, instead of subtracting .06 from the expected returns on the right-hand side of the first three equations, you could have subtracted other numbers (e.g., .04 or zero). If .04 had been used in lieu of .06, the right-hand side of the first three equations would be .11, .13, and .13, respectively, instead of .09, .11, and .11. If zero had been used, the right-hand side would be .15, .17, and .17, respectively.)

For the other portfolio, use the minimum variance portfolio which was computed in Example 4.23 to be:

$$x_1 = .5 \quad x_2 = 0 \quad x_3 = .5$$

Thus, the portfolios on the boundary of the feasible set are described by:

$$x_1 = .4w + .5(1 - w)$$

$$x_2 = .1w$$

$$x_3 = .5w + .5(1 - w) = .5$$

Those with $w > 0$ are on the top half of the boundary and are mean-variance efficient.

---

[11]The exception is at the expected return of the minimum variance portfolio, point V in Exhibit 5.2.

Since the financial markets contain numerous risky investments available to form a portfolio, finding the efficient frontier of risky investments in realistic settings is best left to a computer. Examples in this chapter, like the one above, which are simplified so that these calculations can be performed by hand, illustrate basic principles that you can apply to solve more realistic problems.[12]

5.6 How Useful Is Mean-Variance Analysis for Finding Efficient Portfolios?

One difficulty in employing mean-variance analysis to find mean-variance efficient portfolios is that means and covariances are generally unobservable. The real world requires that they be estimated. Since there is an incredibly large number of stocks and other investments to choose from, the full implementation of mean-variance analysis as a tool for portfolio management seems limited. First, the calculation of the necessary inputs seems to be almost a heroic undertaking, given that almost 10,000 stocks are traded in the U.S. market alone. Moreover, the estimated means and covariances will differ from the true means and covariances for virtually all of these securities.

These considerations do not necessarily limit the applicability of mean-variance analysis to smaller types of problems, such as asset allocation across asset classes (i.e., what fraction of the investor's wealth should be in bonds, stocks, cash, etc.), countries (i.e., what fraction of wealth should be in Japan, Europe, the United States, etc.), or industries. These simpler problems are both more manageable from a computational standpoint and generally have estimated covariances and means closer to their true values because the fundamental "assets" in this case are broad-based portfolios rather than individual stocks.[13] These considerations also do not limit the use of mean-variance analysis for hedging in corporate finance.[14]

The difficulties in applying mean-variance analysis to determine the efficient portfolios of *individual* stocks can be overcome with additional assumptions. These assumptions, when added to those of mean-variance analysis, enable the analyst to deduce the efficient portfolios rather than to compute them from historical covariances and historical means. (We will explore one theory based on additional assumptions, the CAPM, in this chapter.[15])

---

[12]Many software packages, including spreadsheets, can be used to obtain a numerical solution to this type of problem. The solution usually requires inverting the covariance matrix, an important step that the computer uses to solve systems of linear equations. Then sum "weighted" columns of the inverted covariance matrix, which is the same as taking weighted sums of the elements in each row of the matrix, where the "weights" on column i is the risk premium of investment i. Next, rescale the "weighted" sum of the columns, itself a column, so that its entries sum to 1. Entry i of the rescaled column is the weight on investment i in the tangency portfolio. In Microsoft Excel, the function MINVERSE inverts a matrix and the function MMULT multiplies the inverted matrix and the column of risk premia, which is the same as summing weighted columns.

[13]Estimates of portfolio means and standard deviations are more accurate than those for individual stocks because random estimation errors across stocks tend to cancel one another in a portfolio.

[14]The practice of hedging is discussed in Chapter 21.

[15]A second approach known as factor modeling, discussed in Chapter 6, is a statistical method for reducing the problem of estimating covariances to one of manageable size in order to derive insights about optimal portfolios. If the statistical assumptions correspond to reality, the covariance estimates obtained may be precise. Moreover, with this second approach, the mean returns necessary to find the optimal portfolios reduce to a problem of estimating the means of a few broad-based portfolios of large numbers of stocks. As suggested in our discussion of asset allocation, mean-variance analysis is more feasible in this case.

5.7 The Relation between Risk and Expected Return

A secondary benefit of identifying a mean-variance efficient portfolio is that it generates an equation that relates the risk of an asset to its expected return. Knowing the relation between risk and expected return has a variety of applications; among these are the evaluation of the performance of professional fund managers, the determination of required rates of return in order to set fair rates for regulated utilities, and the valuation of corporate investment projects.

As an example of the last application, suppose that Dell Computer wants to expand by developing factories in the Far East. It has estimated the expected future cash flows from such an investment. To determine whether this expansion improves the firm's value, the expected future cash flows from the expansion need to be translated into a value in today's dollars. Dell can compute this by discounting the expected future cash flows at the rate of return required by the financial markets on investments of similar risk.[16]

A popular assumption in the estimation of this required rate of return is that the expansion project has the same required return as Dell's common stock. However, it would be foolish for Dell to estimate this required rate of return by taking the average of Dell's historical stock returns. Dell's stock appreciated in value by more than 20-fold in the seven years following its initial public offering in the late 1980s. It would be highly unusual for this incredible track record to be repeated. In other words, because of its remarkable performance in its first seven years as a publicly traded company, the average historical return of Dell's stock substantially exceeds the expected rate of return required by investors looking ahead.

Because stock returns have such high variances, Dell's problem is common to many corporations. If historical data provide unreliable estimates of the true expected rates of return of the stocks of individual corporations, how do these companies obtain such estimates? Fortunately, the difficulty in estimating means is not shared by measures of risk. Reasonably accurate estimates of risk can be obtained if one knows the tangency portfolio. In this case, a theory that relates the variables that one can estimate well (i.e., the risk measures) to the variables that are problematic to estimate (i.e., expected returns of individual companies) could be useful to companies like Dell. Later parts of this chapter estimate Dell's risk and expected return with such a theory.

Relevant Risk and the Tangency Portfolio

When a risk-free asset exists, the relation between the relevant risk of an investment and its expected return can be derived directly from equation 5.2. Specifically, equation (5.3) is obtained by moving the risk premium of the investment to the right-hand side of equation (5.2):

$$\bar{r} - r_f = \frac{cov(\tilde{r}, \tilde{R}_T)}{var(\tilde{R}_T)}(\bar{R}_T - r_f) \tag{5.3}$$

(For simplicity in notation, we have dropped the *i* subscript.)

Equation (5.3) describes the relation between the expected return of an investment and a measure of its risk. In this case, the relevant measure of risk is the covariance between the returns of the tangency portfolio and the investment.[17]

---

[16]Chapter 10 explains this valuation procedure in great detail.

[17]Section 5.9 presents a similar treatment of risk and expected return in the absence of a risk-free asset.

Example 5.6 illustrates how to apply equation (5.3).

Example 5.6:   Implementing the Risk-Return Equation

The risk-free return is 8 percent. The return of General Motors stock has a covariance with the return of the tangency portfolio that is 50 percent larger than the corresponding covariance for ITT stock. The expected return of ITT stock is 12 percent per year. What is the expected return of General Motors stock?

Answer: The risk premium of ITT stock is 4 percent per year (the expected return minus the risk-free return: 12 percent less 8 percent). General Motors' risk premium must be 50 percent larger or 6 percent per year. Adding the risk-free return to this number yields 14 percent, the expected return of General Motors.

Betas

The first factor in the product on the right-hand of equation (5.3) is commonly referred to as **beta** and has the Greek letter β:

$$\beta = \frac{cov(\tilde{r}, \tilde{R}_T)}{var(\tilde{R}_T)}$$

This notation is used because the right-hand of equation (5.3) also happens to be the formula for the slope coefficient in a regression, which commonly uses β to denote the slope. With this notation, equation (5.3) becomes:

$$\bar{r} - r_f = \beta(\bar{R}_T - r_f) \tag{5.4}$$

The Securities Market Line versus the Mean-Standard Deviation Diagram. Panel A of Exhibit 5.5 on page 160 plots the familiar mean-standard deviation diagram. For the same financial market, panel B to the right of panel A plots what is commonly known as the securities market line. The **securities market line** is a line relating two important attributes for all the investments in the securities market. In equation (5.4), it is the graphical representation of mean versus beta. The four securities singled out in both panels and the tangency portfolio are the same securities in both diagrams.

Note in panel B that the tangency portfolio has a beta of 1 because the numerator and denominator of the ratio used to compute beta are identical for such a portfolio. The risk-free asset necessarily has a beta of zero; being constant, its return cannot covary with anything. Each portfolio on the capital market line (see panel A), a weighted average of the tangency portfolio and the risk free asset,[18] has a location on the securities market line found by taking the same weighted average of the points corresponding to the tangency portfolio and the risk-free asset. What is special about the securities market line, however, is that all investments in panel A lie on the line: both the efficient portfolios on the capital market line and the dominated investments to the right of the capital market line.

Exhibit 5.5 purposely places the two diagrams side by side to illustrate the critical distinction between the securities market line and the mean-standard deviation diagram. The difference between the diagrams in panels A and B is reflected on the horizontal

---

[18]For this weighting of two portfolios, think of the risk-free asset as a portfolio with a weight of 1 on the risk-free asset and 0 on all the other assets.

EXHIBIT 5.5   **The Relation between the Mean-Standard Deviation Diagram and a Mean-Beta Diagram**

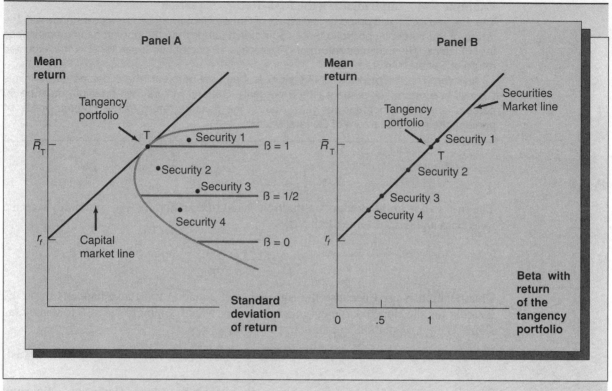

axis. Panel A shows the standard deviation on this axis while panel B shows the beta with the return of the tangency portfolio, which is proportional to the marginal variance. Thus, while investments with the same mean can have different standard deviations, as seen in panel A, they must have the same beta, as seen in panel B. For example, in panel A, all of the points on the grey line to the right of point T, labeled "$\beta = 1$," are portfolios with the same beta as the tangency portfolio. In panel B, all of these portfolios—even though they are distinct in terms of their portfolio weights and standard deviations—plot at exactly the same point as the tangency portfolio. For the same reason, all points on the grey horizontal line to the right of the risk-free asset in the mean-standard deviation diagram, designated "$\beta = 0$" are portfolios with a beta of 0 even though they have positive and differing standard deviations. In the mean-beta diagram, which graphs the securities market line in panel B, these portfolios plot at the same point as r_f.[19]

An Example Illustrating How to Obtain Expected Returns from Betas.   Example 5.7 applies equation (5.4), graphically represented as the securities market line, to estimate expected returns.

---

[19]Because mean return and beta plot on a straight line (see panel B), all investments with the same mean have the same beta and all investments with the same beta have the same mean.

Example 5.7:   Estimating the Expected Return of a Stock Portfolio from its Beta

Firstenberg, Ross, and Zisler (1988) estimated the mean-variance efficient combinations of a well-known stock index, a government bond portfolio, and a real estate index. One of their efficient portfolios, which this example assumes is the tangency portfolio, allocates 80 percent to real estate and 20 percent to government bonds. This tangency portfolio has an expected return of 13 percent per year and a standard deviation of 8.8 percent per year. The beta for the stock index, computed with respect to this tangency portfolio, is .54. Compute the expected return of the stock index, assuming that this 80%/20% mix really is the tangency portfolio when the risk-free rate is 5 percent.

Answer: Applying the formula in equation (5.4) yields:

$$\bar{r} = .05 + .54(.13 - .05) = 9.32\% \text{ per year}$$

Portfolio Betas.   An important property of beta is found in Result 5.4[20]:

Result 5.4   The beta of a portfolio is a portfolio-weighted average of the betas of its individual securities, that is:

$$\beta_p = \sum_{i=1}^{N} x_i \beta_i$$

where

$$\beta_i = \frac{cov(\tilde{r}_i, \tilde{R}_T)}{var(\tilde{R}_T)}$$

Example 5.8 illustrates how to apply the portfolio beta formula in Result 5.4.

Example 5.8:   Calculating a Portfolio Beta

Example 5.7 assumed that the tangency portfolio was allocated 80 percent to real estate and 20 percent to government bonds. The beta for stocks with this tangency portfolio is .54. Compute the beta of a portfolio that is 50 percent invested in the tangency portfolio and 50 percent invested in the stock index (which can be further translated to 40 percent in real estate, 10 percent in government bonds, and 50 percent in stocks).

Answer: As noted earlier, the beta of the tangency portfolio is 1 and the beta for stocks is .54. Applying the formula in Result 5.4, the portfolio-weighted average of the two:

$$\beta_p = .5(1) + .5(.54) = .77$$

Contrasting Betas and Covariances.   Note that betas and covariances are essentially the same measure of marginal variance. Beta is simply the covariance divided by the same constant for every stock. For historical reasons as well as the ease of estimation with regression, beta has become the more popular scaling of marginal variance. In principle, however, both are equally good as measures of marginal risk.

---

[20]Because β_i is merely the covariance of security i with the tangency portfolio divided by a constant, Result 5.4 is a direct extension of Result 4.5 in Chapter 4: the covariance of the return of a portfolio with the return of a stock is the portfolio-weighted average of the covariances of the investments in the portfolio with the stock return.

Marginal Variance versus Total Variance

Previously, this text defined a portfolio's risk as the variance of its return. However, to determine the expected rate of return on an investment, the relevant risk is beta (or covariance) computed with respect to the tangency portfolio.

Beta versus Variance as a Measure of Risk.   Why is it that the beta and not the variance is the relevant measure of risk? An analogy from economics may shed some light on this question. A central tenet of economics is that the market price of a good is equal to the marginal cost of producing one more unit of the good. Thus, the total cost of production or the average cost of production does not matter for pricing—only the *marginal* cost matters. In finance, the marginal variance (i.e., covariance of an investment measured in relation to the optimal portfolio of an investor) determines the incremental risk from adding a small amount of the investment to the portfolio. Therefore, it is not surprising that required rates of return on risky investments are determined by their marginal variances.

Using Marginal Variance Intuition to Understand the Risk-Expected Return Equation.   Now consider the following exercise, which extends the marginal variance exercise developed in Chapter 4. Start with the tangency portfolio, with return $\tilde{R}_T$. Add \$$m$ of stock k to this portfolio per dollar invested in the portfolio. However, instead of financing this purchase with a position in a risk-free asset, finance it with a short position in what will be called "stock k's tracking portfolio." The **tracking portfolio** is a weighted average of the tangency portfolio and the risk-free asset, with weight b on the tangency portfolio. The new portfolio combines:

1. The tangency portfolio.
2. A small additional amount of stock k.
3. A short position in stock k's tracking portfolio, of the same size as the additional purchase of stock k in item 2.

The return of the new portfolio is:

$$\tilde{R} = \tilde{R}_T + m\{\tilde{r}_k - [b\tilde{R}_T + (1-b)r_f)]\} = \tilde{R}_T + m[(\tilde{r}_k - r_f) - b(\tilde{R}_T - r_f)]$$

and its expected return is

$$\bar{R} = \bar{R}_T + m\{\bar{r}_k - [b\bar{R}_T + (1-b)r_f)]\} = \bar{R}_T + m[(\bar{r}_k - r_f) - b(\bar{R}_T - r_f)]$$

Note that the tracking portfolio has a risk premium equal to b times the risk premium of the tangency portfolio and a beta of b computed with respect to the tangency portfolio T. Thus, the additional mean from this adjustment to the tangency portfolio is the difference between the risk premium of stock k and the risk premium of its tracking portfolio, where the latter equals b times the risk premium of the tangency portfolio. If the risk premium of stock k exceeds the risk premium of the tracking portfolio, the new portfolio has a larger mean than the tracking portfolio and vice versa. The additional (or possibly lessened) risk from this adjustment to the tangency portfolio is proportional to the difference between the beta of stock k and the beta of the tracking portfolio, assuming the adjustment is a small one, as the analysis below shows.

Letting σ_T^2 denote $var(\tilde{R}_T)$ and σ_{kT} denote $cov(\tilde{r}_k, \tilde{R}_T)$ the variance of the new portfolio, σ^2, is:

$$\sigma^2 = var\big(\tilde{R}_T + m[(\tilde{r}_k - r_f) - b(\tilde{R}_T - r_f)]\big)$$

$$= \sigma_T^2 + m^2[\sigma_k^2 + b^2\sigma_T^2 - 2b\sigma_{kT}] + 2m[\sigma_{kT} - b\sigma_T^2]$$

The last line is obtained by applying the portfolio variance and covariance formulas, equation (4.9a) and Results 4.4 and 4.5.[21] The derivative of this variance with respect to m is:

$$\frac{d\sigma^2}{dm} = 2m[\sigma_k^2 + b^2\sigma_T^2 - 2b\sigma_{kT}] + 2[\sigma_{kT} - b\sigma_T^2]$$

which, at $m = 0$, has a value of:

$$\frac{d\sigma^2}{dm}\bigg|_{m=0} = 2\sigma_T^2\left[\frac{\sigma_{kT}}{\sigma_T^2} - b\right] = 2\sigma_T^2(\beta_k - b) \tag{5.5}$$

Equation (5.5) implies that adding a small amount of stock k to the tangency portfolio, financed in the manner described above, will:

1. Increase variance if $\beta_k >$ b.
2. Decrease variance if $\beta_k <$ b.
3. Not change variance (for infinitesimal m) if $\beta_k = b$.

These three cases of positive, negative, and zero marginal variance, respectively, correspond to stock k's beta, β_k, being greater, less than, or the same as the beta of its tracking portfolio, namely b.

Let us focus on the case of zero marginal variance, case 3, for which the tracking portfolio is constructed to have the same marginal risk as stock k. Suppose that in this case, where $\beta_k = b$, the risk premium of stock k exceeded the risk premium of the tracking portfolio:

$$\bar{r}_k - r_f > \beta_k(\bar{R}_T - r_f) \tag{5.6}$$

For small m, the addition of stock k to the tangency portfolio—financed by a position in the tracking portfolio with the same marginal variance as stock k—adds no variance to portfolio T but, because of the risk premium inequality, (5.6), it increases the mean.[22] Thus, if (5.6) is true, the addition of stock k, matched by an equal-sized short position in the tracking portfolio, results in a new portfolio that dominates the tangency portfolio. However, the risk premium inequality assumption expressed in (5.6) cannot be true because the tangency portfolio, by definition, cannot be dominated.

---

[21]$var\big(\tilde{R}_T + m[(\tilde{r}_k - r_f) - b(\tilde{R}_T - r_f)]\big)$

$= var(\tilde{R}_T) + var\big(m[(\tilde{r}_k - r_f) - b(\tilde{R}_T - r_f)]\big) + 2cov\big(\tilde{R}_T, m[(\tilde{r}_k - r_f) - b(\tilde{R}_T - r_f)]\big)$

$= \sigma_T^2 + m^2\,var\big((\tilde{r}_k - r_f) - b(\tilde{R}_T - r_f)\big) + 2m\big(cov(\tilde{R}_T, r_k - r_f)\big) - cov\big(\tilde{R}_T, b(\tilde{R}_T - r_f)\big)$

$= \sigma_T^2 + m^2\big[var(\tilde{r}_k) + b^2var(\tilde{R}_T) - 2cov(\tilde{r}_k, b\tilde{R}_T)\big] + 2m[cov(\tilde{R}_T, \tilde{r}_k) - bcov(\tilde{R}_T, \tilde{R}_T)]$

$= \sigma_T^2 + m^2[\sigma_k^2 + b^2\sigma_T^2 - 2b\sigma_{kT}] + 2m[\sigma_{kT} - b\sigma_T^2]$

[22]In this exercise, increasing b to a number slightly above σ_{kT}/σ_T^2, so that the tracking portfolio's marginal variance is larger than stock k's marginal variance, would actually decrease the variance yet still increase the mean. This is a more technically correct (but harder to understand) way of demonstrating the key result in this section.

Now suppose that the risk premium of the tracking portfolio exceeds that of stock k, that is:

$$\bar{r}_k - r_f < \beta_k(\bar{R}_T - r_f) \tag{5.7}$$

Subtraction of sufficiently small amounts of stock k from the tangency portfolio, balanced by an equal-sized long position in the tracking portfolio with the same marginal variance, adds no variance to the tangency portfolio, but by (5.7) increases the mean.[23] Thus, if (5.7) is true, the subtraction of stock k, matched by an opposite tracking portfolio position, as described above, dominates the tangency portfolio. Because the tangency portfolio cannot be dominated, (5.7) cannot hold.

If betas are computed with respect to the tangency portfolio, and it is not possible, as shown above, to observe either

$$\bar{r}_k - r_f > \beta_k(\bar{R}_T - r_f) \quad \text{or} \quad \bar{r}_k - r_f < \beta_k(\bar{R}_T - r_f),$$

then the only remaining possibility is:

$$\bar{r}_k - r_f = \beta_k(\bar{R}_T - r_f)$$

This is the risk-expected return equation and it states that expected returns are linear functions of beta.

Tracking Portfolios in Portfolio Management and as a Theme for Valuation

The last section uses tracking portfolios composed of weighted averages of the tangency portfolio and the risk-free asset to illustrate why the risk-expected return equation has to hold. However, the concept of a tracking portfolio is much broader than that presented earlier. For example, investment professionals use tracking portfolios that differ from those in the last section for the purpose of managing an index fund at a low transaction cost. In addition, this text generalizes the concept of a tracking portfolio to develop valuation models. This section discusses these generalizations of the tracking portfolio concept.

Uses of Tracking Portfolios in Investment Management.   Investment professionals often need to **track**, that is, replicate the return characteristics of large portfolios using a relatively small number of stocks. For example, a number of portfolio managers are asked to create portfolios that "track" the S&P 500 Index in hopes of beating it. In what follows, it will sometimes be important to distinguish between perfect and imperfect tracking.

> *Portfolio A tracks portfolio B perfectly if the difference in the returns of the portfolios is a constant.*

Exhibit 5.6 illustrates the value in 1995 of the S&P 500 and a tracking portfolio that has a higher return.

In a typical tracking strategy, the investment professional selects about 50 stocks that he or she believes are underpriced and then weights each of the underpriced stocks in a portfolio in a way that minimizes the variance of the difference between the return of the managed portfolio and the return of the S&P 500. While such a portfolio may not track the S&P 500 perfectly, it can come close to doing so. As we will see, tracking strategies can lead to important insights about the risk-expected return equation.

---

[23]In this exercise, decreasing *b* to a number slightly less than σ_{kT}/σ_T^2, so that the tracking portfolio's marginal variance is smaller than stock k's marginal variance, would actually decrease the variance, yet still increase the mean.

EXHIBIT 5.6   Value of the S&P 500 and its Tracking Portfolio in 1995

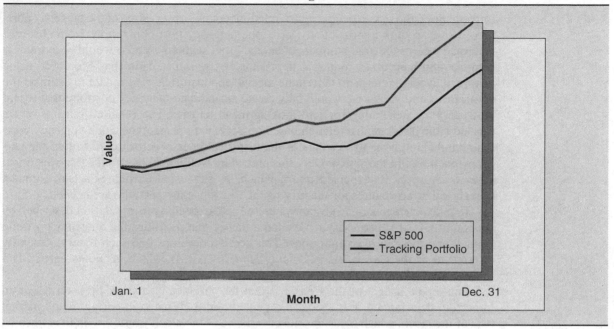

Other Uses of Tracking Portfolios in this Text.   One of the key themes in this text is that it is possible to think about tracking almost any investment. One can track an individual stock, a real asset like a factory, or an index of stocks like the S&P 500. In contrast to the almost perfect tracking of broad-based portfolios like the S&P 500 or of derivatives (which have complicated tracking strategies), the tracking of an individual stock or real asset generally involves substantial tracking error.[24] In these cases, the best tracking portfolio is one that comes as close as possible to matching the returns of the tracked investment. This kind of tracking portfolio minimizes the variance of the tracking error.

In this chapter, where stock k is tracked with a portfolio of the risk-free asset (weight $1 - b$) and the tangency portfolio (weight b), the best tracking portfolio is the one whose tracking weight, b, is the same as the stock's beta, that is:

$$b = \beta_k$$

A tracking portfolio generated with this "best" tracking weight has the same marginal variance as stock k.[25] The main insight derived from this best tracking portfolio is summarized in Result 5.5.

Result 5.5   If a stock and its tracking portfolio have the same *marginal variance* with respect to the tangency portfolio, then the stock and its tracking portfolio must have the same *expected return*. This applies only when the marginal variance is computed with respect to an efficient portfolio. Marginal variances computed with respect to dominated portfolios have no implications for expected returns.

---

[24]The tracking of broad-based portfolios is discussed in Chapter 6, that of derivatives in Chapters 7 and 8.

[25]This conclusion, which implies that tracking portfolios with these weights are optimal hedges, is proved in Chapter 21.

5.8 The Capital Asset Pricing Model

Implementing the risk-expected return relation requires observation of the tangency portfolio. However, it is impossible to derive the tangency portfolio simply from observed historical returns on large numbers of assets. First, such an exercise would be extremely complex and inaccurate, requiring thousands of covariance estimates. Moreover, using historical average returns to determine means, and historical return data to estimate the covariances and variances, would only create a candidate tangency portfolio that would be useless for generating forward-looking mean returns. The required rates of return derived from a risk-return relation based on betas with respect to such a tangency portfolio would simply be the average of the historical rates of return used to find the tangency portfolio. In the case of Dell, this procedure would generate Dell's large historical average return as its expected return which, as suggested earlier, is a bad estimate. Clearly, other procedures for identifying the true tangency portfolio are needed.

To put some economic substance into the risk-expected return relation described by equation (5.4), it is necessary to develop a theory that identifies the tangency portfolio from sound theoretical assumptions. This section develops one such theory, generally referred to as the *Capital Asset Pricing Model* (CAPM), which, as noted earlier, is a model of the relation of risk to expected returns.

The major insight of the CAPM is that the variance of a stock by itself is *not* an important determinant of the stock's expected return. What is important is the market beta of the stock, which measures the covariance of the stock's return with the return on a market index, scaled by the variance of that index.

Assumptions of the CAPM

As noted earlier, the two assumptions of mean-variance analysis are that:

1. Investors care only about the mean and variance of their portfolio's returns.
2. Markets are frictionless.

To develop the CAPM, one additional assumption is needed:

3. Investors have **homogeneous beliefs**, which means that all investors reach the same conclusions about the means and standard deviations of all feasible portfolios.

The assumption of homogeneous beliefs implies that investors will not be trying to outsmart one another and "beat the market" by actively managing their portfolios. On the other hand, the assumption does not imply that investors can merely throw darts to pick their portfolios. A scientific examination of means, variances, and covariances may still be of use, but almost every person will arrive at the same conclusions about the mean and standard deviation of each feasible portfolio's return after his or her own scientific examination.

The Conclusion of the CAPM

From these three assumptions, theorists were able to develop the Capital Asset Pricing Model, which concludes that the tangency portfolio must be the market portfolio. The next section details what this portfolio is and how practitioners implement it in the Capital Asset Pricing Model.

The Market Portfolio

The **market portfolio** is a portfolio where the weight on each asset is the market value (also called the **market capitalization**) of that asset divided by the market value of all risky assets.

Example 5.9:   Computing the Weights of the Market Portfolio

Consider an economy with only three investments: the stocks of Hewlett Packard (HP), IBM, and Digital Equipment (DEC). As of year-end 1995, the approximate prices per share of these three stocks are HP = $83.75, IBM = $90.00, and DEC = $62.60. The approximate number of shares outstanding for the three firms are 513.43 million (HP), 566.67 million (IBM), and 159.74 million (DEC). What are the portfolio weights of the market portfolio?

Answer: The market capitalization of the stocks is:

$$HP = \$83.75 \times 513.43 \text{ million} = \$ \ 43 \text{ billion}$$

$$IBM = \$90.00 \times 566.67 \text{ million} = \$ \ 51 \text{ billion}$$

$$DEC = \$62.60 \times 159.74 \text{ million} = \underline{\$ \ 10 \text{ billion}}$$

$$\text{Total market capitalization} \quad = \$104 \text{ billion}$$

The market portfolio's weights (with decimal approximations) on the three stocks are therefore:

$$HP = \frac{\$43 \text{ billion}}{\$104 \text{ billion}} = .414$$

$$IBM = \frac{\$51 \text{ billion}}{\$104 \text{ billion}} = .490$$

$$DEC = \frac{\$10 \text{ billion}}{\$104 \text{ billion}} = .096$$

In Example 5.9, the return of the market portfolio, $.414\tilde{r}_{HP} + .490\tilde{r}_{IBM} + .096\tilde{r}_{DEC}$, is the relevant return with which one computes the betas of the three stocks if the CAPM is true. The betas determine the expected returns of the three stocks. Of course, the world contains many investment assets, not just three stocks, implying that the actual market portfolio has a weight on every asset in the world.

With all the world's assets to consider, the task of calculating the market portfolio is obviously impractical. As claims to the real assets of corporations, all stocks and corporate bonds listed on all world exchanges and those traded over the counter would have to be included along with all real estate.

Since many of these investments are not traded frequently enough to obtain prices for them, one must use a proxy for the market portfolio. A frequently used proxy is the S&P 500, a **value-weighted portfolio**, meaning that the portfolio weight on each of its 500 typically larger market capitalization stocks—traded on the New York Stock Exchange (NYSE), the American Stock Exchange (AMEX), and the NASDAQ over-the-counter market—is proportional to the market value of that stock. Another commonly used proxy is the value-weighted portfolio of all stocks listed on the NYSE and AMEX. Still, these proxies ignore vast markets (e.g., residential real estate, the Tokyo Stock Exchange, and the Tokyo real estate market), making them poor substitutes for the true market portfolio.

Why the Market Portfolio Is the Tangency Portfolio

Example 5.9 considered a hypothetical world that contained only three risky investments: the stocks of Hewlett Packard, IBM, and Digital Equipment. Suppose that there also is a risk-free asset available for investment and that only two investors exist in this world: Jack and Jill.

What portfolio will Jack select? Mean-variance analysis implies that Jack will hold the tangency portfolio along with either a long or a short position in the risk-free investment. The proportion of his portfolio in the risk-free investment will depend on Jack's aversion to risk. Jill also will invest in some combination of the tangency portfolio and the risk-free investment.

In Example 5.9, the market values of all HP, IBM, and DEC stock are $43 billion, $51 billion and $10 billion, respectively. Since Jack and Jill are the only two investors in the world, their joint holdings of HP, IBM, and DEC also must total $43 billion, $51 billion, and $10 billion. It should be apparent that the tangency portfolio must contain some shares of HP. Otherwise, neither Jack nor Jill will hold the shares, implying that the supply of HP stock ($43 billion) would not equal its demand ($0).

If supply does equal demand and Jack and Jill both hold the tangency portfolio, Jack must hold the same fraction of all the outstanding shares of the three stocks. That is, *if* Jack holds one-half of the 513.43 million shares of HP stock, he must also hold one-half of the 566.67 million shares of IBM stock, and one-half of the 159.74 million shares of DEC. In this case, Jill would own the other half of all three stocks. The respective proportions of their total stock investment spent on each of the three stocks will thus be the market portfolio's proportions; that is, approximately .414, .490, and .096 (see Example 5.9).

To understand why this must be true, consider what would happen if Jack held one-half of the shares of HP, but only one-third of IBM's shares. In this case, the ratio of Jack's portfolio weight on HP to his weight on IBM would *exceed* the .414/.490 ratio of their weights in market portfolio. This implies that Jill would have to hold one-half of the shares of HP and two-thirds of the shares of IBM for supply to equal demand. But then the ratio of Jill's weight on HP to her weight on IBM, being *less than* the .414/.490 ratio of the market portfolio, would differ from Jack's, implying that Jack and Jill could not both be on the capital market line.

In short, because both Jack and Jill hold the tangency portfolio, they hold the risky investments in the exact same proportions. Because their holdings of risky stocks add up to the economy's supply of risky stocks, the market portfolio must also consist of risky investments allocated with these same proportions. It follows that the market portfolio is the tangency portfolio. The same conclusion, summarized in Result 5.6, is reached whether there are two investors in the world or billions.

Result 5.6   Under the assumptions of the CAPM, and if a risk-free asset exists, the market portfolio is the tangency portfolio and, by equation (5.4), the expected returns of assets are determined by:

$$\bar{r} - r_f = \beta(\bar{R}_M - r_f) \tag{5.8}$$

where $\bar{R}_M$ is the mean return of the market portfolio, and β is the beta computed against the return of the market portfolio.

Equation (5.8) is a special case of equation (5.4) with the market portfolio used as the tangency portfolio. By identifying the tangency portfolio, the CAPM provides a risk-return relation that is not only implementable, but is implemented in practice.

Implications for Optimal Investment

In addition to the implementable relation between risk and expected return, described by Equation (5.8), the CAPM also implies a rule for optimal investment:

Result 5.7   Under the assumptions of the CAPM, if a risk-free asset exists, every investor should optimally hold a combination of the market portfolio and a risk-free asset.

According to the CAPM, the major difference between the portfolios of Jack and Jill derives entirely from their differing weights on the risk-free asset. This is demonstrated in Example 5.10.

Example 5.10:   Portfolio Weights that Include the Risk-Free Asset
Consider one-month U.S. Treasury bills as the risk-free asset. One million T-bills are issued for $9,900 each. Jack holds 400,000 T-bills and Jill holds 600,000. If Jack has $60 billion in wealth, what are the portfolio weights of Jack and Jill given the data in the previous example, which indicated that the wealth invested in risky assets is $104 billion?

Answer: The total wealth in the world is the value of the risky assets, $104 billion, plus the value of the T-bills, $9.9 billion, which sum to a total of $113.9 billion. Thus, if Jack has $60 billion, Jill has $53.9 billion. Jack spends $3.96 billion on T-bills, which makes his portfolio weight on T-bills $3.96 billion/$60 billion = .066. Jill spends $5.94 billion on T-bills, making her T-bill portfolio weight approximately .1102. Thus, Jack owns $56.04 billion/$104 billion of the shares of the three risky assets and Jill owns $47.96 billion/$104 billion. After some calculation, the four portfolio weights (respectively, the risk-free asset, HP, IBM, and DEC) for Jack are approximately (.066, .387, .458, .090) and the weights for Jill are (.110, .368, .436, .085).

Note, from Example 5.10, that the last three weights in Jack's and Jill's portfolios, i.e., weights of .387, .458, and .090 (Jack) and .368, .436, and .085 (Jill) on HP, IBM, and DEC, respectively, are the market portfolio's weights if they are rescaled to sum to 1. Obviously, this result follows from both Jack and Jill's portfolios being combinations of the tangency (market) portfolio and the risk-free asset.

To understand the importance of Result 5.7, think again about the inputs needed to find the tangency portfolio. With thousands of securities to choose from, an investor would need to calculate not only thousands of mean returns, but also millions of covariances. Such a daunting task would surely require a professional portfolio manager. However, the CAPM suggests that none of this is necessary; investors can do just as well by investing in the market portfolio.

The 1970s, 1980s, and 1990s witnessed tremendous growth in the use of passively managed index portfolios as vehicles for investment in the pension fund, mutual fund, and life insurance industries. These portfolios attempted to mimic the return behavior of value-weighted portfolios like the S&P 500. One of the major reasons behind this trend was the popularization of the CAPM, which suggested that the mean-standard deviation trade-off from investing in the market portfolio cannot be improved upon.

5.9   Generalizing the Capital Asset Pricing Model

This section examines a variety of generalizations of the CAPM. Most of these generalizations focus on the nonexistence of a risk-free asset or the imposition of some frictions involving the risky or risk-free assets, including no short sales of risky assets, no risk-free borrowing, and differences between risk-free borrowing and lending rates. This section also considers an important multiperiod extension of the CAPM.

What if Short Sales of Risky Assets Are Prohibited?

Our first consideration is whether restricting short sales (including making short sales more costly) alters the conclusion that the market portfolio is mean-variance efficient. Clearly, short sale restrictions affect the set of feasible portfolios. All portfolios with negative weights must now be excluded from the analysis. However, the market portfolio does not have short sales and is still feasible. Hence, if in the absence of short sale restrictions the market portfolio was mean-variance efficient, it has to remain mean-variance efficient when compared with a smaller set of competing feasible portfolios.

In short, our conclusion about the mean-variance efficiency of the market portfolio is unaffected by the short sale restriction, and thus, the risk-expected return relation also is unaffected.

The Market Portfolio's Mean-Standard Deviation Location with No Risk-Free Asset

Earlier, this chapter presented arguments against the existence of a risk-free asset. If no asset is risk-free, our conclusion about the mean-variance efficiency of the market portfolio remains the same. Exhibit 5.7 outlines Jack's and Jill's portfolios on the efficient frontier of risky assets. The market portfolio is simply a wealth-weighted average of these two portfolios. For example, if Jack and Jill each have $180 million in wealth, the market portfolio would be an equal weighting of the two portfolios, lying halfway (vertically) between them, at point $M1$. If Jill has $300 million of the $360 million in total wealth, the market portfolio would be five-sixths of Jill's portfolio and one-sixth of Jack's, thus lying five-sixths of the way vertically toward Jill's portfolio at point $M2$. Two-fund separation (discussed earlier) indicates that if their two portfolios lie on the

EXHIBIT 5.7   The Market Portfolio in the Absence of a Riskless Asset

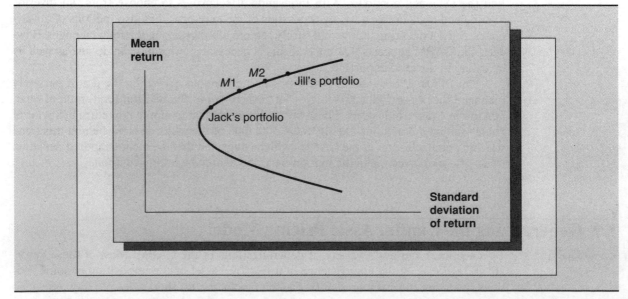

boundary of the feasible set, this wealth-weighted average of their two portfolios also lies on this boundary (compare Exhibit 5.7 with Exhibit 5.2).

The risk-return equation obtained when the market portfolio is mean-variance efficient, but when no risk-free asset exists, is virtually the same as the corresponding equation that results when a risk-free asset does exist. The only difference is that it is necessary to replace the nonexistent risk-free return with another value. This value, $\bar{R}_Z$, is the intercept found by drawing a line tangent to the boundary of the feasible set at the point of the market portfolio (the dashed line in Exhibit 5.8). It represents the mean return of a portfolio that is uncorrelated with the market portfolio.

Why is this so? Recall that the covariance with respect to the market portfolio, or equivalently beta, is a measure of a security's marginal variance with respect to the market portfolio. Equation (5.8) implies that all risky securities with zero betas have the same expected return as the risk-free asset (when a risk-free asset exists). Thus, if there is a riskless asset, all risky portfolios with zero betas lie on the darker blue line in Exhibit 5.8, which plots all the risky portfolios with an expected return equal to the risk-free return. Moreover, one could easily substitute the expected zero β return, $\bar{R}_Z$, for the identical risk-free return in equation (5.8).

When a riskless asset is removed from this picture, hardly anything changes about the portfolios that lie on the darker blue line in Exhibit 5.8. All of these portfolios still have the same expected return. They also have the same β of zero with respect to the portfolio that is tangent to the dashed line, which, by assumption, is the market portfolio. Moreover, all other risky assets still have the same mean return and same β with respect to this portfolio. Hence, the risk-expected return equation remains the same except that the expected zero beta return replaces the nonexistent risk-free return. Indeed, about the only thing that has changed in this diagram, after removing a risk-free asset from the picture, is that all points to the left of the hyperbolic boundary, including the dashed line, are no longer available for investment.

Exhibit 5.9 on page 172 shows the risk-expected return equation without a risk-free asset. This graph is identical to the one obtained with a risk-free asset except that the intercept of the "securities market line" at $\bar{R}_Z$ is actually the expected return of a portfolio with a beta of zero rather than the nonexistent risk-free return. Fittingly, the model without a risk-free asset, developed by Black (1972), is called the **zero-beta model**.

EXHIBIT 5.8   Finding the Expected Zero-Beta Return

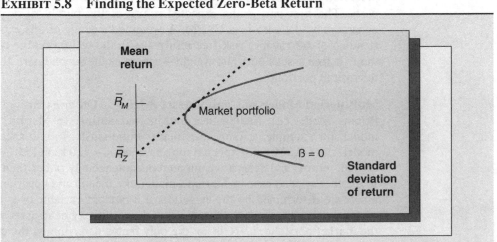

EXHIBIT 5.9   The CAPM Relation between the Mean Return of a Stock and Its Market Beta When No Risk-Free Asset Exists

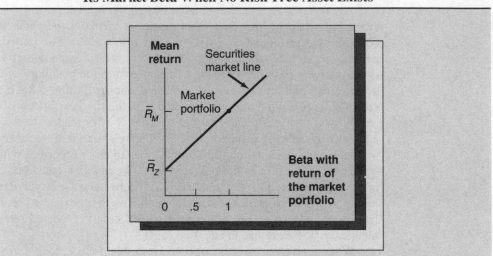

Other Generalizations of the CAPM

Several other relaxations of the assumptions of the original CAPM are important. The same zero-beta pricing result holds for all of these generalizations of the CAPM, although in many cases one cannot use the risk-free return in place of the zero beta return. These include a model developed by Black in which long positions (i.e., lending), but not short sales (i.e., risk-free borrowing) are allowed in the risk-free asset. Brennan (1971) presented a model that has a risk-free borrowing rate larger than the risk-free lending rate. Finally, there are models that prohibit short sales of all assets.

Zero-Beta Models of Capital Asset Pricing.   These restrictions all lead to the same pricing result; that is, equation (5.8) with r_f replaced by the expected return of some zero beta portfolio. In these models, however, any portfolio that includes the risk-free asset lies off of the zero-beta-based securities market line. To compute the expected return predicted by the CAPM for such a portfolio, the portfolio needs to be separated into two parts. The first part is the expected return of the purely risky part of the portfolio generated by the zero-beta CAPM. A weighted average of this expected return and the (lending or borrowing) risk-free return—with the weight on the risk-free return being the risk-free asset's portfolio weight—generates the second part, the expected return of the overall portfolio.

Multiperiod Models of Capital Asset Pricing.   Other extensions of the Capital Asset Pricing Model cast trading in a multiperiod setting. In Merton's (1973) multiperiod model, for example, trading takes place continuously. In one special case of Merton's model, the CAPM risk-expected return equation—equation (5.8)—looks the same, except all returns and betas are computed instantaneously rather than over finite horizons. In another special case of Merton's model, the means and covariances of the returns of assets are determined by the evolution of a random variable over time, $s(t)$, that determines the feasible set in the future. Here the sensitivity of an asset return to the return of the market portfolio, or β, is not the only factor determining the expected return of an asset at a point in time. In addition, the sensitivity of the return to a portfolio that has the maximum correlation with $s(t)$ also determines the expected returns of assets.

5.10 Estimating Betas, Risk-Free Returns, Risk Premiums, and the Market Portfolio

To implement the risk-expected return relation of the Capital Asset Pricing Model, it is necessary to estimate its parameters. These include the risk-free return, beta, the market risk premium, and the market portfolio itself.

Risk-Free or Zero-Beta Returns

Most academic studies of the CAPM have used short-term Treasury bill returns as proxies for the risk-free return. However, as Black, Jensen, and Scholes (1972), among others, have noted, this rate seems to be too low as a zero-beta return. An alternative is to use the zero-beta expected return estimate that comes from fitting the intercept in the risk-expected return equation to all stocks. Interestingly, the risk-free rate employed in derivative securities pricing models, which is the London interbank offered rate (LIBOR),[26] appears to be much closer to this fitted number.

Beta Estimation and Beta Shrinkage

Beta, as mentioned previously, is the notation for the covariance divided by the variance because this ratio is the appropriate slope coefficient in a regression. In practice, one never obtains the true beta, but it is possible to obtain an estimate. Estimation with historical data is easy after recognizing that the ratio of covariance to variance is a slope coefficient, which can be obtained from a linear regression. The left-hand variable in the regression is the return of the stock on which beta is being estimated; the right-hand side is a proxy for the market return (e.g., the return of the S&P 500). Many software packages and calculators have built-in regression routines that will use these data to estimate beta as the regression slope coefficient.

Example 5.11 provides real-world data and illustrates both a beta calculation and the estimation of expected return using beta.

Example 5.11:   Estimating Beta and the Expected Return for Dell Computer

Four years of quarterly returns (in %) for Dell Computer and the S&P 500 are given below:

	Dell				S&P 500			
	Q1	*Q2*	*Q3*	*Q4*	*Q1*	*Q2*	*Q3*	*Q4*
1991	—	—	—	9.04	—	—	—	11.43
1992	41.95	−25.26	57.93	67.68	−2.55	1.97	3.10	5.10
1993	−26.82	−46.62	−11.33	36.09	4.28	.51	2.56	2.31
1994	11.60	4.46	41.94	9.52	−3.81	.41	4.92	−.03
1995	6.71	37.43	41.37	−21.18	9.74	9.49	7.95	5.96

a. What is the annualized expected return required by investors in Dell Computer stock as estimated by averaging the 17 quarterly returns from the end of 1991 through 1995 and multiplying by 4?

---

[26]See Chapter 2.

   b. What is the annualized expected return required by investors in Dell Computer stock as estimated from the CAPM, using the S&P 500 as the market portfolio, 4.9 percent for the risk-free (or zero-beta) return, and the four-year average return of the S&P 500 less 4.9 percent as the market portfolio's risk premium?

   Answer: *a.* Averaging the 17 quarterly returns of Dell and multiplying by 4 generates an annualized expected return of 55.18 percent.

   b. The beta estimated by regressing the 17 returns of Dell on the 17 returns of the S&P 500 is 1.02. The annualized average return of the S&P over the 17 quarters is 14.9 percent. Hence, using equation (5.8), the expected return of Dell is:

$$15.1\% = 4.9\% + 1.02(14.9\% - 4.9\%)$$

Source: Dell figures are from Center for Research in Securities Prices (CRSP); the S&P 500 figures are from Ibbotson and Sinquefeld (1996).

A variety of statistical methods can improve the beta estimate. These methods usually involve taking some weighted average of 1 and the beta estimated with a software package.

Improving the Beta Estimated from Regression

Example 5.11 estimated the beta of Dell Computer with a simple regression of 17 quarterly Dell stock returns on the corresponding returns of a proxy for the market portfolio. The better beta estimates, alluded to above, account for estimation error. One source of estimation error arises simply because Dell's stock returns are volatile; therefore, estimates based on those returns are very imprecise.[27] A second source of estimation error arises because price changes for some stocks (usually the smaller capitalization stocks), seem to lag the changes of other stocks either because of nontrading or stale limit orders, that is, limit orders that were executed as a result of the investor failing to update the order as new information about the stock became available.

To understand the importance of estimation error, consider a case where last year's returns are used to estimate the betas of four very similar firms, denoted as firms A, B, C, and D. The estimated betas are $\beta_A = 1.4$, $\beta_B = .8$, $\beta_C = .6$, and $\beta_D = 1.2$. However, because these are estimated betas, they contain estimation error. As a result, the true betas are probably not as divergent as the estimated betas. Given these estimates, it is likely that stock A has the highest beta and stock C the lowest. Our best guess, however, is that the beta of stock A is overestimated and the beta of stock C is underestimated.[28]

The Bloomberg Adjustment.   Bloomberg, an investment data service, adjusts estimated betas with the following formula:

$$\text{Adjusted beta} = .66 \times \text{Unadjusted beta} + .34$$

---

[27]Just as a coin tossed 10 times can easily have a "heads" outcome 60 percent of the time (or 6 times), even if the true probability of a "heads" outcome is 50 percent, the average historical returns of stocks are rarely equal to their true mean returns.

[28]To understand why this is true, think about your friends who scored 770 on their GMATs or SATs. While it is true that most people who score 770 are smart, scoring that high might also require some luck; thus, those with the best scores may not be quite as smart as their 770 score would indicate. Similarly, the stock with the highest estimated beta in a given group may not really be as risky as its beta would indicate. The stock with the highest estimated beta in a group is likely to have a high estimation error in addition to having a high actual beta.

Exhibit 5.10   Bloomberg Unadjusted and Adjusted Betas

	Unadjusted Beta	Adjusted Beta
Delta Air Lines	0.84	0.89
Procter & Gamble	1.40	1.27
Coca-Cola	0.88	0.92
Gillette	0.90	0.93
Harcourt General	0.74	0.83
Time Warner	1.52	1.35
Citicorp	1.32	1.21
Chrysler	0.77	0.85
Caterpillar	1.00	1.00
Exxon	0.64	0.76

Source: Bloomberg Financial Markets, © 1998. Bloomberg L.P. All Rights Reserved. Data from a Bloomberg machine, Dec. 10, 1996; estimation based on weekly return data from June 7, 1996, to Dec. 6, 1996.

The **Bloomberg adjustment** formula lowers betas that exceed 1 and increases betas that are under 1. Exhibit 5.10 shows adjusted and unadjusted betas for 10 well-known stocks. The Bloomberg adjustment given in Exhibit 5.10 is applied in exactly the same way to all stocks. However, beta estimates can be improved upon by adjusting some stocks more than others. For example, one would expect estimation error to be somewhat larger for small firms than for large firms, which would imply that smaller firms should have a larger adjustment factor. In addition, better beta estimates might result by shrinking the unadjusted estimates toward an industry average beta rather than toward the market average. Further adjustments take into account the firm's leverage ratio and other characteristics possibly related to beta that also improve the precision of the beta estimate.

The BARRA Adjustment.   A number of data services provide beta adjustments of this type to portfolio managers. Perhaps the best known is a firm called BARRA, which was started by a former University of California, Berkeley, finance professor, Barr Rosenberg, who was one of the first to develop ways to improve beta estimates. Rosenberg et al. (1985) showed that using historical betas as predictors of future betas was much less effective than using alternative beta prediction techniques. Rosenberg first used a shrinkage factor similar to what Bloomberg is now using. Rosenberg later refined his prediction technique to incorporate fundamental variables—an industry variable and a number of company descriptors.

Adjusting for the Lagging Reaction of the Prices of Small Company Stocks to Market Portfolio Returns.   It also may be necessary to make additional adjustments to the betas of small firms because the returns of the stocks of small companies tend to react to market returns with a lag. This delayed reaction creates a downward bias in the beta estimates of these smaller capitalization stocks, since only part of the effect of market movements on the returns of these stocks are captured by their contemporaneous covariances. The bias can be significant when one estimates the betas from daily stock returns. For this reason, analysts should avoid daily returns and instead estimate betas with weekly or monthly returns where the effect of delayed reaction tends to be less severe.

However, a paper by Handa, Kothari, and Wasley (1989) suggests that the monthly betas of small capitalization stocks also may be underestimated compared with yearly betas.[29]

The following simple procedure for adjusting the betas of smaller cap stocks can compensate for the lagged adjustment: Add the lagged market return as an additional right-hand-side variable in the beta estimation regression. Then, sum the two slope coefficients in the regression—the slope coefficient on the market return that is contemporaneous with the stock return and the slope coefficient on the lagged market return—to obtain the adjusted beta. One could further refine this adjusted beta with the Bloomberg or BARRA techniques.

A Result to Summarize the Beta Adjustments.   Result 5.8 summarizes this subsection.

Result 5.8   Betas estimated from standard regression packages may not provide the best estimates of a stock's true beta. Better beta estimates can be obtained by taking into account the lead-lag effect in stock returns and the fact that relatively high beta estimates tend to be overestimates and relatively low beta estimates tend to be underestimates.

Estimating the Market Risk Premium

Assuming one knows the composition of the market portfolio, averaging its return over a long historical time series to compute an expected return on the market portfolio has the advantage of generating a better statistical estimate if the market portfolio's expected return also is stable over time. However, some empirical evidence suggests that the mean returns of portfolios like the S&P 500 change over time, providing an argument for the use of a shorter historical time series, although the four years used in Example 5.11 may be too short. In addition, changes in the expected return of the market portfolio appear to be predictable from variables such as the level of interest rates, the aggregate dividend yield, and the realized market return over the previous three to five years. To the extent that a model predicting the market's expected return is accurate and holds over long periods of time, one should estimate the parameters of such a model with as much historical data as possible, and then use current levels of the predictor variables to generate a forecast of the market's expected return.

To compute the market portfolio's risk premium, subtract a risk-free (or zero-beta) return from the expected return estimate. It also is possible to estimate the risk premium directly by averaging the market portfolio's historical **excess returns**, which are its returns in excess of the risk-free return. However, this is sensible only if the risk premium is stable over time. Empirical evidence suggests that the mean of the market return itself is more stable than the mean of the excess return. Hence, we do not recommend averaging historical excess returns to estimate the risk premium.

Identifying the Market Portfolio

Of course, the entire analysis here presumes that the analyst can identify the weights of the market portfolio. Previously, our discussion focused on several common proxies for

---

[29]In the absence of these considerations, the smaller is the return horizon, the more precise is the beta estimate. Our preferred compromise horizon for large firms is weekly data. An alternative is to employ daily data but make a statistical correction to the beta estimation procedure. See Scholes and Williams (1977) and Dimson (1979) for details on these statistical corrections.

the market portfolio, which were selected because, like the market portfolio, they were value-weighted portfolios. However, they compose only a small set of the world's assets. Hence, always keep in mind that these are merely proxies and that the usefulness of the CAPM depends on whether these proxies work or not. The next section discusses the evidence about how well these proxies do as candidates for the tangency portfolio.

5.11 Empirical Tests of the Capital Asset Pricing Model

In Part III of this text the CAPM is used as a tool for obtaining the required rates of return needed to evaluate corporate investment projects. The relevance of CAPM applications is determined by the ability of the theory to accurately predict these rates. Given the importance of this topic, financial economists have conducted hundreds of studies that examine the extent to which the expected returns predicted by the CAPM fit the data. This section describes the results of these studies.

In empirical tests of the CAPM, the returns of low-beta stocks are much too high relative to its predictions, and the returns of high-beta stocks are much too low. More importantly, a number of stock characteristics explain historical average returns much better than the CAPM beta does. These characteristics include, among others, the firm's market capitalization; that is, the market value of the firm's outstanding shares, the ratio of the firm's market value to book value or **market-to-book ratio**, and **momentum**, defined as the stock's return over the previous six months.[30] Interestingly, investment funds exist to exploit all three characteristics. For example, Dimensional Fund Advisors is perhaps the most famous fund to exploit what has come to be known as the small firm effect. The current interpretation of these empirical findings, discussed in greater depth below, is that the CAPM does not properly describe the relation between risk and expected return.

Can the CAPM Really Be Tested?

Applications and tests of the CAPM require the use of market proxies like the S&P 500 because, as noted earlier, the exact composition of the market portfolio is unobservable. In an influential article, Roll (1977) pointed out that the unobservability of the market portfolio made the CAPM inherently untestable. As such, previous tests that used proxies for the market provided almost no evidence that could lead one to either accept or reject the CAPM. Roll's logic was as follows:

1. A portfolio always exists with the property that the expected returns of all securities are related linearly to their betas, calculated with respect to that portfolio. (Equation 5.4 shows this is a mean-variance efficient or tangency portfolio.)
2. Even if the theory is wrong, the portfolio used as a market proxy may turn out to be mean-variance efficient, in which case, the tests will incorrectly support the theory.
3. Alternatively, the proxy may be not be mean-variance efficient even though the theory is correct, in which case, the theory is incorrectly rejected.

---

[30]Momentum investment strategies that use returns from anytime in the past 3 months to the past 12 months seem to work about equally well. The choice of 6 months for our discussion is arbitrary.

Applications of the CAPM in corporate finance and portfolio management share this problem of observability with the tests. Is it possible to apply the models if they cannot be tested and their most crucial components cannot be observed?

Although academics have debated whether the CAPM is testable without arriving at a consensus, the models are applied by practitioners, using various portfolios as proxies for the market. In these industry applications, appropriate expected returns are obtained from any market proxy that is mean-variance efficient, whether the CAPM actually holds or, equivalently, whether the "true" market portfolio is mean-variance efficient. Therefore, the appropriateness of the various applications of the CAPM rests not on whether the CAPM actually holds, but on whether the S&P 500, or whatever market proxy one uses to apply the CAPM, is mean-variance efficient. Purported tests of the CAPM that use these proxies for the market are in fact tests of the mean-variance efficiency of the proxies and are of interest for exactly this reason.

We summarize this discussion as follows:

Result 5.9   Testing the CAPM may be problematic because the market portfolio is not directly observable. Applications of the theories use various proxies for the market. Although the results of empirical tests of the CAPM that use these proxies cannot be considered conclusive, they provide valuable insights about the appropriateness of the theory as implemented with the specific proxies used in the test.

Example 5.12 illustrates why it is important to test the CAPM using proxy portfolios that are applied in practice.

Example 5.12:   Using a Proxy to Estimate the Cost of Capital

Upstart Industries would like to obtain an estimate of the expected rate of return on its stock. Analysts estimate that the stock's beta with respect to the S&P 500 is about 1, and the expected rate of return on the S&P 500 is estimated to be 9.5 percent. Is the expected return on Upstart Industries' stock 9.5 percent?

Answer: If the S&P 500 is a mean-variance efficient portfolio, 9.5 percent is a good estimate of Upstart's expected return, regardless of whether the CAPM is correct. If the S&P 500 is not mean-variance efficient, the estimate will not be valid.

Most tests of the CAPM used the value-weighted portfolio of all NYSE and AMEX stocks as a proxy for the market portfolio. This value-weighted portfolio is highly correlated with the S&P 500 stock index described earlier. If empirical tests strongly reject the mean-variance efficiency of the value-weighted portfolio, then you must be skeptical of applications that use similar portfolios (e.g., S&P 500) to calculate expected returns. However, if these same tests provide strong support for the model, then you can be comfortable with applications that use the S&P 500.

Our view of this debate is that if the true picture of the world is that the portfolio used as a market proxy is mean-variance efficient, then even if the theory is wrong—Roll's situation (2)—we can throw out the CAPM and use the proxy even if there is no initially apparent theoretical justification for its use. The danger is that a hunt for a mean-variance efficient proxy, which is based largely on empirical fit and not on sound theoretical footing, is unlikely to have the same fit in the future. However, some balance between theory and fit may be the best we can do.[31]

---

[31]This will be discussed further in Chapter 6 where inquiries into efficiency are a bit less dismal than those presented here.

Is the Value-Weighted Market Index Mean-Variance Efficient?

To understand the nature of the various tests of the CAPM, it is useful to first contrast the model with the empirical tests that use historical data. The CAPM provides predictions about how the expected rates of return of securities relate to their betas. Unfortunately, the analyst does not observe either the expected returns or the betas. The tests assume that in large samples the average historical return of each stock approximates its expected return and the estimated betas approximate the true betas. Of course, the CAPM will not hold exactly with these estimated betas and estimated expected returns. Research on the CAPM performs statistical tests to determine whether the observed deviations from the model occurred because of estimation error (e.g., the averages of the realized returns may have been very different from the expected returns) or because the model was wrong.

Cross-Sectional Tests of the CAPM

In the early 1970s, extensive tests were conducted to determine if the CAPM was consistent with the observed distribution of the returns of NYSE-listed stocks. One of the earliest procedures used to test the CAPM involved a two-step approach developed by Fama and MacBeth (1973). First, betas were estimated with a set of time-series regressions, one for each security. (In a **time series regression**, each data observation corresponds to a date in time; for example, the returns on IBM stock and the S&P 500 in January 1997 might be the respective left-hand-side and right-hand-side values for a single observation.) Each of these regressions, one for each security j, can be represented by the equation:

$$r_{jt} = \alpha_j + \beta_j R_{Mt} + \epsilon_{jt} \tag{5.9}$$

where

α_j = the regression's intercept

β_j = the regression's slope coefficient

r_{jt} = the month t return of stock j

R_{Mt} = the month t return of the value-weighted portfolio of NYSE and

AMEX stocks

ϵ_{jt} = the month t regression residual for stock j

Exhibit 5.11 on page 180 graphs the data and line of best fit for a beta regression involving the returns of Dell Computer stock, using the quarterly data from the end of 1991 through the end of 1995 (see Example 5.11). The slope of the line of best fit is the beta.[32]

The second step obtains estimates of the intercept and slope coefficient of a single **cross-sectional regression**, in which each data observation corresponds to a stock. (For example, IBM's average return and beta might be the respective left and right hand side values for a single observation.)[33] This equation can be represented algebraically as:

$$\bar{r}_j = \gamma_0 + \gamma_1 \hat{\beta}_j + \gamma_2 CHAR_j + \delta_j \tag{5.10}$$

---

[32]To list the large volume of data in Example 5.11, we used quarterly data. In practice, monthly or even weekly return data would be better.

[33]Fama and MacBeth (1973) used an innovative procedure to overcome a bias in statistical inference arising from correlated residuals in the cross-sectional regression. This involves running one cross-sectional regression for each observation in time, and averaging the slope coefficients. Also, these researchers ran their tests on beta-grouped portfolios rather than on individual stocks.

EXHIBIT 5.11   Dell Computer: Quarterly Returns (Dec. 31, 1991–Dec. 29, 1995)

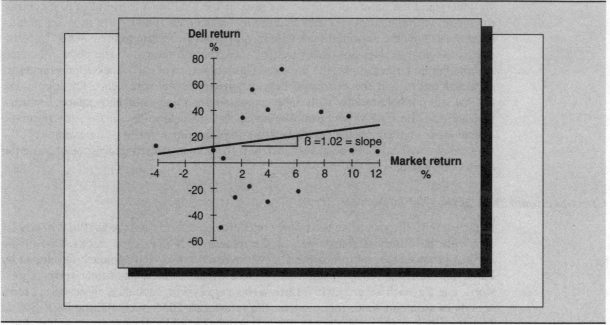

where

$\bar{r}_j$ = average monthly historical return of stock j, each j representing a NYSE-listed stock

$\hat{\beta}_j$ = estimated slope coefficient from the time series regression described in equation (5.9)

CHAR$_j$ = a characteristic of stock j unrelated to the CAPM, like firm size

γ's = intercepts and slope coefficients of the regression

δ_j = stock j regression residual

If the CAPM is true, the second step regression, equation (5.10), should have the following features:

• The intercept, γ_0 should be the risk-free return.
• The slope, γ_1, should be the market portfolio's risk premium.
• γ_2 should be zero since variables other than beta (e.g., return variance or firm size), represented as CHAR$_j$, should not explain the mean returns once beta is accounted for.

Exhibit 5.12, which illustrates hypothetical data and fit for the cross-sectional regression, is indicative of data that is consistent with the CAPM. In particular, the intercept is the risk-free return and the slope is the risk premium of the market portfolio. In contrast, the four panels in Exhibit 5.13 portray data that are inconsistent with the theory. In panel A, the intercept is wrong; in panel B, the slope is wrong; in panel C, securities appear to lie on a curve rather than on a line; in panel D, the deviations of the mean returns from the securities market line are plotted against firm size. The evidence of a relationship between returns (after accounting for beta) and firm size would imply rejection of the CAPM.

EXHIBIT 5.12 Second Step Regression Data Consistent with the CAPM

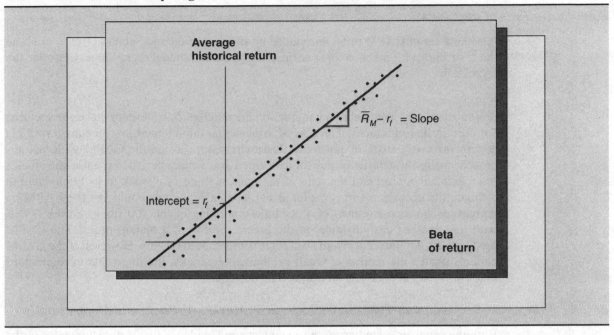

EXHIBIT 5.13 Second Step Regression Data Inconsistent with the CAPM

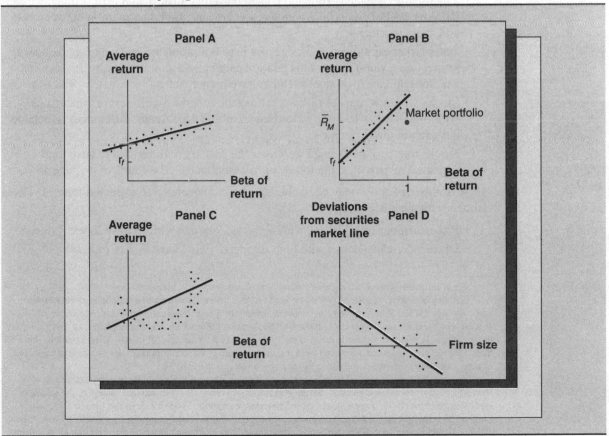

Time-Series Tests of the CAPM

A second set of CAPM tests, introduced by Black, Jensen and Scholes (1972), examine the restrictions on the intercepts of time-series market model regressions. Consider the regression:

$$r_{jt} - r_f = \alpha_j + \beta_j(R_{Mt} - r_f) + z_{jt} \qquad (5.11)$$

It is substantially identical to the regression in equation (5.9)[34] except that excess returns are used in lieu of returns. The CAPM implies that the intercept, α_j, in equation (5.11) is zero for every stock or portfolio. Researchers have tested the CAPM with this approach, using the returns of portfolios formed from characteristics such as the stock's prior beta, firm size, and the ratio of the market value of a stock to its book value to estimate the coefficients in equation (5.11). For example, one could test the CAPM by regressing the excess returns of a portfolio consisting of the 100 stocks on the NYSE with the smallest capitalization on the excess returns of a market proxy. The CAPM predicts that the intercepts from such regressions should be zero. However, if the CAPM underestimates the returns of small-capitalization stocks, the intercepts in regressions that involve small company stocks, will be positive.

Results of the Cross-Sectional and Time-Series Tests: Size, Market-to-Book, and Momentum

Both the time-series and cross-sectional tests find evidence that is not supportive of the CAPM. The following are the most noteworthy violations of the CAPM:

- The relation between estimated beta and average historical return is much weaker than the CAPM suggests. Some researchers have found no relation between beta and average returns.[35]
- The market capitalization or size of a firm is a predictor of its average historical return (see Exhibit 5.14). This relation cannot be accounted for by the fact that smaller capitalization stocks tend to have higher betas.[36]
- Stocks with low market-to-book ratios tend to have higher returns than stocks with high market-to-book ratios (see Exhibit 5.15). Again, differences in beta do not explain this difference.
- Stocks that have performed well over the past six months tend to have high expected returns over the following six months (see Exhibit 5.16 on page 184).

A number of additional stock characteristics are related to expected returns. These characteristics include:

- Price/earnings ratios (firms with high price/earnings ratios have lower returns)
- Dividend yields (stocks with high-dividend yields have higher returns)

---

[34]Betas estimated from both regressions are almost always nearly identical.

[35]Kothari, Shanken, and Sloan (1995) pointed out that the relation between beta and expected return is much stronger when using annual returns instead of monthly returns to estimate betas. Moreover, they argued that the data used to measure market-to-book ratios presents an inaccurate picture of true expected returns because the data vendor is more likely to provide data on successful firms—what is called "backfill bias." However, as Fama and French (1996) countered, size is still an important determinant of expected returns in Kothari, Shanken, and Sloan's data, which violates the CAPM.

[36]The fact that small capitalization stocks have historically outperformed large capitalization stocks seems to be an international phenomena. For example, Ziemba (1991) found that in Japan, the smallest stocks outperformed the largest stocks by 1.2 percent per month, 1965–1987. In the United Kingdom, Levis (1985) found that small capitalization stocks outperformed large capitalization stocks by 0.4 percent, 1958–1982. However, one of the biggest size premiums was in Australia, where Brown et al. (1983) found a premium of 5.73 percent per month from 1958 to 1981.

EXHIBIT 5.14   **Average Annualized Returns, Beta, and Firm Size for Value-Weighted Portfolios of NYSE and AMEX Stocks**
Formed on the Basis of Market Capitalization (Apr. 1951–Dec. 1989)

Size Portfolio	Annualized Mean Return (percent)	Beta	Market Capitalization ($millions)
Smallest	19.8%	1.17	9.7
2	17.8	1.19	23.2
3	16.1	1.15	41.4
4	15.4	1.17	68.0
5	16.0	1.11	109.8
6	14.5	1.05	178.9
7	14.4	1.04	291.4
8	14.8	1.03	502.3
9	13.0	1.01	902.1
Largest	11.9	0.95	3983.0

Source: Reprinted from Gabriel Hawawini and Donald Keim, "On the Predictability of Common Stock Returns, World Wide Evidence," 1995, Chapter 17 in *Handbooks in Operations Research and Management Science,* Vol. 9, *Finance,* edited by R. Jarrow, V. Maximovic, and W. Ziemba, with kind permission of Elsevier Science-NL, Sara Burgerhartstreet 25, 1055 KV Amsterdam, The Netherlands.

EXHIBIT 5.15   **Average Annualized Returns, Market-to-Book Ratios (ME/BE), Beta, and Firm Size for Value-Weighted Portfolios of NYSE and AMEX Stocks**
Formed on the Basis of the Ratio of Market Price/Book Price
(Apr. 1962–Dec. 1989)

ME/BE Portfolio	Annualized Mean Return (percent)	Beta	Market Capitalization ($millions)
Negative	19.9%	1.29	118.6
Lowest > 0	17.9	1.04	260.5
2	17.5	0.95	401.2
3	13.0	0.90	619.5
4	13.4	0.83	667.7
5	11.5	0.90	641.1
6	9.8	0.91	834.6
7	10.3	0.98	752.3
8	11.2	1.02	813.0
9	10.2	1.11	1000.8
Highest	10.9	1.05	1429.8

Source: Reprinted from Gabriel Hawawini and Donald Keim, "On the Predictability of Common Stock Returns, World Wide Evidence," 1995, Chapter 17 in *Handbooks in Operations Research and Management Science,* Vol. 9, *Finance,* edited by R. Jarrow, V. Maximovic, and W. Ziemba, with kind permission of Elsevier Science-NL, Sara Burgerhartstreet 25, 1055 KV Amsterdam, The Netherlands.

- Long-term contrarian strategies (DeBondt and Thaler (1985) found that stocks that did poorly over a three- to five-year period do especially well up to five years in the future)

EXHIBIT 5.16   Average Annualized for Returns for Portfolios Grouped by Six-Month Momentum and Held for Six Months
(Jan. 1965–Dec. 1989)

Momentum-Ranked Portfolio (by decile)	Average Annualized Returns (percent)
Portfolio 1 (minimum momentum)	9.48%
Portfolio 2	13.44
Portfolio 3	15.00
Portfolio 4	14.88
Portfolio 5	15.36
Portfolio 6	16.08
Portfolio 7	16.32
Portfolio 8	17.16
Portfolio 9	18.36
Portfolio 10 (maximum momentum)	20.88
Portfolio 10 minus Portfolio 1	11.40

Source: Reprinted with permission from *The Journal of Finance,* Narasimhan Jegadeesh and Sheridan Titman, "Returns to Buying Winners and Selling Losers: Implications for Stock Market Efficiency," Vol. 48, pp. 65–91.

Fama and French (1992) claimed that after accounting for expected returns based on a stock's capitalization and its market-to-book ratio, the stocks' betas, and the other characteristics—price/earnings ratios and long-term past returns—have almost no ability to explain expected returns across stocks.[37]

Indeed, there may be a negative relation between beta and stock returns after controlling for firm size (more precisely, capitalization). The top row of Exhibit 5.17 presents the returns of three portfolios, the value-weighted portfolio of all stocks (left column), a value-weighted portfolio of stocks ranked by beta in the lowest decile (middle column), and a portfolio of stocks ranked by beta in the highest decile (right column). The figures presented in this row reveal that portfolios of low-beta stocks had returns that were slightly higher than the returns of high-beta stocks. When the portfolios include only small capitalization stocks (middle row), the results are essentially the same, that is, low beta implies only slightly higher returns. However, for the large capitalization stocks (bottom row), there is a large penalty associated with beta. Large capitalization stocks with high betas realized very poor returns over the 1963–1990 time period.

Exhibit 5.18 provides the monthly returns of nine portfolios formed on the basis of capitalization and market-to-book ratios (ME/BE). Reading across the first row, one

---

[37]There is also a size-related "January effect" documented in empirical research by Keim (1983, 1986), Reinganum (1983), and Roll (1982–1983). They have shown that small capitalization firms earn "exceptionally large returns" at the beginning of January each year. There is also evidence suggesting that short-term contrarian strategies realize positive abnormal returns. For the short-horizon returns, Jegadeesh (1990) and Lehmann (1990) found that strategies that pick stocks that did poorly over the past month or week do well in the following month or week.

We believe that shorter horizon return reversals provide evidence on market liquidity, and that large buy and sell orders tend to temporarily move prices away from their fundamental values, perhaps providing opportunities for short-term traders who can profit when the short-term losers bounce back. However, we do not believe that the analysis of the short-term return reversals reveal much about what determines expected rates of return.

EXHIBIT 5.17   Average Annualized Returns Based on Size and Beta Groupings
(July 1963–Dec. 1990)

	All Firms (%)	Low Betas (%)	High Betas (%)
All firms	15.0%	16.1%	13.7%
Small cap firms	18.2	20.5	17.0
Large cap firms	10.7	12.1	6.7

Source: Reprinted with permission from *The Journal of Political Economy,* "The Cross-section of Expected Stock Returns," by Eugene Fama and Kenneth R. French, pp. 425–465, © 1992 by the University of Chicago.

EXHIBIT 5.18   Average Annualized Returns (%) Sorted by Size and Market Equity/Book Equity
(July 1963–Dec. 1990)

	All Firms (%)	High ME/BE (%)	Low ME/BE (%)
All firms	14.8%	7.7%	19.6%
Small cap firms	17.6	8.4	23.0
Large cap firms	10.7	11.2	14.2

Source: Reprinted with permission from *The Journal of Political Economy,* "The Cross-section of Expected Stock Returns," by Eugene Fama and Kenneth R. French, pp. 425–465, © 1992 by the University of Chicago.

sees that for the sample of all firms, low market-to-book stocks realize much higher returns than high market-to-book stocks. However, the lower two rows show that the effect of market-to-book ratios on stock returns is substantially stronger for the small cap firms. What Exhibit 5.18 shows is that an investor who bought and held small capitalization stocks with low market-to-book ratios would have realized a yearly return of close to 23 percent. Compounded over time, a $1,000 investment made at the beginning of 1963 would grow at a 23 percent annual rate, to about $267,000 by the end of 1989.[38]

Result 5.10 summarizes the results of this subsection:

Result 5.10   Research using historical data indicates that cross-sectional differences in stock returns are related to three characteristics: market capitalization, market-to-book ratios, and momentum. Controlling for these factors, these studies find no relation between the CAPM beta and returns over this time period.

Interpreting the CAPM's Empirical Shortcomings

There are two explanations for the poor ability of the CAPM to explain average stock returns. The first explanation has to do with the possibility that the various proxies for the market portfolio do not fully capture all of the relevant risk factors in the economy. According to this explanation, firm characteristics, such as size and market-to-book ratios, are highly correlated with the sensitivities of stocks to risk factors not captured by proxies for the market portfolio. For example, Jagannathan and Wang (1996)

---

[38]This assumes that 23 percent is the growth rate each year. If there is variation in the growth rate, but the average is 23 percent, one ends up with much less than $267,000 at the end of 1989. See the appendix to Chapter 10 for further discussion of the impact of growth rate variation on long-term growth.

suggested that **human capital**—that is, the present value of a person's future wages—is an important component of the market portfolio that is not included in the various market portfolio proxies. Since investors would like to ensure against the possibility of losing their jobs, they are willing to accept a lower rate of return on those stocks that do relatively well in the event of layoffs.[39] In addition, if investors believe that large firms are likely to benefit more or be harmed less than small firms from economic factors that lead to increased layoffs or wage reductions, then they may prefer investing in the larger stocks of the large firms even if the expected returns of large firms are lower.

A second explanation of the CAPM's poor performance is that it is simply a false theory because investors have behavioral biases against classes of stocks that have nothing to do with the mean and marginal risk of the returns on stocks. The smaller capitalization stocks and stocks with lower market-to-book ratios may require a higher expected rate of return if investors shy away from them for behavioral reasons. For example, firms with low market-to-book ratios are generally considered to have poor prospects. Indeed, that is why their market values are so low relative to their book values. By contrast, firms with high market-to-book ratios are considered to be those with the brightest futures.

One behavioral explanation for the higher returns of the distressed, or near-bankrupt, firms is that some portfolio managers find it more costly to lose money on distressed firms. There used to be a saying on Wall Street that "portfolio managers can't get fired buying IBM stock." The basic argument was that if portfolio managers had bought IBM stock in the late 1970s and then lost money it wasn't really their fault. All the other professional money managers were buying IBM stock and the conventional wisdom was that the firm was doing great. Contrast this with Chrysler in the late 1970s. The newspapers were full of stories about Chrysler's imminent demise, and its stock was selling for less than $5 a share. Since it should have been obvious to anyone reading a newspaper that Chrysler was on the verge of bankruptcy, money managers who invested in Chrysler would probably be fired if Chrysler did go bankrupt. What this means is that a money manager might find it riskier, from a personal perspective, to buy a distressed stock even if the actual return distribution is no different than the stock of a financially healthy firm. If this were true, the distressed stock would require a higher expected rate of return.

A more recent situation arose with Microsoft and Apple Computer. In 1995, Microsoft came out with a new operating system which was a critical success and the newspapers were full of articles suggesting that the firm had almost unlimited growth opportunities. Apple, on the other hand, was having problems and a number of newspapers predicted its demise.

What should portfolio managers do in this situation? They may not be willing to invest in Apple, even if—understanding the risks associated with Apple—they believe that the market may have overreacted to its misfortunes. If portfolio managers buy Apple stock and it does poorly, they have to explain why they bought the stock despite all the predictions of the company's demise. On the other hand, if they buy Microsoft stock and it does poorly, they might be blamed less for the poor performance, given all the great publicity that Microsoft was having at the time the stock was purchased. Because of these more personal risks, portfolio managers may require a much higher expected return to invest in Apple than in Microsoft, even if both stocks have the same beta.

---

[39]See Mayers (1972).

A study by Lakonishok, Shleifer, and Vishny (1994), using data from April 1968 to April 1990, examined the long-term success of what they called value and glamour stocks, and reported evidence in favor of the behavioral story over the missing risk factor story. Although they do not select stocks explicitly in terms of market-to-book ratios, their value stocks are generally low market-to-book stocks and their glamour stocks are generally high market-to-book stocks.

The authors provided two important pieces of evidence suggesting that the higher returns of the value stocks are due to some kind of behavioral bias. First, value stocks tend to consistently dominate glamour stocks.[40] If hidden risk factors are driving the expected return difference, then a glamour investment strategy should occasionally beat a value strategy. It is difficult to conclude that a strategy that almost never seems to lose requires a big risk premium. Second, the story of the missing risk factor would be more credible if the value stocks performed relatively poorly during recessions, but they do not.[41]

5.12 Summary and Conclusions

This chapter analyzed various features of the mean-standard deviation diagram, developed a condition for deriving optimal portfolios, and showed that this condition has important implications for valuing financial assets. The chapter also showed that the beta used in this valuation relation, the relation between risk and expected return, is an empty concept unless it is possible to identify the tangency portfolio. The Capital Asset Pricing Model is a theory that identifies the tangency portfolio as the market portfolio, making it a powerful tool for valuing financial assets. As later chapters will illustrate, it also is useful for valuing real assets.

Valuation plays a major role in corporate finance. Part III will discuss that when firms evaluate capital investment projects, they need to come up with some estimate of the project's required rate of return. Moreover, valuation often plays a key role in determining how corporations finance their new investments. Many firms are reluctant to issue equity when they believe their equity is undervalued. To value their own equity, they need an estimate of the expected rate of return on their stock; the Capital Asset Pricing Model is currently one of the most popular methods used to determine this.

The empirical tests of the CAPM contradict its predictions. Indeed, the most recent evidence fails to find a positive relation between the CAPM beta and average rates of returns on stocks from 1960 to 1990, finding instead that stock characteristics, like firm size and market-to-book ratios, provide very good predictions of a stock's return. Does this mean that the CAPM is a useless theory?

One response to the empirical rejection of the CAPM is that there are additional aspects of risk not captured by the market proxies used in the CAPM tests. If this is the case, then the CAPM should be used, but augmented with additional factors that capture those aspects of risk. Chapter 6, which discusses multifactor models, considers this possibility. The other possibility is that the model is fundamentally unsound and that investors do not act nearly as rational as the theory suggests. If this is the case, however, investors should find beta estimates even more valuable because they can be used to construct portfolios that have relatively low risk without giving up anything in the way of expected return.

This chapter provides a unique treatment of the CAPM in its concentration on the more general proposition that the CAPM "works" as a useful financial tool if its market proxy is a mean-variance efficient portfolio and does not work if the proxy is a dominated portfolio. The empirical evidence to date has suggested that the proxies used for the CAPM appear to be dominated. This does not

---

[40]Lakonishok, Shleifer, and Vishny formed value and glamour portfolios in each year between 1968 and 1989 and tracked the performance of the portfolios for the next 1, 3, or 5 years. For every formation year, the value portfolio was worth more than the glamour portfolio after five years. In other words, in this 21-year period, a patient investor would always do better with a value strategy than with a glamour strategy.

[41]Four recessions—December 1969 to November 1970, November 1973 to March 1975, January 1980 to July 1980, and July 1981 to November 1982—took place during the study's sample period. The authors found that value stocks do well during recessions and beat the glamour stocks in three out of four of those recessions.

preclude the possibility that some modification of the proxy may ultimately prove to be useful. As you will see in Chapter 6, research along these lines currently appears to be making great strides.

We also should stress that testing the CAPM requires examining data in the fairly distant past, to a period prior to when Wall Street professionals, portfolio managers, and corporations used the CAPM. However, corporations that are interested in valuing either investment projects or their own stocks have no interest in the historical relevance of the CAPM; they are interested only in whether the model provides good current estimates of required rates of return. As economists, we like to think that investors act as if they are trained in the nuances of modern

portfolio theory even though beta was a relatively unknown Greek letter to the Wall Street of the 1960s. As educators, however, we like to believe that we do make a difference and that our teaching and research has made a difference. Given those beliefs, we at least want to entertain the possibility that current required rates of return reflect the type of risk suggested by the CAPM, even if rates of return did not reflect this type of risk in the past.[42]

---

[42]Some evidence of this is that the size effect has greatly diminished, if it has not disappeared entirely, since the early 1980s, when practitioners began to focus on the academic research in this subject.

Key Concepts

Result 5.1: All portfolios on the mean-variance efficient frontier can be formed as a weighted average of any two portfolios (or funds) on the efficient frontier.

Result 5.2: Under the assumptions of mean-variance analysis, and assuming the existence of a risk-free asset, all investors will select portfolios on the capital market line.

Result 5.3: The ratio of the risk premium of every stock and portfolio to its covariance with the tangency portfolio is constant; that is, denoting the return of the tangency portfolio as $\tilde{R}_T$:

$$\frac{\bar{r}_i - r_f}{cov(\tilde{r}_i, \tilde{R}_T)}$$

is identical for all stocks.

Result 5.4: The beta of a portfolio is a portfolio-weighted average of the betas of its individual securities, that is:

$$\beta_p = \sum_{i=1}^{N} x_i \beta_i$$

where

$$\beta_i = \frac{cov(\tilde{r}_i, \tilde{R}_T)}{var(\tilde{R}_T)}$$

Result 5.5: If a stock and its tracking portfolio have the same *marginal variance* with respect to the tangency portfolio, then the stock and its tracking portfolio must have the same *expected return*. This applies only when the marginal variance is computed with respect to an efficient portfolio. Marginal variances computed with respect to

dominated portfolios have no implications for expected returns.

Result 5.6: Under the assumptions of the CAPM, and if a risk-free asset exists, the market portfolio is the tangency portfolio and, by equation (5.4), the expected returns of assets are determined by:

$$\bar{r} - r_f = \beta(\bar{R}_M - r_f) \qquad (5.8)$$

where $\bar{R}_M$ is the mean return of the market portfolio, and β is the beta computed against the return of the market portfolio.

Result 5.7: Under the assumptions of the CAPM, if a risk-free asset exists, every investor should optimally hold a combination of the market portfolio and a risk-free asset.

Result 5.8: Betas estimated from standard regression packages may not provide the best estimates of a stock's true beta. Better beta estimates can be obtained by taking into account the lead-lag effect in stock returns and the fact that relatively high beta estimates tend to be overestimates and relatively low beta estimates tend to be underestimates.

Result 5.9: Testing the CAPM may be problematic because the market portfolio is not directly observable. Applications of the theories use various proxies for the market. Although the results of empirical tests of the CAPM that use these proxies cannot be considered conclusive, they provide valuable insights about the appropriateness of the theory as implemented with the specific proxies used in the test.

Result 5.10: Research using historical data indicates that cross-sectional differences in stock returns are related to three characteristics: market capitalization, market-to-book ratios, and momentum. Controlling for these factors, these studies find no relation between the CAPM beta and returns over this time period.

Key Terms

Exercises

5.1. Here are some general questions and instructions to test your understanding of the mean standard deviation diagram.
   a. Draw a mean-standard deviation diagram to illustrate combinations of a risky asset and the risk-free asset.
   b. Extend this concept to a diagram of the risk-free asset and all possible risky portfolios.
   c. Why does one line, the capital market line, dominate all other possible portfolio combinations?
   d. Label the capital market line and tangency portfolio.
   e. What condition must hold at the tangency portfolio?

Exercises 5.2–5.9 make use of the following information about the mean returns and covariances for three computer software stocks. The numbers used are hypothetical.

Stock	Covariance with			Mean Return
	Netscape	Microsoft	Novell	
Netscape	.002	.001	0	15%
Microsoft	.001	.002	.001	12
Novell	0	.001	.002	10

5.2. Compute the tangency portfolio weights assuming a risk-free asset yields 5 percent.

5.3. How does your answer to exercise 5.2 change if the risk-free rate is 3 percent? 7 percent?

5.4. Draw a mean-standard deviation diagram and plot Netscape, Microsoft, and Novell on this diagram as well as the three tangency portfolios found in exercises 5.2 and 5.3.

5.5. Show that an equally weighted portfolio of Netscape, Microsoft, and Novell can be improved upon with marginal variance-marginal mean analysis.

5.6. Repeat exercises 5.2 and 5.3, but use a spreadsheet to solve for the tangency portfolio weights of Netscape, Microsoft, and Novell in the three cases. The solution of the system of equations requires you to invert the matrix of covariances above, then post multiply the inverted covariance matrix by the column of risk premia. The solution should be a column of cells, which needs to be rescaled so that the weights sum to 1. *Hint:* See footnote 12.

5.7. a. Compute the betas of Netscape, Microsoft, and Novell with respect to the tangency portfolio found in exercise 5.2.
   b. Then compute the beta of an equally weighted portfolio of the three stocks.

5.8. Using the fact that the hyperbolic boundary of the feasible set of the three stocks is generated by any two portfolios:

    a. Find the boundary portfolio that is uncorrelated with the tangency portfolio in exercise 5.2.

    b. What is the covariance with the tangency portfolio of all inefficient portfolios that have the same mean return as the portfolio found in part *a*?

5.9. What is the covariance of the return of the tangency portfolio from exercise 5.2 with the return of all portfolios that have the same expected return as Netscape?

5.10. Using a spreadsheet, compute the minimum variance and tangency portfolios for the universe of three stocks described below. Assume the risk-free return is 5 percent. Hypothetical data necessary for this calculation are provided in the table below. See exercise 5.6 for detailed instructions.

Stock	Standard Deviation	Mean Return	Correlation with Bell South	Correlation with Caterpillar
Apple	.20	.15	.8	−.1
Bell South	.30	.10	1.0	.2
Caterpillar	.25	.12	.2	1.0

5.11. The Alumina Corporation has the following simplified balance sheet (based on market values)

Assets	Liabilities and Equity
$10 billion	Debt $6 billion
	Common Stock $4 billion

    a. The debt of Alumina, being risk-free, earns the risk-free return of 6 percent per year. The equity of Alumina has a mean return of 12 percent per year, a standard deviation of 30 percent per year, and a beta of .9. Compute the mean return, beta, and standard deviation of the assets of Alumina. *Hint:* View the assets as a portfolio of the debt and equity.

    b. If the CAPM holds, what is the mean return of the market portfolio?

    c. How does your answer to part *a* change if the debt is risky, has returns with a mean of 7 percent, has a standard deviation of 10 percent, a beta of .2, and has a correlation of .3 with the return of the common stock of Alumina?

5.12. The following are the returns for Exxon and the corresponding returns of the S&P 500 market index for each month in 1994.

Month	Exxon Return (%)	S&P 500 Return (%)
January	5.35%	3.35%
February	−1.36	−2.70
March	−3.08	−4.35
April	0.00	1.30
May	−1.64	1.63
June	−7.16	−2.47
July	4.85	3.31
August	1.21	4.07
September	−3.36	−2.41
October	9.35	2.29
November	−2.78	−3.67
December	0.62	1.46

Using a spreadsheet, compute Exxon's beta. Then apply the Bloomberg adjustment to derive the adjusted beta.

5.13. What value must ACYOU Corporation's expected return be in Example 5.4 to prevent us from forming a combination of Henry's portfolio, ACME, ACYOU, and the risk-free asset that is mean-variance superior to Henry's portfolio?

References and Additional Readings

Banz, Rolf W. "The Relationship between Return and Market Value of Common Stocks." *Journal of Financial Economics* 9 (1981), pp. 3–18.

Basu, Sanjay. "The Relationship between Earnings Yield, Market Value, and Return for NYSE Common Stocks: Further Evidence." *Journal of Financial Economics* 12 (1983), pp. 129–56.

Black, Fischer. "Capital Market Equilibrium with Restricted Borrowing." *Journal of Business* 45 (1972), pp. 444–55.

Black, Fischer; Michael C. Jensen; and Myron Scholes. "The Capital Asset Pricing Model: Some Empirical Tests." In *Studies in the Theory of Capital Markets,* M. Jensen, ed. New York: Praeger, 1972.

Bodie, Zvi; Alex Kane; and Alan Marcus. *Investments.* 3d ed. Burr Ridge, IL: Richard D. Irwin, 1996.

Breeden, Douglas. "An Intertemporal Asset Pricing Model with Stochastic Consumption and Investment Opportunities." *Journal of Financial Economics* 7 (1979), pp. 265–96.

Brennan, Michael. "Capital Market Equilibrium with Divergent Lending and Borrowing Rates." *Journal of Financial and Quantitative Analysis* 6 (1971), pp. 1197–1205.

———. "Taxes, Market Valuation and Corporate Financial Policy." *National Tax Journal* 23, December (1970), pp. 417–27.

Brown, Philip; Allan Kleidon; and Terry Marsh. "New Evidence on Size-Related Anomalies in Stock Prices." *Journal of Financial Economics* 12, no. 1 (1983), pp. 33–56.

Chan, K. C., and Nai-fu Chen. "An Unconditional Asset Pricing Test and the Role of Firm Size as an Instrumental Variable for Risk." *Journal of Finance* 43 (1988), pp. 309–25.

Chan, Louis K.; Yasushi Hamao; and Josef Lakonishok. "Fundamentals and Stock Returns in Japan." *Journal of Finance* 46 (1991), pp. 1739–89.

Constantinides, George, and A. G. Malliaris. "Portfolio Theory." Chapter 1 in *Handbooks in Operations Research and Management Science*. Vol. 9, *Finance*. Robert Jarrow, V. Maksimovic, and W. Ziemba, eds. Amsterdam: Elsevier Science Publishers, 1995.

DeBondt, Werner, and Richard Thaler. "Does the Stock Market Overreact?" *Journal of Finance* 40 (1985), pp. 793–805.

Dimson, Elroy. "Risk Measurement When Shares Are Subject to Infrequent Trading." *Journal of Financial Economics* 7, no. 2 (1979), pp. 197–226.

Fama, Eugene. *Foundations of Finance*. New York: Basic Books, 1976.

Fama, Eugene, and Kenneth R. French. "The CAPM Is Wanted, Dead or Alive." *Journal of Finance,* 51, no. 5 (1996), pp. 1947–58.

———. "The Cross-Section of Expected Stock Returns." *Journal of Finance* 47 (1992), pp. 427–65.

Fama, Eugene, and James MacBeth. "Risk, Return, and Equilibrium: Empirical Tests." *Journal of Political Economy* 81 (1973), pp. 607–36.

Firstenberg, Paul; Stephen Ross; and Randall Zisler. "Real Estate: The Whole Story." *Journal of Portfolio Management* 14 (1988), pp. 22–34.

Grinblatt, Mark. "An Analytic Solution for Interest Rate Swap Spreads." Working paper, University of California at Los Angeles, 1995.

Handa, Puneet; S. P. Kothari; and Charles Wasley. "The Relation between the Return Interval and Betas: Implications for the Size Effect." *Journal of Financial Economics* 23 (1989), pp. 79–100.

Hawawini, Gabriel, and Donald Keim. "On the Predictability of Common Stock Returns: World Wide Evidence." Chapter 17 in *Handbooks in Operations Research and Management Science*. Vol. 9, *Finance,* Robert Jarrow, V. Maximovic, and W. Ziemba, eds. Amsterdam: Elsevier Science Publishers, 1995.

Ibbotson, Roger, and Rex Sinquefeld. *Stocks, Bonds, Bills, and Inflation*. Chicago, IL: Ibbotson Associates, 1996.

Jagannathan, Ravi, and Zhenyu Wang. "The Conditional CAPM and the Cross-Section of Expected Returns." *Journal of Finance* 51, no. 1 (March 1996), pp. 3–53.

Jegadeesh, Narasimhan. "Does Market Risk Really Explain the Size Effect? *Journal of Financial and Quantitative Analysis* 27 (1992), pp. 337–51.

———. "Evidence of Predictable Behavior of Security Returns." *Journal of Finance* 45, no. 3 (1990), pp. 881–98.

Jegadeesh, Narasimhan, and Sheridan Titman. "Returns to Buying Winners and Selling Losers: Implications for Stock Market Efficiency." *Journal of Finance* 48 (1993), pp. 65–91.

Keim, Donald. "Size-Related Anomalies and Stock Return Seasonality: Further Empirical Evidence." *Journal of Financial Economics* 12 (1983), pp. 13–32.

———. "The CAPM and Equity Return Regularities." *Financial Analysts Journal* 42, no. 3 (1986), pp. 19–34.

Kothari, S. P.; Jay Shanken; and Richard G. Sloan. "Another Look at the Cross-Section of Expected Stock Returns." *Journal of Finance* 50, no. 1 (1995), pp. 185–224.

Lakonishok, Josef, and Alan C. Shapiro. "Systematic Risk, Total Risk, and Size as Determinants of Stock Market Returns." *Journal of Banking and Finance* 10 (1986), pp. 115–32.

Lakonishok, Josef; Andrei Shleifer; and Robert Vishny. "Contrarian Investment, Extrapolation, and Risk." *Journal of Finance* 49, no. 5 (Dec. 1994), pp. 1541–78.

Lehmann, Bruce. "Fads, Martingales, and Market Efficiency." *Quarterly Journal of Economics* 105 (1990), pp. 1–28.

Levis, M. "Are Small Firms Big Performers?" *Investment Analyst* 76 (1985), pp. 21–27.

Lintner, John. "Security Prices, Risk, and Maximal Gains from Diversification." *Journal of Finance* 20 (1965), pp. 587–615.

Litzenberger, Robert, and Krishna Ramaswamy. "The Effect of Personal Taxes and Dividends on Capital Asset Prices: Theory and Empirical Evidence." *Journal of Financial Economics* 7 (1979), pp. 163–95.

Markowitz, Harry. *Portfolio Selection: Efficient Diversification of Investments.* New York: John Wiley, 1959.

Mayers, David. "Nonmarketable Assets and Capital Market Equilibrium under Uncertainty," in *Studies in the Theory of Capital Markets,* Michael Jensen, ed. New York: Praeger, 1972.

Merton, Robert. "An Intertemporal Capital Asset Pricing Model. *Econometrica* 41 (1973), pp. 867–87.

Reinganum, Marc R. "A Misspecification of Capital Asset Pricing: Empirical Anomalies Based on Earnings, Yields, and Market Values." *Journal of Financial Economics* 9 (1981), pp. 19–46.

———. "The Anomalous Stock Market Behavior of Small Firms in January: Empirical Tests for Tax-Loss Selling Effects." *Journal of Financial Economics* 12 (1983), pp. 89–104.

Roll, Richard W. "Vas Ist Das?" *Journal of Portfolio Management* 9 (1982–1983), pp. 18–28.

———. "A Critique of the Asset Pricing Theory's Tests; Part I: On Past and Potential Testability of the Theory." *Journal of Financial Economics* 4, no. 2 (1977), pp. 129–76.

Rosenberg, Barr; Kenneth Reid; and Ronald Lanstein. "Persuasive Evidence of Market Inefficiency." *Journal of Portfolio Management* 11 (1985), pp. 9–17.

Scholes, Myron, and Joseph Williams. "Estimating Betas from Nonsynchronous Data." *Journal of Financial Economics* 5, no. 3 (1977), pp. 309–27.

Sharpe, William. "Capital Asset Prices: A Theory of Market Equilibrium under Conditions of Risk." *Journal of Finance* 19 (1964), pp. 425–42.

———. *Portfolio Theory and Capital Markets.* New York: McGraw-Hill, 1970.

Stattman, Dennis. "Book Values and Stock Returns." *Chicago MBA: A Journal of Selected Papers* 4 (1980), pp. 25–45.

Ziemba, William. "Japanese Security Market Regularities: Monthly, Turn-of-the-Month, and Year, Holiday and Golden Week Effects." *Japan World Econ.* 3, no. 2 (1991), pp. 119–46.

Factor Models and the Arbitrage Pricing Theory

Learning Objectives

After reading this chapter, you should be able to:

1. Decompose the variance of a security into market-related and nonmarket-related components, as well as common factor and firm-specific components, and comprehend why this variance decomposition is important for valuing financial assets.

2. Identify the expected return, factor betas, factors, and firm-specific components of a security from its factor equation.

3. Explain how the principle of diversification relates to firm-specific risk.

4. Compute the factor betas and expected return for a portfolio given the betas and expected returns of its component securities.

5. Design a portfolio with a specific configuration of factor betas in order to design pure factor portfolios, as well as portfolios that perfectly hedge an investment's endowment of factor risk.

6. State what the arbitrage pricing theory (APT) equation means and what the empirical evidence says about the APT. You also should be able to use your understanding of the APT equation to form arbitrage portfolios when the equation is violated.

In the late 1980s, the theoretical models of Wall Street investment banks revealed that the market prices of many Japanese warrants were too low relative to the prices of the common stock of these same corporations. Subsequently, the banks began to buy the undervalued Japanese warrants whose prices would rise as the Japanese stock market rose in value and vice versa.

To hedge the risk associated with their exposure to the Japanese stock market, many Wall Street banks sold futures contracts on Japanese stock indexes like the Topix or the Nikkei. In spite of these hedging activities, many of these banks still lost a lot of money. In retrospect, the banks could have avoided these losses. An analysis with factor models later revealed how the banks lost money and how they could prevent similar losses from occurring in the future.

This chapter introduces **factor models**, which are equations that break down the returns of securities into two components. A factor model specifies that the return of each risky investment is determined by:

- A relatively small number of **common factors**, which are proxies for those events in the economy that affect a large number of different investments.
- A risk component that is unique to the investment.

For example, changes in IBM's stock price can be partly attributed to a set of **macroeconomic variables**, such as changes in interest rates, inflation, and productivity, which are common factors because they affect the prices of most stocks. In addition, changes in IBM's stock price are affected by the success of new product innovations, cost-cutting efforts, a fire at a manufacturing plant, the discovery of an illegal corporate act, a management change, and so forth. These components of IBM's return are considered **firm-specific components** because they affect only that firm and not the returns of other investments.

In many important applications, it is possible to ignore the firm-specific components of the return variance of large portfolios that are not heavily concentrated in any single stock. The return variances of these portfolios are almost entirely determined by the common factors, and are virtually unaffected by the firm-specific components. Since these are the kinds of portfolios that most investors should and will hold, the risk of a security that is determined by these firm-specific components—firm-specific risk—does not affect the overall desirability or lack of desirability of these types of portfolios.

Although common factors affect the returns of numerous investments, the sensitivities of an investment's returns to the factors differ from investment to investment. For example, the stock price of an electric utility may be much more sensitive to changes in interest rates than that of a computer software firm. These **factor betas**,[1] or **factor sensitivities** as they are sometimes called, are similar to the market betas discussed in the last chapter, which also differ from stock to stock.

Factor models are useful tools for risk analysis, hedging, and portfolio management. The chapter's opening vignette illustrates why it is important to understand the multiple sources of risk that can affect an investment's return.[2] Recall that the Wall Street banks, by acquiring large positions in underpriced Japanese warrants, exposed themselves to fluctuations in the Japanese stock market. To offset this risk, they sold positions in futures on the Topix or Nikkei indexes. To determine the amount of futures to sell, the bankers computed the market betas of their warrant portfolios and sold the appropriate amount of futures so that their combined portfolios of warrants and futures would have market betas of zero.

The strategy of hedging the warrants with futures would eliminate most of the risk if Japanese stocks were sensitive to only one common factor. However, Japanese stocks, like U.S. stocks, are subject to multiple sources of **factor risk**, which is return variability generated by common factors. Some factors tend to affect large and small firms differently. Since the warrant positions were driven more by the performance of small firms and the futures position were driven more by the performance of large firms, the banks were not as well hedged as they originally had thought. The consequences of this poorly conceived hedging strategy were borne out in the late 1980s, when portfolios of large Japanese firms substantially outperformed the portfolios of small Japanese firms. As a consequence, the banks lost more money on their position in warrants than they made on futures.

---

[1]Statisticians also refer to these as factor loadings.

[2]Chapter 21 discusses risk analysis and hedging with factor models in greater depth.

To prevent these losses in the future, some Wall Street banks developed factor models to identify a factor that drives the performance of small firms. They then adjusted the weighting of the individual warrants so that the sensitivity of the portfolio of warrants to the "small firm factor" matched the sensitivity of the futures contract to the small-firm factor. Doing this substantially decreased the risk of their position.

Factor models not only describe how unexpected changes in various macroeconomic variables affect an investment's return, but they also can be used to provide estimates of the expected rate of return of an investment. Section 6.10 uses factor models to derive the **arbitrage pricing theory (APT)**, developed by Ross (1976), which relates the risk of an investment to its expected rate of return. It is termed the *arbitrage pricing theory* because it is based on the principle of no arbitrage.[3]

As a theory, the APT is applied in much the same way as the Capital Asset Pricing Model (CAPM). However, it requires less restrictive assumptions about investor behavior than the CAPM, is more amenable to empirical tests, and in many cases can be applied more easily than the CAPM. The APT has recently become more popular because of the empirical shortcomings of the CAPM described in Chapter 5. Specifically, the stocks of small capitalization firms and the stocks of companies with low market-to-book ratios generally have much higher returns than the CAPM would predict. The hope is that, with APT factors, additional aspects of risk beyond market risk can be taken into account and the high average returns of both the smaller cap stocks and the low market-to-book stocks can be explained.

Although investors often view the CAPM and the APT as competing theories, both can benefit investors as well as corporate finance practitioners. For example, the empirical evidence described at the end of Chapter 5 suggests that applications of the CAPM that use traditional market proxies, such as the S&P 500, fail to explain the cross-sectional pattern of past stock returns. The analysis of factor models in this chapter provides insights into why the CAPM failed and an alternative that would have worked much better in the past. However, the greater flexibility of the APT, which allows it to explain *past* returns much better than the CAPM, comes at a cost. Because the APT is less restrictive than the CAPM, it also provides less guidance about expected *future* rates of return.

6.1 The Market Model: The First Factor Model

The simplest possible factor model is a **one-factor model** which is a factor model with only one factor. It is often convenient to think of this one factor as the market factor and to refer to the model as the **market model**. Intuition for the CAPM is often based on the properties of the market model. However, as this section shows, the CAPM is not necessarily linked to the market model; thus, this intuition for the CAPM is often wrong.

The Market Model Regression

To understand the market model, consider the regression used to estimate market betas in Chapter 5. There we estimated beta as the slope coefficient in a regression of the return of Dell's stock on the return of the S&P 500 and pictured the regression as the

---

[3]As noted in the introduction to Part II, an **arbitrage opportunity**, essentially a money tree, is a set of trades that make money without risk.

line of best fit for the points in Exhibit 5.11. The algebraic expression for the regression is simply equation (5.9) applied specifically to Dell:

$$\tilde{r}_{\text{DELL}} = \alpha_{\text{DELL}} + \beta_{\text{DELL}}\tilde{R}_{\text{S\&P}} + \tilde{\epsilon}_{\text{DELL}} \qquad (6.1)$$

With quarterly data from the end of 1991 through 1995, the estimates are:

α_{DELL} = regression intercept = .31

β_{DELL} = regression slope coefficient (DELL's market beta) = 1.02

$\tilde{\epsilon}_{\text{DELL}}$ = regression residual, which is constructed to have a mean of zero

By the properties of regression, $\tilde{\epsilon}_{\text{DELL}}$ and $\tilde{R}_{\text{S\&P}}$ are uncorrelated.

Ignoring the constant α_{DELL}, equation (6.1) decomposes the uncertain return of Dell into two components:

- A component that can be explained by movements in the market factor. This component is the product of the beta and the S&P return.
- A component that is not due to market movements, the regression residual, $\tilde{\epsilon}_{\text{DELL}}$.

The Market Model Variance Decomposition

Because $\tilde{\epsilon}_{\text{DELL}}$ and $\tilde{R}_{\text{S\&P}}$ are uncorrelated, and because α_{DELL} is a constant that does not affect variances, the variance of the return on Dell stock can be broken down into a corresponding set of two terms[4]:

$$\sigma^2_{\text{DELL}} = var(\beta_{\text{DELL}}\tilde{R}_{\text{S\&P}}) + var(\tilde{\epsilon}_{\text{DELL}}) \qquad (6.2)$$

$$= \beta^2_{\text{DELL}}var(\tilde{R}_{\text{S\&P}}) + var(\tilde{\epsilon}_{\text{DELL}})$$

A Glossary of Risk Terms. The first term on the right-hand side of equation (6.2), $\beta^2_{\text{DELL}}var(\tilde{R}_{\text{S\&P}})$, is referred to variously as Dell's "systematic," "market," or "non-diversifiable" risk. The remaining term, $var(\tilde{\epsilon}_{\text{DELL}})$, is referred to as its "unsystematic," "nonmarket," or "diversifiable" risk.[5] We prefer to use *systematic* and *unsystematic* risk when referring to these terms; referring to these terms as *diversifiable* and *non-diversifiable* is misleading in most instances, as this chapter will show shortly. The following definitions are more precise.

1. The **systematic (market) risk** of a security is the portion of the security's return variance that is explained by market movements. The **unsystematic (nonmarket) risk** is the portion of return variance that cannot be explained by market movements.
2. **Diversifiable risk** is virtually eliminated by holding portfolios with small weights on every security (lest investors put most of their eggs in one basket). Since the weights have to sum to 1, this means that such portfolios, known as **well-diversified portfolios**, contain large numbers of securities. **Nondiversifiable risk** cannot generally be eliminated, even approximately, in portfolios with small weights on large numbers of securities.

---

[4]See the portfolio variance formula, Equation (4.9a), in Chapter 4 for more detail.

[5]Other terms that are synonymous with diversifiable are "unique risk" and "firm-specific risk." We will elaborate on the latter term shortly.

EXHIBIT 6.1   High R-Squared Regression

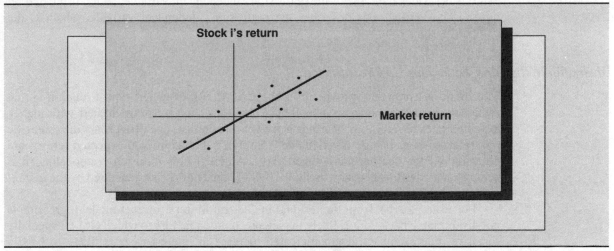

EXHIBIT 6.2   Low R-Squared Regression

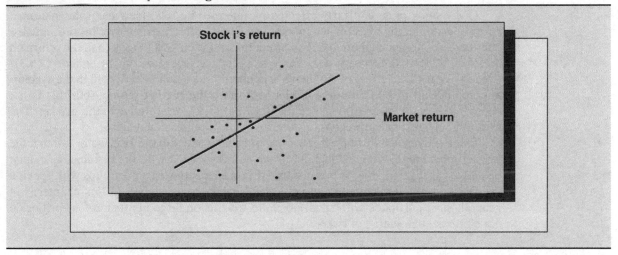

Regression R-squared and Variance Decomposition.   A commonly used statistic from the regression in equation (6.1), known as the **R-squared**,[6] measures the fraction of the return variance owing to systematic risk. First, generalize the regression in equation (6.1) to an arbitrary stock (stock i) and an arbitrary market index with return $\tilde{R}_M$. This yields:

$$\tilde{r}_i = \alpha_i + \beta_i \tilde{R}_M + \tilde{\epsilon}_i \tag{6.3}$$

Exhibits 6.1 and 6.2 graph data points for two such regressions: one for a company with mostly systematic risk (high R-squared in Exhibit 6.1), the other for a company with

---

[6]In the case of Dell, one measures R-squared as the ratio of the first term on the right-hand side of equation (6.2) to the sum of the two terms on the right-hand side. This ratio is a number between 0 and 1. In addition to the interpretation given here, one often refers to R-squared as a measure of how close the regression fits historical data. R-squared is also the square of the correlation coefficient between $\tilde{r}_i$ and $\tilde{R}_M$.

mostly unsystematic risk (low R-squared in Exhibit 6.2). The horizontal axis in both exhibits describes the value of the regression's independent variable, which is the market return. The vertical axis describes the regression's dependent variable, which is the company's stock return.

Diversifiable Risk and Fallacious CAPM Intuition

The intuition commonly provided for the CAPM risk-expected return relation is that systematic risk is nondiversifiable. Thus, investors must be compensated with higher expected rates of return for bearing such risk.[7] In contrast, one often hears unsystematic risk referred to as being "diversifiable," implying that additional expected returns are not required for bearing unsystematic risk. Although this intuition is appealing, it is somewhat misleading because, as shown below, some of the risk generated by the market model residual is not necessarily diversifiable.

For example, risk from the residual in General Motors' market model regression is not diversifiable because it is likely to pick up common factors to which GM is especially sensitive. For example, an unanticipated increase in interest rates is likely to have a negative effect on most stocks. Interest rate risk is nondiversifiable because it is not eliminated by holding well-diversified portfolios. Instead, interest rate risk is a common factor.

GM's stock price is clearly affected by interest rate risk. New car sales plummet when buyers find the rates on automobile loans prohibitively expensive. Indeed, interest rate increases are much more likely to affect the return on GM's stock than the return on the market portfolio. Where does the interest rate effect show up in equation (6.3)? Clearly, some of the effect of the increase in interest rates will be reflected in the systematic component of GM's return—GM's beta times the market return—but this is not enough to explain the additional decline in GM's stock price relative to the market. The rest of the interest rate effect has to show up in GM's regression residual.

Since the change in interest rates, clearly a nondiversifiable risk factor, affects the market model regression residual, all of the risk associated with the residual, $\tilde{\epsilon}_i$, cannot be viewed as diversifiable. While it is true that one can construct portfolios with specific weights that eliminate interest rate risk (with methods developed in this chapter),[8] in general, *most* portfolios with small portfolio weights on large numbers of securities do not eliminate this source of risk.

Residual Correlation and Factor Models

If the market model is to be useful for categorizing diversifiable and nondiversifiable risk, the market portfolio's return must be the only source of correlation between different securities. As discussed above, this generally will not be true. Formally, it must be the case that the return of the ith security can be written as:

$$\tilde{r}_i = \alpha_i + \beta_i \tilde{R}_M + \tilde{\epsilon}_i,$$

where

$\tilde{R}_M$ is the return on the market portfolio

---

[7]Note that the market model regression, which uses realized returns, differs from the CAPM, which uses mean returns. If the CAPM holds, $\alpha_i = (1 - \beta_i)r_f$ in equation (6.3). Exercise 6.9 asks you to prove this.

[8]Factor risk is also eliminated with judicious portfolio weight choices, as will be noted shortly.

$\tilde{\epsilon}_i$ and $\tilde{R}_M$ are uncorrelated

The $\tilde{\epsilon}_i$'s of different securities are mean zero and *uncorrelated* with each other[9]

The fact that the $\tilde{\epsilon}_i$'s of the different stocks are all uncorrelated with each other is the key distinction between the one-factor market model expressed above and the more general "return generating process"—equation (6.3) without the uncorrelated $\tilde{\epsilon}$ assumption—used in discussions of the CAPM.

This "one-factor model" has only one common factor, the market factor, generating returns. Each stock's residual return, $\tilde{\epsilon}_i$, is determined independently of the common factors. Because these $\tilde{\epsilon}_i$'s are uncorrelated, each $\tilde{\epsilon}_i$ represents a change in firm value that is truly firm specific. As the next section shows, firm-specific components of this type have virtually no effect on the variability of the returns of a well-balanced portfolio of a large number of securities. Hence, in the one-factor model, return variability due to firm-specific components, known as **firm-specific risk**, is diversifiable.

Even though the interest rate discussion above suggests that a one-factor market model is unlikely to hold in reality, studying this model helps to clarify the meaning of diversifiable and nondiversifiable risk. After a brief discussion of the mathematics and practical implementation of diversification, this chapter turns to more realistic multifactor models, built upon the intuition of diversifiable versus nondiversifiable risk.

6.2 The Principle of Diversification

Everyone familiar with the cliché, "Don't put all your eggs in one basket," knows that the fraction of heads observed for a coin tossed 1,000 times is more likely to be closer to one-half than a coin tossed 10 times. Yet, coin tossing is not a perfect analogy for investment diversification. Factor models help us break up the returns of securities into two components: a component for which coin tossing as an analogy fails miserably (common factors) and a component for which it works perfectly (the firm-specific components).

Insurance Analogies to Factor Risk and Firm-Specific Risk

To further one's intuition about these two components of risk, think about two different insurance contracts: automobile insurance and health insurance. Automobile accidents are fairly independent events across all insured drivers; thus, the claims on each company are reasonably predictable each year. (Only a million-car crack-up on a fogged interstate highway could prove us wrong.) As a consequence of the perfect diversifiability of these claims, automobile insurance companies tend to charge the expected claim for this diversifiable type of risk (adding a charge for overhead and profit). By contrast, health insurance has a mixture of diversifiable and nondiversifiable risk components. Diseases that require costly use of the medical care system do not tend to afflict large portions of the population simultaneously. As the AIDS epidemic proves, however, health insurance companies cannot completely eliminate some kinds of risk by having a large number of policyholders. Should the HIV virus mutate into a more easily transmittable disease, many major health insurers would be forced into bankruptcy. As a result, insurers should

---

[9]With a finite number of assets, some negligible but nonzero correlation must exist between residuals in the market model because the market portfolio-weighted average of the residuals is identically zero. We do not address this issue because the effect is trivially small.

charge more than the expected loss (i.e., a risk premium) for the financial risk they bear from epidemics.

Factor risk is not diversifiable because the factors are common to many securities. This means that the returns due to each factor's realized values are perfectly correlated across securities. In a one-factor market model, a portfolio with equal weights on a thousand securities, each with the same market model beta, has the same market beta (and thus, the same systematic risk) as each of the portfolio's individual securities.[10] This holds true in more general factor models, as the next section shows. Thus, even the most extreme diversification strategy, such as placing an equal number of eggs in all the baskets, does not reduce that portion of the return variance due to factor risk.

Quantifying the Diversification of Firm-Specific Risk

By contrast, it is relatively straightforward to demonstrate that the $\tilde{\epsilon}$ risk of securities is diversified away in large portfolios because the $\tilde{\epsilon}$'s are uncorrelated across securities. Let us begin with two securities, denoted 1 and 2, each with uncorrelated $\tilde{\epsilon}$'s that have identical variances of, say, .1. By the now familiar variance formula found in equation (4.9a), an equally weighted portfolio of the two securities, that is $x_1 = x_2 = .5$, has the firm-specific variance:

$$var(\tilde{\epsilon}_p) = x_1^2 var(\tilde{\epsilon}_1) + x_2^2 var(\tilde{\epsilon}_2) = .25(.1) + .25(.1) = .25(2)(.1) = .05$$

Thus, a portfolio of two securities halves the firm-specific variance of each of the two securities.

An equally weighted portfolio of 10 securities, each with equal firm-specific variance, has the firm-specific variance:

$$var(\tilde{\epsilon}_p) = x_1^2 var(\tilde{\epsilon}_1) + x_2^2 var(\tilde{\epsilon}_2) + \ldots + x_{10}^2 var(\tilde{\epsilon}_{10})$$

$$= .01(.1) + .01(.1) + \ldots + .01(.1) = .01(10)(.1) = .01$$

This is one-tenth the firm-specific variance of any of the individual securities.

Continuing this process for N securities shows that the firm-specific variance of the portfolio is $1/N$ times the firm-specific variance of any individual security and that the standard deviation is inversely proportional to the square root of N. Exhibit 6.3 summarizes these results by plotting the standard deviation of the firm-specific $\tilde{\epsilon}$ of a portfolio against the number of securities in the portfolio. It becomes obvious that firm-specific risk is rapidly diversified away as the number of securities in the portfolio increases.[11]

A good rule of thumb is that a portfolio with these kinds of weights will have a firm-specific variance inversely proportional to the number of securities. This implies the following result about standard deviations:

Result 6.1   If securities returns follow a factor model (with uncorrelated residuals), portfolios with approximately equal weight on all securities have residuals with standard deviations that are approximately inversely proportional to the square root of the number of securities.

---

[10]See Chapter 5, Result 5.4.

[11]When firm-specific variances are unequal, the portfolio of the N securities that minimizes $var(\tilde{\epsilon}_p)$ has weights that are inversely proportional to the variances of the $\tilde{\epsilon}_i$'s. These weights result in a firm-specific variance for the portfolio that is equal to the product of the inverse of the number of securities in the portfolio times the inverse of the average precision of a security in the portfolio, where the precision of security i is $1/var(\tilde{\epsilon}_i)$. As the number of securities in the portfolio increases, the firm-specific variance rapidly gets smaller with large numbers of securities in this portfolio. Although the inverse of the average precision is not the same as the average variance unless all the variances are equal, the two will probably be reasonably close.

EXHIBIT 6.3   **Firm-Specific Standard Deviation of a Portfolio**

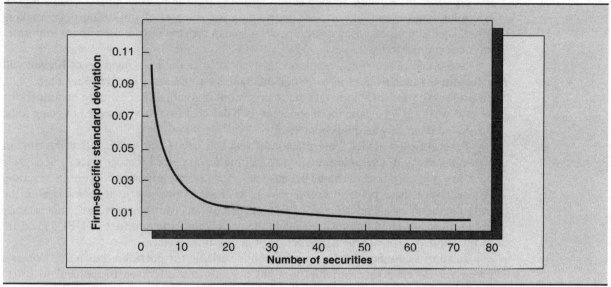

6.3 Multifactor Models

The one-factor market model provides a simple description of stock returns, but unfortunately, it is unrealistic. When stocks are sensitive to interest rate risk as well as to market risk and firm-specific risks, the interest rate risk generates correlation between the market model residuals, implying that more than one common factor generates stock returns.

The Multifactor Model Equation

The algebraic representation of a **multifactor model**, that is, a factor model with more than one element, is given in equation (6.4) below:

$$\tilde{r}_i = \alpha_i + \beta_{i1}\tilde{F}_1 + \beta_{i2}\tilde{F}_2 + \ldots + \beta_{iK}\tilde{F}_K + \tilde{\epsilon}_i \tag{6.4}$$

The assumption behind equation (6.4) is that securities returns are generated by a relatively small number of common factors, each factor symbolized by a subscripted F, for which different stocks have different sensitivities, or β's, along with *uncorrelated* firm-specific components, the ϵ's, which contribute negligible variance in well-diversified portfolios.

Interpreting Common Factors

The F's in equation (6.4) can be thought of as proxies for *new* information about macroeconomic variables, such as industrial production, inflation, interest rates, oil prices, and stock price volatility. Because F's represent new information, they are generally scaled to have means of zero, which also has the convenient benefit of allowing the α's to be interpreted as the mean (or expected) returns of securities.

This information about macroeconomic variables is inferred by participants in financial markets from a variety of sources, including economic announcements, such as the employment report announced one Friday each month by the U.S. Labor Department.

Other important regularly scheduled announcements are the merchandise trade deficit, the producer price index, money supply growth, and the weekly jobless claims report. Irregular news events like the testimony or press releases of important policymaking officials or actions taken by central banks also can provide information about important macroeconomic forces.

Sometimes a seemingly nonfinancial event such as the Iraqi invasion of Kuwait will affect these fundamental forces. When Saddam Hussein's army invaded Kuwait in 1990, oil prices shot up while bond and stock prices fell dramatically. This drop continued for several weeks as it became more apparent each day that Iraqi troops were not going to be dislodged from Kuwait quickly or easily.

Several factor model "interpretations" explain why stock prices fell at the time of Kuwait's invasion. One interpretation is that higher expected import prices for oil may have lowered corporate earnings because oil prices are an important cost of production. Alternatively, these political events may have changed investor expectations about the inflation factor or altered the risk of most securities because of an increase in uncertainty about future inflation, interest rates, and the **gross domestic product (GDP)**, a measure of the value of an economy's production of goods and services.

In sum, a common factor is an economic variable (or portfolio return that acts as a proxy for an economic variable) that has a significant effect on the returns of broad market indexes rather than individual securities alone. The common factors affect returns by changing discount rates or earnings prospects, or both.

6.4 Estimating the Factors

There are three ways to estimate the common factors in a factor model.

1. Use a statistical procedure, such as factor analysis, to determine **factor portfolios**, which are portfolios of securities designed to mimic the factors.
2. Use macroeconomic variables like interest rate changes and changes in economic activity as proxies for the factors.
3. Use firm characteristics associated with higher or lower expected returns to form portfolios that act as proxies for the factors.

Exhibit 6.4 illustrates the advantages and disadvantages of the various methods. We now elaborate on each of these factor-estimation techniques individually.

Using Factor Analysis to Generate Factor Portfolios

Factor analysis is based on the idea that the covariance between stock returns provides information about the common factors generating the returns. Factor structures determine the covariance between stock returns (see Section 6.6). Factor analysis starts with the covariances and discovers which factor structure best explains it.[12]

With only two stocks, it is possible to construct a single factor and a pair of factor betas that explains their covariance perfectly. However, when there are a large number of stocks, the best factor analysis estimates can only approximately explain the covariances, measured from historical returns, between all pairs of stocks. The factors and factor betas generated by factor analysis are those that provide the best possible explanation of the covariances estimated from historical stock returns.

---

[12]This procedure was pioneered in Roll and Ross (1980).

EXHIBIT 6.4   Summary of the Three Different Ways to Construct Factors

Estimation Method	*Advantages*	*Disadvantages*
Factor Analysis A purely statistical procedure for estimating factors and the sensitivity of returns to them	Provides the best estimates of the factors given its assumptions	The assumption that covariances are constant is crucial and is probably violated in reality; does not "name" the factors
Macroeconomic Variables Uses macroeconomic time-series that capture changes in productivity, interest rates, and inflation to act as proxies for the factors generating stock returns	Provides the most intuitive interpretation of the factors	Implies that the appropriate factors are the unanticipated changes in the macrovariables. Unanticipated changes in variables such as aggregate productivity and inflation may be difficult to measure in practice
Firm Characteristics Uses firm characteristics such as firm size, which are known to be related to stock returns, to form factor portfolios	More intuitive than the factor analysis portfolios; formation does not require constant covariances	Portfolios selected on the basis of past return anomalies, which are only factors because they explain historical "accidents," may not be good at explaining expected returns in the future

The advantage of forming factors based on factor analysis is that the factors selected best explain the covariances between all stocks. In theory, if covariances do not change over time the factors derived from factor analysis are exactly the factors desired. However, the downside to factor analysis is that it sheds little insight into which economic variables the factors are linked. Corporate managers would like to be able to relate the riskiness of their firm to factors like interest rate changes and exchange rate changes, but it is difficult to "name" the factors with the purely statistical factor analysis approach. The second problem is that the technique assumes that the return covariances do not change over time. As a result, the technique is severely disadvantaged in its ability to explain, for example, why the expected return of a stock increases following a large decline in its stock price.

Using Macroeconomic Variables to Generate Factors

A second approach for estimating the factors and factor betas is to use macroeconomic variables as proxies for the common factors. This approach takes a large set of macroeconomic variables such as changes in unemployment, inflation, interest rates, oil prices, and so forth. It then limits the number of factors to, say, five, and then examines which five of a larger set of macroeconomic variables best explains the observed pattern of stock returns.

An initial attempt to identify which common factors have the greatest influence on U.S. stock prices was undertaken in empirical research by Chen, Roll, and Ross (1986) and Chan, Chen, and Hsieh (1985). These authors found that the following five factors best explain the correlations between stock returns:

1. Changes in the monthly growth rate of gross domestic product (GDP), which alters investor expectations about future industrial production and corporate earnings,

2. Changes in the default risk premium, measured by the spread between the yields of AAA and Baa bonds of similar maturity. As this spread widens, investors become more concerned about default.

3. Changes in the spread between the yields of long-term and short-term government bonds; that is, the average slope of the term structure of interest rates as measured by the yields on U.S. Treasury notes and bonds. This would affect the discount rates for obtaining present values of future cash flows.

4. Unexpected changes in the price level, as measured by the difference between actual and expected inflation. Unexpectedly high or low inflation alters the values of most contracts. These include contracts with suppliers and distributors, and financial contracts such as a firm's debt instruments.

5. Changes in expected inflation, as measured by changes in the short-term T-bill yield. Changes in expected inflation affect government policy, consumer confidence, and interest rate levels.

One of the main advantages of using the macroeconomic variables approach is that it provides economic intuition about why some stocks have higher expected returns than others. In other words, this approach names the factors. As a result, corporate managers who want APT-based estimates of their cost of capital tend to prefer this approach.[13]

On the other hand, it may be difficult to measure the *unexpected* changes in the macroeconomic variables, which are needed to act as proxies for the factors. As a result, some variables with semipredictable movements, like oil prices, may not show up as factors with this procedure when they really are factors.[14] Another disadvantage is that some potentially important factors may be extremely difficult to quantify. For example, political changes, like the fall of the former Soviet Union, can have a potentially enormous effect on stock returns. However, constructing an index that reflects changes in the world's political environment is difficult.[15]

Using Characteristic-Sorted Portfolios to Estimate the Factors

Factors also can be estimated by using portfolios formed on the basis of the characteristics of firms associated with high and low stock returns. The rationale behind using the characteristic-based proxies for the factors is as follows: If the risk premium (expected return less the risk-free rate) associated with a characteristic, such as size, represents compensation for a specific kind of factor risk, then portfolios consisting of stocks with that characteristic are likely to be highly sensitive to that kind of factor risk.

Given that covariances may change over time, portfolios formed in this way may provide better proxies for these common factors than portfolios formed with factor analysis. They also have the advantage of using the returns of financial securities which,

---

[13]See Chapter 10.

[14]A remedy that was not available at the time of these studies is to use futures prices that can serve as a proxy for common factors like unexpected changes in oil prices.

[15]See Erb, Harvey, and Viskanta (1995) for a discussion of political risk and stock returns.

being largely unpredictable, give this method an advantage over the macroeconomic variables approach in measuring the unexpected changes the factors are supposed to capture. On the other hand, if there is no link between the return premiums of stocks and factor sensitivities, then this method is not picking up true factors that explain covariances, but simply picking out portfolios consisting of stocks that financial markets appear to be mispricing.

6.5 Factor Betas

The magnitudes of a security's factor betas describe how sensitive the security's return is to changes in the common factors.

What Determines Factor Betas?

Consider how the stock prices of General Motors, an automobile manufacturer, and AMC Entertainment, Inc. (AMC), a chain of movie theaters, react differently to factors. Auto sales are linked highly to overall economic activity. Therefore, the returns to holding GM stock should be very sensitive to changes in industrial production. In contrast, movie attendance is not as related to the business cycle as car purchases, so AMC should prove less sensitive to this factor. Hence, GM should have a larger factor beta on the industrial production factor than AMC. If consumers go to more movies during recessions than at other times, substituting cheap theater entertainment for expensive vacations during tough times, AMC might even have a negative factor beta on the industrial production factor.

Factor Models for Portfolios

Multifactor betas, like single-factor betas, have the property that portfolio betas are the portfolio-weighted averages of the betas of the securities in the portfolio (see exercise 6.1). For example, if stock A's beta on the inflation factor is 2 and stock B's is 3, a portfolio that has weights of .5 on stock A and .5 on stock B has a factor beta of 2.5 on this factor.

Result 6.2   The factor beta of a portfolio on a given factor is the portfolio-weighted average of the individual securities' betas on that factor.

Given the K-factor model (or factor model with K distinct factors) of equation (6.4) for each stock i, a portfolio of N securities with weights x_i on stock i and return, $\tilde{R}_p = x_1\tilde{r}_1 + x_2\tilde{r}_2 + \ldots + x_N\tilde{r}_N$, has a factor equation of:

$$\tilde{R}_p = \alpha_p + \beta_{p1}\tilde{F}_1 + \beta_{p2}\tilde{F}_2 + \ldots + \beta_{pK}\tilde{F}_K + \tilde{\epsilon}_p$$

where

$$\alpha_p = x_1\alpha_1 + x_2\alpha_2 + \ldots + x_N\alpha_N$$
$$\beta_{p1} = x_1\beta_{11} + x_2\beta_{21} + \ldots + x_N\beta_{N1}$$
$$\beta_{p2} = x_1\beta_{12} + x_2\beta_{22} + \ldots + x_N\beta_{N2}$$
$$\vdots \qquad \vdots \qquad \vdots \qquad \qquad \vdots$$
$$\beta_{pK} = x_1\beta_{1K} + x_2\beta_{2K} + \ldots + x_N\beta_{NK}$$
$$\tilde{\epsilon}_p = x_1\tilde{\epsilon}_1 + x_2\tilde{\epsilon}_2 + \ldots + x_N\tilde{\epsilon}_N$$

Example 6.1 shows that not only is the factor beta a portfolio-weighted average of the factor betas of the stocks in the portfolio, but also the alphas (α) and the epsilons ($\tilde{\epsilon}$) of the portfolios are the portfolio-weighted averages of the alphas and epsilons of the stocks.

Example 6.1:   Computing Factor Betas for Portfolios

Consider the following two-factor model for the returns of three securities: Apple Computer (security A), Bell Atlantic (security B), and Chrysler (security C).

$$\tilde{r}_A = .03 + \quad \tilde{F}_1 - 4\tilde{F}_2 + \tilde{\epsilon}_A$$

$$\tilde{r}_B = .05 + \quad 3\tilde{F}_1 + 2\tilde{F}_2 + \tilde{\epsilon}_B$$

$$\tilde{r}_C = .10 + 1.5\tilde{F}_1 + 0\tilde{F}_2 + \tilde{\epsilon}_C$$

Using Result 6.2, write out the factor equation for a portfolio that (*a*) equally weights all three securities and (*b*) has weights $x_A = -.5$, $x_B = 1.5$, and $x_C = 0$.

Answer:

(*a*) $\alpha_p = \dfrac{1}{3}(.03) + \dfrac{1}{3}(.05) + \dfrac{1}{3}(.10) = .06$

$\beta_{p1} = \dfrac{1}{3}(1) + \dfrac{1}{3}(3) + \dfrac{1}{3}(1.5) = 1.833$

$\beta_{p2} = \dfrac{1}{3}(-4) + \dfrac{1}{3}(2) + \dfrac{1}{3}(0) = -.667$

Thus:

$$\tilde{R}_p = .06 + 1.833\tilde{F}_1 - .667\tilde{F}_2 + \tilde{\epsilon}_p$$

where

$\tilde{\epsilon}_p$ is an average of the three ϵ's

(*b*) $\alpha_p = -.5(.03) + 1.5(.05) + 0(.10) = .06$
$\beta_{p1} = -.5(1) + 1.5(3) + 0(1.5) = 4$
$\beta_{p2} = -.5(-4) + 1.5(2) + 0(0) = 5$

Thus:

$$\tilde{R}_p = .06 + 4\tilde{F}_1 + 5\tilde{F}_2 + \tilde{\epsilon}_p$$

where

$$\tilde{\epsilon}_p = -.5\tilde{\epsilon}_A + 1.5\tilde{\epsilon}_B$$

6.6 Using Factor Models to Compute Covariances and Variances

This section demonstrates that the correlation or covariance between the returns of any pair of securities is determined by the factor betas of the securities. It then discusses how to use factor betas to compute more accurate covariance estimates. When using mean-variance analysis to identify the tangency and minimum variance investment portfolios, the more accurate the covariance estimate, the better the estimate of the weights of these critical portfolios.

Computing Covariances in a One-Factor Model

Since the $\tilde{\epsilon}$'s in the factor equations described in the last section are assumed to be uncorrelated with each other and the factors, the only source of correlation between securities has to come from the factors. The next example illustrates the calculation of a covariance in a one-factor model.

Example 6.2: Computing Covariances from Factor Betas

The following equations describe the annual returns for two stocks, Acorn Electronics and Banana Software, where $\tilde{F}$ is the change in the GDP growth rate and A and B represent Acorn and Banana, respectively:

$$\tilde{r}_A = .10 + 2\tilde{F} + \tilde{\epsilon}_A$$

$$\tilde{r}_B = .15 + 3\tilde{F} + \tilde{\epsilon}_B$$

The $\tilde{\epsilon}$'s are assumed to be uncorrelated with each other as well as with the GDP factor, and the factor variance is assumed to be .0001. Compute the covariance between the two stock returns.

  Answer: $\sigma_{AB} = cov(.10 + 2\tilde{F} + \tilde{\epsilon}_A, .15 + 3\tilde{F} + \tilde{\epsilon}_B)$
              $= cov(2\tilde{F} + \tilde{\epsilon}_A, 3\tilde{F} + \tilde{\epsilon}_B)$

since constants do not affect covariances. Expanding this covariance, using the principles developed in Chapter 4, yields:

$$\sigma_{AB} = cov(2\tilde{F}, 3\tilde{F}) + cov(2\tilde{F}, \tilde{\epsilon}_B) + cov(\tilde{\epsilon}_A, 3\tilde{F}) + cov(\tilde{\epsilon}_A, \tilde{\epsilon}_B)$$

$$= cov(2\tilde{F}, 3\tilde{F}) + 0 + 0 + 0$$

Thus, the covariance between the returns is the covariance between $2\tilde{F}$ and $3\tilde{F}$, which is $6var(\tilde{F})$, or .0006.

The pair of equations for $\tilde{r}_A$ and $\tilde{r}_B$ in Example 6.2 represents a one-factor model for stocks A and B. Notice the subscripts in this pair of equations. The $\tilde{\epsilon}$'s have the same subscripts as the returns, implying that they represent risks specific to either stock A or B. The value each ϵ takes on provides no information about the value the other ϵ acquires. For example, ϵ_A, taking on the value .2, provides no information about the value of ϵ_B. The GDP factor, represented by $\tilde{F}$, has no A or B subscript, implying that this macroeconomic factor is a common factor affecting both stocks. Since the firm-specific components of these returns are determined independently, they have no effect on the covariance of the returns of these stocks. The common factor provides the sole source of covariation. As a result, the covariance between the stock returns is determined by the variance of the factor and the sensitivity of each stock's return to the factor. The more sensitive the stocks are to the common factor, the greater is the covariance between their returns.

Computing Covariances from Factor Betas in a Multifactor Model

Example 6.3 illustrates how return covariances are calculated within a two-factor model.

Example 6.3: Computing Covariances from Factor Betas in a Two-Factor Model

Consider the returns of three securities (Apple, Bell Atlantic, and Chrysler), given in Example 6.1. Compute the covariances between the returns of each pair of securities, assuming that the two factors are uncorrelated with each other and both factors have variances of .0001.

Answer: Since the two factors, denoted $\tilde{F}_1$ and $\tilde{F}_2$, are uncorrelated with each other, and since the $\tilde{\epsilon}$'s are uncorrelated with each of the two factors and with each other:

$$cov(\tilde{r}_A, \tilde{r}_B) = 3var(\tilde{F}_1) - 8var(\tilde{F}_2) = -.0005$$

$$cov(\tilde{r}_A, \tilde{r}_C) = 1.5var(\tilde{F}_1) = .00015$$

$$cov(r_B, r_C) = 4.5var(\tilde{F}_1) = .00045$$

In Example 6.3, the covariances between the returns of any two securities are determined by the sensitivities of their returns to factor realizations and the variances of the factors. If some of the factors have high variances, or equivalently, if a number of stock returns are particularly sensitive to the factors, then those factors will account for a large portion of the covariance between the stocks' returns. More generally, covariances can be calculated as follows:

Result 6.3   Assume that there are K factors uncorrelated with each other and that the returns of securities i and j are respectively described by the factor models:

$$\tilde{r}_i = \alpha_i + \beta_{i1}\tilde{F}_1 + \beta_{i2}\tilde{F}_2 + \ldots + \beta_{iK}\tilde{F}_K + \tilde{\epsilon}_i$$

$$\tilde{r}_j = \alpha_j + \beta_{j1}\tilde{F}_1 + \beta_{j2}\tilde{F}_2 + \ldots + \beta_{jK}\tilde{F}_K + \tilde{\epsilon}_j$$

Then the covariance between $\tilde{r}_i$ and $\tilde{r}_j$ is:

$$\sigma_{ij} = \beta_{i1}\beta_{j1}var(\tilde{F}_1) + \beta_{i2}\beta_{j2}var(\tilde{F}_2) + \ldots + \beta_{iK}\beta_{jK}var(\tilde{F}_K) \tag{6.5}$$

Result 6.3 states that covariances between securities returns are determined entirely by the variances of the factors and the factor betas. The firm-specific components, $\tilde{\epsilon}_i$ and $\tilde{\epsilon}_j$, play no role in this calculation. If the factors are correlated, the $\tilde{\epsilon}$'s are still irrelevant for covariance calculations. In this case, however, additional terms must be appended to equation (6.5) to account for the covariances between common factors. Specifically, the formula becomes:

$$\sigma_{ij} = \sum_{m=1}^{K} \sum_{n=1}^{K} \beta_{im}\beta_{jn}cov(\tilde{F}_m, \tilde{F}_n)$$

Factor Models and Correlations between Stock Returns

In a multifactor model, the returns of stocks that have similar configurations of factor betas are likely to be highly correlated with each other while those that have differing factor beta patterns are likely to be less correlated with each other.

In an examination of John Deere, General Motors (GM), and Wal-Mart, one is likely to find that the returns of GM (primarily a manufacturer of automobiles) and John Deere (a manufacturer of farm equipment, especially tractors) have the largest correlation while Wal-Mart has less correlation with the other two. Indeed, monthly returns from 1976 through 1995 bear this out. The correlation between GM and John Deere is .406, while Wal-Mart's correlations with these two firms are .299 and .277, respectively.

The greater correlation between John Deere and GM occurs not because they both manufacture transportation equipment—consumer demand for automobiles is not quite the same as the farmers' demand for tractors—but because both companies are highly sensitive to the interest rate factor and the industrial production factor. Wal-Mart, on the other hand, while highly sensitive to the industrial production factor, is not particularly sensitive to the interest rate factor.

Applications of Factor Models to Mean-Variance Analysis

Result 6.3 is used by portfolio managers who estimate covariances to determine optimal portfolio weights. For example, computing the tangency portfolio or the minimum variance portfolio in mean-variance analysis requires the estimation of covariances for each possible pairing of securities. The universe of securities available to most investors is large. The more than 8,000 common stocks listed on the NYSE, AMEX, and NASDAQ markets toward the end of 1996[16] had more than 31,996,000 covariances between different securities in addition to over 8,000 variances. Calculating more than 32 million numbers is a herculean task. If a five-factor model is accurate enough as a description of the covariance process, only five factor betas per security, or 40,000 calculations, would be needed in addition to variance calculations for each of 8,000 securities (and five factors). While 48,000 calculations is a daunting task, it is far less daunting than 32,000,000 calculations.

One of the original reasons for the development of the one-factor market model was to reduce the computational effort needed to determine covariances. Researchers, however, discovered that the market model added more than computational simplicity. The correlations, and consequently the covariances, estimated from the one-factor market model were, on average, better predictors of future correlations than the correlations calculated directly from past data (see Elton, Gruber, and Urich (1978)). The correlations and covariances based on multiple factor models might do even better.[17]

Using Factor Models to Compute Variances

Like the market model, factor models provide a method for breaking down the variance of a security return into the sum of a diversifiable and a nondiversifiable component. For a one-factor model, where:

$$\tilde{r}_i = \alpha + \beta_i\tilde{F} + \tilde{\epsilon}_i$$

$$var(\tilde{r}_i) = \beta_i^2 var(\tilde{F}) + var(\tilde{\epsilon}_i)$$

The first term in the variance equation algebraically defines factor risk; the second term is firm-specific risk. The fraction of risk that is factor related is the R-squared statistic from a regression of the returns of security i on the factor. Result 6.4 summarizes this more generally in a multifactor setting.

Result 6.4   When K factors are uncorrelated with each other and security i is described by the factor model:

$$\tilde{r}_i = \alpha_i + \beta_{i1}\tilde{F}_1 + \beta_{i2}\tilde{F}_2 + \ldots + \beta_{iK}\tilde{F}_K + \tilde{\epsilon}_i$$

the variance of $\tilde{r}_i$ can be decomposed into the sum of $K + 1$ terms:

$$var(\tilde{r}_i) = \beta_{i1}^2 var(\tilde{F}_1) + \beta_{i2}^2 var(\tilde{F}_2) + \ldots + \beta_{iK}^2 var(\tilde{F}_K) + var(\tilde{\epsilon}_i)$$

---

[16]The breakdown for common stock listings in the fall of 1996 was 2,776 NYSE, 936 AMEX, and 3,834 NASDAQ-NMS and 1,231 NASDAQ small cap (non-NMS) issues.

[17]Recall that mean-variance analysis ideally requires the true covariances that generate securities returns. However, just as a fair coin does not turn out to be heads 50 percent of the time in a series of tosses, historical covariances based on a few years of data also will deviate from the true covariances. In the experience of modern science, parsimonious models that capture the underlying structure of a phenomenon are more accurate at prediction than mere extrapolations of data. Here, factor models—to so dominate the inferences drawn from chance correlations based on past data—must be capturing some of the underlying structure of the true covariances.

In this variance decomposition, the sum of the first K terms is the factor risk of the security while the last term is the firm-specific risk. Example 6.4 applies the decomposition given in Result 6.4.

Example 6.4:   Decomposing Variance Risk

Assume that the two factors in Example 6.1 each have a variance of .0001 and that the $\tilde{\epsilon}$'s of the three securities have variances of .0003, .0004, and .0005, respectively. Compute the factor risk and the firm-specific risk of each of the three securities in Example 6.1. Then compute the return variance. The factor equations for the three securities in the example are repeated here.

$$\tilde{r}_A = .03 +\quad \tilde{F}_1 - 4\tilde{F}_2 + \tilde{\epsilon}_A$$

$$\tilde{r}_B = .05 +\quad 3\tilde{F}_1 + 2\tilde{F}_2 + \tilde{\epsilon}_B$$

$$\tilde{r}_C = .10 + 1.5\tilde{F}_1 + 0\tilde{F}_2 + \tilde{\epsilon}_C$$

Answer: The variance equation in Result 6.4 implies:

Security	Factor Risk	Firm-Specific Risk	Return Variance
A	1(.0001) + 16(.0001) = .0017	.0003	.002
B	9(.0001) + 4(.0001) = .0013	.0004	.0017
C	2.25(.0001) + 0 = .000225	.0005	.000725

6.7 Factor Models and Tracking Portfolios

Having learned about several applications of factor models, such as estimating covariances and decomposing variances, we now turn to what is perhaps the most important application of these models: Designing a portfolio that targets a specific factor beta configuration in order to track the risk of a security or portfolio.[18] The tracking application is not only useful for hedging, but it is the foundation of the no-arbitrage risk-return relation derived in Section 6.10.

To illustrate the tracking application, let us suppose that you have the ability to select underpriced stocks and are put in charge of your corporation's pension fund. The CEO of the firm has confidence in you, but he tells you that if the pension fund underperforms the S&P 500 by more than 2 percent in any given month you will be fired! You are considering three strategies.

1. Place the largest portfolio weights on the most underpriced stocks. This strategy would have the highest expected return if you really do have the ability to pick underpriced stocks. The problem is that the portfolio selected in this way may turn out to be much more sensitive than the S&P 500 to a common factor, such as changes in the rate of inflation, and might then underperform the S&P 500 in some months by more than the allowed 2 percent because of news that inflation is diminishing.

2. Put 90 percent of the company's pension fund in an S&P 500 index fund and hope to beat the market with the other 10 percent. This option is of course a lot less

---

[18]Chapter 5 introduced tracking portfolios.

risky, but if you really have superior ability to pick stocks, you would not want to tie 90 percent of your portfolio to the S&P 500 index.

　　3. Pick the stocks that are expected to perform the best, but weight them so that the portfolio closely tracks or mimics the S&P 500. In other words, the weights are chosen so that the portfolio's return is almost perfectly correlated with the S&P 500 return.

Option 3, the tracking strategy, is commonly used by portfolio managers, corporate hedgers, and **arbitrageurs**, who are investors who profit on price discrepancies between securities by simultaneously buying them and selling them short. When returns are generated by a relatively small number of common factors, a tracking portfolio for the S&P 500 is constructed, so that its returns have the same factor betas as the returns of the S&P 500. For example, if the S&P 500 is expected to increase 5 percent when short-term interest rates drop 1 percent, then the tracking portfolio also should increase 5 percent. The tracking portfolio must also be well-diversified, which makes its return relatively insensitive to firm-specific news.

Tracking Portfolios and Corporate Hedging

The methods used by investors to form tracking portfolios also are useful in corporate finance. Many corporate managers would like to hedge a specific set of risks, such as the risks that determine the company's cash flows from foreign operations (see Chapters 20 and 21). For example, assume that Disney, which has extensive operations in Japan, knows that for every 10 percent appreciation in the Japanese yen, its stock declines by 1 percent, and vice versa. Similarly, a weakening of the Japanese economy, which would reduce turnout at the Disney theme park in Tokyo and dampen sales of Disney's videos, might result in Disney's stock price dropping by 5 percent for every 10 percent decline in the growth of Japanese GDP. Hence, Disney has two sources of risk in Japan to worry about: currency risk and a slowing of the Japanese economy.

Disney can hedge these sources of risk by selling short a portfolio that tracks the sensitivity of Disney's equity to these two sources of risk. A short position in such a tracking portfolio, which might be composed of U.S. and Japanese stocks, as well as currency instruments, would (1) appreciate in value by 1 percent for every 10 percent appreciation of the yen and (2) increase in value by 5 percent when Japan experiences a 10 percent decline in the growth of its GDP. A factor model allows Disney to measure the sensitivity of all securities to these two sources of risk and identify the portfolio weights needed to form this type of tracking portfolio.

Capital Allocation Decisions of Corporations and Tracking Portfolios

There is reason to believe that the ability to earn abnormal profits by investing in financial assets—buying an undervalued security and selling short its tracking portfolio—is rare. Admittedly, some arbitrageurs do this for a living. Indeed, the equity investment strategies of some Wall Street investment banks make liberal use of factor models to earn profits in this manner. However, lacking the expertise, financial backing, and information systems of a sophisticated investment house and the ability to undertake large-scale transactions in a timely manner at low cost, an ordinary investor's ability to earn arbitrage profits from the tracking portfolio investment strategy is more fantasy than reality.

For most investors, this means that financial assets are fairly priced and thus do not offer profitable opportunities. In contrast, when it comes to investments in real assets such as factories and office buildings, some corporations have advantages over their competitors. Such real asset investment may yet be fruitful grounds for the earning of true economic profits.

In this vein, the tracking portfolio strategy has value for advising corporations about how to allocate investment capital. A central theme of this text is that corporations create value whenever they allocate capital for real investment projects with returns that exceed those of the project's tracking portfolio in the financial markets. Moreover, the corporation does not have to actually sell short the tracking portfolio from the financial markets to create wealth. That can be achieved by the investors in the corporation's equity securities if they find that such arbitrage is consistent with their plans for selecting optimal portfolios. What is important is that the tracking portfolio be used as an appropriate benchmark for determining whether the investment is undervalued.

Designing Tracking Portfolios

A tracking portfolio is constructed by first measuring the factor betas of the investment one wishes to track. Having identified the target configuration of factor betas, how do we construct a portfolio of financial securities with the target configuration?

Knowledge of how to compute the factor betas of portfolios from the factor betas of the individual investments enables an analyst to design portfolios with any targeted factor beta configuration from a limited number of securities. The only mathematical tool required is the ability to solve systems of linear equations.

A Step-by-Step Recipe.   To design a tracking portfolio, one must follow a sequence of steps.

1. Determine the number of relevant factors.[19]
2. Identify the factors with one of the three methods discussed in Section 6.4 and compute factor betas.
3. Next, set up one equation for each factor beta. On the left-hand side of the equation is the tracking portfolio's factor beta as a function of the portfolio weights. On the right-hand side of the equation is the target factor beta.
4. Then, solve the equations for the tracking portfolio's weights, making sure that the weights sum to 1.

For example, to target the beta with respect to the first factor in a K-factor model, the equation would be:

$$x_1\beta_{11} + x_2\beta_{21} + \ldots + x_N\beta_{N1} = \text{target beta on factor 1}$$

The betas on the left-hand side and target beta on the right-hand side would appear as numbers, and the x's (the portfolio weights), would remain as unknown variables that have to be solved for. The equation targeting the beta with respect to the second factor would be:

$$x_1\beta_{12} + x_2\beta_{22} + \ldots + x_N\beta_{N2} = \text{target beta on factor 2}$$

Proceed in this manner until each factor has one target beta equation. Then, add an additional equation that forces the portfolio weights to sum to 1.

$$x_1 + x_2 + \ldots + x_N = 1$$

---

[19]The number of factors, which can often be found in the finance research literature, is based on statistical tests.

Solving all of these equations for the portfolio weights, $x_1, x_2, \ldots x_N$, designs a tracking portfolio with the proper factor betas.

A Numerical Illustration of the Recipe.   Example 6.5 illustrates how to do this.

Example 6.5:   Designing a Portfolio with Specific Factor Betas

Consider the three stocks in Examples 6.1, 6.3, and 6.4. You are informed that the Wilshire 5000 Index, a broad-based stock index, has a factor beta of 2 on the first factor and a factor beta of 1 on the second factor. Design a portfolio of stocks A, B, and C that has a factor beta of 2 on the first factor and 1 on the second factor.

Answer: To design a portfolio with these characteristics, it is necessary to find portfolio weights, x_A, x_B, x_C, that make the portfolio-weighted averages of the betas equal to the target betas. To make the weights sum to one, x_A, x_B, and x_C must satisfy

$$x_A + x_B + x_C = 1$$

To have a factor beta of 2 on the first factor implies:

$$1x_A + 3x_B + 1.5x_C = 2$$

To have a factor beta of 1 on the second factor implies:

$$-4x_A + 2x_B + 0x_C = 1$$

Substituting the value of x_C from the first equation into the !other two equations implies:

$$(a) \quad 1x_A + 3x_B + 1.5(1 - x_A - x_B) = 2$$
$$(b) \quad\quad\quad -4x_A + 2x_B \quad\quad\quad = 1$$

Equation (a), immediately above, is now solved for x_B. This value, when substituted into equation (b), eliminates x_B from equation (b), so that it now reads:

$$-4x_A + \frac{2}{3}(x_A + 1) = 1$$

This equation has $x_A = -.1$ as its solution. Since equation (a) reduces to:

$$x_B = \frac{x_A + 1}{3}$$

$$x_B = .3$$

implying that:

$$x_C = .8$$

The Number of Securities Needed to Design Portfolios with Specific Target Beta Configurations.   Example 6.5 could have made use of any configuration of target betas on the two factors and derived a solution. Hence, it is possible to design a portfolio with almost any factor beta configuration from a limited number of securities. In a two-factor model, only three securities were needed to create investments with any factor beta pattern. In a five-factor model, six securities would be needed to tailor-design the factor risk. In a K-factor model, $K + 1$ securities would be needed.

An Interesting Target Beta Configuration.   An important application of the design of portfolios with specific factor configurations is the design of *pure factor portfolios*. These portfolios, discussed in the next section, can be thought of as portfolios that track the factors. They make it easier to see that factor models imply a useful risk-return relation.

6.8 Pure Factor Portfolios

This section uses the technique developed in the last section to construct pure factor portfolios. **Pure factor portfolios** are portfolios with a sensitivity of 1 to one of the factors and 0 to the remaining factors. Such portfolios, which have no firm-specific risk, provide an intuitive framework for thinking about the implications of factor models. Some portfolio managers use them as an aid in determining their optimal portfolio.

Constructing Pure Factor Portfolios from More Primitive Securities

In a K-factor model, it is possible to construct K pure factor portfolios, one for each factor, from any $K + 1$ investments that lack firm-specific risk.[20] Example 6.6 illustrates the construction.

Example 6.6:   Finding Weights That Design Pure Factor Portfolios

What are the weights of the two pure factor portfolios constructed from Centocor (c), Genentech (g), and Schering-Plough (s), assuming the following hypothetical factor equations (with factor means of zero) for these three pharmaceutical companies:

$$\tilde{r}_c = .08 + 2\tilde{F}_1 + 3\tilde{F}_2$$

$$\tilde{r}_g = .10 + 3\tilde{F}_1 + 2\tilde{F}_2$$

$$\tilde{r}_s = .10 + 3\tilde{F}_1 + 5\tilde{F}_2$$

Answer: To construct the factor portfolio that is only sensitive to factor 1, find portfolio weights x_1, x_2, and x_3 that result in a portfolio with a target factor beta of one on the first factor:

$$2x_c + 3x_g + 3x_s = 1$$

To generate a factor beta of 0 on the second factor the portfolio weights need to satisfy:

$$3x_c + 2x_g + 5x_s = 0$$

Since $x_c + x_g + x_s = 1$, the substitution for x_s in the two previous equations implies:

$$2x_c + 3x_g + 3(1 - x_c - x_g) = 1$$

$$3x_c + 2x_g + 5(1 - x_c - x_g) = 0$$

or

$$-x_c = -2$$

$$-2x_c - 3x_g = -5$$

Thus, $x_c = 2$, $x_g = \dfrac{1}{3}$, and $x_s = -\dfrac{4}{3}$.

To find factor portfolio 2, set $x_s = 1 - x_c - x_g$ and solve the following:

$$2x_c + 3x_g + 3(1 - x_c - x_g) = 0$$

$$3x_c + 2x_g + 5(1 - x_c - x_g) = 1$$

The solution is $x_c = 3$, $x_g = -\dfrac{2}{3}$, and $x_s = -\dfrac{4}{3}$.

---

[20]Since many investments have firm-specific risk, pure factor portfolios, in practice, may need to be generated from $K + 1$ well-diversified portfolios.

The Risk Premiums of Pure Factor Portfolios

The respective risk premiums of the K factor portfolios in a K-factor model are typically denoted as $\lambda_1, \lambda_2, \ldots \lambda_K$. In other words, the expected return of factor portfolio 1 is $r_f + \lambda_1$, etc. Example 6.7 computes the expected returns and risk premiums of the factor portfolios constructed in Example 6.6.

Example 6.7:   The Factor Equations of Pure Factor Portfolios

Write out the factor equations for the two factor portfolios in Example 6.6 and determine their risk premiums if the risk-free rate is 5 percent.

Answer: The expected return for factor portfolio 1 is the portfolio-weighted average of the expected returns of the individual securities, implying:

$$\alpha_{p1} = 2(.08) + \frac{1}{3}(.10) - \frac{4}{3}(.10) = .06$$

$$\alpha_{p2} = 3(.08) - \frac{2}{3}(.10) - \frac{4}{3}(.10) = .04$$

Thus, the factor equation for factor portfolio 1 is:

$$\tilde{R}_{p1} = .06 + \tilde{F}_1 + 0\tilde{F}_2$$

For factor portfolio 2, the factor equation is:

$$\tilde{R}_{p2} = .04 + 0\tilde{F}_1 + \tilde{F}_2$$

The risk premiums are, respectively:

$$(1) \ \ \lambda_1 = .06 - .05 = .01$$
$$(2) \ \ \lambda_2 = .04 - .05 = -.01$$

What Determines the Risk Premiums of Pure Factor Portfolios?   Pure factor portfolios, being risky, generally have expected returns that differ from the risk-free return. Some factors may carry a positive risk premium; others, such as factor portfolio 2 in Example 6.7, may have a zero or negative risk premium. Whether a factor portfolio has a positive or a negative risk premium depends on the aggregate supply of the factor in the financial markets and the tastes of investors. If the assumptions of the Capital Asset Pricing Model are true, then the risk premiums of the factor portfolios are proportional to their covariances with the return of the market portfolio.[21]

Why the Interest in Pure Factor Portfolios?   From a computational standpoint, it is easier to track an investment with a portfolio of the factor portfolios than with a portfolio of more basic investments, such as individual stocks. For example, an investment that

---

[21]If the factors are uncorrelated with each other, the covariance of a factor with the return of the market portfolio is determined by the market portfolio's factor beta on that factor. In this case, the factor will have a positive risk premium if the market portfolio has a positive factor beta on a factor and vice versa. The economic intuition for this is straightforward: Under the assumptions of the CAPM, investors must be induced to hold the market portfolio so that supply is equal to demand. This is the same as inducing them to hold the factors in exactly the same proportions as they are contained in the market portfolio. Hence, if the market portfolio has a negative beta on a factor, implying that the factor is in negative supply, investors must be induced to short the factor so that the supply of the factor is equal to its demand. To induce an investor to short a factor, the action must carry a reward. If the factor itself has a negative risk premium, short positions in it earn a positive reward. The opposite holds true for factors on which the market portfolio has a positive factor beta.

has a beta of .25 on factor 1 and .5 on factor 2 is tracked by a portfolio with weights of .25 on factor portfolio 1 and .5 on factor portfolio 2. A .25 weight on the risk-free asset is also needed to make the weights sum to one.

The construction of this tracking portfolio is easy because each of the building blocks has only one function: Only the weight on factor portfolio 1 affects the tracking portfolio's factor 1 beta. Only the weight on factor portfolio 2 affects the tracking portfolio's factor 2 beta. The risk-free asset is used only to make the portfolio weights sum to 1, after the other two weights are determined. Thus, it is particularly simple to construct tracking portfolios after first taking the intermediate step of forming factor portfolios. The next section uses this insight.

6.9 Tracking and Arbitrage

The previous sections illustrated how to construct portfolios with any pattern of factor betas from a limited number of securities. With more securities, the additional degrees of freedom in the selection of portfolio weights make the task of targeting a specific factor beta configuration even easier. Because a sufficiently large number of securities in the portfolio makes it likely that these portfolios will have negligible firm-specific risk, it is usually possible to construct portfolios that perfectly track investments that have no firm-specific risk. This is done by forming portfolios of the pure factor portfolios that have the same factor betas as the investment one wishes to track. The factor equations of the tracking portfolio and the tracked investment will be identical except for the α's. By assumption, there are no $\tilde{\epsilon}$ terms in these factor equations. Hence, the return of the tracking portfolio and the tracked investment can, at most, differ by a constant: the difference in their α's, which is the difference in their expected returns.

If the factor betas of the tracking portfolio and the tracked investment are the same but their expected returns differ, then there will be an opportunity for arbitrage. For example, if the tracking portfolio has a higher expected return, then investors can buy that portfolio and short sell the tracked investment and receive risk-free cash in the future without spending any money today.

Using Pure Factor Portfolios to Track the Returns of a Security

Example 6.8 illustrates how to use factor portfolios and the risk-free asset to track the returns of another security.

Example 6.8:   Tracking and Arbitrage with Pure Factor Portfolios
Given a two-factor model, find the combination of a risk-free security with a 5 percent return and the two pure factor portfolios from Example 6.6 that tracks a security with a factor equation of:

$$\tilde{r} = .08 + 2\tilde{F}_1 - .6\tilde{F}_2$$

Then, find the expected return of the tracking portfolio and determine if arbitrage exists. Recall that the factor equations for the two pure factor portfolios (see Example 6.7) were respectively given by:

$$\tilde{R}_{p1} = .06 + \tilde{F}_1 + 0\tilde{F}_2$$
$$\tilde{R}_{p2} = .04 + 0\tilde{F}_1 + \tilde{F}_2$$

Answer: To track the security's two factor betas, place a weight of 2 on factor portfolio 1 and a weight of $-.6$ on factor portfolio 2. Since the weights now sum to 1.4, make this a legitimate portfolio with a weight of $-.4$ on the risk-free asset. The expected return of this portfolio is the portfolio-weighted average of the expected returns of the risk-free asset, factor portfolio 1, and factor portfolio 2, which is:

$$-.4(.05) + 2(.06) - .6(.04) = .076$$

An arbitrage opportunity exists because this expected return of 7.6 percent differs from the 8 percent return of the tracked security, as indicated by the .08 intercept (and the common convention, discussed earlier, that the means of the factors are zero).

The Expected Return of the Tracking Portfolio

In Example 6.8, the tracking portfolio is a weighted average of the two factor portfolios and the risk-free asset. Factor portfolio 1 is used solely to generate the target factor 1 beta. Factor portfolio 2 is used solely to generate the target sensitivity to factor 2. The risk-free asset is used only to make the weights of the tracking portfolio sum to one. Note that the expected return of this tracking portfolio is:

$$\text{Expected return} = (1 - \beta_1 - \beta_2)r_f + \beta_1(r_f + \lambda_1) + \beta_2(r_f + \lambda_2)$$

where β_j is the factor beta of the tracked investment on factor j (and thus also the weight on pure factor portfolio j), and λ_j is the risk premium of factor portfolio j (making $r_f + \lambda_j$ its expected return). The expression above for the expected return is also written in an equivalent form:

$$\text{Expected return} = r_f + \beta_1\lambda_1 + \beta_2\lambda_2$$

Result 6.5 generalizes Example 6.8 as follows:

Result 6.5   An investment with no firm-specific risk and a factor beta of β_j on the jth factor in a K-factor model is tracked by a portfolio with weights of β_1 on factor portfolio 1, β_2 on factor portfolio 2, . . . , β_K on factor portfolio K, and $1 - \sum_{j=1}^{K} \beta_j$ on the risk-free asset. The expected return on this tracking portfolio is therefore:

$$r_f + \beta_1\lambda_1 + \beta_2\lambda_2 + \ldots + \beta_K\lambda_K$$

where $\lambda_1, \lambda_2, \ldots \lambda_K$ denote the risk premiums of the factor portfolios and r_f is the risk-free return.

Decomposing Pure Factor Portfolios into Weights on More Primitive Securities

Factor portfolios are themselves combinations of individual securities, like stocks and bonds. In Example 6.8, the portfolio with weights of $-.4$ on the risk-free security, 2 on factor portfolio 1, and $-.6$ on factor portfolio 2, can be further broken down. Recall from Example 6.6 that factor portfolio 1 has respective weights of $(2, 1/3, -4/3)$ on the three individual securities while the factor portfolio 2 has corresponding weights of $(3, -2/3, -4/3)$. Hence, a weight of 2 on factor portfolio 1 is really a weight of 4 on security c, 2/3 on security g, and $-8/3$ on security s. A weight of $-.6$ on factor portfolio 2 is really a weight of -1.8 on security c, .4 on security g, and .8 on security s. Summing the weights for each security found in Example 6.6 implies that at a more basic level, our tracking portfolio in Example 6.8 consisted of weights of 2.2, 16/15, and $-28/15$ on securities c, g, and s, respectively, plus a weight of $-.4$ on the risk-free asset.[22] Thus, it makes no difference in the last example whether one views the tracking portfolio as being generated by stocks c, g, and s or by pure factor portfolios.

6.10 No Arbitrage and Pricing: The Arbitrage Pricing Theory

Because firm-specific risk is fairly unimportant to investors who hold well-diversified portfolios, it is reasonable at this point to pretend that firm-specific risk does not exist and to analyze the risk of securities by focusing only on their factor betas. If most investors do not have to bear firm-specific risk because they hold well-diversified portfolios, our analysis of the relation between risk and return will be unaffected by this omission.

If two investments perfectly track each other and have different expected returns, then a trader can achieve riskless profits by purchasing the investment with the higher expected return and selling short the investment with the lower expected return. It is possible to demonstrate that such arbitrage opportunities will exist only if securities returns do not satisfy an equation that relates the expected returns of securities to their factor betas. As noted previously, this risk-expected return relation is known as the arbitrage pricing theory (APT).

The Assumptions of the Arbitrage Pricing Theory

The derivation of the APT requires only three assumptions:

1. Returns can be described by a factor model.
2. There are no arbitrage opportunities.
3. There are a large number of securities, so that it is possible to form portfolios that diversify the firm-specific risk of individual stocks. This assumption allows us to pretend that firm-specific risk does not exist.

This section derives the APT. To keep the analysis relatively simple, consider investments with no firm-specific risk.

Arbitrage Pricing Theory with No Firm-Specific Risk

Consider investment i with returns generated by the K-factor model represented by:

$$\tilde{r}_i = \alpha_i + \beta_{i1}\tilde{F}_1 + \beta_{i2}\tilde{F}_2 + \ldots + \beta_{iK}\tilde{F}_K \tag{6.6}$$

Note that equation (6.6) has no $\tilde{\epsilon}_i$ term; thus, there is no firm-specific risk. As noted in the last section, one way to track the return of this investment is to form a portfolio with weights of $1 - \sum_{j=1}^{K} \beta_{ij}$ on the risk free security, β_{i1} on factor portfolio 1, β_{i2} on factor portfolio 2, . . . , and finally β_{iK} on factor portfolio K. Recall that these factor portfolios can be generated either from a relatively small number of securities with no firm-specific risk or from a very large number of securities where the firm-specific risk is diversified away.

---

[22]Moreover, even a risk-free security could have been formed from securities c, g, and s in Example 6.6, so it is possible to break this down to an even more basic level.

The expected return of the portfolio that tracks investment i is:

$$r_f + \beta_{i1}\lambda_1 + \beta_{i2}\lambda_2 + \beta_{iK}\lambda_K$$

where $\lambda_1, \ldots \lambda_K$ are the risk premiums of the factor portfolios.

It should be immediately apparent that an arbitrage opportunity exists—unless the original investment and its tracking portfolio have the same expected return—because a long position in investment; and an offsetting short position in the tracking portfolio has no risk and no cost. For example, if the common stock of Dell Computer is investment i, buying \$1 million of Dell and selling short \$1 million of the tracking portfolio would require no up-front cash. Moreover, since the factor betas of the long and short positions match exactly, any movements in the value of Dell stock due to factors would be completely offset by exactly opposite movements in the value of the short position in the tracking portfolio. Hence, if the expected return of Dell stock exceeds the expected return of Dell's tracking portfolio, an investor obtains a riskless positive cash inflow at the end of the period. For example, if Dell's expected return exceeds the tracking portfolio's by 2 percent, the investor would receive:

$$\$1,000,000 \times .02 = \$20,000$$

Since this cash does not require any up-front money and is obtained without risk, buying Dell and shorting its tracking portfolio represents an arbitrage opportunity. Similarly, if the expected return of Dell stock was smaller than the expected return of the tracking portfolio, a short position in Dell stock and an equal long position in its tracking portfolio would provide an arbitrage opportunity. To prevent arbitrage, the expected return of Dell and its tracking portfolio must be equal.

Result 6.6 states this formally:

Result 6.6   An arbitrage opportunity exists for all investments with no firm-specific risk unless:

$$\bar{r}_i = r_f + \beta_{i1}\lambda_1 + \beta_{i2}\lambda_2 + \ldots + \beta_{iK}\lambda_K \tag{6.7}$$

where $\lambda_1, \ldots \lambda_K$ applies to all investments with no firm-specific risk.

The equation of the arbitrage pricing theory, equation (6.7), is a relation between risk and expected return that must hold in the absence of arbitrage opportunities. On the left-hand side of the equation is the expected return of an investment. On the right-hand side is the expected return of a tracking portfolio with the same factor betas as the investment. Equation (6.7) thus depicts a relationship where there is no arbitrage: The equal sign merely states that the expected return of the investment should be the same as that of its tracking portfolio.

Graphing the APT Risk Return Equation

In the one-factor case, the graph of equation (6.7) observed in Exhibit 6.5, on page 220 is very similar to the graph of the securities market line, depicted in panel B of Exhibit 5.5 in the previous chapter. On one axis is the beta or factor beta of a security; on another axis is its mean return. In this case, the risk-return relation graphs as a straight line. According to the results in this section, if there is no arbitrage, all investments must lie on this line.

In the two-factor case, equation (6.7) graphs as a plane in three dimensions. The location and slope of the plane are determined by the risk-free return, which is the height of the plane above the origin, and the two risk premiums, or λ's of the pure factor portfolios. All investments must lie on this plane if there is no arbitrage (see Exhibit 6.6 on page 220).

EXHIBIT 6.5   **The APT Relation between the Mean Return of a Stock and Its Factor Beta**

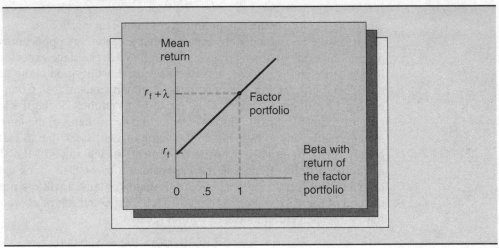

EXHIBIT 6.6   **Relation between the Mean Return of a Stock and Its Factor Betas in a Multifactor Model**

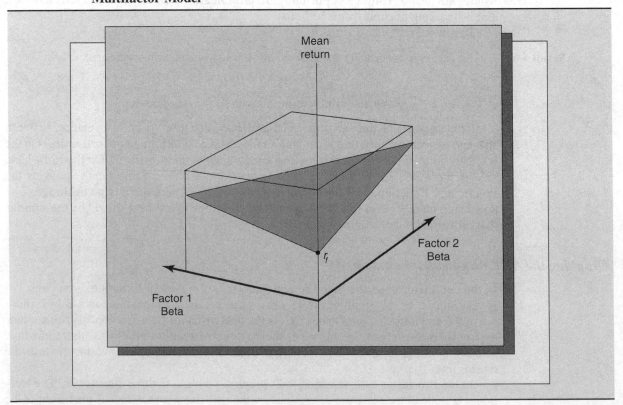

Verifying the Existence of Arbitrage

To learn whether the arbitrage pricing theory holds, do not look at graphs (which is obviously impossible if there are more than two factors) or form tracking portfolios. Instead, given more than $K + 1$ securities in a K-factor model, determine whether a single set of λ's can generate the expected returns of all the securities. One way to assess this is to solve for the K λ's using $K + 1$ securities and see if these λ's fit equation (6.7) for the remaining investments. If they do, the APT holds; if they do not, the APT is violated and there is an arbitrage opportunity (assuming the factor model assumption holds). Example 6.9 illustrates the procedure for testing whether a single set of λ's have this property.

Example 6.9:   Determining Whether Arbitrage Exists

Let the following 2-factor model describe the returns to four securities: three risky securities indexed 1, 2, and 3 and a risk-free security.

$$r_f = .05$$

$$\tilde{r}_1 = .06 + \quad 0\tilde{F}_1 + .02\tilde{F}_2$$

$$\tilde{r}_2 = .08 + .02\tilde{F}_1 + .01\tilde{F}_2$$

$$\tilde{r}_3 = .15 + .04\tilde{F}_1 + .04\tilde{F}_2$$

Is there an arbitrage opportunity?

Answer: The APT risk-expected return equation says:

$$\bar{r}_i = r_f + \beta_{i1}\lambda_1 + \beta_{i2}\lambda_2$$

For securities 1 and 2, this reads:

$$.06 = .05 + \quad 0\lambda_1 + .02\lambda_2$$

and

$$.08 = .05 + .02\lambda_1 + .01\lambda_2$$

The first of these two equations implies $\lambda_2 = .5$. Substituting this value for λ_2 into the second equation gives $\lambda_1 = 1.25$. Using these values for the APT equation of security 3, check to see whether:

$$.15 \text{ equals } [.05 + .04(1.25) + .04(.5)]$$

Since the right-hand side equals .12, which is less than the value on the left-hand side, .15, there is arbitrage. A long position in security 3 (the high expected return security) and an equal short position in its tracking portfolio, formed from securities 1, 2, and the risk-free security, generates arbitrage.

In Example 6.9, if the expected return of security 3 had been equal to .12, there would be no arbitrage. However, because its expected return of .15 exceeded the .12 expected return of its tracking portfolio, the no arbitrage risk-return relation of equation (6.7) is violated. While this provides a prescription for generating arbitrage, it does not determine whether security 3 is underpriced or whether its tracking portfolio is overpriced. Based on this example, all one knows is that security 3 is underpriced *relative* to its tracking portfolio.

An alternative method for identifying the existence of arbitrage is to test directly whether a unique set of λ's generate the expected returns of the securities. In this case, solve for the set of λ's using one group of securities (the number of securities in the set is one plus the number of factors). Then, solve again, using a different group of securities. If the different sets of λ's are the same, there is no arbitrage; if they differ, there is arbitrage. Example 6.10 illustrates this technique.

Example 6.10:   Determining Whether Factor Risk Premiums Are Unique

Use the same data provided in Example 6.9 to determine whether there an arbitrage opportunity by comparing the pair of λ's found in Example 6.9 with the pair of λ's found by using securities 2, 3, and the risk-free asset.

Answer: The APT risk-expected return equation says:

$$\bar{r}_i = r_f + \beta_{i1}\lambda_1 + \beta_{i2}\lambda_2$$

Example 6.9 found that using the risk-free asset and securities 1 and 2 to solve for λ_1 and λ_2 yields:

$$\lambda_1 = 1.25 \quad \text{and} \quad \lambda_2 = .5$$

Using securities 2 and 3 and the risk-free asset to solve for the λ's requires solving the following pair of equations:

$$.08 = .05 + .02\lambda_1 + .01\lambda_2$$

$$.15 = .05 + .04\lambda_1 + .04\lambda_2$$

The first equation of the pair immediately above says $\lambda_2 = 3 - 2\lambda_1$. Substituting this into the second equation and solving for λ_1 yields $\lambda_1 = .5$, which, when substituted back into the first equation, yields $\lambda_2 = 2$. Since this pair of λ's differs from the first pair, the APT equation does not hold and there is arbitrage.

If security 3 in the last example had an expected return of .12, the second pair of λ's would have been identical to the first pair. This would be indicative of no arbitrage.

Exhibits 6.7 and 6.8 illustrate this technique in a slightly more general fashion. They graph the factor risk-premiums that are consistent with the APT risk-expected return equation (6.7) for each of the three risky securities in the last example. The value for λ_1 corresponds to the horizontal axis and the value for λ_2 corresponds to the vertical axis. As you can see, solving systems of equations is identical to finding out where lines cross. The intersection of lines for securities 1 and 2 (2 and 3) represent the first (second) pair of factor risk premiums. In Exhibit 6.7, the intersection point for the lines that correspond to securities 1 and 2, at point A, is not on the line for security 3. To preclude arbitrage, which would be the case if the expected return of security 3 was .12, all three of these lines would have to intersect at the same point, point A in Exhibit 6.8. Any other securities that exist would also require corresponding lines that go through this point.

The Risk-Expected Return Relation for Securities with Firm-Specific Risk

Up to this point, Chapter 6 has examined the risk-expected return relation of portfolios and securities that have no firm-specific risk. With a sufficiently large number of securities, however, the APT risk-expected return equation (6.7) also must hold, at least approximately, for individual securities that contain firm-specific risk.

EXHIBIT 6.7   Risk Premiums (λ_1 & λ_2) That Are Inconsistent with No Arbitrage for Three Securities

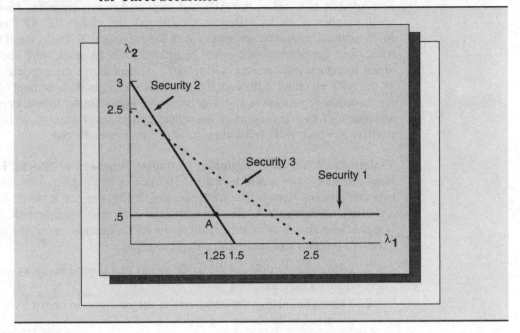

EXHIBIT 6.8   Risk Premiums (λ_1 & λ_2) That Are Consistent with No Arbitrage for Three Securities

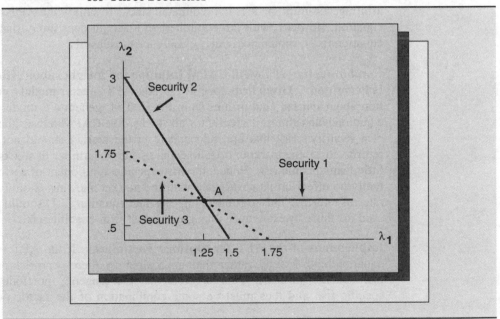

Violations of the APT Equation for a Small Set of Stocks Do Not Imply Arbitrage.
As the last section showed, an arbitrage opportunity exists whenever portfolios without
firm-specific risk violate the APT risk-expected return equation. However, a relatively
small number of stocks with firm-specific risk can violate the APT equation [equation
(6.7)] without providing an opportunity for arbitrage. To understand this, consider the
investment opportunity that would be offered if IBM's stock were underpriced and provided investors with an expected return 5 percent above the expected return expressed
by the APT equation. Although this provides a very good investment opportunity, it does
not necessarily provide a risk-free arbitrage opportunity. Investors who want to take
advantage of this underpricing must hold a significant percent of IBM stock in their
portfolios, which will expose them to IBM's firm-specific risk.

Violations of the APT Equation by Large Numbers of Stocks Imply Arbitrage.
Now consider what would happen if 300 stocks had expected returns that exceed the
expected returns given by the APT equation. If this were so, it would be possible to form
a portfolio of those stocks that virtually eliminates firm-specific risk. Since this diversified portfolio also must be mispriced by the APT equation, an arbitrage opportunity will
exist. An investor can achieve these arbitrage gains by:

1. Forming a portfolio of these 300 stocks that diversifies away almost all of the
   firm-specific risk.
2. Then, eliminating the factor risk of the portfolio in item 1 by taking offsetting
   positions in the factor portfolios.

This argument suggests that the number of securities mispriced by the APT must
not exceed the minimum needed to form a portfolio that virtually eliminates firm-
specific risk. The number that can be mispriced depends on what one means by "virtually eliminate." Completely eliminating firm-specific risk requires an infinite number of
securities. In a realistic setting with a large but finite number of securities, the no-
arbitrage assumption does not require all stocks to satisfy the APT risk-expected return
equation. However, with large numbers of assets, it does imply that the pricing model,
equation (6.7), should hold fairly closely for most assets.

**Combining the APT with CAPM Intuition for Insights about How Much Deviation
Is Permitted.**   Given firm-specific risk, the APT's factor models, combined with intuition about market equilibrium from the CAPM, generate a model in which the APT
equation holds almost perfectly for all stocks. The CAPM tells us that those components
of a security's risk that are independent of the market should not affect its expected
returns. Since the market portfolio contains a large number of stocks, its return contains
little firm-specific risk. Hence, the firm-specific component of a security's risk has virtually no effect on its covariance with the market and thus should not affect expected
rates of return.[23] This argument suggests that equation (6.7) should hold almost exactly
even for those investments with a great deal of firm-specific risk.

Implications of the APT for Optimal Portfolios.   If the APT risk-expected return
equation holds exactly, rather than approximately, there is no risk premium attached to
firm-specific variance. This suggests that the tangency portfolio contains no firm-
specific risk and thus must be some combination of the factor portfolios. Since the

---

[23]This intuition is provided in models by Connor (1984), Dybvig (1983), Grinblatt and Titman (1983),
and Wei (1988).

optimal portfolio for investors is a combination of the tangency portfolio and the risk-free asset, optimal investment portfolios are composed of weightings of the K factor portfolios and the risk-free investment. Such optimal portfolios contain the optimal mix of factor risk, but have no firm-specific risk.

6.11 Estimating Factor Risk Premiums and Factor Betas

Factor risk premiums are needed to implement the APT. Typically, these have been estimated from the average historical risk premiums of factor portfolios, i.e., their historical average returns in excess of the risk-free return. Since historical averages are not true means, considerable statistical error is associated with the factor risk premiums.[24]

To estimate factor betas when factors are prespecified, either as macroeconomic factors or as portfolios tied to firm characteristics, one must use a regression of the historical returns of the security against the historical values of the factors. The slope coefficients in this regression are the factor betas. With a factor analysis implementation of a factor model, both the factor portfolios and the factor betas are generated directly as outputs of the factor analysis procedure. However, the resulting factor betas in this case are still identical to multiple regression slope coefficients from a regression of historical returns against historical values of the factors.

6.12 Empirical Tests of the Arbitrage Pricing Theory

As Chapter 5 noted, some researchers have suggested that market prices do not reflect fundamental long-term values because characteristics like size, market-to-book, and momentum better explain average stock returns than the CAPM beta. As a result, investors can realize superior performance by buying the stocks of small capitalization companies with low market-to-book ratios which have performed well over the past 3 to 12 months. If this were true, it would have important implications for the way corporations make financing decisions as well as for how investors select their portfolios. In an irrational market, for example, corporations may be able to lower their costs of capital by timing their share issues to correspond to periods when the shares are overpriced.

However, not all researchers share this view of financial markets. Others have argued that the return premiums associated with these characteristics arise because stocks with these characteristics are exposed to systematic risk factors. Since this risk is not reflected in the CAPM betas of the stocks, a multifactor model like the APT is needed to explain the returns.

---

[24]We believe that just as beta estimates can be improved with a statistical adjustment, so can factor risk premiums. The insights of the last section, which combine the CAPM with the APT, imply that the risk premiums of the factor portfolios should be their CAPM betas times the risk premium of the market portfolio. To the extent that investors have some confidence in the CAPM risk-expected return relation, they should make some comparison between the risk premiums for the factors that would exist if the CAPM were true and the risk premiums estimated by averaging historical data. For those factors with historical risk premiums that deviate substantially from their CAPM-predicted risk premiums, it is possible to improve the estimated risk premium by taking a weighted average of the historical risk premium and the CAPM-predicted risk premium. The weighting would depend on the relative confidence one has in the historical estimate over the CAPM estimate. To the extent that the factor has been extremely volatile, one has less confidence in the historical estimate of the factor risk premium. To the extent that the CAPM predictions for all risk premiums seem to bear little relation to the historical averages, one has less confidence in the CAPM estimates of the factor risk premiums.

Some researchers have argued that low market-to-book stocks are more sensitive to swings in the business cycle and changes in credit conditions because the companies are more likely to have their financing cut off during an economic downturn, and that the added sensitivity to these economic factors is not reflected in their covariation with the S&P 500. In other words, returns are generated by multiple factors, as described by the APT, and small capitalization and low market-to-book stocks may have high betas on factors underrepresented by the S&P 500.

Unfortunately, the empirical literature on the multifactor APT is not as well developed as the empirical literature on the CAPM, and the results are less conclusive. As a consequence, the debate about whether these effects are driven by psychological behavior or by the sensitivity of stocks to risk factors that researchers have ignored is not yet resolved. With this caveat in mind, the remainder of this section explores what is known about the APT.

Empirical Implications of the APT

Tests of the APT examine the following three implications:

1. The expected return of any portfolio with factor betas all equal to zero is the risk-free rate.
2. The expected returns of securities increase linearly with increases in a given factor beta.
3. No other characteristics of stocks, other than factor betas, determine expected returns.

Evidence from Factor Analysis Studies

Roll and Ross (1980) published one of the first APT tests using factor analysis. Because of the computational limitations of standard statistical factor analysis programs, they were forced to estimate factors on small numbers of stocks. In a test of 42 groups of 30 securities each, they found that in 88.1 percent of the groups there was at least one factor with a nonzero risk premium; in 57.1 percent of the groups, at least two with nonzero risk premiums; and in about one-third of the groups, at least three factors with nonzero risk premiums. Roll and Ross concluded that at least three factors are important for the APT's risk-expected return relation, but probably no more than four are important.

More recent papers used procedures that allow researchers to generate factor portfolios from much larger data sets. These include works by Chen (1983), Connor and Korajczyk (1988), and Lehmann and Modest (1988), which were all particularly interested in whether the factors explain the size effect.[25] Chen claimed that his factors explain the size effect: After controlling for differences in factor sensitivities between large and small firms, the return premium for size becomes negligible. However, Lehmann and Modest argued that there is still a size effect, even after controlling for these differences.

Evidence from Studies with Macroeconomic Factors

Chen, Roll, and Ross (1986), who analyzed a number of macroeconomic factors, found that the factors representing the growth rate in GDP, the yield spread between long- and

---

[25]The market-to-book ratio and the momentum effect had not attracted much academic attention at the time these papers were written.

short-term government bonds and changes in default spreads had significant effects on risk premiums. The two inflation factors had a weaker but still significant effect. They also performed tests using consumption and oil prices as factors and found that neither affected the expected returns of common stocks. In addition, when added to the regression, the return of the market index could not explain expected returns.

Chan, Chen, and Hsieh (1985) examined the size effect in the context of the Chen, Roll, and Ross model. They created 20 size-ranked portfolios and estimated the factor sensitivities of each portfolio to the five Chen, Roll, and Ross factors as well as the equal-weighted NYSE portfolio. They found that the difference in residuals between the portfolio of smallest firms and that of the largest is positive, but not statistically significant. They also conducted a test using the logarithm of firm size as an independent variable and found its coefficient to be insignificantly different from zero in the multifactor model. The authors concluded that the multifactor model explains the size anomaly.

A more recent paper by Jagannathan and Wang (1995) uses some of the Chen, Roll, and Ross macro factors to predict time series changes in the risk premiums associated with the factors and adds an additional macro factor, aggregate labor income, to explain the average stock returns. A number of interesting observations come from the Chan, Chen, and Hsieh (1985) and Jagannathan and Wang (1995) papers, which provide some insights about the small firm effect:

- Small company stock returns appear to be highly correlated with changes in the spread between Baa and default-free bonds.
- The spread seems to be a fairly good predictor of future market returns.
- Small companies have higher market betas when the spread is higher.
- Small company stock returns seem to covary more with per capita labor income than do the returns of large company stocks.

The first and last points imply that it is possible, at least in part, to explain the small-firm effect using a standard APT-type model that identifies the default spread and labor income as systematic factors associated with positive risk premiums. The middle two observations suggest that small firms, in essence, successfully "time the market." In other words, small firms have higher betas when the market risk premium is highest. The explanation of the small firm effect that comes from these studies is that small cap stocks have higher returns than large cap stocks because they are riskier in two aspects: (1) Their returns are more sensitive to short-term business cycle and credit movements that seem to be captured by the spread between high- and low-grade bonds and changes in aggregate labor income; (2) small cap stocks are especially sensitive to movements in the overall market when the market is the most risky. This means that the CAPM beta of the stock of a typical small company underestimates the stock's true risk.

Evidence from Studies That Use Firm Characteristics

Huberman, Kandel, and Stambaugh (1987) formed three factor portfolios based on market capitalization: small firms, medium-sized firms, and large firms. They used the returns of these portfolios as factors to explain the returns of other portfolios formed on the basis of firm size. They found that the size effect could not be captured fully by three size factors. Grinblatt and Titman (1989) extended this approach and included three factor portfolios constructed on the basis of dividend yield, one based on past returns, and four based on firm size to form an eight-portfolio benchmark that they used to evaluate mutual fund performance. More recently, Fama and French (1996) suggested a three-factor model composed of the following three zero-cost (i.e., self-financing) portfolios.

- A long position in the value-weighted index portfolio and a short position in T-bills—the difference between the realized return of the value-weighted market index and the return of Treasury bills.
- A long position in a portfolio of low market-to-book stocks and a short position in high market-to-book stocks.
- A long position in a portfolio of small capitalization stocks and a short position in a portfolio of large capitalization stocks.

Fama and French (1993, 1996a) asserted that the three factors explain most of the risk premiums of stocks, including those that cannot be accounted for by the CAPM. A notable exception is the momentum effect.[26]

Daniel and Titman (1997) reexamined the Fama and French characteristic-based factor portfolios and asked whether the betas associated with the characteristics portfolios or the characteristics themselves determine expected stock returns. In other words, they ask whether high or low expected returns are associated with small firms that have stock return patterns that are similar to large firms and high market-to-book firms that have return patterns that look more like the return patterns of low market-to-book firms. The APT and the CAPM suggest that the return patterns, not the characteristics, determine expected returns. Hence, stocks with return patterns that look like small firms should have expected returns similar to other small firms regardless of whether they are large or small. However, some of the behavioral stories suggest that small firms have high returns for reasons other than risk, so that a small firm that trades like a large firm should still have high expected returns.

The evidence provided by Daniel and Titman indicates that it is the characteristics rather than the factor betas on the characteristic-based factor portfolios that determine expected returns. Specifically, they found that stocks with low market-to-book ratios, but high betas with respect to the market-to-book factor portfolio, tended to have returns similar to other low market-to-book stocks. Similarly, the returns of high market-to-book stocks also were insensitive to their betas with respect to the market-to-book factor portfolios while stocks formed on the basis of size were found to be insensitive to their betas with respect to the size factor portfolio.

6.13 Summary and Conclusions

A factor model is a decomposition of the returns of securities into two categories: (1) a set of components correlated across securities and (2) a component that generates firm-specific risk and is uncorrelated across securities. The components that determine correlations across securities—common factors—are variables that represent some fundamental macroeconomic conditions. The components that are uncorrelated across securities represent firm-specific information.

The firm-specific risk, but not the factor risk, is diversified away in most large well-balanced portfolios.

Through a judicious choice of portfolio weights, however, it is possible to tailor portfolios with any factor beta configuration desired.

The arbitrage pricing theory is based on two ideas: first, that the returns of securities can be described by factor models; and second, that arbitrage opportunities do not exist. Using these two assumptions, it is possible to derive a multifactor version of the CAPM risk-expected return equation which expresses the expected returns of each security as a function of its factor betas. To test and implement the model, one must first identify the actual factors.

---

[26]The momentum effect was discussed in Chapter 5.

There are substantial differences between a multifactor APT and the CAPM that favor use of the APT in lieu of the CAPM. In contrast to the CAPM, the multifactor APT allows for the possibility that investors hold very different risky portfolios. In addition, the assumptions behind the CAPM seem relatively artificial when compared with those of the APT.

In choosing the multifactor APT over the CAPM, one must recognize that the research about what the factors are is still in its infancy. The three methods of implementing the multifactor APT are more successful than the CAPM in explaining historical returns. However, it appears that firm characteristics such as size and market-to-book (directly, as opposed to the indirect characteristic-based factor sensitivities), explain average historical returns more successfully. Until we can better determine what the factors are and which factors explain expected returns, the implications of APT will be fraught with ambiguity and will likely be controversial.

If the CAPM and the APT do not hold in reality, the theories may be quite useful to portfolio managers. Recall that according to the CAPM, the market compensates investors who bear systematic risk by providing higher rates of return. If this hypothesis is false, then portfolio managers can match the S&P 500 in terms of expected returns with a far less risky portfolio by concentrating on stocks with low betas. The evidence in this chapter suggests that in addition to buying low-beta stocks, investors should tilt their portfolios toward smaller cap firms with low market-to-book ratios. However, we stress that these suggestions are based on past evidence which may not be indicative of future events. As you know, economists do reasonably well explaining the past, but are generally a bit shaky when it comes to predicting the future.

Despite any shortcomings these theories exhibit when measured against historical data, the CAPM and APT have become increasingly important tools for evaluating capital investment projects.[27] They provide an increasingly significant framework for corporate financial analysts who can use them appropriately while understanding their limitations.

_____

[27]Chapter 10 discusses how firms can use the CAPM and the APT to calculate their costs of equity capital.

Key Concepts

Result 6.1: If securities returns follow a factor model (with uncorrelated residuals), portfolios with approximately equal weight on all securities have residuals with standard deviations that are approximately inversely proportional to the square root of the number of securities.

Result 6.2: The factor beta of a portfolio on a given factor is the portfolio-weighted average of the individual securities' betas on that factor.

Result 6.3: Assume that there are K factors uncorrelated with each other and that the returns of securities i and j are respectively described by the factor models:

$$\tilde{r}_i = \alpha_i + \beta_{i1}\tilde{F}_1 + \beta_{i2}\tilde{F}_2 + \ldots + \beta_{iK}\tilde{F}_K + \tilde{\epsilon}_i$$

$$\tilde{r}_j = \alpha_j + \beta_{j1}\tilde{F}_1 + \beta_{j2}\tilde{F}_2 + \ldots + \beta_{jK}\tilde{F}_K + \tilde{\epsilon}_j$$

Then the covariance between $\tilde{r}_i$ and $\tilde{r}_j$ is:

$$\sigma_{ij} = \beta_{i1}\beta_{j1}var(\tilde{F}_1) + \beta_{i2}\beta_{j2}var(\tilde{F}_2) + \ldots + \beta_{iK}\beta_{jK}var(\tilde{F}_K)$$

Result 6.4: When K factors are uncorrelated with each other and security i is described by the factor model:

$$\tilde{r}_i = \alpha_i + \beta_{i1}\tilde{F}_1 + \beta_{i2}\tilde{F}_2 + \ldots + \beta_{iK}\tilde{F}_K + \tilde{\epsilon}_i$$

the variance of $\tilde{r}_i$ can be decomposed into the sum of $K + 1$ terms:

$$var(\tilde{r}_i) = \beta_{i1}^2var(\tilde{F}_1) + \beta_{i2}^2var(\tilde{F}_2) + \ldots + \beta_{iK}^2var(\tilde{F}_K) + var(\tilde{\epsilon}_i)$$

Result 6.5: An investment with no firm-specific risk and a factor beta of β_j on the jth factor in a K-factor model is tracked by a portfolio with weights of β_1 on factor portfolio 1, β_2 on factor portfolio 2, . . . , β_K on factor portfolio K, and $1 - \sum_{j=1}^{K} \beta_j$ on the risk-free asset. The expected return of this tracking portfolio is therefore:

$$r_f + \beta_1\lambda_1 + \beta_2\lambda_2 + \ldots + \beta_K\lambda_K$$

where $\lambda_1, \lambda_2, \ldots \lambda_K$ denote the risk premiums of the factor portfolios and r_f is the risk-free return.

Result 6.6: An arbitrage opportunity exists for all investments with no firm-specific risk unless:

$$\bar{r}_i = r_f + \beta_{i1}\lambda_1 + \beta_{i2}\lambda_2 + \ldots + \beta_{iK}\lambda_K$$

where $\lambda_1, \ldots, \lambda_K$ applies to all investments with no firm-specific risk.

Key Terms

Exercises

6.1. Prove that the portfolio-weighted average of a
    stock's sensitivity to a particular factor is the
    same as the covariance between the return of the
    stock and the factor divided by the variance of the
    factor if the factors are uncorrelated with each
    other. Do this with the following steps: (1) Write
    out the factor equation for the portfolio by
    multiplying the factor equations of the individual
    stocks by the portfolio weights and adding.
    (2) Group terms that multiply the same factor.
    (3) Replace the factor betas of the individual stock
    returns by the covariance of the stock return with
    the factor divided by the variance of the factor.
    (4) Show that the portfolio-weighted average of
    the covariances that multiply each factor is the
    portfolio return's covariance with the factor. The
    rest is easy.

6.2. What is the minimum number of factors needed
    to explain the returns of a group of 10 securities
    that are uncorrelated with each other if the
    securities returns have no firm-specific risk?
    Why?

6.3. Consider the following two-factor model for the
    returns of three stocks. Assume that the factors
    and epsilons have means of zero. Also, assume the
    factors have variances of .01 and are uncorrelated
    with each other.

$$\tilde{r}_A = .13 + 6\tilde{F}_1 + 4\tilde{F}_2 + \tilde{\epsilon}_A$$

$$\tilde{r}_B = .15 + 2\tilde{F}_1 + 2\tilde{F}_2 + \tilde{\epsilon}_B$$

$$\tilde{r}_C = .07 + 5\tilde{F}_1 - 1\tilde{F}_2 + \tilde{\epsilon}_C$$

If the $var(\tilde{\epsilon}_A) = .01$ $var(\tilde{\epsilon}_B) = .04$ $var(\tilde{\epsilon}_C) = .02$,
what are the variances of the returns of the three

stocks, as well as the covariances and correlations
between them?

6.4. What are the expected returns of the three stocks
    in exercise 6.3?

6.5. Write out the factor betas, factor equations, and
    expected returns of the following portfolios:

    (1) A portfolio of the three stocks in exercise
        6.3 with $20,000 invested in stock A,
        −$20,000 invested in stock B, and $10,000
        invested in stock C.

    (2) A portfolio consisting of the portfolio
        formed in part (1) of this exercise and
        a $3,000 short position in stock C of
        exercise 6.3.

6.6. How much should be invested in each of the
    stocks in exercise 6.3 to design two portfolios?
    The first portfolio has the following attributes:

    factor 1 beta = 1
    factor 2 beta = 0

    The second portfolio has the attributes:

    factor 1 beta = 0
    factor 2 beta = 1

    Compute the expected returns and risk premiums
    of these two portfolios:

    (1) assuming the risk-free rate is 5 percent per
        year, and

    (2) assuming the risk-free rate is the "zero-beta
        rate" implied by the factor equations for
        the three stocks in exercise 6.3.

6.7. Two stocks, Uni and Due, have returns that follow the one factor model:

$$\tilde{r}_{uni} = .11 + 2\tilde{F} + \tilde{\epsilon}_{uni}$$

$$\tilde{r}_{due} = .17 + 5\tilde{F} + \tilde{\epsilon}_{due}$$

How much should be invested in each of the two securities to design a portfolio that has a factor beta of -3. What is the expected return of this portfolio, assuming that the factors and epsilons have means of zero?

6.8. Describe how you might design a portfolio of the 40 largest stocks that mimic the S&P 500. Why might you prefer to do this instead of investing in all 500 of the S&P 500 stocks?

6.9. Prove that $\alpha_i = (1 - \beta_i)r_f$ in equation (6.3), assuming the CAPM holds. To do this, take expected values of both sides of this equation and match up the values with those of the equation for the CAPM's securities market line.

6.10. Compute the firm-specific variance and firm-specific standard deviation of a portfolio that minimizes the firm-specific variance of a portfolio of 20 stocks. The first 10 stocks have firm-specific variances of .10. The second 10 stocks have firm-specific variances of .05.

References and Additional Readings

Abeysekera, Sarath P., and Arvind Mahajan. "A Test of the APT in Pricing UK Stocks." *Journal of Business Finance & Accounting* 14 (Autumn 1987), pp. 377–91.

Admati, Anat R., and Paul Pfleiderer. "Interpreting the Factor Risk Premia in the Arbitrage Pricing Theory." *Journal of Economic Theory* 35 (1985), pp. 191–95.

Berry, Michael A.; Edwin Burmeister; and Marjorie B. McElroy. "Sorting Out Risks Using Known APT Factors." *Financial Analysts Journal* 44 (Mar./Apr. 1988), pp. 29–42.

Bower, Dorothy; Richard S. Bower; and Dennis E. Logue. "Arbitrage Pricing Theory and Utility Stock Returns." *Journal of Finance* 39 (Sept. 1984), pp. 1041–54.

Brown, Stephen J. "The Number of Factors in Security Returns." *Journal of Finance* 44 (Dec. 1989), pp. 1247–62.

Brown, Stephen J., and Mark I. Weinstein. "A New Approach to Testing Asset Pricing Models: The Bilinear Paradigm." *Journal of Finance* 38 (June 1983), pp. 711–43.

Chan, K. C.; Nai-fu Chen; and David Hsieh. "An Exploratory Investigation of the Firm Size Effect." *Journal of Financial Economics* 14 (Sept. 1985), pp. 451–71.

Chan, Louis K.; Yasushi Hamao; and Josef Lakonishok. "Fundamentals and Stock Returns in Japan." *Journal of Finance* 46 (1991), pp. 1739–89.

Chen, Nai-fu. "Some Empirical Tests of the Theory of Arbitrage Pricing." *Journal of Finance* 38 (Dec. 1983), pp. 1393–1414.

Chen, Nai-fu; Richard Roll; and Stephen A. Ross. "Economic Forces and the Stock Market." *Journal of Business* 59 (July 1986), pp. 383–403.

Cho, D. Chinhyung. "On Testing the Arbitrage Pricing Theory: Inter-Battery Factor Analysis." *Journal of Finance* 39 (Dec. 1984), pp. 1485–1502.

Cho, D. Chinhyung; Edwin J. Elton; and Martin J. Gruber. "On the Robustness of the Roll and Ross Arbitrage Pricing Theory." *Journal of Financial Quantitative Analysis* 19 (Mar. 1984), pp. 1–10.

Cho, D. Chinhyung; Cheol S. Eun; and Lemma W. Senbet. "International Arbitrage Pricing Theory: An Empirical Investigation." *Journal of Finance* 41 (June 1986), pp. 313–29.

Connor, Gregory. "Notes on the Arbitrage Pricing Theory." In *Theory of Valuation: Frontiers of Modern Financial Theory,* Vol. 1, S. Bhattacharya and G. M. Constantinides, eds. Totowa, NJ: Rowman & Littlefield, 1989.

———. "A Unified Beta Pricing Theory." *Journal of Economic Theory* 34 (1984), pp. 13–31.

Connor, Gregory, and Robert Korajczyk. "The Arbitrage Pricing Theory and Multifactor Models of Asset Returns." Chapter 4 in *Handbook in Operations Research and Management Science. Vol. 9: Finance.* Robert Jarrow, V. Maksimovic, and W. Ziemba, eds. Amsterdam: Elsevier Science Publishers, 1995.

———. "Risk and Return in an Equilibrium APT: Application of a New Test Methodology." *Journal of Financial Economics* 21 (Sept. 1988a), pp. 255–89.

Cragg, John G., and Burton G. Malkiel. *Expectations and the Structure of Share Prices.* Chicago: University of Chicago Press, 1982.

Daniel, Kent, and Sheridan Titman. "Evidence on the Characteristics of Cross-Sectional Variation in Stock Returns." *Journal of Finance* 52 (Mar. 1997), pp. 1–33.

Dybvig, Philip H. "An Explicit Bound on Deviations from APT Pricing in a Finite Economy." *Journal of Financial Economics* 12 (Dec. 1983), pp. 483–96.

Dybvig, Philip H., and Stephen A. Ross. "Yes, the APT is Testable." *Journal of Finance* 40 (Sept. 1985), pp. 1173–88.

Elton, Edward J.; Martin J. Gruber; and Thomas J. Urich. "Are Betas Best?" *Journal of Finance* 33 (Dec. 1978), pp. 1375–84.

Erb, Claude; Campbell Harvey; and Tadas Viskanta. "Country Risk and Global Equity Selection." *Journal of Portfolio Management* 21, no. 2 (Winter 1994), pp. 74–83.

Fama, Eugene, and Kenneth French. "The CAPM Is Wanted: Dead or Alive." *Journal of Finance* 51, no. 5 (Dec. 1996b), pp. 1947–58.

———. "Common Risk Factors in the Returns on Stocks and Bonds." *Journal of Financial Economics* 33 (1993), pp. 3–56.

———. "Multifactor Explanations of Asset Pricing Anomalies." *Journal of Finance* 51, no. 1 (Mar. 1996a), pp. 55–84.

Gehr, Adam Jr. "Some Tests of the Arbitrage Pricing Theory," *Journal of the Midwest Finance Association* 7 (1978), pp. 91–106.

Grinblatt, Mark, and Sheridan Titman, "Approximate Factor Structures: Interpretations and Implications for Empirical Test." *Journal of Finance* 40 (Dec. 1985), pp. 1367–73.

———. "Factor Pricing in a Finite Economy." *Journal of Financial Economics* 12 (Dec. 1983), pp. 497–507.

———. "The Relation between Mean-Variance Efficiency and Arbitrage Pricing." *Journal of Business* 60 (Jan. 1987), pp. 97–112.

Gultekin, N. Bulent, and Richard J. Rogalski. "Government Bond Returns, Measurement of Interest Rate Risk, and the Arbitrage Pricing Theory." *Journal of Finance* 40 (Mar. 1985), pp. 43–61.

Hamao, Yasushi. "An Empirical Examination of the Arbitrage Pricing Theory: Using Japanese Data." *Japan World Econ.* 1 (1988), pp. 45–61, reprinted in *Japanese Capital Markets*. Edwin J. Elton and Martin J. Gruber, eds. New York: Harper & Row, 1990.

Huberman, Gur, "Arbitrage Pricing Theory." In *The New Palgrave: Finance*, J. Eatwell, M. Milgate, and P. Newman, eds. New York: Norton, 1989.

———. "A Simple Approach to Arbitrage Pricing." *Journal of Economic Theory* 28 (1982), pp. 183–91.

Huberman, Gur; Shmuel Kandel; and Robert Stambaugh. "Mimicking Portfolios and Exact Arbitrage Pricing." *Journal of Finance* 42, no. 4 (1987), pp. 873–88.

Hughes, Patricia J. "A Test of the Arbitrage Pricing Theory Using Canadian Security Returns." *Canadian Journal of Administrative Science* 1 (1984), pp. 195–214.

Ingersoll, Jonathan E. "Some Results in the Theory of Arbitrage Pricing." *Journal of Finance* 39 (Sept. 1984), pp. 1021–39.

Jagannathan, Ravi, and Zhenyn Wang. "The Conditional CAPM and the Cross-Section of Expected Returns." *Journal of Finance* 51, no. 1 (March 1996), pp. 3–53.

Jobson, J. D. "A Multivariate Linear Regression Test of the Arbitrage Pricing Theory." *Journal of Finance* 37 (Sept. 1981), pp. 1037–42.

Jones, Robert C. "Designing Factor Models for Different Types of Stock." *Financial Analysts Journal* 46 (Mar./Apr. 1990), pp. 25–30.

Kuwahara, Hirohito, and Terry A. Marsh. "The Pricing of Japanese Equity Warrants." *Management Science* 38 (1992), pp. 1610–41.

Lehmann, Bruce N., and David M. Modest. "The Empirical Foundations of the Arbitrage Pricing Theory." *Journal of Financial Economics* 21 (Sept. 1988), pp. 213–54.

Levine, Ross. "An International Arbitrage Pricing Model with PPP Deviations." *Economic Inquiry* 27 (Oct. 1989), pp. 587–99.

Litterman, Robert, and Jose Scheinkman. "Common Factors Affecting Bond Returns." *Journal of Fixed Income* 1 (June 1991), pp. 54–61.

McCulloch, Robert, and Peter E. Rossi. "A Bayesian Approach to Testing the Arbitrage Pricing Theory." *Journal of Econometrics* 49 (1991), pp. 141–168.

McElroy, Marjorie B., and Edwin Brumeister. "Arbitrage Pricing Theory as a Restricted Nonlinear Multivariate Regression Model." *Journal of Business & Economic Statistics* 6 (Jan. 1988), pp. 29–42.

Reinganum, Marc. "The Arbitrage Pricing Theory: Some Simple Tests." *Journal of Finance* 36 (May 1981), pp. 313–22.

Roll, Richard, and Stephen A. Ross. "The Arbitrage Pricing Theory Approach to Strategic Portfolio Planning." *Financial Analysts Journal* (May/June 1984), pp. 14–26.

———. "An Empirical Investigation of the Arbitrage Pricing Theory." *Journal of Finance* 35 (Dec. 1980), pp. 1073–1103.

———. "Regulation, the Capital Asset Pricing Model, and the Arbitrage Pricing Theory." *Public Utilities Fortnightly* (May 26, 1983), pp. 22–28.

Rosenberg, Barr. "Choosing a Multiple Factor Model." *Investment Management Review* (Nov./Dec. 1987), pp. 28–35.

————. "Extra-Market Components of Covariance in Security Returns." *Journal of Financial and Quantitative Analysis* 9 (Mar. 1974), pp. 263–74.

Ross, Stephen A. "The Arbitrage Theory of Capital Asset Pricing." *Journal of Economic Theory* 13 (Dec. 1976), pp. 341–60.

————. "Return, Risk and Arbitrage." In *Risk and Return in Finance,* Irwin Friend and James Bicksler, eds. Cambridge, MA: Ballinger, 1977.

Shanken, Jay. "The Arbitrage Pricing Theory: Is It Testable?' *Journal of Finance* 37 (Dec. 1982), pp. 1129–40.

Shanken, Jay, and Mark I. Weinstein, "Macroeconomic Variables and Asset Pricing: Estimation and Tests." Working paper, University of Rochester, July 1990.

Sharpe, William F. "Factor Models, CAPMs, and the APT." *Journal of Portfolio Management* 11 (Fall 1984), pp. 21–25.

Warga, Arthur. "Experimental Design in Tests of Linear Factor Models." *Journal of Business and Economic Statistics* 7 (Apr. 1989), pp. 191–98.

Wei, K. C. John. "An Asset Pricing Theory Unifying the CAPM and APT." *Journal of Finance* 43 (Sept. 1988), 881–92.

Wei, K. C. John; Cheng Few Lee; and Andrew H. Chen. "Multivariate Regression Tests of the Arbitrage Pricing Theory: The Instrumental Variable Approach." *Review of Quantitative Finance and Accounting* 1 (Mar. 1991), pp. 191–208.

Winkelmann, Michael. "Testing APT for the German Stock Market." In *Proceedings of the 11th Annual Meeting of the European Finance Association,* Manchester, England, Sept. 1984.

Pricing Derivatives

Learning Objectives

After reading this chapter, you should be able to:

1. Explain what a derivative is and how basic derivatives, like futures, forwards, options, and swaps, work.
2. Use the binomial model to construct a derivative's tracking portfolio and understand its importance in valuing the derivative.
3. Understand how to form arbitrage portfolios if a derivative's market price differs from its model price.
4. Use risk-neutral valuation methods to solve for the no-arbitrage prices of any derivative in a binomial framework and understand why risk-neutral solutions to the valuation problems of derivatives are identical to solutions based on tracking portfolios.

Merrill has $250 million loss on unauthorized trading
. . . Executives at Merrill Lynch privately identified the trader as Howard A. Rubin, 36 years old, who had been the firm's head mortgage trader. They said he had far exceeded his limits in acquiring mortgages that were packaged into a particularly risky form of securities. The package involves splitting off the interest payments on the mortgages from the principal and selling each separately. They are known only as interest-only/principal-only securities, or IO/POs . . .
The Wall Street Journal, *April 29, 1987*

The late 1970s and the 1980s saw a Wall Street boom that revolved around the development of new financial products. Virtually all of these products were investments known as derivatives. Derivative securities were introduced in Chapter 4. This chapter provides a more complete analysis. Recall that a *derivative* is an investment whose value today or at some future date is derived entirely from the value of another asset (or a group of other assets), known as the **underlying asset** (assets). Examples of derivatives include interest rate futures contracts; options on futures; mortgage-backed securities; interest rate caps and floors; swap options; commodity-linked bonds; zero-coupon Treasury strips; and all sorts of options, contractual arrangements, and bets related to the values of other more primitive securities.

Derivatives have now entered into the public discourse and political debate, as anyone who has read a newspaper in the first half of the 1990s is aware. Metallgesellschaft AG, Orange County, Gibson Greetings, Procter and Gamble, and Barings Bank, to name a few, received substantial unwanted publicity because of derivative investments that went sour.

Despite these "scandals," derivatives remain popular among investors and corporations because they represent low transaction cost vehicles for managing risk and for betting on the price movements of various securities. For example, Wall Street investors shorted the Nikkei and Topix futures contracts to hedge their purchases of some undervalued Japanese warrants (see Chapter 6). Savings banks, which finance long-term loans with short-term deposits, enter into interest rate swaps to reduce the interest rate risk in their balance sheets. Corporations such as Disney, with substantial revenues from Japan, enter into currency swaps and currency forward rate agreements to eliminate currency risk. Pension fund managers, with large exposure to stock price movements, buy put options on stock indexes to place a floor on their possible losses. Mutual funds that have accumulated large profits may short stock index futures contracts in order to effectively realize capital gains in an appreciating stock market without selling stock, thereby avoiding unnecessary taxes. The list of profitable uses of derivatives is extensive.

The most important use of derivatives is hedging,[1] which requires a sound understanding of how to value derivatives. Derivatives hedging is based on the notion that the change in the value of a derivative investment can offset changes in the value of the underlying asset. However, it is impossible to understand how a derivative's value changes without first understanding what the proper value is.

Some derivatives are straightforward to value and others are complicated. Every year on Wall Street, hundreds of millions of dollars are made and lost by speculators willing to test their skills and their models by placing bets on what they believe are misvalued derivatives. The **principal-only securities (POs)**, discussed in the opening vignette, are among the more complex types of derivatives to value. As their name suggests, POs receive only the principal from a pool of mortgages. In Michael Lewis's book, *Liar's Poker,* the losses of Howie Rubin were tied to his positions in POs, and "no bond plummets faster when interest rates go up than a PO."[2] However, during the derivatives debacle of the 1980s, the mortgage arbitrage group at Salomon Brothers profited immensely from a hedged position in the similarly complicated **interest-only securities (IOs)**, which receive only the interest from pools of mortgages. Not surprisingly, a key player in this group, Greg ("the Hawk") Hawkins, was a former academic and an expert at derivatives valuation.

The major breakthrough in the valuation of derivatives started with a simple call option. At about the same time that options began trading on an organized exchange (in 1973 at the Chicago Board Options Exchange), two finance professors at the Massachusetts Institute of Technology, Fischer Black and Myron Scholes, came out with a formula, commonly known as the Black-Scholes formula, that related the price of a call option to the price of the stock to which the option applies. This formula was the start of a revolution for both academics and practitioners in their approach to finance.

---

[1]Hedging is covered in depth in Part VI.

[2] Michael Lewis, *Liar's Poker: Rising through the Wreckage on Wall Street* (New York: W. W. Norton, 1989), p. 145.

The Black-Scholes model that led to the development of this formula is now part of a family of valuation models, most of which are more sophisticated than the Black-Scholes model. This family, known as derivatives valuation models, is based on the now familiar principle of no arbitrage. No-arbitrage valuation principles can determine the fair market price of almost any derivative. Knowledge of these principles is common in the financial services industry. Therefore, it is often possible to tailor a security that is ideally suited to a corporation's needs and to identify a set of investors who will buy that security. The financial intermediaries such as investment banks that design the security largely concern themselves with what design will be attractive to corporations and investors. These intermediaries do not worry about the risks of taking bets opposite to those of their customers when they "make markets" in these derivatives because they can determine, to a high degree of precision, what the security is worth and hedge risks associated with it.[3]

The analysis of derivatives in this chapter begins by exploring some of the derivatives encountered by the corporate financial manager and the sophisticated investor, followed by an examination of valuation principles that apply to all derivatives.[4]

7.1 Examples of Derivatives

This section introduces a number of derivatives: forwards and futures, swaps, options, corporate bonds, mortgage-backed securities, and structured notes. The section also introduces derivatives that are implicit in real assets.

Forwards and Futures

A **forward contract** represents the obligation to buy (sell) a security or commodity at a prespecified price, known as the **forward price**, at some future date. Forward contracts are inherent in many business contracts and have been in existence for hundreds of years. Exhibit 7.1 illustrates the exchange that takes place at the **maturity date**, or **settlement**

EXHIBIT 7.1   The Exchange of an Asset for Cash in a Forward Contract at Maturity

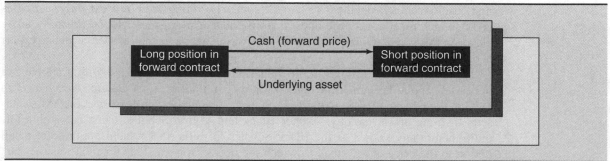

---

[3]An investment bank will often serve as an over-the-counter market maker in the derivative it creates, standing ready to buy the derivative at a bid price and sell it at an ask price.

[4]The valuation of options, one of the most popular derivatives, is covered in some depth in Chapter 8, which also touches briefly on forward prices for some complex assets such as bonds, commodities, and foreign exchange.

date, of the forward contract. At maturity, the person or firm with the long position pays the forward price to the person with the short position, who in turn delivers the asset underlying the forward contract. **Futures contracts** are a special type of forward contract that trade on organized exchanges known as **futures markets**.

Exhibits 7.2 and 7.3 introduce foreign exchange forwards and futures. The "Currency Trading" listing in the *Wall Street Journal* (see Exhibit 7.2) shows 30-, 90-, and 180-day forward currency rates for exchanging dollars for British pounds, Canadian dollars, French francs, German marks, Japanese yen, and Swiss francs. The rates are similar to those provided in the futures market (see Exhibit 7.3 on page 238). For example, the Japanese yen had a foreign exchange rate on Tuesday, August 27, 1996, at 3 P.M. New York time, of 107.71 yen to the U.S. dollar. However, the 180-day forward rate was 104.98 yen to the dollar. This means that one could have agreed at 3 P.M. that day to have exchanged a single U.S. dollar for 104.98 yen 180 days hence. Exhibit 7.3

EXHIBIT 7.2   Currency Trading

CURRENCY TRADING

EXCHANGE RATES

Tuesday, August 27, 1996

The New York foreign exchange selling rates below apply to trading among banks in amounts of $1 million and more, as quoted at 3 p.m. Eastern time by Dow Jones Telerate Inc. and other sources. Retail transactions provide fewer units of foreign currency per dollar.

Country	U.S. $ equiv. Tue	U.S. $ equiv. Mon	Currency per U.S. $ Tue	Currency per U.S. $ Mon
Argentina (Peso)	1.0012	1.0012	.9988	.9988
Australia (Dollar)	.7881	.7910	1.2689	1.2642
Austria (Schilling)	.09622	.09614	10.393	10.401
Bahrain (Dinar)	2.6525	2.6525	.3770	.3770
Belgium (Franc)	.03283	.03286	30.460	30.430
Brazil (Real)	.9844	.9835	1.0158	1.0168
Britain (Pound)	1.5549	1.5578	.6431	.6419
30-Day Forward	1.5545	1.5571	.6433	.6422
90-Day Forward	1.5554	1.5576	.6429	.6420
180-Day Forward	1.5565	1.5577	.6425	.6420
Canada (Dollar)	.7305	.7294	1.3689	1.3710
30-Day Forward	.7313	.7302	1.3674	1.3695
90-Day Forward	.7330	.7318	1.3643	1.3665
180-Day Forward	.7353	.7341	1.3599	1.3623
Chile (Peso)	.002435	.002437	410.65	410.35
China (Renminbi)	.1199	.1199	8.3371	8.3371
Colombia (Peso)	.0009685	.0009685	1032.50	1032.50
Czech. Rep. (Koruna)	....	....		
Commercial rate	.03824	.03810	26.150	26.246
Denmark (Krone)	.1750	.1750	5.7127	5.7130
Ecuador (Sucre)	....	....		
Floating rate	.0003077	.0003071	3250.00	3256.00
Finland (Markka)	.2233	.2230	4.4775	4.4851
France (Franc)	.1976	.1980	5.0600	5.0515
30-Day Forward	.1979	.1983	5.0528	5.0440
90-Day Forward	.1984	.1988	5.0408	5.0305
180-Day Forward	.1992	.1996	5.0207	5.0088
Germany (Mark)	.6765	.6760	1.4782	1.4793
30-Day Forward	.6778	.6772	1.4753	1.4766
90-Day Forward	.6805	.6799	1.4696	1.4709
180-Day Forward	.6849	.6843	1.4600	1.4614
Greece (Drachma)	.004229	.004231	236.44	236.36
Hong Kong (Dollar)	.1293	.1293	7.7323	7.7328
Hungary (Forint)	.006495	.006486	153.96	154.17
India (Rupee)	.02799	.02802	35.730	35.690
Indonesia (Rupiah)	.0004270	.0004270	2342.00	2342.00
Ireland (Punt)	1.6176	1.6197	.6182	.6174
Israel (Shekel)	.3188	.3183	3.1365	3.1415
Italy (Lira)	.0006614	.0006617	1512.00	1511.25
Japan (Yen)	.009284	.009281	107.71	107.75
30-Day Forward	.009325	.009320	107.24	107.29
90-Day Forward	.009402	.009399	106.36	106.39
180-Day Forward	.009526	.009524	104.98	105.00
Jordan (Dinar)	1.4065	1.4065	.7110	.7110
Kuwait (Dinar)	3.3422	3.3422	.2992	.2992
Lebanon (Pound)	.0006400	.0006398	1562.50	1563.00
Malaysia (Ringgit)	.4011	.4012	2.4930	2.4925
Malta (Lira)	2.8090	2.8011	.3560	.3570
Mexico (Peso)				
Floating rate	.1333	.1332	7.5010	7.5070
Netherland (Guilder)	.6035	.6032	1.6569	1.6577
New Zealand (Dollar)	.6914	.6944	1.4463	1.4401
Norway (Krone)	.1559	.1561	6.4133	6.4060
Pakistan (Rupee)	.02846	.02846	35.140	35.140
Peru (new Sol)	.4061	.4074	2.4626	2.4547
Philippines (Peso)	.03818	.03814	26.195	26.221
Poland (Zloty)	.3657	.3662	2.7345	2.7311
Portugal (Escudo)	.006596	.006592	151.61	151.71
Russia (Ruble) (a)	.0001868	.0001873	5352.00	5339.00
Saudi Arabia (Riyal)	.2666	.2666	3.7505	3.7505
Singapore (Dollar)	.7102	.7100	1.4080	1.4085
Slovak Rep. (Koruna)	.03314	.03314	30.175	30.175
South Africa (Rand)	.2211	.2206	4.5225	4.5325
South Korea (Won)	.001221	.001222	818.75	818.05
Spain (Peseta)	.008001	.008000	124.99	125.00
Sweden (Krona)	.1514	.1519	6.6048	6.5822
Switzerland (Franc)	.8378	.8379	1.1936	1.1935
30-Day Forward	.8401	.8401	1.1903	1.1904
90-Day Forward	.8447	.8446	1.1839	1.1840
180-Day Forward	.8486	.8519	1.1784	1.1739
Taiwan (Dollar)	.03640	.03640	27.475	27.473
Thailand (Baht)	.03957	.03954	25.271	25.288
Turkey (Lira)	.00001163	.00001163	85958.50	85997.50
United Arab (Dirham)	.2724	.2724	3.6715	3.6715
Uruguay (New Peso)				
Financial	.1209	.1209	8.2700	8.2700
Venezuela (Bolivar) b	.002105	.002102	475.00	475.65
Brady Rate	.002098	.002098	476.75	476.75
— — —				
SDR	1.4614	1.4603	.6843	.6848
ECU	1.2724	1.2736	....	....

Special Drawing Rights (SDR) are based on exchange rates for the U.S., German, British, French, and Japanese currencies. Source: International Monetary Fund.

European Currency Unit (ECU) is based on a basket of community currencies.

a-fixing, Moscow Interbank Currency Exchange.
b-Changed to market rate effective Apr. 22.

EXHIBIT 7.3   Futures Prices for Currency

CURRENCY

	Open	High	Low	Settle	Change	Lifetime High	Lifetime Low	Open Interest
JAPAN YEN (CME)-12.5 million yen; $ per yen (.00)								
Sept	.9312	.9330	.9289	.9311	+ .0002	1.2085	.8636	71,276
Dec	.9405	.9432	.9405	.9429	+ .0002	1.0500	.9214	6,422
Mr97	.9547	.9547	.9547	.9549	+ .0002	1.0045	.9330	167
June	....	....	....	.9669	+ .0002	.9790	.9465	188
Est vol 8,727; vol Mn 16,851; open int 78,069, −3,420.								
DEUTSCHEMARK (CME)-125,000 marks; $ per mark								
Sept	.6770	.6794	.6764	.6772	+ .0003	.7312	.6497	66,096
Dec	.6821	.6826	.6809	.6812	+ .0003	.7070	.6537	6,183
Mr97	....	....	....	.6858	+ .0003	.6937	.6633	953
Est vol 10,900; vol Mn 11,891; open int 73,242, −2,168.								
CANADIAN DOLLAR (CME)-100,000 dlrs.; $ per Can $								
Sept	.7306	.7322	.7300	.7316	+ .0016	.7490	.7170	35,243
Dec	.7330	.7345	.7330	.7339	+ .0016	.7460	.7130	5,588
Mr97	.7363	.7365	.7363	.7361	+ .0016	.7400	.7117	491
June	.7380	.7386	.7397	.7376	+ .0016	.7405	.7185	695
Sept	....	....	....	.7385	+ .0016	.7380	.7309	118
Est vol 6,386; vol Mn 4,772; open int 42,135, −573.								
BRITISH POUND (CME)-62,500 pds.; $ per pound								
Sept	1.5568	1.5592	1.5526	1.5544	− .0024	1.5840	1.4860	50,773
Dec	1.5584	1.5588	1.5520	1.5540	− .0024	1.5660	1.4850	1,529
Est vol 6,326; vol Mn 5,115; open int 52,311, +278.								
SWISS FRANC (CME)-125,000 francs; $ per franc								
Sept	.8392	.8435	.8380	.8395	+ .0003	.9188	.7917	37,683
Dec	.8488	.8488	.8451	.8465	+ .0003	.8999	.7976	3,434
Mr97	.8554	.8560	.8535	.8541	+ .0003	.8715	.8050+	620
Est vol 7,747; vol Mn 8,273; open int 41,717, +50.								
AUSTRALIAN DOLLAR (CME)-100,000 dlrs.; $ per A.$								
Sept	.7904	.7905	.7861	.7872	− .0028	.7987	.7250	10,489
Dec	.7865	.7865	.7843	.7849	− .0028	.7930	.7665	175
Est vol 534; vol Mn 624; open int 10,699, −85.								
MEXICAN PESO (CME)-500,000 new Mex. peso, $ per MP								
Sept	.13112	.13170	.13112	.13170	+ .0035	.13230	.08600	11,352
Dec	.12390	.12425	.12370	.12425	+ .0030	.12520	09900	7,068
Mr97	.11680	.11730	.11670	.11730	+ .0035	.12240	.10070	1,583
June	.11040	.11090	.11040	.11095	+ .0020	.11550	.10270	415
Est vol 2,921; vol Mn 2,116; open int 20,418, −86.								

Source: Reprinted by permission of *The Wall Street Journal*, © 1996 by Dow Jones & Company. All Rights Reserved Worldwide.

contains data on comparable exchange rate futures. The futures exchange rate with the closest maturity, the March 1997 contract traded on the Chicago Mercantile Exchange, specifies 100 yen is exchangeable for .9549 U.S. dollars, which translates into one U.S. dollar being exchanged for 104.72 Yen. The relatively minor discrepancy between the two, 104.98 vs. 104.72, can be mostly attributed to slight differences in both the quote times and the maturities of the forward contract and the futures contract.

Markets for Forwards and Futures.   The first organized futures trading market, the Chicago Board of Trade, dates back to the U.S. Civil War. Although the Board's early trading records were lost in the Great Chicago Fire of 1871, the earliest futures contracts were probably limited to agricultural commodities that were grown in the Midwest.

Today, futures and forward markets are also well known for the trading of contracts on financial securities, such as Treasury bonds, stock indexes, short-term interest rate instruments, and currencies. Because of their sheer size and the relevance of their prices to the actions of investors, the three most important financial futures markets are those that trade:

- U.S. Treasury bond futures, which allows delivery of almost any treasury bond with 15 years maturity or more remaining.
- Eurodollar futures, which is a cash settled bet on the future value of three-month LIBOR.
- S&P 500 futures, a cash-settled bet on the future level of the S&P 500 stock index.

The most important financial forward market is the interbank forward market for currencies, particularly dollars for yen and dollars for deutsche marks.

In Exhibit 7.4, the rows under "Crude Oil" provide the New York Mercantile Exchange's futures prices (in dollars per barrel) for contracts to buy 1,000 barrels of light sweet crude oil. The column on the far right is the **open interest**, which is the number of contracts outstanding. On August 27, 1996 there were 6,427 May '97 contracts and 24,658 June '97 contracts. Open interest can be thought of as the number of bets between customers about oil prices. The column labeled "Settle" describes the closing price for August 26, 1996. This price is used, along with the previous day's settlement price, to determine how much cash is exchanged between parties to the contract that day. The contracts maturing in mid-May 1997 and mid-June 1997 specify settlement prices of $19.00 and $18.76 per barrel, respectively.

Distinguishing Forwards from Futures.   The essential distinction between a forward and a futures contract lies in the timing of cash flows. With a forward contract, cash is paid for the underlying asset only at the maturity date of the contract. It is useful to think of this cash amount, the forward price, as the sum of

1. What one would pay for immediate delivery of the underlying asset at the maturity date without the forward contract—this is known as the **spot price** at maturity, essentially, the prevailing market price of the underlying asset.
2. The profit (or loss) incurred as a result of having to pay the forward price in lieu of this spot price.

With a futures contract, the price paid at maturity is the spot price. The profit (or loss) is received (paid) on a daily basis instead of in one large amount at the maturity date. The amount the buyer receives from (pays to) the seller of the futures contract is

EXHIBIT 7.4   Futures Prices for Oil

	Open	High	Low	Settle	Change	Lifetime High	Lifetime Low	Open Interest
CRUDE OIL, Light Sweet (NYM) 1,000 bbls.; $ per bbl.								
Oct	21.58	21.87	21.45	21.56	− 0.06	22.55	16.70	84,729
Nov	21.10	21.35	21.00	21.08	− 0.09	21.95	16.68	37,861
Dec	20.66	20.89	20.60	20.63	− 0.07	21.30	16.65	45,477
Ja97	20.22	20.51	20.22	20.23	− 0.07	20.80	16.70	30,170
Feb	19.90	20.15	19.90	19.88	− 0.08	20.35	16.72	21,871
Mar	19.69	19.75	19.63	19.55	− 0.07	20.00	16.75	13,566
Apr	19.40	19.51	19.37	19.26	− 0.07	19.70	16.74	11,098
May	19.12	19.12	19.12	19.00	− 0.07	19.40	16.92	6,427
June	18.85	19.05	18.85	18.76	− 0.07	19.60	16.71	24,658
July	.....	.....	.....	18.58	− 0.07	19.00	16.80	8,647
Aug	18.57	18.57	18.57	18.41	− 0.08	18.75	16.88	4,378
Sept	.....	.....	.....	18.25	− 0.08	18.60	16.71	5,879
Oct	18.24	18.32	18.24	18.09	− 0.09	18.50	16.84	2,685
Nov	.....	.....	.....	17.93	− 0.11	18.31	16.90	5,885
Dec	18.00	18.00	18.00	17.83	− 0.11	19.20	16.80	21,462
Ja98	.....	.....	.....	17.77	− 0.11	18.13	17.04	6,502
Feb	.....	.....	.....	17.71	− 0.12	18.04	17.15	1,735
Mar	.....	.....	.....	17.66	− 0.12	18.07	17.30	1,571
Apr	.....	.....	.....	17.61	− 0.12	17.95	17.38	557
May	.....	.....	.....	17.56	− 0.13	17.90	17.39	367
June	17.78	17.78	17.78	17.52	− 0.13	18.70	17.17	5,921
July	.....	.....	.....	17.48	− 0.14	17.70	17.60	1,055
Aug	.....	.....	.....	17.46	− 0.15	.....	.....	98
Sept	.....	.....	.....	17.46	− 0.15	18.06	17.94	520
Oct	.....	.....	.....	17.46	− 0.15	18.00	17.75	71
Nov	.....	.....	.....	17.47	− 0.15	.....	.....	170
Dec	17.79	17.79	17.74	17.48	− 0.15	19.10	17.05	7,326
Ju99	.....	.....	.....	17.57	− 0.15	18.15	17.90	1,264
Dec	17.95	18.00	17.95	17.70	− 0.15	19.82	17.62	6,842

the one-day appreciation (depreciation) of the futures price. For example, if the futures price of oil rises from $20 a barrel to $22 a barrel from Monday to Tuesday, the buyer of a futures contract on 1,000 barrels receives $2,000 from the seller on Tuesday. This procedure, known as **marking to market**, reduces the risk of default because the amounts that each side has to pay on a daily basis are relatively small. Moreover, it facilitates early detection in the event that one party to the contract lacks sufficient cash to pay for his or her losses.

The marking to market takes place automatically, by transferring funds between the margin accounts of the two investors agreeing to the contact. These **margin accounts** are simply deposits placed with brokers as security against default.

Example 7.1 illustrates how marking-to-market works.

Example 7.1:   Marking to Market with S&P 500 Futures

Trevor has a long position in the March futures contract to buy 1 unit of the S&P 500. Gordon has a short position in the same contract. If the futures price for the March S&P 500 contract is 754 on January 12, but it rises to 757 on January 13, and then falls to 756.2 on January 14, and falls to 755.5 on January 15, describe the cash payments and margin accounts of Trevor's long and Gordon's short position. Assume that each of the margin accounts of Trevor and Gordon initially contains $40.

Answer: The mark-to-market feature implies that the margin accounts of the long and short positions are described by the table below:

Date	Trevor's Long Margin	Change from Day Before	Gordon's Short Margin	Change from Day Before
Jan. 12	$40.0	—	$40.0	—
Jan. 13	$43.0	$3.0	37.0	−$3.0
Jan. 14	$42.2	−.8	37.8	.8
Jan. 15	$41.5	−.7	38.5	.7

With a few exceptions, notably long-term interest rate contracts, the distinction in the timing of cash flows from profits or losses has a negligible effect on the fair market price agreed to in forward and futures contracts.[5] Hence, this text treats forward and futures prices as if they are identical.

Swaps

A **swap** is an agreement between two investors, or **counterparties** as they are sometimes called, to periodically exchange the cash flows of one security for the cash flows of another. The last date of exchange determines the **swap maturity**. For example, a fixed-for-floating **interest rate swap** (see Exhibit 7.5) exchanges the cash flows of a fixed-rate bond for the cash flows of a floating rate bond. The **notional amount** of the swap represents the size of the principal on which interest is calculated.

---

[5]See Grinblatt and Jegadeesh (1996).

EXHIBIT 7.5   The Cash Flows of a Five-Year Semiannual Fixed for Floating Interest Rate Swap: $100 Notional

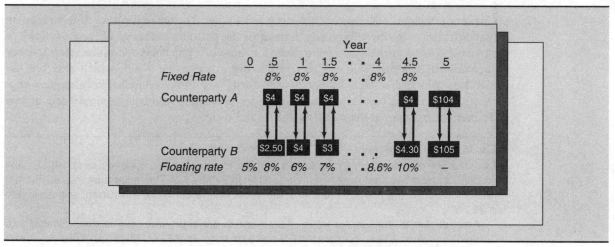

Netting in an Interest Rate Swap.   The cash flows in an interest rate swap are netted so that periodically, typically every six months, only one of two swap counterparties pays cash and the other receives cash. In the typical swap, the floating rate is LIBOR.[6]

Example 7.2 illustrates how netting affects swap payments.

Example 7.2:   Netting Payments in an Interest Rate Swap

If the fixed interest rate in a swap with semiannual payments is 8 percent per year (4 percent for 6 months) and the floating interest rate is 8.6 percent per year, how much does the party who pays the floating rate and receives the fixed rate receive or pay? What would happen to that party if, six months later, the floating interest rate had increased to 10 percent per annum?

Answer: As seen in Exhibit 7.5, at year 4.5, counterparty A swaps its fixed payments of $\$4 \left[= \dfrac{8\%}{2}\$100 \right]$ with counterparty B's floating payments $\left[= \dfrac{\text{floating rate }\%}{2}\$100 \right]$. Counterparty B would thus *pay* \$.30 $\left[= \dfrac{8.6\% - 8\%}{2}\$100 \right]$ per \$100 of notional amount to counterparty A. If interest rates at year 4.5 increase to 10 percent, counterparty B *pays* \$1.00 $\left[= \dfrac{10\% - 8\%}{2}\$100 \right]$ per \$100 of notional amount to counterparty A at year 5.

Growth of the Interest Rate Swap Market.   Interest rate swaps are one of the great derivatives success stories. At the end of 1987, the aggregate notional amount of interest rate swaps outstanding was less than $800 billion. By the end of the decade, that amount had more than doubled. Two years later, at the end of 1992, the aggregate notional amount had grown to almost $4 trillion; one year after that, at the end of 1993, it was over $6 trillion. By the end of 1996, the estimated notional amount of interest rate swaps

---

[6]Swaps are often used in conjunction with interest rate caps and floors, which are also popular derivatives. Caps pay when prevailing interest rates exceed a prespecified rate and floors pay if the prespecified rate exceeds the prevailing rate. See Chapter 2 for further discussion.

exceeded $26 trillion, which is about half of the entire derivatives market—many times the value of all U.S. stocks![7]

Currency Swaps.   A *currency swap* (see Chapter 2) exchanges cash flow streams in two different currencies. Typically, it involves the periodic exchange of the cash flows of a par bond denominated in one currency for those of a par bond denominated in another currency. In contrast with a fixed-for-floating interest rate swap, which nets out the identical principal of the two bonds at maturity and thus exchanges only interest payments, the typical currency swap exchanges principal, which is denominated in two different currencies, at the maturity date of the swap.

Example 7.3:   Payments in a Currency Swap

Describe the exchange of payments in a fixed-for-fixed dollar-yen currency swap with annual payments and a $100 notional amount as shown in Exhibit 7.6. The dollar bond has an interest rate of 7 percent, the yen bond has an interest rate of 5 percent, and the current exchange rate is ¥80/$.

Answer: Here, the interest rates of both bonds are fixed, but each is denominated in a different currency. Thus, counterparty *A* will exchange its $7 [= (7%)$100] fixed payments with counterparty *B*'s fixed payments of ¥400 [= (5%)$100(80¥/$)], as illustrated in Exhibit 7.6.

The typical forward contracts, futures contracts, and swap contracts are self-financing, or **zero-cost instruments**[8]—that is, the terms of these contracts are set so that one party does not have to pay the other party to enter into the contract. In many instances, margin or collateral is put up by both parties, which protects against default in the event of extreme market movements, but this is not the same as paying someone to

---

EXHIBIT 7.6   The Cash Flows of a Five-Year Annual Yen-Dollar Fixed-Rate Currency Swap: $100 Notional

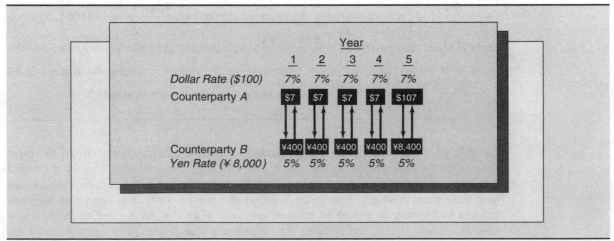

---

[7]*Swaps Monitor,* Dec. 2, 1996.
[8]See Chapter 5 for the first use of the term *self-financing.*

enter into the contract because the terms of the contract are more favorable to one side than the other. There are exceptions to this zero-cost feature, however. Financial contracts can be modified in almost every way imaginable.

Options

Options exist on countless underlying securities. For example, there are swap options, bond options, stock options, and options that are implicit in many securities, such as callable bonds, convertible preferred stock, and caps and floors which are options on interest rates.[9]

As noted in previous chapters, options give their buyers the right *but not the obligation,* to buy (call option) or sell (put option) an underlying security at a prespecified price, known as the **strike price**. The value of the underlying security determines whether the right to buy or sell will be exercised and how much the option is worth when exercised.

Most options have a limited life and expire at some future **expiration date**, denoted as T. Some options, which are called American options (see Chapter 8), permit exercise at any date up to T; others, which are called European options (see Chapter 8), permit exercise only on date T.

Values of Calls and Puts at Expiration.   Exhibit 7.7 on page 244 outlines the values of a call and put at their expiration date, T, as a function of S_T, the value of the underlying asset (e.g., here, a share of stock) at that date. Exhibit 7.7 illustrates that if an option is exercised at T, its value is the difference between the stock price and the strike price (call) or between the strike price and the stock price (put). For example, if the stock is selling at \$105 at the expiration date, a call option with a strike price of \$100 is worth \$5 because holding it is like having a coupon worth \$5 off the going rate. If the stock is selling for \$117, the call option is like a coupon with \$17 marked off. If the stock is selling for \$94, the option is worthless. It is better to buy the stock at the market price than to exercise the option and pay the price specified by the option. Exercise of a put allows the option holder to sell the stock at an unfairly high price. For example, the right to sell a share of stock worth \$48 at a price of \$50 is worth \$2.

Panel A in Exhibit 7.7 (a call) illustrates this point more generally. The horizontal axis represents S_T, the price of the stock at expiration date T, while the vertical axis represents the value of the call at date T. If the price of the stock is below the strike price of the call, the call option will not be exercised. Thus, the call has zero value. If the stock price is greater than the strike price, the value of the call rises one dollar for each dollar increase in the stock price. The value of the call at date T equals the maximum of either zero or S_T less the strike price.

Panel B of Exhibit 7.7 (a put) illustrates that the opposite relation holds between the value of the put and the value of the stock. Recall that the holder of a put possesses the right to *sell* the stock at the strike price. Thus, the value of the put at date T equals the maximum of either zero or the strike price less S_T.

In contrast to forwards, futures, and swaps, options benefit only one side of the contract—the side that receives the option. Hence, the investor who receives an option pays for it up front, regardless of the terms of the option.

---

[9]See Chapter 2.

EXHIBIT 7.7   The Value of a Call Option and a Put Option at Expiration

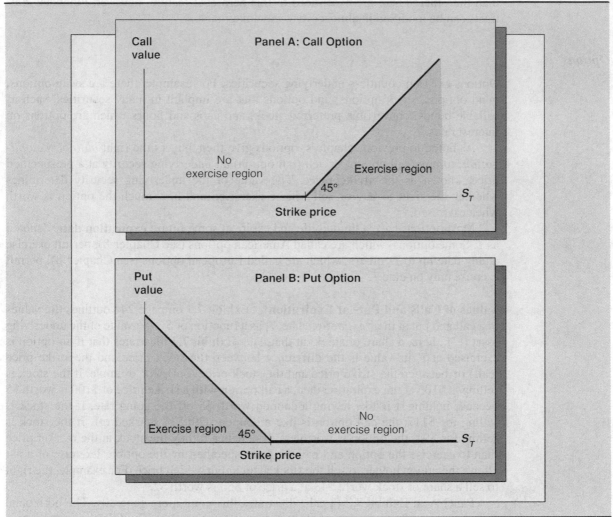

Exchange-Traded Options.   Options are an important segment of the securities markets in the United States; four major options exchanges trade equity options. The Chicago Board Options Exchange (CBOE) is the first and largest such exchange. Of the more than 25 million contracts outstanding on the four major exchanges in 1996, the CBOE had more than 11 million. The other notable exchanges are the American Exchange, which is a division of the American Stock Exchange; the Pacific Exchange, a division of the Pacific Stock Exchange; and the Philadelphia Exchange. Exchange-traded options compose the bulk of traded options, although options on futures contracts, swaps, and bonds also are extremely popular.

The first three columns of *The Wall Street Journal*'s options quotations page (see Exhibit 7.8) reflect the call and put features described above. These columns are labeled "Option/Strike," "Exp.," "Vol.," and "Last." Under AT&T, for example, one finds 53⅜, 55, Jan, 421, 2½, 155, and 3. What does all this mean? It notes that AT&T stock is the underlying risky asset, the strike price is $55 a share, and the expiration date is a

EXHIBIT 7.8 Listed Options Quotations

Tuesday, August 27, 1996

Composite volume and close for actively traded equity and LEAPS, or long-term options, with results for the corresponding put or call contract. Volume figures are unofficial. Open interest is total outstanding for all exchanges and reflects previous trading day. Close when possible is shown for the underlying stock on primary market. **CB**-Chicago Board Options Exchange. **AM**-American Stock Exchange. **PB**-Philadelphia Stock Exchange. **PC**-Pacific Stock Exchange. **NY**-New York Stock Exchange. **XC**-Composite. **p**-Put.

MOST ACTIVE CONTRACTS

Option/Strike				Vol	Exch	Last	Net Chg	a-Close	Open Int
BankAm	Jan 98	60		4,845	CB	24 7/8	+ 1/8	80 5/8	7,138
Intel	Sep	80		3,505	AM	3 3/8	+ 3/8	81 1/2	8,714
Reebok	Sep	30		3,169	AM	5 3/4	+ 1 1/8	35 9/16	10
Compaq	Jan	60		2,942	PC	4 1/8	− 1/4	56 3/4	5,404
AmerOn	Sep	40		2,900	XC	1/4	+ 1/16	30 7/8	4,505
Ph Mor	Sep	90		2,570	AM	3 1/2	+ 11/16	91 7/8	10,810
Seagte	Sep	50	p	2,540	XC	2 3/16	+ 7/16	51	5,034
Dig Eq	Sep	35	p	2,281	XC	15/16	+ 1/16	37 1/4	2,218
Coke	Nov	40		2,064	XC	11 7/8	− 1/4	51 5/8	4,655
Coke	Feb	50		2,000	XC	4 1/2	− 3/8	51 5/8	1,692
WorldCm	Sep	20	p	1,958	PC	5/8	+ 5/16	21	1,405
Arakis	Oct	5		1,801	XC	3/16	− 1/16	2 3/4	16,140
BelrAtl	Oct	55	p	1,782	CB	1 5/16	+ 7/16	57	543
CmpAsoc	Sep	60		1,757	CB	7/8	− 3/8	56 1/8	2,635
Ph Mor	Sep	95		1,636	AM	1 5/16	+ 5/16	91 7/8	14,869
GrdCasn	Nov	15		1,634	XC	3 3/8	+ 1	17 3/8	4,799
Allergan	Oct	35		1,545	PB	4 3/4	− 1/4	38 7/8	15,110
Compaq	Oct	55	p	1,483	PC	2 1/8	...	56 3/4	2,499
Amgen	Sep	55	p	1,475	AM	1/2	+ 1/8	61 5/8	1,220
PepsiCo	Sep	30	p	1,411	CB	7/16	+ 1/8	31	3,722

Option/Strike				Vol	Exch	Last	Net Chg	a-Close	Open Int
Compaq	Jan	50		1,404	PC	9 5/8	− 1/8	56 3/4	7,712
Intrnu	Sep	35		1,365	XC	2 3/8	+ 1 13/16	33 7/8	708
BayNwk	Sep	30		1,325	CB	1 1/8	+ 1/2	28 1/4	12,052
DankaB	Sep	25		1,300	PC	2 7/8	+ 1/8	28 1/4	966
Softkey	Apr	15	p	1,295	XC	3 1/2	...	17 5/16	...
Softkey	Oct	17 1/2	p	1,295	XC	3	...	17 5/16	1,129
Ph Mor	Sep	85	p	1,284	AM	3/4	− 1/4	91 7/8	9,080
L S I	Oct	22 1/2		1,276	CB	1 9/16	− 1/8	22 1/2	2,480
TubMex	Oct	10		1,250	CB	1 3/8	− 5/8	11 1/8	1,103
MicrTc	Sep	20		1,225	XC	2 7/8	...	22 1/2	4,108
BarrickG	Jan 98	25		1,140	AM	6 1/8	− 1/4	27 1/2	3,008
AscendC	Sep	55		1,100	XC	1 13/16	− 1/4	51 1/2	3,693
BayNwk	Dec	35		1,100	CB	1 1/2	+ 7/16	28 1/4	1,286
MblTel	Sep	12 1/2		1,061	CB	2	+ 13/16	14 1/4	2,070
AppleC	Sep	25		1,044	AM	13/16	+ 5/16	24 55/64	3,218
BellSo	Jan	35	p	1,030	AM	1 1/4	+ 3/16	37 1/2	4,707
C-CUBE	Sep	35	p	1,023	XC	1 7/16	− 1 5/16	39 1/4	498
I B M	Sep	115		1,023	CB	1 3/8	− 5/16	111 3/4	10,616
Alza	Oct	30		1,018	PC	9/16	+ 1/16	27 5/8	6,603
GrdCasn	Feb	15		1,013	XC	4 1/2	+ 1 1/4	17 3/8	1,376

Option/Strike		Exp	Call Vol.	Call Last	Put Vol.	Put Last
ACC Cp	55	Dec	30	3 1/2	...	...
ADC Tel	45	Sep	35	7 3/4	7	1/8
53 1/4	50	Sep	88	4	24	15/16
53 1/4	50	Nov	5	4 1/2	30	3 1/2
53 1/4	55	Sep	52	1 1/2	...	...
53 1/4	55	Oct	50	2 3/8	...	...
ADT	20	Sep	94	5/8	...	...
19 5/8	20	Mar	60	2 1/4	...	...
AES Cp	30	Sep	40	5 3/8	...	...
AL Phr	15	Oct	100	1 1/4	...	...
A M R	75	Nov	100	13	...	...
86 3/8	85	Sep	80	3 1/8	...	...
86 3/8	90	Oct	102	2 3/8	...	...
APACT	40	Sep	106	3 7/8	15	1 15/16
A S A	40	Oct	63	1 1/2	...	...
40 3/8	40	Nov	110	2	...	...
ASM Litho	35	Oct	...	...	60	2 7/8
38 3/8	45	Sep	...	...	50	8 1/8
AST Rs	5	Sep	131	5/8	...	...
5 9/16	5	Nov	50	1	...	...
5 9/16	5	Feb	37	1 3/8	...	...
5 9/16	7 1/2	Feb	53	5/8	...	...
AT&T	50	Jan	14	5 1/8	423	1 1/16
53 5/8	55	Sep	118	11/16	25	1 3/4
53 5/8	55	Oct	59	1 1/8	...	...
53 5/8	55	Jan	421	2 1/2	155	3
53 5/8	60	Jan	38	3/4	...	...
53 5/8	60	Apr	34	1 3/8	2	6 7/8
ATC Com	10	Sep	60	7 1/8	...	...
17 11/16	10	Dec	100	7 7/8	...	...
17 11/16	12 1/2	Oct	30	5 3/8	10	1/4
17 11/16	15	Sep	321	3	20	5/16
17 11/16	17 1/2	Sep	351	1 3/8	20	1 1/8
17 11/16	17 1/2	Oct	55	2	...	...
AVX Cp	17 1/2	Sep	...	...	45	7/16
AamesF	40	Sep	265	13 3/4	...	...
52 1/8	45	Dec	130	8 3/4	...	...
52 1/8	50	Sep	541	3	5	1 11/16
Abbt L	45	Nov	37	2 15/16	8	1 1/8
46 3/8	50	Nov	58	3/4	...	...

Option/Strike		Exp.	Call Vol.	Call Last	Put Vol.	Put Last
27 7/8	25	Sep	23	2 5/8	50	1/8
27 7/8	30	Sep	525	3/8	30	2 5/16
27 7/8	30	Dec	103	1 1/2	...	...
Aztar	10	Sep	26	1 1/4	...	...
10 7/8	10	Oct	40	1 5/8	20	7/16
10 7/8	10	Nov	35	1 7/8	...	...
10 7/8	12 1/2	Sep	110	7/16	10	1 13/16
10 7/8	12 1/2	Oct	145	5/8	...	...
10 7/8	12 1/2	Nov	50	7/8	10	1 15/16
BoltBr	25	Jan	30	7/8	...	...
BEC Gp o	5	Sep	35	4 1/4	...	...
BJ Svc	35	Oct	...	...	250	7/8
38	40	Sep	200	3/4	...	...
38	40	Oct	200	1 1/4	...	...
BMC Sft	75	Sep	40	3 1/2	10	3 1/2
74 1/4	75	Nov	1	7	153	6 3/4
BabySst	10	Sep	20	3 1/2	215	5/16
14 5/8	12 1/2	Sep			501	3/4
14 5/8	12 1/2	Oct	...	...	176	1 1/16
14 5/8	15	Sep	40	7/8	134	1 9/16
14 5/8	15	Dec	30	2 1/8	5	2 15/16
14 5/8	17 1/2	Sep	57	3/8	25	2 7/8
BakrHu	30	Oct	102	2 1/4	...	...
30 7/8	32 1/2	Oct	200	1 1/8	20	2 3/16
30 7/8	35	Oct	114	1/2	...	...
BncoFrn	25	Sep	15	1/2	50	2 3/8
23 3/8	25	Oct	57	1	4	2 7/8
BkBost	55	Sep	30	5/8	...	...
53 3/4	55	Nov	43	1 1/2	...	...
BankAm	75	Oct	...	...	138	3/4
BkrsTr	80	Sep	40	1 5/8	...	...
79 1/4	80	Jan	1000	4 1/4	2	4 3/4
BanySy	7 1/2	Feb	30	7/8	...	...
Bard	30	Oct	...	...	35	3/4
Barnet	55	Jan	...	...	50	9/16
65	60	Jan	...	...	50	1 7/16
BarickG	25	Sep	17	2 1/2	100	1/8
27 1/2	25	Oct	145	3	...	...
27 1/2	25	Jan	920	4	53	7/8
27 1/2	30	Sep	30	1/4	...	...

Option/Strike		Exp.	Call Vol.	Call Last	Put Vol.	Put Last
19 3/4	20	Apr	44	3 1/4	...	...
19 3/4	21 1/4	Sep	119	7/16	2	2 1/16
19 3/4	21 1/4	Oct	187	1	10	2 1/2
19 3/4	22 1/2	Sep	56	5/16	...	...
19 3/4	22 1/2	Jan	85	1 13/16	...	...
19 3/4	26 1/4	Oct	88	3/16	...	...
Chryslr	25	Jan	...	...	69	7/8
29	27 1/2	Jan	...	...	30	1 5/8
29	30	Sep	321	1/2	18	1 9/16
29	30	Oct	45	1	...	...
29	30	Jan	46	2	22	3
29	32 1/2	Sep	50	1/8	...	...
29	32 1/2	Oct	66	3/8	...	...
29	32 1/2	Apr	41	1 9/16	...	...
29	35	Oct	85	1/8	...	...
29	35	Jan	103	9/16	5	6 3/8
CIBER	25	Sep	31	2 1/16	...	...
Circon	15	Oct	100	3 1/4	...	...
17 1/2	20	Sep	155	3/16	...	...
Circus	30	Sep	26	3 3/4	...	...
33 1/4	32 1/2	Sep	42	1 1/2	2	1 3/16
33 1/4	35	Dec	46	2 1/8	...	...
Cirrus	12 1/2	Oct	...	...	35	3/8
15 7/8	17 1/2	Oct	35	13/16	100	2 9/16
15 7/8	17 1/2	Dec	114	1 1/2	16	3
15 7/8	20	Dec	30	13/16	5	4 3/4
Cisco	45	Sep	150	10 3/8	...	...
55	45	Oct	10	11 1/2	135	5/8
55	45	Jan	4	13 1/8	30	1 13/16
55	50	Sep	85	5 3/4	470	5/8
55	50	Oct	121	6 7/8	108	1 9/16
55	50	Jan	4	9 3/8	68	3 1/4
55	55	Sep	884	2 7/16	233	2 1/8
55	55	Oct	142	3 7/8	25	3 1/2
55	55	Jan	47	6 3/8	6	5 3/8
55	60	Sep	892	11/16	20	5 3/8
55	60	Oct	208	1 13/16	13	6 7/8
55	60	Jan	60	3 7/8	1	8
55	65	Oct	107	3/4	5	10 5/8
Citicp	75	Jan	...	...	30	1 1/4

Source: Reprinted by permission of *The Wall Street Journal*,

particular date in January 1997. At the close of trading on August 27, 1996, AT&T stock traded at 53 5/8 per share, the call option on AT&T traded at \$2.50, and the put option traded at \$3. The volume of trading—421 calls, each on 100 shares, and 155 puts, each on 100 shares—is reflected in the volume column.

The day of expiration is not printed. Most brokers provide option expiration calendars that contain this information free of charge. Also, it is understood that American options are the type of option traded on exchanges listed in *The Wall Street Journal*.

It is also important to understand other option terminology. The underlying asset of a call or put option that is **in the money** has a current price that is greater (less) than the strike price. The underlying asset of a call or put option that is **out of the money** has a current price that is less (greater) than the strike price. An option **at the money** is one for which the strike price and underlying asset's price are the same.[10] As you can see above, the AT&T option is an out-of-the-money call option, but an in-the-money put option. The September and October 1996 call and put options for Cisco, whose stock is $55 a share, are at the money because their strike prices are identical to Cisco's stock price.

Investors seem to be most interested in options that are slightly out of the money. Hence, most exchange-traded options are initially designed to be slightly out of the money. As the underlying asset's price changes, however, they can evolve into at-the-money or in-the-money options.

You may notice (e.g., under the most active contracts) that most of the equity option volume is concentrated in the options expiring within the next six months. A few stocks have substantial volume in longer dated options, known as **leaps**, but maturities of more than three years for these are rare.

Corporations are not involved in exchange-based trading of options on their stock. These options, like most derivatives, are merely complicated bets between two counterparties. As such, the number of long positions in an option is exactly the same as the number of short positions. This feature also applies to options traded in loosely organized "over-the-counter markets" between institutions like banks, pension funds, and corporations.

Dealing with a single counterparty can be burdensome when liquidating or exercising an option position. If the call or put seller does not perform according to the option contract (i.e., does not deliver the cash or underlying asset required in exercising the option), there is a high probability that a costly lawsuit would ensue. The institutional over-the-counter options markets mitigate this possibility by investigating the creditworthiness of each counterparty before entering into the contract. As a result, different option prices exist for different option sellers, depending on their degree of creditworthiness.

The organized exchanges solve the problem of counterparty default risk differently. Instead of performing the investigation function, each exchange uses a **clearinghouse**, which is a corporation set up by the exchange and its member brokers to act as a counterparty to all option contracts. All options are legal contracts between the investor and the clearinghouse. When an investor exercises an option, the clearinghouse's computer randomly selects one of the outstanding short positions in the option and requires the holder of this short position either to buy or to sell the underlying security at the exercise price under the terms of the investor's contract with the clearinghouse. The clearinghouse mitigates the need for lawsuits by requiring those who short options to put up margin and have their creditworthiness verified by their brokers. In the rare instance of a lawsuit, the clearinghouse is responsible for suing the counterparty.

---

[10]As implied by the terms, an *in the money* option means that exercising the option is profitable (excluding the cost of the option). Similarly, *at the money* and *out of the money* imply that exercising the option produces zero cash flow and negative cash flow, respectively, and thus, exercise should not be undertaken.

The eagerness of investors to place bets with optionlike payoffs determines the number of outstanding exchange-listed options. This number increases by one when an investor places an order to sell an option that he or she does not have and has the broker find a counterparty who wants to buy it at the offered price. In option markets, the procedure for shorting an option is commonly referred to as **writing an option**. Alternatively, the investor can write an option with a market order, which basically requires auctioning the option off to the highest bidder at the highest price the auction can command. When an order to write an option is executed, the clearinghouse acts as the legal intermediary between the two parties, announcing that there is an increase in the number of contracts outstanding. Hence, the mechanism for shorting most options differs from the mechanism for shorting stocks and bonds, which requires some form of borrowing of securities to execute a short sale because the number of outstanding shares is fixed by the original issuer. Conversely, when an investor cancels a long position in an option by selling it and someone else—not necessarily the investor from whom the option was purchased—with a short position simultaneously agrees that this is a fair price at which to close out his or her short position, the clearinghouse closes out its contracts with both parties. This leaves one less option contract outstanding.

Warrants.   Warrants are options, usually calls, that companies issue on their own stock (see Chapter 3). In contrast to exchange-traded options, which are mere bets between investors on the value of a company's underlying stock—in which the corporation never gets involved—warrants are contracts between a corporation and an investor.

Warrants are sources of capital for newer growth firms. They are more common in some countries, like Japan, where the warrants are often linked to a bond issue. In the United States, warrants are most frequently seen in the form of employee stock options in which case the "investor" is the employee (typically, an executive).

Most of the warrants used to finance companies are traded on stock exchanges. These warrants can be sold short by borrowing them from a warrant holder in the same way that the stock is sold short (see Chapter 4).[11] Thus, the number of warrants is fixed for a given issue. Warrants issued as employee compensation are generally not traded.

The major distinction between a warrant and other types of call options is that the company issues additional stock when an investor exercises a warrant. Upon exercise, the stock is sold to the warrant holder at the strike price. Since exercise occurs only when the strike price is less than the current price of the stock, the exercise of the warrant involves the issuance of new shares of stock at bargain prices. The new shares dilute the value of existing shares. Because of this dilution, option pricing models used to value warrants differ from option pricing models used to value exchange-traded options. For example, if IBM is trading at $117 a share, warrants with a strike price of $120 that expire in one year might be worth $10; they are worth slightly more than $10 if one values them with models that do not account for the dilution. Generally, the percent of a corporation's equity represented by warrants is so small that one can ignore the effect of dilution and value them like any other option. Hence, for the example of IBM, the difference between $10 (the value with dilution) and $10.01 (the value assuming no dilution) might be a realistic portrayal of the warrant dilution effect.[12]

---

[11]This is in notable contrast to exchange-traded options where a short position is created along with every long position because both positions merely represent the sides of a "bet" between parties.

[12]It is important to note that exchange-traded options and otherwise identical warrants necessarily have the same value. Hence, if both warrants and identical exchange-traded options exist at the same time, the dilution effect of the warrants must be taken into account in valuing *both* the warrant and the exchange-traded options. However, this is rarely done in practice.

Embedded Options.   In addition to warrants, a number of corporate securities have optionlike components. For example, when a corporation issues a convertible bond, it gives the bondholder the option to exchange the bond for a prespecified number of shares of stock in the corporation. Similarly, many long-term corporate bonds are callable or refundable bonds, which means that the corporation has the option to buy back the bonds at a prespecified price after a certain date.

Options are also implicit in simple equity and simple debt even when they lack a call or conversion feature. One can look at simple equity as a call option on the assets of the firm; thus, it can be valued *in relation to the assets* as a derivative.[13] Similarly, one can look at simple corporate debt as risk-free debt and a put option on the assets of the firm; thus, it can be valued in relation to the assets (or the equity) with the techniques developed in this chapter.

Real Assets

Investors can view many real assets as derivatives. For example, a copper mine can be valued in relation to the price of copper.[14] Sometimes other derivatives, such as options, are implicit in these real assets. For example, the option to shut down a copper mine often needs to be accounted for when valuing a mine. These implicit options also can be valued with the techniques developed here.

Mortgage-Backed Securities

U.S. residential mortgages are generally packaged together into a pool and resold to a bank with a guarantee against default. Pooled mortgages are known as **mortgage pass-throughs** because they pass on the interest and principal payments of the mortgage borrowers (home owners) less servicing and guarantee fees (usually, about 50 to 75 basis points). These guarantees are given by three agencies: the Government National Mortgage Association (GNMA or "Ginnie Mae"), the Federal National Mortgage Association (FNMA or "Fannie Mae"), and the Federal Home Loan Mortgage Corporation (FHLMC or "Freddie Mac"). The latter two buy mortgages from the original lenders and package them.

Once these mortgages are packaged and sold, markets are made chiefly by the same set of dealers who make markets in U.S. Treasury securities. Many mortgage pass-throughs are carved up into a series of derivatives, known as **collateralized mortgage obligations (CMOs)**. The most popular carve-up of this type consists of different **tranches**, which are individual bonds with different rights to the principal payments of the mortgage pass-through. Tranches can be used to design mortgage securities with different amounts of prepayment risk.

A hypothetical series of such mortgage-backed securities might consist of a mortgage pass-through that is carved up into two tranches and an additional bond that serves the purpose of equity. The first tranche has the shortest expected life. It is entitled to all principal payments from the mortgage pass-through until its principal is paid off. Its value is least affected by prepayments on the mortgage. As mortgages prepay—in response to home sales or to mortgage refinancings at lower interest rates—and all of the first-tranche bonds are paid off, the second tranche, which has always received a share

---

[13]See Chapter 8.
[14]See Chapter 11.

of interest payments, will begin to receive principal payments. The second tranche behaves more like a Treasury note or bond because for a while it receives only interest and later receives the principal. Unlike Treasury notes and bonds, however, the interest payments decline over time as prepayments occur and the principal payments are a series of declining payments rather than a single payment at maturity. After this second tranche is paid off, all remaining cash flows are paid to the remaining bond. Hence, the last "equity piece" is more like a zero-coupon bond than a Treasury bond. Depending on the prepayment rate, this cash may flow relatively early or relatively late. Hence, the value of the equity piece is more sensitive to prepayment risk than the other two bonds.

The carve-ups can be fairly exotic. For example, the opening vignette of this chapter featured *IOs* and *POs* as one way to carve up the cash flows. Not only can these carve-ups of the cash flows be valued as derivatives, but—to the extent that variability in the rate of mortgage prepayments depend largely on interest rates—even the mortgage pass-through can be valued as a derivative on the other riskless bonds.

Structured Notes

About 30 percent of the new issues of traded debt securities issued by U.S. corporations in 1995 were in the form of *structured notes* (see Chapter 2), which are bonds of any maturity sold in small amounts by means of a previously shelf-registered offering (see Chapter 1). They are customized for investors in that they often pass on the cash flows of derivative transactions entered into by the issuer.

Examples of structured notes include inverse floaters,[15] which have coupons that decline as interest rates increase; bonds with floating-rate coupons part of the time and fixed-rate coupons at other times; and bonds with coupons that depend on the return of the S&P 500, an exchange rate, a constant times a squared benchmark interest rate, such as LIBOR, or a commodity price. Basically, anything goes.

Why are structured notes so popular? From an economic perspective, structured notes are derivatives. From a legal and public relations standpoint, however, they are bonds, "blessed" by the regulatory authorities, investment banks, and ratings agencies. Some investors, such as state pension funds, may be prohibited from investing in derivatives directly. One hypothesis about the popularity of structured notes is that they permit such investors to enter into a derivatives transaction while appearing to the public like an investor in the conservative bonds of an AAA-rated corporation.

7.2 The Basics of Derivatives Pricing

Derivative securities valuation has two basic components. The first component is the concept of perfect tracking. The second is the principle of no arbitrage. A fair market price for a derivative, obtained from a derivatives valuation model, is simply a no-arbitrage restriction between the tracking portfolio and the derivative.

Perfect Tracking Portfolios

All derivatives valuation models make use of a fundamental idea: *It is always possible to develop a portfolio consisting of the underlying asset and a risk-free asset that perfectly*

---

[15]See the opening vignette in Chapter 22.

tracks the future cash flows of the derivative. As a result, in the absence of arbitrage the derivative must have the same value as the tracking portfolio.[16]

A *perfect tracking portfolio* is a combination of securities that perfectly replicates the future cash flows of another investment.

The perfect tracking, used to value derivatives, stands in marked contrast to the use of tracking portfolios (discussed in Chapters 5 and 6) to develop general models of financial asset valuation. There our concern was with identifying a tracking portfolio with the same systematic risk as the investment being valued. Such tracking portfolios typically generate substantial tracking error. We did not analyze tracking error in Chapters 5 and 6 because the assumptions of those models implied that the tracking error had zero present value and thus could be ignored. This places a high degree of faith in the validity of the assumptions of those models. The success of the derivatives valuation models rests largely on the fact that the derivatives can be almost perfectly tracked, which means that we do not need to make strong assumptions about how tracking error affects value.

No Arbitrage and Valuation

In the absence of tracking error, arbitrage exists if it costs more to buy the tracking portfolio than the derivative, or vice versa. Whenever the derivative is cheaper than the tracking portfolio, arbitrage is achieved by buying the derivative and selling (or shorting) the tracking portfolio. Upon initiating the arbitrage position, cash comes in to the investor because the cash spent on the derivative is less than the cash received from shorting the tracking portfolio. Since the future cash flows of the tracking portfolio and the derivative are identical, buying one and shorting the other means that the future cash flow obligations from the short sales position can be met with the future cash received from the position in the derivative.[17]

Applying the Basic Principles of Derivatives Valuation to Value Forwards

This subsection considers three applications of the basic principles described above, all of which are related to forward contracts.

Valuing a Forward Contract. Models used to value derivatives assume that arbitrage is impossible. Example 7.4 illustrates how to obtain the fair market value of a forward contract using this idea and how to arbitrage a mispriced forward contract.

Example 7.4:   Valuing a Forward Contract on a Share of Stock
Consider the obligation to buy a share of Microsoft stock one year from now for $200. Assume that the stock currently sells for $189 per share and that Microsoft will pay no dividends over the coming year. One-year zero-coupon bonds that pay $100 one year from now currently sell for $92. At what price are you willing to buy or sell this obligation?

---

[16]In this text, the models developed to value derivatives assume that perfect tracking is possible. In practice, however, transaction costs and other market frictions imply that investors can, at best, attain almost perfect tracking of a derivative.

[17]Usually, it is impossible to perfectly track a *mispriced* derivative, although a forward contract is an exception. However, any mispriced derivative that does not converge immediately to its no-arbitrage value can be taken advantage of further to earn additional arbitrage profits, using the tracking portfolio strategy outlined in this chapter.

Answer: Compare the cash flows today and one year from now for two investment strategies. Under strategy 1, the forward contract, the investor acquires today the obligation to buy a share of Microsoft one year from now at a price of $200. Upon paying $200 for the share at that time, the investor immediately sells the share for cash. Strategy 2, the tracking portfolio, involves buying a share of Microsoft today and selling short $200 in face value of 1-year zero-coupon bonds to partly finance the purchase. The stock is sold one year from now to finance (partly or fully) the obligation to pay the $200 owed on the zero-coupon bonds. Denoting the stock value one year from now as the random number $\tilde{S}_1$, the cash inflows and costs from these two strategies are as follows:

	Cost Today	Cash Flow One Year from Today
Strategy 1 (forward)	?	$\tilde{S}_1 - \$200$
Strategy 2 (tracking portfolio)	$189–$184	$\tilde{S}_1 - \$200$

Since strategies 1 and 2 have identical cash flows in the future, they should have the same cost today to prevent arbitrage. Strategy 2 costs $5 today. Strategy 1, the obligation to buy the stock for $200 one year from now, also should cost $5. If it costs less than $5, then going long in strategy 1 and short in strategy 2 (which, when combined, means acquiring the obligation, selling short a share of Microsoft, and buying $200 face amount of the zero-coupon bonds) has a positive cash inflow today and no cash flow consequences in the future. This is arbitrage. If the obligation costs more than $5, then going short in strategy 1 and going long in strategy 2 (short the obligation, buy a share of stock, and short $200 face amount of the zero-coupon bonds) has a positive cash inflow today and no future cash flows.

Result 7.1 generalizes Example 7.4 as follows:

Result 7.1   The no-arbitrage value of a forward contract on a share of stock (the obligation to buy a share of stock at a price of K, T years in the future), assuming the stock pays no dividends prior to T, is:

$$S_0 - \frac{K}{(1 + r_f)^T}$$

where

$$S_0 = \text{current price of the stock}$$

and

$$\frac{K}{(1 + r_f)^T} = \text{the current market price of a default-free zero-coupon bond paying } K,$$
$$T \text{ years in the future}$$

Obtaining Forward Prices for Zero-Cost Forward Contracts.   The value of the forward contract is zero for a contracted price, K, that satisfies:

$$S_0 - \frac{K}{(1 + r_f)^T} = 0$$

namely,

$$K = S_0(1 + r_f)^T$$

The contracted price K, $S_0(1 + r_f)^T$, also is known as the forward price of the stock.[18] Assuming that no money changes hands today as part of the deal, $S_0(1 + r_f)^T$ represents the fair price upon which two parties would agree today for purchasing the non-dividend-paying stock T years in the future. It is fair in the sense that no arbitrage takes place with this agreed upon forward price.

Result 7.2   The forward price for settlement in T years of the purchase of a nondividend-paying stock with a current price of S_0 is:

$$K = S_0(1 + r_f)^T$$

Currency Forward Rates.   Currency forward rates are a variation on Result 7.2. Specifically:

Result 7.3   In the absence of arbitrage, the forward currency rate s_F (e.g., French francs/dollar) is related to the current exchange rate (or **spot rate**), s_0, by the equation:

$$\frac{s_F}{s_0} = \frac{1 + r_{foreign}}{1 + r_{domestic}}$$

where

r = the return (unannualized) on a domestic or foreign risk-free security over the life of the forward agreement, as measured in the respective country's currency

Note that $\dfrac{1 + r_{foreign}}{1 + r_{domestic}} - 1$ is approximately the same as $r_{foreign} - r_{domestic}$. Thus, Result 7.3 implies that the **forward rate discount**[19] relative to the spot rate,

$$\frac{s_F - s_0}{s_0} \left(= \frac{s_F}{s_0} - 1 \right)$$

which represents the percentage discount at which one buys foreign currency in the forward market relative to the spot market, is approximately the same as the interest rate differential. For example, if the one-year interest rate in France is 10 percent and the one-year interest rate in the United States is 8 percent, then a U.S. company can purchase French francs forward for approximately 2 percent less than the spot rate, which is reflected by s_F being about 2 percent larger than s_0.

Result 7.3 is sometimes known as the **covered interest rate parity relation**. This relation describes how forward currency rates are determined by spot currency rates and interest rates in the two countries. Example 7.5 illustrates how to implement the covered interest rate parity relation.

Example 7.5:   The Relation Between Forward Currency Rates and Interest Rates
Assume the Euro-deutsche mark rate (six-month LIBOR) is 4 percent and the Eurodollar rate (six-month LIBOR) is 10 percent and that both rates are default free. What is the six-month forward DM/US$ exchange rate if the current spot rate is DM 1.25/US$? Assume that six months from now is 182 days.

---

[18]As mentioned earlier, "off-market" forward prices, resulting in nonzero-cost contracts, exist. Usually, however, *forward price* refers to the cash required in the future to buy the forward contract's underlying investment under the terms specified in a *zero-cost* contract.

[19]It is a discount instead of a premium because exchange rates are measured as units of foreign currency that can be purchased per unit of domestic currency.

Answer: As noted in Chapter 2, LIBOR is a zero-coupon rate based on an actual/360 day count. Hence:

	Germany	United States
6-month interest rate (unannualized):	$2.02\% = \dfrac{182}{360}4\%$	$5.06\% = \dfrac{182}{360}10\%$

By Result 7.3, the forward rate is $\dfrac{\text{DM } 1.21}{\text{US\$}}\left(=\dfrac{1.0202}{1.0506}1.25\right)$

7.3 Binomial Pricing Models

In derivatives valuation models, the *current* price of the underlying asset determines the price of the derivative *today*. This is a rather surprising result because in most cases the link between the price of the derivative and the price of the corresponding underlying asset is usually obvious only at some future date. For example, the forward contract described in Example 7.4 has a price equal to the difference between the stock price and the agreed upon settlement price, but only at the settlement date one year from now. A call option has a known value at the expiration date of the call when the stock price is known.

Tracking and Valuation: Static versus Dynamic Strategies

The pricing relation of a derivative with an underlying asset in the future translates into a no-arbitrage pricing relation in the present because of the ability to use the underlying asset to perfectly track the derivative's future cash flows. Example 7.4 illustrates an investment strategy in the underlying asset (a share of Microsoft stock) and a risk-free asset (a zero-coupon bond) that tracks the payoff of the derivative at a future date when the relation between their prices is known. In the absence of arbitrage, the tracking strategy must cost the same amount today as the derivative.

The tracking portfolio for a forward contract is particularly simple. As Example 7.4 illustrates, forward contracts are tracked by static investment strategies; that is, buying and holding a position in the underlying asset and a risk-free bond of a particular maturity. The buy and hold strategy tracks the derivative, the forward contract, because the future payoff of the forward contract is a linear function of the underlying asset's future payoff. However, most derivatives have future payoffs that are not linear functions of the payoff of the underlying asset. Tracking such nonlinear derivatives requires a dynamic strategy: The holdings in the underlying asset and the risk-free bond need to change frequently in order to perfectly track the derivative's future payoffs. With a call option on a stock, for example, tracking requires position in the stock and a risk-free bond, where the number of shares of stock in the tracking portfolio goes up as the stock price goes up and decreases as the stock price goes down.

The ability to perfectly track a derivative's payoffs with a dynamic strategy usually depends on a few assumptions.

- The price of the underlying security must change smoothly; that is, it does not make large jumps.

- It must be possible to trade both the derivative and the underlying security continuously.
- Markets must be frictionless (see Chapter 5).[20]

If these assumptions are violated, the results obtained will generally be approximations. One notable exception to this relates to the first two assumptions. If the price of the underlying security follows a very specific process, known as the binomial process, the investor can still perfectly track the derivative's future cash flows.

With the **binomial process**, the underlying security's price moves up or down over time, but can take on only *two* values at the next point at which trading is allowed—hence the name "binomial." This is certainly not a true picture of a security's price process, but it is a better approximation than you first might think and it is very convenient for illustrating how the theory of derivative pricing works. Academics and practitioners have discovered that the dynamic tracking strategies developed from binomial models are usually pretty good at tracking the future payoffs of the derivative. Moreover, the binomial fair market values of most derivatives approximate the fair market values given by more complex models, often to a high degree of accuracy, when the binomial periods are small and numerous.

Binomial Model Tracking of a Structured Bond

Exhibit 7.9 illustrates what are known as binomial trees. The tree at the top represents the possible price paths for the S&P 500, the underlying security. The leftmost point of this tree, 850, represents the value of the S&P 500 today. The lines connecting 850 with the next period represent the two possible paths that the S&P 500 can take. The two values at the end of those lines, 1,000 and 500, represent the two possible values that the S&P 500 can assume one period from today. In the binomial process. one refers to the two outcomes over the next period as the **up state** and the **down state**. Hence, 1,000 and 500 represent the payoffs of the S&P 500 in the up state and down state, respectively.

The middle tree models the price paths for a risk-free security paying 10 percent per period. This security is risk free because each $1.00 invested in the security pays the same amount, $1.10, at the nodes corresponding to both the up and the down states.

The bottom tree models the price paths for the derivative, which in this case is a structured bond. The upper node corresponds to the payoff of the structured bond when the up state occurs (which leads to an S&P 500 value of 1,000); the lower node represents the down state, which corresponds to an S&P value of 500. The structured bond pays $112.50, $100.00 in principal plus 12.5 percent interest at the maturity of the bond one period from now. In addition, if the S&P 500 goes up in value, there is an additional payment of 25 percent of the value of the S&P 500. Since this occurs only in the up state, the payoff of the structured bond at the up state node is $362.50 while the payoff at the down state node is $112.50.

The structured bond pictured in Exhibit 7.9 is a simplified characterization of a number of these bonds. Investors, pension fund managers, who are prohibited from participating directly in the equity markets have attempted to circumvent this restriction

---

[20]Most of the models analyzed here assume that the risk-free rate is constant. If the short-term risk-free return can change over time, perfect tracking can be achieved with more complicated tracking strategies. In many instances, formulas for valuing derivatives (e.g., options) based on these more complex tracking strategies can be derived, but they will differ from those presented here. These extensions of our results are beyond the scope of this text.

Exhibit 7.9   One Period Binomial Trees

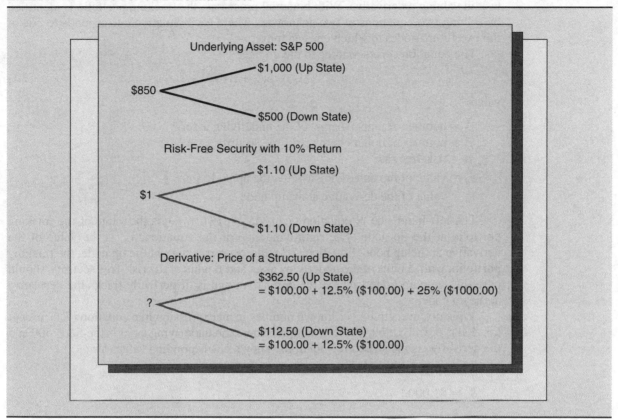

Underlying Asset: S&P 500

$850 → $1,000 (Up State)

$850 → $500 (Down State)

Risk-Free Security with 10% Return

$1 → $1.10 (Up State)

$1 → $1.10 (Down State)

Derivative: Price of a Structured Bond

? → $362.50 (Up State)
= $100.00 + 12.5% ($100.00) + 25% ($1000.00)

? → $112.50 (Down State)
= $100.00 + 12.5% ($100.00)

by investing in corporate debt instruments such as structured bonds that have payoffs tied to stock indexes. Of course, a corporation that issues such a bond needs compensation for the future payments it makes to the bond's investors. Such payments reflect interest and principal, as well as a payoff that enables the investor to enjoy upside participation in the stock market. When an active market for trading such bonds exists, observation of a recent transaction price is usually a sufficient measure of fair value. However, the corporation cannot observe a transaction price for some derivatives, because like many structured bonds, they are not actively traded. The question mark at the leftmost node of the bottom tree in Exhibit 7.9 reflects that a fair value is yet to be determined. The next section computes this fair value using the principle of no arbitrage.

Using Tracking Portfolios to Value Derivatives

Since each node has only two future values attached to it, binomial processes allow perfect tracking of the value of the derivative with a tracking portfolio composed of the underlying security and a risk-free bond. After identifying the tracking portfolio's current value from the known prices of its component securities, the derivative can be valued. This is the easy part because, according to the principle of no arbitrage, the value of the derivative is the same as that of its tracking portfolio.

Identifying the Tracking Portfolio.   Finding the perfect tracking portfolio is the major task in valuing a derivative. With binomial processes, the tracking portfolio is identified by solving two equations in two unknowns, where each equation corresponds to one of the two future nodes to which one can move.

The equation corresponding to the *up node* is:

$$\Delta S_u + \beta(1 + r_f) = V_u \tag{7.1}$$

where

Δ = number of units (shares) of the underlying asset
β = number of dollars in the risk-free security
r_f = risk-free rate
S_u = value of the underlying asset at the up node
V_u = value of the derivative at the up node

The left-hand side of equation (7.1), $\Delta S_u + \beta(1 + r_f)$, is the value of the tracking portfolio at the up node. The right-hand side of the equation, V_u, is the value of the derivative at the up node. Equation (7.1) thus expresses that, at the up node, the tracking portfolio, with Δ units of the underlying asset and β units of the risk-free security, should have the same up-node value as the derivative; that is, it perfectly tracks the derivative at the up node.

Typically, everything is a known number in an expression like equation (7.1), except for Δ and β. In Exhibit 7.9, for example, where the underlying asset is the S&P 500 and the derivative is the structured bond, the known corresponding values are:

r_f = .1
S_u = $1,000

and

V_u = $362.50

Thus, to identify the tracking portfolio for the derivative in Exhibit 7.9 the first equation that needs to be solved is:

$$\$1,000\Delta + \beta(1.1) = \$362.50 \tag{7.1a}$$

Equation (7.1) represents one linear equation with two unknowns, Δ and β. Pair this equation with the corresponding equation for the down node:

$$\Delta S_d + \beta(1 + r_f) = V_d \tag{7.2}$$

For the numbers in Exhibit 7.9, this is:

$$\$500\Delta + \beta(1.1) = \$112.50 \tag{7.2a}$$

Solving equations (7.1) and (7.2) simultaneously yields a unique solution for Δ and β, which is typical when solving two linear equations for two unknown variables.

Example 7.6 illustrates this technique for the numbers given in Exhibit 7.9 and provides some tips on methods for a quick solution.[21]

---

[21]Example 7.6 tracks the structured bond over the period with a static portfolio in the S&P 500 and a riskless security. With multiple periods, readjust these weights as each new period begins to maintain perfect tracking of the option's value. This readjustment is discussed in more detail shortly.

Example 7.6:   Finding the Tracking Portfolio

A unit of the S&P 500 sells for $850 today. One period from now, it can take on one of two values, each associated with a good or bad state. If the good state occurs, it is worth $1,000. If the bad state occurs, it is worth $500. If the risk-free interest rate is 10 percent per period, find the tracking portfolio for a structured bond, which has a value of $362.50 next period if the S&P 500 unit sells for $1000, and $112.50 if the S&P 500 sells for $500.

Answer: A quick way to find the tracking portfolio of the S&P 500 and the risk-free asset is to look at the differences between the up and down node values of both the derivative and the underlying asset. (This is equivalent to subtracting equation (7.2a) from (7.1a) and solving for Δ.) For the derivative, the structured bond, the difference is $250 = $362.50 − $112.50, but for the S&P 500, it is $500 = $1,000 − $500.

Since the tracking portfolio has to have the same $250 difference in outcomes as the derivative, and since the amount of the risk-free security held will not affect this difference, the tracking portfolio has to hold ½ unit of the S&P 500. If it held more than ½ unit, for example, the difference in the tracking portfolio's future values would exceed $250. Given that Δ is ½ unit of the S&P 500 and that β dollars of the risk-free asset is held in addition to this ½ unit, the investor perfectly tracks the derivative's future value only if he or she selects the correct value of β. To determine this value of β, study the two columns on the right-hand side of the table below, which outlines the values of the tracking portfolio and the derivative in the up and down states next period:

	Today's Value	Next Period Value	
		Up State	*Down State*
Tracking portfolio	$\frac{1}{2}$$850 + \beta$	$\frac{1}{2}$$1,000 + 1.1\beta$	$\frac{1}{2}$$500 + 1.1\beta$
Derivative	?	$362.50	$112.50

Comparing the two up-state values in the middle column implies that the amount of the risk-free security needed to perfectly track the derivative next period solves the equation $500 + 1.1\beta = $362.50.

Thus, $\beta = −$137.50/1.1 or −$125. (The minus sign implies that $125 is borrowed at the risk-free rate.) Having already chosen Δ to be ½, this value of β also makes the down-state values of the tracking portfolio and the derivative the same.

Finding the Current Value of the Tracking Portfolio.   The fair market value of the derivative equals the amount it costs to buy the tracking portfolio. Buying Δ shares of the underlying security today at a cost of S per share, and β dollars of the risk-free asset cost $\Delta S + \beta$ in total. Hence, the derivative has a nonarbitrageable price of:

$$V = \Delta S + \beta \tag{7.3}$$

This calculation is demonstrated in Example 7.7.

Example 7.7:   Valuing a Derivative Once the Tracking Portfolio is Known

What is the no-arbitrage value of the derivative in Example 7.6? See Exhibit 7.9 for the numbers to use in this example.

Answer: The tracking portfolio, which requires buying ½ unit of the S&P 500 (for $850 per unit) and borrowing $125 at the risk-free rate costs:

$$\$300 = \frac{1}{2}(\$850) - \$125$$

To prevent arbitrage, the derivative should also cost the same amount.

Result 7.4 summarizes the results of this section.

Result 7.4   To determine the no-arbitrage value of a derivative, find a (possibly dynamic) portfolio of the underlying asset and a risk-free security that perfectly tracks the future payoffs of the derivative. The value of the derivative equals the value of the tracking portfolio.

Risk-Neutral Valuation of Derivatives: The Wall Street Approach

One of the most interesting things about Examples 7.6 and 7.7 is that there was no mention of the probabilities of the up and down states occurring. The probability of the up move determines the mean return of the underlying security, yet the value of the derivative *in relation to the value of the underlying asset* does not depend on this probability.

In addition, it was not necessary to know how risk averse the investor was.[22] If the typical investor is risk neutral, slightly risk averse, highly risk averse, or even risk loving, one obtains the same value for the derivative *in relation to the value of the underlying asset* regardless of investor attitudes toward risk. Of course, whenever arbitrage considerations dictate pricing, risk preferences should not affect the relation between the value of the derivative and the value of the underlying asset. Whether risk neutral, slightly risk averse, or highly risk averse, you would still love to obtain something for nothing. The valuation method expressed in this chapter is simply a way to determine the unique pricing relation that rules this out.

Result 7.5 summarizes this important finding.

Result 7.5   Given the value of the underlying asset, the value of a derivative does not depend on the mean return of the underlying asset or investor risk preferences.

Why Mean Returns and Risk Aversion Do Not Affect the Valuation of Derivatives. The reason that information about probabilities or risk aversion does not enter into the valuation equation is that such information is already captured by the price of the underlying asset on which we base our valuation of the derivative. For example, assume the underlying asset is a stock. Holding risk aversion constant, the more likely the future stock price is up and the less likely the stock price is down, the greater the current stock price will be. Similarly, holding the distribution of future stock price outcomes constant, if the typical investor is more risk averse, the current stock price will be lower. However, the wording of Result 7.5 is about the value of the derivative *given the current stock price*. Thus, Result 7.5 is a statement that, *once the stock price is known*, risk aversion and mean return information are superfluous, not that they are irrelevant.

---

[22]Given two investments with the same expected return but different risk, a risk-averse individual prefers the investment with less risk. To make a risk-averse individual indifferent between the two investments, the riskier investment would have to carry a higher expected return.

An Overview of How the Risk-Neutral Valuation Method is Implemented.   Result 7.5 states that the no-arbitrage price of the derivative in relation to the underlying security is the same, regardless of risk preferences. This serves as the basis for a trick known as the *risk-neutral valuation method,* which is especially useful in valuing the more complicated problems encountered on Wall Street.

The **risk-neutral valuation method** is a two-step procedure for valuing derivatives.

1. Identify *risk-neutral probabilities* that are consistent with investors being risk neutral, given the current value of the underlying asset and its possible future values. **Risk-neutral probabilities** are a set of weights applied to the future values of the underlying asset along each path. The *expected* future asset value generated by these probabilities, when discounted at the risk-free rate, equals the current value of the underlying asset.

2. Multiply each risk-neutral probability by the corresponding future value for the derivative, and discount the sum of these products (i.e., a probability-weighted average of the derivative's possible future values) at the risk-free rate.

The major benefit of the risk-neutral valuation method is that it requires fewer steps to value derivatives than the tracking portfolio method. However, it is not really a different method, but a shortcut for going through the tracking portfolio method's valuation steps, developed in the last section. As such, it is easier to program into a computer and has become a fairly standard tool on Wall Street. Moreover, it has its own useful insights that aid in the understanding of derivatives.

The risk-neutral valuation method obtains derivative prices in the risk preference scenario that is easiest to analyze—that of risk-neutral preferences. While this scenario may not be the most realistic, pretending that everyone is risk neutral is a perfectly valid way to derive the correct no-arbitrage value that applies in all risk preference scenarios.

The next two subsections walk through the two-step procedure in great detail.

Step 1: Obtaining Risk-Neutral Probabilities.   Example 7.6 has a unique probability π of the good state occurring, which implies that the underlying asset, the S&P 500, is expected to appreciate at the risk-free rate. Example 7.8 solves for that probability.

Example 7.8:   Attaching Probabilities to Up and Down Nodes

For Example 7.6, solve for the probability of the up state occurring that is consistent with expected appreciation of the underlying asset at the 10 percent risk-free rate. See Exhibit 7.9 for the numbers to use in this example.

Answer: With a 10 percent risk-free rate per period in Example 7.6, the expected value of the S&P 500 in the next period if investors are risk neutral is 110 percent of the current value, $850. Hence, the risk-neutral probability π that makes the expected future value of the underlying asset 110 percent of today's value solves:

$$\$850(1.1) = \$1,000\pi + \$500(1 - \pi)$$

Thus, $\pi = .87$.

Note from Example 7.8 that .87 is the risk-neutral probability, not the actual probability, of the good state occurring, which remains unspecified. The risk-neutral probability is simply a number consistent with $850 as the current value of the underlying asset and with the assumption that investors are risk neutral, an assumption that may not be true.

The ability to form risk-free investments by having a long position in the tracking portfolio and a short position in the derivative, or vice versa, is what makes it possible to ignore the true probabilities of the up and down state occurring. This is a subtle point. In essence, we are pretending to be in a world that we are not in—a world where all assets are expected to appreciate at the risk-free rate. To do this, throw away the true probabilities of up and down moves and replace them with up and down probabilities that make future values along the binomial tree consistent with risk-neutral preferences.

Step 2: Probability-Weight the Derivative's Future Values and Discount at the Risk-Free Rate.   Once having computed the risk-neutral probabilities for the underlying asset, apply these same probabilities to the future outcomes of the value of the derivative to obtain its risk-neutral expected future value. This is its expected *future* value, assuming that everyone is risk neutral, which is not the same as the derivative's true expected value. Discounting this risk-neutral expected value at the risk-free rate gives the no-arbitrage present value of the derivative.

Example 7.9 demonstrates how to value derivatives using the risk-neutral valuation method.

Example 7.9:   Using Risk-Neutral Probabilities to Value Derivatives
Apply the risk-neutral probabilities of .87 and .13 from Example 7.8 to the cash flows of the derivative of Example 7.6 and discount the resulting risk-neutral expected value at the risk-free rate. See Exhibit 7.9 for the numbers to use in the example.

Answer: .87($362.50) + .13($112.50) yields a risk-neutral expected future value of $330, which has a discounted value of $330/1.1 = $300.

Relating Risk-Neutral Valuation to the Tracking Portfolio Method.   It is indeed remarkable, but not coincidental, as our earlier arguments suggested, that Examples 7.9 and 7.7 arrive at the same answer. Indeed, this will always be the case, as the following result states.

Result 7.6   Valuation of a derivative based on no arbitrage between the tracking portfolio and the derivative is identical to risk-neutral valuation of that derivative.[23]

It is worth repeating that one cannot take the true expected future value of a derivative, discount it at the risk-free rate, and hope to obtain its true present value. The true expected future value is based on the true probabilities, not the risk-neutral probabilities.

A General Formula for Risk-Neutral Probabilities.   One determines risk-neutral probabilities from the returns of the underlying asset at each of the binomial outcomes, and not by the likelihood of each binomial outcome. The risk-neutral probabilities, π, are those probabilities that make the "expected" return of an asset equal the risk-free rate. That is, π must solve:

$$\pi u + (1 - \pi)d = 1 + r_f$$

where

r_f = risk-free rate
u = 1 + per period rate of return of the underlying asset at the up node
d = 1 + per period rate of return of the underlying asset at the down node

---

[23]Another related method of valuing derivatives is the *state price valuation method,* which was derived from research in mathematical economics in the 1950s by Gerard Debreu, a 1986 Nobel Prize winner, and Kenneth Arrow, a 1974 Nobel Prize winner. Since a state price is the risk-neutral probability times the risk-free rate, the state price valuation technique yields the same answers for derivatives as the two other methods discussed earlier.

When rearranged, this says:

$$\pi = \frac{1 + r_f - d}{u - d} \tag{7.4}$$

Risk-Neutral Probabilities and Zero Cost Forward and Futures Prices.   One infers risk-neutral probabilities from the terms and market values of traded financial instruments. Because futures contracts are one class of popularly traded financial instruments with known terms (the futures price) and known market values, it is often useful to infer risk-neutral probabilities from them.

For example, corporations often enter into derivative contracts that involve options on real assets. Indeed, in the next section, we will consider a hypothetical case involving the option to buy jet airplanes. To value this option correctly, using data about the underlying asset, the jet airplane, is a heroic task. For reasons beyond the scope of this text, the future values postulated for an asset like a jet airplane must be adjusted in a complex way to reflect maintenance costs on the plane, revenue from carrying passengers or renting the plane out, obsolescence, and so forth. In addition, the no arbitrage-based valuation relationship derived is hard to envision if one is required to "sell short a jet airplane" to take advantage of an arbitrage.

In these instances, corporations often use forward and futures prices as inputs for their derivative valuation models.[24] Such forwards and futures, while derivatives themselves, can be used to value derivatives for which market prices are harder to come by, like jet airplane options, without any of the complications alluded to above.

In order to use the prices of zero-cost forwards or futures to obtain risk-neutral probabilities, it is necessary to slightly modify the risk-neutral valuation formulas developed above. We begin with futures and later argue that forwards should satisfy the same formula.

Recall that futures prices are set so that the contract has zero fair market value. The amount earned on a futures contract over a period is the change in the futures price. This profit is marked to market in that the cash from this profit is deposited in—or, in case of a loss, taken from—one's margin account at a futures brokerage firm. Thus, a current futures price of F, which can appreciate to F_u in the up state or depreciate to F_d in the down state, corresponds to margin cash inflow $F_u - F$ if the up state occurs, and a negative number, $F_d - F$ (a cash outflow of $F - F_d$) if the down state occurs. In a risk-neutral setting with π as the risk-neutral probability of the up state, the expected cash received at the end of the period is:

$$\pi(F_u - F) + (1 - \pi)(F_d - F)$$

The investor in futures spends no money to receive this expected amount of cash. Thus, in a risk-neutral world, the zero cost of entering into the contract should equal the discounted[25] expected cash received at the end of the period, that is:

$$0 = \frac{\pi(F_u - F) + (1 - \pi)(F_d - F)}{(1 + r_f)}$$

Rearranging this equation implies:

---

[24]Indeed, forward contracts to buy airplanes are fairly common.

[25]The discount rate does not matter here. With a zero-cost contract, expected future profit has to be zero.

Result 7.7   The no-arbitrage futures price is the same as a weighted average of the expected futures prices at the end of the period, where the weights are the risk-neutral probabilities, that is:

$$F = \pi F_u + (1 - \pi)F_d \tag{7.5}$$

If the end of the period is the maturity date of the futures contract, then $F_u = S_u$ and $F_d = S_d$, where S_u and S_d, respectively, are the spot prices underlying the futures contract. Substituting S_u and S_d into the last equation implies that for this special case:

$$F = \pi S_u + (1 - \pi)S_d$$

We can generalize this as follows:

Result 7.8   The no-arbitrage futures price is the risk-neutral expected future spot price at the maturity of the futures contract.

Result 7.8 is a general result that holds in both a multiperiod and single-period setting. For example, a futures contract in January 1998, which is two years from maturity, has a January 1998 futures price equal to the risk-neutral expected spot price in January 2000. Example 7.10 illustrates how futures prices relate to risk-neutral probabilities.

Example 7.10:   Using Risk-Neutral Probabilities to Obtain Futures Prices

Apply the risk-neutral probabilities of .87 and .13 from Example 7.8 to derive the futures price of the S&P 500. Exhibit 7.10, which modifies a part of Exhibit 7.9, should aid in this calculation.
   Answer: Using Result 7.8, the S&P futures price is $935 = .87($1,000) + .13($500). Note that, consistent with Result 7.2, this is the same as $850(1.1), which is the spot price plus the 10 percent risk-free interest on the spot price during one period.

EXHIBIT 7.10   Futures Prices

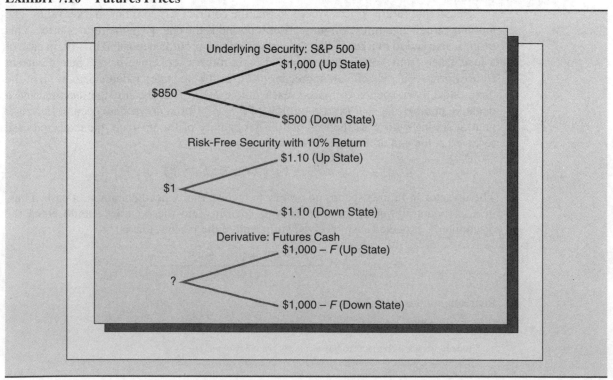

It is also possible to rearrange equation (7.5) to identify the risk-neutral probabilities, π and $1 - \pi$ from futures prices. This yields:

$$\pi = \frac{F - F_d}{F_u - F_d} \tag{7.6}$$

Example 7.11 provides a numerical illustration of this.

Example 7.11:   Using Futures Prices to Determine Risk-Neutral Probabilities

If futures prices for Boeing 777 airplanes can appreciate by 10 percent (up state) or depreciate by 10 percent (down state), compute the risk-neutral probabilities for the up and down states.

Answer: In the up state, $F_u = 1.1F$; in the down state, $F_d = .9F$. Thus, applying equation (7.6), the risk-neutral probability for the up state, $\pi = .5 = \dfrac{F - .9F}{1.1F - .9F}$, making $1 - \pi = .5$ as well.

Earlier in this chapter, we mentioned that futures and forward prices are essentially the same, with the notable exception of long-term interest rate contracts. Hence, the evolution of forward prices for zero-cost contracts could be used just as easily to compute risk-neutral probabilities. This would be important to consider in Example 7.11 because forward prices for airplanes exist, but futures prices do not.

In applying equations (7.5) and (7.6) to forwards rather than futures, it is important to distinguish the evolution of forward prices on new zero-cost contracts from the evolution of the value of a forward contract. For example, in January 1999 American Airlines may enter into a forward contract with Boeing to buy Boeing 777s one year hence (i.e., January 2000), at a prespecified price. Most likely, this prespecified price is set so that the contract has zero up-front cost to American. However, as prices of 777s increase or decrease over the next month, the value of the forward contract becomes positive or negative because the old contract has the *same forward price*. Equations (7.5) and (7.6) would not apply to the value of this contract. Instead, these equations compare the forward price for 777s at the beginning of the month with subsequent forward prices for new contracts to buy 777s *at the maturity of the original contract,* that is, new contracts in subsequent months that mature in January 2000. Such new contracts would be zero-cost contracts.

It is also possible to use the binomial evolution of the *value,* not the *forward price* of the old American Airlines forward contract to determine the risk-neutral probabilities. However, because this contract sometimes has positive and sometimes negative value, one needs to use equation (7.4) for this computation.

It is generally impossible to observe a binomial path for the value of a single forward contract when that contract is not actively traded among investors (and it usually isn't). In contrast, parameters that describe the path of forward prices for new zero-cost contracts are usually easier to observe and estimate.

7.4 Multiperiod Binomial Valuation

Risk-neutral valuation methods can be applied whenever perfect tracking is possible. When continuous and simultaneous trading in the derivative, the underlying security, and a risk-free bond can take place and when the value of the tracking portfolio changes smoothly (i.e., it makes no big jumps) over time, perfect tracking is usually feasible. To the extent that one can trade almost continuously and almost simultaneously in the real world, and to the extent that prices do not move too abruptly, a derivative value obtained from a model based on perfect tracking may be regarded as a very good approximation of the derivative's fair market value.

When large jumps in the value of the tracking portfolio or the derivative can occur, perfect tracking is generally not possible. The binomial process that we have been discussing is an exception where jumps occur and perfect tracking is still possible.

How Restrictive Is the Binomial Process in a Multiperiod Setting?

Initially at least, it appears as though the assumption of a binomial process is quite restrictive—more restrictive in fact than the continuous trading and price movement assumptions that permit tracking. We prefer to discuss tracking with binomial processes instead of continuous processes because the latter, requiring advanced mathematics, is more complex to present. Moreover, binomial processes are not as restrictive as they might at first seem.

Although only two outcomes are permitted for the next period, one can define a period to be as short as one likes and can value assets over multiple periods. Paths for the tracking portfolio when periods are short appear much like the paths seen with the continuous processes. Hence, it is useful to understand how multiperiod binomial valuation works. Another advantage of multiperiod binomial models is that the empirical accuracy of the binomial pricing model increases as time is divided into finer binomial periods implying that there are more binomial steps.

Numerical Example of Multiperiod Binomial Valuation

Example 7.12 determines the current fair market price of a derivative whose value is known two binomial periods later. However, it will be necessary to program a computer or use a spreadsheet to value derivatives over large numbers of short binomial periods.

In Example 7.12, the derivative is an option to buy airplanes. The "underlying asset," basically a financial instrument that helps determine risk-neutral probabilities, is a set of forward contracts on airplanes. The binomial tree for the underlying forward price (above the nodes) and derivative values (below the nodes) is given in Exhibit 7.11.

Example 7.12:   Valuing a Derivative in a Multiperiod Setting

As the financial analyst for American Airlines, you have been asked to analyze Boeing's offer to sell options to buy 200 new 777 airplanes 6 months from now for $83 million per plane. You divide up the 6 months into two 3-month periods and conclude—after analyzing historical forward prices for new 777s—that a reasonable assumption is that new forward prices, currently at $100 million per airplane, can jump up by 10 percent or down by 10 percent in each 3-month period. By this, we mean that new 3-month forward prices tend to be either 10% above or 10% below the new 6-month forward prices observed 3 months earlier. Similarly, spot prices for 777s tend to be 10% above or 10% below the new 3-month forward prices observed 3 months earlier. Thus, the Boeing 777 jet option is worth $38 million per plane if the forward price jumps up twice in a row and $16 million if it jumps up only once in the two periods. If the forward price declines 10 percent in the first 3-month period and declines 10 percent again in the second 3-month period, the option Boeing has offered American will not be exercised because the prespecified 777 purchase price of the option will then be higher than the price American would pay to purchase 777s directly. What is the fair price that American Airlines should be willing to pay for an option to buy one airplane, assuming that the risk-free rate is 0%?

Answer: Exhibit 7.11 graphs above each node the path of the new forward prices that (as described above) are relevant for computing risk-neutral probabilities. Below each node are the option values that one either knows or has to solve for. The leftmost point represents today. Movements to the right along lines connecting the nodes represent possible paths that new zero-cost forward prices can take. If there are two up moves, the forward (and spot) price is $121 million per plane. Two down moves mean it is $81 million per plane. One up and one down move, which occurs along two possible paths, results in a $99 million price per plane.

Solve this problem working backward through the tree diagram, using the risk-neutral valuation technique. Exhibit 7.11 labels the nodes in the tree diagram at the next period as *U* and *D* (for up and down), and as *UU, UD,* and *DD,* for the period after that. Begin with a look at the *U, UU, UD* trio from Exhibit 7.11.

At node *U,* the forward price is $110 million per plane. Using the risk-neutral valuation method, solve for the π that makes $121\pi + 99(1 - \pi) = 110$. Thus, $\pi = .5$. The value of the option at *U* is:

$$.5(\$38 \text{ million}) + .5(\$16 \text{ million}) = \$27 \text{ million}$$

At node *D,* the forward price is $90 million per plane. Solving $99\pi + 81(1 - \pi) = 90$ identifies the risk-neutral probability $\pi = .5$. This makes the option worth:

$$.5(\$16 \text{ million}) + .5(\$0) = \$8 \text{ million}$$

The derivative is worth either $27 million (node *U*) or $8 million (node *D*) at the next trading date. To value it at today's date, multiply these two outcomes by the risk-neutral probabilities. These are again $\pi = .5$ and $1 - \pi = .5$. Thus, the value of the derivative is:

$$\$17.5 \text{ million} = .5(\$27 \text{ million}) + .5(\$8 \text{ million})$$

Algebraic Representation of Two-Period Binomial Valuation

Let us try to represent Example 7.12 algebraically. Let V_{uu}, V_{ud}, and V_{dd} denote the three values of the derivative at the final date. To obtain its node *U* value V_u, Example 7.12 took π (which equals .5) and computed:

$$V_u = \frac{\pi V_{uu} + (1 - \pi)V_{ud}}{1 + r_f}$$

EXHIBIT 7.11   Forward Price Paths (in $ millions) and Derivative Values (in $ millions) in a Two-Period Binomial Tree

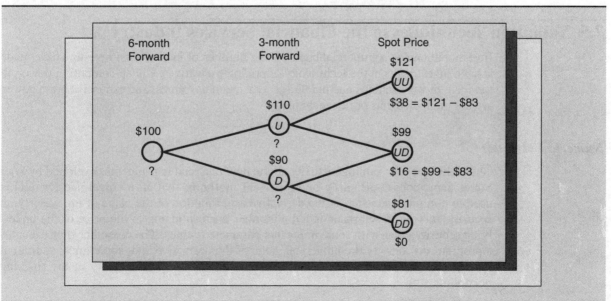

(Since r_f was zero in the example, there is no reason to consider it.) To obtain its node D value V_d, the example computed:

$$V_d = \frac{\pi V_{ud} + (1 - \pi)V_{dd}}{1 + r_f}$$

To solve for today's value V, Example 7.12 computed:

$$V = \frac{\pi V_u + (1 - \pi)V_d}{1 + r_f}$$

$$= \pi \frac{\pi V_{uu} + (1 - \pi)V_{ud}}{1 + r_f} + (1 - \pi)\frac{\pi V_{ud} + (1 - \pi)V_d}{1 + r_f}$$

$$= \frac{\pi^2 V_{uu} + 2\pi(1 - \pi)V_{ud} + (1 - \pi)^2 V_{dd}}{(1 + r_f)^2} \tag{7.7}$$

This is still the discounted expected future value of the derivative with an expected value that is computed with risk-neutral probabilities rather than true probabilities. The risk-neutral probability for the value V_{uu} is the probability of two consecutive up moves, or π^2. The probability of achieving the value V_{ud} is $2\pi(1 - \pi)$, since two paths (down-up or up-down) get you there, each with probability of $\pi(1 - \pi)$. The probability of two down moves is $(1 - \pi)^2$. Thus, the risk-neutral expected value of the derivative two periods from now is the numerator in equation (7.7). Discounting this value by the risk-free rate over two periods yields the present value of the derivative, V. Of course, the same generic result applies when extending the analysis to three periods or more. To value the security today, take the discounted expected future value at the risk-free rate.

Note that in principle, π can vary along the nodes of tree diagrams. However, in Example 7.12, π was the same at every node because u, d, and r_f, which completely determine π, are the same at each node, making π the same at each node. If this was not the case, it is necessary to compute each node's appropriate π from the u, d, and r_f that apply at that node.

7.5 Valuation Techniques in the Financial Services Industry

Investment banks, commercial banks, and a number of institutional investors have made sizable investments in the technology of pricing derivatives. Cheap computing power, in the form of workstations and parallel processing mainframes, and expensive brain power are the main elements of this technology.

Numerical Methods

The techniques for valuing virtually all the new financial instruments developed by Wall Street firms consist primarily of **numerical methods**; that is, no algebraic formula is used to compute the value of the derivative as a function of the value of the underlying security. Instead, a computer is fed a number corresponding to the price of the underlying security along with some important parameter values. The computer then executes a program that derives the numerical value of the derivative and, sometimes, additional information such as the number of shares of the underlying security in the tracking portfolio.

Binomial-like Numerical Methods. These numerical methods fall into several classes. One class is the binomial approach used throughout this chapter. On Wall Street, Salomon Brothers Bond Portfolio Analysis group employs the binomial approach to value callable corporate bonds (see exercise 7.5). This binomial approach also is commonly used in spreadsheets by recent M.B.A. graduates working in corporate finance, sales, and trading, who need to find "quick and dirty" valuation results for many derivatives.

One potential hitch in the binomial method is that it is necessary to specify the values of the underlying security along all nodes in the tree diagram. This requires estimation of u and d, the amounts by which the security can move up and down from each node. There are several ways to simplify the process. First, the binomial method can be used to approximate many kinds of continuous distributions if the time periods are cut into extremely small intervals. One popular continuous distribution is the lognormal distribution. The natural logarithm of the return of a security is normally distributed when the price movements of the security are determined by the lognormal distribution. Once the standard deviation, σ, of this normal distribution is known, u and d are estimated as follows:

$$u = e^{\sigma\sqrt{T/N}}$$

$$d = \frac{1}{u}$$

where

T = number of years to expiration
N = number of binomial periods
e = exponential constant (about 2.7183)

Thus,

$$\sqrt{\frac{T}{N}} = \text{square root of the number of years per binomial period}$$

Depending on the problem, the available computing power, and the time pressures involved, the valuation expert can model the binomial steps, T/N, as anywhere from one day to six months.[26]

Numerical analysis of derivatives with binomial approaches is often modified slightly to account for inefficient computing with the binomial approach. For one, the value of the derivative is affected more by what happens to the underlying asset in the near term and in the middle of the binomial tree, because that is where the risk-neutral probabilities are greatest and risk-free discounting has the least impact on the current value of the derivative. Hence, derivative valuation experts typically modify the binomial method to compute near-term future values and future values in the middle of the binomial tree more intensively and thus more precisely. Often, the tree is modified to a rectangular grid shape.[27]

---

[26]Chapter 8 describes how to estimate σ from historical data.

[27]Other approaches are also available for valuing derivatives. One method, developed by Schwartz (1976), models the process for the underlying security as a continuous process and uses stochastic calculus and no-arbitrage conditions to derive a differential equation for the derivative. It is possible to solve the differential equation with numerical methods that have been devised in mathematics, including the implicit finite difference method. Explicit methods of solving the differential equation are tied directly to the risk-neutral valuation method.

Simulation.   An additional method that Wall Street firms use to value derivatives is **simulation,** a method that uses random numbers obtained from a computer to generate outcomes and then averages the outcomes of some variable to obtain values. Simulations are generally used when the derivative value at each node along the tree diagram depends only on the value of the underlying asset at the node, rather than on the entire historical path followed by the underlying asset. Derivatives that possess this property are known as **path independent derivatives**. These include forwards and European options, but they exclude, for example, mortgages and American put options.

A simulation starts with the initial price of the underlying security. Then, a random number generated by a computer determines the value for the underlying security at the next period. This process continues to the end of the life of the derivative. At that point, a single path for the underlying security over a number of periods has been constructed and an associated path for the derivative (whose value *derives* from the underlying security) has been computed. Usually, one generates derivative values along the single path by discounting back, one period at a time, the terminal value of the derivative. The discounting is made at the short-term risk-free rate, which may itself have its own simulated path!

A second path for the underlying security is then generated, the derivative value is calculated for that path, and an initial derivative value for the second path is computed. This process continues until anywhere from 100 to 100,000 simulated paths have been analyzed. The initial value of the derivative over each path is then averaged to obtain the fair market value of the derivative.

The Risk-Free Rate Used by Wall-Street Firms

All derivative valuation procedures make use of a short-term risk-free return. The most commonly used input is LIBOR. While most academic research focuses on the short-term U.S. Treasury bill rate as "the risk-free rate," this research fails to recognize that only the Treasury can borrow at this rate while arbitrage opportunities between a tracking portfolio and a mispriced derivative may require uncollateralized risk-free borrowing by a high-quality borrower. The rate at which such borrowing takes place is much closer to LIBOR than to the T-bill rate.[28]

7.6 Summary and Conclusions

This chapter examined one of the most fundamental contributions to financial theory: the pricing of derivatives. The price movements of a derivative are perfectly correlated over short time intervals with the price movements of the underlying asset on which it is based. Hence, a portfolio of the underlying asset and a riskless security can be formed that perfectly tracks the future cash flows of the derivative. To prevent arbitrage, the tracking portfolio and the derivative must have the same cost.

The no-arbitrage cost of the derivative can be computed in several ways. One method is direct. It forms the tracking portfolio at some terminal date and works back-

---

[28] A further discussion of this subject is found in Grinblatt (1995). This chapter's results on currency forward rates require longer-term risk-free rates. Implied zero-coupon interest rates in the LIBOR market (known as **Eurocurrency rates**) appear to be the correct interest rates to use for this relation. For horizons in excess of one year, the fixed rate on one side of an interest rate swap that is exchanged for LIBOR provides the correct risk-free rate for the equation in Result 7.3.

ward to determine a portfolio that maintains perfect tracking. The initial cost of the tracking portfolio is the no-arbitrage cost of the derivative. An alternative, but equivalent, approach is the risk-neutral valuation method, which assigns risk-neutral probabilities to the cash flow outcomes of the underlying asset that are consistent with that asset earning, on average, a risk-free return. Applying a risk-free discount rate to the expected future cash flows of the derivative gives its no-arbitrage present value. Both methods lend their unique insights to the problem of valuing derivatives, although the tracking portfolio approach seems to be slightly more intuitive. Computationally, the risk-neutral approach is easier to program.

To keep this presentation relatively simple, we have relied on binomial models, which provide reasonable approximations for the values of most derivatives. The binomial assumptions are usually less restrictive than they might at first seem because the time period for the binomial jump can be as short as one desires. As the time period gets shorter, the number of periods gets larger. A binomial jump to one of two values every minute can result in 2^{60} (more than a billion) possible outcomes at the end of an hour. Defining the time period to be as short as one pleases means that the binomial process can approximate to any degree almost any probability distribution for the return on an investment over almost any horizon.

This chapter mainly focused on the general principles of no-arbitrage valuation, although it applied these principles to value simple derivatives. Many other applications exist. For example, the exercises that follow this chapter value risky bonds, callable bonds, and convertible bonds. The following chapter focuses in depth on one of the most important applications of these principles, option pricing.

Key Concepts

Result 7.1: The no-arbitrage value of a forward contract on a share of stock (the obligation to buy a share of stock at a price of K, T years in the future), assuming the stock pays no dividends prior to T, is:

$$S_0 - \frac{K}{(1 + r_f)^T}$$

where

$$S_0 = \text{current price of the stock}$$

and

$$\frac{K}{(1 + r_f)^T} = \begin{array}{l}\text{the current market price of} \\ \text{a default-free zero-coupon} \\ \text{bond paying } K, T \text{ years} \\ \text{in the future}\end{array}$$

Result 7.2: The forward price for settlement in T years of the purchase of a non-dividend-paying stock with a current price of S_0 is:

$$K = S_0(1 + r_f)^T$$

Result 7.3: In the absence of arbitrage, the forward currency rate s_F (e.g., French francs/dollar) is related to the current exchange rate (or **spot rate**) s_0, by the equation:

$$\frac{s_F}{s_0} = \frac{1 + r_{foreign}}{1 + r_{domestic}}$$

where

$r = $ the return (unannualized) on a domestic or foreign risk-free security over the life of the forward agreement, as measured in the respective country's currency

Result 7.4: To determine the no-arbitrage value of a derivative, find a (possibly dynamic) portfolio of the underlying asset and a risk-free security that perfectly tracks the future payoffs of the derivative. The value of the derivative equals the value of the tracking portfolio.

Result 7.5: Given the value of the underlying asset, the value of a derivative does not depend on the mean return of the underlying asset or investor risk preferences.

Result 7.6: Valuation of a derivative based on no arbitrage between the tracking portfolio and the derivative is identical to risk-neutral valuation of that derivative.

Result 7.7: The no-arbitrage futures price is the same as a weighted average of the expected futures prices at the end of the period, where the weights are the risk-neutral probabilities, that is:

$$F = \pi F_u + (1 - \pi)F_d$$

Result 7.8: The no-arbitrage futures price is the risk-neutral expected future spot price at the maturity of the futures contract.

Key Terms

Exercises

7.1. Using risk-neutral valuation, derive a formula for a derivative that pays cash flows over the next two periods. Assume the risk-free rate is 4 percent per period.

   The underlying asset, which pays no cash flows, has a market value that is modeled by the following tree diagram.

$$\$1 \left\langle \begin{matrix} \$1.10 \left\langle \begin{matrix} \$1.20 \\ \$1.05 \end{matrix} \right. \\ \$\ .95 \left\langle \begin{matrix} \$1.05 \\ \$\ .90 \end{matrix} \right. \end{matrix} \right.$$

The cash flows that correspond to the above tree diagram are:

$$\$0 \left\langle \begin{matrix} \$\ .10 \left\langle \begin{matrix} \$2.20 \\ \$3.05 \end{matrix} \right. \\ \$\ .90 \left\langle \begin{matrix} \$3.05 \\ \$0 \end{matrix} \right. \end{matrix} \right.$$

Find the present value of the derivative.

7.2. A convertible bond can be converted into a specified number of shares of stock at the option of the bondholder. Assume that a convertible bond can be converted to 1.5 shares of stock. A single share of this stock has a price that follows the binomial process:

Date 0   Date 1

$$\$50 \left\langle \begin{matrix} \$80 \\ \$30 \end{matrix} \right.$$

The stock does not pay a dividend between dates 0 and 1.

   If the bondholder never converts the bond to stock, the bond has a date 1 payoff of $100 + x$, where x is the coupon of the bond. The conversion to stock may take place either at date 0 or date 1 (upon revelation of the date 1 stock price).

   The convertible bond is issued at date 0 for $100. What should x, the equilibrium coupon of the convertible bond per $100 at face value, be if the risk-free return is 15 percent and there are no taxes, transaction costs, or arbitrage opportunities? Does the corporation save on interest payments if it issues a convertible bond in lieu of a straight bond? If so, why?

7.3. Value a risky corporate bond, assuming that the risk-free interest rate is 4 percent per period, where a period is defined as six months. The corporate bond has a face value of $100 payable two periods from now and pays a 5 percent coupon per period; that is, interest payments of $5 at the end of both the first period and the second period.

The corporate bond is a derivative of the assets of the issuing firm. Assume that the assets generate sufficient cash to pay off the promised coupon one period from now. In particular, the corporation has set aside a reserve fund of $5/1.04 to pay off the promised coupon of the bond one period from now. Two periods from now, there are three possible states. In one of those states, the assets of the firm arc not worth much and the firm defaults, unable to generate a sufficient amount of cash. Only $50 of the $105 promised payment is made on the bond in this state.

The exhibit below describes the value of the firm's assets (less the amount in the reserve fund maintained for the intermediate coupon) and the cash payoffs of the bond. The nonreserved assets of the firm are currently worth $100. At the *U* and *D* nodes, the reserve fund has been depleted and the remaining assets of the firm are worth $120 and $90, respectively, while they are worth $300, $110, and $50, respectively, in the *UU, UD,* and *DD* states two periods from now.

Paths for the Value of the Firm's Assets (Above the Node) Cash Payoffs of a Risky Bond (Below the Node) in a Two-period Binomial Tree Diagram

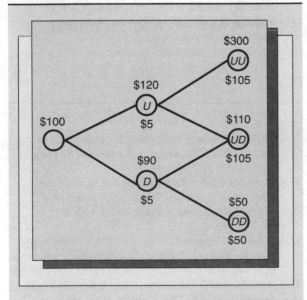

7.4. In many instances, whether a cash flow occurs early or not is a decision of the issuer or holder of the derivative. One example of this is a callable bond, which is a bond that the issuing firm can buy back at a prespecified call price. Valuing a callable bond is complicated because the early call date is not known in advance—it depends on the future path followed by the underlying security. In these cases, it is necessary to compare the value of the security—assuming it is held a while longer—with the value obtained from cash by calling the bond or prematurely exercising the call option. To solve these problems, you must work backward in the binomial tree to make the appropriate comparisons and find the nodes in the tree where intermediate cash flows occur.

Suppose that in the absence of a call, a callable corporate bond with a call price of $100 plus accrued interest has cash flows identical to those of the bond in exercise 7.3. (In this case, accrued interest is the $5 coupon if it is called cum-coupon at the intermediate date and 0 if it is called ex-coupon.) What is the optimal call policy of the issuing firm, assuming that the firm is trying to maximize shareholder wealth? What is the value of the callable bond? *Hint:* Keep in mind that maximizing shareholder wealth is the same as minimizing the value of the bond.

7.5. Consider a stock that can appreciate by 50 percent or depreciate by 50 percent per period. Three periods from now, a stock with an initial value of $32 per share can be worth (1) $108—three up moves; (2) $36—two up moves, one down move; (3) $12—one up move, two down moves; or (4) $4—3 down moves. Three periods from now, a derivative is worth $78 in case (1), $4 in case (2), and $0 otherwise. If the risk-free rate is 10 percent throughout these three periods, describe a portfolio of the stock and a risk-free bond that tracks the payoff of the derivative and requires no future cash outlays. Then, fill in the question marks in the exhibit on page 272, which illustrates the paths of the stock and the derivative. *Hint:* You need to work backward. Use the risk-neutral valuation method to check your work.

Three Period Binomial Tree Diagram Underlying Security's Price Above Node, Derivative Security's Price Below Node

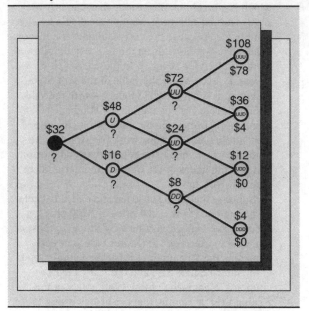

7.6. Consider a forward contract on IBM requiring purchase of a share of IBM stock for $150 in six months. The stock currently sells for $140 a share. Assume that it pays no dividends over the coming six months. Six-month zero-coupon bonds are selling for $98 per $100 of face value.

   a. If the forward is selling for $10.75, is there an arbitrage opportunity? If so, describe exactly how you could take advantage of it.

   b. Assume that three months from now, the stock price has risen to $160 and three-month zero-coupon bonds are selling for $99. How much has the value of your forward contract changed?

7.7. Assume that forward contracts to purchase one share of Sony and Digital Equipment (DEC) at $100 and $40, respectively, in one year are currently selling for $3.00 and $2.20. Assume that neither stock pays a dividend over the coming year, and that one-year zero-coupon bonds are selling for $93 per $100 of face value. The current prices of Sony and DEC are $90 and $35, respectively.

   a. Are there any arbitrage opportunities? If so, describe how to take advantage of them.

   b. What is the price of a forward contract on a portfolio composed of one-half share of Sony and one-half share of DEC, requiring that $70 be paid for the portfolio in one year?

   c. Is this the same as buying one-half of a forward contract on each of Sony and DEC? Why or why not? (Show payoff tables.)

   d. Is it generally true that a forward on a portfolio is the same as a portfolio of forwards? Explain.

7.8. Assume the Eurodollar rate (nine-month LIBOR) is 9 percent and the Eurosterling rate (nine-month LIBOR for the U.K. currency) is 11 percent. What is the nine-month forward $/£ exchange rate if the current spot exchange rate is $1.58/£? (Assume that nine months from now is 274 days.)

7.9. Assume that futures prices for Hewlett-Packard (HP) can appreciate by 15 percent or depreciate by 10 percent and that the risk-free rate is 10 percent over the next period. Price a derivative security on HP that has payoffs of $25 in the up state and −$5 in the down state in the next period, where the actual probability of the up state occurring is 75 percent.

References and Additional Readings

Arrow, Kenneth J. "The Role of Securities in the Optimal Allocation of Risk-Bearing." *Review of Economic Studies* 31 (1964), pp. 91–96.

Balducci, Vince; Kumar Doraiswani; Cal Johnson; and Janet Showers, "Currency Swaps: Corporate Applications and Pricing Methodology," pamphlet. New York: Salomon Brothers, Inc., Bond Portfolio Analysis Group, 1990.

Black, Fischer, and Myron Scholes. "The Pricing of Options and Corporate Liabilities." *Journal of Political Economy* 81 (May–June 1973), pp. 637–59.

Breeden, Douglas T., and Robert H. Litzenberger.

"Prices of State-Contingent Claims Implicit in Option Prices." *Journal of Business* 51 (1978), pp. 621–52.

Cox, J., and S. Ross. "The Valuation of Options for Alternative Stochastic Processes." *Journal of Financial Economics* 3 (Jan.–Mar. 1976), pp. 145–66.

Cox, John C.; Stephen A. Ross; and Mark Rubinstein. "Option Pricing: A Simplified Approach." *Journal of Financial Economics* 7 (Sept. 1979), pp. 229–63.

Cox, John C., and Mark Rubinstein. *Options Markets.* Engelwood Cliffs, NJ: Prentice-Hall, 1985.

Grinblatt, Mark. "An Analytic Solution for Interest Rate

Swap Spreads." Working Paper, University of
California, Los Angeles, 1995.

Grinblatt, Mark, and Narasimhan Jegadeesh. "The
Relative Pricing of Eurodollar Futures and
Forwards." *Journal of Finance* 51, no. 4
(Sept. 1996), pp. 1499–1522.

Grinblatt, Mark and Francis Longstaff. "Financial
Innovation and the Role of Derivative Securities: An
Empirical Analysis of the Treasury Strips
Program," UCLA working paper (1996).

Harrison, Michael J., and David M. Kreps. "Martingales
and Arbitrage in Multiperiod Securities Markets."
Journal of Economic Theory 20 (1979),
pp. 381–408.

Ingersoll, Jonathan. *Theory of Financial Decision
Making.* Totowa, NJ: Rowman & Littlefield, 1987.

Hull, John C. *Options, Futures, and Other Derivatives,*
3d Ed. Upper Saddle River, N.J.: Prentice-Hall,
1997.

Jarrow, Robert, and Stuart Turnbull. *Derivative
Securities.* Cincinnati, Ohio: South-Western
Publishing, 1996.

Lewis, Michael. *Liar's Poker: Rising through the
Wreckage on Wall Street.* New York: W. W. Norton,
1989.

Merton, Robert C. *Continuous Time Finance.* Oxford,
England: Basil Blackwell, 1990.

———. "Theory of Rational Option Pricing." *Bell
Journal of Economics and Management Science*
4 (Spring 1973), pp. 141–83.

Rendelman, Richard J. Jr., and Brit J. Bartter. "Two-State
Option Pricing." *Journal of Finance* 34 (Dec.
1979), pp. 1093–1110.

Ross, Stephen A. "A Simple Approach to the Valuation
of Risky Streams." *Journal of Business* 51 (July
1978) pp. 453–75.

Rubinstein, Mark. "Presidential Address: Implied
Binomial Trees. *Journal of Finance* 49 (July 1994),
pp. 771–818.

Schwartz, Eduardo. "The Valuation of Warrants:
Implementing a New Approach." *Journal of
Financial Economics* 4 (Jan. 1977), pp. 79–93.

Options

Learning Objectives

After reading this chapter, you should be able to:

1. Explain the basic put-call parity formula, how it relates to the value of a forward contract, and the types of options to which put-call parity applies.

2. Relate put-call parity to a boundary condition for the minimum call price and know the implications of this boundary condition for pricing American call options and determining when they should be exercised.

3. Gather the information needed to price a European option with (*a*) the binomial model and (*b*) the Black-Scholes Model, and then implement these models to price an option.

4. Understand the Black Scholes formula in the following form: $S_0 N(d_1) - PV(K)N(d_1 - \sigma\sqrt{T})$. Be able to explain what interpretation to give to $N(d_1)$.

5. Provide examples that illustrate why an American call on a dividend-paying stock or an American put (irrespective of dividend policy) might be exercised prematurely.

6. Understand the effect of volatility on option prices and premature exercise.

In 1980, Chrysler, then on the verge of bankruptcy, received loan guarantees from the U.S. government. As partial payment for the guarantees, Chrysler gave the U.S. government options to buy Chrysler stock for $13 a share until 1990. At the time these options (technically known as "warrants") were issued, Chrysler stock was trading at about $7.50 per share. By mid-1983, however, Chrysler stock had risen to well over $30 a share and in July of that year, Chrysler repaid the guaranteed loans in full.

Lee Iacocca, Chrysler's CEO at the time, argued that the government had not shelled out a dime to provide the loan guarantees and asked that the warrants be returned to Chrysler at little or no cost. However, many congressmen felt that the government had taken a risk by providing the guarantees and if the warrants were to be returned to Chrysler, they should be returned at their full market value. Ultimately, the government decided to hold an auction for the warrants. Determined to recover its warrants, Chrysler participated in the auction, which occurred when Chrysler stock *was trading at about $28 a share. Chrysler's bid, about $22 per warrant, was the winning bid in the auction.*

O ne of the most important applications of the theory of derivatives valuation is the pricing of options. Options, introduced earlier in the text, are ubiquitous in financial markets and, as seen in this chapter and in much of the remainder of this text, are often found implicitly in numerous corporate financial decisions and corporate securities.

Options have long been important to portfolio managers. There are several reasons for this. In recent years, they have also become increasingly important to corporate treasurers. For one, a corporate treasurer needs to be educated about options for proper oversight of the pension funds of the corporation. In addition, the treasurer needs to understand that options can be useful in corporate hedging[1] and are implicit in many securities the corporation issues, such as convertible bonds, mortgages, and callable bonds.[2] Options also are an important form of executive compensation and, in some cases, a form of financing for the firm.

An understanding of option valuation also is critical for any sophisticated financial decision maker. Consider the opening vignette, for example. As compensation for a government loan guarantee—which by itself is an option—Chrysler issued stock options that gave the government the right to buy Chrysler stock at $13 a share. Both Chrysler and the government felt that this agreement (along with some additional compensation that Chrysler provided) was a fair deal at the time. However, as Chrysler recovered in 1983, the value of the loan guarantee declined to zero and the value of the stock options rose. With no active market in which to observe traded prices for the Chrysler options, it was difficult to know exactly how much the options were worth.

This chapter applies the no-arbitrage tracking portfolio approach to derive the "fair market" values of options, like those issued by Chrysler, using both the binomial approach and a continuous-time approach known as the Black-Scholes Model. It then discusses several practical considerations and limitations of the binomial and Black-Scholes option valuation models. Among these is the problem of estimating volatility. The chapter generalizes the Black-Scholes Model to a variety of underlying securities, including bonds and commodities. It concludes with a discussion of the empirical evidence on the Black-Scholes Model.

8.1 A Description of Options and Options Markets

There are two basic types of options, call options and put options. The next subsection elaborates on an additional important classification of options.

European and American Options
• A **European** call (put) **option** is the right to buy (sell) a unit of the underlying asset at the strike price, *at a specific point in time,* the expiration date.
• An **American** call (put) **option** is the right to buy (sell) a unit of the underlying asset *at any time on or before* the expiration date of the option.

---

[1]Hedging is discussed in Chapter 21.

[2]Callable bonds give the corporation the right to redeem the outstanding bonds before maturity by paying a premium to bondholders. Therefore, it is an option which the firm can choose to exercise by "calling" the bonds. Typically, this will occur when interest rates are low. See Chapter 2.

Most of the options that trade on organized exchanges are American options. For example, the Chicago Board Options Exchange (CBOE) trades American options, primarily on stocks and stock indexes like the S&P 100 and the S&P 500. European options traded from the mid-1980s through 1992 on the American Stock Exchange and are often traded in the over-the-counter market as well. Discussions about reintroducing them on the American Stock Exchange took place during the mid-1990s.

European options are easier to value than American options because the analyst need only be concerned about their value at one future date. However, in some circumstances, which will be discussed shortly, both European and American options have the same value. Because of their relative simplicity and because the understanding of European option valuation is often the springboard to understanding the process of valuing American options, this chapter devotes more space to the valuation of European options than to the more popular American options.

The Four Features of Options

Four features characterize a simple option, the offer of the right to buy (call) or the right to sell (put):

1. An underlying risky asset that determines the option's value at some future date.
2. A strike price.
3. An **exercise commencement date**, prior to which the option cannot be exercised.
4. An expiration date beyond which the option can no longer be exercised.

Because European options can be exercised only on their expiration dates, their commencement and expiration dates are the same. American options, which can be exercised at any time on or before their expiration dates, have commencement dates that coincide with their dates of initial issuance.[3] The stock options traded on organized options exchanges in the United States (e.g., call options on IBM stock) are all American options. However, there is a vast over-the-counter market between financial institutions in which options of almost any variety on virtually any underlying asset or portfolio of assets are traded.[4]

8.2 Option Expiration

Exhibit 8.1, first seen in Chapter 7 as Exhibit 7.7, graphs the value of a call and put option at the expiration date against the value of the underlying asset at expiration. In this chapter, we attach some algebra to the graphs of call and put values. For expositional simplicity, we will often refer to the underlying asset as a share of common stock, but our results also apply to options on virtually any financial instrument.

The uncertain future stock price at the expiration date, T, is denoted by S_T. The strike price is denoted by K. The expiration value for the call option is the larger of zero

---

[3]Deferred American options, not discussed here, have issue dates that precede their commencement dates.

[4]Typically, the underlying asset is common stock, a portfolio of stocks, foreign currencies, or futures contracts, but there are many other assets or portfolios of assets on which options can be written. We use the term "asset" loosely here to mean anything that has an uncertain value over time, be it an asset, a liability, a contract, or a commodity.

EXHIBIT 8.1   The Value of a Call Option and a Put Option at Expiration

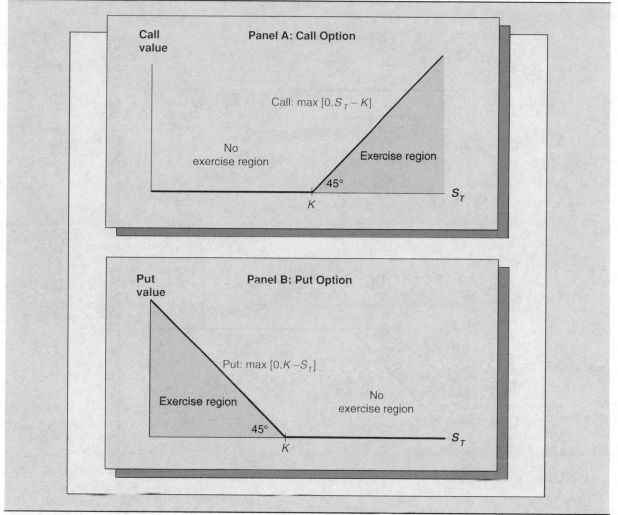

and the difference between the stock price at the expiration date and the strike price, denoted as $\max[0, S_T - K]$. For the put option, the expiration value is $\max[0, K - S_T]$.

Note that the two graphs in Exhibit 8.1 never lie below the horizontal axis. They either coincide with the axis or lie above it on the 45° line. In algebraic terms, the expressions for the future call value, $\max[0, S_T - K]$, and the future put value, $\max[0, K - S_T]$, are never negative. Recall from Chapter 7 that options can never have a negative value because options expire unexercised if option exercise hurts the option holder. The absence of a negative future value for the option and the possibility of a positive future value makes paying for an option worthwhile.

Future cash flows are never positive when writing an option. Exhibit 8.2 illustrates the value at expiration of the short position generated by writing an option. When the call's strike price, K, exceeds the future stock price S_T (or S_T exceeds K for the put), the option expires unexercised. On the other hand, if S_T exceeds K, the call writer has to sell a share of stock for less than its fair value. Similarly, if K exceeds S_T, the put writer has to buy a share of stock for more than it is worth. In all cases, there is no positive future

Exhibit 8.2   The Value of Short Positions in Call and Put Options at Expiration

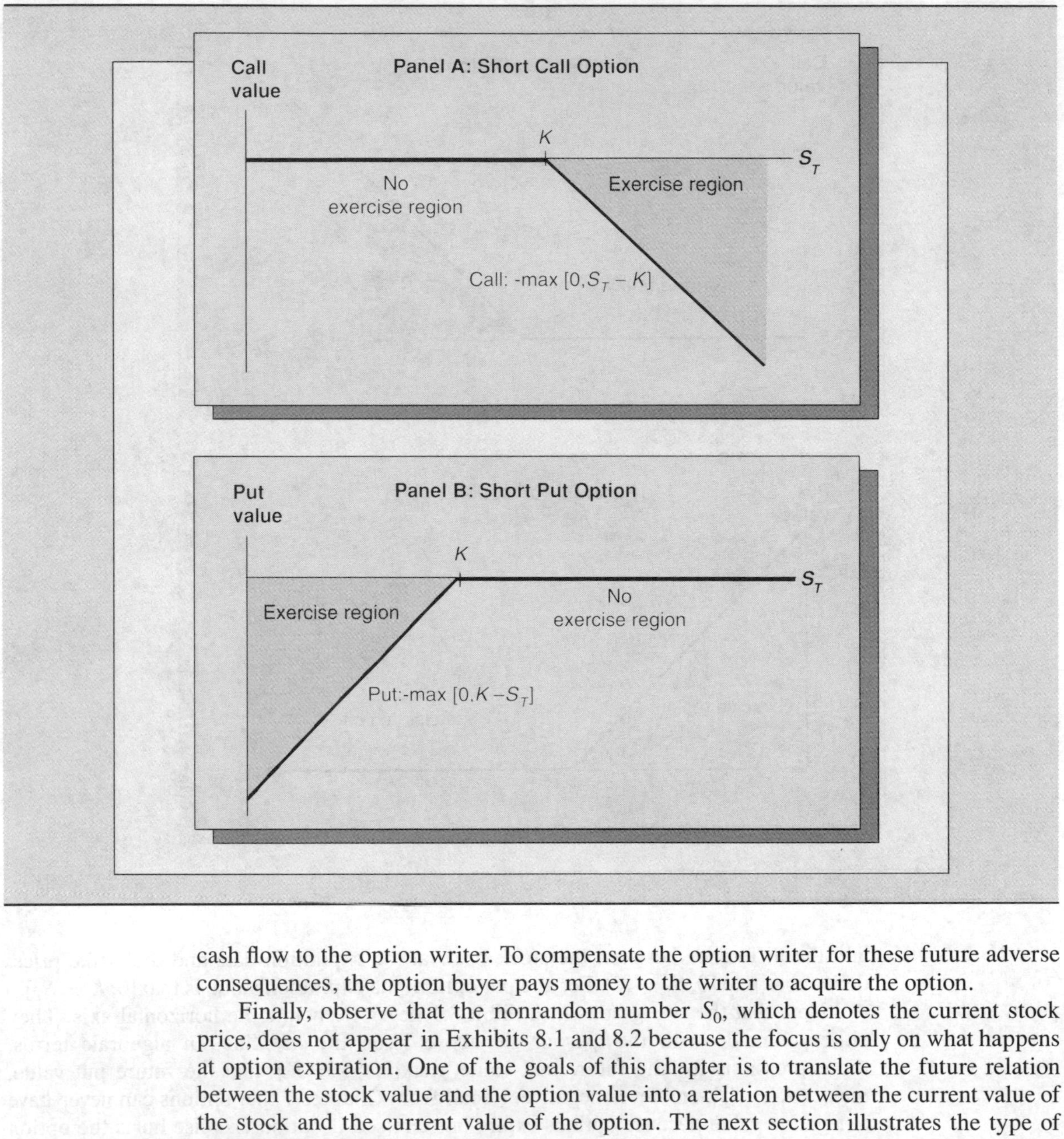

Panel A: Short Call Option

Call value

S_T

K

No exercise region

Exercise region

Call: $-\max[0, S_T - K]$

Panel B: Short Put Option

Put value

S_T

K

Exercise region

No exercise region

Put: $-\max[0, K - S_T]$

cash flow to the option writer. To compensate the option writer for these future adverse consequences, the option buyer pays money to the writer to acquire the option.

Finally, observe that the nonrandom number S_0, which denotes the current stock price, does not appear in Exhibits 8.1 and 8.2 because the focus is only on what happens at option expiration. One of the goals of this chapter is to translate the future relation between the stock value and the option value into a relation between the current value of the stock and the current value of the option. The next section illustrates the type of reasoning used to derive such a relation.

8.3 Put-Call Parity

With some rudimentary understanding of the institutional features of options behind us, we now move on to analyze their valuation. One of the most important insights in option pricing, developed by Stoll (1969), is known as the **put-call parity formula**. This equa-

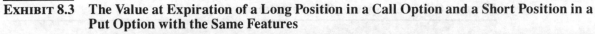

EXHIBIT 8.3   The Value at Expiration of a Long Position in a Call Option and a Short Position in a Put Option with the Same Features

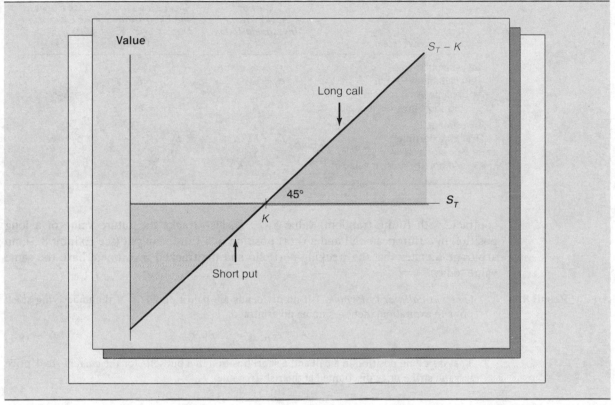

tion relates the prices of European calls to the prices of European puts. However, as this section illustrates, this formula also is important because it has a number of implications that go beyond relating call prices to put prices.

Put-Call Parity and Forward Contracts: Deriving the Formula

Exhibit 8.3 illustrates the value of a long position in a European call option at expiration and a short position in an otherwise identical put option. This combined payoff is identical to the payoff of a forward contract, which is the obligation (not the option) to buy the stock for K at the expiration date.[5]

Result 7.1 in Chapter 7 indicated that the value of a forward contract with a strike price of K on a non-dividend paying stock is $S_0 - K/(1 + r_f)^T$, the difference between the current stock price and the present value of the strike price. The forward contract has this value because it is possible to perfectly track this payoff by purchasing one share of stock and borrowing the present value of K.[6] Since the tracking portfolio for the forward

---

[5]In contrast to options, forward contracts—as obligations to purchase at prespecified prices—can have positive or negative values. Typically, the strike price of a forward contract is set initially, so that the contract has zero value. In this case, the prespecified price is known as the forward price. See Chapter 7 for more detail.

[6]Example 7.4 in Chapter 7 proves this.

EXHIBIT 8.4a   Comparing Two Investments (Algebra)

Investment	Cost of Acquiring the Investment Today (1)	Cash Flows at the Expiration Date if $S_T < K$ (2)	Cash Flows at the Expiration Date if $S_T > K$ (3)
Investment 1:			
Buy call and write put	$c_0 - p_0$	$\tilde{S}_T - K$	$\tilde{S}_T - K$
= Long position in a call	$= \quad c_0$	$= 0$	$= \tilde{S}_T - K$
and short position in a put	$- p_0$	$-(K - \tilde{S}_T)$	-0
Investment 2:			
Tracking portfolio	$S_0 - PV(K)$	$\tilde{S}_T - K$	$\tilde{S}_T - K$
= Buy stock	$= \quad S_0$	$= \quad \tilde{S}_T$	$= \quad \tilde{S}_T$
and borrow present value of K	$-PV(K)$	$-K$	$-K$

contract, with future (random) value $\tilde{S}_T - K$, also tracks the future value of a long position in a European call and a short position in a European put (see Exhibit 8.3), no arbitrage dictates that the tracking portfolio and the tracked investment have the same value today.

Result 8.1   (*The put-call parity formula*.) If no dividends are paid to holders of the underlying stock prior to expiration, then, assuming no arbitrage:

$$c_0 - p_0 = S_0 - PV(K) \tag{8.1}$$

That is, a long position in a call and a short position in a put sells for the current stock price less the strike price discounted at the risk-free rate.

Using Tracking Portfolios to Prove the Formula.   Exhibit 8.4a, which uses algebra, and 8.4b, which uses numbers, illustrate this point further. The columns in the exhibits compare the value of a forward contract implicit in buying a call and writing a put (investment 1) with the value from buying the stock and borrowing the present value of K (investment 2, the tracking portfolio), where K, the strike price of both the call and put options, is assumed to be \$50 in Exhibit 8.4b. Column (1) makes this comparison at the current date. In this column, c_0 denotes the current value of a European call and p_0 the current value of a European put, each with the same time to expiration. Columns (2) and (3) in Exhibit 8.4a make the comparison between investments 1 and 2 at expiration, comparing respectively the future values of investments 1 and 2 in the exercise and no exercise regions. To represent the uncertainty of the future stock price, Exhibit 8.4b assumes three possible future stock prices at expiration: $S_T = 45$, $S_T = 52$, and $S_T = 59$, which correspond to columns (2), (3), and (4), respectively. In Exhibit 8.4b, columns (3) and (4) have option exercise, while column (2) does not.

Since the cash flows at expiration from investments 1 and 2 are both $\tilde{S}_T - K$, irrespective of the future value realized by $\tilde{S}_T$, the present values of investments 1 and 2 observed in column (1) have to be the same if there is no arbitrage. The algebraic statement of this is Equation (8.1).

An Example Illustrating How to Apply the Formula.   Example 8.1 illustrates an application of Result 8.1.

8.4b   Comparing Two Investments (Numbers) with $K = \$50$

Investment	Cost of Acquiring the Investment Today (1)	Cash Flows at the Expiration Date if S at that time is:		
		$45 (2)	$52 (3)	$59 (4)
Investment 1:				
Buy call and write put	$c_0 - p_0$	$-\$5$	$\$2$	$\$9$
= Long position in a call	$= \quad c_0$	$= \quad 0$	$= (\$52 - \$50)$	$= (\$59 - \$50)$
and short position in a put	$-p_0$	$-(\$50 - \$45)$	-0	-0
Investment 2:				
Tracking portfolio	$S_0 - PV(50)$	$-\$5$	$\$2$	$\$9$
= Buy stock	$= \quad S_0$	$= \quad \$45$	$= \quad \$52$	$= \quad \$59$
and borrow present value of K	$-PV(\$50)$	$-\$50$	$-\$50$	$-\$50$

Example 8.1:   Comparing Prices of At-the-Money Calls and Puts

An at-the-money option has a strike price equal to the current stock price. Assuming no dividends, what sells for more: An at-the-money European put or an at-the-money European call?

Answer: From put-call parity, $c_0 - p_0 = S_0 - PV(K)$. If $S_0 = K$, $c_0 - p_0 = K - PV(K) > 0$. Thus, the call sells for more.

Arbitrage When the Formula is Violated.   Example 8.2 demonstrates how to achieve arbitrage when equation (8.1) is violated.

Example 8.2:   Generating Arbitrage Profits When There Is a Violation of Put-Call Parity

Assume that a European call sells for $c_0 = \$2$ and a European put on the same stock ($S_0 = \$45$), with the same strike price ($\$44$), and time to expiration (one year), sells for $p_0 = \$1$. If the one-year, risk-free interest rate is 10 percent, the put-call parity formula is violated, and there is an arbitrage opportunity. Describe it.

Answer: $PV(K) = \$44/1.1 = \$40$. Thus, $c_0 - p_0 = \$1$ is less than $S_0 - PV(K) = \$5$. Therefore, buying a call and writing a put is a cheaper way of producing the cash flows from a forward contract than buying stock and borrowing the present value of K. Pure arbitrage arises from buying the cheap investment and writing the expensive one, that is:

- Buy the call for $2.
- Write the put for $1.
- Sell short the stock and receive $45.
- Invest $40 in the 10 percent risk-free asset.

This strategy results in an initial cash inflow of $4.

- If the stock price exceeds the strike price at expiration, exercise the call, using the proceeds from the risk-free investment to pay for the $44 strike price. Close out the short position in the stock with the share received at exercise. The worthless put expires unexercised. Hence, there are no cash flows and no positions left at expiration, but the original $4 is yours to keep.

- If the stock price at expiration is less than the $44 strike price, the put will be exercised and you, as the put writer, will be forced to receive a share of stock and pay $44 dollars for it. The share you acquire can be used to close out your short position in the stock and the $44 strike price comes out of your risk-free investment. The worthless call expires unexercised. Again, there are no cash flows or positions left at expiration. The original $4 is yours to keep.

Put-Call Parity and a Minimum Value for a Call

The put-call parity formula provides a lower bound for the current value of a call, given the current stock price. Because it is necessary to subtract a nonnegative current put price, p_0, from the current call price, c_0, in order to make $c_0 - p_0 = S_0 - PV(K)$, it follows that:

$$c_0 \geq S_0 - PV(K) \qquad (8.1a)$$

Thus, the minimum value of a call is the current price of the underlying stock, S_0, less the present value of the strike price, $PV(K)$.

Put-Call Parity and the Pricing and Premature Exercise of American Calls

This subsection uses equation (8.1) to demonstrate that the values of American and European call options on nondividend-paying stocks are the same. This is a remarkable result and, at first glance, a bit surprising. American options have all the rights of European options, plus more; thus, values of American options should equal or exceed the values of their otherwise identical European counterparts. In general, American options may be worth more than their European counterparts, as this chapter later demonstrates with puts. What is surprising is that they are *not always* worth more.

Premature Exercise of American Call Options on Stocks with No Dividends Prior to Expiration.   American options are only worth more than European options if the right of premature exercise has value. Prior to expiration, however, the present value of the strike price of any option, European or American, is less than the strike price itself, that is, $PV(K) < K$. Inequality (8.1a)—which, as an extension of the put-call parity formula, assumes no dividends prior to expiration—is therefore the strict inequality

$$c_0 > S_0 - K \qquad (8.1b)$$

prior to expiration, which must hold for both European and American call options. Inequality (8.1b) implies Result 8.2.

Result 8.2   It never pays to exercise an American call option prematurely on a stock that pays no dividends prior to expiration.

One should never prematurely exercise an American call option on a stock that pays no dividends prior to expiration because exercising generates cash of $S_0 - K$, while selling the option gives the seller cash of c_0, which is larger by inequality (8.1b). This suggests that waiting until the expiration date always has some value, at which point exercise of an in-the-money call option should take place.

What if the market price of the call happens to be the same as the call option's exercise value? Example 8.3 shows that there is arbitrage if an American call option on a nondividend-paying stock does not sell for (strictly) more than its premature exercise value prior to expiration.

Example 8.3:   Arbitrage When a Call Sells for its Exercise Value
Consider an American call option with a $40 strike price on Houghton-Mifflin stock. Assume that the stock sells for $45 a share and pays no dividends to expiration. The option sells for $5 one year before expiration. Describe an arbitrage opportunity, assuming the interest rate is 10 percent per year.

Answer: Sell short a share of Houghton-Mifflin stock and use the $45 you receive to buy the option for $5 and place the remaining $40 in a savings account. The initial cash flow from this strategy is zero. If the stock is selling for more than $40 at expiration, exercise the option and use your savings account balance to pay the strike price. Although the stock acquisition is used to close out your short position, the $4 interest ($40 × .1) on the savings account is yours to keep. If the stock price is less than $40 at expiration, buy the stock with funds from the savings account to cancel the short position. The $4 interest in the savings account and the difference between the $40 (initial principal in the savings account) and the stock price is yours to keep.

Holding onto an American call option instead of exercising it prematurely is like buying the option at its current exercise value in exchange for its future exercise value. That is, not exercising the option means giving up the exercise value today in order to maintain the value you will get from exercise at a later date. Hence, the cost of not exercising prematurely (i.e., waiting) is the lost exercise value of the option.

Example 8.3 illustrates that the option to exercise at a later date is more valuable than the immediate exercise of an option. At a cost of $5 an investor can buy the option, sell the stock short, and gain an arbitrage opportunity by exercising the option in the future. It follows that holding onto an option already owned (which is equivalent to buying the $5 option in the example), selling short the stock, and lending money dominates early exercise (see exercise 8.1 at the end of the chapter).

When Premature Exercise of American Call Options Can Occur.   Result 8.2 does not necessarily apply to an underlying security that pays cash prior to expiration. This can clearly be seen in the case of a stock that is about to pay a liquidating dividend. An investor needs to exercise an in-the-money American call option on the stock prior to the **ex-dividend date** of a liquidating dividend, which is the last date one can exercise the option and still receive the dividend.[7] The option is worthless thereafter since it represents the right to buy a share of a company that has no assets. All dividends dissipate some of a company's assets. Hence, for similar reasons even a small dividend with an ex-dividend date shortly before the expiration date of the option could trigger an early exercise of the option.

Early exercise also is possible when the option cannot be valued by the principle of no arbitrage, as would be the case if the investor was prohibited from selling short the tracking portfolio. This issue arises in many executive stock options. Executive stock options awarded to the company's CEO may make the CEO's portfolio more heavily weighted toward the company than prudent mean-variance analysis would dictate it should be. One way to eliminate this diversifiable risk is to sell short the company's stock

---

[7]Ex-dividend dates, which are ex-dates for dividends (see Chapter 2), are determined by the record dates for dividend payments and the settlement procedures of the securities market. The record date is the date that the legal owner of the stock is put on record for purposes of receiving a corporation's dividend payment. On the New York Stock Exchange, an investor is not the legal owner of a stock until three business days after the order has been executed. This makes the ex-date three business days prior to the record date.

(a part of the tracking portfolio), but the CEO and most other top corporate executives who receive such options are prohibited from doing this. Another way is to sell the options, but this too is prohibited. The only way for an executive to diversify is to exercise the option, take the stock, and then sell the stock. Such suboptimal exercise timing, however, does not capture the full value of the executive stock option. Nevertheless, the CEO may be willing to lose a little value to gain some diversification.

Except for these two cases—one in which the underlying asset pays cash prior to expiration and the other, executive stock options, for which arbitraging away violations of inequality (8.1b) is not possible because of market frictions—one should not prematurely exercise a call option.

When dividends or other forms of cash on the underlying asset are paid, the appropriate timing for early exercise is described in the following generalization of Result 8.2:

Result 8.3   An investor does not capture the full value of an American call option by exercising between ex-dividend or (in the case of a bond option) ex-coupon dates.

Only at the ex-dividend date, just prior to the drop in the price of the security caused by the cash distribution, is such early exercise worthwhile.

To understand Result 8.3, consider the following example: Suppose it is your birthday and Aunt Em sends you one share of Intel stock. Uncle Harry, however, gives you a gift certificate entitling you to one share of Intel stock on your next birthday, one year hence. Provided that Intel pays no dividends within the next year, the values of the two gifts are the same. The present value of the deferred gift is the cost of Intel stock today. Putting it differently, in the absence of a dividend, the only rights obtained by receiving a security early is that you will have it at that later date. You might retort that if you wake up tomorrow and think Intel's share price is going down, you will sell Aunt Em's Intel share, but you are forced to receive Uncle Harry's share. However, this is not really so, because at any time you think Intel's share price is headed down, you can sell short Intel stock and use Uncle Harry's gift to close out your short position. In this case, the magnitude and timing of the cash flows from Aunt Em's gift of Intel, which you sell tomorrow, are identical to those from the combination of Uncle Harry's gift certificate and the Intel short position that you execute tomorrow. Hence, you *do not* create value by receiving shares on nondividend-paying stocks early, but you do create value by deferring the payment of the strike price—increasing wealth by the amount of interest collected in the period before exercise.

Thus, with an option or even with a forward contract, paying for the security at the latest date possible makes sense. With an option, however, you have a further incentive to wait: If the security later goes down in value, you can choose not to acquire the security by not exercising the option and, if it goes up, you can exercise the option and acquire the security.

Premature Exercise of American Put Options.   The value from waiting to see how the security turns out also applies to a put option. With a put, however, the option holder receives rather than pays out cash upon exercise, and the earlier the receipt of cash, the better. With a put, an investor trades off the interest earned from receiving cash early against the value gained from waiting to see how things will turn out. A put on a stock that sells for pennies with a strike price of $40 probably should be exercised. At best, waiting can provide only a few more pennies (the stock cannot sell for less than zero), which should easily be covered by the interest on the $40 received.

Relating the Price of an American Call Option to an Otherwise Identical European Call Option.   If it is never prudent to exercise an American call option prior to expiration, then the right of premature exercise has no value. Thus, in cases where this is true (e.g., no dividends) the no-arbitrage prices of American and European call options are the same.

Result 8.4   If the underlying stock pays no dividends prior to expiration, then the no-arbitrage value of American and European call options with the same features are the same.

Put-Call Parity for European Options on Dividend Paying Stocks.   If there are riskless dividends, it is possible to modify the put-call parity relation. In this case, the forward contract with price $c_0 - p_0$ is worth less than the stock minus the present value of the strike price, $S_0 - PV(K)$. Buying a share of stock and borrowing $PV(K)$ now also generates dividends that are not received by the holder of the forward contract (or, equivalently, the long call plus short put position). Hence, while the tracking portfolio and the forward contract have the same value at expiration, their intermediate cash flows do not match. Only the tracking portfolio receives a dividend prior to expiration. Hence, the value of the tracking portfolio (investment 2 in Exhibit 8.4) exceeds the value of the forward contract (investment 1) by the present value of the dividends, denoted $PV(\text{div})$.

Result 8.5   (*Put-call parity formula generalized.*) $c_0 - p_0 = S_0 - PV(K) - PV(\text{div})$. The difference between the no-arbitrage values of a European call and a European put with the same features is the current price of the stock less the sum of the present value of the strike price and the present value of all dividends to expiration.

Example 8.4 applies this formula to illustrate how to compute European put values in relation to the known value of a European call on a dividend-paying stock.

Example 8.4:   Inferring Put Values from Call Values on a Dividend-Paying Stock
Assume that Intel stock currently sells for $100. A European call on Intel has a strike price of $121, expires two years from now, and currently sells for $20. What is the value of the comparable European put? Assume the risk-free rate is 10 percent per year and that Intel is certain to pay a dividend of $2.75 one year from now.
    Answer: From put-call parity,

$$\$20 - p_0 = \$100 - \frac{\$121}{1.1^2} - \frac{\$2.75}{1.1}, \text{ or}$$

$$p_0 = -(\$100 - \$100 - \$2.50 - \$20) = \$22.50$$

Put-Call Parity and Corporate Securities as Options

Important option-based interpretations of corporate securities can be derived from put-call parity. Equity can be thought of as a call option on the assets of the firm.[8] This arises because of the limited liability of corporate equity holders. Consider a simple two-date model (dates 0 and 1) in which a firm has debt with a face value of K to be paid at date 1, assets with a random payoff at date 1, and no dividend payment at or before date 1. In this case, equity holders have a decision to make at date 1. If they pay the face value of the debt (the strike price), they receive the date 1 cash flows of the assets. On the other

---
[8]See Chapter 15 for more information on this subject.

hand, if the assets at date 1 are worth less than the face value of the debt, the firm is bankrupt, and the equity holders walk away from the firm with no personal liability. Viewed from date 0, this is simply a call option to buy the firm's assets from the firm's debt holders.[9]

Since the value of debt plus the value of equity adds up to the total value of assets at date 0, one also can view corporate bonds as a long position in the firm's assets and a short position in a call option on the firm's assets. With S_0 now denoting the current value of the firm's assets, c_0 denoting the current value of its equity, K denoting the face value of the firm's debt, and D as the market value of its debt, the statement that bonds are assets less a call option is represented algebraically as:

$$D = S_0 - c_0$$

However, when using the no-dividend put-call parity formula, $c_0 - p_0 = S_0 - PV(K)$, to substitute for c_0 in this expression, risky corporate debt is:

$$PV(K) - p_0$$

One can draw the following conclusion, which holds even if dividends are paid prior to the debt maturity date:

Result 8.6   It is possible to view equity as a call option on the assets of the firm and to view risky corporate debt as riskless debt worth $PV(K)$ plus a short position in a put option on the assets of the firm ($-p_0$) with a strike price of K.

Because corporate securities are options on the firm's assets, any characteristic of the assets of the firm that affects option values will alter the values of debt and equity. One important characteristic of the underlying asset that affects option values, presented later in this chapter, is the variance of the asset return.

Result 8.6 also implies that the more debt a firm has, the less in the money is the implicit option in equity. Thus, knowing how option risk is affected by the degree to which the option is in or out of the money may shed light on how the mix of debt and equity affects the risk of the firm's debt and equity securities.

Finally, because stock is an option on the assets of the firm, a call option on the stock of a firm is really an option on an option, or a **compound option**.[10] The binomial derivatives valuation methodology developed in Chapter 7 can be used to value compound options.

Put-Call Parity and Portfolio Insurance

In the mid-1980s, the firm of Leland, O'Brien, and Rubinstein, or LOR, invented a successful financial product known as portfolio insurance. **Portfolio insurance** is an option-based investment which, when added to the existing investments of a pension fund or mutual fund, protects the fund's value at a target horizon date against drastic losses.

---

[9]This analysis is easily modified to accommodate riskless dividends. In this case, equity holders have a claim to a riskless dividend plus a call option on the difference between the firm's assets and the present value of the dividend. The dividend-inclusive put-call parity formula can then be used to interpret corporate debt.

[10]The valuation of compound options was first developed in Geske (1979).

LOR noticed that options have the desirable feature of unlimited upside potential with limited downside risk. Exhibit 8.5 demonstrates that if portfolios are composed of

1. a call option, expiring on the future horizon date, with a strike price of K, and
2. riskless zero-coupon bonds worth F, the floor amount, at the option expiration date,

the portfolio's value at the date the options expire would never fall below the value of the riskless bonds, the floor amount, at that date. If the underlying asset of the call option performed poorly, the option would expire unexercised; however, because the call option value in this case is zero, the portfolio value would be the value of the riskless bonds. If the underlying asset performed well, the positive value of the call option would enhance the value of the portfolio beyond its floor value. In essence, this portfolio is insured.

The present value of the two components of an insured portfolio is:

$$c_0 + PV(F)$$

The problem is that the portfolios of pension funds and mutual funds are not composed of riskless zero-coupon bonds and call options. The challenge is how to turn them

EXHIBIT 8.5   Horizon Date Values of the Two Components of an Insured Portfolio

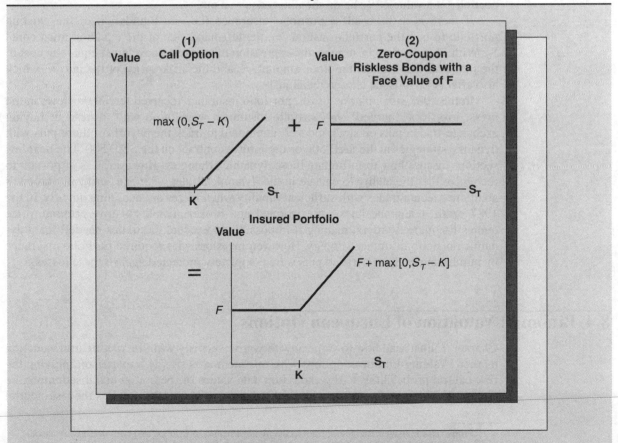

into something with similar payoffs. As conceived by LOR, portfolio insurance is the acquisition of a put on a stock index. The put's strike price determines an absolute floor on losses due to movements in the stock index. The put can be either purchased directly or produced synthetically by creating the put's tracking portfolio (see Chapter 7). Because of the lack of liquidity in put options on stock indexes at desired strike prices and maturities, the tracking portfolio is typically constructed from a dynamic strategy in S&P 500 futures. For a fee, LOR's computers would tailor a strategy to meet a fund's insurance objectives.[11]

To understand how portfolio insurance works, note that the extended put-call parity formula in Result 8.5, $c_0 - p_0 = S_0 - PV(K) - PV(\text{div})$, implies that the *present value* of the desired insured portfolio is:

$$c_0 + PV(F) = S_0 + p_0 - [PV(\text{div}) + PV(K) - PV(F)]$$

where

S_0 = the current value of the uninsured stock portfolio

p_0 = the cost of a put with a strike of K

$PV(\text{div})$ = the present value of the uninsured stock portfolio's dividends

The left-hand side of the equation is the present value of a desired insured portfolio with a floor of F. The right-hand side implies that if an investor starts with an uninsured stock portfolio at a value of S_0, he or she must acquire a put.

If there is to be costless portfolio insurance (i.e., no liquidation of the existing portfolio to buy the portfolio insurance), the left-hand side of the equation must equal S_0. With such costless insurance, the expression in brackets above must equal the cost of the put. This implies that the floor amount, F, and the strike price of the put, K, which also affects p_0, must be chosen judiciously.

In the 1987 stock market crash, portfolio insurance received terrible reviews in the press. Investors "burned" by portfolio insurance were those who, instead of buying exchange-traded puts on stock indexes, attempted to track the payoffs of these puts with dynamic strategies in the S&P 500 or the futures contract on the S&P 500. The next few sections discuss how to formulate these dynamic strategies. However, it is important to recognize that the ability to engage in the dynamic strategy depends critically on one's ability to execute trades with sufficient rapidity when prices are declining quickly. In the 1987 crash, telephone lines were jammed and brokers could not give accurate price quotes for market orders, making it impossible to execute the trades needed for a dynamic portfolio insurance strategy. However, investors who acquired portfolio insurance by purchasing exchange-traded puts were completely protected against these losses.

8.4 Binomial Valuation of European Options

Chapter 7 illustrated how to value any derivative security with the risk-neutral valuation method. Valuing European options with this method is simply a matter of applying the risk-neutral probabilities to the expiration date values of the option and discounting the risk-neutral weighted average at the risk-free rate. This section applies the risk-neutral

---

[11]Proper risk management is important in the management of portfolios and corporations. A casual reading of the business press would have you believe that all derivative securities are extremely risky. Here, however, the acquisition of protective puts can reduce risk by placing a floor on one's losses.

EXHIBIT 8.6   **Tree Diagram for the Value of the Stock (Above Node) and the Call Option (Below Node) Near the Expiration Date**

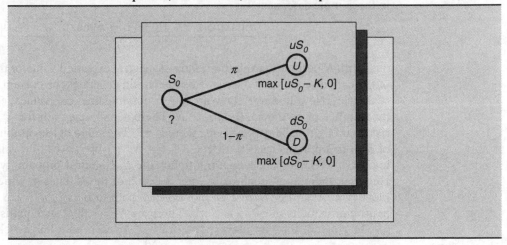

valuation method to algebraic symbols that represent the binomial expiration date values of a European call option in order to derive an analytic formula for valuing European call options. (Put-call parity can be used to obtain the European put formula.) To simplify the algebra, assume that the one-period risk-free rate is constant, and that the ratio of price in the next period to price in this period is always u or d.

This section first analyzes the problem of valuing a European call one period before expiration. It then generalizes the problem to one of valuing a call T periods before expiration. According to Result 8.4, if there are no dividends, the formula obtained also applies to the value of an American call.

Exhibit 8.6 illustrates the investor's view of the tree diagram one period before the option expiration date. Both the values of the stock (above the nodes) and the call option (below the nodes) are represented.[12] We noted in Chapter 7 that it is possible to value the cash flows of any derivative security after computing the risk-neutral probabilities for the stock. The hypothetical probabilities that would exist in a risk-neutral world must make the expected return on the stock equal the risk-free rate. The risk-neutral probabilities for the up and down moves that do this, π and $1 - \pi$, respectively, satisfy:

$$\pi = \frac{1 + r_f - d}{u - d}$$

and

$$1 - \pi = \frac{u - 1 - r_f}{u - d}$$

where

u = ratio of next period's stock price to this period's price if the up state occurs
d = ratio of next period's stock price to this period's price if the down state occurs
r_f = risk-free rate

---

[12]The expiration date prices of the stock and call are at the two circular nodes on the right-hand side of the tree diagram, U and D, in Exhibit 8.6. The prices one period before are at the single node on the left-hand side.

Discounting the risk-neutral expected value of the expiration value of the call at the risk-free rate yields the proper no-arbitrage call value c_0, as a function of the stock price, S_0, in this simple case, namely:

$$c_0 = \frac{\pi \max[uS_0 - K, 0] + (1 - \pi)\max[dS_0 - K, 0]}{1 + r_f}$$

With N periods to expiration, the risk-neutral expected value of the expiration value of the call, discounted at the risk-free rate, again generates the current no-arbitrage value of the call. Now, however, there are $N + 1$ possible final call values, each determined by the number of up moves, $0, 1, \ldots, N$. There is only one path for N up moves, and the risk-neutral probability of arriving there is π^N. The value of the option with a strike price of K at this point is $\max[0, u^N S_0 - K]$. For $N - 1$ up moves, the value of the option is $\max[0, u^{N-1}dS_0 - K]$, which multiplies the risk-neutral probability of $\pi^{N-1}(1 - \pi)$. However, there are N such paths, one for each of the N dates at which the single down move can occur. For $N - 2$ up moves, each path to $\max[0, u^{N-2}d^2S_0 - K]$ has a risk-neutral probability of $\pi^{N-2}(1 - \pi)^2$. There are $N(N - 1)/2$ such paths.

In general, for j up moves, $j = 0, \ldots, N$, each path has a risk-neutral probability of $\pi^j(1 - \pi)^{N-j}$, and there are $\dfrac{N!}{j!(N - j)!}$ such paths to the associated value of $\max[0, u^j d^{N-j}S_0 - K]$.[13] Therefore, the "expected" future value of a European call option, where the expectation uses the risk-neutral probabilities to weight the outcome, is:

$$\sum_{j=0}^{N} \frac{N!}{j!(N - j)!} \pi^j(1 - \pi)^{N-j}\max[0, u^j d^{N-j}S_0 - K]$$

This expression, discounted at the risk-free rate of r_f per binomial period, gives the value of the call option.

Result 8.7   (*The binomial formula.*) The value of a European call option with a strike price of K and N periods to expiration on a stock with no dividends to expiration and a current value of S_0 is:

$$c_0 = \frac{1}{(1 + r_f)^N} \sum_{j=0}^{N} \frac{N!}{j!(N - j)!} \pi^j(1 - \pi)^{N-j}\max[0, u^j d^{N-j}S_0 - K] \tag{8.2}$$

where

r_f = risk-free return per period

π = risk-neutral probability of an up move

u = ratio of the stock price to the prior stock price given that the up state has occurred over a binomial step

d = ratio of the stock price to the prior stock price given that the down state has occurred over a binomial step

Example 8.5 applies this formula numerically.

Example 8.5:   Valuing a European Call Option with the Binomial Formula

Use equation (8.2) to find the value of a three month at-the-money call option on the pharmaceutical company, Centocor, in mid-August 1996. At that time, Centocor was trading at $32 a share. To keep the computations simple, assume that $r_f = 0$, $u = 2$, $d = .5$, and the number of periods (computed as years) $N = 3$.

Answer: Exhibit 8.7 illustrates the tree diagram for Centocor's stock and call option. The stock can have a final value (seen on the right-hand side of the diagram) of $256 (three up

---

[13]The expression $N!$ means $N(N - 1)(N - 2)\ldots 3 \times 2 \times 1$, with the special case of 0! being equal to 1.

**EXHIBIT 8.7   Binomial Tree Diagram for the Value of Centocor Stock (Above Node) and the
Centocor Call Option (Below Node)**

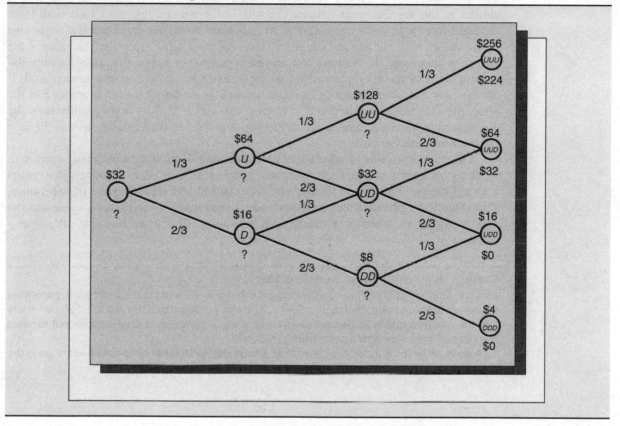

moves to node *UUU*), $64 (two up moves to node *UUD*), $16 (one up move to node *UDD*), or
$4 (0 up moves to node *DDD*). The corresponding values for the option are $224 = $u^3 S_0 - K$,

$32 = $u^2 d S_0 - K$, 0, and 0. Since $\pi = \dfrac{1}{3} = \dfrac{1 + r_f - d}{u - d}$ and $(1 - \pi) = \dfrac{2}{3}$ for these values of *u, d,*
and r_f, the expected future value of the option using risk-neutral probabilities is:

$$\left(\frac{1}{3}\right)^3 (\$256 - \$32) + 3\left(\frac{1}{3}\right)^2 \left(\frac{2}{3}\right)(\$64 - \$32) + 3\left(\frac{1}{3}\right)\left(\frac{2}{3}\right)^2 (\$0) + \left(\frac{2}{3}\right)^3 (\$0) = \$15.41$$

Since the discount rate is 0, $15.41 is also the value of the call option.

8.5 Binomial Valuation of American Options

The last section derived a formula for valuing European calls.[14] This section illustrates
how to use the binomial model to value options that may be prematurely exercised. These
include American puts and American calls on dividend-paying stocks.

---

[14]As suggested earlier, American calls on stocks that pay no dividends until expiration can be valued as
European calls with the method described in the last section.

American Puts

The procedure for modeling American option values with the binomial approach is similar to that for European options. As with European options, work backward from the right-hand side of the tree diagram. At each node in the tree diagram, look at the two future values of the option and use risk-neutral discounting to determine the value of the option at that node. In contrast to European options, however, this value is only the present value of the option provided that the investor holds on to it one more period. If the investor exercises the option at the node, and the underlying asset is worth S at the node, then the value captured is $S - K$ for a call and $K - S$ for a put, rather than the discounted risk-neutral expectation of the values at the two future nodes, as was the case for the European option.

This suggests a way to value the option, assuming that it will be optimally exercised. Working backward, at each node, compare (1) the value from early exercise of the option with (2) the present value of waiting one more period and achieving one of two values. The value to be placed at that decision node is the larger of the exercise value and the present value of waiting. Example 8.6 illustrates this procedure for an American put.

Example 8.6:   Valuing an American Put

Assume that each period, the nondividend-paying stock of Chiron, a drug company, can either double or halve in value, that is, $u = 2$, $d = .5$. If the initial price of the stock is $20 per share and the risk-free rate is 25 percent per period, what is the value of an American put expiring two periods from now with a strike price of $27.50?

Answer: Exhibit 8.8 outlines the path of Chiron's stock and the option. At each node in the diagram, the risk-neutral probabilities solve:

$$\frac{2\pi + .5(1 - \pi)}{1.25} = 1$$

Thus, $\pi = .5$ throughout the problem.

In the final period, at the far right-hand side of the diagram, the stock is worth $80, $20, or $5. From node U, where the stock price is $40 a share, the price can move to $80 (node UU) with an associated put value of $0, or it can move to $20 (node UD), which gives a put value of $7.50. There is no value from early exercise at node U because the $40 stock price exceeds the $27.50 strike price. This means the put option at node U is worth the present value of the $0 and $7.50 outcomes, or:

$$\frac{0\pi + \$7.50(1 - \pi)}{1.25} = \$3.00$$

From node D, where the stock price is $10 a share, early exercise leads to a put value of $17.50. Compare this with the present value from not exercising and waiting one more period, which leads to stock prices of $20 (node UD) and $5 (node DD), and respective put values of $7.50 and $22.50. The present value of these two outcomes is:

$$\frac{\$7.50\pi + \$22.50(1 - \pi)}{1.25} = \$12.00$$

This is less than the value from early exercise. Therefore, the optimal exercise policy is to exercise when the stock price hits $10 at node D.

From the leftmost node, there are two possible subsequent values for the stock. If the stock price rises to $40 a share (node U), the put, worth $3, should not be exercised early. If the stock price declines to $10 a share (node D), the put is worth $17.50, achieved by early exercise. If the market sets a price for the American put, believing it will be optimally exercised, the market value at this point would be $17.50. To value the put at the leftmost node, weight the $3.00 and $17.50 outcomes by the risk-neutral probabilities and discount at the risk-free rate. This value is:

$$\frac{\$3.00\pi + \$17.50(1 - \pi)}{1.25} = \$8.20$$

Early exercise leads to a $7.50 put at this node, which is inferior. Thus, the value of the put is $8.20, and it pays to wait another period before possibly exercising.

Note that even with the possibility of early exercise, it is still possible to track the put option in Example 8.6 with a combination of Chiron stock and a risk-free asset. However, the tracking portfolio here is different than it is for a European put option with comparable features. In tracking the American put, the major difference is due to what happens at node D in Exhibit 8.8, when early exercise is optimal. To track the option value, do not solve for a portfolio of the stock and the risk-free security that has a value of $3.00 if an up move occurs and $12.00 if a down move occurs, solve for the portfolio that has a value of $3.00 if an up move occurs and $17.50 if a down move occurs. This still amounts to solving two equations with two unknowns. With the European option, the variation between the up and down state is −$9.00. With the American option in Example 8.6, the variation is −$14.50. Since the variation in the stock price between nodes U and D is $30 (= $40 − $10), −.3 (= −$9/$30) of a share perfectly tracks a European option and −.483333 (= −14.50/$30) shares perfectly tracks an American option. The associated risk-free investments solve:

$$-.3(\$40) + 1.25x = \$3 \text{ or } x = \$12 \text{ for the European put}$$

$$-.483333(\$40) + 1.25x = \$3 \text{ or } x = \$17.867 \text{ for the American put}$$

This also implies that the European put is worth −.3($20) + $12 = $6, which is $2.20 less than the American put. One can also compute this $2.20 difference by multiplying

EXHIBIT 8.8   Binomial Tree Diagram for the Price of Chiron Stock (Above Node) and an American Put Option (Below Node) with $K = \$27.50$ and $T = 2$

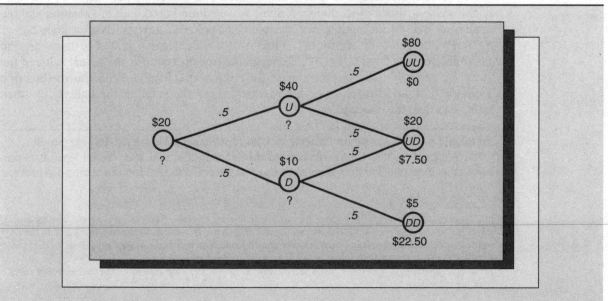

$1 - \pi$ (which is .5) by the $5.50 difference between the nonexercise value and actual value of the American put at node D and discounting back one period at a 25 percent rate.

Valuing American Options on Dividend-Paying Stocks

A stock that pays dividends has two values at the node representing the ex-dividend date: (1) the **cum-dividend value** of the stock, which is the value of the stock prior to the ex-dividend date, and (2) the **ex-dividend value**, the stock price after the ex-dividend date, which is lower by the amount of the dividend, assuming no taxes. At the ex-dividend date, arbitrage forces dictate that the stock price should drop by the amount of the present value of the declared dividend (which is negligibly less than the amount of the dividend since a check generally is mailed a few weeks after the ex-dividend date. Our analysis ignores this small amount of discounting).[15]

It never pays to exercise an American put just prior to the ex-dividend date. For example, if the dividend is $5 per share, a put that is about to be exercised is worth $5 more just after the ex-dividend date than it was prior to it. It makes sense to exercise an American call just prior to the ex-dividend date if one chooses to exercise prematurely at all. If the call is in the money both prior to and after the ex-date of a $5 dividend, the exercise value of the call is $5 higher before the ex-dividend date than after it.

The assumption that dividends are riskless creates a problem if an investor is not careful. For example, it may be impossible to have a risk-free dividend if the ex-date is many periods in the future and large numbers of down moves occur. In taking this "bad path" along the binomial tree, an investor might find that a riskless dividend results in a *negative* ex-dividend value for the stock—which is impossible. There are two ways to model the dividend process that avoid such problems. One approach, which works but is difficult to implement, assumes that the size of the dividend depends on the path that the stock takes. After all, if a stock declines substantially in value, the company may reduce or suspend the dividend. This requires the ability to model the dividend accurately along all paths a stock might take. Such a dividend would be a risky cash flow because the path the stock will follow is unknown in advance.

A second approach is to ignore the dividend and model the path taken by the value of the stock stripped of its dividend rights between the initial date of valuation and the expiration date of the option. For the binomial process, start out with a price $S_0^* = S_0 - PV$(dividends to expiration). Then, select a constant u and d to trace out the binomial tree at all dates t for S_t^*. To obtain the tree diagram for the actual value of the stock S_0, add back the present value of the riskless dividend(s). With this method (see Example 8.7), an investor never has to worry about the value of the underlying stock being less than the dividend.

Example 8.7:   Valuing an American Call Option on a Dividend-Paying Stock

Even though, in reality, Chiron did not pay dividends at the time, assume for illustrative purposes that it did and that the values above each node in Exhibit 8.8 represent the price process

---

[15]If investors know that the price of the stock will drop by less than the dividend amount, buying the stock just before it goes ex-dividend and selling just after it goes ex-dividend means a loss equal to the drop in the stock price, which is more than offset by the dividend received. If the stock drops by more than the dividend, selling short the stock just before it goes ex-dividend and buying it back just after is also an arbitrage opportunity. With taxes, stock prices may fall by less than the amount of the dividend. For more detail, see Chapter 14.

for Chiron stock stripped of its rights to a risk-free dividend of $6.25 paid at nodes *U* and *D* (which is assumed to be the only dividend prior to expiration). (1) Describe the tree diagram for the actual value of the stock, assuming a risk-free rate of 25 percent and (2) value an American call option expiring in the final period with a strike price of $20.

Answer: (1) At the expiration date, on the far right of Exhibit 8.8, the actual stock price and the ex-dividend stock price are the same: The dividend has already been paid! At the intermediate period, each of the two nodes has two values for the stock. Ex-dividend, the values of the stock are $40 and $10 at nodes *U* and *D*, respectively, while the corresponding cum-dividend values are $46.25 and $16.25, derived by adding the $6.25 dividend to the two ex-dividend stock values. Since the present value of the $6.25 dividend is $5.00 one period earlier, the actual stock price at the initial date is:

$$\$25 = \$20 + \frac{\$6.25}{1.25}$$

(2) The value of the option at the intermediate period requires a comparison of its exercise value with its value from waiting until expiration. Exercising just before the ex-dividend date generates $46.25 − $20.00 = $26.25 at the *U* node. The present value from not exercising is the present value of the two subsequent option expiration values, $60 (= $80 − $20) at node *UU* and $0 at node *UD*. Example 8.6 found that the two risk-neutral probabilities are each .5. Hence, this present value is:

$$\frac{\$60\pi + \$0(1 - \pi)}{1.25} = \$24$$

Since $24.00 is less than the value of $26.25 obtained by exercising at node *U*, early exercise just prior to the ex-dividend instant is optimal. At the *D* node, the option is worth 0 since it is out of the money (cum-dividend) at node *D* and is not in the money for either of the two stock values at the nodes *UD* and *DD* at expiration. The initial value of the option is therefore:

$$\frac{\$26.25\pi + \$0(1 - \pi)}{1.25} = \$10.50$$

As in the case of put valuation (see Example 8.6), the American call option in Example 8.7 is worth more than a comparable European call option. If the option in this example had been a European option, it would have been worth $9.60 = [(.5)$24 + (.5)$0]/1.25. This is smaller than the American option value because the right of premature exercise is used at node *U* and therefore has value.

Any suboptimal exercise policy lowers the value of the premature exercise option and transfers wealth from the buyer of the American option to the seller. This issue often arises in corporations, which are well known to exercise the American option implicit in callable bonds that they issue at a much later date than is optimal. Such suboptimal exercise unnecessarily transfers wealth from the corporation's stockholders to its bondholders.

8.6 Black-Scholes Valuation

Up to this point, we have valued derivatives using **discrete models** of stock prices, which consider only a finite number of future outcomes for the stock price and only a finite number of points in time. We now turn our attention to **continuous-time models**. These models allow for an infinite number of stock price outcomes and they can describe the distribution of stock and option prices at any point in time.

Black-Scholes Formula

Chapter 7 noted that if time is divided into large numbers of short periods, a binomial process for stock prices can approximate the continuous time lognormal process for these prices. Here, particular values are selected for u and d which are related to the standard deviation of the stock return, which also is known as the stock's **volatility**. The limiting case where the time periods are infinitesimally small is one where the binomial formula developed in the last section converges to an equation known as the **Black-Scholes formula**:

Result 8.8   (*The Black-Scholes formula*.) If a stock that pays no dividends prior to the expiration of an option has a return that is lognormally distributed, can be continuously traded in frictionless markets, and has a constant variance, then, for a constant risk-free rate,[16] the value of a European call option on that stock with a strike price of K and T years to expiration is given by:

$$c_0 = S_0 N(d_1) - PV(K)N(d_1 - \sigma\sqrt{T}) \tag{8.3}$$

where

$$d_1 = \frac{ln(S_0/PV(K))}{\sigma\sqrt{T}} + \frac{\sigma\sqrt{T}}{2}$$

The Greek letter σ is the annualized standard deviation of the natural logarithm of the stock return, $ln(\ )$ represents the natural logarithm, and $N(z)$ is the probability that a normally distributed variable with a mean of zero and variance of 1 is less than z.

The Black-Scholes formula provides no-arbitrage prices for European call options and American call options on underlying securities with no cash dividends until expiration (because such options should have the same values as European call options with the same features). The Black-Scholes formula also is easily extended to price European puts (see exercise 8.2). Finally, the formula reasonably approximates the values of more complex options. For example, to price a call option on a stock that pays dividends, one can calculate the Black-Scholes values of options expiring at each of the ex-dividend dates and those expiring at the true expiration date. The largest of these option values is a quick and often accurate approximation of the value obtained from more sophisticated option pricing models. This largest value is known as the **pseudo-American value** of the call option.

Example 8.8 illustrates how to use a normal distribution table to compute Black-Scholes values.

Example 8.8:   Computing Black-Scholes Warrant Values for Chrysler

Use the normal distribution table at the end of the book (or a spreadsheet function like NORMSDIST in Microsoft Excel) to calculate the fair market value of the Chrysler warrants described at the beginning of this chapter. Assume that at the time Chrysler is making a bid of $22 for the warrants (1) Chrysler stock is worth $28 a share, (2) Chrysler's stock return

---

[16]The formula also holds if the variance and risk-free rate can change in a predictable way. In the former case, use the average volatility (the square root of the variance) over the life of the option. In the latter case, use the yield associated with the zero-coupon bond maturing at the expiration date of the option. If the risk-free rate or the volatility changes in an unpredictable way, and is not perfectly correlated with the stock price, no risk-free hedge between the stock price and the option exists. Additional securities (such as long- and short-term bonds or other options on the same stock) may be needed to generate this hedge and the Black-Scholes formula would have to be modified accordingly. However, for most short-term options, the modification to the option's value due to unpredictable changes in interest rates is a negligible one.

volatility σ is 30 percent per year (which is 0.3 in decimal form), (3) the risk-free rate is 10 percent per year (annually compounded), (4) the warrants are American options, but no dividends are expected to be paid over the life of the option, and there is no dilution effect, so it is possible to value the warrants as European options, (5) the options expire in exactly seven years, and (6) the strike price is $13.

   Answer: The present value of the strike price is $13/1.1^7 = \$6.67$. The volatility times the square root of time to maturity is the product of 0.3 and the square root of 7, or 0.79. The Black-Scholes equation says that the value of the call is therefore:

$$c_0 = \$28N(d_1) - \$6.67N(d_1 - .79)$$

where

$$d_1 = \frac{ln(\$28/\$6.67)}{.79} + \frac{1}{2}(.79) = 2.21$$

The normal distribution values for d_1 (-2.21) and $d_1 - .79$ (-1.42) in Table B5 in the Appendix indicates that the probability of a standard normal variable being less than 2.21 is .9864, and the probability of it being less than 1.42 is .9222. Thus, the no arbitrage call value is:

$$\$28(.9864) - \$6.67(.9222) = \$21.47$$

The estimate of $21.47 in this example is less than Chrysler's bid of $22.00, which would indicate, if the assumptions used are correct, that Chrysler got a slightly poor deal by winning the auction. While the example ignored the possibility of dividends, the existence of dividends would make the value of this option even lower.

Dividends and the Black-Scholes Model

It is especially important with continuous-time modeling to model the path of the stock price when stripped of its dividend rights if dividends are paid prior to the expiration date of the option. For example, the Black-Scholes Model assumes that the logarithm of the return on the underlying stock is normally distributed. This means that in any finite amount of time, the stock price may be close to zero, albeit with low probability. Subtracting a finite dividend from this low value would result in a negative ex-dividend stock price. Hence, unless one is willing to describe the dividend for each of an infinite number of stock price outcomes in this type of continuous price model, it is important to model the process for the stock stripped of its right to the dividend. This was illustrated with the binomial model earlier, but it is more imperative here.[17]

8.7 Estimating Volatility

The only parameter that requires estimation in the Black-Scholes Model is the volatility σ. This volatility estimate also may be of use in estimating u and d in a binomial model (see Chapter 7).

   There are a number of ways to estimate σ, assuming it is constant. One method is to use historical data, as shown in Exhibit 8.9. Chapter 5 noted that historical estimates of volatility can sometimes be refined; we now analyze this issue.

---

[17]A numerical example illustrating the Black-Scholes valuation of a European option on a dividend-paying stock appears later in this chapter. In terms of the above formula, one merely substitutes the value of the stock stripped of the present value of the dividends to expiration for S_0 in equation (8.3) to arrive at a correct answer. This is simply the current stock price less the risk-free discounted value of the dividend payment.

EXHIBIT 8.9   Computation of the Volatility Estimate for the Black-Scholes Model Using Historical Return Data on Dell Computer

Year–Quarter	Return (%)	Gross Return (%)	Logged Gross Return
1991–4	9.04%	109.04%	.0866
1992–1	41.95	141.95	.3503
1992–2	−25.26	74.74	−.2911
1992–3	57.93	157.93	.4570
1992–4	67.68	167.68	.5169
1993–1	−26.82	73.18	−.3123
1993–2	−46.62	53.38	−.6277
1993–3	−11.33	88.67	−.1203
1993–4	36.09	136.09	.3082
1994–1	11.60	111.60	.1098
1994–2	4.46	104.46	.0436
1994–3	41.94	141.94	.3502
1994–4	9.52	109.52	.0909
1995–1	6.71	106.71	.0649
1995–2	37.43	137.43	.3179
1995–3	41.37	141.37	.3462
1995–4	−21.18	78.82	−.2380
Logged gross return standard deviation		.315681	
Annualized standard deviation, the volatility estimate		.631362	

Using Historical Data

The appropriate volatility computation for the σ in the Black-Scholes Model is based on the volatility of instantaneous returns.

- First, obtain historical returns for the stock the option is written on. The second column of Exhibit 8.9 ("Return") reports the 17 quarterly returns of Dell Computer from the fourth quarter of 1991 through the end of 1995.
- Second, convert the returns to gross returns (100 percent plus the rate of return in percentage form, 1 plus the return in decimal form), as shown in the gross return column of Exhibit 8.9.
- Third, take the natural logarithm of the decimal version of the gross return; that is, divide by 100 if the gross return is in percentage form.
- Fourth, compute the unbiased sample variance of the logged return series and annualize it (as in the last row) by multiplying it by the square root of the ratio of 365 to the number of days in the return interval (e.g., for monthly returns multiply by the square root of twelve).

Using Spreadsheets to Compute the Volatility.   Spreadsheet standard deviation functions typically provide the unbiased estimate of standard deviation.[18] Remember to

---

[18]For example, STDEV in Excel or @STD in Lotus 1-2-3).

annualize the standard deviation obtained from the spreadsheet because the spreadsheet does not know whether the returns were taken weekly, monthly, daily, and so on. In Exhibit 8.9, which was quarterly returns, this adjustment amounts to multiplying the output from the spreadsheet by 2, which is the square root of 4.

Frequency Choice.   Exhibit 8.9 uses quarterly data to estimate the volatility of Dell Computer for the Black-Scholes Model. Statistical theory suggests that one should use returns that are sampled more frequently to obtain more precise volatility estimates; our preference is weekly data. For reasons outlined in Chapter 5, the use of daily data may be inferior because the bid-ask spread tends to make volatility estimates overstate the true volatility of returns.

Improving the Volatility Estimate.   Procedures, similar to those designed to improve beta estimation for the Capital Asset Pricing Model, can improve the volatility estimate. Consider the spectrum of historical estimates of σ for a large number of securities. Those securities with the highest (lowest) estimated volatilities from historical data are more likely to have overestimates (underestimates) of the true volatility because of sampling error. This information can be used to improve volatility estimates. In particular, an improved volatility estimate can be derived by taking a weighting of the average estimated volatility over a large group of securities and the historical volatility estimate for a single security.

The Implied Volatility Approach

An alternative approach for estimating volatility in a security is to look at other options on the same security. If market values for the options exist, there is a unique **implied volatility** that makes the Black-Scholes Model consistent with the market price for a particular option.

Exhibit 8.10 illustrates this concept. The σ at point A, the intersection of the horizontal line, representing the market price of the call option, and the upward sloping line, representing the Black-Scholes value, is the implied volatility. In this graph, it is about 19 percent.

Averaging the implied volatilities of other options on the same security is a common approach to obtaining the volatility necessary for obtaining the Black-Scholes valuation of an option. Since the implied volatilities of the other options are obtained from the Black-Scholes Model, this method implicitly assumes that the other options are priced correctly by that model.

Implied volatility is a concept that is commonly used in options markets, particularly the over-the-counter markets. For example, price quotes are often given to sophisticated customers in terms of implied volatilities because these volatilities change much less frequently than the stock and option prices. A customer or a trader can consider an implied volatility quote and know that tomorrow the same quote is likely to be valid even though the price of the option will be different. This helps the investor who can then use comparison shopping to obtain the best option price since the price changes minute by minute as the investor shops between dealers.

If options of the same maturity but different strike prices have different implied volatilities, arbitrage is possible. This arbitrage requires purchase of the low implied volatility option and writing of the high implied volatility option. The next section explores the arbitrage of mispriced options in more depth.

Exhibit 8.10   The Value of a Call Option as a Function of its Volatility

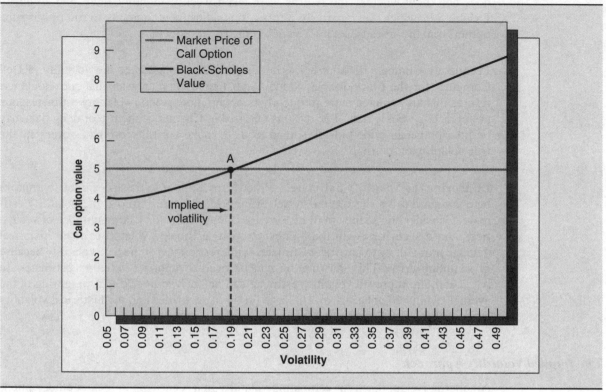

8.8 Black-Scholes Price Sensitivity to Stock Price, Volatility, Interest Rates, and Expiration Time

This section develops some intuition for the Black-Scholes Model by examining whether the call option value in the formula, equation (8.3), increases or decreases as various parameters in the formula change. These parameters are the current stock price S_0, the stock price volatility σ, the risk-free interest rate r_f, and the time to maturity T.

Delta: The Sensitivity to Stock Price Changes

The Greek letter delta (Δ) is commonly used in mathematics to represent a change in something. In finance, **delta** is the change in the value of the derivative security with respect to movements in the stock price, holding everything else constant. The delta of the option is the derivative of the option's price with respect to the stock price, $\frac{\partial c_0}{\partial S_0}$ for a call, $\frac{\partial p_0}{\partial S_0}$ for a put. The derivative of the right-hand side of the Black-Scholes formula, equation (8.3), with respect to S_0, the delta of the call option, is $N(d_1)$. (See exercise 8.4.)

Delta as the Number of Shares of Stock in a Tracking Portfolio.   Delta has many uses. One is in the formation of a tracking portfolio. Delta can be viewed as the number of shares of stock needed in the tracking portfolio. Let x be the number of shares in the tracking portfolio. For a given change in S_0, dS_0, the change in the tracking portfolio is $x dS_0$. Hence, unless x equals $\dfrac{\partial c_0}{\partial S_0}$ for a call or $\dfrac{\partial p_0}{\partial S_0}$ for a put, $x dS_0$ will not be the same as the change in the call or put value, and the tracking of the option payoff with a portfolio of the underlying stock and a risk-free bond will not be perfect.

Because $N(d_1)$ is a probability, the number of shares needed to track the option lies between zero and one. In addition, as time elapses and the stock price changes, d_1 changes, implying that the number of shares of stock in the tracking portfolio needs to change continuously. Thus, the tracking of the option using the Black-Scholes Model, like that for the binomial model, requires dynamically changing the quantities of the stock and risk-free bond in the tracking portfolio. However, these changes are self-financing.

Delta and Arbitrage Strategies.   If the market prices of options differ from their theoretical prices, it is possible to design an arbitrage. Once set up, the arbitrage is self-financing until the arbitrage position is closed out.

As always, arbitrage requires the formation of a tracking portfolio using the underlying assets and a risk-free security. One goes long in the tracking portfolio and short in the option, or vice versa, to achieve arbitrage (see exercise 8.3.)

In the design of the arbitrage, the ratio of the underlying asset position to the option position must be the negative of the partial derivative of the *theoretical* option price with respect to the price of the underlying security. For a call option that is priced by the Black-Scholes formula, this partial derivative is $N(d_1)$, the option's delta.

Delta and the Interpretation of the Black-Scholes Formula.   The interpretation of $N(d_1)$ as the number of shares of stock in the tracking portfolio lends a nice interpretation to the Black-Scholes call option formula. The first part of the Black-Scholes formula in equation (8.3), $S_0 N(d_1)$, is the cost of the shares needed in the tracking portfolio. The second term, $PV(K)N(d_1 - \sigma\sqrt{T})$, represents the number of dollars borrowed at the risk-free rate. The difference in the two terms is the cost of the tracking portfolio. Hence, the Black-Scholes formula is simply an arbitrage relation. The left-hand side of the equation, c_0, is the value of the option. The right-hand side represents the market price of the tracking portfolio.

An examination of the tracking portfolio reveals that call options on stock are equivalent to leveraged positions in stock. When you focus on the capital market line, the more leverage you have, the greater the beta, standard deviation, and expected return, as pointed out in Chapter 5. For this reason, call options per dollar invested are always riskier than the underlying stock per dollar invested.

Black-Scholes Option Values and Stock Volatility

One can use the Black-Scholes formula, equation (8.3), to show that an option's value is increasing in σ, the volatility of the underlying stock. (Refer again to the Black-Scholes call value in Exhibit 8.10, which has a positive slope, and see exercise 8.5.)

Result 8.9   As the volatility of the stock price increases, the values of both put and call options written on the stock increase.

EXHIBIT 8.11   **Effect of Increasing Volatility**

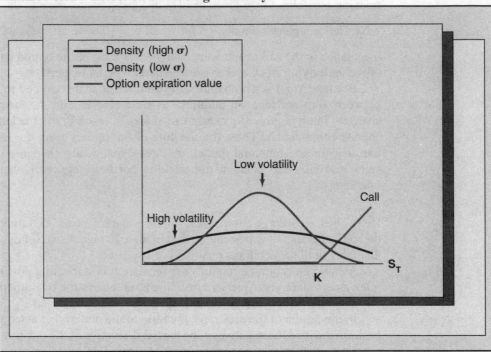

Result 8.9 is a general property of options, holding true for calls and puts and both American and European options. It has a number of implications for the financial behavior of both corporate finance executives and portfolio managers and is a source of equity holder–debt holder conflicts.[19]

    The intuition for this result is that increased volatility spreads the distribution of the future stock price, fattening up both tails of the distribution, as shown in Exhibit 8.11. Good things are happening for a call (put) option when the right (left) tail of the distribution is more likely to occur. It is not good when the left (right) tail of the distribution is more likely to occur, but exercise of the option does *not* take place in this region of outcomes, so it is not so bad either. After a certain point, a fatter tail on the left (right) of the distribution can hurt the investor much less than a fat tail on the right (left) of the distribution can help. The worst that can happen is that an option expires worthless.

Option Values and Time to Option Expiration

European calls on nondividend-paying stocks are more valuable the longer the time to expiration, other things being equal, for two reasons. First, the terminal stock price is more uncertain the longer the time to expiration. Uncertainty, described in our discussion of σ, makes options more valuable. Moreover, given the same strike price, the longer is the time to maturity, the lower is the present value of the strike price paid by the holder of a call option.

---

[19]These conflicts are discussed in Chapter 15.

EXHIBIT 8.12   **Determinants of Current Option and Forward Prices: Effect of a Parameter Increase**

Parameter Increased	Long Forward	American Call	American Put	European Call	European Put
S_0	↑	↑	↓	↑	↓
T	↑	↑	↑	↑	Ambiguous
σ	No effect	↑	↑	↑	↑
r_f	↑	↑	↓	↑	↓

In contrast, the discounting of the strike price makes European puts less valuable. Thus, the combination of the effects of uncertainty and discounting leaves an ambiguous result. European puts can increase or decrease in value the longer the time to expiration. American puts and calls, incidentally, have an unambiguous sensitivity to expiration time. These options have all the rights of their shorter-maturity cousins in addition to the rights of exercise for an even longer period. Hence, the longer the time to expiration, the more valuable are American call and put options, even for dividend-paying stocks.

Option Values and the Risk-Free Interest Rate

The Black-Scholes call option value is increasing in the interest rate r (see exercise 8.6) because the payment of K for the share of stock whose call option is in the money costs less in today's dollars (i.e., it has a lower discounted value) when the interest rate is higher. The opposite is true for a European put. Since one receives cash, puts are less valuable when the interest rate is higher. As noted earlier in this chapter, the timing of stock delivery is irrelevant as long as there are no dividends. Only the present value of the cash payment upon option exercise and whether this cash is paid out (call) or received (put) determines the effect of interest rates on the option value. Once again, this is a general result that holds for European and American options and works the same in the binomial model and the Black-Scholes Model.

A Summary of the Effects of the Parameter Changes

Exhibit 8.12 summarizes the results in this section and includes the impact on the value of a long forward contract (equivalent to a call less a put). These exercises hold constant all the other factors determining option value, except the one in the relevant row.

Two points deserve mention. The effect of an increase in strike price K and the dividend paid is going to have the opposite effect from that of the increase in the stock price described in Exhibit 8.12. It also is interesting to observe what has not been included here because it has no effect. In particular, risk aversion and the expected growth rate of the stock have no effect on option values, which are determined solely by no-arbitrage relations between the option and its tracking portfolio (see Result 7.5 in Chapter 7). When tracking is impossible (e.g., executive stock options), option values are not tied to tracking portfolios. In such cases, considerations like risk aversion or stock growth rates may play a role in option valuation.

8.9 Valuing Options on More Complex Assets

Options exist on many assets. For example, corporations use currency options to hedge their foreign currency exposure. They also use swap options, which are valued in exactly the same manner as bond options, to hedge interest rate risk associated with a callable bond issued in conjunction with interest rate swaps. Option markets exist for semiconductors, agricultural commodities, precious metals, and oil. There are even options on futures contracts for a host of assets underlying the futures contracts.

These options trade on many organized exchanges and over the counter. For example, currency options are traded on the Philadelphia Options Exchange, but large currency option transactions tend to be over the counter, with a bank as one of the parties. Clearly, an understanding of how to value some of these options is important for many finance practitioners.

The Forward Price Version of the Black-Scholes Model

To value options on more complex assets such as currencies, it is important to recognize that the Black-Scholes Model is a special case of a more general model having arguments that depend on (zero-cost) forward prices instead of spot prices. Once you know how to compute the forward price of an underlying asset, it is possible to determine the Black-Scholes value for a European call on the underlying asset.

To transform the Black-Scholes formula into a more general formula that uses forward prices, substitute the no-arbitrage relation from Chapter 7; $S_0 = s_F/(1 + r_f)^T$, where s_F is the forward price of an underlying asset in a forward contract maturing at the option expiration date, into the original Black-Scholes formula, equation (8.3). The Black-Scholes equation can then be rewritten as:

$$c_0 = PV[s_F N(d_1) - KN(d_1 - \sigma\sqrt{T})]$$

where

$$d_1 = \frac{ln(s_F/K)}{\sigma\sqrt{T}} + \frac{\sigma\sqrt{T}}{2}$$

and where

PV is the risk-free discounted value of the expression inside the brackets

This equation looks a bit simpler than the original Black-Scholes formula.

Investors and financial analysts can apply this simpler, more general version of the Black-Scholes formula to value European call options on currencies, bonds,[20] dividend-paying stocks, and commodities.

Computing Forward Prices from Spot Price

In applying the forward price version of the Black-Scholes formula, it is critical to use the appropriate forward price for the underlying asset. The appropriate forward price s_F

---

[20]The Black-Scholes formula assumes that the volatility of the bond price is constant over the life of the option. Since bond volatilities diminish at the approach of the bond's maturity, the formula provides only a decent approximation to the fair market value of an option that is relatively short-lived compared with the maturity of the bond.

represents the price in dollars one agrees to today, but pays at the option expiration date, to acquire one unit of the underlying asset at that expiration date.

The following are a few rules of thumb for calculating forward prices for various underlying assets:

- *Foreign currency.* Multiply the present spot foreign currency rate, expressed as $/fx, (see Chapter 7) by the *present value* of a riskless unit of foreign currency paid at the forward maturity date (where the discounting is at the foreign riskless interest rate). Multiply this value by the *future value* (at the maturity date) of a dollar paid today; that is, multiply by $(1 + r_f)^T$ where T represents the years to maturity.

- *Riskless coupon bond.* Find the present value of the bond when stripped of its coupon rights until maturity; that is, current bond price less PV(coupons). Multiply this value by the future value (at the maturity date) of a dollar paid today. (Depending on how the bond price is quoted, an adjustment to add accrued interest to the quoted price of the bond to obtain the full price may also need to be made, as described in Chapter 2.)

- *Stock with dividend payments.* Find the present value of the stock when stripped of its dividend rights until maturity; that is, current stock price less PV (dividends). Multiply this value by the future value (at the maturity date) of a dollar paid today.

- *Commodity.* Add the present value of the storage costs until maturity to the current price of the commodity. Subtract the present value of the benefits, known as the *convenience yield,* associated with holding an inventory of the commodity to maturity.[21] Multiply this value by the future value, at the maturity date, of a dollar paid today.

Note that all forward prices multiply some adjusted market value of the underlying investment by $(1 + r_f)^T$, where r_f is the riskless rate of interest. Multiplying by one plus the risk-free rate of interest accounts for the cost of holding the investment until maturity. The cost is the lost interest on the dollars spent to acquire the investment. For example, with a stock that pays no dividends, the present value of having the stock in one's possession today as opposed to some future date is the same. However, the longer the investor can postpone paying a prespecified amount for the stock, the better off he or she is. The difference between the forward price and the stock price thus reflects interest to the party with the short position in the forward contract, who is essentially holding the stock for the benefit of the party holding the long position in the forward contract.

The difference between the forward price and the stock price also depends on the benefits and any costs of having the investment in one's possession until forward maturity. With stock, the benefit is the payment of dividends; with bonds, the payment of coupons; with foreign currency, the interest earned in a foreign bank when that currency is deposited; with commodities, the convenience of having an inventory of the commodity less the cost of storage.

Applications of the Forward Price Version of the Black-Scholes Formula

Example 8.9 demonstrates the use of the generalized Black-Scholes formula to value European call options having these more complex underlying assets.

---

[21]See Chapter 21 for a more detailed discussion of convenience yields.

Example 8.9:   Pricing Securities with the Forward Price Version of the Black-Scholes Model

The U.S. dollar risk-free rate is assumed to be 6 percent per year and all σ's are assumed to be 25 percent per year. Use the forward price version of the Black-Scholes Model to compute the value of a European call option to purchase one year from now.

(*a*) 1 DM at a strike price of US$0.50. The current spot exchange rate is US$.40/DM and the one-year risk-free rate is 8 percent in Germany.

(*b*) A 30-year bond with an 8 percent semiannual coupon at a strike price of $100 (full price). The bond is currently selling at a full price of $102 (which includes accrued interest) per $100 of face value and has two scheduled coupons of $4 before option expiration, to be paid six months and one year from now. (At the forward maturity date, the second coupon payment has just been made.)

(*c*) The S&P 500 contract with a strike price of $850. The S&P 500 has a current price of $800 and a present value of next year's dividends of $20.

(*d*) A barrel of oil with a strike price of $20. A barrel of oil currently sells for $18. The present value of next year's storage costs is $1 and the present value of the convenience of having a barrel of oil available over the next year (e.g., if there are long gas lines due to an oil embargo and deplorable government policy) is $1.

Answer: The forward prices are, respectively:

(*a*) $\dfrac{US\$.40(1.06)}{1.08} = US\$.3926$

(*b*) $\$102(1.06) - \$4\sqrt{1.06} - \$4 = \$100.0017$

(*c*) $(\$800 - \$20)(1.06) = \$826.80$

(*d*) $(\$18 + \$1 - \$1)(1.06) = \$19.08$

Plugging these values into the forward price version of the Black-Scholes model yields:

(*a*) $c_0 = \dfrac{\$.3926N(d_1) - \$.5N(d_1 - .25)}{1.06}$ where $d_1 = \dfrac{ln(.3926/.5)}{.25} + .125 = -.84$. Thus, c_0 is approximately $.01.

(*b*) $c_0 = \dfrac{\$100.0017N(d_1) - \$100N(d_1 - .25)}{1.06}$ where $d_1 = \dfrac{ln(100.0017/100)}{.25} + .125 = .13$. Thus, c_0 is approximately $9.39.

(*c*) $c_0 = \dfrac{\$826.80N(d_1) - \$850N(d_1 - .25)}{1.06}$ where $d_1 = \dfrac{ln(826.80/850)}{.25} + .125 = .014$. Thus, c_0 is approximately $68.22.

(*d*) $c_0 = \dfrac{\$19.08N(d_1) - \$20N(d_1 - .25)}{1.06}$ where $d_1 = \dfrac{ln(19.08/20)}{.25} + .125 = -.06$. Thus, c_0 is approximately $1.43.

American Options

The forward price version of the Black-Scholes Model also has implications for American options. For example, the reason American call options on non-dividend-paying stocks sell for the same price as comparable European call options is that the forward price at expiration always exceeds the current stock price, no matter how much time has elapsed since the purchase of the option. If a discrete dividend is about to be paid and the stock is relatively close to expiration, the current cum-dividend price of the stock exceeds the forward price and premature exercise may be worthwhile. If one can be certain that this will not be the case, waiting is worthwhile. One can generalize this result as follows:

Result 8.10   An American call (put) option should not be prematurely exercised if the forward price of the underlying asset at expiration exceeds (is less than) the current price of the underlying asset. As a consequence, if one is certain that over the life of the option this will be the case, American and European options should sell for the same price if there is no arbitrage.

There are several implications of Result 8.10. With call options on the S&P 500 where dividends of different stocks pay off on different days so that the overall dividend stream resembles a continuous flow, American and European call options should sell for the same price if the risk-free rate to expiration exceeds the dividend yield. Also, with bonds where the risk-free rate to option expiration is greater (less) than the coupon yield of the risk-free bond, American and European call (put) options should sell for the same amount as their European counterparts if the option strike price is adjusted for accrued interest (as it usually is, unlike in Example 8.9) so that the coupon stream on the bond is like a continuous flow. This suggests that when the term structure of interest rates (see Chapter 9) is steeply upward (downward) sloping, puts (calls) of the European and American varieties are likely to have the same value.

American Call and Put Currency Options

Result 8.10 also has implications for American currency options on both calls and puts. These implications are given in Result 8.11.

Result 8.11   If the domestic interest rate is greater (less) than the foreign interest rate, the American option to buy (sell) domestic currency in exchange for foreign currency should sell for the same price as the European option to do the same.

8.10 Empirical Biases in the Black-Scholes Formula

The Black-Scholes Model is particularly impressive in the general thrust of its implications about option pricing. Option prices tend to be higher in environments with high interest rates and high volatility. Moreover, you find remarkable similarities when comparing the values of many options, even American options, with the results given by the Black-Scholes Model.

However, after a close look at the prices in the newspaper, it is easy to see that the Black-Scholes formula tends to underestimate the market values of some kinds of options and overestimate others. MacBeth and Merville (1979) used daily closing prices to study actively traded options on six stocks in 1976. Their technique examined the implied volatilities of various options on the same securities and found these volatilities to be inversely related to the strike prices of the options. This meant that the Black-Scholes value, on average, was too high for deep out-of-the-money calls and too low for in-the-money calls. These biases grew larger the further the option was from expiration.

A similar but more rigorous set of tests was conducted by Rubinstein (1985). Using transaction data, he first paired options with similar characteristics. For example, a pairing might consist of two call options on the same stock with two different strike prices, but the same expiration date, that traded within a small interval of time (e.g., 15 minutes). With these pairings, 50 percent of the members of the pair with low strike prices should have higher implied volatilities than their counterparts with high strike prices. Rubinstein also used pairings in which the only difference was the time to expiration. He then evaluated the pairings and found that shorter times to expiration led to higher implied volatility for out-of-the-money calls. This would suggest that the Black-Scholes formula tends to underestimate the values of call options close to expiration relative to call options with longer times to expiration.

Rubinstein also found a strike price bias that was dependent on the period examined. From August 1976 to October 1977, lower strike prices meant higher implied volatility. In this period, the Black-Scholes Model underestimated the values of in-the-money call options and overestimated the values of out-of-the-money call options, which is consistent with the findings of MacBeth and Merville. However, for the period from October 1977 to August 1978, Rubinstein found the opposite result, except for out-of-the-money call options that were close to expiration.

Although these biases were highly statistically significant, Rubinstein concluded that they had little economic significance. In general, Rubinstein found that the biases in the Black-Scholes Model were on the order of a 2 percent deviation from Black-Scholes pricing. Hence, a fairly typical $2 Black-Scholes price would coincide with a $2.04 market price. *This means that the Black-Scholes Model, despite its biases, is still a fairly accurate estimator of the actual prices found in options markets.*

Since these studies were completed, many traders refer to what is known as the **smile effect** (see Exhibit 8.13). If one plots the implied volatility of an option against its strike price, the graph of implied volatility looks like a "smile." This formation suggests that the Black-Scholes Model underprices both deep in-the-money and deep out-of-the-money options relative to near at-the-money options.

EXHIBIT 8.13   Implied Volatility versus Strike Price

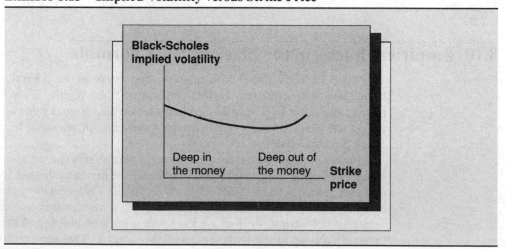

8.11 Summary and Conclusions

This chapter developed the put-call parity formula, relating the prices of European calls to those of European puts, and used it to generate insights into minimum call values, premature exercise policy for American calls, and the relative valuation of American and European calls. The put-call parity formula also provided insights into corporate securities and portfolio insurance.

This chapter also applied the results on derivative

securities valuation from Chapter 7 to price options, using two approaches: the binomial approach and the Black-Scholes approach. The results on European call pricing with these two approaches can be extended to European puts. The put-call parity formula provides a method for translating the pricing results with these models into pricing results for European puts.

The pricing of both American calls on dividend-paying stocks and American puts cannot be derived from European call pricing formulas because it is sometimes optimal to exercise these securities prematurely. This chapter used the binomial method to show how to price these more complicated types of options.

This chapter also discussed a number of issues relating to the implementation of the theory, including (1) the estimation of volatility and its relation to the concept of an implied volatility, (2) extending the pricing formulas to complex underlying securities, and (3) the known empirical biases in option pricing formulas. Despite a few biases in the Black-Scholes option pricing formula, it appears that the formulas work reasonably well when properly implemented.

Key Concepts

Result 8.1: (*The put-call parity formula.*) If no dividends are paid to holders of the underlying stock prior to expiration, then, assuming no arbitrage:

$$c_0 - p_0 = S_0 - PV(K)$$

That is, a long position in a call and a short position in a put sells for the current stock price less the strike price discounted at the risk-free rate.

Result 8.2: It never pays to exercise an American call option prematurely on a stock that pays no dividends prior to expiration.

Result 8.3: An investor does not capture the full value of an American call option by exercising between ex-dividend or (in the case of a bond option) ex-coupon dates.

Result 8.4: If the underlying stock pays no dividends prior to expiration, then the no-arbitrage value of American and European call options with the same features are the same.

Result 8.5: (*Put-call parity formula generalized.*) $c_0 - p_0 = S_0 - PV(K) - PV(\text{div})$. The difference between the no-arbitrage values of a European call and a European put with the same features is the current price of the stock less the sum of the present value of the strike price and the present value of all dividends to expiration.

Result 8.6: It is possible to view equity as a call option on the assets of the firm and to view risky corporate debt as riskless debt worth $PV(K)$ plus a short position in a put option on the assets of the firm $(-p_0)$ with a strike price of K.

Result 8.7: (*The binomial formula.*) The value of a European call option with a strike price of K and N periods to expiration on a stock with no dividends to expiration and a current value of S_0 is:

$$c_0 = \frac{1}{(1 + r_f)^N} \sum_{j=0}^{N} \frac{N!}{j!(N-j)!} \times \pi^j (1 - \pi)^{N-j} \max[0, u^j d^{N-j} S_0 - K]$$

where

r_f = risk-free return per period

π = risk-neutral probability of an up move

u = ratio of the stock price to the prior stock price given that the up state has occurred over a binomial step

d = ratio of the stock price to the prior stock price given that the down state has occurred over a binomial step

Result 8.8: (*The Black-Scholes formula.*) If a stock that pays no dividends prior to the expiration of an option has a return that is lognormally distributed, can be continuously traded in frictionless markets, and has a constant variance, then, for a constant risk-free rate, the value of a European call option on that stock with a strike price of K and T years to expiration is given by:

$$c_0 = S_0 N(d_1) - PV(K) N(d_1 - \sigma\sqrt{T})$$

where

$$d_1 = \frac{ln\big(S_0/PV(K)\big)}{\sigma\sqrt{T}} + \frac{\sigma\sqrt{T}}{2}$$

The Greek letter σ is the annualized standard deviation of the natural logarithm of the stock return, $ln(\ )$ represents the natural logarithm, and $N(z)$ is the probability that a normally distributed variable with a mean of zero and variance of 1 is less than z.

Result 8.9:   As the volatility of the stock price increases, the values of both put and call options written on the stock increase.

Result 8.10:   An American call (put) option should not be prematurely exercised if the forward price of the underlying asset at expiration exceeds (is less than) the current price of the underlying asset. As a consequence,

if one is certain that over the life of the option this will be the case, American and European options should sell for the same price if there is no arbitrage.

Result 8.11:   If the domestic interest rate is greater (less) than the foreign interest rate, the American option to buy (sell) domestic currency in exchange for foreign currency should sell for the same price as the European option to do the same.

Key Terms

American option   275
Black-Scholes formula   296
compound option   286
continuous-time models   295
cum-dividend value   294
delta   300
discrete models   295
European option   275
ex-dividend date   283

ex-dividend value   294
exercise commencement date   276
implied volatility   299
portfolio insurance   286
pseudo-American value   296
put-call parity formula   278
smile effect   308
volatility   296

Exercises

8.1.   You hold an American call option with a $30 strike price on a stock that sells at $35. The option sells for $5 one year before expiration. Compare the cash flows at expiration from (1) exercising the option now and putting the $5 proceeds in a bank account until the expiration date and (2) holding onto the option until expiration, selling short the stock, and placing the $35 you receive into the same bank account.

8.2.   Combine the Black-Scholes formula with the put-call parity formula to derive the Black-Scholes formula for European puts.

8.3.   Intel stock has a volatility of $\sigma = .25$ and a price of $60 a share. A European call option on Intel stock with a strike price of $65 and an expiration time of one year has a price of $10. Using the Black-Scholes Model, describe how you would construct an arbitrage portfolio, assuming that the present value of the strike price is $56. Would the arbitrage portfolio increase or decrease its position in Intel stock if shortly thereafter the stock price of Intel rose to $62 a share?

8.4.   Take the partial derivative of the Black-Scholes value of a call option with respect to the

underlying security's price, S_0. Show that this derivative is positive and equal to $N(d_1)$. *Hint:* First show that $S_0 N'(d_1) - PV(K)N'(d_1 - \sigma \sqrt{T})$ equals zero by using the fact that the derivative of N with respect to d_1, $N'(d_1)$ equals $\dfrac{1}{\sqrt{2\pi}exp(-.5d_1^2)}$.

8.5.   Take the partial derivative of the Black-Scholes value of a call option with respect to the volatility parameter σ. Show that this derivative is positive and equal to $S_0 \sqrt{T}N'(d_1)$.

8.6.   If $PV(K) = \dfrac{K}{(1 + r_f)^T}$, take the partial derivative of the Black-Scholes value of a call option with respect to the interest rate r_f. Show that this derivative is positive and equal to $T \times PV(K)N(d_1 - \sigma \sqrt{T})/(1 + r_f)$.

8.7.   Suppose you observe a European call option on a stock that is priced at less than the value of $S_0 - PV(K) - PV(\text{div})$. What type of transaction should you execute to achieve arbitrage? (Be specific with respect to amounts and avoid using puts in this arbitrage.)

8.8   Consider a position of two purchased calls (AT&T, three months, $K = 30$) and one written put

(AT&T, three months, $K = 30$). What position in AT&T stock will show the same sensitivity to price changes in AT&T stock as the option position described above?

8.9. The present price of an equity share of Strategy Inc. is $50. The stock follows a binomial process where each period the stock either goes up 10 percent or down 10 percent. Compute the fair market value of an American put option on Strategy Inc. stock with a strike price of $50 and two periods to expiration. Assume Strategy Inc. pays no dividends over the next two periods. The risk-free rate is 2 percent per period.

8.10. Steady Corp. has a share value of $50. At-the-money American call options on Steady Corp. with nine months to expiration are trading at $3. Sure Corp. also has a share value of $50. At-the-money American call options on Sure Corp. with nine months to expiration are trading at $3. Suddenly, a merger is announced. Each share in both corporations is exchanged for one share in the combined corporation, "Sure and Steady." After the merger, options formerly on one share of either Sure Corp. or Steady Corp. were converted to options on one share of Sure and Steady. The only change is the difference in the underlying asset. Analyze the likely impact of the merger on the values of the two options before and after the merger. Extend this analysis to the effect of mergers on the equity of firms with debt financing.

8.11. FSA is a privately held firm. As an analyst trying to determine the value of FSA's common stock and bonds, you have estimated the market value of the firm's assets to be $1 million and the standard deviation of the asset return to be .3. The debt of FSA, which consists of zero-coupon bank loans, will come due one year from now at its face value of $1 million. Assuming that the risk-free rate is 5 percent, use the Black-Scholes Model to estimate the value of the firm's equity and debt.

8.12. In the chapter's opening vignette, Chrysler Corporation argued that there was little risk in the government guarantee of Chrysler's debt because Chrysler also was offering a senior claim of Chrysler's assets to the government. In light of this, Chrysler's warrants appear to have been a free gift to the U.S. government that should have been returned to Chrysler in 1983. Evaluate this argument.

8.13. Describe what happens to the amount of stock held in the tracking portfolio for a call (put) as the stock price goes up (down). *Hint:* Prove this by looking at delta.

8.14. Callable bonds appear to have market values that are determined as if the issuing corporation optimally exercises the call option implicit in the bond. You know, however, that these options tend to get exercised past the optimal point. Write up a nontechnical presentation for your boss, the portfolio manager, explaining why arbitrage exists and how to take advantage of it with this investment opportunity.

References and Additional Readings

Black, Fischer. "The Pricing of Commodity Contracts." *Journal of Financial Economics* 3, nos. 1/2 (1976), pp. 167–79.

Black, Fischer, and Myron Scholes. "The Pricing of Options and Corporate Liabilities." *Journal of Political Economy* 81 (May–June 1973), pp. 637–59.

Cox, John C.; Stephen A. Ross; and Mark Rubinstein. "Option Pricing: A Simplified Approach." *Journal of Financial Economics* 7 (Sept. 1979), pp. 229–63.

Cox, John C., and Mark Rubinstein. *Options Markets.* Englewood Cliffs, NJ: Prentice-Hall, 1985.

Galai, Dan, and Ronald Masulis. "The Option Pricing Model and the Risk Factor of Stock." *Journal of Financial Economics* 3, nos. 1/2 (1976), pp. 53–81.

Garman, Mark, and Steven Kohlhagen. "Foreign Currency Option Values." *Journal of International Money and Finance* 2, no. 3 (1983), pp. 231–37.

Geske, Robert. "The Valuation of Compound Options." *Journal of Financial Economics* 7, no. 1 (1979), pp. 63–82.

Geske, Robert, and Herb Johnson. "The American Put Option Valued Analytically." *Journal of Finance* 39, no. 5 (1984), pp. 1511–24.

Grabbe, J. O., "The Pricing of Call and Put Options on Foreign Exchange." *Journal of International Money and Finance* 2, no. 3 (1983), pp. 239–53.

Hull, John C. *Options, Futures, and Other Derivatives.* 3d ed. Upper Saddle River, NJ: Prentice-Hall, 1997.

MacBeth, James D., and Larry J. Merville. "An Empirical Examination of the Black-Scholes Call Option Pricing Model." *Journal of Finance* 34, no. 5 (1979), pp. 1173–86.

Merton, Robert C. "Theory of Rational Option Pricing." *Bell Journal of Economics and Management Science* 4 (Spring 1973), pp. 141–83.

Ramaswamy, Krishna, and Suresh Sundaresan, "The Valuation of Options on Futures Contracts." *Journal of Finance* 40, no. 5 (1985), pp. 1319–40.

Rendelman, Richard J., Jr., and Brit J. Bartter. "Two-State Option Pricing." *Journal of Finance* 34 (Dec. 1979), pp. 1093–1110.

Rubinstein, Mark. "Nonparametric Tests of Alternative Option Pricing Models Using All Reported Trades and Quotes on the 30 Most Active CBOE Option Classes from August 23, 1976 through August 31, 1978." *Journal of Finance* 40, no. 2 (1985), pp. 455–80.

Smith, Clifford. "Option Pricing: A Review." *Journal of Financial Economics* 3, nos. 1/2 (1976), pp. 3–51.

Stoll, Hans. "The Relationship Between Put and Call Option Prices." *Journal of Finance* 24, no. 5 (1969), pp. 801–824.

Whaley, Robert. "On the Valuation of American Call Options on Stocks with Known Dividends." *Journal of Financial Economics* 9, no. 2 (1981), pp. 207–11.

———. "Valuation of American Call Options on Dividend-Paying Stocks: Empirical Tests." *Journal of Financial Economics* 10, no. 1 (1982), pp. 29–58.

PRACTICAL INSIGHTS FOR PART II

Allocating Capital for Real Investment

- Mean-variance analysis can help determine the risk implications of product mixes, mergers and acquisitions, and carve-outs. This requires thinking about the mix of real assets as a portfolio. (Section 4.6)
- Theories to value real assets identify the types of risk that determine discount rates. Most valuation problems will use either the CAPM or APT, which identify market risk and factor risk, respectively, as the relevant risk attributes. (Sections 5.8, 6.10)
- An investment's covariance with other investments is a more important determinant of its discount rate than is the variance of the investment's return. (Section 5.2)
- The CAPM and the APT both suggest that the rate of return required to induce investors to hold an investment is determined by how the investment's return covaries with well-diversified portfolios. However, existing evidence suggests that most of the well-diversified portfolios that have been traditionally used, either in a single factor or a multiple factor implementation, do a poor job of explaining the historical returns of common stocks. While multifactor models do better than single factor models, all model implementations (to varying degrees) have difficulty explaining the historical returns of investments with extreme size, market-to-book ratios, and momentum. These shortcomings need to be accounted for when allocating capital to real investments that fit into these anomalous categories. (Sections 5.12, 6.12)

Financing the Firm

- When issuing debt or equity, the CAPM and APT can provide guidelines about whether the issue is priced fairly. (Sections 5.8, 6.10)
- Because equity can be viewed as a call option on the assets of the firm when there is risky debt financing, the equity of firms with debt is riskier than the equity of firms with no debt (Sections 8.3, 8.8).
- Derivatives valuation theory can be used to value risky debt and equity in relation to one another (Section 8.3)

Knowing Whether and How to Hedge Risk

- The fair market values, not the actual market values, determine appropriate ratios for hedging. These are usually computed from the valuation models for derivatives. (Section 8.8)

- Portfolio mathematics can enable the investor to understand the risk attributes of any mix of real assets, financial assets, and liabilities. (Section 4.6)

Allocating Funds for Financial Investments

- Portfolios generally dominate individual securities as desirable investment positions. (Section 5.2)
- Per dollar invested, leveraged positions are riskier than unleveraged positions. (Section 4.7)
- There is a unique optimal risky portfolio when a risk-free asset exists. The task of an investor is to identify this portfolio. (Section 5.4)
- Mean-Variance Analysis is frequently used as a tool for allocating funds between broad-based portfolios. Because of estimation problems, mean-variance analysis is difficult to use for determining allocations between individual securities. (Section 5.6)
- If the CAPM is true, the optimal portfolio to hold is a broad-based market index. (Section 5.8)
- If the APT is true, the optimal portfolio to hold is a weighted average of the factor portfolios. (Section 6.10)
- Since derivatives are priced relative to other investments, opinions about cash flows do not matter when determining their values. With perfect tracking possible here, mastery of the theories is essential if one wants to earn arbitrage profits from these investments. (Section 7.2)
- Apparent arbitrage profits, if they exist, must arise from market frictions. Hence, to obtain arbitrage profits from derivative investments means that one must be more clever than competitors at overcoming the frictions that allow apparent arbitrage to exist. (Preface to Part II)
- Derivatives can be used to insure a portfolio's value. (Section 8.3)
- The somewhat disappointing empirical evidence on the CAPM and APT may imply an opportunity for portfolio managers to beat the S&P 500 and other benchmarks they are measured against. (Sections 5.8, 6.10)
- Per dollar of investment, call options are riskier than the underlying asset. (Section 8.8)

EXECUTIVE PERSPECTIVE

Myron S. Scholes

At Long-Term Capital Management, financial models are critical to our success. Since we are a liability manager in addition to an asset manager, models are crucial, not only in selecting alternative investments and position sizes, but also in managing the risk of our positions. Indeed, financial models, similar to those developed in Part II of this text, are in everyday use in the firm.

The mean-variance model, developed in Chapters 4 and 5, is one example of this. We, as well as other portfolio managers, must optimize the return-to-risk profile of the portfolio. The mean-variance approach has influenced our optimal capital size and assists us in determining the scale of our positions.

The risk-expected return models presented in Part II, such as the CAPM and the APT, represent another set of useful tools for money management and portfolio optimization. These models have profoundly affected the way investment funds are managed and the way individuals invest and assess performance. For example, passively managed funds, which generally buy and hold a proxy for the market portfolio, have grown dramatically, accounting for more than 20 percent of institutional investment. This has occurred, in part, because of academic writings on the CAPM and, in part, because performance evaluation using these models has shown that professional money managers as a group do not systematically outperform these alternative investment strategies. Investment banks use both debt and equity factor models—extremely important

tools—to determine appropriate hedges to mitigate factor risks. For example, my former employer, Salomon Brothers, uses factor models to determine the appropriate hedges for its equity and debt positions.

All this pales, of course, with the impact of derivatives valuation models, starting with the Black-Scholes option-pricing model that I developed with Fischer Black in the early 1970s. Using the option-pricing technology, investment banks have been able to produce products that customers want. An entire field called financing engineering has emerged in recent years to support these developments. Investment banks use option pricing technology to price sophisticated contracts and to determine the appropriate hedges to mitigate the underlying risks of producing these contracts. Without the option-pricing technology, presented in Chapters 7 and 8, the global financial picture would be far different. In the old world, banks were underwriters, matching those who wanted to buy with those who wanted to offer coarse contracts such as loans, bonds, and stocks. Derivatives have reduced the costs to provide financial services and products that are more finely tuned to the needs of investors and corporations around the world.

Mr. Scholes is currently a principal, co-founder, and limited partner at Long-Term Capital Management, L.P., located in Greenwich, Connecticut. He is also the Frank E. Buck Professor of Finance Emeritus, Stanford University Graduate School of Business.

PART III

Valuing Real Assets

O ne of the major thrusts of this text is that financial managers should use a market-based approach to value cash flows, whether valuing the cash flows of financial assets, like stocks and bonds, or the cash flows of real assets, like factories and machines. To value the real assets of a corporate project, first ask how its cash flows would be valued by a competitive capital market if the project could be spun off and sold as a separate entity. If the separate entity has its own traded stock, it is easy to understand how to choose value-creating real investments: The firm creates value by taking all real investment projects that cost less than what the project can generate from the sale of stock in the project. In this simple world where all investment projects are sold to the capital markets, the criterion for accepting an investment project is the same as that used with any other product a firm might sell. IBM would not sell a computer if the costs were higher than the selling price. Likewise, the company would not create a new division if the costs of doing so were greater than the expected proceeds from taking the division public with a new issue.

Thermo Electron (http://www.thermo.com/index.html), a Boston-area company listed on the New York Stock Exchange, has followed the general strategy of starting new lines of business and turning them into independent public companies with their own publicly traded shares. Thermo Electron benefits from this strategy in two ways. First, by taking its projects public, Thermo Electron learns how financial market participants value its investment projects, which helps the company's managers make better capital allocation decisions. Second, since the compensation of the managers who run the various divisions is based on the stock price of the division, the managers are highly motivated to make decisions that maximize share price.[1]

Thermo Electron obviously views the benefits of this approach to real asset investment as exceeding the costs of taking each of its divisions public, which can be substantial (see Chapter 3). However, Thermo Electron is unusual in this regard. We are unaware of any other firm that follows this strategy.[2] Other firms attempting to address the question, "How much would the financial markets pay for the future cash flows of this investment project?" must recognize that since the sale of stock in the project is only hypothetical, answering this question is much more difficult than it is for Thermo Electron.

---

[1]Chapter 17 discusses this second factor in more detail.

[2]Other firms undertake the same type of equity carve-outs described for Thermo Electron, but none do it with the same frequency or the same intent.

315

To answer this question without actually selling stock in the project, corporate managers must return to the valuation principles developed in Part II. There, we used portfolios to track investments and compared the returns of the tracking portfolios to the returns of the financial assets we wanted to value. This allowed us to value the tracked investment in relation to its tracking portfolio. Models such as the CAPM, the APT, and the binomial derivative pricing model were used to determine relevant tracking portfolios.

The techniques developed in Part III largely piggyback onto these models and principles. The chapters in Part III show how to combine the prices available in financial markets into a single number that managers can compare with investment costs to evaluate whether a real investment increases or diminishes a firm's value. This number is the *present value (PV)* or market price of a portfolio of traded securities that tracks the *future* cash flows of the proposed project. Essentially, a project creates value for a corporation if the cost of investing in the project is less than the cost of investing in a portfolio of financial assets that track the project's future cash flows.

Thus, the *present value* measures the worth of a project's future cash flows at the present time by looking at the market price of identical, or nearly identical, future cash flows obtained from investing in the financial markets. The *net present value (NPV)* of an investment project is the difference between the value of a portfolio of financial instruments that track the project's cash flow, the *PV*, and the cost of implementing the project. Projects that create value are those whose present values exceed their costs. These are called positive *net present value* investments.

In some cases, such as those associated with riskless projects (discussed in Chapter 9), the tracking portfolio will perfectly track the future cash flows of the project. When perfect tracking is possible, the value created by real asset investment is a pure arbitrage gain achievable by taking the project along with an associated short position in the tracking portfolio. Since shorting the project's tracking portfolio from the financial markets offsets the project's future cash flows, a comparison between the date 0 cash flows of the project and the tracking portfolio is the only determinant of arbitrage. Value is created if there is arbitrage, as indicated by a positive *NPV,* and value is destroyed if there is negative *NPV.*

When the project has risky cash flows (see Chapter 10), the tracking portfolios will not perfectly track the project, but the tracking error, comprised entirely of risk that carries no risk premium, will have zero value. Hence, corporations that undertake positive *NPV* projects are, in a sense, creating arbitrage opportunities for shareholders who hold well-diversified portfolios.

The astute reader may wonder if the existence of this kind of arbitrage contradicts the principles on which Part II of this text is based. The valuation of financial assets, developed in Part II, is based on the assumption that *no arbitrage opportunities exist in financial markets.* There is no contradiction here. The perspective we provide on the valuation of real assets is one that allows corporations to create value for their shareholders by generating arbitrage opportunities between the markets for *real assets* and *financial assets.* In other words, we are assuming that it is impossible to make money by buying IBM stock and selling short Microsoft stock. However, Microsoft may be able to make money by investing in a new operating system and financing it by selling its own stock. In other words, financial securities are generally priced right—that is, financial securities are zero-*NPV* projects—but bargains do exist in the market for real assets. Because of its special abilities or circumstances, Microsoft can develop and market a new operating system better than its competitors and, as a result, can create value for its shareholders.

The valuation techniques introduced in Part III can be used as tools for evaluating strategies as well as capital expenditures on projects. For example, a major oil firm would not consider in isolation the opportunity to develop a natural gas field in Thailand. Instead, the firm would be thinking about the strategic implications of an increased presence in Asia, with the natural gas field as only one aspect of that strategy. Chapter 11 discusses how to estimate the value created by these strategic implications and provides broad principles that apply even to cases where quantitative estimation is difficult.

Finally, Chapter 12 focuses on a more real-world setting, introducing corporate tax deductions for debt financing and discussing how the financing of a project may affect the project's *NPV*. This sets the stage for Part IV, where the focus is chiefly on the optimal financial structure of a corporation.

Investing in Risk-Free Projects

Learning Objectives

After reading this chapter, you should be able to:

1. Compute incremental cash flows for projects, which is the basic input in project evaluation.

2. Apply the net present value *(NPV)* criterion to evaluate riskless projects properly both when there are no constraints and when there are constraints that make projects mutually exclusive.

3. Understand how value additivity relates to the proper application of NPV for project evaluation when projects are mutually exclusive.

4. Understand the concept of Economic Value Added (EVA) and the relation between EVA and discounted cash flow.

5. Compute hurdle rates for the internal rate of return *(IRR)* criterion when bond interest rates vary according to bond maturity.

6. Apply the IRR criterion to evaluate projects and be able to distinguish cases for which it is possible to obtain appropriate evaluations with the IRR criterion from those the preclude proper IRR-based evaluations.

A Fortune *magazine cover story, "The Real Key to Creating Wealth," discusses a technique known as Economic Value Added (or EVA™). "Managers who run their businesses according to EVA have hugely increased the value of their companies," the article reported. Companies that have benefited from EVA include CSX, Briggs and Stratton, and Coca-Cola, all of which have witnessed dramatic increases in their stock prices since the adoption of EVA.*

Fortune, September 20, 1993.

Corporations create value for their shareholders by making good real investment decisions. **Real investments** are expenditures that generate cash in the future and, as opposed to financial investments, like stocks and bonds, are not financial instruments that trade in the financial markets. Although one typically thinks about expenditures on plant and equipment as real investment decisions, in reality, almost all corporate decisions can be viewed as real investment decisions.[1]

Real investments range in magnitude from the very small to the very large. A relatively small investment might be the addition of a kitchen in the office of a corporation in order to decrease ongoing catering expenses. A major investment decision would be General Motors' launching of a new division to build its Saturn line of automobiles.

Of course, corporations think quite differently about adding a kitchen than they do about launching a division. There are no strategic implications associated with adding the kitchen and, while uncertainty is associated with the future savings on catering bills, that uncertainty can be safely ignored in most cases. However, the risks and strategic implications linked to launching a division are considerable; thus, major projects need to be evaluated with more sophisticated valuation procedures[2] that properly account for the effect of uncertainty on the project's value.

To be able to evaluate major strategic investments, the manager first needs to master the basic tools of project evaluation. Skill at using these tools comes from learning how to evaluate the more mundane projects, like the kitchen, where the uncertainty about the project's future cash flows can be safely ignored without catastrophic consequences if this oversight leads to an incorrect decision. Later chapters in Part III develop the more sophisticated methods for evaluating strategic investments under uncertainty.

How can a manager determine whether adopting a project creates value for the company's shareholders? For riskless cash flows, this is quite straightforward. The manager simply examines whether the investment project offers an arbitrage opportunity. In essence, the **net present value criterion**, our preferred evaluation technique, measures the arbitrage profits associated with an investment project and recommends projects for which arbitrage profits are positive. A riskless project has future cash flows that are perfectly tracked by a portfolio of riskless bonds of various maturities. Hence, arbitrage profits can be created whenever the project's startup cost is less than the cost of acquiring the tracking portfolio of riskless bonds.

While riskless cash flows rarely occur in practice, this chapter focuses on them exclusively because they illustrate some of the same basic principles required for valuing risky cash flows while keeping the analysis simple. After developing a consistent intuition for real asset valuation, this chapter focuses on complex problems in valuation that arise because of the multiperiod nature of cash flows. One problem arises when discount rates vary with the date of cash flow payment.[3] Another problem is the impact of a

---

[1]For example, firms generally recognize, when hiring a new employee, that the cost of the employee in the initial months may exceed the benefits he provides the firm. However, as the employee acquires skills over time, he is likely to provide benefits that exceed his costs. Similarly, when a firm increases its advertising expenditures, it is sacrificing current profits in the hope of generating more sales and future profits.

[2]**Capital budgeting** procedures, as these valuation procedures are sometimes called, are the decision-making rules used to evaluate real investments. The name derives from the fact that each project adopted by a firm requires that some *capital* be assigned or *budgeted* to the project.

[3]The **term structure of interest rates**—also known as the **yield curve**—is the pattern of yields on riskless bonds, based on their maturity. The term structure if "flat" when riskless bonds of all maturities have the same yield to maturity. See the appendix to this chapter for further discussion.

variety of constraints, such as limited capital and **mutually exclusive projects** (which occur whenever taking one project excludes the possibility of taking any of the other projects).

One of the insights in this chapter is that with riskless cash flows, the net present value method is equivalent to the **discounted cash flow method**, which obtains the *NPV* by discounting *all* cash flows at the rate(s) of return prevalent in the securities markets and adding the discounted cash flows together.

The net present value/discounted cash flow method has been around for a long time. Under sexier names, however, it seems to be rediscovered periodically. One version is **Economic Value Added (EVA™)**, described in the opening vignette, which is a trade-marked product marketed by the consulting firm of New York-based Stern Stewart & Company. EVA is a measure of a company's true economic profitability. Consulting firms such as McKinsey and BCG/Holt have similar products that also are being implemented by a vast number of companies, apparently with substantial success.[4] Part of the success of EVA is due to its use as a tool for managerial performance evaluation.[5] However, an additional benefit is that EVA steers managers away from some of the less appropriate methods of evaluating real investments and toward the adoption of projects with positive net present values.

9.1 Cash Flows

The most important inputs for evaluating a real investment are the incremental cash flows that can be attributed to the investment.

How to Compute Incremental Cash Flows

Incremental cash flows (or **net cash flows**) are the differences between two cash flow patterns: The pattern of cash flows to the firm with the project less the cash flows to the firm without the project (or with some next best alternative). This view of a cash flow allows for synergies and other interactions between any new project and the firm's existing projects.[6]

Example 9.1 illustrates how to compute incremental cash flows.

**Example 9.1:   Incremental Cash Flows as the Cash Flow Difference in
                   Two Scenarios**

Flyaway Air is thinking of acquiring a fleet of new fuel-savings jets. The airline will have the following cash flows if it does not acquire the jets:

---

[4]McKinsey calls their measure *Economic Profits,* and BCG/Holt employs three measures which they call *Cash Value Added* (CVA), *Cash Flow Return on Investment* (CFROI), and *Total Shareholder Return* or *Total Business Return* (TSR or TBR). The methods can differ in the way that they calculate cash flows as well as in how the cost of capital is calculated.

[5]See Chapter 17.

[6]*Cash flow* should not be confused with *earnings*. The major differences between earnings and cash flow include depreciation, which reduces earnings without affecting cash flow, and changes in working capital or fixed capital, which can either increase or decrease a project's cash flow without affecting earnings. This chapter will discuss some of the pitfalls associated with using earnings numbers to value real investments. Chapter 12 discusses how to generate cash flow from earnings.

Cash Flows (in $ millions) at Date			
0	*1*	*2*	*3*
100	140	120	100

If it does acquire the jets, its cash flows will be:

Cash Flows (in $ millions) at Date			
0	*1*	*2*	*3*
80	180	110	130

What are the incremental cash flows of the project?

Answer: The incremental cash flows of the project are given by the difference between the two sets of cash flows:

Cash Flows (in $ millions) at Date			
0	*1*	*2*	*3*
−20	40	−10	30

Real Asset Cash Flows and Financing Cash Flows

The NPV evaluation criterion values the cash flows that stem directly from the real assets of a proposed project, (the **real asset cash flows** of the project), and ignores the cash that flows into the firm when it borrows money or issues shares and flows out of the firm when loans are paid off, debt interest is paid, or shares are repurchased (the **financing cash flows**). This chapter assumes that the financing of the project does not create value; that is, the *NPV* of the financing cash flows is zero. When this occurs, discounting the real asset cash flows is the same as discounting the combined cash flows from both the project and its financing sources.[7]

9.2 Net Present Value

The **net present value (NPV)** of an investment project is the difference between the project's **present value (PV)**, the value of a portfolio of financial instruments that track the project's future cash flows, and the cost of implementing the project.

---

[7]One cannot ignore the financing cash flows when considering the possibility that the firm can create value from its financing decisions by altering the firm's tax liabilities. For this reason Chapter 12, which focuses on taxes and valuation, considers both real asset cash flows and the tax effect of the financing cash flows.

Discounted Cash Flow and Net Present Value

When the cash flows of a project are riskless, they can be tracked perfectly with a combination of default-free bonds. For convenience, this chapter uses zero-coupon bonds, which are bonds that pay cash only at their maturity dates (see Chapter 2) as the securities in the tracking portfolio. This subsection shows that the net present value is the same as the discounted value of the project's cash flows.[8] The discount rates are the yields to maturity of these zero-coupon bonds.

Yield-to-maturity of a Zero-Coupon Bond: the Discount Rate.   The per period *yield-to-maturity* of a zero-coupon bond is the discount rate (compounded once per period) that makes the discounted value of the bond's payment on its maturity date equal to the current market price of the bond, that is, the r_t that makes:

$$B = \frac{F}{(1 + r_t)^t}$$

where

B = current bond price
F = face value of the bond
t = number of periods to the maturity date of the bond

When markets are frictionless, a concept defined in Chapter 4, and if there is no arbitrage, the yields to maturity of all zero-coupon bonds of a given maturity are the same.

A Formula for the Discounted Cash Flow.   We now formally define the Discounted Cash Flow (DCF) of a riskless project. A project has riskless cash flows:

$$C_0, C_1, C_2, \ldots, C_T$$

where

C_t = the (positive or negative) cash flow at date t. Positive numbers represent *cash inflows* (e.g., when a sale is made) and negative numbers represent *cash outflows* (e.g., when labor is paid), which are positive costs.

The **discounted cash flow** of the project is:

$$DCF = C_0 + \frac{C_1}{1 + r_1} + \frac{C_2}{(1 + r_2)^2} + \ldots + \frac{C_T}{(1 + r_T)^T} \tag{9.1}$$

where

r_t = the per period yield to maturity of a default-free zero-coupon bond maturing at date t

A project's discounted cash flow is the sum of all of the discounted future cash flows plus today's cash flow, which is usually negative, since it represents the initial expenditure needed to start the project. The "discounted *future* cash flow stream," equation (9.1) with C_0 omitted on the right-hand side, is often used interchangeably with the term "present value of the project's future cash flows," or simply "project present value."

---

[8]Although this is also true for risky cash flows, in many of these cases, we would not discount cash flows to compute the *NPV* of a risky cash flow stream. See Chapter 11 for further detail.

Similarly, the sum of the present value of the future cash flows plus today's cash flow, referred to as "the net present value of the project," is then used interchangeably with the term "discounted cash flow stream."

Using Different Discount Rates at Different Maturities.   Many formulas compute present values (and net present values) using the same discount rate for cash flows that occur at different times. This simplification makes many formulas appear elegant and simple. However, if default-free bond yields vary as the maturity of the bond changes, the correct approach must use discount rates that vary depending on the timing of the cash flows. These discount rates, often referred to as the **costs of capital**, (or costs of financing), are the yields to maturity of default-free zero-coupon bonds.[9]

Project Evaluation with the Net Present Value Rule

This subsection shows why the NPV rule, "adopt the project when *NPV* is positive," is sensible. Below, we show that the *NPV* rule is consistent with the creation of wealth through arbitrage.

Arbitrage and NPV.   Adopting a project at a cost less than the present value of its future cash flows (i.e., positive *NPV*) means that financing the project by selling short this tracking portfolio leaves surplus cash in the firm today. Since the future cash that needs to be paid out on the shorted tracking portfolio matches the cash flows coming in from the project, the firm that adopts the positive *NPV* project creates wealth risklessly. In short, adopting a riskless project with a positive *NPV* and financing it in this manner is an arbitrage opportunity for the firm.

Hence, when there are no project selection constraints, net present value offers a simple and correct procedure for evaluating real investments:

Result 9.1   The wealth maximizing net present value criterion is that:

- All projects with positive net present values should be accepted.
- All projects with negative net present values should be rejected.

The Relation between Arbitrage, NPV, and DCF.   Below, we use a riskless project tracked by a portfolio of zero-coupon bonds to illustrate the relation between *NPV* and arbitrage. This illustration points out—at least for riskless projects—that net present value and discounted cash flow are the same. Begin by looking at a project with cash flows at two dates, 0 (today) and 1 (one period from now). The algebraic representation of the cash flows of such a project is given in the first row below the following time line:

	Cash Flows at Date	
	0	*1*
Algebra	C_0	C_1
Numbers	−$10 million	$12 million

[9]When cash flows are risky, the appropriate discount rate may reflect a risk premium, as Chapter 10 discusses.

The second row of the time line is a numerical example of the cash flows at the same two dates. Inspection of the time line suggests that a default-free zero-coupon bond, maturing at date 1, with a face value of C_1 ($12 million), perfectly tracks the *future* cash flows of this project. Let:

B = the current market price of such a bond divided by its face value

r = bond's yield-to-maturity (an equivalent way of expressing the bond's price) = $1/B - 1$

For example, if the bond is selling at $0.93 per $1.00 of face value, then B = $0.93 and r = 7.5 percent (approximately). After rearranging the equation $r = 1/B - 1$ to obtain $B = 1/(1 + r)$, note that the issuance of C_1 of these bonds results in a date 0 cash flow of $C_1 B = C_1/(1 + r)$, or numerically, $12 million × .93 = $12 million/1.075, and a cash flow of $-C_1$, or $-$12 million, at date 1.

Hence, a firm that adopts the project and issues C_1 ($12 million) in face value of these bonds has cash flows at dates 0 and 1 summarized by the time line below:

| | **Cash Flows at Date** | |
	0	*1*
Algebra	$C_0 + \dfrac{C_1}{1 + r}$	0
Numbers	$-$10 million $+ \dfrac{\$12 \text{ million}}{1.075}$	0

Since the date 1 cash flow from the combination of project adoption and zero-coupon bond financing is zero, the firm achieves arbitrage if $C_0 + C_1/(1 + r)$, the value under date 0, is positive, which is the case here.

The algebraic symbols or number under date 0 above, the project's *NPV,* is the sum of the discounted cash flows of the project, including the (undiscounted) cash flow at date 0. It also represents the difference between the cost of buying the tracking investment for the project's *future* cash flows, $C_1/(1 + r)$ (or $12,000,000/1.075), and the cost of initiating the project, $-C_0$ ($10 million). If this difference, $C_0 + C_1/(1 + r)$ (or $-$10 million + $12 million/1.075), is positive, the future cash flows of the project can be generated more cheaply by adopting the project (at a cost of $-C_0$) than by investing in the project's tracking investment at a cost of $C_1/(1 + r)$.

Example 9.2 extends this idea to multiple periods.

Example 9.2:   The Relation between Arbitrage and NPV
Consider the cash flows of the project in Example 9.1:

| **Cash Flows (in $ millions) at Date** | | | |
0	*1*	*2*	*3*
-20	40	-10	30

Explain how to finance the project so that the combined future cash flows from the project and its financing are zero. What determines whether this is a good or a bad project?

Answer: The cash flows from the project at dates 1, 2, and 3 can be offset by

(1) issuing, that is selling short, zero-coupon bonds maturing at date 1 with a face value of $40 million,

(2) purchasing zero-coupon bonds maturing at date 2 with a face value of $10 million, and

(3) selling short zero-coupon bonds maturing at date 3 with a face value of $30 million.

The cash flows from this bond portfolio in combination with the project are

Cash Flows at Date			
0	1	2	3
V	0	0	0

where V is the cost of the tracking portfolio less the $20 million initial cost of the project, and thus is the project's *NPV.* Clearly, if V is positive, the project is good because it represents an arbitrage opportunity. If V is negative, it represents a bad project.

All riskless projects can have their future cash flows tracked with a portfolio of zero-coupon bonds. Shorting the tracking portfolio thus offsets the future cash flows of the project. To see this, let $C_1, C_2, \ldots, C_T$ denote the project's cash flows at dates $1, 2, \ldots, T$, respectively. A short position in a zero-coupon bond maturing at date 1 with a face value of C_1 offsets the first cash flow; shorting a zero-coupon bond with a face value of C_2 paid at date 2 offsets the second cash flow; and so forth. A portfolio that is short by these amounts creates a cash flow pattern similar to that in Example 9.2, with zero cash flows at future dates and possibly a nonzero cash flow at date 0.

The logic of the net present value criterion for riskless projects and the equivalence between net present value and discounted cash flow follows immediately. Result 9.2 summarizes our discussion of this issue as follows:

Result 9.2   For a project with riskless cash flows, the *NPV,* that is, the market value of the project's tracking portfolio less the cost of initiating the project, and the discounted value of all present and future cash flows of the project are the same.

Actual Financing Cash Flows Do Not Have to Track the Real Asset's Cash Flows. It is important to understand that even though arbitrage between the market for securities that might finance the project and the real asset market lies behind the logic of the *NPV* rule, the precise form the financing takes does not affect the project's *NPV* in frictionless markets.[10]

---

[10]Chapter 13 shows that investors can always "undo" the cash flow effects of any of the firm's financing arrangements in their personal portfolios. Essentially, they can achieve arbitrage between the securities market and the real asset market, even if the cash flows to investors from the firm's financing of the project do not track the future cash flows from the project. When markets have frictions—taxes, information asymmetries, managerial incentive problems, bankruptcy costs, and so on—the precise form of financing the firm may create value. Chapters 12–18 discuss this issue at length. However, to understand the simple logic of project valuation, we focus for now on frictionless markets and avoid this issue.

Net Present Values Have the Value Additivity Property

A consequence of no arbitrage is that two cash flow streams, when combined, have a value that is the sum of the net present values of the separate cash flow streams. An arbitrage opportunity exists when an investor can purchase two cash flow streams separately, put them together, and sell the combined cash flow stream for more than the sum of the purchase prices of each of them. Arbitrage is also achieved if it is possible to purchase a cash flow stream and break it up into two or more cash flow streams (as in equity carve-outs), and to sell them for more than the original purchase price. The principle that the net present value from combining two (or more) cash flow streams is the sum of the net present values of each cash flow stream is known as **value additivity**. The net present value, which, as seen earlier, is so closely linked to the principle of no arbitrage in financial markets, has the value additivity property.

Moreover, value additivity is apparent from the DCF formula, equation (9.1), which in this chapter is equivalent to *NPV*. If project A has cash flows $C_{A0}, C_{A1}, \ldots C_{AT}$ and project B has cash flows $C_{B0}, C_{B1}, \ldots, C_{BT}$, then, because cash flows only appear in the numerator terms of equation (9.1), $NPV(C_{A0} + C_{B0}, C_{A1} + C_{B1}, \ldots, C_{AT} + C_{BT})$ is the sum of $NPV(C_{A0}, C_{A1}, \ldots, C_{AT})$ and $NPV(C_{B0}, C_{B1}, \ldots, C_{BT})$.

Implications of Value Additivity for Project Adoption and Cancellation. Value additivity implies that the net present value of a firm after project adoption is the value of the firm's cash flows prior to adoption plus the net present value of the adopted project's cash flows. (If one is careful to define the cash flows of the project as incremental cash flows, this is true even when synergies exist between the firm's current projects and the new project.) Value additivity also works in reverse. A firm that cancels a project will find that its new value is its old net present value less the present value of the incremental cash flows from project cancellation. Thus, if the net present value of a project is negative, a firm that has just adopted the project would find that its incremental cash flow pattern for canceling the project and acquiring the tracking bonds is the stream given in the table below, which has a positive value under date 0:

Cash Flows at Date	
0	*1*
$-C_0 - \dfrac{C_1}{1 + r}$	0

This table demonstrates that a negative net present value for adoption of the project implies a positive net present value for canceling the project, once adopted, and vice versa.

Implications of Value Additivity when Evaluating Mutually Exclusive Projects. The value additivity property makes it easy to understand how to properly select the best project from among a group of projects that are mutually exclusive. For example, a firm may choose to configure a manufacturing plant to produce either tractors or trucks, but it cannot use the plant for both. Value additivity implies that the best of these mutually exclusive projects is the one with the largest positive net present value.

One way to understand this is to recognize adopting the project with the cash flows that have the largest *NPV* generates the largest net present value of the firm's aggregated cash flows. This is because value additivity implies that the *NPV* of the firm, a collection of projects, is the sum of the *NPV* of the firm without the adoption of any of the proposed projects plus the *NPV* of the incremental cash flows of whichever project is adopted.

Another way to understand that the project with the largest NPV is the best is that the cost of adopting one of two mutually exclusive projects is the forgone cash flows of the other project, not a zero *NPV* investment in the financial markets. Recall that the concept of incremental cash flows compares the cash flows of the firm with the project with the cash flows of the firm without the project. With mutual exclusivity, not adopting a particular project means that the firm adopts its next best alternative project, provided that the latter has positive *NPV*. Thus, the true incremental cash flows of a particular project are the difference between the cash flows of the project and those of the forgone alternative. By value additivity, or more precisely "subtractivity," the *NPV* of this differenced cash flow stream is the difference between the *NPV*s of the two projects. Example 9.3 illustrates this point.

Example 9.3:   Mutually Exclusive Projects and *NPV*

The law firm of Jacob and Meyer is small and only has the resources to take on one of four cases. The cash flows for each of the four legal projects and their net present values discounted at the rate of 10 percent per period are given below.

	Cash Flows (in $000s) at Date			
	0	1	2	Net Present Value
Project A	−7	11	12.1	13
Project B	−1	22	−12.1	9
Project C	−5	44	−24.2	15
Project D	−1	11	0	9

Which is the best project?

Answer: These cash flows are calculated as the cash flows of the firm with the project less the cash flows of the firm without any of the four projects. Clearly, project C has the highest net present value and should be adopted.

It is possible to calculate the cash flows differently. With mutual exclusivity, the cost of adopting one of the projects is the loss of the others. Hence, computation of the cash flows relative to the best alternative should provide an equally valid calculation. The best alternative to projects A, B, and D is project C. The best alternative to project C is project A. The appropriate cash flow calculation subtracts the cash flows of the best alternative and is described below:

	Cash Flows (in $000s) at Date			Net Present Value (in $000s)
	0	1	2	
Project A (less C)	−2	−33	36.3	−2
Project B (less C)	4	−22	12.1	−6
Project C (less A)	2	33	−36.3	2
Project D (less C)	4	−33	24.2	−6

Only project C has a positive net present value. Thus, selecting the project with the largest positive net present value, as in the first *NPV* calculation, is equivalent to picking the only positive net present value project, when cash flows are computed relative to the best alternative.

Using NPV with Capital Constraints

The last subsection considered the possibility of having mutually exclusive projects because of physical constraints. Among those was the possibility that some important input was in short supply, perhaps land available for building a manufacturing facility or managerial time.

This subsection considers the possibility that the amount of capital the firm can devote to new investments is limited. For truly riskless projects, these **capital constraints** are unlikely to be important because it is almost always possible to obtain outside financing for riskless projects. However, the cash flows of most major projects are uncertain, so the availability of outside capital for these projects may be constrained.

Profitability Index.   We are concerned here with how a corporation, constrained in its choice owing to a limited supply of capital, should allocate the capital that it can raise.[11] Specifically, this subsection introduces an extension of the net present value rule known as the **profitability index**, which is the present value of the project's *future* cash flows divided by $-C_0$, the negative of the initial cash flow, which is the initial cost of the project. In the absence of a capital constraint, the value maximizing rule with the profitability index is one that adopts projects with a profitability index greater than 1 if C_0 is negative. (If C_0 is positive, a firm should adopt projects with a profitability index of less than 1.) This is simply another form of the net present value rule. For example, with annual cash flows, denote:

$$PV = \frac{C_1}{1 + r_1} + \frac{C_2}{(1 + r_2)^2} + \ldots + \frac{C_T}{(1 + r_T)^T}$$

The net present value rule says that one should select projects for which:

$$C_0 + PV > 0$$

or equivalently

$$PV > -C_0$$

or

$$\frac{PV}{-C_0} > 1 \text{ if } C_0 < 0 \text{ and } \frac{PV}{-C_0} < 1 \text{ if } C_0 > 0$$

The profitability index can be particularly useful if C_0 is negative for all projects under consideration and if there is a capital constraint in the initial period. If the projects under consideration can be scaled up or down to any degree, the project with the largest profitability index exceeding 1 is the best. This point is demonstrated in Example 9.4.

---

[11]Parts IV and V of the text explain why these capital constraints exist.

Example 9.4:   The Profitability Index

There is a capital constraint of $10,000 in the initial period. The two scalable projects available for investment are projects B and C from Example 9.3. The cash flows are given below:

	Cash Flow (in $000s) at Date			Net Present Values (in $000s)	Profitability Index
	0	*1*	*2*		
Project B	−1	22	−12.1	9	10
Project C	−5	44	−24.2	15	4

Which is the better project?

Answer: Project B is the best because it gives the biggest "bang per buck." For the maximum initial expenditure of $10,000, it is possible to run 10 B projects, but only 2 C projects. The old net present value rule calculation is deceiving here because it reflects the benefit of adopting only one project. But adopting 10 B projects would yield an *NPV* of $90,000, which exceeds $30,000, the *NPV* from two C projects. The profitability index reflects this because it represents the present value of future cash flows per dollar invested.

Net Profitability Rate.   Perhaps a better representation of the relative profitability of two investments is offered by the **net profitability rate**, where the:

$$\text{Net profitability rate} = (1 + \text{Risk-free rate}) \times (\text{Profitability index}) - 1$$

If C_0 is negative, the net profitability rate represents the additional value next period of all future cash flows per dollar invested in the initial period. It is, in essence, the net present value translated into a rate of return.[12]

Using NPV to Evaluate Projects That Can Be Repeated over Time

Capital allocation takes place in the presence of many different kinds of constraints, so it is often inappropriate to look at projects in isolation. One type of constraint is a space constraint, which would exist, for example, if there was space for only one piece of equipment on the shop floor. Here, the mere fact that projects have different lives may affect the choice of project. Longer-lived projects use space, the scarce input, to a greater degree and should be penalized in some fashion. Example 9.5 demonstrates how to solve a capital allocation problem with a space constraint.

Example 9.5:   Evaluating Projects with Different Lives

Two types of canning machines, denoted A and B, can only be placed in the same corner of a factory. Machine A, the old technology, has a life of two periods. Machine B costs more to purchase, but cans products faster. However, machine B wears out more quickly and has a life of only one year. The delivery and setup of each machine takes place one period after initially paying for it. Immediately upon the setup of either machine, positive cash flows begin to be

---

[12]The net profitability rate amortizes the project's net present value over the first period of the project's life. It can be used to make decisions about the economic profitability of both riskless and risky projects.

produced. The cash flows from each machine and the net present values of their cash flows at a discount rate of 10 percent are as follows:

	Cash Flow (in $millions) at Date			Net Present Value (in $millions)
	0	*1*	*2*	
Machine A	−.8	1.1	1.21	1.2
Machine B		−1.9	3.30	1.1

It appears that machine A is a better choice. Is this true?

Answer: A second picture tells a different story.

	Cash Flow (in $millions) at Date			Net Present Value (in $millions)
	0	*1*	*2*	
Machine A	−.8	1.1	1.21	1.2
First machine B	−1.9	3.3		1.1
Second machine B		−1.9	3.30	1.0
Sum of the two B machines	−1.9	1.4	3.30	2.1

Over the life of machine A, one could have adopted machine B, used it to the end of its useful life, purchased a second machine B, and let it live out its useful life as well. In this case, machine B seems to dominate.

Example 9.5 points out the value of being able to repeat a project over time. One makes an appropriate comparison between repeatable mutually exclusive projects only after finding a common date where, after repeating in time, both projects have lived out their full lives. This date is the least common multiple of the terminal dates of the projects under consideration.

Two other approaches also can help in the selection between repeatable, mutually exclusive projects with different lives. One of these approaches repeats the project in time until infinity. It values the project's cash flows as the sum of the present values of perpetuities. The other approach computes the project's **equivalent annual benefit**; that is, the periodic payment for an annuity that ends at the same date and has the same *NPV* as the project. The project with the largest annual benefit is the best project.

9.3 Economic Value Added (EVA)

This chapter's opening vignette, which described one of the most reprinted articles in the history of *Fortune* magazine, demonstrates that American corporations are wild about EVA and the related measures of true profitability introduced by other consulting firms. EVA was originally conceived as an adjustment to accounting earnings that better measures how firms are performing.[13] However, as this section shows, one of the keys to EVA's success is that its implementation provides a system in which managers are encouraged to take on positive net present value investment projects.

Economic Value Added is simply a way of accounting for the cost of using capital in computing profit. In contrast to accounting earnings, which charge only for the interest paid on debt capital, EVA imposes a charge on both debt and equity capital. Also, while EVA prefers cash flow to accounting earnings, it recognizes that changes in capital affect cash flow. When initiating a project, for example, the project's initial cash flow C_0 is probably negative because of a large capital expenditure on items such as machines, land, and a factory. Similarly, at the termination date of a project, the capital is returned to the firm's investors in the form of cash as the depreciated capital assets are sold for their salvage value. This reduction in capital tends to make the terminal cash flow C_T large even when the project may not be very profitable in its final year. Along the way, there also may be additional capital expenditures, sales of capital equipment, or reductions in the value of the capital due to economic depreciation. By *economic depreciation,* we mean the reduction in the salvage value of the capital, estimated by what the market is willing to pay for the project's capital assets at the end of a period compared with their value when the project is initiated.

One advantage of accounting earnings over cash flow is that the former tends to smooth out the abrupt changes in cash flow due to changes in capital and to present a more stable year-to-year picture of operating profitability. Proponents of EVA advocate that the smoothing (or, to use accounting terminology, *amortization*) of capital expenditures over the life of the project can be achieved in a more economically sensible way.

Specifically, EVA attempts to account for the cash flow impact of capital

where

I_t = the date t book value, adjusted for economic depreciation, of the
      project's capital assets (Special cases: at $t = 0$, it is the purchase price;
      both at $t = -1$, the date before the project begins, and at $t = T$, the
      terminal date at which the assets are sold, $I_t = 0$)

The date t cash flow, C_t is broken into the sum of three components:

$I_{t-1} - I_t$ = the reduction in capital from $t - 1$ to t[14]
    $I_{t-1}r$ = a fair charge for the use of capital from $t - 1$ to t
   EVA_t = a measure of the project's true economic profitability from $t - 1$ to t

Since EVA_t is defined as whatever is left over after accounting for the first two components, the date t Economic Value Added of the cash flow stream is:

$$EVA_t = C_t - (I_{t-1} - I_t) - I_{t-1}r \qquad (9.2a)$$

Note that if one groups the I_{t-1} terms in equation (9.2a) together, then:

$$EVA_t = C_t + I_t - I_{t-1}(1 + r) \qquad (9.2b)$$

There are two special cases. At beginning date 0, since there is no charge for capital until date 1, equation (9.2b) states:

---

[13]The discussion of the accounting rate of return in Section 9.6 illustrates how accounting earnings can mislead corporate managers.

[14]Reduction in capital includes the sale of capital assets as well as economic depreciation. Increases in capital arise from capital expenditures and economic appreciation in the salvage value of a capital asset.

$$EVA_0 = C_0 + I_0$$

At the terminal date T, equation (9.2b) implies:

$$EVA_T = C_T - I_{T-1}(1 + r)$$

because all of the capital is liquidated at the terminal date, implying $I_T = 0$.

Now discount the EVA stream from date 0 through date T, generating

$$\text{Discounted } EVA \text{ stream} = EVA_0 + \frac{EVA_1}{(1 + r)} + \frac{EVA_2}{(1 + r)^2} + \ldots + \frac{EVA_{T-1}}{(1 + r)^{T-1}} + \frac{EVA_T}{(1 + r)^T}$$

Substituting equation (9.2b) into this formula implies:

$$\text{Discounted } EVA \text{ stream} = C_0 + I_0 + \frac{C_1 + I_1 - I_0(1 + r)}{1 + r} + \frac{C_2 + I_2 - I_1(1 + r)}{(1 + r)^2} + \ldots$$

$$+ \frac{C_{T-1} + I_{T-1} - I_{T-2}(1 + r)}{(1 + r)^{T-1}} + \frac{C_T - I_{T-1}(1 + r)}{(1 + r)^T}$$

$$= C_0 + \frac{C_1}{1 + r} + \frac{C_2}{(1 + r)^2} + \ldots + \frac{C_{T-1}}{(1 + r)^{T-1}} + \frac{C_T}{(1 + r)^T}$$

$$= NPV$$

Because the I_t terms, representing capital, cancel one another in the expression for the discounted EVA stream, the discounted EVA stream is the same as the *NPV* of the project!

Example 9.6 illustrates this point numerically.

Example 9.6:   Computing EVAs

Assume that NASA is allowed to select one of three commercial projects for the next space shuttle mission. Each of these projects has industrial spin-offs that will generate cash for NASA over the next two periods. The cash flows and *NPV*s of the projects are described below:

	Cash Flow (in $millions) at Date			NPV at 2% (in $millions)
	0	*1*	*2*	
Project A	−17.0	12	9	3.420
Project B	−16.8	10	11	3.558
Project C	−16.9	11	10	3.50

What are the EVAs and the discounted values of the EVA streams of the three projects? Assume a cost of capital of 2 percent per period and, for simplicity, no changes in capital at date 1. Also assume that the negative cash flow at date 0 is entirely a capital expenditure, implying that $EVA_0 = 0$.

Answer: The EVAs of the three projects occur only at dates 1 and 2. The following table gives the six EVAs and their present values for each project:

	EVA_1 (in $millions)	EVA_2 (in $millions)	$PV(EVA_1) + PV(EVA_2)$ at 2% (in $millions)
Project A	$11.660 = 12 - 17.0(.02)$	$-8.34 = 9 - 17.0(.02) - 17.0$	3.42
Project B	$9.664 = 10 - 16.8(.02)$	$-6.14 = 11 - 16.8(.02) - 16.8$	3.58
Project C	$10.662 = 11 - 16.9(.02)$	$-7.24 = 10 - 16.9(.02) - 16.9$	3.50

Note, as suggested earlier, that the summed discounted values of EVA_1 and EVA_2 for the three projects in Example 9.6 (which assumes $EVA_0 = 0$) are the same as their respective *NPVs*. Result 9.3 states this formally.

Result 9.3   The discounted value of the stream of *EVA*s of a project is the same as the net present value of the project.

9.4 Using *NPV* for Other Corporate Decisions

Although the techniques examined in this chapter have typically been applied only to the evaluation of capital investments, the introduction of EVA has had the effect of getting managers to think about other uses for the net present value rule. These could include labor strategies, pricing strategies, product development strategies, and so forth. To illustrate this point, this section considers two examples. The first, Example 9.7, analyzes a labor decision.

Example 9.7:   Laying Off Workers as an Investment Decision

Ace Farm Equipment is currently suffering from a slowdown in sales and temporary overstaffing. The company can save $600,0000 at the end of each of the next three years if it cuts its workforce by 25 individuals. In four years, however, it expects that its market will improve and that it will have to hire replacements for the 25 individuals who were laid off. Ace estimates that the cost of hiring and training workers is $100,000 per employee, or $2.5 million for the 25 employees. If the discount rate is 10 percent per year, should Ace temporarily cut its workforce?

Answer: The incremental cash flows associated with the layoffs are as follows:

	Cash Flow (in $millions) at End of Year			
	1	2	3	4
	0.6	0.6	0.6	−2.5

$$NPV = -\$2.15 \text{ million} \left(= \frac{\$.6 \text{ million}}{1.1} + \frac{\$.6 \text{ million}}{1.1^2} + \frac{\$.6 \text{ million}}{1.1^3} - \frac{\$2.5 \text{ million}}{1.1^4} \right)$$

The negative *NPV* implies that layoffs destroy shareholder wealth.

Example 9.8 analyzes a project pricing decision.

Example 9.8:   Cutting Product Price as an Investment Decision

Assume that Buzz Beers, a local distributor, currently sells about 10,000 cases of beer per month, which is 15 percent of the Akron market. Buzz Beers management is considering a temporary price cut to attract a larger share of the market. If management chooses to lower beer prices from $4.00 to $3.80 a case, Buzz Beers will expand its market by 50 percent. Elmer Buzz, the CFO, estimates that the beer costs $3.50 per case, so that the company would be making $5,000 per month with the higher price but only $4,500 per month with the lower price. However, the company plans to stick with the lower price for two years and then raise the price to $3.90 per case. Management believes that at this higher price they still will be able to keep their new customers for the subsequent two years, allowing Buzz Beers to generate a monthly cash flow of $6,000 per month in years 3 and 4. If the discount rate is 1 percent per month, should prices be lowered?

Answer: The incremental cash flows are as follows:

	Cash Flow at the End of Month						
1	*2*	...	*24*	*25*	*26*	...	*48*
−$500	−$500	...	−$500	$1,000	$1,000	...	$1,000

$$NPV = \$6,109 = \frac{-\$500}{1.01} + \frac{-\$500}{1.01^2} + \ldots + \frac{-\$500}{1.01^{24}} + \frac{\$1,000}{1.01^{25}} + \frac{\$1,000}{1.01^{26}} + \ldots + \frac{\$1,000}{1.01^{48}}$$

The positive *NPV* means that cutting prices is worthwhile.

9.5 Evaluating Real Investments with the Internal Rate of Return

This text, like most finance texts, recommends the *NPV* method for evaluating investment projects. However, a number of corporate managers base their real investment decisions on the **internal rate of return *(IRR)*** of their investments. The internal rate of return *(IRR)* for a cash flow stream $C_0, C_1, \ldots, C_T$ at dates $0, 1, \ldots, T$, respectively, is the interest rate y that makes the net present value of a project equal zero; that is, the y that solves

$$0 = C_0 + \frac{C_1}{1+y} + \frac{C_2}{(1+y)^2} + \ldots + \frac{C_T}{(1+y)^T} \tag{9.3}$$

Since internal rates of return cannot be less than −100 percent, $1 + y$ is positive.

Intuition for the IRR Method

The **internal rate of return method** for evaluating investment projects compares the *IRR* of a project to a **hurdle rate** to determine whether the project should be taken. In this chapter, where cash flows are riskless, the hurdle rate is always the risk-free rate of interest. For risky projects, the hurdle rate, which is the project's cost of capital (see Chapter 10), may reflect a risk premium.

Projects have several kinds of cash flow patterns. A **later cash flow stream** starts at date 0 with a negative cash flow and then, at some future date, begins to experience positive cash flows for the remaining life of the project. It has this name because all the positive cash flows of the project come later, after a period when the firm has pumped money into the project. A later cash flow stream can be thought of as the cash flow pattern for investing. When investing, high rates of return are good. Thus, a project with a later cash flow stream enables the firm to realize arbitrage profits by taking on the project and shorting the tracking portfolio whenever the project's *IRR* (its multiperiod rate of return) exceeds the appropriate hurdle rate (which is the multiperiod rate of return for the tracking portfolio). Projects with internal rates of return less than the hurdle rates have low rates of return and are rejected.

The reverse cash flow pattern, when all positive cash flows occur first and all negative cash flows occur only after the last positive cash flow, is known as an **early cash flow stream**. This cash flow pattern resembles borrowing; when borrowing, it is better to have a low rate *(IRR)* than a high rate. Hence, the *IRR* rule for this cash flow pattern is to reject projects that have an *IRR* exceeding the hurdle rate and to accept those where the hurdle rate exceeds the *IRR*.

Some cash flow patterns, however, are more problematic because they resemble both investing and borrowing, including those that start out negative, become positive, and then become negative again. Such cash flow patterns create problems for the *IRR* method, as we will see shortly.

Numerical Iteration of the IRR

The computation of the internal rate of return is usually performed using a technique known as **numerical iteration**, which can be viewed as an intelligent "trial-and-error procedure." Iterative procedures begin with an initial guess at a solution for the interest rate y. They then compute the discounted value of the cash flow stream given on the right-hand side of equation (9.3) with that y, and then increase or decrease y depending on whether the right-hand side of equation (9.3) is positive or negative. The procedure generally stops when the discounted value of the present and future cash flows is close enough to zero to satisfy the analyst. Most electronic spreadsheets and financial calculators have built-in programs that compute internal rates of return.

Formulas for computing the internal rate of return directly (i.e., without numerical iteration) exist only in rare cases, such as when a project has cash flows at only a few equally spaced dates. For example, if a project has cash flows only at year 0 and year 1, we can multiply both sides of equation (9.3) by $1 + y$ and solve for y. The resulting equation, $0 = C_0(1 + y) + C_1$, has the solution:

$$y = -\frac{C_1}{C_0} - 1$$

If there are cash flows exactly zero, one, and two periods from now, multiplying both sides of equation (9.3) by $(1 + y)^2$ results in a quadratic equation. This can be solved with the quadratic formula. Most of the time, however, projects have cash flows that occur at more than three dates or are timed more irregularly. In this case, numerical iteration is used to find the *IRR*.

NPV and Examples of IRR

This subsection works through several examples to illustrate the relation between *NPV* and *IRR*.

Examples with One IRR.   Examples 9.9 and 9.10 are simple cases having only one *IRR*.

Example 9.9:   An IRR Calculation and a Comparison with NPV

Joe's Bowling Alley is considering whether to relacquer its lanes, which will generate additional business. The project's cash flows, which occur at dates 0, 1, 2, and 3, are assumed to be riskless and are described by the following table:

Cash Flows (in $000s) at Date			
0	*1*	*2*	*3*
−9	4	5	3

If the yields of riskless zero-coupon bonds maturing at years 1, 2, and 3 are 8 percent, 5 percent, and 6 percent per period, respectively, find the net present value and the internal rate of return of the cash flows.

Answer: The *NPV,* obtained by discounting the cash flows at the zero-coupon yields, is

$$-\$9,000 + \frac{\$4,000}{1.08} + \frac{\$5,000}{1.05^2} + \frac{\$3,000}{1.06^3} = \$1,758$$

The *IRR* is approximately 16.6 percent per period. That is:

$$-\$9,000 + \frac{\$4,000}{1.166} + \frac{\$5,000}{1.166^2} + \frac{\$3,000}{1.166^3} = 0$$

In Example 9.9, the internal rate of return of the project exceeds the rate of return of all of the bonds used to track the project's cash flow. In this case, it is not surprising that the *NPV* is positive. In Example 9.10, the *IRR* is negative.

Example 9.10:   NPV and IRR with Irregular Periods

A contractor is considering whether to take on a renovation project that will take two and one-half years to complete. Under the proposed deal, the contractor has to initially spend more money to pay workers and acquire material than he receives from the customer to start the project. After the initial phase is completed, there is a partial payment for the renovation. A second phase then begins. When the company completes the second phase, the customer makes the final payment. The cash flows of the project are described by the following table:

Years from Now:	0	.5	1.25	2.5
Cash flows (in $000s):	−10	5	−15	18

The respective annualized zero-coupon rates are:

Years to Maturity	.5	1.25	2.5
Yield (%/year):	6%	6%	8%

Find the net present value and internal rate of return of the project.

Answer: The *NPV* of the project is:

$$-\$10{,}000 + \frac{\$5{,}000}{1.06^5} - \frac{\$15{,}000}{1.06^{1.25}} + \frac{\$18{,}000}{1.08^{2.5}} = -\$4{,}240$$

This is a negative number. The *IRR* is approximately −6.10 percent per year or −2 percent per quarter.

In Example 9.10, the negative *IRR* was below the yield on each of the zero coupon bonds used in the project's tracking portfolio and the *NPV* was negative.

An Example with Multiple IRRs.   One reason it was easy to compare the conclusions derived from the *NPV* and *IRR* in Examples 9.9 and 9.10 is that both examples had only one *IRR*. Whenever the cash flows have only one *IRR*, the internal rate of return method and the net present value method usually will result in the same decision. However, the project in Example 9.11, for instance, has multiple internal rates of return, making comparisons between the two methods rather difficult.

Example 9.11:   Multiple Internal Rates of Return

Strip Mine, Inc., is considering a project with cash flows described in the following table.

Cash Flows (in $millions) at Date			
0	*1*	*2*	*3*
−10	41	−30	−1

Compute the *IRR* of this project.
   Answer: This project has two internal rates of return, 213.19 percent and 0 percent, determined by making different initial guesses in the *IRR* program of a financial calculator or spreadsheet.

Exhibit 9.1 outlines the net present value of the project in Example 9.11 as a function of various hypothetical discount rates. The exhibit shows two discount rates at which the *NPV* is zero.

Multiple internal rates of return can (but do not have to, as Example 9.10 illustrates) arise when there is more than one sign reversal in the cash flow pattern. To better understand this concept, let us denote the plus sign (+) if the cash flow is positive and minus (−) if a cash flow is negative. In Example 9.11, the sign pattern is − + − −, which has two sign reversals: one sign reversal occurs between dates 0 and 1, when the cash flow sign switches from negative to positive, the other between dates 1 and 2, when the cash flow sign switches from positive to negative.

In Example 9.11, it is obvious that 0 percent is an internal rate of return because the sum of the cash flows is zero. As the interest rate increases to slightly above zero, the future cash flows have a present value that exceeds $10 million because a small positive discount rate has a larger effect on the negative cash flows at $t = 2$ and $t = 3$ than it does at $t = 1$. With very high interest rates, however, even the cash flow at $t = 1$ is greatly diminished after discounting; and subsequently higher discount rates lower the present value of the future cash flows. Thus, as the interest rate increases, eventually there will be a discount rate that results in an *NPV* of zero. This rate is 213.19 percent.

EXHIBIT 9.1   Net Present Value for Cash Flows in Example 9.11 as a Function of Discount Rates

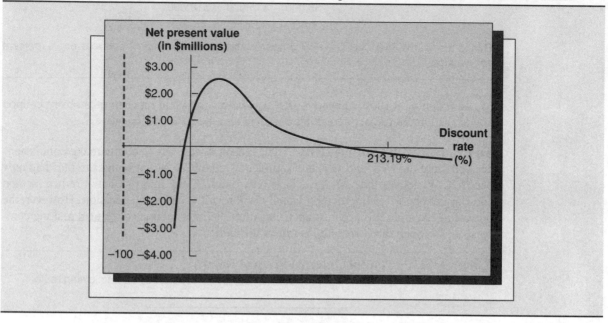

An Example with No IRR.   It is also possible to have no *IRR,* as Example 9.12 illustrates.

Example 9.12:   An Example Where No IRR Exists

A group of statisticians is thinking of taking a 2-period leave from their academic positions to form a consulting firm for analyzing survey data from polls in political campaigns. The project has cash flows described by the following table:

	Cash Flows (in $000s) at Date	
0	*1*	*2*
10	−30	35

Compute its *IRR.*
    Answer: This project has no internal rate of return.

As Exhibit 9.2 illustrates, all positive and negative discount rates (above −100 percent) make the discounted cash flow stream from the project positive. This appears to be a very good project, indeed! If the signs on the cash flows were reversed, all positive and negative discount rates would make the net present value of the project negative. However, there is still no internal rate of return. Thus, the lack of an *IRR* does not indicate whether a project creates or destroys firm value.

EXHIBIT 9.2 Net Present Value for Cash Flows in Example 9.12 as a Function of Discount Rates

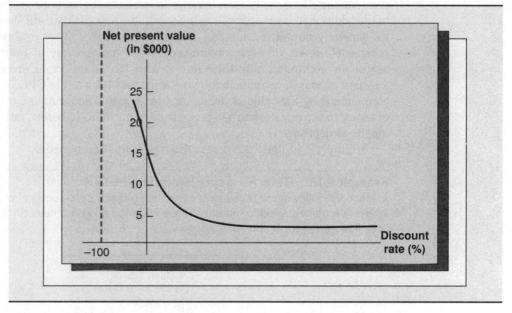

Term Structure Issues

The previous material illustrated problems that arise with the internal rate of return method because of multiple internal rates of return in some cases and none in others. Additional problems exist when the term structure of riskless interest rates is not flat. In this case, there is ambiguity about what the appropriate hurdle rate should be. In general, long-maturity riskless bonds have different yields to maturity than short-maturity riskless bonds, implying that the appropriate hurdle rate should be different for evaluating riskless cash flows occurring at different time periods. Although this creates no problem for the net present value method, it does create difficulties when the internal rate of return method is applied.

Most businesses, confused about what the appropriate *IRR* hurdle rate should be, take a coupon bond of similar maturity to the project and use its yield to maturity as the hurdle rate. This kind of bond has a yield that is a weighted average of the zero coupon yields attached to each of the bond's cash flows. While this may provide a reasonable approximation of the appropriate hurdle rate in a few instances, using the yield of a single-coupon bond as the hurdle rate for the *IRR* comparison generally will not provide the same decision criteria as the net present value method. Result 9.4 outlines a technique for computing a hurdle rate that makes the net present value method and the internal rate of return method equivalent in cases where the *IRR* is applicable, even when the term structure of interest rates is not flat.

Result 9.4   The appropriate hurdle rate for comparison with the *IRR* is that which makes the sum of the discounted *future* cash flows of the project equal to the present (or market) value of those *future* cash flows, as given by the selling price of the tracking portfolio of the future cash flows.

Although the hurdle rate in Result 9.4 generates the same *IRR*-based decision as the net present value method, it requires additional computations. Indeed, an analyst has to compute the *PV* of the project in order to compute the appropriate hurdle rate. Because of the additional work—as well as other pitfalls in its use that will shortly be discussed—we generally do not recommend the *IRR* as an approach for evaluating an investment project. However, in some circumstances, the internal rate of return method may be useful for communicating the value created by taking on an investment project. An assistant treasurer, communicating his or her analysis to the CFO, may have more luck communicating the value of taking on a project by comparing the project's internal rate of return to the rate of return of a comparable portfolio of bonds, rather than by presenting the project's *NPV*.

Example 9.13 illustrates a case that makes this comparison.

Example 9.13:   Term Structure Issues and the IRR

Assume the following for Finalcon's consulting project: Zero-coupon bonds maturing at date 1 have a 6 percent yield to maturity, those maturing at date 2 have an 8 percent yield, while cash flows are given in the table below.

Cash Flows (in $000s) at Date		
0	1	2
−80	40	50

The *NPV* of the project is $602.79, which is positive, indicating a good project. The *IRR* of the project is 7.92 percent. Does the internal rate of return also indicate that it is a good project?

Answer: There is ambiguity about which number the internal rate of return must be compared to. If one compares the *IRR* with 6 percent, it appears to be a good project, but it is a bad project if compared with a hurdle rate of 8 percent.

The appropriate comparison is with some weighted average of 6 percent and 8 percent. That number is another internal rate of return: the yield to maturity of a bond portfolio with payments of $40,000 at date 1 and $50,000 at date 2. In a market with no arbitrage, this bond should sell for its present value, $80,602.79 because

$$\$80,602.79 = \frac{\$40,000}{1.06} + \frac{\$50,000}{(1.08)^2}$$

Its yield to maturity is the number *y* that makes:

$$0 = \$80,602.79 + \frac{\$40,000}{1 + y} + \frac{\$50,000}{(1 + y)^2}$$

which is 7.39 percent. Since the project's internal rate of return, 7.92 percent, exceeds the 7.39 percent *IRR* (or yield to maturity) of the portfolio of zero-coupon bonds that track the future cash flows of the project, it should be accepted.

Cash Flow Sign Patterns and the Number of Internal Rates of Return

Adopting a project only when the internal rate of return exceeds the hurdle rate is consistent with the net present value rule as long as the pattern of cash flows has *one sign reversal* and *cash outflows precede cash inflows*. One example of this is the later cash flow sign pattern (of pluses and minuses) seen below for cash flows at six consecutive dates:

Date 0–5 Time Line					
Cash Flow Sign at Date					
0	*1*	*2*	*3*	*4*	*5*
−	−	+	+	+	+

Later Cash Flow Streams.   While the illustration above has two negative cash flows followed by four positive ones, a later cash flow stream can have an arbitrary number of both negative and positive cash flows. Having only *one* sign reversal, however, means that a later cash flow stream can have only one *IRR*.

The uniqueness of the *IRR* in a later cash flow stream is best demonstrated by looking at the value of the cash flow stream at the date when the sign of the cash flow has just changed. If, for some discount rate, the value of the entire cash flow stream, discounted to that date is zero, then that discount rate corresponds to an *IRR*. Let's look at the value of the cash flow stream at date 2 in the blue-shaded time line above, where the cash flow sign has changed from negative to positive. If the value of the entire stream of the six cash flows is zero at date 2 for discount rate r, then the value of the stream at date 0 is simply the date 2 value divided by $(1 + r)^2$. Thus, if the date 2 value of the six cash flows is zero in the date 0–5 time line, their value at date 0 is also zero, which makes r, by definition, an *IRR*.

Without assigning actual numbers to these cash flows, it is possible to represent schematically the date 2 values of the positive and negative cash flows separately (see Exhibit 9.3 on page 342). Panel A illustrates that the date 2 value of the four positive cash flows in the time line always diminishes as the discount rate increases. Moreover, for a very large discount rate, their date 2 value is close to zero. For a very small discount rate (i.e., close to −100 percent), their date 2 value becomes large.

The opposite is true for the value at date 2 of the two negative cash flows at dates 0 and 1 (see panel B of Exhibit 9.3). Their negative date 2 value is becoming more negative as the discount rate increases. For a very small discount rate (close to −100 percent), the value is small and close to the size of the date 2 cash flow. For a very large discount rate, the date 2 value of the cash flows at dates 0 and 1 is extremely negative. Hence, summing the date 2 values of the positive and negative cash flows (see panel C of Exhibit 9.3), one finds that at low discount rates the sum is large and positive (point *A* in panel C) while at high interest rates it is negative (point *B* in panel C). As one increases the discount rate, the negative date 2 value from the first two cash flows becomes increasingly negative whereas the positive value from the last four cash flows becomes smaller. The *IRR* coincides with the discount rate where the date 2 values of the stream's positive and negative cash flows just offset each other.

Two important insights come from Exhibit 9.3. First, there always is a unique internal rate of return for a later cash flow stream. Second, if discounting *all cash flows* (present and future) with the hurdle rate yields a positive discounted value, the *IRR* is larger than the hurdle rate. In other words, only a larger discount rate achieves a zero discounted value. Conversely, a negative *NPV* implies that the *IRR* lies to the left of the hurdle rate.

EXHIBIT 9.3   Date 2 Values

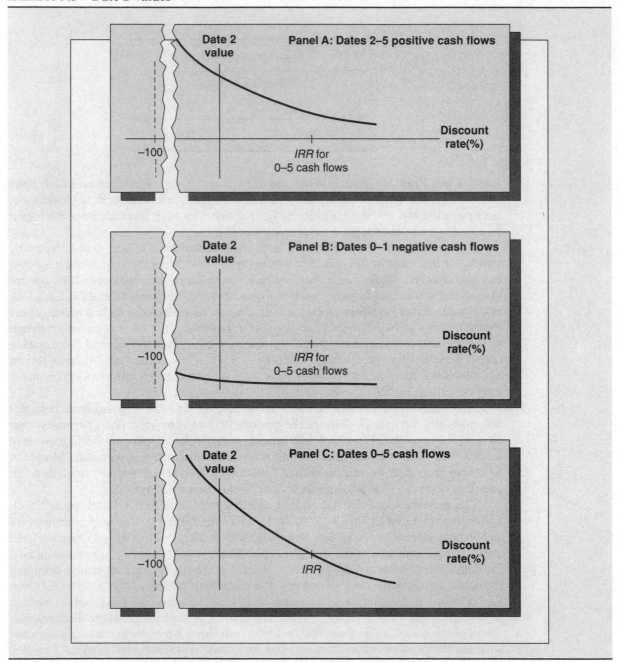

Early Cash Flow Streams.   Examples 9.14 and 9.15 illustrate the intuition developed earlier about how to apply the internal rate of return method, depending on whether the positive portion of the cash flow stream is later or earlier.

Example 9.14:   Implementing the IRR Rule for Investing

Refer to the Joe's Bowling Alley project in Example 9.9, where the stream of cash flows (in $000s) at dates 0, 1, 2, and 3 was $C_0 = -9$, $C_1 = 4$, $C_2 = 5$, and $C_3 = 3$, respectively, with associated zero-coupon yields of 8 percent, 5 percent, and 6 percent at maturity dates 1, 2, and 3, respectively. How does the *IRR* compare with the hurdle rate for the project?

Answer: The yield to maturity (or *IRR*), y, of the bond portfolio that tracks the future cash flows of the project satisfies the equation:

$$\frac{\$4,000}{1.08} + \frac{\$5,000}{1.05^2} + \frac{\$3,000}{1.06^3} = \frac{\$4,000}{(1 + y)} + \frac{\$5,000}{(1 + y)^2} + \frac{\$3,000}{(1 + y)^3}$$

The left-hand side, which equals $10,758, is the present value of the *future* cash flows from the project (which is why the −$9,000 initial cash flow does not appear). It is the project's *NPV* less its initial cash flow. It also represents the price of the portfolio of bonds that tracks the future cash flows of the project. The *IRR*, or y, on the portfolio of bonds is the constant discount rate that makes the portfolio a zero *NPV* investment. This number, about 5.92 percent, represents the hurdle rate for the project. Since the project's internal rate of return, the 16.6 percent found in Example 9.9, exceeds the hurdle rate, one should adopt the project.

Example 9.15:   Implementing the IRR Rule for Borrowing Needs

Consider the cancellation of the project in Example 9.14, "the old project," immediately after Joe's Bowling Alley made the adoption decision. In other words, the decision was made not to relacquer the lanes following the earlier decision to relacquer them. What are the cash flows from canceling the project? How does the *IRR* compare with the hurdle rate in this case?

Answer: The relevant incremental cash flows for the cancellation decision (a project in its own right) are found by subtracting the cash flow position of the bowling alley when it adopted the lane relacquering project from its cash flow position without the project. These cash flows are simply the negatives of the cash flows in Example 9.3: $9,000 at $t = 0$, −$4,000 at $t = 1$, −$5,000 at $t = 2$, and −$3,000 at $t = 3$. The net present value calculation is:

$$\$9,000 - \frac{\$4,000}{1.08} - \frac{\$5,000}{1.05^2} - \frac{\$3,000}{1.06^3} = -\$1,758$$

The internal rate of return and the hurdle rate are still the same, approximately 16.6 percent and 5.92 percent, respectively. Reversing signs does not change the *IRR* calculation! Thus, as in Example 9.14, the *IRR* exceeds the hurdle rate.

In Example 9.15, the net present value rule says that canceling the project, once adopted, is a bad decision. This makes sense because Example 9.14 determined that adopting the project was a good decision. From the standpoint of the *IRR*, it also makes sense. The pattern of cash flows from the cancellation of the project has signs that can be described by the early cash flow pattern $+ - - -$. Like the later cash flows, this pattern has only one sign change and thus has only one *IRR*. Because this cash flow sign pattern is more like borrowing than investing, the appropriate *IRR*-based investment evaluation rule is to *accept* a project when the IRR is *lower* than the hurdle rate and reject it otherwise (as in this case).

The Correct Hurdle Rate with Multiple Hurdle Rates.   The internal rate of return is unique when a cash flow sign pattern exhibits the pattern of an early cash flow stream or a later cash flow stream. Even in these cases, however, there may still be multiple hurdle rates if the term structure of interest rates is not flat. The point of this subsection is that no one should worry about these cases.

For a later cash flow stream where the present values of the *future* cash flows of the project are negative (which can only happen if the stream starts off with two or more negative cash flows), two interest rates can be candidates for the hurdle rate if hurdle rates are computed with the procedure suggested in Result 9.4.[15] A negative *PV* and a negative initial cash flow implies a negative *NPV*. Clearly, the correct hurdle rate is one that results in rejection. Fortunately, both of these hurdle rates will exceed the *IRR*, which thus tells us to reject the project, as Example 9.16 illustrates.[16]

Example 9.16:   Multiple Hurdle Rates

The following time line describes the cash flows of a bad project developed by a team at Idiots, Inc. The appropriate discount rates for riskless cash flows of various maturities are given below the cash flows.

Cash Flows and Discount Rates for Date			
0	1	2	3
−$5	−$10	$5	$5
	4%	5%	6%

Compute the *IRR* and the two hurdle rates for the project.

Answer: The unique *IRR* is −19.81 percent. The hurdle rates are found by first discounting the cash flows from years 1–3, which gives a present value of −$.882. The cash flows of the (zero *NPV*) bond portfolio that tracks the *future* cash flows of the project are therefore:

Tracking Portfolio Cash Flows at Date			
0	1	2	3
$.882	−$10	$5	$5

Note that, in contrast to the cash flows of the project, the cash flows of the tracking portfolio have two sign changes and thus may have more than one *IRR*. The two hurdle rates of the four cash flows of the tracking portfolio are 6.86 percent and 976.04 percent. Both hurdle rates exceed the *IRR*, implying the project should be rejected.

---

[15]As we demonstrate shortly, the reason that two hurdle rates may sometimes arise is that the hurdle rates are themselves internal rates of return of a portfolio of zero-coupon bonds. If this bond portfolio has a cash flow pattern with more than one sign reversal (implying both long and short positions in zero-coupon bonds), it is possible for two internal rates of return to exist. In the following sections, the existence and implications of multiple internal rates of return are described in greater detail.

[16]A similar problem arises with an early cash flow stream when the present value of its future cash flows is positive. In this case, the project has a positive *NPV*. If the project has two hurdle rates because of this, both will exceed the *IRR* and indicate that the project should be adopted. Since a project has a positive *NPV* when it has an early cash flow stream with future cash flows that have a positive present value, the internal rate of return rule in this case makes the correct decision, regardless of which of the two hurdle rates is used.

These considerations suggest the following *IRR* adoption rule for projects with later and early cash flow streams:

Result 9.5   (*The appropriate internal rate of return rule.*) In the absence of constraints, a project with a later cash flow stream should be adopted only if its internal rate of return exceeds the hurdle rate(s). A project with an early cash flow stream should only be adopted if the hurdle rate(s) exceed the internal rate of return of the project.

Sign Reversals and Multiple Internal Rates of Return

The last subsection noted that multiple internal rates of return for the bond portfolio that tracks the project, and thus determines the hurdle rates, do not prevent us from using the *IRR* to determine whether projects with later or early cash flow streams should be adopted. By contrast, the existence of multiple internal rates of return for the project's cash flows has a major impact on one's ability to use the *IRR* for evaluating investments.[17]

A project could have more than one internal rate of return if its cash flows exhibit more than one sign reversal. These multiple sign reversals can arise for many reasons. For example, environmental regulations may require the owner of a strip mine to restore the land to a pristine state after the mine is exhausted. Or the tax authorities may not require a firm to pay the corporate income tax on the sale of a profitable product until one year after the profit is earned. In this case, the last cash flow for the project is merely the tax paid on the last year the project earned profits. The next section illustrates how mutually exclusive projects can create sign reversals, even when the cash flows of the projects per se do not exhibit multiple sign reversals.

In the event of multiple sign reversals like this, many practitioners employ very complicated and often ad hoc adjustments to the internal rate of return calculation. In principle (although rarely in practice), these adjustments can ensure that the *IRR* rule yields the same decisions as the net present value rule. However, it makes little sense to bother with these troublesome procedures when the net present value rule gives the correct answer and is easier to implement.

Mutually Exclusive Projects and the Internal Rate of Return

When selecting one project from a group of alternatives, the net present value rule indicates that the project with the largest positive net present value is the best project.

Do Not Select the Project with the Largest IRR.   It is easy, but foolhardy, to think that one should extend this idea to the internal rate of return criterion and adopt the project with the largest *IRR*. Even if all the projects under consideration are riskless and have the later cash flow stream pattern, each project might have different hurdle rates if the term structure of interest rates is not flat. If the project with a large *IRR* also has a larger hurdle rate than the other projects, how does one decide? Is it then more appropriate to look at the difference between the internal rate of return and the cost of capital or the ratio? Fortunately, it is unnecessary to answer this question because even if all the

---

[17]However, Cantor and Lippman (1983) have shown that multiple internal rates of return can have useful interpretations. Specifically, when lending is possible at a rate of *r* but borrowing is not possible and projects are repeated in time because cash from the first run of the project is needed to fund the second project, and so on, then if discounting at *r* yields a positive *NPV* for the project, the smallest *IRR* above *r* represents the growth rate of the project if the project is repeated in perpetuity.

projects have the same hurdle rate, the largest internal rate of return project is not the best, as Example 9.17 illustrates.

Example 9.17:   Mutually Exclusive Projects and the IRR

Centronics, Inc., has two projects, each with a discount rate of 2 percent per period. The table below describes their cash flows, net present values, and internal rates of return.

	Cash Flows (in $millions) at Date			NPV at 2% (in $millions)	IRR
	0	1	2		
Project A	−10	−16	30	$3.149	10.79%
Project B	−10	2	11	$2.534	15.36%

Given that Centronics must select only one project, should it choose A or B?

Answer: The net present value of project A, about $3.149 million, is higher than the net present value of B, about $2.534 million. Thus, project A is better than project B, even though it has a lower internal rate of return.

The appropriate *IRR*-based procedure for evaluating mutually exclusive projects is similar to that used for the net present value rule: Subtract the cash flows of the next best alternative. If one is lucky and the difference in the cash flow streams of the two projects have an early or later sign pattern, one can choose which of the two projects is better. In Example 9.17, the cash flows of project A less those of project B can be described by the following table:

	Cash Flows (in $millions) at Date			NPV at 2% (in $millions)	IRR
	0	1	2		
Project A − B:	0	−18	19	.615	5.56%

There is only one sign reversal and a later cash flow. The implication is that project A is better than project B because the 5.56 percent *IRR* is higher than the 2 percent hurdle rate.

How Multiple Internal Rates of Return Arise from Mutually Exclusive Projects.
The last subsection showed how differencing the cash flows of two projects might lead to a correct *IRR*-based rule for evaluating mutually exclusive projects. The key concept is that the comparison of the pair leads to a differenced cash flow that has only one sign reversal. If there are many projects, a large number of comparisons of two projects like those described in the last subsection must be made. As Example 9.18 demonstrates, it is highly likely that some of the differenced cash flows will have more than one sign reversal, even if both projects have later or early cash flow sign patterns.

Example 9.18:   Multiple IRRs from Mutually Exclusive Projects

Refer back to Example 9.6, where NASA must select one of three commercial projects for the next space shuttle mission. Each of these projects has industrial spin-offs that will pay off in the next two years. The cash flows, net present values, and internal rates of return of the projects are described below:

	Cash Flow (in $millions) at Date			NPV at 2% (in $millions)	IRR
	0	1	2		
Project A	−17.0	12	9	3.415	16.16%
Project B	−16.8	10	11	3.577	15.98
Project C	−16.9	11	10	3.496	16.07

Which project should NASA select?

Answer: The net present value criterion indicates that project B is the best project, even though it has the *lowest IRR*. The internal rate of return criterion fails because the differences in the cash flows of various pairs of projects have multiple internal rates of return. In this case, there are three pairs of cash flow differences:

	Cash Flow (in $millions) at Date			NPV at 2% (at $millions)	IRR
	0	1	2		
Project A − B	−.2	2	−2	−.162	12.7% and 787.3%
Project A − C	−.1	1	−1	−.081	12.7 and 787.3
Project B − C	.1	−1	1	.081	12.7 and 787.3

The multiple internal rates of return arise from the two sign reversals in the cash flow differences, which—being identical for all three differences—provide no information about the best project.

On the other hand, the net present value, based on cash flow differences, selects project B, which was the project with the highest NPV without cash flow differencing. The reason that cash flow differences alone tell us that project B is the best of the three projects is twofold:

- The difference between the cash flows of projects A and B has a negative *NPV,* indicating A is worse than B.
- The difference between the cash flows of projects B and C has a positive *NPV,* indicating B is better than C.

The net present value criterion tells us to adopt the project with the largest positive net present value. The appropriateness of this rule follows from the value additivity property of the net present value formula. However, the value additivity property does not apply to the *IRR*.

9.6 Popular but Incorrect Procedures for Evaluating Real Investments

Other evaluation methods besides *NPV* and *IRR* exist, including ratio comparisons, exemplified by the price to earnings multiple, and the competitive strategies approach.[18] This section briefly discusses two popular rules of thumb used by managers to evaluate investment projects: the *payback* and the *accounting rate of return* methods.

The Payback Method

The **payback method** evaluates projects based on the number of years needed to recover the initial capital outlay for a project. For example, an investment that costs $1 million and returns $250,000 per year would have a payback of four years. By the payback criterion, this investment would be preferred to a $1 million investment that returned $200,000 per year and thus had a payback of five years.

A major problem with the payback method is that it ignores cash flows that occur after the project is paid off. For example, most of us would prefer the second project over the first if the second project generated $200,000 per year for the next 20 years and the first project generated $250,000 per year for only 5 years and nothing thereafter. There is no reason to ignore cash flows after the payback period except that the payback method provides a simple rule of thumb that may help managers make quick decisions on relatively minor projects.[19] Experienced managers do not need a financial calculator to tell them that a routine minor project with a one-year payback has a positive *NPV*. They know this is almost always the case.

The Accounting Rate of Return Criterion

The **accounting rate of return** criterion evaluates projects by comparing the project's **return on assets**, which is the accounting profit earned on the project divided by the amount invested to acquire the project's assets. The accounting rate of return is then compared with some hurdle rate in the same manner as the internal rate of return decision rule.

Our principle objection to this criterion is that accounting profits are often very different from the cash flows generated by a project. When making a comparison between a project and its tracking portfolio, we understand why it would be inappropriate to use earnings in such a calculation.

The wealth creation associated with the net present value rule is based on the date 0 arbitrage profits from a long position in the project and a short position in the project's tracking portfolio. This combined position is supposed to eliminate all future cash flows to allow a comparison between the date 0 cost of the investment strategy in real assets and the date 0 cost of the tracking portfolio's financial assets as the basis for deciding whether value is created or destroyed. However, all future cash flows are not eliminated in attempting to match the project's earnings with a tracking portfolio. Paying the cash flows on the tracking portfolio to some outside investor requires actual cash, which is not balanced by the reported earnings generated by the project. Earnings differ from cash flows for a number of reasons, including, notably, depreciation.

---

[18] See Chapter 11.

[19] Variations of the payback method, such as discounted payback, also exist. This method suffers from a similar deficiency of ignoring cash flows after the payback period.

9.7 Summary and Conclusions

This chapter focused on the project selection decision. Since projects have cash flows that occur in the future, it is important to have a selection technique that accounts for the greater interest earning capability of cash that arrives sooner. The best way of taking the time value of money into account is to study carefully how investors value existing portfolios of securities with cash flows that are similar to the cash flows of the project.

In assessing investment projects, the net present value rule properly accounts for the time value of money and is easy to implement when the future cash flows are riskless. The net present value rule also is useful for evaluating risky cash flows, as will be seen in later chapters, and it is easily modified to account for various capital constraints. The internal rate of return rule, the other major alternative, also accounts for the time value of money, but it is too fraught with ambiguities to be used appropriately except in special circumstances.

Despite this, the *IRR* rule is still widely used. We have no good explanation for this. It may be that practitioners prefer to think about rates of return rather than about present values when making decisions. However, the net profitability rate, a variation on the net present value rule, is couched in terms of the rate of return and is not as popular as the *IRR*.

Many businesses, aware of the problems inherent in multiple internal rates of return, have adopted procedures that "correct" for the flaws in the *IRR*-based capital allocation criterion. One correction of this type is to compute an internal rate of return by first computing the sum of the discounted future negative cash flows at the hurdle rate and then adding this to the initial cash flow. The adjusted *IRR* is then computed as the rate that makes this sum plus the discounted value of all future positive cash flows (discounted at the adjusted *IRR*) equal to zero. Another correction finds the "internal rate of return" for the project as if only two cash flows existed: an initial cash flow and a cash flow at the terminal date of the project that is equivalent in value to the future cash flows of the project.

These methods are not really internal rate of return methods, but merely variations of the net profitability rate (a different way of expressing the net present value criterion). These adaptations work fine in the absence of particular constraints; however, it is easy to misuse these methods when such constraints exist. For example, the method that computes the value of future cash flows at the project's terminal date essentially spreads the rate of return from the net profitability rate over the life of the project. However, if capital is constrained only in the early stages of a project, this method is unfairly biased toward shorter-term projects.

If may be that firms tend to be overly optimistic about the cash flows that stem from a project. In this case, firms using the net present value rule would favor longer-term projects more than firms using the *IRR* rule or its adaptations. The bias of the net present value rule in favoring longer-term projects occurs because each additional year of overly optimistic cash flows would increase the net present value. However, we think that using an inappropriate rule is a poor way to correct the tendency of a firm's employees to exaggerate cash flow estimates.

Firms use other rules and rules of thumb to evaluate investments. In contrast to the internal rate of return method, which can be justified under some circumstances, the payback and accounting rate of return methods are not sound decision criteria. Specifically, payback and accounting rates of return are based on accounting concepts. Unlike the *IRR* and *NPV* rules, they do not adjust for the time value of money. As a result, they are being used less and less for evaluating major investments. That obviously inferior rules, like payback and accounting rate of return, are used at all for major decision making suggests to us that the commonly used *IRR* rule contains no hidden virtue that makes it superior to *NPV*. We suspect that *IRR* rules, like the accounting-based rules, persist because of habits or ignorance and over time, we expect to see the use of *IRR* diminish.

Key Concepts

Result 9.1: The wealth maximizing net present value criterion is that:

- All projects with positive net present values should be accepted.
- All projects with negative net present values should be rejected.

Result 9.2: For a project with riskless cash flows, the *NPV*, that is, the market value of the project's tracking portfolio less the cost of initiating the project, and the discounted value of all present and future cash flows of the project are the same.

Result 9.3: The discounted value of the stream of *EVA*s of a project is the same as the net present value of the project.

Result 9.4: The appropriate hurdle rate for comparison with the IRR is that which makes the sum of the discounted *future* cash flows of the project equal to the present (or market) value of those *future* cash flows, as given by the selling price of the tracking portfolio of the future cash flows.

Result 9.5: (*The appropriate internal rate of return rule*.) In the absence of constraints, a project with a later cash flow stream should be adopted only if its internal rate of return exceeds the hurdle rate(s). A project with an early cash flow stream should only be adopted if the hurdle rate(s) exceed the internal rate of return of the project.

Key Terms

Exercises

9.1. Your firm has recently reached an expansion phase and is seeking possible new geographic regions to market the newly patented chemical compound Glupto. The five regional projections are as follows:

Years from Now:	Cash Flows (in $millions)					
	0	1	2	3	4	5
Northeast	−95	15	20	25	30	30
Midwest	−75	15	20	20	25	30
Southeast	−60	10	15	20	20	25
West Coast	−35	5	10	10	15	15
Southwest	−20	5	5	6	6	10
Zero-coupon yields (%)		6.5%	7%	7%	7.5%	8%

a. Which regions would be profitable to the firm? Which of the five is most profitable?

b. If current budgeting can support a $100 million expenditure in year 0, what combination of regions is optimal?

c. Assume now that you can expand without regional saturation. With the budget constraint in part *b*, which region is optimal?

9.2. The Wheatena Company is considering the purchase of a new milling machine. What purchase price makes the *NPV* of the project zero? Base your analysis on the following facts:

• The new milling machine will reduce operating expenses by exactly $20,000 per year for 10 years. Each of these cash flow reductions takes place at the end of the year.

• The old milling machine is now 5 years old and has 10 years of scheduled life remaining.

It was purchased for $45,000 and has a current market value of $20,000.

- There are no taxes or inflation.
- The risk-free rate is 10 percent.

Exercises 9.3–9.6 make use of the following information:

Small Corp. is investigating a possible new project, project X, which would affect corporate cash flow as follows:

Cash Flows (in $) of Small Corp. without Project X in Year					
0	1	2	3	4	5
150	175	185	185	195	200

Cash Flows (in $) of Small Corp. with Project X in Year					
0	1	2	3	4	5
110	165	200	205	210	213

9.3. Respond to parts *a* through *d*.
   a. What are the incremental cash flows associated with Small Corp.'s undertaking project X? Are these inflows or outflows, costs or revenue?
   b. What is the *PV* of project X under a flat term structure of 8 percent, compounded annually, irrespective of maturity.
   c. Under these assumptions, what is the hurdle rate? Without further calculation, determine whether the *IRR* for project X is higher or lower than the hurdle rate. (*Hint:* Use part *b*.)
   d. Why might a flat rate structure be unrealistic?

9.4. Describe the equivalent tracking portfolio for project X, giving long and short positions and amounts, under a flat term structure of 8 percent, compounded annually. Conceptually, why are we interested in tracking project X's cash flows with a portfolio of marketable securities?

9.5. Let B_t = price per $100 of face value of a zero-coupon bond maturing at year t. Then, if $B_1 = \$94.00$, $B_2 = \$88.20$, $B_3 = \$81.50$, $B_4 = \$76.00$, and $B_5 = \$73.00$:
   a. Determine zero-coupon rates for years 1 through 5 to the nearest .01 percent.
   b. Consider the tracking portfolio in exercise 9.4. What is the cost or revenue associated with such a portfolio at date 0?
   c. What is the *NPV* of Project X?
   d. How are your answers to parts *b* and *c* related?

9.6. Consider the cash flows associated with undertaking Project X.
   a. Is this an early or later cash flow stream?
   b. Based on the rates in exercise 9.5, what is the hurdle rate? What does such a rate represent?
   c. Calculate the *IRR* for Project X.
   d. Based on the hurdle rate calculated and a comparison with the *IRR*, should Small Corp. undertake the project?
   e. If the sign of each cash flow were reversed, how would the hurdle rate and project *IRR* change? How would Small Corp.'s decision change? Why?

9.7. As a regional managing director of Finco, a U.S.-based investment company, your mandate is to scour the Midwest in search of promising investment opportunities and to recommend *one project* to corporate headquarters in Los Angeles. Your analysts have screened thousands of prospective ventures and passed on the following four projects for your final review:

	Cash Flows (in $millions)					
Years from Now:	0	1	2	3	4	5
Project 1	−40	10	10	15	15	20
Project 2	−25	5	5	10	15	15
Project 3	−20	5	5	5	10	15
Project 4	−15	3	3	6	6	13
Zero-coupon yields (%)	—	5%	5%	6%	6%	5%

   a. Calculate the *NPV*, hurdle rate, and *IRR* for each project. Which project appears most promising?
   b. Determine *NPV*s using pairwise project comparisons to verify your decision from part *a*.
   c. How would your answer change if all projects could be scaled and you have a year 0 budget constraint of $50 million? (*Hint:* Calculate profitability indexes.)

9.8. ABC Metalworks wants to determine which model sheetcutter to purchase. Three choices are available, (1) machine 1 costs the least but must be replaced the most frequently, (2) machine 2 has average cost and average lifespan, and (3) machine 3 costs the most but needs only infrequent replacement. Assume all three machines meet production quality and volume standards. Annual maintenance is inversely proportional to the purchase price (i.e., the cheaper machine requires higher maintenance), and machine replacement, being instantaneous, will not disrupt production.

	Machine 1	Machine 2	Machine 3
Initial cost	$2,000	$3,200	$4,500
Annual maintenance	$ 400	$ 300	$ 200
Life span	2 years	3 years	4 years

a. Under a flat discount rate assumption of 5 percent, calculate the *NPV* for each machine.
b. Which machine makes the most sense for cost efficient production?
c. How does your answer to part *b* change under a flat 6 percent discount rate assumption? Why?

9.9. Investco, a West Coast research company, must decide on the level of computer technology it will buy for its analysis department. Package A, a midlevel technology, would cost $2.5 million for firmwide installation, while package B, a higher-level technology, would cost $3.5 million. Equipped with A-level technology, the firm could generate a cash flow of $1.5 million for two years before the technology would require replacement; with level-B technology, the firm could generate a cash flow of $1.7 million for three years, after which the technology would require replacement. Investco is interested in a six-year planning horizon. Assume the following about discount rates:

Zero-Coupon Yields for Year					
1	2	3	4	5	6
5%	5.5%	6%	6%	6.5%	7%

a. What is the nearest terminal date that is concurrent for both packages? What are the associated cash flows for each package or sequence of packages?
b. What is the optimal decision, given Investco's planning horizon?
c. At approximately what alternative package B price would Investco be indifferent between the two packages?

References and Additional Readings

Brealey, Richard, and Stewart Myers. *Principles of Corporate Finance*, 5th ed. New York: McGraw-Hill, 1996.

Cantor, David G., and Steven A. Lippman. 1983, "Investment Selection with Imperfect Capital Markets." *Econometrica* 51 no. 4 (1983), pp. 1121–44.

Hirshleifer, Jack. *Investment, Interest, and Capital*. Englewood Cliffs, NJ: Prentice Hall, 1970.

Pindyck, Robert S., and Daniel L. Rubinfeld. *Econometric Models and Economic Forecasts*, 3d ed. New York: McGraw-Hill, 1991.

Ross, Stephen; Randolph Westerfield; and Jeffrey Jaffe. *Corporate Finance*. 4th ed. Burr Ridge, IL: Richard D. Irwin, 1996.

9A APPENDIX
THE TERM STRUCTURE OF INTEREST RATES

The term structure of interest rates, or yield curve, mentioned earlier in the chapter, is the pattern of yields to maturity for riskless bonds of all maturities. In the United States, for example, the yields from U.S. Treasury securities usually define the term structure. While Treasury securities of all maturities do not always exist, the concept of a term structure is so important to corporate finance and investment management that rates are computed between the existing maturities by interpolating the rates.

Term Structure Varieties

There are a variety of term structures. The **par yield curve** for the United States represents the yields and interpolated yields of on-the-run coupon-paying Treasury securities of various maturities (see Chapter 2). The **annuity term structure** represents the yields to maturity of riskless bonds with level payments. There also is the **spot term structure**, which represents the yields to maturity of zero-coupon bonds of various maturities.

In contrast to the Treasury term structures, par, annuity, and spot **LIBOR term structures** are derived from the Treasury term structures and swap spreads in the interest rate swap market. Adding the swap spreads to the par yield curve of Treasury securities gives the par LIBOR term structure. This represents a set of almost riskless yields because LIBOR rates are based on corporate credits that are comparable to AA and AAA-rated bonds. LIBOR rates may be preferred to Treasury rates in some instances because many Treasury yields are artificially low due to exceptionally favorable financing.[1]

Uses of Spot Yields and Where They Come From

The DCF approach, as exhibited in equation (9.1), makes use of the spot (or zero-coupon) yield curve. Generally, one obtains a more accurate picture of spot yields by looking at the implied zero-coupon yields of par (straight coupon) bonds than by looking at the yields of zero-coupon bonds.

Forces Driving the Term Structure of Interest Rates

Historically, the yield curve has had many shapes. Moreover, yield curves for different countries can have different shapes at the same time. Sometimes it is upward sloping, sometimes downward sloping, sometimes nearly flat, and sometimes it has bumps in it, particularly at the short end. Exhibit 9A.1 shows graphs of par yield curves at four different points in time.

EXHIBIT 9A.1   Par Yield Curves at Four Different Points in History

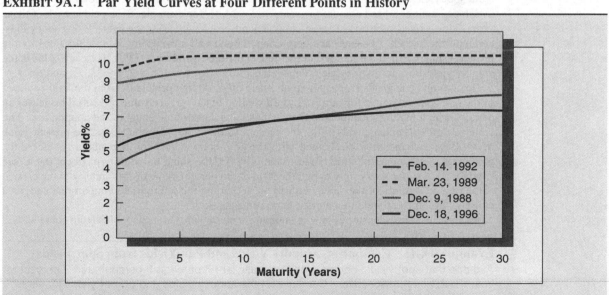

---

[1]See Duffie (1996) or Grinblatt (1995) for a discussion of this issue.

The activities of central banks (e.g., the Federal Reserve System in the United States or the Bundesbank in Germany) generally determine the rates at the short end of the yield curve. Attempts to slow down the economy generally drive up short-term rates while expansionary monetary policy tends to lower short-term rates. Often these policies have an opposite effect at the long end of the yield curve because inflationary expectations often drive the long end of the yield curve. A contractionary monetary policy is often intended to reduce inflation, which reduces long-term yields while simultaneously driving short-term yields upward.

Rates at the short end of the yield curve are generally 30 to 40 percent more volatile than rates at the long end, probably because monetary policy acts primarily at the short end of the curve and is countercyclical. Hence, if long-term prospects are in some sense an average of short-term prospects, and if subsequent short-term prospects tend to reverse mistakes in previous policies or eliminate shocks, then long-term rates will be more stable.

Spot Rates, Annuity Rates, and Par Rates

This subsection discusses how to convert par rates to spot rates and annuity rates, and vice versa. First, it provides a general rule for comparing the three types of term structures, which are graphed in Exhibit 9A.2.

If the term structure of one of the three yield curves (spot, annuity, or par) is consistently upward or downward sloping, the other two yields will slope in the same direction. The spot yield curve will have the steepest slope, the par curve will have the second steepest slope, and the annuity yield curve will have the gentlest slope. If the yield curve is flat, all three yield curves will be identical.[2]

To simplify the analysis of how to translate one type of yield into another, assume that the yields are compounded annually and computed only at years $1, \ldots, T$. Use interpolation to generate approximate yields for fractional years (e.g. 1.5 years or 2.3 years).

Using Spot Yields to Compute Annuity Yields and Par Yields.   Computing annuity yields from spot yields is relatively straightforward. The annuity yield for year t is found by assuming a cash payment of a fixed amount for years $1, 2, \ldots, t$—for example, \$1 is paid at each of those years. This is like a portfolio of t zero-coupon bonds, each with a \$1 face value. Using spot yields, compute the present value of each zero-coupon bond and sum up the t present values. If the present value is P, find the internal rate of return for the cash flows: $-P, 1, 1, \ldots, 1$. This is the annuity yield-to-maturity for date t. Repeat this process for $t = 1, t = 2, t = 3, \ldots$, and $t = T$.

To compute par yields from spot yields, strip off \$100, the principal, from the final payment of the par bond, assumed for purposes of illustration to have a face value of \$100. This leaves an annuity with a maturity identical to the par bond and a cash flow equal to the coupon rate. The annuity's present value equals \$100, the present value of the par bond, less the present value of \$100 paid at maturity, discounted with the zero-coupon rate for that maturity. Since, for par bonds, the coupon rate and yield to maturity are the same on coupon payment dates (see Chapter 2), it is necessary only to find the ratio of the present value of this annuity to the present value of a \$1 annuity of the same maturity to determine the appropriate coupon rate and, as a consequence, the par yield to maturity, in percentage terms.

Example 9A.1 demonstrates how to compute annuity yields and par yields from spot yields.

Example 9A.1:   Computing Annuity Yields and Par Yields from Spot Yields
Assume that spot yields, compounded annually, are 7 percent, 8 percent, and 9 percent for years 1, 2, and 3, respectively. Compute (1) the annuity yields and (2) par yields for years 1, 2, and 3, assuming annual cash flows for these bonds.

---

[2]This relation between the slopes is due to the different timing and size of the cash flows (see Chapter 22) of the three types of bonds.

EXHIBIT 9A.2   Three Types of Yield Curves

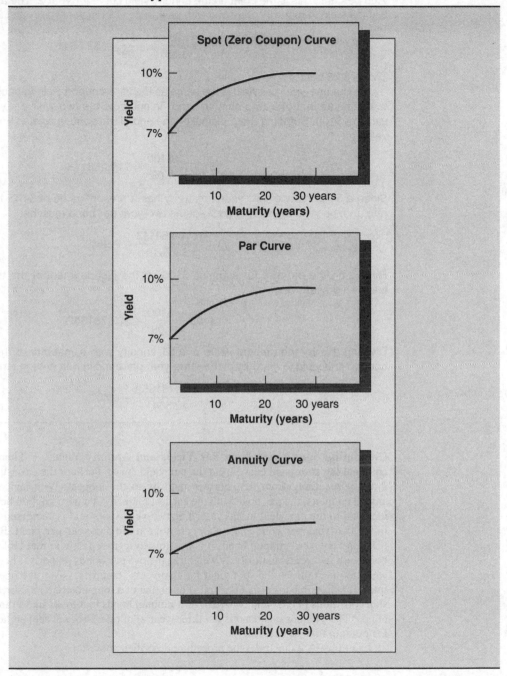

Answer: (1) The annuity yield for year 1 is 7 percent because a one-year annuity with annual payments has only one payment and thus behaves like a zero-coupon bond. The annuity yield for year 2 is found by first computing the present value of a two-year annuity. With $1 payments, such a bond has a value of:

$$\frac{\$1}{1.07} + \frac{\$1}{1.08^2} = \$1.7919$$

The yield to maturity of a bond with a cost of \$1.7919 and payments of \$1 at year 1 and 2 is 7.65 percent. This is the point on the annuity yield curve for year 2. The annuity yield for year 3 is the yield to maturity of a bond with payments of \$1 in years 1, 2, and 3, and a cost of

$$\frac{\$1}{1.07} + \frac{\$1}{1.08^2} + \frac{\$1}{1.09^3} = \$2.5641$$

This is 8.28 percent.

(2) The one-year par yield is the same as the zero-coupon yield because its cash flows are the same as that of a zero-coupon bond. To compute the two-year par yield, assume a face value of \$100. Stripping the principal off the end of the bond leaves an annuity with a present value of:

$$\$100 - \frac{\$100}{1.08^2} = \$14.266118$$

Since a \$1 annuity of two years' maturity has a present value of \$1.7919, both the coupon rate and the yield to maturity (in %) of the two-year par bond must be:

$$\frac{\$14.266118}{\$1.7919} = 7.96\%$$

Repeating the process for stripping \$100 off the last payment of the three-year par bond leaves a present value of:

$$\$100 - \frac{\$100}{1.09^3} = \$22.781652$$

Dividing this by the present value of a \$1 annuity with a maturity of three years gives the coupon and yield to maturity of the three-year par bond in percentage terms:

$$\frac{\$22.781652}{\$2.5641} = 8.88\%$$

Computing Spot Yields from Par Yields and Annuity Yields.   There are many ways to compute the spot yield curve from the par yield curve. Perhaps the easiest way to proceed is to move sequentially from the shortest maturity to the longest. With annual compounding and annual coupons, the par bond with the earliest maturity is a zero-coupon bond. The spot yield is identical to the par yield in this case. The two-year spot yield is computed from a long position in the two-year par bond and a short position in the one-year par bond. Because the one-year par bond is a zero-coupon bond, it is possible to form a portfolio that looks like a zero-coupon bond with two years' maturity by weighting the two par bonds properly. The yield of this properly weighted portfolio is the spot yield for two years' maturity. Given the one- and two-year spot rates, it is possible to form a portfolio consisting of a long position in a three-year par bond and short positions in one- and two-year zero-coupon bonds that looks like a three-year zero coupon bond.[3] The yield of this bond is the three-year spot rate. Proceed sequentially in this manner as far out into time as necessary.

Example 9A.2 illustrates the procedure described above.

Example 9A.2:   Computing Spot Yields from Par Yields
Compute the spot yield curve, assuming annually compounded yields, for years 1, 2, and 3, given par curve yields as follows:

---

[3]See the appendix at the end of the text for cash flows from short positions.

	Maturity in Years		
	1	*2*	*3*
Par yield	9%	8%	7%

All par yields assume coupons paid annually and all yields are compounded annually.

Answer: The one-year spot yield is 9 percent because the one-year par bond is the same as a zero-coupon bond.

The two-year par bond has an 8 percent coupon paid at year 1. As a par bond, its face value is the same as its market value. Assume a face value of $100, although any value will do. The cash flows of this bond are $8 at year 1 and $108 at year 2. The one-year par bond has a cash flow of $109 at year 1. A long position in the two-year $100 par bond and a short position in 8/109 of the one-year $100 par bond has a future cash flow at year 2 in the amount of $108 and no future cash flows at other dates. Thus, the position is equivalent to a two-year zero-coupon bond and, since it has a value of $92.66055 (= $100 − (8/109)$100), the yield of this bond, *r*, satisfies the equation:

$$\$92.66055 = \frac{\$108}{(1 + r)^2}$$

implying *r* = 7.96 percent. Alternatively, knowing that the appropriate discount rate for the $8 coupon of the par bond at year 1 is 9 percent, stripping that coupon leaves a bond with a value of $100 − $8/1.09 = $92.66055, which as seen above, implies a 7.96 percent yield.

To find the year 3 spot rate, strip the two $7 coupons at years 1 and 2 from the par bond. This leaves a bond with a value of

$$\$100 - \frac{\$7}{1.09} - \frac{\$7}{(1.0796)^2} = \$87.5722$$

With a future payoff at year 3 in the amount of $107, and no future cash flows at other dates, the stripped bond now has the payoff of a zero-coupon bond with a 3-year spot yield *r* that solves:

$$\$87.5722 = \frac{\$107}{(1 + r)^3}$$

implying *r* = 6.91 percent.

To compute zero-coupon yields from annuity yields, strip all payments from the annuity except the last one. If the annuity yields are known, the present value of the stripped cash flows and the original annuity is known. This leaves a single future cash flow. The yield to maturity of this cash flow is the spot yield for that maturity.

Example 9A.3 illustrates how to compute spot yields from annuity yields.

Example 9A.3:   Computing Spot Yields from Annuity Yields

If the annuity yields are 7 percent, 7 percent, and 8 percent for years 1, 2, and 3, respectively, compute the spot yields. Assume annual cash flows and annual compounding.

Answer: The first two spot yields are both 7 percent. The first is 7 percent because the annuity is a zero-coupon bond. The second is 7 percent because the annuity yield would be higher (lower) than 7 percent if the spot yield was higher (lower) than 7 percent. (You can prove this with the method we now use.)

The present value of the two-year annuity at 7 percent, using $1 cash flows, is about $1.81. The present value of the three-year annuity at 8 percent is about $2.58. The difference between the values of the two- and three-year annuities is $0.77. For the present value of $1 paid in three years to be $0.77, the 3-year spot yield has to be about 9.15 percent.

Why Spot Yields Should Be Computed from Par Yields.   The term structure of risk-free interest rates given by the Treasury yield curve, is generally computed from on-the-run Treasury bonds. You can think of on-the-run bonds as newborns. They become slightly less interesting to many investors as they become toddlers, and traders begin to lose interest in them as they become children and young adults. As these bonds age, many of them get tucked away into pension accounts and insurance funds to pay off future liabilities. As the actively traded supply of these bonds begins to diminish, it becomes more difficult to use the bonds for short sales. Moreover, the lack of active trading means that investors are never sure whether the price they pay is fair, because the last trading price they observe is often stale.

For this reason, it is useful to focus on the on-the-run bonds to compute a Treasury yield. The prices are fresh, the trading is active, and the opinions of many bond market participants have gone into determining their yields. Even though many zero-coupon Treasury bonds—they are known as Treasury strips—are available, it is still better to infer spot yields from on-the-run par bonds than to compute them directly from the Treasury strips.

While we generally agree with this approach, there is one major caveat. On-the-run Treasury securities do not exist at every maturity. Currently, on-the-run notes and bonds exist for maturities of years 1, 2, 3, 4, 5, 7, 10 and 30 years. What about years 6, 8, 9, and 11–29 years? A similar problem arises if one needs a zero-coupon rate for a fractional horizon such as 3.5 years.

The general procedure to use when maturities for on-the-run securities are missing is to interpolate par yields for the missing maturities and to compute spot rates from the interpolated par yields. While traditional practice typically uses linear interpolation to fill in the missing date, clearly superior nonlinear interpolation procedures also exist which make the yield curve appear to be smooth. These techniques are beyond the scope of this text.

Key Terms for Appendix 9A

Exercises for Appendix 9A

9A.1. A zero-coupon bond maturing two years from now has a yield to maturity of 8 percent (annual compounding). Another zero-coupon bond with the same maturity date has a yield to maturity of 10 percent (annual compounding). Both bonds have a face value of $100.

  a. What are the prices of the zero-coupon bonds?

  b. Describe the cash flows to a long position in the 10 percent zero-coupon bond and a short position in the 8 percent zero-coupon bond.

  c. Are the cash flows in part *b* indicative of arbitrage?

  d. Suppose the 10 percent bond matured in 3 years rather than 2 years. Is there arbitrage now?

9A.2. Compute annuity yields and par yields for years 1, 2, and 3 if spot yields for years 1, 2, and 3 are respectively 4.5 percent, 5 percent, and 5.25 percent. Assume annual compounding for all rates and annual payments for all bonds.

9A.3. Compute spot yields and annuity yields for years 1, 2, 3, and 4 if par yields for years 1, 2, 3, and 4 are, respectively, 4.5 percent, 5 percent, 5.25 percent, and 5.25 percent. Assume annual compounding for all rates and annual payments for all bonds.

References and Additional Readings for Appendix 9A

Duffie, Darrell. "Special Repo Rates." *Journal of Finance* 51 (1996), pp. 493–526.

Grinblatt, Mark. "An Analytic Solution for Interest Rate Swap Spreads." Working paper, University of California, Los Angeles, 1995.

CHAPTER 1

Investing in Risky Projects

Learning Objectives

After reading this chapter you should be able to:

1. Estimate the cost of capital with the CAPM, APT, and dividend discount models.
2. Understand how to implement the comparison approach with the risk-adjusted discount rate method and know its shortcomings.
3. Understand when to use comparison firms and when to use scenarios to obtain present values.
4. Discount expected future cash flows at a risk-adjusted rate and know when to discount the certainty equivalent at a risk-free rate.
5. Identify the certainty equivalent of a risky cash flow, using equilibrium models, risk-free scenarios, and forward prices.

In 1993, the Times Mirror Corporation implemented a new capital allocation system, developed with the aid of the Boston Consulting Group. This system, known as Times Mirror Value Management (TMVM), provided a framework for computing the market values of real investments by discounting cash flows at the cost of capital. The TMVM system committed Times Mirror to base investment decisions systemwide on the discounted value of cash flows rather than on an evaluation of accounting numbers.

In most U.S. firms, managers value risky investments in much the same way that they value riskless investments. First, the manager *forecasts* the future cash flows of the investment and then discounts them at some interest rate. This task, however, is much more difficult for risky investments because (1) the manager needs to know what it means to forecast cash flows when they are risky, and (2) identifying the appropriate discount rate is more complex when cash flows are risky.

One of the lessons of this chapter is that the way one forecasts cash flows determines the discount rate used to obtain present values. This chapter considers two ways to "forecast" a cash flow:

1. Forecast the expected cash flow.
2. Forecast the cash flow adjusted for risk (defined shortly).

First, consider the case (see point 1) where the manager forecasts a stream of expected cash flows for the proposed project. Each **expected cash flow**, generated as the probability-weighted sum of the cash flow in each of a variety of scenarios, could then be discounted with a risk-adjusted discount rate determined by a risk-return model like the CAPM or the APT. Obtaining PV's in this fashion is known as the **risk-adjusted discount rate method**. The TMVM system, described in the chapter's opening vignette, evaluates capital investments in this manner.

As noted above (see point 2), there is another case where managerial forecasts of cash flows are adjusted for risk. As we will see, this does not necessarily present problems when managers are fully aware of the way they are forecasting and understand its implications for the discount rate. However, managers are often unaware of what they are forecasting or how they are adjusting for risk. For example, managers often think they are forecasting expected cash flows when, in reality, their forecasts are not true expectations because they ignore possible events that potentially can make the cash flows zero.

As an illustration of this, consider an energy company, deciding whether to invest hundreds of millions of dollars on a pipeline running through a developing country, knowing that it has a 5 percent chance of losing the entire investment in the event of a change in government. The managers of some energy companies will ignore this threat when they calculate the expected cash flows, but they will increase the discount rate to reflect the higher risk. Instead of employing this ad hoc adjustment to the discount rate, one should adjust the expected cash flows to reflect the possibility of the unfortunate outcome and discount expected cash flows at the appropriate risk-adjusted rate.

In other situations, managers account for the riskiness of a cash flow by reporting a conservative "expected cash flow," that is, they place too much weight on the bad outcomes and too little on the good ones. This procedure, while generally misapplied, has some merit. In some instances, the conservative forecasted cash flow can be viewed as a **certainty equivalent**, or hypothetical riskless cash flow that occurs at the same time and which has the same present value as the risky cash flow being analyzed.[1] Valuing a stream of certainty equivalents with the **certainty equivalent method** involves discounting at the risk-free rate. Thus, for valuation purposes, certainty equivalent cash flows can be treated as if they are certain.

The choice of whether to obtain a present value by discounting an expected cash flow at a risk-adjusted discount rate or by discounting a certainty equivalent cash flow at a risk-free rate depends largely on the information available to value the project. If traded

---

[1]Chapter 7 introduced forward prices for zero-cost financial contracts. The certainty equivalent can be thought of as the preferred terminology for the forward prices of real asset cash flows.

securities exist for companies that have the same line of business as the project, then the beta risk of these comparison securities can be used to identify the appropriate discount rate for the project's expected cash flows. In this case, if the expected cash flows are easier to identify than the certainty equivalents of the cash flows, discounting expected cash flows will be the preferred method.

If it is not possible to identify the beta risk of comparison securities (e.g., because securities in the same line of business are nonexistent), then beta risk needs to be identified from scenarios that allow a statistician to estimate it. In the latter setting, the certainty equivalent method is generally more convenient. In addition, it is sometimes easier to identify certainty equivalent cash flows than expected cash flows, particularly when forward or futures prices exist for commodities that are fundamental to the profitability of the project. In this case, discounting certainty equivalents at a riskless rate of interest would be the preferred method of identifying the present values of real assets.

When applied properly, discounting expected cash flows at a risk-adjusted discount rate and certainty equivalent cash flows at a risk-free discount rate provide the same value for the project's future cash flows. They are equivalent because both methods are applications of the general valuation principle used throughout the text: Identify a tracking portfolio and use its value as an estimate of the value of the asset's future cash flows. Real asset investment should be undertaken only in situations where the financial investments that track the future cash flows of the real asset have a value that exceeds the project's cost.

The approach to valuing risky real assets presented in this chapter is eminently practical. For example, numerous corporations and banks use the two valuation methodologies. Moreover, the chapter analyzes in depth a great number of implementation issues and obstacles.[2]

10.1 Tracking Portfolios and Real Asset Valuation

The discounted cash flow valuation formula (equation (9.1) in Chapter 9) is founded on the tracking portfolio approach. The formula is a statement that the market price of a combination of financial investments that track the future cash flows of the project should be the same as the value of the project's future cash flows.

Although this method is fairly straightforward with riskless cash flows, it is much more difficult to apply to risky projects. A portfolio that perfectly tracks the cash flows of a risky project exists only in special circumstances. One case might be an oil well whose cash flows can be perfectly tracked by a portfolio of forward contracts on oil and some investment in risk-free bonds. Another case is a copper mine, which can be perfectly tracked by a portfolio of copper forward contracts and a risk-free investment.[3] In most cases, however, there will be some *tracking error*; that is, a difference between the cash flows of the tracking portfolio and the cash flows of the project. The analyst who wants to value a project in these cases needs to employ a theory that describes how to generate tracking portfolios for which the tracking error has a present value of zero. The next section elaborates on this point.

---

[2]However, one practical issue of great importance, of which the reader needs to be aware, is not addressed in this chapter: the issue of how corporate taxes affect the valuation of projects financed with debt. Unless the reader is valuing only equity-financed projects or projects with no corporate tax implications, we urge the study of Chapter 12, which addresses this topic.

[3]The oil well and copper mine cases are discussed in Chapter 11.

Asset Pricing Models and the Tracking Portfolio Approach

When tracking error exists, the analyst must appeal to asset pricing models, like the Capital Asset Pricing Model (CAPM) and the arbitrage pricing theory (APT), to derive a project's present value. Specifically, imperfect tracking portfolios can be used for valuation purposes if the tracking error has zero present value, which is the case only when the tracking error is comprised entirely of unsystematic or firm-specific risks.

An Example of How to Use Tracking Portfolios for Valuation.   Consider the cash flows from the following hypothetical project, which, for simplicity, we initially assume can be perfectly tracked by a mix of the market portfolio and the risk-free asset: Faced with the possibility of legalized onshore gambling in Louisiana, the senior management of Hilton Hotels wants to evaluate the prospects for a hotel/casino. To simplify the analysis, focus only on the valuation of a single risky cash flow from the casino to be received by Hilton one year from now. Assume further that this cash flow can take on one of only three values: one in the good state (40 percent probability), the average state (40 percent probability), and the bad state 20 percent probability as shown in the table below. Attached to these states are the future values of the market portfolio per dollar invested.

	Cash Flow Next Year of	
	Hilton Hotel/Casino (in $ millions)	*Market Portfolio (per $1 invested)*
Good state	$12.3	$1.40
Average state	11.3	1.20
Bad state	9.3	.80

If the risk-free rate is 6 percent, the future cash flow of the Hilton Hotel casino can be perfectly tracked by a $10 million investment: $5 million in a risk-free asset and $5 million in the market portfolio. Since a portfolio of financial assets worth $10 million tracks the cash flow of the casino, the value of the casino's future cash flow is $10 million.

Moreover, note that if one were discounting the casino's expected cash flow to obtain a present value, the appropriate discount rate must equal the discount rate for the tracking portfolio's expected cash flow, namely the expected return of the tracking portfolio. This is a weighted average of the expected return of the market portfolio and the risk-free return, where the weights correspond to the respective portfolio weights on the market (β) and risk-free asset ($1 - \beta$) in the tracking portfolio. Discounting the expected cash flow at the tracking portfolio's expected return generates the present value *only if the present value is of the same sign (positive or negative) as the expected cash flow and both the present value and expected cash flow are nonzero.* For example, as either the present value or expected cash flow (but not both) approach zero, the expected return (i.e., the discount rate), approaches (plus or minus) infinity. In such cases, we have to abandon the risk-adjusted discount rate method, and instead use the certainty equivalent method (discussed later in the chapter) to generate present values.

Tracking Error and Present Values.   The perfect tracking seen above arises because we constructed an example where the return on the market portfolio is perfectly correlated with the casino cash flow. Changing any one of the three casino cash flows or three market portfolio cash flows eliminates this perfect correlation. In this case, we would find, at best, that only imperfect tracking is possible.

With imperfect tracking, the mix of the market portfolio and the risk-free asset that best tracks the Hilton cash flow is one that minimizes the variance of the tracking error. Much of this chapter is devoted to illustrating how to obtain this mix. For now, simply assume that the portfolio that best tracks the casino cash flow, in the sense of minimizing the variance of tracking error, is one that contains $5 million of the market portfolio and $5 million of the risk-free asset.

As noted above, since the tracking portfolio has a $10 million value, the value of the casino cash flow also should be $10 million. As Chapter 9 illustrated, this is obvious when there is perfect tracking, given the assumption of no arbitrage. It is useful to review why this also is the case with imperfect tracking (see Chapters 5 and 6). First, valuation requires a tracking portfolio with the same expected future cash flow as that of the real asset it tracks. This implies that the tracking error, measured as the difference between the tracking portfolio's future value and the casino's cash flow, has an expected value of zero. Moreover, the tracking error from a properly designed tracking portfolio represents unsystematic (or diversifiable) risk. Whenever tracking error has no systematic or factor risk and has zero expected value, it has zero present value and can be ignored. Thus, we can often use a tracking portfolio's market value as a fair representation of what a cash flow is worth, even when it tracks the cash flow imperfectly.

In general:

Result 10.1   Whenever a tracking portfolio for the future cash flows of a project generates tracking error with zero systematic (or factor) risk and zero expected value, the market value of the tracking portfolio is the present value of the project's future cash flows.

Implementing the Tracking Portfolio Approach

If the financial manager identifies a tracking portfolio that is mean-variance efficient, valuation is a straightforward task. For example, if the CAPM holds, simply knowing the $5 million (market portfolio) and $5 million (risk-free asset) composition of the Hilton casino tracking portfolio indicates that the project's present value is $10 million. The manager does not need to know the expected return of the market, the risk-free return, or even the expected cash flow of Hilton to compute this present value.

This situation, however, is rare. For example, we might be able to look at traded casino stocks and compute their average beta as .5, but how would we know that $5 million is the correct investment in the market portfolio without first estimating the expected future cash flow and the expected return of the market portfolio?

Estimating Tracking Portfolios without Expected Cash Flows or Returns.   There are a few ways to estimate a tracking portfolio without knowing expected returns or expected cash flows. One way arises when there is perfect or almost perfect tracking.[4] Because tracking error that is zero or close to zero can be ignored, perfect or almost perfect tracking has a further advantage: A financial manager can use any combination of financial assets to track the investment, including those that are not mean-variance efficient. This approach is clearly superior to the CAPM/APT approaches, which generate substantial tracking error because of the restrictive composition of their tracking portfolios but nevertheless imply that the tracking error has zero present value. As a first pass, a manager should try to identify a tracking portfolio with minimum tracking error

---

[4]This alternative is discussed more fully in Chapter 11.

variance and, only when this variance is large, turn to asset pricing models that specify a tangency portfolio as the critical tracking instrument.

Using the Market Portfolio or Factor Portfolios in Computing the Tracking Portfolio.   In most cases, the existence of tracking error necessitates the use of a market portfolio or a set of factor portfolios, combined with a risk-free asset, to track a project. However, the specification of the appropriate mix of financial assets in the tracking portfolio can be complicated.

Linking Financial Asset Tracking to Real Asset Valuation with the SML

Despite this complexity, it is very important to determine, as best as one can, the proper mix of assets in the tracking portfolio, especially when there is tracking error. In this subsection, we use the securities market line to illustrate why being careless about this estimation can be costly.

The returns of risky zero *NPV* investments, such as financial assets, can be graphed as lying on the securities market line (see Chapter 5). This line (see Exhibit 10.1) is based on the risk-expected return relation developed in Chapter 5. Having a cash flow with return beta of β—computed with respect to the tangency portfolio (also discussed in Chapter 5)—means that we can track the cash flow per dollar of present value with a portfolio that has a weight of β on the tangency portfolio and a weight of $1 - \beta$ on the risk-free asset. In the Hilton example, the β of the project return and thus the weight on the market portfolio is ½.

Positive *NPV* projects plot above the securities market line at, for example, point *A*. Conversely, negative *NPV* projects plot below the securities market line at point *B*. Expected returns on the projects in Exhibit 10.1 are computed *using the cost of initiating the project* as the base price in lieu of the *"market" or "present" value* of the future cash flows. Hence, expected returns of real assets can plot above or below the

EXHIBIT 10.1   Real Assets and the Securities Market Line

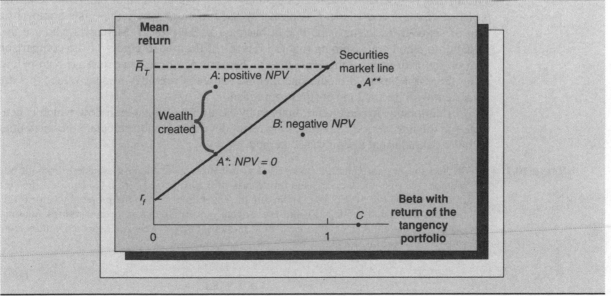

securities market line. When a project's future cash flows are sold to the financial markets (as in the Thermo Electron discussion in the preface to Part III), returns are computed with the present value as the base price. Hence, a positive *NPV* project, like point *A* in Exhibit 10.1, when spun off to the financial markets, would lie at point *A**. The movement from *A* to its counterpart *A** on the securities market line signifies that wealth is created by adopting the project and spinning it off to the securities markets. This wealth arises because the firm can sell those future cash flows for more than it costs to produce them.

The key to recognizing a positive *NPV* project is to know the project's beta. If beta is overestimated—for example, if the project at point *A* is assumed to have a beta at point *C*, and thus is erroneously interpreted as being at point *A***—a positive *NPV* project can mistakenly appear to have a negative *NPV*. It is also possible to underestimate the betas of negative *NPV* projects, which could lead to adoptions of bad projects. Thus, it is very important to understand how to best identify the project's beta. The next section discusses this issue at great length.

10.2 The Risk-Adjusted Discount Rate Method

This section discusses what is perhaps the most popular method for obtaining the present value of the future cash flows of a real asset. The method discounts the expected future cash flows at a rate known as the project's *cost of capital*. The cost of capital of a project is the expected return that investors require for holding an investment with the same risk as the project. To employ this method, one has to estimate the expected cash flow, the expected return of the market (or factor portfolios), and the CAPM beta (or factor betas) of the project return. Also, as noted earlier, the expected cash flow and present value have to be either both positive or both negative.

Defining and Implementing the Risk-Adjusted Discount Rate Method with Given Betas

The method of discounting expected cash flows at a risk-adjusted discount rate, the *risk-adjusted discount rate method,* is primarily used in cases where there is a comparison firm or set of firms in the same line of business as the project. Managers who use this valuation method are assuming that the returns of the traded equity of the comparison firm or set of firms have the same beta as the returns of the project. As shown below, using the risk-adjusted discount rate method generally provides present values that are consistent with the tracking portfolio approach.

For simplicity, we begin our analysis by assuming a single cash flow which is generated in the next period. The following result describes how to calculate present values with the risk-adjusted discount rate method.

Result 10.2   To find the present value of next period's cash flow using the risk-adjusted discount rate method: (1) compute the expected future cash flow next period, $E(\tilde{C})$; (2) compute the beta of the return of the project β; (3) compute the expected return of the project by substituting the beta calculated in step (2) into the tangency portfolio risk-expected return equation; (4) divide the expected future cash flow in step (1) by 1 plus the expected return from step (3). In algebraic terms:

$$PV = \frac{E(\tilde{C})}{1 + r_f + \beta(\bar{R}_T - r_f)} \tag{10.1}$$

Example 10.1 illustrates how to implement the risk-adjusted discount rate method.[5]

Example 10.1:   Computing the Cost of Capital

Hot Shot Computer Corp (HSCC), a wholly owned subsidiary of Novel, Inc., has a β of 1.2 when computed against the tangency portfolio. One year from now, this subsidiary has a .9 probability of being worth $10 per share and a .1 probability of being worth $20 per share. The risk-free rate is 9 percent per year. The tangency portfolio has an expected return of 19 percent per year. What is the present value of a share of HSCC, assuming no dividend payments to the parent firm in the coming year?

Answer: The expected value per share of HSCC one year from now is:

$$\$11 = .9(\$10) + .1(\$20)$$

According to the tangency portfolio risk-expected return equation, the appropriate discount rate is:

$$21\% \text{ per year} = .09 + 1.2(.19 - .09)$$

The subsidiary's present value per share is the share's expected future value divided by 1 plus the appropriate discount rate, or approximately:

$$\$9.09 \text{ per share} = \frac{\$11 \text{ per share}}{1.21}$$

The β in Example 10.1 was given to us. In general, the hallmark of the risk-adjusted discount rate method is that it is implemented with a **comparison approach**, which provides an estimate of the appropriate beta for the project by analyzing the betas of traded comparison securities. In Example 10.1, the comparison approach would have identified the project β of 1.2 by estimating the betas of the traded stocks of comparison firms in the computer industry and using some average of their betas as a proxy for HSCC's β. Implicitly, this comparison approach assumes that the present value is not negative or zero.

The Tracking Portfolio Method Is Implicit in the Risk-Adjusted Discount Rate Method

To understand the relation between the risk-adjusted discount rate method and tracking, assume that the CAPM is applied to value the Hilton casino cash flow considered in the last section. To do this, we discount the expected cash flow, assumed to be $11.3 million, at the discount rate implied by the CAPM.

The average of the betas of the traded equity of a group of comparison casinos is estimated to be .5. Thus, the Hilton casino cash flow is tracked by a portfolio that is invested 50 percent in the market portfolio and 50 percent in the risk-free asset. If the expected return on the market is 20 percent and the risk-free rate is 6 percent, the appropriate discount rate is .06 + .5(.20 − .06) = .13. Hence, the present value of the expected future cash flow is $11.3 million/1.13 = $10 million.

The 13 percent used to discount the $11.3 million expected future cash flow from the Hilton casino is the expected return of the tracking portfolio. Hence, if one buys enough of the tracking portfolio to have an expected future value of $11.3 million, the tracking portfolio will cost $10 million today. This tracking portfolio cost represents $5 million in the market portfolio (50 percent) and $5 million in the risk-free asset

---

[5]Example 10.1 is used to value an entire subsidiary, which is a collection of projects. The risk-adjusted discount rate method also can be used to value a single project.

(50 percent). Thus, the discounted (or present) value of the expected future cash flow is nothing more than the cost of acquiring the tracking portfolio's cash flows ($10 million) while the CAPM beta (.5) represents the proportion of the tracking portfolio allocated to the market portfolio, which is assumed to be the tangency portfolio.

10.3 The Effect of Leverage on Comparisons

Since the risk-adjusted discount rate method uses the traded stocks of comparison firms to estimate the betas of projects, it is important that the beta risk of the equity of the comparison firms be truly comparable. However, it is not enough to merely use firms in the same line of business as the project. Since the amount of debt financing a firm takes on can dramatically affect equity betas, it is necessary to adjust for differing amounts of debt financing in order to make appropriate beta risk comparisons.

In this section, we explore the effect of debt financing, also known as leverage, on the beta and standard deviation of a firm's equity. We begin by performing a financing experiment in which a firm issues risk-free debt, but does not alter the operations of the firm. Hence, the proceeds of the debt issue are used to retire outstanding equity while sales, EBIT, marketing, production, and so forth remain the same.

The Balance Sheet for an All Equity-Financed Firm

Begin with an all equity-financed firm. Exhibit 10.2 illustrates the familiar accounting balance sheet in T-account form. The left-hand side reflects the assets of the firm and the right-hand side reflects the debt (liabilities) and equity. In contrast to an accounting balance sheet, which reflects book values, the T-account in Exhibit 10.2 describes market values. Hence, A represents the market value of the firm's assets and E the market value of the firm's equity. In the absence of leverage, A equals E because the two sides of the balance sheet add up to the same number; that is, they *balance*. This identity implies that the *risk* of A and E in the all equity-financed firm must be the same, whether risk is measured as standard deviation (in which case $\sigma_A = \sigma_E$), or as beta risk (in which case $\beta_A = \beta_E$).

The Balance Sheet for a Firm Partially Financed with Debt

Now, let us introduce debt. In this case, the balance sheet looks like the T-account depicted in Exhibit 10.3. Because the two sides of the balance sheet must balance, $A = D + E$. In other words, the market value of the assets of the firm must equal the sum of the market values of the debt and equity. This makes sense. All of the future cash flows from the assets of the firm must at some point flow to the cash flow claimants. An investor who buys up all the debt and equity of the firm has a right to all the cash flows produced by the assets. Hence, the sum of the market values of the debt and equity must be the same as the market value of the firm's assets.

The Right-Hand Side of the Balance Sheet as a Portfolio

Now, view the right-hand side of the balance sheet in Exhibit 10.3 as a portfolio of investments, with the weight on debt as $D/(D + E)$, and the weight on equity as $E/(D + E)$. To understand the relation between asset risk and equity risk, we now use the portfolio mathematics developed in Chapters 4 and 5 to analyze risk measures of each of the components, A, D, and E. With risk-free debt, all of the risk is born by the equity

EXHIBIT 10.2   Balance Sheet for an All Equity-Financed Firm

Assets	Liabilities and Equity	
	Debt	
		0 (i.e., $D = 0$)
A	Equity	
		E

EXHIBIT 10.3   Balance Sheet for a Firm with Leverage

Assets	Liabilities and Equity	
	Debt	
		D ($D > 0$)
A	Equity	
		E

holders. In this case, σ_D and β_D are both zero for risk-free debt, implying by the portfolio formulas developed earlier:

$$\sigma_A = \frac{D}{D+E}0 + \frac{E}{D+E}\sigma_E$$

and

$$\beta_A = \frac{D}{D+E}0 + \frac{E}{D+E}\beta_E \tag{10.2a}$$

Inverting these equations to place the equity risk measures on the left-hand side results in:

$$\sigma_E = \left(1 + \frac{D}{E}\right)\sigma_A$$

and

$$\beta_E = \left(1 + \frac{D}{E}\right)\beta_A \tag{10.2b}$$

Recall that the experiment performed is one in which altering the mix of financing between debt and equity does not change A, the operating assets of the firm. Hence, equations (10.2a) and (10.2b) imply:

Result 10.3   Increasing the firm's debt (raising D and reducing E) increases the (beta and standard deviation) risk per dollar of equity investment. It will increase linearly in the D/E ratio if the debt is risk free.

Result 10.3 stems from the equivalence of the assets of the firm to a portfolio of the firm's debt and equity, with respective positive portfolio weights of $D/(D + E)$ and $E/(D + E)$. Thus:

$$\tilde{r}_A = \frac{D}{D+E}\tilde{r}_D + \frac{E}{D+E}\tilde{r}_E \tag{10.3a}$$

This also means that each dollar of equity can be thought of as a portfolio-weighted average of the firm's assets and debt, with a long position in the assets and a short position in debt. Here the respective portfolio weights are $(1 + D/E)$ on the assets and $-D/E$ on the debt; that is, upon rearranging equation (10.3a) to place $\tilde{r}_E$ on the left-hand side, we obtain:

$$\tilde{r}_E = \left(1 + \frac{D}{E}\right)\tilde{r}_A - \frac{D}{E}\tilde{r}_D \tag{10.3b}$$

Graphs and Numerical Illustrations of the Effect of Debt on Risk

Exhibit 10.4 illustrates the beta of equity as a function of the **leverage ratio**, D/E. When the debt is risk free, the firm's equity holders bear all of the risk from swings in asset values. By Equation 10.2b, the beta of equity as a function of D/E should graph as a straight line in this case. When debt default is possible, debt holders bear part of the risk, implying that equity holders bear less risk. As a result, the beta risk of equity becomes a curved line.

To explore Result 10.3 further, we illustrate numerically why equity holder (beta or standard deviation) risk per dollar invested increases with leverage. First, note that if a firm's total cash flows are independent of its **capital structure**—that is, its mix of debt and equity financing—the total risk borne by the aggregation of the investors of a firm, debt holders plus equity holders, does not change when the firm changes its capital structure. Thus, an all-equity financed firm with assets that change from a value of $100 million in 1995, to $110 million in 1996, and then to $88 million in 1997, has equity that experiences the same value changes. Per dollar invested, such equity holders experience value changes amounting to a 10 percent increase from 1995 to 1996 and a 20 percent decrease from 1996 to 1997.

However, if the same assets had been financed with $75 million in risk-free debt, implying an initial debt-to-equity ratio of 3, the equity jumps from $25 million (= $100 million − $75 million) in 1995 to $35 million (= $110 million − $75 million) in 1996. The equity increase of 40 percent ($25 million to $35 million) is four times larger per

EXHIBIT 10.4   Equity Beta as a Function of the Firm's Leverage Ratio

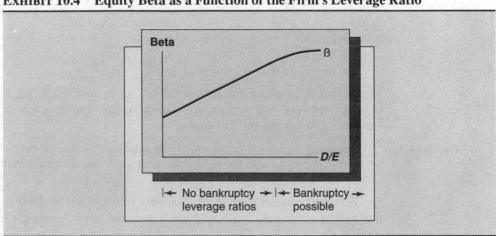

dollar invested than the 10 percent equity increase of the all-equity firm ($100 million to $110 million). Thus, leverage benefits the firm's stockholders when asset values appreciate but, from 1996 to 1997, when the assets drop from $110 million to $88 million, a 20 percent decrease, the equity of the levered firm goes from $35 million in 1996 to $13 million in 1997, a 63 percent decrease.[6]

The Cost of Equity, Cost of Debt, and Cost of Capital as a Function of the Leverage Ratio.   The **cost of equity** for a firm is the expected return required by investors to induce them to hold the equity. Since the firm's equity beta increases linearly as the amount of risk-free debt financing increases, it should not be surprising that the firm's cost of equity capital also increases linearly as a function of the leverage ratio, D/E. Specifically, taking expectations of equation (10.3b) and grouping terms yields:

Result 10.4   The cost of equity $\bar{r}_E = \bar{r}_A + (D/E)(\bar{r}_A - \bar{r}_D)$ increases as the firm's leverage ratio D/E increases. It will increase linearly in the ratio D/E if the debt is default free and if $\bar{r}_A$, the expected return of the firm's assets, does not change as the leverage ratio increases.[7]

In Result 10.4, the expected (and actual) return of a firm's debt $\bar{r}_D$, its **cost of debt**, equals r_f for moderate leverage ratios. As long as the firm's debt is default free, the cost of equity capital increases linearly in the firm's leverage ratio. However, when firms take on extreme amounts of debt, $\bar{r}_D$, the expected return on risky debt, rises as D/E increases. Since debt holders share part of the risk in this case, the cost of equity increases more slowly as D/E rises than it does with default-free debt. Again, the risks of the assets are shared by both debt holders and equity holders when bankruptcy is possible, but they are borne only by equity holders when bankruptcy is not possible.

Exhibit 10.5 summarizes the findings of this section. It plots the cost of equity $\bar{r}_E$, the cost of debt $\bar{r}_D$, and the cost of capital $\bar{r}_A$ as functions of the leverage ratio D/E.

EXHIBIT 10.5   Cost of Debt, Equity, and Capital as a Function of D/E

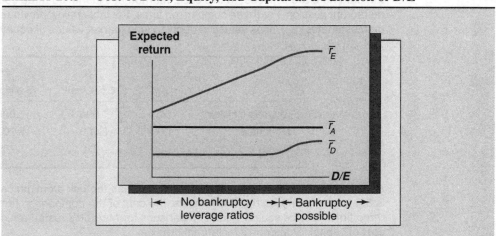

---

[6]The 63 percent decrease for the leveraged firm is not quite four times the 20 percent decrease experienced by the assets because the debt-equity ratio is smaller than three to one in 1996.

[7]Result 10.4 also applies when expected returns are determined by factor betas in a multifactor setting. In this vein, note that interest rate risk, discussed in Chapters 6, 12, and 22, may make the beta of default-free fixed-rate debt non-zero, but only default risk can generate the curvature seen in Exhibits 10.4 and 10.5.

10.4 Implementing the Risk-Adjusted Discount Rate Formula with Comparison Firms

Suppose that the CAPM is correct and that HSCC (from Example 10.1) has operations similar to those of Dell Computer, a stock traded on NASDAQ. HSCC is a wholly owned subsidiary of Novel, Inc., so it is not traded, but Dell is. In this case, it might be possible to use Dell's beta—computed by regressing Dell's past stock returns on the returns of a market proxy—to determine beta and thus, the expected return, for HSCC. However, one needs to be cautious about drawing this connection because the way in which a firm is financed can affect its equity beta, as indicated in Section 10.3. It is important not only for Dell Computer and HSCC to have similar lines of business, but also for both to have similar leverage ratios.

The CAPM, the Comparison Method, and Adjusting for Leverage

If an acquisition (or project) and its comparison firm(s) are financed differently, it may be possible to adjust the comparison firm's beta for the difference in leverage ratios. However, making this type of adjustment can be tricky, especially when one takes corporate taxes into account. We will discuss beta adjustments in the absence of taxes below, and will examine how these adjustments are affected by taxes in Chapter 12.

An Illustration of the Necessary Leverage Adjustment without Taxes.   Example 10.2 illustrates the simpler task of how to adjust for leverage differences in the absence of taxes.

Example 10.2:   Using the Comparison Approach to Obtain Beta and $\bar{r}$

This example is based on a Harvard case about the Marriott Corporation,[8] although much of the data here are fictitious. In this case, Marriott has identified three comparison firms for its restaurant division. For these comparison firms, the table below provides CAPM-based equity beta estimates (β_E), book values of debt (D), and market values of equity (E).

	β_E	D ($ billions)	E ($ billions)
Church's Chicken	.75	.004	.096
McDonald's	1.00	2.300	7.700
Wendy's	1.08	.210	.790

Assume that the risk-free rate is 4 percent per year, the risk premium on the market portfolio is 8.4 percent per year, the CAPM holds, the debt of the comparison firms is risk free, and all three firms provide equally good comparisons for Marriott's restaurant division. Estimate the cost of capital for Marriott's restaurant division.

Answer: Using equation (10.2a), $\beta_A = \dfrac{E}{D+E}\beta_E$, we first find the three firms' asset betas:

---

[8]Ruback (1992).

	β_A
Church's Chicken	$.72 = \dfrac{.096}{.100}.75$
McDonald's	$.77 = \dfrac{7.7}{10}1.00$
Wendy's	$.85 = \dfrac{.79}{1.0}1.08$
Marriott (average of above)	$.78 = \dfrac{.72 + .77 + .85}{3}$

Applying the CAPM risk-expected return equation, using the .78 estimate of Marriott's restaurant asset beta gives the restaurant cost of capital, 10.55 percent per year:

$$.1055 = .04 + .78(.084)$$

In Example 10.2, β_E, the equity beta, determines the cost of equity capital. Recall from the last section that if β_E is positive, this beta and the associated expected return on the equity increase as the leverage of the firm increases. The cash flows that are discounted by the risk-adjusted discount rate method are the cash flows from the project's assets, which do not have debt interest payments subtracted from them. Hence, it is inappropriate to discount these cash flows at a rate used for discounting the cash flows that belong to the leveraged equity of comparison firms.

By multiplying the betas by $E/(D + E)$, Example 10.2 identifies the beta of the portfolio of debt and equity of the comparison firms (with $\beta_D = 0$). Since assets equal debt plus equity, this portfolio beta is indeed the asset beta that generates an appropriate discount rate for the cash flows of the assets.

Weighting the Betas of Comparison Firms.   Note that Example 10.2 averaged the betas of the three comparison firms to estimate the beta of Marriott's restaurant assets. This averaging is appropriate if each comparison firm provides an equally valid estimate of the Marriott restaurant asset beta. However, if some firms provide better comparisons than others, their betas should be weighted more than those of the less closely matched firms. For example, if Church's Chicken was a less appropriate match than McDonald's or Wendy's, we might give the .72 beta of Church's Chicken a lower weight than the betas of McDonald's or Wendy's.

Obtaining a Cost of Capital from the Arbitrage Pricing Theory (APT)

Earlier, we learned that when the tangency portfolio is the market portfolio, the cost of capital—that is, the discount rate in the denominator of the present value formula, equation (10.1)—is obtained from the Capital Asset Pricing Model. An alternative to the CAPM is the Arbitrage Pricing Theory (APT), developed in Chapter 6, which is the correct theory to use when a combination of factor portfolios, instead of the market portfolio, is the tangency portfolio.

The Multifactor APT Version of the Risk-Adjusted Discount Rate Formula. When computing costs of capital using the expected returns generated by the APT [equation (6.7)], the present value for the project's future cash flow is:

$$PV = \frac{E(\tilde{C})}{1 + r_f + \lambda_1\beta_1 + \lambda_2\beta_2 + \ldots + \lambda_K\beta_K} \tag{10.4}$$

The project's net present value is computed by subtracting the project's initial cost from this present value.

The discount rates provided by the APT generally differ from those of the CAPM. Thus, they can generate different capital allocation decisions. The Marriott Corporation, for example, has an APT-based cost of capital of 9.3 percent, resulting in a denominator of 1.093 for equation (10.1).[9] However, Marriott's CAPM-based cost of capital is 10 percent, resulting in a denominator of 1.1 for equation (10.1). If the APT is correct and the CAPM is incorrect, Marriott would be missing out on some good projects by using the higher discount rate from the CAPM. As the following case study illustrates, such differences in the cost of capital between the two models are not uncommon.

Arbitrage Pricing Theory versus Capital Asset Pricing Model

Alcar's APT!, a consulting firm, provides its clients with the costs of equity capital and costs of capital for a variety of firms, using both the CAPM and the APT. The Alcar version of the APT is based on a five-factor model, where the five prespecified factors are changes in:

- Short-term inflation (SINF).
- Long-term inflation (LINF).
- The level of short-term interest rates (INT).
- The premium for default risk (PREM).
- The monthly Gross Domestic Product (GDP).

Exhibit 10.6 presents Alcar's equity expected returns from both the CAPM and APT, as well as the CAPM beta, for nine well-known firms, as of the third quarter of 1995.

EXHIBIT 10.6   Cost of Equity Capital

Firm	CAPM Equity Beta	CAPM Equity Expected Returns (%)	APT Equity Expected Returns (%)	SINF	LINF	INT	PREM	GDP
Chrysler	1.13	11.86%	12.50%	0.67%	1.22%	1.27%	1.06%	1.31%
Coca Cola	1.03	11.42	12.61	0.83	1.25	1.39	0.95	1.22
Con Edison NY	0.60	9.57	10.41	0.52	0.76	0.86	0.56	0.74
CSX Corp	1.24	12.34	11.89	0.57	1.13	1.24	0.82	1.15
Fed Nat Mtg Assn	1.52	13.56	11.79	0.39	1.16	1.31	0.69	1.26
Microsoft Corp	1.05	11.53	8.95	−0.03	0.54	0.61	0.22	0.64
Nat'l Med'l Enterp	1.51	13.49	12.85	0.70	1.36	1.54	0.91	1.36
Northrop	0.98	11.19	8.54	−0.07	0.45	0.49	0.17	0.52
Scott Paper Co	1.19	12.13	13.91	1.00	1.50	1.60	1.31	1.52

Note: column group headers — "CAPM" spans Equity Beta and Equity Expected Returns (%); "Arbitrage Pricing Theory (APT)" spans Equity Expected Returns (%) and "Premiums from Sensitivity to Five Factors" (SINF, LINF, INT, PREM, GDP).

---

[9]Based on third-quarter 1995 data for the Marriott Corporation.

For each row, the sum of the numbers in the five right-hand columns in Exhibit 10.6 represent the APT risk premiums. APT equity expected returns (the costs of equity capital), are computed as the sum of these risk premiums plus the September 7, 1995 risk-free rate of 6.98 percent.

With adjustments for risky debt and taxes, these numbers translate into Exhibit 10.7's comparative costs of capital for the typical existing project of these firms.[10] The difference in the cost of capital computed with the CAPM and APT in Exhibit 10.7 is as large as 2.58 percent per year, as you'll note in the case of Microsoft (2.58% = 11.53% − 8.95%). Many projects that are similar to the existing projects of Microsoft typically have large investments in the early years—primarily wages for programmers and expenses for advertising and promotion—and substantial revenues from sales of software which are not likely to occur until much later, perhaps 5 to 15 years after the initial investment. Therefore, adoption decisions about any prospective project that resembles Microsoft's existing collection of projects will be greatly affected by whether one selects the CAPM or the APT to compute Microsoft's discount rate.

Costs of Capital Computed with Alternatives to CAPM and APT: Dividend Discount Models

The Capital Asset Pricing Model and the Arbitrage Pricing Theory are the two most popular models for determining risk-adjusted discount rates. Although both models are applied in practice, their applications have been criticized because of the difficulties associated with estimating their essential inputs.

Impediments to Using the CAPM and APT.   Specifically, the CAPM requires knowledge of not only the covariance (or beta) of the return of an investment with the return of the market portfolio, but also an estimate of the expected return of the market portfolio. The APT requires multiple factor sensitivities and the corresponding expected returns on multiple factor portfolios.

The Dividend Discount Model.   A number of financial analysts have abandoned the CAPM and APT as tools for risk adjustment and have instead estimated required rates

Exhibit 10.7   CAPM and APT Costs of Capital with Leverage Ratios (D/E) for Nine Firms

Firm	Debt to Equity Ratio (%)	CAPM Cost of Capital (%)	APT Cost of Capital (%)	Difference between APT and CAPM Cost of Capital (%)
Chrysler	143.83%	8.85%	9.11%	0.26%
Coca-Cola	6.36	11.02	12.14	1.12
Consolidated Edison	46.90	7.93	8.51	0.58
CSX Corp.	51.31	9.85	9.55	−0.30
Federal National Mortgage Association	778.74	5.65	5.45	−0.20
Microsoft Corp.	0.00	11.53	8.95	−2.58
National Medical Enterprises	106.55	9.31	9.01	−0.30
Northrop	27.50	10.12	8.04	−2.08
Scott Paper Co.	99.92	8.67	9.56	0.89

---

[10]Adjustments for taxes are discussed in Chapter 12.

of return using analysts' forecasts of future earnings with what is known as the **dividend discount model**—sometimes referred to as the **Gordon Growth Model** because it was first developed by Gordon (1962). According to this model, the equity of a firm with a dividend stream growing at a constant rate can be valued as follows:

$$E = \frac{\text{div}}{(\bar{r}_E - g)} \tag{10.5a}$$

where

E = the firm's equity value

div = next year's expected dividend

$\bar{r}_E$ = the market required rate of return of the firm's stock (its cost of equity capital)

g = the expected growth rate of dividends

Equation (10.5a) is merely the growing perpetuity formula (see Appendix A at the end of the text, equation (A.10)). By rearranging this equation, one sees that the expected rate of return of a stock can be expressed as the sum of the growth rate and the dividend yield:

$$\bar{r}_E = g + \frac{\text{div}}{E} \tag{10.5b}$$

Using Analyst Forecasts to Estimate the Expected Dividend Growth Rate.   To compute the risk-adjusted discount rate for equity from this equation, only g, the expected rate of growth of the firm's dividends, and div$/E$, the firm's dividend yield, need to be estimated.[11] Analysts' forecasts of the growth rate of a firm's earnings provide one estimate for g. Under the assumption that a firm pays a fixed percentage of its earnings as dividends, the expected growth rate in dividends equals the forecasted growth rate in earnings. This growth rate can then be added to the existing dividend yield to derive the expected return on the firm's stock.[12]

For example, suppose that Value Line, an investment advisory service, forecasts a 9.5 percent rate of growth for IBM's earnings. Adding this to the firm's 3.9 percent dividend yield (as of late 1996) implies an expected rate of return on IBM stock of 13.4 percent. To obtain a cost of capital for an IBM-like project, it is necessary to adjust this 13.4 percent rate of return for debt in IBM's capital structure. For example, in the risk-free debt no taxes case of Section 10.2, one can obtain $\bar{r}$ by multiplying $\bar{r}_E$ by $E/(D + E)$.

Using the Plowback Ratio Formula to Estimate the Expected Dividend Growth Rate.   An alternative method for estimating g, the growth rate in dividends, employs accounting data. This method estimates the growth rate as:

$$g = b \times ROE \tag{10.6}$$

---

[11]A historical average of the ratio of dividend per share to prior year stock price per share, sometimes over a period of five years, can be used if the current year's dividend payout is unusual.

[12]Note that using the current dividend yield in equation (10.5b) gives the wrong answer. The formula requires next year's expected dividend in the numerator. Multiplying the current dividend per share by $1 + g$ and dividing by the current stock price gives the appropriate dividend yield estimate.

where

b = the **plowback ratio**, the fraction of earnings retained in the firm

ROE = **book return on equity**, that is, earnings divided by last year's (midyear) book equity[13]

The intuition for this **plowback ratio formula**, equation (10.6), is that the book return on equity (ROE) represents the rate of growth of capital invested in the firm. When a firm has an ROE of 10 percent, every \$1 invested in the firm returns \$1.00 of equity capital and \$0.10 of earnings next year, or \$1.10. If this \$1.10 is entirely reinvested, it will grow another 10 percent to \$1.21 one year later. However, if 75 percent of the earnings are paid out in the form of dividends, implying a plowback ratio of .25, the capital will only grow at a rate of $(1 - .75)(\$.10)$—that is, at 25 percent of the 10 percent growth rate, or 2.5 percent. In this case, at the end of the first year, 75 percent of \$0.10 would be paid out in dividends, implying that only \$1.025 $[= \$1.10 - .75(\$.10)]$ is left in the firm for reinvestment. This would grow to \$1.025(1.1), but if 75 percent of the amount over \$1.025 (the earnings) is paid out as a dividend, the amount to be reinvested is just $\$1.025(1.1) - .75(\$1.025)(.1) = \$1.025^2$. Thus, paying out a fixed proportion of a company's earnings as dividends slows the growth rate of the funds available for reinvestment. Moreover, since earnings and dividends are a constant proportion of the reinvestment amount, their growth rates will be the same as the growth rate of the funds available for investment in the firm.

Assumptions and Pitfalls of the Dividend Discount Model.   The plowback ratio formula, equation (10.6), uses the book return on equity in lieu of the return on new investment, the return that theoretically should be used but which is more difficult to measure accurately. If old assets and new assets have different returns, ROE in the plowback ratio formula should be the *book return of equity for new asset investment*. If the project is a positive *NPV* project, this return on equity will exceed the project's cost of capital.

The implicit assumptions of the dividend discount model's estimate of the cost of capital are that:

- The earnings growth forecasts, whether from analysts or equation (10.6), are unbiased; that is, they do not tend to systematically underestimate or overestimate the earnings growth rate.
- The earnings growth forecasts are based on the same information that investors use to value the firm's stock.
- The firm's earnings and dividends grow at the same constant growth rate, forever.

To the extent that these assumptions are valid, the dividend discount model may provide a better estimate of the expected rate of return on a firm's stock or project than either the CAPM or the APT because it does not require estimates of beta or estimates of the expected return of the market portfolio. However, these assumptions, particularly that of a constant growth rate, are stringent and may not apply to many of the firms or projects that an analyst wants to value.

---

[13]Alternatively, it is possible to use forecasts of next year's earnings divided by this year's (midyear) book equity.

What if No Pure Comparison Firm Exists?

Many firms are large diversified entities that have many lines of business. In this instance, the equity returns of potential comparison firms are distorted by other lines of business that are inappropriate as comparisons. A financial manager in this situation still may be able to obtain an appropriate comparison by forming portfolios of firms that generate a "pure" line of business. The mathematics behind the approach taken in Example 10.3, which illustrates how to create comparison investments in a pure line of business when none initially exists, is similar in spirit to the formation of pure factor portfolios in Chapter 6.

Example 10.3:   Finding a Comparison Firm from a Portfolio of Firms

Assume that Time-Warner is interested in acquiring the ABC television network from Disney. It has estimated the expected incremental future cash flows from acquiring ABC and desires an appropriate beta in order to compute a discount rate to value those cash flows. However, the two major networks that are most comparable, NBC and CBS, are owned by General Electric and Westinghouse—respectively—which have substantial cash flows from other sources. For these comparison firms, the table below presents hypothetical equity betas, debt to asset ratios, and the ratios of the market values of the network assets to all assets:

	β_E	$\dfrac{D}{D+E}$	$\dfrac{Network\ Assets}{All\ Assets} = \dfrac{N}{A}$
General Electric	1.1	.1	.25
Westinghouse	1.3	.4	.50

Estimate the appropriate beta for the ABC acquisition. Assume that the debt of each of the two comparison firms is risk free. Also assume that the non-network assets of General Electric and Westinghouse are substantially similar and thus have the same beta.

Answer: Using equation (10.2a), $\beta_A = [E/(D + E)]\ \beta_E$, first find the asset betas of the two comparison firms. For the two firms, these are, respectively,

$$\beta_A$$

General Electric $.99 = (.9)(1.1)$
Westinghouse $.78 = (.6)(1.3)$

Viewing the comparison firms as portfolios of network and non-network assets, and recognizing that the beta of a portfolio is a portfolio-weighted average of the betas of the portfolio components, implies the following equation:

$$\beta_A = \frac{N}{A} \times (\text{network asset beta}) + \frac{A-N}{A} \times (\text{non-network assets' beta})$$

For the two comparison firms this equation is represented as:

General Electric: $.99 = (.25)\beta_{NETWORK} + (.75)\beta_{NON-NETWORK}$
Westinghouse: $.78 = (.5)\ \beta_{NETWORK} + (.5)\ \beta_{NON-NETWORK}$

Multiplying both sides of the second equation (Westinghouse) by 1.5, subtracting it from the first equation (General Electric), and solving for $\beta_{NETWORK}$ yields $\beta_{NETWORK} = .36$, which is used for the ABC acquisition.

The procedure used in Example 10.3 is based on the idea that portfolio betas are port-folio-weighted averages of the betas of individual securities. If we view firms with multiple lines of business as portfolios of lines of business, it may be possible to infer the betas of the individual lines of business by solving systems of linear equations.

10.5 Pitfalls in Using the Comparison Method

As the discussion below indicates, there are a number of pitfalls to watch for when implementing the comparison approach.

Project Betas are Not the Same as Firm Betas

Most firms use their own cost of capital as a discount rate for evaluating specific investment projects. This could be appropriate, for example, if the analyst is estimating the value of one new Sears outlet: Each Sears store is largely a clone of the others and its risk probably closely matches the overall risk of the Sears corporation, which is basically a collection of these cloned stores. Hence, the cost of capital for Sears as a whole is probably a good discount rate for evaluating the profitability of opening up a Sears store in a new location.

In most cases, however, using the firm's cost of capital as the discount rate for a new project is inappropriate. New projects may have higher beta risk than the firm's mature projects. Still, there is no good rule of thumb. Either a project may be less risky than the firm's existing projects or it may support a higher percentage of debt than the firm as a whole.[14] This would argue for using a lower cost of capital for the project than that experienced by the firm.

Growth Opportunities Are Usually the Source of High Betas

Comparisons are also distorted by what we refer to as "growth opportunities" or "growth options." Consider Wal-Mart, for example. The value of this firm's assets can be regarded as the value of the existing Wal-Mart outlets in addition to the value of any outlets that Wal-Mart may open in the future. The option to open new stores is known as a growth option. Because growth options tend to be most valuable in good times and have implicit leverage (as Chapter 8 noted for call options in general), which tends to increase beta, they contain a great deal of systematic risk. Hence, individual projects can differ in their risk from the firm as a whole because they lack the growth options that are embedded in the firm's stock price.

Sears, however, has been contracting in recent years, so the growth option is probably small, indicating that Sears's cost of capital may be appropriate for valuing a Sears store.[15] On the other hand, Wal-Mart, which has been opening new stores at a phenomenal rate, may have most of its value generated by growth options. An individual Wal-Mart store thus has assets that look quite different from the assets of the Wal-Mart Corporation, which is composed of the relatively low-risk existing stores and high-risk growth options to open new stores. One would be exaggerating the systematic risk of an

---

[14]See Chapter 12.

[15]One must be cautious with this example because Sears also derives substantial profits from in-home remodeling and maintenance, such as carpet cleaning and painting. Also, Sears is currently experiencing a modest turnaround and may soon experience the same comparison problems as Wal-Mart.

individual Wal-Mart store by using the risk of Wal-Mart's stock as the appropriate comparison.

There is no good rule of thumb for adjusting the risk of comparison firms for growth options. Usually, but not always, growing franchises like Starbucks, promising biotech and internet firms such as Amgen or Netscape—which have high price-earnings ratios—or firms with high ratios of market value of equity to book value of equity have valuable growth options. However, the systematic risk of these growth options, which is the risk that is relevant for discounting, depends on how strongly the growth is tied to the health of the economy. The stronger the tie to the health of the economy, the riskier the growth option.

With a company like Amgen, whose success depends largely on successful clinical trials and approval by the Food and Drug Administration, the growth options are tied less directly to the health of the economy. For this reason, the beta of Amgen's growth options may be low. On the other hand, the potential advertising and subscription revenues of Netscape, or the willingness of individuals to regularly pay more than $4 for their morning coffee and pastry at Starbucks, are probably tied to the health of the economy—implying relatively high betas for the growth options of Netscape and Starbucks.

Multiperiod Risk-Adjusted Discount Rates

Virtually all projects have cash flows over multiple periods. Traditionally, multiperiod valuation problems have been viewed as simple extensions of the one-period analysis.

The Approach Used by Practitioners.   To value the multiperiod cash flow *stream* from a project, practitioners typically use the following approach:

1. Estimate the equity beta from a comparison firm using historical data, typically of weekly or monthly frequency. Usually, the comparison firm is the firm doing the project.
2. Compute the expected return using the risk-expected return formula of choice (CAPM or APT) with parameters estimated from historical data.
3. Adjust for leverage and taxes[16] to obtain a cost of capital.
4. Use the cost of capital as a single discount rate for each period in the way that we used the risk-free rate (assuming a flat term structure) in Chapter 9 to discount multiperiod cash flows.

Example 10.4 illustrates this approach.

Example 10.4:   Applying a One-Period Cost of Capital to Multiyear Cash Flows
Example 10.2 identified three comparison firms for Marriott's restaurant division and from these estimated 10.55 percent per year as the cost of capital for Marriott. Assume that Marriott's restaurant division is expected to produce $5 million in cash flows at the end of this year and that this number will grow by 5 percent per year forever. At what price is Marriott willing to sell its restaurant division?

Answer: The present value, using a risk-adjusted discount rate of 10.55 percent per year, is:

---

[16]See Chapter 12.

$$PV = \frac{\$5 \text{ million}}{1.1055} + \frac{\$5 \text{ million}(1.05)}{1.1055^2} + \frac{\$5 \text{ million}(1.05)^2}{1.1055^3} + \cdots$$

Recognizing this as a growing perpetuity (see equation (A.10) in Appendix A at the end of the text), the restaurant division's value would be:

$$PV = \frac{\$5 \text{ million}}{.1055 - .05} = \$90.09 \text{ million}$$

Pitfalls in Using the Practitioner Approach.   Using a single cost of capital to discount each of the expected future cash flows—the approach taken in Example 10.4—is popular with analysts because it is simpler than using a different discount rate for each individual cash flow. However, in many cases a single cost of capital tends to misvalue cash flows.

This can be true even when cash flows are riskless. Chapter 9 emphasized that analysts should discount the cash flows in different years at different discount rates. For example, if the rate on a default-free zero-coupon bond maturing in the year 2002 is 7 percent, then a certain cash flow occurring in 2002 must be discounted at a 7 percent rate. Similarly, if the rate on a default-free zero-coupon bond maturing in 2010 is 9 percent, then cash flows occurring in 2010 also must be discounted at 9 percent. Hence, if analysts used a single discount rate of 8 percent, the near-term cash flows would be undervalued while the cash flows in the more distant future would be overvalued.[17]

The same lesson applies to risky projects. In seeking a comparison firm for the cash flows of its restaurant division, Marriott can use the 10.55 percent expected rate of return of comparison stocks only if the cash flows of its restaurant division, at each horizon, have expected values and market (or factor) risk identical to those of the tracking portfolio. For example, if the expected cash flows of Church's Chicken and Wendy's have faster growth rates than the cash flows of Marriott's restaurant division, then they represent an inappropriate comparison and should not be used in the tracking portfolio.

Long-Term Risk-Free Rate, Short-Term Risk-Free Rate, or Zero-Beta Rate?   The expected rate of return of the firms comparable to Marriott's restaurant division—McDonald's, Wendy's, and Church's Chicken—are based on risk-expected return models like the CAPM and APT. A portfolio of these comparison firms is assumed to track the Marriott restaurant cash flows. In turn, the cost of capital for a given comparison firm is a statement that the firm is tracked by a weighted average of the risk-free asset and the market portfolio (or factor portfolios). For these risk-expected return formulas, *there is no theoretical reason to select a short-term risk-free rate over a long-term risk-free rate, or vice versa*. Moreover, the decision about which horizon to use for the risk-free return in these formulas is not at all tied to the horizon of the cash flow one is trying to value.

In general, the use of the long-term versus the short-term risk-free rate in the CAPM or APT risk-expected return relation depends on practical considerations, not on the horizon of the cash flow. As an illustration, consider the valuation of a long-horizon certain cash flow. It is very clear that the yield of a default-free zero coupon bond of matched horizon provides the appropriate rate for discounting the certain cash flow. As Chapter 9 emphasized, this discounting is equivalent to finding a tracking portfolio,

---

[17]With a riskless cash flow stream, it is possible that all of the overvaluations and undervaluations would cancel out if the single 8 percent discount rate were used. However, this would only be true if (1) the project's cash flows were identical to those of the tracking portfolio and (2) the internal rate of return of the tracking portfolio was 8 percent.

comprised entirely of a default-free zero-coupon bond, that *perfectly tracks the certain cash flow. For practical reasons,* valuation with perfect tracking is generally more accurate than valuation using the market portfolio or factor portfolios.

Thus, for a long horizon, the beta of the certain cash flow, measured over long horizons, is zero, and the risk-free rate is the long-term riskless rate. However, if one believes the CAPM is correct, it is also appropriate to track a long-horizon certain cash flow with *short-horizon* riskless bond and the market portfolio.

Since, over short intervals of time, the values of both the certain cash flow and the market portfolio tend to decrease when expected inflation increases, and vice versa, the certain cash flow is likely to have a positive beta when measured against the short-term return of the market portfolio. Indeed, a typical default-free long-term zero coupon bond has a beta, measured over short horizons, of about .2. With a market risk premium of 8 percent per year, this generates a reasonable forecast of the typical 1.5 to 2 percent higher yield of default-free long-term bonds over short-term bonds. Thus, the beta of .2 obtained from regressions using short-horizon returns suggests that the long-horizon certain cash flow of the long-term bond, and by extension the long-term certain cash flow of any real asset, is tracked by a portfolio that is 20 percent invested in the market portfolio and 80 percent invested in a rollover position in short-term riskless bonds.

Note that the beta of the cash flow of the long-term bond above depends on the maturity of the debt used in the tracking portfolio. The bond cash flow's short-horizon CAPM beta of .2 identifies the best mix of the market portfolio and a short-term risk-free asset that, with rollovers in the position, tracks the long-horizon certain cash flow. However, the weight of .2 on the market portfolio and .8 on the short-term risk-free asset changes to 0 and 1, respectively, when the market portfolio is combined with a long-term risk-free asset.

While technically correct, the short-horizon CAPM-based method of valuing a riskless long-horizon cash flow has substantial tracking error. Because of the difference in tracking error with the two approaches, it is preferable to use a long-horizon riskless bond as the sole instrument in the tracking portfolio for a long-term riskless cash flow and to avoid the CAPM-based approach altogether.

The same considerations apply in evaluating a risky long-horizon cash flow. Whether it is better to include a long-term risk-free bond or a short-term risk-free bond in the tracking portfolio depends on which bond generates a better tracking portfolio. The better approach is whichever one has a present value closer to zero for the tracking error. This is partly determined by the amount of tracking error and partly by how closely the risk-expected return relation described by the tracking portfolio approximates reality.

In contrast with a riskless cash flow, the decision about using a long-term or a short-term risk-free rate in valuing a risky cash flow that cannot be perfectly tracked is less clear-cut. In this case, which of the two imperfect tracking portfolios to use—market portfolio and short-term risk-free investment or market portfolio and long-term risk-free investment *(with a different mix of the two in each pairing)*—is an empirical issue best left to the analyst's judgment. Given our ambivalence on this topic, we are fortunate to be able to present a compromise position: the two-factor APT allows the tracking of a future cash flow with a short-term risk-free investment, a long-term risk-free investment, and a proxy for the market portfolio—if these are indeed the appropriate factors. If including each one of these three financial assets improves the tracking ability of the overall tracking portfolio, then such a tracking portfolio would be superior to one that leaves out either of the two risk-free investments.

Cash Flow Horizon and Beta Risk.   The last subsection illustrated that the horizon of the returns used in the tracking portfolio may affect the computed beta for a cash flow of a given horizon. This subsection considers whether beta risk is fundamentally different for cash flows in the near future than for cash flows in the distant future. In practice, financial analysts who implement the risk-adjusted discount rate method almost always use the same beta for every cash flow in a cash flow stream. Below, we argue that in many cases this practical shortcut leads to major valuation errors.

The prices of comparison stocks represent the present values of the cash flow streams. Unless the cash flow pattern of the comparison stream matches well with the stream of cash flows being valued, the beta risk of comparison firms may not provide an appropriate discount rate for the project.[18]

This applies doubly to individual cash flows. A single cash flow, 10 years out, is unlikely to have the same beta risk as a firm in the same line of business. The risk of the comparison firm depends on the risk of each of its future cash flows. Hence, the beta of the comparison firm is, in essence, a blend of the betas of each of the cash flows in its cash flow stream.

There are no hard-and-fast rules for how betas vary with the cash flow horizon. For some projects, the initial cash flows are relatively safe, but the cash flows in the future depend much more on market returns. In this case, other things equal, it is best to use a lower discount rate for the shorter-horizon cash flows. In other cases, long-horizon cash flows tend to have less systematic risk than similar cash flows of short horizons because many cash flows are highly correlated with the contemporaneous returns of traded securities and the health of the economy at the time the cash flow is produced, but are not significantly correlated with cumulative past returns.

For example, the cash flows of a brokerage firm such as Merrill Lynch are primarily determined by same-year and prior-year transaction volume, which is highly correlated with the market return. This would imply that the returns of the market over the next 8 years probably have little impact on Merrill Lynch's brokerage cash flows 10 years from now. As a consequence, Merrill Lynch's year 10 cash flow should be discounted back to year 8 at a risky rate of interest, and from year 8 to date 0 discounted at a much lower rate of interest, like the risk-free rate.

For example, suppose the risk-free rate over all horizons was 8 percent per year and the risky rate was 15 percent per year. The per year discount rate for the year 10 cash flow should be the geometric mean of eight years of 8 percent returns and two years of 15 percent returns or:

$$[(1.08)^8(1.15)^2]^{1/10} - 1$$

More generally, the **geometric mean** of T returns, $\tilde{r}_1, \tilde{r}_2, \ldots, \tilde{r}_T$ is

$$[(1 + \tilde{r}_1) \times (1 + \tilde{r}_2) \times \ldots \times (1 + \tilde{r}_T)]^{1/T} - 1$$

This is the short-horizon rate of return which, when compounded, gives the return over the long horizon.

Competitive considerations also suggest that long-horizon cash flows contain relatively little systematic (or factor) risk. When market returns are high, business is often good. However, good times often encourage entry into the market by competitors who can erode profits in subsequent years. Hence, if the economy is doing well in year 5 and General Motors is selling a record number of Chevy Suburban sport utility vehicles in that year, Ford, Chrysler, Toyota, and Mitsubishi also might decide to expand their sport

---

[18]This remains an issue whether we believe that an appropriate tracking portfolio (i.e., a tracking portfolio with zero-*PV* tracking error) is composed of a long-horizon riskless bond and the market portfolio (or factor portfolios) or whether it is composed of a short-horizon riskless bond rolled over each period and the market portfolio (or factor portfolios).

utility line to include an eight-seat, 8,000-pound vehicle like the Suburban. By the time year 10 rolls around, the competitors' products will be eroding GM's profits in this line of vehicles. This means that although the year 5 market return is positively correlated with the year 5 cash flow for the Suburban project, it may actually be negatively correlated with the year 10 cash flow. Hence, the year 10 cash flow may not be highly sensitive to the cumulative 10-year return of the market portfolio.

Empirical Failures of the CAPM and APT

The tracking portfolio metaphor applies even if one questions the validity of the CAPM and APT. If, after reading the empirical evidence in Chapters 5 and 6, one believes that market-to-book ratios and firm size are better determinants of a stock's *future* expected rate of return than market betas or factor betas, then the expected return of each comparison firm is identical to that of a portfolio of firms with similar firm size and market-to-book ratios. In the case of Marriott, this means that the average historical returns of firm size and market-to-book matched portfolios would be good estimates for the expected returns of McDonald's, Church's Chicken, and Wendy's.

In early 1996, for example, the McDonald's Corporation had a market-to-book ratio of about 4.5 and a market capitalization of about $35 billion. If the average historical return of a portfolio of firms with this same market-to-book ratio and market capitalization is 15 percent per year, then the appropriate required return for projects with the same risk as McDonald's is 15 percent per year. Because this is only an estimate of the project's cost of capital, we may want to do the same computation for Church's Chicken and Wendy's, averaging their required rates of return with McDonald's 15 percent per year estimate to obtain a more statistically precise estimate of the cost of capital for Marriott's restaurant division.[19]

On the other hand, if one believes that the empirical evidence from the past is the result of a psychological fad, a statistical accident, poor research, or some other anomaly that is unlikely to repeat in the future, then one should be more cautious in discarding CAPM- or APT-based expected return estimates.

What if No Comparable Line of Business Exists?

Using comparisons to identify beta risk is fine if portfolios of traded assets exist. However, for some real assets there is no suitable comparison line of business in which to search for the components of a tracking portfolio. In October 1996, for example, NASA announced a $7 billion deal with Lockheed Martin and Rockwell International, effectively privatizing the operation of the space shuttle. To value such a deal either from the perspective of NASA or the two companies, one would need to estimate beta risk, yet no comparison firm to the NASA space shuttle existed. In instances like this, beta risk can be computed by estimating the project's cash flows in each of many scenarios. Each scenario is associated with a particular realization of the return of the tangency portfolio.

Using Scenarios to Estimate Betas for the Risk-Adjusted Discount Rate Method.
Example 10.5 illustrates one way to estimate betas with scenarios. As we shall shortly see, there are some pitfalls to this approach.

---

[19]For simplicity, we have ignored the usual adjustments for leverage that need to be made.

Example 10.5:   Estimating Betas with Scenarios

The Adonis Travel Agency wishes to estimate the present value of next year's cash flow from the purchase of 10 new airline reservation computers, at a cost of $10,000 per computer. The new computers, which are faster than the current ones at the agency, are expected to increase the number of reservations that each agent can handle. For simplicity, assume that the additional cash flows associated with the increase in booking capacity are all received one year from now. The size of the increase is tied to the state of the economy. Over the next year, three possible economic scenarios, described in the following table, are considered:

Outcome	Probability	Market Return (%)	Incremental Cash Flow in One Year	Return on Computers
Recovery	$\frac{3}{4}$	25%	$150,000	$50\% = \dfrac{\$150{,}000 - \$100{,}000}{\$100{,}000}$
Recession	$\frac{3}{16}$	−1	35,000	$-65\% = \dfrac{\$35{,}000 - \$100{,}000}{\$100{,}000}$
Depression	$\frac{1}{16}$	−15	5,000	$-95\% = \dfrac{\$5{,}000 - \$100{,}000}{\$100{,}000}$

What is the present value of the additional cash flow one year from now if the risk-free return over the next year is 8.625 percent and the CAPM determines the expected returns of traded securities?

Answer: The market portfolio's expected return is:

$$17.625\% = \frac{3}{4}(25\%) + \frac{3}{16}(-1\%) + \frac{1}{16}(-15\%)$$

The variance of the market return is:

$$.017236 = \frac{3}{4}(.25 - .17625)^2 + \frac{3}{16}(-.01 - .17625)^2 + \frac{1}{16}(-.15 - .17625)^2$$

The expected return of the incremental cash flow is:

$$19.375\% = \frac{3}{4}(50\%) + \frac{3}{16}(-65\%) + \frac{1}{16}(-95\%)$$

The covariance of the cash flow return with the return of the market portfolio is:

$$.0697 = \frac{3}{4}(.5 - .19375)(.25 - .17625) + \frac{3}{16}(-.65 - .19375)(-.01 - .17625)$$

$$+ \frac{1}{16}(-.95 - .19375)(-.15 - .17625)$$

This yields a return beta (β) of:

$$4.045 = \frac{.0697}{.017236}$$

With a cost of $100,000 and a return of 19.375 percent, the expected cash flow, $E(\tilde{C})$, is

$$\$119{,}375 = \$100{,}000(1 + .19375)$$

Thus, by the risk-adjusted discount rate formula:

$$PV = \frac{\$119{,}375}{1 + .08625 + 4.045(.17625 - .08625)} = \$82{,}311$$

In Example 10.5, adoption of the new computer system is a negative *NPV* project because the $100,000 cost exceeds the benefit of $82,311. These calculations were based on beta estimates that generate the correct project adoption/rejection decision in simple cases. However, these betas are not really correct. As discussed below, the *true* beta in Example 10.5 is actually lower than the beta *of the return of project*.

Why Betas of Returns Are Not the Correct Betas for the Project.   The beta computed in Example 10.5 is not the true beta because the project returns for which this beta is computed have a base price of $100,000 instead of a base price equal to the project's present value, which is lower than $100,000. The securities market line relation between beta and expected return holds for the returns of financial assets, which are zero *NPV* investments and, by extension, all real asset investments that are zero *NPV*.

Suppose that instead of computing beta with scenarios, we computed scenarios for a portfolio of financial securities that perfectly track the cash flow of the Adonis Travel Agency project. Example 10.5 resorted to the scenario computation of beta because a comparison firm, needed to generate a tracking portfolio, did not exist. However, it is instructive to examine what the beta computation would be if a comparison-based tracking portfolio did exist.

The Adonis Travel Agency project has a negative *NPV*, but the hypothetical comparison-based tracking portfolio has a zero *NPV*. To indicate that the project has a negative *NPV*, the cost of the tracking portfolio (i.e., the project's *PV*) has to be *smaller* than $100,000. Hence, in each of the three scenarios of Example 10.5, the tracking portfolio's **gross return**, which is the return plus 100 percent, would be larger than the gross return of the project.

Exhibit 10.8, along with the observation in the Adonis example that $-C_0 = \$100,000$, demonstrates that the gross return of the project in each of the three scenarios is

$$\frac{PV}{-C_0} \times \text{(the gross return of the tracking portfolio)}$$

Recall from Chapter 9 that $PV/(-C_0)$ is the profitability index. Since, in this example, the profitability index is less than one, the gross returns of the hypothetical tracking portfolio are of larger scale, and thus have a larger beta, than the project's gross returns.[20] More generally, we have the following result:

Result 10.5   The betas of the actual returns of projects equal the project's profitability index times the appropriate beta needed to compute the true present value of the project. Since the profitability index exceeds 1 for positive *NPV* projects and is below 1 for negative *NPV* projects, this error in beta computation does not affect project selection in the absence of project selection constraints.

One can take only momentary comfort in the fact that the erroneous beta and, consequently, the erroneous present value computed from project returns do not alter the decision about whether a real investment should be accepted or rejected. The discussion below points out that incorrect capital allocation decisions will be made with mutually exclusive projects if one does not make corrections for return betas of negative *NPV* projects that are too low and those of positive *NPV* projects that are too high.

---

[20]We know from Chapter 4 that the covariance of a constant times the return of stock i with the return of stock j is the constant times the covariance of the returns of stocks i and j.

EXHIBIT 10.8   Gross Returns of the Project and Its Tracking Portfolio for Example 10.4

Outcome	*Probability*	*Project Return + 100%*	*Tracking Portfolio Return + 100%*
Recovery	$\dfrac{3}{4}$	$150\% = \dfrac{\$150{,}000}{\$100{,}000}$	$\dfrac{\$150{,}000}{PV}$
Recession	$\dfrac{3}{16}$	$35\% = \dfrac{\$35{,}000}{\$100{,}000}$	$\dfrac{\$35{,}000}{PV}$
Depression	$\dfrac{1}{16}$	$5\% = \dfrac{\$5{,}000}{\$100{,}000}$	$\dfrac{\$5{,}000}{PV}$

Properties of the Correct Beta and Correct Present Value.   How one computes a correct beta and present value is not immediately obvious. For example, it is tempting to think that one could do this for Example 10.5 by using the *PV* of $82,311 as the base number for computing returns and their betas. However, since this *PV* is still higher than the true *PV* of the project, it too is inappropriate as a base number. Also, the profitability index that, at least in theory, could be used as a divisor to generate the correct beta and thus the correct *PV* requires that the analyst first know the correct *PV*. While correct in theory, the adjustment implied by Result 10.5 obviously is impractical.

The correct *PV* has the following property: if the analyst made a lucky guess and selected the correct *PV* number, the returns (generated by using that *PV* as a base number) would have a beta and an associated discount rate from the CAPM or APT that would generate the original *PV* as the discounted expected future cash flow. A general formula for identifying this *PV* appears in Section 10.6 on the certainty equivalent method where the formula identifying the *PV* does not use a risk-adjusted discount rate.

Mutually Exclusive Projects.   If no comparison firms exist in the same line of business, forcing the use of scenarios to compute the betas for the risk-adjusted discount rate formula, Result 10.5 points out that the project's return betas will be misestimated by a factor equal to the project's profitability index, $PV/(-C_0)$. This can lead to the wrong choice among a set of mutually exclusive projects, as Example 10.6 demonstrates.

Example 10.6:   Mutually Exclusive Projects—Pitfalls in Applying Risk-Adjusted Discount Rates with Scenarios

The Adonis Travel Agency, discussed in Example 10.5, has a choice between two new software reservation systems for its new computers: One is produced by United Airlines, the other by American Airlines. Both new reservation systems have positive net present values and thus profitability indexes above 1. The actual returns of United's system have a beta of 1 while the actual returns of American's system have a beta of 1.5. Both have an expected incremental future cash flow of $40,000 one year from now. The cost of initiating United's system is $17,679.56 while that of American's system is $16,555.43. Assume that the CAPM holds, that the one-year risk-free rate is 8.625 percent, and that the one-year market risk premium is 9 percent. John Adonis, the son of the owner and, more importantly, the graduate of a rather backward M.B.A. program that does not use this text, thinks that United's system has a higher net present value. He argues that the risk-adjusted discount rate formula implies that the net present value of United's system is about:

$$\$16{,}327 = \frac{\$40{,}000}{1 + .08625 + (1).09} - \$17{,}679.56$$

The *NPV* of American's system is:

$$\$16,198 = \frac{\$40,000}{1 + .08625 + (1.5).09} - \$16,555.43$$

which is smaller. Is John Adonis correct in his analysis?

Answer: Suppose that the United reservation computer system has a profitability index of 2.0 and the American system has a profitability index of 2.1. By Result 10.5, the betas computed for the United and American systems are too high. The true betas are thus .5 (= ½) for the United system and .7143 (= 1.5/2.1) for the American system. Hence, the true *PV* of the United system (assuming the CAPM holds) is about:

$$\$17,680 = \frac{\$40,000}{1 + .08625 + (.5).09} - \$17,679.56$$

while that of American's system is:

$$\$18,211 = \frac{\$40,000}{1 + .08625 + (.7143).09} - \$16,555.43$$

Thus, in contrast to Mr. Adonis's assertion, American's reservation system has the higher *NPV* if the profitability index assumptions are correct. However, note that the profitability indexes of 2.0 and 2.1 are exactly the correct "guesses" because they are consistent with what the true profitability indexes turned out to be. Thus, the profitability indexes of 2.0 and 2.1 for United and American respectively are not really assumptions, but rather truths about the projects' profitabilities. Clearly, John Adonis is wrong and needs to read this text.

Chapter 9 emphasized that mutually exclusive projects should be chosen on the basis of the largest *NPV,* which is an arithmetic difference between the *PV* of the project's future cash flows and its initial cost. However, the way in which the *PV*s of positive *NPV* projects are distorted—through the use of the project returns to compute betas for the risk-adjusted discounted rate formula—is a rather complicated function of the true *PV* and the project's initial cost. The distortion is certainly not an arithmetic difference. Hence, it should not be surprising that it is possible to construct examples such as Example 10.6 where the naive manager may select the wrong project by using the risk-adjusted discount rate method.

10.6 Estimating Beta from Scenarios: The Certainty Equivalent Method

Hypothetical examples like Example 10.6 can illustrate the problem of using scenarios with the risk-adjusted discount rate method. In analyzing a real-world project, however, financial managers face a significant challenge whenever projects are mutually exclusive and it is difficult to identify a comparison tracking portfolio. Managers do not know the true *PV* unless they know the beta computed using a base cost that makes the project a zero-*NPV* investment. However, they cannot know this true project return beta unless they know the true *PV*. This section suggests a way out of this quandary. The method introduced is also applicable in cases where the present value is not of the same sign as the expected cash flow.

Defining the Certainty Equivalent Method

As noted earlier, the certainty equivalent method is closely related to the risk-adjusted discount rate method. However, instead of discounting expected cash flows at risk-adjusted discount rates, certainty equivalent cash flows are discounted using risk-free interest rates.

To understand what a certainty equivalent cash flow is, consider a project that pays off either $100, $200, or $300 next year, depending on the state of the economy. If these three states of the economy are equally likely, the expected cash flow is $200. Because of risk aversion, however, a project that paid $200 for certain would be preferred to this project. In other words, the certainty equivalent cash flow for this hypothetical project is less than $200—the project's expected cash flow. On the other hand, we know that this risky project is more valuable than a project with a guaranteed payoff of $100, the project's lowest cash flow. The certainty equivalent cash flow is thus some certain amount between $100 and $200 that would make the manager indifferent between taking the certain cash flow and taking the risky cash flow.[21] Specifically, the certainty equivalent of a risky cash flow paid at future date t is the riskless cash flow paid at date t that has the same present value as the risky cash flow.

Finding the present value of a stream of certainty equivalent cash flows is straightforward. Simply discount the certainty equivalent cash flows at the relevant risk-free rates, exactly as riskless cash flows were discounted in Chapter 9. The *certainty equivalent method* first obtains the certainty equivalent of the future cash flow. It then discounts the certainty equivalent back to date 0 at the risk free rate.

The difference between the risk-adjusted discount rate method and the certainty equivalent method is simply a matter of where the risk adjustment occurs. Recall that the present value of a cash flow can be expressed as the ratio of the projected cash flow to 1 plus the discount rate. *With the certainty equivalent method, the numerator of that ratio, the certainty equivalent cash flow, is adjusted for risk and discounted at a risk-free interest rate in the ratio's denominator. By contrast, the risk-adjusted discount rate method places the expected cash flow in the numerator and discounts it in the ratio's denominator at a risk-adjusted interest rate.* Either method is theoretically acceptable; it is appropriate to risk-adjust in either the numerator or the denominator of the present value expression. The preferred method depends on the practical considerations emphasized throughout the chapter.

Identifying the Certainty Equivalent from Models of Risk and Return

Denote $CE(\tilde{C})$ as the certainty equivalent of uncertain future cash flow $\tilde{C}$ and $E(\tilde{C})$ as the cash flow mean, Result 10.6 describes how to compute certainty equivalents from a risk-expected return model.

Result 10.6   To obtain a certainty equivalent, subtract the product of the cash flow beta and the tangency portfolio risk premium from the expected cash flow, that is:

$$CE(\tilde{C}) = E(\tilde{C}) - b(\overline{R}_T - r_f)$$

where

$$b = \frac{\text{cov}(\tilde{C}, \tilde{R}_T)}{\sigma_T^2}$$

The Cash Flow Beta and its Interpretation.   Result 10.6 adjusts for risk with the cash flow beta, denoted as b. The **cash flow beta** is the covariance of the *future cash flow*

---

[21]In rare cases, specifically projects with negative betas, the certainty equivalent may exceed the expected cash flow.

(not the return on the cash flow), with the return of the tangency portfolio, divided by the variance of the return of the tangency portfolio, that is:

$$b = \frac{\text{cov}(\tilde{C}, \tilde{R}_T)}{\sigma_T^2}$$

This risk measure is the amount of the tangency portfolio that must be held to track, as best as possible, the future cash flow. In contrast to the return beta (β), which is used with the risk-adjusted discount rate method, the cash flow beta (b) can be computed directly after forming scenarios, as we will illustrate shortly. Since obtaining this cash flow beta does not require prior knowledge of the present value, *the certainty equivalent is a superior vehicle for identifying present values when return and cash flow estimation in scenarios is the only method available for generating risk measures.*

The Certainty Equivalent Present Value Formula and Its Interpretation.   To obtain the present value, discount the certainty equivalent at the risk-free rate. Combining this finding with Result 10.6 generates the following result:

Result 10.7   *(The certainty equivalent present value formula.) PV*, the present value of next period's cash flow, can be found by (1) computing $E(\tilde{C})$ the expected future cash flow and the beta of the future cash flow, (2) subtracting the product of this beta and the risk premium of the tangency portfolio from the expected future cash flow, and (3) dividing by (1 + the risk-free return), that is:

$$PV = \frac{E(\tilde{C}) - b(\bar{R}_T - r_f)}{1 + r_f}$$

Thus, the certainty equivalent present value formula first adjusts for the risk-premium component and then for the time value of money. To compute the net present value, subtract the initial cost of the project $-C_0$ from this present value.

One interpretation of the certainty equivalent formula in Result 10.6 comes from recognizing that b, the cash flow beta, is the tracking portfolio's dollar investment in the tangency portfolio. The tangency portfolio earns an extra expected return (i.e., a risk premium) because of risk. Specifically, $\bar{R}_T - r_f$ is the future additional amount earned per dollar invested in the tangency portfolio because of the tangency portfolio's systematic (or factor) risk. For an investment of b dollars in the tangency portfolio, the additional expected cash flow (in dollars) from the project's systematic (or factor) risk is thus:

$$b(\bar{R}_T - r_f)$$

Hence, subtracting $b(\bar{R}_T - r_f)$ from the expected cash flow $E(\tilde{C})$ yields:

$$E(\tilde{C}) - b(\bar{R}_T - r_f)$$

This represents the cash flow that would be generated if the project had a cash flow beta of zero or, alternatively, if the future cash flow were risk free.

An Illustration of a Present Value Computation when the Cash Flow Beta Is Given.   Example 10.7 illustrates how to compute present values given cash flow betas.

Example 10.7:   Computing the Cost of Capital

Hot Shot Computer Corp (HSCC), a wholly owned subsidiary of Novel, Inc., first seen in Example 10.1, has a cash flow beta (b) of $10.91 when computed against the tangency portfolio. One year from now, this subsidiary has a .9 probability of being worth $10 per share and a .1 probability of being worth $20 per share. The risk-free rate is 9 percent per year. The tangency portfolio has an expected return of 19 percent per year. What is the present value of HSCC, assuming no dividend payments to the parent firm in the coming year?

Answer: The expected value of HSCC one year from now is:

$$\$11 \text{ per share} = .9(\$10) + .1(\$20)$$

The numerator in the certainty equivalent formula, the certainty equivalent, is thus:

$$\$9.91 = \$11 - \$10.91(.19 - .09)$$

The subsidiary's present value is its certainty equivalent divided by 1 plus the risk-free rate or

$$\text{approximately } \$9.09 \text{ per share} = \frac{\$9.91 \text{ per share}}{1.09}$$

Cash Flow Betas and Return Betas.   The answer in Example 10.7 is identical to the answer given in Example 10.1 because Example 10.7 uses a cash flow beta consistent with the return beta from Example 10.1. Note that in Example 10.1, β is the beta of a comparison financial security, which is a zero NPV investment. The cash flow beta $b = \$9.09\beta$; that is, the ratio of the cash flow beta to the return beta (as computed for a cost of $9.09), equals the project's present value:

$$PV = \frac{b}{\beta}$$

This equation is not valid if $PV \leq 0$ (and expected cash flow is non-negative).

The CAPM, Scenarios, and the Certainty Equivalent Method

The last subsection suggested that scenarios provide one way to identify cash flow betas and present values with the certainty equivalent method. Example 10.8 illustrates how to implement this scenario method, assuming that the market portfolio is the tangency portfolio.

Example 10.8:   Present Values with the Certainty Equivalent Method

The Adonis Travel Agency, examined in Examples 10.5 and 10.6, wishes to estimate the present value of the cash flow from purchasing 10 new airline reservation computers. The new computers, which are faster than the current ones in place at the agency, are expected to increase the number of reservations each agent can handle. For simplicity, assume that all the additional cash flows associated with the increase in booking capacity are received one year from now. The size of the increase is tied to the state of the economy. Over the next year, three possible economic scenarios are considered, which are described in the following table, taken from Example 10.5:

Outcome	Probability	Market Return (%)	Incremental Cash in One Year
Recovery	$\frac{3}{4}$	25%	$150,000
Recession	$\frac{3}{16}$	−1	35,000
Depression	$\frac{1}{16}$	−15	5,000

What is the present value of the additional cash flow one year from now if the risk-free return over the next year is 8.625 percent and the CAPM determines the expected returns of traded securities?

Answer: The risk premium of the market portfolio is:

$$\bar{R}_M - r_f = \frac{3}{4}(.25) + \frac{3}{16}(-.01) + \frac{1}{16}(-.15) - .08625 = .09$$

while the variance of the market return (computed in Example 10.5) is .017236.

The expected incremental cash flow is:

$$\$119{,}375 = \frac{3}{4}(\$150{,}000) + \frac{3}{16}(\$35{,}000) + \frac{1}{16}(\$5{,}000)$$

The covariance of the cash flow with the return of the market portfolio:

$$\text{cov}(\tilde{C}, \tilde{R}_m) = \$1{,}000\left[\frac{3}{4}(150)(.25) + \frac{3}{16}(35)(-.01) + \frac{1}{16}(5)(-.15)\right] - (\$119{,}375)(.17625)$$

$$= \$28{,}012.5 - \$21{,}039.84375 = \$6{,}972.65625$$

which generates a cash flow beta of $\dfrac{\$6{,}972.65625}{.017236}$. Substituting these values into the certainty equivalent formula leaves a present value of approximately:

$$PV = \frac{\$119{,}375 - \left[\dfrac{\$6{,}972.65625}{.017236}\right](.09)}{1 + .08625} = \$76{,}379$$

Example 10.8 is based on the same numbers as Example 10.5, where, using the risk-adjusted discount rate method, we found an erroneous present value for the Adonis Travel computer cash flow of $82,311. The latter number was too high because negative *NPV* projects have underestimated return betas.

Example 10.8 demonstrates that the certainty equivalent method gives the true present value of $76,379. The last section and Example 10.6, using the same travel agency, emphasized the importance of knowing this true present value for mutually exclusive projects.

The APT and the Certainty Equivalent Method

To obtain the certainty equivalent in the one-factor APT, subtract from the expected future cash flow the product of (1) the factor loading of the future cash flow and (2) the risk premium of the factor. If there is more than one factor, sum these products over all factors and then subtract.[22] Then discount this certainty equivalent at the risk-free rate to obtain the present value, that is:

$$PV = \frac{E(\tilde{C}) - (\lambda_1 b_1 + \lambda_2 b_2 + \ldots + \lambda_K b_K)}{1 + r_f}$$

where b_j $(j = 1, \ldots, K)$ is the factor loading of the *future cash flow* (not the cash flow return) on the jth factor. The symbol b_j represents the number of dollars invested in the

---

[22]In the multifactor case, the cash flow factor loading will be its multiple regression coefficient against the factor and it will be its covariance with the factor divided by the factor variance only if the factors are uncorrelated.

*j*th factor portfolio that best tracks the cash flow of the project. The amount subtracted from $E(\tilde{C})$ in the numerator of this ratio is thus the additional expected cash flow due to the factor risk of the project.

The Relation between the Certainty Equivalent Formula and the Tracking Portfolio Approach

Recall the Hilton casino illustration from Sections 10.1 and 10.2, which ascribed a present value of $10.0 million to an expected cash flow of $11.3 million from Louisiana gambling. Hilton's tracking portfolio for the casino consisted of $5 million invested in the market portfolio, which has a risk premium of 14 percent (= 20% − 6%), and $5 million invested in a risk-free asset, which has a return of 6 percent. As suggested in the previous subsection, the amount invested in the tangency portfolio (in this case, the market portfolio) is the cash flow beta (*b*). Hence, the Hilton casino cash flow beta is $5 million. Using this cash flow beta in the certainty equivalent formula (see Result 10.6) yields a certainty equivalent (the numerator) of $11.3 million − $5.0 million(.14) = $10.6 million and thus a present value (see Result 10.7) of $10 million (= $10.6 million/1.06).

In practice, one first obtains the cash flow beta, $5 million, from scenarios, and only then is it possible to recognize this as the amount of the tracking portfolio invested in the market portfolio. To keep the tracking as close as possible, the expected cash flow from the tracking portfolio of financial securities must be the same as the expected cash flow from the casino. (Can you explain why?) Hence, in deriving this tracking portfolio, it is important to know that the expected cash flow from the casino was $11.3 million. Then, solving for the risk-free investment, *x*, in combination with a $5 million investment in the market portfolio, yields an expected future cash flow of $11.3 million, which pins down the risk-free investment. Algebraically, *x* solves:

$$\$11,300,000 = x(1.06) + \$5,000,000 \,(1.2), \text{ or}$$
$$x = \$5,000,000$$

The certainty equivalent method gives the same present values as the tracking portfolio approach used earlier. Indeed, the certainty equivalent is derived from the tracking portfolio approach as evidenced by the fact that cash flow beta *b* is the tracking portfolio's expenditure on the market (or tangency) portfolio.

10.7 Obtaining Certainty Equivalents with Risk-free Scenarios

The CAPM and APT implementations of the certainty equivalent method require knowledge of the composition of a portfolio that tracks the evaluated investment's cash flow. Moreover, to obtain the certainty equivalent of the cash flow, the manager must:

1. Compute two items: the expected cash flow and its adjustment for risk based on the cash flow's covariance with the return of the tangency portfolio.
2. Obtain the difference between these two items.

It would clearly be advantageous if the manager could estimate the certainty equivalent without having to estimate both the expected value and risk of the cash flow.

A Description of the Risk-Free Scenario Method

An alternative computational approach to the certainty equivalent, which we call the risk-free scenario method, provides the manager with a simple way to estimate the certainty equivalent cash flow. The **risk-free scenario method** generates the certainty equivalent with a typically conservative cash flow forecast under a scenario where all assets are expected to appreciate at the risk-free rate. In other words, the certainty equivalent cash flow is assumed to be the expected cash flow in situations where the tangency portfolio return equals the risk-free rate.

Distributions for Which the Risk-Free Scenario Method Works. This method works when the returns of the tangency portfolio and the future cash flows of the project have specific distributions. Specifically, it must be a distribution where the expectation of the future cash flow, given the return of a mean-variance efficient portfolio, is a linear function of the return of the tangency portfolio.

Algebraically, this can be expressed as follows:

$$E(\tilde{C} \mid \text{given the return } R_T) = a + bR_T$$

The values of a and b, the intercept and cash flow beta, respectively, do not change for different outcomes of the return of the tangency portfolio. This is basically the assumption of linear regression and it is satisfied by, among other distributions, the normal distribution. The key feature of this distributional assumption is that the error in the cash flow forecast is distributed independently of the tangency portfolio's return.

Inputs for the Risk-Free Scenario Method. The risk-free scenario method uses as its input an estimate of the project's cash flows, assuming that the return of the tangency portfolio, and thus the tracking portfolio, equals the risk-free return. In other words, instead of asking the engineers and marketing research managers to estimate the expected cash flows of a project, the analyst asks them to come up with what they think the cash flows would be in a scenario where the tracking portfolio (e.g., a combination of the market portfolio and a risk-free asset if the CAPM holds) has a return that equals the risk-free rate. As shown below, eliciting this kind of information is useful because, under the conditions noted above, these **conditional expected cash flows**—that is, expected cash flows conditional on the tracking portfolio return equaling the risk-free return—can be viewed as the cash flow's certainty equivalent. To see this, regress $\tilde{r}$, the *actual* excess returns of any zero-*NPV* investment (return less the risk-free rate), on the actual excess return of the tangency portfolio. The resulting equation is:

$$\tilde{r} - r_f = \alpha + \beta(\tilde{R}_T - r_f) + \tilde{\epsilon} \tag{10.7}$$

where (for each particular outcome of the return of the tangency portfolio):

$$E(\tilde{\epsilon}) = 0$$

Equation (10.7) indicates that high beta investments are expected to outperform low beta investments in scenarios where the tangency portfolio return exceeds the risk-free return. The opposite is true in scenarios where the risk-free return exceeds the tangency portfolio's return. However, when the tangency portfolio return equals the risk-free return, the expected returns of all zero-*NPV* investments are equal to α (alpha), irrespective of their betas. Moreover, it is possible to show that the intercept (α) is 0 in equation (10.7) by first calculating the expected values of both sides of the equation and noting, from the risk-expected return equation (5.4), that

$$\bar{r} = r_f + \beta(\bar{R}_T - r_f) \tag{10.8}$$

Hence, letting $\alpha = 0$, as implied by equation (10.8), the expectation of the left-hand side of equation (10.7) in the risk-free scenario is 0, and thus:

$$E(\tilde{r} \mid \text{given } \tilde{R}_T = r_f) = r_f$$

Obtaining PVs with the Risk-Free Scenario Method.   This analysis demonstrates that when the return of the tangency portfolio equals the risk-free return, all zero-*NPV* investments are expected to appreciate at the risk-free rate. In this risk-free scenario, a project's expected future value is

$$E(\tilde{C} \mid \text{given risk-free scenario}) = (1 + r_f)PV$$

Thus, once the product $(1 + r_f)PV$ is estimated, the analyst can determine the *PV* by discounting the expected cash flow for the risk-free scenario, $E(\tilde{C} \mid \text{given risk-free scenario})$, at the risk-free rate.

Result 10.8   *(Estimating the certainty equivalent with a risk-free scenario.)* If it is possible to estimate the expected future cash flow of an investment or project under a scenario where all securities are expected to appreciate at the risk-free return, then the present value of the cash flow is computed by discounting the expected cash flow for the risk-free scenario at the risk-free rate.

Tracking Portfolios and the Risk-Free Scenario Method.   If the CAPM applies, the implicit tracking portfolio used in Result 10.8 is a combination of the market portfolio and a risk-free asset. However, there is no need to estimate betas or to identify the tangency portfolio used in the tracking portfolio if it is possible to forecast the future cash flow under a scenario where all securities are expected to appreciate at the risk-free rate. Moreover, the task of estimating the cash flows for all possible scenarios and weighting by the probabilities of the scenarios is eliminated with the risk-free scenario method.

The only scenario where cash flow forecasts are needed is one in which all securities are expected to earn the risk-free return. Because the tangency portfolio return equals its expected return in the average scenario, and the tangency portfolio's expected return is larger than the risk-free return, the risk-free scenario is more pessimistic than the average scenario.

An Illustration of How to Implement the Risk-Free Scenario Method.   Example 10.9 illustrates how to implement the risk-free scenario method.

Example 10.9:   Valuation with the Risk-Free Scenario Method

The McGirwin Company is evaluating a project with a one-year life that has uncertain cash flows at the end of the first year. Its managers estimate that the project will generate a cash flow of $100,000 at the end of year 1 under a scenario where all securities are expected to earn the risk-free return of 5 percent per year. What is the present value of this risky project? For what costs should the project be accepted or rejected?

Answer: $100,000 is the certainty equivalent of the future cash flows. Discounting this at a rate of 5 percent yields $100,000/1.05 or $95,238. Therefore, if the project costs less than $95,328, McGirwin managers should accept it. If it costs more than $95,328, they should reject it.

Advantages of the Risk-Free Scenario Method.   As a practical matter, the advantage of employing the risk-free scenario method is obvious. In the risk-free scenario, investors expect the stock held by shareholders in the manager's own firm and the stock in all other firms in the industry to appreciate at the risk free rate (with dividends reinvested). For this moderately pessimistic scenario, the manager may find it easier to estimate the future cash flow of the project than to estimate both its expected value over all scenarios and its covariance with the tangency portfolio, assuming that it is possible to even identify the tangency portfolio.

In theory, the present value obtained with the risk-free scenario method should be the same as that obtained with the traditional certainty equivalent method. In practice, however, there is no reason for these methods to generate either identical certainty equivalents or identical present values because the estimates of cash flows for risk-free scenarios and estimates of cash flow betas for traditional certainty equivalent approaches are imperfect.[23]

Implementing the Risk-Free Scenario Method in a Multiperiod Setting

The risk-free scenario method avoids many of the problems faced by more traditional methods in a multiperiod setting (see Section 10.5). To illustrate the multiperiod use of the risk-free scenario method, assume that yields on one-year, five-year, and 10-year risk-free zero-coupon bonds are respectively 5, 6, and 7 percent. Consider a computer operating system designed by Microsoft; it has a life of 10 years and will have three major versions: version 8.0 (sold at the end of year 1), 9.0 (sold at the end of year 5), and version 10.0 (sold at the end of year 10). For simplicity, assume that so much software pirating is going on between these major revisions of the software product that the cash flows between revisions are essentially zero.

To obtain the present value of the three future cash flows, it is necessary to obtain estimates of the year 1, year 5, and year 10 cash flows under their respective risk-free scenarios. These cash flow estimates are not easily obtained but, as we show below, are probably no more difficult to obtain than estimates of the year 1, year 5, and year 10 *expected* cash flows.

To obtain the risk-free scenario estimate for year 1, envision an estimate of the cash flow under a scenario in which all assets, with dividends reinvested, are expected to appreciate by 5 percent, the one-year risk-free rate. The present value of the year 1 cash flow is that estimate discounted back one year at a rate of 5 percent. To obtain the risk-free scenario estimate for year 5, envision what the year 5 cash flow would be if all assets, with dividends reinvested, are expected to appreciate at a rate of 6 percent per year for these 5 years, the yield on a five-year risk-free bond. The present value of the year 5 cash flow is that estimate discounted back five years at a rate of 6 percent. To obtain the risk-free scenario estimate for year 10, envision what the year 10 cash flow would be if all assets, with dividends reinvested, are expected to appreciate at a rate of 7 percent per year for these 10 years, the yield on a 10-year risk-free bond. The present value is this estimate, discounted back 10 years at a rate of 7 percent per year.

When the mean-variance efficient (i.e., tangency) portfolio appreciates at the risk-free rate, all securities are expected to appreciate at the risk-free rate, including the stock of Microsoft. Thus, a reasonable procedure for estimating the cash flows for the risk-free scenarios at the three horizons is to forecast the cash flow as a multiple of Microsoft's future stock price and compute what the price of Microsoft's stock and the project cash flow would be when Microsoft's stock appreciates at a risk-free rate.[24]

---

[23]The major drawback to the risk-free scenario method is that it will only provide the true present value if the distribution of the return of the tangency portfolio and the cash flow belong to certain families of distributions, including the bivariate normal distribution. If the distribution of the cash flow and the return of the tangency portfolio is one in which the conditional expectation is nonlinear, the forecast under this scenario is not the same as the certainty equivalent.

[24]This multiple could differ for different horizons, but in the example we will assume it does not change with the horizon.

This forecast will be the true certainty equivalent if the error in the cash flow forecast is distributed independently of the return of the mean-variance efficient portfolio for that horizon. For simplicity, assume that Microsoft will not pay any dividends over the next 10 years. For companies that pay dividends, forecast the stock value with all dividends reinvested.

If Microsoft is currently trading at $100 a share, it will trade at $105 a share one year from now in a risk-free scenario, given a risk-free rate of 5 percent per year. Over a five-year period, Microsoft will trade at $133.82 if it appreciates at the five-year risk-free rate, 6 percent per year. In 10 years, it will trade at $196.72 if it appreciates at the 10-year risk-free rate, 7 percent per year.

Assume that Microsoft's managers believe the operating system is expected to generate cash equal to 10 million times Microsoft's stock price per share. Hence, the new operating system is expected to generate $1.05 billion at the end of year 1 if Microsoft stock with dividends reinvested is then selling at $105 a share, $1.3382 billion at the end of year 5 if Microsoft stock sells for $133.28 a share at that point, and $1.9672 billion at the end of year 10 if Microsoft stock sells for $196.72 at that point.

The present value of the operating system is then:

$$PV = \frac{\$1.05 \text{ billion}}{1.05} + \frac{\$1.3382 \text{ billion}}{(1.06)^5} + \frac{\$1.9672 \text{ billion}}{(1.07)^{10}}$$

$$= \frac{\$1.05 \text{ billion}}{1.05} + \frac{\$1.3382 \text{ billion}}{1.3382} + \frac{\$1.9672 \text{ billion}}{1.9672}$$

$$= \$3 \text{ billion}$$

Example 10.10 presents another illustration of the risk-free scenario method.

Example 10.10:   Multiperiod Valuation with the Risk-Free Scenario Method

Omegatron, a game software company, wants to value the cash flows of its new Doombo game at years 5 and 10. Assume the following:

- Cash flow forecast errors are noise; that is, they are distributed independently of everything.
- The year 5 cash flow of Doombo has an expected value of $39 million if its five-year stock return, with dividends reinvested in Doombo stock, is 30 percent over the 5 years
- The year 10 cash flow of Doombo has an expected value of $80 million if an investment in its stock (with all dividends reinvested) doubles over 10 years.
- At date 0, $1.00 buys $1.30 in face value of a risk-free, five-year zero-coupon bond.
- At date 0, $1.00 buys $2.00 in face value of a risk-free, ten-year zero-coupon bond.

What are the present values of the two cash flows?

Answer: Applying the certainty equivalent formula, the present value of the year 5 cash flow is:

$$\$30 \text{ million} = \frac{\$39 \text{ million}}{1.30}$$

and the year 10 cash flow's present value is

$$\$40 \text{ million} = \frac{\$80 \text{ million}}{2.00}$$

The cash flow estimate in Example 10.10 is trickier than it may seem at first. The long-term appreciation in the stock is assumed to equal the appreciation of a risk-free security. This does not mean that the stock has to appreciate year by year at the same rate as the risk-free security. Like the tortoise and the hare, the stock can start off faster than the risk-free security, then slow down, or vice versa, just as long as they end up in the same place at the same time. In a risk-free scenario, the manager knows that the geometric mean of the stock return is the risk-free rate, but he does not know the pattern of short-horizon returns by which that geometric mean is achieved. Each pattern could generate a different project cash flow. In this case, it is important to analyze and weigh the likelihood of paths in order to arrive at the expected cash flow under the scenarios in which the stock's geometric mean return for the tangency portfolio is the risk-free rate.

The firm's own stock price is not the only candidate to use for a risk-free scenario; other traded securities or portfolios of securities are perfectly adequate substitutes. Generally, using more securities and portfolios makes it more likely that the cash flow forecast error will be distributed independently of the return of the mean-variance efficient portfolio.

The ease with which the risk-free scenario method is applied in a multiperiod setting gives it a major advantage over the risk-adjusted discount rate method or the traditional certainty equivalent method. When it can be applied, we believe that the risk-free scenario method generates better approximations to the true present values than those estimated with more traditional methods.

Providing Certainty Equivalents without Knowing It

In many instances, the cash flow for the risk-free scenario is provided unwittingly by analysts or managers. This situation usually arises when the manager wants to be conservative in his forecast, knowing that the cash flow is risky and the forecast is imprecise.

For example, consider a financial analyst working at a hypothetical company that we will call Elliot Hand Tools. The engineers have designed a new hand drill and have calculated the costs of setting up a plant to manufacture this product. After the engineers calculate the manufacturing costs per unit, the market research department estimates a projected selling price and the number of units that they think Elliot Hand Tools can sell. Based on all of this information, the financial analyst forecasts a stream of future cash flows and then evaluates whether the company should go through with the project.

To discount the cash flows stream, the financial analyst has to know a bit about how the cash flows were estimated. If the engineers and marketing researchers decide to give conservative estimates because the cash flows are so risky, then the cash flow stream may be better thought of as a certainty equivalent that should be discounted at the risk-free rate. The analyst would not want to discount such risk-adjusted cash flows at a risk-adjusted discount rate. However, the analyst must also be aware that the conservative estimates of the engineers and marketing researchers may not be the precise certainty equivalent.

10.8 Computing Certainty Equivalents from Prices in Financial Markets

In some cases, prices from financial markets provide information that analysts can use to project future cash flows.

Forward Prices

Forward prices are related to estimates of the future spot prices of different currencies and commodities. As Chapter 7 pointed out, however, the forward price represents the certainty equivalent of the uncertain future price rather than its expected value. Whenever forward prices are available for future cash flows, use the certainty equivalent method for valuation. Such forward prices effectively translate data from the complex world of risky cash flows to the much simpler world of riskless cash flows, which were considered in Chapter 9.

Example 10.11 illustrates how to value cattle using this method.

Example 10.11:   Present Values with Certainty Equivalents from Futures Prices

Farmer John is considering the purchase of live cattle that will be ready for slaughter six months from now, at which point their aggregate weight will be 100,000 pounds. The asking price for the cattle is $50,000 and it will cost $10,000 to buy feed and medication for all the cattle. The (unannualized) risk-free interest rate over this six-month period is 3 percent, and the only source of uncertainty associated with this transaction is the future market price of cattle. However, on the Chicago Mercantile Exchange, we observe a six-month forward price for cattle of $0.70 per pound. Should Farmer John buy the cattle?

Answer: $70,000 is the certainty equivalent for the cattle revenue produced by the farm in six months. A comparison of the present value of that amount, $67,961 = $70,000/1.03, with the cost of the cattle, the feed, and the medication, $60,000, implies that Farmer John should purchase the cattle because the project has a positive *NPV* of $7,961.

Tracking Portfolios That Contain Forward Contracts

It would be difficult to calculate an expected cash flow and to apply the risk-adjusted discount rate approach in Example 10.11. In this case, the tracking portfolio approach provides an equivalent answer; the appropriate tracking portfolio would be a forward contract to sell 100,000 pounds of live cattle along with $70,000/1.03 in a risk-free investment with a return of 3 percent. Since the forward contract has zero value (see Chapter 7), the value of that tracking portfolio is $70,000/1.03, which is the present value of the future cash flows.[25]

10.9 Summary and Conclusions

This chapter analyzed the rules for computing the market values of the future cash flows of risky investment projects. Academics often recommend and practitioners implement two equivalent discounted cash flow methods—the risk-adjusted discount rate method and the certainty equivalent method—to value future cash flows. As a simple practical approach, we also recommend a particular implementation—the risk-free scenario method—of the certainty equivalent method.

The major theme of this chapter is that practical rather than theoretical considerations dictate which valuation approach to use and how to implement it. The risk-adjusted discount rate method, which obtains the discount rate (i.e., the cost of capital) from commonly used theories of risk and return, such as the CAPM and APT, is impractical when the betas of comparison firms are hard to estimate. Also, a variety of nuances require adjustments to the beta estimates. These adjustments can make this

---

[25]Chapter 11 further examines how to identify present values from futures and forward prices.

seemingly simple valuation method extremely complicated. In cases where comparison firms do not exist and scenarios are required to estimate risk, practical considerations dictate that the certainty equivalent method is the better valuation method to use. Once the cash flow's certainty equivalent is obtained, there are no further nuances and complications to watch out for. Hence, whenever observable forward prices or internal estimation procedures lead to certainty equivalents, the certainty equivalent is the preferred valuation method.

Despite a thorough treatment of real asset valuation in the last two chapters, our coverage of this important topic remains incomplete; a number of additional issues that have a major impact on the capital allocation decision remain. Chapter 11 studies the impact of growth options and other strategic options. It also explores an alternative valuation approach that is quite popular in a number of practical settings: the ratio comparison approach. Chapters 12–14 analyze financing and dividend policies and their impact on corporate tax liabilities in deciding between projects. The effect of capital structure and dividend policy on incentives for choosing positive *NPV* projects, as well as bankruptcy costs, are studied in the latter half of Part IV. Managerial incentives and information asymmetries are dealt with in Part V of the text.

Key Concepts

Result 10.1: Whenever a tracking portfolio for the future cash flows of a project generates tracking error with zero systematic (or factor) risk and zero expected value, the market value of the tracking portfolio is the present value of the project's future cash flows.

Result 10.2: To find the present value of next period's cash flow using the risk-adjusted discount rate method: (1) compute the expected future cash flow next period, $E(\tilde{C})$; (2) compute the beta of the return of the project, β; (3) compute the expected return of the project by substituting the beta calculated in step (2) into the tangency portfolio risk-expected return equation; (4) divide the expected future cash flow in step (1) by 1 plus the expected return from step (3). In algebraic terms:

$$PV = \frac{E(\tilde{C})}{1 + r_f + \beta(\bar{R}_T - r_f)}$$

Result 10.3: Increasing the firm's debt (raising D and reducing E) increases the (beta and standard deviation) risk per dollar of equity investment. It will increase linearly in the D/E ratio if the debt is risk free.

Result 10.4: The cost of equity

$$\bar{r}_E = \bar{r}_A + (D/E)(\bar{r}_A - \bar{r}_D)$$

increases as the firm's leverage ratio D/E increases. It will increase linearly in the ratio D/E if the debt is default free and if $\bar{r}_A$, the expected return of the firm's assets,

does not change as the leverage ratio increases.

Result 10.5: The betas of the actual returns of projects equal the project's profitability index times the appropriate beta needed to compute the true present value of the project. Since the profitability index exceeds 1 for positive *NPV* projects and is below 1 for negative *NPV* projects, this error in beta computation does not affect project selection in the absence of project selection constraints.

Result 10.6: To obtain a certainty equivalent, subtract the product of the cash flow beta and the tangency portfolio risk premium from the expected cash flow, that is:

$$CE(\tilde{C}) = E(\tilde{C}) - b(\bar{R}_T - r_f)$$

where

$$b = \frac{\text{cov}(\tilde{C}, \bar{R}_T)}{\sigma_T^2}$$

Result 10.7: *(The certainty equivalent present value formula.)* PV, the present value of next period's cash flow, can be found by (1) computing $E(\tilde{C})$ the expected future cash flow and the beta of the future cash flow, (2) subtracting the product of this beta and the risk premium of the tangency portfolio from the expected future cash flow, and (3) dividing by (1 + the risk-free return), that is:

$$PV = \frac{E(\tilde{C}) - b(\bar{R}_T - r_f)}{1 + r_f}$$

Result 10.8: *(Estimating the certainty equivalent with a risk-free scenario.)* If it is possible to estimate the expected future cash flow of an investment or project under a scenario where all securities are expected to appreciate at the risk-free return, then the present value of the cash flow is computed by discounting the expected cash flow for the risk-free scenario at the risk-free rate.

Key Terms

book return on equity   377
capital structure   370
cash flow beta   389
certainty equivalent   361
certainty equivalent method   361
comparison approach   367
conditional expected cash flows   394
cost of debt   371
cost of equity   371

dividend discount model (Gordon Growth Model)   376
expected cash flows   361
geometric mean   383
gross return   386
leverage ratio   370
plowback ratio   377
plowback ratio formula   377
risk-adjusted discount rate method   361
risk-free scenario method   394

Exercises

10.1. A project has an expected cash flow of $1 million one year from now. The standard deviation of this cash flow is $250,000. If the expected return of the market portfolio is 10 percent, the risk-free rate is 5 percent, the standard deviation of the market return is 5 percent, and the correlation between this future cash flow and the return on the market is .5, what is the present value of the cash flow? Assume the CAPM holds. *Hint:* Use the certainty equivalent method.

Exercises 10.2–10.6 make use of the following information.

Assume that Marriott's restaurant division has the following joint distribution with the market return:

Market Scenario	Probability	Market Return (%)	Year 1 Restaurant Cash Flow Forecast
Bad	.25	−15	$40 million
Good	.50	5	$50 million
Great	.25	25	$60 million

Assume also that the CAPM holds.

10.2. Compute the expected year 1 restaurant cash flow for Marriott.

10.3. Find the covariance of the cash flow with the market return and its cash flow beta.

10.4. Assuming that historical data suggests that the market risk premium is 8.4 percent per year and the market standard deviation is 40 percent per year, find the certainty equivalent of the year 1 cash flow. What are the advantages and disadvantages of using such historical data for market inputs as opposed to inputs from a set of scenarios, like those given in the table above exercise 10.2?

10.5. Discount your answer in exercise 10.4 at a risk-free rate of 4 percent per year to obtain the present value.

10.6. Explain why the answer to exercise 10.5 differs from the answer in Example 10.2.

10.7. Start with the risk-adjusted discount rate formula. Derive the certainty equivalent formula by rearranging terms and noting that the $b = \beta \times PV$.

10.8. In Section 10.3's illustration, asset values increased 10 percent from 1995 to 1996, from $100 million to $110 million.
  a. Compute the percentage increase in the value of equity if the firm is financed with $50 million in debt.
  b. Compute the leverage ratio of this firm in 1996.

10.9.   Explain intuitively why the certainty equivalent of a cash flow with a negative beta exceeds the cash flow's expected value.

Exercises 10.10–10.14 make use of the following data.

In 1989, General Motors (GM) was evaluating the acquisition of Hughes Aircraft Corporation. Recognizing that the appropriate discount rate for the projected cash flows of Hughes was different than its own cost of capital, GM assumed that Hughes had approximately the same risk as Lockheed or Northrop, which had low-risk defense contracts and products that were similar to Hughes. Specifically, assume the following inputs:

Comparison	β_E	D/E
GM	1.20	.40
Lockheed	0.90	.90
Northrop	0.85	.70

Target $\frac{D}{E}$ for Hughes's acquisition = 1

Hughes's expected real asset cash flow next year = $300 million

Growth rate of Hughes's cash flows = 5 percent per year

Appropriate discount rate on debt (riskless rate) = 8 percent

Expected return of the tangency portfolio = 14 percent

10.10. Analyze the Hughes acquisition (which never took place) by first computing the betas of the comparison firms, Lockheed and Northrop, as if they were all equity financed. Assume no taxes.

10.11. Compute the beta of the assets of the Hughes acquisition, assuming no taxes, by taking the average of the asset betas of Lockheed and Northrop.

10.12. Compute the cost of capital for the Hughes acquisition, assuming no taxes.

10.13. Compute the value of Hughes with the cost of capital estimated in exercise 10.12.

10.14. Compute the value of Hughes if GM's cost of capital is used as a discount rate instead of the cost of capital computed from the comparison firms.

10.15. In a two-factor APT model, Dell Computer has a factor beta of 1.15 on the first factor portfolio, which is highly correlated with the change in GDP, and a factor beta of −.3 on the second factor portfolio, which is highly correlated with interest rate changes. If the risk-free rate is 5 percent per year, the first factor portfolio has a risk-premium of 2 percent per year and the second has a risk premium of −.5 percent per year,

   a. Compute the cost of capital for the HSCC project that uses Dell as the appropriate comparison firm. Assume no taxes and no need for leverage adjustments.

   b. What is the present value of an expected $1 million HSCC cash flow one year from now, assuming that Dell is the appropriate comparison? Assume no taxes and no need for leverage adjustments.

   c. What is the cash flow beta and the certainty equivalent for the HSCC project?

10.16. Risk-free rates at horizons of one year, two years, and three years are 6.00 percent per year, 6.25 percent per year, and 6.75 percent per year, respectively. The manager of the space shuttle at Rockwell International forecasts respective cash flows of $200 million, $250 million, and $300 million for these three years under the risk-free scenario. Value each of these cash flows separately.

References and Additional Readings

Brennan, Michael. "The Term Structure of Discount Rates." *Financial Management* 26 (Spring 1997), pp. 81–90.

Copeland, Tim; Tim Koller; and Jack Murrin. *Valuation: Measuring and Managing the Value of Companies.* New York: John Wiley, 1994.

Cornell, Bradford. *Corporate Valuation: Tools for Effective Appraisal and Decision Making.* Burr Ridge, IL: Business One Irwin, 1993.

Cornell, Bradford, and Simon Cheng. "Using the DCF Approach to Analyze Cross-Sectional Variation in Expected Returns." Working paper, University of California, Los Angeles, 1995.

Damodoran, Aswath. *Investment Valuation.* New York: John Wiley, 1996.

Elton, Edwin; Martin Gruber; and Jiangping Mei. "Cost of Capital Using Arbitrage Pricing Theory: A Case Study of Nine New York Utilities." *Financial*

Markets, Institutions, and Instruments 3, no. 3 (1994), pp. 46–73.

Gordon, Myron. *The Investment Financing and Valuation of the Corporation*. Burr Ridge, IL: Richard D. Irwin, 1962.

Harris, Robert. "Using Analysts' Growth Forecasts to Estimate Shareholder Required Rate of Return." *Financial Management* 15, no. 1 (1986), pp. 58–67.

Rappaport, Alfred. *Creating Shareholder Value: The New Standard for Business Performance*. New York: Free Press, 1986.

Ross, Stephen A. "Mutual Fund Separation in Financial Theory—The Separating Distributions." *Journal of Economic Theory* 17, no. 2 (1978), pp. 254–86.

Ruback, Richard. "Marriott Corporation: The Cost of Capital." Harvard Case Study 289-047. In *Case Problems in Finance*, William Fruhan et al., eds. Burr Ridge, IL: Richard D. Irwin, 1992.

Rubinstein, Mark. "A Mean-Variance Synthesis of Corporate Financial Theory." *Journal of Finance* 28, no. 1 (1973), pp. 167–181.

Sick, Gordon. *Capital Budgeting*. Burr Ridge, IL: Richard D. Irwin. In press.

———. "A Certainty Equivalent Approach to Capital Budgeting." *Financial Management*. Winter 1986, pp. 23–32.

Shapiro, Alan. "Creating Shareholder Value." Working paper, University of Southern California, 1995.

APPENDIX 10A
STATISTICAL ISSUES IN ESTIMATING THE COST OF CAPITAL FOR THE RISK-ADJUSTED DISCOUNT RATE METHOD

The implementation of the risk-adjusted discount rate method uses an estimate of the cost of capital. Error in the cost of capital estimate can arise from several sources, including:

- Having the wrong comparison firm (or portfolio) for computing beta.
- Using historical data to estimate beta, which does not estimate beta perfectly.
- Adjusting for leverage with estimated leverage ratios instead of true leverage ratios.[1]
- Knowing that inherent flaws are in the model of how to adjust equity risk for leverage (for reasons discussed in Chapter 12 and Part IV of the text).
- Having an improper model of how risk relates to return.

The mere fact that errors exist in the cost of capital estimate means that the process of estimation itself leads the firm to reject good projects and to accept bad projects. In the presence of such cost of capital estimation error, it would be desirable to have a valuation procedure that leads to an unbiased estimate of the present value, implying that the expected *NPV* of an estimated positive *NPV* project is still positive and that the expected *NPV* of a negative *NPV* project is negative. However, an estimation procedure that yields unbiased estimates of the cost of capital is a procedure that generates biased present values.

Estimation Error and Denominator-Based Biases in Present Value Estimates

Assume that the true cost of capital is $\bar{r}$ and the estimated cost of capital is $\bar{r} + \tilde{e}$, the true cost of capital plus an error where the expected error $E(\tilde{e}) = 0$. Then, if the expected cash flow is $E(\tilde{C})$, the expected present value estimate for the cash flow is:

$$E(PV) = E\left[\frac{E(\tilde{C})}{1 + \bar{r} + \tilde{e}}\right]$$

This is approximately equal to the sum of the true present value:

$$\frac{E(\tilde{C})}{1 + \bar{r}}$$

and the product of the discounted expected cash flow and the discounted variance of the discount rate estimation error:

$$\left[\frac{E(\tilde{C})}{1 + \bar{r}}\right]\left[\frac{\text{var}(\tilde{e})}{1 + \bar{r}}\right]$$

which generates an expected present value estimate of:

$$E(PV) = \left[\frac{E(\tilde{C})}{1 + \bar{r}}\right]\left[1 + \frac{\text{var}(\tilde{e})}{1 + \bar{r}}\right]$$

Since the first factor in brackets, $\frac{E(\tilde{C})}{1 + \bar{r}}$, is the true present value and the second factor, $1 + \frac{\text{var}(\tilde{e})}{1 + \bar{r}}$, is greater than 1, the expected present value estimate is larger than the true present value.

---

[1]For example, data on the market value of debt are not readily available.

The upward bias in the present value estimate arises because the denominator of a ratio is estimated with error and the numerator tends to be positive. An upward adjustment to the discount rate can eliminate the upward bias in the present value estimate. The degree of the adjustment depends on one's (admittedly ballpark) estimate for var($\tilde{e}$), the estimation error variance of the cost of capital.

The recommended bias correction is to *increase the estimated discount rate by an amount equal to the estimated variance of the error divided by 1 plus the estimated discount rate,* that is, $\dfrac{\text{var}(\tilde{e})}{1 + \bar{r} + \tilde{e}}$. The estimate of present value of the cash flow would then be:

$$\frac{E(\tilde{C})}{\left[\dfrac{1 + \bar{r} + \tilde{e} + \text{var}(\tilde{e})}{1 + r + \tilde{e}}\right]}$$

Example 10A.1 illustrates the procedure.

Example 10A.1:   Obtaining Unbiased PVs from an Unbiased Cost of Capital Estimate

In Example 10.2, the three comparison firms for Marriott's restaurant division were used to generate 10.55 percent as the division's cost of capital. Assume that this cost of capital estimate has a standard deviation of 3 percent per year. What is the best discount rate to use for a six-month cash flow for Marriott's restaurant division?

Answer: If the standard deviation is .03 per year, the variance is .0009. Hence, it is appropriate to increase the estimated discount rate from 10.55 percent to:

$$10.63\% = 10.55\% + \frac{.09\%}{1.1055}$$

For reasons that will be explained in the next subsection, one should implement this upward adjustment to the cost of capital adjustment only for short-horizon cash flows.

Geometric versus Arithmetic Means and the Compounding-Based Bias

The previous subsection demonstrated that, on average, estimated present values tend to be higher than true present values. To correct for this bias, one should increase the estimate of the cost of capital. In a multiperiod setting, estimated present values tend to be too low rather than too high. This occurs because, as Section 10.5 noted, the financial manager generally compounds an imprecise cost of capital to discount a long-horizon cash flow in a multiperiod setting. The size of this overestimate depends on the number of times the estimated discount rate is compounded. The bias also depends on the size of the estimation error.

The type of bias described in this subsection does not arise if the discount rate is not compounded. There is no compounding of the discount rate whenever the cash flow has the same horizon as the returns used to estimate beta. Hence, in Example 10A.1, a financial manager using six-month returns as the basis for estimating the cost of capital for Marriott's restaurant division needs only to adjust the cost of capital upward for the denominator-based bias described in the last subsection. The opposite bias, from compounding the cost of capital, does not exist in this case.

On the other hand (see Example 10A.1), if Marriott's financial manager uses monthly returns to estimate the monthly cost of capital as .8393 percent per month ($= 1.1055^{1/12} - 1$), a present value would be obtained by first compounding the monthly rate six times (i.e., 1.008393^6) and then discounting the six-month expected cash flow $E(\tilde{C})$ with the formula:

$$PV = \frac{E(\tilde{C})}{1.008393^6} = \frac{E(\tilde{C})}{1.1055^{1/2}}$$

EXHIBIT 10A.1   The Bias in Compounded Average Returns

	Ending Digit of Year in Decade	S&P 500 Returns (%)		
		1960s	*1970s*	*1980s*
	0	0.47%	4.01%	32.42%
	1	26.89	14.31	−4.91
	2	−8.73	18.98	21.41
	3	22.80	−14.66	22.51
	4	16.48	−26.47	6.24
	5	12.45	37.20	32.16
	6	−10.06	23.84	18.47
	7	23.98	−7.18	5.23
	8	11.06	6.56	16.81
	9	−8.50	18.44	31.49
Average annual return (%)		8.68	7.50	31.64
Average return compounded for 10 years		129.96	106.16	431.55
Actual 10-year return (%)		112.07	76.68	403.53

Source: Ibbotson Associates, *Bonds, Bill, Stocks, and Inflation: 1995 Yearbook*.

In this case, if the compounding-based bias just balances or is larger than the opposite, denominator-based bias, there may be no need to adjust the cost of capital at all or, possibly, the cost of capital may require a downward adjustment to correct for the stronger bias generated by compounding.

To understand the rough magnitude of the compounding-based bias, assume that expected returns do not change with the horizon of the cash flow; for example, if the expected one-year return on an investment is 10 percent per year, its expected 10-year return is $1.1^{10} − 1$. Although this seems to suggest that it is sufficient to collect data that estimates annual mean returns and to adjust the mean for the appropriate horizon with the standard compound interest formula, it would be the wrong thing to do. Why is this the case?

One statistical estimate of the annual mean return is the **arithmetic sample mean**, which looks at annual returns and then averages them. Exhibit 10A.1 illustrates the arithmetic mean returns for the S&P 500 Index, a portfolio of stocks, over three decades: the 1960s, 1970s, and 1980s. These are averages of the 10 yearly returns in each decade. Below these average annual returns are the compounded 10-year returns computed from the averages. Note that the actual 10-year return, directly below the 10-year compounded return, is always less than the compounded return computed from the arithmetic averages.

A general property of the arithmetic sample mean is that, when compounded, it always overestimates the true return. Hence, while the arithmetic sample mean is a good estimate of the one-period mean return, errors in the estimate are greatly magnified when the analyst compounds the sample mean to produce an estimate of the long-horizon mean. A little algebra illustrates this bias with greater generality. Suppose that an asset has returns in two consecutive years denoted as $\tilde{r}_1$ and $\tilde{r}_2$. One dollar invested over two years in the asset would earn:

$$(1 + \tilde{r}_1)(1 + \tilde{r}_2) = \left[1 + \frac{\tilde{r}_1 + \tilde{r}_2}{2} + \frac{\tilde{r}_1 - \tilde{r}_2}{2} \right]\left[1 + \frac{\tilde{r}_1 + \tilde{r}_2}{2} - \frac{\tilde{r}_1 - \tilde{r}_2}{2} \right]$$

$$= \left[1 + \frac{\tilde{r}_1 + \tilde{r}_2}{2} \right]^2 - \left[\frac{\tilde{r}_1 - \tilde{r}_2}{2} \right]^2$$

Taking the one-period sample mean, $\dfrac{\tilde{r}_1 + \tilde{r}_2}{2}$, and compounding it over two periods indicates that one dollar earns:

$$\left[1 + \frac{\tilde{r}_1 + \tilde{r}_2}{2}\right]^2$$

which exceeds the actual amount earned over the two periods by $\left[\dfrac{\tilde{r}_1 - \tilde{r}_2}{2}\right]^2$. This overestimate of the long-run return occurs because any positive deviations of the sample mean from the true mean are exacerbated more than negative deviations as a result of compounding. Thus, it may be important to reduce the estimated cost of capital to eliminate the bias.

The cost of capital adjustment that achieves unbiased present values depends on the frequency with which means are estimated, the length of time over which data are available, and the horizon of the cash flow. If the horizon of the cash flow is fairly long, it may be better to estimate the per period mean as the geometric mean (discussed earlier in this chapter), instead of the arithmetic mean. For short-horizon returns, the arithmetic mean may provide a better estimate. Blume (1974) argued that there is an appropriate weighting of the arithmetic mean and the geometric mean that provides the correct estimate of the long-run mean return on a comparison investment. The following considerations determine the weights:

- If pairs of consecutive returns are negatively correlated, more weight should be placed on the geometric mean.
- If a great number of small-return horizons are averaged to obtain the arithmetic mean (e.g., a day, a week), more weight should be placed on the geometric mean.
- If the horizon of the cash flow is long term, more weight should be placed on the geometric mean.

These insights apply even when the short-horizon expected return is obtained with an equilibrium model that relates expected return to beta risk. For example, the three considerations concerning the appropriate weighting of arithmetic and geometric means still apply in estimating the expected return of the tangency portfolio. Moreover, because of error in estimating beta along with the expected return of the tangency portfolio, the short-horizon cost of capital of a stock is estimated with error. As a result, adjustments need to be made to the cost of capital to correct for the compounding-based bias in present values.

The compounding-based bias is avoided only if one estimates returns by averaging (or estimating a risk-return model like the CAPM), over periods of the same length as the cash flow horizon. For example, if the horizon of the cash flow is five years, an estimate of the five-year expected return of an investment, obtained by averaging the five-year returns during 1980–85, 1981–86, 1982–1987, and so on is not subject to the compounding-based bias. Hence, an unbiased present value estimate of a cash flow five years out in this case requires an upward adjustment to the cost-of-capital estimate to compensate for the denominator-based bias, but it would not require an adjustment for the bias induced by compounding.

Key Term

arithmetic sample mean   406

References and Additional Readings

Blume, Marshall. "Unbiased Estimators of Long-Run Expected Rates of Return." *Journal of the American Statistical Association* 69 (Sept. 1974), pp. 634–38.

Ibbotson Associates. *Bonds, Bills, Stocks, and Inflation: 1995 Yearbook*. Chicago: Ibbotson Associates, 1995.

CHAPTER
11

Allocating Capital and Corporate Strategy

Learning Objectives

After reading this chapter, you should be able to:

1. Identify the sources of positive net present value.
2. Implement the derivatives valuation methodology to value projects, the options inherent in mines and vacant land, and the options to wait or to expand a project. Know the effect of these options on a firm's choice to diversify and select different production techniques than its competitors.
3. Use the ratio comparison approach to value real assets, and in the case of price/earnings ratios, how to adjust the ratio to make appropriate comparisons between firms with different leverage ratios.
4. Compare the virtues and pitfalls of the competitive analysis approach to evaluate real investments and how to apply it.

"My father and I started a cosmetic cream factory in the late 1940s. At the time, no company could supply us with plastic caps of adequate quality for cream jars, so we had to start a plastic business. Plastic caps alone were not sufficient to run the plastic-molding plant, so we added combs, toothbrushes, and soap boxes. This plastic business also led us to manufacture electric fan blades and telephone cases, which in turn led us to manufacture electrical and electronic products and telecommunication equipment. The plastics business also took us into oil refining which needed a tanker-shipping company. The oil-refining company alone was paying an insurance premium amounting to more than half the total revenue of the then largest insurance company in Korea. Thus an insurance company was started. This natural step-by-step evolution through related businesses resulted in the Lucky-Goldstar group as we see it today. For the future, we will base our growth primarily on chemicals, energy, and electronics. Our chemical business will continue to expand toward fine chemicals and genetic engineering while the electronics business will grow in the direction of semiconductor manufacturing, fiber optic telecommunications, and eventually satellite telecommunications."

Koo Cha-kyung, CEO, Lucky Star Chaebol.

Chapters 9 and 10 examined the traditional discounted cash flow (DCF) method for valuing real assets. DCF is useful in many cases, but it does not get to the heart of how intimately linked capital allocation is to long-term corporate strategy. This chapter's opening vignette, a quotation from the CEO of the Lucky Star Chaebol conglomerate in Korea, illustrates the way in which past investment projects generate future as well as current opportunities—an important consideration that DCF rarely takes into account.

This chapter presents a variety of advanced valuation techniques that remedy some of the deficiencies inherent in traditional DCF. The main emphasis will be on techniques that emphasize the role that the adoption of projects plays in the overall long-term strategy of a corporation. Among these advanced techniques are:

- A **derivatives valuation approach**, which refers to the application of the derivatives valuation methodology introduced in Chapters 7 and 8 to value real assets.
- A **ratio comparison approach**, which values an investment at approximately the same ratio of value to a salient economic variable as an existing comparable investment for which the same ratio is observable.
- A **competitive analysis approach**, which attributes positive net present value to any project of a firm that can identify its competitive advantages and a negative *NPV* to any project where competitors have the advantages.

These alternatives to the traditional discounted cash flow method sometimes have the added advantage of providing more accurate estimates of the future cash flows than those obtained from the DCF method. In many cases, observed market prices provide information about the future cash flows of a project which also is useful for valuing the project. For example, the futures price for copper, used to value a copper mine with the derivatives valuation approach, provides information about the expected future profits of a copper mine and can be used to compute the certainty equivalent of a copper mine's cash flows. Or the ratio of Compaq's stock price to current earnings—using the ratio comparison approach—may provide information about how the market assesses the future potential of the personal computer business.

Some of these advanced techniques, particularly the derivatives valuation approach, also make an explicit attempt to value new opportunities typically missed in the direct cash flow forecasts of traditional valuation methods. These opportunities, which arise as a result of undertaking the project, are known as **strategic options**.

The consensus among academics in finance is that the values of these strategic options are large and often the source of most of the positive net present value inherent in projects. In commenting on the DCF-based TMVM system to Times Mirror (see Chapter 10's opening vignette), for example, several UCLA professors noted, "It is crucial to bear in mind that investments that generate *strategic options* will be unfairly penalized by this technique. More sophisticated methods could be used to supplement TMVM when such options are identified. Such options may be prevalent in many of Times Mirror's divisions. . . ."

In a few industries and in some strategic arenas, these advanced valuation techniques have had a major impact on the way projects are evaluated. The derivatives valuation approach, for example, has taken the oil industry by storm, and the ratio comparison approach has been common in the real estate industry for a while. In valuing potential acquisitions, the competitive analysis approach now plays a major role. For example, the

1996 acquisition of Duracell by Gillette was based in part on the competitive analysis approach.[1]

11.1 Sources of Positive Net Present Value

It is worthwhile to step back and ask where positive net present value *(NPV)* projects come from. To a large extent, firms are in positions to generate positive net present value projects because of situations arising from prior investments. For example, in the early and mid 1990s, Microsoft was in the best position to profit from an investment in a new operating system (Windows 95) and to compete with Netscape to become the dominant Internet browser because it already had a large customer base owing to its DOS and Windows 3.1 programs.

In valuing potential investment projects, most firms do not adequately recognize that the adoption of an investment project generates future investment opportunities that often are quite valuable. Firms typically evaluate projects by discounting only the cash flows directly tied to the project under consideration, thereby underestimating the project's total value. However, the most successful corporations, like Microsoft, grow and prosper as a result of new opportunities serendipitously arising from the company's past investment decisions.

Result 11.1   New opportunities for a firm often arise as a result of information and relationships developed in its past investment projects. Therefore, firms should evaluate investment projects on the basis of their potential to generate valuable information and to develop important relationships, as well as on the basis of the direct cash flows they generate.

Unocal's Pipeline Yadana Project
Consider Unocal's current investments in southeast Asia. Unocal, the California-based oil company, has been doing business with both the Burmese and Thai governments for many years. From the contacts developed in its various business ventures, the company learned that Thailand's rapidly growing economy had brought about a severe shortage of electrical power in Bangkok, Thailand's capital. Unocal also was aware of a substantial natural gas field (the Yadana natural gas field) in Burma (Myanmar), which borders Thailand. Potentially, the natural gas in Burma could be used to power an electrical generator in Bangkok, but transporting the gas from Burma to Thailand would require a pipeline costing more than $1 billion. Such a project would not only require a firm with the substantial financial resources and expertise needed to build a pipeline, but also with the experience and contacts required to deal with the officials of two governments.

Unocal was in an excellent position to exploit a profitable investment opportunity because it had the expertise and connections developed from the company's prior investments. In other words, Unocal ultimately was able to initiate a positive *NPV* pipeline project because its prior investments generated advantages that its competitors lacked.

Sources of Competitive Advantage

In general, the ability to generate profits in a competitive market are due to the advantages one firm has over its competitors.[2] These competitive advantages arise for a variety of reasons. First, there may be **barriers to entry**, or obstacles, that prevent competition by other firms from eroding profits. Consider Merck, which has patents on a large number

---

[1]This acquisition is discussed in Chapter 19.

[2]For a detailed description of these advantages and a plethora of real-world illustrations, see Shapiro (1985).

of drugs, giving the company a temporary monopoly[3] on the production and sale of these drugs which is enforced by the U.S. government and international agreements. There also may be **economies of scale**, which arise when per unit production costs decline with the scale of production, thus making producers of large quantities of a good more efficient than small producers. Economies of scale give firms with a large market share a sustainable advantage. There also are **economies of scope**, which arise when a certain product or service can be supplied more efficiently by a firm that makes a related product. Economies of scope manifest themselves in the superior knowledge, marketing system, or production technology that are acquired only by first producing a related product.

Economies of Scope, Discounted Cash Flow, and Options

Much of the discussion in this chapter focuses on economies of scope because they are the most important source of competitive advantage for a firm. If some of the positive cash flows that firms achieve from projects are positive only because of the economies of scope generated by earlier investments, then these positive cash flows should have been attributed to the earlier related investments. In evaluating the earlier investments, however, we noted earlier that most firms unnecessarily limit their analysis to the investment's direct cash flows and rarely consider the indirect cash flows that might subsequently follow.

An implication of this limited analysis is that the discounted cash flow method leads to bad decisions. As currently implemented, DCF is biased against long-term projects because it ignores many aspects of long-term investment projects that cannot easily be quantified.[4] Managers who use the discounted cash flow method tend to focus on what can easily be quantified, and thus, tend to ignore the indirect cash flows.[5]

Take the hypothetical case of General Motors considering whether to engage in a joint venture with Shougang Steel to produce automobiles in China. It is possible to arrive at some estimate of the joint venture's cash flows, but the working relationship between a U.S. and Chinese firm may have other benefits that go beyond the cash flows of any particular project. After establishing a working relationship with Shougang, General Motors might, for example, have the opportunity to engage in additional joint projects. Because these opportunities may subsequently prove to be valuable, they need to be considered when calculating the cash flows of the original investment project. But making a precise calculation of the value of subsequent opportunities is a heroic task. This chapter develops an approach, based on the derivatives valuation methodology, that at least can provide rules of thumb about when subsequent opportunities are likely to significantly enhance a project's value, and may even provide "ballpark quantitative estimates," of the degree of this enhancement.

Option Pricing Theory as a Tool for Quantifying Economies of Scope

Because subsequent opportunities will only be pursued further if they prove to be valuable, they are options that the firm possesses. Most investment projects include an optionlike component. In addition to the option to pursue additional projects, financial

---

[3]As of 1996, drug patents were only valid for 17 years, but in reality, imitation drugs that carefully avoid violating the letter of the law often appear within 5 to 10 years of a patent filing.

[4]Hayes and Abernathy (1980) present the details of this argument.

[5]It is wrong, however, to assert that the discounted cash flow method is flawed as a result of this short-term focus because the method itself does not tell us to ignore indirect long-term cash flows that stem from a project.

managers also need to recognize that the adoption of almost any project contains other important options—among them, options to cancel, downsize, or expand the project. The decision about exercising these types of options at a later date can be viewed as an investment project in the same way that GM's potential future projects with Shougang Steel are considered projects.

The analysis of whether to "exercise the option" and enter into these new projects will depend on underlying economic variables such as the demand for the product, the level of interest rates, the health of the economy, the success of competitors, the political climate, and so forth. These underlying variables affect the values of many traded securities, including the company's own stock. Hence, if it is possible to model how the project and other traded securities are affected by underlying securities, it is possible to use the derivatives valuation techniques (developed in Chapter 7) to value the indirect cash flows. Even in cases where the modeling is very crude and one can obtain only a few guiding rules of thumb about the nature of the strategic option, it is important to consider such options when valuing an investment project. These options contribute to the value of any investment project in which management has flexibility in future implementation.

11.2 Valuing Strategic Options with the Derivatives Valuation Methodology

The term *strategic options* is an appropriate label for the opportunities that arise from the ability to alter a project midcourse or to enter into new projects as a result of some investment. There are two reasons for this. First, strategic options represent strategies that the firm has an option to pursue only by taking on the earlier project; that is, unless the firm undertakes the earlier project, there is no possibility of obtaining the cash flows from the strategic option. Second, strategic options are valued with the same option pricing methodology developed in Chapter 7 (and applied to options in Chapter 8). This section analyzes the application of this pricing methodology for the valuation of real assets.

We indicated in Chapter 7 that a derivative is an investment whose value is determined by the value of another investment. One example is a stock option, which has a value determined by the price of the underlying stock. Another example is a forward contract to purchase copper for a specific price at a specific date in the future. The techniques used to value derivatives also can be used to value projects in relation to some underlying financial asset(s). In the following sections, we will illustrate the use of the derivatives valuation methodology to value:

- A mine with no strategic options.
- A mine with an abandonment option.
- Vacant land.
- The option to delay the start of a project.
- The option to expand capacity.
- Flexibility in production technology.

Valuing a Mine with No Strategic Options

The valuation of natural resource investments (e.g., oil wells and copper mines) illustrates how to implement the derivatives valuation approach developed in this chapter. This subsection focuses on a copper mine. The choice of a mine stems from the unambiguous connection to an underlying asset, a forward contract on a metal, and the popularity, in practice, of the derivatives valuation approach among natural resource firms. For example, the trade literature on energy is filled with articles on strategic options. In addition, large diversified energy companies like Enron ($10 billion market capitalization in 1996), which trade raw and processed energy products such as natural gas and electricity, have profited from sophisticated valuation models that employ this methodology.

This subsection first examines how to use derivatives valuation techniques to value a copper mine when no strategic options exist. In the absence of strategic options, the approach to mine valuation is identical to the certainty equivalent method discussed in Chapter 10.

The cash flows of a copper mine can be tracked by financial assets since the mine's value is largely determined by the price of copper. Suppose that some of the copper in the mine will be extracted at date 1 and the remainder at date 2. If the extraction costs are known or can be contracted for in advance, then the cash flows from this mine are contingent only on the price of copper. The date 1 and date 2 cash flows from the mine, C_1 and C_2, respectively, can be expressed as:

$$C_1 = p_1 Q_1 - K_1$$
$$C_2 = p_2 Q_2 - K_2$$

where

p_1 = date 1 copper price

p_2 = date 2 copper price

Q_1 = date 1 quantity of copper extracted

Q_2 = date 2 quantity of copper extracted

K_1 = date 1 cost of extraction

K_2 = date 2 cost of extraction

Only p_1 and p_2 are assumed to be unknown at the adoption decision time, date 0.

Profits from holding a forward contract on copper also are determined only by the price of copper. Exhibit 11.1 illustrates the cash flows of forward contracts to exchange Q_t units of copper for cash at future date t.[6]

It is possible to use the forward prices from copper forward contracts maturing at dates 1 and 2 to value the copper mine. To see this, note that the respective cash flows at dates 1 and 2 from operating the mine, $p_1 Q_1 - K_1$ and $p_2 Q_2 - K_2$, are exactly the same as the future cash flows incurred by holding the following tracking portfolio:

1. A forward contract to purchase Q_1 units of copper at date 1 at the current forward price of F_1 per unit, and a second forward contract to purchase Q_2 units of copper at date 2 at the current forward price of F_2 per unit.

2. A risk-free zero-coupon bond paying $F_1 Q_1 - K_1$ in year 1, and a second risk-free zero-coupon bond paying $F_2 Q_2 - K_2$ at date 2.

Since F_1 and F_2 represent the current forward prices, the contracts have zero value at date 0 and thus the first item 1 in the tracking portfolio (see above) costs nothing. The

---

[6]The absence of a cash flow at the initiation of these contracts is another way of saying that the future exchange price of these contracts is set to a value that makes the contracts have zero present value.

EXHIBIT 11.1   Cash Flows of Forward Contracts to Exchange Q_t Units of Copper for Cash at Future Date t

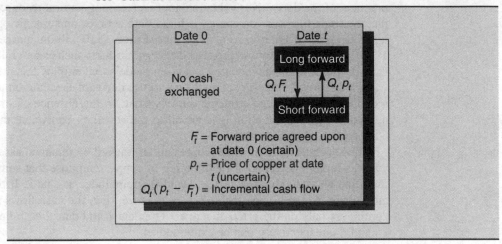

present value of the uncertain cash flows from the mine equal the present value of the zero-coupon bonds in item 2. The value of the mine thus equals:

$$PV = \frac{F_1 Q_1 - K_1}{(1 + r_1)} + \frac{F_2 Q_2 - K_2}{(1 + r_2)^2}$$

where

r_t = the yield to maturity of zero-coupon bonds maturing at date t ($t = 1, 2$)

$F_t Q_t - K_t$ = the future payment of the zero-coupon bond maturing at date t
       ($t = 1, 2$)

Example 11.1 implements this valuation procedure numerically.

Example 11.1:   Valuing a Copper Mine

Lincoln Copper Company has a mine that will produce a total of 75,000 pounds of copper: 25,000 pounds of copper at the end of the first year and 50,000 pounds of copper at end of the second year. Extraction costs are always $0.10 per pound. The current forward prices are $0.65 per pound for a one-year contract and $0.60 per pound for a two-year contract. The annually compounded risk-free rates are 5 percent for one-year zero-coupon bonds and 6 percent for two-year zero-coupon bonds.

What is the present value of the cash flows from the mine, assuming that payments for the mined copper are received at the end of each year?

Answer: Mine value $= \dfrac{\$.65(25{,}000) - \$.10(25{,}000)}{1 + .05} + \dfrac{\$.60(50{,}000) - \$.10(50{,}000)}{(1 + .06)^2}$

$= \$35{,}345$

The valuation of the copper mine in Example 11.1 is based on identifying the cost of a combination of investments traded in the financial market that *perfectly* track the copper mine's future cash flows at years 1 and 2. As Exhibit 11.2 illustrates, the forward contracts (items *a* and *b*), in combination with a series of zero-coupon bonds maturing at

EXHIBIT 11.2   **Cash Flows of Copper Mine versus Portfolio of Forward Contracts and Zero-Coupon Bonds**

F_1 = Year 1 forward price = $.65 per pound
F_2 = Year 2 forward price = $.60 per pound

Investment	Beginning of Year 0	Beginning of Year 1	Beginning of Year 2
Copper Mine	PV Unknown	$25,000(p_1 - .10)$	$50,000(p_2 - .10)$
a. Forward contract to buy 25,000 pounds of copper at beginning of year 1	$0	$25,000(p_1 - .65)$	$0
b. Forward contract to buy 50,000 pounds of copper at beginning of year 2	$0	$0	$50,000(p_2 - .60)$
c. Buy zero-coupon bonds; Maturity = year 1 Face amount = $25,000(.65 - .10)$	$-\dfrac{\$25,000(.65 - .10)}{1.06}$	$25,000(.65 - .10)$	$0
d. Buy zero-coupon bonds; Maturity = year 2 Face amount = $50,000(.60 - .10)$	$-\dfrac{\$50,000(.60 - .10)}{1.08}$	$0	$50,000(.60 - .10)$
Total: $a + b + c + d$	$-\$35,345$	$25,000(p_1 - .10)$	$50,000(p_1 - .10)$

two different dates (items c and d), produce cash flows (bottom row, two right-hand columns) identical to those of the copper mine. The tracking portfolio costs $35,345, which is the value attributed to the identical future cash flows of the copper mine.[7]

Valuing a Mine with an Abandonment Option

The analysis of mine valuation assumed that the amount of copper to be extracted was known with certainty and was not controllable. In other words, the owner of the mine would not or could not alter the production decision as economic conditions changed.

In the real world, copper mine owners close their mines when the price of copper becomes too low to make mining profitable and speed up production when copper prices recover to the point where mining is profitable. The opportunity to alter production in this way is an example of a strategic option, and it enhances the value of the mine.

---

[7]This analysis assumes that copper production takes place on the dates that forward contracts mature. In reality, copper production is a continuous process, spread out over an entire period. To obtain a reasonable approximation of the value of a continuous mining process, assume that the present value of these spread-out cash flows is the same as the present value computed as if all production takes place at the "average date." For example, to compute the present value of all cash flows in the first year, assume that all first-year cash flows take place six months from now. Similarly, all second-year cash flows occur 18 months from now.

When forward contracts that settle 6 months and 18 months from now do not exist, the hypothetical forward price—found from linearly interpolating the forward prices that surround the target extraction date—generates a satisfactory mine value with the tracking procedure described above. For example, given four-month and eight-month forward contracts, with respective forward prices of $1.40 per pound and $1.20 per pound, it would be reasonable to assume that a six-month forward contract, if one existed, would have a forward price of about $1.30 per pound.

A Binomial Illustration of the Brennan-Schwartz Method.   Consider a copper mine that generates a cash flow equal to the maximum of 0 and $(p_1 Q_1 - K_1)$ in year 1 and nothing thereafter. In this case, the mine owner is in effect willing to buy copper at its extraction cost as long as this cost is less than the value of the copper. This is an option that is exercised (i.e., to mine the copper) or not exercised (i.e., to shut down the mine), depending upon whether the price of the copper p_1 is sufficiently high to cover the cost of extraction. Indeed, the cash flows from the mine are exactly equal to the cash flows of an option to purchase Q_1 units of copper at an exercise price of K_1. If it were possible to observe the value of a call option to purchase copper, one would know the value of the mine. In most investments of this type, unfortunately, the type of traded option that tracks the real investment does not exist.

Brennan and Schwartz (1985) developed a method for valuing mines that takes into account the owner's options to reduce and increase production, but does not require the observation of the market price of an option to purchase the mineral being mined. The inputs used in their valuation method are the current forward price of the mineral, the volatility of the price of the mineral, and the risk-free rate of interest.

Although the Brennan and Schwartz method is complex, it can be approximated with the binomial approach developed in Chapters 7 and 8. The technique used in valuing derivative assets assumes that the future price movements of the underlying asset (e.g., copper) follow a binomial process in which the price of the asset takes on one of only two possible values after one time period: a high value or a low value. The derivative asset—in this case, the copper mine—also takes on only one of two possible values at the end of the time period. Thus, the future value of the copper mine can be tracked by a portfolio of two traded investments which, according to the no-arbitrage assumption, implies that the value of the mine is simply the cost of the tracking portfolio. Example 11.2 illustrates how to compare the tracking portfolio with the mine to derive the mine's value.

Example 11.2:   Valuing a Copper Mine with a Shutdown Option

Penny Copper Mining's Brazilian mine will produce 75,000 pounds of copper one year from now if economic conditions are favorable. Penny's managers forecast two possible outcomes for copper prices then: $0.50 per pound if demand is low and $0.90 per pound if demand is high. The year 1 forward price is currently $0.60 per pound, implying that a forward contract has a negative future cash flow of −$0.10 per pound next year if demand is low and a positive future cash flow of $0.30 per pound if demand is high. The risk-free one-year interest rate is 5 percent. The extraction costs are $0.80 per pound, so if demand turns out to be low, the firm will shut down the mine. What is the value of this mine?

Answer: Exhibit 11.3 illustrates the payoffs from the mine in two scenarios and can be used to find the portfolio of forward contracts and risk-free zero-coupon bonds that track the mine's future cash flows in either copper price scenario.

Scenario 1 (Low copper price = $0.50 per pound): In this scenario, the copper mine will shut down and be worth zero. The equation that the tracking portfolio is worth zero in the event that copper prices are low is:

$$x(\$.50 - \$.60) + y(1.05) = \$0$$

where

  x = pounds of copper purchased forward
  y = dollars invested in zero-coupon bonds today that mature in one year

Scenario 2 (High copper price = $0.90 per pound): In this scenario, the copper mine will be profitable. It will earn $0.10 per pound of copper mined and it thus pays to produce at

EXHIBIT 11.3   Payoffs of a Copper Mine with a Shutdown Option

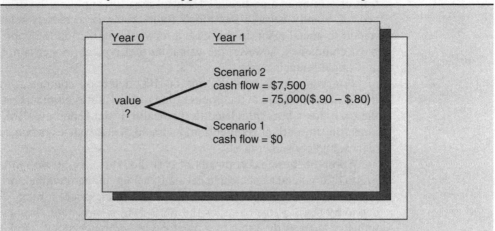

maximum capacity. The cash flow in this scenario is $7,500 = 75,000($.90 − $.80). The equation that the same tracking portfolio also yields $7,500 if copper prices are high is:

$$x(\$.90 - \$.60) + y(1.05) = \$7,500$$

Simultaneously solving the equations for scenarios 1 and 2 gives the tracking portfolio:

x = 18,750 pounds of copper received from a one-year forward contract

y = $1,786 invested in zero-coupon bonds

The value of this tracking portfolio is $1,786. Therefore, the copper mine must also have a value of $1,786.

Practical Considerations.   While useful for showing how to value a real asset with an option, Example 11.2 contains simplifications that make mine valuation simpler than it is in the real world. First, it assumes that if the copper is not extracted at the end of the period, it cannot be extracted in the future. More realistic copper mine valuations should not limit the mining to a specific date by which the copper must be extracted. There are procedures for valuing mines in this case, where the option to extract is perpetual.

Exchange Options and Volatility.   Another practical consideration in valuing a copper mine is that the extraction cost, as well as the price of copper, is generally uncertain. The copper mine is thus analogous to an **exchange option**, which is the option to exchange one item (e.g., asset, liability, or commodity) for another. Margrabe (1978) first valued this type of option by noting that the underlying price for the option value was the ratio of the prices of the two items being exchanged. In this case, the copper mine owner has the option to exchange the extraction costs for the copper; the relevant variable that determines the value of the copper mine is the ratio of the copper price to the extraction costs. As the volatility of this ratio increases, the value of the mine increases. Result 11.2 summarizes this discussion as follows:

Result 11.2   A mine can be viewed as an option to extract (or purchase) minerals at a strike price equal to the cost of extraction. Like a stock option, the option to extract the minerals has a value that increases with both the volatility of the mineral price and the volatility of the extraction cost.

Generalizing the Derivatives Valuation Approach to Other Industries.   The valuation of a mine is a particularly fruitful area for applying the derivatives valuation approach, chiefly because the mine's future value is so closely related to the value of a traded financial asset, in this case a forward contract on the copper being mined. For most companies, however, the valuation of a typical project is not so closely linked to any single financial asset.

For example, a proposed line of IBM notebook computers may have future cash flows that are related to the prices of long-term futures contracts on semiconductors, but the cash flows also are related to the health of the economy, IBM's reputation, interest rates, the strength of competition, technological advances, advances in production efficiency, and consumer tastes.

Some of these determinants of cash flow are closely tied to a financial asset or a group of financial assets which certainly belong in the tracking portfolio. For example, a proxy for IBM's reputation such as IBM's stock price, a proxy for the health of the economy such as the value of the S&P 500, a proxy for the health of the computer industry such as the value of a portfolio of computer stocks, and a host of interest rate futures contracts are possible candidates for the IBM project's tracking portfolio.

In contrast to the tracking of the mine, however, the IBM notebook line's tracking portfolio probably generates substantial tracking error. This is partly because some important cash flow determinants of the notebook line are not properly captured by the prices of any financial assets, and partly because estimating the weights of the various financial assets in the tracking portfolio is more complex than it was in the mine valuation case.

These obstacles to implementing the derivatives valuation approach in more general cases does not imply that the financial analyst should not attempt the implementation. Even when the quantitative estimates are imprecise, important lessons can be learned from such an exercise. Illustrations of these lessons are provided throughout the remainder of this chapter.

Risk-Neutral Valuation.   Chapter 7 indicated that the tracking portfolio approach to valuation is equivalent to valuation with "risk-neutral" probabilities. Applying risk-neutral probabilities to the cash flows of the mine and discounting the risk-neutral expected cash flow at the risk-free rate would have yielded the same answer. These risk-neutral probabilities are implicitly given by the prices of traded investments—in the last example, by the prices of a copper forward contract and a risk-free zero-coupon bond. To illustrate the use of the risk-neutral valuation technique, the next section values land.

Valuing Vacant Land

Vacant land has value because it represents an option to turn the vacant land into developed land. For example, a particular plot of land may have potential use for condominiums, an office building, or a shopping mall. In the future, the developer will have an incentive to develop the property for the use that maximizes the difference between the value of the project's future revenues and its construction costs. However, the best possible future use for the land may not be known at the present time.

The derivatives valuation approach can be used to determine the worth of an option to construct one of a number of possible buildings with strike prices equal to the building's construction costs. One can value this option, and thus the land, by first computing the risk-neutral probabilities associated with various outcomes. Example 11.3, adapted from Titman (1985), uses the binomial approach to obtain the risk-neutral probabilities necessary to value vacant land. One derives these probabilities from the observed market prices of traded investments (e.g., the price of condominiums and the risk-free rate of interest).

Calculating these risk-neutral probabilities requires solving for probabilities that generate expected cash flows for traded assets which equal their certainty equivalent cash flows. In other words, with the correct risk-neutral probabilities, the expected cash flows of traded assets, discounted at the risk-free rate, will equal the observed market price of the traded asset. Then, to determine the real asset's present value, apply these same risk-neutral probabilities to the cash flows of the real asset being valued and discount the risk-neutral expected cash flow at the risk-free rate, as Example 11.3 illustrates.

Example 11.3:   Valuing Vacant Land

An investor owns a lot that is suitable for either six or nine condominium units. The per unit construction costs of the building with six units are $80,000 and with nine units $90,000. Construction costs are the same whether construction takes place this year or next. The current market price of each unit is $100,000. The per year rental rate is $8,000 per unit (net of expenses), and the risk-free rate of interest is 12 percent per year. If market conditions are favorable next year, each condominium will sell for $120,000; if conditions are unfavorable, each will sell for only $90,000. What is the value of the lot?

Answer: At the present time, building nine condominium units yields $90,000 profit [= 9($100,000 − $90,000)] while building six units yields $120,000 profit [= 6($100,000 − $80,000)]. Hence, a six-unit building is best if building now. However, if the investor chooses to wait one year to build, he will receive the payoffs illustrated in panel A of Exhibit 11.4 on page 420, which shows that by waiting a year and constructing a nine-unit building if market conditions are favorable, the investor will realize a total profit of $270,000. He will construct a six-unit building and realize a total profit of $60,000 if unfavorable market conditions prevail. If the present value of this pair of cash flows is larger than the $120,000 profit from building a six-unit building now, waiting is the best alternative. Assuming that the investor waits, the value of the lot is computed by valuing the two possible cash flow outcomes, $270,000 (favorable conditions) and $60,000 (unfavorable conditions).

To calculate the present value of this cash flow pair, first compute the risk-neutral probabilities, π and $(1 - \pi)$, associated with the two states. As the binomial tree in panel B of Exhibit 11.4 shows, a $100,000 investment in a condominium this year yields a year-end value of either $120,000 plus $8,000 in rent or $90,000 plus $8,000 in rent, depending on market conditions. This implies that the risk-neutral probabilities must satisfy:

$$\$100,000 = \frac{\pi\$128,000 + (1 - \pi)\$98,000}{1.12}$$

which is solved by $\pi = \dfrac{7}{15}$.

Discounting next year's expected cash flows at the risk-free rate of 12 percent, seen in panel C, with expectations computed using the risk neutral "probabilities," gives the current value of the land under the assumption that it will remain vacant until next year. This current value is:

$$\frac{\left(\dfrac{7}{15}\right)\$270,000 + \left(\dfrac{8}{15}\right)\$60,000}{1.12} = \$141,071$$

Since $141,071 is greater than the $120,000 profit that would be realized by building a six-unit condominium immediately, it is better to keep the land vacant. The value of the vacant land is $141,071.

EXHIBIT 11.4   Binomial Trees for Land Valuation

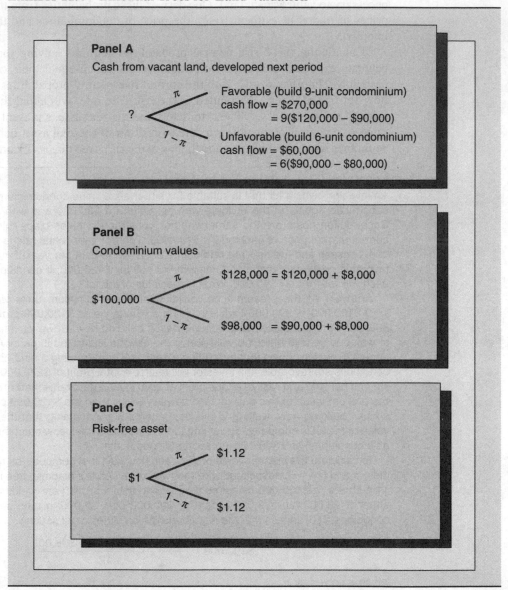

Panel A

Cash from vacant land, developed next period

?

π → Favorable (build 9-unit condominium)
cash flow = $270,000
= 9($120,000 − $90,000)

1 − π → Unfavorable (build 6-unit condominium)
cash flow = $60,000
= 6($90,000 − $80,000)

Panel B

Condominium values

$100,000

π → $128,000 = $120,000 + $8,000

1 − π → $98,000 = $90,000 + $8,000

Panel C

Risk-free asset

$1

π → $1.12

1 − π → $1.12

Example 11.3 values vacant land as an option to build different kinds of structures, depending on market conditions. How realistic is this? Chapter 8 indicated that option values are increasing in the volatility of the underlying asset—in this case, developed land. In a study of commercial properties in the Chicago area, Quigg (1993) found that land was indeed more valuable with greater uncertainty. Result 11.3 summarizes this view as follows:

Result 11.3   Vacant land can be viewed as an option to purchase developed land where the exercise price is the cost of developing a building on the land. Like stock options, this more complicated type of option has a value that is increasing in the degree of uncertainty about the value (and type) of development.

Titman (1985) shows that development restrictions, such as ceilings on building height or density, may reduce uncertainty, leading to both a lower value for vacant land and a greater desire to exercise the option—that is, to develop the land. This curious phenomenon—that development restrictions may lead to more development—arises because the benefit of waiting is the greatest force keeping vacant landholders from exercising the development option. The benefit of waiting is larger when the degree of uncertainty about the option's terminal value is greater, as Chapter 8 noted.

The valuation approach used here works because vacant land has payoffs like an option and because the possibility of arbitrage keeps prices in line. Example 11.4 illustrates how to achieve arbitrage if the real estate market places a different price on the value of the land than on the price derived from risk-neutral valuation.

Example 11.4:   Arbitraging Mispriced Real Estate

If the land in Example 11.3 sells for $120,000, show how investors can earn arbitrage profits by purchasing the land and hedging the risk by selling short the condominium units.

Answer: One achieves risk-free arbitrage by purchasing the land, selling short seven condominium units, and spending $626/1.12 on risk-free, zero-coupon bonds maturing in one year. The present value of seven condominium units completely hedges the risk from owning the vacant land, since the difference between the value of the units in the favorable and unfavorable states, $210,000 (= 7 × ($120,000 − $90,000)), exactly offsets the difference in land values in the two states ($270,000 − $60,000).

The arbitrage opportunity is summarized as follows:

Investment	Cash Inflow Today (in $000s)	Cash in Favorable State Next Year (in $000s)	Cash in Unfavorable State Next Year (in $000s)
Short 7 condos	$700	−$840−$56	−$630−$56
Buy vacant land	−$120	$270	$ 60
Buy risk-free bonds	−$626/1.12	$626	$626
Total	$21.07	$ 0	$ 0

The investment in Example 11.4 yields a risk-free gain of $21,071. Because this kind of gain cannot exist in equilibrium, investors will bid up the price of the land from $120,000 to its equilibrium value of $141,071.

It is tempting to argue that arbitrage is impossible in the situation described in Example 11.4 because it is impossible to sell short seven condominium units. However, someone who already owns similar condominium units could sell seven of them, and buy both the vacant land and the risk free-asset. At the margin, this looks like an arbitrage opportunity because the change in cash flows associated with this decision is riskless and yields positive cash today.

Valuing the Option to Delay the Start of a Manufacturing Project

Strategic options affect a variety of investment decisions. The condominium example in the last subsection illustrated the value of delay, which permitted some flexibility in the size of the condominium structure. Delay has value because it allows the developer to construct the condominium building with the size best suited for economic conditions. The optimal building size cannot be known until economic conditions unfold over time.

Usually, delay also is beneficial in deciding whether to adopt a project. When a firm accepts a project, it exercises the strategic option to delay and, hence, loses the value from waiting. The value of waiting makes it imprudent to exercise an American call option on a nondividend-paying stock prior to the option's expiration date (see Chapter 8). This lesson should not be forgotten when dealing with the strategic options of a real asset. While the future cash flows of a real asset may not exactly mimic the future cash flows of an American call option, the generic lesson is the same: For the call option, delay exercise until the last possible moment. For the real asset, it is often better to delay accepting a project even when the project currently has a positive "net present value," as computed by discounting its direct cash flows.

To understand why this value from delay arises, think about each project as a combination of two or more mutually exclusive investments that are defined by the time they are first implemented. For example, investment 1 might be to initiate the project immediately, while investment 2 is to wait one year and then initiate the project only if economic conditions are favorable. Initiating the project immediately may be a positive net present value *(NPV)* investment, but the *NPV* of waiting one year may be higher.[8]

Viewed from this perspective, it might make sense to turn down positive net present value projects, at least temporarily, as Example 11.5 illustrates. In this example, it pays to turn down the positive *NPV* project at year 0, and in year 1 adopt the project if the good state occurs, and reject the project if the bad state occurs.

Example 11.5:   Creating Value by Rejecting a "Positive NPV Project"

Acme Industries is considering building a plant. After an initial investment of $100 million, the plant will be completed in one year and then have the series of annual cash flows shown in Exhibit 11.5. Acme's managers can decide to immediately invest the $100 million, or they can wait until next year to decide whether to build or not.

If the project is built immediately, panel A in Exhibit 11.5 shows that after a year of start-up procedures, next year's cash flow will be $10 million, but a perpetual annual cash flow stream of either $15 million or $2.5 million will occur each year thereafter, depending on whether the economy is good or bad one year from now. If the project is delayed, panel B of Exhibit 11.5 shows that the first year's initial $10 million cash flow will be lost and only the perpetual cash flow stream of $2.5 million or $15 million, beginning two years hence, will be captured, depending on the state of the economy in year 1. Assuming that the risk-free interest rate is 5 percent per year and that $1.00 invested in the market portfolio today will be worth either $1.30 (if the economy does well) and $0.80 (if the economy does poorly), compute the *NPV* of the project and decide whether or not it pays to wait.

Answer: View the decision to wait or build now as two mutually exclusive projects with the higher *NPV* project winning out. Each of the two projects can be valued as a derivative asset using the binomial option valuation methodology. First, compute the value of the plant if Acme builds it immediately.

If the market return is good, the plant has a year 1 value of $10 million plus the value of the perpetuity, that is:

$$\$10 \text{ million} + \frac{\$15 \text{ million}}{.05} = \$310 \text{ million}$$

---

[8]Ingersoll and Ross (1992) note that even if the manager knows that cash flows will not change as a result of waiting to invest, the present values of cash flows will change because interest rates are always changing. Hence, every project can be viewed as an option on interest rates.

EXHIBIT 11.5   Cash Flows for ACME's Factory Timing Decision in Example 11.5

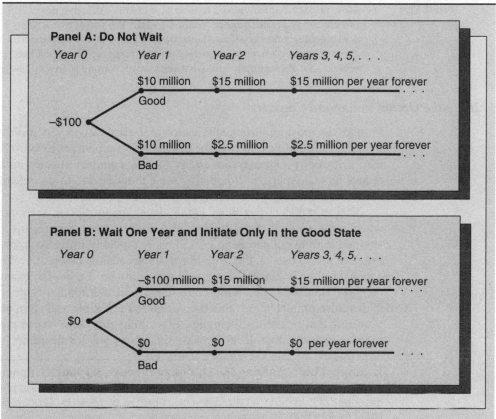

Panel A: Do Not Wait

Year 0	Year 1	Year 2	Years 3, 4, 5, . . .
	$10 million	$15 million	$15 million per year forever
	Good		
−$100			
	$10 million	$2.5 million	$2.5 million per year forever
	Bad		

Panel B: Wait One Year and Initiate Only in the Good State

Year 0	Year 1	Year 2	Years 3, 4, 5, . . .
	−$100 million	$15 million	$15 million per year forever
	Good		
$0			
	$0	$0	$0 per year forever
	Bad		

If the market return is bad, the year 1 value is:

$$\$10 \text{ million} + \frac{\$2.5 \text{ million}}{.05} = \$60 \text{ million}$$

To compute the present value, calculate the risk-neutral probabilities, π and $1 - \pi$, associated with the valuation of the market portfolio. These solve:

$$\$1.00 = \frac{\pi(\$1.30) + (1 - \pi)(\$.80)}{1.05}$$

implying that $\pi = .5$. Applying the probabilities π and $1 - \pi$ to the relevant values in the two states yields a present value for the plant of:

$$\frac{(.5)\$310 \text{ million} + (.5)\$60 \text{ million}}{1.05} = \$176.19 \text{ million}$$

Since this is greater than the $100 million cost of building the plant, the project has a positive net present value of $76.19 million (= $176.19 million − $100 million).

The alternative of waiting one year and then investing in the plant only if the favorable outcome occurs results in a net present value of:

$$.5 \times \frac{\$15 \text{ million}/.05 - \$100 \text{ million}}{1.05} = \$95.24 \text{ million}$$

Since $95.24 million exceeds $76.19 million, the alternative of waiting is preferred.

Example 11.5 illustrates the following point:

Result 11.4   Most projects can be viewed as a set of mutually exclusive projects. For example, taking the project today is one project, waiting to take the project next year is another project, and waiting three years is yet another project. Firms may pass up the first project, that is, initiate the capital investment immediately, even if doing so has a positive net present value. They will do so if the mutually exclusive alternative, waiting to invest, has a higher *NPV*.

Valuing the Option to Expand Capacity

Perhaps the most important application of the derivatives valuation approach is assessing the importance of flexibility in the design of investment projects. In an uncertain environment, flexibility—such as the ability to take a project already initiated and expand it, reduce its scale (perhaps liquidating some of its assets), or completely abandon it—is an option, and each option available enhances the project's value.

One example of flexibility is the abandonment option seen earlier in this chapter when we discussed the valuation of a copper mine. There, the mine owner simply stopped mining copper at no cost. This is probably unrealistic, as flexibility generally imposes some costs on the firm. For example, scaling down or scaling up the capacity of a project already started often requires additional cash—for example, severance payments or shutdown costs with scaling down and additional machinery with scaling up. It is therefore important to value the option to be flexible and compare it with the cost of acquiring that flexibility. Example 11.6 demonstrates how to use the binomial approach to value investment projects that have this more complex flexibility.

Example 11.6:   Valuing the Option to Increase a Plant's Capacity

Acme Industries is considering building a plant that will have a value after two years which is described in Exhibit 11.6. The cash flows from the plant will be $200 million following two good years (point *D*), $150 million following one good and one bad year (point *E*), and $100 million (point *F*) following two bad years. The initial cost of the plant is $140 million (point *A*). After one year, however, if the state of the economy looks good, the firm has the option to double the plant's capacity by investing another $140 million.

EXHIBIT 11.6   Cash Flows if There Is No Capacity Change at Year 1

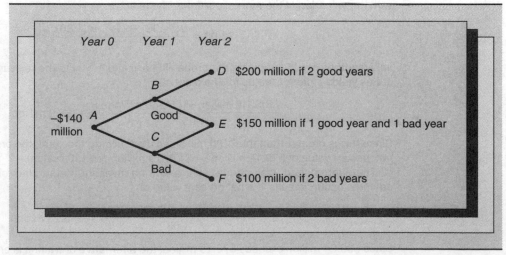

Exhibit 11.7 shows that doubling the plant's capacity will have the effect of doubling the cash flows to either $400 million or $300 million in its final year (compare the two point *D*s and points *E* and *E*1 in Exhibits 11.6 and 11.7). Assume a risk-free rate of 5 percent per year and that $1.00 invested in the market portfolio today yields future values, depending on the state of the economy, shown by the tree diagram in Exhibit 11.8. The corresponding risk-neutral probabilities, π and $1 - \pi$, attached to the nodes in the tree consistent with these prices have been computed and appear next to the branches in the tree diagram in Exhibit 11.8.

Compute the value of building a plant under two scenarios: In scenario 1, the option to double the plant's capacity is ignored; in scenario 2, it is not ignored.

Exhibit 11.7   Cash Flows if Plant Capacity Is Doubled at Good Node in Year 1

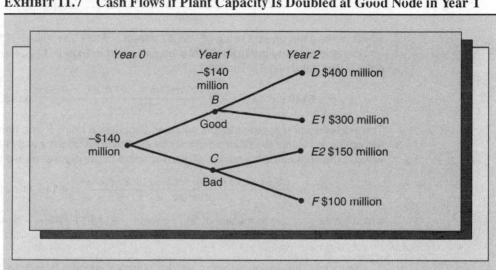

Exhibit 11.8   Market Portfolio Payoffs for Determining Risk Neutral Probabilities in Example 11.6

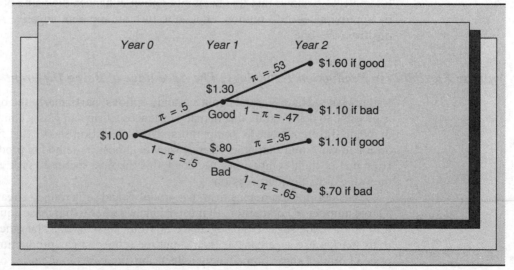

Answer: *Scenario 1:* Applying the risk-neutral probabilities, π and $1 - \pi$, from Exhibit 11.8 to compute expectations and discounting at the 5 percent per year risk-free rate implies that the value of the plant at point *B* (the good node) in Exhibit 11.6 is:

$$\frac{(.53)\$200 \text{ million} + (.47)\$150 \text{ million}}{1.05} = \$168.10 \text{ million}$$

The value of the plant at point *C* (the bad node), in Exhibit 11.6 is:

$$\frac{(.35)\$150 \text{ million} + (.65)\$100 \text{ million}}{1.05} = \$111.90 \text{ million}$$

The value of the plant at point *A* (the initial node) is thus:

$$\frac{(.5)\$168.10 \text{ million} + (.5)\$111.90 \text{ million}}{1.05} = \$133.33 \text{ million}$$

which yields a net present value of $-\$6.67$ million $= \$133.33$ million $- \$140$ million.

Scenario 2: Using the risk-neutral probabilities from Exhibit 11.8, the value of the plant at point *B* (the good node) in Exhibit 11.7 is:

$$-\$140 \text{ million} + \frac{(.53)\$400 \text{ million} + (.47)\$300 \text{ million}}{1.05} = \$196.19 \text{ million}$$

The $-\$140$ million appears in this equation because at point *B*, the firm takes advantage of the option to double the plant's capacity by spending an additional $140 million. The point *C* value is the same as in scenario 1. Thus, the value of the plant at date 0 is:

$$\frac{(.5)\$196.19 \text{ million} + (.5)\$111.90 \text{ million}}{1.05} = \$146.71 \text{ million}$$

which yields a net present value of $6.71 million $= \$146.71$ million $- \$140$ million.

Ignoring the option to increase the plant's capacity (scenario 1 in Example 11.6) results in a $140 million cost that exceeds the present value of its future cash flows ($133 million). Thus, a naive forecast of the cash flows of the plant makes it appear as though building the plant destroys value. However, unless Acme builds the plant at year 0, it can never take advantage of the option to increase capacity. Scenario 2 in Example 11.6 shows that this flexibility option enhances the value of building the plant by approximately $13 million, enough to turn an apparent negative *NPV* project into a positive *NPV* one.

Valuing Flexibility in Production Technology: The Advantage of Being Different

Using what we have learned about strategic options, particularly the option to expand, it is possible to demonstrate that in many instances a firm can gain a competitive advantage by being different from its competitors. This subsection shows that firms that have the option to vary their output levels may want to choose a method of production that differs from that of their competitors. By doing this the firm increases risk, thereby increasing the value of its flexibility option.

Consider, for example, a firm that produces and sells refined sugar in a market with a large number of competitors. It must decide whether to purchase equipment that allows it to produce the sugar from sugarcane or from sugar beets. The other sugar producers in its market use sugarcane as their input for refined sugar production. As a result, the price of refined sugar immediately reflects any increases in the price of sugarcane. However, because the competing firms currently do not use sugar beets as an input, fluctuations in the price of sugar beets are not as tied to the price of refined sugar as is the price of sugarcane.

A firm that lacks flexibility about how much sugar it will be producing will want to design its facilities to use the input with the lowest present value of its costs. However, as Example 11.7 shows, if the firm has a plant that gives it the option to increase production, the added uncertainty linked to using an input (sugar beets) that differs from the inputs used by competitors (sugarcane) can be valuable.

Example 11.7:   The Effect of Capacity Expansion on the Choice to be Different

The tree diagram in panel A of Exhibit 11.9 on page 428 illustrates some of our assumptions, namely:

- In a good economy, the cost of producing refined sugar with sugarcane is $0.60 per pound and the cost of using sugar beets is $0.54 per pound.

- In a bad economy, the cost of producing refined sugar with sugarcane falls to $0.40 per pound. However, the demand for sugar beets is somewhat less cyclical than sugarcane because it is not generally used to produce refined sugar. Thus, the cost of producing refined sugar with sugar beets falls somewhat less to $0.50 per pound.

- The risk-neutral probabilities associated with each of these two states of the economy (seen next to the branches of the tree diagram in panel A of Exhibit 11.9) are assumed to be .5.

- The price of refined sugar is always $0.03 per pound greater than the cost of production using sugarcane, which is reasonable because virtually all producers use sugarcane as their input.

Assuming that the fixed cost of building a sugarcane and sugar beet plant are the same, which method of producing refined sugar is better when (*a*) capacity is fixed, or (*b*) capacity is flexible in that the firm is committed to producing at least 1 million pounds of refined sugar in the plant but, at a cost of $40,000, the firm can double capacity to 2 million pounds upon discovering the state of the economy?

Answer: (*a*) Capacity is fixed. Using the risk-neutral probabilities of .5 and .5 to compute expectations, the expected production costs, from panel A in Exhibit 11.9, are $0.50 per pound [= .5($.60/lb.) + .5($.40/lb.)] for sugarcane and $0.52 per pound [= .5($.54/lb.) + .5($.50/lb.)] for sugar beets. Hence, sugarcane is the better input.

(*b*) Capacity can be doubled. If the firm uses sugarcane as its input, then the firm will earn $30,000 from selling 1 million pounds of sugar in both the good and bad economies, as seen in panel C of Exhibit 11.9. Since the cost of additional capacity, $40,000, exceeds the profit from expanded capacity, $30,000, a firm using sugarcane will choose not to exercise its option to double capacity. However, if the firm chooses to use sugar beets as its input, it will earn $0.09 per pound if the good state of the economy occurs because the price of refined sugar in this state of the economy is $0.63 per pound while production costs are $0.54 per pound. The firm will therefore make $90,000 on the first 1 million pounds of production. By exercising its option to double production, the firm makes $90,000 − $40,000 = $50,000 on the second 1 million pounds of production. Hence, as seen in panel B of Exhibit 11.9, the total profit in the good economy is $140,000. In the bad economy, the firm using the sugar beet input loses $70,000 at the lower refined sugar price of $0.43 per pound. Despite this loss, however, the firm's expected profit using sugar beets is $35,000, which exceeds the expected profits it achieves using sugarcane as its input. Thus, with the capacity to expand, sugar beets represent the superior raw input for production of refined sugar.

What is the intuition for the conclusion in Example 11.7 that sugar beets are a better raw input than sugarcane, despite their being more expensive on average? For the sugar

EXHIBIT 11.9   Production of Refined Sugar

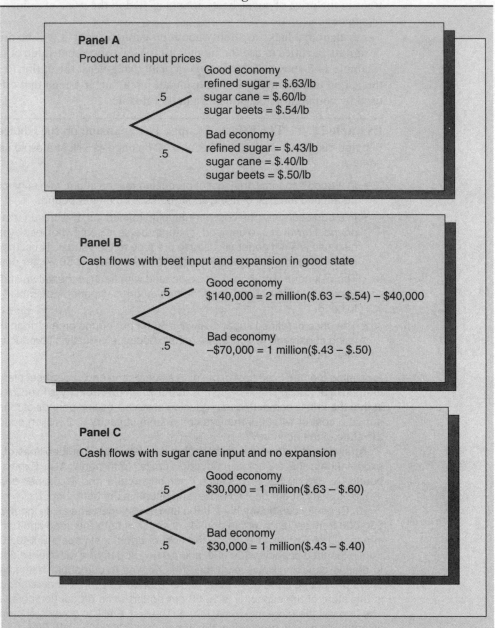

Panel A

Product and input prices

.5
Good economy
refined sugar = $.63/lb
sugar cane = $.60/lb
sugar beets = $.54/lb

.5
Bad economy
refined sugar = $.43/lb
sugar cane = $.40/lb
sugar beets = $.50/lb

Panel B

Cash flows with beet input and expansion in good state

.5
Good economy
$140,000 = 2 million($.63 − $.54) − $40,000

.5
Bad economy
−$70,000 = 1 million($.43 − $.50)

Panel C

Cash flows with sugar cane input and no expansion

.5
Good economy
$30,000 = 1 million($.63 − $.60)

.5
Bad economy
$30,000 = 1 million($.43 − $.40)

beet input, the lower output price in the bad economy reflects the drop in the price of sugarcane, the dominant raw material for producing refined sugar. Because output prices are correlated with the price of the dominant input, sugarcane producers who use *sugarcane* as the raw input generate profits that are partly insured against swings in the economy. However, producers who use *sugar beets* as the raw input in the production of refined sugar experience only a small decline in their input price when prices for refined sugar and sugarcane drop dramatically. Refined sugar production using *sugar beets* as the raw input is thus subject to wild swings in profit—earning $140,000 in the good economy and losing $70,000 in the bad economy. While this might seem like a disadvantage, it can be turned into an advantage if options such as the option to expand capacity exist. This is simply an application of the principle learned in Chapter 8 that options become more valuable when there is more volatility to the underlying asset.[9]

It is important to emphasize that the benefits of being different are not a principle, only a possibility. Had the numbers in Example 11.7 been different, one could easily have concluded that sugarcane manufacturing was still the cheaper method despite the option to increase capacity. Irrespective of which production method in the last example is cheap, however, one always would conclude that the advantage associated with being different is greater when there is more uncertainty and when the firm has greater flexibility to expand.

11.3 The Ratio Comparison Approach

A popular way that investment bankers and analysts value firms, projects, or assets is to compare them with other traded firms, projects, or assets. One of the best examples of this occurs in the field of real estate. The standard discounted cash flow method often is used to value real estate, but it is not the principal method. For example, most commercial real estate is valued relative to comparable real estate that recently sold. A building should sell for $20 million if it has twice the annual cash flow (rent revenues less maintenance costs) as a building across the street that recently sold for $10 million. The implicit assumption is that the cash flows of the two buildings will grow at the same rate, so that two times the cash flows of the comparable building tracks the future cash flows of the subject building. Hence, if the value of the tracked investment sells for the same price as its tracking investment, it has to sell for twice the selling price of the comparable building.

While the current annual cash flows of the building being valued may be twice that of the comparable building, this method is reasonable only if all future cash flows of the subject building are going to be twice as large as those of the comparable building. When this is not a reasonable assumption, other variables besides current cash flows might better summarize all future cash flows and thus serve as better proxies for generating the tracking investment.

For example, investment bankers consider a multiple of the forecasted annual earnings of comparison firms when valuing the initial public offering (IPO) of a company's common stock.[10] Earnings are often smoothed proxies for long-run cash flows and may work better as proxies than the current cash flow in determining the tracking portfolio. In some cases, these comparisons are based on book values or replacement values. For example, it is common to describe the prices of **real estate investment trusts (REITs)**, which are real estate portfolios that list and trade like shares of stock on an exchange, as a percentage of the book values of their assets. Other variables besides cash flow, earnings, and book value also are used in valuation. For example, a multiple of the number

---

[9]The risk-free return is not mentioned in Example 11.7 because it does not affect any of the conclusions. The production method with the largest risk-neutral expected profit is also the method with the largest present value.

[10]To price a firm that is going public, the firm's investment bankers generally will try to project the earnings of the firm and then come up with an earnings multiple by analyzing the price/earnings ratios of comparison firms. This provides an initial estimate of the firm's value which is likely to be adjusted for any specific risks of the IPO and unusual market conditions.

of subscribers is typically used to estimate the prices of nontraded cable television companies. Stock analysts value money management firms as a fraction of the amount of assets they have under management. Newspapers and magazines are valued relative to their advertising revenue and circulation.

These approaches to valuation assume that a new investment should sell for at approximately the same ratio of price to some salient economic variable as an existing investment with an observable ratio, which is why this approach is called the *ratio comparison approach*. This section illustrates the ratio comparison approach by using the ratio of price to earnings, *P/NI*, where *NI* stands for net income (that is, earnings) on the accounting income statement.[11] However, the examples above show that it is possible to use alternative numbers for earnings—sales revenue, book value, subscribers, monthly rents, advertising lines, or cash flow—as the denominator for this comparison.

The Price/Earnings Ratio Method

With the **price/earnings ratio method**, one obtains the present value of a project's future cash flows as follows:

Result 11.5   *(The Price/Earnings Ratio Method.)* The present value of the future cash flows of a project can be found by (1) obtaining the appropriate price/earnings ratio for the project from comparison investment for which this ratio is known and (2) multiplying the price/earnings ratio from the comparison by the first year's net income of the project. In a similar vein, a company should adopt a project when the ratio of its initial cost to earnings is lower than the price to earnings ratio of the comparison investment. (Alternative ratio comparison methods simply substitute a different economic variable for earnings.)

Subtracting the cost of initiating the project from this present value *(PV)* yields the net present value *(NPV)*. A company should adopt a project whenever the project's *NPV* is positive, which occurs when the project produces the future cash flow stream more cheaply than the comparable investment. Expressed another way, if the cost-to-earnings ratio of the project is less than the price/earnings ratio of a comparison investment, the project is a bargain.

Keep in mind that prices incorporate both the appropriate discount rate as well as the appropriate earnings growth rate. As a result, the price/earnings ratio method may avoid some of the difficulties in estimating either discount rates or growth rates. The price/earnings ratio method assumes, however, that the comparison investment on which the price/earnings multiple is based has the same discount rate and earnings growth as the project being valued. This is a a safe assumption in some settings, but it may be inappropriate in others.

When Comparison Investments Are Hidden in Multibusiness Firms

Finding an investment with an observable value that is comparable to, for example, a specialty steel plant, is more difficult than finding something comparable to an office building. Therefore, it may be necessary to examine combinations of the traded securities of a number of firms to identify an appropriate comparison investment. This approach is similar to the identification of beta risk when the betas of comparison firms are generated

---

[11]This is sometimes referred to as the P/E ratio, but we often use the variable *E* in the text to represent the market value of equity, so we employ *P/NI*.

by multiple lines of business. (See Chapter 10, Example 10.3.) When using price/earnings ratios to value projects, it may be necessary to use the following result:

Result 11.6   The price/earnings ratio of a portfolio of stocks 1 and 2 is a weighted average of the price/earnings ratios of stocks 1 and 2, where the weights are the fraction of earnings generated, respectively, by stocks 1 and 2. Algebraically:

$$\frac{P}{NI} = w_1 \frac{P_1}{NI_1} + w_2 \frac{P_2}{NI_2}$$

where

P/NI = price/earnings ratio of the portfolio
P_i/NI_i = price/earnings ratio of stock i (i = 1 or 2)
w_i = fraction of portfolio earnings from stock i.[12]

To apply this result to the specialty steel plant, consider a situation where the only potential comparison firm producing specialty steel also is in the oil business. How does an analyst filter out the impact of the oil business on the price/earnings ratio of the comparison firm?

Result 11.6 implies that the comparison firm in combination with a firm producing similar oil-related products might be a pure specialty steel portfolio, which can be used to determine the appropriate price/earnings ratio for valuing the specialty steel division. Example 11.8 illustrates how to do this.

Example 11.8:   Price/Earnings Ratio Comparisons with Multiple Lines of Business

Chrysler is considering the opportunity to enter the passenger bus market. Assume that General Motors (GM) currently produces similar buses from which it realizes 10 percent of its earnings. The rest of GM's cash flows come from automobile lines that are essentially the same as Chrysler's.

If GM's price/earnings ratio is 9.7, and if the price/earnings ratio of its automobile division, is (as seems reasonable) assumed to be the same as the price/earnings ratio of Chrysler, which is 10, what is the implied price/earnings ratio for the bus division?

Answer: Ninety percent of GM's earnings have a price/earnings ratio of 10, 10 percent of the earnings have a price/earnings ratio of x, and the total GM value is 9.7 times the company's total earnings. Viewing GM as a portfolio of a pure automobile business and a pure bus business, and applying Result 11.6, implies that x must solve:

$$.9(10) + .1x = 9.7$$

Thus, $x = 7$.

If the cost of the bus plant in Example 11.8 is less than seven times the initial earnings of the plant, and if it is realistic to assume that those earnings will grow at the same rate

---

[12]This result is derived by noting that:

$$P = P_1 + P_2 = \left(\frac{NI_1}{NI}\right)\left(\frac{P_1}{NI_1}\right)NI + \left(\frac{NI_2}{NI}\right)\left(\frac{P_2}{NI_2}\right)NI, \text{ implying}$$

$$\frac{P}{NI} = \left(\frac{NI_1}{NI}\right)\left(\frac{P_1}{NI_1}\right) + \left(\frac{NI_2}{NI}\right)\left(\frac{P_2}{NI_2}\right) = w_1\left(\frac{P_1}{NI_1}\right) + w_2\left(\frac{P_2}{NI_2}\right)$$

and have the same risk as the General Motors' bus plant, then Chrysler should accept the project.

The Effect of Earnings Growth and Accounting Methodology on Price/Earnings Ratios

The price/earnings ratio method is useful in many circumstances, yet it has drawbacks. As mentioned earlier, the earnings of the project and the comparison portfolio must have similar growth rates. For example, if the earnings of the comparison portfolio are growing at a faster rate than those of the project, the price/earnings ratio method is invalid because the value of the comparison portfolio will be enhanced by the faster growth rate. Even if the project costs little to initiate and seems to have a favorable cost-to-earnings ratio compared to the price/earnings ratios available from similar investments, the project could destroy value if the low cost does not make up for the project's low earnings growth rate.

Analysts who use the price/earnings ratio method also must be especially careful that the earnings calculations reflect the true economic earnings of the firm. For example, accounting changes, such as one-time write-downs, can dramatically affect the reported earnings of firms without affecting their cash flows or their market values. Analysts who naively use reported earnings to calculate the appropriate value of a project will substantially misvalue the project. For this reason, some analysts who employ the price/earnings ratio method use EVA or similar measures of adjusted earnings in lieu of earnings per se.

In general, the valuation expert must be aware of how accounting earnings differ from true economic earnings; specifically, how accrual accounting, working capital changes, and depreciation affect reported earnings. To address these concerns, some analysts use the price-to-cash-flow ratio in lieu of the price/earnings ratio. However, it is also easy to distort the comparison with the price-to-cash-flow ratio. For example, a comparison firm may find itself cash rich simply because a major customer decides to obtain an income tax deduction by paying its bill at the end of the year instead of at the beginning of the new year. Customers who speed up the payment of their bills by a few days have a negligible effect on the comparison firm's present value, but they may substantially increase the reported cash flow in the relevant tax year and reduce the cash flow in the year after.

The Effect of Leverage on Price/Earnings Ratios

In order to use the price/earnings ratio method to make capital allocation decisions, it also is important to understand how leverage affects a firm's net income per share (EPS) and, consequently, its price/earnings ratio. Hence, when evaluating a project using the price/earnings ratio method, the manager must calculate the earnings of the project using the assumption that the project is financed with the same ratio of debt to equity—the leverage ratio—as the comparison firm. As this chapter will demonstrate shortly, an increase in leverage, holding the firm's operations and total value constant, will increase or decrease the firm's net income per share and price/earnings ratio, depending on the relative size of the price/earnings ratio and the reciprocal of the yield on debt borrowing.

When Leverage Increases the Price/Earnings Ratio.   Example 11.9 illustrates a hypothetical case where leverage increases the *P/NI* ratio.

Example 11.9: A Case When Leverage Increases the Price/Earnings Ratio

The information below applies to Micro Technologies at the beginning of its fiscal year:

Assets (book value)	$500,000,000
Liabilities (book value)	$100,000,000
Equity (book and market value)	$400,000,000
Number of shares outstanding	40,000,000
Equity per share (book and market value)	$10 = \dfrac{\$400,000,000}{40,000,000}$
Expected net income	$20,000,000
Expected *EPS*	$.50 = \dfrac{\$20,000,000}{40,000,000}$
$\dfrac{P}{NI}$	$20 = \dfrac{\$10}{\$.50}$
ROE	$5.0\% = \dfrac{NI}{P} = \dfrac{\$20,000,000}{\$400,000,000}$

Assume that Micro Technologies issues $100 million in debt at the beginning of the year at a rate of 6 percent, and that equity is decreased by the same amount through a repurchase of 10 million shares at $10 each (i.e., assuming market value equals book value). Assuming no taxes and thus no response in stock price per share to the increase in leverage, how does the debt issue affect Micro's balance sheet account and expected financial performance for the year?

   Answer: As a result of the debt issuance, resulting in a $100 million increase in liabilities and a $100 million decrease in equity, Micro's balance sheet accounts and expected financial performance for the year will be as follows:

Assets (book value)	$500,000,000
Liabilities (book value)	$200,000,000
Equity (book and market value)	$300,000,000
Number of shares outstanding	30,000,000
Equity per share (book and market value)	$10 = \dfrac{\$300,000,000}{30,000,000}$
Expected net income	$14,000,000 $= \$20,000,000 - (\$100,000,000)(.06)$
Expected *EPS*	$.47 = \dfrac{\$14}{30}$
$\dfrac{P}{NI}$	$21.28 = \dfrac{\$10}{\$.47}$
ROE	$4.7\% = \dfrac{NI}{P} = \dfrac{\$14,000,000}{\$300,000,000}$

   Example 11.9 illustrates that the increased debt reduces Micro Technologies' *EPS*. Since there was no share price response to the debt increase, the reduction in *EPS* led to

an increase in the firm's price/earnings ratio. We provide a more realistic example of the effect of leverage on price/earnings ratios below.

The Effect of a Leveraged Acquisition on Maytag's Price/Earnings Ratios

The Maytag Corporation dramatically increased its leverage in the late 1980s. From year-end 1987 to year-end 1989, the company's long-term debt as a percent of total capital (long-term debt plus book equity) rose from 23.3 percent to 46.8 percent. Exhibit 11.10 provides some relevant financial information for the Maytag Corporation over these years.

Maytag's increased debt level, due primarily to the debt financing of its acquisition of Chicago Pacific Corporation in January 1989, resulted in a significant increase in interest expense during 1989 (from $19.7 million in 1988 to $83.4 million in 1989). Following this increase in leverage, the firm's *EPS* decreased substantially.

The increase in Maytag's price/earnings ratio may have been due to increased interest expense caused by the leverage taken on to acquire Chicago Pacific. Example 11.10 illustrates how to filter out the drop in Maytag's earnings that is due to the increase in its leverage.

Example 11.10:   The Impact of Leverage on Maytag's Earnings per Share

Assume that Maytag chooses to maintain its 1987 ratio of long-term debt to capital, 23.3 percent. Ignoring taxes, calculate what Maytag's 1989 *EPS* would have been without any change in the company's leverage.

Answer: Holding all other decisions of the firm constant, Maytag's financial data for 1989 would have been as follows:

	Maytag Corporation Financial Statement	
	Actual 1989 Data	*With No Leverage Change*
Long-term debt (*LTD*) ($ millions)	$ 877	$ 437
Long-term debt + book equity (*LTD + BE*) ($ millions)	$1,875	$1,875
Leverage ratio $\dfrac{LTD}{LTD + BE}$	46.8%	23.3%
Earnings ($ millions)	$ 131	$ 166*
Number of shares outstanding	105,560,000	126,047,576†
Earnings per share	$ 1.24‡	$ 1.32

Notes to Financial Data

*Earnings would have been $35 million higher due to the decreased interest cost. Assuming an interest rate of 8 percent on the additional debt in the actual data, earnings in the hypothetical situation would be (in millions): $131 + ($877 − $437) × .08 = $166.

†Assuming the issuance of $437 million in equity at the average 1989 share price of $21.34 (on 20,487,576 shares), to substitute for the debt issuance.

‡Value Line's *EPS* of $1.27 is based on earnings divided by the average number of shares outstanding throughout the 1989 fiscal year. The *EPS* of $1.24 is based on Value Line's aggregate earnings over end-of-year shares outstanding. The $0.08 increase in *EPS* due to leverage should be approximately the same with either method of computing *EPS*.

Example 11.10 illustrates that Maytag's *EPS* was reduced from $1.32 to $1.24 because it had increased its leverage ratio. Hence, only a small part, $0.08, of the large decrease in actual *EPS* from 1988 to 1989 is due to leverage.

EXHIBIT 11.10   Selected Financial Information for the Maytag Corporation

	EPS	Interest Expense ($ millions)	Interest Coverage Ratio*	ROE (%)	Price/Earnings	Value ($ billions)
1986	$1.51	$12.0	18.5	25.1%	14.7	$1.9
1987	1.91	10.8	25.3	33.4	13.5	2.0
1988	1.77	19.7	11.9	29.6	13.0	1.8
1989	1.27	83.4	3.5	16.1	16.8	2.3

*See the preface to Part IV of the text for more detail about interest coverage ratios.
Source: Value Line Investment Survey, Dec. 21, 1990.

A Case Where Leverage Decreases the Price/Earnings Ratio.   If a firm's stock price is high because earnings are expected to grow at an exceptionally fast rate, then an increase in leverage could decrease the price/earnings ratio, as Example 11.11 demonstrates.

Example 11.11:   Leverage Can Decrease the Price/Earnings Ratio

The Gamma Feron Biotech Company, currently an all-equity firm, has 1 million shares of stock trading at $25 a share and a price/earnings ratio (using next year's expected earnings in the denominator) of 12.5. The company plans to reinvest 50 percent of its earnings in the company and to pay the remaining 50 percent as dividends.

First, calculate next year's expected earnings. Then compute the growth rate of earnings, assuming that the $25 share price is consistent with the dividend discount model (discussed in Chapter 10) at a cost of capital of 10 percent per year. Finally, assume that there are no taxes, and compute the effect on earnings and the price/earnings ratio of a leveraged recapitalization (see Chapter 2), in which 50 percent of the company's shares are retired in a purchase financed with risk-free debt earning interest at 6 percent per year. Assume that the price per share does not change as a consequence of the leveraged recapitalization.

Answer: Next year's expected **unlevered earnings** (income from the firm's operations, assuming that the firm is all equity financed, also EBI), are $2 per share which implies a dividend of $1 per share at a 50 percent reinvestment rate. The dividend discount model says that the price per share, $P = div/(\bar{r}_E - g)$, or $25 = 1/(.1 - g)$, implying $g = 6$ percent per year. As a result of the leveraged recapitalization, the price remains at $25 per share, but the earnings drop to:

$$NI \text{ per share} = \frac{\text{Unlevered earnings} - \text{Debt interest}}{\text{Number of shares outstanding}}$$

$$= \frac{\$2 \text{ million} - .06(\$12.5 \text{ million})}{.5 \text{ million}} = \$2.50 \text{ per share, which generates}$$

$$\frac{\text{Price}}{\text{Earnings}} = 10$$

In Example 11.11, the debt issue decreased Gamma Feron's price/earnings ratio from 12.5 to 10. If debt is default free, so that debt interest is always paid, more leverage will decrease the price/earnings ratio whenever the ratio of unlevered earnings to price exceeds the yield r_D on the risk-free debt. (If there had been corporate taxes in Example 11.11, the comparison would have to be made with the after-tax cost of debt,

$r_D \times (1 - \text{tax rate})$.) In this case, the 8 percent ratio of unlevered earnings to price, ($2/$25), exceeds the 6 percent yield on Gamma Feron's debt. Thus, every dollar of equity retired in the leveraged recapitalization leaves remaining shareholders with extra earnings of $0.08. However, each retired dollar of equity is exchanged for a dollar of debt that soaks up only $0.06. The remaining equity shares have $0.02 more earnings remaining per dollar of debt exchanged for equity, implying, with a constant price per share, that the price/earnings ratio increases.

What Determines Whether Leverage Increases or Decreases the Price/Earnings Ratio?   The general principle is formally stated as follows:

Result 11.7   Assume the market value of the firm's assets is unaffected by its leverage ratio. Also assume that all debt is risk free. Then, if the ratio of price to earnings of an all-equity firm is larger than $1/r_D$, where r_D is the interest on the firm's (assumed) risk-free perpetual debt, then an increase in leverage increases the price/earnings ratio. If the price/earnings ratio of an all-equity firm is less than $1/r_D$, then the increase in leverage lowers the price/earnings ratio of the firm.

To prove this result, simply write out the price/earnings ratio, assuming risk-free perpetual debt, where:

A = the market value of the assets

X = unlevered earnings

A/X = the price/earnings ratio of an all-equity firm

The ratio of the market value of equity to the firm's total net income (assuming zero taxes) is:

$$\frac{\text{Price}}{\text{Earnings}} = \frac{A - D}{X - r_D D} \tag{11.1}$$

$$= \frac{1}{r_D} \left[\frac{\left(\dfrac{A/X}{1/r_D}\right) X - r_D D}{X - r_D D} \right]$$

Note that the expression in brackets in equation (11.1) is either larger or smaller than 1, depending on the relative size of A/X and $1/r_D$. An increase in D, which moves the expression in brackets closer to 1, decreases the price/earnings ratio when $A/X < 1/r_D$ and increases it otherwise.

Adjusting for Leverage Differences

If one uses a comparison firm's price/earnings ratio to value a particular project, it is important to value the project with the **unleveraged price/earnings ratio**, which is the ratio that would exist if the comparison investment were all equity financed, rather than the leveraged price/earnings ratio that one observes. One values the project as the product of the unlevered earnings of the project and the unleveraged price/earnings ratio of the comparison. That is,

$$PV_{\text{project}} = \left(\frac{A}{X}\right)_{\text{comparison}} \times (X)_{\text{project}}$$

To "unlever" a price/earnings ratio, use equation (11.1) in reverse. First, substitute the measured price/earnings ratio on the left-hand side and then solve for the A/X, the unleveraged price/earnings ratio that makes equation (11.1) hold.[13] With corporate taxes, multiply the denominator expression in brackets, $X - r_D D$, by $1 - corporate\ tax\ rate$ before solving for A/X.

11.4 The Competitive Analysis Approach

Earlier this chapter discussed how financial analysis tools can be used to clarify the thinking of a corporation's long-run strategic planners. This section turns the tables somewhat by discussing how issues typically considered by strategic planners can be used to analyze the value created by specific projects.

Determining a Division's Contribution to Firm Value

In many cases, it is impossible to unravel the contribution of a particular division to a firm's value. For example, trying to obtain the appropriate price/earnings ratio for an investment in toothpaste production by examining the financial statements of multiproduct companies like Proctor & Gamble or American Home Products is pointless: Their toothpaste divisions account for only a small part of the performance reported in their consolidated financial statements. However, with a great deal of confidence, one can assert that toothpaste is a product that will continue to be used in the future. In addition, it is likely that a firm probably has a positive net present value project if it either can produce toothpaste more cheaply or sell it more effectively than its competitors. If this is not the case, the project's net present value is probably negative. In other words, the *NPV* of a project is ultimately determined by a firm's advantages relative to those of its competition. A firm that can accurately assess its competitive advantages may find that this is the best method of assessing the *NPV* of a project.

Result 11.8   *(The Competitive Analysis Approach.)* Firms in a competitive market should realize that they can only achieve a positive *NPV* from a project if they have some advantage over their competitors. When other firms have competitive advantages, the project has a negative NPV.

Disadvantages of the Competitive Analysis Approach

Like any of the other valuation methods, the competitive analysis approach has its pitfalls. In the early 1980s, for example, most oil firms were spending more to explore for oil than the oil was worth. Because the competitive analysis approach implicitly assumes value-maximizing competitors, it could lead a value-maximizing firm astray when this assumption is false. A manager of a firm with non-value-maximizing competitors might accurately project the demand for oil in the foreseeable future and correctly ascertain that it has a competitive advantage in its production (e.g., lower costs). The manager might assume that, even if oil prices declined, less efficient competitors would stop production before the price level dropped to a point where the firm starts to incur losses. Given these assumptions, the competitive analysis approach suggests that oil exploration is a good investment. However, if other firms are in the oil business for reasons other than value-maximization (e.g., company pride), the manager may find that

---

[13]See Exercise 11.10 for an algebraic solution to this problem.

as oil prices decline competitors do not exit or, possibly, even increase production, believing they can survive a "price war" and drive prices even lower. This type of market would be unattractive, even for the lowest-cost firm.[14]

11.5 When to Use the Different Approaches

Part III of the text has discussed a number of different approaches to real asset valuation. The approaches in Chapters 9 and 10 include discounted cash flow, using the risk-adjusted discount rate and certainty equivalent approaches, and internal rate of return. This chapter has discussed the derivatives, ratio comparison, and competitive analysis approaches. Which approach or set of approaches should a manager use?

Can these Approaches Be Used at All?

Determining whether one of these approaches can be used at all provides partial guidance. For instance, the intuition gained from the examples that employ the derivatives valuation approach in this chapter is always going to be useful, but this advanced valuation technique is not always applied easily. For example, the strategic options associated with many investment projects are difficult to specify before the project is actually initiated. Moreover, it frequently is impossible to estimate the random process (e.g., the binomial tree) that generates the future asset prices that determine the investment's present value. This makes it difficult to apply the derivatives valuation approach literally. On the other hand, it is difficult in many cases to estimate the expected or certainty equivalent cash flows of an investment, so the discounted cash flow method also may be difficult to implement reliably.

Valuing Asset Classes versus Specific Assets

In addition, when asking questions like, "Is real estate a good investment?" the derivatives valuation and the ratio comparison approaches cannot be used. These approaches are based on a comparison between highly similar investments and reveal little about the relative pricing of widely disparate classes of assets, so they are not effective for identifying whether broad asset classes are mispriced.

To determine the attractiveness of real estate investments as a group, one would have to determine the risk of a broad-based portfolio of real estate investments and assess whether the financial markets are appropriately pricing that risk. Therefore, it is best for this purpose to use a model—either the CAPM or the APT—that makes statements about the risk-return relation across asset classes. In contrast, given the empirical shortcomings of the CAPM and APT (see Chapters 5 and 6), one should look to alternatives in more specific cases when they are available. For example, it would be inappropriate to use the CAPM and APT to value an office building when a suitable comparable office building exists.

Tracking Error Considerations

The tracking portfolio metaphor may be useful in determining the best valuation approach. The Capital Asset Pricing Model argues that every investment should be tracked

---

[14]In the early 1980s most major oil firms continued to explore for oil despite these price signals from the market. As a result, many of these firms were taken over in order to end the unprofitable exploration in which these firms were engaged. See Chapter 19 for further detail on this.

with a weighted average of the market portfolio and a risk-free asset. Tracking with the CAPM has to be highly imperfect considering the dissimilarities between a particular office building and the market portfolio. Financial analysts who use the CAPM to value a real asset rely on the insight that the CAPM-based tracking error has a zero present value to conclude that the valuation is correct. If the CAPM as a theory is untrue or untrue in certain circumstances, this conclusion is unwarranted. We already know that the tracking error does not have zero present value for stocks with low market-to-book ratios, small market capitalizations, and high past returns. Thus, there is no reason to have similar confidence in the tracking error for any particular investment project.

In contrast, the cash flows from a portfolio composed of a comparable office building and the risk-free asset tracks the evaluated building's cash flows more closely than a combination of the market portfolio and a risk-free asset. In this case, there is no theoretical reason to believe that the tracking error will have zero present value. However, if the tracking error is so small as to be negligible, one obtains a better present value by using the comparable office building in a ratio comparison than by using the CAPM.

Other Considerations

While the ratio comparison approach and the competitive analysis approach seem easy to implement and implicitly account for the strategic options embedded in most projects, they are limited by the degree to which the comparison investments and firms exhibit rationality, either in their pricing (e.g., in the price/earnings approach[15]) or in their behavior (e.g., in the competitive analysis approach). Moreover, it may be difficult to ensure that the comparison investment (or firm) is truly an appropriate comparison and to take into account all factors for which there are differences between the comparison entity and the project.

The practical focus we emphasize here suggests that using any single approach discussed in this chapter need not preclude a manager from also valuing a project with a second method when it is practical to apply an alternative. Indeed, it probably makes sense to value major investment projects using two or three approaches.

11.6 Summary and Conclusions

A good portion of this chapter focused on using the derivatives valuation approach to value projects with strategic options. This approach requires making a number of simplifying assumptions that may not be particularly realistic (e.g. the assumption that cash flows evolve along a binomial tree). As a result, one should consider the calculated values as rough estimates rather than as exact quantities. Nevertheless, though the pricing of strategic options is still an inexact science, the methods described in this chapter provide useful intuition about the kinds of projects that are likely to be more valuable or to have large components of value missed by the discounted cash flow method.

Among the intuitive lessons to remember are:

- Strategic options exist whenever management has any flexibility regarding the implementation of a project.
- Options to change the scale of a project, abandon it, or drastically change its implementation in the future need to be considered. The more different a firm is from its competitors, the more valuable the options (e.g., the option to expand).
- The existence of these options improves the value of an investment project. If management ignores such options, the project will be undervalued. Hence, a

---

[15]For example, the purchaser of the comparison office building across the street might have paid too much for the property.

manager who computes a zero or slightly negative *NPV* for a project with the standard discounted cash flow method can feel confident about adopting the project. The cash flows arising from strategic options that were missed due to their indirect nature will push the *NPV* of the project well into the positive range.

- The values of most options increase with the maturity of the option. This suggests that strategic options are generally more valuable for longer-term projects. Standard discounted cash flow methods, which tend to ignore such options, may underestimate the value of long-term projects more than they underestimate the value of short-term projects. If decision makers ignore such options in their valuation analysis, long-term projects will be undervalued more than short-term projects.

- The greater the uncertainty about the future value of the underlying investment, the greater the option's value. This suggests that strategic options are more valuable the higher the risk of the project, indicating that it is probably beneficial to build more flexibility into projects with more uncertain future cash flows. Traditional discounted cash flow methods that ignore strategic options are likely to undervalue high-risk projects more than low-risk projects, so it is important for decision makers to be careful before rejecting high-risk projects.

In addition to the derivatives valuation approach, this chapter studied two other methods for analyzing capital allocation: the ratio comparison approach and the competitive analysis approach.

All three valuation methods, like nearly every valuation method for valuing financial assets or real assets studied in this text, are based on comparisons between assets. Each asset is tracked, sometimes approximately, by a portfolio of other assets. Financial valuation is simply a way of connecting the value of an asset that has a known price to the asset being valued.

What if the manager believes that the market is incorrect? For example, if managers think that the comparable office building is undervalued or the underlying copper price is too low, should they use their superior information and accept investment projects that the market incorrectly undervalues but which are overvalued relative to their tracking portfolios? Generally, the answer to this question is no. If the cost of a prospective investment exceeds the cost of its tracking portfolio, it is clearly better to buy the tracking portfolio rather than take the investment. This is true regardless of the market's assessment—correct or incorrect—of the value of the tracking portfolio.

In sum, the advantages of this chapter's valuation methods over the standard discounted cash flow method (developed in Chapters 9 and 10) largely have to do with deficiencies in the way the standard discounted cash flow method is implemented. Two general rules often ignored by practitioners who use the standard discounted cash flow method should be emphasized.

- Because decision makers are ultimately trying to evaluate the market value of a project, financial managers should use observable market prices as much as possible. Don't rely on estimated market values when actual market prices can be observed.

- Managers should think in terms of investment strategies instead of isolated individual investment projects. Most projects are flexible in their implementation and often provide the firm with additional profitable investment opportunities in the future. Consider these options, which add value to an investment strategy, when evaluating investment projects.

Key Concepts

Result 11.1: New opportunities for a firm often arise as a result of information and relationships developed in its past investment projects. Therefore, firms should evaluate investment projects on the basis of their potential to generate valuable information and to develop important relationships as well as on the basis of the direct cash flows they generate.

Result 11.2: A mine can be viewed as an option to extract (or purchase) minerals at a strike price equal to the cost of extraction. Like a stock option, the option to extract the minerals has a value that increases with both the volatility of the mineral price and the volatility of the extraction cost.

Result 11.3: Vacant land can be viewed as an option to purchase developed land where the exercise price is the cost of developing a building on the land. Like stock options, this more complicated type of option has a value that is increasing in the degree of uncertainty about the value (and type) of development.

Result 11.4: Most projects can be viewed as a set of mutually exclusive projects. For example, taking the project today is one project, waiting to take the project next year is another project, and waiting three years is yet another project. Firms may pass up the first project, that is, initiate the capital investment immediately, even if doing so has a positive net present value. They will do so if the mutually exclusive alternative, waiting to invest, has a higher *NPV*.

Result 11.5: *(The Price/Earnings Ratio Method.)* The present value of the future cash flows of a project can be found by (1) obtaining the appropriate price/earnings ratio for the project from a comparison investment for which this ratio is known and (2) multiplying the price/earnings ratio from the comparison by the first year's net income of the project. In a similar vein, a company should adopt a project when the ratio of its initial cost to earnings is lower than the price to earnings ratio of the comparison investment. (Alternative ratio comparison methods simply substitute a different economic variable for earnings.)

Result 11.6: The price/earnings ratio of a portfolio of stocks 1 and 2 is a weighted average of the price/earnings ratios of stocks 1 and 2, where the weights are the fraction of earnings generated, respectively, by stocks 1 and 2. Algebraically:

$$\frac{P}{NI} = w_1 \frac{P_1}{NI_1} + w_2 \frac{P_2}{NI_2}$$

where

$\dfrac{P}{NI}$ = price/earnings ratio of the portfolio

$\dfrac{P_i}{NI_i}$ = price/earnings ratio of stock i ($i = 1$ or 2)

w_i = fraction of portfolio earnings from stock i

Result 11.7: Assume the market value of the firm's assets is unaffected by its leverage ratio. Also assume that all debt is risk free. Then, if the ratio of price to earnings of an all-equity firm is larger than $1/r_D$, where r_D is the interest on the firm's (assumed) risk-free perpetual debt, then an increase in leverage increases the price/earnings ratio. If the price/earnings ratio of an all-equity firm is less than $1/r_D$, then the increase in leverage lowers the price/earnings ratio of the firm.

Result 11.8: *(The Competitive Analysis Approach.)* Firms in a competitive market should realize that they can only realize a positive *NPV* from a project if they have some advantage over their competitors. When other firms have a competitive advantage the project has a negative *NPV*.

Key Terms

Exercises

11.1. Maytag merges with Whirlpool. Assume that Maytag's price/earnings ratio is 20 and Whirlpool's is 15. If Maytag accounts for 60 percent of the earnings of the merged firm, and if there are no synergies between the two merged firms, what is the price/earnings ratio of the merged firm?

11.2. The XYZ firm can invest in a new DRAM chip factory for $500 million. The factory, which must be invested in today, has cash flows two years from now that depend on the state of the economy. The cash flows when the factory is running at full capacity are described by the following tree diagram:

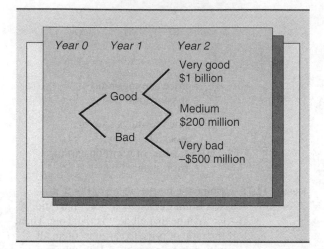

In year 1, the firm has the option of running the plant at less than full capacity. In this case, workers are laid off, production of memory chips is scaled down, and the subsequent cash flows are half of what they would be when the plant is running at full capacity.

An alternative use for the firm's funds is investment in the market portfolio. In the states that correspond to the branches of the tree above, $1 invested in the market portfolio grows as follows:

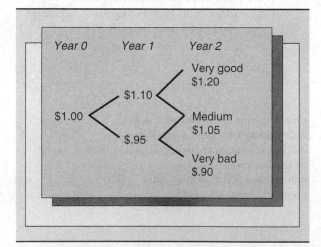

Assume that the risk-free rate is 5 percent per year, compounded annually. Compute the project's present value (*a*) with the option to scale down and (*b*) without the option to scale down. Compute the difference between these two values, which is the value of the option.

11.3. Vacant land has been zoned for either one 10,000-square-foot five-unit condominium or two single-family homes, each with 3,000 square feet. The cost of constructing the single-family homes is $100 per square foot and the cost of constructing the condominium is $120 per square foot. If the real estate market does well next year, the homes can be sold for $300 per square foot and the condominiums for $230 per square foot. If the market performs poorly, the homes can be sold for $200 per square foot and the condos for $140 per square foot. Today, the homes could be sold for $225 per square foot and the condos for $180 per square foot. First-year rental rates (paid at the end of the year) on the condos and homes are 20 percent and 10 percent, respectively, of the initial sales prices.

a. What is the implied risk-free rate, assuming that short selling is allowed?

b. What is the value of the vacant land, assuming that building construction will take place immediately or one year from now? What is the best building alternative?

11.4. A silver mine has reserves of 25,000 troy ounces of silver. For simplicity, assume the following schedule for extraction, ore purification, and sale of the silver ore:

Extraction and Sale Date	Troy Ounces
Today	10,000
One year from now	10,000
Two years from now	5,000

Also assume the following:

- The mine, which will exhaust its supply of silver ore in two years, is assumed to have no salvage value.
- The current price of silver is $4 per troy ounce.
- Today's forward price for silver settled one year from now is $4.20 per troy ounce.
- Today's forward price for silver settled two years from now is $4.50 per troy ounce.
- The cost of extraction, ore purification, and selling is $2 per troy ounce now and at any point over the next two years.
- The risk-free return is 5 percent per year.

What is the value of the silver mine?

11.5. Widget production and sales take place over a one-year cycle. For simplicity, assume that all costs (revenues) are paid (received) at the end of the one-year cycle.

A factory with a life of three years (from today) has a capacity to produce 1 million widgets each year (which are to be sold at the end of each year of production). Widgets produced within the last year have just been sold.

Each year, production costs can either rise or decline by 50 percent from the previous year's cost. Over the coming year, widgets will be produced at a cost of $2 per widget. Unlike production costs, which vary from year to year, the revenue from selling widgets is stable. Assume that in the coming year and in all future years the widget selling price is $4 per widget.

The performance of a portfolio of stocks in the widget industry depends entirely on expected future production costs. When widget production costs increase by 50 percent from date t to date $t + 1$, the return on the industry portfolio over the same interval of time is assumed to be -30 percent. If the production costs decline by 50 percent, the portfolio return is assumed to be 40 percent over that time period.

Assume that the factory producing the widgets is to be closed down and sold for its salvage value whenever the cost of extraction per widget exceeds the selling price of a widget. This closure occurs at the beginning of the production year.

Value the factory, assuming that its salvage value is zero and that the risk-free return is 12 percent per year.

11.6. The futures closing prices on the New York Mercantile Exchange from *The Wall Street Journal* published on August 28, 1996 (for August 27 closing prices) specify that futures prices per barrel for light sweet crude oil delivered monthly from mid-October 1996 through mid-December 1998 are, respectively, $21.56, $21.08, $20.63, $20.23, $19.88, $19.55, $19.26, $19.00, $18.76, $18.58, $18.41, $18.25, $18.09, $17.93, $17.83, $17.77, $17.71, $17.66, $17.61, $17.56, $17.52, $17.48, $17.46, $17.46, $17.46, $17.47, and $17.48. Compute the August 27, 1996, value of an oil well that produces 1000 barrels of light sweet crude oil per month for the months October 1996 through December 1998, after which the well will be dry. Assume that there are no options to increase or decrease production and that the cost of producing each barrel of oil and shipping it to market is $2.00 per barrel. Also assume that the risk-free return is 5 percent per year, compounded annually.

11.7. Compute the risk-neutral probabilities attached to the two states—high demand and low demand—in Example 11.2. Show that applying these probabilities to value the mine provides the same answer for scenarios 1 and 2 as given in Example 11.2

11.8. Although there is no empirical evidence to strongly support this hypothesis, some financial journalists have claimed that American managers are shortsighted and overly risk averse, preferring to take on relatively safe projects that pay off quickly instead of taking on longer-term projects with less certain payoffs. Assume the journalists are correct.

a. Explain why managers who use a single discount rate for valuing projects are likely to have a systematic bias against longer-term projects if the systematic risk of the cash flows of many long-term investment projects declines over time.

b. Discuss how the presence of strategic investment options affects the decisions to adopt long-term over short-term investments.

11.9. Porter and Spence (1982) pointed out that firms may want to overinvest in production capacity to show a commitment to maintain their market share to competitors. In their model, excess plant capacity would not be a positive net present value project if the cash flows were calculated taking the competitors actions as given. However, since competitors are less likely to enter a market when the incumbent firm has excess capacity, the added capacity may be worthwhile even if it is never used. Comment on whether this strategic consideration should be taken into account when analyzing an investment project.

11.10. Solve for the unlevered price/earnings ratio, A/X, by rearranging equation (11.1).

References and Additional Readings

Aguilar, Francis, and Dong-Seng Cho. "Gold Star Co. Ltd." Case 9-385-264, Harvard Business School, 1985.

Brennan, Michael, and Eduardo Schwartz. "Evaluating Natural Resource Investments." *Journal of Business* 58 (April 1985), pp. 135–57.

———. "A New Approach to Evaluating Natural Resource Investments." *Midland Corporate Finance Journal* 3 (Spring 1985). (A less technical version of the previous entry.)

Dixit, Avinash, and Robert Pindyck. *Investment under Uncertainty*. Princeton, NJ: Princeton University Press, 1994.

Ekern S. "An Option Pricing Approach to Evaluating Petroleum Projects." *Energy Economics* 10 (1985), pp. 91–99.

Fine, Charles H., and Robert M. Freund. "Optimal Investment in Product-Flexible Manufacturing Capacity." *Management Science* 36 (April 1990), pp. 449–66.

Hayes, Robert, and William Abernathy. "Managing Our Way to Economic Decline." *Harvard Business Review* 58 (July–Aug. 1980), pp. 67–77.

Ingersoll, Jonathan E., and Stephen A. Ross. "Waiting to Invest: Investment and Uncertainty." *Journal of Business* 65 (Jan. 1992), pp. 1–29.

Jacoby, Henry D., and David G. Laughton. "Project Evaluation: A Practical Asset Pricing Method." *Energy Journal* 13 (1992), pp. 19–47.

Kogut, Bruce, and Nalin Kulatilaka. "Operating Flexibility, Global Manufacturing, and the Option Value of a Multinational Network." *Management Science* 40, no. 1. (1993), pp. 123–39.

Kulatilaka, Nalin, and Alan J. Marcus. "General Formulation of Corporate Real Options." *Research in Finance* 7 (1988), pp. 183–99.

Lerner, Eugene, and Arnold Rappaport. "Limit DCF in Capital Budgeting." *Harvard Business Review* 46 (Sept.–Oct. 1968), pp. 133–39.

Lohrenz, Joh, and R. N. Dickens. "Option Theory for Evaluation of Oil and Gas Assets: The Upsides and Downsides." *Proceedings of the Society of Petroleum Engineers,* 1993, pp. 179–88.

Majd, Saman, and Robert S. Pindyck. "Time to Build, Option Value, and Investment Decisions." *Journal of Financial Economics* 18 (Mar. 1987), pp. 7–27.

Margrabe, William. "The Value of an Option to Exchange One Asset for Another." *Journal of Finance* 33, no. 1 (1978), pp. 177–86.

McDonald, Robert, and Daniel Siegel. "Investment and the Valuation of Firms When There Is an Option to Shut Down." *International Economic Review* 26, no. 2 (1985), pp. 331–49.

———. "The Value of Waiting to Invest." *Quarterly Journal of Economics* 101, no. 4 (1986), pp. 707–27.

Milgrom, Paul, and John Roberts. *Economics, Organization and Management*. Englewood Cliffs, NJ: Prentice-Hall, 1992.

Myers, Stewart C. "Determinants of Corporate Borrowing." *Journal of Financial Economics* 5 (Nov. 1977), pp. 147–75.

———. "Finance Theory and Financial Strategy." *Interfaces* 14 (Jan.–Feb. 1984), pp. 126–37.

Paddock, James L.; Daniel R. Siegel; and James L. Smith. "Option Valuation of Claims on Real Assets: The Case of Offshore Petroleum Leases." *Quarterly Journal of Economics* 103 (Aug. 1988), pp. 479–508.

Pakes, Ariel. "Patents as Options: Some Estimates of the Value of Holding European Patent Stocks." *Econometrica* 54 (July 1986), pp. 755–84.

Porter, Michael, and Michael Spence. "The Capacity Expansion Process in a Growing Oligopoly: The Case of Corn Wet Milling." In John McCall, ed., *The Economics of Information and Uncertainty*. Chicago: University of Chicago Press, 1982.

Quigg, Laura. "Empirical Testing of Real Option-Pricing Models." *Journal of Finance* 48 (June 1993), pp. 621–39.

Rappaport, Alfred. "Forging a Common Framework." *Harvard Business Review* 70 (May–June, 1992), pp. 84–91.

Shapiro, Alan. "Corporate Strategy and the Capital Budgeting Decision." *Midland Corporate Finance Journal* 3, no. 1 (Spring 1985), pp. 22–36.

Stibolt, R. D., and John Lehman. "The Value of a Seismic Option." *Proceedings of the Society of Petroleum Engineers,* 1993, pp. 25–32.

Titman, Sheridan. "Urban Land Prices under Uncertainty." *American Economic Review* 75, no. 3 (June 1985), pp. 505–14.

Triantis, Alexander J., and James E. Hodder. "Valuing Flexibility as a Complex Option." *Journal of Finance* 45 (June 1990) pp. 549–65.

Trigerogis, Lenos. *Real Options*. Cambridge, Massachusetts: MIT Press, 1996.

Corporate Taxes and the Impact of Financing on Real Asset Valuation

_____

Learning Objectives

After reading this chapter, you should be able to:

1. Understand the effect of leverage on the cost of equity and the beta of the firm when there is a corporate tax deduction for interest payments.

2. Apply the adjusted present value method (APV) to value real assets.

3. Understand the weighted average cost of capital (WACC) and the effect of leverage on the WACC when there is a corporate tax deduction for interest payments.

4. Understand how debt affects the payoffs of projects to equity holders.

In 1995, Los Angeles, the second largest metropolitan area in the United States and a major world media market, found itself without a professional football team. The Raiders of the American Football Conference and the Rams of the National Football Conference departed after the 1994 season for the seemingly less attractive markets of Oakland and St. Louis, respectively. Not only were the markets and media exposure in these cities inferior to those of Los Angeles, but there was the complication for the Raiders of competing against the successful and popular San Francisco 49ers, the dominant football franchise since the mid-1980s. Since pure economics, based on market size, makes these decisions seemingly irrational, some other inducements were responsible for these moves.

U p to this point in the text, we have assumed that firms can create value only on the asset (left-hand) side of their balance sheets. In reality, however, firms also create value on the liability (right-hand) side because the design of the financing of investment projects can create value for the firm. The best example of this is that debt interest payments are tax deductible, implying that debt financing is somewhat cheaper than equity financing if additional debt does not add substantial financial distress costs. Another example would be subsidized loans, such as those received by the Raiders and Rams to entice them to move. This chapter takes as given the mix of debt and equity financing for a project and asks how to value investments, taking into account the way in which they are financed.[1]

Two valuation methods, both extensions of the methods discussed in Chapter 10, can be used to account for the additional cash flows that arise from the project's debt financing. The first method, the **adjusted present value (APV) method**, introduced in Myers (1974), generates present values that account for the debt interest tax shield and other loan subsidies by:

1. Forecasting a project's after-tax cash flows, assuming that the project is financed entirely with equity.
2. Valuing the cash flows in step 1, assuming that the project is financed entirely with equity. Any method of computing present values (PVs) discussed in Chapters 10 or 11 can be used for this step.
3. Adding to the value obtained in step 2 the value generated as a result of the tax shield and other subsidies from the project's debt financing.

The second method, known as the **weighted average cost of capital (WACC) method**, is a generalization of the risk-adjusted discount rate method, designed to account for the cost of debt and equity financing from the firm's perspective. It generates present values by:

1. Estimating a project's *expected* after-tax cash flows, assuming that the project is financed entirely with equity.
2. Valuing the expected cash flows in step 1 by discounting them at a single risk-adjusted discount rate that varies with the degree of debt financing that can be attributed to the project.

The result below summarizes these points formally.

Result 12.1   Analysts use two popular methods to evaluate capital investment projects: the APV method and the WACC method. Both methods use as their starting points the after-tax cash flows generated by the project, assuming that the project is financed entirely by equity. The APV method calculates the net present value (NPV) of the all-equity-financed project and adds the value of the tax (and any other) benefits of debt. The WACC method accounts for any benefits of debt by adjusting the discount rate.

Although corporations use the WACC method more than the APV method, most academics believe the APV method is the better approach for evaluating most capital investments and that the APV approach will grow in popularity over time. The advantage of the APV method is that it calculates separately the value created by the project and the value created by the financing. For this reason, it is often referred to as **valuation by components**. It also fits in nicely with the alternative approaches discussed in Chapter 11, such as the derivatives valuation and ratio comparison approaches. Moreover, unlike the WACC, the APV can be used when debt levels or tax rates change over time.

---

[1]Part IV addresses the implications of this observation on the optimal financial structure of a firm.

The WACC method may be conceptually easier to understand because it discounts only one set of cash flows while the APV method discounts separately the cash flows of the project and the cash flows of the tax savings or other debt subsidies. In addition, the WACC method is used more widely, so that analysts presenting a WACC-based valuation will be able to communicate their analysis to others more easily. It is important to have a firm understanding of both approaches—the APV method because it is an easier, more flexible approach, and the WACC method because it is more widely used and understood.

The location decisions of the Raiders and Rams, discussed in the chapter's opening vignette, were driven by huge enticements, including packages of subsidized loans, rents, and free stadium renovations offered by Oakland and St. Louis. The renovations included expensive corporate skyboxes, from which 100 percent of the revenue would go to the team. In the case of the Raiders, $85 million in improvements were targeted for the Oakland Coliseum, which was to add 175 luxury suites and locker rooms.[2] In deciding to relocate, the owners of these teams must have weighed these additional transfers of wealth against the traditional considerations of population size and media coverage, which favored the Los Angeles location.

A financial analyst needs to value the subsidies offered by St. Louis and Oakland and determine whether the present value of the subsidies exceeds the net additional value of a Los Angeles location in the absence of these subsidies. While we are unfamiliar with the methods used by the owners of the Rams and Raiders to weigh these factors, the APV method provides the best way to account for these subsidies. The APV method accounts for all subsidies by discounting the cash flows associated with those subsidies at the discount rate that is appropriate for the risk of the cash flows, *irrespective of where they came from*. For example, the APV method would treat the cash flows from the subsidized rents in a similar manner to the incremental cash flows that are generated by subsidized loans. By contrast, the WACC method draws a distinction between subsidies that are related to the project's financing and those that are not related to financing. Thus, with the WACC method, the loan subsidies offered to the football teams would affect the discount rate applied to the remaining cash flows, but would not affect the size of the expected cash flows that are discounted.

To simplify the analysis, this chapter ignores personal taxes.[3] It is also important to emphasize that this chapter considers as given the amount of debt financing the firm will optimally add when taking the project, which we call the project's **debt capacity**.[4]

12.1 Corporate Taxes and the Evaluation of Equity-Financed Capital Expenditures

Substantial groundwork must be laid before either the APV or the WACC method can be implemented in a practical setting. First, one must estimate the future cash flows of a project, typically from accounting earnings data. Then, one needs to estimate a discount rate. We noted in Chapter 10 that risk determines discount rates and that it is important to make a leverage-based adjustment to the beta risk used to estimate the discount rate of a comparison firm. However, the formula for the leverage-based adjustment for beta risk given in Chapter 10 assumed no taxes. This section analyzes how risk is affected by financing when there is a corporate tax deduction for interest payments. Understanding

[2]The final cost was $100 million.
[3]Personal taxes are discussed in Chapters 13 and 14.
[4]The analysis of debt capacity is discussed in Parts IV and V.

how to adjust risk for different degrees of leverage in the presence of corporate taxes is necessary to identify the discount rate for an all-equity financed project. This discount rate is implemented in the second step of the APV method. In addition, knowledge of the effect of leverage on risk will later prove useful when studying the WACC method.

After-Tax Real Asset Cash Flows

The first step in evaluating a prospective investment project is to estimate its future **after-tax real asset cash flows**; that is, cash flows stemming directly from the project itself rather than from its financing. The after-tax real asset cash flows ignore (1) interest payments associated with any debt financing the project may have and (2) any interest-based tax deductions that stem from debt financing. It is important to recognize that this chapter assumes that the firm's mix of debt and equity financing does not affect the firm's after-tax real asset cash flows.[5] Under this assumption, real asset cash flows can be computed as the after-tax cash flows of the project, assuming that it is financed entirely with equity. For this reason, after-tax real asset cash flows are sometimes referred to as *unlevered* after-tax cash flows.

Computing After-Tax Real Asset Cash Flows from EBIT.   To translate earnings before interest and taxes, or EBIT, into after-tax real asset cash flows, note that EBIT is:

- Reduced by depreciation and amortization,[6] which affects earnings but not cash flows.
- Not affected by increases in working capital,[7] which reduce cash flows.
- Not affected by purchases of capital assets (capital expenditures), which decrease cash flows, nor by sales of capital assets, which increase cash flows, except when such sales generate realized capital gains and losses.
- Computed before taxes, but taxes reduce after-tax real asset cash flow.
- Is equivalent to taxable earnings under the hypothetical assumption that the project is financed entirely with equity.

Thus, to obtain the after-tax real asset cash flows of a business or project from EBIT, one applies the formula:

$$
\begin{aligned}
\text{After-tax real asset cash flows} = \ &\text{EBIT} \\
&+ \text{depreciation and amortization} \\
&- \text{change in working capital} \\
&- \text{capital expenditures} \\
&+ \text{sales of capital assets} \\
&- \text{realized capital gains} \\
&+ \text{realized capital losses} \\
&- \text{EBIT} \times \text{tax rate}
\end{aligned}
$$

---

[5]Chapters 15–18 relax this assumption.

[6]*Amortization* generally refers to depreciation of intangible assets.

[7]*Working capital* is current assets, typically accounts receivable and inventory, less current liabilities, typically accounts payable. A sale paid for by increasing accounts receivable results in less cash than a cash sale and an inventory expansion paid with cash results in a cash outflow.

Computing After-Tax Real Asset Cash Flows from Pretax Cash Flows.   To illustrate the future after-tax real asset cash flows that one discounts for valuation purposes, consider the decision facing Chemicals, Inc.: Whether to purchase a hydrogenerator for $500,000. For tax purposes, the hydrogenerator is depreciated over five years; in reality it will last eight years and generate pretax real asset cash flows—after-tax real asset cash flows plus EBIT × tax rate—of $100,000 per year. Exhibit 12.1 displays the future after-tax real asset cash flows of the hydrogenerator, assuming a 34 percent corporate tax rate and pretax real asset cash flows that are the same as earnings before interest, taxes, depreciation, and amortization (EBITDA). Thus, Exhibit 12.1 assumes that there are no changes in working capital and no capital expenditures or sales.

The $500,000 cost of acquiring the hydrogenerator is not listed in Exhibit 12.1 because it is not a future cash flow and (except for its effect on depreciation, and thus taxes), it does not affect the present value of the *future* cash flows of the project. However, as Example 12.1 illustrates, the $500,000 cost is relevant to the decision of whether the project should be adopted because it enters into the net present value *(NPV)* calculation.

Example 12.1:   Using a Risk-Adjusted Discount Rate on After-Tax Cash Flows
If the appropriate cost of capital for evaluating the after-tax real asset cash flows of the hydrogenerator project (see Exhibit 12.1) is 10 percent, what is the project's net present value assuming all-equity financing?

Answer: The present value of the future after-tax real asset cash flows of the project is

$$PV = \$480,992 = \frac{\$100,000}{1.1} + \frac{\$100,000}{1.1^2} + \frac{\$100,000}{1.1^3} + \frac{\$100,000}{1.1^4}$$

$$+ \frac{\$100,000}{1.1^5} + \frac{\$66,000}{1.1^6} + \frac{\$66,000}{1.1^7} + \frac{\$66,000}{1.1^8}$$

Subtracting the $500,000 initial cost of the project from the present value of $480,992 leaves a net present value of:

$$NPV = PV - \text{Initial cost} = -\$19,008$$

Since this is negative, Chemicals, Inc., should reject the project.

EXHIBIT 12.1   Pretax and After-Tax Real Asset Cash Flows for Chemicals, Inc.

Year	Pretax Cash Flow (a)	Depreciation (b)	Taxes (at 34%) (c) = [(a) − (b)] × .34	After-Tax Real Asset Cash Flow (d) = (a) − (c)
1	$100,000	$100,000	0	$100,000
2	100,000	100,000	0	100,000
3	100,000	100,000	0	100,000
4	100,000	100,000	0	100,000
5	100,000	100,000	0	100,000
6	100,000	0	$34,000	66,000
7	100,000	0	34,000	66,000
8	100,000	0	34,000	66,000

Incremental Cash Flows.   After-tax real asset cash flows for the Chemicals, Inc., project are computed by examining the incremental effect of the project on the after-tax cash flows of the firm, assuming all-equity financing. As discussed in Chapter 9, the incremental effect is the total after-tax real asset cash flows of the firm achieved with the project less the cash flows that would be achieved if the project is turned down.

In the first five years of the project, the incremental cash flows are the pretax cash flows of the project because the depreciation of the machine eliminates the taxes associated with the earnings of the project. Once the depreciation tax shield is used up, however, the annual $100,000 in earnings must be reduced by 34 percent to reflect the additional tax payments that the firm will make as a consequence of having taken on the project.

Inflation.   Chemicals, Inc., has pretax cash flows that are constant over time (see Exhibit 12.1). In an inflationary economic environment, however, one typically expects both revenues and costs, and thus cash flows, to increase over time. The nominal discount rates—that is, the rates obtained from the financial markets directly—apply to nominal cash flows, the observed cash flows, which grow with inflation. However, it is possible to forecast **inflation-adjusted cash flows**, which take out the component of growth due to inflation. Indeed, if there is inflation in the economy, this appears to be what Chemicals, Inc., has done because its cash flow forecasts are constant over time.

When inflation-adjusted cash flow forecasts are employed, they need to be discounted at **real discount rates**, which are the rates of appreciation of the asset's tracking portfolio less the appreciation due to inflation. If i is the rate of inflation per period, and r is the appropriate nominal discount rate obtained from comparison firms in the bond and stock markets, the real discount rate per period is:

$$r_{\text{real}} = \frac{1 + r_{\text{nominal}}}{1 + i} - 1$$

To convert the date t nominal cash flow, C_t, to an inflation-adjusted cash flow, C_t^{IA}, use the formula:

$$C_t^{\text{IA}} = \frac{C_t}{(1 + i)^t}$$

The present value of the inflation-adjusted cash flow, using the real rate for discounting back t periods, is:

$$PV = \frac{C_t^{\text{IA}}}{(1 + r_{\text{real}})^t}$$

$$= \frac{\left[\dfrac{C_t}{(1 + i)^t}\right]}{(1 + r_{\text{real}})^t} = \frac{C_t}{(1 + r_{\text{nominal}})^t}$$

The present value equality implies that discounting nominal cash flows at nominal discount rates or inflation-adjusted cash flows at the appropriately computed real interest rates generates the same present value.

Debt Interest and Taxes.   The taxes associated with the after-tax real asset cash flows are not the true taxes paid unless the project is all-equity financed. If there is debt interest and a debt interest tax deduction, the actual after-tax flows of the project will be higher than those computed for Chemicals, Inc., in the previous example. One needs to account for this debt interest tax subsidy to obtain the true present value and net present value of any project that is partly financed with debt. How to properly do this will be the focus of the rest of this chapter.

The Cost of Capital

Example 12.1 assumed that the discount rate was 10 percent. Where did this 10 percent discount rate come from?

Distinguishing the Unlevered Cost of Capital from the WACC.   For an all-equity-financed, or "unlevered" firm, the appropriate risk-adjusted discount rate for a project that has the same risk as the overall firm is the firm's unlevered cost of capital. This required rate of return is the same as the expected rate of return on the unlevered firm's equity, as described in Chapter 10. Chapter 10 referred to this discount rate as "the cost of capital." In the presence of corporate tax deductions for debt interest, we need to be concerned with two costs of capital. The **unlevered cost of capital** is the expected return on the equity of the firm if the firm was financed entirely with equity. The *weighted average cost of capital* is a weighted average of the after-tax expected return paid by the firm on its debt and equity. In the absence of a debt tax shield, debt subsidy, or other market frictions that favor one form of financing over another, the two concepts of cost of capital are the same and, as seen in Chapter 10, there is no need to distinguish between them. In this chapter, however, the two concepts necessarily differ because the focus is on the impact of corporate taxes.

Note that the expected return paid by the firm from issuing equity is the same as the expected return to the investor who holds the equity security. This point—that the expected rate of return the firm pays for the use of the capital is the same as the expected rate of return the investor receives for providing the capital—is not true, in general. When a third party, such as the government taxing authority, favors one form of financing over another, the cost of the favored form of financing will differ from the expected return to investors. For example, the tax deductibility of interest implies that the cost of debt financing to a corporation (as measured by the after-tax return paid by the corporation) may be less than the rate of return on a firm's debt received by the firm's debt investors. This point, which drives the distinction between the two cost of capital concepts, will be an important one to explore when analyzing debt financing at a later point in this chapter.

Why it Is Important to Calculate the Unlevered Cost of Capital for a Levered Firm.
It is straightforward to evaluate an equity-financed project that is a scale replication of a comparison all-equity firm. In this case, the project is a miniaturized version of the comparison firm's equity, implying that the project's cost of capital is the expected rate of return on the comparison firm's equity. Chapter 10 described a variety of techniques for estimating this expected rate of return. For example, if the CAPM applies, measuring the comparison firm's market beta and using this beta in the CAPM risk-expected return formula is one way to generate the project's cost of capital.

However, the inclusion of debt financing complicates this analysis. To value an all-equity-financed project when the comparison firm has debt financing, it is necessary to calculate the required rate of return on the comparison firm's equity in the hypothetical case of a comparison firm being all equity financed. Moreover, when the project adds to the ability of the firm adopting the project to take on tax-advantaged debt, it is necessary to understand how shifting the comparison firm's debt affects the risk of the comparison firm's equity. While Chapter 10 studied this issue in the absence of taxes, a real-world

EXHIBIT 12.2   Balance Sheet for a Firm with Leverage When Debt Interest Is Corporate Tax Deductible

Assets		Liabilities and Equity	
Tax Assets *(TXA)*		Debt	
	T_cD		D
Operating Assets *(OA)*		Equity	
	$D + E - T_cD$		E

application of the valuation techniques developed in this text requires us to account for the effect of taxes.

The Risk of the Components of the Firm's Balance Sheet with Tax-Deductible Debt Interest

A financial manager who employs either the WACC or the APV method needs to understand how debt financing and taxes affect the risks of various components of the firm's balance sheet. To develop this understanding we return to the simplified balance sheet of Chapter 10. Exhibit 12.2, which mirrors Exhibit 10.3 of Chapter 10, presents the two sides of the balance sheet of a firm for which there is a corporate tax deduction for debt interest payments, but no personal taxes. Exhibit 12.2 illustrates that the assets of the firm contain two components. One is the **operating assets** *(OA)*, the value of which is the present value of the after-tax real asset cash flows; the other is the **tax-savings asset** *(TXA)*, which is driven entirely by the liability side of the firm's balance sheet. The more debt the firm has, the bigger this tax savings. Note that the two sides of the balance sheet must add up to the same number—that is, balance—implying that the value of the operating assets can be viewed as the sum of the debt and equity, $D + E$, less the value of the tax-savings assets.[8]

Viewing the assets of the firm with value A as a portfolio of the operating assets with value *OA* and tax assets with value *TXA* implies that the beta of the assets is the portfolio-weighted average of the betas of the operating and tax-savings assets. That is

$$\beta_A = \frac{OA}{D + E}\beta_{OA} + \frac{TXA}{D + E}\beta_{TXA} \tag{12.1}$$

where

$$\beta_{TXA} = \text{beta risk of the tax-savings assets}$$

$$\beta_{OA} = \text{beta risk of the operating assets}$$

Static Perpetual Risk-Free Debt. Let T_c denote the effective corporate tax rate. Exhibit 12.2 has the firm's tax-savings asset value expressed as

$$TXA = T_cD \tag{12.2}$$

and thus

$$OA = D + E - T_cD \tag{12.3}$$

---

[8]More generally, TXA can be viewed as the present value of *any* debt financing subsidy.

The values for TXA and OA both in Exhibit 12.2 and in equations (12.2) and (12.3) are developed in a model by Hamada (1972). If the firm issues default-free perpetuities with aggregate face amount of D and interest payments equal to the risk-free rate, each interest payment of Dr_f, saves $T_c Dr_f$ in taxes in the year it is paid. The present value of the tax savings from the interest payments (see Appendix A at the end of the text, equation (A.7), for the formula for the present value of a perpetuity) is

$$T_c D = \frac{T_c Dr_f}{r_f}$$

The same present value is also achieved when the risk-free rate changes over time and the firm rolls over one-period risk-free debt.

The Hamada model assumes that the tax shield is riskless and thus, each period's tax deduction arising from an interest payment should be discounted back to date 0 at the risk-free rate. This implies that the beta of the tax assets in the Hamada model is zero. Using this observation, and substituting equations (12.2) and (12.3) into equation (12.1) yields

$$\beta_A = \left[\frac{D + E - T_c D}{D + E} \right] \beta_{OA} \tag{12.4}$$

In the typical case where the beta of the operating assets of the firm, β_{OA}, is positive, equation (12.4) states that the beta of the combined operating and tax savings assets, β_A, must decline with an increase in leverage to reflect the addition of the risk-free tax savings. To see this, note that the portfolio weight on β_{OA}, $\dfrac{D + E - T_c D}{D + E}$, which equals $1 - \dfrac{T_c D}{D + E}$, declines as the leverage ratio $\dfrac{D}{D + E}$ increases, reflecting the fact that risk-free tax savings assets compose a larger proportion of the firm's assets as leverage increases.

The key assumptions that lead to this result are: (1) The debt is perpetual, in other words, it is either a perpetuity or consists of rolled over short-term debt positions. (2) The debt is default-free and pays the risk-free rate. (3) The face value of the debt and the tax rate do not change over time. The third assumption distinguishes the Hamada model from other models that will be discussed later in this chapter.

Equity Betas and Asset Betas.   Equity betas are also affected by taxes. Chapter 10 indicated that (assuming risk-free debt), the equity beta is:

$$\beta_E = \left(1 + \frac{D}{E} \right) \beta_A \tag{12.5}$$

Substituting the right-hand side of equation (12.4) for β_A in equation (12.5) gives:

$$\beta_E = \left(1 + \frac{D}{E} \right) \left[\frac{D + E - T_c D}{D + E} \right] \beta_{OA}$$

With a little simplification, this equation, which is based on the Hamada model, reads:

$$\beta_E = \left[1 + (1 - T_c) \frac{D}{E} \right] \beta_{OA} \tag{12.6}$$

Assuming that β_{OA} does not change with leverage,[9] equation (12.6) states that for a given debt increase, the beta of the firm's equity increases less the larger is the corporate tax rate, and increases the most when there are no taxes. Reversing this equation also allows us to identify β_{OA} from β_E, which is often a necessary step in the implementation of the APV method.

Identifying the Unlevered Cost of Capital

Chapter 10 suggested that one could value a project with an identified risk-adjusted discount rate from the equity returns of comparison firms. This necessarily entailed adjusting the equity betas and associated expected returns of the comparison firms for the effect of leverage.[10] However, the unlevering procedure described in Chapter 10 assumed no taxes. With corporate tax deductions for interest, the procedure for identifying the unlevered cost of capital for a project is very similar to the procedure used in Chapter 10. However, the formula for unlevering the betas must be modified whenever the betas of tax-savings assets *(TXA)* differ from the betas of operating assets *(OA)*.

The formula for unlevering the equity betas of comparison firms in the presence of corporate taxes is embedded in equation (12.6) which, when reversed, reads:

$$\beta_{OA} = \frac{\beta_E}{\left[1 + (1 - T_c)\dfrac{D}{E} \right]} \tag{12.7}$$

Since β_{OA} is the same as the beta of the firm (as well as the beta of its equity) assuming that the firm is all-equity financed, substituting β_{OA} into a risk-expected return formula gives the desired unlevered cost of capital.

The Marriott Example Revisited.   Example 12.2 reworks Example 10.2 of Chapter 10 to account for corporate taxes.

Example 12.2:   Using the Comparison Method to Obtain Beta and $\bar{r}$ with Taxes
Recall from Example 10.2 that Marriott identified three comparison firms for its restaurant division. For these comparison firms, equity beta estimates (β_E), book values of debt (*D*), and market values of equity (*E*) have been identified as follows:

Comparison Firm	β_E	D (in $ billions)	E (in $ billions)
Church's Chicken	.75	.004	.096
McDonald's	1.00	2.300	7.700
Wendy's	1.08	.210	.790

Estimate the unlevered cost of capital for Marriott's restaurant division. Assume that the risk-free rate is 4 percent per year, the risk premium on the market portfolio is 8.4 percent per year, the corporate tax rate is 34 percent, the CAPM holds, the debt of the comparison firms is risk free, and all three firms are equally good as comparisons for Marriott's restaurant division.

Answer: Using equation (12.7), first find the operating asset betas of the three firms, then average.

---

[9]Chapters 15–18 relax this assumption.

[10]This comparison firm can be the firm adopting the project if the project is similar in operating risk to the firm's existing projects.

Comparison Firm	β_{OA}
Church's Chicken	$.73 = \dfrac{.75}{1 + .66\left(\dfrac{.004}{.096}\right)}$
McDonald's	$.84 = \dfrac{1.00}{1 + .66\left(\dfrac{2.3}{7.7}\right)}$
Wendy's	$.92 = \dfrac{1.08}{1 + .66\left(\dfrac{.21}{.79}\right)}$
Marriott (average of above)	$.83 = \dfrac{.73 + .84 + .92}{3}$

Applying the CAPM risk-expected return equation using this estimate of Marriott's restaurant operating asset beta gives the restaurant unlevered cost of capital, 10.97 percent per year, since:

$$.1097 = .04 + .83(.084)$$

Example 12.2, using the same comparison firms as Example 10.2, concludes that $\beta_{OA} = .83$ and that the unlevered cost of capital is 10.97 percent. This is larger than the respective unlevered beta and cost of capital in Example 10.2, namely .78 and 10.55 percent. The reason is that risk-free tax-savings assets partly offset the increase in observed equity betas that is generated by the leverage of the three comparison firms. Thus, the reduction in beta arising from the unleveraging equation is not as great here as it was in the absence of taxes.

The Hamada Formula Is Not Always Correct.   If the firm uses debt in a flexible manner, the Hamada formulas for leveraging and unleveraging equity betas, represented in equations (12.6) and (12.7), are not correct. For example, if the firm issues debt as the value of the operating assets rises and retires debt as the value of the operating assets falls, then equity betas will move more in response to leverage changes than equation (12.6) suggests they should. As this chapter later shows, in the extreme case where the issuance and retirement of debt is perfectly positively correlated with the value of the operating assets, the correct formula for leveraging and unleveraging equity betas is the same as in the no-tax case. However, if firms tend to retire debt when they are doing well, then the Hamada formula overstates the impact of leverage on equity betas. The tendency of firms to retire debt when they do well, which is especially common following leveraged recapitalizations, is consistent with Kaplan and Stein's (1990) observation that equity betas are less sensitive to changes in leverage than predicted by equation (12.6).

12.2 The Adjusted Present Value Method

Our recommended approach for valuing investment projects with corporate taxes is the adjusted present value (APV) method. The left-hand side of Exhibit 12.2 illustrates how the APV method is used in a setting with corporate tax deductions for interest payments. First, one values the lower left-hand side of the T-account, the operating assets, which by definition is the after-tax value of the assets, assuming all-equity financing. One way to do this is to discount expected future real asset cash flows at the required rate of return for equity financing with risk equal to β_{OA}. Then, one values the upper half of the left-hand side of the T-account, the tax assets, which are generated by the debt financing of the firm. A different discount rate generally would be used to value the tax-savings assets. For example, in Exhibit 12.2, where such assets are assumed to be risk free, the risk-free rate would be the appropriate discount rate. Finally, the two present values, those of the operating assets and the tax-savings assets, are added together to generate the project's present value.

Three Sources of Value Creation for Shareholders

Exhibit 12.3 depicts three sources of value to the shareholders of a firm that adopts an investment project:

1. The *NPV* of the project's after-tax real asset cash flows.
2. The *NPV* of subsidies due to the financing of the project.
3. Transfers to shareholders from existing debt holders due to the financing of the project.

Net Present Value of After-Tax Real Asset Cash Flows.   The main source of value from an investment project is from the operating assets themselves, portrayed in the left-hand box of Exhibit 12.3. To obtain this value, compute the net present value of the after-tax cash flows from the project, assuming that the project is all equity financed.

Net Present Value of Financing Subsidies.   The middle box in Exhibit 12.3 illustrates that the project's financing can create value for the firm. Although the reduction in corporate taxes linked to debt financing may be the most important source of value created by financing (as measured relative to the all-equity financing case), it is not the only source. For example, to lure Nissan's automobile assembly plant to Smyrna, Tennessee, the state offered debt financing at reduced rates.

EXHIBIT 12.3   Sources of Value Creation to Shareholders

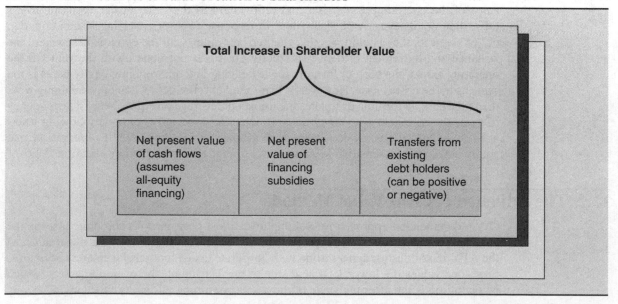

In addition to direct debt subsidies, small market inefficiencies, arising perhaps from regulations, can generate financing bargains. For example, consider a group of investors with a taste for highly leveraged positions in certain stocks. If regulations preclude these investors from borrowing sufficient funds to buy these stocks,[11] it might be possible for a firm to create value by issuing overpriced warrants to these investors. While financing bargains of this type sometimes exists, it is important to be skeptical about them. In the 1980s, for example, a number of Japanese firms issued bonds with attached warrants, thinking that they were getting a financing bargain, but academic studies suggest that these warrants were underpriced, not overpriced.[12] Also, it is important to emphasize that these subsidies will artificially make a project more attractive than it really is, and thus should not be counted, if the subsidies can be earned without undertaking the project.

Transfers from Existing Debt Holders.   The third source of value to shareholders, illustrated in the right-hand box of Exhibit 12.3, is transfers of wealth from existing debt holders to equity holders. For example, the selection of high-risk projects can transfer wealth from existing debt holders to equity holders while the selection of safe projects can do the reverse. In addition, new debt financing can sometimes extract wealth from old debt financing to the benefit of equity holders. Although the APV method was not originally designed to account for such transfers, it can be used to take these transfers into account. We consider this issue later in this chapter and in Chapter 15.

Debt Capacity

The notion that the debt tax shield creates value suggests, holding all else equal, that firms should be financed entirely with debt. Some might argue that Michael Milken learned this lesson very well while studying at the Wharton School and built an industry around this idea. However, there are limits to the amount of debt that firms can issue and costs that offset the tax benefits of debt financing. Some of these limits and costs arise because the probability of bankruptcy is tied to the amount of debt a firm has and bankruptcy can be costly. Other limits to debt financing may arise because of frictions in the capital markets. For the moment, we need to know only that each firm has a specific debt capacity, which is the amount of debt that management decides is in the firm's best interest. A project's debt capacity is the marginal amount by which a firm's debt capacity increases as a direct result of taking on the project.

Dynamic versus Static Debt Capacity.   Debt capacity need not be a fixed amount of debt, but for simplicity we will often treat it as such. In general, however, we would expect debt capacity to be dynamic; that is, to change over time, sometimes depending on the profitability of the firm or the project. Thus, a project may initially be financed entirely with internal funds, but become debt financed at a later date when the firm finds it more convenient or less costly to issue the debt. In such instances, this dynamic sequence of debt financing must be taken into account in determining the corporate tax subsidy. As we will see, this is much easier to do with the APV method than with the WACC method.

What Determines Debt Capacity?   Debt capacity is determined by management's view of the difference between the present value of the benefits of debt (e.g., tax-

---

[11]Regulation T in the United States effectively prevents such borrowing.

[12]See Kuwahara and Marsh (1992).

advantaged interest deductions) and the present value of the disadvantages of debt (e.g., bankruptcy costs). The debt capacity of a project may depend on both the characteristics of the project and the characteristics of the firm.[13]

The APV Method Is Versatile and Usable with Many Valuation Techniques

The APV method can be used in conjunction with any valuation technique that generates a present value for the after-tax real asset cash flows. Hence, the APV method is appropriate to consider in conjunction with the risk-adjusted discount rate method, the certainty equivalent method, the derivatives valuation approach, or the ratio comparison approach.

The APV and the Risk-Adjusted Discount Rate Method in Complicated Tax Situations.   The APV method is also ideally suited to complicated tax situations. Consider, for example, a project that initially has a great deal of nondebt tax deductions because of accelerated depreciation write-offs or tax credits for research and development expenses. For a firm that is marginally profitable, such a project might initially add little to the firm's ability to employ debt financing. Later, however, when cash flows materialize, there is a substantial increase in the amount of debt that the project can support. The changes in the financing of the project cause its cost of capital to change over time, which makes calculating the project's *NPV* with the WACC method somewhat tedious and perhaps impossible. However, it is fairly straightforward to value such a project with the APV method, as Example 12.3 illustrates.

Example 12.3:   Applying the APV Method to Value a Project

United Technologies (UT) is considering a project that has a cost of capital of 14 percent if it is financed entirely with equity. The project is expected to generate after-tax real asset cash flows in the next four years as follows:

Cash Flows (in $ millions) at End of			
Year 1	*Year 2*	*Year 3*	*Year 4*
$100	$100	$1,000	$1,000

Since the project generates large tax deductions in the first two years, UT will initially finance the project exclusively with equity. However, at the start of year 3 the firm will repurchase some of its equity and borrow $2 billion to finance the project for the last two years of its life. The borrowing (and discount) rate at this time will be 8 percent per year and the corporate tax rate will be 34 percent. What is the present value of the project, given this plan for debt financing?

Answer: To value this project, first calculate its present value when financed entirely with equity:

$$PV\begin{pmatrix} \text{after-tax} \\ \text{real asset} \\ \text{cash flows} \end{pmatrix} = \frac{\$100 \text{ million}}{1.14} + \frac{\$100 \text{ million}}{1.14^2} + \frac{\$1,000 \text{ million}}{1.14^3} + \frac{\$1,000 \text{ million}}{1.14^4}$$

$$= \$87.72 \text{ million} + \$76.95 \text{ million} + \$674.97 \text{ million} + \$592.08 \text{ million}$$

$$= \$1,431.72 \text{ million}$$

---

[13]The issues important for determining a firm's optimal debt capacity are discussed in later chapters.

To this amount, add the present value of the tax shields generated by the debt financing:

$$PV(\text{tax shields}) = \frac{.34(.08 \times \$2 \text{ billion})}{1.08^3} + \frac{.34(.08 \times \$2 \text{ billion})}{1.08^4}$$

$$= \$83.17 \text{ million}$$

Thus, the present value of the levered project from both its operating and financing aspects is:

$$PV(\text{real asset cash flow and tax shields}) = \$1,431.72 \text{ million} + \$83.17 \text{ million}$$

$$= \$1,514.89 \text{ million}$$

The Discount Rate for Risky Debt Tax Shields.   Most applications of the APV assume that the debt tax savings can be discounted at the risk-free rate. However, the tax savings from debt will not be risk free and should not be discounted at the risk-free rate if the firm's financing plans are flexible or if there is a chance that the firm may not be able to generate cash flows large enough to take full advantage of the interest tax shield.[14] Safeway's approach to this issue is examined below.

Safeway and Debt Tax Shields

Safeway Inc. is a California-based food retailer with more than 1,000 stores in the United States and Canada. In the 1980s, management bought out Safeway for $5.3 billion. The buyout was part of a trend in the 1980s, during which a number of firms went private with transactions known as *leveraged buyouts* (LBOs) that greatly increased their debt ratios (see Chapter 2). The high debt loads of the privatized firms were temporary measures, designed to force changes in the operating policies of the firms, that would be paid down over time from company profits. In Safeway's case, the debt was paid down quickly—from profits as well as from subsequent equity offerings.

In cases like Safeway, the tax savings from debt were uncertain. If Safeway had not performed poorly, it would not have paid down its debt and its debt-based tax savings would have been larger than if it had performed well. Thus, debt tax shields increase when a firm performs poorly, at least for many LBO-financed firms. Because performance is tied partly to the overall health of the economy, debt tax shields in this kind of situation tend to have negative betas, implying that the tax shields should be discounted at a rate less than the risk-free rate. However, if Safeway had performed poorly, it would not have had sufficient earnings to utilize its debt tax shields, which would have reduced its tax savings. This loss of debt tax shields tends to increase the beta of the tax assets. Without a careful analysis of Safeway's future real asset cash flows and financing plans, it is impossible to determine which of the two effects dominates: the tendency to pay down debt after performing well or the inability to fully use debt tax shields when earnings are negative. When the debt level of the project is fixed but the utilization of the debt tax shield is uncertain, the underutilized tax shields, which generate positive betas, are the only consideration. In this case, it would be appropriate to discount the tax shields at a rate somewhere between the cost of capital used

---

[14]U.S. tax law has varied over time in the degree to which earnings losses can be carried forward or backward into different tax years to offset profits and reduce taxes. The ability to transfer losses through time allows firms to better utilize debt tax shields, but rarely to the full extent, because (1) there are limits to the numbers of years a loss can be carried forward or backward, (2) it is always possible that all of the tax years to which the loss can be transferred have insufficient profits to offset the loss, and (3) the time value of money is not properly adjusted for in these transfers of losses. For example, deferring a loss generated by a debt interest payment to a future profitable year implies that interest payments realize only the present value of a future tax deduction, which is less than the tax impact of the interest payment if the company had been profitable in the tax year the interest payment was incurred.

to discount the firm's real asset cash flows and the risk-free rate. The expected return derived from the beta of the debt financing is a reasonable proxy for this discount rate.

Example 12.4 illustrates how to use such a discount rate to implement the APV method.

Example 12.4:   Computing NPVs When the Debt Tax Shield Is Risky

The managers of the Engoleum Corporation are considering the possibility of buying new molding equipment at a cost of $100 million. The equipment is expected to generate after-tax cash flows of $20 million per year for the next 10 years. Analysts estimate that the beta of these cash flows, β_{OA}, is close to 1 and that the expected return on the market is 13 percent. Although the risk-free rate is 5 percent, the firm's borrowing rate is 8 percent. Assume that the project adds $80 million to the firm's debt capacity for the life of the project and that the corporate tax rate is 30 percent. To calculate the present value of the debt interest tax savings associated with the project, the analyst must account for the spread that exists between the risk-free rate and the firm's promised debt yield. The spread between the risk-free rate and the firm's borrowing rate reflects the debt holders' belief that they might not be paid in full, which implies that the debt tax shield may not be fully utilized. Assuming that the company will use, on average, only 75 percent of the debt interest tax shields and that the beta of the firm's debt is .25, calculate the project's NPV.

Answer: The present value of the firm's after-tax real asset cash flows is:

$$\$108.52 \text{ million} = \frac{\$20 \text{ million}}{1.13} + \frac{\$20 \text{ million}}{1.13^2} + \ldots + \frac{\$20 \text{ million}}{1.13^{10}}$$

The debt interest tax shield adds $1.92 million ($= .08 \times .30 \times \$80$ million) to cash flows each year if it is fully utilized, and thus is expected to add 75 percent of this amount or $1.44 million per year. We conjecture that the beta of these tax savings is somewhat less than the beta of the firm's cash flows and probably resembles the beta of the firm's debt, .25. Thus, the required rate of return on the tax savings is given by the CAPM formula:

$$.07 = .05 + .25 \times (.13 - .05)$$

This implies a present value for the tax savings of:

$$\$10.11 \text{ million} = \frac{\$1.44 \text{ million}}{1.07} + \frac{\$1.44 \text{ million}}{1.07^2} + \ldots + \frac{\$1.44 \text{ million}}{1.07^{10}}$$

Adding the two *PV*s and subtracting the $100 million cost leaves an *NPV* of:

$$NPV = \$18.63 \text{ million} = \$108.52 \text{ million} + \$10.11 \text{ million} - \$100 \text{ million}$$

As Example 12.4 illustrates, calculating the present value of debt tax shields may be complex when there is uncertainty about the extent to which the firm will utilize them. As the Safeway discussion indicated, uncertainty about the evolution over time of the debt capacity of the project or the firm increases this complexity even more. In such cases, we recommend that analysts use the derivatives valuation approach (see Chapter 11) to value the debt tax shields.

The APV and the Certainty Equivalent Method.   Chapter 10 noted that analysts should use—and often do use—a certainty equivalent method to evaluate risky investment projects. One implementation of this method, the risk-free scenario method, requires a forecast of expected cash flows that is conditional on the market return being equal to the risk-free rate (assuming the CAPM is true). This conditional expectation, which should be somewhat lower than the unconditional expectation typically used, provides the certainty equivalent cash flow. Discounting this certainty equivalent cash flow at the risk-free rate yields the present value of the risky cash flow.

Combined with the APV method, the certainty equivalent method provides perhaps the simplest method for evaluating risky projects, at least in cases where the debt tax shields are certain. When the debt tax shields are certain, one simply adds the debt tax shields to the certainty equivalent cash flows of the project and discounts the sum at the risk-free rate. Example 12.5 illustrates this method.

Example 12.5:   Using the APV Method with the Certainty Equivalent Method

Emruss Ltd. is considering the purchase of a mold to make a new, improved dish drainer. The mold costs $150,000 and lasts five years, after which it has zero salvage value. Analysts estimate the after-tax expected real asset cash flows to be $50,000 per year for the next five years and zero thereafter. The certainty equivalent cash flows are given in the table below:

Cash Flows (in $000s) at End of				
Year 1	Year 2	Year 3	Year 4	Year 5
$45	$40	$35	$30	$25

The mold adds $100,000 to the firm's debt capacity in years 1 and 2, $50,000 in years 3 and 4, and zero in year 5. If Emruss has a borrowing rate of 6 percent and a tax rate of 50 percent, and will use its tax shields with certainty, what is the *NPV* of this investment if the risk-free rate is 5 percent?

Answer: Note first that the certainty equivalent cash flow declines over time even if the expected cash flows stay constant since a scenario where the five-year return on the market equals the risk-free rate represents a much more unfavorable scenario than a one-year return equal to the risk-free rate. To these certainty equivalent cash flows, add the tax savings associated with debt financing. These savings will be $3,000 in years 1 and 2, and $1,500 in years 3 and 4. Hence, the total certainty equivalent cash flows for the project are shown in the table below:

Cash Flows (in $000s) at End of				
Year 1	Year 2	Year 3	Year 4	Year 5
$48.0	$43.0	$36.5	$31.5	$25.0

Discounting these cash flows at 5 percent generates the present value of the project and results in a positive *NPV* since:

$$NPV = -\$150,000 + \frac{\$48,000}{1.05} + \frac{\$43,000}{1.05^2} + \frac{\$36,500}{1.05^3} + \frac{\$31,500}{1.05^4} + \frac{\$25,000}{1.05^5}$$

$$= -\$150,000 + \$45,714 + \$39,002 + \$31,530 + \$25,915 + \$19,588 = \$11,750$$

(See exercise 12.12 which asks for a calculation of the *NPV* if the project has zero debt capacity.)

When the tax shields are uncertain, a financial analyst also must calculate their certainty equivalents. However, doing so is not a straightforward task. For example, the risk-free scenario method assumes that the distribution of outcomes is symmetrical, but the distribution of tax savings is rarely so. Although tax savings can be lost in the worst states of the economy, the firm can do no better than to use all of the tax shields in the best states of the economy. Under the scenario in which the market return equals the risk-free rate, the company may use all of its available debt tax shields. This does not mean, however, that the certainty equivalent tax savings is equal to the entire tax savings. Instead, the certainty equivalent tax savings always should be somewhat less than the entire tax savings to account for the firm's inability to use all of the debt interest expense as a tax deduction in the most unfavorable states of the economy.

Combining the APV and the Derivatives Valuation Approaches.   It should now be apparent that most major investment projects involve strategic future choices that are not easy to evaluate using traditional valuation methods. As the discussion above indicates, the financing choice also is a strategic variable in many cases, because firms have the option to increase or decrease their reliance on debt financing. While this strategic tax-related option creates value for the firm, valuation of the interest tax shield is complex. Fortunately, the APV method works extremely well with the derivatives valuation approach, as Example 12.6 illustrates:

Example 12.6:   Using the APV Method with the Derivatives Valuation Approach
Reconsider Example 11.6 in Chapter 11, which featured Acme Industries, a company with the option to expand its plant's capacity during good times. The initial cost of the plant was $140 million and the cost of the expansion was an additional $140 million. The risk-free rate was 5 percent per period. Assume the following:

- For tax purposes, Acme will expense at year 2 (when the project's income is realized), both the $140 million initial cost and, provided it expands capacity, the additional $140 million in expansion costs.
- Acme is generating plenty of taxable earnings over the next few years and will be able to take advantage of any tax losses if the project turns out to be unprofitable.
- Acme is financed initially with $100 million in debt, but it can issue an additional $200 million in debt if the good state of the economy occurs and the firm expands capacity.
- The interest rate on the debt is 10 percent and the marginal tax rate is 50 percent.

What is the value of the project? How much of that value can be attributed to the firm's debt capacity?

  Answer: The pretax cash flows are given in Exhibit 11.7 in Chapter 11. Following two good years, the project's after-tax cash flows (accounting for the impact of financing) are:

$$\text{(Pre-tax cash flow)} - \text{(Earnings)} \times \text{(Tax rate), or}$$

$$\$400 \text{ million} - (\$400 \text{ million} - \$280 \text{ million} - .1 \times \$300 \text{ million}) \times .5 = \$355 \text{ million}$$

With an initial good year followed by a bad year, and assuming that the firm can use the entire tax shield, the project has after-tax cash flows of:

$$\$300 \text{ million} - (\$300 \text{ million} - \$280 \text{ million} - .1 \times \$300 \text{ million}) \times .5 = \$305 \text{ million}$$

If the initial year is bad and the plant is not expanded, again assuming that Acme can use the tax shields, the after-tax cash flows in the two states at year 2 (points E_2 and F) are:

$$\$150 \text{ million} - (\$150 \text{ million} - \$140 \text{ million} - .1 \times \$100 \text{ million}) \times .5 = \$150 \text{ million}$$

$$\$100 \text{ million} - (\$100 \text{ million} - \$140 \text{ milllion} - .1 \times \$100 \text{ million}) \times .5 = \$125 \text{ million}$$

Applying the risk-neutral probabilities given in Exhibit 11.8, the project's after-tax present value is determined as follows:

The value of the project at the "good" node is now:

$$-\$140 \text{ million} + \frac{\$355 \text{ million}(.53) + \$305 \text{ million}(.47)}{1.05} = \$175.71 \text{ million}$$

The value of the project at the "bad" node is now:

$$\frac{\$150 \text{ million}(.35) + \$125 \text{ million}(.65)}{1.05} = \$127.38 \text{ million}$$

The net present value of the project at the initial node is then:

$$\frac{\$175.71 \text{ million}(.5) + \$127.38 \text{ million}(.5)}{1.05} - \$140 \text{ million} = \$4.33 \text{ million}$$

It is also possible to compute the project's *NPV* under the assumption that the project adds nothing to the firm's debt capacity. In this case, the *NPV* is negative. The difference between (1) the *NPV* calculated with the debt capacity, and (2) the *NPV* ignoring the debt capacity, provides the value created by the debt tax shield. (See exercise 12.11.)

The APV and the Ratio Comparison Approach.   Chapter 11 noted that investment bankers and analysts often value firms and projects by examining various ratios for comparison firms or other investments. Popular ratios for the comparison include price to earnings, price to book value, price to cash flow, and price to sales revenue.

The APV method is well suited to be used along with any of the ratio comparison approaches. If the project being evaluated supports a higher debt level than that used by the comparison firm, then the value of the additional tax shields is an important component of the project's value. The APV method adds or subtracts the value associated with the difference between the tax benefits of the project and the comparison firm. Example 12.7 illustrates this point.

**Example 12.7:   Implementing the APV Method with the
                    Price Earnings Ratio Approach**

Hewlett Packard is thinking about developing a workstation. It projects that the cost of development will be $100 million and that the expected earnings in the first year of the project will be $15 million. Thereafter, the earnings will grow at about the same rate as those of Sun Microsystems, which currently produces a similar workstation. Sun, which is almost exclusively financed with equity, has a current price to earnings ratio of 6.5. Is the project acceptable?

Answer: If the project were financed almost exclusively with equity, as Sun Microsystems is, then the market value of this project would be:

$$\$97.5 \text{ million} = \$15 \text{ million} \times 6.5$$

If this were the case, Hewlett-Packard should reject the project, since the *NPV* is −$2.5 million, but given Hewlett-Packard's reputation and stability, its managers believe that the project's debt capacity is $30 million. If the present value of the tax benefits from this debt financing exceeds $2.5 million, Hewlett-Packard should accept the project.

Summary of the Applicability of the APV Method.   Result 12.2 summarizes this section.

Result 12.2   Firms can use the APV method along with most valuation approaches. In all cases, the project's value is the sum of (1) the project's value, evaluated under the assumption that it is all equity financed, and (2) the value of the tax shields or other debt subsidies. However, the derivatives valuation approach and the certainty equivalent method often make it convenient to value the tax shields and the after-tax real asset cash flows separately. For projects with strategic options, we recommend using the derivatives valuation approach. For projects that do not have embedded options, we recommend using the certainty equivalent method or the ratio comparison approach.

12.3 The Weighted Average Cost of Capital

In contrast to the APV method, the WACC method adjusts the discount rate rather than the after-tax cash flows to account for the effect of debt and taxes. The adjusted discount rate, which is applied to the expected after-tax real asset cash flows, is the weighted average cost of capital of the project, to be explained shortly. Most large firms use some variant of the *firm's* weighted average cost of capital to evaluate their capital expenditures. There are practical reasons for doing so. In any given year, a large corporation may evaluate hundreds of different projects from various divisions and it would be costly to come up with a different discount rate for each project. Using the firm's weighted average cost of capital, however, is inappropriate for valuing projects with different risks and different debt capacities than those of the firm as a whole. As the subsection below indicates, obtaining a WACC to discount the cash flows of an entire business is generally simpler than obtaining a WACC for an individual project.

Valuing a Business with the WACC Method When a Debt Tax Shield Exists

Consider the case of ExMart, currently an all-equity firm. Martin Chang is interested in purchasing ExMart, financing 50 percent of the purchase with debt and the remaining 50 percent with equity. To value ExMart, it is necessary to estimate its expected future after-tax real asset cash flows and discount them at the appropriate weighted average cost of capital. This discount rate reflects Chang's various sources of capital. Mathematically this can be expressed as:

$$\text{WACC} = w_E \bar{r}_E + w_D (1 - T_c) \bar{r}_D \tag{12.8}$$

where

WACC = weighted average cost of capital

$w_E = \dfrac{E}{D + E}$ = market value of equity over market value of all financing

$w_D = \dfrac{D}{D + E}$ = market value of debt over market value of all financing

T_c = marginal corporate tax rate when interest is fully tax deductible

      (or, more generally, the debt financing subsidy in percentage terms)

The costs of the financing components are:

$\bar{r}_E$ = the expected return on equity to investors

$\bar{r}_D$ = the expected return on debt to investors

The last two expected returns $\bar{r}_E$ and $\bar{r}_D$ represent the expected rates of return that investors require as compensation for the riskiness of the firm's equity and debt securities.

The term $\bar{r}_D(1 - T_c)$, the expected after-tax *cost of debt* to the firm, differs from $\bar{r}_D$ because every dollar of interest paid to the debt holders represents a deduction on the corporate income tax statement that would not be available with equity financing.

Example 12.8 provides an illustrative calculation of the WACC.

Example 12.8:   Computing a Weighted Average Cost of Capital

Mr. Chang believes that the required rate of return on ExMart equity when it is 50 percent levered will be 12 percent per year. Since ExMart is a very stable business, it will be able to borrow at the risk-free rate of 8 percent per year. If the marginal corporate tax rate is 25 percent, what is the WACC for ExMart?

Answer: WACC = $.5 \times .12 + .5(1 - .25) \times .08 = .09$ or 9%

WACC Components: The Cost of Equity Financing

One input for calculating the WACC is $\bar{r}_E$, the required expected rate of return on the equity (see Chapter 10), which also is known as the *cost of equity* financing. This rate of return can be determined in many ways. Typically, one uses expected return formulas from the Capital Asset Pricing Model, the arbitrage pricing theory, or the dividend discount model to compute $\bar{r}_E$. With the CAPM and APT, equity betas estimated from historical return data are used in the formulas. Note that the expected rate of return of a firm's equity obtained with these methods is the relevant cost of equity financing, whether or not there are tax advantages to debt financing.

WACC Components: The Cost of Debt Financing

The methods used to estimate $\bar{r}_D$, the pretax cost of debt, which is the other major input in the WACC formula, are generally not the same as those used to calculate the cost of equity capital.

Default-Free Debt.   Practitioners typically assume that the firm's pretax cost of debt is the yield to maturity of the firm's debt. (The yield to maturity, being certain, lacks the bar over r_D in contrast to the expected value of an uncertain return, $\bar{r}_D$.) The yield to maturity provides a fairly accurate estimate of a firm's pretax cost of debt when the debt is highly rated and not callable or convertible. (Chapter 2 notes that default rates on investment-grade debt are negligible.) Example 12.9 illustrates how to use the CAPM to calculate the WACC of a firm with debt of this type.

Example 12.9:   Computing the After-Tax Cost of Debt and WACC When Default Is Unlikely

The financing of United Technologies (UT) consists of 20 percent debt and 80 percent equity. With so little debt, the firm is able to borrow at the risk-free rate of 8 percent per year. The interest expense is tax deductible and the corporate tax rate is 34 percent. Assuming that the CAPM holds, the expected return of the market portfolio is 14 percent, and the beta of the firm's equity is 1.2, what is the WACC of United Technologies?

Answer: Using the CAPM, UT's cost of equity is:

$$\bar{r}_E = 8\% + 1.2(14\% - 8\%) = 15.2\%$$

The firm's cost of debt in this case is:

$$r_D(1 - T_c) = 8\% \ (1 - .34)$$

Therefore, using equation (12.8):

$$WACC = w_E \bar{r}_E + w_D r_D (1 - T_c)$$

$$= .8 \times 15.2\% + .2 \times 8\% \times .66$$

$$= 13.2\%$$

Risky Debt. Using the *promised yield* times *one* minus the corporate rate *tax* as the cost of debt may be appropriate for relatively risk-free debt. Generally, however, this after-tax yield is not the cost of debt capital for highly levered firms. For firms with risky debt, the promised return on the debt (i.e., the yield to maturity) is larger than the debt's expected return because of the possibility of default.

Expected rather than promised debt returns are the WACC inputs because the WACC method, as a debt- and tax-based generalization of the risk-adjusted discount rate method, is designed to discount *expected* cash flows. As Chapter 10 noted, the risk-adjusted discount rate method requires that expected cash flows be discounted at expected rates of return. Since these expected cash flows are the same as the expected cash flows to debt and equity holders on the right-hand side of the balance sheet, they can be appropriately discounted at a portfolio-weighted average of the expected returns of debt and equity.

Using the yield to maturity, a promised rather than an expected return for debt, overstates the pretax cost of any debt financing with nonnegligible default risk. Partially offsetting this, however, are the tax shields of highly levered firms that often go unused. Indeed, when using the more appropriate expected debt return $\bar{r}_D$ as the pretax cost of debt, a value different from the marginal corporate tax rate should be used for T_c when the firm may not fully use its debt tax shields. In this instance, the appropriate value to use for T_c in the WACC formula may be higher or lower than the corporate tax rate, depending on the relation between the promised yield of the debt, the expected return of the debt, the frequency with which the firm is unprofitable, and the likely timing of default.

In simple cases where the debt interest tax deduction is either fully used or fully unused, and where the probability of full use is the same at any point in time *in perpetuity,* the T_c input for the WACC is given by the equation:

$$T_c = \frac{\text{Corporate tax rate} \times \text{Probability of utilization} \times \text{Promised yield to maturity}}{\bar{r}_D}$$

The tax gain variable, T_c, is thus higher than the corporate tax rate if the product of the probability of utilization and the promised yield to maturity exceeds $\bar{r}_D$, and lower otherwise. In these instances, one needs only to compute the numerator in the above formula, which equals $\bar{r}_D T_c$, and subtract it from $\bar{r}_D$ to obtain the after-tax cost of debt $\bar{r}_D (1 - T_c)$.

For example, suppose the promised yield on the debt is 14 percent and the corporate tax rate is 34 percent. With a probability of .75, the firm enjoys the full tax benefit of the 14 percent debt interest payment and with a probability of .25, it enjoys no tax benefit from debt interest payments. In this case, each dollar of debt has an expected tax benefit of 3.57 percent [= .75(.34)14%]. Subtracting 3.57 percent from $\bar{r}_D$ yields the after-tax cost of debt to the firm, $\bar{r}_D (1 - T_c)$. When $\bar{r}_D$ exceeds 10.5 percent, T_c is less than the corporate tax rate of 34 percent, and if $\bar{r}_D$ is less than 10.5 percent, T_c is greater than the corporate tax rate.

In cases where the probability of utilizing the tax shield changes over time, T_c may differ from the value given in the above ratio. To illustrate this point, consider high-yield debt. Firms that issue high-yield debt tend to have low default rates in the early years after debt issue. In these early years, the tax deduction for profitable firms issuing high-yield debt is based on the actual debt interest payments which early on are likely to be larger than the promised interest payments of firms issuing safer debt. Default for firms issuing high-yield debt reduces or even reverses the tax advantages of debt (because of a possible taxable capital gain to the firm), but tends to occur many years after issuance, and typically at a time when the firm's tax bracket is zero. Thus, for firms issuing high-yield debt, events that are relatively tax disadvantageous tend to be deferred and the tax benefit of paying high coupons on the high-yield debt tends to be immediate. The timing of the debt tax benefit provides a larger tax benefit to the high-yield debt than to safe debt. This timing also implies that the appropriate T_c for the WACC formula is greater than the T_c given in the last equation.

Although risky debt in the example has a T_c that is underestimated by the above formula, one also can generate cases for which the opposite is true. The complexity of adjusting the WACC method to account for the timing of taxation punctuates our reasons for preferring the APV method to analyze the debt tax shield in complicated scenarios.

Computing the Expected Return of Risky Debt.   Let us return now to the issue of computing $\bar{r}_D$, the expected return on debt, which the WACC method requires as the pretax cost of debt. Two popular methods are used to identify expected returns on risky debt and both tend to give similar values for $\bar{r}_D$. The first method subtracts expected losses owing to default from the promised yield (weighted by the no default probability) to generate the pretax cost of debt financing. For example, the promised yield on a high-yield bond may be 14 percent; however, if 4 percent of these bonds default in a given year with the bondholders recovering about 60 percent of their original investment, and thus losing 40 percent, the expected return on the bonds is:

$$.96(14\%) + .04(-40\%) = 11.84\%$$

The second method uses either the Capital Asset Pricing Model or APT to calculate the expected return of debt. Estimated betas for junk debt range from about .3 to about .5.[15] Assuming a 6 percent risk premium on the market, the CAPM would project a 1.8 percent ($= .3 \times 6\%$) to 3 percent ($= .5 \times 6\%$) spread between the expected returns of a junk bond and a default-free bond.

Example 12.10 provides an estimate of the cost of debt capital that accounts for default and the loss of tax benefits arising from negative net income and default.

Example 12.10:   Calculating the Cost of Debt for Highly Levered Firms

RJR Nabisco has issued high-yield bonds to finance its LBO. Assume that the outstanding bonds currently have a 14 percent per year yield to maturity, a beta of .5, and interest payments that are tax deductible with a probability of .75. If the risk-free rate is 8 percent per year, the expected return of the market portfolio is 14 percent, and the corporate tax rate is 34 percent, what is the after-tax cost of debt to RJR Nabisco?

Answer: Using the CAPM, the expected return on the RJR bonds is:

$$8\% + .5(14\% - 8\%) = 11\%$$

(To check whether this estimated default premium of 3 percent ($= 14\% - 11\%$) is sensible, see whether the product of the expected default rate and the recovery rate is 3 percent.)

---

[15]In contrast, investment-grade debt typically has a beta of about .2.

To calculate the after-tax cost of debt, note that when RJR has sufficient income to take advantage of the tax shield, it enjoys a tax savings of 4.76 percent ($= 14\% \times .34$). With .75 as the probability of utilization, the expected tax savings per dollar of debt equals 3.57 percent ($= 4.76\% \times .75$), so RJR's after-tax cost of debt is 7.43 percent ($= 11\% - 3.57\%$).

Determining the Costs of Debt and Equity from Expected Rates of Return at Project Adoption Time

For a firm, the relevant pretax cost of debt capital $\bar{r}_D$ or the cost of equity capital $\bar{r}_E$ is the expected rate of return of the respective sources of capital at the time the firm decides to adopt the project rather than the actual cost that the firm incurred to obtain the funds. Example 12.11 illustrates this distinction.

Example 12.11:   Cost of Capital Is Based on Foregone Financial Market Investments

Suppose that the CFO of Textron, in anticipation of future capital requirements, decided in December 1998 to float a AAA $100 million, 20-year bond at an annual interest rate of 9 percent. By April 1999, interest rates on 20-year AAA bonds had increased to 10 percent. What is Textron's cost of debt capital?

Answer: In April 1999, Textron would not want to take a risk-free project yielding 9.5 percent even though it had previously borrowed at 9 percent. It could do better by repurchasing its outstanding bonds. Given the increase in interest rates, the bonds would have fallen to a level that provides investors with a 10 percent return, which is Textron's pretax cost of debt capital. Thus, Textron's cost of debt capital is 10 percent.

The Effect of Leverage on a Firm's WACC When There Are No Taxes

In determining the relevant discount rate for a firm's expected future real asset cash flows, a manager needs to know how leverage affects the firm's WACC. A naive manager might note that the cost of debt is typically less than the cost of equity, so that an increase in the proportion of debt financing would reduce its weighted average cost of capital. However, this logic ignores the fact that an increase in a firm's debt level also increases the risk of its equity and (usually also its) debt and therefore raises the required return of each source of financing. In the absence of taxes, the increase in the risk of the two sources of capital is exactly offset by a shift in the WACC formula's weights toward the cheaper source of financing, leaving the WACC unchanged. Result 12.3 states this formally.

Result 12.3   In the absence of taxes, the WACC of a firm is independent of how it is financed.

Result 12.3 implies what this chapter suggested earlier: in the absence of taxes, the WACC is the same as the unlevered cost of capital.

Deriving Leverage's Impact on the WACC.   To demonstrate Result 12.3, return to the accounting identity that the market value of the assets of the firm equals the market value of the firm's debt and equity. One implication of this identity, first discussed in Chapter 10, is that the beta of the firm's portfolio of debt and equity is the same as the beta of its assets:

$$\beta_A = \frac{E}{D + E}\beta_E + \frac{D}{D + E}\beta_D$$

This equation can be rearranged to view equity as a portfolio that is long in the assets and short in the debt:

$$\beta_E = \left(1 + \frac{D}{E}\right)\beta_A - \frac{D}{E}\beta_D \tag{12.9}$$

Substituting equation (12.9) into the now familiar risk return equation implies

$$\bar{r}_E = r_f + \left[\left(1 + \frac{D}{E}\right)\beta_A - \frac{D}{E}\beta_D\right](\bar{R}_T - r_f) \tag{12.10}$$

Note from the corresponding risk return equation for debt that:

$$\bar{r}_D = r_f + \beta_D(\bar{R}_T - r_f) \tag{12.11}$$

Second, substitute equations (12.10) and (12.11) into the WACC equation (12.8), with $T_c = 0$, obtaining:

$$\text{WACC} = \frac{E}{D + E}\left\{r_f + \left[\left(1 + \frac{D}{E}\right)\beta_A - \frac{D}{E}\beta_D\right](\bar{R}_T - r_f)\right\} + \frac{D}{D + E}[r_f + \beta_D(\bar{R}_T - r_f)]$$

$$= r_f + \beta_A(\bar{R}_T - r_f) \tag{12.12}$$

As long as a shift in the firm's leverage ratio D/E does not change (1) r_f, the risk-free return, (2) $\bar{R}_T - r_f$, the risk premium of the tangency portfolio, or (3) β_A, the beta of the return of the firm's assets with the tangency portfolio, the leverage shift will not alter the firm's WACC. Conditions (1) and (2) will certainly hold in most cases, since a change in a single firm's leverage ratio can only have a negligible effect on the expected returns of the risk-free asset and the tangency portfolio.

The conclusion reached in Result 12.3, which is another version of the "Modigliani-Miller Theorem" (examined in detail in Chapter 13), says in essence that, in the absence of taxes and other frictions that might alter either β_A or expected future cash flows, the financing mix is irrelevant for valuation.

Example 12.12:   The Effect of Debt on the WACC without Corporate Taxes
Divided Technologies has no debt financing and has an equity beta of .5. Assume that the risk-free rate is 8 percent, the CAPM holds, the expected rate of return of the market portfolio is 14 percent, and there are no corporate taxes. If the firm can repurchase one-third of its outstanding shares and finance the repurchase by issuing risk-free debt carrying an 8 percent interest rate, what will be the effect of a debt-financed share repurchase on its WACC?

Answer: The cost of capital of Divided Technologies before issuing risk-free debt is its cost of equity:

$$8\% + .5(14\% - 8\%) = 11\%$$

After the repurchase, Divided Technologies has a 1 to 2 debt to equity ratio, making $1 + D/E = 1.5$. As a consequence, equation (12.9) implies that Divided Technologies' equity beta will increase from .5 to .75 so its cost of equity capital will increase from 11 percent to 12.5 percent. The WACC's (2/3, 1/3) weighted average of the 12.5 percent cost of equity and the 8 percent cost of debt will be 11 percent. This is the same WACC that Divided Technologies had before the debt was issued..

Graphing the WACC, the Cost of Debt and the Cost of Equity.   Exhibit 12.4 graphs the WACC, the cost of equity capital, and the cost of debt capital as a function of the leverage ratio, D/E, based on the figures given for Divided Technologies in Example 12.12. The WACC is a weighted average of the cost of equity, the upwardly sloping line beginning at 11 percent, and the cost of debt, the horizontal line at 8 percent. The WACC line is horizontal because, as D/E increases, the WACC weight $D/(D + E)$ on the

EXHIBIT 12.4   WACC, Cost of Equity, and Cost of Debt vs. $\dfrac{D}{E}$ with No Taxes

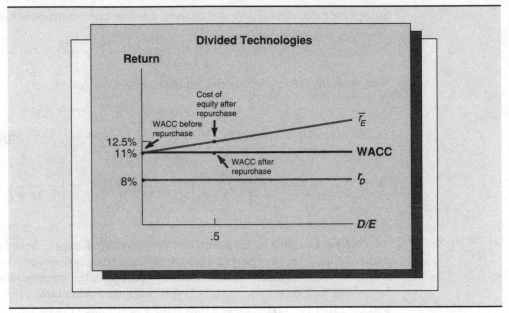

8 percent horizontal line r_D increases while the complementary weight on the upward sloping cost of equity line decreases.

If the cost of equity did not increase as leverage increases, the WACC would decline as leverage increases. However, as D/E increases, which means a movement to the right on the graph, the increase in $\bar{r}_E$ exactly offsets the effect from placing greater weight on the lower cost of debt line, resulting in a horizontal (blue) line for the WACC. *When the WACC line is horizontal, it means that the WACC is unaffected by leverage.*

The Effect of Leverage on a Firm's WACC with a Debt Interest Corporate Tax Deduction

The picture of the WACC in Exhibit 12.4 changes when a tax gain is associated with leverage. With corporate taxes, the WACC declines with an increase in debt because, relative to all-equity financing, part of the cost of financing is borne by the government. Substituting equations (12.10) and (12.11) into the WACC equation (12.8) yields

$$\text{WACC} = r_f + \beta_A(\bar{R}_T - r_f) - \frac{D}{D + E} T_c \bar{r}_D \tag{12.13}$$

which is similar to equation (12.12) except for the third term on the right-hand side. This third term is the portion of equation (12.8) that contains the terms that multiply (the now nonzero) T_c. Substituting the right hand side of equation (12.1) for β_A in equation (12.13) and simplifying implies that

$$\text{WACC} = r_f + \beta_{OA}(\bar{R}_T - r_f) - \frac{TXA}{D + E}(\beta_{OA} - \beta_{TXA})(\bar{R}_T - r_f) - \frac{D}{D + E} T_c \bar{r}_D$$

$$= \bar{r}^* - \frac{TXA}{D + E}(\beta_{OA} - \beta_{TXA})(\bar{R}_T - r_f) - \frac{D}{D + E} T_c \bar{r}_D \tag{12.14}$$

where

$$\bar{r}^* = r_f + \beta_{OA}(\bar{R}_T - r_f)$$

$\bar{r}*$ is the unlevered cost of capital, which not only is the discount rate used in the APV method to discount expected after-tax real asset cash flows, but is the WACC and cost of equity for an all equity financed firm (or project).

Equation (12.14)[16] implies the following result:

Result 12.4   When debt interest is tax deductible, and the beta of the tax savings assets does not exceed the beta of the operating assets, the WACC will be declining as the firm's leverage ratio, D/E, increases.

The Adjusted Cost of Capital Formula.   In the Hamada model, with static perpetual debt, both debt and its tax shield are risk-free, implying $\bar{r}_D = r_f$, $\beta_D = 0$, and $TXA = T_c D$. In this case, equation (12.14) reduces to Modigliani and Miller's (1963) **adjusted cost of capital formula**, which gives the firm's WACC as a function of its debt to value ratio:

$$\text{WACC} = \bar{r}* \left[1 - T_c \frac{D}{D + E} \right] \tag{12.15}$$

An application of equation (12.15) is provided in Example 12.13.

Example 12.13:   The Effect of Leverage on the WACC with Corporate Taxes

Example 12.9 found that United Technologies (UT), with liabilities consisting of 20 percent debt and 80 percent equity, had a WACC of 13.2 percent when the corporate tax rate was 34 percent. In a financial restructuring designed to raise to 40 percent the proportion of UT financed with debt, UT issues debt and buys back its equity with the proceeds. Compute the firm's new WACC given the assumptions of the Hamada model.

Answer: To calculate the firm's new cost of capital, first estimate UT's unlevered cost of capital. From equation (12.15), a WACC of 13.2 percent with 20 percent debt financing corresponds to an $\bar{r}*$ that satsifies:

$$.132 = \bar{r}*[1 - (.34)(.20)]$$

Therefore, $\bar{r}* = .1416$. Plugging this value into equation (12.15) at a 40 percent $\frac{D}{D + E}$ ratio leaves a WACC satisfying:

$$\text{WACC} = .1416[1 - (.34)(.4)] = .122$$

Therefore, the new WACC is 12.2 percent.

Graphing the WACC, Cost of Debt, and Cost of Equity with Corporate Taxes. Exhibit 12.5 graphs United Technologies' WACC, cost of equity capital, and cost of debt capital as a function of the leverage ratio D/E, when the corporate tax rate is 34 percent, based on the figures in Example 12.13. Note, as suggested earlier, that as D/E increases, more weight is placed on the bottom horizontal line, $r_D(1 - T_c)$, in the computation of the WACC. However, in contrast to the no-tax case, the increase in $\bar{r}_E$ as D/E increases is insufficient to offset the additional weight on the lower debt cost $r_D(1 - T_c)$. Hence, unlike the pattern shown in Exhibit 12.4, the WACC in Exhibit 12.5 declines from the starting point of 14.2 percent ($= \bar{r}*$) as D/E increases. The WACC continues to decline as D/E increases, up to the point where the firm eliminates all corporate taxes. Thereafter the WACC is flat.

---

[16]Equation (12.14) applies to risky debt as long as one adjusts T_c to account for nonuse of the tax shields, as discussed earlier in the chapter.

EXHIBIT 12.5   WACC, Cost of Equity, and Cost of Debt vs. $\dfrac{D}{E}$ with Corporate Taxes

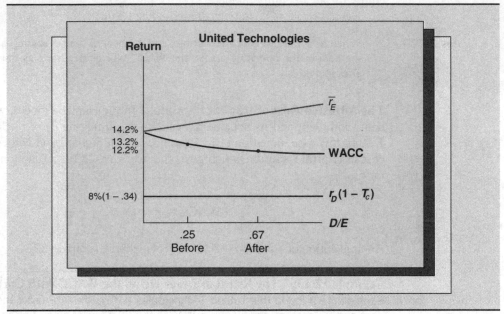

Dynamic Perpetual Risk-Free Debt.   If the firm wants to maintain a given ratio of debt to equity, it will need to issue new debt and repurchase equity as the firm's (or project's) value rises and issue equity to retire debt as the value of the firm (or project) falls. Such a dynamic debt issuance and repurchase strategy, even with default-free debt, leads to a dynamic value for D; that is, D changes over time.

In the Miles and Ezzell (1980, 1985) model, D is perfectly correlated with the value of the operating assets of the firm and thus the tax savings from debt issuance are perfectly correlated with the prior period's value of the operating assets. This implies that, at least approximately,

$$\beta_{TXA} = \beta_{OA}$$

As periods become arbitrarily short, this equality between the betas of the tax savings assets and the operating assets holds exactly, rather than approximately, in which case equation (12.14) reduces to

$$\text{WACC} = \bar{r}^* - \frac{D}{D+E}T_c\bar{r}_D$$

Dynamic updating of debt to maintain a constant leverage ratio has implications for both the WACC and the APV methods because it affects asset betas and thus, the formulas for leveraging and unleveraging equity betas. The Miles and Ezzell model, for example, which assumes risk-free debt, implies that only the tax shield associated with the first interest payment, which has a present value of $T_cDr_f/(1 + r_f)$ is riskless and the remainder of the tax shield has the same beta risk as the operating assets. Thus, the beta of all the assets is a portfolio weighted average of 0 and β_{OA} with the portfolio weight on 0 being $T_cDr_f/(1 + r_f)$, that is

$$\beta_A = \left[1 - \left(\frac{T_c D}{D + E} \right) \left(\frac{r_f}{1 + r_f} \right) \right] \beta_{OA}$$

When the updating interval is short, the term in brackets is very close to one, and thus, this formula says that with dynamic updating of debt, the beta of the assets and the beta of the operating assets are approximately the same. As periods become arbitrarily short, the value of the first debt interest payment becomes infinitesimal and the two betas become exactly the same. As suggested earlier, this implies that the no tax versions of equations (12.6) and (12.7) can be used to adjust equity betas for leverage when taxes exist, provided that the firm dynamically maintains a constant ratio of D to E.

One Period Projects.   If a project lasts only one period, there is only a single interest payment. In this case, the present value of the tax shield, $T_c D r_f / (1 + r_f)$, is the same as the present value of the riskless component of the tax shield in the Miles and Ezzell model. Thus, the beta of the assets when there is debt that lasts only a single period is the same as that in the Miles and Ezzell model. In general, the Miles and Ezzell formulas for the WACC and the beta of equity apply to one-period projects. This is because the fraction of the assets that is risk-free is identical in the two cases.

Which Set of Formulas Should Be Used?   If the operating assets of the firm have a significant risk premium, the models of Hamada and Miles/Ezzell generate different WACCs, as well as different formulas for leverage adjustments of equity betas. Dynamic updating of debt and equity to maintain a constant leverage ratio, as in Miles and Ezzell, tends to generate a larger WACC than with a debt issue that is never repurchased or added to, as in the Hamada model.

Many firms, particularly those with low to moderate amounts of leverage, try to maintain a target debt to equity ratio, but update rather slowly, perhaps because the cost of frequently issuing and repurchasing debt and equity is prohibitive. For such firms, truth lies somewhere between the models of Hamada and Miles/Ezzell. The weighting of the two models depends on which behavioral assumption the firm conforms to better. Large firms, firms with existing shelf registrations, and those with a history of repurchasing equity are likely to be more active in dynamically updating. Also, for projects with short lives, truth is probably closer to that given by the Miles and Ezzell formulas (with the caveat that comparison firms are perpetual).

However, we noted earlier that for many highly leveraged firms, it is possible that the tax assets have a negative beta. Equation (12.14) implies that for firms and projects with this property, it is important to use even a lower WACC and more gentle equity beta adjustments for leverage than those suggested by the Hamada model.

Evaluating Individual Projects with the WACC Method

The appropriate discount rate for a particular project must reflect the risk and debt capacity of the project rather than the risk and debt capacity of the firm as a whole. While the tracking portfolio analysis in Chapter 10 emphasized this in great detail, some financial managers believe that they are losing money whenever a project returns less than the firm's WACC. Examples 12.14 and 12.15 provide an additional perspective on why this line of thinking is fallacious by examining an extreme case where a risky firm is evaluating a project that has no risk.

Riskless Project, Riskless Financing.   In Example 12.14, the project has riskless cash flows. The project's financing also is riskless, composed of debt with tax-deductible interest payments. In this case, analysts can evaluate the project directly by comparing the project's proceeds with its financing costs. In contrast to the analysis of riskless projects in Chapter 9, however, the analyst now has to account for the debt tax shield.

Example 12.14:   Profiting from a Project That Earns Less than the Firm's WACC
Applied Micro Devices (AMD) currently spends $213,333 a year leasing its office space. Because lease payments are tax deductible at a 25 percent corporate tax rate, the firm spends about $160,000 per year [= $213,333 × (1 − .25)] on an after-tax basis to lease the building. The firm has no debt and has an equity beta of 2. Assuming an expected market return of 14 percent and a risk-free rate of 8 percent, its CAPM-based cost of capital is 20 percent. Suppose that AMD has the opportunity to buy its office space for $1 million. The office building is a relatively risk-free investment. The firm can finance 100 percent of the purchase with tax-deductible mortgage payments. The mortgage rate is only slightly higher than the risk-free rate. How does AMD determine whether to buy the building or continue to lease it?

Answer: It makes sense to buy rather than lease if the cost of owning the office space is less than the cost of leasing it. Clearly, it would be inappropriate to use the firm's cost of capital of 20 percent to calculate the cost of owning the building. Since owning the building is assumed to be a risk-free investment and the firm can finance it with a mortgage having a rate equal to the risk-free rate, the after-tax mortgage rate would be:

$$6\% \; [= .08(1 - .25)]$$

The after-tax cost of the mortgage would be:

$$\$60,000 \text{ per year } [= .06(\$1,000,000)]$$

This is about $100,000 per year less than the after-tax lease payments. Hence, the firm is better off if it buys the building rather than leases it.

The comparison here is equivalent to discounting the $160,000 per year in after-tax lease payments at the 6 percent after-tax discount rate and seeing whether the discounted payments exceed $1,000,000. In this case the present value of the lease payments in perpetuity is $2,666,667 (= $160,000/.06), which exceeds the $1,000,000 cost of the cheaper alternative, buying the building. If the firm had used its 20 percent cost of capital to discount the cash flows from the lease payments, the present value of the perpetual lease payments becomes $800,000 (= $160,000/.2). With the 20 percent cost of capital as the discount rate, AMD would have concluded incorrectly that leasing was the cheaper alternative.

Riskless Project, Risky Equity Financing.   Example 12.15 is more difficult to analyze because the risk-free project is financed by an equity offering. The expected cost of new equity financing is higher than the expected return of the project. However, as we will see in this example, the risk-free rate is still the appropriate marginal, or incremental, cost of raising capital for the project.

The relevant measure for the cost of capital of a project is the firm's **marginal cost of capital**, or the amount by which the firm's total cost of financing will increase if it raises an additional amount of capital to finance the project. In Example 12.14, this amount was apparent because the firm's original capital was composed entirely of equity and risk-free debt was used to finance the building. However, Example 12.15 shows that even if the company funds the new investment with equity, the same concept applies: *The marginal cost of capital for the project reflects the risk of the project and not the risk of the firm as a whole.*

Example 12.15:   The Marginal Weighted Average Cost of Capital

Assume that United Technologies (UT) is an all-equity firm, has a market value of $1 million, and has a beta of 2. Given the expected rate of return on the market of 14 percent and the risk-free rate of 8 percent, its cost of capital is 20 percent. The firm is considering a project that costs $1 million, but is risk free. Since UT generates no taxable income, it finances the project by issuing additional equity. How does the company determine whether to accept or reject the project? To simplify the example, assume that both existing projects and the new project have perpetual cash flows with expected values that do not change with the cash flow horizon.

Answer: Discount the project's cash flows at the 8 percent return and see whether the discounted value exceeds $1 million. This is equivalent to valuing the firm's cash flows, both with and without the project, using the appropriate WACC in each case.

To understand this point, note that at a 20 percent return, shareholders expect to earn $200,000 per year from UT's existing projects on the $1 million invested in the firm. Assume, for the moment, that the new project is a zero-*NPV* project. If management decides to go forward with the project, the total risk of UT will decline as its risk falls from a beta of 2 to a beta of 1, which is the average of the betas of the firm's existing assets and the beta of the new project. With a beta of 1, UT's cost of capital would then be 14 percent, the same as the market portfolio's expected return. With this return, shareholders expect to earn $280,000 per year on the $2 million invested in the firm. This is indeed what UT's shareholders will receive if the incremental cash flows from the new project are $80,000 per year. Thus, UT's shareholders are indifferent about whether to adopt the project if it provides exactly $80,000 per year in incremental expected cash flow. Note that discounting the $80,000 per year at 8 percent results in a $1 million present value and a zero net present value. Thus, 8 percent is the correct discount rate to use for the project's incremental cash flows.

If the project's expected cash flows exceed $80,000 per year, implying that UT's investors prefer project adoption, then the 8 percent discount rate will indicate that UT's project has a positive *NPV.* Analogously, if the expected cash flows are less than $80,000 per year, the 8 percent discount rate will indicate a negative *NPV* project.

Example 12.15 illustrates that the marginal cost of capital, that is the project's WACC, provides the appropriate hurdle rate for determining whether a project should be selected. We also know from the value additivity concept, discussed in Chapter 9, that the value created by an investment project equals the *NPV* of the project, calculated here by discounting the project's cash flows at the *project's* WACC and subtracting from this value the initial expenditure on the project.

The Importance of Using a Marginal Weighted Average Cost of Capital.   In Examples 12.14 and 12.15, shareholders gain from selecting risk-free projects whose rates of return exceed the risk-free rate, but which return less than the firm's weighted average cost of capital. In Example 12.14, the project could be financed by risk-free borrowing, so that accepting the project represented an arbitrage gain. The increase in cash flows from the project exceeded the cash outflow from the financing. In Example 12.15, an all-equity-financed firm used additional equity financing to fund the project. In this case, the project created value for the firm by lowering its risk and thus the required WACC. Practitioners who think the firm can never make money by earning an 8 percent return when the firm as a whole pays 12 percent on its capital are forgetting to consider how the firm's risk is affected by adopting the project.

Computing a Project WACC from Comparison Firms.   The last two examples illustrate that the WACC of a firm is the relevant discount rate for the *incremental* cash flows of one of its projects only when the project has exactly the same risk profile as the entire firm. In other words, the project must (1) have the same beta and (2) contribute the same proportion as the entire firm to the firm's debt capacity. If these conditions do not hold, firms can apply the WACC method by finding another firm with the same risk profile and financial structure as the project being valued and using the WACC of the comparison firm to discount the expected real asset cash flows of the project. Example 12.16 illustrates how this is done, adjusting nonmatching firms so they will match.

Example 12.16   Adjusting Comparison Firm WACCs for Leverage

This extends Example 12.2, where the unlevered cost of capital for the Marriott restaurant division was found to be 10.97 percent per year when the corporate tax rate is 34 percent. Compute the WACC for Marriott's restaurant division, assuming that the division's debt capacity implies a target $D/E = .4$ and static perpetual debt, as in the Hamada model.

Answer: There are two ways to solve this problem. This example uses the adjusted cost of capital formula, equation (12.15). Exercise 12.8 focuses on applying the WACC formula, equation (12.8), directly. Note that $\dfrac{D}{D+E} = \dfrac{D/E}{1 + D/E}$. Hence, $\dfrac{D}{D+E} = .2857 = \dfrac{.4}{1 + .4}$. Substituting this into equation (12.15) at the target $\dfrac{D}{D+E}$ of .2857 yields a WACC of:

$$9.9\% = .1097[1 - .34(.2857)]$$

12.4 Discounting Cash Flows to Equity Holders

The valuation approaches discussed in Part III value the cash flows of real assets. These cash flows accrue to the debt holders as well as to the equity holders. The decision rules that arise from these valuation approaches select projects that maximize the total value of the firm's outstanding claims; that is, the value of its debt plus the value of its equity. In a number of instances, this decision rule conflicts with the objective of maximizing the value of the firm's equity.

Positive NPV Projects Can Reduce Share Prices When Transfers to Debt Holders Occur

For example, the last section illustrated two risk-free projects and showed that discounting them at a risk-free rate was appropriate. This approach was correct as long as the objective is to maximize firm value. However, maximizing firm value is not always the same as maximizing the firm's stock price. The adoption of a positive *NPV* project can transfer equity holders to debt holders, which adversely affects share prices. Example 12.17 points out that when these conflicts exist, discounting cash flows at a risk-free rate may not be consistent with maximizing the firm's stock price.

Example 12.17:   When Discounting Riskless Cash Flows at a Risk-Free Rate Is Wrong

Anna Kramer, a recent Wharton graduate, is evaluating a project for Unitron that is virtually riskless and returns 12 percent per year. Given that the risk-free borrowing rate is currently at 10 percent, she recommends to her supervisor that the company undertake the project because its return exceeds the cost of capital for a riskless project. Her supervisor, Harold McGovern, a 1952 Wharton graduate, thinks that the company should reject the project. He notes that Unitron, which is highly levered, has a BBB debt rating and cannot borrow at the 10 percent rate assumed in Kramer's analysis. How can Unitron make money, he asks, if it borrows at 13 percent to fund an investment that yields only 12 percent? Kramer finds it difficult to answer this question. On the one hand, she has been taught that risk-free projects should be discounted at the risk-free rate. However, when taking the project's financing mix into account, the project generates negative cash flows to the firm's equity holders. Who is right?

Answer: McGovern is correct if you believe the firm's goal is to maximize its share price. On the other hand, to maximize the value of the firm, as would be the case if the firm was also beholden to bankers and other debt holders, Kramer's point is correct.

In the last example, the cash flows from the Unitron project that accrue to the equity holders are negative with certainty. This implies that the value to the equity holders must necessarily be negative. However, since these certain returns of the project exceed the risk-free return, the project must create value for someone. In this example, the project creates value for existing debt holders. The addition of a riskless project reduced the overall risk of the firm, which in turn increases the amount that the debt holders expect to recover in the event of default.[17]

Example 12.17 illustrates that it is not enough to ask whether a project generates a value that exceeds its cost. Instead, the analyst has to ask whether the value created accrues to the firm's equity holders or its debt holders. In Example 12.15, where the firm had no debt, the marginal WACC generated a project selection rule that maximized share price. However, when a firm is partly financed with debt, as in Example 12.17, discounting expected real asset cash flows with the marginal WACC measures a value that accrues to debt holders as well as equity holders.

Computing Cash Flow to Equity Holders

For the firm as a whole, **cash flow to equity holders** is pre-tax real asset cash flow less payments to debt holders less taxes. Computing a project's incremental cash flows to equity holders is similar to the computation of incremental real asset cash flow described in Chapter 9. First, compute the cash flows equity holders receive (from all of the firm's existing projects) if the new project is not adopted; then, subtract this from the cash flows to the *same* shareholders, assuming that the project is adopted. This difference is the project's incremental cash flow to equity holders.

While it is easy to state how to compute incremental cash flow, it is not simple to implement this computation in practice. Analysts typically avoid the complexities by computing the cash flow to equity holders as the difference between the incremental after-tax real asset cash flows of the project and the after-tax interest payments associated with the project's debt financing. While this approach is appropriate with **non-recourse debt**, also called **project financing**, which is debt with claims only to the project's cash flows, it is inappropriate with debt whose claims are not limited in this manner. To see why this approach is incorrect, assume no taxes, and, in a 2-date model, with today being date 0, let

C_{OLD} = date 1 real asset cash flow of the firm without the project

C_{NEW} = date 1 real asset cash flow of the firm with the project

$C = C_{NEW} - C_{OLD}$ = date 1 incremental real asset cash flow of the project

D_{OLD} = date *0* debt financing of the firm before project adoption

D_{NEW} = date *0* debt financing of the firm after project adoption and

$D = D_{NEW} - D_{OLD}$ = Debt capacity of the project.

y = promised yield-to-maturity on all debt financing the firm has (old and new)

---

[17]Chapter 15 will discuss this in detail. As Chapter 15 points out, the opposite is also true: For equity holders, high-risk projects are more attractive than comparable *NPV* low-risk projects when the firm's debt is risky.

The simple call option view of equity correctly computes the date 1 incremental cash flows to equity holders as

$$max(0, C_{NEW} - (1 + y)D_{NEW}) - max(0, C_{OLD} - (1 + y)D_{OLD})$$

Whenever either C_{NEW} or C_{OLD} is uncertain, this difference is not the same, nor does it have the same expectation, as the cash flow to equity holders that would be calculated with non-recourse debt, namely:

$$max(0, C - (1 + y)D) = max(0, C_{NEW} - C_{OLD} - (1 + y)(D_{NEW} - D_{OLD})$$

In particular, because of the option-like payoffs to equity holders, projects with incremental real asset cash flows that are more highly correlated with the cash flows of existing projects generate larger present values for cash flow to equity holders, other things being equal.

Valuing Cash Flow to Equity Holders

To calculate the *net present value of a project to equity holders,* the analyst must determine the appropriate discount rate for the cash flow to equity holders. Since these cash flows are often highly levered, they probably have betas that are substantially larger than those used to discount real asset cash flows. However, because options that are valued with dynamic tracking strategies necessarily enter into these calculations, it is very cumbersome to use a CAPM- or APT-based risk-adjusted discount rate approach to value these options. In our view, the derivatives valuation approach would be the preferred valuation approach whenever these options are likely to affect the valuation to a significant degree.

Example 12.18 illustrates the use of the derivatives valuation approach.

Example 12.18:   Valuing Cash Flow to Equity Holders with Derivatives Valuation
In a two-date binomial model, assume that Unitron, from Example 12.17, has existing projects that generate a firm worth $110 million at date 1 if the up state occurs and $71.5 million if the down state occurs. Assuming no taxes, a risk-free rate of 10 percent, and risk-neutral probabilities of ½ attached to each of the two states, Unitron's date 0 value is $82.5 million (= [.5($110 million) + .5($71.5 million)]/1.1). Unitron currently has debt maturing at date 1 with a face value of $77 million and a date 0 market value of $67.5 million (= [.5($77 million) + .5($71.5 million)]/1.1) and equity with a market value of $15 million (= [.5($110 million − $77 million) + .5($0)]/1.1).

Anna Kramer identifies a riskless project that will cost Unitron $28.23 million and will produce a cash flow of $31.62 million at date 1, providing a 12 percent return. The project will be entirely financed with debt that is equal in seniority to Unitron's existing debt. Compute the effect of the adoption of this project on the value of Unitron's existing debt and on the value of its equity.

Answer: After adopting the project, Unitron's date 1 cash flows will be $141.62 million (= $110 million + $31.62 million) in the up state and $103.12 million (= $71.5 million + $31.62 million) in the down state. This generates a new firm value of $111.25 million (= [.5($141.62 million) + .5($103.12 million)]/1.1). Since the new debt holders payment of $28.23 million is a fair market price for their debt, the existing debt and equity holders now have claims worth $83.02 million. The additional $0.52 million in value for the existing debt and equity holders ($83.02 million versus $82.5 million), is simply the net present value of the project (= −$28.23 million + $31.62 million/1.1).

In order for $28.23 million to be the fair market price of the new debt, the promised payments on the new debt, F, which capture the fraction F/(F + $77 million) of the firm's assets in default, must satisfy \$28.23 million $\left(= \left[.5F + .5 \dfrac{F}{F + \$77 \text{ million}} (\$103.12 \text{ million}) \right] / 1.1 \right)$ implying F = \$31.90 million, and a debt yield (for both old and new debt of 13 percent (= [\$31.90 million − \$28.23 million]/\$28.23 million).

However, with promised payments to debt holders at \$108,90 million (= \$77 million + \$31.90 million) if the project is adopted, the value of the shares of the equity holders is only \$14.87 million (= [.5(\$141.62 million − \$108.90 million) + .5(\$0)]/1.1).

Thus, the adoption of the project destroys \$.13 million in equity value. This \$.13 million is transferred to the existing debt holders along with the .5 million positive NPV.

The loss in equity value, seen in Example 12.18, occurs whether the project is financed with debt or equity or any mix of the two. The *NPV* to equity holders criterion rejects the project whercas the *NPV* to the firm criterion says adopt the project because equity is the most junior cash flow claimant in the event of debt default.

Derivatives Valuation versus the Risk-Adjusted Discount Rate Method

Example 12.18 illustrates the importance of using the derivatives valuation approach when wealth transfers, generated by debt default, are significant considerations in project evaluation. It is true that traditional approaches, like the risk-adjusted discount rate method, can be easily applied to value cash flows to equity holders when the options arising because of default play a negligible role in valuation. However, as the next result points out, project present values computed with the WACC method and those computed by discounting cash flows to equity holders are identical in the absence of such default considerations.

Result 12.5   In the absence of default, the present value of a project's future aftcr-tax real asset cash flows, discounted at the WACC, is identical to the present value of cash flows to equity holders discounted at the cost of equity. Hence, in the absence of default, the *NPV*s generated with both present value calculations select and reject the same projects. When debt default is a significant consideration, projects that increase firm value may not increase the values of the shares held by equity holders and vice versa. However, in these cases, it is more appropriate to analyze the values of cash flows with the derivatives valuation approach.

12.5 Summary and Conclusions

Previous chapters examined how risk affects a firm's cost of capital and its capital allocation decisions in the absence of taxes. This chapter showed how taxes also can have an important effect. Two methods of accounting for the valuation effect of debt and taxes were introduced: the weighted average cost of capital (WACC) method and the adjusted present value (APV) method. Some analysts prefer the WACC method to the APV approach since it is the more commonly used approach. However, the WACC method is appropriate only in limited circumstances. For example, if the debt capacity of a project changes over time, the WACC method is difficult to apply. In addition, in contrast to the APV framework, the WACC method cannot easily be adapted to evaluate investments with stra-

tegic options. For this reason, the APV method should be implemented for all major investments, although corporations may want to be aware of their WACC and use that method to evaluate smaller projects.

The discussion up to this point has indicated that the financing and the risk of an investment project determine its value. Different projects generate cash flows with different levels of risk, but there has been little discussion about why different projects add more or less to a firm's debt capacity. At this point, one might conclude that firms should use as much debt as possible since doing so creates value. However, there are costs associated with debt financing that offset these tax advantages, which is the subject of Part IV.

Key Concepts

Result 12.1: Analysts use two popular methods to evaluate capital investment projects: the APV method and the WACC method. Both methods use as their starting point the after-tax cash flows generated by the project, assuming that the project is financed entirely by equity. The APV method calculates the net present value (*NPV*) of the all-equity financed project and adds the value of the tax (and any other) benefits of debt. The WACC method accounts for any benefits of debt by adjusting the discount rate.

Result 12.2: Firms can use the APV method along with most valuation approaches. In all cases, the project's value is the sum of (1) the project's value, evaluated under the assumption that it is all equity financed, and (2) the value of the tax shields or other debt subsidies. However, the derivatives valuation approach and the certainty equivalent method often make it convenient to value the tax shields and the after-tax real asset cash flows separately. For projects with strategic options, we recommend using the derivatives valuation approach. For projects that do not have

embedded options, we recommend using the certainty equivalent method or the ratio comparison approach.

Result 12.3: In the absence of taxes, the WACC of a firm is independent of how it is financed.

Result 12.4: When debt interest is tax deductible, and the beta of the tax savings assets does not exceed the beta of the operating assets, the WACC will be declining as the firm's leverage ratio, *D/E*, increases.

Result 12.5: In the absence of default, the present value of a project's future after-tax real asset cash flows, discounted at the WACC, is identical to the present value of cash flows to equity holders discounted at the cost of equity. Hence, in the absence of default, the *NPV*s generated with both present value calculations select and reject the same projects. When debt default is a significant consideration, projects that increase firm value may not increase the values of the shares held by equity holders and vice versa. However, in these cases, it is more appropriate to analyze the values of cash flows with the derivatives valuation approach.

Key Terms

adjusted cost of capital formula   471
adjusted present value (APV) method   446
after-tax real asset cash flows   448
cash flow to equity holders   477
debt capacity   447
inflation-adjusted cash flows   450
marginal cost of capital   474

non-recourse debt (project financing)   477
operating assets   452
real discount rates   450
tax-savings asset (TXA)   452
unlevered cost of capital   451
valuation by components   446
weighted average cost of capital (WACC) method   446

Exercises

Exercises 12.1–12.7 make use of the following data:

In 1989, General Motors (GM) was evaluating the acquisition of Hughes Aircraft Corporation. Recognizing that the appropriate WACC for discounting the projected cash flows for Hughes was different from General Motors' WACC, GM assumed that Hughes was of

approximately the same risk as Lockheed or Northrop, which had low-risk defense contracts and products that were similar to those of Hughes. Specifically, assume the Hamada model of debt interest tax shields and the following inputs:

Comparison Firm	β_E	D/E
GM	1.20	.40
Lockheed	.90	.90
Northrop	.85	.70

Target $\dfrac{D}{E}$ for acquisition of Hughes's = 1

Hughes's expected after-tax real asset cash flow next year = $300 million

Growth rate of cash flows for Hughes = 5% per year

Marginal corporate tax rate = 34%

Appropriate discount rate on debt: riskless rate = 8%

Expected return of the tangency portfolio = 14%

12.1. Analyze the Hughes acquisition (which never took place) by first computing the betas of the comparison firms, Lockheed and Northrop, as if they were all equity financed. *Hint:* Use equation (12.7) to obtain β_{OA} from β_E.

12.2. Compute β_{OA}, the beta of the operating assets of the Hughes acquisition by taking the average of the betas of the operating assets of Lockheed and Northrop.

12.3. Compute the β_E for the Hughes acquisition at the target debt level.

12.4. Compute the WACC for the Hughes acquisition.

12.5. Compute the value of Hughes with the WACC from exercise 12.4.

12.6. Compute the value of Hughes if the WACC of GM at its existing leverage ratio is used instead of the WACC computed from the comparison firms (see exercise 12.4).

12.7. Apply the APV method. First, compute the value of the operating assets of the Hughes acquisition. Next, compute the present value of the tax shield. Finally, add the two numbers.

12.8. Compute the WACC of Marriott's restaurant division in Example 12.16 by doing the following:
   a. Compute the β_E of Marriott's restaurant division using equation (12.6).
   b. Apply the CAPM's risk expected return equation to obtain the restaurant $\bar{r}_E$, assuming a risk-free rate of 4 percent and a market risk premium of 8.4 percent.
   c. Estimate the WACC, using equation (12.8).
   d. Compare this WACC to the WACC in Example 12.16. If they are not the same, you made a mistake.

12.9. GT Associates have plans to start a widget company financed with 60 percent debt and 40 percent equity. Other widget companies are financed with 25 percent debt and 75 percent equity and have equity betas of 1.5. GT's borrowing costs will be 14 percent, the risk-free rate is 8 percent, and the expected rate of return on the market is 15 percent. The tax rate is 50 percent. Compute the equity beta and WACC for GT Associates.

12.10. The HTT Company is considering a new product. The new product has a five-year life. Sales and net income after taxes for the new product are estimated in the following table:

Year	Net Sales (in $000s)	Net Income after Taxes (in $000s)
1	$1,000	$ 40
2	2,000	75
3	4,000	155
4	6,000	310
5	2,000	75

The equipment to produce the new product costs $500,000. The $500,000 would be borrowed at an interest rate of 14 percent. However, the machine adds only $300,000 to the firm's debt capacity in years 1, 2, and 3, and only $200,000 in years 4 and 5.

Although net income includes the depreciation deduction, it does not include the interest deduction (i.e., it assumes that the equipment is financed with equity). The equipment can be depreciated on a straight-line basis over a five-year life at $100,000 per year. The equipment is expected to be sold for $100,000 in 5 years.

Net working capital (NWC) required to support the new product is estimated to be equal to 10 percent of net sales of the new product. The NWC will be needed at the start of the year. This means that if sales were $1 in year 1, the NWC needed to support this one dollar of sales would be committed at the beginning of year 1. The company's discount rate for the after-tax cash flows associated with this new product is 18 percent and the tax rate is 40 percent.

What is the net present value of this project?

12.11. Compute the value of the debt tax shield for Acme Industries in Example 12.6.

12.12. Compute the net present value of the mold in Example 12.5, assuming that the debt capacity of the project is zero.

12.13. Use the risk-neutral valuation method to directly show that the risk-neutral discounted value of the existing debt of Unitron is $636,000 higher if the project in Example 12.18 is adopted.

References and Additional Readings

Benninga, Simon, and Oded Sarig. *Corporate Finance: A Valuation Approach*. New York: McGraw-Hill, 1997.

Copeland, Tom; Tim Koller; and Jack Murrin. *Valuation: Measuring and Managing the Value of Companies*. New York: John Wiley, 1994.

Cornell, Bradford. *Corporate Valuation: Tools for Effective Appraisal and Decision Making*. Burr Ridge, IL: Business One Irwin, 1993.

Damodaran, Aswath. *Investment Valuation*. New York: John Wiley, 1996.

Kaplan, Steven, and Jeremy Stein. "How Risky Is the Debt of Highly Leveraged Transactions?" *Journal of Financial Economics* 27, no. 1 (1990), pp. 215–46.

Kuwahara, Hiroto, and Terry Marsh. "The Pricing of Japanese Equity Warrants." *Management Science* 38, no. 11 (1992), pp. 1610–41.

Miles, James, and John Ezzell. "The Weighted Average Cost of Capital, Perfect Capital Markets, and Project Life: A Clarification." *Journal of Financial and Quantitative Analysis* 15, no. 3 (1980), pp. 719–30.

———. "Reformulating Tax Shield Valuation: A Note." *Journal of Finance* 40, no. 5 (1985), pp. 1485–92.

Miller, Merton H. "Debt and Taxes." *Journal of Finance* 32, no. 2 (1977), pp. 261–75.

Modigliani, Franco, and Merton Miller. "Corporate Income Taxes and the Cost of Capital: A Correction." *American Economic Review* 53, no. 3 (1963), pp. 433–92.

———. "The Cost of Capital, Corporate Finance and the Theory of Investment." *American Economic Review* 48, no. 3 (1958), pp. 261–97.

Myers, Stewart C. "Interactions of Corporate Financing and Investment Decisions—Implications for Capital Budgeting." *Journal of Finance* 29, no. 1 (1974), pp. 1–25.

Sick, Gordon. *Capital Budgeting*. Burr Ridge, IL: Richard D. Irwin, in press.

PRACTICAL INSIGHTS

Allocating Capital for Real Investment

- Firms create value by implementing real investment projects that generate returns that are tracked by combinations of financial instruments with values that exceed the projects' costs. (Introduction to Chapter 9)
- The expected return of a project's tracking portfolio is the appropriate discount rate to use to value the project. (Sections 9.2, 10.1, and 10.2)
- When choosing between mutually exclusive investments, pick the project with the highest NPV. With capital constraints, the project with the highest NPV is the best. (Section 9.2)
- Projects with the highest NPV also have the highest EVA.™ (Section 9.3)
- The NPV rule is useful for evaluating many different corporate decisions in addition to capital investments. (Section 9.4)
- The Internal Rate of Return (or IRR) is a useful concept for projects that can be described as consisting of an initial negative cash flow, the cost of the project, and a subsequent series of positive cash flows. In this case, projects with internal rates of return that exceed the expected rate of return on an appropriate tracking portfolio create value for the firm. (Section 9.5)
- Projects with future cash flows that alternate between positive and negative values may have more than one IRR. For these projects, the IRR generally is not a useful concept. (Section 9.5)
- IRRs are not very useful when choosing between mutually exclusive projects. (Section 9.5)
- Generally, a project with a negative PV cannot be valued with the risk-adjusted discount rate method. (Sections 10.1 and 10.2)
- Analysts often examine the return characteristics of publicly traded firms with real investments that are similar to the real investments being evaluated to determine the appropriate tracking portfolio and discount rate. (Sections 10.2, 10.3, and 10.4)
- The APT and the CAPM require knowledge of betas and the expected returns on the relevant tracking portfolios. Analysts without good estimates for these inputs sometimes use a dividend discount model to compute discount rates. (Section 10.4)
- A common mistake made by many firms is to use the firm's own cost of capital rather than the expected return of the appropriate tracking portfolio to value the cash flows of a project. (Sections 10.5 and 12.3)
- Publicly traded firms consist of assets in place and

growth opportunities. Their betas are weighted averages of the risks associated with these two sources of value. Growth opportunities generally have much higher betas than do assets in place. Therefore, the beta of a growth firm is likely to be substantially higher than the betas of their assets in place. Analysts should consider this when using the comparison firm approach to estimate the cost of capital for a project. (Section 10.5)
- Financial analysts tend to use a single discount rate to evaluate an investment to simplify their analysis. However, more accurate valuations can be achieved by accounting for the fact that different expected cash flows should be discounted at different rates. (Section 10.5)
- If a project's cash flows tend to decline over time following unusually large cash flow increases, and vice versa, then expected cash flows generated far in the future should be discounted at lower rates than the cash flows occurring in the near future. (Section 10.5)
- It is often easier to evaluate projects by discounting certainty equivalent cash flows at risk-free rates than by discounting expected cash flows at risk-adjusted discount rates. (Section 10.6)
- For projects that generate cash flows over many years, the estimate of the cash flows in a risk-free scenario may be the best way to obtain their certainty equivalents and their present values. (Section 10.7)
- Positive NPV investment opportunities often arise as a result of past investments. When evaluating prospective investments, consider the fact that additional investment opportunities may be created as a result of this investment. Option pricing theory may be useful for evaluating these potential opportunities. (Section 11.1)
- Option pricing theory has proved to be especially useful for evaluating natural resource investments, like copper mines and oil fields. (Section 11.2)
- Most real investments contain options. Firms have the option to delay the project's initiation date, expand the project, downsize it, and liquidate the project. Option pricing models are useful for evaluating all of these options. (Section 11.2)
- More flexible manufacturing processes provide the firm with more options. These options are more valuable in more uncertain environments. (Section 11.2)
- Information from the option markets and the forward and futures markets often provide useful information for evaluating investment projects. (Sections 10.7 and 11.2)

- When future cash flows are difficult to estimate, the financial ratios of comparable firms, like price/earnings ratios and market/book ratios, may be the best way to value an investment project. Price/earnings ratios are often used to evaluate real estate investments and to value IPOs. (Section 11.3)

- When interest payments are tax deductible, the value of an investment project depends in part on its debt capacity. (Section 12.1)

- Both the APV and the WACC methods account for the debt tax shield when they value a project. Although the WACC method is currently more popular, the APV method is the superior method. (Sections 12.2 and 12.3)

- The APV method can be combined with every approach for valuing real assets. The WACC method can only be used when discounting expected cash flows at risk-adjusted discount rates. (Sections 12.2 and 12.3)

- A common mistake is to use the yield on a risky bond as the cost of debt capital. The appropriate cost of debt, the expected return on the bond, is generally less than the yield on a risky bond. (Section 12.3)

- The APV and WACC methods assume that the manager wishes to maximize the combined value of the firm's outstanding debt and equity. For highly levered firms, projects that improve the value of the firm may negatively affect the value of the firm's stock. Analysts may, therefore, want to evaluate the project cash flows that accrue to the firm's equity holders when such a possibility exists. However, this is sometimes difficult to do with traditional discounting methods. (Section 12.4)

Financing the Firm

- National and local governments often subsidize debt financing, either indirectly through the tax system or directly by giving cheap financing to attract investments that they view favorably. Firms should take advantage of these financing bargains and account for them when valuing investment projects. (Sections 12.1, 12.2, and 12.3)

- When debt is tax deductible, the firm's weighted average cost of capital is reduced if the firm uses more debt financing. (Section 12.3)

EXECUTIVE PERSPECTIVE

Thomas E. Copeland

The investment decision is the driving force behind the value of companies. Nothing is more important. The decision may involve growing the company via a capital expenditure, an investment in working capital, or a commitment for an acquisition. Or, the decision may imply shrinking the company via a divestment, an equity carveout, or a spinoff.

Chapters 9 through 12 are a thoroughly modern and fresh exposition of the approach to making investment decisions based on the fundamental economic role of one price. The reader is introduced to the idea that the value of a capital project can be estimated by building a tracking portfolio of marketable securities that has similar payoffs to the actual investment itself. Hence, the value of the project is equal to the value of its perfect substitute, a tracking portfolio, whose securities have observable market prices. This idea has been the foundation of securities pricing on Wall Street for over two decades and is introduced here for the first time in a corporate finance textbook. And, it's about time!

Throughout this capital budgeting part of the book, Grinblatt and Titman use simple numerical examples to illustrate fundamental investment theory. Their approach makes it very easy to understand. And, because the pre-

sentation is so new and fresh, practitioners will find their mental horizons expanded. For example, Chapter 11 contains capital budgeting material on real options. This is the most important breakthrough in thinking about investment decisions in decades! The authors convincingly demonstrate how traditional net present value methods are inadequate when flexibility is important. This same chapter also covers ratio approaches to valuation and a competitive analysis approach. Any investment banker will be interested in their explanation of how financial leverage may increase or decrease price earnings ratios.

Chapter 12 compares the two most widely advocated cash flow valuation approaches—the adjusted present value method and the traditional approach, which discounts enterprise cash flows at the weighted average cost of capital. Although mathematically equivalent, the two approaches differ in their ease of use—another fact that will be useful for today's practitioners.

Mr. Copeland currently is director of corporate financial services at McKinsey & Company where he is co-leader of the firm's finance practice. Previously, Mr. Copeland was a professor of finance at UCLA's Anderson Graduate School of Management where he served as Chairman of the Finance Group and Vice-Chairman of the graduate school.

PART IV Capital Structure

Firms raise investment funds in a number of ways. They can borrow from banks and other financial institutions or they can issue various kinds of debt, preferred stock, and common equity. A firm's mix of these different sources of capital is referred to as its *capital structure*.

Part III pointed out that the capital structure of a corporation can affect capital allocation decisions. In that part of the text, a firm's capital structure and the financing mix of its investment projects were taken as given. Part IV examines how corporate capital structures are determined.

If a firm's capital structure includes a great deal of debt, then the firm is said to be highly leveraged. The term *leverage* is used because a high debt ratio allows a relatively small percentage change in a firm's earnings (before interest, taxes, depreciation, and amortization) (EBITDA) to translate into a large percentage change in the firm's net income.

The extent to which a firm is leveraged is measured in a number of different ways (see Exhibit IV.1). The first two *debt-to-value ratios* measure the portion of a firm's capitalization financed with debt. The market value of debt is often difficult to calculate since a large percent of corporate debt takes the form of either privately placed bonds or bank loans which do not generally trade. As a result, the amount of debt in a firm's capital structure, the numerators in these expressions, is generally measured at its book value. The denominator in these expressions represents book debt plus either the market value (row 1) or the book value (row 2) of the firm's equity.[1] Because the market value of equity measures the firm's discounted *future* cash flows, ratios with market values in the denominator are good measures of the firm's future ability to meet its interest payments. Because the book value of equity is determined by how well the firm has done in the past, the ratio of debt to the book value of equity is not as reliable an indicator of the firm's ability to meet its interest payments. However, it does indicate how a firm has historically financed its new investments.

An additional measure of leverage is the firm's *interest coverage ratio,* which is the ratio of EBITDA to interest payments. The interest coverage ratio is an indicator of a firm's *current* ability to meet its interest payments.

---

[1]Debt-to-equity ratios, D/E, also are frequently observed, with E measured either as a market value or a book value.

EXHIBIT IV.1   Common Leverage Measures

Leverage Measure	What is Measured
$\dfrac{\text{Debt}}{\text{Debt} + \text{market value of equity}}$	Measures long-term ability to meet interest payments
$\dfrac{\text{Debt}}{\text{Total book assets}}$	Measures historical financing of investments
$\dfrac{\text{EBITDA}}{\text{Interest}}$	Measures ability to meet current interest payments

Exhibit IV.2 provides the financial ratios described in Exhibit IV.1 for a sample of 15 well-known U.S. corporations. It shows that high-tech companies like Hewlett-Packard and Raytheon tend to rely little on debt financing; their debt-to-value ratios indicate that less than 20 percent of their total capital consists of debt. The most highly leveraged companies on this list are Boston Edison, an electric utility; Delta Air Lines; and Safeway, a supermarket chain. Safeway's leverage ratio actually declined significantly from the late 1980s, following the company's purchase by management in a leveraged buyout. Since a number of supermarkets undertook leveraged buyouts in the 1980s, firms in that industry are often highly leveraged. Airlines and electric utilities, as groups, also are relatively highly levered. For the airlines, however, the high level of debt may be temporary, reflecting accumulated losses during the late 1980s and early 1990s. For example, the first column's debt-to-market value ratio of Delta Air Lines was lower in the past: less than 30 percent in 1990 and less than 25 percent in 1985.

Part IV will explain why firms like Safeway choose to be highly levered while firms like Hewlett-Packard and Raytheon use little debt financing. The starting point for this discussion is the *Modigliani-Miller Theorem,* which states that in the absence of taxes and other market frictions (e.g., transaction costs), the capital structure choice does not affect firm values. According to this theorem, managers should place all of their effort into making the real investment decisions described in Part III; how these real investments are actually financed is a matter of indifference.

Of course, the real world is very different from the frictionless markets model set forth by Modigliani and Miller; in reality, managers can create value for their corporations by making astute financing decisions. Chapters 13 and 14 discuss how taxes affect financing choices. The key insight is that when interest payments, but not dividends, are tax deductible, debt is a less expensive form of financing than equity. However, the corporate tax advantage of debt can be somewhat mitigated by the personal tax advantages of equity financing. In particular, the returns that accrue to equity holders are often treated as capital gains, which are more lightly taxed than the interest income paid to the firm's debt holders. In addition, because equity holders must pay personal taxes on dividend income, they may be better off if the firm finances its investments with retained earnings instead of paying a dividend and financing new investment with borrowing.

The discussion of project valuation and taxes in Chapter 12 is closely related to the discussion of capital structure and taxes in Chapters 13 and 14. The various methods introduced in Chapter 12 to calculate the *NPV* of a project were based on a world with corporate taxes but no personal taxes. However, as the following chapters illustrate, if personal taxes are relevant, these methods need to be revised.

EXHIBIT IV.2   Financial Ratios of Selected U.S. Corporations, 1993

Company Name	Debt / (Debt + Mkt Equity)	Debt / Total Book Assets	EBITDA / Interest
AT&T	20%	29%	16.36
Boeing	15	13	14.37
Boston Edison	49	42	3.49
John Deere	40	37	2.47
Delta Air Lines	53	32	1.08
Disney	9	20	14.09
General Motors	61	37	2.98
Hewlett-Packard	13	17	21.67
McDonalds	15	31	7.18
3M	6	12	59.70
Philip Morris	27	35	6.72
Raytheon	9	12	37.88
Safeway Stores	55	53	3.06
Texaco	27	26	4.70
Wal-Mart	14	36	7.54

Source: Standard and Poor's Compustat Data 1994.

Chapters 15 and 16 describe how contracting and transactions costs can affect the capital structure choice. In the world of Modigliani and Miller, a firm that goes bankrupt has its assets transferred costlessly from equity holders to debt holders. Their model also assumes that the real investment and operating decisions of the firm can be made independently of this potential transfer of ownership, which is likely to be the case in the absence of contracting and transaction costs. In reality, however, legal costs are associated with this transfer. Perhaps more importantly, managerial incentives in a firm close to bankruptcy will change in ways that can create substantial costs to the firm. Because of these potential costs, firms tend to limit their use of debt financing despite its tax advantages.

Our goal in Part IV is to provide guidelines for managers in situations where all parties have a shared objective to maximize the wealth of shareholders. However, the maximization of shareholder wealth may not be the objective of all managers because of the transaction and contracting costs alluded to above. Part V examines how financial decisions are made when managers have differing objectives from those of shareholders, which will complete the analysis of capital structure.

How Taxes Affect Financing Choices

Learning Objectives

After reading this chapter, you should be able to:

1. Understand that in the absence of taxes, transaction costs, and other market frictions, capital structure can affect firm values *only* when the debt-equity choice affects cash flows (the Modigliani-Miller Theorem).

2. Explain how corporate taxes provide incentives for firms to use debt financing as well as how they affect the decision to buy or lease capital assets.

3. Understand why personal taxes provide an incentive for firms to use equity financing.

4. Explain how nondebt tax shields, such as depreciation deductions and R&D expenses, affect the capital structure choice.

5. Use the yields on municipal bonds to quantify the total tax gain associated with a leverage change.

6. Understand how inflation affects the capital structure choice.

After World War II, the U.S. airline industry expanded, and some airlines issued additional equity to fund their expansions. Jack Frye, then CEO of TWA, thought that TWA also should issue equity to fund its expansion. However, Howard Hughes, TWA's largest shareholder, disagreed. Partly because of this disagreement, Frye was replaced as CEO.

In a Civil Aeronautics Board hearing in 1959 concerning Howard Hughes's control of TWA, Hughes explained his position at the earlier time: "My position was [that] . . . debt financing was very attractive. Interest rates were low, and interest could be paid out of basic earnings before taxation. Equity financing, to leave a satisfied stockholder, probably should have returned something between 7 and 10 percent, and that would have been required to be paid out of earnings after taxation." [1]

---

[1] Robert W. Rummel, *Howard Hughes and TWA* (Washington, DC: Smithsonian Institution Press, 1991), p. 128.

C hapter 12 discussed how taxes and a firm's financial structure can interact to affect
     its real investment decisions. The following two chapters take one step backward
and examine how taxes affect the proportions of debt and equity used to finance a firm.
To understand how taxes affect a firm's financing choices, one must first understand what
financing choices would be like without taxes. Hence, the springboard for discussion
of this topic is the no-tax capital structure irrelevance theorem offered by Franco
Modigliani and Merton Miller.

The **Modigliani-Miller Theorem**, which was largely responsible for both authors
winning Nobel Prizes in economics, states that if the capital structure decision has no
effect on the cash flows generated by a firm, the decision also will have no effect—in the
absence of transaction costs—on the total value of the firm's debt and equity. This means
that a manager who is contemplating whether it is cheaper to finance the firm primarily
with junk bonds (i.e., very high-yield, high-risk debt) or with equity and perhaps a small
amount of high-quality debt should stop worrying: Neither financing decision is superior
to the other!

The premise of the Modigliani-Miller Theorem, that capital structure has no effect
on cash flows, is not true in the real world. Because the interest on debt is tax deductible,
the after-tax cash flows of firms increase when they include more debt in their capital
structures, leading firms to favor debt over equity financing. However, the capital structure choice becomes more complicated when considering personal as well as corporate
taxes. Personal taxes tend to favor the use of equity in a firm's capital structure since a
large portion of the returns on stock are taxed at the capital gains rate, which is generally
more favorable than the ordinary tax rate that applies to interest income.

13.1 The Modigliani-Miller Theorem

The first step in understanding the firm's capital structure choice is the Modigliani-Miller
Theorem. Much of the rest of this chapter—indeed, much of the rest of this text—will
build results based on this theorem.

Slicing the Cash Flows of the Firm

Exhibit 13.1 illustrates the total cash flows of a firm as a pie chart and the various claims
on those cash flows as slices of the pie. Pie 1 illustrates the case in which all of the cash
flows accrue to debt holders and equity holders; the way that the pie is sliced does not
affect the total cash flows available. This is the assumption of the Modigliani-Miller
Theorem.

Pies 2 and 3 illustrate how a firm's capital structure affects the total cash flows to its
debt and equity holders. Pie 2 has a piece removed for tax payments to the government.
Again, how the pie is sliced does not affect its the total size. However, the owners of
the firm are not interested in the total size of the pie. They are interested only in those
cash flows they can sell to security holders, that is, the debt and equity portions. Hence,
the owners would like to minimize the size of the slice going to the government, which
they cannot sell. When more of the pie is allocated to the debt holders, less is allocated
to the government, implying that the combined debt and equity slices increase.

Finally, pie 3 includes an additional piece that reflects the possibility that part of the
pie is wasted. In other words, a slice of the pie is lost because of inefficiency, lost
opportunities, or avoidable costs. Chapters 15 through 18 describe various reasons why
the size of this wasted slice may be determined partly by how a firm is financed.

EXHIBIT 13.1   Slicing the Cash Flows of the Firm

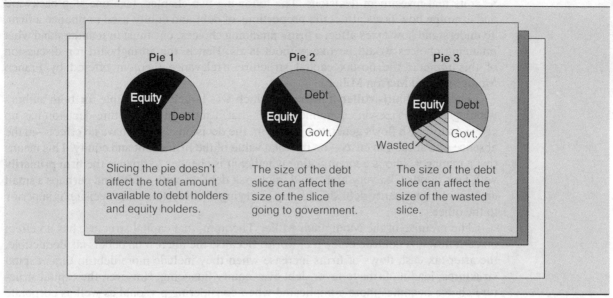

This section considers the case illustrated by pie 1, where the total *future* cash flows of the firm are unaffected by the debt-equity mix. If the total cash flows are unaffected by the debt-equity mix, the total *value* of a firm's debt and equity also is unaffected by their mix, as we will now show.

Proof of the Modigliani-Miller Theorem

Modigliani and Miller (1958) proved the irrelevance theorem by showing that if two firms are identical except for their capital structures, an opportunity to earn arbitrage profits exists if the total values of the two firms are not the same. To illustrate this, assume that two firms exist for one year, produce identical real asset cash flows at the end of that year, , and then liquidate. However, the firms are financed differently: company U is unleveraged (i.e., it has no debt) and company L is leveraged (i.e., it has some debt in its capital structure).

Exhibit 13.2 presents the cash flows of companies U and L, the split of the cash flows between debt and equity, and the present values of the cash flows. Since company U has no debt, its uncertain cash flow $\tilde{X}$ is split only among the firm's equity holders. Thus, the current value of company U, or V_U, is the same as the value of its equity. Company L, in contrast, has a debt obligation in one year of $(1 + r_D)D$ dollars. If, for simplicity, we assume that the debt is riskless, and r_D is equal to the riskless rate, company L's debt holders will receive $(1 + r_D)D$ at the end of the year and its equity holders will receive the remaining $\tilde{X} - (1 + r_D)D$ dollars. The current value of company L, or V_L, is the current value of its outstanding debt D plus its equity E_L.

According to the Modigliani-Miller Theorem, V_U must equal $D + E_L$, which can be seen by applying the tracking approach to valuation introduced in Part II. Since company U's equity is perfectly tracked by company L's debt plus equity, the value of company U's equity must equal the combined value of company L's debt plus equity. If these values are unequal, an opportunity to earn arbitrage profits exists.

EXHIBIT 13.2   Liability Cash Flows and Their Market Values for Two Firms with Different Capital Structures

	Company U		Company L	
	Future Cash Flow	*Current Value*	*Future Cash Flow*	*Current Value*
Debt	0	0	$(1 + r_D)D$	D
Equity	$\tilde{X}$	V_U	$\tilde{X} - (1 + r_D)D$	E_L
Total	$\tilde{X}$	V_U	$\tilde{X}$	$V_L = D + E_L$

Earning Arbitrage Profits When the Modigliani-Miller Theorem Fails to Hold.   To illustrate this arbitrage opportunity, first consider the case where the value of company U is greater than the value of company L ($V_U > D + E_L$). Suppose, for example, that company U has an equity value of $100 million and company L has an equity value of $60 million and a debt value of $30 million. If this were the case, a shrewd investor could profit by buying, for example, 10 percent of the outstanding shares (equity) of company L (costing $6 million) and 10 percent ($3 million) of its outstanding debt, and selling short 10 percent (or $10 million) of the shares (equity) of company U.

Assuming that the investor receives the proceeds of the short sale, this transaction yields a net cash inflow of $1 million [$10 million − ($6 million + $3 million)]. However, when cash flows are realized at year-end, the investor will receive $.1(\tilde{X} - (1 + r_D)D) + .1(1 + r_D)D$ in cash from company L's stock and bonds and must pay out $.1\tilde{X}$ to cover the short sale of company U's stock. Thus, the net combined future cash flow from these transactions is $.1(\tilde{X} - (1 + r_D)D) + .1(1 + r_D)D - .1\tilde{X}$, which is zero, regardless of the future value that $\tilde{X}$ realizes. In other words, the transaction generates cash for the investor at the beginning of the period, but requires nothing from the investor at the end of the period. Similar opportunities for arbitrage exist if company U has a lower value than company L, that is, $V_U < D + E_L$. Since we assume that such arbitrage opportunities cannot exist, the total value of the two firms must be the same regardless of how they are financed.

Example 13.1 illustrates this type of arbitrage opportunity in a simple case where the firm's cash flows can take on one of only two possible values.

Example 13.1:   An Arbitrage Opportunity if the Modigliani-Miller Theorem Is False

Assume:

- Company U is financed totally with equity and is worth $100 million.
- An otherwise identical company L is financed with $40 million in equity plus $50 million (market value) in riskless debt that offers a 10 percent interest rate. Thus, the bonds pay $55 million (= $5 million in interest plus $50 million in principal) at the end of the year.
- If the economy is weak, cash flows for each company will be $80 million; if the economy is strong, cash flows for each company will be $200 million.

Show how a shrewd investor would profit from this violation of the Modigliani-Miller Theorem.

Answer: The shrewd investor can profit by purchasing 10 percent of company L's equity ($4 million) and 10 percent of its outstanding debt ($5 million) while selling short 10 percent of the shares of company U. The investor would then realize an immediate cash inflow of $1 million (= .10 ($100 million − $40 million − $50 million). However, as the following table shows, the investor would have no net obligations at the end of the year, so the initial $1 million inflow can be considered a risk-free profit.

	Cash Flow to Investor (in $ millions) at		
	Beginning of Year	End of Year	
		Weak Economy	Strong Economy
Short sale of U equity	$10	($8.0)	($20.0)
Purchase of L equity	(4)	2.5	14.5
Purchase of L debt	(5)	5.5	5.5
Net cash inflow	$ 1	$0.0	$ 0.0

The year-end equity figures for company L are, by definition, the total cash flows for company L less the principal and interest payments to debt holders.

Stating the Modigliani-Miller Theorem Explicitly.   Example 13.1 illustrates how a shrewd investor can realize arbitrage profits when the Modigliani-Miller Theorem is violated. Result 13.1 states explicitly the assumptions and the implications of this theorem.

Result 13.1   *(The Modigliani-Miller Theorem.)* Assuming: (1) a firm's total cash flows to security holders are independent of how it is financed, (2) there are no transaction costs, and (3) no arbitrage opportunities exist in the economy, then, the total market value of the firm, which is the same as the sum of the market values of the items on the right-hand side of the balance sheet (i.e., its debt and equity), is independent of how it is financed.

Assumptions of the Modigliani-Miller Theorem

Result 13.1 indicates that the capital structure irrelevance theorem holds only under some restrictive assumptions. The Modigliani-Miller theorem is, however, important because it provides a framework that allows managers to focus on those factors that are important determinants of the optimal capital structure choice. Examining the different assumptions of the theorem provides important insights into how the capital structure decision affects firm values.

The Key Assumption.   The first assumption of the Modigliani-Miller Theorem—that the sum of all future cash flows distributed to the firm's debt and equity investors is unaffected by capital structure—is really the key, and it will be the focus of much of the remainder of this text. In reality, capital structure can affect a firm's cash flows for a number of reasons. This chapter focuses on how capital structure can affect a firm's total cash flows by altering its tax liabilities.[2]

The Importance of Transaction Costs.   The second assumption, no transaction costs, was used throughout Parts II and III of the text. However, transaction costs play a special

---

[2]Chapters 15–18 examine how the financing mix affects a firm's investment choices and the efficiency of its operations.

role here that requires some additional discussion. In the absence of transaction costs, the cash flows to investors from any new security that a firm issues can be tracked by other securities that already exist in the market.[3] This means that the issuing firm is not really offering the investing public a pattern of returns that they could not otherwise obtain. However, transaction costs limit the availability of return patterns that can be obtained in the market and sometimes provide firms with an opportunity to improve their value by issuing special securities that investors desire.

For example, in the early 1990s in Hong Kong, there was a strong demand for warrants because they provide investors with highly leveraged positions with limited downside risk. In the absence of transaction costs, warrants are not special securities because they can be tracked with a dynamic strategy involving the underlying stock and the risk-free asset (see Chapter 8). However, if transaction costs are high, tracking a warrant with a dynamic strategy may be impossible. As a result, Hong Kong firms were able to take advantage of the demand for option-like payoffs by issuing warrants at prices exceeding the theoretical Black/Scholes prices discussed in Chapter 8. For similar reasons, a firm might be able, in some instance, to obtain relatively attractive financing with a convertible bond.

The Absence of Arbitrage.   The final Modigliani-Miller assumption, no arbitrage, is made throughout the text. Analyzing any sort of decision that affects a corporation's value requires some framework for determining valuation. The Modigliani-Miller Theorem is consistent with all pricing models that satisfy the most basic assumption in asset pricing: Equilibrium prices cannot provide opportunities for riskless arbitrage profits.

13.2 How an Individual Investor Can "Undo" a Firm's Capital Structure Choice

The proof of the Modigliani-Miller Theorem described in the last section implicitly assumes that firms with identical cash flows but different capital structures exist. An alternative way to prove the Modigliani-Miller Theorem is to demonstrate that, under its assumptions, a firm's shareholders are indifferent to a change in its capital structure. This is illustrated in Example 13.2.

Example 13.2:   Undoing Elco's Capital Structure Change

Elco is considering a change in its capital structure. Prior to the change, the firm's stock sells for $100 per share, and the firm has 1,000 shares outstanding. The firm also is financed with riskless zero-coupon debt maturing in one year, and having a current market value of $D = \$10,000$.

Stanley Kowalski currently owns 100 shares of Elco stock (10 percent of its equity). In the absence of a capital structure change, Stanley's payoff next year will equal:

$$.1(\tilde{X} - (1 + r_D)\$10,000) = .1\tilde{X} - (1 + r_D)\$1,000$$

Here $\tilde{X}$ is the firm's cash flows and r_D is the risk-free interest rate to be paid to debt holders, so that the firm's future debt service obligation is $(1 + r_D)\$10,000$. The firm plans to repurchase 500 shares of its outstanding stock for $50,000 and will finance the equity repurchase by issuing $50,000 in risk-free debt.

---

[3]This tracking does not have to be perfect. For example, if the CAPM holds, the Modigliani-Miller Theorem still applies. The key is that investors cannot be made better off by the issuance of a new security.

First, show what Stanley's payoff will be if he does nothing to counteract the firm's actions. Then show how he, as an individual investor, can undo in his personal portfolio any change in the firm's leverage, so that he can attain the same cash flows he would have received without the leverage change.

Answer: If Stanley chooses not to alter his portfolio, his share of Elco's cash flow next period will be:

$$.2(\tilde{X} - (1 + r_D)\$60,000)$$

because he would own 20 percent (= 100/500) of the firm's outstanding shares if half of the shares were repurchased. He would then have a riskier investment than he held previously, which he may or may not prefer.

However, if Stanley sells 50 shares of his stock, using the proceeds to buy \$5,000 in bonds, he will once again own 10 percent (= 50/500) of the firm's shares and will realize a return equal to:

$$.1[\tilde{X} - (1 + r_D)\$60,000] + (1 + r_D)\$5,000 = .1\tilde{X} - (1 + r_D)\$1,000$$

Example 13.2 illustrates how shareholders can undo the effect of a change in a firm's capital structure by making offsetting changes to their own portfolio. The shareholder can achieve the same cash flow pattern and continue to control the same percent of the firm's shares. Thus, without transaction costs, the shareholder is indifferent to changes in the firm's capital structure.

13.3 How Risky Debt Affects the Modigliani-Miller Theorem

Up to this point, we have assumed that all debt is riskless; that is, there is no bankruptcy. This section discusses situations in which firms can go bankrupt, thus making their debt risky.

The Modigliani-Miller Theorem with Costless Bankruptcy

The assumptions of the Modigliani-Miller Theorem permit bankruptcy, but no bankruptcy costs. In other words, the theorem assumes that when a firm goes bankrupt, control of the firm's assets move costlessly from the equity holders to the debt holders.[4]

To understand what we mean by costless bankruptcy, return to Example 13.2 in which the payoff to Stanley Kowalski, who owns 10 percent of Elco's shares, is 10 percent of the cash flow less Elco's debt obligations:

$$.1[\tilde{X} - (1 + r_{DS})\$10,000]$$

where r_{DS} is the promised interest rate to be paid to the original or senior debt holders.

If the debt in Example 13.2 had been risky, the cash flow described in the above expression would be the payoff to shareholders *only if this quantity is positive*. Because stockholders enjoy limited liability, they receive nothing if the debt obligation exceeds the cash flows for the period; in this case, debt holders receive the entire cash flow $\tilde{X}$ of the firm, assuming no bankruptcy costs. The debt is risky because in these instances, the entire cash flow can still be considerably less than the promised debt payment.

---

[4]Of course, this assumption in unrealistic. Lawyers are very much involved in the bankruptcy process and they are expensive. The various costs of bankruptcy are discussed in detail in Chapter 15.

Leverage Increases and Wealth Transfers

When bankruptcy can occur, we must be more explicit about what we mean when we say that the capital structure decision is irrelevant. The possibility of bankruptcy implies that capital structure changes can result in transfers of wealth between the firm's equity holders and its debt holders. Hence, a change in a firm's debt-equity mix can affect its share price even if the change does not affect the sum of the firm's debt and equity values.

The potential for wealth transfers from existing debt holders to the firm's equity holders depends on whether the new debt must be subordinated. In bankruptcy proceedings, *subordinated debt* (see Chapter 2) has a claim to the assets of the firm only after the debt with higher priority has been fully paid off. As we will show, if a new debt issue is not subordinated to the old debt, the new debt can generate a transfer of wealth from the existing debt holders to the equity holders. However, if the debt is subordinated, shareholders will continue to be indifferent to a capital structure change.

The Effect of Leverage Changes When New Debt Is Subordinated to Existing Debt. To understand the effect of a capital structure change when debt is risky, consider again the possibility that Elco issues $50,000 in new debt and uses the proceeds to repurchase 500 shares. Assume initially that the new debt is junior to existing debt in the event of bankruptcy, which means that the new debt is subordinated to the old debt, and, as a consequence, its coupon rate, r_{DJ}, is greater than r_{DS}, the rate on senior debt.

Exhibit 13.3 illustrates that Mr. Kowalski can, in effect, undo the effects of additional risky debt in Elco's capital structure by buying $5,000 of the new debt and selling 50 shares. This leaves him with 50 shares (100 shares less the 50 sold) and $5,000 of the new subordinated debt.

Note that in each scenario of Exhibit 13.3 the cash flow is identical to what Mr. Kowalski would have received as a shareholder, given the firm's original capital structure. In scenarios A and B—where the firm has sufficient cash to pay off its obligations to senior debt holders—the investor achieves the same cash flow he or she would have achieved as an equity holder, given the firm's original capital structure, that is, $.1[\tilde{X} - (1 + r_{DS})10,000]$. In scenario C, the state in which the firm has insufficient cash flows to pay off its senior debt, an equity holder would have received nothing even in the

---

EXHIBIT 13.3   Undoing the Effects of Additional Risky Debt When New Debt Is Subordinated to Old Debt

Investment	Cash Flows		
	Scenario A	*Scenario B*	*Scenario C*
	Cash flow exceeds all debt obligations: $\tilde{X} > (1 + r_{DS})\$10,000$ $+ (1 + r_{DJ})\$50,000$	Cash flow exceeds senior debt obligation but not subordinated debt obligation	Senior debt obligation exceeds cash flow: $\tilde{X} < (1 + r_{DS})\$10,000$
50 shares of stock	$.1[\tilde{X} - (1 + r_{DS})\$10,000]$ $- .1[(1 + r_{DJ})\$50,000]$	0	0
$5,000 of new debt	$.1(1 + r_{DJ})\$50,000$	$.1[\tilde{X} - (1 + r_{DS})\$10,000]$	0
Total	$.1[\tilde{X} - (1 + r_{DS})\$10,000]$	$.1[\tilde{X} - (1 + r_{DS})\$10,000]$	0

Note: r_{DS} represents the promised interest rate on the senior debt and r_{DJ} is the promised interest rate on the junior subordinated debt.

absence of a new debt issue. Now the investor still receives nothing as an investor holding both equity and subordinated debt.

Result 13.2 summarizes the main points about how capital structure changes affect debt and equity holders when new debt is subordinated to existing debt.

Result 13.2   If a firm's original debt holders have a senior claim in the event of bankruptcy, then the values of both the firm's stock and its existing debt are invariant to changes in the firm's capital structure under the assumptions listed in Result 13.1.

What Occurs When New Debt Is Not Subordinated to Old Debt?   When firms have new debt subordinated to old debt r_{DS}, the promised yield on the old debt must be less than r_{DJ}, the promised yield on the new debt, because of the greater default risk of the new debt. If the new debt is not subordinated to the old debt, the new debt holders share proportionately the cash flow of the bankrupt firm with the original debt holders. In this case, the promised yield on the new debt is lower than when it is subordinated because it is less risky. However, the original debt holders are made worse off when the new debt is issued.

This cost to the original debt holders is a benefit to the stockholders. To understand this, consider again the case analyzed in Exhibit 13.3, except now assume that the new debt is subordinated. Assume again that the investor undoes the capital structure increase by selling 50 shares of stock and buying $5,000 of new debt. In scenario A, the investor still receives the same cash flow that would have been achieved under the original capital structure. Under scenarios B and C where the firm is bankrupt, however, the investor receives greater cash flows than Exhibit 13.3 specifies because the new debt the investor holds now receives a proportional share of the bankruptcy proceeds.

Result 13.3   If a firm's original debt holders do not have a senior claim in the event of bankruptcy, a new debt issue can decrease the value of existing debt. Under the assumptions listed in Result 13.1, however, the loss to the old debt holders would be offset by a gain to the equity holders, making the total value of the firm invariant to this type of capital structure change.

During the 1980s, a number of firms increased their debt ratios substantially, most dramatically in leveraged buyout transactions that took public companies private. In a number of these transactions, the transfer of wealth from the original debt holders to the equity holders was quite large. In the RJR Nabisco leveraged buyout, for example, some existing bonds lost about 20 percent of their value.[5]

13.4 How Corporate Taxes Affect the Capital Structure Choice

Financial managers spend a great deal of time making decisions about their firms' capital structures. In addition, stock prices react dramatically when firms make major changes in their capital structures.[6] This suggests that it probably would be unwise to stick with the conclusion that the capital structure decision is irrelevant.

The apparent relevance of the capital structure decision suggests that some of the assumptions underlying the Modigliani-Miller Theorem are unrealistic and that relaxing them may have important implications for the firm's capital structure choice. The most obviously unrealistic assumption is that of no taxes. Taxes have a major effect on the cash flows of firms and, as a result, strongly influence their capital structure decisions. The preceding two sections indicated that, in the absence of taxes, a firm's value does not

---

[5]Studies by Asquith and Wizman (1990) and Warga and Welch (1993) indicate that bondholders lost money in a number of other leveraged buyouts.

[6]Stock price reactions to corporate events like capital structure changes are discussed in Chapter 18.

depend on its capital structure. It follows that, in the absence of other market frictions, minimizing the amount paid in taxes maximizes the cash flows to the firm's equity holders and debt holders, thereby maximizing the firm's total value.

Howard Hughes's perceptive analysis of the tax benefits of debt financing, described in the chapter's opening vignette, predated the academic discussion of debt and taxes by several years. This section explores the types of tax benefits he mentioned in more detail; specifically considering situations in which there are (1) corporate taxes, (2) tax-deductible interest expenses, and (3) no personal taxes.[7]

How Debt Affects After-Tax Cash Flows

If the corporate tax rate is T_c, a firm with pretax real asset cash flows of $\tilde{X}$ and interest payments of rD has taxable income of $\tilde{X} - r_D D$ and pays a corporate tax of $(\tilde{X} - r_D D)T_c$. Since interest expense is tax deductible, a firm can reduce its tax liabilities and thus increase the amount it distributes to its security holders by issuing additional debt. Therefore, in the absence of personal taxes, transaction costs, and bankruptcy costs, and holding the total cash flow generated by the firm constant, the value-maximizing capital structure includes enough debt to eliminate the firm's tax liabilities.

To examine how debt affects firm values in the presence of corporate taxes, assume that the firm is financed with a combination of equity and a risk-free perpetuity bond (see Chapter 2), which pays interest at a fixed rate of r_D forever. The year t after-tax cash flows for such a firm is the sum of the after-(corporate) tax payments to its debt and equity holders, as expressed in the following equation:

$$\tilde{C}_t = (\tilde{X}_t - r_D D)(1 - T_c) + r_D D \tag{13.1}$$

This expression assumes that all of the firm's period t cash flow, $(\tilde{X}_t - r_D D)$, is taxable income.

By rearranging terms, the firm's cash flows can be expressed as the sum of the after-tax cash flows that the firm would have achieved if it were an all-equity firm plus the cash flows it achieves because of the tax gain from debt:

$$\tilde{C}_t = \tilde{X}_t(1 - T_c) + r_D D T_c \tag{13.2}$$

How Debt Affects the Value of the Firm

As Chapter 12 showed, the value of the firm is the present value of the after-tax cash flows expressed in equation (13.2). To determine how the value of the firm changes with a change in leverage, note that $\tilde{X}_t(1 - T_c)$ is the period t cash flow that would be achieved by an unleveraged firm. Therefore, the present value of this series of cash flows, $\tilde{X}_1(1 - T_c), \tilde{X}_2(1 - T_c), \ldots$, must equal the value of the firm had it been unlevered (V_U). In addition, recall that with static perpetual debt the present value of the firm's yearly tax savings $r_D D T_c$ is $T_c D$. This implies the following result:

Result 13.4   Assume that the pretax cash flows of the firm are unaffected by a change in a firm's capital structure, and that there are no transaction costs or opportunities for arbitrage. If the corporate tax rate is T_c, then the value of a levered firm with static risk-free perpetual debt is the value of an otherwise equivalent unlevered firm plus the product of the corporate tax rate and the market value of the firm's debt, that is:

$$V_L = V_U + T_c D \tag{13.3}$$

---

[7]The effect of personal taxes on the capital structure choice will be explored later in this chapter and in Chapter 14.

As equation (13.3) illustrates, the value of the firm increases with leverage by the amount T_cD, which is the tax gain to leverage.[8]

To illustrate how tax-deductible debt can increase the cash flows to shareholders as well as increase firm value, Example 13.3 recalculates the answer to Example 13.2, assuming that there are corporate taxes.

Example 13.3:   The Effect of Corporate Taxes on Cash Flows to Equity and Debt Holders

Recall from Example 13.2 that Stanley Kowalski held 10 percent of the firm's equity and that the firm was increasing its debt level from $10,000 to $60,000. In this example the firm uses perpetuity bonds instead of zero-coupon bonds for debt financing.

Compute Stanley's cash flow (1) in the original low-leverage scenario and (2) in the high-leverage scenario in which the investor attempts to undo the firm's capital structure change by selling half of his shares and using the proceeds to buy $5,000 in bonds. Assume there is a corporate tax on earnings at a rate of T_c.

Answer: The after-tax cash flow to the investor given the initial low level of debt is:

$$\tilde{C}_{\text{low lev}} = .1[\tilde{X} - r_D\$10{,}000](1 - T_c)$$

A leverage increase of $50,000 that is offset by a change in the investor's portfolio will now yield after-tax cash flows to the investor of:

$$\tilde{C}_{\text{high lev}} = .1[\tilde{X} - r_D\$60{,}000](1 - T_c)] + r_D\$5{,}000$$
$$= .1[\tilde{X} - r_D\$10{,}000](1 - T_c) + r_DT_c\$5{,}000$$

Hence, if, as in Example 13.3, a firm increases its debt level by adding $5,000 in bonds, an equity investor in the firm can increase his cash flow by $r_DT_c\$5{,}000$ without increasing the risk of his portfolio. Moreover, if a firm increases its debt level further, its investors will be able to generate higher cash flows, again without increasing risk. This implies the following result:

Result 13.5   Assume that the pretax cash flows of the firm are unaffected by a change in a firm's capital structure, and there are no transaction costs or opportunities for arbitrage. With corporate taxes but no personal taxes, a firm's optimal capital structure will include enough debt to completely eliminate the firm's tax liabilities.

Example 13.4 illustrates the tax gains associated with leverage with a hypothetical leverage increase by RJR Nabisco in 1987, prior to its leveraged buyout.

Example 13.4:   Recapitalizing RJR Nabisco

In 1987, RJR Nabisco earned $2,304 million before interest and taxes, out of which $488 million was paid out in interest and $735 million was paid out in taxes. Suppose that RJR chose to recapitalize by distributing to its *shareholders* $5 billion in 9.4 percent notes, requiring $470 million in annual interest payments. Assuming that the investment choice and the pretax real asset cash flows of the firm are unchanged, how would this additional $470 million affect the cash flows to a tax-exempt shareholder?

---

[8]As long as the firm maintains a certain proportion of debt in its capital structure, either by rolling over debt or issuing perpetuities, the present value of the tax gain is still T_cD. This gain does not depend on the real asset cash flows of the firm as long as the firm is profitable enough to pay taxes, because the present value of the after-tax real asset cash flows is independent of the firm's capital structure. Because the real asset cash flows do not affect the tax gain, adding time subscripts to the real asset cash flows and earnings of the firm does not lend anything to the analysis. Henceforth, we will drop them.

Answer: From RJR's annual report, we compute the following:

	1987 (in $millions)	Recapitalization (in $millions)
EBIT	$2,304	$2,304
− Net interest expenses	− 488	− 958
EBT	1,816	1,346
− Taxes (rate = 40.5%)	− 735	− 545
Net income	1,081	801
Gain from extraordinary item	128	128
Net profits (a)	1,209	929
Net investment (b)	739	739
Dividends [(a) − (b)]	470	190
CF to shareholders (from stock and bonds)	470	660
	($1.88/share)	($2.64/share)

The difference in the cash flows between the two scenarios, $190 million (= $660 − $470) equals the tax savings from the debt, .405 × .094 × $5 billion.

13.5 How Personal Taxes Affect Capital Structure

A tax-exempt investor, such as a pension fund, is indifferent about whether the cash flows of a firm come in the form of interest on debt, dividends on equity, or capital gains on equity as long as the form of payment does not affect the return on the investment. Since the total after-tax corporate cash flows of firms are larger when cash flows are paid out in the form of debt interest payments instead of retained or paid as dividends, tax-exempt shareholders will prefer firms to have high leverage. However, investors who pay personal taxes prefer to receive income in the form of capital gains because capital gains can always be deferred and, in many countries, are taxed at lower rates than interest or dividend income. This preference for capital gains income can lead some taxable investors to prefer firms with less leverage.

Relevant Features of the U.S. Tax Code

To understand how personal taxes affect the choice of whether to raise external funds with debt or equity,[9] it is important to review a number of relevant features of the U.S. tax code, which are summarized below:

---

[9]Note that the analysis that follows is somewhat incomplete because it does not consider the choice between financing investment with internally generated equity (i.e., retained earnings) and the alternative of paying out the earnings as a dividend and funding the investment with debt. The analysis also ignores the personal tax effects of changing a firm's leverage ratio. For example, the RJR recapitalization (see Example 13.4) would have important personal tax implications for some shareholders. These remaining personal tax issues are considered in Chapter 14.

- Capital gains are generally taxed at a lower rate than ordinary income, and the tax is deferred until the gain is realized.[10] As a result, the average tax rate on stock income T_E, which generally has a capital gains component, is less than the average tax rate on debt income T_D, which is taxed as ordinary income; that is, $T_E < T_D$.

- Interest expenses are tax deductible. However, since dividends are viewed as distributions of profits rather than expenses of doing business, they are not tax deductible in the United States.

- Corporations have a number of **nondebt tax shields** These are tax deductions for items like depreciation, R&D expenses, and so forth. Because these deductions do not exactly reflect the firm's true economic costs, there is generally a difference between the pretax cash flows available to investors in the firm's securities and earnings before interest and taxes (*EBIT*).

The Effect of Personal Taxes on Debt and Equity Rates of Return

We first examine how personal taxes affect the expected rates of return required to induce investors to hold debt securities instead of equity securities. In general, debt is less risky than equity and thus requires a lower expected rate of return. To simplify this analysis, we assume risk-free debt with a promised coupon and return of r_D and risk neutrality, so that the expected return of equity, $\bar{r}_E$, which more generally can be viewed as a pretax risk-adjusted (or zero-beta) expected return, differs from r_D only because of taxes.

Which Investors Prefer Debt and Which Prefer Equity.   In the absence of taxes and other market frictions, the expected return of zero-beta equity equals the return on riskless debt (see Chapter 5). With taxes, however, it is necessary to account for the fact that the returns to equity, which often come in the form of capital gains, are generally taxed less heavily than the returns to debt. To compensate taxable investors for its relative tax disadvantage, the pretax return on debt should exceed the pre-tax risk-adjusted expected return on equity.

This pretax return difference leads tax-exempt investors to prefer debt to equity. However, if the return difference is not too large, investors in the highest tax brackets should prefer equity to debt. Other investors will be indifferent between holding debt and equity. The personal tax rates on debt and equity of these indifferent investors satisfy the following condition:

$$r_D(1 - T_D) = \bar{r}_E(1 - T_E) \tag{13.4}$$

so that the after-tax expected return is the same for each security. If $r_D(1 - T_D) > \bar{r}_E(1 - T_E)$ for a particular investor—that is, the after-tax return to debt exceeds the after-tax expected return to equity—the investor will prefer debt to equity. If the inequality is reversed, the investor will prefer equity to debt. If T_E is proportional to T_D, as is often the case, there is a tendency for investors in low tax brackets to hold debt and investors in high tax brackets to hold equity.

---

[10]Capital gains tax rates change from year to year as well as from country to country. For example, Hong Kong and Taiwan have no tax on capital gains. In the United States, the tax rate on capital gains has been as low as 40 percent of the ordinary income tax rate; in 1996 the highest federal tax rate on capital gains income was 28.0 percent while the highest rate on dividend and interest income was 39.6 percent. There also are state taxes on capital gains and interest and dividend income which could affect the attractiveness of debt and equity financing. State taxes differ from state to state and will not be considered in this text.

EXHIBIT 13.4   The Earnings Stream

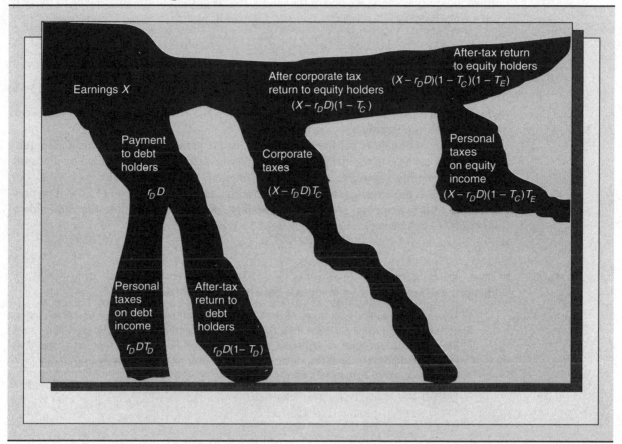

Earnings X

Payment to debt holders
$r_D D$

After corporate tax return to equity holders
$(X - r_D D)(1 - T_C)$

After-tax return to equity holders
$(X - r_D D)(1 - T_C)(1 - T_E)$

Corporate taxes
$(X - r_D D)T_C$

Personal taxes on equity income
$(X - r_D D)(1 - T_C)T_E$

Personal taxes on debt income
$r_D D T_D$

After-tax return to debt holders
$r_D D(1 - T_D)$

The Analysis When Investors Have Identical Tax Rates.   To understand how personal taxes affect the choice between issuing debt and issuing equity, consider the total cash flows accruing to the firm's debt and equity investors, who, for simplicity, are assumed to have the same personal tax rates, T_D and T_E. The after-tax cash flow C that these investors receive is determined by corporate taxes, personal taxes, and the way in which the firm is financed. Exhibit 13.4 illustrates this as a stream of cash that starts with all of the firm's realized pretax cash flows X and branches out into smaller streams which reflect the cash distributed to debt and equity holders, and to the government in the form of taxes. To keep this illustration simple, Exhibit 13.4 assumes that the firm pays out all of its earnings, and that its earnings before interest and taxes (*EBIT*) exceed its promised interest payment, $r_D D$.

As Exhibit 13.4 illustrates, some of the cash, $r_D D$, is diverted into a branch of the stream labeled "Payment to debt holders." This branch of the stream reaches a fork where some of the cash flows go to the government in the form of personal taxes on the debt interest payments while the rest goes to the debt holders as an after-tax return.

The upper branch of the stream carries the pretax cash that flows to the equity holders. Part of this cash, $(X - r_D D)T_c$, is diverted to the government in the form of corporate taxes. The remainder of the firm's cash flows, $(X - r_D D)(1 - T_c)$, flows to the firm's equity holders, where $(X - r_D D)(1 - T_c)T_E$ is diverted to the branch labeled "Personal taxes on equity income," with the rest going to equity holders as an after-tax return.

By summing the branches labeled after-tax return to debt holders and after-tax return to equity holders, we derive the total after-tax cash flow stream flowing to the debt and equity holders:

$$C = (X - r_D D)(1 - T_c)(1 - T_E) + r_D D(1 - T_D) \tag{13.5a}$$

By rearranging terms, equation (13.5a) can be rewritten as:

$$\tilde{C} = \tilde{X}(1 - T_c)(1 - T_D) + r_D D[(1 - T_D) - (1 - T_c)(1 - T_E)] \tag{13.5b}$$

where the last part of equation (13.5b), $r_D D[(1 - T_D) - (1 - T_c)(1 - T_E)]$, represents the tax gain from leverage.

If the level of debt is permanently fixed, this tax gain can be viewed as a perpetuity that accrues tax free to the firm's debt and equity investors. It can be valued by discounting the perpetuity payments at the after-(personal) tax rate on debt $r_D(1 - T_D)$ or, equivalently, at the after-(personal) tax return on equity (see equation (13.4)). The present value of this perpetual stream of tax savings, obtained by dividing the right side of equation (13.5b) by $r_D(1 - T_D)$, is gD where g is given by:

$$g = 1 - \left[\frac{(1 - T_c)(1 - T_E)}{1 - T_D} \right] \tag{13.6}$$

This generalizes Result 13.4 to include the effect of personal taxes.

Result 13.6   Assume that the pretax cash flows of the firm are unaffected by a change in a firm's capital structure, and that there are no transaction costs or opportunities for arbitrage. If investors all have personal tax rates on debt and equity returns of T_D and T_E, respectively, and if the corporate tax rate is T_c, then the value of a levered firm exceeds the value of an otherwise equivalent unlevered firm by gD, that is:

$$V_L = V_U + gD,$$

where

$$g = 1 - \left[\frac{(1 - T_c)(1 - T_E)}{1 - T_D} \right]$$

If g in equation (13.6) is positive, firms will want to issue enough debt to eliminate their tax liability; if g is negative, firms will want to include no debt in their capital structures. Firms will be indifferent about their debt level if g is zero, which is the case when the following equality holds:

$$(1 - T_D) = (1 - T_c)(1 - T_E) \tag{13.7}$$

When this equality holds, each investor pays directly in personal taxes and indirectly through the corporate tax the same amount in taxes for every pretax dollar that the firm earns. This holds regardless of whether the earnings are distributed in the form of interest payments to debt holders or accrue as capital gains to stockholders. Thus, the investor is indifferent about the capital structure choice.

An Analysis with Many Investors.   Result 13.6 was derived assuming that all investors are in the same personal tax bracket. Evaluating the tax advantage of debt financing becomes more complicated when investors have different marginal tax rates. However, it is possible to gain insight into the capital structure choice in this case by (1) analyzing an investor with tax rates that make him or her indifferent between holding debt or equity securities and (2) evaluating the firm's after-tax cost of capital, using debt versus equity financing.

As shown below, the *firm's* (risk-adjusted) after-tax cost of capital will be the same for debt and equity if equation (13.7) holds for this indifferent investor. To prove this, combine equation (13.7), which provides the condition for the firm to be indifferent between debt and equity, with equation (13.4), which provides the condition for an investor to be indifferent between holding debt or equity, to yield:

$$r_D(1 - T_c) = \bar{r}_E \tag{13.8}$$

The left-hand side of the equation is the *firm's* after-(corporate) tax cost of debt; the right-hand side its after-tax (and pretax) cost of equity. Thus, equation (13.8) states that the (risk-adjusted) after-tax cost of capital is the same for debt and equity whenever the investor who is indifferent between holding debt and equity has personal tax rates that make the firm indifferent about debt versus equity financing.

How Personal Taxes Affect the Capital Structure Choice: The Miller Equilibrium

In his 1976 presidential address to the American Finance Association, "Debt and Taxes," Merton Miller presented a model where, in equilibrium, firms are indifferent between financing their new investments by issuing debt or issuing equity. This model is called the **Miller equilibrium**. In the Miller equilibrium, equation (13.8) holds, so that the after-tax cost of debt equals the cost of equity financing.

To understand Miller's argument, we will first look at the demand by investors for debt and equity instruments. We then consider the incentive of firms to supply these instruments. The equilibrium in this market is determined at the point where the amount of debt and equity supplied by firms equals the amount of each instrument demanded by investors at the instruments' equilibrium rates of return.

To understand the Miller equilibrium, recall that if the pretax costs of debt and equity are equivalent on a risk-adjusted basis, debt is cheaper on an after–corporate tax basis. This is the case considered in Chapter 12 where a firm's weighted average cost of capital was shown to decline as the firm added debt to its capital structure. In this case, if there are no offsetting costs associated with debt financing, firms have an incentive to increase their debt levels and will do so by issuing debt to repurchase their own shares.

As Exhibit 13.5 illustrates, the Miller equilibrium assumes that the supply curve for debt, the light blue line, is flat. Since Miller assumes that there are no costs associated with debt financing (e.g., no bankruptcy costs), firms will use debt financing exclusively if the cost of debt, $r_D(1 - T_c)$, is less than the cost of equity, $\bar{r}_E$, and they will use equity financing exclusively otherwise.

Tax exempt investors are willing to invest their entire portfolio in debt as long as its expected rate of return exceeds the expected rate of return of equity. The demand curve for debt, the dark blue line, would then be flat up to the point where the supply of funds from tax-exempt investors is exhausted. To induce taxable investors to hold debt instruments, a return premium must be offered because debt is a tax-disadvantaged instrument from their perspective. Hence, the demand curve slopes upward after the point at which the tax-exempt investors are fully invested, reflecting the fact that investors in higher tax brackets require increasingly higher debt returns to hold debt instead of equity.

To understand the Miller equilibrium, consider first the case where the pretax (risk-adjusted) returns on debt and equity are the same. In this case, firms have an incentive to increase leverage and will continue to replace equity with debt financing, moving up the demand curve and increasing the return they offer to debt investors until the after-tax cost of debt equals the cost of equity. This point is reached at the intersection of the supply and demand curves in Exhibit 13.5.

EXHIBIT 13.5   Miller Equilibrium

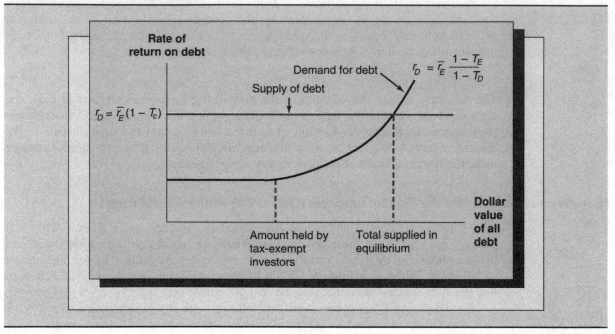

In this equilibrium, the investor who is indifferent between holding debt and equity must have tax rates that satisfy equation (13.4), $r_D(1 - T_D) = \bar{r}_E(1 - T_E)$, and the equilibrium rates from the supply curve, $r_D(1 - T_c) = \bar{r}_E$, must be satisfied. By combining the above equations, we see that the tax rates for the indifferent investor satisfy:

$$(1 - T_D) = (1 - T_c)(1 - T_E)$$

In other words, from the perspective of the investor who is indifferent between holding debt and equity, there is no tax gain from leverage for the firm.

The conditions that must be satisfied for the existence of the equilibrium described above are described in Result 13.7.

Result 13.7   *(The Miller equilibrium.)* If the following assumptions hold:

- the interest deduction for debt always reduces taxes at the margin, that is, firms experience positive earnings after paying interest;
- $(1 - T_D)$ is less than $(1 - T_c)(1 - T_E)$ for some investors, that is, investors who prefer equity to debt;
- there are no costs such as bankruptcy costs associated with increasing debt levels,

then in equilibrium, $g = 0$, that is, $(1 - T_D) = (1 - T_c)(1 - T_E)$ and $r_D(1 - T_c) = \bar{r}_E$. This implies that firms should be indifferent about leverage when both corporate taxes and personal taxes are taken into account.

Discussion of the Miller Equilibrium.   In the Miller equilibrium, the total supply of debt in the economy is determined at the intersection of the supply and demand curves illustrated in Exhibit 13.5. However, the amount of debt supplied by each firm is a matter of indifference.

That such an important decision is a matter of indifference is not unusual in economics. Consider a group of farmers who can produce either apples or oranges. If competition eliminates economic rents from both products, the farmers will be indifferent about which product to produce. However, consumer tastes will determine the mix of apples and oranges produced in the entire economy. Similarly, in the Miller equilibrium, competition implies that the relative advantages associated with issuing debt and equity securities vanish, making firms ultimately indifferent about which to issue. Again, consumer tastes—in this case, investor tastes for receiving ordinary income instead of capital gains—determine the mix of debt and equity in the economy as a whole.

Capital Structure Choices When Taxable Earnings Are Low

The assumption of the Miller model, that firms can always utilize their interest tax shields, is unrealistic for many firms. Many firms have extremely low taxable earnings even before taking into account the interest tax deduction. For example, many start-up firms with substantial R&D and depreciation deductions, and very little current revenues, have no taxable earnings.

Since firms with low taxable earnings will not always be able to take advantage of the tax gain associated with leverage, they will prefer equity financing if the returns on equity and debt satisfy equation (13.8) for those firms that will be paying corporate taxes with certainty; that is, $\bar{r}_E = (1 - T_c)r_D$, where T_c is the corporate tax rate for those firms that will be paying the full corporate tax rate. In other words, firms that are indifferent between debt and equity when they are assured of using the debt tax deduction will prefer equity financing when they are uncertain about being able to use the tax deduction. To induce such firms to issue debt, (1) the (risk-adjusted) after-tax cost of debt must be less than the (risk-adjusted) cost of equity when the firm can use the debt tax shield.[11] In addition, if firms are to include equity in their capital structures, (2) the cost of debt financing must be greater than the cost of equity financing when the firm cannot take advantage of the interest tax deduction. Statements (1) and (2) imply:

$$r_D > \bar{r}_E > (1 - T_c)\bar{r}_D \qquad (13.9)$$

The inequality $\bar{r}_E > (1 - T_c)\bar{r}_D$ implies that a firm that has positive taxable income $(X > r_D D)$ would have achieved a lower cost of capital if it had issued more debt. However, the inequality $r_D > \bar{r}_E$ implies that a firm with negative taxable income $(X < r_D D)$, which cannot take advantage of the interest tax deduction, would have achieved a lower cost of capital had it issued more equity.

If the inequalities in equation (13.9) are satisfied, firms will have an optimal capital structure consisting of both debt and equity. Under certainty, the optimal capital structure includes just enough debt to eliminate the firm's taxable earnings $(X = r_D D)$. When firms are uncertain about their taxable earnings, their optimal debt levels can be determined by weighing the costs associated with using higher-cost debt in situations where the firm cannot use the interest tax shield against the benefit of having a lower after-tax cost of capital in situations where the firm can use the full debt tax shield.

This point is illustrated below.

Prodist and Pharmcorp
Consider two firms that initially have equal amounts of debt.

- The first firm, Prodist, is engaged primarily in production and distribution while the second firm, Pharmcorp, is a pharmaceutical company with high R&D expenditures.

---

[11]See DeAngelo and Masulis (1980) for a discussion of this point.

- Assume that each firm currently has equal revenues and wishes to raise $14 million in new capital with either debt or equity. (For simplicity, rule out the possibility of a debt-equity mix.)
- Assume that Pharmcorp's taxable income is negative because the firm has high R&D expenditures. However, Prodist has no nondebt tax shields; therefore, it has a positive taxable income. When evaluating whether to issue debt or equity, the firms take into account the following information:

$$\bar{r}_D = 12\%$$
$$\bar{r}_E = 10\%$$
$$\text{Capital to be raised} = \$14,000,000$$
$$T_c = 34\%$$

Therefore, $\bar{r}_D(12\%) > \bar{r}_E(10\%) > (1 - T_c)\bar{r}_D(7.92\%)$.

Exhibit 13.6 illustrates how the capital structure choices of Prodist and Pharmco affect the cash flows to the original shareholders of each firm, assuming that the firms held no previous debt. Exhibit 13.6 shows the after-tax cash flows available to the equity holders when the two firms issue debt and when they issue equity. In this scenario, Pharmco equity holders are better off if the firm issues equity because they receive $54,600 instead of $54,320, whereas Prodist's shareholders are better off if the firm issues debt because they receive $35,851 instead of $35,560. The companies make different decisions because Prodist receives the tax shield benefit of debt and Pharmco does not.

Exhibit 13.6 assumes that Pharmco's negative taxable earnings and Prodist's positive taxable earnings are certain. Of course, earnings are likely to be uncertain in the real world. Nevertheless, since Pharmco has high R&D expenditures at any given debt level, the possibility of its having negative taxable income during some period is much more likely than it would be for Prodist. As a result, Pharmco's optimal capital structure is likely to include less debt than that of Prodist.

EXHIBIT 13.6   Debt-Equity Trade-Offs for a Distribution Company and a Pharmaceutical Company

Item	Prodist (Distribution Company)		Pharmcorp (Pharmaceutical Company)	
	Debt (in $000s)	*Equity (in $000s)*	*Debt (in $000s)*	*Equity (in $000s)*
	$ 56,000	$ 56,000	$ 56,000	$ 56,000
− Nondebt tax shields	0	0	− 58,000	− 58,000
EBIT	56,000	56,000	− 2,000	− 2,000
− Interest expense	− 1,680	0	− 1,680	0
Taxable income	54,320	56,000	− 3,680	− 2,000
− Corporate tax ($T_c = 34\%$)	− 18,469	− 19,040	0	
Net income	35,851	36,960	− 3,680	− 2,000
Return to new shareholders (10% of $14,000)	0	− 1,400	0	− 1,400
Tax shields subtracted earlier for tax purposes			58,000	58,000
Cash flows available to original shareholders	$ 35,851	$ 35,560	$ 54,320	$ 54,600

Given that firms with nondebt tax shields, such as large depreciation and research and development expenditures, are more likely to have negative taxable income at any given debt level, they should have lower debt levels than firms without nondebt tax shields. Nondebt tax shields are probably an important determinant of the capital structures of biotech firms such as Amgen which may have substantial value but very little taxable earnings in the near future. However, nondebt tax shields are probably not relevant to the capital structure choice of a firm like AT&T with a long history of positive taxable earnings. If AT&T were to realize negative taxable income in the present year, it could use the losses to offset past earnings and receive an immediate refund. If the tax losses are very large, it could defer them to offset future earnings. Thus, it would be extremely unlikely for AT&T to lose the tax benefits associated with debt financing.[12] Hence, from a pure tax standpoint, AT&T may be better off issuing debt to fund its new investment. However, start-up firms with large depreciation write-offs and R&D expenditures may have negative or only slightly positive taxable incomes for a long period of time. Since these firms may not be able to take advantage of available tax credits even if they can be deferred for many years, they will be better off financing their investments with equity instead of debt.

Result 13.8 summarizes the implications of the above discussion.

Result 13.8   Assume there is a tax gain from leverage, but the taxable earnings of firms are low relative to their total values.

- Firms will want to use debt financing up to the point where they eliminate their entire corporate tax liabilities, but they will not want to borrow beyond that point.
- With uncertainty, firms will pick the debt ratio that weighs the benefits associated with the debt tax shield, when it can be used, against the higher cost of debt in cases where the debt tax shield cannot be used.
- Firms with more nondebt tax shields are likely to use less debt financing.

13.6 Taxes and Preferred Stock

Chapter 3 noted that preferred stock is similar to a bond because it has a fixed payout. In contrast to bonds, however, preferred shareholders cannot force the firm into bankruptcy if the firm fails to meet its dividend obligation. Although the claims of a preferred stockholder are always junior to the claims of the firm's debt holders in the event of bankruptcy, such claims are senior to the claims of the firm's common stockholders. The common stockholders cannot receive a dividend until the preferred dividends (including all past dividends) are paid. In addition, preferred shareholders, unlike debt holders, often have voting rights.

Perhaps one of the most important differences between preferred stock and bonds is that the dividends of preferred stock are not tax deductible while the coupon payments of a bond are. This has led some analysts to conclude that subordinated bonds provide cheaper financing than preferred stock. However, a feature of the U.S. tax code provides an incentive for the use of preferred stock. For corporate holders, preferred dividends (as well as common dividends) carry a 70 percent tax exclusion. In other words, if a

---

[12]Current tax laws allow a firm to carry back the net losses in its current year as far as three years. When there is not enough income in the previous three years to allow the loss carryback, the firm can carry forward those losses for up to 15 years to offset future taxable profits.

corporation owns the preferred stock of another corporation, only 30 percent of the dividend received by the original corporation is taxable. Consequently, the required yield on a firm's preferred stock is often less than the yield on its bonds, despite the bond's senior status in the event of bankruptcy. Example 13.5 illustrates this point.

Example 13.5:   The Effect of Taxes on the Decision to Invest in Preferred Stock
Connolly Partners, Inc., seeks to invest excess funds in either the straight bonds or preferred stock of Pacific Gas and Electric (PG&E). In March 1990, a 10.125 percent PG&E bond had a yield to maturity of 9.79 percent. The 10.18 percent preferred stock, although riskier, was yielding a 9.4 percent dividend. If Connolly's marginal tax rate is 34 percent, which alternative will it prefer?

Answer: Connolly Partners will receive an after-tax yield of 6.46 percent (.66 × 9.79%) if it invests in the bonds and an after-tax yield of 8.44 percent [(9.4% × .30 × .66) + (9.4% × .70)] in the preferred stock. In this case, the preferential tax treatment gives the firm an incentive to invest in preferred stock even though the preferred stock is riskier and has a lower yield.

A firm that is certain to have positive taxable earnings will have a lower after-tax cost of capital if it issues a bond instead of preferred stock. However, if the firm is likely to have negative taxable earnings for several years in the future, the interest tax deduction will have no value, and preferred stock will provide the lower cost of capital. By issuing preferred stock when it cannot use the interest tax deduction, the firm is, in a sense, selling the tax deduction that it cannot use to another firm that does have taxable income. The firm that buys the preferred stock is willing to offer a more favorable borrowing rate because only 30 percent of the preferred dividend is taxable.

13.7 Taxes and Municipal Bonds

The largest shareholders in a corporation are likely to be either tax-exempt investors or individuals who pay the maximum personal tax rate. Recall that tax-exempt investors experience an increase in their cash flows when the firms whose shares they own increase their leverage. If these investors find the additional risk associated with the leverage increase undesirable, they can undo it by selling some of their stock and buying the corporation's bonds. However, the analysis in Section 13.5 suggests that shareholders in a high tax bracket have an offsetting personal tax cost associated with an increase in the firm's leverage. As a result, conflicts between the interests of taxable and tax-exempt shareholders are likely.

In general, the taxable and tax-exempt shareholders will not agree about the correct policy for a corporation if each group votes as shareholders. However, our analysis may have exaggerated the personal tax costs associated with debt for shareholders in the maximum tax brackets because it ignores the ability of taxable investors to lower their personal tax burdens by holding tax-exempt municipal bonds in lieu of corporate bonds. Historically, yields on tax-exempt municipal bonds, while less than corporate bond yields, have generally been substantially greater than the after-tax yields on corporate bonds for investors in high tax brackets (see Exhibit 13.7). This suggests that corporations can probably increase the after-tax cash flow to their high-tax-bracket shareholders, as well as their low tax bracket shareholders, by increasing leverage, with shareholders undoing or, offsetting, this increase, if they so desire, by selling shares and increasing their tax-exempt bond holdings.

Exhibit 13.7   Historical Yields on AAA Taxable and Tax-Exempt Bonds

Year	Municipal Bond Yield (%)	Corporate Bond Yield (%)	T_c	$(1 - T_c) \times (Corp. Bond Yield)(\%)$
1960	4.1%	4.6%	0.48	2.4%
1970	5.2	7.6	0.48	4.0
1980	9.4	13.2	0.46	7.1
1990	6.6	9.1	0.34	6.0
1995	5.4	6.8	0.34	4.5

To illustrate this point, reconsider Example 13.3 where the investor initially holds 10 percent of the firm's equity and in the absence of corporate taxes realizes a cash flow of:

$$.1[\tilde{X} - r_D\$10,000]$$

With corporate taxes, the cash flow to the investor will be:

$$.1[\tilde{X} - r_D\$10,000](1 - T_c)$$

Assume once again that the firm wishes to increase its leverage, so it repurchases 500 outstanding shares at $100 per share and issues $50,000 in corporate bonds. In the no-tax example, the investor was able to undo the effect of this increase in leverage on his or her personal portfolio by selling 50 shares of the firm's stock and buying $5,000 of the new corporate bonds. However, given personal taxes, the individual may be better off using the proceeds from the sale of $5,000 in stock to buy municipal bonds with returns of r_m rather than the corporate bonds. If the firm increases its leverage and the investor undoes the effect of this action by buying tax-free municipal bonds, he or she will receive an after-tax cash flow of:

$$.1[\tilde{X} - r_D\$60,000](1 - T_c)(1 - T_E) + r_m\$5,000$$

Rearranging terms in the above expression yields the following expression for the after-tax cash flows of a taxable investor holding stock plus municipal bonds:

$$.1\tilde{X}(1 - T_c)(1 - T_E) - .1r_D(\$10,000)(1 - T_c)(1 - T_E) + [r_m - r_D(1 - T_c)(1 - T_E)]\,(\$5,000)$$

where the bracketed term $[r_m - r_D(1 - T_c)(1 - T_E)]\ \$5,000$ is the gain in after-tax cash flows from this transaction.

Exhibit 13.7 shows that this bracketed term has been positive for at least the last 30 years. Hence, even investors in the highest tax bracket could have higher after-tax cash flows if the firms in which they held equity had higher debt-to-equity ratios.

13.8 The Effect of Inflation on the Tax Gain from Leverage

Recall that the last part of equation (13.5b) had an expression for the yearly saving associated with increased leverage. Note that $r_D D[(1 - T_D) - (1 - T_c)(1 - T_E)]$, the tax gain, increases as the interest rate on corporate debt increases. Although interest rates for corporate borrowers can change for a number of reasons, the most notable cause is a change in the expected rate of inflation. If investors expect inflation to be high, nominal borrowing costs will also be high, reflecting the decreased purchasing power of the dollars used to repay the loans.

Fisher's (1930) well-known theory of interest rate changes postulates a one-to-one relation between interest rates and expected inflation; that is, if inflation is expected to be one percentage point higher, the nominal interest rate also increases by approximately one percentage point.[13] This suggests that an increase in inflation increases the tax gain associated with leverage for firms that will be able to use the interest tax deductions. Higher rates of inflation imply higher nominal borrowing costs which, in turn, create higher tax deductions. Example 13.6 illustrates how increases in inflation can reduce taxable income and hence reduce taxes.

Example 13.6:   The Effect of Inflation on Prodist's Corporate Taxes
Prodist (see Exhibit 13.6) has a large amount of taxable income. It raised $140 million with 12 percent notes. Show the impact of a 4 percent increase in inflation, assuming that this increases the rate on the notes to 16 percent and that the inflation-adjusted, cash flows are unchanged.

Answer: The assumed inflation increases Prodist's tax shield from $16.8 million to $22.4 million, as shown below:

	Cash Flows (in $millions) Given		
	Low Inflation	*High Inflation*	*Difference*
Inflation-adjusted cash flows	$ 56.00	$ 56.00	—
− Interest expense (= Tax shields)	− 16.80	− 22.40	+ $5.6
Taxable income	39.20	33.60	− $5.6
Corporate tax (34%)	13.33	11.42	$1.9

In this case, the increase in inflation of 4 percent leads to a $5.6 million increase in tax shields for the same amount of debt. While this suggests that inflation encourages higher leverage ratios, this is true only when a firm can take advantage of all of its tax shields. By increasing the magnitude of the tax deduction for each dollar of debt, inflation reduces the amount of debt needed to eliminate the firm's taxable income. Since firms have no tax incentive to borrow beyond this point, firms that previously had little taxable income may reduce their leverage ratios when inflation increases.

13.9 Are There Tax Advantages to Leasing?

Up to this point, we have assumed that firms finance their capital assets by raising either debt or equity capital. This section considers the tax advantages and disadvantages associated with a third financing possibility: leasing the capital assets.

---

[13]See Chapter 12.

Operating Leases and Capital Leases

As Chapter 2 discussed, an *operating lease* is an agreement to obtain the services of an asset for a period that generally represents only a small part of the asset's useful life. For example, one might lease a car for three years. At the end of this period, the lease may or may not be extended. In a *financial lease* (also known as a *capital lease*), the lease agreement extends over most of the asset's useful life.

The decision to enter into an operating lease generally relates to the transaction costs associated with buying and selling the assets. For example, leasing rather than buying a car makes sense if you need a car for only two months. Other issues relevant to the "lease versus buy" decision include information about the resale value of an asset, potential renegotiation problems at the end of the lease (e.g., you might want to keep the asset longer), and incentive problems (e.g., you might be likely to drive a car differently if you leased rather than bought it).

The above considerations are much less relevant for financial leases, which should be considered more or less as a financing alternative that is equivalent to buying the asset with borrowed funds. The major difference between buying an asset with borrowed funds and leasing the equipment relates to the timing of payments, which in turn affects the tax treatment of the two alternatives.

The After-Tax Costs of Leasing and Buying Capital Assets

In general, an organization in a low tax bracket has an incentive to lease equipment from organizations in higher tax brackets. To understand this, consider the issues faced by the University of California, Los Angeles (UCLA) when its business school moved into a new building in 1995. Although the university did not consider the option of leasing the building rather than buying it, examining the tax advantages of this alternative is instructive. We will assume that if the building is owned, it is funded with an amortizing mortgage over the 50-year life of the building, which we assume is worthless after 50 years. To simplify the illustration, the amortization of the mortgage (i.e., its schedule of debt repayments) is assumed to be identical to the *economic depreciation* of the building. Because UCLA is a tax-exempt institution, calculating its costs of renting versus owning the building is straightforward. Its yearly costs of owning the building are:

$$\text{Cost of owning} = \text{debt repayment} + \text{interest cost} \qquad (13.10)$$

Leasing Costs in a Competitive Market.   If the leasing market is competitive, the costs of the *lessor,* who owns the building, must be passed on to the *lessee,* who rents the building, in this case, UCLA. To calculate the cost of leasing the building, assume that the lessor pays taxes at a rate T_c and charges a lease rate that just compensates for these costs, so that each year its after-tax lease revenues equal its after-tax costs.

$$(\text{Lease payment}) \times (1 - T_c) = \text{debt repayment} + (\text{interest cost}) \times (1 - T_c)$$
$$- (\text{depreciation deduction}) \times T_c.$$

This equation can be solved to determine the yearly lease payments that allow the lessor to break even in each year:

$$\text{Lease payment} = \frac{\text{debt repayment} - (\text{depreciation deduction}) \times T_c}{1 - T_c} + \text{interest cost} \quad (13.11)$$

When Is Leasing Cheaper than Buying?   Consider first the case where the building is *depreciated for tax purposes* at the same rate that the mortgage amortizes; that is, tax depreciation equals actual depreciation. Assume also that the mortgage is paid off over time, so that the loan's value always equals the depreciated value of the building. Under these assumptions, debt repayment and the depreciation deduction are equal, so that equation (13.11) can be rewritten as:

$$\text{Lease payment} = \text{debt repayment} + \text{interest cost} \qquad (13.12)$$

A comparison of equations (13.10) and (13.12) implies that each annual lease payment equals the annual cost of owning the building in this case. This implies that a lessor who can take advantage of **accelerated depreciation**—depreciation for tax purposes at a rate that initially occurs faster than economic depreciation (and accordingly, faster than the debt repayment in the lease's early years) would profit from the lease payment stream given in equation (13.12). This is because, holding the sum of an undiscounted stream of tax benefits constant, the sooner the tax benefits occur, the greater is their present value. Hence, if the lease payments specified in equation (13.12) make the asset purchase and attached lease a zero *NPV* investment for an investor who cannot enjoy accelerated depreciation, the hastened tax benefits from accelerated depreciation must make the same investment a positive *NPV* one.

Such an investor could easily afford to lower UCLA's lease payments on the building and still turn a profit. UCLA, being tax-exempt, and thus unable to enjoy the tax benefits from depreciating the building, would thus find it cheaper to lease from such an investor rather than to buy the building outright. The lesson is as follows:

Result 13.9   For low tax bracket investors, it is often cheaper to lease an asset than to buy it.

The tax advantage of leasing instead of buying applies not only to tax-exempt institutions, but also to any institution or corporation that is taxed at a rate less than the full corporate tax rate. Corporations that are temporarily in a zero marginal tax bracket often use leases for exactly this reason. Earlier, we suggested that such firms should use a higher portion of equity financing to minimize the unused tax benefits. A better solution, however, may be to lease equipment which might allow some of the tax benefits, in essence, to be sold to other tax-paying corporations.

Given this analysis, why did UCLA buy rather than lease its new building? In theory, UCLA can sell its new building to a taxable investor, invest the proceeds in bonds, and lease the building back at a rate that is less than the amount it receives in interest payments. The difference between the lease payments and the interest proceeds would come from the tax benefits that UCLA would in effect be selling to the lessor.

Since most of the money for the UCLA building was donated, it might be difficult to structure a deal that involved a lease. In addition, the IRS might not recognize this transaction as a *true lease* for tax purposes and might disallow the lessor's tax deductions. Whether a lease is considered a true lease for tax purposes depends on the intent of the parties. Specifically, if the IRS rules that UCLA, in effect, owns the building— that is, it receives all the benefits and takes all the risks associated with ownership—then the lessor's depreciation benefits may not be allowed.

To qualify for the tax advantages of leasing, the lessor must take on some of the risk associated with the appreciation or the depreciation of the asset being leased. As noted earlier, however, incentive problems can arise when the lessee's behavior affects the asset's value. The lessor will charge the lessee for the costs arising from these incentive problems, which may offset the tax advantages of leasing.

13.10 The Empirical Implications of the Analysis of Debt and Taxes

We have suggested in this chapter that taxes play an important role in determining the debt-equity mix of U.S. corporations. Firms that are generating substantial taxable earnings before interest and taxes (*EBIT*) should use a substantial amount of debt financing to take advantage of the tax deductibility of the interest payments. However, firms with substantial amounts of other tax shields, such as depreciation deductions and R&D expenses, are likely to have much lower *EBIT* relative to their values and would thus choose lower debt-equity ratios. Hence, in a comparison across firms, there should be a negative correlation between a firm's nondebt tax shields and its debt ratio.

Do Firms with More Taxable Earnings Use More Debt Financing?

In reality, we do not observe a positive cross-sectional relation between *EBIT* and debt ratios (see, for example, Titman and Wessels (1988)). Indeed, those firms that generate the largest amount of taxable earnings tend to have the lowest debt ratios, which is the opposite of what we might expect from the analysis in this chapter. This negative correlation between *EBIT* and debt-equity ratios probably arises because firms only rarely issue new equity, which implies the following[14]:

- Nondebt tax shields and the use of debt financing are positively correlated because firms tend to finance most major capital expenditures, which generate investment tax credits and depreciation deductions, with debt.
- Firms that perform poorly (i.e., have low or negative *EBIT*) tend to accumulate debt to meet their expenses.

The above observations, however, do not rule out the possibility that firms take taxes into account when they consider whether or not to issue equity. Indeed, a study by Mackie-Mason (1990) found that firms do consider the tax benefits when they decide between issuing substantial amounts of either new debt or new equity. Firms that are unable to use their interest deductions are much more likely to issue equity than debt. In contrast, firms that have significant taxable earnings are more likely to issue debt.

How the Tax Reform Act of 1986 Affected Capital Structure Choice

Changes in the tax code also provide a way to judge the importance of taxes. Givoly, Hayn, Ofer, and Sarig (1992) examined how the Tax Reform Act of 1986, which reduced the level of nondebt tax shields for most companies, affected capital structures in the years following the tax change.[15] They found that corporations that lost the most nondebt tax shields under the 1986 act increased their debt levels more than firms that were less affected by the new tax law. This evidence provides further support to the Mackie-Mason finding that taxes play a key role in determining the optimal capital structure of firms.

---

[14]There are personal tax as well as information explanations for this behavior. See Chapters 14, 16, and 18.

[15]In addition to reducing both corporate and personal income taxes, the Tax Reform Act of 1986 substantially reduced or eliminated most tax shields. Most notably, the act eliminated investment tax credits and reduced the amount that buildings and equipment could be depreciated for tax purposes.

13.11 Summary and Conclusions

This chapter analyzed how taxes affect the capital structures of firms. In the absence of taxes and other market imperfections, the value of a firm is independent of how it is financed. However, the interest tax deduction makes debt financing less expensive than equity financing, which implies that in the absence of personal taxes and other market frictions, firms should use sufficient debt to eliminate their entire corporate tax liabilities.

Personal taxes somewhat offset the tax advantage of debt financing. Because equity returns (often taxed as capital gains) are taxed at a more favorable personal rate than debt, the pretax (risk-adjusted) expected rate of return on equity may be lower than the pretax (risk-adjusted) expected rate of return on debt. When considering personal as well as corporate taxes, it is possible that the risk-adjusted after-tax costs of debt and equity are equal. However, current tax rates along with the observed gap between the rates on taxable corporate bonds and tax-exempt municipal bonds suggest that, in reality, there is still a tax advantage to debt financing.

Although the analysis up to this point presents a fairly complete discussion of the corporate tax advantages of debt financing, the discussion of personal taxes remains incomplete. Chapter 14, which completes our analysis of taxes, analyzes how personal taxes affect a firm's dividend policy. The effect of taxes on dividend policy can have an important effect on its capital structure because earnings that are not distributed to shareholders are retained within the firm and add to its equity base. Indeed, most new equity on corporate balance sheets comes from retained earnings rather than new equity issues. Hence, no discussion of the effect of taxes on capital structure is complete without considering the effect of taxes on dividend policy.

Of course, taxes are only one aspect of a corporation's capital structure choice. Corporate executives often express concerns about the ability of their firms to meet debt obligations and about how debt financing affects their firms' access to investment capital in the future. More recently, executives have started to consider the beneficial role that debt has on management incentives, and the information conveyed to stockholders by their financing decisions. These and other topics are discussed in future chapters.

Key Concepts

Result 13.1: *(The Modigliani-Miller Theorem.)* Assuming: (1) a firm's total cash flows to security holders are independent of how it is financed; (2) there are no transaction costs; and (3) no arbitrage opportunities exist in the economy, then the total market value of the firm, which is the same as the sum of the market values of the items on the right-hand side of the balance sheet (i.e., its debt and equity), is independent of how it is financed.

Result 13.2: If a firm's original debt holders have a senior claim in the event of bankruptcy, then the values of both the firm's stock and its existing debt are invariant to changes in the firm's capital structure under the assumptions listed in Result 13.1.

Result 13.3: If a firm's original debt holders do not have a senior claim in the event of bankruptcy, a new debt issue can decrease the value of existing debt. Under the assumptions listed in Result 13.1, however, the loss of the old debt holders would be offset by a gain to the equity holders, making the total value of the firm invariant to this type of capital structure change.

Result 13.4: Assume that the pretax cash flows of the firm are unaffected by a change in a firm's capital structure, and that there are no transaction costs or opportunities for arbitrage. If the corporate tax rate is T_c, then the value of a levered firm with static risk-free perpetual debt is the value of an otherwise equivalent unlevered firm plus the product of the corporate tax rate and the market value of the firm's debt, that is:

$$V_L = V_U + T_c D$$

Result 13.5: Assume that the pretax cash flows of the firm are unaffected by a change in a firm's capital structure, and that there are no transaction costs or opportunities for arbitrage. With corporate taxes but no personal taxes, a firm's optimal capital structure will include enough debt to completely eliminate the firm's tax liabilities.

Result 13.6: Assume that the pretax cash flows of the firm are unaffected by a change in a firm's capital structure, and that there are no transaction costs of opportunities for arbitrage. If investors all have personal tax rates on debt and equity returns of T_D and T_E, respectively, and if the corporate tax rate is T_c, then the value of a levered firm exceeds the value of an otherwise equivalent unlevered firm by gD, that is:

$$V_L = V_U + gD,$$

where

$$g = 1 - \left[\frac{(1 - T_c)(1 - T_E)}{1 - T_D}\right]$$

Result 13.7: *(The Miller equilibrium model.)* If the following assumptions hold:

- the interest deduction for debt always reduces taxes at the margin, that is, firms experience positive earnings after paying interest;
- $(1 - T_D)$ is less than $(1 - T_c)(1 - T_E)$ for some investors, that is, some investors prefer equity to debt;
- there are no costs such as bankruptcy costs associated with increasing debt levels,

then in equilibrium, $g = 0$, that is, $(1 - T_D) = (1 - T_c)(1 - T_E)$ and $r_D(1 - T_c) = \bar{r}_E$. This implies that firms should be indifferent about leverage when both corporate taxes and personal taxes are taken into account.

Result 13.8: Assume there is a tax gain from leverage, but the taxable earnings of firms are low relative to their total values.

- Firms will want to use debt financing up to the point where they eliminate their entire corporate tax liabilities, but they will not want to borrow beyond that point.
- With uncertainty, firms will pick the debt ratio that weighs the benefits associated with the debt tax shield, when it can be used, against the higher cost of debt in cases where the debt tax shield cannot be used.
- Firms with more nondebt tax shields are likely to use less debt financing.

Result 13.9: For low tax bracket investors, it is often cheaper to lease an asset than to buy it.

Key Terms

accelerated depreciation   512
Miller equilibrium   503

Modigliani-Miller Theorem   489
nondebt tax shields   500

Exercises

13.1.   Suppose $r_D = 12\%$ $\bar{r}_E = 10\%$ $T_c = 33\%$ $T_D = 20\%$.
   a. What is the marginal tax rate on stock income T_E which would make an investor indifferent in terms of after-tax returns between holding stock or bonds? Assume all betas are zero.
   b. What is the probability that a firm will not utilize its tax shield if, on the margin, the firm is indifferent between issuing a little more debt or equity?

13.2.   Consider a single period binomial setting where the riskless interest rate is zero, and there are no taxes. A firm consists of a machine that will produce cash flows of $210 if the economy is good and $80 if the economy is bad. The good and bad states occur with equal risk-neutral probability. Initially, the firm has 100 shares outstanding and debt with a face value of $50 due at the end of the period. What is the share price of the firm?

13.3.   Suppose the firm in exercise 13.2 unexpectedly announces that it will issue additional debt, with the same seniority as existing debt and a face value of $50. The firm will use the entire proceeds to repurchase some of the outstanding shares.
   a. What is the market price of the new debt?
   b. Just after the announcement, what will the price of a share jump to?
   c. Show how a shareholder with 20 percent of the shares outstanding is better off as a result of this transaction when he or she undoes the leverage change.
   d. Show how the Modigliani-Miller Theorem still holds.

13.4.   Assume that the real riskless interest rate is zero and the corporate tax rate is 33 percent. IGWT Industries can borrow at the riskless interest rate. It will have an inflation-adjusted *EBIT* next year of $200 million. It would like to borrow $50 million today. Its only deductions will be interest payments (if any).

    a. What are its interest payments, taxable income, tax payments, and income left for shareholders in a no-inflation environment?

    b. Suppose there is inflation of 10 percent per year, but the real interest rate stays at zero. This means that investors now will require a sure payment of $1.10 next year for each $1.00 loaned today. Repeat part *a*, assuming that *EBIT* is affected by inflation.

    c. In which environment is the inflation-adjusted income left for shareholders higher? Why?

13.5. As owner of 10 percent of ABC Industries, you have control of its capital structure decision. The current corporate tax rate is 34 percent and your personal tax rate is 31 percent. Assume that the returns to stockholders accrue as nontaxable capital gains. ABC currently has no debt and can finance the repurchase of 10 percent of its outstanding shares by borrowing $100 million at the risk free rate of 10 percent. The AAA (tax-free) municipal bond rate is 8 percent. If you hold your 10 percent of the firm constant and buy the municipal bonds, what is your after-tax gain from this transaction?

13.6. Explain how inflation affects the capital structure decision. Does inflation affect the capital structure choice differently for different firms?

13.7. Assume the corporate tax rate is 50 percent, AAA corporate bonds are trading at a yield of 9 percent, and municipal bonds are trading at a yield of 6 percent. How can the shareholders of an AAA-rated firm gain by increasing the leverage of their firm without increasing the leverage of their personal portfolio? Assume the probability of bankruptcy is zero.

13.8. During the early 1990s, most new airplanes were leased by the airlines. This was not true during the early and mid-1980s. Explain why.

13.9. Restaurant chains like McDonald's sometimes franchise their restaurants and sometimes own them outright. The franchised restaurants are usually owned by individuals who hold them in subchapter S corporations which pass income through directly to the owners. There is no corporate tax on this income, but the owner must pay personal taxes on the income.

    a. From the perspective of the owner of the franchise, is there a tax advantage to debt financing?

    b. Which organizational form is better from the perspective of tax minimization: corporate ownership of the individual restaurants or franchises?

13.10 Real estate investment trusts (REITs) are companies set up to manage investment properties like office buildings and apartment houses. REITs are not subject to corporate taxes and are required to pass through 95 percent of their income to their shareholders who are taxed at the personal level. How do we expect taxes to affect the capital structure choice of REITs?

References and Additional Readings

Asquith, Paul, and Thierry Wizman. "Event Risk, Covenants, and Bondholder Returns in Leveraged Buyouts." *Journal of Financial Economics* 27 (1990), pp. 195–213.

DeAngelo, Harry, and Ronald Masulis. "Optimal Capital Structure under Corporate and Personal Taxes." *Journal of Financial Economics* 8 (1980), pp. 3–29.

Fisher, Irving. *The Theory of Interest.* 1930. Reprint, New York: Augustus Kelly, 1965.

Givoly, Dan; Carla Hayn; Aharon Ofer; and Oded Sarig. "Taxes and Capital Structure: Evidence from Firm's Response to the Tax Reform Act of 1986." *Review of Financial Studies* 5 (1992), pp. 331–55.

MacKie-Mason, Jeffrey K. "Do Taxes Affect Corporate Financing Decisions?" *Journal of Finance* 45 (1990), pp. 1471–95.

Miller, Merton. "Debt and Taxes." *Journal of Finance* 32 (1977), pp. 261–75.

Modigliani, Franco, and Merton H. Miller. "A Comment on the Modigliani-Miller Cost of Capital Thesis: Reply." *American Economic Review* 59, no. 4 (1969), pp. 592–95.

———. "Corporate Income Taxes and the Cost of Capital: A Correction." *American Economic Review* 53, no. 3 (1963), pp. 433–92.

———. "The Cost of Capital, Corporation Finance, and the Theory of Investment." *American Economic Review* 48, no. 3 (1958), pp. 261–97.

Titman, Sheridan, and Roberto Wessels. "The Determinants of Capital Structure Choice." *Journal of Finance* 43 (1988), pp. 1–20.

Warga, Arthur, and Ivo Welch. "Bondholder Losses in Leveraged Buyouts." *Review of Financial Studies* 6 (1993), pp. 959–82.

CHAPTER 14

How Taxes Affect Dividends and Share Repurchases

Learning Objectives

After reading this chapter, you should be able to:

1. Explain why, in the absence of personal taxes, there is an equivalence between dividends and share repurchases and why tax-paying investors prefer a share repurchase to a dividend payment.

2. Provide reasons for why firms pay taxed dividends instead of repurchasing shares.

3. Understand the difference between the classical tax system, which exists in the United States, and the imputation system, which exists in a number of other countries, and how these differences affect capital structures and dividend policies.

4. Understand empirical evidence about how expected stock returns relate to dividend yields.

5. Describe how personal taxes on dividend distributions can lead to distortions in both investment and financing decisions.

At the end of 1994, Kirk Kerkorian held 32 million shares of Chrysler, representing 9.2 percent of Chrysler's equity, and worth $1.57 billion. While Kerkorian expressed "high regard" for the management of Chrysler, he found its most recent stock price performance "very disappointing." Indeed, although Chrysler's stock price had increased by almost 400 percent since Kerkorian first started buying the stock in 1991, it began to fall during the last three quarters of 1994. In November, Kerkorian was quoted as saying: "It is essential that the company take positive steps to enhance shareholder value.[1]

To understand Kerkorian's disappointment, it is important to realize that Chrysler's stock price dropped from 63½ in January 1994 to 45⅛ in mid-November 1994. This drop represented a loss of $588 million for Kerkorian, which was more than the value of his original investment.

---

[1]"Kerkorian Pushes Chrysler to Improve Shareholder Value Update," *Bloomberg Business News,* Nov. 14, 1994.

Kerkorian's major objection was that Chrysler had accumulated about $7.5 billion in cash at the end of 1994, with projections of further cash increases to more than $8.6 billion by the end of 1995 and $11.3 billion by the end of 1996. Nevertheless, Chrysler maintained that it needed the large cash reserves to "weather the next recession."

In an effort to boost Chrysler's stock price, Kerkorian proposed in November 1994 that Chrysler:

- *Boost its dividends.*
- *Declare a two-for-one stock split.*
- *Undertake a stock repurchase plan.*
- *Remove its poison pill takeover defenses and allow him to increase his holdings.*

Dividend policy, which specifies a firm's policy about the distribution of cash to its shareholders, is perhaps the topic which financial economists have the most trouble discussing with corporate managers. Academics cite the **Miller-Modigliani dividend irrelevancy theorem** which states that, except for tax and transaction cost considerations, dividend policy is irrelevant. Corporate managers, however, who sometimes spend long hours considering their dividend choices, think that this irrelevance proposition is crazy. This difference of opinion persists despite numerous articles on the subject in professional and academic journals as well as academic forums that bring together participants from both academia and business.

The communication gap between financial economists and corporate managers stems, at least in part, from the fact that the two groups often consider different issues when they think about dividend policy. When corporate managers talk about optimal dividend policies, they are to a large extent really discussing the investment and cash payout policies of their firms. Managers are asking whether earnings could be better invested within the firm rather than outside the firm. They also think about how dividend policies affect their leverage ratios, and about the trade-offs between financing new investments with internally generated equity versus increasing dividends and funding the new investments with debt. In the Chrysler case described in this chapter's opening vignette, the company's managers are presumably considering how much cash to keep within the corporation and how much to distribute to shareholders.

Financial economists view the dividend choice from a narrower perspective, stressing that a firm's dividend choice need not be related to either its investment decisions or its leverage decision. Financial economists believe that any analysis of a firm's dividend policy should hold the firm's investment decisions and its capital structure choice constant. When they talk about Chrysler's dividend policy, they assume that a certain amount of cash will be paid out and ask whether Chrysler should distribute the cash by paying a dividend or by repurchasing shares.

As this chapter later shows, when investment choices and leverage ratios are held constant, the only alternative to paying a dividend is for the firm to use the funds to repurchase shares. Hence, most of the academic literature on dividend policy considers the pros and cons of paying dividends versus repurchasing shares. For example, the Miller-Modigliani dividend irrelevancy theorem does not say that the choice between paying dividends and retaining the earnings to either pay off debt or to fund new investment is a matter of indifference. Rather, it merely says that in the absence of tax and transaction cost considerations, the way in which the earnings are distributed to shareholders, that is, the choice between paying a dividend and repurchasing shares, does not affect shareholders.

This chapter analyzes how taxes and transaction costs affect the way firms distribute cash to their shareholders. It shows that share repurchases are the better alternative for most investors who must pay personal taxes. However, some tax-exempt investors may prefer receiving cash distributions in the form of dividends because of their lower transaction costs. The chapter also examines how personal taxes and transaction costs can make internally generated funds less expensive than externally generated funds. As a result, personal taxes and transaction costs affect how firms are financed as well as how investment choices are made.[2]

14.1 How Much of U.S. Corporate Earnings Is Distributed to Shareholders?

Have Dividend Payout Ratios Changed over Time?

Exhibit 14.1 on page 520 presents historical data on yearly aggregate after-tax earnings and dividends for U.S. corporations. The "Dividends ÷ Earnings" column of this exhibit indicates that U.S. corporations paid out, on average, approximately 50 percent of their earnings to shareholders in the form of cash dividends from 1971 to 1992. However, the ratio of dividends to profits, the **dividend payout ratio**, tends to decrease in years when earnings increase (e.g., 1984) and increase in years when earnings decrease (e.g., 1982). This means that at least in the aggregate, firms tend to smooth their dividends, adjusting them only partially to earnings increases and decreases. Lintner (1956) discovered that individual firms also tend to smooth their dividends. He found that managers aim to have steadily increasing dividends and, as a result, only slowly adjust dividends to increases in earnings.

Aggregate Share Repurchases and Dividends

Share repurchases provide firms with an alternative to cash dividends as a way to distribute earnings to shareholders. Firms acquire shares by either buying them on the open market or making a tender offer for a block of shares. Many countries outside the United States do not allow firms to buy back their own shares, and this practice was not done on a large scale in the United States prior to 1973.[3] The stock buybacks in the early 1970s were started subsequent to President Nixon's imposition of wage and price controls in 1971. Among the price controls were restrictions on dividend payouts. As a result, the only option available to firms that wished to substantially increase the cash distributed to shareholders was to repurchase their own shares.

Bagwell and Shoven (1989) reported that the first large share repurchase by a major corporation was the $1.4 billion repurchase by IBM in 1977, which represented close to half of the aggregate dollar volume of repurchases in that year. By the mid- to late-1980s, repurchases had increased substantially. Exhibit 14.2 on page 521 shows that during the late 1980s, large U.S. firms distributed about 70 percent as much cash in repurchases as they distributed in dividends. Many well-known companies, such as Union Carbide, Goodyear, Teledyne, and Exxon repurchased over half of their outstanding shares.

---

[2]In addition, as Chapter 20 discusses, the taxes and transaction costs associated with distributing cash also provide an important motive for why firms hedge their cash flows.

[3]Only recently have a number of other countries, like Hong Kong and a number of European countries, begun to allow firms to repurchase their own shares.

EXHIBIT 14.1   After-Tax Earnings and Dividends for All Corporations, 1971–92

Year	After-Tax Corporate Earnings (in $ billions)	Dividends (in $ billions)	Dividends ÷ Earnings (%)
1971	53	24	45%
1972	61	26	42
1973	67	30	45
1974	53	30	58
1975	71	30	42
1976	83	36	43
1977	103	41	40
1978	116	46	40
1979	115	52	46
1980	93	59	64
1981	101	69	69
1982	88	70	79
1983	135	81	60
1984	170	83	49
1985	184	92	50
1986	165	110	67
1987	193	106	55
1988	228	115	51
1989	221	135	61
1990	242	153	63
1991	240	137	57
1992	261	150	57

Source: Based on Table B-88 from the 1994 *Economic Report of the President,* as shown in Allen and Michaely (1995).

Dividend Policies of Selected U.S. Firms

Exhibit 14.3 on page 522 provides a representative sample of well-known U.S. corporations and their **dividend yields**, the ratio of the dividend per share and the price per share, and *dividend payout ratios,* the ratio of the dividend per share and the earnings per share (income before extraordinary items) for 1993. The exhibit reveals major differences in the dividend policies of various types of firms. The high-tech growth firms have both low dividend yields and low payout ratios. In 1993, Microsoft paid no dividends while Hewlett Packard had a payout ratio of less than 20 percent and a yield of only 1.14 percent. On the other hand, utilities usually pay out a sizable portion of their earnings in dividends. In 1993, Boston Edison paid out almost 65 percent of its earnings in dividends, which gave its stock a dividend yield of 5.71 percent. AT&T, whose business has evolved from that of a regulated utility to more of a high-tech growth company, has seen its dividend yield fall from nearly 5.0 percent in 1985 to about 2.5 percent in 1993; its payout ratio fell from about 80 percent to less than 45 percent during this same period.

EXHIBIT 14.2   Aggregate Share Repurchases and Dividends

Year	Repurchases (in $ millions)	Dividends (in $ millions)
1973	$ 8,050	$48,373
1974	3,992	47,794
1975	2,168	46,576
1976	3,506	50,516
1977	6,886	56,979
1978	7,263	58,260
1979	8,676	59,778
1980	9,844	61,759
1981	7,788	57,584
1982	13,090	59,888
1983	11,711	60,331
1984	34,974	55,255
1985	51,239	60,438
1986	46,523	65,461
1987	56,608	67,330
1988	51,931	77,454
1989	46,751	68,106
1990	39,187	66,697
1991	21,742	64,181

Source: Based on Tables 1 and 2 of Dunsby (1993), as shown in Allen and Michaely (1995). Data are from the 1,000 largest firms (by book value of assets) from the combined industrial and research files on Compustat for each year. Amounts are in millions of 1991 dollars. Repurchases are cash spent on common equity and preferred shares. Dividends are cash dividends declared on common equity.

14.2 Distribution Policy in Frictionless Markets

The Accounting Identity for Sources and Uses of Corporate Cash Flow

Exhibit 14.4 on page 423 summarizes the various uses of a corporation's after-tax cash flow. After paying interest expenses, the cash flows of a firm must go to funding new investment, paying off debt, repurchasing stock, or paying dividends. The sources and uses of a corporation's after-tax cash flows must be equal, as expressed in equation (14.1):

$$\text{After-tax cash flow} = \text{Investment} - \text{Change in debt} + \text{Interest payments} \quad (14.1)$$
$$- \text{Change in equity} + \text{Dividends}$$

Chapters 9 to 13 examined the corporation's internal investment decisions and debt-equity choices. If one holds these decisions as fixed, the company's dividend choice is simply one of allocating what is left over from cash flows after investment and financing decisions are made. Various market frictions, such as taxes and transaction costs, affect all of the above decisions, which in turn affect a firm's dividend policy.

Exhibit 14.3   Selected Dividend Yields and Payout Ratios, 1993

Company	Dividend Yield (%)	Payout Ratio (%)
AT&T	2.51%	44.92%
Apple Computer	1.64	64.39
Bank of Boston	1.74	15.40
Boeing	2.31	27.34
Boston Edison	5.71	64.90
Deere	2.70	92.74
Disney	0.54	18.35
Dow Chemical	4.58	110.82
General Motors	1.46	23.36
Hewlett-Packard	1.14	19.32
McDonalds	0.74	13.82
Microsoft	0	0
Minnesota Mining & Mfg.	3.05	56.45
Philip Morris	4.67	63.91
Safeway	0	0
Texaco	4.94	65.84
USX	0	0
Wal-Mart	0.52	12.81

Note: These ratios were calculated with data taken from COMPUSTAT.

Before considering how market frictions affect dividend policy, we examine a simple case where there are no transaction costs and no taxes, and where the dividend choice conveys no information to investors.[4] The analysis of this case serves as a useful benchmark for understanding the more realistic settings examined later. We will start with the case in which the firm knows how much cash it would like to distribute, but has not decided whether to distribute the cash by paying a dividend or by repurchasing shares.

The Miller-Modigliani Dividend Irrelevancy Theorem

In their classic article, Miller and Modigliani (1961) examined a firm that wanted to distribute a fixed amount of cash to its shareholders either by repurchasing shares or by paying a cash dividend. The authors assumed that the choice between these two alternatives would affect neither the firm's investment decisions nor its operations. Given these assumptions, they demonstrated that, in the absence of personal taxes and transaction costs, the choice between paying a dividend and repurchasing shares is a matter of indifference. Shareholders are indifferent and firm values are unaffected by which of the two methods is used. Result 14.1 summarizes the Miller-Modigliani dividend irrelevancy theorem.

---

[4]Chapter 18 examines how information considerations affect dividend policy.

EXHIBIT 14.4   Uses of Corporate Cash

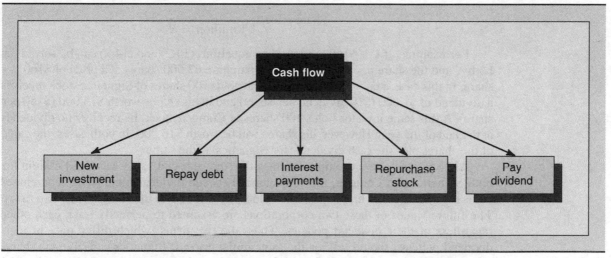

Result 14.1   *(The Miller-Modigliani dividend irrelevancy theorem.)* Consider the choice between paying a dividend and using an equivalent amount of money to repurchase shares. Assume:

- There are no tax considerations.
- There are no transaction costs.
- The investment, financing, and operating policies of the firm are held fixed.

Then the choice between paying dividends and repurchasing shares is a matter of indifference to shareholders.

A Proof of the Miller-Modigliani Theorem.   To understand Result 14.1, consider two similar biotech firms with different dividend policies:

- One firm, Signetics, has announced that it will pay a $10 million dividend next year.
- The other firm, Comgen, has announced that it will repurchase $10 million in outstanding shares.
- The firms will each be worth somewhere between $100 million or $200 million at the end of the year, depending on industry conditions.
- The future values of the two firms (after paying dividends or repurchasing shares), denoted by *V,* are the same.
- Each firm initially has 1 million shares outstanding.

These assumptions imply that a share of Signetics stock will sell for one millionth of *V* at the end of the year, implying that if *V* is $150 million, each share will be worth $150. Calculating the year-end value of Comgen stock is slightly more complicated. Comgen will repurchase *N* shares for $10 million, implying:

$$\text{Share price} \times N = \$10 \text{ million} \tag{14.2}$$

Since the year-end value of Comgen equals V, its share price must satisfy:

$$\text{Share price} = \frac{V}{1 \text{ million} - N} \qquad (14.3)$$

For example, if V is $150 million, then equations (14.2) and (14.3) can be solved for both N and the share price. Comgen will repurchase 62,500 shares at a price of $160 per share. In this case, a tax-exempt investor who holds 100 shares of Signetics stock receives a dividend of $1,000 ($10 dividend per share) and holds shares worth $15,000 ($150 per share). If this same investor holds 100 shares of Comgen stock, he receives no dividends at the end of the year. However, his shares will be worth $16,000. In both cases, the value of the shares plus the cash dividend (for Signetics) is the same.

Although the above example assumes that the year-end value was $150 million for both Signetics and Comgen, the equivalence between dividends and share repurchases holds regardless of the firms' year-end values, as long as it is the same for the two firms. The future values of these two corporations are assumed to perfectly track each other regardless of their dividend policies. Thus, the two firms, which differ only in their dividend policies, should sell for the same initial price. If Signetics and Comgen shares sell for different prices, there will be an arbitrage opportunity, as Example 14.1 illustrates.

Example 14.1:   Arbitrage Opportunities that Arise When the Miller-Modigliani Theorem Does Not Hold

Suppose that Signetics stock was selling at $130 a share and Comgen was selling at $128 a share. What can the investor do to realize an arbitrage gain?

Answer: An investor who buys 100 shares of Comgen for $128 a share and sells short 100 shares of Signetics at $130 a share will realize an initial $200 cash inflow. This $200 is free money; there will be no net outflow at the end of the year.

For example, assume that both companies are going to be worth either $100 million or $200 million next year. The Comgen shares will then be worth either $200 per share or $100 per share, depending on industry conditions. The Signetics shares will be worth either $90 per share or $190 per share, depending on the state of the economy, plus a dividend of $10 per share. Hence, the year-end value of this arbitrage portfolio is zero, regardless of the state of the economy.

Example 14.1 shows that if two firms are equivalent except for their dividend policies, their values should be the same in the absence of taxes and transaction costs. If the values are not the same, smart investors can realize arbitrage profits.

Kerkorian and Chrysler

Consider the Kerkorian and Chrysler situation examined in the opening vignette to this chapter. Exhibit 14.5 compares the effects on Kerkorian's position under the following alternatives:

- Chrysler pays out $1 billion as a special dividend.
- Chrysler repurchases $1 billion of its own stock.

To simplify the numbers, assume that Chrysler stock is selling at $50 per share, that the company has 350 million shares outstanding, and that Kerkorian wishes to maintain 10 percent control of the firm.

If Chrysler pays a dividend, Kerkorian receives a $100 million dividend and ends up with shares worth $1.65 billion. If Chrysler repurchases shares, Kerkorian will sell 2 million shares to bring his stake back to 10 percent. At a selling price of $50 per share, the stock

EXHIBIT 14.5   Chrysler's Choice: Dividends or Share Repurchase

	Prior to Transaction (in $ millions)	Pay $1 Billion in Dividends (in $ millions)	Repurchase $1 Billion of Stock (in $ millions)
Total assets (other than cash)	$ 9,800	$ 9,800	$ 9,800
Cash	7,700	6,700	6,700
Equity value	$17,500	$16,500	$16,500
Dividends		$ 1,000	
Shares outstanding	350	350	330
Stock value per share	$ 50.00	$ 47.14	$ 50.00
Dividends per share		$ 2.86	
Kerkorian stock value (in $ millions)	$ 1,750	$ 1,650	$ 1,650
Kerkorian dividends (in $ millions)		$ 100	
Kerkorian's proceeds from selling shares			$100 ($50 × 2)

sale will bring Kerkorian $100 million, and his stock position will be worth $1.65 billion. Ignoring taxes and transaction costs, Kerkorian is indifferent between the two alternatives.[5]

Optimal Payout Policy in the Absence of Taxes and Transaction Costs

This section considers the trade-off between distributing earnings to shareholders, either by paying a dividend or repurchasing shares, and retaining the earnings to increase internal investment. The previous subsections indicated that, in the absence of taxes and transaction costs, dividends and share repurchases are equivalent. Therefore, a distinction between the two methods of distribution at this point is unnecessary.

Result 14.2 specifies the assumptions made up to this point, along with their implications for the corporation's choice between distributing or retaining the earnings.

Result 14.2   Consider the choice between paying out earnings to shareholders versus retaining the earnings for investment. Assume:

1. There are no tax considerations.
2. There are no transaction costs.
3. The choice between paying a dividend and retaining the earnings for reinvestment within the firm does not convey any information to shareholders.
4. The firm is financed completely with equity.

Then a dividend payout will either increase or decrease firm value, depending on whether there are positive net present value (NPV) investments that could be funded by retaining

---

[5]Accounting considerations also may lead firms to prefer share repurchases over dividends. Compared with dividends, share repurchases generally increase both earnings per share and return on shareholder's equity.

the money within the firm. If there are no positive *NPV* investments, the money should be paid out.

Result 14.2 restates the more fundamental point discussed in Part III of this text. With frictionless capital markets, firms should accept all positive *NPV* projects and reject all negative ones. However, as we see below, this will not necessarily be the case when taxes and transaction costs are present.

14.3 The Effect of Taxes and Transaction Costs on Distribution Policy

Any discussion of tax reform in Washington almost always includes a discussion about the double taxation of corporate profits. As discussed in Chapter 13, corporations first pay corporate taxes on their earnings, and shareholders pay tax again on the distributed profits. Example 14.2 illustrates that from a shareholder's perspective, the effective tax on corporations can be considerable[6]:

Example 14.2:   The Effective Tax Rate on MGI's Profits

MGI earned $100 million in pretax profits in 1996. Its corporate tax rate is 34 percent. Joe Gecko, who owns 10 percent of the firm's shares, has a personal marginal tax rate of 33.33 percent. From Gecko's perspective, what is the effective tax rate on MGI's profits if its entire after-tax profits are distributed as a dividend?

   Answer: MGI will pay $34 million in corporate taxes and distribute $66 million to shareholders in the form of a dividend. Gecko thus receives $6.6 million in dividends and pays $2.2 million in personal taxes, leaving him with $4.4 million after taxes from his $10 million share of the firm's pretax profits. From Gecko's perspective, the effective tax rate on corporate profits is 56 percent [= ($3.4 million + $2.2 million)/$10 million].

A Comparison of the Classical and Imputation Tax Systems

A number of countries outside the United States have changed their tax systems to eliminate the double taxation of corporate profits. Greece and Norway, for example, allow dividends to be deducted from corporate taxes and thus treat dividends and interest payments symmetrically. Australia, Canada, France, Germany, Italy, and the United Kingdom have introduced an **imputation system**, under which investors who receive taxable dividends get a tax credit for part or all of the taxes paid by the corporation. This tax credit at least partly offsets the personal taxes these investors must pay on dividend income.

The discussion in this section focuses on what is known as the **classical tax system** which is observed in the United States. In a classical tax system, dividends are taxed as ordinary income and capital gains are generally taxed at a lower rate than ordinary income. As of 1997, the maximum federal tax rate on dividends and other ordinary

---

[6]There are other ownership forms that are not double taxed. For example, most small firms in the United States are incorporated as subchapter S corporations, which are not taxed at the corporate level but which pass through their earnings directly to shareholders who pay a personal tax on the income. Subchapter S corporations allow only a limited number of shareholders and thus cannot be used for larger firms. Most real estate firms are set up as master limited partnerships or real estate investment trusts, which also pass through all earnings directly to shareholders and are not taxed at the firm level.

EXHIBIT 14.6   Tax Consequences: Dividend versus Share Repurchase (in $ millions)

Dividend Alternative	
Dividend	$100.0
Tax rate	× 39.6%
Immediate tax liability	$ 39.6
Share Repurchase Alternative	
Proceeds from sale of 2 million shares	$100.0
Less original cost (at $38/share)	− 76.0
Taxable capital gain	$ 24.0
Tax rate	× 28.0%
Immediate tax liability	$ 6.7

income was 39.6 percent and the capital gains rate was 28 percent.[7] Shareholders do not receive tax credits, offsetting the taxes paid by corporations, implying that the classical tax system effectively double taxes corporate profits.

Financial economists and policymakers have expressed concern about the adverse consequences of the classical tax system and suggested that the United States move to an imputation system. In particular, under the classical system the cost of funding investments through retained earnings is lower than the cost of funding investment by issuing new equity. As a result, new firms with promising opportunities but insufficient amounts of internally generated cash will find it more expensive to fund their investment needs than more mature firms with less promising opportunities.

How Taxes Affect Dividend Policy

Personal taxes on dividends can profoundly affect a firm's choice between paying dividends and repurchasing shares. Because the pretax proceeds from both strategies are equal, the only difference between the two methods of cash distribution is the amount of the tax liability generated by each.

The Tax Disadvantage of Dividends.   Exhibit 14.6 details the immediate tax consequences to an individual investor, like Kerkorian, if Chrysler chooses to distribute $1 billion in the form of a dividend or as a share repurchase. It assumes that the investor currently owns 10 percent of the outstanding shares and plans on maintaining the 10 percent ownership. It also assumes that the shares, if repurchased, will be repurchased at a price of $50 a share and that they were originally purchased at a price of $38 a share.

Although the *immediate* tax liability is considerably higher with the dividend alternative, the *future* tax liability incurred by shareholders when their shares are eventually

---

[7]Until 1982, the tax on dividend income in the United States could be as high as 70 percent while capital gains were taxed at 50 percent of the ordinary rate. With the passage of the Tax Equity and Fiscal Responsibility Act of 1982, the maximum tax on dividends fell to 50 percent and that on capital gains was reduced to 20 percent.

sold is higher when shares are repurchased. This is because the share prices drop by the amount of the dividend when a dividend is paid, making the future capital gains lower for shareholders who purchased stock prior to the dividend. However, the total amount paid in taxes (and its present value) is still considerably lower with the repurchase alternative.

Result 14.3   In the United States, taxes favor share repurchases over dividends. The gain associated with a share repurchase over a cash dividend depends on:

- The difference between the capital gains rate and the ordinary tax rate.
- The tax basis of the shares, that is, the price at which the shares were purchased.
- The timing of the sale of the shares (if soon, the gain is less).

Can Individual Investors Avoid the Dividend Tax?   Miller and Scholes (1978) claimed that individual investors should be indifferent between repurchases and dividends because they can avoid the tax on dividends. Their dividend tax avoidance scheme is quite simple: Individuals borrow money that they invest in tax-deferred insurance annuities. In theory, the interest on the loan is tax deductible and can offset the taxable dividend income. However, the tax on the insurance annuity can be deferred indefinitely. These transactions are illustrated in Example 14.3:

Example 14.3:   Deferring the Dividend Tax

Elliot Jackson has $12,000 in dividend income. How can he defer the taxes on this dividend if he can borrow at 6 percent and insurance annuities pay an interest rate of 6 percent?

Answer: Elliot should borrow $200,000 at 6 percent and invest the proceeds in a tax-deferred insurance annuity. By doing this, the tax on the $12,000 dividend is deferred (since the dividend is offset by the $12,000 interest payment) until the money is withdrawn from the insurance annuity.

In reality, individual investors rarely avoid the dividend tax in the way that Miller and Scholes suggests. Indeed, Feenberg (1981) found that individual investors paid over $8 billion dollars in taxes on dividend income in 1977. Similar findings by Peterson, Peterson, and Ang (1985) indicated that individual tax returns included over $33 billion of dividend income in 1979, which was slightly more than two-thirds of the total amount of dividends paid by U.S. corporations. Thus, since shareholders seem unable to avoid taxes on dividends, the argument of Miller and Scholes fails to explain why corporations continue to pay dividends given the tax advantages of share repurchases.

The Miller and Scholes insights may be useful for individuals wishing to reduce their own taxes. However, deferring taxes may be more difficult in practice than in theory. It requires, for example, that investors be able to borrow on the same terms that they invest in the insurance annuity, matching investment horizon as well as rates. It also assumes that there are no costs associated with such transactions.

Dividend Clienteles

The tax advantages of a share repurchase do not apply to all investors. A large percentage of investors are tax exempt (e.g., pension funds and university endowments). As previously demonstrated, these investors are indifferent between receiving dividends or having the firm repurchase shares when there are no transaction costs. In reality, however, transaction costs do exist. Shareholders and the firm must pay brokerage fees as part of a share repurchase. Also shares repurchased with a tender offer usually carry underwriting fees and registration costs. Although these transaction costs are small relative to the tax gains enjoyed by taxable investors with repurchases, they might lead tax-exempt investors to prefer dividends.

As Chapter 13 noted, corporations that hold shares in other corporations may also prefer dividends to share repurchases since only 30 percent of their dividend income is taxable while their capital gains are fully taxed. Large investors who hold their shares within a corporate form (e.g., Kerkorian's Tracinda Corporation) also may prefer dividends to a share repurchase. In addition, many individuals and institutions that receive income from trust funds may prefer higher dividend-paying stocks if the beneficiary of the trust is allowed to spend the income but not the principal of the trust.

Some authors have suggested that different firms have different dividend payout ratios to appeal to different **investor clienteles**; that is, the different groups of investors with different tastes for receiving dividend income. Firms that pay no dividends are likely to attract individual investors in high tax brackets while firms that pay large dividends are likely to attract tax-exempt institutions, individual investors in low marginal tax brackets, and corporations attracted by the dividend tax preference.

Empirical tests by Pettit (1977) and Lewellen, Stanley, Lease, and Schlarbaum (1978) provide evidence that the dividend yields of investors' portfolios are indeed related to their marginal tax rates. Investors with high marginal tax rates tend to select stocks with low dividend yields and investors with low or zero marginal tax rates tend to select stocks with high dividend yields. Firms, however, do not appear to vary their dividends in order to satisfy the demands of different tax clienteles. Dividend policies of similar firms usually exhibit great similarity. This makes it extremely difficult for investors to specialize in terms of dividend yields for their portfolios and still diversify their portfolios adequately. For example, an investor in a high tax bracket would find it very difficult to find a utility with a low dividend yield while an investor with a desire for dividends would find it equally difficult to find a biotech firm with a high dividend yield.

Why Do Corporations Pay Out So Much in Taxed Dividends?

The previous subsection suggested that some investors prefer dividends to share repurchases while others prefer share repurchases to dividends. However, the dividend tax borne by the taxable investor is likely to be larger than the transaction costs associated with a repurchase, suggesting that corporate values would probably increase if firms cut their dividends and repurchased shares instead. This has led a number of financial economists to suggest that the dividend policy of U.S. firms is somewhat of a puzzle.[8]

To understand why U.S. dividend policy is so puzzling, consider the situation in the United States during the 1960s and 1970s. The majority of investors during this period were individual investors, many of whom paid taxes at marginal tax rates as high as 70 percent. For these investors, the tax advantage of a share repurchase over a dividend was very large, but repurchases were very uncommon at that time (see Exhibit 14.2). While we can only speculate on why U.S. firms paid out so much in tax-disadvantaged dividends at that time, our best guess is that the decisions of financial managers at that time were simply wrong and that most shareholders would have been better off if corporations had cut dividends and, instead, repurchased shares.

---

[8]See Black (1976) for further discussion of this dividend puzzle.

The increase in repurchase activity that began in the 1980s supports the hypothesis that most managers previously had misunderstood the relation between dividends and share repurchases and were changing their behavior to reflect their improved understanding of the tax advantage of share repurchases. Of course, other changes may have been taking place in the 1980s that would have made repurchases more attractive than dividends. However, the tax law changes in 1982 and 1986, which substantially decreased the tax disadvantage of dividends, should have had the opposite effect. In addition, the percentage of stock held by tax-exempt institutions greatly increased over this period, increasing the percentage of shareholders who might prefer dividends to share repurchases. These two changes had the effect of making dividends a relatively more attractive vehicle for paying out corporate cash than they previously were. Yet, share repurchases were, and still are, becoming increasingly popular.

14.4 How Dividend Policy Affects Expected Stock Returns

We have asserted that share repurchases provide a better method of distributing cash than dividends because most investors prefer capital gains income to an equivalent dividend taxed at a higher rate. Stocks with higher dividend yields, to compensate investors for their tax disadvantage, should offer higher expected returns than similar stocks with lower dividend yields. Thus, firms with higher dividend yields, but equivalent cash flows, have lower values, reflecting the higher rates that apply to their cash flows.

Researchers have taken two approaches to evaluate the effect of dividend yield on expected stock returns. The first approach measures stock returns around the date that the stock trades ex-dividend. Recall from Chapter 8 that the *ex-dividend date* (or the ex-date) is the first date on which purchasers of new shares will not be entitled to receive the forthcoming dividend. For example, a dividend paid on February 15 may have an ex-dividend date of February 5, which means that purchasers of stock on and after February 5 will not receive the dividend. Since investors who purchase the stock prior to the ex-dividend date (February 4 or earlier in this example) receive the dividend while those who purchase stock on or after this date do not, the decline in the stock price on the ex-dividend date provides a measure of how much the market values the dividend. The second approach measures how dividend yield affects expected returns cross-sectionally.

Ex-Dividend Stock Price Movements

Consider Example 14.4, which assumes that a dividend is taxed at an investor's personal income tax rate and that capital gains are not taxed at all.

**Example 14.4:   The Decision to Purchase Stock Before or After the
Ex-Dividend Date**

Trevtex Corporation plans to pay a dividend of $1 per share. Tomorrow is the ex-dividend date, so investors who purchase the stock tomorrow will not receive the dividend. Assume Trevtex is selling for $20.00 per share today and is expected to sell for $19.20 per share tomorrow. Should an investor with a 33 percent marginal tax rate, who is not taxed on capital gains, purchase the stock today and receive the dividend or should the investor wait one day and purchase it without the dividend?

Answer: The net cost per share of buying the stock with the dividend is $20 minus $1 for the dividend plus the tax the investor must pay on the dividend. For an investor with a 33 percent marginal tax rate, this net cost is $19.33 per share. Hence, purchasing the stock ex-dividend for $19.20 per share would be preferred to purchasing the stock for $20 per share just prior to the ex-dividend date, which has a net cost of $19.33. However, a tax-exempt investor would prefer to purchase the stock prior to the ex-dividend date since the net cost per share is $19 (= $20 − $1).

Example 14.4 illustrates that a $1 dividend may be worth less than $1 because of personal taxes that investors must pay on the dividends. As a result, stock prices will drop by less than the amount of the dividend on the ex-dividend date. For instance, the stock price would fall $0.67 after the payment of a $1.00 dividend if the marginal investor, who would be indifferent between buying either before or after the ex-dividend date, had a 33 percent tax rate on dividends, assuming that there is no tax on capital gains.

Empirical Evidence on Price Drops on Ex-Dividend Dates.   Elton and Gruber (1970) examined the price movements around the ex-dividend dates of listed stocks from April 1966 to the end of March 1967. They found that, on average, the stock price decline was 77.7 percent of the dividend, implying that shareholders place a value of only slightly more than $0.77 on a dividend of $1.00. The authors also found that the percentage price drop was related to the size of the dividend. For dividends greater than 5 percent of the stock price, the price drop on the ex-dividend date exceeded, on average, 90 percent of the dividend. For the smallest dividends, however, the price drop on the ex-dividend date was closer to 50 percent of the dividend.

Elton and Gruber interpreted the differential price drop as evidence of the investor clientele effect. Because the marginal investor in a stock with a high dividend yield is likely to have a low marginal tax rate, the after-tax value of the dividend should be relatively close to the amount of the payout. However, the marginal buyer of a stock with a low dividend yield is likely to have a high marginal tax rate and thus will place a much lower value on the dividends.

Non-Tax-Based Explanations for the Magnitudes of the Ex-Dividend Date Price Drops.   A second explanation for the differential price drop was suggested by Kalay (1982). To understand this explanation, consider first the case where there are no trans-action costs. In this case, if the stock price drop was not close to the amount of the dividend, traders would have an opportunity to earn arbitrage profits. In Example 14.2, traders could buy the stock at $20.00, receive the $1.00 dividend, and sell the stock the next day for $19.20. Because the capital loss from the price drop is fully tax deductible at the personal income tax rate for short-term traders, this transaction yields an after-tax as well as a pretax gain. This arbitrage gain will exist as long as the price does not drop by the full amount of the dividend.

Consider next the case where there is a $0.10 per share transaction cost. In this case, the price need not drop the full $1.00, but it must drop at least $0.90, or 90 percent of the dividend, to preclude arbitrage. However, on a $0.40 dividend, the price needs to drop only $0.30, or 75 percent of the dividend, to preclude arbitrage. Hence, for smaller dividends, smaller percentage price drops are needed to preclude arbitrage, which is exactly what Elton and Gruber observed.

Other evidence leads us to suspect that the observed behavior of stock prices on ex-dividend dates may have nothing to do with taxes. First, the kind of behavior observed on the ex-dividend date in the United States seems to be an international phenomenon, even where dividends are not tax disadvantaged. In Hong Kong, where dividends are not taxed, stock price changes on ex-dividend dates are similar to those observed in the

United States. In addition, stock prices also fall by much less than the amount of the dividend on the ex-dividend dates of stock dividends. Since stock dividends are not taxed, one cannot use a tax-based story to explain the stock price behavior around the time of ex-dividend dates for stock dividends.[9]

The Cross-Sectional Relation between Dividend Yields and Stock Returns

If a firm's dividend policy is determined independently of its investment and operating decisions, the firm's future cash flows also are independent of its dividend policy. In this case, dividend policy can only affect the value of a firm by affecting the expected returns that investors use to discount those cash flows. For example, if dividends are taxed more heavily than capital gains, then, as noted earlier, investors must be compensated for this added tax by obtaining higher pretax returns on high-dividend yielding stocks. (They would not hold shares in such stocks and supply would not equal demand if this were not true.)

Stocks with high dividend yields do, in fact, have higher returns, on average, than stocks with low dividend yields. However, Blume (1980) documented that the relationship between returns and dividend yield is actually U-shaped. Stocks with zero dividend yields have substantially higher expected returns than stocks with low dividend yields, but for stocks that do pay dividends, expected returns increase with dividend yields. This finding is consistent with the idea that stocks with zero dividend yields are extremely risky, but for firms that pay dividends, higher dividends require higher expected returns because of their tax disadvantage.

To test whether a return premium is associated with high-yield stocks, a number of studies estimate cross-sectional regressions of the following general form[10]:

$$R_j = a + \gamma_1 \beta_j + \gamma_2 D_j + \epsilon_j \tag{14.4}$$

where

β_j = the firm's beta
D_j = the expected dividend yield[11]
ϵ_j = the error term.

The hypothesis is that γ_2, which measures the effect of dividend yield on required returns, is positive to reflect the tax disadvantage of dividend payments, and that γ_1, the coefficient of beta, is positive to reflect the effect of systematic risk on returns. Most of these studies found that the coefficient of the expected dividend yield was positive, which they interpreted as evidence favoring a tax effect.

---

[9]Studies by Eades, Hess and Kim (1984) and Grinblatt, Masulis, and Titman (1984) document positive returns on ex-dates for stock dividends and stock splits.

[10]The first study to test this specification was Brennan (1970), who concluded that there was a return premium associated with stocks that have high dividend yields.

[11]The expected dividend yield rather than the actual dividend yield must be used in these regressions because of the information content of the dividend choice. For example, a firm that pays a high dividend in a given year is likely to have a high return in that year because of the favorable information conveyed by the dividend increase (which we will discuss in detail in Chapter 18). Miller and Scholes (1982) pointed out that this information effect was ignored in the early studies on this topic and, as a result, the purported finding of a tax effect was spurious. However, Litzenberger and Ramaswamy (1982) measured an expected dividend yield, using information available prior to the time the returns were measured, and found the coefficient of the expected dividend yield to be positive and statistically significant, supporting the hypothesis of a tax-related preference for capital gains.

These interpretations assume that the beta estimates used as independent variables in the regression in equation (14.4) provide an adequate estimate of the stocks' risks. However, as discussed in Chapter 5, finance academics find weak support for the idea that market betas provide a good measure of the kind of risk that investors wish to avoid. Distinguishing between tax and risk effects is further compounded by the relation of the dividend yield to other firm characteristics that are likely to be related to risk and expected returns. For example, Keim (1985) showed that both firms paying no dividends and firms paying large dividends were primarily small firms. This suggests that the expected dividend yield may be acting as a proxy for firm size in the regression shown in equation (14.4). In addition to being related to firm size, dividend yield is correlated with a firm's expected future investment needs and its profitability—both attributes that are likely to affect the riskiness of a firm's stock.

Result 14.4   Stocks with high dividend yields are fundamentally different from stocks with low dividend yields in terms of their characteristics and their risk profiles. Therefore, it is nearly impossible to assess whether the relation between dividend yield and expected returns is due to taxes or risk.

Since it may be impossible to detect whether paying dividends increases a firm's required expected rate of return, one cannot be certain that a policy of substituting share repurchases for dividends will have a lasting effect on the firm's share price. Although some articles by finance academics claim that dividends increase a stock's required rate of return, these studies are open to interpretation.

Citizens Utilities

Citizens Utilities provides an interesting case study for examining the effect of dividend yields on prices. From 1955 until 1989, Citizens Utilities had two classes of common stock that differed only in their dividend policy: Series A stock paid a stock dividend (which is not taxed) and series B stock paid a cash dividend (which generates personal income tax liabilities for shareholders). The company's charter required the stock dividend on series A stock to be *at least* of equal value to the cash dividend on series B stock. The stock dividends were, on average, about 10 percent higher than the cash dividends.

In the absence of taxes, the two stocks should trade at an average price ratio comparable to their dividend ratio. Taxable investors, however, would then prefer the series A stock which pays no taxable dividend. This suggests that the price of series A stock should exceed 1.1 times the price of the series B stock because the untaxed stock dividend paid by the series A stock is 10 percent higher than the taxed cash dividend paid by the series B stock. As shown by Long (1978), the price of series A stock before 1976 was somewhat less than 1.1 times that of the series B stock, but in the period examined by Poterba (1986), 1976–84, the ratio of the prices was about equal to 1.1. This evidence suggests that investors in Citizens Utilities stock prices were not influenced by these tax considerations. Furthermore, a study by Hubbard and Michaely (1995) showed that the relationship between the prices of the two classes of Citizens Utilities stock was largely unaffected by the Tax Reform Act of 1986 which substantially influenced the relative value of dividends and capital gains to taxable investors.[12]

While dividends may have had no effect on Citizens Utilities stock prices, we cannot generalize this finding to all firms. Since the two classes of Citizen's stock are essentially the

---

[12]That series B (cash dividend) shares in the early time period were priced to yield less than the series A (stock dividend) shares probably reflected the fact that the stock dividends were initially higher than the cash dividends, implying that the stock dividends were likely to fall relative to the cash dividends. Indeed, the dividends on series A and B shares are currently identical and their prices are the same. (Both share classes currently pay stock dividends, but Citizens Utilities provides a service to its series B shareholders whereby it sells the stock dividends and distributes the cash proceeds to the shareholders.)

same, any large difference in their prices presents an opportunity for arbitrage by tax-exempt investors. Indeed, the arbitrage argument described in Example 14.1 can be applied to show that in the absence of transaction costs the stock prices must be identical. This opportunity for arbitrage would not exist for other stocks, indicating that one might observe two closely related, but not identical, stocks with different dividends providing very different expected returns.

14.5 How Dividend Taxes Affect Financing and Investment Choices

Although it is very difficult to determine whether the taxation of dividends is reflected in stock returns, it is true that some investors incur a tax penalty when they receive dividends. In addition, firms impose taxes and transaction costs on their shareholders when they distribute excess cash by repurchasing shares. These taxes and transaction costs can distort investment and financing choices.

Dividends, Taxes, and Financing Choices

This subsection reexamines the capital structure decision from the perspective of a firm that subjects its stockholders to personal tax liabilities when it distributes a portion of its earnings to them. Recall from Chapter 13 that firms operating within the U.S. tax system should prefer debt to equity financing. However, the analysis there largely ignored the distinction between internally generated and externally generated equity. This distinction is quite important, however, if distributed earnings are taxed at high personal rates, as the discussion below illustrates.

Should Microsoft Increase Its Leverage?

Bill Gates, founder and CEO of Microsoft, recognizes that there is a tax gain from debt financing and that Microsoft can increase the firm's leverage, either by repurchasing shares or by paying a dividend, and funding more of the firm's investment needs from debt securities without running any significant risk of bankruptcy. This would increase firm value by lowering its corporate tax bite.

Gates currently owns about 24 percent of the company's shares. Assume that he would like to retain this percentage of ownership. The corporate tax rate is currently 35 percent and Gates's personal tax rate is 40 percent on ordinary income and 28 percent on capital gains. Different shareholders may have different opinions about whether the firm should pay a large dividend, repurchase shares, or continue with its policy of retaining most of its earnings to fund its investments internally. For example, tax-exempt institutions definitely would prefer that the firm repurchase shares or pay a dividend to increase its debt, at least to the point where there is some risk of bankruptcy. However, Bill Gates may personally prefer keeping the firm underleveraged. If the firm uses a large dividend to distribute its retained earnings, Gates will have to pay 40 percent of the distribution in taxes. Because of the lower capital gains tax, he would prefer a share repurchase over a dividend. However, if Gates is going to keep his percentage ownership of the firm constant he will have to sell some of his shares, forcing him to realize the capital gains on his shares. As we will show, Gates's incentive to have Microsoft distribute cash to increase its leverage depends on the difference between his personal rate and Microsoft's corporate tax rate. If the corporate tax rate is less than the personal rate, he will prefer retaining the earnings rather than distributing them. However, as stated in the next result, for the reasons discussed in Chapter 13, he will still have a tax preference for debt financing over issuing new equity.

Result 14.5   The combination of the corporate tax deductibility of interest payments and the personal taxes on dividends implies that firms may prefer:

- Financing new investments with retained earnings over issuing debt.
- Issuing debt to issuing equity.

The Pecking Order of Financing Choices.   Consistent with Result 14.5, an in-depth study of large corporations by Gordon Donaldson (1961) found that managers prefer funding investment, first, with retained earnings, second, after the supply of retained earnings has been exhausted, with debt, and finally, when it is imprudent for the firm to borrow additional amounts, by issuing outside equity. This financing hierarchy is known as the **pecking order of financing choices.**[13]

Debt, Taxes, and How Capital Structures Change Over Time.   Result 14.5 indicates that as profitable firms mature, and require less external capital, they are likely to reduce their leverage. Hence, when there is a tax advantage associated with debt financing and a tax disadvantage associated with dividends, forward-looking firms initially should be highly leveraged and then should pay down their debt with internally generated earnings. If the tax costs of distributing future corporate earnings are sufficiently high, a firm initially might want to take on more debt than is needed to eliminate its corporate income taxes, even if it requires the firm to bear some risks of financial distress. As the firm matures, it will find it advantageous to reduce its leverage ratio by using retained earnings to pay down debt, thereby eliminating the need to pay highly taxed dividends. Perhaps the strategy of firms that initiate leveraged buyouts and then pay down their debt over time is motivated in part by these tax considerations.

Dividends, Taxes, and Investment Distortions

The personal tax on dividends also affects a firm's choice between paying out earnings and retaining them for internal investment. This section illustrates that shareholders who are taxed differently on their dividend income favor different investment policies for their firms.

The Investment Policy Favored by Tax-Paying Shareholders.   Assume that you own shares in Continental Corporation and have a marginal personal income tax rate of 50 percent. Suppose that Continental Corporation must decide whether to pay out an additional $1 million in dividends or to retain the earnings for internal investment. As the holder of 10 percent of the outstanding shares, you have a major say in the decision and need to consider the possibilities seriously. Your advisors calculate that over the next five years the firm will earn 6 percent after corporate taxes with certainty on the $1 million and that these earnings will be distributed to the shareholders in addition to the dividends they would have received otherwise. At the end of the five years, the $1 million retained this year will be distributed to shareholders. In essence, the choice for shareholders is whether to defer the $1 million dividend for five years and receive as compensation for this deferral, additional annual dividends of $60,000 per year (= $1 million × .06) in the interim period.

   This investment possibility does not seem particularly attractive at first glance because the rate of return on five-year U.S. Treasury bonds is 7 percent. Your tax advisors, however, suggest that, given your 50 percent marginal tax rate, you are better off if the money is retained within the corporation. After taxes, your $100,000 dividend

---

[13]Non-tax-based explanations for this pecking order behavior are described in Chapters 16 and 18.

EXHIBIT 14.7   After-Tax Cash Flows for a Taxable Investor

Alternative 1: Investment of after-tax dividend of $50,000 in Treasury bonds.

After-Tax Cash Flows

Year 1	Year 2	Year 3	Year 4	Year 5	Principal Payment
$1,750	$1,750	$1,750	$1,750	$1,750	$50,000

Alternative 2: Retain earnings and invest internally for five years, which returns 6 percent to stockholders per year with a final dividend in year 5.

After-Tax Cash Flows

Year 1	Year 2	Year 3	Year 4	Year 5	Deferred Dividend
$3,000	$3,000	$3,000	$3,000	$3,000	$50,000

(10 percent of the $1 million distribution) would be worth only $50,000, which generates only $1,750 per year after taxes if invested at 7 percent.

The after-tax cash flows from these alternatives appear in Exhibit 14.7.

The after-tax cash flows on the internally invested retained earnings, alternative 2, are higher than those on the distributed dividends, alternative 1. A return is earned on the *entire* $1 million of earnings kept within the firm rather than on *half* this amount on earnings that are distributed. As a result, tax-paying investors tend to prefer retaining the earnings within the firm rather than receiving a cash dividend.

The Investment Policy Favored by Tax-Exempt Shareholders.   Tax-exempt institutions would evaluate these alternatives quite differently. From their perspective, assuming the same 10 percent ownership of the outstanding shares, cash flows would be as specified in Exhibit 14.8.

Thus, from the perspective of a tax-exempt institution, a cash dividend, alternative 1, would be preferred.

Summary of How Personal Taxes Influences Investment Choices.   In general, investors prefer retained earnings over a cash dividend if:

(1 − corporate tax rate) × (pretax risk-adjusted rate of return within the corporation)   (14.5)
> (1 − personal tax rate) × (pretax risk-adjusted rate of return outside the corporation)

Otherwise, investors would prefer the cash dividend.

Inequality (14.5) can be contrasted with the requirement that investment projects funded with externally raised equity must earn an after-tax rate of return that exceeds the rate of return investors can earn in the financial markets:

(1 − corporate tax rate)
× (pretax risk-adjusted rate of return within the corporation)
> pretax rate of return outside the corporation   (14.6)

EXHIBIT 14.8   Cash Flows for a Tax Exempt Investor

Alternative 1: Investment of $100,000 dividend in Treasury bonds.

Cash Flows

Year 1	Year 2	Year 3	Year 4	Year 5	Principal Payment
$7,000	$7,000	$7,000	$7,000	$7,000	$100,000

Alternative 2: Retain earnings and invest internally for five years, which returns 6 percent to stockholders per year with a final dividend in year 5.

Cash Flows

Year 1	Year 2	Year 3	Year 4	Year 5	Deferred Dividend
$6,000	$6,000	$6,000	$6,000	$6,000	$100,000

Result 14.6 follows from a comparison of equations (14.5) and (14.6).

Result 14.6   Tax-exempt and tax-paying shareholders agree about which projects a firm should fund from external equity issues, but may disagree about which projects should be financed from retained earnings. In particular:

- Tax-exempt shareholders require the same expected return for internally financed projects as they do for externally financed projects.
- Tax-paying shareholders prefer that firms use lower required rates of return for internally financed projects if the alternative is paying taxable dividends.

Disagreements at Microsoft

Consider a corporation, like Microsoft, which by 1996 had accumulated over $10 billion in *excess* cash (i.e., cash not currently needed for debt repayment or investment). Equation (14.6) suggests that tax-exempt institutional investors prefer the firm to pay out the cash as a dividend. However, equation (14.5) suggests that Bill Gates, Microsoft's CEO, and other shareholders with higher marginal tax rates than the corporation, prefer to have the corporation retain the earnings and invest the money in Treasury bonds. Shareholders with the same marginal tax rate as the corporation will be indifferent between the two alternatives.

Although companies like Microsoft sometimes invest excess cash in T-bonds and equivalent instruments, Gates may prefer alternative uses for these funds. For example, Gates may prefer to diversify his portfolio by using Microsoft to buy another company's stock instead of buying the stock with his personal money. Since U.S. corporations are taxed on only 30 percent of the dividend income they receive from other corporations, they can often earn a higher after-tax rate of return by buying the common or preferred shares of other companies than they can earn from holding debt instruments like T-bonds.[14]

---

[14]Until 1987, corporations were taxed on only 15 percent of their dividend income. This was raised to 20 percent in 1987 and 30 percent in 1988. Corporations that own between 20 and 80 percent of the stock of the dividend-paying companies are taxed on 20 percent of the dividends. Firms that own over 80 percent of another firm's stock are not taxed on the dividends.

Recall from Chapter 13 that because corporations are taxed on only 30 percent of the dividends they receive from other corporations, many U.S. firms invest their excess cash in preferred stock rather than corporate or Treasury bonds. As Chapter 3 noted, financial institutions recently designed a number of variations of preferred stock that take advantage of this tax preference. As a result, the tendency of corporations to invest their excess cash in preferred stock has increased since the mid-1980s. Because firms can invest their excess cash in preferred stock that is taxed at a lower rate, they find it more attractive to reduce dividends and invest their earnings internally.

14.6 Summary and Conclusions

This chapter analyzed two methods by which firms distribute earnings to their shareholders: dividends and share repurchases. In the absence of taxes and transaction costs, the two methods of distributing cash are virtually identical. However, taxable U.S. investors prefer share repurchases.

The chapter presented a few hypotheses that might explain why corporations have paid out so much in tax-disadvantaged dividends instead of repurchasing their shares, yet none of the explanations are entirely convincing. We are still puzzled by the significant amount of dividends that U.S. corporations pay, and believe that tax-paying shareholders would be better off if firms increased their share repurchase programs and simultaneously cut their dividends. Firms may continue to pay dividends because managers observe an increase in their stock prices when they announce dividend increases. However, we do not believe that the positive stock price response to dividend increases provides a good rationale for paying a dividend.[15]

Other inexplicable puzzles also relate to dividend policy and taxes. First, a number of U.S. firms implemented share repurchase programs in the 1980s. This occurred even as U.S. tax laws were changing to lessen the tax disadvantage of dividends relative to share repurchases. Second, there are large differences across countries in both the tax treatment of dividends and the ability of firms to repurchase shares. However, we do not observe systematic differences in dividend yields across countries that correspond to these tax and institutional differences.[16]

Our analysis of the payout of dividends and taxes suggests that stocks with high dividend yields should offer higher expected returns to attract tax-paying investors. Unfortunately, testing this proposition has turned out to be difficult. Historically, stocks with high dividend yields have had higher returns than stocks with low dividend yields, but we cannot conclude that the return premium represents compensation for taxes. Since dividend policies are highly correlated with investment policies cross-sectionally, it also is likely that dividend policies are highly correlated with systematic risk. Therefore, it may be impossible to distinguish whether stocks with high dividend yields require higher rates of return because they are tax disadvantaged or whether they receive higher rates of return because they are in some ways riskier. As Chapter 5 discussed, most recent empirical tests of asset pricing have failed to document a relation between systematic risk and expected returns, which makes us less sanguine about the possibility of determining how dividends affect expected returns.

---

[15]This topic is discussed in Chapter 18.

[16]As an example, individual investors in Japan pay a tax of only 20 percent on dividend income. Less than 25 percent of all shares are held by individuals, however, and most other shareholders pay no taxes on dividends. In Japan, average dividend payout ratios are between 40 percent and 50 percent of earnings, about the same as in the United States, but dividend yields are much lower in Japan given their much higher price/earnings ratios.

Key Concepts

Result 14.1: *(The Miller-Modigliani dividend irrelevancy theorem.)* Consider the choice between paying a dividend and using an equivalent amount of money to repurchase shares. Assume:

- There are no tax considerations.
- There are no transaction costs.
- The investment, financing, and operating policies of the firm are held fixed.

Then the choice between paying dividends and repurchasing shares is a matter of indifference to shareholders.

Result 14.2: Consider the choice between paying out earnings to shareholders versus retaining the earnings for investment. Assume:

1. There are no tax considerations.
2. There are no transaction costs.
3. The choice between paying a dividend and retaining the earnings for reinvestment within the firm does not convey any information to shareholders.
4. The firm is financed completely with equity.

Then a dividend payout will either increase or decrease firm value, depending on whether there are positive net present value (*NPV*) investments that could be funded by retaining the money within the firm. If there are no positive *NPV* investments, the money should be paid out.

Result 14.3: In the United States, taxes favor share repurchases over dividends. The gain associated with a share repurchase over a cash dividend depends on:

- The difference between the capital gains rate and the ordinary tax rate.
- The tax basis of the shares, that is, the price at which the shares were purchased.

- The timing of the sale of the shares (if soon, the gain is less).

Result 14.4: Stocks with high dividend yields are fundamentally different from stocks with low dividend yields in terms of their characteristics and their risk profiles. Therefore, it is nearly impossible to assess whether the relation between dividend yield and expected returns is due to taxes or risk.

Result 14.5: The combination of the corporate tax deductibility of interest payments and the personal taxes on dividends implies that firms may prefer:

- Financing new investments with retained earnings over issuing debt.
- Issuing debt to issuing equity.

Result 14.6: Tax-exempt and tax-paying shareholders agree about which projects a firm should fund from external equity issues, but may disagree about which projects should be financed from retained earnings. In particular:

- Tax-exempt shareholders require the same expected return for internally financed projects as they do for externally financed projects.
- Tax-paying shareholders prefer that firms use lower required rates of return for internally financed projects if the alternative is paying taxable dividends.

Key Terms

classical tax system   526
dividend payout ratio   519
dividend policy   518
dividend yields   520

imputation system   526
investor clienteles   529
Miller-Modigliani dividend irrelevancy theorem   518
pecking order of financing choices   535

Exercises

14.1. Explain why the proportion of earnings distributed in the form of a share repurchase has increased substantially over the past 15 years.

14.2. You are considering buying IBM stock which is trading today at $98 a share. IBM is going

ex-dividend tomorrow, paying out $2.00 per share. If you believe the stock will drop to $96.50 following the dividend, should you buy the stock before or after the dividend payment? Explain how your answer depends on the tax rate on ordinary income, capital gains, and your expected holding period.

14.3. The Tax Reform Act of 1986 removed the tax preference for capital gains. Does this eliminate the tax preference for share repurchases over dividends?

14.4. Hot Shot Uranium Mines is issuing stock for the first time and needs to determine an initial proportion of debt and equity. In its first years, the firm will have substantial tax write-offs as it amortizes the uranium in the mine. In later years, however, it will have high taxable earnings. Make a proposal regarding the firm's optimal capital structure and future payout policy.

14.5. Suppose you are a manager who wants to retain as much as possible of the firm's earnings in order to increase the size of the firm. How would you react to proposals to repurchase shares that would make it less costly to distribute cash to shareholders? How does your reaction relate to your answer in exercise 14.1?

14.6. Hunter Industries has generated $1 million in excess of its investment needs. The firm can invest the excess cash in Treasury bonds at 8 percent or distribute the cash to shareholders as a dividend. Assume that the corporate tax rate is 40 percent and that the firm is owned by three different kinds of taxpayers: The first type is tax exempt, the second type has a 25 percent marginal tax rate, and the third type has a 40 percent marginal tax rate. Describe the decision preferred by the three different investors, indicating the reasons for the decision and providing calculations to show your conclusions. Next, consider the possibility that the firm can invest in preferred stock that pays

7 percent per year. Describe how this would affect Hunter's decision, given the 70 percent dividend exclusion for corporate investors.

14.7. Suppose that the capital gains tax rate is expected to increase in three years. How would this affect Bill Gates's decision on whether Microsoft should use some of the company's excess cash to repurchase shares?

14.8 The XYZ Corporation has an expected dividend of $4 one period from now. This dividend is expected to grow by 2 percent per period.

   a. What is the value of a share of stock, assuming that the appropriate discount rate for expected future dividends is 10 percent per period? For your answer, assume that the effective personal tax rate on dividends is 40 percent and the effective personal tax rate on capital gains and share repurchases is zero.

   b. The XYZ Corporation announces that it will stop paying dividends. Instead, the company will engage in a stock repurchase plan under which future cash that would previously have been earmarked for dividend payments will now be used exclusively for stock repurchases. Assuming no information effects, what should the new price of a share of XYZ stock be when market participants first learn of this announcement?

14.9 Alpha Corporation earned $150 million in before-tax profits in 1996. Its corporate tax rate is 35 percent. Daniel Reptella, who owns 20 percent of the firm's shares, has a personal marginal tax rate of 40 percent. From Daniel's perspective, what is the effective tax rate on Alpha's profits if its entire after-tax profits are distributed as a dividend?

References and Additional Readings

Aharony, Joseph, and Itzhak Swary. "Quarterly Dividend and Earnings Announcements and Stockholders' Returns: An Empirical Analysis." *Journal of Finance* 35, no. 1 (1980), pp. 1–12.

Allen, Franklin, and Roni Michaely. "Dividend Policy." Chapter 25 in *Handbooks in Operations Research and Management Science: Volume 9, Finance,* Robert Jarrow, V. Maksimovic, and W. Ziemba, eds. Amsterdam, The Netherlands: Elsevier Science, B.V., 1995.

Bagwell, Laurie Simon, and John Shoven. "Cash Distributions to Shareholders." *Journal of Economic Perspectives* 3, no. 3 (1989), pp. 129–40.

Black, Fischer. "The Dividend Puzzle." *Journal of Portfolio Management* (1976), pp. 5–8.

Black, Fischer, and Myron Scholes. "The Effects of Dividend Yield and Dividend Policy on Common Stock Prices and Returns." *Journal of Financial Economics* 1 (1974), pp. 1–22.

Blume, Marshall. "Stock Return and Dividend Yield: Some More Evidence." *Review of Economics and Statistics* 62 (1980), pp. 567–77.

Brennan, Michael. "Taxes, Market Valuation, and Corporate Financial Policy." *National Tax Journal* 23 (1970), pp. 417–27.

Chen, Nai-fu; Bruce Grundy; and Robert F. Stambaugh. "Changing Risk, Changing Risk Premiums, and

Dividend Yield Effects." *Journal of Business* 63 (1990), pp. S51–S70.

Donaldson, Gordon. *Corporate Debt Capacity: A Study of Corporate Debt Policy and the Determination of Corporate Debt Capacity.* Boston: Harvard Graduate School of Business Administration, 1961.

Dunsby, Adam. "Share Repurchases and Corporate Distributions: An Empirical Study." Working paper, University of Pennsylvania, Philadelphia, 1993.

Eades, Kenneth; Patrick Hess; and Han Kim. "On Interpreting Security Returns during the Ex-Dividend Period." *Journal of Financial Economics* 13, no. 1 (1984), pp. 3–34.

Elton, Edward, and Martin Gruber. "Marginal Stockholders' Tax Rates and the Clientele Effect." *Review of Economic and Statistics* 52 (1970), pp. 68–74.

Fama, Eugene, and Harvey Babiak. "Dividend Policy: An Empirical Analysis." *Journal of the American Statistical Association* 63 (December 1968), pp. 1132–61.

Feenberg, Daniel. "Does the Investment Interest Limitation Explain the Existence of Dividends?" *Journal of Financial Economics* 9, no. 3 (1981), pp. 265–70.

Grinblatt, Mark; Ronald Masulis; and Sheridan Titman. "The Valuation Effects of Stock Splits and Stock Dividends." *Journal of Financial Economics* 13, no. 4 (1984), pp. 461–90.

Hubbard, Jeff, and Roni Michaely. "Do Investors Ignore Dividend Taxation? A Reexamination of the Citizens Utilities Case." Working paper, Cornell University, Ithaca, New York, 1995.

Kalay, Avner. "Stockholder-Bondholder Conflict and Dividend Constraints." *Journal of Financial Economics* 10, no. 2 (1982), pp. 211–33.

Keim, Don. "Dividend Yields and Stock Returns: Implications of Abnormal January Returns." *Journal of Financial Economics* 14 (1985), pp. 473–89.

Kose, John, and Joseph Williams. "Dividends, Dilution, and Taxes." *Journal of Finance* 40, no. 4 (1985), pp. 1053–70.

Lewellen, Wilbur; Kenneth Stanley; Ronald Lease; and Garry Schlarbaum. "Some Direct Evidence on the Dividend Clientele Phenomenon." *Journal of Finance* 33, no. 5 (1978), pp. 1385–99.

Lintner, John. "Distribution of Incomes of Corporations among Dividends, Retained Earnings, and Taxes." *American Economic Review* 46 (May 1956), pp. 97–113.

Litzenberger, Robert, and Krishna Ramaswamy. "The Effects of Dividends on Common Stock Prices: Tax Effects or Information Effects?" *Journal of Finance* 37, no. 2 (1982), pp. 429–43.

Long, John B., Jr. "The Market Valuation of Cash Dividends: A Case to Consider." *Journal of Financial Economics* 6, no. 2/3 (1978), pp. 235–64.

Michaely, Roni. "Ex-Dividend Day Stock Price Behavior: The Case of the 1986 Tax Reform Act." *Journal of Finance* 46 (1991), pp. 845–60.

Miller, Merton, and Franco Modigliani. "Dividend Policy, Growth and the Value of Shares." *Journal of Business* 34 (October 1961), pp. 411–33.

Miller, Merton, and Myron Scholes. "Dividends and Taxes." *Journal of Financial Economics* 6, no. 4 (1978), pp. 333–64.

———. "Dividends and Taxes: Empirical Evidence." *Journal of Political Economy* 90 (1982), pp. 1118–41.

Peterson, Pamela; David Peterson; and James Ang. "Direct Evidence on the Marginal Rate of Taxation on Dividend Income." *Journal of Financial Economics* 14 (1985), pp. 267–82.

Pettit, Richardson. "Taxes, Transaction Costs and the Clientele Effect of Dividends." *Journal of Financial Economics* 5, no. 3 (1977), pp. 419–36.

Poterba, James. "The Market Valuation of Cash Dividends: The Citizens Utilities Case Reconsidered." *Journal of Financial Economics* 15 (1986), pp. 395–406.

Bankruptcy Costs and Debt Holder–Equity Holder Conflicts

Learning Objectives

After reading this chapter you should be able to:

1. Understand the effect of direct bankruptcy costs on borrowing rates and capital structure choices.
2. Describe the factors contributing to the conflicts of interest between debt holders and equity holders.
3. Explain how debt can cause equity holders to take on projects that are too risky and to pass up positive *NPV* projects.
4. Identify various situations in which debt holders and equity holders may disagree on the liquidation decision.
5. Understand how bond covenants, bank loans, privately placed debt, and convertible bonds can mitigate some of these debt holder–equity holder conflicts.
6. Describe how conflicts between debt holders and equity holders affect capital structure choices.

By May 1992, Terex Corporation, a producer of tractor trailers and earth-moving machines, had experienced several quarters of depressed and sometimes negative operating income. Its stock had fallen 60 percent in the past two years. Many investors saw the company as having a significant risk of default, although such default was not "imminent." Randolph Lenz, the company's chairman, chief executive, and owner of 53 percent of the shares, decided that Terex would undertake a leveraged acquisition despite these problems. Upon the announcement that it would acquire the forklift division of Clark Equipment for $95 million, Terex's stock rose from 11⅝ to 12. Although investors may have seen the increased risk as positive for the company's stock, the acquisition target was extremely speculative, causing the value of Terex's existing bonds to fall substantially.

U p to this point, we have examined the firm's capital structure decision within a simplified setting which either ruled out the possibility of bankruptcy or, alternatively, assumed that if bankruptcy occurs, the assets of the corporation would transfer costlessly from equity holders to debt holders. This chapter moves beyond these simplifying assumptions and examines the capital structure choice in a world where bankruptcy imposes costs on the firm.

Treasurers of bankrupt firms who saw their firm's stock price fall almost to zero might claim that bankruptcy is extremely costly. However, while debt financing may have significantly contributed to the bankruptcy, most of the loss in firm value leading up to the bankruptcy cannot be attributed to debt financing per se but to misfortunes affecting the firm's actual business operations. Only those costs attributed either directly or indirectly to the event of bankruptcy or, more generally, to the threat of bankruptcy are relevant to a firm's capital structure decision. Therefore, as long as bankruptcy or the threat of bankruptcy does not affect the cash flows available to the firm's security holders, the possibility of bankruptcy is irrelevant to a firm's capital structure decision.

The extent to which bankruptcy reduces the cash flows of firms has been debated extensively in the academic literature. The reductions in cash flows related to bankruptcy or the threat of bankruptcy are generally classified as either direct bankruptcy costs or indirect bankruptcy costs. **Direct bankruptcy costs** relate to the legal process involved in reorganizing a bankrupt firm. **Indirect bankruptcy costs** are not directly related to the reorganization and can arise among **financially distressed firms**, or those firms that are close to bankruptcy, but which may never actually go bankrupt. As shown later in this chapter and in Chapter 16, most indirect bankruptcy costs arise because financial distress creates a tendency for firms to engage in actions that are harmful to their debt holders and **nonfinancial stakeholders** such as customers, employees, and suppliers. As a result of these harmful actions, a financially distressed firm may find it difficult to obtain credit and may find it more costly in other ways to efficiently carry out its day-to-day business.

This chapter focuses on the conflicts of interest that can arise between a firm's debt holders and equity holders. In the chapter's opening vignette, for example, Terex's acquisition of Clark Equipment may have been made with the interests of Terex's stockholders in mind. Although this acquisition indeed benefited stockholders, it resulted in a reduction in the value of Terex's outstanding bonds and therefore was not in the best interests of the company's debt holders.

When these conflicts exist, the net present value (*NPV*) of a project, calculated by discounting the cash flows to equity holders, can be substantially different from the *NPV* calculated with either the APV or WACC method. For example, Chapter 12 illustrated how the *NPV* of the equity holders' cash flows from a relatively safe investment project could be negative, even though the *NPV* of the total cash flows to both debt holders and equity holders is positive. In other words, firms that operate solely in the interests of their equity holders, thereby ignoring the interests of their debt holders, may pass up value-creating projects. In addition, these firms may take on excessively risky projects that benefit equity holders but lower the value of the firm's debt.

This chapter argues that the equity holders of a firm ultimately can be hurt by the firm's tendency to ignore the interests of its debt holders. This tendency may result in a firm's inability to obtain debt financing at attractive terms and, in some cases, it may prevent a firm from obtaining any debt financing at all. One solution to this problem (discussed later in the chapter) is to design the debt so that it minimizes the potential for conflict. This can be accomplished through convertibility features and debt covenants (see Chapter 2), which are terms included in many debt contracts to limit a firm's investment and financing choices. Because these solutions are imperfect, however, firms generally will want to limit the amount of debt in their capital structure even when there are substantial tax benefits to debt financing.

Most of the key issues in this chapter are developed with a set of simple numerical examples. Unless specified otherwise, valuation in these examples assumes risk neutrality, no direct bankruptcy costs, no taxes, and a risk-free rate of zero.

15.1 Bankruptcy

The U.S. Bankruptcy Code

Firms that are unable to make required payments to their creditors can file for either a **Chapter 7** bankruptcy,[1] which leads to the liquidation of the firm's assets in the settlement of the creditors' claims, or a **Chapter 11** bankruptcy, which allows the firm to restructure its debt and equity claims and continue to operate.

Chapter 7 Bankruptcy.   In a Chapter 7 bankruptcy, the bankruptcy court selects a trustee from outside the company who liquidates the assets of the firm and distributes the proceeds to the debt holders. Any proceeds from the liquidation that remain after settling the debt holders' claims are then distributed to the company's shareholders. Under Chapter 7, these proceeds are divided among the claim holders according to the **absolute priority rule**, which states that debt holders must be paid in full before equity holders receive any proceeds of the bankruptcy. The rule also states that secured debt holders must be paid before unsecured debt holders and that the more senior of the unsecured debt holders must be paid in full before the more junior debt holders.

Chapter 11 Bankruptcy.   Chapter 11 bankruptcies are much more complicated than Chapter 7 bankruptcies. Under Chapter 11, the claims of debt and equity holders cannot be settled with cash realized from the liquidation of assets. Rather, the debt and equity holders receive new financial claims in exchange for their existing claims. For example, debt holders often end up with equity in the newly reorganized firm that emerges from a Chapter 11 bankruptcy.

Almost all bankruptcies of large corporations start out as Chapter 11 bankruptcies and become Chapter 7 bankruptcies only when the various claimants fail to agree on a **reorganization plan**, which specifies how the new financial claims are to be distributed among the claim holders. After filing for a Chapter 11 bankruptcy, the corporation has 120 days to submit a reorganization plan, which creditors can either accept or reject.[2] If creditors reject the offer or the corporation fails to submit a reorganization plan, the judge overseeing the bankruptcy case can give the corporation an extension during which it must come up with an acceptable plan or ask the creditors to come up with their own reorganization plan. In most cases, at least one extension is granted.

To determine the acceptability of a plan, each class of **impaired creditors**—the creditors who will not be paid in full—as well as the equity holders must vote on it. For a specific class of creditors (e.g., convertible bondholders) to accept the plan, a simple majority of the claimants and those who hold two-thirds of the dollar amount of the claims must vote favorably. A class of stockholders exhibit approval for the plan when at least two-thirds of the firm's shares vote to accept it.

If all classes of claimants accept the plan, the court will approve it. However, it may not be necessary to have all classes of claimants approve the plan. The court may confirm

---

[1]In reality, it is often the creditors who file for Chapter 7 bankruptcy.

[2]Judges frequently extend this 120-day period.

the plan over the objections of the dissenting classes if it judges the plan to be nondiscriminatory, fair, and equitable. A plan that is forced on dissenting claimants is known as a **cramdown**. A necessary condition for a cramdown is that the dissenters receive at least what they would receive under a Chapter 7 liquidation.

The absolute priority rule is often violated in a Chapter 11 settlement.[3] Junior debt holders and equity holders often receive a share of the bankruptcy proceeds even when senior debt holders are not paid in full. Senior debt holders allow these deviations from the absolute priority rule to facilitate a timely settlement of the bankruptcy and to avoid future lawsuits. For example, junior debt holders often sue the bankrupt firm's bank for taking actions that may have caused the firm to go into bankruptcy. In an attempt to settle those lawsuits, the banks often allow these more junior claimants to receive a portion of the bankruptcy settlement.

The Direct Costs of Bankruptcy

If the bankruptcy process is relatively costless, the possibility of bankruptcy does not affect a firm's capital structure decision. Recall from Chapter 13 that the Modigliani-Miller Theorem does not require that there be no bankruptcy, only that the bankruptcy be costless.

There are, however, a number of costs directly related to bankruptcy, including the time management spends dealing with creditors and the additional time creditors spend with the managers of a bankrupt firm. Legal expenses, court costs, and advisory fees also are direct costs of bankruptcy. For example, when Macy's department store went bankrupt in 1992, it spent an estimated $100 million on "lawyers, accountants, investment bankers, and other highly paid advisors."[4] The $100 million represented approximately 2 to 3 percent of the firm's estimated value at the time. Macy's emerged from Chapter 11 bankruptcy in mid-1994 as a division of Federated Department Stores. The two and one-half years that Macy's spent in bankruptcy proceedings was slightly more than the average time spent in bankruptcy.[5]

Estimates of the Direct Costs of Bankruptcy.   The 2 to 3 percent of assets that Macy's lost due to direct bankruptcy costs is fairly typical for large U.S. corporations. Warner (1977) estimated that direct costs of bankruptcy for large railroads, although substantial in magnitude, are quite small relative to the size of the firms, averaging only 5.3 percent of their (already diminished) debt and equity values just prior to the bankruptcy filings. A study of more recent bankruptcies of large firms by Weiss (1990) determined that direct costs averaged about 3.1 percent of the total value of the debt and equity of the bankrupt firms.

Because most of the direct costs of bankruptcy are the same for both small and large firms, the bankruptcy costs of small firms, as a proportion of the value of their assets, are much larger. For small firms, these costs may be fairly large, perhaps 20–25 percent of a firm's value.[6] However, even these high percentages suggest that the direct costs of bankruptcy add very little to a firm's borrowing costs except in cases where bankruptcy is quite likely. This is because these costs (1) are percentages of an already diminished firm value and (2) must be multiplied by the probability of bankruptcy, and then discounted, to determine their impact on borrowing costs.

---

[3]See Franks and Torous (1989).
[4]*The Economist,* May 21, 1994.
[5]Hotchkiss (1995) reported that on average firms in her sample spent 19.5 months in bankruptcy.
[6]See Ang, Chua, and McConnell (1982) and Altman (1984).

Who Bears the Bankruptcy Costs?   Under the absolute priority rule, most of a firm's value in the event of bankruptcy is transferred to its debt holders. Since the direct costs of bankruptcy diminish the value of the firm, most direct bankruptcy costs are thus ultimately borne by the firm's debt holders.

Why should managers, who represent the interests of the firm's equity holders, be concerned about the costs borne by debt holders? While equity holders are not directly concerned with costs that may be imposed on their firm's lenders, they are concerned about the rates at which the firm can borrow. Since lenders realize they will be bearing costs in the event of bankruptcy, they will demand a *default premium* on the interest rate they charge the firm which reflects the probability of the firm's bankruptcy. In paying this default premium, shareholders are, in effect, paying the expected bankruptcy costs whenever they issue risky debt. Therefore, they must consider this premium to be a cost that offsets other advantages associated with debt financing.

Example 15.1:   How Bankruptcy Affects Borrowing Costs

Westlake Corporation would like to borrow $1 million for one year. There is a 90 percent chance that the loan will be repaid in full and a 10 percent chance that the firm will be bankrupt at the end of the year. In the event that the firm is bankrupt, its assets can be sold for $600,000. However, the legal costs of seizing Westlake's assets will cost the bank $100,000. How much will a bank charge for the loan if it prices loans to companies like Westlake to earn, on average, 10 percent? How is the interest rate charged on the loan affected by the potential bankruptcy costs?

Answer: To realize its 10 percent expected return, the bank needs to receive, on average, $1.1 million at the end of the year. If Westlake is bankrupt, the bank will receive only $500,000. Hence, to receive $1.1 million, on average, it must receive $1.167 million if the firm is not bankrupt (since .1 × $.5 million + .9 × $1.167 million = $1.1 million). In other words, the bank must charge 16.7 percent on the loan. If there were no costs associated with bankruptcy, the bank would recover $600,000 instead of $500,000 in the event of bankruptcy, and it would then need to charge only 15.6 percent on the loan.

The general principle to remember from Example 15.1 is that lenders are likely to anticipate future events and thus require compensation for the costs they expect to bear.

Result 15.1   Lenders charge an interest premium that reflects the expected costs they must bear in the event of default. Therefore, shareholders indirectly bear the expected costs of bankruptcy and must consider these costs when choosing their optimal capital structures.

15.2 Debt Holder–Equity Holder Conflicts: An Indirect Bankruptcy Cost

If direct bankruptcy costs were the only costs associated with debt financing, it would be difficult to justify the relatively low debt ratios of firms like AT&T which have long histories of generating taxable earnings and could presumably lower their costs of capital by increasing their leverage. The expected present value of the direct costs of bankruptcy are incorporated into the firm's borrowing costs. Therefore, these direct costs cannot exceed the present value of the yearly difference between the firm's borrowing rate and the comparable default-free rates of interest (e.g., the rates on Treasury bonds). The difference between AT&T's borrowing rate and the default-free interest rate is small— about 0.5 to 1.0 percent. This suggests that the direct costs of bankruptcy should have a trivial effect on AT&T's capital structure decision. Moreover, a large part of the difference in borrowing rates may be due to the favorable tax treatment and greater liquidity of government bonds.

To justify why many firms continue to use more costly equity financing, one must consider the indirect costs of bankruptcy. Indirect costs often arise because of the threat of bankruptcy and are relevant even if the firm never defaults on its obligations. Because of this, we often refer to them as **financial distress costs**. The threat of bankruptcy affects a firm's relationships with its lenders and in other ways affects its ability to operate. The rest of this chapter addresses how the threat of bankruptcy affects a firm's relationship with its lenders and the indirect bankruptcy costs that result.[7]

Equity Holder Incentives

The incentives of equity holders to maximize the value of their shares are not necessarily consistent with the incentive to maximize the total value of the firm's debt and equity. Indeed, shareholders of a leveraged firm often have an incentive to implement investment strategies that reduce the value of the firm's outstanding debt. To understand this concept, remember that the total value of a firm equals the value of its debt plus the value of its equity. Therefore, strategies that decrease the value of a firm's debt without reducing its total value increase the firm's share price. Equity holders have an incentive to carry out these kinds of strategies if permitted to do so. Similarly, they also may implement strategies that *reduce* the total value of the firm's debt and equity claims if these strategies transfer a sufficient amount from the debt holders to the equity holders. The implications of this point are summarized in Result 15.2.

Result 15.2   Firms acting to maximize their stock prices make different decisions when they have debt in their capital structures than when they are financed completely with equity.

Who Bears the Costs of the Incentive Problem?   Before considering specific strategies that enable equity holders to gain at the expense of debt holders, note that sophisticated lenders will anticipate the equity holders' incentives to implement strategies of self-interest and will determine the interest rates they charge on their loans accordingly. A lender who anticipates that equity holders will take actions in the future that reduce the value of the lender's claims will charge higher interest rates. In this way, the equity holders bear the expected costs of their future adverse incentives in the form of higher interest rates at the time they borrow. As a result, firms have an incentive to convince their lenders that they will not engage in such behavior and that they will instead act to maximize the total value of the firm: the value of their debt plus the value of their equity. However, firms may have difficulty committing credibly to a policy of maximizing the firm's total value rather than the value of their shares.

How Equity Holders Can Expropriate Debtholder Wealth.   The firm's equity holders can expropriate wealth from its debt holders in a number of ways. For example, they could instruct the firm's managers to sell off all of its assets and pay the proceeds of this liquidation as a dividend to the shareholders, leaving the debt holders with valueless paper. Lenders, aware that equity holders might implement this type of action, demand covenants, or contracts between the borrower and lender that preclude such actions.[8]

---

[7]Indirect bankruptcy costs that arise for other reasons are examined in Chapter 16.

[8]In reality, regulations exist to prevent a firm from expropriating wealth from the firm's debt holders by paying out all of its cash as a liquidating dividend. However, lenders still must be aware of the incentive of equity holders to pay out excessive amounts of cash.

However, as we will discuss in section 15.3, debt covenants cannot solve all of the potential conflicts that can arise between equity holders and debt holders.

The various distortions in investment strategies that might arise because of conflicts of interest between equity holders and debt holders can be placed into one of the following categories:

- The **debt overhang problem**: Equity holders may *underinvest,* that is, pass up profitable (positive *NPV*) investments because the firm's existing debt captures most of the project's benefits. This is sometimes referred to as the **underinvestment problem**.
- The **asset substitution problem**: Equity holders have a tendency to take on overly risky projects.
- The **shortsighted investment problem**: Equity holders will have a tendency to pass up profitable investment projects that pay off over a long time horizon in favor of less profitable (lower *NPV*) projects that pay off more quickly.
- The **reluctance to liquidate problem**: Equity holders may want to keep a firm operating when its liquidation value exceeds its operating value.

Each of these possibilities will be considered in the following subsections.

The Debt Overhang Problem

Chapter 12 noted that, with risky debt, the *NPV* calculated by discounting the total cash flows generated by a project at the project's weighted average cost of capital can substantially differ from the *NPV* of the cash flows to equity holders. Recall from Example 12.17 that Unitron had a riskless project that yielded 12 percent per year. Given that the risk-free rate was assumed to be 10 percent per year, Unitron can create value by taking this project because the project generates cash flows that exceed those of another investment, the risk-free asset, which costs the same and perfectly tracks the project. However, this value is realized by Unitron's shareholders only when the firm can borrow at the risk-free rate. Since Example 12.17 assumed that Unitron's borrowing rate was 13 percent, Unitron shareholders would be worse off if the project was selected. By taking the project, Unitron shareholders would realize a cash inflow of 12 percent per year, which would be financed by a cash outflow of 13 percent per year. Thus, Unitron's shareholders would lose 1 percent of this project's cost in every period.

Discounting Cash Flows to Equity Holders versus Discounting Total Cash Flows. The Unitron project was a positive *NPV* project as traditionally defined. However, the net cash flows to the firm's stockholders, after financing the project, are always negative, so it follows that the net present value of the project must be negative from the shareholders' perspective. This example illustrates that it is important to distinguish between net present values to the firm and the net present value of the project that accrues to the firm's shareholders.

Result 15.3   Selecting projects with positive net present values can at times reduce the value of a leveraged firm's stock.

In the Unitron example, the risk-free project will create value, as the traditional net present value rule indicates. However, the project creates value for the firm's debt holders rather than its equity holders. By adding the safe project, the firm becomes somewhat less risky, and if the firm does go bankrupt, debt holders are likely to have more assets to

EXHIBIT 15.1   Lily Pharmaceuticals Research

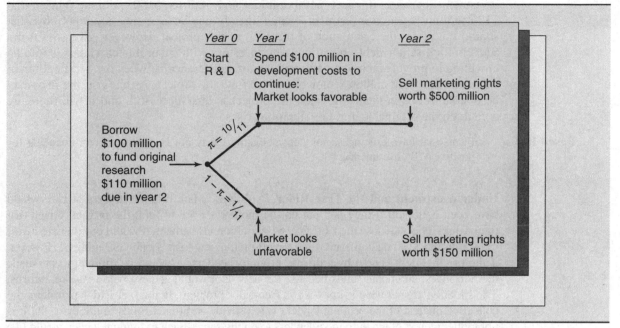

divide up. Hence, debt holders would like the firm to take the project, but equity holders would like the firm to pass it up.

Underinvestment as a Consequence of Debt Overhang.   Unitron examplifies the underinvestment that is generated by *debt overhang*.[9] This problem arises when a firm's existing debt load causes it to pass up positive *NPV* projects because borrowing is too costly, or, as in the illustration below, impossible.

To examine the debt overhang problem in more depth, consider Lily Pharmaceuticals Research, a recent start-up firm shown in Exhibit 15.1. Lily recently spent $100 million to undertake research on a new drug to prevent facial wrinkles. Assume that if the market for this drug looks favorable (see the upper branch of Exhibit 15.1), the firm can spend an additional $100 million to further develop the drug, receive FDA approval, and bring it to market. If this happens, which we assume will happen 10 out of 11 times, Lily, one year later, can sell the marketing rights to the drug for $500 million. However, if the market looks less favorable (see the lower branch of the exhibit—1 out of 11 times), then the company will have a drug with marketing rights worth only $150 million after spending the additional $100 million.

To finance this research, Lily issued a bond with a covenant specifying that any additional debt the firm issues must have lower priority in the event of bankruptcy. To simplify this example, assume that investors are risk neutral and that the appropriate expected rate of return on bonds is zero. However, as shown below, the firm will default on this obligation when the market is unfavorable, which occurs 1 in 11 times. Therefore, to raise the $100 million, Lily must promise to pay $110 million in the future to compensate investors for the possibility that they may not be paid.

---

[9]Myers (1977) originally described this underinvestment problem.

In the less favorable situation, continuing with the project is still a positive *NPV* investment because it costs $100 million and returns $150 million. The initial $100 million research investment, which already has been spent, is a sunk cost that should not affect the calculation of the *NPV* of this project. However, given the firm's $110 million senior debt obligation, new investors with subordinated claims would be unwilling to provide more than $40 million—the difference between the $150 million in value and the $110 million senior claim—to fund the project. As a result, the firm may be unable to obtain financing when the project is less successful, and it will therefore default on the original loan if this situation arises.

Result 15.4   Firms that have existing senior debt obligations may not be able to obtain financing for positive *NPV* investments.

Underinvestment and the Free Rider Problem.   The original lenders at Lily would have been better off if they had put up the money needed to fund the project. Given that they would otherwise lose their original $100 million investment, it would pay them to invest the additional $100 million even if the payoff on the new loan is only $40 million. However, if the original debt is held by a diffuse group of lenders, it would be difficult to persuade them to invest additional funds because the new debt would achieve below-market returns. The situation creates what is known as a free-rider problem. In the **free-rider problem**, the collective interest of the original lenders is to provide additional funds to the firm, but it is not in the interest of the individual lenders to do the same. Each individual lender would like to free ride on the decision of other lenders to bail out the firm.[10]

How the Seniority Structure of Debt Affects the Debt Overhang Problem.   The debt overhang problem in the Lily example arose because Lily's existing debt had protective covenants that prevented the company from issuing new debt senior to the existing debt. Financing the R&D with unprotected debt would have allowed the firm to finance the additional investment with new debt that would be senior to the original debt.[11] If existing debt is unprotected, new debt can be issued to fund the project as long as the project's value exceeds the new debt obligation. If Lily's original debt financing was not senior, a new riskless senior debt obligation of $100 million could be issued to fund the $100 million investment, leaving $50 million for the original debt holders when the senior obligation is paid.

Unfortunately, while using unprotected debt solves the underinvestment problem analyzed in the Lily example, it can cause additional problems that are likely to make this alternative unattractive. In particular, it provides firms with an incentive to raise additional senior debt when they do not really need it. In addition, unprotected debt increases the incentive of firms to take on overly risky projects, as we discuss later in this chapter.

How the Debt Overhang Problem Affects Dividend Policy.   The Lily example assumed that the firm needs to raise money from external sources. However, most firms have internally generated funds available for investments and often must address the relevant decision of whether to distribute the funds to shareholders as a dividend or a share repurchase or, alternatively, use the money to fund additional investment.

---

[10]Later in this chapter, when discussing how to resolve incentive conflicts between debt holders and equity holders, we analyze how a banking relation may help a firm solve this free-rider problem and mitigate the effect of debt overhang.

[11]The relevance of debt seniority rules for the debt overhang problem is considered in Stulz and Johnson (1985).

When an investment is financed from a firm's retained earnings, the tendency to underinvest becomes even more clear. To illustrate this, consider Chan Partners Ltd., which purchased a $100 million office building in Phoenix. Chan's group provided a down payment of $20 million and financed the rest with a bullet mortgage, requiring payments of $8 million per year for 10 years with $80 million in principal due at the end of 10 years. At the time of purchase, Chan's group knew that the building was going to generate $12 million in annual rent and require $3 million a year in maintenance to maintain the building's value.

Two years after buying the building, the Phoenix office market suffered a serious decline and the building's value fell to $70 million. Fortunately, the Chan group had long-term leases so their rental income was not seriously affected. However, the group's incentive to pay out the rental income as cash to the partners rather than to use the cash to maintain the building was affected by this downturn. Since the partners believed that the group was quite likely to default on the final $80 million repayment of principal, they had an incentive to distribute (to the partners) as much cash as possible before the final repayment date, without regard for how their actions would affect the building's value.

The partners considered cutting their annual maintenance budget from $3 million to $2 million, which increased the amount distributed to the partners by $1 million per year. However, cutting the maintenance budget would lower the building's value by $18 million by the time the final mortgage payment becomes due in eight years. The partners generally would not consider saving $1 million per year over an eight-year period if it meant reducing the building's value by $18 million. However, the $1 million annual savings would be distributed directly to the partners, so if the market for Phoenix office buildings fails to turn around, the $18 million loss in value would be borne by the holders of the mortgage. As a result, maintaining the building properly—which is clearly a positive net present value project when considering the interests of debt as well as equity claimants—might not be done if the decision is made without regard for the lenders.

Result 15.5   With risky debt, equity holders have an incentive to pass up internally financed positive net present value projects when the funds can be paid out to equity holders as a dividend.

Using Loan Covenants to Mitigate the Underinvestment Problem.   Most commercial mortgages contain covenants that protect the lender from the kind of behavior described in the Chan situation. The covenants can be written in one of two ways. The first specifies that the partners maintain the building appropriately. The second eliminates the incentive to cut maintenance by restricting the payout to the partners. This second approach works because the partners have no incentive to underinvest in maintenance if they are unable to immediately pass on the cost savings to themselves.

The first alternative is impractical because it is very difficult to specify in most corporate loan contracts exactly what kind of investments a firm must undertake. As a result, most corporate loans and privately placed bonds have some kind of restriction on the amount of funds the firm can pay out in dividends or, equivalently, the dollar amount of shares that can be repurchased per year. This is also true for most public bonds that are not investment grade.

Typically, bond and loan covenants specify dividend restrictions as a function of a firm's earnings. For example, a corporation may be required to retain at least 50 percent of its earnings. The disadvantage of this kind of covenant is that it provides an incentive for firms to artificially inflate their earnings so that they can pay out more in dividends. In the Chan illustration, for example, a reduction in building maintenance services would lead to an increase in reported earnings since maintenance is generally expensed. This would allow the firm to pay out more in dividends. Hence, dividend restrictions tied to corporate earnings may not keep firms from cutting back on items such as maintenance and service; these may be good investments for the firm, but they have the effect of initially reducing reported income.

Empirical Evidence on Dividends and Investment Distortions.   While dividend distortions of this kind seem to be important in theory, there is no empirical evidence that suggests that investment distortions of this kind are prevalent.[12] This may be because the tendency to increase payouts and underinvest is not particularly important when the probability of bankruptcy is low or because covenants are effective at limiting these distortions. With respect to the latter hypothesis, there is empirical evidence that for firms in financial distress, dividend covenants seem to be effective in forcing dividend cuts.[13]

The Shortsighted Investment Problem

A popular topic for financial journalists in the late 1980s was the perceived shortsightedness of American businesses. A common claim was that shortsightedness was worsened by the increased use of debt financing by some firms; highly leveraged firms prefer projects that pay off quickly since short-term projects allow them to meet their near-term debt obligations more easily.

By extending the analysis in the preceding subsection, we can see how future debt obligations can make firms shortsighted; in other words, debt can lead firms to favor lower *NPV* investment projects that pay off quickly over higher *NPV* projects with lower initial cash flows. The intuition for this is rooted in the debt overhang problem. Firms with large debt obligations need to pay high borrowing rates on new subordinated debt used to refinance the portion of their existing debt that is maturing. Thus, firms have an incentive to generate cash quickly to minimize the amount of debt that they will need to refinance at high rates.

To illustrate this possibility, consider the case of Applied Textronics, which has debt obligations that are due both next year and in two years. The firm has a bond obligation of $100 million due next year and $40 million due the following year. The firm is considering two equally costly projects:

- A long-term project with positive cash flows next year and the following year.
- A short-term project that generates positive cash flows next year and zero cash flows thereafter.

Assume that the risk-free rate of interest is zero, both cash flows are certain, and the present value of the long-term project exceeds the present value of the short-term project.

The year 1 (and only) cash flow for the short-term project is $50 million while cash flows are $20 million in year 1 and $40 million in year 2 for the long-term project (see Exhibit 15.2). The firm also can forecast with certainty the $50 million in cash flows from its existing investment projects next year. However, the firm's cash flows from its existing investments in year 2 are uncertain. The cash flow is $60 million in the favorable state of the economy and $10 million in the unfavorable state of the economy. The probability of each state of the economy is 50 percent.

If Applied Textronics chooses the short-term project, it will be able to meet its $100 million debt obligations next year; its year 1 cash flows of $50 million from its

---

[12]Long, Malitz, and Sefcik (1994) found no evidence that firms significantly increase their dividends following an increase in their outstanding debt. However, there is some evidence that bond prices react negatively when firms announce large increases in their dividends. See Dhillon and Johnson (1994).

[13]This issue was examined in a study of financially distressed firms by DeAngelo and DeAngelo (1990).

EXHIBIT 15.2   Applied Textronics Cash Flows

	Debt Due	From Existing Assets	From Short-Term Project	From Long-Term Project
Year 1	$100 million	$50 million	$50 million	$20 million
Year 2	40 million	60 million in favorable state; 10 million in unfavorable state	0 million	40 million

existing assets plus the $50 million from the new investment equals the size of the year 1 debt obligation. If the firm takes the long-term project, however, it will generate total cash flows of only $70 million (= $50 million + $20 million) in year 1 and will thus require an additional $30 million in new debt to meet its year 1 debt obligation. If this new debt is subordinated to the old debt, the firm must offer to pay the new lenders $50 million at the end of the following year in order to raise the $30 million. This is true because the lenders will receive, on average, only $30 million if $50 million is promised (i.e., the $50 million promised in the favorable state and $10 million in the unfavorable state—the $50 million in cash less the $40 million senior debt obligation).

The amounts given in Exhibit 15.2 indicate that Applied Textronics will be unable to meet its year 2 debt obligations if the unfavorable state of the economy occurs, regardless of whether the firm chooses the long-term or short-term project. If the short-term project is selected, the firm has only $10 million in cash and a $40 million obligation. If the long-term project is selected, the firm has $50 million in cash, but a $90 million obligation (i.e., the existing $40 million plus the new $50 million obligation). In either case, the firm's equity will be worth zero in the unfavorable state of the economy.

If the firm takes the long-term project, the firm's equity will be worth $10 million in the favorable state of the economy [$40 million + $60 million − ($40 million + $50 million)]. If the firm takes the short-term project, its equity value in the favorable state of the economy will be $20 million ($60 million − $40 million). Hence, the firm's equity holders are better off selecting the short-term project even though it has a lower *NPV*.

How do the shareholders benefit from taking the lower *NPV* investment? Since the firm's existing debt holders are made worse off when the firm selects the short-term project, the gain to the equity holders comes at the expense of the original debt holders whose debt is due at the end of year 2. These debt holders have been paid in full in the unfavorable state of the economy if the firm takes the long-term project, but they receive only $10 million of their $40 million obligation in the unfavorable state of the economy when the short-term project is selected. This insight is summarized below.

Result 15.6   Firms with high debt obligations tend to pass up high *NPV* projects in favor of lower *NPV* projects that pay off sooner.

The Asset Substitution Problem

This subsection describes an additional problem that might arise when firms are financed with debt. Debt provides an incentive for firms to take on unnecessary risk, substituting riskier investment projects for less risky projects. We call this the *asset substitution problem*.[14]

---

[14]A large academic literature discusses the asset substitution problem. Jensen and Meckling (1976) and Galai and Masulis (1976) were the original contributors to the literature.

Option pricing theory provides one way to think about the asset substitution problem. Recall from Chapter 8 that the payoff to equity holders is similar to the payoff from a call option on the firm's assets. Equity holders can realize an unlimited upside, but in the event of an unfavorable outcome, they can do no worse than lose their entire investment because they have limited liability. Hence, the payoff to the equity holders will be either the firm's cash flows less its debt obligation (when cash flows from assets exceed the debt obligation), or zero (when the debt obligation exceeds the cash flows).

The implication of the option pricing model—that option values increase with increases in the volatility of the underlying stock—can thus be applied to show that a firm's equity will be more valuable if it chooses more risky investments. However, a firm's debt, which can be viewed as the combination of the firm's assets along with a short position in a call option on those assets, becomes less valuable if the firm's investments become riskier. Hence, by increasing a firm's risk, equity holders transfer wealth from the debt holders to themselves.

The Incentives of a Firm to Take Higher Risks: The Case of Unistar

Consider Unistar, a firm that has decided to manufacture memory chips and has borrowed the money to build a factory. Unistar's managers now have to decide on one of two designs for the production process. Although the two processes look nearly identical to the firm's bankers and each costs $70 million, Unistar's management knows that process 2 involves much more risk than process 1.

Lenders are aware of the two alternatives and can forecast the possible payoffs of each, but they cannot observe which process the firm will decide upon until after they lend the money. To simplify the analysis, assume as before that investors are all risk neutral and thus want to maximize expected returns. Also assume that the risk-free interest rate is zero. Thus, the present values of the projects are their expected payoffs.

The projects have different payoffs, depending on whether the state of the economy is favorable or unfavorable. These payoffs, which are equally likely to occur, are given in Exhibit 15.3.

From the perspective of an all-equity firm, process 1 is the better alternative. It achieves a $5 million *NPV*, the $75 million expected value minus the $70 million cost, while process 2 achieves zero *NPV* since the costs and expected values are both $70 million.

Assume that the firm uses debt to finance $40 million of the $70 million to be invested and to raise the other $30 million from internal sources. Exhibit 15.4 presents a summary of the payoffs to the firm's equity holders *after repayment of the $40 million debt obligation*.

The payoffs shown in Exhibit 15.4 equal the payoffs in Exhibit 15.3 less the $40 million debt obligation, with one important exception. The equity holders' payoff in the unfavorable state of the economy for process 2 is given as 0 instead of −$15 million

EXHIBIT 15.3   Unistar's Alternative Payoffs

	Cash Flow if State of the Economy Is		
	Unfavorable (p = .5)	*Favorable (p = .5)*	*Expected Value*
Process 1	$50 million	$100 million	$75 million
Process 2	25 million	115 million	70 million

(= $25 million − $40 million) because limited liability implies that equity holders can do no worse than receive zero. Given these payoffs, the equity holders' expected payoff of $37.5 million from process 2 exceeds their payoff of $35.0 million from process 1. Result 15.7 summarizes the concept illustrated by this example.

Result 15.7   The equity holders of a levered firm may prefer a high-risk, low (or even negative) *NPV* project to a low-risk, high *NPV* project.

How Do Lenders Respond to Shareholder Incentives?

If lenders naively believe that process 1 (the higher *NPV* project described in Exhibit 15.3) will be selected, they will provide the debt financing assumed above. However, sophisticated lenders should understand Unistar's incentives to take the riskier project, process 2, and realize that in this situation they would not be making a sensible loan. Specifically, if lenders anticipate that Unistar will select the high-risk project when it has a $40 million loan obligation, they will realize that their loan would have default risk and that they will receive only $25 million of the $40 million promised debt payment if the bad state of the economy occurs. Thus, their loan has an expected value of only $32.5 million (0.5 × $25 million + 0.5 × $40 million). Hence, the lenders would be unwilling to provide $40 million today for the uncertain promise of obtaining $40 million in the future.

If lenders contribute only $32.5 million now for $40 million promised in the future, the firm's equity holders would have to contribute $37.5 million to fund the project. As shown in Exhibit 15.4, equity holders would then receive only $35.0 million, on average, when process 1 is selected, so they would expect to lose money in this case. Exhibit 15.4 shows that process 2 provides equity holders with $37.50 million, on average, which exactly equals their costs. Thus, Unistar fails to gain from the high-risk, low *NPV* project and is unable to realize the gain from the positive *NPV* project.

If the equity holders were able to commit to taking process 1, lenders would be willing to contribute $40 million for the $40 million obligation because (with the lowest cash flow from process 1 being $50 million) they would be repaid with certainty. Equity holders would then need to put up only the remaining $30 million needed, creating for them a $5 million surplus (= $35 million − $30 million). However, if lenders find it difficult to monitor a firm's investments, it may not be easy for Unistar to include loan covenants that allow it to commit credibly to process 1. The lenders would realize that Unistar's equity holders will try to convince them that they (the equity holders) will select process 1. But if this process cannot be verified, the equity holders have an incentive to choose process 2 after lenders and the company finalize the terms of the loan. Hence, the terms of the loan will reflect the risks associated with process 2, not process 1. The equity holders, therefore, bear the costs associated with their distorted incentives.

EXHIBIT 15.4   Unistar's Payoffs to Equity Holders When the Debt Obligation Is $40 Million

	Cash Flow if State of the Economy Is		
	Unfavorable (p = .5)	*Favorable (p = .5)*	*Expected Value*
Process 1	$10 million	$60 million	$35.0 million
Process 2	0 million	75 million	37.5 million

Result 15.8   With sophisticated lenders, equity holders must bear the costs that arise because of their tendency to substitute high-risk, low *NPV* projects for low-risk, high *NPV* projects.

The Unistar example points out that if the firm raised $32.5 million by issuing a bond with a face value of $40.0 million, the negative *NPV* project would be taken and the equity holders could not realize the gains from the positive *NPV* project. This can be considered a cost of having risky debt. If Unistar had instead raised only $25 million in debt, it would have had no problem. Lenders would be willing to lend this amount because, no matter which project Unistar chooses, lenders would receive their $25 million with certainty. If the company chose process 1, equity holders would receive an expected payoff of $50 million [0.5 × ($50 million − $25 million) + 0.5 × ($100 million − $25 million)]. If the company chose process 2, equity holders would have an expected payoff of $45 million [= .5 × ($0) + .5 × ($115 million − $25 million)]. Since equity holders would have contributed $45 million in either case, they would prefer process 1 and would capture the $5 million gain from process 1. These issues are illustrated in Example 15.2.

Example 15.2:   The Cost Associated with the Asset Substitution Problem

Unoit Industries has two mutually exclusive $50 million investment opportunities, R and S, which it plans to fund with debt. Project S pays off $60 million for certain, and project R pays off only $20 million when the economy is poor and $90 million when the economy is good.

   a. What is the *NPV* of each project, assuming the economy is equally likely to be favorable or unfavorable and the risk-adjusted discount rate is 0 percent?

Suppose Unoit can raise the $50 million by issuing a bond with a face value of $50 million (because the lender naively believes the company will take the safe project).

   b. Which project will Unoit shareholders prefer?
   c. What is the expected payoff to the naive lenders?

Now suppose the lenders are sophisticated.

   d. Which project will the company select, and what do the shareholders gain?

Answer:

   a. NPV_S = .5($60 million + $60 million) − $50 million = $10 million
       NPV_R = .5($20 million + $90 million) − $50 million = $5 million
   b. With naive bondholders, the payoff to equity holders with project S is:

   .5($60 million − $50 million) + .5($60 million − $50 million) = $10 million

   The payoff to equity holders with project R is:

   .5($0) + .5($90 million − $50 million) = $20 million

   Thus, if the executives act in the interest of shareholders, they will choose project R.

   c. Given that project R is chosen, the naive lenders do not receive full payment in the poor state of the economy; they receive only .5($20 million) + .5($50 million) = $35 million, on average.

   d. Sophisticated lenders aware of both projects will realize that equity holders have an incentive to invest in the riskier project. For the $50 million loan, they will require a future payment of $80 million. With the selection of project R, they receive an expected payoff of .5($20 million) + .5($80 million) = $50 million, so they recover their investment. In this situation, the payoff to equity holders selecting project R is .5(0) + .5($90 million − $80 million) = $5 million. The payoff is zero if project S is selected because in neither state of the economy can the obligation be met. Thus, equity holders will select project R despite its lower *NPV.* If they had been able to commit to taking project S, equity holders would have created $10 million instead of $5 million in value.

Asset Substitutions with Government-Insured Debt: The Case of S&Ls.   The fact that debt can lead firms to select extremely risky projects does not by itself create a cost of debt financing. Indeed, in the 1980s a number of savings and loans (S&Ls) initially created value for their shareholders by investing in commercial real estate investments and other risky ventures that may not have had positive *NPV*s. These investments were funded with debt that was raised in the form of insured deposits. The shareholders would have received large gains if the investments had turned out well. However, some of the losses that occurred when the investments turned bad were shared by the government, which insured the deposits. Unfortunately, commercial real estate did very poorly in the late 1980s, so that many of the investments made by the S&Ls did turn out to be unsuccessful.

One reason why taking added risks was very attractive to the S&Ls was that deposit insurance and, as a result, the borrowing costs of the S&Ls did not accurately reflect the risks that the S&Ls were taking with these investments. The Federal Savings and Loan Insurance Corporation (FSLIC), the agency that insured the deposits, charged the same rate for insuring the deposits of all S&Ls. More sophisticated lenders would have been unwilling to provide the debt financing that these S&Ls were indirectly receiving from the U.S. government in the form of insured deposits.

Credit Rationing.   The tendency to increase risk when a firm's debt obligations increase also implies that an increase in interest rates adversely affects a firm's project choice. Some economists have argued that because of the tendency to increase risk, some banks ration credit rather than increase borrowing rates when credit conditions tighten.[15] In such situations, lenders may choose not to lend to certain firms regardless of the rate of interest the firms are willing to pay. The choice not to lend stems from the lenders' belief that firms will respond to higher interest obligations by choosing riskier investments. The following discussion illustrates how a firm that is able to obtain credit when interest rates are low may be denied credit when interest rates are high.

The Multi-Universal Corporation has an opportunity to take on one of two $100 million projects which the firm's lenders cannot distinguish from one another. For simplicity, again assume that investors are risk neutral and the risk-free rate of interest is initially zero percent. The payoffs for the two projects are the same if a bad outcome is realized ($50 million), but the payoff is higher with a good outcome if the company takes on project B ($150 million) rather than project A ($130 million). The probability of a good outcome is only 20 percent if the company selects project B, but it is 80 percent if it selects project A. These payoffs and their probabilities are summarized in Exhibit 15.5.

The *NPV* of project A is $14 million (= $114 million − $100 million). The *NPV* of project B is −$30 million (= $70 million − $100 million). If the firm can convince the lender that it will take project A, then it will be able to obtain the required $100 million financing by issuing a zero-coupon bond that pays $112.5 million at year-end when the

---

[15]See for example Stiglitz and Weiss (1981).

EXHIBIT 15.5   Multi-Universal's Project Payoffs

	Cash Flow if State of the Economy Is		Probability of Good	Expected Value
	Good	Bad		
Project A	$130 million	$50 million	0.8	$114 million
Project B	150 million	50 million	0.2	70 million

payoffs are realized. As the following equation shows, a zero-coupon bond that promises $112.5 million provides the lender with the expectation of:

$$\$100.0 \text{ million} = 0.8 \times \$112.5 \text{ million} + 0.2 \times \$50.0 \text{ million}$$

With a zero discount rate, the firm will select the less risky project (project A) because the expected payoff to the firm's stockholders from taking project A is:

$$0.8 \times (\$130 \text{ million} - \$112.5 \text{ million}) = \$14 \text{ million}$$

The expected payoff from taking project B is:

$$0.2 \times (\$150 \text{ million} - \$112.5 \text{ million}) = \$7.5 \text{ million}$$

Now consider what happens if the risk-free rate of interest increases to 12 percent and the payoffs of the projects remain the same. Lenders who believe that the company will take the safe project (project A) will now demand a $127.5 million promised payment for a $100.0 million loan, because a $127.5 promised payment is required for the lender to receive the $112.0 million needed, on average, to achieve a 12 percent expected rate of return. That is,

$$\$112 \text{ million} = 0.8 \times \$127.5 \text{ million} + 0.2 \times \$50 \text{ million}$$

However, as seen below, with a promised payment of this magnitude, the firm will prefer project B, the more risky project, because it creates a higher return for the equity holders.

With 12 percent being the debt's expected return, the expected payoff to the equity holders from selecting project A is:

$$0.8 \times (\$130 \text{ million} - \$127.5 \text{ million}) = \$2.0 \text{ million}$$

The expected payoff from project B is:

$$0.2 \times (\$150 \text{ million} - \$127.5 \text{ million}) = \$4.5 \text{ million}$$

Realizing that the company will select the more risky project in these circumstances, the lender would not be willing to offer a $100.0 million loan for a $127.5 million promised payment since it will not, on average, achieve the 12 percent risk-free return on its investment. In this case, there is no promised interest payment that will induce the bank to lend money to the firm because even the maximum debt obligation that the firm can possibly pay, $150 million, is insufficient to yield the lender an expected 12 percent return. This example illustrates the following result.

Result 15.9   Firms with the potential to select high-risk projects may be unable to obtain debt financing at any borrowing rate when risk-free interest rates are high.

The effect of the level of interest rates on the ability of firms to obtain debt financing is further illustrated in Example 15.3.

Example 15.3:   Interest Rate Changes, Risk Incentives, and Credit Rationing

The Little Cook Corporation is choosing between project T, which introduces a traditional "triple patty" greasy hamburger, and project E, which introduces a healthy, low-fat emu burger. Project T costs $100 million in marketing, training of cooks, and so forth, and yields cash flows for the next year of $115 million with certainty. Project E also costs $100 million but, because of the controversial nature of the meat, has only a limited probability of success. The marketing experts at Little Cook estimate that there is only a 1 in 3 chance that emu meat will be accepted and the project will be successful.

If project E is successful, it will yield cash flows over the next year of $142 million. If it fails, cash flows will only be $60 million. The following table summarizes the projects available to Little Cook.

	Project Cost	Success Payoff	Failure Payoff	Success Probability
Project T	$100 million	$115 million	—	1
Project E	100 million	142 million	$60 million	1/3

a. Suppose the discount rate is zero. What is the *NPV* of each project?

b. Would lenders be willing to make a $100 million loan for a bond with a face value of $100 million? Which project would Little Cook take?

c. Suppose the discount rate is 10 percent, so that lenders require a bond with a face value of $110 million to make a *riskless* loan of $100 million. Would rational lenders make such a loan to Little Cook?

d. What would the face value need to be in order for bondholders to receive a fair return?

Answer:

a. *NPV*(T) = $115 million − $100 million = $15 million

$NPV(E) = \frac{1}{3}$($142 million) $+ \frac{2}{3}$($60 million) − $100 million = −$12.667 million

b. With such a bond, the expected payoff to equity from project T is:

$$\text{\$115 million} - \text{\$100 million} = \text{\$15 million}$$

and the expected payoff to equity holders if Little Cook chooses project E is:

$$\frac{1}{3}(\text{\$142 million} - \text{\$100 million}) + \frac{2}{3}(\text{\$0}) = \text{\$14 million}$$

Thus, equity holders would choose project T. When the company selects project T, lenders receive their $100 million for sure and thus are willing to make the loan. With zero interest rates, Little Cook can realize the gains from the positive *NPV* project.

c. With a bond having a face value of $110 million, the expected payoff to shareholders from project T is:

$$\text{\$115 million} - \text{\$110 million} = \text{\$5 million}$$

The expected payoff to shareholders if the company selects project E is:

$$\frac{1}{3}(\text{\$142 million} - \text{\$110 million}) + \frac{2}{3}(\text{\$0}) = \text{\$10.667 million}$$

Thus, shareholders would select project E. If they select project E, the lenders expect to receive only

$$\frac{1}{3} (\$110 \text{ million}) + \frac{2}{3} (\$60 \text{ million}) = \$76.667 \text{ million}$$

which is less than the $110 million they require for the loan of $100 million, so they will not make the loan.

d. Given that project E is chosen, the lender will require a payment of F in the good state for a loan of $100 million, where F solves the following:

$$\frac{1}{3} (F) + \frac{2}{3} (\$60 \text{ million}) = \$110 \text{ million}$$

Solving this yields F = $210 million. But such a large promised payment is not feasible. With a $210 millon loan obligation, Little Cook would always default and equity would receive nothing. Thus, neither project will be taken. Because of the increase in interest rates, Little Cook cannot profit from the positive *NPV* project.

The Reluctance to Liquidate Problem

One of the most difficult decisions a firm must make is whether to remain in business. It must decide whether to continue to operate or to dismantle the business and sell its property and equipment for its liquidation value. Like the investment decision, the liquidation decision is affected by how much debt the firm has outstanding. In addition, the decision to liquidate can be affected by the firm's bankruptcy status.

Liquidation Costs versus Bankruptcy Costs.   Because bankruptcy and liquidation often occur together *liquidation costs* are sometimes considered a direct cost of bankruptcy and, hence, are an important determinant of a firm's capital structure. However, as we pointed out at the beginning of this chapter, bankruptcy does not necessarily imply liquidation. Indeed, in many Chapter 11 bankruptcies, firms are reorganized and continue operating.

Generally, it is in the interests of both debt holders and equity holders to reorganize and to continue operating a bankrupt firm if its *going-concern value* exceeds its liquidation value. As a result, firms that liquidate in bankruptcy generally do so because the net proceeds from liquidation exceed the present value of the expected cash flows that the firm would generate if it were to continue operating. Given that bankruptcy is likely to lead firms to liquidate when it is optimal to do so, liquidation costs should not be viewed as a relevant bankruptcy cost in determining the firm's optimal capital structure.[16]

How Capital Structure Affects Liquidation Policy.   Although bankruptcy need not cause a firm to liquidate when it is worth more as a going concern, capital structure can still affect liquidation policy. Managers of financially sound firms, as representatives of their stockholders, have an incentive to continue operating their firm even when the liquidation values of the firm exceed its operating values.[17] To understand why this is likely to be true, remember that equity holders, as the firm's most junior claimant, receive proceeds from the liquidation only after all other claimants have been satisfied. Therefore, if the face value of a firm's debt exceeds the firm's liquidation value, equity holders are likely to receive nothing in a liquidation. In addition, compared to the payoff from continuing to operate, liquidation provides a relatively safe payoff. Therefore,

---

[16]See Haugen and Senbet (1978) for further elaboration of this point.

[17]See Titman (1984) and Gertner and Sharfstein (1991) for further discussion of this point.

liquidation will be less attractive to equity holders than the riskier alternative of continuing to operate. This is analogous to the decision not to exercise an out-of-the-money option, again viewing equity as a call option on the value of the firm—the option is worth nothing if exercised, but it still might pay off in the future.

Managers, of course, have a direct interest in keeping the firm operating, even when the firm's liquidation value exceeds its operating value, because they are likely to lose their jobs if the firm liquidates. Hence, they have a strong incentive to continue operating as long as they control the firm. In the event of bankruptcy, managers and equity holders lose much of their control to representatives of debt holders who have an interest in liquidating the firm if doing so enhances the firm's value. As a result, whether a firm liquidates depends on who has the power to make that decision.

The Financial Distress of Eastern Airlines.   Consider the problem faced by Eastern Airlines when it was on the verge of bankruptcy during a recession in 1989. Suppose it had a $500 million debt obligation and that its *going concern* value would be worth $600 million if the economy recovered (a 50 percent probability), but the company would be forced to liquidate and receive proceeds of only $200 million if the recession continued. Alternatively, it could liquidate immediately and receive $480 million.

Eastern's equity holders would clearly prefer to keep the airline going in this situation since there would be nothing left for them in a liquidation once debt holders were paid off. If the firm can keep going until the economy turns around, equity holders would realize a value of $100 million ($600 million − $500 million). The debt holders, however, prefer to have the airline liquidate its assets immediately! Debt holders realize that there is a 50 percent chance that they will be paid in full if the economy recovers. However, there also is a 50 percent chance that most of the liquidation value will be dissipated if the debt holders wait to liquidate, leaving them with only $200 million. The case of Eastern Airlines illustrates the following result:

Result 15.10   Since debt holders have priority in the event of liquidation, they have a stronger interest in liquidating the assets of a distressed firm than the firm's equity holders, who realize the possible upside benefits that may be realized if the firm continues to operate. As a result, a firm's financial structure partially determines the conditions under which it liquidates.

Bankruptcy and Liquidation Decisions of Firms with More Than One Class of Debt.   When a firm has more than one class of debt (e.g., junior and senior debt) the determinants of its bankruptcy and liquidation decisions become considerably more complicated. For the purpose of this discussion, assume that a firm will go bankrupt if the following conditions hold:

- It has insufficient cash flow to meet its debt obligations.
- It is unable to borrow a sufficient amount to meet its debt obligations.

One might think that the above conditions imply that a firm would be bankrupt if it were not generating sufficient cash flow to meet its current debt obligations and if it is not expecting improvements in the future. As shown below, however, this is not necessarily true, and such a firm might continue to operate as a going concern even when its liquidation value greatly exceeds its *going concern* value.

To understand how a firm can remain in business under these conditions, consider the differing incentives of the firm's equity holders and debt holders in the event of a financial crisis. Equity holders have an incentive to delay bankruptcy and an even greater incentive to delay liquidation. The value of the equity holders' claims, with their optionlike characteristics, increases as its time to maturity lengthens. For this reason, management, when acting in the equity holders' interests, will want to avoid defaulting on the company's debt obligations. Defaulting would make all of the firm's current obligations come due immediately, which in effect would eliminate the option value of the equity claims.

For similar reasons, junior creditors also may be reluctant to force a firm into bankruptcy since their claims also have option-like features.[18] In many cases, these creditors may find it in their interest to lend additional money to a firm in financial distress to keep it from going bankrupt. Thus, a bank may be willing to make a new loan—which by itself is not a good investment—if doing so increases the value of its past loans to the firm.

Consider, for example, the case of Emruss Industries which has no cash flow in the current period, but will have cash flows of $1.5 million next year if the economy is favorable and $0.5 million if the economy is unfavorable. Assuming risk neutrality, a zero discount rate, and equal probabilities of the two events, the operating value of the firm is $1.0 million. Also assume that if the firm were liquidated immediately, it would generate $1.2 million in proceeds. Hence, if the firm were financed entirely with equity, equity holders would choose to have the firm liquidated immediately.

Emruss's capital structure, described in Exhibit 15.6, consists of both debt and equity. The firm has a $1,000,000 senior debt obligation due next year with a $150,000 coupon payment due immediately. In addition, Emruss has borrowed money from a venture capitalist to whom it owes $200,000 which is due next year. The debt to the venture capitalist is junior to the $1 million senior debt.

Emruss will be forced into bankruptcy if it cannot meet its $150,000 current obligation. If this happens, all of its debt obligations become due immediately and the debt holders will take control of the firm. Exhibit 15.7 shows that debt holders will choose to liquidate the firm in this situation because in an immediate liquidation they are paid in full. However, if the firm does liquidate, the stockholders receive nothing from the liquidation proceeds and only $50,000 of the venture capitalist's *junior claim* is paid (the $1,200,000 liquidation value less the senior $1,150,000 debt obligation).

Both Emruss's shareholders and its venture capitalist have an incentive to keep the firm going even though the firm's total value is maximized by immediately liquidating its assets. Given its weak condition, Emruss is willing to promise to pay the venture capitalist $100,000 in interest for a one-year loan that provides an additional $150,000 in financing. Although the 67 percent *promised* interest rate sounds outrageous, the venture capitalist will be repaid only half of the time, so the expected rate of return on the new loan is actually negative. However, the venture capitalist cannot view this loan in isolation. By making the loan, the venture capitalist has a 50 percent chance of being paid the $200,000 owed on the original loan (in the favorable state of the economy) rather than receiving $50,000 immediately from the liquidation proceeds.

Exhibit 15.8 illustrates the payoffs to the debt holders, the venture capitalist, and the equity holders if the venture capitalist provides the needed cash infusion. Consider first the incentives of the venture capitalist. The exhibit, which combines the two loans from the venture capitalist as a single package, shows that offering the new loan entails an immediate outlay of $150,000 and a payoff of $450,000 in the favorable state of the economy and nothing in the unfavorable state. Comparing this payoff stream with the alternative of receiving the $50,000 liquidation payoff immediately, we see that the net

---

[18]See Bulow and Shoven (1978) for further discussion.

EXHIBIT 15.6   Emruss's Debt Obligations

	Debt Obligations	
	Immediate	*Next Year*
Debt holders	$150,000	$1,000,000
Venture capitalist	0	200,000

EXHIBIT 15.7   Liquidation Proceeds for Emruss

Payoff in the Event of Liquidation	
Debt holders	$1,150,000
Venture capitalist	50,000
Stockholders	0

EXHIBIT 15.8   Payoffs in the Event of a Cash Infusion

	Next Year States of the Economy		
	Immediate	*Favorable*	*Unfavorable*
Debt holders	$150,000	$1,000,000	$500,000
Venture capitalist	−150,000	450,000	0
Stockholders	0	50,000	0

cost of offering the loan rather than allowing the firm to liquidate is $200,000 ($150,000 in new financing plus $50,000 in forgone liquidation proceeds). Since a 50 percent chance of receiving $450,000 is worth more than the $200,000 investment, the venture capitalist would find it worthwhile to make the loan.

Note that the senior debt holders in the Emruss example are made worse off when the more junior venture capitalist injects additional capital into the firm, even though the additional capital also has a junior claim. The debt holders receive only $500,000 next year if the firm continues to operate and the unfavorable state of the economy occurs. However, they would have been paid in full if the firm had liquidated. Emruss was able to obtain this cash infusion more easily since it had a venture capitalist who also had the incentive to keep the firm going. However, the firm also could have kept going, at least in theory, to the detriment of its senior lenders, by issuing new equity. Example 15.4 illustrates this idea:

Example 15.4:   The Incentive to Issue Equity to Avoid Liquidation
Consider Emruss Industries' financial condition, as described in Exhibit 15.6. Now assume that it does not have the loan obligation to the venture capitalist. Assuming risk neutrality, interest rates of zero, and frictionless capital markets, will Emruss issue equity to meet the immediate debt obligation?

Answer: If Emruss does not meet the debt obligation, its equity will have a value of zero. If Emruss raises the $150,000 to meet the coupon payment, its equity will be worth zero if the unfavorable state of the economy is realized and $500,000 ($1,500,000 − $1,000,000) if the favorable state of the economy is realized. The value of the firm's equity will be worth $250,000 if the firm obtains a $150,000 equity infusion. Therefore, the firm can issue equity worth $150,000, making its existing equity worth $100,000.

Note that equity holders and other junior claimants have claims resembling options which may be virtually worthless if bankruptcy occurs. They thus have an incentive to put more money into the firm if it allows them to extend the life of their claims, in hopes that the claims eventually will have value. This is especially true when asset values are highly volatile. Because of this incentive to keep their options alive, the firm described in Example 15.4 was able to raise funds to continue operating despite having a liquidation value that exceeded its going concern value. Equity holders benefited from this at the expense of the firm's senior debt holders.

15.3 How Chapter 11 Bankruptcy Mitigates Debt Holder–Equity Holder Incentive Problems

This section discusses how some of the problems that arise because of the debt holder–equity holder conflict can be mitigated in a Chapter 11 bankruptcy. Consider again Lily Pharmaceuticals, described in Exhibit 15.1, which passed up a positive *NPV* investment because of the debt overhang problem. Recall that firms suffer from debt overhang when they have a substantial amount of existing debt with protective covenants that prevent them from issuing additional debt that is senior to the existing debt.

By declaring Chapter 11 bankruptcy, a firm like Lily may be able to obtain additional financing that is senior to existing debt. The new debt obtained under Chapter 11 is called **debtor-in-possession (DIP) financing**. DIP financing allows bankrupt corporations to raise the money necessary to fund investments that are required for its continued operation. In other words, Chapter 11 allows a bankrupt firm to obtain permission to violate the debt covenant that otherwise would keep the firm from obtaining additional funds.

The Lily example provides some insights into why the federal bankruptcy code allows for Chapter 11 bankruptcies. The original lenders to Lily are actually better off because the weakening of their seniority allows the firm to make a good investment. Of course, the firm could have avoided the Chapter 11 filing if its original debt was unprotected. However, debt holders would not want to grant the firm an unrestricted ability to issue new senior debt. By allowing the firm to issue senior claims only under extreme situations, Chapter 11 bankruptcies can create some of the advantages of unprotected debt while avoiding some of the disadvantages. Of course, these advantages have to be weighed against the efficiency losses and legal costs of going through the bankruptcy process.

Some of the efficiency losses in bankruptcy arise because the provision to obtain DIP financing can allow a firm to continue operating when it would be better off liquidating. As the last section showed, junior creditors have an incentive to keep a distressed firm operating if they stand to receive little from the firm's liquidation. If the senior debt has covenants that keep the firm from borrowing an additional amount, the distressed firm is likely to be forced into bankruptcy. However, once the firm has declared Chapter 11 bankruptcy, it can obtain DIP financing which allows the firm to continue operating. This buys time and benefits the more junior claimants, but it may keep a dying firm alive that would be worth more if it were liquidated.

Result 15.11   In Chapter 11 bankruptcy, firms are able to obtain debtor-in-possession (DIP) financing. To some extent, this provision of the bankruptcy code mitigates the debt overhang/underinvestment problem. However, the provision also may allow some firms to continue operating when they would be better off liquidating.

15.4 How Can Firms Minimize Debt Holder–Equity Holder Incentive Problems?

Chapter 11 bankruptcy may lessen some of the costs associated with conflicts between debt holders and equity holders, but bankruptcy would probably not be a manager's preferred way to deal with the problem. This section examines other solutions to these incentive problems. As discussed earlier, equity holders should be motivated to control their incentive problems, since ultimately they must bear the costs that such problems create.

The simplest solution to debt holder–equity holder incentive problems is to eliminate the debt holders. The problems are of course eliminated if the firm is all equity financed. However, there are offsetting advantages to the inclusion of debt in a firm's capital structure. Some of these benefits of debt (e.g., tax advantages) were discussed in earlier chapters. Other benefits will be discussed in Chapters 17 and 18. Therefore, firms have incentives to include debt in their capital structures and to design their debt in ways that minimize the potential conflicts between borrowers and lenders.

The following discussion briefly describes five ways that owners of a firm can minimize the incentive costs associated with debt financing. These are:

- Protective covenants.
- Bank and privately placed debt.
- The use of short-term instead of long-term debt.
- Security design.
- Management compensation contracts.

Protective Covenants

Earlier this chapter discussed protective covenants that specify the seniority of the debt as well as covenants that specify the amount that firms can distribute to shareholders as a dividend or repurchase. In addition, covenants that require the firm to satisfy restrictions on various accounting ratios, such as the debt/equity ratio, interest coverage, and working capital, are often observed. Other covenants restrict the sale of assets. Firms that violate these covenants are in **technical default**, which means that debt holders can demand repayment even if the firm has not missed an interest payment. (See Chapter 2 for additional detail.)

What Covenants Do We Observe?   In their study of bond covenants, Smith and Warner (1979) reported that about 90 percent of a sample of bonds issued in 1974 and 1975 restricted the issuance of additional debt, 23 percent restricted dividends,

39 percent placed constraints on merger activity, and about 35 percent placed restrictions on how a firm can sell its assets. These covenants provide some protection to the original bondholders against the tendency of a firm's management to undertake high-risk investment projects in the future. Junior debt holders, who have the lowest priority of repayment if a firm defaults, would have an incentive to withhold financing if they think the firm is likely to be taking on excessively risky projects. However, the covenants are much weaker than might be expected given the potential conflicts described earlier in this chapter.

Covenants that directly limit the types of projects that firms can undertake are less common. For example, in a study of bonds issued by large U.S. corporations, McDaniel (1986) found almost no restrictions on the ability of firms to increase their risk. This is because it is very difficult to specify in a contract the exact types of investments that are allowed over the 20- to 30-year life of a bond. In many cases, subtle changes in a production technology (e.g., making the plant more labor intensive) can lead to important changes in risk. Even if it were possible to write contracts to prevent such changes, firms may find that the costs of limiting management's flexibility would exceed the benefits of limiting the bondholders' risk.

Covenants on Investment-Grade versus Non-Investment-Grade Debt.   The studies mentioned above focused mainly on the bonds of major companies with high credit ratings. Since these firms have relatively low leverage, the debt holder–equity holder conflicts described in this chapter are unlikely to be severe. For this reason, investment-grade bonds generally have relatively weak covenants.

In contrast, the potential for debt holder–equity holder conflicts in firms that issue noninvestment-grade (i.e., high-yield or junk) bonds is high. Hence, noninvestment-grade bonds often have substantial covenants that limit the issuing firm's operating strategies. In 1992, for example, Continental Medical Systems issued $200 million of senior subordinated notes. The prospectus for these notes included nearly 100 pages of covenants describing what the firm could and could not do. The covenants addressed a number of issues, including:

- The issuance of additional debt.
- Changes in control of the corporation.
- Limitation of dividends and share repurchases.
- The sale of assets.
- Maintenance of properties.
- The provision for insurance.

Covenants Cannot Solve All Problems.   Some of the incentive problems would be especially difficult to eliminate with contractual provisions. At the outset, for example, the debt overhang problem leads firms to pass up positive *NPV* investments. While it is plausible that contracts can be written to preclude certain projects, we don't believe it is possible to include debt covenants that prevent firms from turning down positive *NPV* projects that lower the value of the firm's common stock. A second potential conflict concerns how an infusion of equity can help the original shareholders by allowing the firm to keep operating at the expense of the debt holders, who prefer the firm to liquidate. In this case, the gain to the equity holders is less than the loss to the debt holders, which suggests that it would be beneficial to prevent an equity infusion of this type. In reality, however, firms would not want to rule out equity infusions because generally, equity issues that fund positive *NPV* projects benefit both debt holders and equity holders.

McDaniel (1986) argued that the covenants of bonds issued in the 1960s, 1970s, and the early 1980s were entirely inadequate because they were written at a time when actions such as leveraged recapitalizations were far less common.[19] The author argued that in many cases bondholders had implicit agreements with management that subsequently were violated. If McDaniel is correct, one might expect to find that bonds issued more recently are better protected. Indeed, Lehn and Poulsen (1992) found that about 30 percent of a sample of bonds issued in 1989 included covenants that explicitly protected bondholders from the risks of takeovers and recapitalizations. Moreover, they found that firms that are better candidates for takeovers tend to have covenants that restrict takeovers and leveraged recapitalizations.

It should be noted that while debt covenants may solve some incentive problems, they come with costs. They can be costly to write and enforce, and they can limit a firm's flexibility. Thus, publicly traded investment-grade debt rarely has covenants that could trigger a technical default. However, covenants of this type are observed in private debt, whose holders can more easily monitor covenant compliance, and in noninvestment-grade debt, which is more subject to the kinds of concerns discussed in this chapter.

Bank and Privately Placed Debt

Recall that debt financing can cause either debt overhang or asset substitution, depending upon the circumstances. Bond covenants that affect the firm's ability to issue debt that is senior to existing debt can affect the firm's tendency to experience these problems. As mentioned in Section 15.2, the ability to issue debt that is senior to existing debt eliminates the debt overhang problem, but it also increases the asset substitution problem.

The use of bank debt may be advantageous because it solves the free-rider problem that contributes to the debt overhang problem. Recall the situation described in Section 15.2 in which the debt holders as a group benefit from infusing new capital into a corporation, but individual debt holders do not find it in their interests to provide capital by themselves. The problem arises because the new debt by itself is not a good investment, but the capital infusion increases the value of the existing debt. It is possible to eliminate this free-rider problem if the firm has only one lender, such as a bank, which can take into account how its new loans affect the value of its existing loans.

Bank debt and, to a lesser extent, debt that is privately placed with insurance companies and pension funds, have additional advantages over publicly traded bonds when the incentives to increase risk are most severe. Banks and other private providers of debt capital are better able to monitor the investment decisions of firms and enforce protective covenants. In addition, more stringent covenants can be imposed on private debt because it is much easier to renegotiate and to enforce a covenant with a bank than with a group of bondholders. Consequently, bank loan covenants limit flexibility far less than equivalent bond covenants.

A number of articles have argued that the conflict between debt holders and equity holders in Japan and Germany is less of a problem than it is in the United States because large banks not only provide most of the debt financing for firms but also own large holdings of the firms' stocks (see Chapter 1). Because the banks own both debt and equity claims, they have incentives to endorse policies that transfer wealth between the different claimants. However, banking regulations in the United States limit the amounts of stock a bank can hold, which precludes this solution.

---

[19]A *leveraged recapitalization* refers to greatly increasing a firm's leverage and simultaneously selling off a large fraction of its assets. See Chapter 2 for more detail.

Despite the advantages of bank debt, its importance has been diminishing over time in the United States and Japan. Increasingly, firms in both countries have been going to the bond and commercial paper markets to raise debt capital. In 1975, more than 90 percent of corporate debt in Japan was held by banks. By 1992, that figure had fallen to less than 50 percent, in part due to deregulation.[20] In both countries, the firms raising their debt capital through the public markets instead of through banks are primarily the larger, higher quality, less risky firms which are less likely to be subject to the types of financial distress costs discussed in this chapter. For these firms, the benefits of bank debt are insufficient to justify the added costs associated with bank loans—costs that are passed on to the borrower in the form of higher interest payments.

The Use of Short-Term versus Long-Term Debt

Most of the debt holder–equity holder conflicts discussed in this chapter are more severe when firms use long-term rather than short-term debt financing. To understand why this is true, recall that these conflicts arise because shareholders have an incentive to implement investment strategies that are advantageous to them by lowering the value of the firm's outstanding debt. However, the value of short-term debt is much less sensitive to changes in a firm's investment strategy than the value of long-term debt.

Mitigating the Debt Overhang Problem.   Myers (1977) noted that it is possible to eliminate the debt overhang problem if the firm's existing debt matures prior to the time when it must raise additional debt to fund a new project. To understand this, consider again the example of Unitron, which had a risk-free project yielding 12 percent when the risk-free rate was 10 percent. The firm passed up the project because its borrowing costs were high enough to exceed the project's return. If the firm's debt was all short-term, there would have been no debt overhang problem. In this case, the interest payment on all of the firm's debt would have been renegotiated simultaneously with the selection of the new project. Thus, the addition of a risk-free project, which would lower the overall risk of the firm, also would lower the firm's borrowing costs, making it attractive for the firm to accept the project.

Mitigating the Asset Substitution Problem.   The use of short-term debt also makes it more difficult for equity holders to gain at the expense of debt holders by selecting riskier projects. Consider the case of a firm that must decide whether to design its production facilities so that the process is more or less risky. The equity holders of a highly leveraged firm may prefer the risky project because the upside potential is higher and they share any downside risk with the debt holders. However, if the firm's debt is primarily short term, the incentive to increase asset risk diminishes. With short-term financing, the lending rate is renegotiated after completion of the production process, which largely eliminates a firm's ability to gain at the expense of its lenders.

Disadvantages of Short-Term Debt.   Of course, there also is a downside to funding long-term projects with short-term debt. With short-term financing, unexpected increases in interest rates could potentially bankrupt a highly leveraged firm. This has led some authors to advocate short-term borrowing coupled with hedging interest rate risk in the futures and swap markets.[21]

---

[20]Source: Hoshi, Scharfstein, and Kashyap (1993).

[21]These issues are discussed in greater detail in Chapter 20.

Security Design: The Use of Convertibles

A convertible bond provides its holder with the option to exchange bonds for a pre-specified number of the issuing firm's shares (see Chapter 2). Some analysts view a convertible bond as a combination of a call option on the firm's stock and a straight bond. While this description is not altogether correct, it does provide useful intuition. Recall that options, and thus the option element in the convertible bond, become more valuable as the volatility of the firm's stock increases. This increase in the value of the option component can offset the decrease in the value of the convertible's straight bond component that occurs when the firm's volatility increases.

Designing a Convertible Bond to Make its Value Insensitive to Volatility Changes. Depending on the relative importance of the option and straight bond components, the convertible bond can either increase or decrease in value with an increase in the firm's overall level of risk. Some researchers have suggested that it may be possible to design a convertible bond so that its value is insensitive to changes in the volatility of the firm.[22] The stockholders of a firm financed with such debt would therefore have no incentive to select high-risk projects since they would gain nothing from the bondholders unless the projects have positive *NPVs*.

Empirical Evidence on Convertible Issuance.   Empirical evidence by Mikkelson (1981) tends to support this rationale about why firms issue convertible bonds. Mikkelson found that highly-leveraged, high-growth firms were the most likely to issue convertible bonds. These firms are likely to have the highest probability of bankruptcy, so the effect of risk on the value of their straight bonds and stock is probably the greatest. In addition, these firms are likely to have the most flexibility about future investments and the greatest ability to increase risk. Mikkelson also found that the maturities of the convertible bonds were generally longer than the maturities of straight bonds. This probably reflects the inability of growth firms, because of incentive problems, to obtain long-term financing with straight debt.

Management Compensation Contracts

Up to this point, we have assumed that managers make investment choices that maximize their firm's share price. However, managers often have other objectives.[23] For example, sometimes they are under more pressure to please their debt holders than their equity holders. This can be seen in some highly leveraged U.S. firms, which depend on banks to finance their day-to-day operations, and in countries like Germany and Japan, where the banks have greater influence over managers.

In addition, some of the natural tendencies of managers are more aligned with the interests of debt holders than equity holders. First, relative to other shareholders, managers generally have a much larger portion of their wealth tied up in the firms they manage and thus are likely to act as though they are more risk averse. This would increase their tendency to take on less risky and diversifying investments which might counteract the incentive to take on too much risk. Second, prestige and power go hand in hand with operating a growing firm, providing an incentive for managers to overinvest. The incentive to overinvest probably counteracts the equity-controlled firm's incentive

---

[22]See Brennan and Schwartz (1986) and Green (1984).
[23]These will be discussed extensively in Chapter 17.

underinvest, which derives from the debt overhang problem. Thus, managers may make choices that benefit debt holders at the expense of equity holders.

It is worth emphasizing that it is not in the shareholder's best long-term interests to have managers who act purely in the interests of either debt holders or shareholders. To maximize the firm's current value, a firm must commit its managers to make future choices that are in the combined best interest of all claimants, maximizing the combined value of the firm's debt and equity. A firm will be able to borrow at more attractive rates if the manager can assure the lender that the interests of the debt holders as well as those of the equity holders will be considered when investment choices are made. This means that firms have an incentive to compensate managers in ways that make them sensitive to the welfare of both debt holders and equity holders.

15.5 Empirical Implications for Financing Choices

The preceding discussion carries important implications regarding which firms should have high leverage and which should have low leverage. This section reviews empirical evidence about the extent to which the issues described in this chapter affect observed capital structure choices.

How Investment Opportunities Influence Financing Choices

Since debt financing distorts investment incentives, firms with substantial investment opportunities should be more conservative in their use of debt financing. Existing cross-sectional empirical studies tend to support this hypothesis. The variables used to measure future investment opportunities include, among other things, research and development expenditures, because the point of most research is to develop new opportunities, and the ratio of the firm's market value to its book value, because market value measures the combined value of a firm's existing assets and future opportunities while book value measures only the value of existing assets.

Consistent with the discussion in this chapter, both of these variables are negatively related to the amount of debt included in a firm's capital structure.[24] Firms that have high R&D expenditures and high market values relative to their book values tend to include little debt in their capital structures.[25] Consistent with the discussion in Section 15.4, empirical studies find that firms with good future opportunities tend to prefer short-term to long-term debt.[26]

How Financing Choices Influence Investment Choices

A second type of study examines whether highly leveraged firms invest less than firms with lower debt/equity ratios. Lang, Ofek, and Stulz (1996) concluded that more highly leveraged firms tend to invest less than firms with lower leverage ratios. The authors argued that this reflects the fact that firms with poor investment opportunities choose to be highly leveraged as well as the fact that debt inhibits a firm's ability to invest. In other

---

[24]See Bradley, Jarrell and Kim (1984), Long and Malitz (1985), Titman and Wessels (1988), and Smith and Watts (1992).

[25]Other explanations for these findings are discussed in Chapter 16.

[26]See for example, Barclay and Smith (1995), Stohs and Mauer (1996), and Opler and Guedes (1996).

words, poor investment opportunities can cause firms to be more highly leveraged, and high leverage might cause firms to invest less.

Direct evidence about how debt financing leads firms to invest less comes from the study's analysis of the investment behavior of the noncore business segments of diversified firms. The basic idea is that a company like Mobil Oil would select its debt ratio based on the fundamentals of the oil industry. However, the firm's debt ratio could have inadvertently affected the investment choice of Montgomery Ward, a retail firm that used to be owned by Mobil. The Lang, Ofek, and Stulz study found that, on average, the level of investment in the noncore business segments of diversified firms decreased when the overall leverage of the firms increased, supporting the idea that debt causes firms to invest less.[27]

Firm Size and Financing Choices

Two reasons explain why the debt holder–equity holder conflict may be worse for small firms:

1. Small firms may be more flexible and thus better able to increase the risk of their investment projects.
2. The top managers of small firms are more likely to be major shareholders, which gives them a greater incentive to make choices that benefit equity holders at the expense of debt holders.

These arguments suggest that small firms should exhibit lower debt ratios. This, however, does not seem to be the case. However, small firms do tend to choose debt instruments that minimize conflicts between debt holders and equity holders. In particular, their long-term debt is more likely to be convertible and a greater proportion of their total debt financing tends to be short-term debt.[28]

Small firms also may avoid long-term debt because of the transaction costs of issuing long-term bonds in relatively small amounts. As shown in Chapter 1 (see Exhibit 1.7), the transaction costs of a $500 million bond issue averages about 1.64 percent of the total dollar amount while a $10 million bond issue may entail transaction costs of about 4.39 percent of the total. As a result, smaller firms may opt for less expensive loans from banks, which have lower fixed transaction costs than bond issues, but which tend to provide only short-term financing.

Evidence from Japan

As noted earlier, the debt holder–equity holder conflicts are not likely to be as severe in Japan as they are in the United States.[29] In Japan, banks play a much larger role in the financing of corporations. They hold both corporate debt and stock in the companies to which they lend, and their representatives typically sit on corporate boards of directors. Thus, debt holders have more control of the day-to-day operations of companies in Japan, and, with bank debt more prevalent, free-rider problems have less relevance in Japan. This suggests that variables like R&D expenditures, which serve as a proxy for future investment opportunities, may be less related to financial leverage ratios in Japan than in the United States. Prowse (1990) found that the negative relationship between R&D

---

[27]Lamont (1997) examined similar issues, using detailed data on the investment choices within the oil industry, and arrived at similar conclusions.

[28]See Titman and Wessels (1988).

[29]See Chapter 1 for more detail on the Japanese financial system.

expenditures and leverage is weak in Japan. These findings stand in sharp contrast to those in the United States.

A study by Flath (1993) provides further evidence about how Japanese banks mitigate the debt holder–equity holder conflicts. He found that, as in the United States, Japanese growth firms, which potentially have the greatest conflicts, are generally less highly levered than other Japanese firms. However, Japanese growth firms that have a banking-owner relationship, characterized by the bank's holding a significant fraction of the firm's stock, tend to be more levered than their counterparts without a banking relationship of this type. His evidence suggests that because banks are able to exercise more control when they hold more shares, they can better protect their interests and can thus offer greater amounts of debt financing in situations where potential conflict exists.

15.6 Summary and Conclusions

This chapter discussed some of the costs a firm might bear in the event that it becomes too highly leveraged. We began with a brief discussion of the direct legal and administrative costs of bankruptcy, which are likely to be a relatively small proportion of the assets of most large corporations. The chapter's main focus was on the indirect costs of financial distress that arise because of conflicts of interest between debt holders and equity holders. These conflicts of interest create the following investment distortions:

- Highly leveraged firms tend to pass up positive net present value investment projects.
- Debt creates an incentive for firms to increase risk.
- Debt creates an incentive for firms to take on projects that pay off quickly, leading them to pass up projects with higher net present values that take longer to pay off.
- Debt creates an incentive for shareholders to keep a firm operating when it might be worth more if it were liquidated.

To the extent that lenders anticipate how debt distorts investment incentives, equity holders will bear the costs of the investment distortions caused by their firm's financial structure. A firm with an incentive to make investment decisions that reduce the value of its debt will be subject to higher borrowing costs and may at times be unable to obtain debt financing. Given this, firms have an incentive to design their financial structures and in other ways position themselves to minimize these investment distortions.

This chapter provided the following suggestions for firms wishing to minimize the costs associated with investment distortions that arise from debt financing.

- Use debt covenants that limit dividend payouts, the amount of new debt financing, and investments substantially outside the firm's main line of business.
- Use short-term debt instead of long-term debt.
- Use bank debt (or private placements) instead of public bonds.
- Use convertible debt or bonds with attached warrants.
- Design management compensation contracts that eliminate the incentives of managers to distort investments.

The last suggestion requires further elaboration. Lenders may be more concerned about the preferences of managers than of shareholders. Therefore, the underinvestment problem may not be significant if managers have a preference to overinvest to maximize the growth rates of their firms. Chapter 17, which takes a more careful look at these large management-run firms, concludes that the kinds of distortions created by debt financing can sometimes be beneficial rather than costly.

Key Concepts

Result 15.1: Lenders charge an interest premium that reflects the expected costs they must bear in the event of default. Therefore, shareholders indirectly bear the expected costs of bankruptcy and must consider these costs when choosing their optimal capital structures.

Result 15.2: Firms acting to maximize their stock prices make different decisions when they have debt in their capital structures than when they are financed completely with equity.

Result 15.3: Selecting projects with positive net present values can at times reduce the value of a leveraged firm's stock.

Result 15.4: Firms that have existing senior debt obligations may not be able to obtain financing for positive *NPV* investments.

Result 15.5: With risky debt, equity holders have an incentive to pass up internally financed positive net present value projects when the funds can be paid out to equity holders as a dividend.

Result 15.6: Firms with high debt obligations tend to pass up high *NPV* projects in favor of lower *NPV* projects that pay off sooner.

Result 15.7: The equity holders of a levered firm may prefer a high-risk, low (or even negative) *NPV* project to a low-risk, high *NPV* project.

Result 15.8: With sophisticated lenders, equity holders must bear the costs that arise because of their tendency to substitute high-risk, low

NPV projects for low-risk, high *NPV* projects.

Result 15.9: Firms with the potential to select high-risk projects may be unable to obtain debt financing at any borrowing rate when risk-free interest rates are high.

Result 15.10: Since debt holders have priority in the event of liquidation, they have a stronger interest in liquidating the assets of a distressed firm than the firm's equity holders, who realize the possible upside benefits that may be realized if the firm continues to operate. As a result, a firm's financial structure partially determines the conditions under which it liquidates.

Result 15.11: In Chapter 11 bankruptcy, firms are able to obtain debtor-in-possession (DIP) financing. To some extent, this provision of the bankruptcy code mitigates the debt overhang/underinvestment problem. However, the provision also may allow some firms to continue operating when they would be better off liquidating.

Key Terms

absolute priority rule   544
asset substitution problem   548
Chapter 7   544
Chapter 11   544
cramdown   545
debtor-in-possession (DIP) financing   564
debt overhang problem   548
direct bankruptcy costs   543
financial distress costs   547
financially distressed firms   543

free-rider problem   550
impaired creditors   544
indirect bankruptcy costs   543
nonfinancial stakeholders   543
reluctance to liquidate problem   548
reorganization plan   544
shortsighted investment problem   548
technical default   565
underinvestment problem   548

Exercises

15.1. A firm has $100 million in cash on hand and a debt obligation of $100 million due in the next period. With this cash, it can take on one of two projects—A or B—which cost $100 million each. Assume that the firm cannot raise any additional outside funds. If the economy is favorable, project A will pay $120 million and project B will pay $101 million. If the economy is unfavorable, project A will pay $60 million and project B will pay $101 million. Assume that investors are risk neutral, there are no taxes or direct costs of

bankruptcy, the riskless interest rate is zero, and the probability of each state is .5.
  a. What is the *NPV* of each project?
  b. Which project will equity holders want the managers to take? Why?

15.2. Nigel decides he can make zippers at night for one period and will have cash flows next period of $210 if the economy is favorable, and $66 if the economy is unfavorable. One-third of these proceeds must be paid out in taxes if the firm is all equity financed; however, because of the tax advantage of debt, Nigel saves $0.05 in taxes for every $1.00 of debt financing that he uses. Assume investors are risk neutral, the riskless rate is 10 percent per period, and the probability of each state is .5. Also assume that if Nigel's firm goes bankrupt and debt holders take over, the legal fees and other bankruptcy costs total $20.

    a. If Nigel organizes his firm as all equity, what will it be worth?

    b. Suppose Nigel's firm sold a zero-coupon bond worth $44 at maturity next period. How much would the firm receive for the debt?

    c. With the debt level above, how much would the equity be worth?

    d. How much would the firm be worth?

    e. Would the firm be worth more if it had a debt obligation of $70 next period?

15.3. A firm has a senior bond obligation of $20 due this period and $100 next period. It also has a subordinated loan of $40 owed to Jack and Jill and due next period. It has no projects to provide cash flows this period. Therefore, if the firm cannot get a loan of $20, it must liquidate. The firm has a current liquidation value of $120. If the firm does not liquidate, it can take one of two projects with no additional investment. If it takes project A, it will receive cash flows of $135 next period, for sure. If the firm takes project B, it will receive either cash flows of $161 or $69 with equal probability. Assume risk neutrality, a zero interest rate, no direct bankruptcy costs, and no taxes.

    a. What has a higher *PV*: liquidating, project A, or project B?

    b. Should Jack and Jill agree to loan the firm the $20 it needs to stay operating if they receive a (subordinated) bond with a face value of $20.50?

    c. If the firm does receive the loan from Jack and Jill, which project will the managers choose if they act in the interest of the equity holders?

15.4. Hiroko Fashion Corporation (HFC) can pursue either project Dress, or project Cosmetic with possible payoffs at year-end as follows:

	Bad Economy (prob. = 30%) (in $ millions)	Good Economy (prob. = 70%) (in $ millions)
Project Dress	$2	$9
Project Cosmetic	7	6

Each project costs $6 million at the beginning of the year. Assume there are no taxes, there are no direct bankruptcy costs, all investors are risk neutral, and the risk-free interest rate is zero.

    a. Which project should HFC pursue if it is all equity financed? Why?

    b. If HFC has a $5 million bond obligation at the end of the year, which project would its stockholders want to pursue? Why?

15.5. Sigma Design, a computer interface start-up firm with no tangible assets, has invested $50,000 in R&D. The success of the R&D effort as well as the state of the economy will be observed in one year. If the R&D is successful (*prob.* = 90%), Sigma requires a $53,000 investment to start manufacturing. If the economy is favorable (*prob.* = 90%), the project is worth $153,000, and if it is unfavorable, the project will have a value of $61,000. Demonstrate how the value of Sigma is affected by whether or not it was originally financed with debt or equity. Assume no taxes, no direct bankruptcy costs, all investors are risk neutral, and the risk-free interest rate is zero.

15.6. In Japan, financial institutions hold significant equity interests in the borrowing firms. How does this affect the costs of financial distress and bankruptcy?

15.7. Describe the relation between the risk-adjusted expected return on common stock and the expected risk-adjusted return on corporate bonds in an economy where stock returns are taxed more favorably than bond returns, interest payments are tax deductible, and bankruptcy costs are important determinants of a firm's capital structure choice.

15.8. ABC Corp., which currently has no assets, is considering two projects that each cost $100. Project A pays off $120 next year in the good state of the economy and $90 in the bad state of the economy. Project B pays off $140 next year in the good state of the economy and $60 in the bad state of the economy. If the two states are equally likely, there are no taxes or direct bankruptcy costs, the risk-free rate of interest is zero, and investors are all risk neutral, which project would stockholders prefer if the firm is 100 percent equity financed? Which project would shareholders prefer if the firm has an $85 bond obligation due next year?

15.9. Suppose you are hired as a consultant for Tailways, Inc., just after a recapitalization that increased the firm's debt-to-assets ratio to

80 percent. The firm has the opportunity to take on a risk-free project yielding 10 percent, which you must analyze. You note that the risk-free rate is 8 percent and apply what you learned from Chapters 9 and 10 about taking positive net present value projects; that is, accept those projects which generate expected returns that exceed the appropriate risk-adjusted discount rate of the project. You recommend that Tailways take the project.

Unfortunately, your client is not impressed with your recommendation. Because Tailways is highly leveraged and is in risk of default, its borrowing rate is 4 percent greater than the risk-free rate. After reviewing your recommendation, the company CEO has asked you to explain how this "positive net present value project" can make him money when he is forced to borrow at 12 percent to fund a project yielding 10 percent. You wonder how you bungled an assignment as simple as evaluating a risk-free project. What have you done wrong?

15.10. In the event of bankruptcy, the control of a firm passes from the equity holders to the debt holders. Describe differences in the preferences of the equity holders and debt holders and how decisions following bankruptcy proceedings are likely to change.

15.11. Why are debt holder–equity holder incentive problems less severe for firms that borrow short term rather than long term?

15.12. Consider the case of Ajax Manufacturing which just completed an R&D project on widgets that required a $70 million bond obligation. The R&D effort resulted in an investment opportunity that will cost $75 million and generate cash flows of $85 million in the event of a recession (*prob.* = 20%) and $150 million if economic conditions are favorable (*prob.* = 80%). What is the *NPV* of the project assuming no taxes, no direct bankruptcy costs, risk neutrality, and a risk-free interest rate of zero? Can the firm fund the project if the original debt is a senior obligation that doesn't allow the firm to issue additional debt?

15.13. Assume now that if Ajax Manufacturing (see exercise 15.12) uses a more capital-intensive manufacturing process, it can produce a greater number of widgets at a lower variable cost. Given the greater fixed costs, the cash flows are only $5 million in an unfavorable economy with the capital-intensive process but are $170 million in a favorable economy. Hence, equity holders would receive $100 million in the good state of the economy ($170 million − $70 million) and zero in a recession because $5 million is less than the $70 million debt obligation. Can the firm issue equity to fund the project?

15.14. With debtor in possession (DIP) financing, bankrupt firms are able to obtain additional amounts of debt that is senior to the firm's existing debt. Explain how the firm's existing debt holders can benefit from this.

15.15. You have been hired as a bond analyst for Bull Sterns. A highly leveraged firm, Emax Industries, has switched to a more flexible management process that enables it to change its investment strategy more quickly. How do you expect this change in the management process to affect bond values?

References and Additional Readings

Altman, Edward. "A Further Empirical Investigation of the Bankruptcy Cost Question." *Journal of Finance* 39, no. 6 (1984), pp. 1067–89.

Ang, James; Jess Chua; and John McConnell. "The Administrative Costs of Bankruptcy: A Note." *Journal of Finance* 37, no. 1 (1982), pp. 219–26.

Barclay, Michael, and Clifford Smith. "The Maturity Structure of Corporate Debt." *Journal of Finance* 50, 1995, pp. 609–31.

Bradley, Michael; Gregg Jarrell; E. Han Kim. "On the Existence of an Optimal Capital Structure: Theory and Evidence." *Journal of Finance* 39, no. 3 (1984), pp. 857–78.

Brennan, Michael, and Eduardo Schwartz. "The Case for Convertibles." Reprinted in J. Stern and D. Chew, Jr., *The Revolution in Corporate Finance.* New York: Basil Blackwell Inc., 1986.

Bulow, Jeremy, and John Shoven. "The Bankruptcy Decision." *Bell Journal of Economics* 9, no. 3 (1978), pp. 437–56.

DeAngelo, Harry, and Linda DeAngelo. "Dividend Policy and Financial Distress: An Empirical Investigation of Troubled NYSE Firms." *Journal of Finance* 45, no. 5 (1990), pp. 1415–32.

Dhillon, U., and Herb Johnson. "The Effect of Dividend Changes on Stock and Bond Prices." *Journal of Finance* 49 (March 1994), pp. 281–89.

Flath, David. "Shareholding in Keiretsu, Japan's Financial Groups." *Review of Economics and Statistics* 75, no. 2 (May 1993), pp. 249–57.

Franks, Julian, and Walter Torous. "An Empirical Investigation of U.S. Firms in Reorganization." *Journal of Finance* 44, (1989), pp. 747–70.

Gertner, Robert, and David Scharfstein. "A Theory of Workouts and the Effects of Reorganization Law." *Journal of Finance* 46 (1991), pp. 1189–1222.

Guedes, Jose, and Tim Opler. "The Determinants of the Maturity of Corporate Debt Issues." *Journal of Finance* 51 (1996), pp. 1809–33.

Galai, Dan, and Ronald Masulis. "The Option Pricing Model and the Risk Factor of Stock." *Journal of Financial Economics* 3, nos. 1/2 (1976), pp. 53–81.

Green, Richard. "Investment Incentives, Debt, and Warrants." *Journal of Financial Economics* 13 (1984), pp. 115–36.

Haugen, Robert, and Lemma Senbet. "The Insignificance of Bankruptcy Costs to the Theory of Optimal Capital Structure." *Journal of Finance* 33, no. 2 (1978), pp. 383–93.

Hoshi, T.; David Scharfstein; and Anil Kashyap. "The Choice between Public and Private Debt: An Analysis of Post-Deregulation Corporate Financing in Japan." *NBER Working Paper* 4421 (August 1993).

Hotchkiss, Edith. "Postbankruptcy Performance and Management Turnover." *Journal of Finance* 50 (1995), pp. 3–21.

Jensen, Michael, and William Meckling. "Theory of the Firm: Managerial Behavior, Agency Costs, and Ownership Structure." *Journal of Financial Economics* (October 1976), pp. 305–60.

Kahl, Matthias. "Dynamic Liquidation, Adjustment of Capital Structure, and the Costs of Financial Distress." Working Paper, University of Pennsylvania, 1997.

Lang, Larry; Eli Ofek; and Rene Stulz. "Leverage, Investment, and Firm Growth." *Journal of Financial Economics* 40 (1996), pp. 3–29.

Lamont, Owen. "Cash Flow and Investment: Evidence from Internal Capital Markets." *Journal of Finance* 52, no. 1 (March 1997), pp. 83–109.

Lehn, Kenneth, and Annette Poulsen. "Contractual Resolution of Bondholder-Stockholder Conflicts in Leveraged Buyouts." *Journal of Law and Economics* 34, no. 2 (October 1992) Part 2, pp. 645–73.

Long, Michael, and Irene Malitz. "Investment Patterns and Financial Leverage." In B. Friedman, ed., *Corporate Capital Structure in the United States.* Chicago: University of Chicago Press, 1985.

Long, Michael, and Irene Malitz. "The Investment-Financing Nexus: Some Empirical Evidence." *Midland Finance Journal* (Fall 1985), pp. 53–59.

Long, Michael; Irene Malitz; and Stephen Sefcik. "An Empirical Examination of Dividend Policy Following Debt Issues." *Journal of Financial and Quantitative Analysis* (March 1994), pp. 131–44.

McDaniel, M. "Bondholders and Corporate Governance." *Business Lawyer* 41 (1986), pp. 413–60.

Mikkelson, Wayne. "Convertible Calls and Security Returns." *Journal of Financial Economics* 9, no. 3 (1981), pp. 237–64.

Myers, Stewart. "Interactions of Corporate Financing and Investment Decisions—Implications for Capital Budgeting." *Journal of Finance* 29, no. 1 (1977), pp. 1–25.

Prowse, Stephen. "Institutional Investment Patterns and Corporate Financial Behavior in the United States and Japan." *Journal of Financial Economics* 27, no. 1 (1990), pp. 43–66.

Smith, Clifford, and Jerry Warner. "On Financial Contracting: An Analysis of Bond Covenants." *Journal of Financial Economics* 7, no. 2 (1979), pp. 117–62.

Smith, Clifford, and Ross Watts. "The Investment Opportunity Set and Corporate Financing, Dividend, and Compensation Policies." *Journal of Financial Economics* 32, no. 3 (December 1992), pp. 263–92.

Stiglitz, Joseph, and Andrew Weiss. "Credit Rationing in Markets with Imperfect Information." *American Economic Review* 71, no. 3 (June 1981), pp. 393–410.

Stohs, Mark, and David Mauer. "The Determinants of Corporate Debt Maturity Structure." *Journal of Business* 69 (1996), pp. 279–312.

Stulz, Rene, and H. Johnson. "An Analysis of Secured Debt." *Journal of Financial Economics* 14, no. 4 (December 1985), pp. 501–21.

Titman, Sheridan. "The Effect Of Capital Structure on the Firm's Liquidation Decision." *Journal of Financial Economics* 13 (1984), pp. 137–52.

CHAPTER 16

Capital Structure and Corporate Strategy

Learning Objectives

After reading this chapter you should be able to:

1. Describe how a firm's financial situation is likely to affect its sales and its ability to attract employees and suppliers.
2. Understand how financial distress can benefit some firms by inducing employees, suppliers, and governments to make financial concessions to the firm.
3. Explain how a firm's financial condition affects the way its competitors price their products.
4. Describe how the past profitability of a firm affects its current capital structure.
5. Understand empirical research relating a firm's characteristics to its capital structure choices.

Massey-Ferguson, International Harvester, and John Deere & Company were the three largest producers of heavy farm equipment in North America in the 1970s, capturing virtually the entire market on that continent. In 1976, Massey-Ferguson had about 34 percent of the market, International Harvester about 28 percent, and John Deere about 38 percent. International Harvester and Massey-Ferguson were relatively highly leveraged at this time and Massey-Ferguson in particular had a large amount of short-term debt. John Deere, in contrast, was somewhat more conservatively financed.

In 1979, the Federal Reserve Board raised interest rates to unprecedented levels in an attempt to reduce inflation. This contributed to a large drop in the demand for farm equipment because the interest rate increase raised the cost of financing purchases of farm equipment, like tractors. The interest rate increase simultaneously increased the farm equipment makers' cost of servicing their short-term debt. As a result, Massey-Ferguson and International Harvester found it difficult to meet their debt payments. However, John Deere, being more conservatively financed, continued to make its debt payments in a timely fashion. Customer concerns about the long-term viability of International Harvester and Massey-Ferguson contributed to the downfall of these two companies, and John Deere gained at their expense. By 1980, John Deere's market

577

share increased to almost 50 percent while that of Massey-Ferguson fell to 28 percent and International Harvester fell to 22 percent.[1]

Chapter 15 discussed direct bankruptcy costs (e.g., legal and administrative expenses) as well as the indirect bankruptcy costs that arise because of conflicts of interest between equity holders and debt holders. These indirect costs can occur whenever a firm faces financial difficulties, or what we have been calling financial distress, regardless of whether the firm eventually becomes bankrupt.

Financial distress costs that arise because of debt holder–equity holder conflicts may explain why emerging growth firms like Amgen and Sun Microsystems use so little debt. As the previous chapter illustrated, lenders are unlikely to provide significant amounts of debt capital to these emerging growth firms at attractive terms because of the way that debt distorts the firm's investment incentives. For most of the largest firms in the United States, however, the indirect bankruptcy costs stemming from the conflicts between debt holders and equity holders do not appear to be a major deterrent to debt financing. Many of these large firms have access to eager lenders, willing to provide them with additional debt financing on reasonable terms.

This chapter builds on the framework developed in Chapter 15 and examines other financial distress costs that limit the desire to use debt financing. The financial distress costs examined in this chapter, in contrast to those considered in Chapter 15, explain why many firms choose to maintain low debt ratios even when lenders are willing to provide debt capital at attractive terms.

Consider, for example, the IBM of the 1970s, which had little long-term debt and could have borrowed substantially more at AAA rates. The company also was paying a substantial amount in taxes, suggesting that from a tax perspective the firm would certainly have been better off with more debt. Costs associated with debt holder–equity holder conflicts were apparently not an important issue to IBM because lenders were willing to provide debt at attractive terms. Clearly, lenders were not concerned about IBM changing its investment strategy in a way that would do them serious harm.

The ideas presented in the last three chapters suggest that IBM could have improved its value in the 1970s by increasing its leverage ratio. However, if IBM had chosen to be much more highly leveraged, it would have faced serious financial difficulties in the early 1990s. We will suggest in this chapter that financial distress would have been especially costly for IBM, and that a highly leveraged IBM might not have survived.

The first topic addressed here is how financial distress can affect the ability of a firm like IBM to operate its business profitably. Would a financially distressed IBM lose customers in the same way that International Harvester and Massey-Ferguson (described in the chapter's opening vignette) lost customers when they became financially distressed? How would financial difficulties affect IBM's ability to attract and retain key employees? Would it affect the quality of service provided by its suppliers? How would competitors react to IBM's financial difficulties?

To address these types of questions, we present the "stakeholders" theory of capital structure. **Nonfinancial stakeholders** are the associates of a firm, such as customers, employees, suppliers, and the community in which the firm operates, who do not have debt or equity stakes in the firm, but nonetheless, have a stake in the financial health of the firm. The **stakeholder theory** of capital structure suggests that the way in which a firm and its nonfinancial stakeholders interact is an important determinant of the firm's

---

[1]For more information on the Massey-Ferguson case, see *Case Problems in Finance,* 10th ed. (Burr Ridge, IL: Richard D. Irwin, 1992), p. 175.

optimal capital structure. We argue that these nonfinancial stakeholders may be less willing to do business with a firm that is financially distressed; and that this is especially true for a firm like IBM which sells computers. Indeed, in discussing the bankruptcy of Wang, a computer firm, *The Wall Street Journal* reported: "The biggest challenge any marketer can face [is] selling the products of a company that is on the ropes."[2] Because of this, firms may choose to be conservatively financed even when they can obtain substantial amounts of debt financing at attractive rates.

The interaction between how a corporation is financed and how it is viewed by its stakeholders suggests that the capital structure decision must be incorporated into the overall corporate strategy of the firm. For example, a firm that wants to project a reputation as a stable firm that produces quality products does not want to be too highly leveraged. Similarly, the way that a firm interacts with its suppliers and employees and how it competes within its industry determine its capital structure choice.

Dynamic aspects of the capital structure decision are also discussed in this chapter. Our analysis describes how a firm's history affects its current capital structure. In IBM's case, for example, the firm used almost no debt financing until the 1980s, partially because the firm was so profitable that it was able to fund most of its investments from retained earnings. However, its leverage ratio subsequently increased as it accumulated losses in the early 1990s. IBM could have counteracted this leverage increase by issuing equity, but for a variety of reasons it chose not to do this. As discussed in Chapter 14, taxes may have played some role in this decision. This chapter, as well as Chapters 17 and 18, will discuss other reasons that might explain why IBM did not issue equity to counteract the leverage effect of these losses.

Finally, the chapter analyzes the empirical evidence on these theories of capital structure, which appears to lend support to them.

16.1 The Stakeholder Theory of Capital Structure

Previous chapters examined the firm as a combination of different investments that need to be financed. This analysis largely ignored the nature of the investments and the overall environment in which the firm must operate. This chapter takes that environment more seriously and considers how financial decisions interact with the overall strategy of the firm.

Exhibit 16.1 illustrates how the environment in which a firm conducts business affects the firm's overall corporate strategy, which includes its capital structure choice. This environment includes the firm's nonfinancial stakeholders, who one way or the other have business dealings with the firm, and the firm's competitors. This section and the next examine how the nonfinancial stakeholders affect the firm's capital structure choice. Section 16.3 examines how the competitive environment affects capital structure choices.

Nonfinancial Stakeholders

As defined earlier, the nonfinancial stakeholders of a firm include those parties other than the debt and equity holders who have a stake in the financial health of the firm. These include the:

- Firm's customers.
- Firm's suppliers.

---

[2]*The Wall Street Journal*, Oct. 18, 1989.

EXHIBIT 16.1

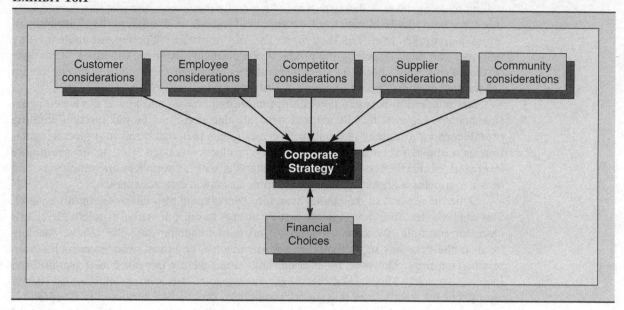

· Firm's employees.
· Overall community in which the firm operates.

These stakeholders can be hurt by a firm's financial difficulties, examples of which are described below. Customers may receive inferior products that are difficult to service, suppliers may lose business, employees may lose jobs, and the overall economies of entire communities can be disrupted.

Because of the costs they potentially bear in the event of a firm's financial distress, nonfinancial stakeholders will be less interested, all else being equal, in doing business with a firm having financial difficulties. This understandable reluctance to do business with a distressed firm creates a cost that can deter a firm from undertaking excessive debt financing even when lenders are willing to provide it on favorable terms.

How the Costs Imposed on Stakeholders Affect the Capital Structure Choice

To understand why nonfinancial stakeholders are concerned about a firm's financial health, it is first important to understand why there might be a connection between the firm's financial health and the decisions a firm might make that affect its stakeholders.[3] Consider first the firm's liquidation decision.

The Connection between Bankruptcy and Liquidation.   Recall from Chapter 15 that when equity holders, the last to get paid in a liquidation, control a leveraged firm, they may not want the firm to liquidate its assets, even if the firm's liquidation value exceeds its *going concern* value. Furthermore, managers who fear losing their jobs often resist liquidations, even those that are in the interests of equity holders.[4] However, the bias in

---

[3]The arguments in this subsection are based on the theoretical work in Titman (1984).
[4]This topic will be discussed in more detail in Chapter 17.

favor of keeping a bankrupt firm operating is not as great when the lenders share in the decision process. Indeed, because lenders get paid first from liquidation proceeds, they tend to prefer a liquidation. This means that a financially distressed firm, given its high probability of bankruptcy, is much more likely to liquidate than a financially healthy firm.

Liquidation Costs Imposed on Stakeholders.   The connection between a firm's financial structure and its liquidation choice is important because frequently there are spill-over costs imposed on the nonfinancial stakeholders of a firm that goes out of business. Consider the costs that would have been imposed on Chrysler's stakeholders had the company gone out of business when it had financial difficulties in the late 1970s. Chrysler's customers would have found it much more difficult to have their cars repaired if the company was no longer producing spare parts. Similarly, employees and suppliers with specific human or physical capital also would have found the firm's liquidation costly because of the loss of jobs and so forth.

The more sophisticated stakeholders anticipate the costs of doing business with a firm that may subsequently liquidate. To avoid any potential costs to them from a firm's liquidation, these stakeholders will avoid doing business with a firm that is experiencing financial distress. Customers will not be willing to pay as much for the products of such a firm and, in some cases, will avoid purchasing from it altogether. Indeed, Lee Iacocca said that because of Chrysler's need for government loan guarantees, "its share of new car sales dropped nearly two percentage points because potential buyers feared the company would go bankrupt."[5] In addition, *The Wall Street Journal* reported that a financially distressed International Harvester, discussed in the chapter's opening vignette, lost customers because of their concerns "about getting parts and service."[6] Similarly, employees and suppliers will be less willing to do business with such a firm and therefore will demand higher wages and charge higher prices. As a result, the revenues of a distressed firm are likely to decline, while its costs are likely to increase. Example 16.1 illustrates that such considerations may lead firms to choose equity financing over debt financing, even when there is a large tax advantage with using debt.

Example 16.1:   The Trade-Off between Tax Gains and the Effect of Debt on Product Prices

Suppose that Apple produces computers at a cost of $2,000 and sells them at $2,400. Given this $400 operating profit, the firm is generating large taxable earnings. Apple is considering a large increase in financial leverage that will increase the firm's probability of bankruptcy from zero to 10 percent, but will save the firm $58 million per years in taxes as a result of the interest tax deduction.

Although this is a financial decision, the financial managers decided to consult with the firm's marketing department prior to increasing Apple's leverage. The marketing managers argue that it will be more difficult to sell computers if consumers believe that bankruptcy is even a remote possibility. Their computers are worth $2,400 if customers can be assured of Apple's continued support of upgrades and new software in the future. However, if Apple were to go bankrupt, the customers' computers would be worth only $1,200. Hence, if customers thought the probability of bankruptcy was 10 percent, and valued computers as probability-weighted averages of their values when Apple, respectively, is solvent and bankrupt, then they would be willing to pay only $2,280 for the computers [$2,280 = .9($2,400) + .1($1,200)]. If Apple expects to sell 1 million computers per year, should it take on this added leverage?

---

[5]*The Wall Street Journal,* July 23, 1981.
[6]Ibid., Oct. 11, 1982.

Answer: The added leverage will save Apple $58 million per year in taxes. However, the company's pretax profits will be reduced $120 million per year because the added debt reduces the firm's revenues and profits. With a marginal tax rate of 40 percent, the firm is better off not taking on the added debt.

Estimating the Financial Distress Costs.   Example 16.1 illustrates how Apple Computer might have incorporated the costs of financial distress into the calculations of its optimal debt ratio. In reality, quantifying these costs is extremely difficult and depends on rough estimates. Example 16.2 provides a rough estimate of the financial distress costs imposed on Chrysler during its financial crisis in the late 1970s.

Example 16.2:   Chrysler's Financial Distress Costs

In the late 1970s, a financially distressed Chrysler would have defaulted on its debt had the government not intervened. In 1979, Chrysler offered rebates on its cars and trucks to attract customers who might have avoided Chrysler vehicles because of the company's financial distress.

A rough estimate of part of the cost of the firm's financial distress can be obtained by multiplying the average rebate times the number of cars sold. In 1979, Chrysler sold 1,438,000 cars and trucks. Assuming that a $300 rebate, on average, was given for each car and truck sold, estimate the cost of financial distress to Chrysler.

Answer: Multiplying the 1,438,000 cars sold times the $300 loss per car amounts to a total loss of $431 million in 1979 due to financial distress.

The $431 million loss owing to Chrysler's financial distress was almost as large as the entire market value of the firm's equity (in 1979, Chrysler's equity was worth $768 million), and it is clearly much more important than any of the direct costs of bankruptcy. However, the financial distress costs estimated in Example 16.2 underestimate the total costs because they do not take into account the lost sales due to customer concerns.

Financial Distress and the Credibility of Implicit Claims[7]

Nonfinancial stakeholders may be concerned about a firm's financial health even when liquidation is unlikely. Chapter 15 discussed how high leverage ratios can make a firm shortsighted in many of its investment decisions. What concerns a firm's nonfinancial stakeholders in this regard is how debt affects the firm's incentive to continue to invest in upholding its reputation for dealing honestly with employees and suppliers, for providing quality products to its customers, and for its overall integrity.

In normal circumstances, firms have an incentive to maintain a good reputation to ensure their long-run profitability. However, the incentive to be short-term oriented in times of financial distress applies to investments in reputation as well as in physical assets. Under financial distress, the long-run value of a good reputation may be less important to managers than the short-run need to generate enough cash to avoid bankruptcy. For this reason, a firm may lower the quality of its products or cut corners in other ways to raise cash to meet its immediate debt obligations. Example 16.3 illustrates this kind of situation.

---

[7]The arguments in this subsection are based on the theoretical work in Maksimovic and Titman (1991); see also the discussions in Shapiro and Titman (1985) and Cornell and Shapiro (1987).

Example 16.3:   Borrowing Costs and Product Quality

Handy Andy Cookies has earned a reputation for producing the best chocolate-chip cookies in the business and, as a result, is able to charge a premium price. The value of maintaining this reputation is clear. Lowering quality will save the firm money and boost profits by $20 million next year, but in later years, as the company's reputation erodes, profits will fall dramatically. Andy calculates that if the firm loses its reputation, it will lose $4 million per year over a nine-year period before it can regain its reputation. Based on these calculations, Andy concludes that, under normal circumstances, the firm is better off producing high-quality cookies. However, Handy Andy currently is having financial difficulties and will need to raise $20 million "in some way" before the end of the year. Because of the firm's financial difficulties, its borrowing rate will be 16 percent instead of the usual 10 percent. How do the financial difficulties affect Handy Andy Cookies' quality choice?

Answer: Producing a high-quality product can be considered an investment that costs $20 million and yields $4 million per year for nine years. The internal rate of return of that investment is 13.7 percent. Under normal circumstances, Andy would produce high-quality cookies since the rate of return from doing so exceeds the firm's 10 percent cost of capital. However, if borrowing costs increase to 16 percent, shareholders will be better off if the firm produces low-quality cookies.

Eastern Airlines

Eastern Airlines offers one of the best examples of alleged quality cutting by a firm in financial distress. During its period of financial distress (1987–90), Eastern was accused by its unions of cutting back on safety in order to save money. The company was indicted—and later pleaded guilty to three counts—for maintenance violations. The indictment stated that the violations occurred "as a result of unreasonable demands, pressure and intimidation put on [maintenance personnel] by Eastern's upper management to keep the aircraft in flight at all costs. . . ."[8] In other words, Eastern may have compromised safety in its cost-cutting efforts to keep from going under.

Unfortunately for Eastern Airlines and other firms in similar circumstances, rational customers understand this incentive and thus will not pay as much for the products of firms facing financial distress. Eastern, for example, experienced lower revenues per seat mile than its competitors during the period of financial distress since travelers tended to avoid the airline whenever they could; potential employees and suppliers concerned about being treated fairly also were less willing to do business with the firm.

As the Eastern Airlines case illustrates, being close to bankruptcy can make it very difficult for some firms to carry out their business. However, there exist other firms that need to be even more vigilant about maintaining a pristine credit rating. As the following case illustrates, the nature of some businesses require that participants maintain AAA bond ratings.

Salomon Swapco, Inc.: The Importance of an AAA Credit Rating

In the early 1990s, after a couple of tough years, a number of Wall Street firms observed that their interest rate swap business was "drying up." After the dissolution of Drexel, Burnham, Lambert in 1990, many healthy companies and financial institutions were afraid to enter into contracts with Wall Street firms with less than AA or AAA credit ratings. When corporations enter into interest rate swaps with an investment bank, they are primarily concerned with hedging interest rate risk, and they do not want to monitor the creditworthiness of their investment bank counterparty. As a result, AAA-rated corporations like American International Group, an insurance company, were making great inroads into the interest rate swap business.

---

[8]Jack E. Robinson, *Freefall: The Needless Destruction of Eastern Airlines and the Valiant Struggle to Save It* (New York: HarperCollins, 1992).

Merrill Lynch addressed this issue by creating MLDP, the first derivative products subsidiary. Their solution was to inject equity capital into the subsidiary—enough to lower the leverage ratio to one that would earn a AAA rating. However, from Merrill's perspective, this was a very expensive solution.

Salomon Brothers, with only an A credit rating from Moody's and Standard and Poor's, came up with an ingenious way to compete effectively in the swap market without recapitalizing the entire firm. In November 1992, it incorporated Salomon Swapco, Inc., with the intention of obtaining for this new subsidiary a AAA credit rating. The subsidiary would enter into swap transactions with those Salomon customers who had reservations about entering into contracts with a firm with less than a AAA credit rating. The subsidiary would then enter into an offsetting swap transaction with its parent company, Salomon Brothers Holding Company, Inc. Hence, if Swapco lost $1 million in the transaction with the customer, it would make $1 million on the offsetting transaction with Salomon Brothers Holding Company. Salomon Brothers Holding Company would post collateral on its transactions with Swapco, immunizing it from the credit risk of the holding company. Because of the offsetting transaction, Swapco's value was affected only by the likelihood of default on transactions with its customers, most of whom were extremely creditworthy, and was not affected by interest rate risk on its swap transactions. Because of this lack of market risk from interest rate movements, the rating agencies required Salomon to place only a small amount of capital in Swapco as a cushion against default. Swapco was awarded a AAA rating in early 1993 and entered into its first transaction in March 1993. Two and a half years later, in October 1995, Swapco had almost $100 billion in swap transactions on its books.

Whom Would You Rather Work For?

Although we mentioned briefly that employees are important nonfinancial stakeholders, our examples up to this point have analyzed the effect of debt on a firm's customers. However, a number of readers of this text will probably be looking for a job soon and may want to consider how career prospects at a prospective employer relate to that employer's financial structure. Perhaps, readers already have worked harder to get interviews with firms that appear to be financially strong and to avoid those firms that appear to be having financial difficulties. They now should have a better understanding of why this strategy makes sense.

As discussed earlier in this chapter, a highly leveraged firm is more likely to go bankrupt and a bankrupt firm is more likely to liquidate. However, this is only one reason—and probably not the most important—that explains why a highly leveraged firm may be a less attractive employer. Because of the debt overhang problem (see Chapter 15), firms that are more highly leveraged tend to invest less, which means they may be less willing to take on new opportunities and thus may offer their employees less opportunity for advancement.

The theoretical relation between employment and capital structure was confirmed empirically by Sharpe (1994). Sharpe examined employment growth rates and found that the cyclical nature of a firm's labor force was related positively to its degree of financial leverage. In other words, companies with very low leverage were much more likely to employ a larger workforce through a recession than companies with high leverage, which were more likely to reduce their workforce in response to modest declines in demand.

The success of a corporation depends largely on the quality of management that it attracts, and many of the best managers choose to work for a company that provides better future opportunities over one that pays more but offers fewer opportunities for advancement. Because of this, a high debt ratio may be very costly for a firm that is trying to attract the best talent. However, as we discuss in the next section, a firm that is not planning on attracting a large number of new managers in the future may find it advantageous to have a relatively high debt ratio.

Summary of the Stakeholder Theory

The Texaco-Pennzoil Litigation: Quantifying Financial Distress Costs

In 1984, Texaco and Pennzoil became involved in a prolonged legal dispute involving the takeover of Getty Oil. Texaco had purchased a large block of Getty Oil stock despite an agreement dated one week prior in which Getty Oil was to sell its stock to Pennzoil. As one of the terms of the Texaco purchase, Texaco had agreed to indemnify Getty Oil against any legal liability for the violation of the Pennzoil agreement. The initial jury award to Pennzoil, including accrued interest, was $12 billion, which would have forced Texaco into bankruptcy. The judgment was appealed, however, and the legal battle continued until 1987, when a settlement of $3 billion was reached. At the time of the jury's announcement, there was substantial uncertainty about how much Texaco would have to pay Pennzoil if Texaco actually went through with the bankruptcy. However, the gain to Pennzoil from the ultimate settlement should have approximately equaled the loss to Texaco.

This case provides a unique way to gauge the combined direct and indirect expected costs of bankruptcy. If the market expected that there would be no bankruptcy costs, then Pennzoil's stock should have increased in value at the time of the award announcement by an amount approximately equal to the amount that Texaco's stock declined. For example, if investors thought that Texaco would ultimately pay Pennzoil $5 billion dollars, we would expect the value of Pennzoil to increase by $5 billion dollars and the value of Texaco to decrease by $5 billion dollars.

Cutler and Summers (1988) studied the changes in market value of the two firms through the course of the legal battle and found that Pennzoil stock gained much less than Texaco's stock declined, implying that the combined values of the two firms declined. The net loss in combined market values of the two companies was more than $3 billion, which one might view as the market's assessment of the expected cost of Texaco's bankruptcy.

The $3 billion decline in combined shareholder value is too large to be attributed to the direct costs of bankruptcy. We believe the drop in the combined value of the two firms reflected two factors. The first is the costs of financial distress discussed in this chapter. Second, the market may have been concerned about how wisely Pennzoil would invest its cash windfall. When managers receive cash windfalls, they tend to increase their level of investment beyond what would be considered optimal.[9]

The discussion in this section suggests that financial distress can be costly for a firm because it affects how the firm is viewed by its customers, employees, suppliers, and any other firms or individuals that in some way have a stake in its success. The stakeholders' views are especially important for firms whose products need future servicing (e.g., automobiles and computers) or whose product quality is important but difficult to observe (e.g., prescription drugs). Financial distress also will be costly for firms that require their employees and suppliers to invest in product-specific training and physical capital. On the other hand, firms that produce nondurable goods (e.g., agricultural products) or provide services that are not particularly specialized (e.g., hotel rooms) probably have low financial distress costs. The main results in this section are summarized below.

Result 16.1   A firm's liquidation choice and its decisions relating to the quality of its product and fairness to employees and suppliers depend on its financial condition. As a result, a firm's financial condition can affect how it is perceived in terms of being a reliable supplier, customer, and employer.

Financial distress is especially costly for firms characterized by:

1. Products with quality that is important yet unobservable.
2. Products that require future servicing.
3. Stakeholders who require specialized capital or training.

---

[9]This topic will be discussed in more detail in Chapter 17.

These types of firms should have relatively less debt in their capital structures.

Financial distress should be less costly for firms that sell nondurable goods and services, that are less specialized, and whose quality can easily be assessed. These firms should have relatively more debt in their capital structures.

The stakeholder theory explains why some firms choose not to borrow when lenders are willing to provide debt financing at attractive terms. The presence of debt reduces the firm's profits even if bankruptcy never occurs. Indeed, some firms cannot be viable if their probabilities of bankruptcy become too high. In such cases, the stakeholders' fear that the firm may ultimately fail can actually cause the firm to fail.

16.2 The Benefits of Financial Distress with Committed Stakeholders

The last section emphasized that when stakeholders commit resources to doing business with a firm, they are effectively betting on the long-term viability of that firm. If the firm does well, the stakeholders will do well; if the firm does poorly, the stakeholders are likely to be hurt financially.

This section examines how debt affects the relationship between a firm and its stakeholders following the stakeholders' commitment of resources to the firm. Consider, for example, a firm that must invest in specialized equipment to supply a product to a specific customer. Such a firm will be concerned about its customer's financial status before committing itself to this investment, but the dynamics of the relationship with the customer changes considerably once the investment is made. After specialized investments in human or physical capital have been made, the relationships between customers and suppliers, employees and employers, and governments and corporations develop into bilateral monopoly relationships. In bilateral monopolies, the terms of trade (e.g., prices and wages) between the parties are open to negotiation. In such cases, the financial distress of a firm may provide it with a negotiating advantage because suppliers and employees must then consider how their wage and price demands affect the firm's future viability.

Bargaining with Unions

One of the best examples of the influence of debt on bargaining outcomes is the relationship between a large firm and the union representing the firm's employees. By increasing leverage, the firm can reduce its employees' demands by exploiting their fear that a wage increase will push the firm towards bankruptcy. Without attractive alternative sources of employment, unionized employees gain less from achieving higher wages if the higher wages substantially increase the probability that the firm will become bankrupt. Hence, high debt ratios may effectively facilitate employee concessions during business downturns.[10]

Example 16.4 illustrates how debt financing can affect the way that a firm bargains with its unions.

Example 16.4:   Debt and Bargaining Power

Bergland Auto Parts will be renegotiating its wage contracts within 12 months. The union is aggressive and would like to increase wages from $15 per hour to $22 per hour. Management recognizes that an increase in wages of this magnitude will lower profits from $80 million to

---

[10]Bronars and Deere (1991), Dasgupta and Sengupta (1993), and Perroti and Spier (1994) describe how leverage can be used to improve bargaining outcomes.

$30 million. How can Bergland increase its bargaining power so that the union will not demand more than $20 per hour, which lowers profits to $35 million?

Answer: One solution would be for Bergland to issue enough debt and repurchase shares with the proceeds, so that the increased debt requires $35 million in additional interest payments. Profits will then decline to $45 million prior to the renegotiated loan contract. The union recognizes that with this additional debt the firm will be unable to meet its debt payments if forced to pay $22 per hour, and the firm will be put in a fairly unstable position, that is, zero profit, if forced to pay $20 per hour. Any wage demand above $20 per hour generates losses and would not be sustainable in the long run.

Result 16.2   Financial distress can benefit some firms by improving their bargaining positions with their stakeholders.

Chrysler's financial distress in the late 1970s illustrates the potential benefits as well as the costs of financial distress. As a consequence of its financial distress, Chrysler had to sell its cars at a lower price, which reflected the potential problems associated with servicing the product of a bankrupt company. Contrary to the discussion in the last section, however, financial distress did not force Chrysler to increase wages to compensate employees for their greater job uncertainty. Instead, Chrysler used its financial distress to its advantage to force employees to make wage concessions. In this sense, financial distress was beneficial to the firm.

Although Chrysler may have benefited from financial distress in its negotiations with unions, it is unlikely, given the firm's costs of financial distress, that the company purposely put itself in such a position. However, Frank Lorenzo, the former CEO of Texas Air, has been accused of purposely putting firms in financial distress in order to obtain wage concessions.

Bankruptcy and Wage Contracts at Texas Air

Texas Air acquired Continental Airlines and Eastern Airlines in highly leveraged transactions. In 1983, Continental was able to use bankruptcy to abrogate its labor contracts and obtain lower wages since the airline was not considered viable with its original wage structure and the new debt level. Perhaps because of this controversial use of bankruptcy, a law was passed in 1984 that made it more difficult for bankrupt firms to abrogate union contracts. For this and other reasons, Lorenzo was not as successful at obtaining wage concessions at Eastern, and the firm went bankrupt in 1989.[11]

Bargaining with the Government

Both local and national communities can sometimes be thought of as stakeholders that can be hurt in the event of the demise of a major corporation. For example, the automobile plant shutdowns in the 1980s had a negative ripple effect throughout Michigan, affecting movie theaters, retailers, restaurants, and a number of other local establishments that had no direct links to the auto industry. Because of these spillover costs, both national and local governments have provided subsidies, such as loan guarantees, to a number of distressed firms to keep them from failing. The U.S. government guaranteed loans to Chrysler and received warrants in return (see Chapter 8). Massey-Ferguson, described in this chapter's opening vignette, received guarantees from the Canadian

---

[11]Eastern's demise was obviously not in the interest of the union employees, most of whom lost their jobs. However, the unions may have benefited from their refusal to go along with Lorenzo's "high leverage" negotiating ploy. By allowing Eastern to fail, the unions probably made the strategy of increasing debt to obtain union concessions appear more risky and less attractive to other airlines that might be considering the strategy in the future.

government on a preferred stock issue in return for a promise not to lay off workers in Canada. In both cases, the financial distress was beneficial to the firms because it allowed them to obtain below-market financing that they otherwise would not have obtained.

We believe that the costs of financial distress for Chrysler and Massey-Ferguson largely outweigh the benefits of the government subsidies. However, the potential government subsidy is definitely a consideration that will tilt firms toward using more debt financing. It should be stressed that governments subsidize failing firms not because of their concern for the firm's debt holders, but because of their concern for nonfinancial stakeholders such as organized union employees who may have political importance. Since the combined political power of the stakeholders of relatively small firms is not likely to be great, only the largest firms should expect government subsidies in the event of financial distress.

16.3 Capital Structure and Competitive Strategy

Having explored how a firm's interactions with its customers, suppliers, employees, and the government affect its financing, we now introduce another player into our analysis: the firm's competitors. This section describes how leverage can affect the competitiveness of an industry and how this in turn is taken into account by firms selecting their leverage ratios.

Chapter 15 discussed how leverage affects a firm's incentives to take on risky projects and to liquidate its business. If these investment and exit decisions influence the actions of a firm's competitors, then the firm's leverage choice may be a strategic tool that allows it to achieve a competitive advantage.

To understand the strategic role of the capital structure choice, it is necessary to understand the importance of a firm's ability to commit to a strategy that it might later want to change. An excellent example of this is a market leader's commitment to maintain an 80 percent market share. Carrying out such a commitment would be costly if one of its competitors chose to contest the market leader and capture a larger share of the market for itself. In this case, a price war is likely to result, creating losses for the market leader and its competitor.

A competitor that believes the market leader will fight to keep its market share will be reluctant to aggressively expand its own market share. Hence, the market leader can capture a strategic advantage if it credibly commits to protecting its market share aggressively. However, the competitor may not believe that the market leader's commitment is credible and may believe instead that, faced with an aggressive competitor, the market leader will acquiesce and give up market share rather than struggle through a costly price war.

Does Debt Make Firms More or Less Aggressive Competitors?

Some academic research has argued that firms can benefit from debt if high debt ratios allow them to commit to an aggressive output policy that they otherwise would not be able to carry out.[12] For example, a firm may wish to send a message to its competitors that it plans to increase its production. If the competitors ignore this message, the added production is likely to reduce the price of the output and, thus, reduce profits to both the

---

[12]See Brander and Lewis (1986) and Maksimovic (1986).

firm and its competitors. However, if the message is credible, the competitor may accommodate the firm by reducing its output instead of engaging in a price war. In this case, the aggressive policy does increase the firm's profits.

How can a high debt ratio help a firm send a credible message that will convince competitors that it will indeed increase output? As demonstrated in Chapter 15, increasing leverage increases a firm's tendency to take on risks. In an uncertain environment, increasing output generally augments profits when product demand is high but diminishes profits when demand is low, thereby increasing the firm's risk. Hence, the greater a firm's leverage, the greater its incentive to produce at a high level of output. Competitors, observing a firm's high leverage ratio, will realize that the firm is going to produce at a high level. Not wishing to drive the price down to the point where no firm profits, the competitors may accommodate the firm's high output by producing at a low level.

Will debt always make a firm act more aggressively? As we also discussed in Chapter 15, debt financing can lead firms to reduce their level of investment, which can make them act less aggressively. Consider, for example, a firm that competes for market share by either lowering its price or increasing its advertising. The firm is likely to suffer reduced profits in the short run by carrying out either strategy, but it should realize greater profits in the long run from gaining a higher market share. Cutting prices or advertising to gain market share should thus be viewed as an investment, implying that the incentive to increase market share will depend on the discount rate, which (from the perspective of equity holders) will be higher for a highly leveraged firm because of the debt overhang problem. Thus, higher debt implies higher discount rates, which in turn makes firms less aggressive in their competition for market share. We summarize this discussion as follows:

Result 16.3   Leverage affects the competitive dynamics of an industry. In some situations, leverage makes firms more aggressive competitors, in others less aggressive.

Eastern Airlines Revisited

When Eastern Airlines went bankrupt, other airlines expressed concern about Eastern's aggressive pricing strategy. To fill vacant seats, Eastern cut fares. Other airlines felt obliged to at least partially match this fare cutting, resulting in substantially lower profits for Eastern and its competitors. In response to the "disruption in pricing" brought about by bankrupt airlines, executives at major airlines aggressively lobbied Congress to change the bankruptcy laws that allowed bankrupt airlines to continue operating.

Our analysis of stakeholder costs along with the incentive distortions created by highly leveraged firms provides some insights into the issues raised by airline bankruptcies. Recall, for example, the discussion regarding passenger concerns about the quality of service on a bankrupt airline. Because of these concerns, a bankrupt or financially distressed airline would have to charge significantly lower prices to attract customers than a financially healthy airline could charge. The executives of healthy airlines claim that they were forced to match those price cuts, which probably was not completely true, because most passengers prefer healthy airlines even if their prices are somewhat higher. Nevertheless, the pricing behavior of the bankrupt airlines probably did contribute to the downward pressure on prices, and we agree with those executives who called for a faster resolution of airline bankruptcies.

The discussion in Chapter 15 explained why the managers of a bankrupt airline had an incentive to keep the airline operating as long as possible. Neither equity holders nor management has an incentive to shut down a financially distressed airline because the proceeds of a liquidation would go almost entirely to the firms' debt holders, particularly the most senior creditors. In addition, the airlines would have an incentive to keep prices low to increase the number of seats they fill for each flight because it would be difficult to justify to the bankruptcy judge that the airline should remain in operation if the planes were flying with most of their seats empty.

Debt and Predation

A firm's leverage ratio will also affect the strategies of its competitors. Specifically, a highly leveraged firm might be especially vulnerable to **predation** from more conservatively financed competitors.[13] In other words, a competitor might purposely lower its prices in an attempt to drive the highly leveraged firm out of business. This could be to the competitor's advantage in the long run if doing so bankrupts its more highly leveraged rival—forcing it to exit the market.

The predatory policy of the conservatively financed firm is especially effective in industries where customers and other stakeholders are concerned about the long-term viability of the firms with which they do business. For example, a producer of specialized computer equipment might be driven from the market more easily by an aggressive competitor than a producer of a breakfast cereal. If the computer equipment producer's customers believe that the firm is likely to go bankrupt and might not be able to service its products, these customers will stop purchasing the products, making the belief self-fulfilling. It would be much more difficult to scare off the customers of a company making breakfast cereal, so predatory pricing to force out highly levered firms in this industry is likely to be less effective.

Empirical Studies of the Relationship between Debt Financing and Market Share

Although some theoretical arguments suggest that highly leveraged firms can become more aggressive, leading them to increase market share, the empirical evidence more strongly supports the idea that high leverage tends to generate losses in market share. For example, Opler and Titman (1994) found that highly leveraged firms lose market share to their more conservatively financed rivals during industry downturns, when high leverage is likely to lead to financial distress.

There are at least three reasons for why high debt ratios might cause firms to lose market share:

1. The financially distressed firm faces debt overhang and, as a result, may invest less, be forced to sell off assets, and reduce its selling efforts in other ways.

2. Because of concerns about its long-term viability and the quality of its product, a highly leveraged firm may find it difficult to retain and attract customers.

3. Rivals may view a highly leveraged firm as a less formidable competitor and seize the opportunity to steal its customers and perhaps eliminate it.

Evidence on Why Distressed Firms Lose Market Share.   There is evidence to support all three of these reasons. First, distressed firms tend to sell off assets and cut back on their level of investment.[14] Second, the more highly leveraged firms with high R&D expenditures have the greatest tendency to lose market share during industry downturns.[15] High R&D firms tend to produce more specialized products, and as a result, their customers are more concerned about their long-term viability. Hence, the correlation between R&D expenditures and the tendency of highly leveraged firms to lose market share supports the stakeholder theory.

There is also evidence to suggest that the third reason is relevant. For example, Opler and Titman (1994) found that the tendency of highly leveraged firms to lose market share

---

[13]Bolton and Scharfstein (1990) consider a model where a less leveraged firm prices aggressively to drive a more leveraged firm from the market.

[14]See studies by Asquith, Gertner and Scharfstein (1994) and Lang, Poulsen and Stulz (1995).

[15]See Opler and Titman (1994).

during industry downturns is related to the number of competitors in the industry. In industries with few competitors, the highly leveraged firms lose the most market share, which supports the idea that a firm with a significant market share will invite predators when it is financially weakened. In the more competitive industries, individual firms have fairly small market shares and do not present such inviting targets when they are financially distressed.

Changes in Market Share Following Substantial Leverage Increases.   Although modest amounts of debt probably affect competition only during industry downturns, extremely large increases in debt can have an almost immediate effect. To explore this possibility, Phillips (1995) and Chevalier (1995a, b) examined how very large capital structure changes affect the competitive dynamics of an industry. Phillips examined four different industries in which one or more of the largest firms substantially increased its leverage. In three of the four industries, the leverage increase led to corresponding decreases in output and increases in prices. In these cases, the industries became less competitive. In the fourth case, the leverage increase resulted in greater output and lower prices.

Chevalier examined in great detail one industry, retail supermarkets, a particularly interesting industry to study for two reasons. First, a number of supermarket chains initiated leveraged buyouts (LBOs) in the 1980s, substantially increasing their leverage, while others remained conservatively financed. In addition, the widespread use of electronic checkout scanners have made data for individual product price at individual stores readily available. The study of the entry, exit, and expansion behavior of supermarket chains in 85 metropolitan areas [Chevalier (1995a)] demonstrated that rival firms are more likely to enter and expand in a local market if a large share of the incumbent firms have undertaken LBOs. In other words, highly leveraged stores are viewed as less formidable competitive rivals.

In her other study [(1995b)], Chevalier found that the firm initiating LBOs charged higher prices than their less leveraged rivals in the same city, suggesting that the less leveraged firms, being less cash constrained, were more willing to build market share than the more highly leveraged LBO firms.

16.4 Dynamic Capital Structure Considerations

Up to this point, we have discussed the capital structure decision within a simple, static context. The discussion assumed that firms initially would choose their preferred capital structure and later would bear the consequences. If the firm's overall business subsequently did well, the managers who took on a large amount of debt would be pleased with this decision because the firm would enjoy the tax benefits of debt and probably would avoid the negative aspects of debt financing. However, if the firm's business did very poorly, its managers would regret having chosen such a high debt ratio because negative aspects of debt would then be relevant and the firm might not be able to utilize the tax benefits of debt. According to the **static capital structure theory**, which assumes that capital structures are optimized period by period, firms weigh the costs of having too much debt when they are doing poorly against the tax benefits of debt when they are doing well to arrive at their optimal capital structures.

Section 16.5 presents some empirical evidence to support the various static theories presented so far. Before these tests can be discussed, however, we must consider that managers do not, in reality, optimize their capital structures period by period as these theories suggest, but determine their capital structures as the result of a dynamic process that accounts for the costs associated with capital structure adjustments. Hence, at any given point in time, a firm may deviate from its long-term optimal or target debt ratio.

The Pecking Order of Financing Choices

Dynamic capital structure theory, the dynamic process that governs the capital structure choice, is still not well understood by financial economists. As a starting point in our explanation of what is understood, consider again (see also Chapter 14) what Donaldson (1961) called the pecking order of financing choices, which describes how managers make their financing decisions. A summary of this pecking order includes the following observations:

1. Firms prefer to finance investments with retained earnings rather than outside sources of funds.
2. Because of their preference to finance investment from retained earnings, firms adapt their dividend policies to reflect their anticipated investment needs.
3. Because of a reluctance to substantially change their dividend policy and because of fluctuations in their cash flows and investment requirements, retained earnings may be more or less than a firm's investment needs. If the firm has excess cash, it will tend to pay off its debt prior to repurchasing shares. If external financing is required, firms tend to issue the safest security first. They begin with straight debt, next issue convertible bonds, and issue equity only as a last resort.

A substantial amount of empirical evidence verifies Donaldson's behavioral description. Most notably, extremely profitable firms tend to use a substantial amount of their excess profits to pay down debt rather than to repurchase equity. In addition, less profitable firms that need outside capital tend to use debt to fund their investment needs. As a result, firms that were profitable in the past have relatively low debt ratios while those that were relatively less profitable in the past have relatively high debt ratios. The main difference between what one might expect to observe from the static trade-off models and what is observed is that firms generally do not issue equity when they are having financial difficulties. The reluctance of firms to issue equity, as Donaldson observed, appears to be greatest when firms need the equity capital the most.

A number of explanations are offered for this pecking order behavior, including:

1. Taxes and transaction costs favor funding new investment with retained earnings and debt over issuing new equity (see Chapter 14).
2. Managers generally can raise debt capital without the approval of the board of directors. However, issuing equity generally requires board approval and hence more outside scrutiny (see Chapter 17).
3. Issuing equity conveys negative information to investors (see Chapter 18).
4. A firm having financial difficulties may want to maintain a high leverage ratio in the hope of gaining concessions from its employees and suppliers (see Section 16.2).
5. The debt overhang problem makes stock issues less attractive for a financially distressed firm (see Chapter 15).

We believe that a combination of all of the above reasons explains this observed pecking order behavior. The first reason was discussed in detail in Chapter 14; the others are described in more detail below.

An Explanation Based on Management Incentives

The second reason is based on the idea that managers personally benefit from having their firms relatively unleveraged. As discussed earlier, one reason managers might prefer lower debt ratios is that less leveraged firms invest more than highly leveraged firms, creating greater opportunities for the managers. Therefore, managers prefer to use retained earnings instead of debt to fund new investments; they probably would prefer to issue equity as well, except that an equity issue requires the approval of the board of directors and thus leads to more scrutiny. Managers may be especially reluctant to issue equity when the firm is doing poorly, because it is precisely during this time that managers are most reluctant to be scrutinized.[16]

An Explanation Based on Managers Having More Information than Investors

The third explanation of Donaldson's observation of the pecking order is based on Myers and Majluf's (1984) information-based model. The basic idea is that managers are reluctant to issue stock when they believe their shares are undervalued.[17] Because of this, investors often see an equity issue as an indication that managers believe the company's stock is overvalued, which in turn implies that the stock price will fall when the company announces it will issue new shares.

An Explanation Based on the Stakeholder Theory

In general, most nonfinancial stakeholders are pleased to see the firm issue equity. For example, employees will find their jobs more secure and their bargaining power improved if the firm has less leverage. However, that does not necessarily mean that the stockholders will find that issuing equity is in their interest. More profitable firms may anticipate expanding and, as a result, will want to maintain low debt ratios to attract the best employees and to appear as attractive as possible to potential strategic partners. Less profitable firms may plan on shrinking in size and could do so more efficiently with a higher leverage ratio. When a firm is shrinking, it might want to renegotiate contracts with suppliers and employees; and as discussed earlier, the firm may be in a better position to ask for concessions if it is highly leveraged and is having financial difficulties.

An Explanation Based on Debt Holder–Equity Holder Conflicts

The firm's financial claimants (i.e., debt holders and equity holders) also may disagree about the attractiveness of issuing equity. Chapter 15 noted that a firm with a substantial amount of long-term debt may have little incentive to issue equity after a series of losses. If bankruptcy costs are borne primarily by the firm's debt holders, the equity holders benefit little from an infusion of new equity. Indeed, share prices will decline when firms replace debt with equity because decreasing the firm's leverage increases the value of

---

[16]Zweibel (1996) presents a theoretical argument similar to this discussion.
[17]This topic is explained in detail in Chapter 18.

existing debt and transfers wealth from the equity holders to the debt holders. An exception to this general rule occurs when reducing leverage significantly cuts the costs of financial distress and thus significantly increases the total value of the firm. We discuss this possibility in more detail below.

In extreme cases, a financially distressed firm may be unable to raise equity capital. For example, during the 1980s, Kent Steel Corporation saw the value of its assets fall by 70 percent. It required a $50 million capital infusion for maintenance costs in order to remain in business for another year. While Kent Steel's managers would have preferred to issue equity, the firm was simply too far gone. The firm had debt obligations with a face value of $120 million; however, with a market value of less than $70 million for the entire firm, the debt was selling at a large discount.

In cases like Kent Steel, the firm cannot get out of financial distress simply by issuing equity. As Example 16.5 illustrates, avoiding financial distress requires that the lenders either forgive some of their debt or provide the firm with an additional infusion of cash.

Example 16.5:   Can Financially Distressed Firms Issue Equity?

Gentry, Inc., is having financial difficulties and although it has not yet defaulted, its bonds are selling at 50 percent of their face values. The current value of the firm is $600 million, which consists of $50 million in equity and $550 million (market value) in bonds. These bonds have a face value of $1.1 billion, with $100 million due within six months and $1 billion due in two years. Can Gentry issue stock to raise the funds needed to meet its $100 million debt obligation, assuming that the bonds gain 10 percent in value as a result of this equity infusion?

Answer: Probably not. Although Gentry is close to bankruptcy, its equity still retains some value because investors believe that there is a slight chance that the firm can be turned around. In this case, the equity should be thought of as an out-of-the-money option. It will probably expire worthless; however, while there is a sizable upside if the firm does manage to survive for the next two years, this does not mean that the firm can issue new stock at the current stock price.

The $100 million equity infusion, which is going to pay the debt obligation, increases the value of the firm by $100 million, since paying off debt is a zero *NPV* investment. This infusion makes the bonds more valuable because it increases the likelihood that they will be repaid in full. Since the bonds gain $55 million in value as a result of this infusion, the post-issue value of all of the firm's equity must be only $95 million. Hence, investors will not be willing to put up an additional $100 million in equity.

Example 16.5 describes a firm that is unable to issue new equity because debt holders capture a large part of the gain associated with the recapitalization. If the recapitalization does not make the firm more valuable, then an equity infusion hurts equity holders by transferring value from them to the debt holders. In many cases, however, a financially distressed firm does become more valuable after a recapitalization, in which case both equity holders and debt holders can benefit. This will happen, for example, when a firm is unable to sell its products or is losing key employees because of its financial difficulties. Since financial distress reduces the current cash flows to equity holders, it provides an incentive for a firm to issue new stock, which can increase the value of the firm's existing equity as well as its debt. Example 16.6 illustrates this point.

Example 16.6:   Issuing Equity to Improve Customer Confidence

Consider again the case of Gentry, Inc., but now assume that one reason for its low value is that its customers have lost faith in the firm's ability to produce quality products because of its financial distress. Although the assets of the firm are currently valued at $600 million, the equity infusion will restore customer confidence and Gentry's asset value (prior to the $100 million debt payment) will increase to $900 million. Under this scenario, is it possible for the firm to issue equity $100 million in equity?

Answer: Yes. The proceeds from the issue are not fully dissipated by an improvement in the value of the firm's debt. If the debt increases in value by less than $200 million as a result of the equity infusion and restored customer confidence, it follows that the post-issue equity value of the firm will exceed $150 million, implying that the stock can be issued and that the original stockholders will benefit from the recapitalization.

Example 16.6 shows that when there are high costs associated with financial distress, equity holders will have an incentive to recapitalize. However, if it is costly to repurchase or issue debt or equity, firms that have relatively low financial distress costs will have their leverage ratios determined to a large extent by their past history. That is, we expect a firm's current debt-to-equity ratio to be low if its past earnings were high, and its leverage ratio to be substantially higher if its past earnings were negative. This argument suggests the following result.

Result 16.4   If the costs of changing a firm's capital structure are sufficiently high, a firm's capital structure is determined in part by its past history. This means that:

- Very profitable firms are likely to experience increased equity values and thus lower leverage ratios.
- Unprofitable firms may experience lower equity values and perhaps increased debt, and thus higher leverage ratios.

16.5 Empirical Evidence on the Capital Structure Choice

Chapters 13 through 16 discuss a variety of theories about the costs and benefits of debt financing. Taken together, these theories help explain why firms select the capital structures that they do. In sum, the theories suggest a trade-off between the tax benefits of debt and a variety of costs as well as some benefits of incurring financial distress. This section examines some of the empirical tests of these theories.

One of the earliest empirical findings was that firms in the same industry tend to choose similar capital structures. In the United States, for example, financial services firms tend to have high leverage ratios while makers of scientific equipment tend to have low leverage ratios. These findings provide evidence that the optimal capital structures of firms vary from industry to industry, reflecting the differential costs and benefits of debt which presumably are related to a firm's line of business. This evidence, however, is consistent with any theory that proposes a trade-off between the costs and benefits of debt financing, and it may even be consistent with capital structure irrelevance. In essence, the evidence may simply indicate that firms like to use industry norms to select their debt ratios. Because the use of industry norms is not harmful to firm value if capital structure is irrelevant, there is no reason to rule it out.

A number of empirical studies have documented evidence more supportive of the trade-off theories.[18] The evidence indicates that debt ratios are systematically linked to variables related to the costs of bankruptcy and financial distress (see Exhibit 16.2). Past

---

[18]See Bradley, Jarrell, and Kim (1984); Long and Malitz (1985); and Titman and Wessels (1988). International evidence is presented by Rajan and Zingales (1995).

Exhibit 16.2   Summary of Empirical Evidence on the Capital Structure Choice

Variables	*Relation to Leverage Ratio*	*Explanation*
EBIT/total assets (profitability)	Strong negative relation.	Pecking order description.
R&D/sales	Strong negative relation.	• Tax reasons.
Selling expenses/sales		• Specialized assets and products imply greater stakeholder costs and potentially more conflicts between debt holders and equity holders.
Market value/book value		
Machines and equipment producers (dummy variable)	Less highly leveraged.	Customer avoidance of purchasing durable goods of distressed firms.
Unionization[a]	Highly unionized industries are more leveraged.	Leverage increases the firm's bargaining power.
Size	Small firms use more short-term debt.	• Transaction costs of issuing long-term debt. • Adverse incentive costs associated with long-term debt.[b]

[a]See Bronars and Deere (1991).
[b]This explanation was discussed in Chapter 15.

research finds that observed debt ratios are negatively related to the firms' past profitability, research and development expenditures, and advertising and selling expenses. In addition, firms in industries that produce durable goods, like machines and equipment, are usually less leveraged then firms that produce nondurables; and more unionized firms are usually more leveraged than less unionized firms. Small firms use about the same amount of long-term debt as larger firms, but small firms use significantly more short-term debt.

The negative relation between operating profit and leverage is found in numerous studies and holds in many countries outside of the United States.[19] This relation reflects the pecking order of financing behavior. When firms have substantial operating profits, they tend to pay down debt before paying out dividends and repurchasing shares. When firms have insufficient profits to cover investment needs, they tend to borrow rather than issue stock to cover losses.

There are a number of explanations for the negative relation of R&D and selling expenses to leverage. First, firms with large R&D and selling expenses may have little taxable earnings and hence, may only be able to utilize rarely, if at all, debt tax shields (see Chapter 13). In addition, firms with high R&D and selling expenses are likely to be growth firms that produce specialized products. To the extent that these are indeed growth firms, these firms are not likely to have access to sizable amounts of debt financ-

---

[19]See Rajan and Zingales (1995).

ing because of the debt holder–equity holder conflicts described in Chapter 15. The tendency of these growth firms to borrow short term provides further support for this idea because short-term debt creates fewer conflicts than long-term debt. Moreover, since firms with high R&D and selling expenses produce more specialized products, their nonfinancial stakeholders are more likely to require investments in specialized human and physical capital. Hence, the stakeholder theory also suggests that these firms should have low leverage ratios. For similar reasons, firms that produce machines and equipment requiring future maintenance tend to have relatively low leverage ratios.

The fact that unionized firms are more highly leveraged relates to our earlier discussion (see section 16.2) about how committed stakeholders generate an environment of bilateral monopoly, characterized by negotiation. As we discussed earlier, unionized firms may prefer to take on more debt because it allows them to bargain more effectively with their unions.

16.6 Summary and Conclusions

The previous chapters examined a variety of costs and benefits of debt financing that firms must consider when they make their financing decisions. The discussion has suggested which firms should be financed more heavily with debt and which should include very little debt in their capital structures. For example, producers of nondurable goods (e.g., tobacco or cookies) that do little research and development generally have relatively high debt ratios. These firms are likely to have low costs associated with financial distress because their customers and other stakeholders are not likely to be especially concerned about their long-run viability. The potential for such firms to substantially increase the risk of their investments is also limited, so that borrowers are willing to lend to them at attractive terms. Such firms also are likely to generate high taxable earnings because they usually have minimal tax shields and, as a result, can fully utilize their interest tax deductions.

Producers of high-technology durable goods (e.g., computers and other scientific equipment) generally are not highly leveraged. These firms have the highest costs associated with financial distress because their stakeholders are very concerned about their long-term viability. In addition, the potential for taking on risky projects is present for such firms, making lenders reluctant to supply large amounts of debt capital. These firms also have lower taxable earnings, relative to their values, and hence, can utilize only limited amounts of debt tax shields.

Although the types of products a firm sells and other aspects of its overall strategy have an important influence on its financial structure, a firm's capital structure is also determined by its history. Firms that were profitable in the recent past generally use some of the profit to repay debt; as a result, they become relatively unleveraged. In contrast, firms that suffer substantial losses generally accumulate debt; as a result, they become highly leveraged.

Bankruptcy rates would be substantially lower if firms issued equity instead of debt subsequent to incurring substantial losses. This chapter has provided several explanations for why firms do not do this. For example, issuing equity in these situations can result in a substantial transfer of wealth from the firm's equity holders to its debt holders. In addition, issuing equity might make it more difficult for the firm to bargain effectively with its employees and suppliers; perhaps by keeping the threat of bankruptcy high, employees and suppliers will make concessions that make the firm more competitive. Additional explanations based on managerial incentives and information considerations will be discussed in more detail in Part V.

This chapter completes Part IV, which was devoted exclusively to issues of capital structure and dividend policy. The chapters in this part provided a fairly thorough discussion of how financial managers make capital structure choices in an ideal world where shareholders and managers are equally informed about the prospects of their firms and agree that the objective of the firm is to maximize shareholder value. While this provides a useful framework for thinking about how one should choose the optimal financing mix for a firm, it provides an incomplete description of how these decisions are made in practice.

In reality, top managers may have an incentive to finance their firms in ways that do not maximize the value of their stock. For example, managers may choose conservative financial structures because of personal aversions to placing their firms in financial distress. In other cases, managers may choose high debt ratios to convey favorable information to their shareholders; that is, they signal their confidence in the firm's ability to generate sufficient earnings to repay the debt. These issues are addressed in Part V.

Key Concepts

Result 16.1: A firm's liquidation choice and its decisions relating to the quality of its product and fairness to employees and suppliers depend on its financial condition. As a result, a firm's financial condition can affect how it is perceived in terms of being a reliable supplier, customer, and employer.

Financial distress is especially costly for firms characterized by:

1. Products with quality that is important yet unobservable.
2. Products that require future servicing.
3. Stakeholders who require specialized capital or training.

These types of firms should have relatively less debt in their capital structures.

Financial distress should be less costly for firms that sell nondurable goods and services, that are less specialized, and whose quality can easily be assessed. These firms should have relatively more debt in their capital structures.

Result 16.2: Financial distress can benefit some firms by improving their bargaining positions with their stakeholders.

Result 16.3: Leverage affects the competitive dynamics of an industry. In some situations, leverage makes firms more aggressive competitors, in others less aggressive.

Result 16.4: If the costs of changing a firm's capital structure are sufficiently high, a firm's capital structure is determined in part by its past history. This means that:

- Very profitable firms are likely to experience increased equity values and thus lower leverage ratios.
- Unprofitable firms may experience lower equity values and perhaps increased debt, and thus higher leverage ratios.

Key Terms

dynamic capital structure theory   592
nonfinancial stakeholders   578
predation   590

stakeholder theory   579
static capital structure theory   591

Exercises

16.1. What are the differences between direct and indirect bankruptcy costs? Who bears these costs? Explain your answer by referring to a real situation from the recent past.

16.2. As a potential employee, why might you be interested in the employer's capital structure?

16.3. Compare qualitatively the indirect bankruptcy costs of operating a franchised hotel to that of running a high-tech start-up computer firm.

16.4. You are the manager of a company that produces automobiles. A union contract will come up for renegotiation in two months and you wish to increase your firm's bargaining power prior to hearing the union's initial demands. The union is likely to ask for a 25 percent increase from existing wage levels of $20 per hour for the 1,000 workers at your company. Workers typically work 2000 hours per year. The firm has $100 million of debt outstanding at an interest rate of 10 percent annually, and an equity market value of $200 million. Income before interest is $20 million per year. Assume no taxes.

What specific financing strategies would you implement and why?

16.5. BCD Manufacturing is considering repurchasing 40 percent of its common stock. Management estimates the tax savings from such a move to be $48 million, based on the addition of $1 billion of debt at a rate of 12 percent with a 40 percent marginal tax rate. However, the company's suppliers are unhappy with the decision and are threatening to revoke the company's net-30 day credit terms, which will cost the firm an additional 2 percent on its $1.5 billion inventory. Should management go ahead with the repurchase? Why or why not?

16.6. Carcinogens-R-Us and Lung Decay, two cigarette producers of comparable size, are struggling for market share in a declining market. Carcinogens-R-Us has just undergone a leveraged buyout and is able to meet its fixed charges with its existing market share, but it may be forced into bankruptcy if it loses market share. As a manager of Lung Decay, how would you establish your pricing policy? If Carcinogens-R-Us enters bankruptcy, it would either (*a*) be forced to liquidate, (*b*) lose market share due to customer concerns, or (*c*) emerge recapitalized with no harm to market share. How would these three possibilities affect your decision?

16.7. Comparing the indirect costs of bankruptcy, explain why IBM includes very little debt in its capital structure while Marriott Corporation uses a fairly large amount of debt.

16.8. Describe the trade-offs involved when firms decide how to price their products. What are the costs and benefits of raising prices? How do interest rates affect the decision? How do leverage ratios affect the decision?

16.9. Weston Tractor is a cyclical business that is forced to lay off workers during downturns. The CEO estimates that they saved $50 million during the last recession by laying off excess workers. However, the company had additional expenses of $70 million three years later when it had to retrain the new workers. The firm is currently facing a similar situation. The risk-free rate is 10 percent, but Weston's current borrowing rate is 16 percent. Should Weston lay off the workers? If Weston was less highly leveraged, it would be able to borrow at 11 percent. How would this affect the firm's decision? Discuss how a prospective employee would react upon learning that Weston was substantially increasing its leverage.

16.10. Compass Computers has suffered an unexpected loss and is currently having financial difficulties. Explain why Compass may choose not to issue equity to solve its financial problems. If Compass does not issue equity, should it change its product market strategy to account for the firm's weaker financial health?

16.11. As the CEO of Mega Corp., which do you prefer: a competitor with high leverage or one with low leverage? Under what conditions will you act more or less aggressively if your competitor is highly leveraged?

16.12. Compton Industries currently has 2 million shares outstanding at $3 per share. Because the company is having financial difficulties, it also has $50 million in face value of long-term outstanding debt that is selling at only 60 percent of its face value. As Compton's CEO, you estimate that you will need a cash inflow of $10 million within six months to meet your payroll. Since covenants in the existing debt preclude further debt financing, you are forced to consider an equity offering. Is such an offering possible, assuming the equity issue would result in a 20 percent increase in the value of the debt? Explain why.

References and Additional Readings

Asquith, Paul; Robert Gertner; and David Scharfstein. "Anatomy of Financial Distress: An Examination of Junk-Bond Issuers." *Quarterly Journal of Economics* 109, no. 3 (1994), pp. 625–58.

Barclay, Michael J., and Clifford W. Smith, Jr. "The Maturity Structure of Corporate Debt." *Journal of Finance* 50, no. 2 (1995), pp. 609–31.

Bolton, Patrick, and David Scharfstein. "A Theory of Predation Based on Agency Problems in Financial Contracting." *American Economic Review* 80 (1990), pp. 93–106.

Bradley, Michael; Gregory Jarrell; and E. Han Kim. "On the Existence of an Optimal Capital Structure: Theory and Evidence." *Journal of Finance* 39, no. 3 (1984), pp. 857–78.

Brander, James A., and Tracy R. Lewis. "Oligopoly and Financial Structure: The Limited Liability Effect." *American Economic Review* 76 (1986), pp. 956–70.

Bronars, Stephen G., and D. R. Deere. "The Threat of Unionization, the Use of Debt, and the Preservation of Shareholder Wealth." *Quarterly Journal of Economics* 106, no. 1 (1991), pp. 231–54.

Chevalier, Judith A. "Capital Structure and Product Market Competition: An Empirical Study of Supermarket LBOs." *American Economic Review* 85 (1995a), pp. 206–56.

———. "Do LBO Supermarkets Charge More? An Empirical Analysis of the Effects of LBOs on Supermarket Pricing." *Journal of Finance* 50 (1995b), pp. 1095–1112.

Cornell, Bradford, and Alan Shapiro. "Corporate Stakeholders and Corporate Finance." *Financial Management* 16 (1987), pp. 5–14.

Cutler, David M., and Lawrence H. Summers. "The Costs of Conflict Resolution and Financial Distress: Evidence from the Texaco-Pennzoil Litigation." *Rand Journal of Economics* 19 (1988), pp. 157–72.

Dasgupta, Sudipto, and Kunal Sengupta. "Sunk Investment, Bargaining, and Choice of Capital Structure." *International Economic Review* 34, no. 1 (1993), pp. 203–20.

Donaldson, Gordon. *Corporate Debt Capacity: A Study of Corporate Debt Policy and the Determination of Corporate Debt Capacity.* Boston: Harvard Graduate School of Business Administration, 1961.

Fischer, Edwin O.; Robert Heinkel; and Josef Zechner. "Dynamic Capital Structure Choice: Theory and Tests." *Journal of Finance* 44 (1989), pp. 19–40.

Harris, Milton, and Arthur Raviv. "The Theory of Capital Structure." *Journal of Finance* 46 (1991), pp. 297–356.

Jensen, Michael, and William Meckling. "The Theory of the Firm: Managerial Behavior, Agency Costs and Ownership Structure." *Journal of Financial Economics* 3 (1976), pp. 305–60.

Lang, Larry H.; Annette Poulsen; and René M. Stulz. "Asset Sales, Firm Performance, and the Agency Costs of Managerial Discretion." *Journal of Financial Economics* 37, no. 1 (1995), pp. 3–37.

Long, Michael, and Irene Malitz. "The Investment-Financing Nexus: Some Empirical Evidence." *Midland Corporate Finance Journal* 3 (Spring 1985), pp. 53–59.

———. "Investment Patterns and Financial Leverage." In *Corporate Capital Structure in the United States.* Benjamin Friedman, ed., Chicago: University of Chicago Press, 1985.

Mackie-Mason, Jeffrey K. "Do Taxes Affect Corporate Financing Decisions?" *Journal of Finance* 45 (1990), pp. 1471–95.

Maksimovic, Vojislav. "Optimal Capital Structure in Oligopolies." Ph.D. dissertation, Harvard University, 1986.

Maksimovic, Vojislav, and Sheridan Titman. "Financial Reputation and Reputation for Product Quality." *Review of Financial Studies* 2 (1991), pp. 175–200.

Miller, Merton, "Debt and Taxes." *Journal of Finance* 32 (1977), pp. 261–75.

Myers, Stewart C. "The Capital Structure Puzzle." *Journal of Finance* 39 (1984), pp. 575–92.

Myers, Stewart C., and Nicholas Majluf. "Corporate Financing and Investment Decisions When Firms Have Information that Investors Do Not Have." *Journal of Financial Economics* 13 (1984), pp. 187–221.

Opler, Tim, and Sheridan Titman. "Financial Distress and Corporate Performance." *Journal of Finance* 49 (1994), pp. 1015–40.

Perotti, Enrico, and Kathy E. Spier. "Capital Structure as a Bargaining Tool: The Role of Leverage in Contract Renegotiation." *American Economic Review* 83, no. 5 (1994), pp. 1131–41.

Phillips, Gordon M. "Increased Debt and Industry Product Markets." *Journal of Financial Economics* 37, no. 2 (1995), pp. 189–238.

Rajan, Raghuram G., and Luigi Zingales. "What Do We Know about Capital Structure? Some Evidence from International Data." *Journal of Finance* 50, no. 5 (1995), pp. 1421–60.

Shapiro, Alan, and Sheridan Titman. "An Integrated Approach to Corporate Risk Management." *Midland Corporate Finance Journal* 3 (Summer 1985), pp. 41–56.

Sharpe, Steven. "Financial Market Imperfections, Firm Leverage, and the Cyclicality of Employment." *American Economic Review* 84 (1995), pp. 1060–74.

Titman, Sheridan. "The Effect of Capital Structure on the Firm's Liquidation Decision." *Journal of Financial Economics* 13 (1984), pp. 137–52.

Titman, Sheridan, and Roberto Wessels. "The Determinants of Capital Structure Choice." *Journal of Finance* 43 (1988), pp. 1–20.

Zweibel, Jeffrey. "Dynamic Capital Structure under Managerial Entrenchment." *American Economic Review* 86 (1996), pp. 1197–1215.

PRACTICAL INSIGHTS FOR PART IV

Allocating Capital for Real Investment

- Investment projects that generate substantial nondebt tax shields, like depreciation deductions, generally contribute less to a firm's debt capacity and, therefore, require higher discount rates. (Section 13.5)
- For firms with taxable shareholders, investment projects that can be financed from retained earnings require a lower cost of capital than projects that require the issuance of new equity. (Section 14.5)
- Managers who wish to maximize shareholder value, as opposed to total firm value, will use higher discount rates when their firms become more highly levered. (Section 15.2)
- Because of potential incentive problems, firms that are highly levered may not be able to borrow additional money to fund positive net present value investment projects. (Section 15.2)
- Because financial distress costs are higher in industries that produce more specialized products that may require future servicing, those industries use less debt financing and as a result, require higher costs of capital. (Section 16.1)

Financing the Firm

- Since interest payments are tax deductible, corporate taxes induce firms to use more debt financing than they would use otherwise. In the absence of other considerations, firms would include sufficient debt in their capital structures to eliminate their corporate tax liability. (Section 13.4)
- Personal tax considerations lead to lower debt ratios for two reasons: First, part of the return to equity holders comes in the form of capital gains which are more lightly taxed than interest payments that are taxed as ordinary income. Second, there is a tax disadvantage associated with paying out retained earnings to shareholders, which would increase leverage. (Sections 13.5 and 14.3)
- Firms without taxable earnings, but which do not wish to issue common stock, may obtain a lower cost of capital by issuing preferred stock rather than debt. (Section 13.6)
- If the personal tax rates of equity holders are higher than corporate rates, retained earnings offers the cheapest form of financing, debt offers the second cheapest form of financing, and equity provides the most expensive capital. (Section 14.5)

- Profitable firms might choose to be initially overlevered and then use their profits to pay down their debt over time. (Section 14.5)
- Shareholders with different marginal tax rates will generally disagree about the firm's optimal debt ratio and dividend policy. (Section 14.5)
- Taxable shareholders will prefer firms to distribute earnings by repurchasing shares rather than by paying dividends. (Section 14.3)
- Taxes play much less of a role in determining capital structure and dividend choices in countries with dividend imputation systems. (Section 14.3)
- Firms with substantial future investment opportunities should use relatively less debt financing than more mature companies whose values consist mainly of the assets they currently have in place. (Section 15.2)
- The direct costs associated with bankruptcy as well as the indirect costs associated with debt holder–equity holder conflicts will be reflected in the firm's required interest payments on its debt. These costs should not be a deterrent to using debt financing if lenders are willing to provide debt at reasonable interest rates. (Section 15.2)
- When there is a substantial potential for debt holder–equity holder incentive problems, convertible debt, short-term debt and bank loans are better sources of debt capital than straight long-term bonds. (Section 15.4)
- Firms that sell specialized products that require future servicing should be less levered than firms that sell commodities. (Section 16.1)
- Holding all else equal, we expect that a less levered firm will provide better future opportunities for employees than a more highly levered firm. (Section 16.1)
- Financial distress, and hence debt financing, may be beneficial if it allows firms to obtain concessions from employees, suppliers, and governments. (Section 16.2)
- Firms often lose market share subsequent to large increases in their debt ratio. (Section 16.3)
- Financially distressed firms can sometimes reduce their financial difficulties by issuing new equity. However, issuing equity in these situations transfers wealth from shareholders to long-term debt holders and puts the firm in a worse bargaining position with employees and suppliers. (Section 16.4)

Allocating Funds for Financial Investments

- High tax bracket individuals should tilt their portfolio toward stocks that pay low dividends and should hold tax exempt municipal bonds. (Sections 13.5, 14.3, and 14.4)

- Tax exempt investors should hold taxable bonds and stocks with high dividend yields. (Sections 13.5, 14.3, and 14.4)

- Investors with high marginal tax rates should time their transactions so that they purchase stocks just after the dividend ex dates and sell them just before the dividend ex dates. Tax exempt investors should do just the opposite: Buying just before the ex dates and selling just after the ex dates. (Section 14.4)

EXECUTIVE PERSPECTIVE

Roberts W. Brokaw III

My experience as an investment banker has brought me into contact with senior company managers and their financial advisors, who are quite sophisticated in effecting specific transactions. However, these financial decision makers often are very deal-driven, which allows them to miss the big view—the impact of the deal on the overall capital structure of the firm. This shortfall occurs because of two basic realities: (1) a transaction's direct consequences are easier to measure than its indirect ones; and (2) the good academic work on how debt and equity costs interact is poorly understood or inconsistently applied.

Chapters 13 through 16 provide a solid basis for remedying this shortfall. In other areas of finance, such as portfolio management, the structuring and valuation of complex securities, and arbitrage, theory has contributed much to practice in recent years. However, while the capital markets have shown an impressive ability to utilize "security-specific" theory, progress has been much slower in management's application of corporate finance theory to capital structure.

Once the bankers have completed their part of a transaction, companies are left to assess their optimal capital structure. Management has the continuing responsibility to weigh the many matters impacting this task, including identifying funding requirements, business risks and opportunities, certainty of operating forecasts, tax position, and potential changes in corporate strategy. Within this context, the decision maker must be knowledgeable about a bewildering range of new financing vehicles and asset disposition alternatives, all in the context of ever-changing capital markets.

Exceptional value can be created for financial managers who understand and apply the concepts described in this part of the book. These concepts might not lend themselves to the same precision as, say, the 50 basis points that could be saved from using debt derivatives in a synthetic fixed-rate financing. But, that is just the point!

Applying lessons learned in these chapters can make 50 basis points on one deal look like chump change.

Most nonfinancial companies' capital structures include equity predominantly (as measured by market value). An improved understanding of equity's cost dynamics is at the heart of the challenge to financial managers today. Equity is more expensive than debt; it serves as the main cushion that makes debt "cheap"; it can be at odds with lenders; and its cost is usually nondeductible for tax purposes. Here, there is an imperfect fit among theory, reality, and practice—a combination which assures that modest improvements toward optimizing the capital structure will reap high marginal returns.

Grinblatt and Titman provide important techniques and guideposts by leading the reader through the basics, starting with the most easily understood concept—the tax impact of financings and distributions to shareholders. Next, they develop the idea of the inherent conflict between lenders and owners of an enterprise, as well as the related consequences of financial distress. This emerging area of theory has important implications, not only for overall leverage, but also for the design of new issues and repair of weakened balance sheets. Finally, the authors reach beyond discussion of the securities themselves to describe an important area affected by and impacting upon capital structure—corporate strategy. This matter is at the heart of how a company is run and of the value it creates. Chapter 16 underscores the importance to a company of having a consistent, disciplined, informed view of capital structure policy—one that is not discouraged by the complexity and relative imprecision of some of the tasks related to its determination.

Mr. Brokaw is currently a managing director and head of the Investment Banking Division's Corporate Finance Group at PaineWebber Incorporated. In addition to these duties, Mr. Brokaw is also adjunct professor of finance at New York University's Stern School of Business.

Incentives, Information, and Corporate Control

Up to this point, we have explored financial strategies that firms can employ to enhance the value of their shares. In reality, however, financial managers do not always make the decisions that maximize the stock prices of their firms. To understand how financial decisions *actually are made,* we have to understand how managerial incentives can differ from shareholder incentives.

Part V takes a closer look at how managers actually make financial decisions. Chapter 17 examines managerial incentive in detail, paying particular attention to the general belief among managers that they must satisfy a broad constituency that includes shareholders as only one of many relevant players. For example, managers generally view their employees as important constituents, so they typically arc somewhat averse to making decisions that jeopardize their employees' jobs. They also are interested in their own job security and future prospects; as a result, managers may take on negative net present value investments that allow their firms to grow and may also include less than the optimal amount of debt in their capital structures.

Although these incentive issues probably cannot be eliminated, financial markets have evolved in recent years in ways that lessen the more significant problems. In most companies, for example, the debt-equity choice is a decision made at the board of directors' level. Hence, firms with active outside board members—that is, members of the board of directors who are not employees of the company—can force managers to select a debt ratio higher than that which the managers would personally prefer. In addition, outside board members might want to see the firm more highly levered than would be optimal in the absence of managerial incentive problems, since the added debt burden may mitigate the incentives of managers to overinvest.

A more direct way to align the incentives of managers and shareholders, which is also examined in Chapter 17, is to make the pay of managers more sensitive to the performance of their stock prices. The threat of outside takeovers, examined in Chapter 19, also helps to align the interests of managers and shareholders. As Chapter 18 notes, however, many types of performance-based compensation, such as executive stock options, and the threat of outside takeovers, can make managers overly concerned about the current share prices of their firms. When this is the case, managers may take actions that convey favorable information to investors that temporarily boosts share prices at the expense of lowering the intrinsic or long-term values of their firms.

The incentives of managers to make financial decisions that convey favorable information to investors is examined in Chapter 18. We argue, for example, that managers may want to distribute cash to shareholders, in the form of either dividends or share repurchases, because cash distributions signal that firms are generating cash, thus resulting in favorable stock price responses. Similarly, leverage increases signal that managers are confident that they can take advantage of the debt tax shield and are not overly concerned about incurring the costs of financial distress. Hence, when firms announce an increase in their debt ratios, stock prices generally respond favorably.

An important lesson of Chapter 18 is that the stock price response to the announcement of a financial decision may provide misleading information about how investors view the particular decision. For example, managers may believe that their shareholders prefer higher dividends because share prices reacts favorably to dividend increases. In reality, however, shareholders may react favorably to dividend increases because of the favorable information the decision conveys, even though investors dislike the tax consequences of the higher dividends. A second important lesson of this chapter is that there may be negative consequences associated with making managers overly concerned about boosting the current stock price of their firm.

Chapter 19, which examines mergers and acquisitions and their effect on the control of firms, applies the material used throughout this text. For example, an understanding of the incentive and information issues examined in Chapters 17 and 18 is particularly important for individuals who evaluate mergers and acquisitions. In some cases, mergers and acquisitions mitigate the incentive and information problems; in other cases, however, mergers can worsen these problems. In addition, many of the tax issues discussed in Chapters 12 through 14 and the valuation techniques developed in Part III prove to be important in the evaluation and structuring of merger and acquisition deals.

It should be noted that both risk aversion and the time value of money, which were central to our analysis of asset pricing in the first half of this text, provide an unnecessary layer of complication to the analysis of how information and incentive problems affect corporate behavior. Hence, unless specified otherwise, the discussion and examples in Part V assume that investors are risk neutral and the interest rate is zero, or equivalently, that the present value of a future cash flow equals its expected future value.

How Managerial Incentives Affect Financial Decisions

Learning Objectives

After reading this chapter, you should be able to:

1. Distinguish between managerial incentives and shareholder incentives.
2. Understand how the differences between manager and shareholder incentives affect the ownership structure, capital structure, and investment policies of firms.
3. Describe ways to design compensation contracts that minimize manager-shareholder incentive problems.

Armand Hammer founded and ran Occidental Petroleum until his death in 1990 at the age of 92. Although he is generally credited with creating a highly successful oil company, during the last decade of his life he pursued strategies that were widely criticized and that resulted in dismal share price performance for Occidental while the stocks of other oil companies tripled in value. A particularly visible example of Hammer's decision making that many stockholders opposed was the building of an art museum for Hammer's art collection at a cost of $120 million to shareholders.

One event illustrates the extent to which Armand Hammer influenced the value of Occidental Petroleum's stock. When it became known, on November 10, 1989, that Hammer had entered the intensive care unit of the UCLA Medical Center, the rumor spread that the 91-year-old chairman was critically ill. Based on this rumor, the price of Occidental stock increased from $28 to $31 per share, representing a total gain in shareholder value of approximately $300 million. Given Hammer's age, his medical problems could not have been totally unexpected, so this $300 million increase in market value probably underestimates the extent to which Hammer was harming the company's value. The following Monday, it was reported that Hammer had gone into the hospital for a routine adjustment to his pacemaker. The price of Occidental stock reacted to this information by falling $2 per share, giving up most of its earlier gain.

U p to this point, we have presented a fairly simplistic view of how corporate decisions are made. The previous chapters considered financial decisions within the context of a firm whose shareholders know as much about the business as the managers and whose managers act in the interests of shareholders. In most cases, these assumptions provide a useful framework for understanding how investment and financing decisions *should* be made to create value for shareholders. However, given the conflicts of interest between managers and shareholders, this framework does not provide a good general description of how these financial decisions are *actually* made.

This chapter has two purposes. The first purpose is to provide a more realistic picture of how financial decisions are *actually made* by firms, taking into account the potential incentive problems that can exist between managers and shareholders. The second purpose is to reexamine how financial decisions *should be made* in this more realistic setting, accounting for inherent manager-shareholder conflicts.

One can take two views as to why management decisions might deviate from those that maximize firm values. The first, more cynical, view is that managers take advantage of their positions and engage in actions that allow them to benefit personally at the expense of shareholders. The chapter's opening vignette, which described Armand Hammer's use of Occidental Petroleum's funds to build a museum for his personal art collection, is an oft-cited example that might fit into this category. Although the popular press has emphasized this cynical view of the management-shareholder conflict, we emphasize a different view: that managers view their positions as serving a broader constituency than just shareholders.

The most important source of conflict between managers and shareholders arises from the sense of loyalty most managers feel toward their employees and other stakeholders. For example, managers generally find it unpleasant to lay off employees, and similarly, find it rewarding to offer their employees good career opportunities. Indeed, many Americans believe that taking care of employees—not maximizing stock prices—should be the primary goal of U.S. corporations. A poll taken by Yankelovich in 1996 "showed that 51 percent of Americans think a corporation's top obligation is to its employees, while 17 percent think stockholders deserve highest priority."[1]

Perhaps the most important implication of both the cynical view and the stakeholder view is that managers may choose investment and financing strategies that do not maximize the firm's value. For example, to enhance their own opportunities as well as those of their employees, managers may bias their investment and financing decisions in ways that reduce risk and increase the firm's growth rate. To accomplish these goals, a manager may accept negative net present value projects that increase the size and diversity of the firm and use less than the value-maximizing level of debt financing.

Since managers and shareholders do not always have the same interests, financial decisions can be viewed from a number of perspectives. For example, the previous chapters viewed financial decisions from the perspective of a firm run by value-maximizing managers. This chapter views the financial decisions from two different perspectives: (1) from the perspective of a manager with incentives to reduce risk and enhance growth, and (2) from the perspective of a large shareholder, or perhaps a board member, who can influence the firm's overall strategy but cannot control the day-to-day decisions made by the firm's managers.

These large outside shareholders may influence a firm's capital structure decision, since they can readily observe the capital structure choice, but they may not be able to

---

[1]*The Wall Street Journal*, May 21, 1996.

influence the firm's investment choices. This chapter addresses the question of how outside shareholders should exert their influence on the capital structure choice in order to *indirectly* influence the manager's investment choice. This chapter also examines ways of compensating managers so that these incentive problems are minimized.[2]

17.1 The Separation of Ownership and Control

Most large corporations are effectively controlled by managers who hold a relatively small amount of their firm's shares. To borrow from the influential book by Berle and Means (1932), there is a separation between ownership and control in large corporations. This separation causes problems because the interests of managers are not generally aligned with those of shareholders.

Whom Do Managers Represent?

Shareholders are interested in maximizing the value of their shares. Managers, however, generally see stockholders as just one of many potential constituents. Donaldson and Lorsch (1983) suggested that top executives see themselves as representatives of three separate constituencies, including both financial and nonfinancial stakeholders:

1. Investors (e.g., the company's shareholders and debt holders).
2. Customers and suppliers.
3. Employees.

In making decisions, managers tend to trade off the interests of all three groups rather than simply maximize shareholder value. Of course, when decisions do not affect the well-being of a firm's customers, suppliers, and employees, there is no conflict. In reality, however, this is rarely ever the case.

The tendency of managers to consider the interests of all of the firm's stakeholders is somewhat natural given that executives spend most of their typical day dealing with customers, suppliers, and employees, and building personal relationships with these individuals. They spend much less time interacting with shareholders, although the time spent with institutional shareholders is certainly increasing.

What Factors Influence Managerial Incentives?

A number of factors influence the extent to which managers act in the interests of shareholders. For example, as the length of time a CEO stays on the job increases, the loyalty to the individuals whom he or she must deal with on a day-to-day basis also increases. This makes it more difficult for the executive to make tough decisions that might improve the firm's stock price at the expense of customers and employees.

Imagine, for example, the dilemma faced by an executive who has the opportunity to substantially improve her firm's value by restructuring the firm. Should she act in the interests of the institutional shareholders who bought the stock last month and plan to sell it after the restructuring is completed, or should she act in the interests of the employees with whom she has worked for many years and who may be forced into early retirement if the restructuring is implemented?

---

[2]Later chapters examine how incentive issues affect both merger and acquisition strategies (Chapter 19) and risk management strategies (Chapter 20).

The proportion of the company's stock owned by managers also determines the extent to which management's interests deviate from those of shareholders. Jensen and Meckling (1976) provided an intuitive explanation of why a manager who owns more shares will act more in the interests of shareholders. If the manager owns only 5 percent of the firm's shares, each dollar of perquisites, or unnecessary expenditures that benefit the manager personally, costs him or her only $0.05, with the other $0.95 borne by other shareholders. For example, a $1 million corporate jet will, in essence, have a personal cost to the manager of only $50,000. Because of this, the manager is likely to use corporate resources inefficiently, consuming in ways that would not occur if the cost of the consumed resources were paid from the manager's personal funds.

Result 17.1   Management interests are likely to deviate from shareholder interests in a number of ways. The extent of this deviation is likely to be related to the amount of time the managers have spent on the job and the number of shares they own.

How Management Incentive Problems Hurt Shareholder Value

The Armand Hammer and Occidental Petroleum illustration in the chapter's opening vignette provides a poignant example of how management incentive problems can affect shareholder wealth. Although the Hammer episode is an extreme example of the extent to which shareholder wealth can be destroyed by a self-interested manager, share prices tend to respond favorably when entrenched executives leave their positions unexpectedly. Articles in *Newsweek* and *The Wall Street Journal* provide several examples of firms that experienced much larger price run-ups subsequent to the deaths of their CEOs.[3]

Unexpected retirements also can lead to a positive stock price response. For example, when Fred Hartley announced on June 7, 1988, that he was stepping down as CEO of Unocal, the company's stock price increased 3.8 percent, a one-day gain in shareholder value of about $150 million. In the subsequent year, Unocal's stock price nearly doubled.

One interpretation of the positive stock price reactions to CEO retirements and deaths is that investors believe that a new CEO, with fewer ties to the firm's other managers, may be more willing to make the kind of tough decisions that might be required to improve share values. In 1989, for example, the price of Campbell Soup's stock increased 20 percent upon the death of Campbell Soup's chairman, John Dorrance, Jr. Shortly thereafter, a new and more aggressive management team restructured the firm, and, among other things, closed down Campbell's original soup plant in Camden, New Jersey.

Why Shareholders Cannot Control Managers

Given the large anticipated gains in share prices linked to changing the policies of managers like Armand Hammer and Fred Hartley, it is surprising that stockholders were unable to force them to act in ways that maximized the firm's share prices or to force them to resign earlier. In neither case did the individuals own a large amount of stock. Armand Hammer and Fred Hartley owned less than 0.5 percent of their companies' outstanding shares, which is typical for large U.S. corporations. Jensen and Murphy (1990) reported that in 1986, the median percentage of inside shareholdings for 746 CEOs in the Forbes compensation survey was 0.25 percent, with 80 percent of this sample holding less than 1.4 percent of the shares in their firms.

---

[3]"Deathwatch Investments," *Newsweek,* Apr. 24, 1989; "Death Watches Are Unseemly but Common," *The Wall Street Journal,* Aug. 6, 1996; see also an interesting study by Johnson et al. (1985), documenting positive stock price responses to the unexpected deaths of CEOs.

As a group, outside shareholders generally cannot force managers to maximize share prices because their ownership is too diffuse. This creates the kind of free-rider problem described in Chapter 15. In this case, the free-rider problem arises because it is not in the interest of any individual shareholder to take actions that discipline a non-value-maximizing manager, even though it is in the interests of all shareholders as a group to have this manager removed.

Shareholders who want to challenge the policies of management must stage **proxy fights**, which require organizing shareholders to oust the incumbent board of directors by electing a new board that supports an alternative policy. Proxy fights are very expensive and outsiders who attempt to organize outside shareholders to vote against incumbent management usually don't win them. Carl Icahn, for example, spent over $5 million on his unsuccessful proxy fight to take over Texaco. While the aggregate benefits to all shareholders involved in such a proxy fight may very well exceed their costs, the individual bearing the costs usually receives only a fraction of the benefits. The remainder of the benefiting shareholders are thus free riders. Given that this is true, it isn't surprising that proxy fights rarely occur.

Why Is Ownership So Diffuse if It Leads to Less Efficient Management?   Chapters 4 and 5 noted that investors have an incentive to hold diversified portfolios. Indeed, the Capital Asset Pricing Model suggests that all investors hold the same market portfolio, implying that an investor's shareholdings in any individual firm must be extremely small. However, the preceding discussion suggests the possibility of an inherent conflict between the desire to hold diversified portfolios and the ability of shareholders to control management.

An individual investor who wishes to obtain enough shares to control management would generally have to hold an undiversified portfolio. Although the investor would benefit by getting management to make value-maximizing decisions, he or she would bear significant costs by holding an undiversified portfolio. Hence, investors face a trade-off between diversification and control. The undiversified investor, however, shares the benefits of control (the higher stock price) with other shareholders, but must bear alone the cost of having an undiversified portfolio, as Example 17.1 illustrates.

Example 17.1:   The Trade-Off between Diversification and Improved Monitoring
John believes that he can take control of Axel Corporation and improve its value by $60 million over the next five years. He can do this by investing his entire wealth of $60 million to purchase 20 percent of Axel's outstanding shares. Axel's stock has a standard deviation of about 40 percent per year, which is about twice the standard deviation of the market portfolio. Should John go ahead with this investment?

Answer: Assume that Axel realizes the $60 million increase in value in five years if John gains control. For a $300 million company, this is equivalent to an additional 20 percent return over five years, which is less than 4 percent per year. It's likely that John could realize a much higher expected return with the same level of total risk with a leveraged position in the market portfolio. The gains from increased monitoring that arise from holding a large stake, therefore, are not enough to offset the costs of having an undiversified portfolio.

Result 17.2   Firms with concentrated ownership are likely to be better *monitored* and thus better managed. However, shareholders who take large equity stakes may be inadequately diversified. All shareholders benefit from better management; however, the costs of having a less diversified portfolio are borne only by the large shareholders. As a result, ownership is likely to be less concentrated than it should be, given mean-variance efficiency considerations.

Can Financial Institutions Mitigate the Free-Rider Problem?   The importance of holding a diversified portfolio explains why individual investors rarely choose to take positions that are large enough to allow them to adequately monitor and control management. However, the diversification motive does not explain why institutions do not arise to provide such monitoring services. For example, one can imagine an economy in which investors pool their money and buy into large, relatively diversified mutual funds. Given their large size, these mutual funds could in theory take individual positions that are large enough to influence management, yet still remain reasonably diversified. For example a $50 billion mutual fund, such as the Fidelity Magellan Fund, might put $1 billion into each of 50 different stocks. If a number of different funds formed portfolios in such a way and communicated with one another, as a group they would be able to effectively monitor management.

As noted in Chapter 1, Roe (1994) argued that regulations adopted in the 1930s, such as the Glass-Steagall Act, prevented U.S. financial institutions from playing this role. This is in contrast with the situation in Germany and Japan where banks hold significant amounts of equity and exert control over managers. Although mutual funds and insurance companies in the United States hold significant amounts of stock, regulations keep them from owning more than 5 percent of the stock of any individual firm and exerting any explicit control over corporate decisions.

Pension funds, the other major institutional holders of common stock, have only recently begun to exert much influence on corporate behavior. The reluctance of private pension funds to exert influence on corporate managers is not surprising. For example, the managers of IBM would not like to see the company's pension fund second-guessing the management of another firm. Doing so might set a precedent that would give the pension funds at other corporations the idea that they should meddle in IBM's affairs. However, pension funds for public employees have no similar disincentive keeping them from acting as active monitors of management. Indeed, a number of large pension funds—most notably CALPERS, the large pension fund for California's public employees—have recently taken on a more active role in their relationship with corporate management. As we discuss below, there has recently been much more pressure on U.S. managers to act in the interests of their shareholders, partly because of the growing importance of public pension funds.

Changes in Corporate Governance

A number of changes took place between the mid-1980s and the early 1990s that made managers more responsive to the interests of shareholders. These include a more active takeover market, an increased usage of executive incentive plans (e.g., stock options) that increase the link between management compensation and corporate performance, and more active institutional shareholders (e.g., CALPERS) who have demonstrated a growing tendency to vote against management.[4]

The active role of institutional investors was sparked, in part, by two Security and Exchange Commission rule changes in the early 1990s. The first change, which required fuller disclosure of executive compensation packages, put managers under greater pressure to perform up to their level of compensation. The second change made it easier for shareholders to get information about other shareholders, which substantially reduced the costs of staging a proxy fight.

---

[4]We discuss the use of executive stock options later in this chapter (as well as in Chapter 8) and the takeover market in Chapter 19.

In this changing environment, eight prominent CEOs lost their jobs in 1993, including John Akers of IBM, Kay Whitmore of Eastman Kodak, John Sculley of Apple Computer, Paul Lego of Westinghouse Electric, and James Robinson III of American Express. American Express is a particularly good example of the recent use of clout by institutional investors.

American Express lost about 50 percent of its value between 1989 and the end of 1992. As a result, Harvey Golub, the chairman of American Express, replaced James Robinson, its CEO. However, Robinson stayed on as chairman of the board and chief executive of the Shearson Lehmann Brothers brokerage and investment banking unit of American Express. On January 28, 1993, Golub met with about a dozen of American Express's largest institutional investors who had expressed their displeasure with Robinson's continued role in the company. The next day, Robinson resigned.[5]

17.2 Management Shareholdings and Market Value

Despite the diversification motive suggested by portfolio theory, the ownership of shares in many corporations is actually quite concentrated. Demsetz and Lehn (1985) and Morck, Shleifer, and Vishny (1988) documented that, for many firms, there exists a large individual shareholder or an institution that owns a significant percent of the outstanding shares. Many of the large shareholders were company founders; for example, Henry Singleton, a founder of Teledyne, owns close to 20 percent of that company's stock, and the Nordstrom family owns close to 40 percent of Nordstrom Inc., the department store chain. Other notable examples of company founders maintaining large shareholdings are Bill Gates of Microsoft and the Walton family of Wal-Mart. Outside the United States, large ownership stakes by company founders are more common.

The Effect of Management Shareholdings on Stock Prices

As Chapter 14 discussed, tax reasons might explain why Bill Gates may choose not to sell his Microsoft stock to diversify his portfolio. An entrepreneur like Bill Gates may also be concerned about how the sale of his stock would affect the firm's share price. By selling shares, an entrepreneur may be indirectly communicating unfavorable information to the firm's shareholders. Holding a large number of shares tells investors that the entrepreneur is confident about the firm's prospects and that he or she plans on implementing a strategy that maximizes the value of the company's shares. (See Chapter 18 for more discussion of this issue.)

Demsetz and Lehn suggested that executives in industries with the greatest potential for incentive problems retain the largest share of ownership in their firms. For example, Exhibit 17.1, which appears on page 622, shows that the CEOs of media companies, which are likely to be fraught with incentive problems, typically hold a relatively large fraction of the firms that they manage. In contrast, the top managers of companies that are monitored more easily are likely to own a smaller fraction of the firms they work for.

Example 17.2 illustrates the trade-off between the benefits of retaining shares to improve incentives and the diversification benefits of selling shares.

---

[5]"Good-Bye to Berle & Means," *Forbes*, Jan. 3, 1994.

Example 17.2:   Inside Ownership and Firm Value
Bates Productions is owned exclusively by John Bates who would like to sell a significant fraction of the firm in an IPO. Bates's investment bankers have asserted that the value of Bates Productions is tied very closely to the efforts of John Bates. They believe the firm is worth $100 million based on the way it is currently operating. They also believe that if Bates sells over 50 percent of the shares in the IPO, they will value the company at only $80 million because investors will not be assured that Bates will put in the same effort that he had been expending in the past. However, if Bates retains two-thirds of the shares, the investment bankers believe they can price the firm at about $90 million. What should John Bates do?

Answer: If John Bates sells half of the firm, he will end up with $40 million in cash and shares worth $40 million. However, if he sells one-third of the firm, he will end up with $30 million in cash and shares worth $60 million. The amount that he should sell depends not only on the value of his cash and shares but also on his aversion to effort (we are assuming that he will put in less effort if he owns less stock) and his aversion to risk.

Result 17.3   Entrepreneurs may obtain a better price for their shares if they commit to holding a larger fraction of the firm's outstanding shares. The entrepreneur's incentives to hold shares is higher for those firms with the largest incentives to "consume on the job." The incentive to hold shares is also related to risk aversion.

Empirical studies by Downes and Heinkel (1982) and Ritter (1984) provide evidence that when entrepreneurs retain a higher stake in their firms when they go public, they do indeed get higher prices for the shares they sell. The following subsection reviews a number of empirical studies that examine the relation between management ownership stakes and firm values for larger, more established firms.

Management Shareholdings and Firm Value: The Empirical Evidence

Morck, Shleifer, and Vishny (1988) examined the relation between market values and management shareholdings in a sample of Fortune 500 firms. They found that, for relatively small shareholdings, firms with higher concentrations of management ownership have higher market values relative to their book values. However, as management's holdings rise above 5 percent, the firms become less valuable. This suggests that as the managers' holdings become too large, managers become entrenched, allowing them more freedom to pursue their own agendas instead of value-maximizing policies.[6]

Unfortunately, it is difficult to interpret the evidence on the relation between value creation and ownership concentration because the ratio of a firm's market value to its book value, which is used in these studies as a measure of value creation, measures more than how well the firm is managed. For example, firms with substantial intangible assets, such as patents and brand names, may have high market-to-book ratios even if they are poorly managed. Similarly, well-managed firms may have relatively low market-to-book ratios because they own few intangible assets. Perhaps, management ownership is related to market-to-book ratios because there are more benefits associated with controlling companies with more intangible assets. We would expect, for instance, that it would be a great deal more fun to own a controlling interest in a baseball team or a movie studio, where most assets are intangible, than a copper mine, where most assets are tangible.

---

[6]McConnell and Servaes (1990), Hermalin and Weisbach (1991), and Kole (1995) provide further evidence that share prices increase with the concentration of management holdings, but, beyond a certain point, increased management ownership can depress firm values.

Measuring the value created by managers is much easier in the case of **closed-end mutual funds**, which are publicly traded mutual funds with a fixed number of shares that can be bought and sold on the open market rather than bought and redeemed directly from the fund at their net asset values, as is the case for **open-end mutual funds**. The ratio of the share price of the closed-end mutual fund and the net asset value per share of the portfolio it holds provides an excellent measure of the value created by the fund's managers, since the net asset value of the fund provides a good measure of the market value that could be achieved without the manager (e.g., if the fund were liquidated). If investors believe a fund is badly managed or that it generates excessive expenses, they will not be willing to pay the full net asset value of the shares. Indeed, there have been many cases of closed-end funds selling at more than a 25 percent discount.

Barclay, Holderness, and Pontiff (1993) found that the average discount was 14.2 percent for closed-end funds with a large shareholder but only 4.1 percent for funds without a large shareholder. This evidence indicates that large shareholders tend to depress values, suggesting that the negative affects of management ownership in this case outweighed the positive benefits.[7]

17.3 How Management Control Distorts Investment Decisions

The separation between the ownership and control of corporations has a number of implications about how investment decisions are made. This section examines the investment choices from two perspectives: (1) a self-interested manager who controls most of the firm's investment choice, and (2) a large outside shareholder who has influence over the firm's strategy for investing, but only indirect control over specific investment choices.

The Investment Choices Managers Prefer

An important premise of this chapter is that there are significant benefits associated with controlling a large corporation, and that top executives prefer investment choices that enhance and preserve those benefits. As discussed below, a firm's investment choice can affect control benefits in a number of ways.

Making Investments that Fit the Manager's Expertise.   If benefits from controlling a corporation are sufficiently large, a CEO's desire to remain on the job will also be very large, providing the CEO with an incentive to bias financing and investment decisions in a manner that makes it more difficult to replace him in the future [see Shleifer and Vishny (1989)]. To become entrenched, managers may choose to make irreversible investments in businesses for which they have a particular expertise, so that they will not become expendable in the future. For this reason, oil firms may have continued to invest in oil exploration in the early 1980s despite falling oil prices.

Managers also may wish to rely on implicit contracts and personal relationships in their business dealings to make it more difficult for potential replacements to complete

---

[7]The authors of this study noted that, in many cases, individuals purchase large blocks of shares in closed-end funds and improve the fund's value either by forcing managers to liquidate the funds or, alternatively, by turning the fund into an open-end fund. Since those cases where large shareholders improve value will not exist in a sample of existing closed-end funds, one should not conclude from the evidence in this study that large shareholders always diminish the value of closed-end funds.

the deals that they initiated. Consider, for example, the threat by Steven Spielberg in the late 1980s to stop making movies with Warner Brothers if its CEO back then, Stephen Ross, left the company. This of course made Ross's job much more secure and probably allowed him to extract greater perquisites than he might otherwise have obtained.

Making Investments that Pay Off Early.   An additional consideration is that managers may want to make investments that help the current stock price of the firm even when they hurt it in long run. Having favorable financial results in the short run may allow a manager to raise capital at more favorable rates and, perhaps, to both increase his compensation and reduce the chance that he will lose his job. Chapter 18 describes how these advantages can create a tendency for managers to select projects with a short payback period over higher *NPV* investments that require a longer payback period.

Making Investments that Minimize the Manager's Risk.   The high personal cost of a firm's bankruptcy provides an additional bias to the investment and financing choices of managers. Gilson (1990) reported that only 43 percent of the chief executive officers and 46 percent of the directors keep their jobs subsequent to the bankruptcy of their firms.

The fear of bankruptcy may be one reason why managers often prefer large empires to small empires and, hence, often choose to expand their companies faster than they should, investing more of the company's earnings and distributing less in dividends than is optimal for value maximization. The tendency of managers to overinvest the firm's internally generated cash can be illustrated by the situation at RJR Nabisco prior to its leveraged buyout (LBO) in 1988. About one and one-half years prior to its LBO, RJR Nabisco's baking unit devised a plan to completely revamp and modernize its baking facilities at a cost of $2.8 billion. The annual savings from this modernization would have been only $148 million, providing a pretax return of only about 5 percent.[8] After the LBO, which substantially cut the resources available for investment, the modernization plan was scaled back considerably.

Managers also may have a tendency to be more risk averse in their choice of investments than they should be, especially in terms of their treatment of those risks that shareholders can avoid through diversification. Only systematic risk matters to shareholders. From the manager's perspective, however, unsystematic risk as well as systematic risk may be of importance because both affect the probability of the firm getting into financial trouble and ultimately the probability of the manager retaining his or her job. This same logic suggests that managers also may prefer less than the value-maximizing level of debt in their capital structures.

Summarizing Management Investment Distortions.   Result 17.4 summarizes the preceding discussion about the ways in which investments chosen by managers may differ from investments selected purely on the basis of value maximization.

Result 17.4   Managers may prefer investments that enhance their own human capital and minimize risk. This implies that:

- Managers may prefer larger, more diversified firms.
- Managers may prefer investments that pay off more quickly than those that would maximize the value of their shares.

---

[8]*The Wall Street Journal,* Mar. 14, 1989.

Outside Shareholders and Managerial Discretion

Up to this point, we have assumed that managers control the investment choice. However, large *outside* shareholders, knowing that managers have a tendency to skew decisions in directions that benefit them personally, have an incentive to reduce management's discretion. These outside shareholders may favor investments in fixed assets and other technologies that limit the manager's future discretion.

Allied Industries

Consider the hypothetical example of Allied Industries, a conglomerate with business units in a number of industries. Its CEO and major shareholder, John Osborne, has appointed James Brandon to run its farm machinery division. Brandon is a good choice for this position because he understands farm machinery better than anyone in the world. As a champion of quality, he represents a commitment to customers that Allied's farm machinery will be the best on the market.

Unfortunately, Brandon's commitment to quality is also his biggest weakness. Osborne is worried that Brandon will spend too much money to produce the "perfect" tractor when an "almost perfect" tractor would still be the best on the market.

Before completely turning over the division to Brandon, Osborne must decide between two production processes: a labor-intensive process and a capital-intensive process. The labor-intensive process requires more upfront training costs, but the yearly cost of the capital-intensive process is actually the higher of the two processes given the high maintenance costs of the machinery. Osborne would certainly prefer the labor-intensive process if he were running the farm equipment division himself. In addition to its lower costs, the labor-intensive process provides the flexibility to improve the quality of the product by increasing costs. However, since he wishes to delegate all future decisions to Brandon, he believes that the capital-intensive technology will be the better alternative because he does not wish to give Brandon too much discretion in choosing the quality of the product.

Trading Off the Benefits and Costs of Discretion.   The Allied Industries example illustrated a negative aspect of flexibility. However, as Chapter 11 noted, under uncertainty, flexible investment designs can add value to a firm since flexibility increases a firm's operating options. The value of that flexibility is greater, the greater is the uncertainty. Hence, the costs associated with having to limit flexibility because of incentive problems is greater, the greater the level of uncertainty. With sufficient uncertainty, it is better for the outside shareholders to expend more effort monitoring management but also to allow managers greater flexibility and discretion. However, when there is very little uncertainty, the outside shareholders may want to limit the manager's flexibility. In sum, we have the following result:

Result 17.5   Allowing management discretion has benefits as well as costs.

- The benefits of discretion are greater in more uncertain environments.
- The costs of discretion are greater when the interests of managers and shareholders do not coincide.

Therefore, we might expect to find more concentrated ownership and more managerial discretion in firms facing more uncertain environments.

17.4 Capital Structure and Managerial Control

As noted earlier, a manager may prefer less than the optimal level of debt because additional debt increases the risk of bankruptcy and limits a manager's discretion. In some circumstances, however, outside shareholders might view these factors as advantages. The added debt may prevent a manager from expanding the firm more rapidly than would be optimal. Moreover, since higher debt ratios increase the threat of bankruptcy, which managers are anxious to avoid, increased debt can induce management to avoid policies they might personally prefer but which reduce firm value.[9] The basic idea is that the fear of losing one's job is a good motivator. In an article in *Business Week*, Holiday Corporation Chairman Michael D. Rose expressed the advantage of debt financing clearly:

> When you get higher levels of debt it really sharpens your focus . . . It makes for better managers since there is less margin for error.[10]

Therefore, the shareholders of a firm that is run by "self-interested" management may prefer a higher leverage ratio than one would find in firms that are managed in the shareholders' interest.

The Relation between Shareholder Control and Leverage

Mehran (1992) provided evidence supporting the idea that control by outside shareholders affects how firms are financed. In his sample of 124 manufacturing firms, Mehran found a positive relation between a firm's leverage ratio and:

- The percentage of total executive compensation tied to performance.
- The percentage of equity owned by managers.
- The percentage of investment bankers on the board of directors.
- The percentage of equity owned by large individual investors.

In other words, firms tend to be more highly levered if they are managed by individuals with a strong interest in improving current stock prices or if they are monitored by board members or large shareholders who have those interests.

Result 17.6   Shareholders prefer a higher leverage ratio than that preferred by management. As a result, firms that are more strongly influenced by shareholders have higher leverage ratios.

How Leverage Affects the Level of Investment

Chapter 15 discussed how debt financing could limit the amount that a firm invests. However, if management has a tendency to overinvest, then limiting management's ability to invest may enhance firm value.[11]

Tom and Charley's Victorian Rehab: Using Debt to Limit Future Investments
To understand why an investor might want to use debt to limit a firm's investment opportunities, consider the case of Tom and Charley, former college roommates. One afternoon Tom, who had become an architect, called Charley, an investment banker, with a proposal to buy an old Victorian house to convert into apartment units. Tom estimated that the total cost of the house and the rehabilitation would be about $200,000. As the project's architect, Tom would receive a small fee from the profits, and he would have complete control over the project once it was financed. Charley was asked to come up with the best financing alternatives.

Charley carefully calculated the project's net present value. After considering several possible scenarios, he concluded that Tom's assessment of the project's potential was reasonably accurate. Charley then considered financing alternatives and settled on a fixed-rate

---

[9]This argument was made by Grossman and Hart (1982).
[10]"Learning to Live with Leverage," *Business Week*, Nov. 7, 1988.
[11]See Jensen (1986) and Stulz (1990).

mortgage as the best alternative. The next question was to determine how much to borrow and how much of their own money to invest in the project.

Both Tom and Charley have $25,000 to invest in the project. Tom would prefer to invest his entire $25,000 since his alternative is to put the money in a bank CD paying 7.5 percent interest and the mortgage rate would be 9 percent. Charley has no good alternatives for his $25,000, but he has one reservation about putting up such a large down payment on the house. With a large down payment, the monthly payments would be much lower, so Tom would face much less pressure to cut costs and increase cash flows. With a large equity investment, Charley also could easily secure an additional loan to make further renovations. Although Charley trusts Tom completely, he realizes that Tom has the tendency to make his projects perfect, regardless of costs. For this reason, Charley believes that the project should have a smaller down payment and a larger loan.

This example illustrates one very important point:

Result 17.7   A large debt obligation limits management's ability to use corporate resources in ways that do not benefit investors.

Selecting the Debt Ratio that Allows a Firm to Invest Optimally.

Chapter 15 discussed how too much debt may force a firm to pass up some positive net present value projects. The *debt overhang problem* indicates that a firm that chooses a high debt ratio will find the costs of obtaining additional funds high, reducing the amount that equity holders will want the firm to invest. The analysis in this section suggests that outside shareholders may be able to use this debt overhang problem to their advantage. When managers have a tendency to overinvest, debt financing can be used to mitigate that tendency.[12] Example 17.3 illustrates how this can be done.

Example 17.3:   Selecting the Debt Ratio that Leads to the Optimal Investment Strategy

Consider a firm that is financed with an initial investment of $100 million. In exactly one year, it must decide whether to go ahead with a project that requires an additional $100 million investment. The present values (at year 1) of the payoffs from taking or not taking the additional investment in three future states of the economy are given in the following table:

	Value (in $ millions) When State of the Economy Is		
	Good	*Medium*	*Bad*
Value with investment	$250	$175	$125
Value without investment	50	50	50

One year from now, if in either the good or medium states, the additional investment has a positive *NPV;* that is, it creates more than $100 million in value in the good and medium states. In the bad state, however, where only $75 million ($125 million − $50 million) is created by taking the investment, the additional investment has a negative *NPV.*

Assume that when financing the investment at date 0, the original entrepreneurs understand that the manager they hire will want to fund the new investment at year 1, even if it has a negative *NPV.* How should they finance the original investment to ensure that the firm can raise sufficient funds only when the additional investment has a positive *NPV* at year 1?

Answer: If the original $100 million investment is financed completely with equity, the additional investment can be funded by issuing debt even in the bad state of the economy. To

---

[12]These ideas were developed in Jensen (1986), Stulz (1990), and Hart and Moore (1995).

keep the managers from funding the additional investment in the bad state of the economy, the firm can finance *part* of the original investment with senior debt, which requires that additional debt be of lower priority. Note that if the original investment at date 0 is financed *completely* with senior debt, the firm will be unable to finance the additional $100 million dollar investment in the medium state of the economy. (Since the original $100 million dollar investment must be paid first in the medium state of the economy, only $75 million is left to pay the new investors.) In this case, a positive *NPV* project is passed up. On the other hand, if the firm issues more than $25 million in senior debt but less than $75 million, it will be able to finance the project in the good and medium states of the economy, but not in the bad state of the economy.

The outside shareholders in Example 17.3 were able to induce the firm's managers to invest exactly the right amount by selecting the appropriate debt ratio. In reality, however, things may not work out as nicely. For one thing, Example 17.3 ignores the possibility that the firm also has internally generated funds to invest in the project. This does not necessarily cause a problem if the firm generates cash in those states of the economy in which it has positive *NPV* investments. However, as Example 17.4 illustrates, if the firm generates a substantial amount of cash when its investments have negative *NPV*s, it may not be possible to induce managers to invest the optimal amount in every state of the economy by simply selecting the appropriate capital structure.

Example 17.4:   Can Financing Choices Always Be Used to Achieve the Optimal Investment Strategy?

Consider, again, Example 17.3 with the added assumption that the firm also generates funds internally. The cash flows and payoffs in the different states of the economy are described below.

	Value (in $ millions) When State of the Economy Is		
	Good	*Medium*	*Bad*
Value with investment	$250	$175	$125
Value without investment	50	50	50
Internal cash flow	100	25	100

Is it possible for the firm to select a debt ratio that allows the firm to fund the investment in the medium and good state of the economy but not in the bad state of the economy?

Answer: It is not possible. The firm can be kept from financing what would be a negative *NPV* project in the bad state of the economy by taking on a $100 million short-term debt obligation due when the initial cash flows are realized and an additional $26 million in senior debt (or any amount above $25 million) due in the following year, which prevents the firm from borrowing additional amounts. However, with these debt obligations, the firm also will be unable to finance the firm's expansion in the medium state of the economy even though doing so is a positive *NPV* investment. If the debt obligations are lowered to allow the firm to finance its investments in the medium state of the economy, then the firm also will be able to finance its operations in the bad state of the economy.

Result 17.8   A firm's debt level is a determinant of how much the firm will invest in the future and it can be used to move the firm toward investing the appropriate amount. In general, however, capital structure cannot by itself induce managers to invest optimally.

A Monitoring Role for Banks

Examples 17.3 and 17.4 assumed that the firm's debt could not be renegotiated, which is a reasonable assumption if the firm's debt is held by diffuse debt holders. In this regard, bank debt may have an advantage over public bonds since it is possible for the firm to reduce free-rider and information problems if it is dealing with one banker instead of a large number of bondholders. Therefore, a banker may be able to mitigate the over-investment-underinvestment problems described in the examples above by evaluating the firm's projects and deciding selectively whether to offer additional credit.

In Example 17.4, an underinvestment problem in the medium state of the economy will arise if the firm issues $100 million in short-term debt as well as $26 million in senior debt. The assumption made in this example was that the debt could not be renegotiated even though debt holders would be better off in the medium state of the economy if they forgave a portion of the firm's debt obligation. However, if a bank owns the debt, it will have an incentive to renegotiate the loan in the medium state of the economy: Otherwise, the firm will go bankrupt and lose a positive *NPV* project, which would increase the value of the bank's claim. The problem considered in Example 17.4 can thus be solved by having the firm take on enough bank debt to prevent it from taking on the negative *NPV* project in the bad state of the economy and by allowing the firm to renegotiate the debt obligation in the medium state of the economy.

Bank financing also may be beneficial when it is necessary to monitor management. The free-rider problem which keeps individual shareholders from monitoring the firm also probably keeps individual debt holders from doing much monitoring. This is especially true for firms with low leverage ratios since, in this case, the debt holders are likely to be paid in full even if management does poorly. However, if a firm is highly leveraged and bankruptcy appears likely, the debt holders will have an incentive to monitor management, especially if they have concentrated holdings.

Bank lending is particularly suited to serve this function since financial institutions have the resources to hold a large fraction of a firm's debt and are capable of monitoring management. Delegating the monitoring of management to their *fixed* claimants (debt holders) rather than their residual claimants (equity holders) also reduces the asset substitution problem discussed in Chapter 15 (i.e., the incentive of a firm's management to choose risky projects that transfer wealth from debt holders to equity holders). However, if debt holders have more influence over management than equity holders, then managers, acting in the interests of their debt holders, may be too conservative in their investment choices.

Another advantage of borrowing through a commercial bank arises for firms with proprietary information. For example, a firm may be able to exploit favorable market conditions only if competitors remain unaware of the situation. Hence, a public debt offering, which reveals this information, places a firm at a competitive disadvantage. However, if this information can be revealed confidentially to the lender, a firm can obtain funds at attractive terms without revealing its information to competitors.

17.5 Executive Compensation

In the economics research literature, the relationship between owners and management is classified as a **principal-agent relationship**, with stockholders considered the **principals** and management as the **agents** hired by the principals to take actions on their behalf. The main focus of this literature is on ways to compensate agents in order to motivate them to work for the benefit of the principals.

The Agency Problem

Perhaps the earliest discussions of agency problems involved the relationship between a tenant farmer (the agent), whose effort cannot be directly observed, and the owner of the farm (the principal). To motivate the tenant farmer to work hard, the amount of compensation must be tied to the farm's output. However, because the crop yield is determined by unobservable soil conditions and unexpected weather, as well as by the farmer's effort, tying the farmer's compensation too strongly to the farm's output may not be optimal. Doing so would expose the farmer to uncontrollable risks which can be borne more efficiently by the owner of the farm because he may be able to diversify away much of this risk. As a result, there is a trade-off between the incentive benefits of tying compensation to output and the disadvantages of subjecting the tenant farmer to excessive risk over which the tenant has no control.

Two Components of an Agency Problem.   The tenant farmer discussion above illustrates the two essential features of an agency problem: uncertainty that the agent cannot control and a lack of information on the part of the principal. If the principal were able to observe the actions of the agent and if there were no free-rider problem, there would be no incentive problems. The principal could simply force the agent to work in his or her interests. The agent who refused could be fired. In addition, if the agent were not averse to bearing the risk of a particular project or, alternatively, if there were no risk that the agent could not control, the principal could motivate the agent to make value-maximizing choices by having the agent bear all of the risks associated with his or her actions. In short, if a manger were not averse to risk and had the capital, the best situation would be one in which the manager owned all of the firm's stock.

Measuring Inputs versus Measuring Outputs.   The agency problem can be substantially alleviated if the principal can accurately observe the agent's actions. The principal can do this in one of two ways: (1) closely monitor the agent to ensure that he or she works the specified number of hours at the required level of intensity; that is, to measure the agent's labor *input;* or (2) indirectly measure the agent's actions by observing the agent's *output*.

Prior to the mid-1970s, most large U.S. corporations tried to solve the agency problem by measuring inputs. Systems were put in place to monitor managers to make sure that they were doing their jobs appropriately. Since the mid-1970s, there has been a trend towards evaluating and compensating managers based on outputs.

Designing Optimal Incentive Contracts.   A firm's profits are determined by a number of factors. Some of these factors are under the manager's control, but others are not. In general, well-designed compensation contracts minimize the extent to which managers can be penalized by factors outside of their control. For example, the tenant farmer should be penalized less for exhibiting low output in years of little rainfall than for poor performance in years of abundant rainfall. Hence, information about rainfall can be used to reduce the agent's risk and improve the relationship between the tenant farmer and the landowner.

In applying this logic to management compensation contracts, one would conclude that a manager's compensation should not be tied simply to the firm's stock price or earnings performance but to the amount that the firm's stock return or earnings exceed the return on the market in general or to the performance of other firms in the industry.[13]

Minimizing Agency Costs.   **Agency costs** represent the difference between the value of an actual firm and the value of a hypothetical firm which would exist in a more perfect world where management and shareholder incentives are perfectly aligned. The discussion in this subsection provides ways that firms can minimize agency costs. These are summarized in Result 17.9:

Result 17.9   Agency problems arise because of imperfect information and risk aversion. Agency costs thus can be reduced by improving information flows and by reducing risk. To minimize the risk borne by managers, optimal compensation contracts should eliminate as much extraneous risk (or risk unrelated to the manager's efforts) as possible.

Is Executive Pay Closely Tied to Performance?

Executives receive compensation from a number of sources. Part of their pay is fixed, part is contingent on corporate profits, and part is contingent on improvements in the stock price of their companies. Anecdotal evidence suggests that executive pay became much more tied to firm performance during the 1980s and 1990s. However, there is some disagreement about how sensitive CEO compensation is to performance.

The Jensen and Murphy Evidence.   In their *Harvard Business Review* article, Michael Jensen and Kevin Murphy (1990) argued that executive compensation is not nearly as performance sensitive as it should be. They examined the compensation and share ownership of 2,505 CEOs from 1974 to 1988 and calculated how much the compensation of the CEOs increased with each $1,000 increase in the value of their companies. Exhibit 17.1 on page 622 presents some of the CEOs from the Jensen and Murphy study with the best and the worst incentive pay.

In companies like Times Mirror, Digital Equipment, and Walt Disney, the CEO's wealth is highly linked to their companies' performance.[14] Michael Eisner at Disney made well over $100 million while turning Disney's fortunes around. On the other hand, Kenneth Olsen probably lost that much money as Digital Equipment's prospects diminished. However, these companies are exceptions. In most companies, the CEO shares a small percentage of the gains and losses of a company, although the dollar amount may still be fairly large. As Exhibit 17.1 demonstrates, the compensation of CEOs of companies like Exxon, AT&T, and IBM are largely insensitive to changes in the values of these firms. For example, if an executive at one of these companies purchased an extra $10 million corporate jet, he or she would be penalized only about $2,500 in lost compensation.

The Boschen and Smith Evidence.   Boschen and Smith (1995) examined how the stock returns of a company affect the future as well as the current compensation of its

---

[13]This point was made in Diamond and Verrecchia (1982).

[14]It is interesting that the CEOs of media companies have compensation contracts that are tied more closely to performance than most other CEOs. Perhaps, CEOs in media companies have more opportunities to "consume on the job" and are more difficult to monitor.

EXHIBIT 17.1   CEOs with the Best and Worst Incentives

CEOs of Large Companies with the Best Incentive Pay

| Company | CEO | Total Effects on CEO Wealth (Over Two Years) Corresponding to Each $1,000 Change in Shareholder Wealth | | |
		Change in All Pay-Related Wealth	Change in the Value of Stock Owned	Change in Total CEO Wealth
MCA	Lew R. Wasserman	$ 0.05	$70.10	$70.15
Times Mirror	Robert F. Erburu	3.29	45.39	48.67
CBS	Laurence A. Tisch	1.79	31.58	33.37
Digital Equipment	Kenneth H. Olsen	1.00	19.06	20.07
Walt Disney	Michael D. Eisner	15.62	2.88	18.50

CEOs of Large Companies with the Worst Incentive Pay

| Company | CEO | Total Effects on CEO Wealth (Over Two Years) Corresponding to Each $1,000 Change in Shareholder Wealth | | |
		Change in All Pay-Related Wealth	Change in the Value of Stock Owned	Change in Total CEO Wealth
Sears Roebuck	Edward A. Brennan	$0.17	$0.20	$0.37
Exxon	Lawrence G. Rawl	0.14	0.11	0.25
AT&T	Robert A. Allen	0.19	0.04	0.24
IBM	John F. Akers	0.13	0.06	0.19
Eastman Kodak	Colby H. Chandler	0.09	0.08	0.17

Note: These observations come from a sample of CEOs in the 250 largest companies, ranked by 1988 sales.
Source: Jensen and Murphy (1990).

CEO. This study concluded that the Jensen and Murphy evidence substantially underestimates the sensitivity of CEO pay to performance.

To understand why it is important to consider the CEO's future compensation, consider a CEO who was promised a bonus in each of the next five years equal to 30 percent of the amount by which the company's earnings exceeded a certain level. If the CEO took actions that doubled earnings in his or her first year, the stock price would probably increase substantially upon the announcement of the higher earnings, reflecting not only this year's earnings but also the higher earnings predicted in the future. In this case, one would observe only a weak relation between the CEO's compensation in a given year and the firm's stock return in that year. In the first year of the contract, the firm's stock price would increase substantially and the CEO would receive a bonus reflecting the higher earnings in that year. In subsequent years, however, one would not expect the firm's stock price to respond to favorable earnings since the expectation of good earnings was already reflected in the stock price at the end of the first year. However, the CEO would continue to receive the same bonus he or she received in the first year. Hence, the correlation between the firm's stock returns in a given year and the CEO's compensation in that year would not be particularly strong. However, if one looked across firms, one might find a relation between stock returns and compensation levels cumulated over many years. Boschen and Smith found that the cumulative response of pay to performance is about 10 times as large as the pay-to-performance sensitivity found by comparing stock returns and compensation levels in individual years.

Cross-Sectional Differences in Pay-for-Performance Sensitivity.   One would expect that the pay-for-performance sensitivity is greatest for firms whose incentive problems are expected to be the greatest. As we have seen, the CEOs of the media companies have compensation contracts that arc tied more closely to performance than those of CEOs of most other companies. In addition, because the CEOs of growth companies generally have more discretion than the CEOs of more mature companies, a number of authors have argued that the compensation of growth company CEOs should be more closely tied to their companies' performance. However, the empirical evidence on this is somewhat mixed.[15]

How Does Firm Value Relate to the Use of Performance-Based Pay?

If performance-based compensation improves incentives, then firms that implement incentive-compensation programs should realize higher values. Empirical studies, which have documented the positive reaction of stock prices to the adoption of performance-based executive compensation plans, tend to support this hypothesis. For example, Tehranian and Waegelein (1985) examined stock returns at the time of the adoption of 42 performance-based compensation plans during the 1970s. They found that stock prices increased about 20 percent, on average, from seven months before the announcement of the adoption of the plans until the adoption date. A more recent study by Mehran (1995) looked cross-sectionally at the relationship between the ratio of the market-to-book value of a firm's shares and the extent of performance-based compensation for top management. He found that these two variables are positively correlated, indicating that, on average, firms using more performance-based compensation have higher stock prices.

Unfortunately, it is difficult to infer causality from these studies. Performance-based compensation is associated with higher stock prices; however, it is difficult to tell whether this compensation causes stock prices to be higher or, alternatively, whether managers are more willing to adopt performance contracts after observing increases in their stock prices. Perhaps it would be easier to sell managers on the idea of adopting performance-based compensation if the managers would have made more money in the recent past had the plan been adopted earlier. In addition, managers are more willing to adopt performance-based compensation plans when they have special information suggesting that the firm may be undervalued.

---

[15]Clinch (1991), Smith and Watts (1992), and Gaver and Gaver (1993) found that equity and options are used more extensively in the compensation of executives in growth firms. However, Bizjak, Brickley, and Coles (1993) and Gaver and Gaver (1995) found no significant relation between growth opportunities and compensation in their samples.

Example 17.5 illustrates why the adoption of a performance-based compensation plan conveys information to investors.

Example 17.5:   The Information Conveyed from Adopting a Performance-Based Compensation Plan

Consider the CEOs of two firms, Jack and Peggy, each with stocks priced at $20 per share. Jack has favorable proprietary information that leads him to believe that his stock is really worth $30 per share. Peggy has unfavorable proprietary information that leads her to believe that her stock is worth only $15 per share. Both CEOs are considering proposals that would lower their fixed salary in exchange for stock options exercisable in one year at $20 per share. Which manager would be more inclined to accept such an offer? How would agreeing to a performance-based incentive plan affect the company's stock price?

Answer: Jack is more willing than Peggy to adopt the performance plan because his proprietary information implies that the expected value of the options on his firm is higher. If investors understand these incentives, they will view Jack's acceptance of the performance plan as good news and bid up the price of his firm's stock.

As Example 17.5 illustrates, stock prices may react positively to the adoption of a performance-based compensation plan even if the plan has no effect on the managers' productivity.

Is Executive Compensation Tied to Relative Performance?

Recall from Result 17.9 that compensation contracts should be designed to eliminate as much extraneous risk as possible. One way to eliminate extraneous risk is with a **relative performance contract**, which determines executive compensation according to how well the executive's firm performs relative to some benchmark such as the performance of the firm's competitors. The relative performance contract would thus eliminate the risks that affect all of a firm's competitors equally.

Although relative performance contracts are still rare, they have been used at some innovative firms. Lambert and Larker (1986) discussed Johnson Controls, which in 1983 implemented an incentive plan that paid its two most senior executives a yearly bonus computed by multiplying a base amount ($100,000 and $300,000) times a percentage between 0 and 150. The determination of this percentage was based each year on the ratio of the average annual shareholder return for Johnson Controls for the previous 10 years to the average return over the same time period for a peer group of Fortune 500 firms. Each of these yearly bonuses was then invested in a hypothetical portfolio of Johnson Controls stock. The value of this portfolio was then paid out at the end of seven years.

To the best of our knowledge, an extreme form of the relative performance contract—where the CEO's compensation is based on the firm's performance relative to that of its direct competitors—has not been implemented at any major corporation. Such a contract has the desired feature of reducing the effect of risk elements that affect all industry participants, which probably are not within the CEO's control, while rewarding the executive only when he or she beats the relevant competition. The disadvantage of this type of contract is its undesirable side effect of providing the CEO with an incentive to take actions that reduce its competitor's profits, even if doing so doesn't help his or her own firm. For example, a firm that utilizes this type of relative performance contract may compete more aggressively for market share since the costs imposed on competitors from being aggressive improves the CEO's compensation, even if the gain in market share does not improve profits. The consequences are that if all industry participants instituted relative performance contracts of this type, industry competition would be more aggressive and profits would likely be lower for all firms in the industry. Perhaps this is one reason we do not observe explicit relative performance compensation contracts.

Result 17.10   Relative performance contracts, which reward managers for performing better than either the entire market or, alternatively, the firms in their industry, have an advantage and a disadvantage.

   • The advantage is that the contracts eliminate the effect of some of the risks that are beyond the manager's control.

   • The disadvantage is that the contracts may cause firms to compete too aggressively, which would reduce industry profits.

Stock-Based versus Earnings-Based Performance Pay

Performance-based compensation contracts come in two distinct forms: *stock-based compensation contracts,* which include executive stock options (see Chapter 8) and other contracts that provide an executive with a payoff tied directly to the firm's share price, and earnings or cash flow-based compensation contracts, based on nonmarket variables like earnings, cash flow, and adjusted cash flow numbers like Stern Stewart's Economic Value Added (EVA™), discussed in Chapter 9.

Stock-Based Compensation.   The advantage of stock-based compensation is that it motivates the manager to improve stock prices, which is exactly what shareholders would like the manager to do. However, there also are disadvantages associated with stock-based compensation which lead us to believe that earnings or cash flow-based compensation might be preferred in many cases.

The first disadvantage of stock-based compensation is that stock prices change from day to day for reasons outside the control of top managers (e.g., changes in interest rates). The second disadvantage is that stock prices move because of changes in expectations as well as realizations. This second disadvantage is illustrated in Example 17.6.

Example 17.6:   Using Stock Returns to Evaluate Management Quality
Consider two CEOs, Ben and Alex, who are hired at the same time to manage competing toy companies. Investors initially have an extremely favorable opinion of Ben and expect his company, the Coy Toy Company, to do well. However, investors initially are extremely skeptical about Alex's qualifications and the prospects of his company, Toyco. How will the stock market react over the next few years if the two toy companies do equally well?
   Answer: If both companies do equally well, Coy Toy will have performed worse than expected and Toyco will have performed better than expected. Hence, Toyco's stock price will perform much better, merely due to the improved opinion of Toyco's future.

In general, companies would like to compensate managers based on how much they contribute to shareholder value. As Example 17.6 illustrates, however, stock prices reflect how well the managers did relative to expectations. Hence, with stock-based compensation plans, managers are penalized when investors have favorable expectations and are helped when investors have unfavorable expectations.

Earnings-Based Compensation.   The principal advantage of compensating managers on the basis of earnings and cash flows is that the numbers are generally available for the individual business units of a firm as well as for nontraded companies that cannot easily base compensation on an observable stock price. However, compensating managers based on earnings and cash flows also has its drawbacks. First, it is difficult to calculate the cash flow number that would be appropriate to use for evaluating performance. For example, one cannot simply base the executive's compensation on total earnings or cash flows because this will provide an incentive to increase the *scale* of the corporation's operations, even if doing so requires the firm to take on negative net present value projects. Hence, there is a need to adjust the cash flows for the amount of capital employed, which is likely to change from period to period. In addition, both cash flow and earnings numbers that can be pulled easily from a firm's income statements are accounting numbers which include various adjustments for inventory valuation methods, pension fund liabilities, and so forth, and might not provide a true measure of the economic cash flows that a firm ideally would use to determine a manager's compensation.

Value-Based Management.   The idea that managers in individual business units should be compensated according to the contribution of their units to overall firm value attracted substantial attention in the 1990s and has generated large revenues for consultants. Consultants like Marakon Associates, Stern Stewart, McKinsey, and Boston Consulting Group/Holt have developed what they call **value-based management** methods to adjust accounting cash flows so that they more accurately measure the economic cash flows that are most useful in compensating managers.[16] Each of the above methods share the insight that managers create value by making positive net present value choices and reward managers for making such choices. As discussed in Chapter 9, these methods calculate the value created by a particular business unit by subtracting a charge for the amount of capital employed from the cash flows of each unit. The methods can differ in the way that cash flows and the cost of capital are calculated.

The advantage of a value-based management compensation method over stock-based compensation methods is summarized below:

Result 17.11   Stock-based compensation has the advantage that it motivates managers to improve share prices. However, stock prices change for reasons outside of a manager's control and only partially reflect the efforts of a manager who heads an individual business unit in a diversified corporation. A cash flow-based compensation plan that appropriately adjusts for capital costs may provide the best method for motivating managers in these cases.

Compensation Issues, Mergers, and Spin-Offs

The discussion in the last subsection suggests that although stock-based compensation contracts might prove useful for motivating top management, they are less useful as a device for motivating the head of a business unit that has little influence on the firm's overall profitability. For example, the efforts of Compaq's CEO are better reflected in the price of the company's stock than the efforts of his counterpart in the personal computer division of a multidivisional firm such as IBM. This puts IBM at a comparative disadvantage to Compaq in motivating the managers in its PC group because their compensation cannot be structured as easily to reflect the results of their efforts. This is especially true when the economic cash flows of the individual business units are hard to measure.

Spin-offs and Divestitures.   Schipper and Smith (1986) and Aron (1991), among others, have argued that these motivational issues are one reason firms sometimes choose

---

[16]Chapter 9 discusses the products offered by various consultants.

to **spin off** a division—transforming the division into a new company by distributing shares of the new company to the firm's existing shareholders—or **divest**—that is, sell individual divisions, making them independent operating firms. Announcements of spin-offs and divestitures usually lead to a favorable reaction in stock prices. In a sample of 93 spin-off announcements between 1963 and 1981, Schipper and Smith found that stock prices increased 2.84 percent, on average, when the spin-offs were announced.

Cusatis, Miles, and Woolridge (1994) described the case of Quaker Oats spinning off Fisher Price, its toy subsidiary in 1991. Fisher Price reported losses of $37.3 million and $33.6 million in the two years prior to the spin-off, but in its first two years as a public company, Fisher Price showed profits of $17.3 million and $41.3 million, respectively. The authors attributed at least part of the strong operating performance of the new company to the financial incentives of the officers and directors, 14 of whom held 6.2 percent of the outstanding shares as of March 23, 1993. While these individuals might have held stock in Quaker Oats prior to the spin-off, the connection between their efforts and the resulting payoff would have been much less direct, so the incentive effects would have been substantially reduced.

Result 17.12   Improved management incentives provide one motivation for corporate spin-offs and divestitures. Similarly, conglomerate mergers may weaken the incentives of executives at the various divisions.

Mergers.   Chapter 19 describes various operating synergies that offset the incentive problems that arise from combining firms in a merger. In cases where both the synergies and the incentive problems are large, a partial takeover may be warranted. In a partial takeover, the acquiring firm buys a controlling interest in the target, possibly to take advantage of synergies, but it leaves a number of shares outstanding on the market. These remaining shares make it possible to compensate the partially owned subsidiary's management more efficiently. Partial takeovers of this kind are common in many countries outside the United States but are less common within the United States.

17.6 Summary and Conclusions

This chapter examined why the financial decisions of managers often deviate from those predicted by the theories presented in Parts III and IV. We first described the type of conflicts that are likely to arise between the interests of shareholders and managers. Some of these conflicts arise because managers simply prefer more pleasant to less pleasant tasks. Other conflicts arise because managers have an incentive to steer their firms in directions that enhance their own career opportunities and limit their risks. Finally, top executives are likely to develop more of a loyalty to their employees, suppliers, and customers, whom they interact with on a day-to-day basis, than to their investors, with whom they are in much less frequent contact.

Since the 1980s, a number of changes have reduced these incentive problems, thus improving the profitability of major corporations. One innovation was the greater use of executive stock options and other contracts contingent on stock price, which link the pay of top executives directly to the performance of their companies' stock. Another change was the increased use of debt financing, which creates pressure on managers to improve productivity while reducing their ability to initiate wasteful investments. A third change was the greater participation of institutional investors. A final change was a more active takeover market, which made it more difficult for underperforming managers to keep control of their firms.

We should emphasize that the agency models of management behavior are somewhat cynical and do not entirely capture management behavior. Brennan (1994) and others have expressed concern that the way we teach students about self-interested managers may, in fact, be self-fulfilling, convincing students that self-interested behavior is the appropriate norm. Indeed, Frank, Gilovich, and Regan (1993) reviewed experiments which implied that undergraduate students trained as economists are much less likely than other students to cooperate for the common good.

The fact that the interests of managers and shareholders differ doesn't mean that managers are purely self-interested or greedy. Indeed, the greatest source of management-shareholder conflict probably arises from the loyalty of managers to their employees. Most managers will try to keep a sick or disabled employee on the payroll—at the expense of the firm's shareholders—out of concern for the employee and his or her family rather than because of any personal benefit to the manager. Clearly, there are notable exceptions, but we have no reason to suspect that management incentives are anything but noble. However, when evaluating financial decisions, we must take into account that these incentives are not always aligned with those of shareholders.

Key Concepts

Result 17.1: Management interests are likely to deviate from shareholder interests in a number of ways. The extent of this deviation is likely to be related to the amount of time the managers have spent on the job and the number of shares they own.

Result 17.2: Firms with concentrated ownership are likely to be better *monitored* and thus better managed. However, shareholders who take large equity stakes may be inadequately diversified. All shareholders benefit from better management; however, the costs of having a less diversified portfolio are borne only by the large shareholders. As a result, ownership is likely to be less concentrated than it should be, given mean-variance efficiency considerations.

Result 17.3: Entrepreneurs may obtain a better price for their shares if they commit to holding a larger fraction of the firm's outstanding shares. The entrepreneur's incentives to hold shares is higher for those firms with the largest incentives to "consume on the job." The incentive to hold shares is also related to risk aversion.

Result 17.4: Managers may prefer investments that enhance their own human capital and minimize risk. This implies that:

- Managers may prefer larger, more diversified firms.
- Managers may prefer investments that pay off more quickly than those that would maximize the value of their shares.

Result 17.5: Allowing management discretion has benefits as well as costs.

- The benefits of discretion are greater in more uncertain environments.

- The costs of discretion are greater when the interests of managers and shareholders do not coincide.

Therefore, we might expect to find more concentrated ownership and more managerial discretion in firms facing more uncertain environments.

Result 17.6: Shareholders prefer a higher leverage ratio than that preferred by management. As a result, firms that are more strongly influenced by shareholders have higher leverage ratios.

Result 17.7: A large debt obligation limits management's ability to use corporate resources in ways that do not benefit investors.

Result 17.8: A firm's debt level is a determinant of how much the firm will invest in the future and it can be used to move the firm toward investing the appropriate amount. In general, however, capital structure cannot by itself induce managers to invest optimally.

Result 17.9: Agency problems arise because of imperfect information and risk aversion. Agency costs thus can be reduced by improving information flows and by reducing risk. To minimize the risk borne by managers, optimal compensation contracts should eliminate as much extraneous risk (or risk unrelated to the manager's efforts) as possible.

Result 17.10: Relative performance contracts, which reward managers for performing better than either the entire market or, alternatively, the firms in their industry, have an advantage and a disadvantage.

- The advantage is that the contracts eliminate the effect of some of the risks that are beyond the manager's control.

- The disadvantage is that the contracts may cause firms to compete too aggressively, which would reduce industry profits.

Result 17.11: Stock-based compensation has the advantage that it motivates managers to improve share prices. However, stock prices change for reasons outside of a manager's control and only partially reflect the efforts of a manager who heads

an individual business unit in a diversified corporation. A cash flow-based compensation plan that appropriately adjusts for capital costs may provide the best method for motivating managers in these cases.

Result 17.12: Improved management incentives provide one motivation for corporate spin-offs and divestitures. Similarly, conglomerate mergers may weaken the incentives of executives at the various divisions.

Key Terms

agency costs   621
agents   619
closed-end mutual funds   613
divest   627
open-end mutual funds   613
principal-agent relationship   619

principals   619
proxy fights   609
relative performance contract   624
spin-off   627
value-based management   626

Exercises

17.1. Discuss why managers might tend to want their organizations to grow.

17.2. Discuss the factors that determine whether firms are likely to have large ownership concentrations.

17.3. John Jacobs, the CEO of High Tech Industries owns 51 percent of the shares of his $50 million company. The firm is starting a new project that requires $25 million in new equity capital. Jacobs is considering two ways to fund the project. The first is to issue $25 million in new equity. The second is to form a partially owned subsidiary of High Tech, which would be called Super Tech, and have the subsidiary issue the equity. Under the second proposal, Super Tech would be 55 percent owned by High Tech and 45 percent owned by new shareholders. Describe how the incentives of the managers of the new business and John Jacobs are likely to be affected by the two proposals.

17.4. Consider three similar firms that differ only in the extent to which they are controlled by their board of directors. In firm 1, the board has complete control of the investment decisions, operating

decisions, and financing choices. In firm 2, the board is unable to monitor investment and operating decisions, but they do control financing decisions. In firm 3, the board has very little control over either investment, operating, or financing decisions. Describe how debt ratios are likely to differ in the three firms.

17.5. As a Washington policy analyst, you are asked to comment on a proposed law that would make it more difficult for large outside shareholders to extract private benefits from the partial control they can exert over management. How would such a law affect the incentives of outside shareholders to monitor management?

17.6. You are a member of the compensation committee of the board of directors for both Chrysler and Chevron. How should the compensation contracts for the CEOs of these two companies differ?

17.7. The tendency of firms to use stock-based compensation is higher for firms with higher market-to-book ratios. Provide two explanations for this empirical observation.

References and Additional Readings

Aron, Debra. "Using the Capital Market as a Monitor: Corporate Spin-Offs in an Agency Framework." *Rand Journal of Economics* 22 (1991), pp. 505–18.

Barclay, Michael; Clifford Holderness; and Jeffrey Pontiff. "Private Benefits from Block Ownership and Discounts on Closed-End Funds." *Journal of Financial Economics* 33, no. 3 (1993), pp. 263–91.

Berle, A. Jr., and G. Means. *The Modern Corporation and Private Property.* New York: Macmillan, 1932.

Bizjak, John; James Brickley; and Jeffrey Coles. "Stock-Based Incentive Compensation and Investment Behavior." *Journal of Accounting and Economics* 16, pp. 349–72.

Brennan, Michael. "Incentives, Rationality, and Society." *Continental Bank Journal of Applied Corporate Finance* 7, no. 2 (1994), pp. 31–45.

Clinch, Greg. "Employee Compensation and Firms' Research and Development Activity." *Journal of Accounting Research* 29 (1991), pp. 59–78.

Cusatis, Patrick; James Miles; and Randall Woolridge. "Some New Evidence that Spinoffs Create Value." *Journal of Applied Corporate Finance* 7 (Summer 1994), pp. 100–07.

Demsetz, Harold, and Kenneth Lehn. "The Structure of Corporate Ownership." *Journal of Political Economy* 93, no. 6 (1985), pp. 1155–77.

Diamond, Douglas, and Robert Verrechia. "Optimal Managerial Contracts and Equilibrium Security Prices." *Journal of Finance* 37 (1982), pp. 275–87.

Donaldson, Gordon, and Jay Lorsch. *Decision Making at the Top: The Shaping of Strategic Direction.* New York: Basic Books, 1983.

Downes, David, and Robert Heinkel. "Signaling and the Valuation of Unseasoned New Issues." *Journal of Finance* 37, no. 1 (1982), pp. 1–10.

Frank, Robert H.; Thomas Gilovich; and Dennis T. Regan. "Does Studying Economics Inhibit Cooperation?" *Journal of Economic Perspectives* 7, no. 2 (1993), pp. 159–71.

Gaver, Jennifer J., and Kenneth M. Gaver. "Additional Evidence on the Association between the Investment Opportunity Set and Corporate Financing, Dividend, and Compensation Policies." *Journal of Accounting and Economics* 16 (1993), pp. 125–50.

———. "Compensation Policy and the Investment Opportunity Set." *Financial Management* 24 (1995), pp. 19–32.

Gilson, Stuart. "Bankruptcy, Boards, Banks and Blockholders: Evidence on Changes in Corporate Ownership and Control When Firms Default." *Journal of Financial Economics* 27 (1990), pp. 355–88.

———. "Management Turnover and Financial Distress." *Journal of Financial Economics* 25 (1989), pp. 241–62.

Grossman, Sanford, and Oliver Hart. "Corporate Financial Structure and Managerial Incentives." In *The Economics of Information and Uncertainty,* John McCall, ed. Chicago: University of Chicago Press, 1982.

Hart, Oliver, and John Moore. "Debt and Seniority: An Analysis of the Role of Hard Claims in Constraining Management." *American Economic Review* 85 (1995), pp. 567–85.

Hermalin, Benjamin, and Michael Weisbach. "The Effects of Board Compensation and Direct Incentives on Firm Performance." *Financial Management* 20 (1991), pp. 101–12.

Holderness, Clifford, and Dennis Sheehan. "The Role of Majority Shareholders in Publicly Held Corporations." *Journal of Financial Economics* 20 (1988), pp. 317–46.

Hoshi, Takeo; Anil Kashap; and David Sharfstein. "The Role of Banks in Reducing the Costs of Financial Distress in Japan." *Quarterly Journal of Economics* 106, no. 1 (1991), pp. 33–60.

Jensen, Michael. "Agency Cost of Free Cash Flow, Corporate Finance and Takeovers." *American Economic Review* 76 (1986), pp. 323–39.

Jensen, Michael, and William Meckling. "Theory of the Firm: Managerial Behavior, Agency Costs and Ownership Structure." *Journal of Financial Economics* (1976), pp. 305–60.

Jensen, Michael C., and Kevin J. Murphy. "CEO Incentives—It's Not How Much You Pay, but How." *Harvard Business Review* 90, no. 3 (1990), pp. 138–53.

———. "Performance Pay and Top-Management Incentives." *Journal of Political Economy* 98, no. 2 (1990), pp. 225–64.

Johnson, Bruce; Robert Magee; Nandu Nagarajan; and Harry Newman. "Analysis of the Stock Price Reaction to Sudden Executive Deaths: Implications for the Managerial Labor Market." *Journal of Accounting* 7 (1985), pp. 151–74.

Kole, Stacey. "Measuring Managerial Equity Ownership: A Comparison of Sources of Ownership Data." *Journal of Corporate Finance* 1 (1995), pp. 413–35.

Lambert, Richard A., and David F. Larker. "Golden Parachutes, Executive Decisionmaking and Shareholder Wealth." *Journal of Accounting and Economics* 7, nos. 1–3 (1986), pp. 179–203.

McConnell, John, and Henri Servaes. "Additional Evidence on Equity Ownership and Corporate Value." *Journal of Financial Economics* 27 (1990), pp. 595–612.

Mehran, Hamid. "Executive Compensation Structure, Ownership, and Firm Performance." *Journal of Financial Economics* 38, no. 2 (1995), pp. 163–84.

———. "Executive Incentive Plans, Corporate Control, and Capital Structure." *Journal of Financial and Quantitative Analysis* 27 (December 1992), pp. 539–60.

Morck, Robert; Andrei Shleifer; and Robert Vishny. "Management Ownership and Market Valuation: An Empirical Analysis." *Journal of Financial Economics* 20, nos. 1–2 (1988), pp. 293–316.

Myers, Stewart C. "The Capital Structure Puzzle." *Journal of Finance* 39 (1984), pp. 575–92.

Myers, Stewart C., and Nicholas Majluf. "Corporate Financing and Investment Decisions When Firms Have Information that Investors Do Not Have." *Journal of Financial Economics* 13 (1984), pp. 187–221.

———."Determinants of Corporate Borrowing." *Journal of Financial Economics* 5 (1977), pp. 147–75.

Prowse, Stephen. "Institutional Investment Patterns and Corporate Financial Behavior in the United States and Japan." *Journal of Financial Economics* 27, no. 1 (1990), pp. 43–66.

Ritter, Jay. "Signaling and the Valuation of Unseasoned New Issues: A Comment." *Journal of Finance* 39, no. 4 (1984), pp. 1231–37.

Roe, Mark. *Strong Managers, Weak Owners: The Political Roots of American Corporate Finance.* Princeton, NJ: Princeton University Press, 1994.

Schipper, Katherine, and Abbie Smith. "A Comparison of Equity Carve-Outs and Seasoned Equity Offerings: Share Price Effects and Corporate Restructuring." *Journal of Financial Economics* 15, nos. 1–2 (1986), pp. 153–86.

Shleifer, Andrei, and Robert W. Vishny. "Management Entrenchment: The Case of Manager-Specific Investments." *Journal of Financial Economics* 25, no. 1 (1989), pp. 123–39.

Smith, Clifford W., Jr., and Ross L. Watts. "The Investment Opportunity Set and Corporate Financing, Dividend, and Compensation Policies." *Journal of Financial Economics* 32 (December 1992), pp. 263–92.

Stulz, René. "Managerial Discretion and Optimal Financing Policies." *Journal of Financial Economics* 26 (1990), pp. 3–27.

Tehranian, Hassan, and James F. Waegelein. "Market Reaction to Short-Term Executive Compensation Plan Adoption." *Journal of Accounting and Economics* 7, nos. 1–3 (1985), pp. 131–44.

The Information Conveyed by Financial Decisions

Learning Objectives

After reading this chapter you should be able to:

1. Understand how financial decisions are affected by managers who are better informed than outside shareholders about firm values.
2. Identify situations in which managers have an incentive to distort accounting information.
3. Explain how financial decisions about the firm's dividend choice, capital structure, and real investments affect stock prices.
4. Interpret the empirical evidence about the reaction of stock prices to various financing and investing decisions.

On July 10, 1984, ITT announced a 64 percent cut in its quarterly dividend from $0.69 to $0.25 per share. Rand Araskog, CEO of ITT, said that the directors approved the dividend cut to save $232 million, enabling the firm to continue to fund its investment in high-technology products and services. The market greeted this announcement with a 32 percent price drop in ITT stock from $31 to $21\frac{1}{8} per share, implying a reduction in shareholder value of about $1 billion.[1]

The magnitude of the decline in ITT's stock price, described in the chapter's opening vignette, is certainly unusual. However, stock prices often move 10 to 15 percent when firms announce changes in their investment, dividend, or financing choices, implying that decisions like these convey information to investors which cause them to reevaluate, and thus revalue, the firm.

---

[1]See Woolridge and Gosh (1985) for more discussion on this particular case.

This chapter provides a framework that will help you to decipher the messages conveyed by financial decisions and to understand how information considerations affect financial decisions. The discussion in this chapter is based on the premise that top managers have proprietary information that enables them to derive more accurate internal valuations of their companies than the investor valuations determined in the market. In other words, managers may have information, which cannot be directly disclosed, about whether the firm's stock is either undervalued or overvalued.

Managers may not be able to disclose their information to the firm's stockholders for a variety of reasons:

- The information may be valuable to the firm's competitors.
- Firms run the risk of being sued by investors if they make forecasts that later turn out to be inaccurate.
- Managers may prefer not to disclose unfavorable information.
- The information may be difficult to quantify or substantiate.

If direct disclosures provide imperfect and incomplete information, then investors will incorporate indirect evidence into their evaluations. In particular, investors will attempt to decipher the information content of observable management decisions. These information-revealing decisions, or **signals**, might include decisions related to the firm's capital expenditures, financing choices, dividends, stock splits, and management shareholdings. For example, an increase in company shareholdings by IBM's top executives might signal that management is optimistic about the firm's prospects. In many instances, an indirect signal of this type can provide more credible information than a direct disclosure. As it is often said, "Actions speak louder than words."

It is natural to assume that managers take the market's expected reaction into account when making major decisions. This is especially true when the ability of managers to keep their jobs, maintain their autonomy, and increase their pay depends, in part, on the performance of their firm's stock. If managers have a strong incentive to increase the current stock prices of their firms, they will bias their decisions toward actions that reveal the most favorable information to investors. As we will demonstrate, these actions will not, in general, maximize the intrinsic or long-term value of the firm. In other words, managers may sometimes make value reducing decisions because they convey favorable information.

An important lesson of this chapter is that a distinction must be made between management decisions that *create* value and decisions that simply signal favorable information to shareholders. In many cases, value-creating decisions signal unfavorable information and result in stock price declines, and value-destroying decisions signal favorable information and result in stock price increases. For example, ITT's decision to cut its dividend would be considered value creating if the cash savings were used for positive net present value investments. However, as this chapter discusses, the dividend cut might signal unfavorable information about the firm's ability to generate cash from its existing operations.

If bad decisions sometimes convey favorable information, one must be careful when interpreting stock price reactions to corporate announcements. For example, a company might think that its shareholders prefer higher dividends because its stock price always reacts favorably when a dividend increase is announced. However, as shown later in the chapter, stock prices can respond favorably to a dividend increase because the increase conveys favorable information, even when most shareholders actually prefer the lower dividend.

18.1 Management Incentives When Managers Have Better Information than Shareholders

Most of the discussion in this text assumes that managers should act to maximize their firm's share price. However, if there is a difference between what managers believe their firm's shares are worth and the market price of those shares, then the appropriate goal of the managers needs further elaboration. Should managers act to maximize the current market price of the firm's shares, which reflects only public information, or should they act to maximize what they believe is the firm's long-term expected value, which reflects the managers' private information?

In some cases, there is no conflict between these two objectives, even when there is a difference between the firm's long-term expected value, which we refer to as the **intrinsic value**, and its current market value. However, as shown later in this chapter, when a decision conveys information that analysts use to value a firm's stock, decisions that maximize the firm's stock price may not be in the best long-term interests of shareholders. When this is the case, different shareholders will not necessarily agree on how managers should choose between these conflicting objectives.

Shareholders who plan to hold onto their shares for a long time prefer managers to make decisions that maximize the expected value of the shares at the future date when these shareholders plan to sell. This of course assumes that managers correctly assess the firm's intrinsic value and are not, for example, overly optimistic. However, shareholders who plan to sell their shares in the near future prefer managers to take actions that improve the firm's current share price irrespective of how this affects the firm's intrinsic or long-run value. Thus, there is an inherent conflict between the interests of long-term and short-term shareholders.

Conflicts between Short-Term and Long-Term Share Price Maximization

Exhibit 18.1 illustrates that managers have a number of competing pressures that determine how a firm's current share price and its intrinsic value enter the decision criteria. If a manager expects to be a long-term player at the firm and intends to continue to hold stock and options in the firm, then he or she is likely to want to maximize the firm's intrinsic value. However, most managers also are concerned about the firm's current stock price. The concern for current stock prices can arise for several reasons.

- Managers may plan to issue additional equity or sell some of their own stock in the near future.
- Managers may be concerned about the acquisition of the firm by an outsider at a price that is less than the firm's intrinsic value.
- Managerial compensation may be directly or indirectly tied to the current stock price of the firm.
- The ability to attract customers and other outside stakeholders may be related to outsiders' perceptions of the firm's value.

Although managers usually have an incentive to increase the firm's current stock price, the degree to which they are willing to sacrifice intrinsic value varies. Indeed, managers also might want to temporarily lower the current stock price of their firms, as we illustrate in the next section.

Given these inevitable conflicting incentives, we might best view a manager's objec-

Exhibit 18.1   Conflicting Incentives That Motivate Management

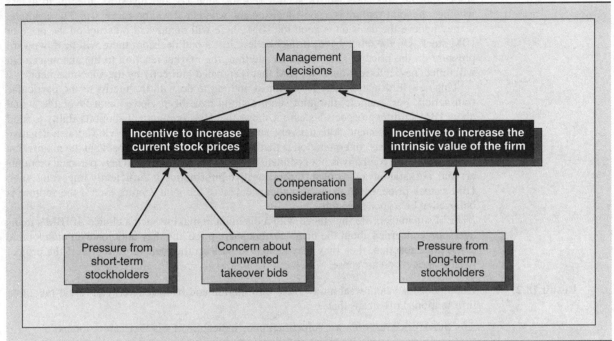

tive function as one of maximizing a weighted average of the firm's current stock price and intrinsic value, as shown below:

$$w_C S_C + w_I S_I$$

where w_C and w_I are the weights given by management to the importance of S_C and S_I, the firm's current and intrinsic values of its stock, respectively.

Result 18.1   Management incentives are influenced by a desire to increase the firm's current share price and its intrinsic value. The weight that managers place on these conflicting incentives is determined by, among other things, the manager's compensation and the security of the manager's job.

Example 18.1 illustrates how the weights on current and intrinsic value are determined.

Example 18.1:   The Trade-Off between Current Value and Intrinsic Value
John Jones, CEO of Tremont Corporation, has just exercised 10,000 stock options and now owns 20,000 shares of Tremont stock. He plans on selling the 10,000 shares within the next month and will hold the remaining 10,000 shares indefinitely. Assuming that his salary is fixed, describe how Jones's objective function would weight current value and intrinsic value.
   Answer: Jones would weight current value and intrinsic value equally. In other words, he would be willing to make a decision that reduces Tremont's long-term or intrinsic stock price by $1 per share if it increased its current stock price by more than $1 per share.

The Joint Venture of IBM, Motorola, and Apple Computer
The joint venture between IBM, Motorola, and Apple Computer to collaborate on new personal computers and workstations (the power PC chip) provides an example of how

corporate decisions can provide information that is potentially relevant for pricing a firm's stock. On the announcement of such a venture, analysts and investors attempt to assess whether the joint venture is a good decision and whether it will be successful. For example, if they believe the decision is good for IBM, there will be upward pressure on the price of IBM stock. On the other hand, if they believe it is a bad decision, there will be downward pressure on the price of IBM stock. In addition, the market reaction to the announcement will reflect new information about IBM that is signaled indirectly by the announcement.

This new information may have almost nothing to do with the merits of the particular transaction. For example, the joint venture could have been viewed as a favorable signal about IBM's future prospects because it shows that IBM is confident about its ability to fund a major new investment. Alternatively, such an investment might be viewed as a negative signal if the analysts' interpretation is that IBM has unfavorable prospects in the mainframe business and the company is not confident about its ability to develop new personal computers and workstations on its own. If this negative information is sufficiently important, then IBM's stock price will drop on the announcement of the joint venture even if the venture is believed to be a good decision.

IBM's managers are thus faced with a dilemma in making such a choice. If IBM's managers are concerned about the firm's current share price and they anticipate an unfavorable stock price reaction, then they may choose to pass up the joint venture even if the project itself makes economic sense.

Result 18.2   Good decisions can reveal unfavorable information and bad decisions can reveal favorable information. This means that:

- Stock price reactions are sometimes poor indicators of whether a decision has a positive or a negative effect on a firm's intrinsic value.
- Managers who are concerned about the current share prices of their firms may bias their decisions in ways that reduce the intrinsic values of their firms.

18.2 Earnings Manipulation

The focus of the chapter is on how information considerations affect financing and investing choices. However, it is instructive to look first at how these considerations affect how firms report their earnings.

Recent accounting research suggests that managers sometimes manipulate the earnings numbers of their firms in ways that increase reported income in the current year at the expense of reporting lower earnings in the future. Managers have some discretion over the firm's accounting methods, which allows them to shift reported income from the future to the current year and vice versa. For example, if the firm elects to use straight-line depreciation, reported earnings are initially higher since the initial depreciation expenses are lower than they would be with accelerated depreciation. However, the opposite is true in later years: Accelerated depreciation methods cause reported earnings in the later years to be higher than they would be with straight-line depreciation. Similarly, the choice of inventory valuation methods—that is, LIFO (last in, first out) or FIFO (first in, first out)—affects current and future earnings, depending on whether input prices are rising or falling.

These accounting methods are typically disclosed in a company's public financial statements. However, other undisclosed accounting-related decisions also affect earnings. For example, managers have discretion in coming up with a number of estimates, including the service lives and salvage values of depreciable assets, lives of intangibles, uncollectible rate on accounts receivable, cost of warranty plans, the degree of completion when the percentage-of-completion method is used for certain assets, the actuarial cost basis for a pension plan, and the interest rates for capitalized leases and pension accounting. As illustrated below, accounting changes can have dramatic effects on reported earnings.

The Management of Reported Earnings by General Motors[2]

Between 1985 and 1989, General Motors reported slightly rising earnings despite the decline in its car and truck sales. Although the efforts of General Motors to streamline its operations may have contributed to this earnings increase, accounting changes also affected its reported earnings.

In 1986, General Motors raised the expected rate of return on its existing pension assets, which allowed it to reduce the amount that it was required to add to the fund in the current and subsequent years. This increased reported profits in 1986 by about $195 million. In 1987, General Motors increased the estimated useful life of its plant and equipment, which reduced depreciation and amortization charges in that year, thus increasing its reported earnings by about $1.2 billion.

Incentives to Increase or Decrease Accounting Earnings

Firms show the greatest tendency to artificially inflate accounting earnings when managers have the most to gain from increasing share prices. For example, Teoh, Welch, and Wong (1997a, 1997b) found that firms make discretionary accounting choices that temporarily increase reported earnings prior to both initial and seasoned public offerings of equity. In these cases, managers are especially interested in improving the firm's current stock price because they want to maximize the proceeds from the equity issues.

Occasionally, managers also manipulate their earnings downward when they want their firms to appear weaker than they really are. For example, Liberty and Zimmerman (1986) found that some firms manipulated their earnings downward prior to union negotiations, and Jones (1991) found strong evidence of managers manipulating their company's earnings downward prior to appealing to the government for help against foreign competitors.

18.3 Shortsighted Investment Choices

Savvy investors and analysts, understanding the incentives of firms to manipulate their earnings numbers, are generally reluctant to take the reported earnings numbers at face value. Some analysts have a preference for evaluating firms based on cash flow rather than earnings numbers, which are less subject to accounting manipulation. However, firms also make real investment and operating decisions that affect the cash flow numbers, as well as earnings, and managers may be motivated to bias these decisions in ways that make the firm look better in the short run, but which hurt the firm in the long run.

Management's Reluctance to Undertake Long-Term Investments

A number of financial economists have argued that the incentive of managers to increase current share prices makes managers reluctant to take on long-term investment projects that generate low initial cash flows.[3] The reluctance to take on long-term projects arises

---

[2]This example is based on the discussion in Louis Lowenstein, *Sense and Non-Sense in Corporate Finance,* Reading, MA: Addison Wesley, 1991.

because investors understand that managers have an incentive to falsely claim that their investment projects have substantial payoffs several years down the road. However, investors have no way of knowing whether the managers are telling the truth about future payoffs or whether they are simply making long-term promises to cover up their current poor performance. As a result, the market price of a firm's stock tends to react negatively to poor performance in the current period, generally ignoring management claims of big payoffs in the future. While this is not a problem for managers who are interested only in the intrinsic value of their shares, it creates problems for other managers who have incentives to keep their current share prices high. This problem is illustrated in Example 18.2.

Example 18.2:   The Incentive to Choose Projects that Pay Off More Quickly

Micro Industries has available two long-term investment strategies and a short-term strategy. The cash flows and their present values are described below.

	Cash Flows (in $ millions) at		
	Year 1	Years 2–10 (annual cash flow)	Value at Year 1
1. Good long-term strategy	$40	$80	$600
2. Short-term strategy	60	50	400
3. Bad long-term strategy	40	40	300

Micro Industries is not considering the third strategy, because its present value of $300 million is obviously an inferior choice. This third strategy creates a problem for Micro, however, because investors are aware of this strategy, but are skeptical about whether Micro can generate the kind of returns reflected in strategies 1 and 2 described above. As a result, if the good long-term strategy is selected, Micro's year 1 market price will be only $300 million, reflecting the market's belief that the cash flows of the third strategy will be realized. However, the market price will rise to $600 million the following year when the first annual cash flow of $80 million is observed. If the short-term strategy is selected, investors will realize its potential when the year 1 cash flow of $60 million is observed and they will value the firm at $400 million. Which project should management select?

Answer: If management is concerned only with maximizing the firm's intrinsic value, it should select the good long-term strategy. However, if managers place sufficient weight on having a high stock price in year 1, they should take the short-term strategy because the year 1 market price in year 1 will then be $400 million rather than $300 million.

In Example 18.2, management may be reluctant to select the superior long-term strategy because the initial cash flows lead investors to believe that the company's future profits will be much lower than they will be in reality. However, by choosing the lower-valued short-term strategy, investors immediately recognize the firm's ability to generate better than expected cash flows and thus reward it by immediately boosting its stock price. The insights of this example are summarized in the following result.

Result 18.3   Managers will select projects that pay off quickly over possibly higher *NPV* projects that pay out over longer periods if they place significant weight on increasing their firm's current stock price.

---

[3]Management's incentive to be shortsighted in making investment choices is analyzed in Stein (1989), Narayaran (1985), and Brennan (1990).

What Determines a Manager's Incentive to Be Shortsighted?

The tendency of managers to implement strategies with better long-term payoffs increases as the weight that managers place on maximizing the current or near-term stock price declines. To understand this, consider again Example 18.2 and assume that management places a 75 percent weight on the year 1 value of the firm and a 25 percent weight on its intrinsic value, implying that the weighted average payoff from the long-term strategy (.75 × $300 million + .25 × $600 million) is $375 million, which is less than the $400 million payoff from picking the short-term strategy. However, if management weights intrinsic value and current share prices equally, then the long-term strategy will be selected because the weighted average value from the strategy is $450 million (.5 × $300 million + .5 × $600 million), which exceeds the value of the short-term strategy.

A number of policymakers and journalists have argued that the incentive to be shortsighted, as Example 18.2 illustrates, applies more to U.S. managers than to Japanese managers because the former place greater weight on the current share prices of their firms. The basic argument for this tendency is that U.S. managers are monitored more closely by institutional investors, are more subject to takeover threats, and have a larger part of their compensation tied to the short-term performance of their firms. The problem is compounded by the tendency of Americans to change jobs more often than the Japanese. Some writers have claimed that these factors have tended to make U.S. firms less willing to make long-term investments that ensure their long-term competitiveness.[4]

18.4 The Information Content of Dividend and Share Repurchase Announcements

This section examines the information conveyed by dividend and share repurchase announcements. As this chapter's opening vignette illustrates, dividend changes can lead to dramatic changes in stock prices.

Empirical Evidence on Stock Returns at the Time of Dividend Announcements

When firms announce dividend increases, their stock prices generally increase about 2 percent [see Aharony and Swary (1980)]. Announcements of the initiation of quarterly dividend payouts by firms that previously paid no dividends generate even larger stock price reactions [see Asquith and Mullins (1983), Healy and Palepu (1988), and Michaely, Thaler, and Womack (1995)]. Moreover, stock prices generally experience similar declines when firms announce dividend decreases or omissions, falling about 9.5 percent, on average, at the announcement of an omission [Healy and Palepu (1988)].

Result 18.4   Stock prices increase, on average, when firms increase dividends and decrease, on average, when they decrease dividends.

As a corporate executive, you might interpret a positive stock price reaction to an announced dividend increase as evidence that investors consider the dividend increase to be a good decision. This evidence, however, does not necessarily imply that dividend increases improve the intrinsic value of firms. Financial decisions that convey favorable information to the market tend to increase stock prices even when the decisions are bad

---

[4]Kaplan (1994) provides evidence at odds with this basic belief. He suggests that Japanese managers also may be strongly motivated to improve the short-term performance of the firms they manage.

for the firm's future profitability. As shown below, dividend increases can destroy intrinsic values, but they can still result in positive stock price responses because they signal favorable information.

A Dividend Signaling Model

Although there have been a number of signaling-based explanations for the positive stock price response to dividend increases, we will describe only one model.[5] This model, which we believe is the most intuitive, is based on the cash flow sources and uses equality [see equation (14.1) in Chapter 14]:

$$\frac{\text{After-tax}}{\text{cash flow}} = \frac{\text{new}}{\text{investment}} - \frac{\text{change in}}{\text{debt}} + \frac{\text{interest}}{\text{payments}} - \frac{\text{change in}}{\text{equity}} + \text{dividends}$$

Information Observed by Investors.   The following argument assumes that investors cannot observe true earnings because managers can manipulate accounting numbers in ways that investors may not be able to unravel. In addition, items such as the firm's investment in equipment maintenance or expenditures to update its customer database are not disclosed and generally cannot be observed by outsiders.

Although investors cannot observe how much the firm actually invests, assume that they do know how much the firm should invest to maximize value. For example, analysts may know that a firm like Johnson Trucking should spend $10 million on modernizing its fleet of trucks even though the company's actual investment in modernization is unobservable. Investors might, therefore, be fooled if Johnson Trucking increases its reported earnings artificially in a given year by cutting back its maintenance expenditures from $10 million to $8 million.

The Information Content of a Dividend Change.   Consider a case where the manager has no incentive to increase the firm's current share price and, in contrast to our argument above, assume that analysts correctly infer that the manager chooses the optimal level of investment. In this case, the cash flows can be observed indirectly from the changes in the levels of debt and equity financing, interest payments, dividends, and the inferred level of investment. As Example 18.3 illustrates, an increase in dividends, with the level of investment and financing held constant, would imply an equivalent increase in cash flow and, hence, an increase in the firm's value.

Example 18.3:   The Information Content of Dividend Payouts
Analysts observe that Johnson Trucking has not changed its level of debt or equity. They also have observed that Johnson has paid out $10 million in dividends over the past year and they believe that the firm has invested $15 million of its cash flow back into the business. From this information, what do the analysts infer about the firm's cash flows?
    Answer: Since the level of debt and equity financing has not changed, the level of dividends plus investment must equal the cash flow. The analysts would thus infer that Johnson's cash flows were $25 million.

Example 18.3 suggests that an increase in dividends from $10 million to $15 million would imply that Johnson Trucking's cash flow increased from $25 million to $30 million. This would be considered good news by shareholders and would result in an in-

---

[5]This discussion is based on Miller and Rock (1985).

crease in the firm's stock price. Hence, a dividend change may convey important information to shareholders even if managers are not explicitly trying to use dividends as a signaling tool.

Dividend Signaling and Underinvestment.   A manager faced with the situation in Example 18.3 would choose the optimal level of investment if he or she was interested solely in maximizing the intrinsic value of the firm. However, as suggested above, a manager who has an incentive to temporarily boost stock prices may want to cut back on unobserved investment and use the proceeds to increase the distribution to shareholders. Hence, an incentive to convey favorable information to shareholders will generally lead to observable payouts that are too high and unobservable investment expenditures that are too low. Example 18.4 illustrates this possibility.

Example 18.4:   Dividend Signaling and Underinvestment

Johnson Trucking is deciding whether to pay out $10 million (option 1), $15 million (option 2), or $20 million (option 3) in dividends. As in Example 18.3, a $10 million dividend, which allows reinvestment of $15 million, will maximize the intrinsic value of the stock. Higher dividends, on the other hand, will increase the current share price but, because of the cut in investment, will reduce the firm's intrinsic value. The following table provides the firm's intrinsic values and current market values associated with the different dividend alternatives.

	Option 1 $10 million dividend $15 million invested	Option 2 $15 million dividend $10 million invested	Option 3 $20 million dividend $5 million invested
Intrinsic value	$220 million	$210 million	$200 million
Market value	190 million	210 million	215 million

If managers want to maximize an equally weighted average of the firm's current market value and intrinsic value, what are they likely to decide?

Answer: The $15 million dividend (option 2) is the best option given the managers' preferences. However, if they place significantly more weight on intrinsic value, they will prefer the lower dividend; if they place more weight on current market value, they will prefer the higher dividend.

Example 18.4 shows that Johnson Trucking's market value and intrinsic values are equal when the firm pays out $15 million in dividends (option 2), suggesting that the market correctly inferred that the firm would invest only $10 million and correctly priced the stock. In other words, the $15 million dividend signals the firm's value because analysts and investors correctly infer management's incentive to increase the firm's current market value at the expense of its intrinsic value. If the firm had paid out more dividends and invested less than analysts expected, there would have been a deviation between the firm's current stock price and its intrinsic value.

To understand this point, consider what would happen if analysts view managers as having little incentive to increase the firm's current stock price at the expense of its intrinsic value when, in reality, their incentive to increase the stock price (perhaps because of a takeover threat) was quite large. In such a case, a large dividend would be incorrectly interpreted as evidence of increased cash flow when, in reality, the cash for the dividend was generated by decreasing investment expenditures.

Do Positive Stock Price Responses Imply that a Decision Creates Value?   In Example 18.4, the higher dividends (options 2 and 3) use funds that would have been used more productively within the firm. However, analysts still view the higher dividend payments as good news, because they reveal that the firm has more cash—and perhaps greater earnings potential—than the analysts had previously believed. In this case, the stock price will react favorably to a dividend increase because of the information it conveys, even though it is a bad decision. Similarly, stock prices may react unfavorably to good decisions. If a firm is experiencing a cash shortfall, it may be in the firm's best interests to cut its dividend payout. However, the announcement of a dividend cut would reveal the firm's difficulties, so the market is likely to react negatively to the announcement.

Result 18.5   An increased dividend implies, holding all else constant, higher cash flows and hence higher stock prices. By cutting investments in items that cannot be readily observed by analysts, firms can increase reported earnings and dividends, thereby increasing their stock prices. A manager's incentive to temporarily boost the firm's stock price may thus lead the firm to pass up positive net present value investments.

Result 18.5 indicates that share price increases that occur when firms announce dividend increases do not imply that investors like the higher dividend payout. Although the dividend increase conveys favorable information, it doesn't necessarily create value for shareholders. Hence, the observed stock price response to dividend increases is a misguided rationale for increasing dividends.

Share Repurchases versus Dividends.   Chapter 14 indicates that, in the absence of taxes and transaction costs, dividends and share repurchases are essentially identical. A share repurchase should also convey the same information as a dividend because, in both cases, cash is distributed to shareholders, revealing to investors that the firm has generated a sizable cash flow.

Indeed, Dann (1981) and Vermaelen (1981) documented impressive share price responses to share repurchase announcements, suggesting that the repurchase alternative conveys the same favorable information to investors as a dividend payment. Dann found that, on average, firms that repurchase shares with tender offers experience about a 16 percent return on the announcement date. In his sample, the tender offers were made at a premium that averaged about 22 percent above the stock price just prior to the offer. The number of shares repurchased averaged about 15 percent of the outstanding shares, taking the premium into account, which represented, on average, 19 percent of the outstanding equity of these firms.

Given the large number of shares repurchased in these tender offers, it is not surprising that the stock price reaction of a share repurchase is much greater than the price reaction to a dividend increase. When firms want to repurchase smaller amounts of their stock (e.g., 3 to 7 percent of their outstanding shares), they usually buy the shares on the open market. The stock returns at the time of the announcements of open market repurchase announcements are about 3 percent, which is comparable to the returns from the initiation of a new dividend. As Example 18.5 illustrates, a number of reasons explain why stock prices do not react as much to open market repurchases as they do to tender offers.

Example 18.5:   Share Price Response to an Open Market Repurchase
On September 12, 1988, Lotus Development Corporation announced that it would repurchase up to 15 percent of its outstanding shares in the open market. The stock reacted by increasing from $17 to $18 per share. While the price increase was somewhat higher than the average

increase for an open market repurchase, the number of shares Lotus planned to repurchase was substantially higher than the average. Indeed, the planned repurchase was about as large as the typical tender offer repurchase in which stock prices generally have a much greater reaction. Why didn't Lotus's stock price react more?

Answer: While various explanations can be offered about why Lotus's stock price didn't react more favorably to the repurchase announcement, we emphasize the following:

1. The announcement of an intention to repurchase a quantity of shares on the open market is not a firm commitment. Lotus could have repurchased fewer shares.

2. In a tender offer, management offers to repurchase shares at a price substantially above the prevailing stock price. This provides an additional signal of the stock's value since the firm would be substantially overpaying for its stock if the current price was not substantially below the stock's intrinsic value. In open market repurchases, no premium is offered.

Whittaker and FPL: Simultaneous Dividend Cuts and Share Repurchases

For tax reasons, it makes sense to substitute a share repurchase for a dividend. In theory, such a transaction should not convey information to investors if the amount of the repurchase is identical to the amount of the dividend cut. However, the market may view the dividend cut positively if investors place a value upon receiving income in the form of more lightly taxed capital gains. Alternatively, stock prices may react negatively if the market views the share repurchase as a one-time event and the dividend cut as permanent.

Unfortunately, there are few examples of firms substituting share repurchases for dividend payments. However, Woolridge and Gosh (1985) reported that on July 24, 1984, Whittaker Corporation announced a cut in its cash dividend from $0.40 to $0.15 per share and at the same time, instigated a share repurchase plan. On the announcement, the share price increased $0.125 to $18.625, suggesting that a dividend cut packaged with a share repurchase is not necessarily bad news.

Similarly, Soter, Brigham, and Evanson (1996), reported that on May 9, 1994, Florida Power and Light (FPL) announced a 32 percent dividend reduction along with its intention to repurchase up to 10 million shares over the next three years. In adopting this change in dividend policy, the company noted the personal tax advantages of the substitution of share repurchases for dividend payments. On the day of the announcement, the company's stock price fell from $31.88 to $27.50, a drop of almost 14 percent. However, the drop in stock prices was quickly reversed; Soter, Brigham, and Evanson reported that "as analysts digested the news and considered the reasons for the reduction, they concluded that the action was not a signal of financial distress. . . . On May 31, FPL 's stock closed at $32.17."

Result 18.6   It is unlikely that signaling considerations explain why firms pay dividends rather than repurchase shares.

Dividend Policy and Investment Incentives

The argument in the last section assumed that investors could correctly infer the firm's investment expenditures even though the investments are not directly observable. This assumption requires that investors understand the investment opportunities of the firm as well as the degree of emphasis that managers place on maximizing the firm's current share price compared with maximizing the firm's intrinsic value. If investors know management's incentives and understand the firm's investment opportunities, they can accurately infer how much the firm will invest. The only unobservable factor in the equation of sources and uses of funds would then be after-tax cash flow, which can be inferred from the observed dividends, interest payments, and changes in debt and equity financing.

In reality, investors and analysts are usually unable to make accurate inferences about a firm's investment opportunities or how much managers want to invest. As a result, the dividend choice conveys information about both the opportunities and incentives to invest as well as the firm's cash flows. This implies that a firm's unanticipated dividend cut could provide a mixed signal. A dividend cut could mean that the firm was less profitable; alternatively, the cut could mean that the firm had good opportunities and planned on investing more than investors had previously anticipated.

Can Dividend Cuts Signal Improved Investment Opportunities?   A dividend cut that is interpreted to mean an increase in investment expenditures can be either good news or bad news, depending on whether investors believe that the firm will be investing in positive or negative net present value projects. Woolridge and Gosh (1985) argued that if firms can effectively communicate to investors that an announced dividend cut is motivated by a desire to conserve cash to fund good investments, their stock prices will not react unfavorably. To illustrate this point, the authors highlighted the April 11, 1975, announcement by Ford Motor Company of a cut in its quarterly dividend from $0.80 to $0.60 per share. This announcement, accompanied by a statement by Henry Ford II that the cut would "conserve sufficient cash to finance products that can add to profitability in future years," generated a 1.9 percent increase in Ford's stock price. However, as our chapter's opening vignette on ITT's dividend cut indicates, investors are often skeptical about such statements. As a result, stock prices usually fall when firms announce dividend cuts.

Dividend Cuts and the Incentive to Overinvest.   Arguing that a dividend cut is made to increase funds for investment will of course elicit a favorable price response only if shareholders believe the firm will invest the money in positive net present value projects. As discussed in Chapter 17, managers may overinvest because they prefer to see their firms grow. Thus, a signal indicating that management plans to increase investment can be considered both bad news and good news. As a result, stock price responses to dividend increases and decreases should depend on the investment opportunities available to the firm. Investors would thus view a dividend increase more favorably when firms have poorer investment opportunities.

Result 18.7   A dividend increase or decrease can provide information to investors about:

- The firm's cash flows.
- Management's investment intentions.

In the latter case, if investors believe that an increased level of investment is motivated by improved prospects, they will view the dividend cut favorably. However, if investors believe that managers will make negative net present value investments, they will interpret a dividend cut as bad news.

The findings in Lang and Litzenberger (1989) support the hypothesis that investors view dividend cuts more favorably when firms have better investment prospects and view dividend increases more favorably when investment prospects are poorer.[6] They examined the stock price reactions to announced dividend increases and decreases for stocks that differed according to the relation between their market values (MV) and their

---

[6]Litzenberger and Lang's sample of daily returns consisted of 429 dividend change announcements that met two criteria: (1) the absolute value of the percentage dividend change was greater than 10 percent and (2) data on market and book values were available.

book values (*BV*). Firms with market values that *exceed* their book values are believed to have favorable investment opportunities while those with market values that are *less than* their book values are believed to have unfavorable investment opportunities.

Lang and Litzenberger's sample was divided into four groups.

1. Firms with *MV* > *BV* with dividend increases.
2. Firms with *MV* > *BV* with dividend decreases.
3. Firms with *MV* < *BV* with dividend increases.
4. Firms with *MV* < *BV* with dividend decreases.

As Exhibit 18.2 shows, a dividend increase created only a slight stock price increase for firms believed to have favorable investment opportunities (i.e., *MV* > *BV*). Likewise, a dividend decrease generated only a slight stock price decrease. In contrast, dividend increases and decreases resulted in much larger stock price responses for firms believed to have unfavorable investment opportunities (i.e., *MV* < *BV*). This evidence suggests that dividend changes are viewed as signals of the firm's level of future investment.

Denis, Denis, and Savin (1994) provide an alternative interpretation of the observed differences in the stock price reaction of high and low *MV/BV* firms to dividend changes. They pointed out that high *MV/BV* firms generally have lower dividend yields and greater growth potential, which implies two things:

1. Increases in the dividends of high *MV/BV* firms are less likely to be viewed as a surprise.
2. High *MV/BV* firms are likely to attract investors who are less interested in dividends.

To understand the first point, recall equation (10.5b) from Chapter 10. This equation, based on the dividend discount model, states that the cost of capital is the sum of (1) the dividend yield and (2) the dividend growth rate. Hence, holding the risk of the firm (and thus the cost of capital) constant, low dividend yields imply high dividend growth rates and vice versa. The second point is an implication of dividend clienteles, discussed in Chapter 14. Both of these factors suggest that high *MV/BV* firms will react less to dividend increases than low *MV/BV* firms even in the absence of the incentive problems discussed by Lang and Litzenberger.

Denis, Denis, and Savin demonstrated that after accounting for differences in dividend yields and the size of the dividend change, high and low *MV/BV* firms react similarly to dividend changes. In addition, they found that following dividend increases, stock market analysts increase their earnings forecasts more for low *MV/BV* firms than for

EXHIBIT 18.2   Average Daily Returns on Dividend Announcement Days, 1979–84

	Dividend Increase	Dividend Decrease	Difference in Absolute Values for Increases and Decreases
MV > *BV*	0.003[a]	−0.003	0.000
MV < *BV*	0.008[a]	−0.027[a]	0.019[a]
Difference	0.005[a]	−0.024[a]	0.019[a]

[a]Statistically different from zero.
Source: Lang and LItzenberger (1989).

high *MV/BV* firms. Based on this evidence, they concluded that stock prices respond to dividend changes because of the information the announcements convey about the firm's future earnings. Their evidence does not support the idea that stock prices respond because dividend changes provide information about the firms' future investment choices.

Dividends Attract Attention

An additional possibility is that a firm's dividend increase or initiation results in a stock price increase simply because it attracts attention to the firm. To understand why investors generally view decisions that attract attention as good news, one must consider the conditions under which the managers of a firm would put the firm under greater scrutiny. If the firm is undervalued, increased scrutiny is likely to lead to a positive adjustment in the firm's stock price, but if the firm is overvalued, the increased scrutiny is likely to lead to a negative adjustment in the firm's stock price. Hence, the incentive to attract attention is greatest for those firms that are the most undervalued, which suggests that one might expect to see positive stock price reactions to any announcements that attract considerable attention.

The positive stock price reactions observed at the time stock dividends and stock splits are announced support the idea that stock prices respond to announcements of managerial decisions that do no more than attract attention to the firm.[7] Unlike cash dividends, stock dividends and splits affect neither the firm's cash flows nor its investment alternatives. Yet, observed stock returns at the time of stock dividend and stock split announcements are of approximately the same magnitude as the returns at the time increases in cash dividends are announced.

18.5 The Information Content of the Debt-Equity Choice

This section examines the type of information conveyed to investors by a firm's debt-equity choice. The section discusses two reasons why the debt-equity choice conveys information to investors. First, because of financial distress costs, managers will avoid increasing a firm's leverage ratio if they have information indicating that the firm could have future financial difficulties. Hence, a debt issue can be viewed as a signal that managers are confident about the firm's ability to repay the debt. The second reason has to do with the reluctance of managers to issue what they believe are underpriced shares. Hence, an equity issue might be viewed as a signal that the firm's shares are not underpriced and therefore may be overpriced.

A Signaling Model Based on the Tax Gain/Financial Distress Cost Trade-Off

To understand why the debt-equity choice conveys information, assume, as a first approximation, that firms select their capital structures by trading off the tax benefits of debt financing (see Chapter 13) against the various costs of financial distress (see Chapters 15 and 16). In this setting, firms desire higher debt levels when expected cash flows

---

[7]Grinblatt, Masulis, and Titman (1984), who proposed this "attention model," provided evidence that stock returns around the time of stock dividend and stock split announcements are of approximately the same magnitude as stock returns around the time of dividend increases. For further discussion and evidence relating to this hypothesis, see Brennan and Hughes (1991).

are higher because they can better utilize the tax benefits of debt. In addition, for any given debt level, the probability of incurring the costs of financial distress is lower if expected cash flows are higher.

Because expected future cash flows determine the firm's optimal capital structure, the capital structure choice is likely to convey information to shareholders. While the information content of the capital structure decision would not affect the decisions of managers concerned only with intrinsic value, it would affect the decisions of managers who also are concerned about the current share prices of their firms. Indeed, managers whose objectives are heavily weighted toward the maximization of current share price are likely to avoid reducing leverage even when doing so improves the intrinsic value of their shares. They may similarly choose to increase leverage beyond the point that maximizes intrinsic value.[8]

Result 18.8   An increase in a firm's debt ratio is considered a favorable signal because it indicates that managers believe the firm will be generating taxable earnings in the future and that they are not overly concerned about incurring financial distress costs. Managers understand that their firm's stock price is likely to respond favorably to higher leverage ratios and may thus have an incentive to select higher leverage ratios than they would otherwise prefer.

CUC International Borrows to Pay a Special Dividend[9]

In March 1989, CUC International's board of directors ratified a leveraged recapitalization plan, that involved the payout of a special dividend of $5 per share, financed in part by a loan from GE Capital. The total size of the dividend payment ($100 million) represented over half of the market value of CUC's equity prior to the announcement. Walter Forbes, the company's chairman and CEO, admitted that part of the motivation for the recapitalization was the favorable signal of an increased debt ratio. Forbes said:

> We judged that borrowing a moderate amount of debt to finance the special dividend would add an appropriate amount of leverage to our capital structure as well as providing, through the repayment of the debt, a clear signal of CUC's ability to generate cash.

It is clear that one of CUC International's motivations for increasing its debt ratio was to send a signal to investors. However, an investor may question whether such a signal is credible given that the motivation for the debt increase was to boost the firm's stock price. The following result describes conditions under which a financial signal conveys favorable information credibly:

Result 18.9   For a financial decision to credibly convey favorable information to investors, firms with poor prospects must find it costly to mimic the decisions made by firms with favorable prospects.

The Credibility of the Debt-Equity Signal.   As Example 18.6 illustrates, issuing debt satisfies the requirement for a credible signal, as specified in Result 18.9, because additional debt is likely to have a much greater effect on the probability of bankruptcy for firms with unfavorable future prospects than it is for firms with favorable prospects.

Example 18.6:   The Information Content of Leverage Changes

Analysts following Prairie Technologies are uncertain about Prairie's success in reducing its production costs. If it has been successful, Prairie's future earnings are expected to range

---

[8]Ross (1977) developed a theory of capital structure along these lines.
[9]This case study is based on Paul Healy and Krishna Palepu, "Using Capital Structure to Communicate with Investors: The Case of CUC International," *Journal of Applied Corporate Finance* (Winter 1996), pp. 30–44.

from $50 million to $60 million. However, if the company has not been successful, its earnings will be in the range of $25 million to $30 million. Prairie then announces a debt for equity swap that increases its interest payments by $40 million. What information is conveyed by this decision?

Answer: Analysts can infer that the cost reductions have been successful. Otherwise, such an increase in leverage would expose the firm to substantial bankruptcy risk and the associated financial distress costs. Hence, the market responds to the announcement by bidding up Prairie's stock price. Since the firm is certain to have the cash flow to meet these interest payments, the signal did not reduce Prairie's long-term value.

Example 18.6 illustrates the situation in which a firm with favorable prospects signals its value by increasing its level of debt financing without risking bankruptcy. In more realistic cases, a firm that wishes to signal its value will have to take on much more debt than it otherwise would have found optimal.

Consider, for example, a firm whose managers have strong incentives to increase current stock prices and would be willing to take on a high debt level to achieve this goal. As a result, outside investors will not find moderately high leverage ratios to be credible signals of high values. Hence, if the firm does have favorable prospects, it will have to use much more debt financing than it would otherwise use in order to convince investors of its higher value. We illustrate this concept in Example 18.7.

Example 18.7:   CEO Incentives and the Credibility of Financial Signals

Textron's CEO knows that the firm's assets are worth either $500 million, $400 million, or $300 million, depending on the demand for their product (each possibility is equally likely). Since managerial information will ultimately be revealed, the average of these three numbers, or $400 million, is the firm's intrinsic value. However, investors are not as optimistic about the firm's future earnings as the CEO and believe that the firm will have respective values of $450 million, $350 million, or $250 million in the three product demand scenarios given above, implying that the firm's current value is $350 million (assuming no financial distress costs). The $50 million discrepancy between the firm's intrinsic value and its current value presents a problem in that Textron's CEO plans on selling a large block of stock in the near future. As a consequence, before selling the stock, the CEO would like to signal to investors that Textron's value is $50 million higher than investors currently believe it is.

The CEO has announced his beliefs about Textron's prospects and investors know that the only alternative to their own beliefs is the more optimistic beliefs of the CEO. However, the mere announcement of more optimistic beliefs is not a very credible signal to investors. They know the CEO would be delighted to witness a temporary increase in Textron's stock price before unloading his block of shares.

Assume that the CEO has announced his intention to sell half of his shares and thus weights intrinsic value and current value equally. Also assume that financial distress costs reduce the value of the firm by $60 million in whichever product demand scenario such distress occurs. The CEO has concluded that he may be able to credibly signal the more optimistic prospects by issuing sufficient debt and using the proceeds to retire equity. From the CEO's perspective, the issuance of debt with a promised payment in excess of $400 million is precluded. There is no need to risk financial distress that reduces intrinsic value by more than one gains in current value (net of financial distress costs). Moreover, debt financing with a promised payment of less than $250 million would not be a very credible signal in that—using either investor beliefs or the more optimistic CEO beliefs—financial distress never occurs.

Analyze what happens to investor beliefs if the CEO issues debt (and retires an equivalent amount of equity) with a promised payment (1) between $250 million and $350 million or (2) between $350 million and $400 million.

Answer: (1) Debt issuance between $250 million and $350 million is not a credible signal to investors that the higher firm values will be realized. Since Textron's CEO weights the current and intrinsic values of Textron equally, he would be willing to take on this amount of debt if doing so would signal the higher value, even if this signal were false. To see this, note that the CEO gains $50 million in current market value and loses only $20 million ($\frac{1}{3} \times$ $60 million) in intrinsic value from being financially distressed in the lowest product demand scenario. Investors, aware of the incentive to be tricked by a CEO who sees cash flows as pessimistically as they do will not believe that a debt signal of this magnitude is credible.

(2) A debt obligation between $350 million and $400 million would put the firm in financial distress $\frac{2}{3}$ of the time if investor beliefs are correct but only $\frac{1}{3}$ of the time if the more optimistic announced beliefs of the CEO were true. No CEO with pessimistic beliefs would take on this much debt since, even if investor beliefs change to those announced by the CEO, the gain to current value (net of financial distress costs) is $30 million ($50 million less $\frac{1}{3}$ of $60 million), while the loss in intrinsic value to the deceptive manager is $40 million ($\frac{2}{3}$ of $60 million). By contrast, the loss in intrinsic value to a manager who truly holds optimistic beliefs is $20 million ($\frac{1}{3}$ of $60 million). Thus, the signal of debt is credible in this case because managers with optimistic beliefs find it profitable to issue debt in amounts between $350 million and $400 million at the same time that managers with pessimistic beliefs find it unprofitable to signal by mimicking the same action.

The amount of debt financing a firm must use to credibly signal a high value depends on its manager's incentive to increase the firm's current stock price. To understand this, consider two CEOs, Jane and Janet. Jane, who plans to retire soon and sell her holdings of her firm's stock, has a strong incentive to temporarily increase her firm's stock price. Janet, on the other hand, plans to stay on as CEO for 10 years at her firm. She also is interested in boosting her firm's current share price, but she is much more concerned about the firm's long-term success and, in addition, is worried about losing her job if the firm has trouble meeting future interest payments.

The interpretation of the signal offered by a leverage increase depends on whether the firm one is looking at is run by a CEO like Jane or a CEO like Janet. When Janet increases her firm's leverage, investors will infer that she is confident that the firm will be able to generate the cash flows to pay back the debt. They understand that she has little incentive to give a false signal, but she has a lot to lose if the firm subsequently fails to make the required interest payments. Investors are likely to react much differently to a leverage increase initiated by Jane. They understand that Jane has a strong incentive to appear optimistic, even when she isn't, and that the cost to her of overleveraging her firm is not substantial. Hence, an equivalent leverage increase will result in a lower stock price response to the leverage signal for Jane's firm than for Janet's.

Adverse Selection Theory

Consider a health insurance company offering two different policies. One policy is very expensive, but it pays 100 percent of all of your medical bills. The second policy is much less expensive, but it pays only 80 percent of your medical bills. How do you expect individuals to choose between the two policies?

Most economists predict that individuals will not *randomly select* between the policies. Rather, we will observe what economists call adverse selection. In the health insurance example, **adverse selection** means that individuals will select their best actions based on their private information. Hence, the more expensive policy will attract the least healthy individuals. An additional example of adverse selection, described in a seminal article by Akerlof (1970), is the adverse selection or problem of "lemons" connected with the sale of used cars. Akerlof argued that cars depreciate so much in their first year largely because people who have the most incentive to sell their cars after only one year are those with lemons, or faulty cars. Buyers, taking into account this adverse selection of used cars, are thus unwilling to pay as much for a used car as for a new car, which is less likely to be a lemon.

Adverse selection also is important when firms issue new equity. Managers have the greatest incentive to sell stock when the stock is a lemon. This means that the incentive to issue equity is highest when management believes that the firm's stock price exceeds its intrinsic value. At these times, equity provides relatively inexpensive financing (i.e., the expected return on equity is relatively low) and a new issue would thus increase the intrinsic value of existing shares. In contrast, issuing shares of stock at a price lower than what management believes they are worth provides relatively expensive financing and dilutes the intrinsic value of the firm's existing shares.

Adverse Selection Problems When Insiders Sell Shares.   The incentive to retain rather than issue underpriced shares can be viewed within the context of an entrepreneur who is motivated to take his firm public in order to sell shares and diversify his portfolio.[10] To understand how an entrepreneur decides how many shares to sell, consider the situation faced by Bill Gates at the time of Microsoft's initial public offering. In reaching a decision of whether or not to sell some of his own shares, Gates has to consider:

- The diversification benefits of selling shares.
- The tax costs of selling shares (see Chapter 14).
- Whether the shares are undervalued or overvalued.

If Gates values diversification and the tax costs are not great, he will sell shares if he believes they are not substantially undervalued. Indeed, if he believes the shares are overvalued, he will sell them even though he places no value on diversification. Conversely, if Gates believes the shares are substantially undervalued, he will choose not to sell any shares even if he is extremely risk averse.

Since investors understand Gates's incentives, they monitor his tendency to sell off shares when they value Microsoft stock (both at the IPO and subsequently, in the secondary market). If Gates were to sell off almost all of his shares, which he would do to diversify optimally, Microsoft's stock would probably fall substantially because it would signal to investors that Gates no longer believes that Microsoft stock is an extraordinary investment. Gates thus faces a trade-off. By holding more shares, he provides a more favorable signal about Microsoft's prospects, which keeps the share price relatively high. However, this forces him to be less diversified than he would like to be.

Owing to the adverse selection problem, a corporate insider like Bill Gates needs a good reason to sell his shares. To understand this argument, review the issues involved in buying a used car. If you know that the car's owner is moving overseas, you might think the adverse selection problem is minimal and feel comfortable about buying the car. Similarly, if investors believe that Gates is extremely risk averse and therefore motivated to sell his shares, they will be less concerned about the adverse selection problem and be more willing to buy his shares. On the other hand, if investors believe that Gates is not very risk averse but is extremely averse to paying taxes, they would be much less willing to buy his shares.

---

[10]These issues were first addressed in Leland and Pyle (1977).

Several decades ago, Howard Hughes (whose sophistication with corporate finance theory was documented in Chapter 13's opening vignette), sold a substantial fraction of his holdings in TWA stock. The stock price of TWA did not plummet in response to the sale because Hughes was able to credibly convince the market that he was selling TWA stock to remedy a "cash crunch" that he was personally experiencing, and not because of any adverse information he held about TWA.

Adverse Selection Problems When Firms Raise Money for New Investments.[11]
Firms often issue equity to raise capital to fund new investment. In the same way that it is easier to sell your car when you can convince would-be buyers that you are moving overseas, it is easier to convince investors that your stock is not overvalued if you can demonstrate that you are raising capital to fund an attractive investment project.

However, the adverse selection problem cannot always be solved by revealing the potential of a favorable investment. As a result, firms sometimes pass up good investments because of their reluctance to finance projects by issuing underpriced shares. The conditions under which a firm will pass up a positive *NPV* investment are seen in the following equations, which compare the intrinsic values of a firm's shares with and without new investment that is financed by issuing equity.

$$\text{Share value taking the project} = \frac{PV \text{ of assets in place} + PV \text{ of new investment}}{\text{Number of original shares} + \text{Number of new shares}}$$

$$\text{Share value not taking the project} = \frac{PV \text{ of assets in place}}{\text{Number of original shares}}$$

The equations show that a firm may reduce the intrinsic value of its shares if the *PV* of the new investment is low relative to the number of shares it must issue. To understand this, consider a case where management believes the firm has assets worth $100 million with 1 million shares outstanding, suggesting that the firm's intrinsic value is $100 per share if it does not take any new investments. If this firm's stock is selling at only $70 per share, it will have to issue an additional 1 million shares to raise $70 million for a project that has a value of $90 million. The firm's share value after taking the project would then be:

$$\frac{\$100 \text{ million} + \$90 \text{ million}}{1 \text{ million} + 1 \text{ million}} = \$95 \text{ per share}$$

Hence, the firm reduces the intrinsic value of its shares by $5 per share by taking on a positive *NPV* project. Although the project has a positive *NPV,* the financing for the project has a negative *NPV.* This possibility is illustrated further in Example 18.8.

Example 18.8:   Issuing Equity When Managers Know More than Investors
Olympus Corporation is currently selling at $50 a share and has 1 million shares outstanding. The $50 share price reflects its current business, valued at $40 million, and an opportunity to take on an investment valued at $30 million, which costs only $20 million. The opportunity can be viewed as an asset with a $10 million *NPV.*

The management of Olympus has discovered a vast amount of oil, worth $50 million, on its property. This fact is unknown to shareholders and thus is not reflected in Olympus's current share price. If information about this oil were known to shareholders, its shares would sell for $100 a share. Unfortunately, management has no way to reveal this information directly to the market, so management expects that its shares will be undervalued for some time.

---

[11]The discussion in this subsection is based on Myers and Majluf (1984).

Suppose that the firm funds its new investment by issuing 400,000 shares at $50 a share. How will this affect the intrinsic value of the firm's existing shares?

Answer: If the firm passes up the project, its shares will be worth $90 each [($40 million + $50 million)/1 million] when the information about the oil is revealed. However, if the project is taken and is financed with an equity issue, the firm's total value will be $120 million ($40 million + $30 million + $50 million) and the total number of shares outstanding will be 1.4 million. The per share value will thus be only $85.71 ($120 ÷ 1.4) if Olympus issues shares and takes the project. Thus, the firm will choose not to invest in the positive *NPV* project if it requires issuing underpriced equity.

Using Debt Financing to Mitigate the Adverse Selection Problem.   Example 18.8 illustrates why managers may choose not to issue equity when they believe that their firm's shares are underpriced. However, the example ignores the possibility that the firm can finance the project with debt. If the project can be financed with riskless debt, then the firm should take the project as long as it has a positive *NPV*. In this case, the share's intrinsic value will be equal to:

$$\text{Share value: financing project with riskless debt} = \frac{\text{Value of original assets} + NPV \text{ of new project}}{\text{Number of shares}}$$

This value clearly increases when the company commits to a positive *NPV* project. However, the firm may still pass up the project if it is forced to issue risky debt that exposes it to the possibility of incurring financial distress costs. In this case, a firm must compare the costs of deviating from its optimal capital structure and the associated financial distress costs with the *NPV* of the particular investment project. Given this comparison, some positive *NPV* investment projects will be passed up while others will be financed with debt, causing the firm to become at least temporarily overlevered.

Similarly, one could show that firms have an incentive to take on negative net present value projects and to become underlevered if it allowed them to issue overpriced securities. Because investors and analysts understand these incentives, issuing equity is considered to be an indication that a firm is overvalued. As a result, announcements of equity issues have a negative effect on a firm's stock price, which has the further effect of reducing the incentive of firms to issue equity because, even if the firm were correctly priced prior to the announcement of a stock issue, the firm's stock is likely to be underpriced at the time of the offering.

This discussion suggests that managers will prefer debt to equity financing when they have a substantial amount of private information. In Example 18.8, Olympus Corporation would have been able to realize a share price of $100 if it could have financed the investment with risk-free debt. If lenders are unwilling to lend the firm additional amounts (see Chapter 15) or if the firm is unwilling to borrow more because of the financial distress costs (see Chapter 16), then undervalued firms may choose to pass up positive net present value investments.

Result 18.10   A firm may pass up a positive net present value investment project if it requires issuing underpriced equity. Since debt holders are fixed claimants, a firm's debt is less likely to be substantially undervalued. As a result, firms may have a bias toward financing new projects with debt rather than equity. With sufficiently high financial distress costs, however, firms may be better off passing up the investment rather than financing it with debt.

Adverse Selection and the Use of Preferred Stock.   The dilution and financial distress problems that can arise when an underpriced firm finances a new project may be mitigated by issuing preferred stock. Recall from Chapter 3 that preferred stock is similar to a bond because it has a fixed payout. However, if a firm fails to meet its dividend obligation, preferred shareholders cannot force it into bankruptcy. Hence, preferred stock will not create the problems associated with financial distress. In addition, since preferred stock offers a fixed claim, it is not likely to be as underpriced as common stock, so the dilution costs of issuing underpriced shares are much less of a problem.

For these reasons, preferred stock is a good security for firms to issue when they are having financial difficulties that they believe are temporary. If investors do not agree that the difficulties are temporary, the stock may be underpriced, so issuing common equity may dilute the value of existing shares. In such a situation, the firm may not have taxable earnings, making debt financing less attractive. Furthermore, additional debt financing may lead to a drop in the firm's credit rating, which could create problems with the firm's nonfinancial stakeholders.

Preferred stock may be the best financing alternative in this situation because it is unlikely to be as undervalued as common stock, given its senior status and fixed dividend, and it does not increase the risk of bankruptcy as would happen when additional debt is issued.

Result 18.11   When firms are experiencing financial difficulties, they prefer equity to debt financing for a number of reasons. In particular, the tax advantages of having debt may be less and the potential for suffering financial distress costs may be greater. Issuing common stock in these situations may be a problem, however, given the negative information conveyed by an equity offering. Hence, a preferred issue may offer the best source of capital.

Empirical Implications of the Adverse Selection Theory.   The adverse selection theory explains a number of observations about how firms externally finance themselves. First, the reluctance of managers to issue underpriced stock helps explain why stock prices react unfavorably when firms announce their intention to issue equity. As we discuss in more detail in the section below, stock prices drop about 2 percent, on average, when firms announce the issue of new equity. The adverse selection theory also provides an explanation for Donaldson's pecking order of financing choices (see Chapters 14 and 16). Donaldson observed that firms prefer first to finance investment with retained earnings; then, when they need outside funding, they prefer to issue debt instead of equity. The adverse selection theory explains the reluctance of firms to issue equity and, in addition, suggests that firms prefer to use their retained earnings to finance investment expenditures because this allows them to retain the capacity to borrow in the future.

18.6 Empirical Evidence

Exhibit 18.3 provides a brief overview of three types of signaling theories that provide insights about financial decision making and the reaction of stock prices when firms make financing and dividend changes. This section discusses some of the empirical implications of those theories. We start by reviewing academic studies that examine empirically the stock price responses to these financial decisions. We will then discuss some of the evidence relating to the effect of information issues on investment choices.

What Is an Event Study?

Academic research that examines stock price responses to the announcement of particular information is generally referred to as an **event study**. For example, the event studies of dividend initiation announcements discussed previously were carried out as follows:

EXHIBIT 18.3   Signaling Theories and Their Implications

Theory	*Explanation*	*Empirical Implications*
Issuing equity dilutes current shareholders.[a]	Management, representing existing shareholders, is reluctant to issue underpriced shares. This reluctance results in either underinvestment or excessive leverage.	Selling shares to outside investors conveys unfavorable information and results in a stock price decline. Similarly, share repurchases result in stock price increases.
Distributing cash to outside investors reveals the firm's earnings capacity.[b]	Cash outflows through dividends, repurchases, or debt retirements reveal that the firm has been and is expected to continue generating sufficient cash flows.	Dividends, repurchases, and debt retirements convey favorable information and result in stock price increases. Equity and debt issues convey unfavorable information.
The capital structure choice reveals management's assessment of the firm's future prospects.[c]	Increased debt signals that firms are confident that they can meet higher interest payments and that they have sufficient EBIT to use the interest tax shields.	Increased leverage conveys favorable information and is associated with positive stock price responses.

[a]See Leland and Pyle (1977) and Myers and Majluf (1984).
[b]See Miller and Rock (1985).
[c]See Ross (1977).

The researchers first collected the dates when a sample of firms announced that they would be initiating new dividends. The stock returns on the announcement dates and the days immediately before and after the event were averaged across all firms in the sample. For example, researchers might find that the average return for a sample of stocks on the day of a dividend initiation announcement was 3.0 percent, the average return on the day before the announcement was 1.2 percent, and the average return on the day after the announcement was 0.2 percent.

It is typical to find significant returns on the day(s) prior to a major announcement because information sometimes leaks out early or the press is slow to report the announcements. Therefore, researchers sometimes add the returns from the day(s) immediately before the announcement to the return on the announcement date itself to gauge the event's total price impact. For example, one might say that the dividend initiation event led to an average return of 4.2 percent, the 3.0 percent return on the event date plus the 1.2 percent return on the day prior to the announcement. With efficient markets, one expects to see insignificant returns after the announcements.

As discussed below, there is evidence that the market underreacts to some information events, and, consequently, some researchers also analyze returns on the days following the event. Events where such underreaction occurs are known as **efficient markets anomalies** because the associated stock price reactions seem to violate the efficient markets hypothesis. At this juncture, we do not have a good explanation for why such anomalies occur, although some research has suggested that flawed methodological design may account for some of the observed underreaction.

EXHIBIT 18.4   Stock Market Response to Pure Capital Structure Changes

Type of Transaction	Security Issued	Security Retired	Average Sample Size	Two-Day Announcement Period Return (%)
Leverage-Increasing Transactions				
Stock repurchase[a]	Debt	Common	45	21.9%
Exchange offer[b]	Debt	Common	52	14.0
Exchange offer[b]	Preferred	Common	9	8.3
Exchange offer[b]	Debt	Preferred	24	2.2
Exchange offer[c]	Income bonds	Preferred	24	2.2
Transactions with No Change in Leverage				
Exchange offer[d]	Debt	Debt	36	0.6°
Security sale[e]	Debt	Debt	83	0.2°
Leverage-Reducing Transactions				
Conversion-forcing call[e]	Common	Convertible debt	57	−0.4°
Conversion-forcing call[e]	Common	Preferred	113	−2.1
Security sale[f]	Convertible debt	Convertible bond	15	−2.4
Exchange offer[b]	Common	Debt	30	−2.6
Exchange offer[b]	Preferred	Preferred	9	−7.7
Security sale[f]	Common	Debt	12	−4.2
Exchange offer[b]	Common	Debt	20	−9.9

Note: Exhibits 18.4 and 18.5 are slightly altered versions of tables reported in Smith (1986).
Sources:
[a]Masulis (1980).
[b]Masulis (1983). These returns include announcement days of both the original offer and, for about 40 percent of the sample, a second announcement of specific terms of the exchange.
[c]McConnell and Schlarbaum (1981).
[d]Dietrich (1984).
[e]Mikkelson (1981).
[f]Eckbo (1986) and Mikkelson and Partch (1986).
°Not statistically different from zero.

In some event studies, researchers average market-adjusted excess returns instead of averaging total returns on the event dates. A **market-adjusted excess return** is the stock's return less the stock's beta times the market return on that date. For example, the market-adjusted excess return of a stock whose beta equaled 1 would be the return on the event day less the market return for that day. For relatively small samples, market adjustments are important because, by coincidence, particular announcements may be made on days when market returns are high. For large samples, however, it is unlikely that market returns will be either unusually high or unusually low on announcement dates, so that adjusting the returns for market movements makes little difference in these cases.

Event Study Evidence

Capital Structure Changes.   Firms sometimes make capital structure changes that have no immediate effect on the asset side of their balance sheets. For example, a firm may issue equity and use the proceeds to pay down debt. Exhibit 18.4 summarizes a

EXHIBIT 18.5   Stock Price Reactions to Security Sales

Type of Announcement	Average Sample Size	Two-Day Announcement Period Return
Security Sales		
Common stock[a]	262	−1.6
Preferred stock[b]	102	0.1[x]
Convertible preferred[c]	30	−1.4[x]
Straight debt[d]	221	−0.2
Convertible debt[d]	80	−2.1

Sources:
[a]Asquith and Mullins (1986), Masulis and Korwar (1986), Mikkelson and Partch (1986), Schipper and Smith (1986), and Pettway and Radcliff (1985).
[b]Linn and Pinegar (1988) and Mikkelson and Partch (1986).
[c]Linn and Pinegar 1988).
[d]Dann and Mikkelson (1984), Eckbo (1986), and Mikkelson and Partch (1986).
[x]Interpreted by the authors as insignificantly different from zero.

number of event studies that examine average stock price movements around the time of the announcements of these pure capital structure changes.

The evidence summarized in Exhibit 18.4 indicates that leverage-increasing events tend to increase stock prices and leverage decreasing events tend to decrease stock prices. For example, Masulis (1983) found that at the time of the announcement of **exchange offers** (in which common stock is retired and debt is issued), stock prices increased about 14 percent, on average. He also found that announcements of leverage-decreasing exchange offers brought stock prices down 9.9 percent. This evidence supports the idea that higher leverage is a signal that managers are confident about their ability to meet the higher interest payments.

Issuing Securities.   Exhibit 18.5 summarizes a number of event studies that examine stock price reactions to the announcements of new security issues. It shows that raising capital is viewed as a negative signal. For example, the announcement of the issuance of common stock results in a stock price decline, on average, of about 1.7 percent. This evidence supports the idea that firms seek outside equity when they think they can obtain cheap financing (i.e., issue overpriced stock) and the idea that by raising outside capital, firms reveal that they have generated insufficient capital internally.

In a sense, firms raising new debt are sending a mixed signal. They are seeking funds, which investors consider bad news, but they are increasing leverage, which investors believe is good news. As a result, when firms announce that they will issue straight bonds, their stock prices generally react very little. However, issuing convertible bonds, an instrument that shares debt and equity characteristics, results in negative stock price reactions.

Explanations for the Event Study Results.   These empirical findings are consistent with the adverse selection theory, which states that firms are reluctant to issue common stock when they believe their shares are underpriced. When firms do issue shares or, alternatively, exchange shares for bonds, management generally believes that the shares are probably either priced about right or overpriced. Analysts and investors observing the announcement of a share issue will then infer that management is not as optimistic as they had earlier thought, which is a bad signal about current share prices.

Since convertible bonds have a strong equity-like component, the adverse selection theory also can explain why the stock market generally reacts negatively when they are issued. On the other hand, short-term bank debt is least subject to adverse selection. Firms that believe that their stock is undervalued and that their credit ratings will improve in the future have the greatest incentive to borrow short term.[12] As a result, investors usually see short-term borrowing as a favorable signal and, as James (1987) showed, stock prices generally respond favorably when firms increase their bank debt.

The adverse selection theory also explains the stock price increases around the announcements of share repurchases and exchange offers that reduce the number of outstanding shares. Since management has the greatest incentive to reduce the total number of outstanding shares when their firm's stock is underpriced, these announcements convey favorable information to the market.

The discussion of taxes and financial distress costs provides an additional explanation for why stock prices rise when firms increase their debt levels. Managers would be less willing to replace equity financing with debt if they thought they were not going to generate sufficient income to utilize the tax benefits of the debt or if they thought repaying the debt would create problems. Thus, when firms increase their leverage, investors are likely to believe that management is unconcerned about either financial distress or having excess tax shields. Since this usually implies that managers are optimistic, leverage increases should be viewed as good news for shareholders.

The events considered in this section may also be signals of the intentions as well as the information of managers. For example, as Chapter 17 discussed, managers may have an incentive to overinvest, taking negative net present value projects that benefit them personally. Shareholders may see a distribution of cash or an increase in leverage as a signal that managers do not plan on initiating what the shareholders view as wasteful investment.

A Summary of the Event Study Findings.   Result 18.12 provides a summary and interpretation of some of the more notable event study findings.

Result 18.12   On average, stock prices react favorably to:

- Announcements that firms will be distributing cash to shareholders.
- Announcements that firms will increase their leverage.

Stock prices react negatively, on average, to:

- Announcements that firms will be raising cash.
- Announcements that firms will decrease their leverage.

These announcement returns can be explained by the information theories presented in this chapter and the incentive theories presented in Chapter 17.

Differential Announcement Date Returns.   Recall from this chapter's discussion of adverse selection that the information conveyed by an equity or debt issue depends on the manager's perceived motivation for issuing the particular financial instrument. For example, if investors believe that a firm is already overleveraged and cannot easily finance new investments with debt, then they are likely to view an equity offer less negatively and a debt offering as evidence that managers believe their stock is undervalued. In contrast, investors are likely to view an equity offering as especially negative in cases

---

[12]This idea is developed in much greater detail in Flannery (1986) and Diamond (1991).

where the firm could easily raise debt capital. In such instances, investors may conclude that managers issued equity because they believe their stock is overvalued.

To examine these possibilities, Bayless and Chaplinsky (1991) developed a model based on variables such as a firm's tax-paying status, a firm's debt ratio relative to its historical average ratio, and other firm characteristics to predict which firms are the most likely to issue equity and which are the most likely to issue debt. They compare the stock market responses around the time that debt and equity issues are announced to determine how expectations regarding the financing instrument that the firm is likely to issue affect stock returns.

The evidence in this study is consistent with the predictions of the theory of adverse selection. Stock returns around the time of equity announcement are more negative for firms that are expected to use debt financing and less negative for firms expected to issue equity.

Postannouncement Drift.   The event studies described in this section assume that markets are efficient and that stock prices react fully to the information event under consideration. However, some recent studies have shown that in a surprising number of cases, the market substantially underreacts to important information. This was first shown in the context of earnings announcements, where research indicates that stock prices react favorably to announcements of unexpectedly good earnings, but tend to underreact to this information. As a result, investors can profit by buying stocks immediately after the announcements of unexpected good earnings and selling the stocks of firms whose earnings fall below expectations.[13]

Michaely, Thaler, and Womack (1995) found that stock prices underreact to the announcement of both dividend initiations and omissions. They found market-adjusted excess returns averaged about 15 percent over the two years following a dividend initiation and about −15 percent following a dividend omission. This means that, historically, the market has substantially underreacted to these dividend events.

Loughran and Ritter (1995) and Ikenberry, Lakonishok, and Vermaelen (1995) documented similar results for equity issues and share repurchases. Stocks realize negative returns over the five years following an equity issue and positive returns over the four years following share repurchases. These results suggest that firms have historically been able to time the equity market successfully, issuing stock when it is overpriced and repurchasing stock when it is underpriced.

Result 18.13   Recent evidence suggests that the market underreacts to the information revealed by earnings reports and announcements of some financial decisions. In the past, investors could have generated substantial profits by buying stocks following favorable announcements and selling stocks following unfavorable announcements.

We stress that most financial economists are generally skeptical about purported market inefficiencies and tend to believe that the observed return premium associated with simple trading strategies compensates for some sort of risk. However, no convincing risk-based explanations for the investment strategies described in Result 18.13 have been proposed. Of course, even a market that was inefficient in the past may not continue to be so in the future. We thus urge readers who plan to implement trading strategies to take advantage of these apparent inefficiencies to exercise caution.

---

[13]Studies that document these abnormal post earnings announcement returns include, Foster, Olsen and Shevlin (1984) and Bernard and Thomas (1989, 1990).

How Does the Availability of Cash Affect Investment Expenditures?

According to the adverse selection theory, firms will sometimes choose not to issue equity and will instead pass up positive net present value investments when they are unable to borrow. Therefore, the theory suggests that a firm's borrowing capacity and the availability of cash may be important determinants of its investment expenditures. The effect of the availability of cash on investment choices is illustrated in the following discussion with Dan Franchi, the assistant treasurer at Unocal. When asked how changes in cash flow affect Unocal's investment expenditures, Franchi replied:

> If oil prices were to drop $4 per barrel, Unocal would cut back funding for capital expenditures . . . because of the lack of available cash, not because the projects became considerably worse. The additional projects that are taken when cash flows are high are projects that would have been attractive anyway, but would have been delayed if we had insufficient internal funds.[14]

Unocal generally does not consider common stock issuance to be an attractive alternative for raising investment capital in the event of a cash shortfall caused by a drop in oil prices. In addition, the company is generally unwilling to fund new investments with debt if it means lowering its credit rating. Franchi indicated that the company was concerned that a weakened credit rating would put Unocal at a competitive disadvantage in attracting business overseas:

> We feel that over the long term, we're going to be competing with companies overseas that tend to have A credit ratings. As a BBB company, we would be at a competitive disadvantage in the long term. Potentially, when a foreign government decides who they would like to have working on a project, they could be looking at the financial strengths of the company. And they would be more likely to want to work with a company that is more financially sound. For example, all else equal, the Chinese government would rather enter a long-term arrangement with a AAA company than a BBB company.[15]

Empirical Evidence in the United States.   A substantial amount of empirical evidence suggests that there is a fairly widespread tendency of firms to determine their level of investment expenditures at least partially based on the availability of cash flow, as the adverse selection theory predicts. Meyer and Kuh (1957), Fazzari, Hubbard, and Petersen (1988), and others documented that year-to-year changes in firms' capital expenditures are highly correlated with changes in their cash flows (net earnings plus depreciation), but they are much less correlated with changes in their stock prices. Fazzari, Hubbard, and Petersen found that the tendency to link new investment expenditures to the availability of cash flows is greater for firms that pay low dividends, which are more likely to be cash constrained. Such firms generally have greater investment needs than firms that pay higher dividends, which presumably generate more cash flow than is required for their relatively low investment needs.

Empirical Evidence in Japan.   The relation between cash flows and investment for U.S. firms also holds for some firms in Japan. The investment expenditures of Japanese firms was analyzed by Hoshi, Kashap, and Scharfstein (1991) in a study that examined the differences between firms associated with a keiretsu family and independent firms. As Chapter 1 noted, a *keiretsu* family is a group of firms with interlocking ownership

---

[14]Dan Franchi, telephone conversation with one of the authors, May 2, 1995.
[15]Ibid.

structures, which prefer to do business with each other rather than with firms outside the group. The *keiritsu* firms are usually headed by a large bank which supplies a major portion of the debt as well as some of the equity capital to the firms. The interlocking ownership structure of these *keiritsu* firms makes it virtually impossible for outsiders to mount a successful hostile takeover of one of them. In addition, the close ties with a major bank means, on the one hand, that the mangers are more closely scrutinized by the suppliers of capital but, on the other hand, that the *keiritsu* firms enjoy greater access to capital when they have investment projects that enhance the value of the firm. Not surprisingly, the investment expenditures of the *keiritsu* firms are much less tied to their cash flows and much more tied to their stock prices than either U.S. firms or independent Japanese firms.

18.7 Summary and Conclusions

Often, a firm's managers possess information that outside investors lack. This chapter examined how these differences in information influence financial decisions. The analysis suggested that if managers' objectives place significant weight on the current share price, these information differences will distort financial decisions in important ways. For example, firms will tend to invest less and bias their investments toward projects that pay off more quickly. Firms also will pay out higher dividends and choose to be more highly levered than they would otherwise be.

Since the distortions that arise from these information differences are costly, managers have an incentive to take steps that minimize the distortions. One way to reduce these information-related costs is to increase the information available to analysts and investors, thus decreasing management's information advantage. Doing this reduces the extent to which outside investors must rely on indirect indicators of value, such as dividends and debt ratios, that management can manipulate to the firm's long-term detriment. One also could reduce the severity of the information problem by designing compensation packages that reduce a manager's incentive to increase the firm's current stock price.

It is unrealistic, however, to think that the distortions caused by information differences can be eliminated completely. The competitive disadvantage of making too much information about the firm public limit the amount that firms should disclose. Moreover, as Chapter 17 emphasized, offsetting incentive problems exist when managers are indifferent to their firm's current stock price. In reality, firms need to strike a balance between the motivational benefits of having a fluid job market that requires compensation based on short-term performance and the costs associated with the potential shortsightedness that such compensation plans promote.

Key Concepts

Result 18.1: Management incentives are influenced by a desire to increase the firm's current share price and its intrinsic value. The weight that managers place on these conflicting incentives is determined by, among other things, the manager's compensation and the security of the manager's job.

Result 18.2: Good decisions can reveal unfavorable information and bad decisions can reveal favorable information. This means that:

• Stock price reactions are sometimes poor indicators of whether a decision has a positive or a negative effect on a firm's intrinsic value.

• Managers who are concerned about the current share prices of their firms may bias their decisions in ways that reduce the intrinsic values of their firms.

Result 18.3: Managers will select projects that pay off quickly over possibly higher *NPV* projects that pay out over longer periods if they place significant weight on increasing their firm's current stock price.

Result 18.4: Stock prices increase, on average, when firms increase dividends and decrease, on average, when they decrease dividends.

Result 18.5: An increased dividend implies, holding all else constant, higher cash flows and hence higher stock prices. By cutting investments in items that cannot be readily observed by analysts, firms can increase reported earnings and dividends, thereby increasing their stock prices. A manager's incentive to temporarily boost the firm's stock price may thus lead the firm to pass up positive net present value investments.

Result 18.6: It is unlikely that signaling considerations explain why firms pay dividends rather than repurchase shares.

Result 18.7: A dividend increase or decrease can provide information to investors about:

- The firm's cash flows.
- Management's investment intentions.

In the latter case, if investors believe that an increased level of investment is motivated by improved prospects, they will view the dividend cut favorably. However, if investors believe that managers will make negative net present value investments, they will interpret a dividend cut as bad news.

Result 18.8: An increase in a firm's debt ratio is considered a favorable signal because it indicates that managers believe the firm will be generating taxable earnings in the future and that they are not overly concerned about incurring financial distress costs. Managers understand that their firm's stock price is likely to respond favorably to higher leverage ratios and may thus have an incentive to select higher leverage ratios than they would otherwise prefer.

Result 18.9: For a financial decision to credibly convey favorable information to investors, firms with poor prospects must find it costly to mimic the decisions made by firms with favorable prospects.

Result 18.10: A firm may pass up a positive net present value investment project if it requires issuing underpriced equity. Since debt holders are fixed claimants, a firm's debt is less likely to be substantially undervalued. As a result, firms may have a bias toward financing new projects with debt rather than equity. With sufficiently high financial distress costs, however, firms may be better off passing up the investment rather than financing it with debt.

Result 18.11: When firms are experiencing financial difficulties, they prefer equity to debt financing for a number of reasons. In particular, the tax advantages of having debt may be less and the potential for suffering financial distress costs may be greater. Issuing common stock in these situations may be a problem, however, given the negative information conveyed by an equity offering. Hence, a preferred issue may offer the best source of capital.

Result 18.12: On average, stock prices react favorably to:

- Announcements that firms will be distributing cash to shareholders.
- Announcements that firms will increase their leverage.

Stock prices react negatively, on average, to:

- Announcements that firms will be raising cash.
- Announcements that firms will decrease their leverage.

These announcement returns can be explained by the information theories presented in this chapter and the incentive theories presented in Chapter 17.

Result 18.13: Recent evidence suggests that the market underreacts to the information revealed by earnings reports and announcements of some financial decisions. In the past, investors could have generated substantial profits by buying stocks following favorable announcements and selling stocks following unfavorable announcements.

Key Terms

adverse selection   649
efficient markets anomalies   654
event study   653
exchange offers   656

intrinsic value   634
market-adjusted excess return   655
signals   633

Exercises

18.1.   Describe how a firm's investment decisions might be made differently if its management is highly concerned about the firm's current stock price.

18.2.   Why might a firm choose to increase its debt level in response to favorable information about its future prospects?

18.3.   Classical finance theory suggests that firms take projects with positive *NPV*s regardless of the amount of cash the firm has available. However, empirical evidence suggests that the amount that firms invest is heavily dependent on their available cash flows. Why might this be?

18.4.   Why might a manager close to retirement select a higher debt ratio than a manager far from retirement?

18.5.   ABC Industries is considering an investment that requires the firm to issue new equity. The project will cost $100, but will add $120 to the firm's value. Although management believes the firm's value is $1,000 without the new project, outside investors value the firm at $600 without the project. If the firm currently has 100 shares outstanding, how many new shares must it issue to finance the project? Now assume that the true value of the firm will become known to the market shortly after the new equity has been issued. What will the firm's stock price be at this time if it chooses to finance this new investment? What will the stock price be if it chooses to pass up the investment?

18.6.   As economies develop, disclosure laws generally get tougher and accounting information becomes more informative. Briefly describe how such changes in the quality of information affect the incentives of firms to be financed by either debt or equity.

18.7.   If it was known that management was selling shares at the same time as it was increasing leverage, how would this affect the credibility of the signal? Why? What other actions or motivations by management could affect the credibility of such a signal?

18.8.   The following table describes management's view of Abracadabra Corporation's future cash flows

along with the consensus view of outside analysts.

	Cash Flows		
State of the Economy:	*Low*	*Average*	*High*
Management's beliefs	$400	$500	$600
Analysts' beliefs	300	400	500
Cost of distress	100	150	200

If the analysts can be convinced that managements' beliefs are correct, the firm's value will increase by $200. Assume that there is no tax or other benefits from debt apart from the information the debt may convey. However, if the promised interest payments exceed the cash flows, the firm will lose $100, $150, or $200 because of financial distress, depending on the state of the economy.

Assuming that management wants to maximize the intrinsic value of the firm, how much debt will the firm take on? Now consider the possibility that management's incentives place an equal weight on the firm's intrinsic value and its current value. How much debt must the firm take on to credibly convince the analysts that their cash flow estimates are wrong? (*Hint:* Consider management's incentive to mislead analysts if the analysts original projections are correct.)

18.9.   Analysts project that Infotech, an information services company, will have the following financial data for equally probable high and low states:

	Value	
State:	*Low*	*High*
Cash	$100	$100
Fixed asset value	200	300
Growth opportunity *NPV*	100	100

The firm is currently financed entirely with equity. The growth opportunity consists of a positive *NPV* project with a required initial investment of $200 and a value of $300. Management, knowing with 100 percent certainty whether the firm is in the high or low state, has a choice of taking the project and issuing debt, taking the project and issuing equity, or not taking the project and doing nothing. Examine the payoffs to current shareholders in the high and low states for each of these three decisions. What if management is unable to issue debt?

18.10. Mr. Chan and Mr. Smith are the CEOs of similar textile manufacturing firms. Chan is 64 years old and plans to retire next year. Smith is 52 years old and expects to remain with the firm for some time. Both firms have just announced 10 percent increases in their earnings. Which firm should expect the greatest stock price increase? Explain.

18.11. Gordon Wu (the largest shareholder of Hopewell) has just announced that he is planning to issue out-of-the-money covered warrants on 10 percent of Hopewell's outstanding stock. Does this announcement make you more or less optimistic about Hopewell's future profits? Does it affect your assessment of Hopewell's volatility?

18.12. When firms increase leverage with exchange offers, what generally happens to their stock prices? Why might this be?

18.13. Divided Industries recently announced a substantial increase in its dividend payout. Stockholders complained because the increased dividend would place an added tax burden on them. Subsequent to the announcement, however, the stock price of Divided Industries increased 10 percent. Does this stock price increase indicate that the market viewed the dividend increase as a good decision?

18.14. Explain why the threat of hostile takeovers can make firms more short-term oriented?

18.15. Show in Example 18.7 that it never pays to issue debt in excess of $400 million.

References and Additional Readings

Aharony, Joseph, and Itzhak Swary. "Quarterly Dividend and Earnings Announcements and Stockholders' Returns: An Empirical Analysis." *Journal of Finance* 35, no. 1 (1980), pp. 1–12.

Akerlof, George A. "The Market for 'Lemons': Quality Uncertainty and the Market Mechanism." *Quarterly Journal of Economics* 84, no. 3 (1970), pp. 488–500.

Asquith, Paul, and David W. Mullins, Jr. "Equity Issues and Offering Dilution." *Journal of Financial Economics* 15, nos. 1–2 (1986), pp. 61–89.

———. "The Impact of Initiating Dividend Payments on Shareholders' Wealth." *Journal of Business* 56, no. 1 (1983), pp. 77–96.

Bayless, Michael, and Susan Chaplinsky. "Expectations of Security Types and the Information Content of Debt and Equity Offers." *Journal of Financial Intermediation* 1 (1991), pp. 195–214.

Bernard, Victor, and Jacob Thomas. "Evidence that Stock Prices Do Not Fully Reflect Implications of Current Earnings for Future Earnings." *Journal of Accounting and Economics* 13 (1990), pp. 305–40.

———. "Post-Earnings-Announcement Drift: Delayed Price Response or Risk Premium?" *Journal of Accounting Research* 27 (1989), Supplement pp. 1–48.

Bhattacharya, Sudipto. "Imperfect Information, Dividend Policy, and 'The Bird-in-Hand Policy'

Fallacy." *Bell Journal of Economics* 10 (Spring 1979), pp. 259–70.

Brennan, Michael. "Latent Assets." *Journal of Finance* 45 (1990), pp. 709–30.

Brennan, Michael and Patricia Hughes. "Stock Prices and the Supply of Information." *Journal of Finance* 46 (1991), pp. 1665–91.

Charest, Guy. "Dividend Information, Stock Returns and Market Efficiency—II." *Journal of Financial Economics* 6 (1978), pp. 297–330.

Dann, Larry Y. "Common Stock Repurchases: An Analysis of Returns to Bondholders and Stockholders." *Journal of Financial Economics* 9, no. 2 (1981), pp. 113–38.

Dann, Larry Y., and Wayne H. Mikkelson. "Convertible Debt Issuance, Capital Structure Change and Financing-Related Information: Some New Evidence." *Journal of Financial Economics* 13, no. 2 (1984), pp. 157–86.

Denis, David J.; Diane K. Denis; and Atula Sarin. "The Information Content of Dividend Changes: Cash Flow Signaling, Overinvestment, and Dividend Clienteles." *Journal of Financial and Quantitative Analysis* 29 (1994), pp. 567–87.

Diamond, Douglas W. "Debt Maturity Structure and Liquidity Risk." *Quarterly Journal of Economics* 106, no. 3 (1991), pp. 709–37.

Dietrich, J. Richard. "Effects of Early Bond Refunding:

An Empirical Investigation of Security Returns." *Journal of Accounting and Economics* 6, no. 1 (1984), pp. 67–96.

Donaldson, Gordon. *Corporate Debt Capacity: A Study of Corporate Debt Policy and the Determination of Corporate Debt Capacity.* Boston: Harvard Graduate School of Business Administration, 1961.

Eckbo, B. Espen. "Valuation Effects of Corporate Debt Offerings." *Journal of Financial Economics* 15, nos. 1–2 (1986), pp. 119–51.

Fazzari, Steven; R. Glenn Hubbard; and Bruce Petersen. "Financing Constraints and Corporate Investment." *Brookings Papers on Economic Activity* 19, no. 1 (1988), pp. 141–206.

Flannery, Mark J. "Asymmetric Information and Risky Debt Maturity Choice." *Journal of Finance* 41, no. 1 (1986), pp. 19–37.

Foster, George; Chris Olsen; and Terry Shevlin. "Earnings Releases, Anomolies, and the Behavior of Security Returns." *Accounting Review* 59 (1984), pp. 574–603.

Grinblatt, Mark; Ronald Masulis; and Sheridan Titman. "The Valuation Effects of Stock Splits and Stock Dividends." *Journal of Financial Economics* 13, no. 4 (1984), pp. 461–90.

Healy, Paul M., and Krishna G. Palepu. "Earnings Information Conveyed by Dividend Initiations and Omissions." *Journal of Financial Economics* 21, no. 2 (1988), pp. 149–75.

Hoshi, T.; Anil Kashap; and David Scharfstein. "Corporate Structure, Liquidity and Investment: Evidence from Japanese Industrial Groups." *Quarterly Journal of Economics.* 106 (1991), pp. 33–60.

Ikenberry, David; Joseph Lakonishok; and Theo Vermaelen. "Market Underreaction to Open Market Share Repurchases." *Journal of Financial Economics* 39, nos. 2–3 (1995), pp. 181–208.

James, Christopher. "Some Evidence on the Uniqueness of Bank Loans." *Journal of Financial Economics* 19, no. 2 (1987), pp. 217–35.

Jones, Jennifer. "Earnings Management during Import Relief Investigation." *Journal of Accounting Research* 29, no. 2 (Autumn 1991), pp. 193–228.

Kaplan, Steven. "Top Executive Rewards and Firm Performance: A Comparison of Japan and the United States." *Journal of Political Economy* 102, no. 3 (1994), pp. 510–46.

Lang, Larry H. P., and Robert H. Litzenberger. "Dividend Announcements: Cash Flow Signaling vs. Free Cash Flow Hypothesis." *Journal of Financial Economics* 24, no. 1 (1989), pp. 181–92.

Leland, Hayne, and David Pyle. "Informational Asymmetries, Financial Structure and Financial Intermediation." *Journal of Finance* 32, no. 2 (1977), pp. 317–87.

Liberty, S., and J. Zimmerman. "Labor Union Contract Negotiations and Accounting Choices." *Accounting Review* 61, no. 4 (1986), pp. 692–712.

Linn, Scott C., and Michael J. Pinegar. "The Effect of Issuing Preferred Stock on Common and Preferred Stockholder Wealth." *Journal of Financial Economics* 22, no. 1 (1988), pp. 155–84.

Loughran, Timothy, and Jay Ritter. "The New Issues Puzzle." *Journal of Finance* 50 (1995), pp. 23–52.

Masulis, Ronald W. "The Effects of Capital Structure Change on Security Prices: A Study of Exchange Offers." *Journal of Financial Economics* 8, no. 2 (1980), pp. 139–77.

———. "The Impact of Capital Structure Change on Firm Value: Some Estimates." *Journal of Finance* 38, no. 1 (1983), pp. 107–26.

Masulis, Ronald W., and Ashok N. Korwar. "Seasoned Equity Offerings: An Empirical Investigation." *Journal of Financial Economics* 15, nos. 1–2 (1986), pp. 91–118.

McConnell, John J., and Gary G. Schlarbaum. "Evidence on the Impact of Exchange Offers on Security Prices: The Case of Income Bonds." *Journal of Business* 54, no. 1 (1981), pp. 65–85.

Meyer, John Robert, and Edwin Kuh. *The Investment Decision.* Cambridge: Harvard University Press, 1957.

Michaely, Roni; Richard Thaler; and Kent Womack. "Price Reactions to Dividend Initiations and Omissions: Overreaction or Drift?" *Journal of Finance* 50, no. 2 (1995), pp. 573–608.

Mikkelson, Wayne H., "Convertible Calls and Security Returns." *Journal of Financial Economics* 9, no. 3 (1981), pp. 237–64.

Mikkelson, Wayne H., and Megan M. Partch. "Valuation Effects of Security Offerance and the Issuance Process." *Journal of Financial Economics* 15, nos. 1–2 (1986), pp. 31–60.

Miller, Merton, and Kevin Rock. "Dividend Policy under Asymmetric Information." *Journal of Finance* 40, no. 4 (1985), pp. 1031–51.

Myers, Stewart C., "The Capital Structure Puzzle." *Journal of Finance* 39 (1984), pp. 575–92.

Myers, Stewart C., and Nicholas S. Majluf. "Corporate Financing and Investment Decisions When Firms Have Information that Investors Do Not Have." *Journal of Financial Economics* 13, no. 2 (1984), pp. 187–221.

Narayanan, M. P. "Managerial Incentives for Short-Term Results." *Journal of Finance* 40, no. 5 (1985), pp. 1469–84.

Pettway, Richard H., and Robert C. Radcliff. "Impacts of

New Equity Sales upon Electric Utility Share Prices." *Financial Management* 14, no. 1 (1985), pp. 16–25.

Ross, Stephen. "The Determinants of Financial Structure: The Incentive Signalling Approach." *Bell Journal of Economics* 8, no. 1 (1977), 23–40.

Schipper, Katherine, and Abbie Smith. "A Comparison of Equity Carve-Outs and Seasoned Equity Offerings: Share Price Effects and Corporate Restructuring." *Journal of Financial Economics* 15, nos. 1–2 (1986), pp. 153–86.

Seyhun, H. Nejat. "Insiders' Profits, Costs of Trading, and Market Efficiency." *Journal of Financial Economics* 16, no. 2 (June 1986), pp. 189–212.

Smith, Clifford W., Jr. "Raising Capital: Theory and Evidence." *Midland Corporate Finance Journal* 4, no. 4 (1986), pp. 4–22.

Sotor, Dennis; Eugene Brigham; and Paul Evanson. "The Dividend Cut 'Heard Round the World': The Case of FPL." *Journal of Applied Corporate Finance* 9 (1996), pp. 4–14.

Spence, Michael. "Job Market Signalling." *Quarterly Journal of Economics* 87 (1973), pp. 355–74.

Stein, Jeremy C. "Efficient Capital Markets, Inefficient Firms: A Model of Myopic Corporate Behavior." *Quarterly Journal of Economics* 104, no. 4 (1989), pp. 655–69.

Teoh, Siew Hong; Ivo Welch; and T. J. Wong. "Earnings Management and the Long-Run Market Performance of Initial Public Offerings." UCLA Finance Working Paper (1997a).

———. "Earnings Management and the Underperformance of Seasoned Equity Offerings." UCLA Finance Working Paper (1997b).

Vermaelen, Theo. "Common Stock Repurchases and Market Signaling: An Empirical Study." *Journal of Financial Economics* 9, no. 2 (1981), pp. 138–83

Woolridge, J. Randall, and Chinmoy Ghosh. "Dividend Cuts: Do They Always Signal Bad News?" *Midland Corporate Finance Journal* 3, no. 2 (1985), pp. 20–32.

Mergers and Acquisitions

Learning Objectives

After reading this chapter, you should be able to:

1. Understand how taxes, operating synergies, and management incentive conflicts can provide incentives for mergers and acquisitions.
2. Discuss the advantages and disadvantages of corporate diversification.
3. Know how and why the stock prices of bidders and targets react around the time of acquisition announcements.
4. Describe the empirical evidence regarding the gains from mergers and acquisitions.
5. Apply the tools developed in Chapters 9–12 to value potential acquisitions and the ideas developed in Chapters 13–18 to understand how such acquisitions should be financed.
6. Describe how acquiring firms determine their bidding strategies and how the targets of unwanted takeovers defend themselves.

On October 18, 1988, Philip Morris, a tobacco and food company, announced its intention to acquire Kraft, a food company. Philip Morris's stock price responded to this announcement by falling from $100 a share to $95.50. Two days later, Ross Johnson, RJR Nabisco's CEO, announced plans to take his firm private in a leveraged buyout, resulting in a large increase in RJR's stock price. As part of the plan, RJR would sell off its food divisions and increase the firm's focus on tobacco. In response to the RJR announcement, Philip Morris's stock price rebounded to $99 a share, which analysts attributed to investors' believing that Philip Morris might abandon its bid for Kraft and instead initiate a leveraged buyout, just as RJR Nabisco was doing.

A **merger** is a transaction that combines two firms into one new firm. An **acquisition** is the purchase of one firm by another firm. In some cases, two organizations are combined into one and one less stock is publicly traded. In others, such as leveraged buyouts (LBOs), there is a transfer of ownership of a single firm. Despite the formal distinction we have drawn between a merger and an acquisition, the two terms are often used interchangeably.

From the Modigliani-Miller Theorem (see Chapter 13) we learned that, with perfect capital markets, value can neither be created nor destroyed by repackaging a firm's securities as long as the repackaging leaves the total cash flows of the firms unchanged. Similarly, any merger or acquisition that has no effect on the after-tax cash flows of either firm, will not create or destroy value. This means that in order for a merger or acquisition (M&A) to create value, the after-tax cash flows of the combined firm must exceed the sum of the after-tax cash flows of the individual firms before the merger.

Although sometimes one observes what we call a "merger of equals," in most cases the parties in a merger can be classified as an **acquiring firm**, or bidder, which initiates the offer, and a **target firm**, or acquired firm, which receives the offer. In most cases, the acquiring firm offers to buy the target's shares at a substantial premium over the target's prevailing stock price. For example, when IBM acquired Lotus in 1995, its $3.4 billion offer was approximately double Lotus's market value prior to the offer. Although this **takeover premium**, the difference between the prior stock price and the amount offered, is somewhat larger than average, it is not unusually large. Takeover premiums generally range from 50 percent to 100 percent of the target firm's share price before the acquisition.

What motivates acquiring firms to offer such large premiums to acquire existing companies? Is it possible that a change in the ownership of a firm can create the kind of value implied by these takeover premiums?

This chapter presents several potential ways in which value can be created by combining two firms. However, it is also possible that the acquiring firm is willing to pay a premium for a target because the bidder's management believes the target is worth more than its current market value. For example, the bidder may have private information that the firm owns valuable assets which are not reported on its balance sheet. Large premiums also may reflect either managerial mistakes or nonvalue-maximizing incentives. For example, the bidder's management may want to buy the target because expanding or diversifying the firm may generate larger salaries, more perks, and greater job security.

In addition to analyzing what motivates mergers and acquisitions from both theoretical and empirical perspectives, it is important to understand mergers and acquisitions from an institutional perspective. As such, this chapter begins with a discussion of the history of mergers and develops a taxonomy for classifying mergers and acquisitions.

19.1 A History of Mergers and Acquisitions

Merger and acquisition (M & A) activity has increased substantially since the mid-1960s. In 1967, the total dollar value of all corporate mergers and acquisitions was under $20 billion. In 1995, the total dollar volume of U.S. mergers and acquisitions exceeded $300 billion. Exhibit 19.1 on page 668, which lists the largest acquisitions completed before 1995, indicates that all of the largest deals were accomplished fairly recently. The largest deal ever was the $26.4 billion takeover of RJR Nabisco by Kohlberg Kravis Roberts in 1988. In addition, a number of very large deals were proposed or completed after 1995 and are not reported in Exhibit 19.1. These include British Telecom's proposed $20 billion purchase of MCI, Disney's $19 billion purchase of Capital Cities/ABC, Westinghouse's $5 billion purchase of CBS, Time Warner's $6.8 billion purchase of Turner Broadcasting Systems, Chemical Bank's $10 billion merger with Chase Manhattan, and Raytheon's $9.5 billion acquisition of Hughes Electronics's defense unit from General Motors.

EXHIBIT 19.1   **Largest Completed U.S. Mergers and Acquisitions of All Time**

Acquirer	Target	Target Industry	Value (in $ billions)	Date
Kohlberg Kravis Roberts	RJR Nabisco	Food, tobacco	$24.72	4/89
AT&T	McCaw Cellular Communications	Telecommunications	18.92	9/94
Chevron	Gulf	Oil and gas	13.30	6/84
Philip Morris	Kraft	Food	12.64	12/88
Time	Warner Communications	Motion pictures, recordings	12.64	1/90
Bristol-Myers	Squibb	Pharmaceuticals	12.53	10/89
Texaco	Getty Oil	Oil and gas	10.13	2/84
Merger Partners: Martin Marietta and Lockhead Martin		Aerospace, defense	10.00	3/95
Viacom	Paramount Communications	Motion pictures, publishing	9.60	7/94
American Home Products	American Cyanamid	Pharmaceuticals	9.56	12/94
Beecham Group	SmithKline Beckman	Pharmaceuticals	8.28	7/89
Viacom	Blockbuster Entertainment	Video rentals, music retailing	7.97	9/94
British Petroleum Co. PLC	Standard Oil of Ohio (remaining 45%)	Oil and gas	7.56	6/87
AT&T	NCR	Computers	7.53	9/91
Dow Chemical	Marion Laboratories (67%)	Pharmaceuticals	7.08	12/89
DuPont	Conoco	Oil and gas	6.92	9/81
Matsushita Electric Industrial	MCA	Motion pictures	6.89	1/91
GTE	Contel	Telecommunications	6.75	3/91
Compeau	Federated Department Stores	Department stores	6.51	7/88

Source: *Mergers & Acquisitions* Sept./Oct. 1995. Reprinted by permission of IDD Enterprises LP, © 1995 by *Mergers & Acquisitions*.

Exhibit 19.2 graphs the total market value of completed mergers and acquisitions in each year from 1967 to 1995. The exhibit shows that the size of M&A activity started to increase substantially around 1980. There was a slowdown in this market starting around 1989, but by 1992 the takeover market was again on the upswing and it has been strong throughout the 1990s.

The increased takeover activity that started in the 1980s can be attributed to a number of factors, most notably the emergence of the high-yield (junk) bond market that was used to finance a number of the acquisitions, and the permissive stance toward mergers by the Justice Department during the Reagan administration. In addition, major changes in certain industries, such as increased foreign competition and the deregulation of transportation, communications, and financial services, brought about a need for a change in the way companies do business. The temporary decline in M&A activity at the end of the 1980s coincided with a recession and the collapse of the junk bond market.

Exhibit 19.2   Dollar Volume of Mergers and Acquisitions by Year

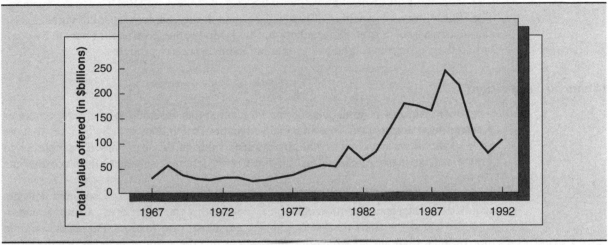

Source: *Mergerstat Review* and W. T. Grimm.

19.2 Types of Mergers and Acquisitions

There are probably almost as many types of mergers and acquisitions as there are bidders and targets. However, investment bankers find it useful to define three different categories of M&A transactions:

- Strategic acquisitions.
- Financial acquisitions.
- Conglomerate acquisitions.

Acquisitions also are often categorized as being friendly or hostile. An offer made directly to the firm's management or its board of directors is characterized as a **friendly takeover**. However, the managers of the target firm often object to being taken over, forcing the bidding firm to make a hostile offer for the target firm.

In a **hostile takeover**, the acquirer often bypasses the target's management and approaches the target company's shareholders directly with a tender offer for the purchase of their shares. A **tender offer** is an offer to purchase a certain number of shares at a specific price and on a specific date, generally for cash. Although a tender offer is usually associated with a hostile takeover, it also is used in friendly takeovers when the target's management approves the offer before it is presented to shareholders.

Strategic Acquisitions

A **strategic acquisition** involves **operating synergies**, meaning that the two firms are more profitable combined than separate. Since the late 1980s, the number of strategic acquisitions has been on the rise and they are now the dominant form of acquisition.

The operating synergies in a strategic acquisition may occur because the combining firms were former competitors. Alternatively, one firm may have products or talents that fit well with those of another firm. For example, IBM's purchase of Lotus in 1995 can be characterized as a strategic acquisition. IBM believed that Lotus's software products (in particular, Lotus Notes) fit well with the overall strategy of IBM's software business. The Philip Morris acquisition of Kraft, described in the chapter's opening vignette, also can be considered a strategic acquisition. Philip Morris and Kraft could benefit by combining their efforts in selling and promoting their respective products.

Financial Acquisitions

Investment bankers generally classify an acquisition that includes no operating synergies as a **financial acquisition**. In a financial acquisition, the bidder usually believes that the price of the target firm is less than the intrinsic value of the firm's assets. In contrast to strategic acquisitions, financial acquisitions have declined substantially since the late 1980s.

A financial acquisition is sometimes motivated by the tax gains associated with the acquisition. Alternatively, the acquirer may believe that the target firm's assets are undervalued because the stock market is ignoring important information. The most common motivation for a financial acquisition, however, is that the acquirer believes that the target firm is undervalued relative to its assets because it is badly managed. In most cases, a financial acquisition motivated by the acquirer's dismal view of target management is hostile. This type of acquisition is sometimes referred to as a **disciplinary takeover**.

For example, T. Boone Pickens, the CEO of Mesa Petroleum, made a bid for Gulf Oil in 1983. Pickens's motivation was that Gulf management was expending substantial resources exploring for oil at a time when the price of oil made exploration unprofitable. He believed that Gulf's stock was priced low because of this unprofitable investment in oil exploration and that a change of management could change this policy. Although Pickens failed in his takeover attempt, Gulf was subsequently acquired by Chevron, which substantially curtailed its exploration activity.

Financial acquisitions are often structured as leveraged buyouts (LBOs). In most leveraged buyouts, an individual or a group, often led by a firm's own management, arranges to buy a public company and take it private. Thus, all of the publicly traded shares are purchased and the firm ceases to be a public company. These are referred to as *leveraged* buyouts because the transactions are financed mainly with debt.

Because the acquirers in LBOs have no other assets, there are no potential synergies. Hence, operating improvements must come from better management and improved incentives. Kohlberg Kravis and Roberts's leveraged buyout of RJR Nabisco is the most well known example of this type of acquisition.

Conglomerate Acquisitions

A third type of acquisition, a **conglomerate** (or **diversifying**) **acquisition**, involves firms with no apparent potential for operating synergies. In this sense, the conglomerate acquisition is similar to the financial acquisition described above. However, conglomerate acquisitions are more likely to be motivated by **financial synergies**, which lower a firm's cost of capital, thus creating value even when the operations of merged firms do not benefit from the combination. As we will discuss below, financial synergies can arise because of taxes as well as because of the information and incentive problems discussed in Chapters 15–18.

Most of the mergers that occurred in the United States during the 1950s, 1960s, and 1970s were conglomerate mergers. A popular explanation for the predominance of conglomerate mergers during that time was that regulators would not approve most strategic combinations because of antitrust considerations. However, some authors have noted that conglomerate acquisitions have also been common in countries without strong antitrust regulations.[1] They have become much less common in the 1980s and 1990s, reflecting either the loosening of antitrust rules that have allowed more strategic combinations or an increase in the efficiency of financial markets, which could have the effect of reducing the financial synergies associated with a merger.

A number of large U.S. corporations were built up in the 1960s through conglomerate acquisitions. For example, ITT (International Telephone and Telegraph) was originally a communications company that developed and ran telephone systems in Europe and Latin America. After ITT's profits had been shaken by political risk, such as the nationalization of ITT's telephone system in Cuba, the CEO, Harold Geneen, recommended in an internal document in 1963 that ITT adopt a policy of acquiring U.S. companies. The first major purchase by ITT was Avis Rent-a-Car, which was followed by both big and small names. Bramwell Business College; the Nancy Taylor Secretarial Finishing School of Chicago; Apcoa, the car-parking company; Continental Baking; Pennsylvania Glass & Sand; Transportation Displays, the billboard rental company; Hartford Insurance group; Howard Sams, the publisher; Levitt, the home construction company; and Sheraton Hotels are just a few of ITT's acquisitions. This diversification strategy did not stop at the U.S. border. In France, for example, ITT acquired a pump maker, two television set manufacturers, a lighting company, a contractor, and a business school.

Many of the conglomerate acquisitions of the 1960s and 1970s proved to be unsuccessful. Indeed, many of the disciplinary takeovers in the 1980s were initiated to break up conglomerates formed earlier. For example, the RJR Nabisco leveraged buyout, described in the chapter's opening vignette, was first proposed as a bustup takeover. The original plan was to separate the food and tobacco businesses. As it turned out, some but not all of the food businesses were sold after the RJR Nabisco LBO. ITT has also been the target of unwanted takeovers. Perhaps to preempt such takeovers, ITT has sold off a number of the divisions acquired over the past 20 years. In 1996, ITT split into three separate companies: an insurance business; an auto-parts and industrial products company; and a hotel, casino, and entertainment company.

Summary of Mergers and Acquisitions

Exhibit 19.3 on page 672 summarizes the three categories of acquisitions discussed in this section. Note that individual acquisitions do not necessarily fit neatly into any one box. For example, Philip Morris's acquisition of Kraft is generally categorized as a strategic acquisition. However, Philip Morris might have believed that an important source of value in the acquisition was that Kraft was undervalued because of poor management. If this were the case, the acquisition could also be categorized as a financial acquisition.

19.3 Sources of Takeover Gains

The previous section categorized takeovers according to the sources of takeover gains. This section examines the various sources in more detail. Result 19.1 summarizes the four main sources of takeover gains that were discussed briefly in the previous section:

---

[1]See for example, Matsusaka (1996) and Comment and Jarrell (1995).

Exhibit 19.3   Types of Acquisitions

Type of Aquisition	Primary Motivation	Hostile or Friendly	Trend
Strategic	Operating synergies	Usually friendly	Increasing importance in the 1990s
Financial	Taxes, incentive improvements	Often hostile	Mainly a phenomenon of the 1980s
Conglomerate	Financial synergies, taxes, and incentives	Hostile or friendly	Mainly a phenomenon of the 1960s and 1970s

Result 19.1   The main sources of takeover gains include:

- Taxes.
- Operating synergies.
- Target incentive problems.
- Financial synergies.

We discuss each of these sources in turn.

Tax Motivations

Tax laws change substantially from year to year and differ from country to country. As a result, we can provide only a brief overview of the relevant tax issues in this chapter. Congress passed two very important tax acts during the 1980s which had important effects on the U.S. takeover market during that decade. These were the Tax Equity and Fiscal Responsibility Act of 1982 and the Tax Reform Act of 1986.

The Tax Equity and Fiscal Responsibility Act of 1982 and Basis Step-Up.   Of the major tax inducements to takeovers, the ability to step up the tax basis on acquired assets (i.e., increase their book values) became somewhat more attractive after the Tax Act of 1982. **Stepping up the basis** of the acquired firm's depreciable assets increases the depreciation tax shields of the assets, which in some cases creates substantial tax savings for the acquiring firm. One good example of this was the $2.6 billion acquisition of Electronic Data Systems by General Motors. As a result of this buyout, General Motors claimed a $2 billion dollar write-up of depreciable assets that produced a $400 million tax deduction annually for five years.

The Tax Reform Act of 1986 and Basis Step-Up.   The Tax Reform Act of 1986 specifies that firms that elect to write up the value of their depreciable assets are taxed on the increase in the tax basis. Under this tax law, for example, the $2 billion write-up of Electronic Data Systems' intangible assets would be considered taxable income in the year of the write-up. As a consequence, taxable income is realized sooner. For example, if General Motors were in the 50 percent tax bracket, it would pay an additional $1 billion in taxes in the year of the merger as a result of this write-up and would then reduce its taxes by $200 million in each of the next five years. Since this is equivalent to an interest-free loan to the IRS, the asset write-up is no longer attractive and, as a result, is rarely done. An exception might occur when the firm currently has no taxable income and has tax loss carry-forwards that it could potentially lose.

The Tax Gain from Leverage.   Additional tax savings arise in cases where the acquisitions are funded primarily with debt. The tax gain associated with these leverage-increasing combinations can be thought of as a financial synergy. As Chapter 13 discussed, a tax gain is associated with leverage because of the tax deductibility of debt interest payments. However, it is important to ask whether or not a takeover is required to accomplish this leverage increase before attributing this leverage-related tax gain to an acquisition.

The typical takeover results in increased leverage for several reasons. First, the combined firm is likely to be better diversified than the separate firms and thus is less likely to have financial difficulties or find itself with excess tax shields for any given level of debt financing. A second possibility is that the target and the bidder are underleveraged and use the takeover as a means of increasing their combined debt-to-equity ratio. The firms may have been underleveraged because of the incentive reasons discussed in Chapter 17 or, as Chapter 14 discussed, because of the personal tax costs associated with increasing leverage.

Taking Advantage of Otherwise Unusable Tax Losses: The Effect of the 1986 Act.
A second tax advantage that was associated with acquisitions in the past occurred when one of the two parties in a merger had past losses. When the firms are combined, the losses of the unprofitable firm become valuable tax shields that could be used to offset the taxes of the profitable firm. However, the acquiring firm can no longer use past losses of the acquired firm to offset its current and future profits, as it could prior to 1986.

We thus draw the following conclusion:

Result 19.2   Prior to the implementation of the Tax Reform Act of 1986, the U.S. Tax Code encouraged corporations to acquire other corporations. Taxes currently play a much less important role in motivating U.S. acquisitions. In some cases, however, mergers increase the combined capacity of merged firms to utilize tax-favored debt.

Operating Synergies

In order for mergers to generate operating synergies, the uniting of two firms must either improve productivity or cuts costs so that the cash flows of the combined firm exceed the combined cash flows of the individual firms. By definition, a target firm that provides such synergies is worth more to a potential acquirer than it is worth operating as an independent company.

Sources and Examples of Operating Synergies.   There are a number of potential sources of operating synergy. For example, a **vertical merger**—that is, a merger between a supplier and a customer—can eliminate various coordination and bargaining problems between the supplier and the customer.[2] DuPont's 1981 purchase of Conoco, for example, may have been motivated in part by DuPont's heavy use of oil for its petrochemicals. The gains from a **horizontal merger**, a merger between competitors, can include a less competitive product market as well as cost savings that occur when, for example, firms combine research and development facilities, combine sales forces, or dispose of underutilized computers and sales outlets.

For example, the Bristol-Myers's 1989 acquisition of Squibb which created the Bristol-Myers Squibb Company, allowed the merged firm to cut operating costs by combining jobs in sales and R&D to reduce their operating costs.[3] Another frequently mentioned synergy

---

[2]For a discussion of these coordination and bargaining problems, see Klein, Crawford, and Alchian (1978) and Grossman and Hart (1986).

[3]*The Wall Street Journal*, Feb. 9, 1990.

comes from combining distribution networks. On the announcement of Gillette's and Duracell's intention to merge, Charles R. Perrin, Duracell's chief executive, stated, "We were searching for ways to get broader distribution, and we've found our answer in Gillette." Gillette has a major presence in developing countries like China, India, and Brazil, and hopes to use its marketing presence there to sell Duracell batteries.[4]

Additional operating synergies arise when the merged firm can benefit from the ability to transfer resources from one division to another. For example, both RJR Nabisco and Philip Morris had extremely profitable tobacco businesses, but their future prospects were uncertain. Domestic demand was likely to fall in the future as the health hazards from smoking became more apparent. The magnitude of this future drop, however, was very uncertain. Offsetting this was a booming, but also uncertain, foreign demand for American cigarettes.

Although both companies believed that they had developed effective organizations, especially in marketing, they felt compelled to take steps to protect this organizational capital in the event of a sharp decline in cigarette demand. Both firms solved this problem through the purchase of packaged food companies, which also require effective marketing organizations—organizations that are similar to those of the tobacco companies. If it turned out that demand for tobacco increased substantially while demand for food products declined, a combined firm could easily transfer personnel from the packaged food division to the tobacco division. Likewise, if the demand for tobacco fell and the demand for packaged food increased, the reverse transfer could be initiated. As uncertainty increases, this option to transfer resources becomes increasingly valuable (see Chapter 11).

Measuring Operating Synergies.   Although there is substantial anecdotal evidence that operating synergies can be large, it is difficult to measure empirically the extent to which mergers have generated operating synergies, for reasons to be discussed shortly. Moreover, it is difficult to use the available empirical data to determine the extent to which value is created from operating synergies instead of other sources, such as tax savings or incentive improvements.

Management Incentive Issues and Takeovers

Chapter 17 described a number of ways in which the interests of managers can deviate from the interests of shareholders. Disciplinary takeovers are generally intended to correct these nonvalue-maximizing policies.

Disciplinary Takeovers and Leveraged Buyouts.   In the early 1980s, integrated oil producers spent roughly $20 per barrel to explore for new oil reserves (thus maintaining their large oil exploration activities) when proven oil reserves could in effect be bought by taking over existing firms for around $6 per barrel. For example, Gulf Oil, mentioned earlier, was spending over one-third of its oil and gas revenues on negative *NPV* oil exploration, causing Gulf's stock to trade at a price substantially below the value of its assets. In 1984 Chevron took over Gulf and the combined Gulf/Chevron exploration budget was cut substantially after the merger. In this case, the merger created value because it led to less oil exploration.

Disciplinary takeovers are usually hostile, often lead to the breakup of large diversified corporations, and result in job losses for a number of the target firm's top managers.

---

[4]*Boston Globe*, Sept. 13, 1996.

For these reasons, disciplinary takeovers are more controversial than synergy-motivated strategic acquisitions. Disciplinary takeovers are particularly controversial when the acquirer, often referred to as the **raider**, is a relatively thinly capitalized individual or firm seeking to acquire a much bigger enterprise using debt financing. These takeovers are generally structured as leveraged buyouts (LBOs).

LBO financing also has been used, albeit in a friendly way, by the top managers of firms who wish to buy their own firms and take them private. This type of buyout is referred to as a **management buyout (MBO)**. In contrast to the disciplinary takeover, the firm's top managers remain the same after an MBO.

In MBOs as well as in hostile LBOs that do not involve management, we do not observe a union of two firms, so there can be no synergies. The gain from these takeovers then has to come from either tax savings or management improvements. Proponents of LBOs argue that firm value can still be improved by changing management incentives, even when the top managers are not replaced. These proponents argue that it is the change in ownership rather than the change in the actual managers that creates value in these transactions.

The changes in ownership structure can result in dramatic changes in management incentives following LBOs. Specifically, executives who had previously owned less than 1 percent of the firm often find themselves owning more than 10 percent; with additional stock options, they have the opportunity to accumulate substantially more stock in the event that the firm does well. Although the potential gain to executives is clearly greater following an LBO, there also is much less protection on the downside. Given the high leverage ratio of the post-LBO firm, the margin of error is much lower. If the firm is not successful, it will soon be bankrupt and the top executives will lose everything. Hence, following LBOs, executives have a much greater incentive to make the firm more profitable.

An excellent example of an incentive problem that was corrected after an LBO was reported in the description of the RJR Nabisco LBO in *Barbarians at the Gate*. The head of the Nabisco unit, John Greeniaus, reportedly told Paul Raether, general partner at Kohlberg Kravis Roberts (KKR), that operating profits at Nabisco could be increased 40 percent if necessary. He argued that prior to the buyout there was no incentive to increase earnings more than 12 percent in any single year because his biggest incentive was to keep earnings predictable. As a result, money was spent on excess promotion and marketing to keep earnings down in good years—to provide slack—so that in bad years, the company wouldn't have to report large drops in earnings.[5]

Incentives and Wealth Transfers.   When firms are acquired, losers as well as winners emerge. For example, when KKR took over RJR Nabisco in a leveraged buyout, existing RJR Nabisco bonds lost 16 percent of their value because of the perceived increase in the probability of their default. Employees, however, are often the more visible losers in takeovers. Critics of these takeovers have argued that a large part of the observed gain in many hostile takeovers comes at the expense of the target's employees, either through layoffs or salary reductions. For example, Shleifer and Summers (1988) calculated that almost the entire premium offered by Carl Icahn in his takeover of TWA could be justified by the salary reductions imposed on TWA's union employees.

The relation between hostile takeovers and employee layoffs may simply reflect the need for a different type of manager at different stages of a corporation's growth. To

---

[5]Bryan Burroughs and John Helyar, *Barbarians at the Gate: The Fall of RJR Nabisco* (New York: HarperCollins, 1993).

build an effective organization, a growing firm requires managers who are good team players and who have a sincere interest in helping other individuals develop the skills needed to make the firm prosper. In most cases, however, the individuals best suited for nurturing and developing others are not particularly well suited to fire these same employees when downsizing is necessary. "Nice-guy," team-playing managers will find themselves recipients of unwanted takeover offers as a consequence of their reluctance to downsize their organizations. When these hostile bids are successful, "more ruthless" managers (e.g., Carl Icahn at TWA or Frank Lorenzo at Eastern Airlines[6]), are better suited to carry out the task of shrinking the organization.

Investors recognize that most managers are reluctant to cut jobs, and they bid up the stock prices of firms that bring in CEOs with a reputation for cutting costs by cutting jobs. For example, when it was announced that Albert Dunlap was hired in July 1996 to be CEO of Sunbeam, Sunbeam's stock price increased by almost 40 percent. Dunlap earned the nickname "Chainsaw" Dunlap for his ruthless job cutting in eight different restructurings. When Dunlap was previously CEO of Scott Paper, over 11,000 jobs were cut in 1994 and 1995, and the firm's stock price more than doubled.[7]

It should be noted, however, that policymakers and journalists may have overemphasized the relation between takeovers and job losses. First, many takeovers resulted in more efficient organizations and increased employment. Second, the downsizing that occurred subsequent to many hostile takeovers also occurred at firms that were not taken over. Indeed, at Scott Paper, the job cuts occurred before, not after, their takeover by Kimberly Clark. Hence, one should not necessarily view the takeovers as the cause of the job losses. Instead, takeovers should be viewed as one means by which inefficient organizations downsize.

Bidder Incentive Problems.   Takeovers can be a symptom as well as a cure for managerial incentive problems. Recall from Chapter 17 that managers often have the incentive to take on projects that benefit them personally even when they do not improve stock prices. For example, managers in declining industries may want to protect their jobs by acquiring firms in industries with better long-term prospects. In addition, some managers may simply want to manage bigger enterprises, and the takeover market may be the most expedient way to accomplish this goal.

Lang, Stulz, and Walkling (1991) suggested that firms acquiring other firms for non-value-maximizing reasons are characterized by low stock prices relative to their book values and cash flows. Such bidder firms are currently profitable, but their low market-to-book ratios (as well as related ratios) indicate that they are not expected to do particularly well in the future. Lang, Stulz, and Walkling found that when firms with these characteristics announce their intentions to acquire another firm, their stock prices generally decline. They interpret these stock price declines to mean that the market considers the acquisitions to be either unwise or based on management incentives that are inconsistent with value maximization.

Mitchell and Lehn (1990) also examined what they call "bad bidders," which they identify as firms that experience large stock price declines when they announce plans for a major acquisition. They find that a large number of these bad bidders subsequently became targets of disciplinary takeovers. Mitchell and Lehn argue that one motivation of takeovers is to oust managers who have a tendency to make bad acquisitions. Bhagat,

---

[6]See Chapter 16 for further discussion of Eastern Airlines.
[7]Scott Paper was subsequently taken over by Kimberly Clark at the end of 1995.

Shleifer, and Vishny (1990) showed that the target in many of these disciplinary take-overs is broken up and some of the former bad acquisitions are sold off.

Financial Synergies

A common argument in support of diversification is that lowering the risk of a firm's stock increases its attractiveness to investors and thereby reduces the firm's cost of capital. However, both the Capital Asset Pricing Model (CAPM) and the Arbitrage Pricing Theory (APT) suggest that investors are unlikely to be willing to pay a premium for the reduced risk of a diversified firm, since they can easily form a well-diversified portfolio on their own by holding the stocks of a number of different firms in different industries (see Chapters 5 and 6). Hence, for a diversification strategy to increase the value of a firm's shares, it must do more than simply reduce risk. Diversification must create either operating synergies or financial synergies.

The discussion of optimal capital structure in the previous chapters provides some intuition about possible financial synergies. We have already discussed the financial synergies associated with the tax gains to leverage. Since diversification reduces the risk of bankruptcy for any given level of debt, it can increase the amount of debt in the firm's optimal capital structure, which in turn can lower the firm's cost of capital.

Financial synergies also can arise because of the personal taxes on cash distributions (see Chapter 14). Consider, for example, Joe's Pizza House, which is generating significant cash but has no investment opportunities, and Bob's Biotech, which has excellent investment opportunities but no internally generated cash. With perfect capital markets, capital will flow costlessly from Joe, who has only negative *NPV* projects, to Bob, who has projects with high *NPV*s. Personal taxes, however, significantly impede this flow since the dividends paid from Joe's profits are taxed before they are reinvested in Bob's Biotech. These personal taxes can be avoided if the two firms merge to form Bob and Joe's Biotech Pizza.

Information and incentive problems provide additional impediments to the flow of capital from Joe to Bob (see Chapters 15–18). Because of these problems, firms with investment requirements that significantly exceed internally generated funds may have to pass up positive net present value projects, while cash-rich firms tend to overinvest, taking on negative net present value projects. This suggests, at least in theory, that there is a potential to create value by combining the cash-rich firms having excess investment capital with the cash-starved firms that are underinvesting. This is illustrated in Example 19.1.

Example 19.1:   The Advantage of Internal Capital Markets

TWT Technologies, based on proprietary technology that it has developed, has an investment opportunity that requires it to raise $100 million in capital. TWT Technologies is currently priced at $22 a share. However, John Jacobs, its CEO and largest shareholder, believes that this technology will be very successful and that the company's shares will be worth $40 a share when it demonstrates the technology publicly. Unfortunately, because competitors may attempt to clone the technology after seeing it demonstrated, TWT cannot demonstrate the technology prior to raising the capital. What are the company's financing options?

Answer: It clearly is not attractive to TWT to issue stock at $22 a share if Jacobs believes the shares will soon be worth $40. However, the firm may be too risky to issue debt, and its ability to license the technology later will be more limited if the firm has difficulties meeting its debt obligations. Perhaps, its best opportunity would be to find a cash-rich firm with which to merge.

Result 19.3   Conglomerates can provide funding for investment projects that independent (smaller) firms would not have been able to fund using outside capital markets. To the extent that positive *NPV* projects receive funding they would not have otherwise received, conglomerates create value.

Example 19.1 and Result 19.3 suggest that the capital allocation process within a firm can allocate capital more efficiently than outside capital markets when firms have proprietary information that they do not wish to disclose. TWT Technologies' possession of proprietary information suggests another advantage associated with diversification. An independent firm like TWT Technologies might be obligated to reveal information to its investors.[8] However, the disclosure of information to investors also reveals it to competitors, which could put the firm at a competitive disadvantage. Even if the proprietary information is not revealed directly, competitors can certainly observe the firm's financial performance, enticing new competitors when the performance is exceptional. This problem would be much less severe if TWT were a small division of a large conglomerate, where proprietary information can be more easily hidden.

Is an Acquisition Required to Realize Tax Gains, Operating Synergies, Incentive Gains, or Diversification?

To evaluate the benefits of an acquisition, a financial analyst needs to do more than simply compare the costs and benefits of combining two firms with the current situation where the two firms have no relationship. The executives in the two companies also should investigate whether the gains from combining the firms can be achieved more efficiently in some other way. For example, to estimate the tax gains from the increased leverage associated with an acquisition, it is important to account for the possibility that the firm could increase leverage in another way, such as by repurchasing its shares.

Similarly, one must consider whether achieving operating synergies between two firms requires them to merge. For example, the executives at Duracell and Gillette should have considered whether the benefits of having Duracell use Gillette's distributors outside the United States required a merger of the firms. A possible alternative might be some kind of joint marketing agreement that allows Gillette to sell batteries through its international distribution channels and to receive a commission on each battery sold.

Of course, writing a long-term joint marketing agreement can be complicated because of the large number of unforeseen circumstances that could arise in the future. The contract would have to specify what would happen if another company devised a better battery that Gillette also might want to sell. This would certainly hurt Duracell, but Gillette may not want to preclude such possibilities. Similarly, Gillette might be concerned that, after investing resources into promoting Duracell batteries, Duracell may find that it can market its batteries without Gillette. To protect against this contingency, Gillette could insist on a long-term contract that makes it the exclusive marketing agent for Duracell. On the other hand, Duracell might be concerned about Gillette's incentive to expend the appropriate level of effort to market the batteries once Duracell has signed a contract that gives it no alternative.

In some cases, these incentive problems are best solved with a very explicit contract that specifies how both parties are to act under all relevant contingencies. In other cases,

---

[8] Managers may want to reveal information to investors even if their firms do not want to raise new capital. First, managerial compensation may be linked to the firm's stock price. Second, managers can be sued for failing to reveal information.

however, it is impossible to know all the relevant contingencies in advance, making it impossible to write a contract that satisfies the concerns of both parties. In such cases, a merger may be preferred.

We should stress that a merger does not necessarily solve all incentive problems. The Duracell people and the Gillette people may still bicker about who gets credit for battery sales in Brazil after a Duracell/Gillette merger; such conflicts within a firm can create the same costs and conflicts that arise between firms.[9] In addition, as we will discuss in next two sections, additional costs and benefits associated with combining firms also must be taken into account.

19.4 The Disadvantages of Mergers and Acquisitions

The preceding section described a number of benefits associated with mergers and acquisitions, but there can also be offsetting disadvantages. The prevailing view of mergers has changed substantially over time. Investors and analysts have become more skeptical about potential gains from M & A and more aware of the potential downside of combining two firms. This change in the prevailing view is especially true for the pure conglomerate acquisitions. In the 1960s, conglomerate acquisitions were in fashion and acquiring firms were rewarded with rising stock prices. The kind of logic illustrated in Example 19.1 was generally accepted by the market. However, for the reasons discussed below, diversifying takeovers have been viewed much more negatively since the 1980s.

Conglomerates Can Misallocate Capital

Combining two firms can destroy value if the managers of the combined firm use the added flexibility to transfer resources between the two firms to subsidize money-losing lines of businesses that alternatively could be shut down. Subsidization of this sort is likely to occur if the firm's top management is reluctant to cut jobs or has other reasons to keep a losing business in operation. For example, the CEO may not want to admit that a past decision was a mistake. Hence, the information asymmetries and incentive problems that can lead financial markets to allocate capital inefficiently also create even greater problems when managers allocate capital internally. Robert D. Kennedy, chairman of Union Carbide, a company that was involved in a number of conglomerate acquisitions, summarized this point as follows:

> All that stuff about balancing the cash generators and the cash users sounded great on paper. But it never worked. When corporate management gets into the business of allocating resources between businesses crying for cash, it makes mistakes.[10]

Mergers Can Reduce the Information Contained in Stock Prices

When two firms combine, there is generally one less publicly traded stock. This can create a cost if stock prices convey information that helps managers to allocate resources. For example, McDonalds may have interpreted the rise in its stock price in the early 1990s to improving opportunities in the growing economies of Southeast Asia. This "stock market opinion" might have led McDonalds to expand its efforts in that part of

---

[9]See Grossman and Hart (1986) for further discussion along these lines.
[10]"Learning to Live with Leverage," *Business Week,* Nov. 7, 1988.

the world. However, if McDonalds were instead part of a large conglomerate, its executives would not have been able to observe market prices and would have had to make their investment decisions based on more subjective information.

As Chapter 17 noted, the information from stock prices also is useful for compensating and evaluating management. We observed that it is much easier to tie the compensation of Compaq's CEO to his performance than it is to tie pay to performance for the head of IBM's PC division because there is no observable stock price for IBM's PC division. In addition to providing motivation, Compaq's stock price provides a signal to shareholders of their CEO's effectiveness. In contrast, IBM's stock price contains much less information about the success of any of its individual divisions.

A Summary of the Gains and Costs of Diversification

The past two sections have covered the advantages and disadvantages of purely diversifying takeovers. These are summarized in the following result:

Result 19.4   The advantages of diversification can be described as follows:

- Diversification enhances the flexibility of the organization.
- The internal capital market avoids some of the information problems inherent in an external capital market.
- Diversification reduces the probability of bankruptcy for any given level of debt and increases the firm's debt capacity.
- Competitors find it more difficult to uncover proprietary information from diversified firms.
- Diversification is advantageous if it allows the firm to utilize its organization more effectively.

The disadvantages of diversification can be described as follows:

- Diversification can eliminate a valuable source of information which may, among other things, make it difficult to compensate the division heads of large diversified firms efficiently.
- Managers may find it difficult to cut back optimally on losing divisions when they can subsidize the losers out of the profits from their winners.

19.5 Empirical Evidence on Takeover Gains for Non-LBO Takeovers

A number of academics and policymakers have asked whether, on average, mergers create value. In other words, are the various financial and operating synergies discussed in this chapter real, or are purported synergies merely a convenient rationale offered by managers attempting to expand their empires? This section reviews a number of studies that attempt to measure the value created by mergers.

Three types of studies have sought to determine the extent to which non-LBO takeovers are value enhancing. The first type analyzes stock returns around the time of the announcements of tender offers and merger offers, and it attributes the gains and losses in stock prices to expected gains associated with combining the firms, improving management, or identifying undervalued assets. The second type of study looks more specifically at whether diversified firms are either more or less valuable than less diversified firms. The third type of study examines accounting data to determine the change, if any, in the profitability of the target firm's business after it has been absorbed by the bidder.

Stock Returns around the Time of Takeover Announcements

Stock market studies look at the returns of both bidding firms and target firms. The sum of the two returns determines whether mergers create value.

Returns of Target Firms.   Stock market evidence strongly indicates that target shareholders gain from a successful takeover. This is not surprising given that target shareholders require a premium as an inducement to sell their shares to the acquiring firm. Jensen and Ruback (1983) reported that, on average, target shares increase in price from about 16 to 30 percent around the date of the announcement of a tender offer. More recent evidence by Jarrell, Brickley, and Netter (1988) found that these returns increased substantially during the 1980s to an average of about 53 percent. Jensen and Ruback (1983) reported that the average return to target firms in negotiated merger offers is only about 10 percent.

Returns of Bidder Firms.   Returns to bidders around tender offer announcements are sometimes positive and sometimes negative, and the average returns vary considerably over time. Jarrell and Poulsen (1989) reported that the announcement return to bidders in tender offers dropped from a statistically significant 5 percent gain in the 1960s to an insignificant 1 percent loss in the 1980s. This finding can be attributed in part to regulations that are disadvantageous to the bidder and perhaps to increased competition among bidders for specific targets. One also can interpret this finding as an indication that either the number of bad takeovers has been increasing or bidders have been paying too much in recent years.

Summary of Bidder and Target Returns.   Adding the bidder and target returns implies that, on average, there is a net gain to shareholders around the time of the merger announcement. Bradley, Desai, and Kim (1988) found that successful tender offers increased the combined values of the merging firms an average of 7.4 percent or $117 million (stated in 1984 dollars), which suggests that mergers are, on average, value enhancing.

Result 19.5 summarizes how stock prices react at the time of takeover announcements.

Result 19.5   Stock price reactions to takeover bids can be described as follows:

- The stock prices of target firms almost always react favorably to merger and tender offer bids.
- The bidder's stock price sometimes goes up and sometimes goes down, depending on the circumstances.
- The combined market values of the shares of the target and bidder go up, on average, around the time of the announced bids.

Interpreting the Stock Return Evidence.   As Chapter 18 discussed, the stock price reaction on the announcement of a corporate decision cannot be attributed solely to how the decision affects the firm's profitability. The stock returns of the bidder at the time of the announcement of the bid may tell us more about how the market is reassessing the bidder's business than it does about the value of the acquisition. Indeed, stock prices may react favorably to the announcement of an acquisition, even when investors believe the acquisition harms shareholders.

For example, a tender offer, especially one for cash, may indicate that the bidding firm has been highly profitable in the past, given that it had accumulated the financial ability to make the offer. Hence, the bidding firm's stock price may increase even if the market views the acquisition as a negative *NPV* project. Indeed, stock prices react very favorably to a firm purchasing its own stock because of the information this decision conveys, even though a share repurchase is a zero *NPV* investment. Given that the stock price reaction around the time of the announcement of an offer for another firm's stock is generally much weaker, one might conclude that the market, on average, views these acquisitions as negative *NPV* investments.

Stock Returns and the Means of Payment.   The way in which a bidder pays for the target can have a major effect on how the bidder's stock reacts to the announced bid. Franks, Harris, and Mayer (1989) and Travlos (1987) demonstrated that average bidder returns differ significantly, depending on whether the bidder offers cash or shares of its own stock in exchange for the target's shares. For example, Travlos found that in U.S. acquisitions financed by an exchange of stock, the bidding firm's stock prices fell 1.47 percent, on average, on the two days around the offer's announcement. Franks, Harris, and Mayer found a similar negative return for equity-financed bidders in both the United States and the United Kingdom. Both studies found that the market price of the bidder reacted favorably to announcements of cash acquisitions, but the returns, on average, were quite small. The returns on the two days around the announcement of a cash offer, as reported by Travlos, were only marginally different from zero (0.24 percent) and the monthly returns around the announcements of cash offers reported in Franks, Harris, and Mayer were 2.0 percent in the United States and 0.7 percent in the United Kingdom.

Chapter 18 provides two explanations for why bidders who make cash offers experience higher returns. Bidders offer stock when they believe their own stock is overvalued, but they issue cash when they believe their own stock is undervalued. In addition, a cash offer may signal that the bidder is able to obtain the financial backing of a bank or other financial institution. A stock offer may then signal that the banks refused to provide the bidder with financial backing, reflecting badly on the bidder's financial strength.

Result 19.6   The bidder's stock price reacts more favorably, on average, when the bidder makes a cash offer rather than an offer to exchange stock. This may reflect the relatively negative information about the bidder's existing business signaled by the offer to exchange stock.

Information Conveyed about the Target.   A bidding firm does not only reveal information about itself when bidding for another company. If the financial markets believe that a bidder has special information about a target, then a bid also is likely to convey information to the market about the value of the target as a stand-alone company. One can obtain insights about the extent to which special information about a target is revealed by examining stock price reactions when offers are terminated.

Share prices tend to decline subsequent to the failure of an initial bid, but the prices generally stay considerably above the stock price for the target that existed before the bid [see Bradley (1980), Dodd (1980), and Bradley, Desai and Kim (1983)]. This evidence could indicate that the bidders have some special information because, if the gains were all due to either improved management or synergies, the stock price theoretically should drop back to its original level after a failed bid.

Bradley, Desai, and Kim suggested a different interpretation. They pointed out that the relatively small decline in share prices when initial bids fail may not occur because the initial bid signaled that the firm was undervalued, but because most failed targets do eventually get taken over. Indeed, a failed bid is often due to a better offer; therefore, the stock price may eventually exceed the price level attained after the initial acquisition announcement. The authors found that one to five years after the first price-raising bid the average share prices of targets of unsuccessful tender offers that were not subsequently acquired by other firms returned to the level that existed before the initial offer. This would suggest that the bidder generally had no special information and that undervalued assets were not the motivation for the takeovers.

In the Bradley, Desai, and Kim sample, only 26 of 371 target firms (about 7 percent) were not acquired once they were "put into play," making it difficult to make strong inferences about the motivation of the initial bidders—whether the bidders felt they could actually improve the values of the firms or believed that the firms were undervalued. The 7 percent of firms not ultimately acquired may have realized negative returns following the offer for a number of different reasons. For example, fighting the takeover may have been very costly and destructive of firm value. Accordingly, a drop in stock prices may have occurred even for well-managed firms. It also is possible that these target firms were not eventually taken over because their assets were later found to be less valuable than the acquiring firm originally thought. This is not inconsistent with the hypothesis that the 93 percent that were taken over were undervalued.

Empirical Evidence on the Gains to Diversification

Whether there are gains associated with takeovers depends, in part, on whether diversification helps or hurts firm values. A number of empirical studies have documented that U.S. corporations increased their level of diversification from the early 1960s to the mid-1970s, in many cases through acquisitions. Starting in the late 1970s, U.S. firms decreased their level of diversification and continued to do so throughout the 1980s and 1990s, as many of the earlier acquisitions were spun off or divested.[11]

A number of empirical studies have examined whether diversification increases or decreases firm values. Lang and Stulz (1994) and Berger and Ofek (1995) found that the market places lower values on more diversified firms. Comment and Jarrell (1995), who examined changes in diversification during the 1980s, found that firms destroy value when they diversify and create value when they sell off divisions and become more focused. Servaes (1996) determined that the market's attitude toward diversification changes over time. In contrast with the earlier findings of diversification discounts in the 1980s, Servaes found no significant valuation penalty associated with diversification in the 1970s. However, he did find significant diversification penalties in the 1960s, as well as the 1980s.

A study by Morck, Shleifer, and Vishny (1990) provided evidence consistent with the change in attitudes about diversification during the 1970s and 1980s.[12] Their study related the stock returns of bidders around the announcement dates of acquisition bids to characteristics of both the bidder and the target, measuring the extent to which the firms were in related lines of business. They found that bidder stock returns for diversifying acquisitions (i.e., unrelated firms) were lower in the 1980s, when they were negative, than they were in the 1970s. For nondiversifying acquisitions, however, bidder stock returns increased somewhat in the 1980s. The difference in the announcement price returns for diversifying and nondiversifying acquisitions was only 1.31 percent in the 1970s, but it was 6.97 percent in the 1980s.

---

[11]See Comment and Jarrell (1995) and Servaes (1996).

[12]A related study by Matsusaka (1993) found that the stock prices of conglomerates responded positively in the 1960s when they announced acquisitions, but responded negatively to similar announcements in the 1980s.

Accounting Studies

Because stock price reactions reflect the information conveyed by an offer, it is difficult to use stock returns to draw inferences about the operating synergies or the economic efficiency generated by a merger. For this reason, some researchers have examined accounting data to draw inferences about the underlying economic impact of a merger.

Evidence of Negative Postmerger Performance.   In their comprehensive study, Ravenscraft and Scherer (1987) investigated over 5,000 mergers occurring between 1950 and 1975. Using accounting data for each of the different lines of business in which the firms were involved, they calculated and compared the postmerger performances of acquired firms with the performance of nonacquired control groups in the same industry. On average, they found significant declines in the postmerger profitability of the acquired portions of those firms.

The Wealth Transfer Interpretation.   The evidence in the Ravenscraft and Scherer study is inconsistent with the view that mergers create value. However, the interpretation of these results has been the subject of much disagreement. First, the validity of the results depends on the accuracy of the accounting numbers, which have been questioned by a number of authors. Second, the mergers may be creating value even if the targets appear to be doing poorly after the takeover. This will be the case if enough wealth is transferred from the acquired firm to the acquirer. For example, Texas Air acquired Eastern Airlines in 1986 for $600 million. Subsequent to the Eastern bankruptcy, some of Eastern's creditors suggested that wealth was transferred from Eastern to Texas Air. After only four months, Eastern sold a number of jumbo jets (at what some considered to be favorable prices) to Continental (also owned by Texas Air) and sold Eastern's reservation system to the parent firm. Finally, the accounting performance of acquired firms will appear to be unfavorable if the targets are generally firms with poor prospects. Although these firms perform poorly subsequent to being taken over, they might have performed even worse had they remained independent.

Tobin's *q* and the Interpretation of Mediocre Accounting Performance.   Hasbrouck (1985) offered support for the view that targets frequently are firms in decline. Hasbrouck assessed each firm's **Tobin's *q*,** the ratio of the market value of the stock to the replacement value of the firm's assets, which can be viewed as a measure of managerial performance. Well-managed firms have a high Tobin's *q* value; poorly managed firms have a low Tobin's *q*. Hasbrouck found that target companies have relatively low values of Tobin's *q*, which suggests that target shares are often selling at a value below their replacement cost. In addition, several studies [see, for example, Asquith (1983)], have found that targets tend to experience negative risk-adjusted returns in the years prior to the merger. Hence, relative to either their past stock prices or their replacement values, target share prices are low at the time of the initial offer, indicating that investors were somewhat pessimistic about the target's prospects as a stand-alone entity. This suggests that the subsequent mediocre postmerger accounting performance of firms may have occurred even if the acquisition had not taken place.

More Recent Evidence.   Healy, Palepu, and Ruback (1992) examined 50 large mergers between 1979 and 1983 and found improvements in both sales and profits of the combined firms following the mergers. This evidence suggests that the mergers of the early 1980s may have been quite different from those of the 1960s and 1970s examined by

Ravenscraft and Scherer. As mentioned earlier, the motivation for many of the mergers of the 1960s and 1970s was diversification, and there can be efficiency losses associated with diversification. However, diversification was a less important motivation for mergers in the 1980s, a decade when many takeovers were motivated by the potential gains from improving managerial incentives. The Healy, Palepu, and Ruback evidence suggests that in many cases productivity did improve as a result of the takeovers.

19.6 Empirical Evidence on the Gains from Leveraged Buyouts (LBOs)

Starting in the late 1970s, a number of large publicly traded firms were taken over in highly leveraged transactions that transformed the public companies into privately held firms. The announcements of those LBOs generally resulted in dramatic increases in the stock price of the target firm, which suggests that LBOs create substantial value. However, because these LBOs did not involve the combination of two firms, the kind of synergies discussed previously do not apply. Most analysts point to improved management incentives as the motivation of LBOs.

How Leveraged Buyouts Affect Stock Prices

A variety of studies have examined the premiums offered in LBOs as well as the stock returns when the LBO transactions are first announced. These studies find that the average price paid in an LBO was 40 to 60 percent above the market price of the stocks one to two months prior to the offers. Around the time of the announcements of these offers, the stock price increased about 20 percent, on average.

Characteristics of Higher Premium Targets.   Lehn and Poulsen (1989) found that higher premiums were offered for firms with high cash flows, relatively low growth opportunities, and high tax liabilities relative to their equity values. The higher premiums for the high-cash flow/low-growth firms support the idea that there are larger gains associated with levering up firms with these characteristics (e.g., leverage reduces their tendency to overinvest). The relation between the tax liabilities and the premium suggests that part of the tax gain from the LBO transaction is passed along to the original shareholders.

Competing Bids.   The presence of competing bids also affects the premium offered in LBOs. Lowenstein (1985) studied 28 LBOs, finding that those with less than three competing bids received an average premium of 50 percent while those with more than three competing bids received an average premium of 69 percent. Of the 15 large LBOs examined by Amihud (1990), the 6 without competing bids offered an average premium of 30.7 percent while those with competition offered an average premium of 52.2 percent.

Cash Flow Changes Following Leveraged Buyouts

A number of studies have examined operating changes following LBOs. These studies, summarized in Exhibit 19.4 on page 686, examined changes in a number of variables that provide insights about how LBOs affect a firm's performance.

The results summarized in Exhibit 19.4 indicate that the magnitude of the cash flow improvements following LBOs declined in the latter half of the 1980s. For example, Kaplan (1989) found that from 1980 to 1986, cash flows increased, on average, by

EXHIBIT 19.4   Summary of Changes in Firm Operations after LBOs*

Variable	Kaplan (1989)	Muscarella and Vetsuypens (1990)	Opler (1993)	Smith (1990)
Cash flow/sales	20.1%	23.5%	8.8%	18%
Sales per employee	NA	3.1%	16.7%	18%
Taxes	NA	NA	−90.5%	−80%
Investment/sales	−31.6%	−11.4%	−46.7%	−25%
Employees	0.9%	−0.6%	−0.7%	−22%
R&D/sales	NA	NA	0.0%	−75%
Time period studied	1980–86	1976–87	1986–89	1976–86
Number of LBOs	37	43	46	18
Window in years (before, after)	(−1, 2)	Variable	Variable	(−1, 2)

NA means statistic not available or not computed.
*Expressed as a percent increase or decrease.

20.1 percent following an LBO. However, Opler (1993) found an average improvement in cash flows of only 8.8 percent for LBOs initiated between 1986 and 1989. One explanation for this decline in the performance of LBOs is that the success of the earlier deals attracted a number of new investors, resulting in "too much money chasing too few good deals," which in turn led to buyouts of firms with less potential for improvement.

Additional evidence suggests that LBOs occurring in later years were priced higher and were more highly levered, leading to much higher default rates on LBO debt. Kaplan and Stein (1993) found that *none* of the 24 LBOs in their sample initiated between 1980 and 1983 subsequently defaulted on their debt. However, defaults claimed 46.7 percent of the LBOs initiated in 1986, 30.0 percent of those initiated in 1987, 16.1 percent of those initiated in 1988, and 20.0 percent of those initiated in 1989. Despite their high default rates, the firms that initiated these later LBOs still tended to show improvements in productivity. In many cases, however, the productivity gains were not sufficient to justify their high prices and the firms did not generate sufficient cash flows to pay off the high levels of debt incurred in the LBOs.

Productivity Increases Following LBOs.   Exhibit 19.4, which summarizes four LBO studies, provides evidence that at least part of the post-LBO increase in cash flows is due to increased productivity. The three studies that measured the average change in the value of sales per employee (labor productivity) found that labor productivity increases after LBOs. A study by Lichtenberg and Siegel (1990), using plant-level data, provides additional evidence about the sources of productivity improvements. They documented significant post-LBO reductions in the ratio of white-collar to blue-collar labor, reflecting perhaps a reduction in excess overhead. In addition, Smith (1990) found strong evidence that working capital is reduced after LBOs.

The Direction of Causation for the LBO Cash Flow Improvement.   The increase in cash flows following LBOs may not solely reflect improvements resulting from the LBOs. Perhaps firms that undergo leveraged buyouts would have shown similar improvements without the LBOs. Managers and LBO sponsors are unlikely to consider an LBO of a firm for which business prospects are forecasted to be unfavorable. Therefore, firms that undergo LBOs are likely to experience subsequent increases in their cash flows even without productivity improvements. While some of the observed increase in the cash flows of LBOs probably can be explained by the selection process of LBO candidates, we are unaware of any convincing evidence on this.

Cost Deferral as an Explanation for the LBO Cash Flow Improvement.   Another explanation for the observed increase in cash flows following LBOs is that higher leverage ratios provide managers with an incentive to increase cash flows in the short run at the expense of their long-run cash flows (see Chapter 15). Critics of leveraged buyouts say that after initiating a leveraged buyout, firms improve their cash flows in the short run by deferring maintenance, cutting R&D, and reducing advertising and promotion budgets. If these actions were the prime cause of the observed increase in cash flows, then one would expect the increase to be reversed later. Although we believe that some of the increase in cash flows can be explained in this way, we again are unaware of any convincing evidence that suggests that part of the short-term gain in cash flows come at the expense of long-term cash flows.

Smith (1990), Lichtenberg and Siegel (1990), and Opler (1993) found that post-LBO research and development expenditures do not generally decline. However, this may not be particularly relevant since most firms that have done LBOs belong to industries that conduct little R&D. Smith (1990) also found no significant reductions in advertising or maintenance following LBOs, but she is cautious about interpreting these results because of the limited size of her sample.

Result 19.7   On average, cash flows of firms improve following leveraged buyouts. Three possible explanations for these improvements are:

- Productivity gains.
- Initiation of LBOs by firms with improving prospects.
- The incentives of leveraged firms to accelerate cash flows, sometimes at the expense of long-run cash flows.

While we expect all three factors to contribute to the observed increase in cash flows, existing empirical evidence suggests that a major part of the increase is due to productivity gains.

19.7 Valuing Acquisitions

Evaluating a potential merger candidate requires a great deal of care. These acquisitions generally are very large transactions which have important effects on the operating strategy and the financial structure of the acquiring firm.

A number of firms now have "M&A" departments devoted entirely to discovering and analyzing acquisition candidates. Evaluating a potential acquisition is similar in most respects to analyzing the net present value of any other investment project a firm may be considering. Hence, the techniques discussed in Chapters 9 through 12 also apply to evaluating acquisition candidates. There are, however, some subtle differences. Most importantly, publicly traded acquisition candidates have an observable stock price that provides an estimate of the market's evaluation of the present value of the firm's cash flows. This information allows the acquiring firm to estimate more accurately the present value of the cash flows from a potential acquisition than it can for most other investment projects.

Valuing Synergies

Obviously, an analyst cannot rely exclusively on a potential acquisition's current stock price to determine the company's value. An acquiring firm will have to offer a premium over the target company's current stock price to purchase the firm, indicating that there has to be additional value created by combining the firms. In other words, there must be synergies that make the value of the target to the acquirer greater than the market value of the target on its own. The present value of the synergies must be added to the value of the firm's cash flows, given its current operations, to arrive at the present value of the acquisition.

In many cases, these synergies arise because of a reduction in the fixed costs of the combined firm. If these cost savings occur with certainty or, equivalently, are determined independently of the market portfolio's return (assuming the CAPM holds), then valuing the target is straightforward, as Example 19.2 illustrates.

Example 19.2:   Valuing Isolated Industries

Isolated Industries is currently selling for $22 a share and has 1 million shares outstanding. Since analysts do not expect the firm to be a takeover target, $22 a share is also its current operating value. However, United Technologies is considering the acquisition of Isolated Industries. It believes that by combining sales forces, it can eliminate 10 salesmen at a savings of $500,000 per year. They expect this savings to be permanent and certain. If the discount rate is 10 percent, how much is Isolated Industries worth to United Technologies?

Answer: The present value of the perpetual savings from combining the sales forces is $5 million (= $500,000/.1) or $5 per share. Hence, United Technologies would be willing to pay up to $27 per share for Isolated Industries.

Example 19.2 was simple because it assumed that the synergies were certain and thus quite easy to value. The example also assumed that the firm's stock price could be used to obtain a value for Isolated Industries as a stand-alone entity which, in general, will not be the case. The target's stock price will exceed the present value of the firm's future cash flows, given its current operating structure, if it reflects the possibility that the firm may eventually be taken over at a premium. Assuming risk neutrality and a zero discount rate, we can express the firm's current stock price as:

Current stock price = Current operating value
        + (Expected takeover premium) × (Takeover probability)

Equivalently, the current operating value of the firm can be expressed as:

Current operating value = Current stock price
        − (Expected takeover premium) × (Takeover probability)

A Guide to the Valuation of Synergies

Valuing acquisitions draws upon the techniques for evaluating real investment projects described in Chapters 9 to 12. However, acquisitions tend to be much larger than the capital investments that firms typically undertake, so firms should go into more depth in their valuation. They should evaluate a variety of scenarios and consider the various embedded options that exist in most firms (see Chapter 11). We suggest that acquiring firms take the following steps to evaluate prospective targets.

Step 1: Value the Target as a Stand-Alone Firm.   Valuing the target as a stand-alone entity provides the analyst with a useful reality check for determining the value created by the acquisition. Such a valuation requires estimates of future cash flows and the appropriate rates for discounting the cash flows. The value obtained in this manner should be compared with the target firm's stock price.

Step 2: Calibrate the Valuation Model.   The analyst needs to explain any difference between the estimated value of the target and the target's preacquisition stock price. As mentioned above, stock prices may reflect takeover probabilities and takeover premiums as well as the stand-alone value of the target. Also, stock prices may not incorporate proprietary information that the acquiring firm's analysts may have obtained about the target's asset values during the course of their investigations. In many cases, especially in friendly takeovers, the acquiring firm has access to information that is unavailable to other investors. For example, the target's management may provide proprietary information when negotiating a selling price. The acquirer also may have come across new information in the course of its own investigation. When buying an entire company, the importance of collecting accurate information is greater than it is when buying even large numbers of shares. Hence, it is plausible that the acquirer might value the target better than the financial markets.

If the acquiring firm's analysts believe they do not have superior information, and the difference between their estimated value of the target and the target stock price cannot be explained by information about a possible takeover, they must conclude that their valuation is flawed. In other words, analysts are valuing the firm using assumptions about future cash flows and discount rates that differ from the assumptions implied by market prices. At this point, the analysts will have to revise their assumptions about cash flows and discount rates. Getting these assumptions right at this stage of the analysis is important because these assumptions also may be used to value the synergies.

Step 3: Value the Synergies.   To evaluate what the target is worth to the acquiring firm, analysts must value the synergies associated with combining the target and the acquirer. Doing this requires estimates of the cash flows generated because of the synergies along with the appropriate discount rates. To simplify the analysis, assume that some synergies are virtually certain while others are risky. For example, synergies that come from tax savings or reductions in fixed costs are often of a lower-risk category—while those related to increased sales or reductions in variable costs should be related to the risk of either the acquirer or the target, or perhaps both.

The future cash flows and the discount rates used in the stand-alone valuation model are likely to be used in valuing risky synergies. For example, to value a 10 percent increase in the target's cash flows that will be generated for the first five years following a takeover requires both the preacquisition discount rate and the cash flows of the target. Valuing the synergies also may require an estimate of the acquiring firm's cost of capital and expected cash flows. Hence, the acquiring firm also will want to use the procedures outlined in steps 1 and 2 to value its own stock and calibrate its cost of capital and cash flows.

As Example 19.3 illustrates, the synergies generated by a takeover should, in many cases, be discounted at a weighted average of the discount rates of the two merging organizations.

Example 19.3:   Valuing the Marketing Synergies from Kraft and Philip Morris
Assume that by combining sales forces Kraft and Philip Morris both increase their pretax profits by 10 percent per year. What discount rate should be used to value this synergy?

   Answer: Since the gain in each year is proportional to the preacquisition cash flows of both firms, the appropriate discount rate is a weighted average of the two firm's costs of capital.

Example 19.3 illustrates a case with marketing synergies that affect both parties to the merger equally. However, this will not always be the case. In the Gillette takeover of Duracell, the synergy was Duracell's use of Gillette's distribution network. If this is expected to result in a proportional increase in Duracell's profits, but not Gillette's, then one would use Duracell's cost of capital to value the synergy.

Because Duracell's ability to enter new markets is the major gain from the merger, one might want to consider valuing the synergies as a strategic option, using the derivatives valuation methodology, rather than the risk-adjusted discount rate method. Recall from Chapter 11 that strategic options exist whenever flexibility exists in the implementation of an investment. When a firm expands into a new market, it has the option to expand further if prospects turn out to be more favorable than originally anticipated, and to exit if the situation turns out to be unfavorable. In these situations, an investment may be substantially undervalued when such options are ignored.

Step 4: Value the Acquisition.   The acquisition can be valued by simply adding the stand-alone value of the target to the synergies being produced. In general, we would suggest acquiring the target if it can be purchased for a price that is less than this sum. However, as discussed in Chapters 9–12, we also have to take into account mutually exclusive projects that may also have positive net present values as well as a possible option to delay making the acquisition.

Hilton Buys Welch Hotels

Welch Hotels, a hypothetical company, is a relatively small chain with 23 hotels in Germany. Of the 2 million shares outstanding, more than 30 percent are owned by the Welch family, who started the hotel chain. The remaining 70 percent of Welch's shares trade on the Frankfurt Stock Exchange. On October 3, Wolfgang Welch, the hotel's founder, announced that he wished to retire and would seek an international hotel company to buy the firm. Following this surprise announcement, the stock price of Welch Hotels jumped from DM 60 to DM 72 per share, or DM 144 million for the entire chain, indicating that the market believed that an international hotel would place a higher value on the firm than its stand-alone value.

The Hilton Hotel Corporation hired Gordon Elliot, an investment banker, to evaluate this potential opportunity. Hilton executives believe that with the unification of Europe and the emerging markets in Eastern Europe, they would benefit from an increased presence in Germany. Since Hilton hotels are known internationally, Hilton's management believes that they can create value with such an acquisition. Specifically, they believe that Hilton is much better positioned to attract international business travelers who value the Hilton name but know nothing about Welch. An added bonus of the acquisition would be increased recognition of Hilton hotels. By increasing their visibility within Germany, Hilton management hopes to increase the number of German businessmen that stay in their hotels when they travel outside Germany.

To value Welch Hotels, Elliot first values the hotel as a stand-alone business. To this, he adds the value created by its combination with Hilton. Elliot examines the projected cash flows of the corporation provided by Welch's top management and by the stock market analysts who follow the company. He finds that his cash flow forecasts, those of the analysts, and those of Welch's management are pretty much the same. These estimates suggest that the after-tax real asset cash flow that will accrue over the current year is DM 12 million and that this value will increase, on average, at 2 percent per year. Based on these projected cash flows and the company's value of DM 120 million before the proposed takeover, Elliot infers that if the company's pretakeover value of DM 120 million does not represent an anticipated takeover premium, the *WACC* for Welch Hotels is 12 percent—obtained by solving for the discount rate in the growing perpetuity formula [see equation (A.10) in Appendix A at the end of the text], $PV = C/(r - g)$, where for this illustration

PV = firm value = DM 120 million
C = end of year expected after-tax real asset cash flow = DM 12 million
g = growth rate of expected cash flow = 2%

and

$r = WACC$

Elliot believes that this *WACC* is consistent with the hotel's risk, which supports his assumption that the value of the firm before the takeover represents the value of the hotel chain as a stand-alone business.

Elliot estimates that because of increased occupancy rates and more aggressive pricing generated as a result of Hilton's reputation and its worldwide reservation network, Welch Hotels will increase its expected after-tax cash flows more than the 2 percent per year that it would have achieved as a stand-alone firm. He assumes that the expected after-tax cash flows will increase 3 percent in years 2 and 3, and 5 percent thereafter. In other words, the expected after-tax cash flows after the takeover can be expressed as follows:

Cash Flows (in DM millions) at End-of-Year			
1	*2*	*3*	*4*
DM 12	DM 12(1.03)	DM 12$(1.03)^2$	DM 12$(1.03)^2$ (1.05)

The cash flows will increase by 5 percent in each year past year 4.

Since the incremental cash flows depend on the state of the German economy, they have the same risk as the original cash flows, so the firm's cash flows after the takeover can be discounted at the 12 percent cost of capital used to value the firm as a stand alone business. This assumes that the tax effects on the *WACC* from both the financing mix and the cross-border transaction can be ignored.

To find the present value of this stream of cash flows, first calculate the end of year 4 value of the cash flows from year 4 on as:

$$V_4 = \text{DM } 12(1.03)^2 (1.05) \text{ million} + \frac{\text{DM } 12(1.03)^2 (1.05)^2 \text{ million}}{.12 - .05} = \text{DM } 214 \text{ million}$$

The present value of the Welch Hotels is thus:

$$\frac{\text{DM } 12 \text{ million}}{1.12} + \frac{\text{DM } 12(1.03) \text{ million}}{1.12^2} + \frac{\text{DM } 12(1.03)^2 \text{ million}}{1.12^3} + \frac{\text{DM } 214 \text{ million}}{1.12^4}$$
$$= \text{DM } 163 \text{ million.}$$

Valuing the spillover benefits that accrue to Hilton Hotels outside Germany is somewhat more difficult. Elliot estimates that by buying the chain of Welch Hotels, 10,000 German individuals will come into contact with the Hilton name every day. He estimates that the cost of buying that sort of advertising would cost about DM 500,000 per year, which he expects will remain fixed indefinitely. Since the benefits associated with that kind of publicity are determined by the demand for Hilton's hotels outside Germany, Elliot discounts the projected benefits of this publicity at Hilton's weighted average cost of capital, which is 10 percent. Assuming that this DM 500,000 stream is perpetual, the value is DM 500,000/.1 = DM 5 million. Adding this to the value of the hotel after the takeover provides a value of Welch Hotels to Hilton of DM 168 million. Given that this amount is substantially above the current market price of DM 144 million for Welch Hotels, Elliot recommends that Hilton proceed with an offer that is slightly higher than the current market price.

19.8 Financing Acquisitions

Major acquisitions are financed in a number of ways. When the acquiring firm purchases the target with cash, it usually will have to borrow or issue new debt. Alternatively, the acquirer may purchase the target by offering target shareholders its own stock in exchange for the target's stock. In making the decision on how to finance an acquisition, managers should consider the following:

1. Tax implications.
2. Accounting implications.
3. Capital structure implications.
4. Information effects.

Tax Implications of the Financing of a Merger or an Acquisition

In a merger, the acquiring firm must decide whether to offer stock, cash, or a combination of each for the shares of the target firm. The decision is often made because of tax considerations. Three tax considerations can affect the choice:

- The potential capital gains tax liability of the acquired firm's shareholders.
- The ability to write up the value of the purchased assets.
- The tax gains from leverage.

The Capital Gains Tax Liability.   All else being equal, the target shareholders generally prefer a stock offer to cash for tax reasons because they do not need to pay a capital gains tax on the appreciation of their shares if they receive the acquirer's stock rather than cash for their shares. Moreover, they maintain the option to receive cash by selling the shares they receive from the acquiring firms. In a cash offer, they have no such option and are forced to realize a taxable gain.

Since the shareholders of acquired firms may have a tax preference for equity-funded acquisitions, one might expect them to require lower premiums for equity-funded offers. The empirical evidence indicates that this is indeed true. Travlos (1987); Franks, Harris, and Mayer (1988); and Huang and Walkling (1987) found that premiums in equity-exchange offers are much lower than in cases where the shareholders of the acquired firm are offered cash for their shares.[13] Franks, Harris, and Mayer reported that the differences in these premiums are reflected in a return to the acquired firm in the announcement month of 25.4 percent for cash offers in the United States (30.2 percent in the United Kingdom) and 11.1 percent for stock offers in the United States (15.1 percent in the United Kingdom).

Stepping up the Basis Prior to the Tax Act of 1986.   From the acquiring firm's perspective, the cash offer was preferred prior to 1986 because it allowed the firm to write up the tax basis of the acquired firm's assets, while an acquisition that used the acquiring firm's stock would not allow such an asset write-up. As noted in Section 19.3, after 1986, the basis is stepped up in a cash offer, but the associated capital gains liability more than outweighs the tax advantage of the basis step-up for depreciation.

---

[13]This also could reflect the fact that hostile offers are generally cash offers.

Accounting Implications of the Financing of a Merger or an Acquisition

If a merger is financed with an exchange of stock, it may qualify for **pooling of interests accounting treatment** under which the items on the balance sheets of the two firms are added together, and the merged firm's reported income would simply be the sum of the income of the two separate firms. For example, if Alpha has a book value of $3 million and Beta has a book value of $2 million, then the merged firm, Alphabeta, will have a book value of $5 million.

If an acquisition is made with cash, the acquisition must be treated as a **purchase of assets**. Under the purchase method of accounting, the acquiring firm is assumed to have purchased the assets of the acquired firm at the purchase price. This means that if Alpha purchases Beta for $3 million, the combined book value of the merged firm will be $6 million rather than $5 million, with the additional $1 million reported on the merged firm's balance sheet as goodwill.

The choice between pooling and purchase accounting has no cash implications for the merged firm, but it is of interest to managers because it affects reported earnings. In the Wells Fargo merger with First Interstate Bank in 1995, a purchase accounting transaction, earnings per share declined as a result of the accounting treatment. A manager involved in the merger told us that at least part of the $10 million in fees paid to investment banks was compensation for convincing stock analysts that the drop in earnings per share was due to the accounting treatment of the merger, not to some fundamental drop-off in the banking business of the merged firms.

The decline in earnings per share in a purchase transaction occurs because the additional goodwill generated on the merged firm's balance sheet needs to be amortized, usually over 40 years, but occasionally over a shorter horizon. Reported income is lower because the amortization charges are deducted from reported income. If the $1 million in goodwill in the hypothetical merger between Alpha and Beta was amortized over 40 years, the merged firm's reported income would be reduced by $25,000 in each of the following 40 years. This change in reported income has no effect on the merged firm's cash flows and therefore should not affect market value. However, since various contracts such as bond covenants and management compensation contracts may be based on reported income, and since analysts are perceived by some firms as being confused about what the impact of the accounting treatment on earnings should be, the accounting treatment of a merger is likely to be of interest to a manager and may influence how a deal is structured.

Most acquirers prefer to use pooling accounting because it results in higher earnings, but they also may want to realize the tax benefits from increased leverage that would result from a cash offer. One might think that the acquirer could achieve the best of both worlds either by repurchasing its own shares following the acquisition or by having the target firm repurchase a substantial fraction of its shares prior to the merger. However, a requirement that must be satisfied to qualify for pooling of interest accounting treatment is that the common equity interests of neither of the merged firms change materially in the two years before and after the merger. Either of the above actions would violate this requirement and force the acquirer to use the purchase of assets accounting method.

Aware of the perceived preference for pooling accounting treatment, potential target firms sometimes repurchase shares to deter unwanted hostile offers. In some of these cases, target managers agree later to accept a more attractive offer, and then take steps that allow the acquirer to use pooling of interest accounting. For example, the target can undo the effects of a repurchase by reissuing the repurchased shares.

The Use of Pooling Accounting in AT&T's Acquisition of NCR

AT&T's $7.5 billion acquisition of NCR in 1991 illustrates the effect that accounting choices can have on mergers.[14] Lys and Vincent (1995) reported that in response to AT&T's hostile offer, NCR established an employee stock ownership plan (ESOP) that controlled approximately 8 percent of the firm's common stock and declared a $1 per share special dividend. Both of these actions qualified as changes in NCR's equity interest, which precluded the use of pooling accounting. NCR also had repurchased shares in 1989 and 1990 which also would be a problem.

AT&T was concerned about the effect of the acquisition on the firm's reported earnings if it was forced to use purchase accounting. Lys and Vincent estimated that if AT&T and NCR were combined with pooling accounting, the earnings per share would have been $2.42 in 1990, but with purchase accounting, the reported earnings per share would have been only $1.97. It should be stressed, however, that this difference in reported earnings would have had no effect on AT&T's taxable income and it would not affect its cash flows.

After AT&T increased its offer, NCR management agreed to be taken over. Part of the increase was specifically tied to steps that NCR needed to take to satisfy the requirements for pooling of interest accounting. For example, *The Wall Street Journal* reported on March 25, 1991, that AT&T was willing to pay "another $5 a share if AT&T pays in stock and can treat the acquisition as a pooling of interests, avoiding certain accounting charges."

To satisfy the conditions for pooling of interest accounting treatment, NCR had to cut its regular dividend, to offset the prior special dividend, and reissue the shares that were previously repurchased. Lys and Vincent estimated that the transaction cost of reissuing the shares was about $50 million and that AT&T was forced to pay an additional $450 million in order to get NCR management to make the changes that allowed them to adopt pooling of interest accounting. Apparently, AT&T placed a very high value on having what it considered the more favorable accounting treatment which pooling of interest accounting provided.

Capital Structure Implications in the Financing of a Merger or an Acquisition

The financing of a takeover is partially determined by its effect on the firm's overall capital structure. As Chapters 14 and 16 discussed, firms that made profitable cash-generating investments in that past, but which have few profitable new investment opportunities, tend to use their cash to pay down debt and become underleveraged over time. Section 19.3 mentioned that firms in these situations often finance acquisitions with debt to move toward their long-run optimal debt ratio. On the other hand, firms that are overleveraged, perhaps because of previous debt-financed acquisitions, may have an incentive to finance new acquisitions by exchanging stock.

Information Effects from the Financing of a Merger or an Acquisition

When management believes that the shares of their own firm are underpriced, they are less likely to want to finance investments by issuing new equity (see Chapter 18). This logic applies to acquisitions of other companies as well as investment in capital equipment. Eckbo, Giammarino, and Heinkel (1990) suggest that uncertainty about the target's value also tends to lead firms to make stock offers rather than cash offers. Stock offers have the advantage that the firm ultimately pays more for the good acquisitions than for the bad acquisitions since the acquirer's stock price is likely to perform better after making a good acquisition.

---

[14]Information on the AT&T-NCR merger is based on an article by Lys and Vincent (1995).

19.9 Bidding Strategies in Hostile Takeovers

In many of the hostile takeovers of the 1980s, the bidder initially attempted to buy less than 100 percent of the target's shares. There are two reasons for this. First, the bidder might think that it is unnecessary to acquire all of the outstanding shares to make the changes required to improve the firm's value. Second, some shareholders may not be willing to sell their shares at any price. For example, the target's managers are unlikely to sell their shares if such a sale allows the firm to be taken over and the managers lose their jobs as a consequence.

The Free-Rider Problem

To simplify the following discussion, assume that the bidder can effectively take over a firm by accumulating over 50 percent of the target firm's shares. We assume that the bidder buys the shares and uses the voting rights of those shares to appoint a new CEO who implements the changes that increase the value of the bidder's original stake. By following this procedure, the bidder can avoid, in theory, the free-rider problem discussed in Chapter 17; that is, if shareholders are all small, none of them will find it in their interest to go to the expense of replacing a non-value-maximizing management team. However, if one of the smaller shareholders can accumulate enough shares to become a large shareholder, then this free-rider problem can be reduced.

Unfortunately, reducing the free-rider problem in this way is not always possible. We will show that the bidder's ability to take over a target at a price that allows the bidder to offset his costs depends on how the bidder treats those shareholders who refuse to sell their shares. If the firm is able to force the bidder to offer nontendering shareholders the post-takeover fair market value of their shares, then hostile takeovers may not be profitable.

Conditional Tender Offers. Suppose that John Douglas discovers that Alpha Corporation, currently selling for $20 a share, can be run more efficiently. Under Douglas's management Alpha will be worth $30 a share. Douglas would like to buy enough shares to gain control of the firm and then make the improvements that will raise the firm's share price. Assume that Douglas offers to buy shares in a **conditional tender offer**, which is an offer to purchase a specific number of shares at a specific price. The offer is considered conditional because the buyer is not required to purchase any shares if the specific number of shares is not tendered.

Assume that Douglas chooses to make a conditional tender offer for 51 percent of the outstanding shares at a price of $25 a share. He figures that he is giving the shareholders a good premium over their original $20 per share value and that he will gain $5 per share after implementing his improvements. Would you expect target shareholders to tender their shares at this price?

To determine whether shareholders will tender their shares, compare the value shareholders will receive if they tender with the value they receive if they do not tender. Exhibit 19.5 on page 696 presents these amounts. If the offer is successful, shareholders who tender their shares receive $25 a share. However, the shareholders realize that if Douglas is willing to pay $25 a share for the stock, it must be worth more than that after he gains control, so they are better off not tendering their shares. In this case, the shareholders who do not tender will have shares worth $30 a share and will thus be better

EXHIBIT 19.5   Values Realized from Tendering versus Not Tendering Shares

	Value if Shareholder Tenders	*Value if Shareholder Doesn't Tender*
Bid succeeds	$25/share	$30/share
Bid fails	20/share	20/share

off than those shareholders who do tender. In the event that less than 51 percent of the shares are tendered and the offer fails, shareholders will retain their shares whether or not they tendered, and all shares will be worth only $20. Hence, small shareholders who believe that their decision has no effect on the outcome of the offer have an incentive *not* to tender their shares.

Of course, what is rational for an individual shareholder may be bad for the shareholders as a group. If no one tenders, the shareholders are left with shares worth only $20 rather than the $25 (or $30) per share they would have received if more than half of them had tendered. This argument indicates that if most of the shareholders are small, tender offers will fail unless an offer equal to the target's post-takeover value is made. But at this price, the bidder cannot make a profit unless the value of the shares to the bidder is greater than their value to the original shareholders after the takeover.[15] Again, we see that significant value improvements may fail to be implemented because of the small shareholders' incentives to free-ride on the efforts of others.

Result 19.8   Small shareholders will not tender their shares if they are offered less than the post-takeover value of the shares. As a result, takeovers that could potentially lead to substantial value improvements may fail.

The above reasoning can be extended to situations where Douglas makes what is known as an **unconditional offer** or an **any-or-all offer**, which requires Douglas to purchase the tendered shares even if he fails to attract enough tendered shares to gain control of the firm.

Solutions to the Free-Rider Problem

In reality, acquiring firms find ways to get around the free-rider problem discussed in the last subsection. First, the acquiring firm may have secretly accumulated shares on the open market and will profit on those shares when the target is taken over. Second, target shareholders may be induced to tender their shares if the bidder can convince them that they will not share in the profits that arise from the bidder's value improvements.

Buying Shares on the Open Market.   During the 1980s, many bidders secretly accumulated shares on the open market prior to making a bid. However, U.S. regulations require purchasers to file a 13D report to the Securities and Exchange Commission in which they must state their intentions as soon as their holdings reach 5 percent of the outstanding shares. At that point, the share price will reflect that the firm is a takeover target and shareholders will again be unwilling to sell their shares for less than their value after the takeover. However, by purchasing some shares at $20 per share, Douglas

---

[15]The above argument was originally suggested in Grossman and Hart (1980).

may find it worthwhile to tender for a controlling block of additional shares even if he must pay the value of the shares after the takeover. This strategy is illustrated in Example 19.4.

Example 19.4:   Share Tendering Strategies

Alpha Corporation has 10 million shares outstanding that are currently selling for $20 per share. Douglas believes the shares will be worth $30 if he controls 51 percent of the shares and implements some changes. The costs of mounting the takeover are expected to be $4 million. Can he take over Alpha profitably?

Answer: Douglas may be able to buy 5 percent of the shares for $20 per share. However, after reaching the 5 percent threshold, he will have to make a tender offer for an additional 46 percent of the shares for $30 per share. Although, he will not gain on the shares purchased through the tender offer, he will realize a $10 per share profit on the 5 percent of the shares he purchases on the open market. His total profits on these shares will be $5 million, which exceeds his costs of $4 million, implying that a takeover will be profitable.

In many cases, the potential gain on a bidder's original stake is not sufficient to compensate for the costs of making the bid. Douglas would be much more willing to bid if he could profit from the shares that he purchases in the tender offer as well as those that he secretly accumulates prior to the bid. In order to do this, he will have to induce shareholders to tender their shares at a price which is less than $30 a share. How can he do this?

Secret Share Accumulation by Risk Arbitrageurs as a Way to Resolve the Free-Rider Problem.   Recall from Result 19.8 that only *small* shareholders will choose not to tender if the offer price is less than the value of the shares after the takeover. Large shareholders, who could affect the success or failure of the offer, may be willing to tender their shares at a price below their post-takeover value. This possibility is illustrated in Example 19.5:

Example 19.5:   The Advantage of Accumulating Shares Prior to a Tender Offer

Suppose that Joe Raider accumulated 15 percent of Alpha stock following Douglas's tender offer to purchase shares for $26. Joe believes that the stock will be worth $30 per share if the offer succeeds, but only $20 per share if the offer fails. If Joe tenders his shares, the offer will succeed for sure. However, if he doesn't tender his shares, the offer has a 50 percent probability of failure. Should Joe tender?

Answer: If Joe tenders his shares he will get $26 per share for sure. If he doesn't tender his shares, he will get .5 × $20 + .5 × $30 = $25 per share, on average. He is better off tendering his shares.

Example 19.5 illustrates that so-called risk arbitrageurs like Joe Raider, who buy shares of prospective targets on the open market in hopes of profiting when the shares are tendered, can increase the likelihood of an offer. The presence of these individuals can allow the bidder to increase his profits by tendering for shares at a price below their post-takeover value.[16]

---

[16]We would like to note, however, that the term risk arbitrageur is really misleading. As we discussed previously, an arbitrageur, by definition, makes money without taking risks, i.e., he or she does not place bets. Individuals who are often referred to as risk arbitrageurs earn their livings by placing bets on the outcomes of takeover battles. This activity certainly involves risks.

The Free-Rider Problem When There Are Gains Captured Directly by the Bidder.
Up to this point, we have assumed that the post-takeover value of the shares is worth the
same amount to the target shareholders and to the bidder. If, however, the bidder values
control of the firm, he or she may place a value on the target shares that exceeds the
post-takeover value to target shareholders. This will occur when some of the gains from
the takeover can be captured directly by the bidder and not by the target.

An alleged example of this occurred when Frank Lorenzo, the owner of Texas Air,
took over Eastern Airlines. After the takeover, Eastern sold a number of assets (most
notably its reservation system) to Texas Air at what was alleged to be a reduced price.
When transfers of this kind can be initiated, the value of the target to the bidder exceeds
the post-takeover value of the shares. Example 19.6 illustrates this possibility.

Example 19.6:   How Wealth Transfers Facilitate Takeovers

Suppose that part of the gain from the takeover of Alpha Corporation comes from the sale of
its insecticide division to the Beta Corporation, which Douglas also owns. Since the division
will be sold to Beta at an attractive price, the post-takeover value of Alpha will be only $27 per
share. In this case, can Douglas gain on the shares that are tendered?

Answer: Shareholders realize that their shares will be worth only $27 per share if the firm
is taken over. Therefore, they would be willing to tender their shares at $27 per share. As a
result, Douglas will be able to earn a profit of $3 on each share that is tendered. The profit
comes from the appreciation of his Beta stock, not from a gain on the Alpha stock that he
purchases.

Two-Tiered Offers as a Way of Resolving the Free Rider Problem.   In most takeovers, the bidder expects eventually to purchase all of the target's outstanding shares.
This could create a substantial holdout problem if there was no way to force remaining
shareholders to sell their shares. In reality, however, if a sufficient number of target
shareholders agree to merge the target firm with the bidding firm, the minority shareholders can be forced to sell their shares.[17]

In what has come to be known as a **two-tiered offer**, the bidder offers a price in the
initial tender offer for a specified number of shares and simultaneously announces plans
to acquire the remaining shares at a specified price in what is known as a **follow-up
merger**. In almost all cases, cash is used in the tender offer, but securities, worth less
than the cash offered in the first-tier offer, generally are offered in the second tier. As a
consequence, shareholders are induced to tender their shares to the bidder. Example 19.7
illustrates why these two-tiered offers are sometimes considered coercive.

Example 19.7:   Coercive Two-Tier Offers

Buccaneers Inc. has made a $25 per share tender offer for 51 percent of Purity Corporation's
shares. If the offer is successful and at least 51 percent of the shares are tendered, the firms
will be merged. The shares not tendered in the first tier will receive a combination of bonds
and preferred stock valued at $22 per share. As a shareholder, you believe the shares are
actually worth as much as $30 per share and would like the takeover to fail. Should you tender
your shares?

Answer: We will assume that you are a small shareholder and, as such, do not affect the
success or failure of the offer. Your payoffs in the event of the success or failure of the offer
are given in the table below.

---

[17]In LBOs, the bidding firm is a shell company, created for the purpose of merging with the target.

	Value if Shareholder Tenders	Value if Shareholder Doesn't Tender
Bid succeeds	$25/share	$22/share
Bid fails	30/share	30/share

As the above numbers indicate, you should tender your shares regardless of what you think they are worth. If the bid succeeds, you are better off having tendered. If the bid fails, you are indifferent.

As Example 19.7 illustrates, two-tiered offers can be coercive because they force some shareholders to tender their shares at prices they believe are inadequate. In theory, by making the second-tier offer sufficiently low, a bidder can successfully take over a firm at a price that all shareholders find unacceptable. There are, however, legal restrictions that limit how low the second-tier price can be. Although the bidder is not legally required to provide the target shareholders who do not tender with an amount that compensates them for all of the synergies brought about by the merger, the bidder is required to pay "fair value" for the target shares in the follow-up merger.

In many takeovers that occurred in the 1980s, second-tier offers were substantially lower than first-tier offers. However, most companies currently have what is known as **fair price amendments** in their corporate charters which require the second-tier price to be equal to the first-tier price. Most states also have laws that require second-tier prices to be at least equal to first-tier prices.

19.10 Management Defenses

Incumbent managers have come up with a number of defensive strategies to fight off unwanted takeover attempts. These include the following:

- Paying **greenmail**, or buying back the bidder's stock at a substantial premium over its market price on condition that the bidder suspend his or her bid.
- Creating **staggered board terms** and **supermajority rules**, which can keep a bidder from taking over the firm even if he or she accumulates more than 50 percent of the target firm's shares.
- Introducing **poison pills**, which provide valuable rights to target shareholders who choose not to tender their shares.
- Lobbying for antitakeover legislation.

Greenmail

Stock prices generally drop when firms pay greenmail to large shareholders who are trying to take over the firm. In 1984, for example, David Murdoch, who owned about 5 percent of Occidental Petroleum's stock, put pressure on Occidental's management to take actions to improve the value of its stock. Rather than change its policies, the firm bought Murdoch's shares at a substantial premium over their market price. They paid

$40.10 for shares that had a market price of $28.75 just prior to the announcement of the purchase. In other words, they paid a premium of 42 percent over the market price for Murdoch's shares, giving him a gain of over $56 million. On the announcement of the repurchase, the share price of Occidental dropped $0.875, indicating a reduction in the market value of the firm of more than $80 million. This $80 million loss underestimates the true drop in the firm's market value created by this buyout since the price of Occidental's stock declined prior to the announcement of the buyback once shareholders began to anticipate—not only that Murdoch might receive a $56 million gift—but, more importantly, that he would be unsuccessful in getting the firm to change its policies.

Staggered Boards and Supermajority Rules

An acquirer does not necessarily gain control of a target firm after acquiring over 50 percent of its stock. Many corporations have supermajority rules that require shareholder approval by at least a two-thirds vote and sometimes as much as 90 percent of the shares before a change in control can be implemented. In most cases, the board of directors can override the supermajority provision, but gaining control of the board can be difficult. Board members are often elected to three-year terms which are generally staggered, so that in any given year, only one-third of the board members are elected.

Poison Pills

Poison pills, first introduced in the mid-1980s, are the most effective takeover defense and thus warrant the most discussion. Poison pills are rights or securities that a firm issues to its shareholders, giving them valuable benefits in the event that a significant number of its shares are acquired. There are many varieties of poison pills, but all share the basic attribute that they involve a transfer from the bidder to shareholders who do not tender their shares, thereby increasing the cost of the acquisition and decreasing the incentives for target shareholders to tender at any given price.

Flipover Rights Plans.   The most popular poison pill defense is generally referred to as the **flipover rights plan**.[18] Under this plan, target shareholders receive the right to purchase the acquiring firm's stock at a substantial discount in the event of a merger. For example, if Alpha Corporation acquires Beta shares and then proceeds with a merger, existing Beta shareholders will receive rights to purchase Alpha stock at 50 percent of its value in the event the merger is consummated. This would make the merger prohibitively expensive for Alpha, which would be reluctant to proceed with the merger unless the poison pill was rescinded. In most cases, poison pills can be rescinded by the board of directors at a trivial cost to allow mergers which they believe are in the shareholders' interest to be implemented.

How Effective Are Poison Pills?   Poison pills have been effective in allowing managers to delay unwanted takeovers and to bargain more effectively with potential acquirers. However, they do not always make managers completely immune to unwanted takeovers. In many cases, bidders have taken target managers to court and have forced them to remove a poison pill. Comment and Schwert (1995) concluded that although poison pills have undoubtably deterred some takeovers, these cases are relatively rare.

---

[18]For more information on poison pill defenses, see Weston, Chung, and Hoag (1990).

Their evidence suggests that the decline in takeovers in the late 1980s and early 1990s was not due to poison pills and antitakeover laws, but to the demise of the junk bond market and the credit crunch at commercial banks that occurred at about the same time. The boom in the takeover market in the mid-1990s, when credit markets recovered, provides further support for this claim.

Antitakeover Laws

A further deterrent to hostile takeovers were the antitakeover laws passed by various states in the late 1980s. Many of these laws prevent an investor who obtains a large proportion of the target's outstanding shares (e.g., 20 percent), from voting those shares. Other laws allow directors to consider the interests of nonfinancial stakeholders like employees and the community when considering a takeover offer. Directors are thus free to turn down an offer that provides a substantial premium over the current share price if they believe, for example, that the takeover will result in layoffs.

Are Takeover Defenses Good for Shareholders?

There has been an active debate about how good or bad these defensive actions are for shareholders. On the one hand, it is argued that takeover defenses do no more than keep entrenched managers in power. A defensive action that prevents the success of an offer of $50 per share cannot be in the interests of shareholders if it results in the firm staying independent with a share price of $40. However, defensive actions sometimes result in the bidder making a higher offer which, of course, benefits target shareholders. For example, a bidder who would otherwise bid $50 per share may be willing to raise his bid to $55 to prevent management resistance.

Evidence on the reaction of stock prices to management defensive actions has been mixed. In some cases, share prices increase following the announcement of a defensive action while in others the price decreases. Jarrell and Poulsen (1987) documented that antitakeover amendments, on average, lead to negative changes in the price of the target stock. However, the stock price reaction is not always negative and is, on average, positive when a large percentage of the firm is held by institutional investors who presumably are better able to block a proposed amendment that hurts shareholder value. This evidence is consistent with the hypothesis that the majority of antitakeover amendments hurt target shareholders, but on occasion their implementation may be in the shareholders' interests.

19.11 Summary and Conclusions

This chapter illustrates how the tools developed throughout this text can be used to analyze mergers and acquisitions. Acquisitions require the valuation of an existing business, which can be performed with the tools developed in Chapters 9 through 12. In addition, acquisitions need to be financed, so our analysis of the capital structure decisions in Chapters 13 to 18 also is applicable. The management incentive issues discussed in Chapter 17 are especially important for understanding the takeover market. Some acquisitions are motivated by value

improvements created by correcting incentive problems. However, many bad acquisitions were motivated by bad incentives.

In summary, we suggest that managers consider the following checklist for evaluating a merger or acquisition proposal:

- Evaluate and quantify the real operating synergies of the acquisition. Is a merger the best way of achieving these synergies?

- Evaluate and quantify the tax benefits of the merger. Is a merger required to achieve these tax benefits?
- Evaluate how management incentives are affected by the merger. Will the acquisition correct an incentive problem, or will it create new incentive problems?

Based on an analysis of the empirical evidence, we cannot say whether mergers, on average, create value. Certainly, some mergers have created value while others were either mistakes or bad decisions. Of course, many of the mistakes were due to unforeseen circumstances and were unavoidable. However, we believe that other mergers and acquisitions were due to misguided notions about the value of diversification, misaligned incentives of the acquiring firm's management, and poor judgment. Fortunately, past experience has taught us a great deal about how mergers can create value, and we believe firms can apply this knowledge to make sound acquisition decisions.

Key Concepts

Result 19.1   The main sources of takeover gains include:

- Taxes.
- Operating synergies.
- Target incentive problems.
- Financial synergies.

Result 19.2   Prior to the implementation of the Tax Reform Act of 1986, the U.S. Tax Code encouraged corporations to acquire other corporations. Taxes currently play a much less important role in motivating U.S. acquisitions. In some cases, however, mergers increase the combined capacity of merged firms to utilize tax-favored debt.

Result 19.3   Conglomerates can provide funding for investment projects that independent (smaller) firms would not have been able to fund using outside capital markets. To the extent that positive *NPV* projects receive funding they would not have otherwise received, conglomerates create value.

Result 19.4   The advantages of diversification can be described as follows:

- Diversification enhances the flexibility of the organization.
- The internal capital market avoids some of the information problems inherent in an external capital market.
- Diversification reduces the probability of bankruptcy for any given level of debt and increases the firm's debt capacity.
- Competitors find it more difficult to uncover proprietary information from diversified firms.
- Diversification is advantageous if it allows the firm to utilize its organization more effectively.

The disadvantages of diversification can be described as follows:

- Diversification can eliminate a valuable source of information which may, among other things, make it difficult to compensate the division heads of large diversified firms efficiently.
- Managers may find it difficult to cut back optimally on losing divisions when they can subsidize the losers out of the profits from their winners.

Result 19.5   Stock price reactions to takeover bids can be described as follows:

- The stock prices of target firms almost always react favorably to merger and tender offer bids.
- The bidder's stock price sometimes goes up and sometimes goes down, depending on the circumstances.
- The combined market values of the shares of the target and bidder go up, on average, around the time of the announced bids.

Result 19.6   The bidder's stock price reacts more favorably, on average, when the bidder makes a cash offer rather than an offer to exchange stock. This may reflect the relatively negative information about the bidder's existing business signaled by the offer to exchange stock.

Result 19.7   On average, cash flows of firms improve following leveraged buyouts. Three possible explanations for these improvements are:

- Productivity gains.
- Initiation of LBOs by firms with improving prospects.

- The incentives of leveraged firms to accelerate cash flows, sometimes at the expense of long-run cash flows.

  While we expect all three factors to contribute to the observed increase in cash flows, existing empirical evidence suggests that a major part of the increase is due to productivity gains.

Result 19.8 Small shareholders will not tender their shares if they are offered less than the post-takeover value of the shares. As a result, takeovers that could potentially lead to substantial value improvements may fail.

Key Terms

acquiring firm   667
acquisition   666
conditional tender offer   695
conglomerate (diversifying) acquisition   670
disciplinary takeover   670
fair price amendments   699
financial acquisition   670
financial synergies   670
flipover rights plan   700
follow-up merger   698
friendly takeover   669
greenmail   699
horizontal merger   673
hostile takeover   669
management buyout (MBO)   675
merger   666

operating synergies   669
poison pills   699
pooling of interest accounting treatment   693
purchase of assets   693
raider   675
staggered board terms   699
stepping up the basis   672
strategic acquisition   669
supermajority rules   699
takeover premium   667
target firm   667
tender offer   669
Tobin's q 684
two-tiered offer   698
unconditional (any-or-all) offer   696
vertical merger   673

Exercises

19.1. Jacobs Industries is currently selling for $25 a share and pays a dividend of $2 a share per year. Analysts expect the earnings and dividends to grow 4 percent per year into the foreseeable future. The company has 1 million shares outstanding. John Jacobs, the CEO, would like to take the firm private in a leveraged buyout. Following the buyout, the firm is expected to cut operating costs, which will result in a 10 percent improvement in earnings. In addition, the firm will cut administrative fixed costs by $200,000 per year and save $500,000 per year on taxes for the next 10 years. Assuming that the risk-free interest rate is 5 percent, and that Jacobs Industries cost of capital is 12 percent per year, what value would you put on Jacobs Industries following the LBO?

19.2. Refer to exercise 19.1. Explain why John Jacobs is likely to make these changes following an LBO, but would not make the changes in the absence of an LBO.

19.3. What type of firm would you prefer to work for: a diversified firm or a very focused firm? What does your answer to the above question tell you about one of the advantages or disadvantages of diversification?

19.4. Diversified Industries has made a bid to purchase Cigmatics Inc., offering to exchange two Diversified shares for 1 share of Cigmatics. When this bid is announced, Diversified Industries' shares drop 5 percent. Henry Clavett, the CEO, has asked you to interpret what this decline in stock prices means. Does it imply that Cigmatics is a bad acquisition?

19.5. Leveraged buyouts are observed mainly in industries with relatively stable cash flows and products that are not highly specialized. Explain why.

19.6. When a firm with an extremely high price/earnings ratio purchases a firm with a very low price/

earnings ratio in an exchange of stock, its earnings per share will increase. Do you think firms are more likely to acquire other firms when it results in an increase in their earnings per share? Is it beneficial to shareholders to initiate a takeover for these reasons?

19.7. Tobacco companies have a large potential liability. In the future, they may be subject to extremely large product liability lawsuits. Discuss how this affects the incentives of tobacco companies to merge with food companies.

19.8. One of the stated benefits of a management buyout is the improvement in management incentives. In many cases, however, the top managers do not change after the buyout. Explain why.

19.9. Why do think AT&T was willing to spend $500 million to get pooling of interest accounting treatment in its acquisition of NCR?

References and Additional Readings

Amihud, Yakov, and Baruch Lev. "Risk Reduction as a Managerial Motive for Conglomerate Mergers." *Bell Journal of Economics* 12 (1981), pp. 605–17.

Asquith, Paul. "Merger Bids, Uncertainty, and Stockholder Returns." *Journal of Financial Economics* 11, no. 1 (1983), pp. 51–83.

Berger, Philip, and Eli Ofek. "Diversification's Effect on Firm Value." *Journal of Financial Economics* 37 (1995), pp. 39–65.

Bhagat, Sanjay; Andrei Shleifer; and Robert Vishny. "Hostile Takeovers in the 1980s: The Return to Corporate Specialization." *Brookings Papers on Economic Activity: Microeconomics, Special Issue* (1990), pp. 1–72.

Bhide, Amar. "Reversing Corporate Diversification." *Journal of Applied Corporate Finance* 5 (1990), pp. 70–81.

Bradley, Michael. "Interfirm Tender Offers and the Market for Corporate Control." *Journal of Business* 53, no. 4 (1980), pp. 345–76.

Bradley, Michael; Anand Desai; and E. Han Kim. "The Rationale behind Interfirm Tender Offers." *Journal of Financial Economics* 11, no. 1 (1983), pp. 183–206.

———. "Synergistic Gains from Corporate Acquisitions and Their Division between the Stockholders of Target and Acquiring Firms." *Journal of Financial Economics* 21, no. 1 (1988), pp. 3–40.

Comment, Robert, and Gregg A. Jarrell. "Corporate Focus and Stock Returns." *Journal of Financial Economics* 37 (1995), pp. 67–87.

Comment, Robert, and G. William Schwert. "Poison or Placebo? Evidence on the Deterrence and Wealth Effects of Modern Antitakeover Measures." *Journal of Financial Economics* 39 (1995), pp. 3–44.

Dodd, Peter. "Merger Proposals, Management Discretion and Stockholder Wealth." *Journal of Financial Economics* 8, no. 2 (1980), pp. 105–38.

Eckbo, B. Espen; Ronald M. Giammarino; and Robert L. Heinkel. "Asymmetric Information and the Medium of Exchange in Takeovers: Theory and Tests." *Review of Financial Studies* 3, no. 4 (1990), pp. 651–75.

Franks, Julian R.; Robert S. Harris; and Colin Mayer. "Means of Payment in Takeovers: Results for the U.K. and U.S." unpublished manuscript, 1987.

Grossman, Sanford J., and Oliver D. Hart. "Takeover Bids, the Free-Rider Problem and the Theory of the Corporation." *Bell Journal of Economics* 11 (Spring 1980), pp. 42–64.

———. "The Costs and Benefits of Ownership: A Theory of Vertical and Lateral Integration." *Journal of Political Economy* 94 (1986), pp. 691–719.

Hasbrouck, Joel. "The Characteristics of Takeover Targets." *Journal of Banking And Finance* 9, no. 3 (1985), pp. 351–62.

Healy, Paul; Krishna Palepu; and Richard Ruback. "Does Corporate Performance Improve after Mergers?" *Journal of Financial Economics* 31 (1992), pp. 135–76.

Huang, Yen-Sheng, and Ralph A. Walkling. "Target Abnormal Returns Associated with Acquisition Announcements: Payment, Acquisition Form, and Managerial Resistance." *Journal of Financial Economics* 19, no. 2 (1987), pp. 329–50.

Hirshleifer, David. "Mergers and Acquisitions: Strategic and Informational Issues." Chapter 26 in *Handbooks in Operations Research and Management Science: Volume 9 Finance,* Robert Jarrow, V. Maksimovic, and W. Ziemba, eds. Amsterdam, The Netherlands: Elsevier Science, B.V., 1995, pp. 839–85.

Jarrell, Gregg, and Annette Poulsen, "Returns to Acquiring Firms in Tender Offers: Evidence from Three Decades." *Financial Management* 18 (1989), pp. 12–19.

————. "Shark Repellents and Stock Prices: The Effects of Antitakeover Amendments since 1980." *Journal of Financial Economics* 19 (1987), pp. 127–68.

Jarrell, Gregg A.; James Brickley; and Jeffrey Netter. "The Market for Corporate Control: The Empirical Evidence since 1980." *Journal of Economic Perspectives* 2, no. 1 (1988), pp. 49–68.

Jensen, Michael C., "Agency Costs of Free Cash Flow, Corporate Finance, and Takeovers." *American Economic Review* 76 (1986), pp. 323–29.

————. "Selections from the Senate and House Hearings on LBOs and Corporate Debt." *Journal of Applied Corporate Finance* 2, no. 1 (1989), pp. 35–44.

Jensen, Michael C., and Richard Ruback. "The Market for Corporate Control: The Scientific Evidence." *Journal of Financial Economics* 11 (1983), pp. 5–50.

Kaplan, Steven. "The Effects of Management Buyouts on Operating Performance and Value." *Journal of Financial Economics* 24 (1989), pp. 217–54.

Kaplan, Steven, and Jeremy Stein. "The Evolution of Buyout Pricing and Financial Structure in the 1980s." *Quarterly Journal of Economics* 108 (1993), pp. 313–57.

Kaplan, Steven, and Michael Weisbach. "The Success of Acquisitions: Evidence from Divestitures." *Journal of Finance* 47 (1992), pp. 107–38.

Klein, April. "The Timing and Substance of Divestiture Announcements: Individual, Simultaneous and Cumulative Effects." *Journal of Finance* 41 (1986), pp. 685–97.

Klein, Ben; Robert Crawford; and Armen Alchian. "Vertical Integration, Appropriable Rents and the Competitive Contracting Process." *Journal of Law and Economics* 21 (1978), pp. 297–326.

Lang, Larry, and Rene M. Stulz. "Tobin's *q*, Corporate Diversification and Firm Performance." *Journal of Political Economy* 102 (1994), pp. 1248–80.

Lang, Larry; Rene Stulz; and Ralph Walkling. "A Test of the Free Cash Flow Hypothesis: The Case of Bidder Returns." *Journal of Financial Economics* 29 (1991), pp. 315–36.

Lehn, Kenneth, and Annette Poulsen. "Free Cash Flow and Stockholder Gains in Going Private Transactions." *Journal of Finance* 44 (1989), pp. 771–88.

Lichtenberg, Frank R., and Donald Siegel. "The Effects of Leveraged Buyouts on Productivity and Related Aspects of Firm Behavior." *Journal of Financial Economics* 27, no. 1 (1990), pp. 165–94.

Lowenstein, Louis. "Management Buyouts." *Columbia Law Review* 85 (1985), pp. 730–84.

Lys, Thomas, and Linda Vincent. "An Analysis of Value Destruction in AT&T's Acquisition of NCR." *Journal of Financial Economics* 39 (1995), pp. 353–78.

Matsusaka, John. "Did Tough Antitrust Enforcement Cause the Diversification of American Corporations?" *Journal of Financial and Quantitative Analysis* 31, no. 2 (1996), pp. 283–94.

Mitchell, Mark L., and Kenneth Lehn. "Do Bad Bidders Make Good Targets?" *Journal of Applied Corporate Finance* 3, no. 2 (1990), pp. 60–69.

Morck, Randall; Andrei Shleifer; and Robert W. Vishny. "Do Managerial Objectives Drive Bad Acquisitions?" *Journal of Finance* 45 (1990), pp. 31–48.

Muscarella, Chris, and Michael Vetsuypens. "Efficiency and Organizational Change: A Study of Reverse LBOs." *Journal of Finance* 45 (1990), pp. 1389–1414.

Opler, Tim C. "Operating Performance in Leveraged Buyouts: Evidence from 1985–1989." *Financial Management* 21, no. 1 (1993), pp. 27–34.

Ravenscraft, David J., and F. M. Scherer. *Mergers, Selloffs, and Economic Efficiency.* Washington, DC: Brookings Institution, 1987.

Rock, Kevin. "Gulf Oil Corporation—Takeover." Harvard Case 9-285-053.

Sampson, Anthony. *The Sovereign State of ITT.* New York: Stein and Day, 1973.

Servaes, Henri. "The Value of Diversification during Conglomerate Merger Waves," *Journal of Finance* 51 (1996), pp. 1201–25.

Shleifer, Andrei, and Lawrence Summers. "Breach of Trust in Hostile Takeovers." Chapter 2 in *Corporate Takeovers: Causes and Consequences.* A. J. Auerbach, ed. Chicago: University of Chicago Press, 1988.

Smith, Abbie J. "Corporate Ownership Structure and Performance: The Case of Management Buyouts." *Journal of Financial Economics* 27, no. 1 (1990), pp. 143–64.

Travlos, Nickolaos G. "Corporate Takeover Bids, Methods of Payment, and Bidding Firms' Stock Returns." *Journal of Finance* 42, no. 4 (1987), pp. 943–63.

Weston J. Fred; Kwang S. Chung; and Susan E. Hoag. *Mergers, Restructuring, and Corporate Control.* Englewood Cliffs, NJ: Prentice Hall, 1990.

PRACTICAL INSIGHTS FOR PART V

Allocating Capital for Real Investment

- Managers, acting in their own interests, often invest more than shareholders would like. (Section 17.3)
- Managers and large shareholders sometimes prefer diversifying investments that reduce the probability of the firm going bankrupt over higher *NPV* investments that provide less diversification. (Section 17.3)
- Managers may choose investment projects that pay off quickly over projects with higher *NPV*s that take longer to pay off if increasing the firm's current share price is an important consideration for them. (Section 18.3)
- Managers who wish to temporarily boost their stock prices may underinvest in positive *NPV* projects that cannot be readily observed by shareholders and instead use the cash savings to pay a dividend or repurchase shares. (Section 18.4)
- Managers sometimes have information that indicates that their debt and equity is not fairly priced, which implies that their financing alternatives may not have zero *NPV*s. Managers may, therefore, pass up positive *NPV* investments if they must be financed by negative *NPV* instruments. (Section 18.5)
- Corporate takeovers can create value through tax savings, operating synergies, financial synergies, and by correcting incentive problems. (Section 19.3)
- Because of various capital market imperfections, conglomerates sometimes do better than the capital markets in allocating investment capital. However, markets better allocate capital when market prices contain useful information that managers do not have and when there exist conflicts between managers' and shareholders' interests. (Section 19.3)

Financing the Firm

- In most major corporations, the debt-equity choice is made by the board of directors but investment choices are made by management. If the board understands the tendency of management to overinvest, they might want to offset this tendency by increasing the firm's debt to equity ratio. (Section 17.3)
- Managers should not use stock price reactions to corporate actions, like dividend and leverage changes, to evaluate how the market views the decision. The market may be reacting to the information conveyed by the decision rather than to whether the decision is value-enhancing. For example, the market may react positively to the announcement of a cash financed

acquisition, if investors are surprised by the firm's ability to raise the cash for the acquisition. This may be the case even when the acquisition itself is a negative *NPV* investment. (Section 18.1)
- If the firm's board of directors and its management believe that the firm is undervalued, they might choose to increase the firm's debt ratio to convince investors that its value is higher. Increasing leverage provides a favorable signal for two reasons: First, it demonstrates that managers (who personally find financial distress costly) are confident that they can generate the cash needed to meet the higher debt obligation. Second, the firm sends the signal that its shares are a "good investment" when it increases its leverage by repurchasing shares. (Section 18.5)
- When a firm is doing poorly, there is generally a lot of uncertainty about its true value. A firm's stock price would be likely to react very negatively in this situation if the firm issued equity. A manager might also consider debt financing very unattractive in this situation because of the threat of bankruptcy and perhaps less need for the tax benefits of debt. For these reasons, we often observe firms issuing preferred stock in these situations. (Section 18.5)
- Firms often use their stock to finance major acquisitions. One advantage of this is that it allows the firm to use pooling of interest accounting. This financing option is less attractive when the acquirer believes its own stock is undervalued. (Section 19.8)

Allocating Funds for Financial Investments

- Decisions that lead to higher leverage ratios generally result in higher stock prices. Decisions that lead to lower leverage ratios generally result in lower stock prices. (Section 18.6)
- Increased dividends and share repurchases generally result in higher stock prices. Dividend cuts and equity issues generally result in lower stock prices. (Section 18.6)
- Empirical evidence suggests that stock prices underreact to some corporate announcements, like dividend and capital structure changes. Investors may be able to profit by buying stocks following announcements that convey positive information and selling stocks following announcements that convey negative information. (Section 18.6)

EXECUTIVE PERSPECTIVE

Lisa Price

In my experience as a banker, I frequently encounter transaction and valuation issues that reinforce many principles addressed in Part V of this book. Understanding how taxes, management incentives, accounting considerations, and operating synergies motivate acquisitions is critical to identifying potential business combinations, valuing acquisition targets, and structuring transactions. Part V of the text discusses these and related issues clearly and comprehensively, combining academic principles with actual experience to provide relevant guidelines for today's financial managers.

Chapters 17 through 19 describe the economic and strategic rationale for mergers and acquisitions. Historically, events such as economic shifts in demand or supply and the maturation of industries have created opportunities to realize operating synergies through the combination of companies, frequently driving a wave of industry consolidation. For example, the defense sector has recently witnessed this effect on an unprecedented scale due to budgetary pressures in Washington and the reduced role of the U.S. military forces in the post–Cold War era. Bear Stearns has recently represented several major defense companies in acquisitions as they sought to build critical mass and scale to allow them to maintain long-term market position and cost competitiveness. Such transactions occur as the defense sector attempts to "right-size." Similarly, transactions that we completed in the technology and telecommunications sectors were motivated by strategic considerations resulting from technological acceleration and uncertainty, a changing regulatory environment, and an increasingly global marketplace. Mergers and acquisitions have allowed companies to build scale and scope, fill in gaps in technologies, share research and development and other overlapping costs, and access greater capital to support top-line growth opportunities.

Grinblatt and Titman point out how important it is not only to identify operating synergies when evaluating an acquisition target, but also to quantify their impact on value and, consequently, the premium that a buyer would pay. In practice, the value created is shared by the buyer and seller. The amount of synergies received by the selling shareholders generally depends on the type of synergy, whether the buyer or seller is primarily responsible for its creation, the competitive dynamics in the selling process, and the mix of acquisition consideration received.

In a low-premium, stock-for-stock transaction, synergies are primarily realized through the seller's ongoing participation in the acquirer's stock. In a cash transaction, synergies are realized explicitly through the premium.

When Bear Stearns advised Martin Marietta in its stock-for-stock merger with Lockheed in 1994, Martin Marietta shareholders initially received a 20 percent premium and also had continuing upside participation in the combined Lockheed Martin's stock. By contrast, Raytheon, in its 1995 cash acquisition of E-Systems, paid an approximate 40 percent premium and E-Systems' shareholders received no continuing interest in the combination.

Consistent with issues raised in Chapter 19, I have also found tax considerations to be very important in structuring transactions. In 1997, Bear Stearns advised Raytheon in its $9.5 billion acquisition of Hughes Electronics' defense unit from General Motors. Persuading GM to sell its defense operations required considerable effort to create a structure to permit the disposition on a tax-free basis.

Part V indicates that an acquirer's choice of cash or stock as acquisition currency depends on a number of factors, including the acquirer's financial flexibility, accounting-related issues, tax considerations, and the proposed governance provisions of the transaction. Often, companies pursue stock transactions to achieve tax-free treatment for shareholders or to qualify for pooling-of-interests accounting to avoid ongoing goodwill amortization charges that reduce reported earnings. These were the concerns of Bell Atlantic and NYNEX when they agreed to a stock-for-stock merger in 1997.

The ability of the combined company to service additional debt is also critical in determining the acquisition currency. For example, a high-growth technology company may prefer to use stock rather than cash to minimize its ongoing fixed charges and maintain future financial flexibility.

Additionally, the choice of cash or stock reflects the proposed governance of the combined company. In stock-for-stock mergers, the shareholders and management of the acquired company frequently have significant ongoing influence in the combined entity through board representation or management roles. Cash acquisitions, on the other hand, are more commonly associated with "change-of-control" transactions in which the acquired management has no meaningful influence after combination. In 1996, for example, Bear Stearns represented Lockheed Martin in its $9.4 billion acquisition of Loral's defense operations. Initial discussions contemplated a stock-for-stock transaction with "merger-of-equals" governance. When discussions evolved to consider a reduced role for Loral management in the combined company as well as the spinoff to Loral shareholders of one of its operating units, Loral Space, the transaction was restructured as a cash acquisition.

The issues that I have addressed here highlight just a few of the principles that Grinblatt and Titman discuss in Part V. The theoretical discussion, supported by practical examples offered in the book, I believe, will provide a good foundation for understanding the issues and intrica-cies of mergers and acquisitions and should be useful to anyone pursuing a career in this field.

Ms. Price is currently managing director of Bear Stearns, specializing in strategic and tactical mergers and acquisitions. Previously, Ms. Price was with Nestlé U.S.A. and Dean Witter Reynolds.

PART VI Risk Management

Prior to the late 1980s, the typical textbook on corporate finance contained virtually no mention of risk management, and, indeed, most corporations exhibited little interest in this topic. Now, however, risk management has become one of the most important responsibilities of the treasurers in large corporations throughout the world.

As an illustration of this trend, consider the lead article in the August 17, 1993, edition of *The Wall Street Journal,* entitled, "Managing Risk: Corporate Treasurers Adopt Hedging Plans with Some Wariness." The article notes that ". . . derivatives help most corporations using them," and then goes on to quote a managing director from Credit Suisse who observed that "although many companies use derivatives for capital raising . . . they are just beginning to use them for broader risk-management purposes." Today, the large firm that does not devote substantial financial expertise to risk management is a rare exception.

Risk management entails assessing and managing, through the use of financial derivatives, insurance, and other activities, the corporation's exposure to various sources of risk. Hence, risk management specialists need a sound understanding of derivative securities (see Chapters 7 and 8), tools for estimating the risk exposure of their firm (see Chapter 6), and an understanding of which risks should and should not be hedged.

Chapter 20, the first chapter in Part VI, describes the various motivations for firms to expend funds to reduce their exposures to various sources of risk. These hedging motivations relate closely to the issues examined in Parts IV and V: minimization of taxes, reducing financial distress costs, matching cash flows with investment needs, and reducing incentive problems. We argue in this chapter that the motivation to hedge determines which risks the firms should hedge as well as how they should organize their hedging operations. In particular, Chapter 20 discusses the differences among firms in their motivations for hedging. Depending on these motivations, some firms seek to hedge cash flow (or earnings) risk while others seek to hedge against changes in firm values.

Chapters 21 and 22 focus more on the implementation of risk management, analyzing how firms can alter or eliminate their exposure to risk by acquiring various financial instruments. Chapter 21 is largely devoted to managing currency and commodity risk while Chapter 22 focuses on interest rate risk. Interest rate risk deserves unique treatment because interest rates, as discount factors, affect the present values of cash flows, even when they do not affect the cash flows directly.

Risk management requires a firm to first estimate its risk exposure. For example, an oil firm might want to know how much its earnings will decline next year if oil prices

709

drop $3 a barrel. A financial institution is similarly interested in how changes in interest rates affect the value of its loan portfolio. Both Chapters 21 and 22 discuss how such risk exposure is measured, using some familiar tools developed in previous chapters, including factor models, regression, and theoretical derivative pricing relationships. The two chapters also introduce popular ways to measure risk, like value at risk (VAR), and discuss various ways of measuring interest rate risk through concepts like duration, DV01, and yield betas.

After estimating its risk exposure, the firm might want to consider various alternatives for eliminating the risk. If financial assets exist that exactly track the risk exposure, then risk can be eliminated or at least altered with offsetting positions in these assets. Both Chapters 21 and 22 discuss how to hedge with a variety of financial instruments that track a firm's risk.

CHAPTER 20

Risk Management and Corporate Strategy

Learning Objectives

After reading this chapter, you should be able to:

1. Understand the different motivations for corporate hedging.
2. Explain which firms should be the most interested in hedging.
3. Understand which risks firms should hedge.
4. Understand the different motivations for foreign currency and interest rate risk management.

Intel Corporation incurs most of its expenses in the United States where it performs the bulk of its R&D and most of its manufacturing, but the company generates revenues throughout the world. Intel is subject to substantial currency risk because of the relatively long time between its quotation of a price to a customer and the customer's payment for the products. Intel's policy has been to actively hedge the currency exposures that arise in these situations.

Corporations throughout the world are devoting increasing amounts of resources to **risk management**. Risk management entails assessing and managing the corporation's exposure to various sources of risk through the use of financial derivatives, insurance, and other activities.

Previous chapters assumed that a firm's **risk profile**—that is, the kinds of risks they are exposed to—are taken as given. This chapter moves back one step and examines how firms determine their risk profiles. For example, if Intel chose not to **hedge**, or take offsetting positions, to eliminate its deutsche mark exposure arising from its sales in Germany, Intel's stock would probably show some sensitivity to movements in the deutsche mark relative to the U.S. dollar. By hedging that exposure, Intel's stock is less sensitive to those sorts of currency movements.

The idea that corporations should manage exposure to various sources of risk is relatively new, but it is becoming increasingly important. In contrast to the past, when the chief financial officer (CFO) of a corporation would spend a small portion of his time on hedging, many corporations now have entire departments devoted to hedging and risk management. A survey conducted for a group of financial institutions known as the

Group of Thirty (1993) reported that over 80 percent of the surveyed corporations considered derivatives either very important (44 percent) or imperative (37 percent) in controlling risk. Of the respondents, 87 percent used interest rate swaps, 64 percent currency swaps, 78 percent forward foreign exchange contracts, 40 percent interest rate options, and 31 percent currency options.

The trend toward greater attention to risk management is due to a number of factors, most notably, the increased volatility of interest rates and exchange rates,[1] and the increased importance of multinational corporations. In addition, the growing understanding of derivative instruments (see Chapters 7 and 8) has also contributed to their increased acceptance as tools for risk management.

The motivation for risk management comes from a variety of sources: taxes, financial distress costs, executive incentives, and other important issues discussed in earlier chapters. Understanding these motives is important because they provide insights into which risks should be hedged and how a firm's hedging operations should be organized.

20.1 Risk Management and the Modigliani-Miller Theorem

Many of the major financial innovations of the 1980s were associated with the markets for derivative securities, such as options, forward contracts, swap contracts, and futures. These contracts provide relatively inexpensive and efficient ways for corporations and investors to bundle and unbundle various aspects of risk, allowing those who are least able to bear the risks to pass them off to others who can bear them more efficiently.

To understand this, return to the factor model introduced in Chapter 6 to reexamine the stock returns of ABC Corporation. We will express those returns as:

$$\tilde{r}_{ABC} = \alpha_{ABC} + \beta_{ABC,1}\tilde{F}_1 + \beta_{ABC,2}\tilde{F}_2 + \ldots + \beta_{ABC,K}\tilde{F}_K + \tilde{\epsilon}_{ABC} \tag{20.1}$$

where

$\tilde{F}$'s represent macroeconomic factors like interest rate movements, currency
   changes, oil price changes, and changes in the aggregate economy
β's represent the stock's sensitivity to those factors, or factor betas
$\tilde{\epsilon}$ is firm-specific risk

A stock's sensitivity to factor risk as well as firm-specific risk is determined by the firm's capital expenditure and operating decisions, (e.g., whether to locate a plant in North Carolina or Malaysia) and its financial decisions (e.g., whether to borrow in U.S. dollars or Japanese yen).

Factor risk is generally not diversifiable, but often it can be hedged by taking offsetting positions in financial derivatives. *Firm-specific risk* is just the opposite; it is generally diversifiable but cannot be hedged with derivative contracts. It is possible, however, to hedge many sources of firm-specific risk with insurance contracts. For example, a fire insurance contract provides a good hedge against the losses incurred as a result of a fire.

The Investor's Hedging Choice

Before analyzing the hedging choice of firms, it is instructive to first consider the possibility that individual investors hedge on their own. Assume that the investor observes

---

[1]Interest rates increased substantially in October 1979 when Federal Reserve Chairman Paul Volker announced that the Federal Reserve Board would no longer attempt to control interest rates. Similarly, the volatility of foreign currency rates increased dramatically after 1973 when foreign exchange rates began to float.

the factor sensitivities of the different investments and constructs an evenly balanced portfolio which diversifies away firm-specific risk and is weighted to give the investor his or her preferred exposure to the various sources of risk, as represented by a particular configuration of factor betas.

Recall that the betas or factor sensitivities of the portfolio are the weighted averages of the sensitivities of the different securities held in the portfolio. In addition to buying and selling stocks and bonds with the appropriate risk profiles, the investor may use derivatives to more directly alter the portfolio's exposure to particular sources of systematic risk. For example, if $\tilde{F}_2$ in equation (20.1) represents uncertain movements in oil prices, investors can directly change the exposures of their portfolios to oil price movements by buying or selling oil price futures or forward contracts.

Derivatives like forwards and futures are indeed used by many investors in exactly this manner. However, the most important users of derivative instruments are corporations and financial institutions, like banks, that want to alter the risk profiles of their firms.

Implications of the Modigliani-Miller Theorem for Hedging

To understand why a firm like Exxon would want to change its risk exposure, we must first return to the Modigliani-Miller Theorem (see Chapter 13). This theorem states that in the absence of taxes and other market frictions, the capital structure decision is irrelevant. In other words, financial decisions cannot create value for a firm unless they in some way affect either a firm's ability to operate its business or its incentives to invest in the future.

The Modigliani-Miller Theorem was applied initially to the analysis of the firm's debt-equity choice. However, the theorem is really much more general and can be applied to the analysis of all aspects of the firm's financial strategy. This would include, for example, a firm's choice of borrowing at a fixed rate or a floating rate; issuing bonds with promised payments denominated in British pounds or U.S. dollars; or issuing bonds with payments linked to the price of oil or some other commodity. In all cases, these choices affect firm values only when there are relevant market frictions like taxes, transaction costs, and financial distress costs. The Modigliani-Miller Theorem also applies to other financial contracts and instruments. Firms can benefit from futures, forwards, and swap contracts, but only in the presence of these same frictions.

The Modigliani-Miller Theorem can be proved by showing that individual investors can use "homemade" leverage on their own accounts to undo or duplicate any leverage choice made by the firms they own. It is also possible to apply this theorem to show that, in the absence of market frictions, shareholders are indifferent between hedging on their own accounts and having their firms do the hedging for them. For example, given frictionless markets, shareholders realize identical returns if IBM hedges its exposure to changes in the dollar-pound exchange rate or if, alternatively, IBM chooses not to hedge and the shareholders do the hedging in their personal accounts. In other words, investors can form portfolios with the same factor risk and the same expected returns regardless of how firms hedge. As a result, in frictionless markets where the operations side of the firm are held fixed, investors gain nothing from the hedging choices of the firm.

Result 20.1   If hedging choices do not affect cash flows from real assets, then, in the absence of taxes and transaction costs, hedging decisions do not affect firm values.

Relaxing the Modigliani-Miller Assumptions

To understand why firms hedge, we must reevaluate the assumptions underlying the Modigliani-Miller Theorem and ask which assumptions are likely to be unrealistic. Our method for understanding why firms hedge is thus similar to the method employed in Chapters 13 through 18 to understand the firm's capital structure choice, and we draw heavily from the analysis in those chapters.

The frictionless markets assumption of the theorem implies that investors and corporations have equal access to hedging instruments, and that there are no transaction costs. In reality, corporations are often in a much better position to hedge certain risks than their shareholders. For example, most institutional and individual investors would find it costly to learn how to hedge a food company's exposure to changes in the price of palm oil even though markets for such hedging instruments exist. In addition, corporate executives are much more knowledgeable than shareholders about their firm's risk exposures and thus are in a much better position to know how much to hedge.[2]

Nevertheless, the difficulties faced by shareholders who wish to hedge their portfolio are probably not a prime reason or motivation for why large firms, owned primarily by diversified investors, choose to hedge. Although these difficult-to-hedge risks may affect the volatilities of individual stocks, most volatility is diversified away in large portfolios.[3] Thus, hedging is unlikely to reduce a firm's cost of capital significantly. If hedging cannot reduce the discount rate a firm applies to value its cash flows, then hedging must increase expected cash flows if it is to improve firm values.

Result 20.2   Hedging is unlikely to improve firm values if it does no more than reduce the variance of a firm's future cash flows. To improve firm values, hedging also must increase expected cash flows.

20.2 Why Do Firms Hedge?

Shortly after Iraq's invasion of Kuwait on August 2, 1990, the price of oil went up substantially. Within months of the invasion, jet fuel prices more than doubled, increasing Continental Airlines' fuel bill by $81 million a month. On December 3, 1990, Continental Airlines filed for Chapter 11 bankruptcy, citing rising fuel costs as the primary cause.[4]

If it were the rising fuel costs that bankrupted Continental, then the bankruptcy would have been avoided if Continental had hedged the risk associated with increased oil prices by making forward purchases of jet fuel prior to the Iraqi invasion. In retrospect, Continental's managers wished that they had hedged. However, the issue addressed in this section is whether or not Continental should have hedged knowing only what they knew prior to the Iraqi invasion.

---

[2]The fact that investors may not have the same access that corporations have to forward and futures markets is sometimes offered as a rationale for why firms often do not hedge and sometimes speculate. For example, most oil firms are very sensitive to oil price changes, yet hedge very little of that risk. One rationale for this is that the forward and futures prices of oil are generally too low, making the cost of hedging too high for the corporations. In a Modigliani and Miller world, the futures and forward prices are irrelevant because investors are indifferent between having the oil companies take the oil price risk, or having the investors take the oil price risk directly by buying the oil price forwards and futures (which in this case, the firms would be selling). However, in reality, most investors are unable to invest directly in oil forward and futures contracts, implying that the only way that these investors can buy exposure to oil is to buy oil stocks that choose not to hedge.

[3]Although hedging nondiversifiable risks, like interest rate movements, can affect a firm's cost of capital, it should still have no effect on the firm's value. In this case, the reduction in the cost of capital should be offset exactly by the effect of the hedge on cash flows.

[4]*The Wall Street Journal*, Dec. 4, 1990.

A Simple Analogy

In our everyday life, individuals make choices that reduce risk. For example, when the authors of this text travel from UCLA to the Los Angeles Airport, they can choose between taking the San Diego Freeway or taking city streets. Most of the time they take the freeway because it is generally faster. However, travel time on the freeway varies considerably at rush hour, depending on traffic conditions. Traveling the freeway between 4:00 and 6:00 P.M. takes anywhere between 30 minutes and an hour, with an expected time of 40 minutes. With certainty, it takes 50 minutes to get to the airport on city streets.

Even though, on average, it takes longer to go by the city streets, they prefer this more certain route during rush hour because the loss from getting a bad outcome on the risky route (e.g., missing their plane) far outweighs the gain of getting a good outcome on this route (e.g., having enough time to get a drink before the flight leaves). Generally speaking, it is this type of asymmetry between gains and losses that lead us to make choices that reduce risk.

As we will show, similar asymmetries between losses and gains lead corporations to make choices that reduce their risks. This will be true even if the corporation is owned by stockholders who are risk neutral and thus prefer to maximize expected return. We describe the sources of these asymmetries below.

How Does Hedging Increase Expected Cash Flows?

The rest of this chapter will examine various ways that firms can increase their expected cash flows by implementing risk management programs. The primary benefits of hedging are related to taxes and to other market frictions discussed in Parts IV and V. Specifically, we will discuss the following benefits associated with hedging:

1. Hedging can decrease a firm's expected tax payments.
2. Hedging can reduce the costs of financial distress.
3. Hedging allows firms to better plan for their future capital needs and reduce their need to gain access to outside capital markets.
4. Hedging can be used to improve the design of management compensation contracts and it allows firms to evaluate their top executives more accurately.
5. Hedging can improve the quality of the decisions made.

The gain from hedging in items (1) through (3) arises because the loss in the corporation's value from receiving one dollar less in profit is greater than the gain in value from one dollar more in profit. For example, the third motivation is based on the idea that the cost of not having enough internal capital available to fund a corporation's investment needs is greater than the benefits of having more than enough capital. Example 20.1 illustrates how this asymmetry between gains and losses motivates firms to hedge. Note that this example, as well as other examples in this chapter (unless specified otherwise) assume risk neutrality and a risk-free rate of zero. We use these assumptions, not just for expositional simplicity, but to show that firms have incentives to reduce risk even when investors have no aversion to risk.

Example 20.1:   How Hedging Creates Value

United Shoes sells U.S.-made shoes in the United Kingdom. Because of this, the firm's value is greater when the U.S. dollar is less valuable relative to the British pound. Suppose that it is equally likely that the British pound will be worth US$1.40, US$1.50, or US$1.60

next year. Under these alternatives, United Shoes is worth either US$105 million, US$140 million, or US$160 million. By purchasing pounds in the forward market at the current forward price of US$1.52, the firm will realize for certain a value of US$138 million next year. Should United Shoes enter into the forward contract?

Answer: The US$138 million realized by hedging exceeds the US$135 million the firm would realize, on average, by not hedging. In this case, the firm benefits by hedging.

In Example 20.1, United Shoes was willing to take an unfair bet, paying $1.52 for British pounds that would be worth only $1.50, on average, to reduce uncertainty. United Shoes was willing to take this bet because movements in exchange rates that lower profits hurt the firm more than the firm is helped by equal-sized exchange rate changes in the opposite direction help it; that is, exchange rate uncertainty decreases United Shoe's expected value. Thus, the firm could improve its expected value by reducing this uncertainty.

In general, whenever a firm is hurt more by a negative realization of an economic variable (e.g., an exchange rate change) than it is helped by a positive realization, the firm can increase its value by hedging. The following sections describe various situations where we might expect the costs of negative realizations to exceed the benefits of positive realizations. Each situation provides a motivation for why firms hedge.

How Hedging Reduces Taxes

Taxes play a key role in most financial decisions, and hedging is no different. Tax gains often accrue from hedging because of an asymmetry between the tax treatment of gains and losses. A U.S. corporation that has earned $100 million will pay about $34 million in federal income taxes. However, if that same corporation loses $100 million, the IRS will rebate its share of the losses only up to the amount of taxes the firm paid in the past three years.[5] Hence, the firm loses more value from a $100 million pretax loss than it gains in value from a $100 million pretax gain. Example 20.2 illustrates how firms can gain from hedging risks in situations of this kind.[6]

Example 20.2:   Taxes and Hedging

Cogen Pharmaceuticals sells a large fraction of its arthritis drugs in France for which it receives payments in francs. Given that its costs are denominated in U.S. dollars, the firm's taxable earnings are subject to currency risk. Currency fluctuations are the firm's only source of risk, so the firm's pretax hedged and unhedged positions in two equally possible exchange rate scenarios can be described as follows:

Pretax Income for Two Equally Likely Scenarios (in $millions)			
	Weak Dollar	*Strong Dollar*	*Average*
Unhedged	$100	−$20	$40
Hedged	35	35	35

---

[5]Tax losses also can be carried forward, but the present value of the future tax savings is less than the value of receiving the tax rebate immediately.

[6]Smith and Stulz (1985) discuss how hedging can be used by a corporation to reduce its expected tax liabilities.

The firm will thus achieve higher average pretax profits if it chooses not to hedge. Assume, however, that there is a 40 percent profits tax, but no tax deduction on losses. Show that the expected after-tax profits will be higher if the firm chooses to hedge:

Answer:

After-Tax Income for Two Equally Likely Scenarios (in $millions)			
	Weak Dollar	*Strong Dollar*	*Average*
Unhedged	$60	−$20	$20
Hedged	21	21	21

Result 20.3   Because of asymmetric treatment of gains and losses, firms may reduce their expected tax liabilities by hedging.

Hedging to Avoid Financial Distress Costs

Chapters 15 and 16 examined why financial distress can be costly. Distress costs include costs arising from conflicts between debt holders and equity holders and those arising from the reluctance of many of the firm's most important stakeholders (e.g., customers and suppliers) to do business with a firm having financial difficulties. By hedging its risks, a firm can increase its value by reducing its probability of facing financial distress in the future.

An Example Based on the Stakeholder Theory of Financial Distress.   Consider, for example, Microtronics, a medium-sized manufacturer of scientific equipment, which needs to borrow $100 million to refinance an existing loan. Its operating value next year is assumed to depend on two factors: the health of the U.S. economy and the dollar/yen exchange rate. Microtronics' value is highest when (1) the U.S. economy is strong, since the demand for scientific equipment will then be strong, and (2) when the dollar is weak relative to the yen, which increases the dollar costs of Microtronics' Japanese competitors.

To evaluate Microtronics' loan application, the lender's analysts have calculated the firm's operating values under two equally possible scenarios. The analysts have assumed that the firm is unhedged and that customers maintain their confidence in the firm. These operating values are described in Exhibit 20.1.

If the economy is weak but the dollar strong, the firm's value ($95 million) will be less than its debt obligation ($100 million). The bank is particularly concerned about the weak economy because the $95 million value of the firm in this scenario assumes that customers maintain their confidence in the firm. As Chapter 16 noted, consumers of

EXHIBIT 20.1   Microtronics' Value in a Strong and in a Weak Economy*

	Strong Economy	*Weak Economy*
Strong dollar	$150 million	$ 95 million
Weak dollar	200 million	125 million

*Assumes the firm is unhedged and that customer confidence is high.

EXHIBIT 20.2   Microtronics' Value in a Strong and Weak Economy*

	Strong Economy	*Weak Economy*
Strong dollar	$165 million	$110 million
Weak dollar	185 million	110 million

*Assumes that currency risk is hedged.

scientific equipment are reluctant to purchase from a firm with financial difficulties because of potential difficulties in obtaining spare parts and service. Thus, if Microtronics is unable to meet its debt obligations, its value in this scenario will be considerably less than the $95 million it would be worth if the firm were solvent. If the firm loses its customer base because of its financial distress, the bank may find it difficult to recover even a small fraction of what it is owed on the loan.

By hedging some of its currency risk (i.e., by selling yen forwards or futures), Microtronics is betting that the yen will weaken relative to the dollar. Such a bet increases the firm's value in scenarios in which the yen is weak relative to the dollar and the firm is at a competitive disadvantage relative to its Japanese competitors. Hedging currency risk, in effect, transfers value from the scenarios where the dollar is weak to scenarios where the dollar is strong. If Microtronics hedges in a way that transfers $15 million from the weak-dollar scenario to the strong-dollar scenario, its values in the four scenarios would be as shown in Exhibit 20.2.

If Microtronics is hedged in this way, the bank is assured of being paid back in all four scenarios and the firm will not be exposed to the costs of bankruptcy. Hence, in the strong-dollar, weak economy scenario, hedging has eliminated the discrepancy between the actual value of the firm and the value of the firm when customer confidence is maintained.

Exhibit 20.3, which plots the distribution of profits with and without hedging, illustrates the potential advantages of hedging. The firm illustrated in this exhibit has a debt obligation of $20 million and will suffer financial distress costs if it cannot meet this obligation. The probability of not meeting the obligation is seen as the areas, to the left of $20 million, under the two curves. Since this illustration assumes that hedging is costly, the mean of the unhedged distribution is greater than the mean of the hedged distribution. However, since the unhedged distribution has a larger variance, the area to the left of $20 million is greater than the corresponding area for the hedged distribution. In other words, hedging reduces the probability of financial distress.

Hedging does not always reduce the probability of financial distress. If the cost of hedging is sufficiently large, and if hedging reduces variance very little, then hedging may actually increase the probability of financial distress. Instances where this would occur are very unusual. However, if it is costly, then hedging may not be worthwhile for firms with very low financial distress costs.

Result 20.4   Firms that are subject to high financial distress costs have greater incentives to hedge.

Hedging to Increase the Tax Shield from Debt Capacity.   The Microtronics example suggests that hedging reduces the expected costs of financial distress for any given debt level. As hedging opportunities improve, however, firms can choose more highly levered capital structures and take advantage of the tax and other advantages of debt financing

EXHIBIT 20.3

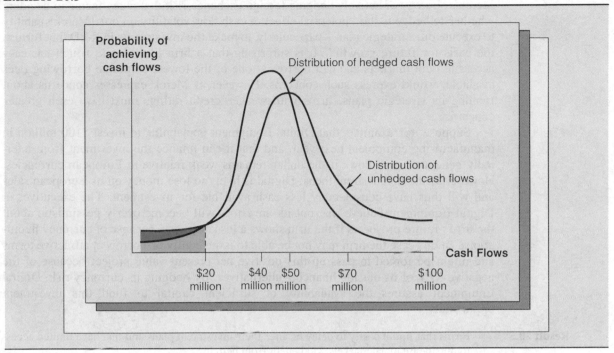

(see Chapters 13 to 18). To understand why hedging allows a firm to take on more debt financing, consider again our analogy about the choice between taking the freeway or taking city streets to the airport. Taking the freeway requires travelers to allow at least an hour to get to the airport in order to be certain of catching the flight. However, when the slower but more certain option of taking city streets is available, travelers can leave 10 minutes later even though, on average, this route takes 10 minutes longer. Similarly, a firm that hedges its risks will be able to take on more debt while keeping its probability of financial distress within a reasonable level.

Hedging to Help Firms Plan for Their Capital Needs

Internal Financing, Underinvestment, and Overinvestment.   Chapters 14, 16, and 18 explained why corporations view internal sources of equity capital as cheaper than external sources. Recall that the lower costs of internal funds arise for information reasons as well as because of taxes and transaction costs. Empirical evidence suggests that because of the difference between the costs of internal and external capital, investment expenditures by firms correspond closely to their cash flows. Firms thus have a tendency to overinvest or underinvest, depending on the availability of internally generated cash flows. The reliance on internally generated cash can be especially costly to firms that need to plan their investments in advance but have highly variable cash flows. To the extent that hedging reduces this variability in cash flows, it can increase the value of the firm.[7]

---

[7]This is discussed in more detail in Lessard (1990) and Froot, Scharfstein, and Stein (1993).

Consistent with this view, Lewent and Kearney (1990) noted in their explanation of Merck's strategy of actively hedging foreign exchange risk that a key factor in deciding whether to hedge is the "potential effect of cash flow volatility on our [Merck's] ability to execute our strategic plan—particularly, to make the investments in R&D that furnish the basis for future growth." It is surprising that a firm like Merck, which has easy access to debt markets and can borrow at one of the lowest corporate borrowing rates available, would express such concerns. However, if Merck expresses concerns about funding its strategic plans, firms with weaker credit ratings must have even greater concerns.

Suppose, for example, that Digital Equipment is planning to invest $100 million in manufacturing equipment next year, and that it can finance the investment from internally generated cash flows if the dollar remains weak relative to European currencies. However, if the dollar strengthens, Digital is likely to lose money on its European sales and will thus have considerably less cash available for investment. The executives at Digital Equipment believe that outside investors will become overly pessimistic about the firm's future prospects if the firm shows a loss next year because of currency fluctuations. In this case the firm may not be able to issue equity or borrow at attractive terms and might be forced to pass up this positive net present value project because of the negative *NPV* of its outside financing alternatives. By hedging its currency risk, Digital Equipment assures the availability of sufficient capital to fund this investment opportunity.

Result 20.5   Firms that find it costly to delay or alter their investment plans and that have limited access to outside financial markets will benefit from hedging.

The Desirability of Partial Hedging.   If either the investment requirements or the costs and benefits of obtaining external financing are determined by the risk factor the firm wishes to hedge, a firm may not want to completely hedge the risk. For example, an oil firm may want to increase its exploration budget when oil prices are high. If the firm can raise capital on more favorable terms after having shown increased earnings, it will want to maintain some exposure to the risks of oil price fluctuations, so that its earnings look good when there is a need for outside capital. Such a firm would not choose to completely eliminate its exposure to oil price movements, but it still would like to hedge risks to guarantee sufficient investment funds in the event of substantial oil price declines.

Example 20.3:   National Petroleum's Partial Hedge

National Petroleum currently has 3 million barrels of oil in reserves that will be extracted within the next three years at the rate of 1 million barrels of oil per year. Extraction costs are $6 per barrel and are expected to remain stable for the next three years. The current price of oil is $22 per barrel. Given current conditions, National is no longer exploring for new oil, but the company plans to reassess the situation after three years. If oil prices exceed $30 per barrel, National will reestablish its exploration operations, which will require a capital investment of $35 million.

Forward contracts for the delivery of oil in one, two, and three years are available at a price of $24 per barrel. National has overhead costs of about $3 million per year and interest costs of $8 million per year. The firm will suffer significant financial distress-related costs if it cannot meet these fixed obligations should oil prices fall significantly. How much should National hedge?

Answer: National would like to hedge its oil price risk in a way that guarantees it will generate at least $11 million from its operations, so that it can cover its fixed costs and interest obligations. National can accomplish this by selling its entire supply of oil on the forward markets, which would guarantee cash flows of $18 million in each year. However, if the firm is completely hedged, it will not accumulate enough internally generated capital to fund new exploration efforts if oil prices exceed $30 per barrel. For this reason, National should hedge only enough to avoid financial distress, so that it has more money available if oil prices rise.

As Example 20.3 illustrates, the fact that oil companies have greater investment needs when oil prices are higher provides one explanation for why these companies generally hedge very little of their oil price risk. As we discuss in Chapter 21, this also provides a motivation for the use of options to hedge oil price risk since they can be used to guarantee sufficient profits to avoid financial distress while allowing the firm to benefit from very high oil prices. The incentive of oil firms to hedge may also be reduced by the fact that the forward price of oil has generally been less than, rather than greater than, the spot price of oil, and as a result, there has historically been a positive expected cost of hedging (see footnote 2 for further discussion).

How Hedging Improves Executive Compensation Contracts and Performance Evaluation

Chapter 17 discussed conflicts of interest between shareholders and management and ways to design executive compensation contracts that minimize the costs of these conflicts. Recall that executive compensation should be designed to expose managers to the risk associated with factors they control (e.g., success at cutting costs) while minimizing exposure to risks they do not control (e.g., changes in interest rates). This suggests that a well-designed compensation package will not leave a risk-averse executive exposed to the risks of currency fluctuations, interest rate changes, and other factors over which the executive has no control.

Consider, for example, an Irish electronics company which sells most of its products in the United States. Its costs are mainly in Irish pounds, but its revenues are predominately in U.S. dollars. If the dollar strengthens against the pound (i.e., if the company receives more pounds for every dollar it receives), then the company's profits increase since its revenues improve while its costs (in pounds) remain constant. Obviously, shareholders benefit from this, but it makes no sense to reward the company's top executives for this unexpected increase in profits because the exchange rate change is completely outside of their control. It also makes no sense to penalize the executives for a decline in profits owing to a weakening of the dollar. The shareholders would like to eliminate as much risk that managers cannot control so they can increase the managers' exposures to the risks they do control.

It is no doubt difficult to design a compensation package that eliminates a manager's exposure to all hedgeable risks. Doing this would create an excessively complicated contract and require prior knowledge of exactly how interest rates, currency movements, and other hedgeable risks affect earnings and firm values, and how these relationships change over time. Corporations, however, may be better able to accomplish this objective with much simpler performance-based contracts if they allow their managers to hedge the appropriate risks and compensate them in a way that gives them the incentive to hedge.

An additional, but related, advantage of implementing a hedging program is that by requiring its managers to hedge, a firm will be able to evaluate its executives more accurately. Earnings become a more accurate indicator of managerial performance when extraneous noise in the earnings (i.e., outside the managers' control) is eliminated. Unhedged risks provide managers with additional excuses when earnings are poor. A common excuse might be that "the earnings would have been much better if the dollar hadn't weakened." Unhedged risks might also mask poor performance when managers are lucky enough to realize gains resulting from favorable currency or interest rate changes.

Evaluating the Management at International Chemicals

Despite being a relatively small chemical company, International Chemicals (IC) is a true multinational. It has production facilities in France, the United States, and Malaysia and sells its products throughout the world. Despite IC's diversification, its earnings have been extremely volatile, particularly so in 1992. Management explained the poor performance in that year, especially in the firm's European sales, as the result of the rapid decline in the British pound, which fell by over 20 percent relative to the U.S. dollar. Because of the pound's decline, International Chemicals was at a serious disadvantage relative to its most important competitor, which is located in the United Kingdom.

The board of directors of International Chemicals found management's explanation plausible. However, board members wondered how much of the record performance in earlier years could be attributed to favorable shifts in exchange rates rather than the hard work and clever decisions of the company's top managers. A senior director raised the following concern: How can we evaluate our top managers with such volatile currencies? When they do poorly, they can almost always point to losses due to currencies moving against them. When they do well, we will always suspect that they were lucky and that currencies moved in a favorable direction.

In response to this concern, one of the directors made the following proposal: At the end of each year, the next year's earnings would be projected. The managers would receive a bonus if the earnings projection were exceeded, but there would be an even greater penalty for doing worse than the projection. The penalty for failure in meeting the projection would provide management with an incentive to use the futures market to hedge currency risks, so that unfavorable currency movements would not cause them to fall below their projections. The directors making the proposal believed that by motivating management to hedge the effects of currency movements, it would be much easier to assess the quality of management's performance.

One of the newer board members questioned the wisdom of this hedging policy. Shouldn't the board encourage managers to take positions in currencies that are expected to appreciate? The response of the senior board member was quite forceful. "We are in the chemical business, not the foreign exchange trading business. It is unlikely that our financial managers would have any better knowledge about currency movements than the bankers and professional speculators they would be "betting against" when executing such trades. In the absence of special information, a commodity or currency position is at best a zero net present value investment which should be avoided."

The senior manager also provided an additional advantage of implementing the new corporate hedging policy: Managers who are confident about their abilities will be attracted to firms that can evaluate their performance more accurately. Because a firm that chooses not to hedge its risks might be regarded as one that is less able to evaluate its managers, it may tend to attract managers who are less confident about their abilities and who prefer some noise in the evaluation process.[8]

Result 20.6   The gains from hedging are greater when it is more difficult to evaluate and monitor management.

Disney's Motivation to Hedge

Executives at Disney believe that by reducing the volatility of their profits from individual business units they are better able to evaluate the business unit managers and assess the profitability of their different lines of business. The executives also believe that if the overall

---

[8]Theoretical articles by DeMarzo and Duffie (1995) and Breeden and Vishwanathan (1996) explore how information issues affect hedging choices.

firm is hedged, analysts will find the firm's profits more easy to interpret and predict, so that the firm's stock price will reflect the firm's true value more accurately.

As part of their evaluation system, the top executives at Disney's central headquarters and the top managers of the individual units agree on a target for each unit's operating profits in the next evaluation period. Managers must then implement a strategy that minimizes their chances of not meeting the target. As part of this strategy, the individual units initiate transactions with Disney's treasury group to hedge their exposures to currency fluctuations and other sources of hedgeable risks. The treasury group in turn would hedge their exposures in the derivatives markets.[9]

How Hedging Improves Decision Making

The Disney discussion suggests that an active risk management program can improve management's decision-making process by reducing the profit volatility of individual business units. Less volatile profits for a company's business units provide management at the firm's central headquarters with better information about where to allocate capital and which managers are the most deserving of promotions.

Using Futures Prices to Allocate Capital. Firms with sophisticated risk management groups have further advantages derived from their greater understanding of market prices, which they can utilize to make better capital allocation decisions. As Chapter 10 discussed, futures prices, viewed as certainty equivalents, provide an assessment of the current value of pork bellies delivered in one year, enabling a farmer to make intelligent decisions about whether to increase hog production. If the farmer's costs are less than the futures price, he can increase his production and sell the futures contracts to lock in his gains. If the costs exceed the futures price, then the farmer should probably cut his production.

Although we believe that futures markets generally lead managers to make better decisions, managers sometimes ignore new price information after hedging and, as a result, often make serious mistakes. This is what we call the fallacy of sunk costs, which Example 20.4 illustrates:

Example 20.4:   Hedging and Production Choices: A Pitfall

Omega Chemicals sells a lemon-scented detergent base that is used by producers of both laundry detergent and dish-washing soap. Lemon oil is one of its most expensive ingredients and its price is volatile. To hedge this price risk, Omega made a forward purchase of 300,000 pounds of lemon oil at $4.50 per pound for delivery over the next 12 months. Subsequent to this purchase, the price of lemon oil increased to $6.25 per pound because of political uncertainties in one of the major exporting countries. Omega's management views this as a prime opportunity to aggressively increase its market share given its "cost advantage" over its leading competitor, whose management chose not to hedge and thus must pay $6.25 per pound for the lemon oil. Do you agree with management's logic?

Answer: Omega is much better off as a result of its forward purchase of lemon oil. However, the opportunity costs associated with the input of one pound of lemon oil is $6.25 rather than $4.50. Although it will be purchasing the lemon oil for $4.50 per pound, Omega could, if it wished, sell the lemon oil on the open market for $6.25. Hence, although the company made over $500,000 on the forward purchase, its opportunity costs have increased just as much as those of its competitors.

---

[9]The material on Disney is based on the discussion by Ken Frier, vice president for financial risk management, at the UCLA Risk Management Conference, March 30, 1996.

When making pricing and other operating decisions, managers must rely on opportunity costs instead of historical costs. Managers who understand this should be able to greatly improve their operating and investment decisions when futures and forward markets exist for either their inputs or outputs.

Using Information from Insurance Premiums to Allocate Capital.   One way to value the uncertain negative cash flows associated with adverse events is to use insurance premiums to obtain certainty equivalents. However, as the discussion below illustrates, there are risks that are best left uninsured.

British Petroleum's Insurance Choices

British Petroleum (BP), recognizing that hedging risks can result in better decision making, revised its corporate insurance strategy in a somewhat unconventional way.[10] The conventional wisdom is that corporations should insure large risks but not small risks because small risks should average out over time and can be diversified within the firm. British Petroleum, however, has decided to take the opposite approach: to insure its small risks but not its large risks. The reason has absolutely nothing to do with the motivations for hedging described earlier. Instead, British Petroleum's rationale relates to how hedging affects decision making.

To understand BP's rationale, consider the issues involved in deciding whether to spend $50 million on new refining capacity. There are a number of uncertain but insurable expenses associated with such an operation. For example, unintentional oil spills, caused by fires or natural disasters, raise the potential for lawsuits, and on-the-job injuries might cause employee lawsuits. If these uncertain costs were uninsured, the calculation of the net present value of the oil refining project would require BP's management to calculate the expected value of those uncertain losses as well as the corresponding discount rates.

The top executives of British Petroleum believe that insurance companies may be better able than BP management to calculate the present values of these insurable losses. One reason has to do with incentives. Conceivably, a situation might arise in which a manager may want to approve a marginal project and thus might tend to understate the potential losses from fires and natural disasters. The second reason has to do with expertise. Insurance companies are probably in a better position to assess the expected losses from fires and other risks they insure as part of their regular business.

For more unusual and larger risks, BP probably has the better information. One might expect that it would have better information about the chances of incurring hundreds of millions of dollars in damages from an explosion in one of its oil tankers, caused by negligence. Because the oil giant can better assess these risks, it is difficult and expensive to insure against them. Insurance companies are concerned with the adverse selection problem (see Chapter 18), which in this context implies that firms have an incentive to insure those risks that insurance companies underprice. Understanding these incentives, insurance companies use extremely pessimistic assumptions in assessing risks when they are at an informational disadvantage compared with the firm's management. As a result, insurance quotes for these large risks are often unattractive to the firm.

Result 20.7   Firms have an incentive to insure or hedge risks that insurance companies and markets can better assess. Doing this improves decision making. Firms will absorb internally those risks over which they have the comparative advantage in evaluating.

20.3 The Motivation to Hedge Affects What Is Hedged

The previous section noted that hedging can improve the values of firms for a number of reasons. In designing their risk management strategies, firms should consider each of

---

[10]British Petroleum's insurance strategy is discussed in detail in Doherty and Smith (1993).

the individual reasons for hedging. For example, firms would like to minimize taxes as well as the costs of financial distress, and they also would like a risk management system that improves the quality of their management. Unfortunately, it may be difficult to do all of these things simultaneously. A firm's taxable income is not the same as the income that it reports to shareholders, so minimizing the volatility of its taxable income will not always minimize the volatility of its reported income. More importantly, a hedge that minimizes the volatility of a firm's earnings will not always effectively insure against longer-term changes in the firm's value, which is likely to be more important if there is concern about financial distress in the future.

Consider, for example, a Hong Kong textile firm which we will call Canton International. The firm manufactures a variety of shirts that it sells mainly in Europe. The firm is partially owned by one of Hong Kong's wealthiest families, the Chans, who also own a construction business and other small manufacturing firms. The Chan family fully delegates the management of Canton International to a group of executives whom they have recently hired. The Chans have let it be known, however, that the new managers will be replaced if they do not perform well within the next two years.

The Chan family can best assess their managers if they require them to completely hedge the firm's foreign exchange risk over the next two years. They would prefer to avoid replacing the managers because of poor performance if the problems were due entirely to unfavorable and unexpected movements in exchange rates. Likewise, they would not want to retain a poor-quality management team that was lucky enough to experience favorable movements in exchange rates. These objectives suggest that the Chans should require their management team to minimize the volatility of the firm's *earnings* over the next two years.

Unfortunately, this objective may only partially solve a second concern of the Chan family. Canton International is a highly levered firm with a $100 million note due at the end of five years. To minimize the chances of default, which would greatly embarrass the family, the Chans would like to instruct management to enter into forward contracts that minimize their chances of defaulting on this note. However, implementing a hedge that minimizes the chances of default will probably require larger positions in the forward and futures markets than would be required to minimize uncertainty over the next two years because the firm's *value* represents the discounted value of all future cash flows, not just the cash flows accruing in the next two years.

Result 20.8   If a firm's main motivation for hedging is to better assess the quality of management, the firm will probably want to hedge its earnings or cash flow rather than its value. However, if the firm is hedging to avoid the costs of financial distress, it should implement a hedging strategy that takes into account both the variance of its value and the variance of its cash flows.

20.4 How Should Companies Organize Their Hedging Activities?

In addition to understanding whether to hedge and how to hedge, firms must consider the organization of their risk management activities. Should risk management be centralized, operating out of the firm's treasury department, or should hedging be performed at the level of the individual divisions? The answer to this question depends on the level of expertise in the various divisions, the availability of information about the divisions' exposures, the transaction costs of hedging, and the motivation for hedging.

At present, most risk management programs are implemented at the corporate rather than the divisional level. One reason for this has to do with the costs of trading. In illiquid markets, trading costs can be high, and it might make sense to consolidate trading. Consolidating allows the exposures of each of the business units to be netted against one another. Corporate managers then execute trades in the financial markets to hedge only the firm's aggregate exposure. A second reason has to do with the relative newness of the field of risk management and the likelihood of limited expertise in it at the divisional level. A final reason is the fixed costs associated with setting up a risk management department.

As risk management expertise becomes more widespread and the futures and swap markets become more liquid, we expect to see hedging performed more at the divisional level. This is especially true when the principal motivation for hedging has to do with improving management incentives. Division heads, who have the best information about risk exposures in their divisions, ultimately should be responsible for hedging those risk exposures. Divisions also may want to hedge to assure themselves of investment funds if investment funds from corporate headquarters are tied in some way to the divisional profits. If, however, a firm's principal motivation for hedging has to do with either lowering expected tax liabilities or reducing the probability of bankruptcy, then most hedging should be carried out at the corporate level.

Result 20.9   Corporations should organize their hedging in a way that reflects why they are hedging. Most hedging motivations suggest that hedging should be carried out at the corporate level. However, the improvement in management incentives that can be realized with a risk management program are best achieved when the individual divisions are responsible for hedging.

20.5 Do Risk Management Departments Always Hedge?

Until now, our analysis has assumed that the purpose of a risk management department is to reduce the risks of a firm's cash flows. However, some corporations view risk management departments as "profit centers" and have encouraged them to generate profits by speculating rather than hedging. Indeed, a number of firms have generated large profits by speculating in currencies and interest rates. We think that in most cases, these efforts are seriously misguided. There have been a number of highly publicized cases where managers, thinking that they had special information, bet heavily in futures markets—and lost. For example, in 1994 Procter and Gamble *gambled* that U.S. and German interest rates would fall and lost $157 million on two interest rate swap contracts.[11]

Certainly, cases do arise where firms have special information that leads them to speculate instead of hedge. For example, Nestlé is one of the biggest buyers of cocoa in the world and, as a result, it may have special information that allows the company to better predict cocoa prices. Although Nestlé will want to buy cocoa futures to hedge its anticipated future purchases, occasionally it will want to use its special information to speculate. Suppose, for example, that Nestlé anticipates that its needs will be less than normal over the next six months, resulting in a decline in cocoa prices. In this case, Nestlé might choose to sell rather than buy cocoa futures.

The above example is somewhat atypical because only in exceptional cases do managers have superior information about future price changes. For example, we are very skeptical of corporate treasurers who claim to have superior information about foreign exchange and use that information to speculate in those markets.

---

[11]*The Wall Street Journal,* Apr. 14, 1994.

Result 20.10   Managers have private information only in exceptional cases. Given this, they almost always should be hedging rather than speculating.

20.6   How Hedging Affects the Firm's Stakeholders

Up to this point, we have examined hedging from the perspective of managers who are trying to maximize total firm value (i.e., the value of the debt plus the value of the equity). As Chapters 15 and 17 discussed, however, managers have competing pressures and may not choose to maximize total firm value. Perhaps the instances where firms were observed to be speculating rather than hedging arose because management's objective was *not* to maximize total firm value. In this section, we explore the effect of hedging on the debt holders and equity holders separately, and how hedging can affect other stakeholders of the firm.

How Hedging Affects Debt Holders and Equity Holders

Chapter 8 described how equity can be viewed as a call option on the firm's value. To the extent that hedging reduces volatility without increasing firm value, it reduces the value of this option, transferring value from equity holders to debt holders. From an equity holder's perspective, the value-maximizing benefits of hedging may be reduced, and possibly even reversed, by this transfer. The actions of managers to hedge in these circumstances certainly would not endear them to these equity holders. However, a firm's bankers and bondholders would certainly like the firm to hedge.

How Hedging Affects Employees and Customers

The interests of most of a firm's employees are closer to the interests of debt holders than to equity holders. Their jobs and reputations are at risk in the event of bankruptcy, and they may not realize substantial benefits if the firm does extremely well. Managers who look out for the interest of their employees would then have an incentive to hedge. Customers generally like to see a firm that will honor its warranties, supply replacement parts, and generate additional products that will enhance the value of existing products. Since firms in financial distress are less likely to make choices that benefit their customers, hedging also benefits a firm's customers.

Hedging and Managerial Incentives

The discussion in the previous subsection suggests that managers who are loyal to their employees and customers may want to hedge more than the firm's shareholders would like them to. In this subsection, we will discuss other reasons why the managers' incentives to hedge may differ from those of shareholders.

Managerial Incentives to Hedge.   Consider the case of an entrepreneur, like Bill Gates at Microsoft, who starts a successful business and continues to hold a sizable fraction of the firm's shares. Gates is probably more concerned about Microsoft's risk than other shareholders because he is much less diversified than they are. As a result, Gates might want Microsoft to hedge to reduce his personal risks even when doing so has no effect on the firm's expected cash flows. In this case, and in the absence of transaction costs, Gates is indifferent between hedging on his personal account and hedging through the corporation. However, it might be more efficient to have the transaction costs borne by Microsoft, which has a trained staff of risk management experts, rather than by Gates personally.

Managerial Incentives to Speculate.   Managers also may have an incentive to speculate when the firm would be better off hedging. As noted in the previous section, this sometimes happens when managers have misguided notions that they possess superior information about future trends in currency and commodity prices. In addition, managers may have an incentive to speculate if they are compensated with executive stock options, which are worth more when stock price volatility is higher. Longer-term considerations may provide managers with even more incentives to take speculative risks and choose not to hedge. Managers who realize a favorable outcome as a result of a risky strategy are likely to receive an attractive bonus and, in addition, be promoted and have many more opportunities in the future. As long as their upside potential exceeds their downside risk, managers will want to speculate rather than hedge.

The case of Nick Leeson and the bankruptcy of Barings Bank illustrates how perverse management incentives, along with a lack of oversight, can lead to disaster. By making a series of enormous speculative bets on Japanese stock index futures, Leeson managed to lose US$1.4 billion for his firm, Barings Bank, which ultimately led to the firm's demise in 1994. If these trades had been successful and Barings had earned instead of lost over a billion dollars, Leeson would have received a generous bonus and enjoyed increased opportunities and prestige within the firm. The upside associated with this risky strategy was clearly quite high. Perhaps, Leeson believed that all he had to lose in the event of a bad outcome was his job. Unfortunately, Leeson lost not only his job, but was sentenced to six years in a Singapore jail.

Before concluding this section, we should stress that the Barings case, the Proctor and Gamble case discussed in the last section, as well as the Metallgesellschaft case[12] attracted a great deal of attention because of the huge losses created by the improper use of derivatives. However, these cases should not be viewed as typical. Our understanding is that most managers use derivative instruments to hedge rather than to speculate and, as a result, add value to their corporations. Unfortunately, well-run corporations that use risk management tools effectively to benefit their shareholders are not nearly as newsworthy as their counterparts that take ill-advised positions which bankrupt their firms.

20.7 The Motivation to Manage Interest Rate Risk

Until now, we have discussed the motivations for risk management in general terms, without reference to the particular sources of risk. In reality, however, a firm's motivation to hedge interest rate risk, which is closely tied to the capital structure choice, may be quite different than its incentive to hedge either commodity or foreign exchange risk.

Our earlier discussion of capital structure (Chapters 13–18), covered the issues surrounding the firm's choice between debt and equity financing in great detail. However, the choice between debt and equity financing is only the first step that firms must take when they determine the overall makeup of their liabilities. Beause they affect who owns and controls the firm, decisions relating to the level of equity financing (e.g., whether to issue new shares or repurchase existing shares) are important decisions and are typically

---

[12]Metallgesellschaft is discussed in Chapter 21.

made at the highest levels of the corporation, generally the board of directors, suggesting that a treasurer's staff is unlikely to face these types of decisions on a day-to-day basis. However, the nature of a firm's debt is something that the treasurer's staff faces on a continuing basis. For example, people who perform the treasury function are continually making choices about whether to borrow at fixed or floating rates, or whether to roll over short-term commercial paper. In addition, they must decide whether to borrow in the domestic currency, in a foreign currency or perhaps with commodity-linked bonds, such as those whose principal is tied to the price of oil. These decisions all affect the firm's **liability stream**, which is the stream of interest costs that a firm will be paying in the future.

We can view all of the above as **liability management** decisions because they affect the nature of the firm's liabilities. However, the decisions can be viewed equivalently as risk management choices, because the decisions affect the firm's exposure to various sources of risk. In general, when a firm determines its exposure to interest rates, commodities, and foreign exchange through its borrowing choices without using derivatives, we think of these choices as *liability management* choices. When the firm alters these risk exposures with the aid of derivatives, we refer to this as *risk management*. However since, in many cases, a firm might be close to being indifferent between, for example, (1) borrowing in dollars and swapping the dollar debt for a yen obligation, and (2) simply borrowing in yen, this distinction between liability management and risk management becomes largely irrelevant.

Alternative Liability Streams

It is useful to think about the different liability streams that a U.S. firm can create when it is restricted to borrowing only in U.S. dollars. We further simplify this analysis by assuming that there are only two possible maturities for the debt: short term and long term. One might want to think of short-term debt as debt due in one year and long-term debt as debt due in five years.

Whether the firm is borrowing short term or long term, its cost of borrowing will consist of the sum of a risk-free component, r, which we can think of as a Treasury bond rate, and a default spread, d, which is determined by the firm's credit rating. As we will see below, the firm can create four separate liability streams, depending on whether the firm borrows short term or long term and whether it chooses to hedge its interest rate exposure.

If the firm chooses to roll over short-term debt, its liability structure can be described by the following equation:

$$i_{st} = r_{st} + d_{st} \tag{20.2}$$

where

i_{st} = the firm's short-term borrowing cost for period t, which is composed of:

r_{st} = the default-free short-term interest rate for period t

d_{st} = the default spread for period t

Note that the t subscripts indicate that short-term borrowing rates and the firm's credit rating change over time.

If the firm instead chooses to borrow long term at a fixed rate, then its liability structure can be described as:

$$i_l = r_l + d_l \tag{20.3}$$

where

r_l = the long-term interest rate

d_l = the default premium

Since these rates are fixed for the life of the loan, they do not have the t subscript.

The third approach involves a floating-rate loan. Firms may be able to obtain the floating-rate loans directly from their banks or they can obtain the loans by borrowing long term and swapping a default-free fixed-rate obligation for a default-free floating-rate obligation (see Chapter 7). In either case, the floating-rate liability can be described by:

$$i_{ft} = r_{st} + d_l \qquad (20.4)$$

where i_{ft} = firm's period t borrowing rate on the long-term floating rate loan

This liability stream subjects the firm to interest rate risk (i.e., changes in r_{st}), but not to risk relating to changes in its credit rating.

The final possibility is a liability stream, i_{ht} that hedges the risk of changing levels of the default-free interest rate, r_{st}, but which leaves the firm exposed to changes in its credit rating or default spread.

$$i_{ht} = r_l + d_{st} \qquad (20.5)$$

Firms were unable to create the liability stream described by equation (20.5) prior to the introduction of interest rate swaps and interest rate futures. Before the introduction of these instruments, borrowing short term implied exposure to interest rate risk and credit risk, while borrowing long term implied exposure to neither. Indeed, the principal advantage of these derivative instruments is that they allow firms to separate their exposures to interest rate risk and changes in their credit ratings. In particular, the liability stream described in equation (20.5) can be created by borrowing short term and swapping a floating- for fixed-rate obligation. Details on how to implement such a transaction are found in Chapter 21.

Result 20.11   A firm's liability stream can be decomposed into two components: one that reflects default-free interest rates and one that reflects the firm's credit rating. When a firm borrows at a fixed rate, both components are fixed. When it rolls over short-term instruments, the liability streams fluctuate with both kinds of risks.

Derivative instruments allow firms to separate these two sources of risk: to create liability streams that are sensitive to interest rates but not their credit ratings, as described in equation (20.4), and to create liability streams that are sensitive to their credit ratings but not interest rates, as described in equation (20.5).

How Do Corporations Choose between Different Liability Streams?[13]

To understand how corporations decide between the various liability streams, consider the two components of their borrowing costs separately. We will first think about how firms should structure their liabilities in terms of their exposure to changing levels of interest rates. Then we will consider how firms decide on their exposure to changes in credit risk. To determine the optimal exposure of their liabilities to interest rate risk, firms must first think about the interest rate exposure they face on the asset side of their balance sheets. In other words, firms must ask whether their ability to make a profit is tied in any way to the overall interest rates in the economy.

---

[13]For more detailed analysis of the issues in this section, see Titman (1992).

Matching the Interest Rate Risk of Assets and Liabilities.   The opening vignette to Chapter 16 provides a vivid illustration of the risks connected with ignoring interest rate exposure on the asset side of a firm's balance sheet. Recall that Massey-Ferguson, a manufacturer of tractors, was highly levered and had a substantial amount of short-term debt financing. When interest rates increased at the end of 1979, farmers found it difficult to buy and finance new tractors, causing Massey-Ferguson's sales and operating income to drop substantially. In other words, the asset side of Massey-Ferguson's balance sheet was extremely sensitive to changes in interest rates and, as a result, the company had a severe mismatch in the interest rate sensitivity of its assets and liabilities. An increase in interest rates, which made its short-term debt more expensive to service, coincided with a drop in the firm's cash flows, which compounded the problem and resulted in the firm facing severe financial distress. As a consequence of financial distress, Massey-Ferguson was forced to downsize considerably and thousands of employees lost their jobs. Perhaps those jobs could have been saved if Massey-Ferguson had done a better job of matching the interest rate exposure of its assets and debt.

Decomposing Interest Rates into Real and Inflation Components.   When thinking about a firm's interest rate exposure, consider that interest rates are composed of a real component and an expected inflation component, that is, the Fisher decomposition (discussed in Chapters 12 and 13). In many cases, a firm's cash flows are unaffected by changes in the real interest rate, but they are affected by changes in the inflation rate. For example, a manufacturer of furniture may see its nominal profits increase when the general price level in the economy increases if the prices that it charges and its labor costs increase at the overall rate of inflation. The furniture manufacturer might then prefer to have a floating-rate liability structure because it does not want to run the risk of being locked into high long-term interest rates when inflation is reduced.

The experience many firms faced in 1982 provides a valuable lesson about the risks connected with locking in long-term interest rates when inflation is uncertain. In the early 1980s, interest rates were very high and many firms were locked into fixed obligations with rates in excess of 15 percent. The high rates did not seem excessive at the time since inflation was running at well over 10 percent per year. Firms were counting on paying back expensive loans with cheaper dollars in the future. However, policies to reduce inflation appeared to be successful by the middle of 1982, substantially increasing the real cost of existing fixed-rate loans. Short-term rates dropped substantially in 1982, so that firms with a substantial amount of floating rate debt did much better than firms that were stuck with fixed-rate obligations.

Result 20.12   If changes in interest rates mainly reflect changes in the rate of inflation and if a firm's operating profits generally increase with the rate of inflation, then the firm will want its liabilities to be exposed to interest rate risk. If, however, interest rate changes are not primarily due to changes in inflation (i.e., real interest rates change) and if the firm's ability to sell its product is affected by the level of real interest rates, then the firm will want to minimize the exposure of its liabilities to interest rate changes.

Hedging Exposure to Credit Rate Changes.   In addition to evaluating a firm's interest rate exposure, we must ask how exposed the firm is to changes in its own credit rating. In general, a firm would like to limit its exposure to changes in its own credit rating since lenders almost always require larger default spreads when firms can least afford to pay the higher interest rates. Firms prefer financing alternatives that keep their default spreads fixed, such as long-term fixed-rate loans or floating-rate loans. However, two factors offset this tendency.

The first factor arises when there is disagreement about the firm's true financial condition. For example, the lender might believe that the firm will face financial difficulties in the future, but the borrower believes that its credit rating is likely to improve in the future. In this case, the borrower may not want to lock in what it considers an unfavorable default spread, preferring instead to borrow short term in hopes that its credit rating will improve in the future. The second factor arises because of the conflicts between debt holders and equity holders discussed in Chapter 15. Recall that a lender who is concerned that the firm will take on excessively risky investments (i.e., the asset substitution problem) is not willing to provide long-term financing on favorable terms. Both of these factors imply that the firm takes on greater exposure to changes in its own credit rating than it would otherwise want, because the costs associated with long-term debt are simply too high. As we discuss in Chapter 21, in these situations, firms often roll over short-term debt and use interest rates swaps to insulate the firm's borrowing costs from the effect of changing interest rates, thereby creating the liability stream described in equation (20.5).

20.8 Foreign Exchange Risk Management

Multinational corporations must pay particular attention to managing their currency risk. Changes in currency rates affect a firm's cash flows as well as its accounting profits. Currency rate changes also affect a company's market and book values.

Types of Foreign Exchange Risk

The various risks associated with changes in the value of currencies are generally divided into three categories: transaction risk, translation risk, and economic risk, which Exhibit 20.4 defines.

Exhibit 20.4   Categories of Currency Risk

	Transaction Risk	*Translation Risk*	*Economic Risk*
Descriptions	Associated with individual transactions denominated in foreign currencies: imports, exports, foreign assets, and loans	Arising from the translation of balance sheets and income statements in foreign currencies to the currency of the parent company for financial reporting purposes	Associated with losing competitive advantage due to exchange rate movements
Examples	A U.S. company imports parts from Japan. The U.S. company is exposed to the risk of the yen strengthening and, as a result, the dollar price of parts increasing.	A U.S. enterprise has a German subsidiary. The U.S. enterprise is exposed to the risk of the deutsche mark weakening, and the value of the subsidiary's assets, liabilities, and profit contributions decreasing in dollar terms in consolidated financial statements.	A U.S. and a Japanese company are competing in Britain. If the yen weakens against the pound and the dollar-pound exchange rate remains constant, the Japanese company can lower its prices in Britain without losing yen income, thus obtaining a competitive advantage over the U.S. company.

Transaction Risk.   To summarize, **transaction risk** represents only the immediate effect on cash flow of an exchange rate change. Exposure to transaction risk arises when a company buys or sells a good, priced in a foreign currency, on credit. Suppose, for example, that IBM sells computers for DM 10 million when the DM is worth US$0.60, with payment required in six months. If the DM depreciates in six months and is worth only US$0.50, IBM will receive the equivalent of US$5 million rather than the US$6 million it had originally expected to receive.

It is quite easy for firms to hedge against transaction risk. For example, IBM could simply require payment in U.S. dollars, which would effectively shift the transaction risk onto its German customer. Alternatively, IBM could enter into a forward contract to sell DM 10 million at a prespecified dollar/deutsche mark exchange rate, with delivery in six months, to lock in the revenues from its sale in U.S. dollars.

Hedges of this type are quite straightforward and are commonly observed in businesses throughout the world. However, they control only the short-term implications of exchange rate changes. For example, IBM's profits in Germany are likely to decline if the deutsche mark weakened unless the company raised the price of its computers in deutsche marks to its German customers. As a result, there are long-run implications of currency changes that are not hedged when risk management is restricted to individual transactions.

In the terminology described in Exhibit 20.4, the economic risk connected with currency changes is much larger than the transaction risk because it takes into account the long-term consequences of the change in currency value.

Translation Risk.   **Translation risk** occurs because a foreign subsidiary's financial statements must be translated into the home country's currency as part of the consolidated statements of the parent. For example, suppose IBM purchased a firm in the United Kingdom for £100 million when the pound was worth US$1.90. The British firm is then set up as a wholly owned subsidiary of IBM with a book value of US$190 million. Subsequently, the dollar strengthens, so that the pound is worth US$1.60. FASB Rule 52 requires that IBM restate its balance sheet to account for this currency change, so that the book value of the subsidiary becomes US$160 million.[14]

Why is translation risk important? First, changes in value associated with exchange rate changes often reflect real economic changes that affect the future profitability of the firm. Translation risk may, however, be an important consideration even when the firm's inflation-adjusted cash flows are unaffected by a change in the exchange rate, as long as the firm has contracts written with terms that are contingent on the firm's book value. For example, firms often have loan covenants that require it to keep its debt-to-book-value ratio above a certain level. In such cases, exchange rate changes that create a drop in the book value of a foreign subsidiary create violations of loan covenants. Since covenant violations can result in real costs, firms may find it beneficial to hedge against such possibilities.

Economic Risk.   What are the determinants of **economic risk**? Or, what are the factors that determine how changes in exchange rates affect the fundamentals of a firm's business. These factors include the following:

---

[14]The gain or loss on the translation of foreign currency in a firm's financial statements is not recognized in current net income, but is reported as a separate component of stockholders' equity. The amounts accumulated in this separate component of stockholders' equity are realized on the sale or liquidation of the investment in the foreign entity.

- Differences between the location of the production facilities and where the product is sold.
- Location of competitors.
- Determinants of input prices: Are they determined in international markets or local markets?

It is easy to see how a firm with a large percentage of its sales overseas is exposed to currency fluctuations. However, even firms that sell only in the United States are subject to currency risk if they import some of their supplies or have foreign competitors.

Why Do Exchange Rates Change?

To understand foreign exchange hedging in greater detail, it is important to think about why exchange rates change over time. Perhaps the most important contributor to exchange rate changes is the difference in the inflation rates of two countries. For example, suppose the British pound is initially worth US$1.50. If the inflation rate in the United Kingdom is 10 percent over the next year while the inflation rate in the United States is zero—and nothing else changes during this time period—then the British pound is likely to fall in value by 10 percent to US$1.35. In this case, the **nominal exchange rate**, which measures the U.S. dollar price of British pounds, changes by 10 percent, but the **real exchange rate**, which measures the relative price of British and U.S. goods, remains unchanged. An American tourist in the United Kingdom will find British goods and services selling at the same price in terms of U.S. dollars as they were selling for in the previous year.

The Case of No Real Effects.   If you believe that differential inflation rates are the primary cause of exchange rate movements, would you need to hedge against unexpected changes? If your main concern is economic risk or transaction risk, there would be no need for your firm to hedge. The firm is subject to neither risk. This point is illustrated in Example 20.5.

Example 20.5:   Currency Risk and Inflation

Textronics will buy three million circuit boards from a small firm in Taiwan in about one year. Each circuit board is currently priced at NT$100, which is equivalent to about US$4 in current exchange rates. Suppose Taiwan has an uncertain monetary policy and could experience either inflation or deflation, which can cause currency movements of as much as 10 percent. Is Textronics exposed to currency risk?

Answer: If inflation is the only cause of exchange rate changes, then Textronics is not exposed to currency risk. A 10 percent increase in the Taiwan price level will result in a price increase of circuit boards to NT$110. However, the inflation will simultaneously result in a drop in the value of the Taiwan dollar to US$.036. The U.S. dollar price that Textronics pays for the circuit boards is thus unchanged.

In Example 20.5, Textronics was simply purchasing an item from a foreign company. Suppose now that Textronics sets up a plant in Taiwan to produce the circuit boards. In this case, an exchange rate change driven purely by inflation can have real effects because it can affect how the firm's Taiwanese assets are represented on its balance sheets which could, in turn, affect bond covenants and other contracts.

Inflation Differences Tend to Generate Real Effects.   Of course, it is rare when different inflation rates in two countries are not also generating real effects in the two countries. For example, when oil was discovered in the North Sea off Britain's coast, the British pound strengthened because, at the prevailing exchange rate, the United Kingdom was expected to have an excess of exports (especially oil) over imports. In this case, the strengthening of the pound did affect relative prices. A U.S. tourist in the United Kingdom after the oil discovery would find that prices calculated in U.S. dollars had increased. Since the real, or inflation-adjusted, exchange rate changed, a U.S. firm that imported materials from the United Kingdom would see its costs increase. If the production costs of the British firm in British pounds stayed the same, the firm's price in pounds also would stay the same, which implies that U.S. dollar prices would increase if the pound strengthened. A U.S. firm would be exposed to currency risk in this case.

Result 20.13	Exchange rate movements can be decomposed into those caused by differences in the inflation rates in the home country and the foreign country, and those caused by changes in real exchange rates. In most cases, the incentive is to hedge against real exchange rate changes rather than the component of exchange rate changes that is driven by inflation differences between the two countries.

Exhibit 20.5 documents both real and nominal exchange rate movements from 1985 to 1993 for five countries: Indonesia, Japan, Spain, Thailand, and Turkey. It is important to note that nominal exchange rates changed dramatically over this time period for countries experiencing high levels of inflation. However, the real exchange rates, which are more important for multinational firms, are somewhat less volatile over longer periods of time.

The exchange rates shown in Exhibit 20.5 represent the number of units of the local currency that can be exchanged for each U.S. dollar. For example, the 1985 exchange rate for Turkey is 576.86, which means that 576.86 Turkish liras could be exchanged for US$1.00 on the spot market at the end of 1985. The consumer price index (CPI) for each year relates the price levels of each country to the price levels for 1990. An index value of 100 means that the price level is identical to the prices in that country in 1990. For example, the CPI of 114.00 for Thailand in 1993 means that prices were 14 percent higher in 1993 than they were in 1990.

The right-hand column summarizes the real exchange rate for each selected currency, or the equivalent purchasing power that must be exchanged from one currency to another. To determine the purchasing power being exchanged in the spot market, adjustments must be made for the rate of inflation in each evaluated country and in the United States. To accomplish this adjustment, the spot exchange rate is divided by the local CPI and multiplied by the U.S. CPI, resulting in the real exchange rate. Because all the local consumer price indexes and the U.S. CPI are stated with a 1990 basis, the real exchange rate reported is also relative to 1990 prices.

In 1985, for example, Turkey's spot exchange rate was TL 576.86 per US$. However, the 1985 Turkish lira had 8.35 times the purchasing power of the 1990 lira (100/11.77). Meanwhile, the 1985 dollar had only 1.21 times the purchasing power of the 1990 dollar. To take into account the disparities in the inflation rates of the two countries, divide the spot rate of TL 576.86 by the local CPI of 11.77 and multiply by the U.S. CPI of 82.40 to find the real exchange rate. In this case, the exchange rate for 1985 is equivalent to TL 4,038.51 per US$ in 1990. As you can see from Exhibit 20.5, the real exchange rate between Turkey and the United States dropped between 1985 and 1990. In other words,

EXHIBIT 20.5   Real and Nominal Exchange Rates in Five Countries*

		Indonesia		
		Consumer Price Indexes		*Real Exchange Rate* $\left(\dfrac{\text{1990 Rupiah per}}{\text{1990 Dollar}}\right)$
Year	*Rupiah Exchange Rate*	*Indonesia CPI*	*U.S. CPI*	
1985	1,125.00	69.76	82.40	1,328.84
1990	1,901.00	100.00	100.00	1,901.00
1993	2,110.00	128.51	110.60	1,815.94

		Japan		
		Consumer Price Indexes		*Real Exchange Rate* $\left(\dfrac{\text{1990 Yen per}}{\text{1990 Dollar}}\right)$
Year	*Yen Exchange Rate*	*Japan CPI*	*U.S. CPI*	
1985	200.50	93.50	82.40	176.70
1990	134.40	100.00	100.00	134.40
1993	111.85	106.40	110.60	116.27

		Spain		
		Consumer Price Indexes		*Real Exchange Rate* $\left(\dfrac{\text{1990 Peseta per}}{\text{1990 Dollar}}\right)$
Year	*Peseta Exchange Rate*	*Spain CPI*	*U.S. CPI*	
1985	154.15	73.10	82.40	173.76
1990	96.91	100.00	100.00	96.91
1993	142.21	117.30	110.60	134.09

		Thailand		
		Consumer Price Indexes		*Real Exchange Rate* $\left(\dfrac{\text{1990 Baht per}}{\text{1990 Dollar}}\right)$
Year	*Baht Exchange Rate*	*Thailand CPI*	*U.S. CPI*	
1985	26.65	82.70	82.40	26.55
1990	25.29	100.00	100.00	25.29
1993	25.54	114.00	110.60	24.78

		Turkey		
		Consumer Price Indexes		*Real Exchange Rate* $\left(\dfrac{\text{1990 Lira per}}{\text{1990 Dollar}}\right)$
Year	*Lira Exchange Rate*	*Turkey CPI*	*U.S. CPI*	
1985	576.86	11.77	82.40	4,038.51
1990	2,930.07	100.00	100.00	2,930.07
1993	14,472.50	468.84	110.60	3,414.08

*Based on authors' calculations, using data from the International Financial Statistics (IFS) database.

the U.S. dollar costs of goods and services in Turkey increased at a higher rate than the U.S. dollar cost of goods and services in the United States.

Hedging When Both Inflation Differences and Real Effects Drive Exchange Rate Changes.   Whenever exchange rates can change for purely monetary reasons as well as for real reasons, it is difficult to implement effective hedges. To understand this, consider again the case where a firm needs to purchase an input that will be priced in British pounds. By buying the pounds in the forward market, the firm effectively hedges against changes in the value of the pound that are unrelated to price level changes. However, if the pound fell 10 percent in value because a monetary shift caused a 10 percent increase in British prices, then the firm's loss on its foreign exchange contracts would not be offset by a decrease in the price of the inputs.

For the most part, short-term exchange rate changes can be considered as real changes, indicating that short-term hedges should be effective. This follows from the fact that, over short intervals, exchange rates fluctuate more than inflation rates. Over long periods, however, inflation accounts for a large part of exchange rate movements. Perhaps this explains why firms tend to actively hedge short-term currency fluctuations, but tend to ignore the effect of long-term fluctuations.

Why Most Firms Do Not Hedge Economic Risk

Most major multinational firms hedge transaction and translation currency risk, at least partially. However, most firms do not hedge long-term economic risk. Hedging the long-term economic consequences of an exchange rate change is substantially more complicated than hedging either transaction or translation risk. The biggest problem with implementing such a hedging strategy is in estimating both the current and the long-term effects of exchange rate changes on the firm's cash flows. Consider, for example, the case of a U.S. firm like IBM, which manufactures computers in the United States for sale in France. What is the effect of a change in the U.S. dollar/French franc exchange rate on IBM's long-term profitability?

To answer this question, one must first ascertain whether the change in the French franc can be attributed to a general change in price levels, so that the inflation-adjusted or real exchange rate remains constant. As mentioned above, if the real exchange rate remains constant, then a nominal exchange rate change is likely to have only a minor effect on IBM's cash flows. However, changes in real exchange rates can have a significant effect on these cash flows.

Consider what happens when the U.S. dollar strengthens against the French franc, making the computers more expensive in francs. If the franc weakened because of general inflation in France, so that the inflation-adjusted exchange rate remained constant, then the price of computers in France, relative to other prices, would not have changed. In this case, demand for IBM computers would not be affected by the change in exchange rates. Contrast this case with one in which the real exchange rate does change, raising the relative price of IBM computers in France and lowering the demand for them. IBM's cash flows in France (calculated in U.S. dollars) would probably decrease in this case since it would either sell fewer computers at the same U.S. dollar price or, alternatively, be forced by competitors to cut its U.S. dollar price for computers.

As these arguments suggest, one of the major difficulties in assessing the effect of exchange rate changes on cash flows has to do with predicting the cause of the exchange rate movement. If we cannot predict whether future exchange rate fluctuations are associated with relative price changes, then forward and futures contracts provide imperfect hedges. This is illustrated in Example 20.6.

Example 20.6:   Hedging Real Changes in the Yen

Suppose that American Lumber sells a significant quantity of prefabricated housing units in Japan. These units sell for ¥10,000 per square foot, with the market price increasing at the Japanese inflation rate. The exchange rate is currently ¥100 per US$. Analysts predict that it will trade in the range of ¥90 per US$ to ¥110 per US$ over the next 12 months, depending on the differences in the Japanese and U.S. inflation rates as well as productivity changes that can be reflected in trade imbalances. Forward prices are also at ¥100 per US$. Is it possible for American Lumber to create a hedge to guarantee a U.S. dollar price of $100 per square foot for the prefab units?

Answer: It is not possible to create such a hedge. To understand this, suppose that Japan experiences 5 percent deflation, causing housing unit prices to fall to ¥9,500. Although this would normally cause the yen to depreciate, suppose that a simultaneous increase in Japanese productivity, which tends to strengthen the yen, offset the effect of inflation on exchange rates exactly, so that the exchange rate stayed at ¥100 per US$. In this case, American Lumber will sell prefab units at $95 per square foot and will break even on its hedging activities regardless of its forward positions.

Result 20.14   When exchange rates changes can be generated by both real and nominal changes, it may be impossible for firms to effectively hedge their long-term economic exposures.

When it is difficult to hedge in the derivatives markets, firms sometimes undertake what is known as operational hedging, which involves changing the structure of the firm's operations. [See Chowdhry and Howe (1997) for details.]

20.9 Which Firms Hedge? The Empirical Evidence

A number of empirical studies have compared the characteristics of firms that use derivatives to firms that do not. Although research on this topic is still evolving, a number of patterns are worth considering.

Larger Firms Are More Likely to Use Derivatives than Smaller Firms

A number of studies have found that larger firms are more likely to use derivatives than smaller firms.[15] The fact that smaller firms are less likely to use derivatives than larger firms is inconsistent with the view that smaller firms generally face higher risks of bankruptcy and thus have more to gain from hedging. However, the fixed costs of setting up a hedging operation and their lower level of sophistication probably explains why smaller firms are less likely to hedge. Indeed, Dolde (1993) found that among firms that have implemented hedging operations, the larger firms tend to hedge less completely than the smaller firms, leaving themselves more exposed to interest rate and currency risks. In other words, size is a barrier to setting up a hedging operation, but among firms that do hedge, smaller firms facing greater risks of bankruptcy hedge more completely.

---

[15]See Nance, Smith, and Smithson (1993); Dolde (1993); and Geczy, Minton, and Schrand (1997).

Firms with More Growth Opportunities Are More Likely to Use Derivatives

Nance, Smith, and Smithson (1993) and Geczy, Minton, and Schrand (1997) provided evidence that firms with greater growth opportunities are more likely to use derivatives. In particular, firms with higher R&D expenditures and higher market-to-book ratios are more likely to use derivatives than companies that spend less on R&D, have lower market-to-book ratios, and, therefore, probably have fewer investment opportunities. This evidence is consistent with the idea that firms hedge to ensure that they have enough cash to fund their investment opportunities internally.

A number of other reasons explain why R&D-intensive firms with high market-to-book ratios are more likely to use derivatives. As Chapter 16 discussed, firms with these characteristics generally have higher financial distress costs, suggesting that they should hedge to ensure that they will meet their debt obligations. Furthermore, because R&D expenditures are tax deductible, these firms are likely to have lower taxable earnings, implying that the tax argument discussed earlier in this chapter applies more to firms with high R&D expenditures.

Highly Levered Firms Are More Likely to Use Derivatives

Nance, Smith, and Smithson (1993); Block and Gallagher (1986); and Wall and Pringle (1989) found weak evidence that firms with more leveraged capital structures hedge more. The positive relation between leverage ratios and the tendency to hedge is consistent with the view that firms hedge to avoid financial distress costs. However, the weakness of the evidence probably reflects the tendency of firms with high financial distress costs, which have the most to gain from hedging, to have the lowest leverage ratios. For example, as discussed in Chapter 16, high R&D firms tend to use little debt and also tend to hedge because of their potential costs of financial distress.

Geczy, Minton, and Schrand (1997) found no significant relation between the debt ratios of most firms and their tendency to use derivatives. However, among those firms with high R&D expenditures and high market-to-book ratios, firms with more leverage are more likely to hedge. This implies that firms that suffer the highest costs of financial distress are more likely to hedge when they are highly levered.

Risk Management Practices in the Gold Mining Industry

The studies described above examined hedging choices across a number of different industries. A study by Tufano (1996) looked in greater detail at the risk management practices within a single industry, gold mining. Within a single industry, proxies for financial distress costs, financing constraints, and investment opportunities will probably vary much less than they do across industries. Consequently, differences in the hedging strategies across firms within a single industry are likely to be related to differences in the incentives and tastes of the top executives.

The evidence described in the Tufano study indicates that management incentives and tastes do have an important effect on the risk management practices in the gold mining industry. Specifically, managers who hold large amounts of their firm's stock tend to use forward and futures contracts to hedge more of their firm's gold price risk. Thus, managers who are personally the most exposed to gold price risk choose to hedge more of the risk. However, those who own relatively more stock options tend to hedge less, which may reflect the greater value of the options when volatility is increased. Tufano also found that firms with CFOs hired more recently hedge a greater portion of their exposure than firms with CFOs who have been on the job longer.

20.10 Summary and Conclusions

While we believe, as a general guideline, that most firms can benefit by hedging, the gains of hedging differ across firms. Firms can gain from hedging that reduces their probability of being financially distressed, especially in those industries where financial distress costs are the highest. There are also tax reasons for distressed firms to hedge, and gains that come from the fact that a firm's reported cash flows and profits are more informative when the firm has hedged out extraneous risks.

This chapter also considered situations where firms should not hedge. When excellent investment opportunities tend to arise at times when existing assets (unhedged) are most profitable, they may be better off remaining unhedged or only partially hedged. For example, an oil firm is likely to find more high *NPV* exploration projects when oil prices and hence unhedged profits are the highest. An oil firm would not want to completely hedge away the variability in profits because that would leave it short of funds when favorable investment opportunities exist.

In addition, firms may choose not to hedge those risks about which they have private information or which they partially control. In this respect, firm are similar to individuals buying auto insurance. The safest drivers choose to be underinsured since they regard insurance as overpriced. Recognizing this tendency, insurance companies raise the rates for drivers wanting full insurance. In most cases, these considerations do not affect whether firms hedge in derivatives markets because firms are unlikely to have important private information about currency and commodity price movements. However, these considerations do affect whether firms insure against firm-specific risk or choose liability streams that leave them exposed to changes in their own credit ratings. For the same reason that the safest drivers often choose to be underinsured,

managers who believe that their firms are a much safer risk than their credit rating reflects will choose to borrow short term in hopes that their credit rating will improve in the future. In other words, the safest firms will be overexposed to the risks connected with changes in their credit rating.

Our discussion of both foreign exchange and liability risk management indicated that implementing a sound risk management strategy requires a good understanding of the relations between interest rate changes, exchange rate changes, and inflation. The appropriate interest rate hedging strategy depends on the extent to which interest rate volatility is due to changes in the rate of inflation. Similarly, the appropriate foreign exchange hedging strategy depends on the extent to which currency fluctuations are due to differences between domestic and foreign inflation rates.

This chapter presented our view of how firms can use risk management tools to maximize firm value, which may differ from current practice. This difference is due in part to the limited experience many managers have in dealing with derivatives markets and risk management problems. This inexperience is exacerbated by potential incentive problems (see Chapter 17). For example, if managers get a large share of their compensation from stock options—to solve one kind of incentive problem—they may choose to speculate rather than hedge, since option values increase with risk.

Again, we must stress that risk management, like all corporate finance decisions, cannot be viewed in isolation. Corporations must view their risk management choices as part of an overall strategy that includes their choice of capital structure and executive compensation as well as considerations of overall product market strategy.

Key Concepts

Result 20.1: If hedging choices do not affect cash flows from real assets, then, in the absence of taxes and transaction costs, hedging decisions do not affect firm values.

Result 20.2: Hedging is unlikely to improve firm values if it does no more than reduce the variance of a firm's future cash flows. To improve firm values, hedging also must increase expected cash flows.

Result 20.3: Because of asymmetric treatment of gains and losses, firms may reduce their expected tax liabilities by hedging.

Result 20.4: Firms that are subject to high financial distress costs have greater incentives to hedge.

Result 20.5: Firms that find it costly to delay or alter their investment plans and that have limited access to outside financial markets will benefit from hedging.

Result 20.6: The gains from hedging are greater when it is more difficult to evaluate and monitor management.

Result 20.7: Firms have an incentive to insure or hedge risks that insurance companies and markets can better assess. Doing this improves decision making. Firms will absorb internally those risks over which they have the comparative advantage in evaluating.

Result 20.8: If a firm's main motivation for hedging is to better assess the quality of management, the firm will probably want to hedge its earnings or cash flow rather than its value. However, if the firm is hedging to avoid the costs of financial distress, it should implement a hedging strategy that takes into account both the variance of its value and the variance of its cash flows.

Result 20.9: Corporations should organize their hedging in a way that reflects why they are hedging. Most hedging motivations suggest that hedging should be carried out at the corporate level. However, the improvement in management incentives that can be realized with a risk management program are best achieved when the individual divisions are responsible for hedging.

Result 20.10: Managers have private information only in exceptional cases. Given this, they almost always should be hedging rather than speculating.

Result 20.11: A firm's liability stream can be decomposed into two components: one that reflects default-free interest rates and one that reflects the firm's credit rating. When a firm borrows at a fixed rate, both components are fixed. When it rolls over short-term instruments, the liability streams fluctuate with both kinds of risks.

Derivative instruments allow firms to separate these two sources of risk: to create liability streams that are sensitive to interest rates but not their credit ratings, as described in equation (20.4), and to create liability streams that are sensitive to their credit ratings but not interest rates, as described in equation (20.5).

Result 20.12: If changes in interest rates mainly reflect changes in the rate of inflation and if a firm's operating profits generally increase with the rate of inflation, then the firm will want its liabilities to be exposed to interest rate risk. If, however, interest rate changes are not primarily due to changes in inflation (i.e., real interest rates change) and if the firm's ability to sell its product is affected by the level of real interest rates, then the firm will want to minimize the exposure of its liabilities to interest rate changes.

Result 20.13: Exchange rate movements can be decomposed into those caused by differences in the inflation rates in the home country and the foreign country, and those caused by changes in real exchange rates. In most cases, the incentive is to hedge against real exchange rate changes rather than the component of exchange rate changes that is driven by inflation differences between the two countries.

Result 20.14: When exchange rates changes can be generated by both real and nominal changes, it may be impossible for firms to effectively hedge their long-term economic exposures.

Key Terms

economic risk   733
hedge   711
liability management   729
liability stream   729
nominal exchange rate   734
real exchange rate   734
risk management   711
risk profile   711
transaction risk   733
translation risk   733

Exercises

20.1. Small firms currently hedge less than large firms. Why is this? Do you expect smaller firms to start hedging more in the future? Explain.

20.2. Why is it harder to hedge currency risks in countries with volatile inflation rates?

20.3. Whistler Resorts is a Canadian ski resort just north of Vancouver, British Columbia. Discuss the resort's exposure to exchange rate risk.

20.4. It is now much easier to hedge risks than it was in the past. How should this affect a firm's optimal capital structure? Why?

20.5. The XYZ corporation manufactures in both Turkey and Japan for export to the United States. Japan has a stable monetary policy and, as a result, its inflation is easy to predict. Monetary policy in Turkey is much less predictable. In which of the two countries can XYZ more easily hedge against

the risk that manufacturing costs, measured in U.S. dollars, will become significantly more expensive? Why?

20.6. Purchasing power parity (PPP) implies that real exchange rates remain constant. If PPP holds, do firms need to hedge their long-term foreign exchange exposure? Explain.

20.7. Oil firms hedge only part of their exposure to oil price movements. Why might that be a good idea?

20.8. Harwood Outboard manufactures outboard motors for relatively inexpensive motor boats. The firm is optimistic about its long-term outlook, but its bond rating is only BB. Describe how you would manage Harwood's liability stream if you believed that within two years Harwood's credit rating would improve to A.

References and Additional Readings

Block, S. B., and T. J. Gallagher. "The Use of Interest Rate Futures and Options by Corporate Financial Managers." *Financial Management* 15 (1986), pp. 73–78.

Breeden, Douglas, and S. Vishwanathan. "Why Do Firms Hedge? An Asymmetric Information Model." Duke University working paper, 1996.

Chowdhry, Bhagwan, and Jonathan Howe. "Corporate Risk Management for Multinational Corporations: Financial and Operational Hedging Policies." UCLA Finance working paper, 1997.

DeMarzo, Peter, and Darrell Duffie. "Corporate Incentives for Hedging and Hedge Accounting." *Review of Financial Studies* 8 (1995), pp. 743–71.

Doherty, Neal, and Clifford Smith. "Corporate Insurance Strategy: The Case of British Petroleum." *Journal of Applied Corporate Finance*, 6, no. 3 (Fall 1993), pp. 4–15.

Dolde, Walter. "Use and Effectiveness of Foreign Exchange and Interest Rate Risk Management in Large Firms." University of Connecticut working paper, 1993.

Froot, Ken; David Scharfstein; and Jeremy Stein. "Risk Management: Coordinating Corporate Investment and Financing Policies." *Journal of Finance* 48, (1993), pp. 1629–58.

Geczy, Christopher; Bernadette Minton; and Catherine Schrand. "Why Firms Use Currency Derivatives." *Journal of Finance* 52 (September 1997).

Lessard, Don. "Global Competition and Corporate Finance in the 1990s." *Continental Bank Journal of Applied Corporate Finance* 3 (1991), pp. 59–72.

Lewent, Judy C., and A. John Kearney. "Identifying, Measuring, and Hedging Currency Risk at Merck." *Continental Bank Journal of Applied Corporate Finance* 2 (1990), pp. 19–28.

Nance, Deana R.; Clifford W. Smith; and Charles W. Smithson. "On the Determinants of Corporate Hedging." *Journal of Finance* 48 (1993), pp. 267–84.

Rawls, S. Waite, and Charles W. Smithson. "Strategic Risk Management." *Continental Bank Journal of Applied Corporate Finance* 2 (1990), pp. 6–18.

Shapiro, Alan, and Sheridan Titman. "An Integrated Approach to Corporate Risk Management." *Midland Corporate Finance Journal* 3 (1985), pp. 41–56.

Smith, Clifford W., and Rene Stulz. "The Determinants of Firms' Hedging Policies." *Journal of Financial and Quantitative Analysis* 20 (December 1985), pp. 391–405.

Titman, Sheridan. "Interest Rate Swaps and Corporate Financing Choices." *Journal of Finance* 47 (1992), pp. 1503–16.

Tufano, Peter. "Who Manages Risk? An Empirical Examination of Risk Management Practices in the Gold Mining Industry." *Journal of Finance* 51 (September 1996), pp. 1097–1137.

Wall, Larry D., and John Pringle. "Alternative Explanations of Interest Rate Swaps: An Empirical Analysis." *Financial Management* 18 (1989), pp. 59–73.

The Practice of Hedging

Learning Objectives

After reading this chapter, you should be able to:

1. Describe the factor beta, standard deviation, and value-at-risk methods of estimating risk exposure.
2. Use forwards, futures, swaps, and options to generate hedges.
3. Apply the covered interest rate parity relation in foreign exchange markets to develop currency hedges.
4. Understand why and how to tail a hedge with futures and forwards.
5. Use regression and factor models to determine hedge ratios.
6. Describe the relation between hedging with regression, minimum-variance hedging, and mean-variance analysis.

In the early 1990s, Metallgesellschaft AG, one of Germany's largest conglomerates, possessed considerable refinery capacity through a 51 percent-owned subsidiary. Promises to sell heating oil from its subsidiary's refineries to its customers at guaranteed prices over the subsequent 10 years exposed the company to considerable oil price risk. To offset the risk arising from these promises, management at Metallgesellschaft decided to purchase crude oil futures contracts on the New York Mercantile Exchange. In September 1993, oil prices dropped precipitously and Metallgesellschaft began to receive margin calls on its futures contracts. The cash required to meet these margin calls soon exceeded the company's revenues from its sales of heating oil and Metallgesellschaft was forced to liquidate much of its futures position, resulting in $1.34 billion in capital losses. As a consequence of this hedging fiasco, senior management was replaced, and academics began to study what went wrong. The consensus was that Metallgesellschaft had the wrong hedge ratio—so wrong that its futures position increased rather than decreased the firm's exposure to oil price risk.

The risks a firm faces in its operations, often called its **exposures**, include, for example, exposures to interest rate risk, currency risk, business cycle risk, inflation risk, commodity price risk, and industry risk. This chapter develops an understanding of how to **hedge**, or reduce these risk exposures.

Risk exposures are closely tied to the factor betas in factor models. Most of the analysis of factor models in Chapter 6 focused on equity returns. In this context, **value hedging**, the acquisition of financial instruments that alter the factor betas of the firm's equity return in order to reduce the firm's equity return risks, is particularly pertinent. However, as Chapter 20 noted, some firms focus on the risk of their near-term cash flows rather than on the risk of their equity return. Reducing *cash flow risk exposure* requires **cash flow hedging**,[1] which is the acquisition of financial instruments to reduce the *cash flow factor betas* of the firm (see Chapter 10). To minimize risk exposure, one acquires financial instruments that set these factor betas to zero. Alternatively, targeting a risk exposure involves setting the factor beta to a **target beta** level. The mathematics of these two tasks is similar.

Numerous financial instruments are used for hedging. These instruments include forward contracts, futures contracts, options, swaps, and bonds. The size of the position per unit of the underlying asset or commodity that achieves minimum risk is known as the **hedge ratio**.[2] This ratio is often difficult to estimate. The proper instrument for hedging also may require complex analysis. In the Metallgesellschaft discussion in the chapter's opening vignette, for example, futures were ineffective instruments for hedging exposure to oil price risk. Metallgesellschaft's price guarantees to its customers, which generated its oil price risk exposure, were long-term contracts. Metallgesellschaft, however, hedged this long-term exposure by rolling over a series of short-term futures contracts. As this chapter later shows, it is not possible to perfectly hedge long-term oil price commitments by rolling over a series of short-term futures contracts. In principle, however, Metallgesellschaft could have better hedged its price commitments with more complex derivative securities or with a more sophisticated hedging strategy.

Although this chapter touches briefly on the topic of interest rate risk, it leaves the detailed analysis of interest rate risk to the next chapter. For the most part, we will use commodity risk—risk exposure due to changing commodity prices—and currency risk—risk exposure due to changing exchange rates—as illustrative cases to address the basics of hedging.

The first part of the chapter discusses the measurement of risk exposure. The second part assumes that the firm has measured its risk exposure properly and desires merely to find the proper hedge ratio to minimize its exposure.

21.1 Measuring Risk Exposure

Exposures are measured in a variety of ways, but as Chapter 20 and the discussion above noted, one can generally view an exposure as a factor beta, similar to the factor betas discussed in Chapter 6. This section discusses the measurement of risk exposure with factor models.

Assume that currency and interest rate risk are the two factors that most trouble a firm doing business in Japan. The firm can measure the exposure of a future cash flow to

---

[1]As an alternative to cash flows, firms also focus on hedging the risk of their future earnings.

[2]While the analysis in Chapter 20 did not indicate that firms should minimize risk exposure, this chapter, for simplicity of exposition, focuses on how to implement hedging that minimize exposure to risk factors. Our results can easily be generalized to target any desired set of risk exposures.

these two factors by estimating a factor model. Assume that the estimation of the factor model generates the equation:

$$\tilde{C} = 30 + 2\tilde{F}_{curr} - 4\tilde{F}_{int} + \tilde{\epsilon}$$

where

$\tilde{C}$ = cash flow (in \$ millions)
$\tilde{F}_{curr}$ = percentage change in the ¥/\$ exchange rate over the coming year
$\tilde{F}_{int}$ = percentage change in the short-term interest rate over the coming year

The 2 and −4 in the equation are the sensitivities of the cash flow to the exchange rate and interest rates, respectively, or the *cash flow's factor betas*. The $\tilde{\epsilon}$ term represents the risks of the cash flow not captured by these two risk factors.

Using Regression to Estimate the Risk Exposure

The **regression method**, one of the most popular tools for analyzing risk and developing hedges, examines how the unhedged cash flows of the firm performed historically in relation to a risk factor. Specifically, it estimates the factor betas as slope coefficients from regressions of historical returns or cash flows on the risk factors.

Measuring Risk Exposure with Simulations

The **simulation method**, or the use of scenario analysis which was first introduced in Chapter 10, is a forward-looking method of estimating risk exposure. In rapidly changing industries, the simulation method is superior to regression estimation using historical data, which is backward looking.

Implementation with Scenarios.   To implement the simulation method, a manager needs to forecast earnings or cash flows for a variety of factor realizations. With exchange rate risk, for example, a manager would implement this method by specifying a wide range of different exchange rate scenarios. Each scenario estimates the profits or cash flows that would occur under a variety of assumptions about industry demand and competitor and supplier responses.

Simulation versus Regression.   Although simulations require much more judgment on the part of the analyst, they do not require that the past history of the firm provide the best estimate of the future. In reality, this can be very important in a changing environment. For example, one would not want to derive an estimate of General Motors' (GM's) deutsche mark exposure solely from regressions that make use of data from the past 10 years. Competition from German automakers has diminished considerably over this historical period and it is unlikely that a firm's future exposure to the deutsche mark will be as important as its past exposure.

Modifying Initial Estimates Obtained from Regression.   The simulation method for exchange rate risk simply asks the manager to estimate the firm's future costs and revenues under different exchange rate scenarios to obtain profit (or cash flow). Regression may provide useful inputs for these estimates, but the manager is not limited to the regression results for these estimates. He or she also could incorporate assumptions about the sensitivity of the demand for a product to its price as well as expected competitor responses to exchange rate changes. In addition, the regression analysis specifies a linear relation between the determinants of profits (or cash flows) and exchange rate changes which is unlikely to be true in reality. The manager will want to modify the regression-based estimates to account for any nonlinearities in the statistical relationships.

For example, General Motors might assume that German automakers will maintain the same U.S. dollar prices for their cars when faced with a small increase in the value of the deutsche mark, giving up some profit to maintain market share. If this is the case, GM would not benefit from a small increase in the value of the deutsche mark. However, if the deutsche mark strengthens significantly, German automakers may find it preferable to abandon certain U.S. markets, an action that would greatly benefit General Motors.

Similar arguments can be made about a weakening of the deutsche mark, which provides an advantage to the German automakers. A slight weakening may have no effect on the prices U.S. dealers pay for German cars, perhaps because German automakers are concerned about having to later raise prices if the deutsche mark subsequently strengthens. However, if the deutsche mark weakens considerably, giving German automakers a large cost advantage, they might exploit the opportunity to expand market share, which would significantly reduce General Motors' profits.

Prespecification of Factor Betas from Theoretical Relations

In some cases, factor betas can be prespecified using knowledge of theory. For example, the commitments of Metallgesellschaft to sell heating oil at predetermined prices can be viewed as forward contracts. If the risk factor is the price of oil in 10 years, the factor beta of a 10-year forward contract to such a risk factor must be 1.

Volatility as a Measure of Risk Exposure

Corporate managers often like to summarize risk exposure with a single number. For this reason, the standard deviation is often used to summarize the risk impact of a collection of factor betas. Extending the analysis of Chapter 6 to correlated factors, the formula for the variance of the factor risk of an investment is:

$$\sigma^2 = \sum_{m=1}^{K} \sum_{n=1}^{K} \beta_m \beta_n cov(\tilde{F}_m, \tilde{F}_n)$$

where

β_m = factor beta on factor m
β_n = factor beta on factor n

The volatility (i.e., standard deviation) of the cash flow or value due to factor risk is the square root of this.

Example 21.1 illustrates how to implement this formula.

Example 21.1:   Computing Factor-Based Volatility for a Cash Flow
Assume that a firm has a cash flow one year from now (in $ millions) that follows the factor model:

$$\tilde{C} = 30 + 2\tilde{F}_{curr} - 4\tilde{F}_{int} + \tilde{\epsilon}$$

where the currency factor, $\tilde{F}_{curr}$, is the percentage change in the ¥/$US exchange rate over the next year and the interest rate factor, $\tilde{F}_{int}$, is the percentage change in three-month LIBOR from now until one year from now. Assume that the variance of the currency factor is estimated to be .011, the variance of the interest rate factor is approximately .022, and the covariance between the two is .004. What is the factor-based volatility of the cash flow?

Answer: Using the variance formula above, the factor based variance is:

$$\sigma^2 = 4(.011) - 8(.004) - 8(.004) + 16(.022) = .332$$

The square root of this number, the volatility, is .576 (expressed in $ millions).

Clearly, the estimates of variances and covariances of the risk factors are critical for obtaining a good estimate of the volatility. One procedure for estimating the covariances and variance of risk factors is to compute historical variances and covariances. However, financial institutions that make use of volatility recognize that variances and covariances tend to change over time, so they have developed more sophisticated estimation procedures.

J. P. Morgan, for example, in its RiskMetrics™ covariance matrix (Website: http://www.jpmorgan.com), forecasts variances as weighted averages of the previous variance forecast and of the latest deviation from the forecast. This model is a special case of a procedure, Generalized Autoregressive Conditional Heteroskedastic (GARCH) estimation, developed in the economics statistics literature.[3]

Value at Risk as a Measure of Risk Exposure

Perhaps the most popular way to measure risk exposure today is **value at risk (VAR)**, defined as the worst loss possible under *normal market conditions* for a given time horizon. For example, an investment position that loses a maximum of $100 million over the next year, no more than 1 percent of the time, will be viewed by some managers as having a value at risk of $100 million for the next year.

Value at risk is determined by the time interval under consideration as well as by what the manager regards as normal market conditions. A position with a value at risk of $100 million over the next year will have considerably less value at risk over a shorter horizon, say over the next month. Similarly, a manager who considers abnormally bad market conditions to be those that occur less than 5 percent of the time will have less value at risk than a manager who is willing to ignore only those losses that, because of their astounding magnitude, occur less than 1 percent of the time.

The importance of both the significance level (5 percent or 1 percent as the typical thresholds for determining abnormal market conditions) and the time horizon are illustrated when representing value at risk in a diagram using the distribution of profits and losses. Exhibit 21.1 illustrates the value at risk at the 5 percent significance level for a transaction with zero expected profit. The time horizon affects the shape of the distribution curve. The longer the time horizon, the more uncertain the profits, and the more spread out is the normal distribution curve. This should shift point A—the boundary of the 5 percent area under the curve's left tail—to the left, increasing VAR. The threshold for the area in the tail (5 percent versus 1 percent) matters, too, as a shift to a 1 percent tail as the threshold moves point A to the left, thereby increasing VAR.

---

[3]However, until recently GARCH estimation was virtually impossible to implement when there are five or more risk factors. Ledoit and Santa-Clara (1997) developed a procedure to derive GARCH forecasts of variances and covariances when there are numerous risk factors.

EXHIBIT 21.1   Probability Distribution and Value at Risk

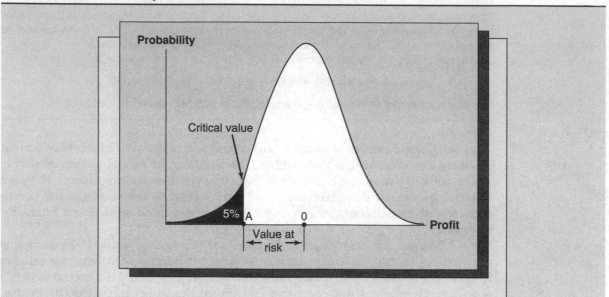

Value at risk is the standard methodology used for measuring the risk to the value of a portfolio of derivatives or other securities. There is a regulatory impetus for this. In late 1996, the Bank for International Settlements, the U.S. Securities and Exchange Commission, and the Federal Reserve Board proposed that the institutions they supervise use this risk measure as a standard for certain activities. An analogous methodology applied to cash flows, known as **cash flow at risk (*CAR*)**, is becoming an increasingly important concept for corporations.

Estimating *VAR* and *CAR* from Standard Deviations.   *VAR* and *CAR* are simple translations of the standard deviation if the value or cash flow is normally distributed. For example,

$$VAR(5\% \text{ significance level}) = 1.65\ \sigma$$

where σ is the standard deviation of the value. The same formula applies to *CAR*, except that σ is the standard deviation of the cash flow.

The 1.65 in the above equation is obtained from a normal distribution table, such as that found in Table B.5 in Appendix B at the end of this text. In particular, note that $N(-1.65)$ is approximately .05 in such a table. More generally, let x be the value or cash flow which makes the probability that a normally distributed value or cash flow with a mean of zero and a standard deviation of σ is less than p percent, that is, $N(x) = p\%$. Then, *VAR* or *CAR* is $-x\sigma$.

Example 21.2 illustrates how to transform a σ to a *CAR*.

Example 21.2:   Computing *CAR* from Standard Deviations Assuming a Normal Distribution

In Example 21.1, the standard deviation of the cash flow was approximately $576,200. What is the cash flow at risk at the 5 percent significance level assuming that the cash flow is normally distributed?

   Answer: 1.65($576,200) = $950,720.

Estimating *VAR* or *CAR* Using Simulation.   When *CAR* is estimated, simulation usually is preferred to the standard deviation formula as an estimation procedure. Given prespecified factor betas, the cash flow is then simulated from the factor equation for the factor values observed over a given historical period. The *CAR* is then the difference between the average cash flow and the fifth percentile outcome over the historical period.

21.2 Hedging Short-Term Commitments with Maturity-Matched Forward Contracts

Forward contracts are among the most popular tools for hedging. We begin with a review of forward contracts. Next, we analyze a firm, such as Metallgesellschaft, which is exposed to oil price risk. We assume that it wants to minimize that risk by using forward contracts that mature on the same date as the obligation the company wishes to hedge.

Review of Forward Contracts

As discussed in Chapter 7, a *forward contract* is an agreement to buy or sell a security, currency, or commodity at a prespecified price, known as the *forward price,* at some future date. In contrast, the **spot market** for a commodity is the market for immediate delivery and payment. The amount paid for the commodity in the spot market is the *spot price* or, in the case of currencies, the *spot rate.* Generally, the forward price is set so that the contract is a zero–present value (zero-*PV*) investment; thus, no cash need exchange hands at the contract's inception. An exception to this takes place in what is known as an *off-market contract.* Generally, when a reference is made to the market's forward price, it is to the forward price of a generic zero-*PV* contract.

How Forward-Date Obligations Create Risk

Metallgesellschaft sought to mitigate oil price exposure from a series of forward contracts which, in essence, locked in the selling price at which its customers could purchase heating oil. Forward contracts are inherent in many business contracts and have been around for hundreds of years. It is not surprising that Metallgesellschaft would enter into forward contracts as part of its business strategy.

In the absence of these commitments, Metallgesellschaft's profit was tied only to the spread between the prices of heating oil and crude oil because the company was a purchaser of crude oil and a supplier of heating oil. However, by locking in its customers' heating oil prices, Metallgesellschaft exposed itself to fluctuations in the price of crude oil. These fluctuations are much more volatile than the spread between the price of heating oil and the price of crude oil. Hence, to minimize its oil price exposure, the company needed to lock in the crude oil prices it pays to its suppliers. An additional series of crude oil forward contracts seemed to be a natural vehicle by which Metallgesellschaft could offset the effect of locking in the prices at which it sold its heating oil.

Using Forwards to Eliminate the Oil Price Risk of Forward Obligations

The future payoff at date T of the long forward contract for oil is the difference between an uncertain number, $\tilde{S}_T$, the future spot price of oil, and a certain number K, the forward price agreed upon today.

Combining a Forward Commitment to Sell with the Acquisition of a Forward Contract.   Consider an oil refiner that needs to buy crude oil and, like Metallgesellschaft, has locked in the price of its output. The operations of this business produce a constant gross revenue of G, but require the purchase of oil at date T at the then prevailing oil price, $\tilde{S}_T$. The combination of the risk of this business operation, which has a cash inflow of $G - \tilde{S}_T$, and the forward contract, which at maturity has a cash inflow of $\tilde{S}_T - K$, eliminates the oil price risk. This is illustrated in Exhibit 21.2 by the horizontal line (with the height of $G - K$, which is the sum of cash flow from operations (line AB) and the cash flow from the forward (line CD). In this case, the firm can comfortably acquire oil in the spot market at date T, and it knows that the price it pays, $\tilde{S}_T$, will be hedged by the gains or losses on the forward contract, as Example 21.3 indicates.[4]

Example 21.3:   Hedging Oil Price Risk with a Maturity-Matched Forward Contract

Assume that Metallgesellschaft has an obligation to deliver 1.25 million barrels of oil one year out at a fixed price of $25 per barrel. How can it hedge this obligation in the forward market and eliminate its exposure to crude oil prices?

Answer: The cash needed to acquire the oil to meet this obligation is uncertain. Metallgesellschaft can eliminate the variability in its profit arising from this uncertainty *by acquiring 1.25 million barrels of oil for forward delivery one year from now. If the date 0 forward* price is less than $25 per barrel, Metallgesellschaft will profit with certainty. If the price is greater than $25 per barrel, it will lose money with certainty. In either case, its profit (or loss) from operations and hedging will be known at date 0.

The Information in Forward Prices.   In addition to being useful hedging instruments, forward contracts provide critical information about profitability through the prices associated with them. Regardless of Metallgesellschaft's opinion about the spot oil price one year from now, the company loses money, in a present value sense, if it charges its customers less than the forward oil price and makes money if it charges its customers more than that oil price.

During the Persian Gulf War of 1990–91, when spot oil prices were close to $40 a barrel, several financial intermediaries began to introduce oil-linked bonds. One set of these bonds, which had a maturity of about 2 years, carried a relatively high rate of interest and paid principal equal to the minimum of (1) four times the price of oil at maturity and (2) $100. The bonds were selling at approximately $100 each. Many investors looked at these bonds and found them attractive because of their high interest rate and the belief that, at $40 a barrel, it was virtually a sure thing that the bond would pay off $100 in principal in two years. However, to understand the risk of not getting back the $100 principal on these bonds, it was important that investors look at the two-year

---

[4]It is also possible to view a forward contract as simply locking in a price for oil needed for operations in the future. Obviously, this eliminates oil price risk. In many instances, however, the commodity delivered in the forward market is not precisely suited for the oil refiner's operations. Delivery might be at an inconvenient location or the oil might not be the right grade for the refiner's operations. In these cases, the cash flow algebra used above tells us that if a slightly different product exists in the spot market, the forward contract described above will do a good job of hedging its price risk. The oil received as a result of the maturation of the forward contract may be sold to a third party. The oil needed for future operations, which may be slightly different in quality, delivery location, and so forth, can be bought in the spot market from a fourth party at approximately the same price. In this case, the position in the forward contract still hedges oil price risk albeit imperfectly. Further discussion of this topic is covered under cross-hedging in Section 21.9.

EXHIBIT 21.2   Hedging Business Risk with a Forward Contract

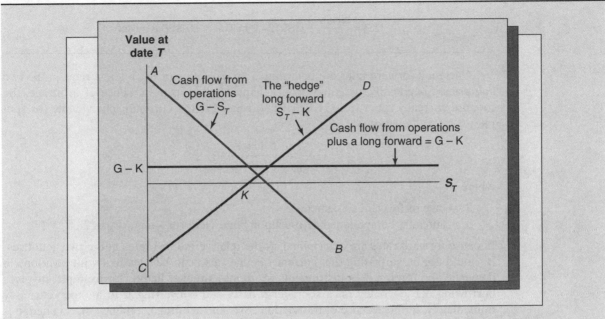

forward price for oil (which was about $23 a barrel) rather than the $40 spot price. Four times the two-year forward price equals $92, which indicates that the return of $100 in principal was much less of a sure thing.

Using Forward Contracts to Hedge Currency Obligations

The last subsection illustrated how to use forward contracts to hedge commodity price risk, in that case, oil. Corporations and financial institutions also commonly use forward contracts to hedge currency risk. Corporations generally enter into currency forward contracts with their commercial banker. Such contracts are customized for the amount and required maturity date and can be purchased in almost all major currencies. Maturities can range from a few days to several years (long-dated forwards), although the average maturity is one year.

Because forward contracts are fairly simple and can be customized, they are the hedging tool most commonly used by corporate foreign exchange managers. Example 21.4 illustrates a typical foreign exchange hedge with currency forwards.

Example 21.4:   Hedging Currency Risk with a Currency Forward Contract

Assume that Disney wants to hedge the currency risk associated with the expected losses of Euro-Disneyland (outside Paris) over the next year. The expected loss is 1 billion French francs. How can Disney accomplish this, assuming that the current French franc/U.S. dollar spot rate is FFr 5 per US$ and the forward rate for currency exchanged six months from now is FFr 5.15/US$?

Answer: To approximate the FFr billion loss spread evenly over the entire year, assume that the entire loss occurs in six months. Thus, if Disney agrees to buy FFr 1 billion six months from now, it will have to pay US$1 billion/5.15 or approximately US$194.2 million. The US$194.2 million is the locked-in loss. If the dollar depreciates to FFr 4 per US$ six months from now, the FFr 1 billion loss becomes $250 million, but this is offset by a gain of US\$55.8 million on the forward contract:

$$\text{US\$}\frac{1\ \text{billion}}{4} - \text{US\$194.2 million} = \text{US\$55.8 million}$$

Currency forward rates are determined by the ratios of the interest rates in the two countries. Specifically, we know from Chapter 7 that in the absence of arbitrage, the forward currency rate s_F (e.g., FFr/US\$) is related to the current exchange rate (or spot rate) s_0 by the equation:

$$\frac{s_F}{s_0} = \left(\frac{1 + r_{\text{foreign}}}{1 + r_{\text{domestic}}}\right)^T$$

where

T = date of forward settlement

r = annually compounded zero-coupon bond yield for a maturity of T

Because forward rates are determined by the relative interest rates in the two countries, it should not be surprising that currency hedges also can be executed with positions in domestic and foreign debt instruments. A **money market hedge**, for example, involves borrowing one currency on a short-term basis and converting it to another currency immediately. In the absence of transaction costs and arbitrage, a money market hedge is exactly like a forward contract. Also like a forward contract, it eliminates the uncertainty associated with exchange rate changes.[5]

Example 21.5:   Hedging with a Money Market Hedge

How can Disney (see Example 21.4) use a money market hedge to ensure that the expected FFr 1 billion loss from Euro-Disneyland over the next year will not grow larger in U.S. dollars as a consequence of a depreciating dollar? Assume as before that the current spot rate is FFr 5 per US\$. To be consistent with the six-month forward rate of FFr 5.15 per US\$, it is necessary to assume that six-month dollar LIBOR is 6 percent per annum, while six-month French franc LIBOR is 12.114 percent per annum, and six months is 182 days.

Answer: The money market hedge requires the following three steps:

1. Borrow U.S. dollars in the LIBOR market today for six months.
2. Exchange the U.S. dollars for French francs.
3. Invest the French francs for six months in Euro-French franc deposits.

In six months, the maturing US\$ LIBOR loan will require repayment in dollars, while the maturing FFr LIBOR investment will provide the necessary French francs that the U.S. company wanted to purchase. Hence, if the dollars borrowed in step 1 is:

$$\text{US\$188.46 million} = \frac{\text{US\$1 billion}}{5\left[1 + .12114\left(\dfrac{182}{360}\right)\right]}$$

Exactly 1 billion FFr will be received in six months and the Eurodollar loan in step 1 will require payment of:

$$\text{US\$194.2 million} = \text{US\$188.46 million} \times \left[1 + .06\left(\frac{182}{360}\right)\right]$$

---

[5]The equivalence of hedging with forward contracts and a money market hedge is known as the covered interest parity relation. See Chapter 7 for more detail.

Note that the US$194.2 million payout in six months is the same amount locked in as a loss with the forward rate because the interest rates chosen were consistent with the covered interest parity relation.

21.3 Hedging Short-Term Commitments with Maturity-Matched Futures Contracts

This section investigates how to hedge obligations that generate risk exposure with futures contracts that mature on the same date as the obligation. As we will see, there is an important difference between hedging with futures and hedging with forwards.

Review of Futures Contracts, Marking to Market, and Futures Prices

In contrast to forward contracts, which can be tailored to the individual needs of the corporation, futures contracts are standardized. For example, currency futures contracts on the International Monetary Market, a currency futures market owned by the Chicago Mercantile Exchange, are limited to standard lot sizes, which differ between currencies, have standard maturity dates (quarterly), and involve only a selected number of major currencies.[6]

Recall that the essential distinction between a forward and a futures contract lies in the timing of their cash flows. With a futures contract, profit (or loss) is received (paid) on a daily basis, instead of being paid in one large sum at the maturity date as the forward contract does.

Because each party to a futures contract keeps a small amount of cash on deposit (i.e., margin) with a broker to cover potential losses, brokers automatically execute the daily cash transfer, requiring only occasional notification to the two parties when margin funds are running low. If the futures price increases from the previous day's price, cash is taken from the accounts of investors who have short positions in the contract and placed in the accounts of those with long positions in the contract. If the futures price goes down, the reverse happens.

This procedure, known as *marking to market* (see Chapter 7), has a negligible effect on the fair market price of the futures relative to the forwards (with the notable exception of long-term interest rate contracts). This means that forwards and futures contracts can be treated the same, for the most part, for valuation purposes. Despite this valuation similarity, the next subsection points out that futures and forwards cannot be treated as if they are the same for hedging purposes.

Tailing the Futures Hedge

It is easy to become confused about how to hedge with futures because, as we shall see, futures hedges require *tailing* (defined shortly). The futures position in a tailed futures hedge is smaller than it is in a hedge that uses forward contracts because it needs to account for the interest earned on the marked-to-market cash. The proper way to perform tailing on a hedge is a source of confusion for many practitioners, and it has caused grief for a number of corporations. Therefore, we need to go through the logic of futures hedge tailing carefully.

---

[6]In early 1997, the currencies available for exchange against the U.S. dollar in this market were the Japanese yen, German mark, Canadian dollar, British pound, Swiss franc, French franc, Mexican peso, Brazilian real, and Australian dollar.

No Arbitrage Futures and Forward Prices.   Assume that gold trades at $400 an ounce. Now compute the futures price for gold. Recall from Chapter 7 that for an investment that pays no dividends, the no-arbitrage T-year forward price—and, because their values are approximately the same, the T-year futures prices—is given by the equation:

$$F = S_0(1 + r_f)^T$$

where

F = futures price
S_0 = today's spot price of the underlying investment
r_f = annually compounded yield on a T-year zero coupon bond

The futures price for gold delivered one year from now, with a risk-free interest rate of 10 percent per year, would have a futures price of $440 [= $400(1.1)] per ounce of gold.

Creating a Perfect Futures Hedge.   Suppose you own an ounce of gold that you wish to sell in one year. To fix the selling price today by selling futures contracts, it is necessary to *tail* your hedge. That is, you should sell less than one ounce in futures for each ounce that you plan to sell in one year.

Why is selling a futures contract on one ounce of gold overhedging in this case? Well, picture what would happen if the spot price of gold instantly changed today from $400 per ounce to $401 per ounce. As line *a* of Exhibit 21.3 illustrates, the gold futures price would then change from $440 to $441.10 per ounce. Hence, selling one futures contract to hedge the change in the price of gold would overhedge the gold price risk. As the gold price jumps from $400 to $401 per ounce, we gain $1 from holding one ounce of gold, but lose $1.10 from having sold a futures contract on one ounce of gold.

Selling less than one futures contract remedies this overhedging problem. Specifically, for a sale of 1/1.1 futures contracts, the loss on the futures contracts associated with the $1 gold price increase would be $(1/1.1) \times \$1.10$ or $1.00, which would exactly

EXHIBIT 21.3   Hedging a Decline in the Price of Gold with Futures and Forwards

Position	*(1)* Position Value at Initial Gold Price of $400/oz. ($\Rightarrow$ Zero PV forward and futures price = $440)	*(2)* Position Value if Gold Price Rises to $401/oz ($\Rightarrow$ Zero PV forward and futures price = $441.10)	*(3)* Mark-to-Market Cash	*(4)* Gain from Position = (2) + (3) − (1)
Hold 1 oz gold	$400	$401	$ 0	$ 1
Sell 1 futures contract	0	0	−1.1	−1.1
Sell 1/1.1 futures contracts	0	0	−1	−1
Sell 1 forward contract	0	−1 = 440/1.1 − 401	0	−1
a. Hold 1 oz of gold and sell 1 futures contract	400	401	−1.1	−.1
b. Hold 1 oz of gold and sell 1/1.1 futures contracts	400	401	−1	0
c. Hold 1 oz of gold and sell 1 forward contract	400	400 = 401 − 1	0	0

offset the $1.00 gain from holding one ounce of gold. This is shown in line *b* of Exhibit 21.3. The practice of selling less than one financial contract to hedge one unit of the spot asset is known as **tailing the hedge**.

Contrasting the Futures Hedge with the Forward Hedge.   In our gold example, the no-arbitrage forward price, like the future price, is initially $440. This makes the forward contract, like the futures contract, a zero-*PV* investment. It seems curious that the minimum-risk hedge with the forward contract, where the hedge ratio is one-to-one, should *always* differ from the hedge ratio with futures contract. Note, however, that the forward contract, in contrast with the futures contract, need not have a zero present value after the contract terms are set. This difference explains why futures hedges require tailing, but (maturity-matched) forward hedges do not.

Consider what happens to the present values of the two sides of the forward contract when the price of gold instantly jumps from $400 to $401 on the first day of the contract. The present value of the forward contract's risk-free payment of $440 at a 10 percent discount rate remains the same (i.e., $400), but this payment is exchanged for gold that has a present value of $401 after the $1 price increase. Thus, the forward contract's present value jumps from zero to $1. In other words, instantaneous changes in the price of gold do not affect the present value of the cash payout of the forward contract, but they do affect the present value of the gold received and, hence, the forward contract's value, on a one-for-one basis.

In other words, if the price of gold increases from $400 to $401 per ounce, the forward contract, formerly a zero-*PV* investment, becomes an investment with a positive *PV* of $1. As line *c* of Exhibit 21.3 illustrates, immediately after the increase the closing out of *one short position* in a forward contract, which loses $1 in value, exactly offsets the $1 gain from holding one ounce of gold.

Result 21.1 summarizes the distinction between hedging with futures and hedging with forwards.

Result 21.1   Futures hedges must be tailed to account for the interest earned on the cash that is exchanged as a consequence of the futures mark-to-market feature. Such tailed hedges require holding less of the futures contract the further one is from the maturity date of the contract. The magnitude of the tail relative to an otherwise identical forward contract hedge depends on the amount of interest earned (on a dollar paid at the date of the hedge) to the maturity date of the futures contract.

21.4 Hedging and Convenience Yields

The forward price of gold is generally close to its spot price times one plus the risk-free return to the forward maturity date. In this respect, gold is very similar to a stock that pays no dividend.[7] Since the entire return from holding a stock that pays no dividend comes from capital appreciation, the present value of receiving a non-dividend-paying stock in the future must be the current price of the stock. As Chapter 8 noted, this is not true for stocks that pay a dividend. The forward price of dividend-paying stocks is less than their current price by an amount equal to the present value of the dividends that will be paid between the current date and the settlement date of the forward contract.

---

[7]There is some dispute about this among academics and practitioners. Central banks are willing to pay money to lease gold. This may imply that gold is more like a stock that pays dividends. Other researchers have argued that this lease value is tied to default risk.

From a valuation perspective, most commodities are like dividend-paying stock because there is a benefit to owning them aside from their potential for price appreciation. The direct benefit from owning such commodities is called a convenience yield. A **convenience yield** is a benefit from holding an inventory of the commodity net of its direct storage costs that arises because it is more convenient to have the inventory on hand than to have to purchase the commodity every time it is needed. For commodities with these convenience yields, the number of the futures or forward contracts used to hedge the commodity would vary depending on the date of the future obligation.

When Convenience Yields Do Not Affect Hedge Ratios

Convenience yields do not affect forward or futures hedge ratios when the maturity of the future obligation one is trying to hedge matches the maturity of the futures or forward contract used as the hedging instrument. This point is an obvious one with forward hedges. Example 21.3, for instance, shows that a forward obligation is offset exactly with an opposite position in a maturity-matched forward contract with the same terms as the forward obligation. Example 21.3 is based on oil, a commodity that has long been known to have a convenience yield; Example 21.6 illustrates this point for the same commodity with a futures contract for oil.

Example 21.6:   Hedging Oil Price Risk with a Futures Contract

Assume that Metallgesellschaft has an obligation to deliver 1.25 million barrels of oil one year out at a fixed price of $25 per barrel. How can it hedge this obligation in the futures market if the risk-free rate is 10 percent per year?

Answer: Since forward contracts to buy 1.25 million barrels hedged this same obligation in Example 21.3, tailed positions in futures contracts to buy 1.25/1.1 million barrels also would hedge this obligation. The number of futures contracts would increase every day to reflect the shortening maturity of the contract.

Whenever the obligation is a forward contract and risk therefore is eliminated with an offsetting opposite forward contract, the futures contract can generate the same perfect hedge provided that it is tailed for interest earned on the marked-to-market cash, just as in the gold illustration in Exhibit 21.3.

When there is a mismatch in the maturity of the hedging instrument and the obligation to be hedged, the convenience yield affects the hedge ratio whether the hedge is executed with forward contracts or futures contracts. Before analyzing this issue, it is important first to understand what determines convenience yields.

How Supply and Demand for Convenience Determine Convenience Yields

Consider the gasoline that is used to fill up the tank in your automobile. When you go to the gas station, you fill up your tank instead of pumping a single gallon of gas into the tank because it is convenient not to stop at a gas station every 25 miles or risk running out of gas. There is a small cost to this convenience: The gasoline in the tank, on average, is not appreciating in value, whereas the money used to pay for the gas might have earned interest (or you might have owed less interest on a credit card balance) if it had been in the bank instead of in the tank.

It also would be convenient to have even greater inventories of gasoline. You would rarely have to stop at a gas station if you could dig holes in your backyard and keep gasoline storage tanks there, have extra storage tanks in your car, or have a gasoline tanker truck follow you wherever you drive. You don't do this because it would be prohibitively costly.

If storage of large amounts of gasoline were free, you would probably choose to store the gasoline. Note that *free* means not only free of the direct costs of storage, but also free in the sense that interest earned from holding gasoline (in terms of its expected price appreciation, adjusted for systematic risk) would be comparable to that earned from cash deposited in the bank. Of course, this situation is not possible even if the direct costs of storage were zero. If everyone stored gasoline to an unlimited degree, the price of gasoline would be bid upward, making its return smaller than the interest on cash deposited in the bank.

In essence, the demand for convenience and the supply of convenience, which depend on the cost of supplying convenience, determine the inventory of any commodity. For supply to equal demand, the difference between the expected price appreciation of the commodity and that of any other investment of identical risk must be the difference in their net convenience yields (the latter being the value of convenience less direct storage costs as a proportion of the commodity's price). For simplicity of exposition, we will refer to the net convenience yield as the convenience yield.

Hedging the Risk from Holding Spot Positions in Commodities with Convenience Yields

Convenience yields tend to reduce forward prices, other things being equal. Consider, for example, the forward prices of crude oil. Refineries with oil inventories earn a convenience yield (that exceeds the cost of storage) because they avoid the risk of having to shut down the refinery if supplies are interrupted. Assume that crude oil has a convenience yield of 2 percent per year. If oil is currently selling at $25 a barrel and the risk-free rate is 10 percent per year, then the no-arbitrage futures and forward price for oil delivered one year from now is:

$$\$26.96 \text{ per barrel} = \frac{\$25(1.1)}{1.02}$$

More generally, if the commodity's convenience yield to the forward commitment's maturity date is y, and F_0 is the no-arbitrage forward price that would apply in the absence of a convenience yield, the forward price for the commodity should be:

$$\frac{F_0}{1 + y}$$

The division of F_0 by *one plus the convenience yield* affects hedge ratios when there is a mismatch between the maturity of the futures and the date of the position one is trying to hedge. For example, when trying to use forwards or futures to perfectly hedge the oil price risk from holding an inventory of oil, the convenience yield would affect the hedge ratio used. As Exhibit 21.4 on page 758 illustrates, an increase in the current price of oil from $25 per barrel in column (1) to $30 per barrel in column (2)—which results in a zero-*PV* futures and forward price of $32.35—would be offset by a short position in 1.02/1.1 futures contracts (row *a*) or 1.02 forward contracts (row *b*).

Hence, the 2 percent convenience yield makes oil a very different commodity than gold, which we believe has very little or no convenience yield. In contrast with gold, the present value of the obligation to buy a barrel of oil one year from now is less volatile than the value of the purchase of a barrel of oil today. A purchase of oil one year from now is, in essence, equivalent to a purchase of 1/1.02 barrels of oil today, in terms of risk.

Exhibit 21.4   **Hedging a Decline in the Price of Oil with a 2 Percent Convenience Yield–Current Oil Position**

Position	*(1)* Position Value at Initial Oil Price of \$25/Barrel ($\Rightarrow$ Zero PV Forward and Futures Price = \$26.96)	*(2)* Position Value if Oil Price Rises to \$30/barrel ($\Rightarrow$ Zero PV Forward and Futures Price = \$32.35)	*(3)* Mark-to-Market Cash	*(4)* Gain from Position (2) + (3) − (1)
Hold 1 barrel oil	\$25	\$30	\$ 0	\$ 5
Sell 1 futures contract	0	0	−5.4	−5.4
Sell 1.02/1.1 futures contracts	0	0	−5	−5
Sell 1 forward contract	0	$-4.9 = \dfrac{26.96 - 32.35}{1.1}$	0	−4.9
Sell 1.02 forward contracts	0	$-5 = 1.02(-4.9)$	0	−5
Hold 1 barrel of oil and sell 1 futures contract	25	\$30	−5.4	−.4
Hold 1 barrel of oil and sell 1 forward contract	25	$25.1 = 30 - 4.9$	0	.1
a. Hold 1 barrel of oil and sell 1.02/1.1 futures contracts	25	\$30	−5	0
b. Hold 1 barrel of oil and sell 1.02 forward contracts	25	$25 = 30 - 1.02(4.9)$	0	0

It is important to recognize that this risk comparison assumes that the convenience yield is constant. If the convenience yield tends to increase as the price of commodity increases and vice versa, then the purchase of oil one year from now is even less risky in comparison with the purchase of oil today, as we show in the next section.

21.5 Hedging Long-Dated Commitments with Short-Maturing Futures or Forward Contracts

A fundamental hedging problem faced by many corporations arises because most financial instruments, particularly futures, have relatively short maturities. Corporate commitments, on the other hand, are often long term. Even when longer maturities exist for the desired hedging instruments, it is difficult to use them for sizable hedging tasks because very little trading takes place in the longer maturing financial instruments. The sheer market impact of a hedge would make hedging prohibitively costly. Corporations with long-dated obligations thus tend to hedge them by using the shorter maturing futures or forwards.

As we show below, for the special case where convenience yields are constant, a perfect hedge can be implemented with short-term futures and forward contracts. This perfect hedging can be extended to the case where changes in the convenience yield are perfectly correlated with changes in the price of the commodity. However, because this assumption of perfect correlation is unrealistic, it is generally not possible to perfectly hedge a long-term obligation by rolling over a series of shorter term forward or futures contracts.

Maturity, Risk, and Hedging in the Presence of a Constant Convenience Yield

To understand the hedging of long-dated commitments with shorter-maturing futures and forwards, it is necessary to link the risk of each commitment and hedging instrument to the risk of holding the commodity. For example, assuming that oil has a convenience yield of 2 percent per year, the forward commitment to buy a barrel of oil *10 years from now* is equivalent in risk to a position in $1/1.02^{10}$ barrels of oil purchased today. Similarly, a commitment to buy oil *one year from now* is equivalent in risk to a position in $1/1.02$ barrels of oil purchased today. Hence, to perfectly hedge the obligation to buy a barrel of oil 10 years from now by selling a forward contract to purchase oil one year from now, sell:

$$\frac{1}{1.02^9} = \frac{1/1.02^{10}}{1/1.02} = .837$$

forward contracts maturing one year from now.

Rollovers at the Forward Maturity Date.   As each day passes, it is unnecessary to alter the position in the one-year forward contract. For example, one-half year from now, the obligation to buy oil long term would be 9.5 years away, while the short-term forward would be 0.5 years from maturity. Hence, the proper number of short-term forward contracts being sold still would be:

$$\frac{1}{1.02^9} = \frac{1/1.02^{9.5}}{1/1.02^{.5}}$$

However, as the year elapses and the short-term forward contract matures, it is important to roll over the old contract and enter into a new one-year forward contract. For this new contract, the obligation would be nine years out. At this point, selling:

$$\frac{1}{1.02^8} = \frac{1/1.02^9}{1/1.02} = .853$$

of the new one-year forward contracts perfectly hedges the risk of the (now) nine-year-out obligation. Altering the number of offsetting forward contracts at the maturity date of the short-term hedging instrument is a form of tailing the hedge, similar to the tailing observed earlier with long-dated futures contracts.

Exhibit 21.5 on page 760 illustrates the use of this tailed rollover strategy for hedging. The exhibit indicates that at each annual rollover date of the series of short-term forward contracts, the number of forward contracts sold that would perfectly hedge the obligation increases until in the final year—because of the matched maturity between the commitment and the hedging instrument—the perfect hedge involves selling exactly one forward contract.

Futures Hedges.   Earlier, we noted that a one-year futures contract is more risky than a one-year forward contract because of the mark-to-market feature of the futures. With a 10 percent risk-free rate, each one-year futures contract is equivalent in risk to $1/1.1$ one-year forward contracts. Hence, for the illustration above, a perfect futures hedge would involve selling:

$$\frac{1}{1.02^9(1.1)} = .761$$

EXHIBIT 21.5   **Hedging a Long-Term Obligation with Short-Maturing Forwards Rolled Over at Maturity (Positive Convenience Yield)**

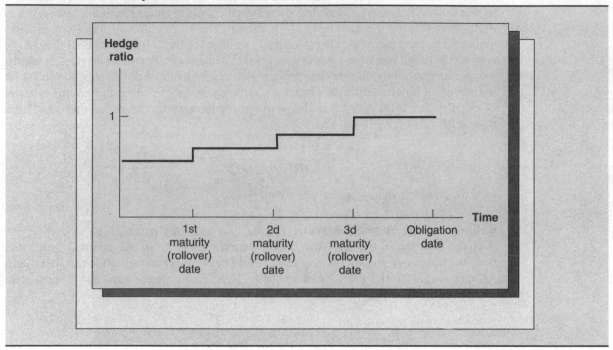

one-year futures contracts at the outset. However, as each day elapses in that first year, it is necessary to tail the futures hedge because it is getting closer to the forward contract in terms of its risk. For example, one-half year from now, the obligation to buy oil long term would be 9.5 years away implying that the number of short-term futures contracts being sold would have to equal:

$$\frac{1}{1.02^9(1.1^{.5})} = \frac{1/1.02^{9.5}}{1/1.02^{.5}} \div 1.1^{.5} = .798$$

Thus, as Result 21.2 noted, the hedge ratio for a hedge involving a futures contract is always changing, both when there is and when there is not a convenience yield to holding the underlying commodity. Exhibit 21.6 illustrates the process of hedging with the futures rollover strategy. Note the difference between the hedge ratios from this exhibit and those in Exhibit 21.5; in particular, note the difference in the way the hedge ratios evolve between rollover dates.

Example 21.7 applies these insights to a hypothetical hedging problem faced by Metallgesellschaft.

Example 21.7:   Hedging Oil Price Risk with Short-Dated Futures and Forwards
Assume that Metallgesellschaft has an obligation to deliver 1.25 million barrels of oil one year out at a fixed price of $25 per barrel.

  a. How can it hedge this obligation in the forward or futures markets, using forwards and futures maturing one month from now and then rolling over into new one-month forwards and futures as these mature? Assume that the convenience yield is 5 percent per year and the risk-free interest rate is 10 percent per year, both compounded annually.

EXHIBIT 21.6   **Hedging a Long-Term Obligation with Short-Maturing Futures Rolled Over at Maturity (Positive Convenience Yield)**

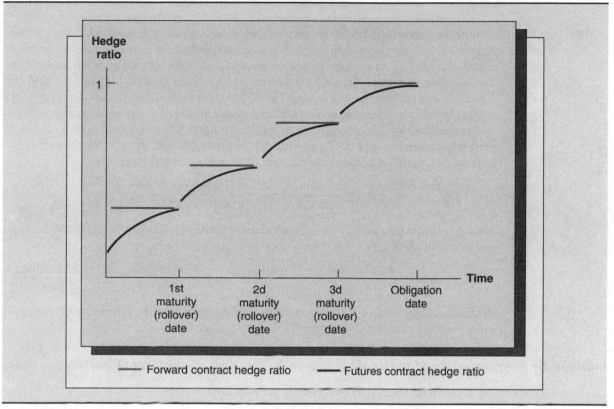

b. How would your answer change if you want to hedge against the change in value from owning 1.25 million barrels of oil?

Answer:

a. The sum of 1 plus the one-month convenience yield per dollar invested is $1.05^{1/12}$. Hence, the forward hedge would buy 1.25 million/$1.05^{11/12}$ barrels of oil one-month forward. In the futures market, one would buy futures to acquire 1.25 million/$[(1.05^{11/12})(1.1^{1/12})]$ barrels of oil.

b. The convenience yield makes the risk from holding 1.25 million barrels of oil greater than the risk associated with the present value of the obligation to receive 1.25 million barrels in one year. The risk-minimizing hedge would be to sell $1.05^{1/12} \times 1.25$ million barrels of oil for one-month forward delivery. A futures position to sell $(1.05/1.1)^{1/12} \times 1.25$ million barrels of oil also eliminates the oil price risk.

Quantitative Estimates of the Oil Futures Stack Hedge Error

Mello and Parsons (1995) constructed a simulation model for Metallgesellschaft's hedging problem. Their model assumes that Metallgesellschaft has an obligation to deliver 1.25 million barrels of oil at a fixed price on a monthly basis for the next 10 years. This amounts to delivery obligations of 150 million barrels of oil at a fixed price. Mello and

Parsons reported that Metallgesellschaft used what is known as a rolling stack of short-term futures contracts to undertake this hedge. With a **rolling stack**, the obligation to sell (buy) a commodity is offset with a series of short-term futures or forward contracts to buy (sell) the same amount of the commodity. Metallgesellschaft's commitment to sell 150 million barrels of oil at a preset price is hedged with a rolling stack (albeit imperfectly) that takes a position in short-term futures contracts to buy 150 million barrels of oil. As the futures contracts expire, they are replaced with futures contracts in amounts that maintain a one-to-one relation between the futures contracts to buy oil and the forward commitment to sell oil. Mello and Parsons assumed that the convenience yield of oil is 0.565 percent per month and the risk-free rate is 0.565 percent per month. Based on the analysis above, the obligation to sell 1.25 million barrels of oil at month t could be perfectly hedged by purchasing one-month futures contracts that are rolled over. If the convenience yield is constant, the number of futures contracts should be:

$$\frac{1.25 \text{ million}}{1.00565^t} = \frac{1.25 \text{ million}}{(1.00565^{t-1})(1.0565)}$$

For the obligation at each of the 120 months, the annuity formula gives a futures position (in barrels of oil) of

$$108.7 \text{ million} = \frac{1.25 \text{ million}}{1.00565} + \frac{1.25 \text{ million}}{1.00565^2} + \ldots + \frac{1.25 \text{ million}}{1.00565^t} + \ldots + \frac{1.25 \text{ million}}{1.00565^{120}}$$

Hence, a rolling stack of 150 million barrels overhedges the risky obligation of Metallgesellschaft by a considerable degree.

Intuition for Hedging with a Maturity Mismatch in the Presence of a Constant Convenience Yield

We summarize the results of this section as follows:

Result 21.2   Long-dated obligations hedged with short-term forward agreements need to be tailed if the underlying commitment has a convenience yield. The degree of the tail depends on the convenience yield earned between the maturity date of the forward instrument used to hedge and the date of the long-term obligation. When hedging with futures, a greater degree of tailing is needed (see Result 21.1).

Result 21.2 derives from the fact that a convenience yield makes the receipt of a commodity at a future date less risky than receiving the same commodity now. Just as 50 percent of an investor's risk disappears when he sells 50 percent of his shares of stock in a company or if the stock has a dividend equal to 50 percent of its value, so does a 50 percent convenience yield reduce the risk of a commodity received in the future by 50 percent. Because y percent of risk disappears with a y percent convenience yield, eliminating the risk of a forward commitment by taking on a position in a (more risky) underlying (spot) commodity requires less than a one-to-one hedge ratio when the commodity has a convenience yield.

Perfect hedging of long-dated obligations with short-term forwards (or futures) has a less than one-to-one hedge ratio because perfect hedging is a matter of matching up risks. The short-dated forward (or futures) contract is more like the underlying commodity, which has more risk than the long-term obligation. The closer the maturity date of the forward, the closer the hedge ratio in a perfect hedge is to the "less-than-one" ratio for hedging the obligation by holding the underlying commodity. The longer the maturity of the forward contract, the more the forward contract looks like the forward commitment and the closer the hedge ratio is to one.

Convenience Yield Risk Generated by Correlation between Spot Prices and Convenience Yields

The analysis up to this point has assumed that the convenience yield was constant. Generally, however, the convenience yield is uncertain and correlated with the price of the commodity. This subsection examines the effect of the correlation on the hedge ratios.

It is not difficult to see that convenience yields are generally positively related to the price of the underlying commodity. In the late spring of 1996, for example, gasoline prices in the United States rose over a matter of weeks by approximately 25 percent. Industry forecasters suggested that this was caused by a temporary shortage of gasoline and higher than expected demand, but that gasoline prices would be coming down by the end of the summer.

Earlier, we argued that gasoline consumers fill up their tanks for the convenience of not having to stop again. However, when gasoline prices rose in the summer of 1996, some motorists did not fill up their tanks when they were empty. Instead, they put in five gallons at a time, hoping that in a few days the price of gasoline would come down. Because gasoline prices were *expected* to depreciate, the cost of convenience went up. After all, storing an inventory is not very profitable when the inventory value is declining. Note, however, that the convenience yield of gasoline also went up at this time because the convenience benefit of that last gallon in a 5-gallon fill-up is a little higher than the convenience of the last gallon in a 15-gallon fill-up.[8]

Generally, the size of a commodity's convenience yield fluctuates inversely with the aggregate inventory of a commodity, which, in turn, is driven by supply and demand shocks. A necessary ingredient for a convenience yield, that is, for there to be a benefit from holding inventory, is that there must be some transaction cost, above and beyond the ordinary cost of the commodity, to acquire the commodity at certain times. A gasoline station may pay the ordinary price for gasoline when the supplier's tanker truck shows up on its weekly route. However, if between its regular deliveries, the gasoline station requires a special delivery of gasoline because demand was exceptionally high, the supplier may impose a surcharge. This surcharge reflects the tanker truck driver's inability to deliver gasoline using the most efficient route possible. At times of low aggregate inventory nationwide, e.g., the summer driving season, the benefit of a large inventory of gasoline—gasoline's convenience yield—is high.

Hedge ratios are further reduced by convenience yields that tend to increase whenever the price of the commodity increases. The intuition for this insight, as with Result 21.2, is based on a comparison of the risk of the commodity's present value at different dates. In particular, the following result suggests that a convenience yield that increases a lot as spot prices increase tends to dampen the change in the long-term forward prices more than when the convenience yield exhibits only a mild increase in response to a spot price increase.

Result 21.3   The greater the sensitivity of the convenience yield to the commodity's spot price, the less risky the long-dated obligation is to buy or sell a commodity.

The positive correlation between the convenience yield and the commodity's spot price means that the convenience yield acts as a hedge against spot price movements. Usually,

---

[8]Some motorists of course continued to put as much gasoline in their tanks as they had before the price increase. These motorists always place a high value on the convenience of gasoline. However, these motorists were never the marginal investor in determining the convenience yield in the marketplace. Rather, it was the motorists who were willing to cut their inventory of gasoline who determined the price of convenience in the marketplace.

the convenience yield is high when the commodity price is high and vice versa. Thus, a more realistic picture of the convenience yield suggests that in hedging long-dated commitments with short-term forwards or futures, the hedge ratio should be smaller than the ratio computed for a convenience yield that is assumed to be certain.

The exact computation of the hedge ratio in cases where the convenience yield changes depends on the process that generates the underlying commodity's spot price, which is tied to the fluctuating convenience yield.[9]

We summarize the results of this subsection as follows:

Result 21.4   The greater the sensitivity of the convenience yield to the price of the underlying commodity, the lower the hedge ratio when hedging long-dated obligations with short-term forward agreements. When hedging with futures, a further tail is needed (see Result 21.1).

In simple models, sensitivity as used in Results 21.3 and 21.4 can be thought of as the covariance between changes in the convenience yield and changes in the commodity's price. Alternatively, one can view sensitivity as the slope coefficient from regressing changes in the convenience yield on changes in the commodity's price.

Basis Risk

When hedging an obligation with a rollover position, there is an additional consideration known as basis risk. The **basis** at date t of a futures contract, B_t, is the difference between the futures (or forward) price and the spot price,

$$B_t = F_t - S_t$$

Basis risk is the degree to which fluctuations in the basis are unpredictable given perfect foresight about the path the price takes in the future. Since the basis is simply the difference between the futures (or forward) price and the spot price, basis risk is also the degree to which the futures (or forward) price is unpredictable, given perfect foresight about the path the spot price will take.

Sources of Basis Risk.   Basis risk may arise because investors are irrational or face market frictions that prevent them from arbitraging a mispriced futures or forward contract. We are somewhat skeptical about this as a cause of basis risk, especially as it applies to financial markets from about the late 1980s on. Basis risk may also arise because changes in interest rates are unpredictable. While this eliminates the ability to arbitrage any deviation from the futures-spot pricing relation, the effect on the pricing relation and on hedge ratios has to be negligible. [See Grinblatt and Jegadeesh (1996), for example.] Finally, basis risk may arise because of variability in convenience yields that is not determined by changes in the spot price of the commodity. Convenience yield risk of this type is unhedgeable and eliminates, not only the ability to perfectly hedge long-term obligations with short term forwards, but also the ability to arbitrage deviations from the forward spot pricing relation. It is largely this unhedgeable convenience yield risk that the analyst needs to be concerned about when estimating hedge ratios.

How Unhedgeable Convenience Yield Risk Affects Hedge Ratios.   Thinking about convenience yields in the same way one thinks about dividend yields aids in understanding the effect of unhedgeable convenience yield risk on the variance minimizing hedge ratio. Recall from Chapter 10 that the stock price is the present value of future dividends.

---

[9]The interested reader is referred to Gibson and Schwartz (1990) and Ross (1996).

Hence, the stock price 10 years out is the present value (*PV*) of the dividends from year 10 onward, while the stock price 1 year out is the *PV* of the dividends from year 1 onward. The difference is the *PV* of the dividends paid from years 1 through 10. Now, consider the hedge of a forward obligation to pay the year 10 stock price offset with a 1-year forward contract on the stock and examine how variable the *PV*s of the two hedge components are over time. The variability of the *PV* of the 1-year forward contract, which is entirely due to changes in *PV* of the stock price 1 year out, exceeds the variability in the *PV* of the 10-year forward obligation, which stems entirely from the *PV* of the year 10 stock price. The difference in variability is the variability in the *PV* of the dividends paid from years 1 through 10. There is a portion of this that cannot be hedged because it is unrelated to the stock price. As this chapter's prior and subsequent analysis shows (e.g., Section 21.9), when the hedging instrument is more volatile than the obligation, the hedge ratio is generally lower, implying:

Result 21.5   The greater the unhedgeable convenience yield risk, the lower is the hedge ratio for hedging a long-term obligation with a short term forward or futures contract.

When hedging with a rollover strategy, the largest risk arises at the rollover dates of the short-term contracts. At these dates, the benefit of convenience embedded in the value of the hedging instrument drops abruptly as a result of the change in the forward maturity date. By contrast, the risk from changes in the convenience yield over small intervals of time is orders of magnitude smaller.

Situations Where Basis Risk Does Not Affect Hedge Ratios.   Basis risk does not affect the size of the minimum variance hedge ratio when hedging a long-dated commitment with a comparably long-dated forward contract on the same underlying commodity or asset. In this case, the forward contract and the forward obligation are essentially the same investment, implying a hedge ratio of one. As long as there is no arbitrage at the maturity date, $F_T = S_T$ and any basis risk that occurs before the maturity date are irrelevant.

21.6 Hedging with Swaps

The last section noted that many financial contracts have a shorter term than the commitments they try to hedge. The success of the swap market is due in part to swaps typically having longer-term maturities than the contracts offered in the futures and forward markets.

Review of Swaps

Swaps, discussed in detail in Chapter 7, are agreements to periodically exchange the cash flows of one security for the cash flows of another. In addition to specifying the terms of the exchange and the frequency with which exchanges take place, the swap contract specifies a notional amount of the swap. This amount represents the size of the principal on which the cash flow exchange takes place. The most common swaps are *interest rate swaps,* which exchange the cash flows of fixed- for floating-rate bonds, and *currency swaps,* which exchange the cash flows of bonds denominated in two different currencies.

Swaps can be used to hedge a variety of risks. For example, corporations often employ basket swaps to hedge currency risk. **Basket swaps** are currency swaps that exchange one currency for a basket of currencies. Typically, this basket of currencies is weighted to match the foreign currency exposure of the corporation.

Hedging with Interest Rate Swaps

Banc One's use of interest rate swaps described by Backus, Klapper, and Telmer (1994) illustrates how swaps are used for risk management. According to a 1991 issue of *Bankers Magazine,* Banc One viewed itself as the McDonald's of retail banking. Banc One's franchises, which consisted originally of a set of acquired Midwestern banks, grew in the 1980s and early 1990s to include banks in the West, Southwest, and East. All of these "franchises" have decentralized management whose decisions resulted in a situation in which the collective assets of the franchises are more short term than their liabilities. As a consequence, Banc One's liabilities are more sensitive to interest rate movements than its assets.[10]

Backus, Klapper, and Telmer computed that a 1 percent decline in interest rates in the early 1990s resulted in an equity decline of about $180 million for Banc One. As a result of this interest rate sensitivity, headquarters management at Banc One assumed positions in interest rate derivatives in the 1990s, using mainly interest rate swaps with a notional amount of almost $40 billion. Banc One reported that a 1 percent decline in interest rates decreased net income by 12.3 percent without the swaps, but increased net income by 3.3 percent with the swaps.

The Interest Rate Risk of an Interest Rate Swap.   The key to interest rate hedging with interest rate swaps is that the floating side of the swap has virtually no sensitivity to interest rate risk, while the fixed side has the same kind of interest rate risk as a fixed-rate bond. Hence, a swap to pay a fixed rate of interest and receive a floating rate of interest generates the same interest rate sensitivity as the issuance of a fixed-rate bond. Conversely, a swap to pay a floating interest rate and receive a fixed interest rate generates the same interest rate sensitivity as the purchase of a fixed-rate bond. As a result, an interest rate swap can effectively change positions in fixed-rate bonds into positions in floating-rate bonds and vice versa. Ignoring credit risk considerations, rolled over positions in short-term debt have the same risks as floating-rate debt. Thus, interest rate swaps can also be thought of as vehicles for converting short-term debt into long-term debt and vice versa.

Converting Fixed to Floating.   If the value of the assets of a firm are insensitive to interest rates, financing with a fixed-rate debt instrument creates interest rate exposure, increasing equity value when interest rates rise and decreasing equity value when interest rates fall. An interest rate swap can effectively convert the fixed-rate liability into a floating-rate liability, as Example 21.8 illustrates.

**Example 21.8:   Using Swaps to Convert a Floating Rate into a
                              Fixed-Rate Liability**

Assume that First Federal Bank has issued a 5-year $1 million fixed rate bond at the 5-year Treasury rate + 200 basis points (bp), paid semiannually, with principal due in five years. First Federal would like to convert this into a floating-rate loan. How can it achieve this?

Answer: First Federal should enter into a $1 million national swap to receive a fixed rate equal to the 5-year Treasury yield plus 200bp and pay LIBOR plus a spread. The receipt of the Treasury yield plus 200bp effectively cancels out the fixed-rate payments on the First Federal bond. The payment of the floating rate on the swap is all that remains.

---

[10]In contrast to Banc One, in the absence of hedging most large banks have income that increases in response to an interest rate decrease.

The **swap spread** for a five-year swap is the number of basis points in excess of the five-year on-the-run Treasury yield that the payer of the fixed rate must pay in exchange for LIBOR. Hence, in Example 21.8, if the swap spread for First Federal is 50bp, the bank would convert a five-year fixed-rate loan at the five-year Treasury yield plus 200bp into a floating-rate loan at LIBOR + 150bp (= 200bp − 50bp).

Converting Short-Term Debt to Long-Term Debt.   If the assets of the firm are highly sensitive to interest rate risk, the firm might desire fixed-rate debt financing to offset this risk. However, as Chapter 20 discussed, a firm may expect its credit risk to improve, and thus prefer rolling over short-term debt. The firm could then use a swap to hedge the interest rate risk that arises with this strategy. This possibility is examined in Example 21.9.

Example 21.9:   Hedging Interest Rate Risk

Kaiser Automotives needs to finance a project that requires $100 million for five years. The firm can obtain a fixed-rate loan for the five-year period with an interest rate of 10 percent which is three percentage points above the five-year Treasury note rate. Alternatively, Kaiser can roll over one-year bank loans to finance the project. Its current borrowing cost from such a loan is 9 percent, which is three percentage points above the one-year Treasury note rate. The bank has also agreed to enter into a swap contract with Kaiser in which the bank pays Kaiser the interest rate on one-year Treasury notes, and Kaiser pays the bank 7.3 percent, which is the interest rate on five-year Treasury notes plus 30 basis points. Kaiser is aware that the demand for automobiles is closely tied to changes in interest rates and that it can ill afford to be exposed to interest rate risk. However, it also believes that its cost of long-term debt, 10 percent, is much too high given the firm's current prospects. It believes that within a year, its credit rating will improve and its borrowing costs will decline. What should Kaiser do, and what are the risks?

Answer: Kaiser does not want to be exposed to interest rate risk, but it does want to bet on its own credit rating. It can do this by rolling over short-term loans and entering into the interest rate swap with a national amount of $100 million. With this combined transaction, the firm's initial borrowing cost will be 9% − 6% + 7.3% = 10.3%, which is slightly higher than the cost of borrowing with a fixed-rate loan. However, if Kaiser's credit rating does improve next year so that its default spread is reduced from 3 percent to 2 percent, its borrowing cost will drop from 10.3 percent to 9.3 percent and will not be subject to changes in default-free interest rates. Of course, Kaiser's projections may be wrong and its credit rating may not improve, in which case the firm would have been better off borrowing at a fixed rate.

Note that in Example 21.9, Kaiser is still exposed to interest rate risk on the asset side of its balance sheet. Because of this, its default spread may be correlated with changes in the interest rates. Specifically, Kaiser might be concerned that a large increase in interest rates could lead to a drop in its sales, which in turn causes its credit rating to decline. In this sense, the swap transaction described in the example does not totally insulate the firm's borrowing costs from the effect of changing interest rates.

Hedging with Currency Swaps

Currency swaps can be used to create foreign debt synthetically. As the last line of Exhibit 21.7 on page 768 indicates, the cash outflows of foreign debt can be synthesized by combining domestic debt (outflows in row *a*) with a swap to pay foreign currency and receive domestic currency (net outflows as row *c* less row *b*).

EXHIBIT 21.7   Creating Synthetic Foreign Debt

	Year					
	1	*2*	*3*	...	*9*	*10*
Net Cash Flows of $1 Million U.S.$ Debt						
a. Outflows (in millions)	$.09	$.09	$.09		$.09	$1.09
Future Cash Flows from 10-Year Currency Swap $1 Million Notional Amount						
b. Inflows (in millions)	$.09	$.09	$.09	...	$.09	$1.09
c. Outflows (in millions)	¥16.00	¥16.00	¥16.00	...	¥16.00	¥216.00
Total outflows of domestic debt plus swap (in millions) $a + c - b$	¥16.	¥16	¥16	...	¥.16	¥216

Creating Synthetic Foreign Debt to Hedge Foreign Asset Cash Inflows.   Allen (1987) suggested that Disney's profits from Tokyo Disneyland (net of its yen financing liabilities) created an exposure to yen currency risk for Disney in the mid-1980s. This yen-denominated cash inflow was estimated at ¥6 billion per year and growing. Disney could eliminate this yen exposure by issuing yen-denominated debt to a Japanese bank, but management saw this as prohibitively expensive. A comparable strategy, albeit not exactly the one Disney followed, would have the company issue U.S. dollar-denominated debt and enter into a currency swap.

Creating Synthetic Domestic Debt to Save on Financing Costs.   Sometimes, firms wish to issue domestic debt to hedge the interest rate risk of domestic assets. Example 21.9 illustrates that currency swaps also can be used to create domestic debt synthetically. If a company's debt issue is well received in a foreign country, the transaction can result in lower debt financing costs.

Example 21.9:   Using Currency Swaps to Create Domestic Debt

Assume that Motorola can issue a 5 million Swiss franc five-year straight-coupon bond at a yield of 5 percent. In the United States, its comparable dollar straight-coupon debt issues are financed at 8 percent. In the currency swap market, Motorola can swap the payments of 5 percent Swiss franc bonds for those of 7 percent U.S. dollar bonds. How can Motorola get a US$4 million loan synthetically at a yield of 7 percent? Assume that the current exchange rate is 1.25 Swiss francs to the dollar.

Answer:

1. Issue 5 million Swiss franc (SFr) notes at 5 percent.

2. Enter into a five-year US$4 million notional currency swap in which payments equivalent to the semiannual payments from the 5 percent Swiss franc notes (SFr 125,000) are received. In exchange, Motorola pays 7 percent in dollars (US$140,000 semiannually) and an additional US$4 million at the maturity of the swap. The cash received in Swiss francs on the swap funds the payment on the Swiss franc notes (interest and SFr 5 million principal), leaving only the U.S. dollar payments on one side of the swap as Motorola's obligation.

Example 21.9 shows that Motorola saves 100bp on its financing costs, or about US$40,000 per year, because Swiss franc investors are treating Motorola relatively more favorably than U.S. dollar investors. There are a variety of explanations for this, but one reason simply is that Motorola may be offering Swiss investors a unique opportunity to diversify their bond portfolios. Because the number of Swiss companies issuing bonds (e.g., Nestlé), is relatively small and because the transaction costs of investing in bonds denominated in foreign currency (and then converting back to Swiss francs) may be prohibitively large, Swiss investors may be willing to pay a premium for Motorola bonds.

21.7 Hedging with Options

Options are used in two ways to hedge risk. In the first, a **covered option strategy**, one option is issued or bought per unit of the asset or liability generating the risk exposure. The resulting one-to-one hedge ratio places either a floor on losses or a cap on gains. With the alternative, **delta hedging**, one first computes the option's delta where delta (Δ) is the number of units of the underlying asset in the option's tracking portfolio (see Chapter 7). Then, options in the quantity $1/\Delta$ are issued or bought per unit of the asset or liability generating the risk exposure, delta hedging can, at least theoretically, eliminate all risk. Such hedging typically has a greater than one-to-one hedge ratio because Δ is generally between 0 and 1.

Why Option Hedging Is Desirable

For a variety of reasons, the payoff from an option hedge is sometimes preferred to the payoff from hedged positions with futures or forwards. For example, a covered option hedge can be used when managers want to partake in some upside risk. Portfolio insurance (see Chapter 8), which offers this desirable payoff, can be created by acquiring put options to partly offset the risk from holding assets.

Alternatively, options may be appropriate when the risk being hedged has some option-like component. For example, many companies purchase swap options when they enter into swaps that are designed to offset the interest rate risk of callable bonds issued by the firm. Once the bond is called by the issuing firm, the interest rate swap that formerly hedged the bond now hedges nothing. The interest rate swap now creates rather than mitigates interest rate risk. In such a case, the previously purchased swap option can be exercised when the bond is called to eliminate the risk from the interest rate swap.[11]

Metallgesellschaft represents another case where option-based hedging may have been useful. If heating oil prices declined substantially, Metallgesellschaft may have had to deal with a set of irate customers who demanded renegotiation of their contracts to purchase heating oil at exorbitant prices. Faced with this option-like risk, Metallgesellschaft might have found a more suitable hedge by issuing call options on oil instead of selling oil futures.

As Chapter 20 noted, options may be particularly useful in cases where firms would like to hedge to minimize the probability of financial distress, but do not want to eliminate all of the upside associated with favorable outcomes. For instance, in Example 20.3,

---

[11]In many cases, such option exercise is suboptimal. Chapter 8 indicated that there are correct rules for when to exercise an option early and a time to defer exercise. The time at which the investor should optimally exercise a swap option often depends on interest rate risk alone, while the exercise of a call provision of a bond often occurs because the credit health of the company has improved. Hence, the call of a bond by the issuing firm does not mean that the firm should exercise its swap option if it is trying to maximize the option's value.

National Petroleum wanted to eliminate the possibility of financial distress but also wished to have sufficient cash flow in the event of an oil price increase to internally fund new exploration. Oil options are particularly useful in such cases because they place a floor on the company's oil revenues while allowing them to generate higher revenues, and hence fund more exploration activity, as oil prices rise above the strike price of the options.

Covered Option Hedging: Caps and Floors

The use of a single option in combination with a single position in the underlying asset (or liability) implicitly creates what is known as a *cap* or a *floor,* first discussed in Chapter 2. A floor, illustrated in panel A of Exhibit 21.8, can be thought of as a call option in combination with a risk-free security. It eliminates some downside risk—namely, all values below the floor value—so one generally pays more to acquire a floor-like position than a comparable payoff without a floor. A cap, illustrated in panel B of Exhibit 21.8, can be thought of as a short position in a put option plus a risk-free security. It eliminates some upside volatility—eliminating all outcomes above the cap value—and thus costs less (or one is paid more) than the comparable payoff without the cap.

Put-Call Parity. The put-call parity relation discussed in Chapter 8 is useful for understanding the construction of caps and floors. A floor is created by buying an option on some underlying value or exposure of a firm. For example, if the value of the firm decreases when the price of oil declines, buying a put on oil prices creates insurance against the loss in the value of the firm that results from oil prices declining too much. If the value of the firm decreases when the price of oil increases (e.g., when oil is a major input, not an output, in the production process), buying a call creates insurance against the loss in firm value that results from oil prices rising too much.

Consider now a firm whose future value at date T, V_T, can be represented as a constant value a plus the product of a coefficient b and the price of oil S_T, that is:

$$V_T = a + bS_T, \tag{21.1}$$

EXHIBIT 21.8   Floors and Caps

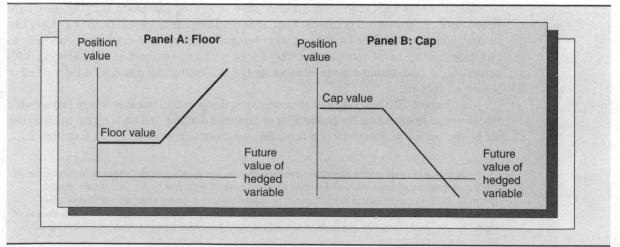

then b is positive when there is a positive relation between oil prices and firm values; b is negative when there is a negative relation between oil prices and firm value. In Chapter 8's discussion of put-call parity, we learned that the future difference between the date T value of a call and a put is:

$$c_T - p_T = S_T - K$$

or

$$S_T = c_T - p_T + K \tag{21.2}$$

We now show how to create floor values or cap values that are related to the option strike price of K.

Creating Floors. Substituting equation (21.2) into equation (21.1) tells us that the firm's value at a given future date T is:

$$V_T = a + bK + bc_T - bp_T \tag{21.3}$$

The expression $a + bK$ can be thought of as a risk-free bond. With a positive value for b, acquiring b puts at a cost of bp_0 converts the firm's date T value from that shown in equation (21.3) to:

$$V_T^* = a + bK - bp_0 (1 + r_f)^T + bc_T$$

where r_f denotes the risk-free interest rate per period.

This payoff is like a call option plus a risk-free bond, where the risk-free bond has the payoff:

$$a + bK - bp_0 (1 + r_f)^T$$

The floor value of $a + bK - bp_0 (1 + r_f)^T$ is generated when S_T is small in this case. If b is negative, buying $-b$ calls, a positive number of calls, makes the firm value:

$$V_T^* = a + bK + bc_0 (1 + r_f)^T - bp_T$$

Since b is negative, this is like having a risk-free bond plus a positive number of puts. In this case, the floor value of $a + bK + bc_0 (1 + r_f)^T$ takes effect when S_T is large.

Example 21.10 provides a numerical illustration of how to create a floor by acquiring options.

Example 21.10:   Using Options to Create Floors on Losses

Assume that Metallgesellschaft has an obligation to deliver 1.25 million barrels of oil one year from now at a fixed price of $25 per barrel. If oil prices rise to $45 a barrel, Metallgesellschaft loses $20 per barrel on this promise. How can Metallgesellschaft insure itself against oil prices exceeding $30 per barrel, yet profit if oil prices decline, as its analysts are forecasting?

Answer: Acquiring a call option to buy 1.25 million barrels of oil one year from now at $30 per barrel will cap oil prices for Metallgesellschaft at $30 per barrel, and put a floor on Metallgesellschaft's losses should oil prices rise.

Creating Caps. Caps are constructed by shorting options. Starting with the firm value shown in equation (21.3), shorting b calls when b is positive generates a new firm value of:

$$V_T^* = a + bK + bc_0 (1 + r_f)^T - bp_T$$

This has the payoff of a risk-free bond and a short position in puts. This new value is capped at $a + bK + bc_0 (1 + r_f)^T$ because the short put position can never have a positive value and the remaining terms on the right-hand side of the equation, the cap value, are nonrandom.

Similarly, with b negative, shorting $-b$ puts, a positive number of puts, creates a firm value of:

$$V_T^* = a + bK - bp_0 (1 + r_f)^T + bc_T$$

This has the payoff of a risk-free bond and a short position in calls. The new firm value is now capped at $a + bK - bp_0 (1 + r_f)^T$ because the short call position can never have a positive value and the remaining terms on the right-hand side of the equation, the cap value, are nonrandom.

Currency Caps and Floors.   Multinational companies often use currency option contracts to hedge transaction exposure. Options on spot currency are traded on organized exchanges, such as the Philadelphia Stock Exchange, while options on currency futures trade on the Chicago Mercantile Exchange. Options also trade over the counter through large commercial banks and other financial institutions.

Options on foreign currencies provide corporate foreign exchange managers with a unique hedging alternative to the forward or the futures contract. The purchase of options can create a floor. Selling options creates a cap. Options to buy a portfolio of currencies, known as **basket options**, are also popular because—with a diversified, and thus less volatile, basket of currencies underlying the option—they are less expensive than buying a portfolio of single currency options.

Example 21.11 illustrates how to use a single currency option to create a floor on foreign currency exposure.

Example 21.11:   Using Currency Options to Create Floors on Losses

Return to the hypothetical case of Disney from Example 21.4, which needs to hedge the FFr 1 billion expected loss spread out over the next year. As the earlier example pointed out, this is similar to a FFr 1 billion loss six months from now. How can Disney use currency options to ensure that a six-month drop in the value of the dollar below FFr 5.15 per US\$ will not make the dollar loss even larger?

Answer: Acquiring call options to buy 1 billion French francs with strike prices of US\$.1942 per FFr (which is FFr 5.15 per US\$) creates a floor on the dollar loss. The option allows the firm to lock in the cost of purchasing French francs for up to six months at a specified price (the strike price).

Contrast the option in Example 21.11 with a forward contract. If FFr 1 billion was purchased with a six-month forward contract at FFr 5.15 per US\$ and the value of the dollar increases from FFr 5 to FFr 6, the firm would be bound by the terms of the forward contract and would not benefit from a dramatic rise in the dollar vis-à-vis the franc.

Assume that a six-month call option to buy FFr 1 billion at the forward price of US\$.1942 per FFr costs US\$10,000 (or equivalently FFr 50,000 at FFr 5 per US\$). Such a call option insures against a drop in the dollar below the forward rate of FFr 5.15 per US\$. The option costs US\$10,000, which contrasts with the forward contract, which costs nothing, because it enables a company like Disney to earn additional dollar profits if the U.S. dollar appreciates against the French franc. This $10,000 cost must be weighed against the benefit of being able to partake in an increase in the value of the dollar (versus the franc).

It is interesting to note that the reference to calls or puts with currency options is discretionary: the right to *buy* deutsche marks in exchange for a prespecified number of dollars (a call) can also be viewed as the right to *sell* dollars in exchange for a prespecified number of deutsche marks (a put). While both views of the option are correct, this dual view raises the question of which risk-free interest rate to use for valuation: the domestic interest rate or the foreign rate? With foreign exchange options, the *interest rate differential* between the two countries ultimately determines option values. In addition, it is this differential that determines whether American currency options should be exercised prior to their maturity date.[12]

Delta Hedging with Options

The caps and floors created above leave risk on one side—upside or downside risk. However, as Chapter 8 indicated, options are tracked by a dynamic portfolio of the underlying security and riskless bonds. The tracking portfolio's investment in the underlying security, the option's delta, referred to here as the **spot delta**, can be used in a dynamic trading strategy to eliminate all risk exposure from the underlying asset or liability.

Spot Delta versus Forward Delta.   In the context of hedging currency or commodity risk associated with some future obligation, it is sometimes useful to think of options as a dynamic portfolio of forward contracts in the underlying security and riskless bonds. The **forward delta** represents the number of forward contracts that track the option. In the case of a non-dividend-paying stock, the forward delta and the spot delta of the option are the same. This means that if two-thirds of a share of stock are in the option's stock-bond tracking portfolio, then two-thirds of a forward contract on a share of stock are in the option's forward contract-bond tracking portfolio.[13] However, if the stock pays dividends or if the underlying asset is a commodity with a convenience yield or a currency with an interest rate that exceeds the interest rate on the currency with which the strike price is paid, then the forward delta generally exceeds the spot delta.

Delta Hedging with the Forward Delta.   We now illustrate how to apply forward deltas to perfectly hedge risk. The use of forward deltas allows us to skirt the issue of how convenience yields affect delta hedging. Consider once again a firm with a future value of $a + b\tilde{S}_T$, where $\tilde{S}_T$ is the price of a barrel of oil. If Δ (delta) represents the number of *forward* barrels of oil that track one option, and β is the number of risk-free dollars implicit in the option's tracking portfolio, then shorting b/Δ options creates a firm with a riskless future value of:

$$V_T^* = a + (1 + r_f)^T \times \text{(option cost)} + b\tilde{S}_T - (b/\Delta)\Delta\tilde{S}_T - (1 + r_f)^T \times \beta b/\Delta$$
$$= a + (1 + r_f)^T \times \text{(option cost)} - (1 + r_f)^T \times \beta b/\Delta$$

The firm also may use options to alter the risk exposure from a commodity like oil, for example, without completely eliminating the exposure. For the case above, shorting fewer than b/Δ options reduces but does not eliminate risk.

---

[12]The interested reader is referred to Margrabe (1978), who values exchange options. Subsequent researchers have pointed out that European options to buy currency can be viewed as a special case of exchange options.

[13]The risk-free bond position in the two tracking portfolios always differs.

Example 21.12 assumes that Metallgesellschaft's *b* is 1.25 million, which is the number of barrels of oil generated by Metallgesellschaft's delivery agreement. It enters into option agreements to completely eliminate its exposure to oil price risk.

Example 21.12:   Using an Option's Delta to Perfectly Hedge Oil Price Risk

Assume that Metallgesellschaft has an obligation to deliver 1.25 million barrels of oil one year from now at a fixed price of $25 per barrel. European options to buy oil in one year at a price of $30 per barrel have a forward delta (according to the Black-Scholes formula of Chapter 8) of .25. How many of these options should Metallgesellschaft buy to eliminate oil price risk generated by the delivery agreement?

Answer: Acquiring call options to buy 5 million barrels of oil one year from now at $30 a barrel eliminates oil price risk. Each option has the same sensitivity to oil price changes as one-fourth of a forward contract to deliver a barrel of oil. Thus, the firm needs four times the number of options relative to forward contracts to perfectly hedge this risk.

Delta Hedges Are Self-Financing.   The option hedging strategy in Example 21.12 is a dynamic strategy that hedges only instantaneous changes in oil prices. As oil prices change, the forward delta changes, implying that the number of options required for the hedge needs to change. While an increase in the delta implies that cash is needed to acquire additional options as the delta rises, the additional cash is balanced by the profit on the present value of the promise to deliver 1.25 million barrels of oil at $25 a barrel. The reverse is true as well.

We summarize the results of this subsection as follows:

Result 21.6   If a firm's exposure to a risk factor is eliminated by acquiring *b* forward contracts, then the firm also can eliminate that risk exposure, if an option's forward delta is Δ, by acquiring b/Δ options.

21.8   Factor-Based Hedging

This section discusses how the factor betas of commitments and financial instruments can be used for risk management.

Computing Factor Betas for Cash Flow Combinations

One of the most useful things about factor models is the additivity property of factor betas. To compute the aggregated factor sensitivities of combinations of cash flows, add their respective factor betas. Example 21.13 illustrates the computation.

Example 21.13:   Computing Factor Loadings for Combinations of Cash Flows

Consider the following two factor models for the cash flows of projects a, b, and c, which are part of the ABC corporation. (Intercepts and coefficients are in millions of dollars.)

$$\tilde{C}_a = 3 \ + \tilde{F}_{curr} \ \ \ - 4\tilde{F}_{int} + \tilde{\epsilon}_a$$
$$\tilde{C}_b = 5 \ + 3\tilde{F}_{curr} + 2\tilde{F}_{int} + \tilde{\epsilon}_b$$
$$\tilde{C}_c = 10 + 1.5\tilde{F}_{curr} + 0\tilde{F}_{int} + \tilde{\epsilon}_c$$

Write out the factor equations for (1) the combination of all three projects and (2) a super-project that involves doubling the size of project a and combining it with project b alone.

Answers:

(1) $\alpha_p = 3 + 5 + 10 = 18$

$\beta_{p,curr} = 1 + 3 + 1.5 = 5.5$

$\beta_{p,int} = -4 + 2 = -2$

So $\tilde{C}_p$, the cash flow of the collection of projects, satisfies the factor equation:

$$\tilde{C}_p = 18 + 5.5\tilde{F}_{curr} - 2\tilde{F}_{int} + \tilde{\epsilon}_p,$$

where $\tilde{\epsilon}_p$ is the sum of the three ϵ's.

(2) $\alpha_p = 2(3) + 5 = 11$

$\beta_{p,curr} = 2(1) + 3 = 5$

$\beta_{p,int} = 2(-4) + 2 = -6$

Thus,

$$\tilde{C}_p = 11 + 5\tilde{F}_{curr} - 6\tilde{F}_{int} + \tilde{\epsilon}_p,$$

where

$$\tilde{\epsilon}_p = 2\tilde{\epsilon}_a + \tilde{\epsilon}_b$$

The additivity property of factor models makes it easy to compute the risk impact of adding any financial instrument to a firm's cash flow. When combining the cash flow from a real asset with the cash flow from a financial instrument, add their respective betas together to obtain the impact on the risk of the firm.

Computing Hedge Ratios

The last subsection noted that the sum of the cash flow factor betas, factor by factor, yields the cash flow betas of the aggregated cash flows. This means that the quantities of various financial instruments which perfectly hedge the factor risk exposures have exactly the opposite sensitivity to the factors that the firm has. Therefore, the computation of such quantities is generally a straightforward mathematical calculation, as Example 21.14 illustrates.

Example 21.14:   Eliminating Factor Loadings with Portfolios of Factor Portfolios
Consider the following 2-factor model, which describes, per dollar of investment, how the cash flows of the projects of the Family School Alliance Corp. (FSA) relate to the currency and interest rate factors:

$$\tilde{C}_{FSA} = .3 + \tilde{F}_{curr} - 4\tilde{F}_{int} + \tilde{\epsilon}_{FSA}$$

Assume that pure factor portfolios can be constructed (see Chapter 6) that perfectly track the factors. How many dollars need to be invested in the pure factor portfolio for currency (*curr*) and the pure factor portfolio for interest rates (*int*) to perfectly hedge the factor risk of FSA?

Answer: Per dollar of real investment, if FSA sells short $1 of the pure factor portfolio for currency risk and buys $4 of the pure factor portfolio for interest rates, it will eliminate all factor sensitivity.

Result 21.7   Factor risk in cash flows is eliminated by acquiring a portfolio of financial instruments with factor betas exactly the opposite of the factor betas for the firm's cash flows.

Direct Hedge Ratio Computations: Solving Systems of Equations

As Chapter 6 noted, pure factor portfolios often must be constructed from portfolios of more basic financial instruments. In this case, factor hedging can be implemented using the more basic financial instruments, as Example 21.15 illustrates.

Example 21.15:   Eliminating Factor Loadings with Portfolios of
Financial Instruments

Consider a two-factor model, where the two factors are interest rate movements and changes in inflation. Assume that the Noah's Bagel Company has a future cash flow with factor betas of 2.5 on the interest rate factor and 4.5 on the inflation factor. Noah's would like to eliminate its sensitivity to both factors by acquiring financial securities, yet it does not wish to use its own cash to do this.

Noah's contacts its investment bank and learns that it can (1) enter into a five-year interest rate swap contract, (2) purchase 30-year government bonds, and (3) acquire a sizable chunk of shares in DESPERATE, Inc. Investment 1, the swap contract, has no up-front cost and, per contract, has a factor equation for its future value described by:

$$\tilde{C}_1 = 5 - 5\tilde{F}_{INT} - 3\tilde{F}_{INF}$$

Investment 2, the 30-year corporate bond, per million dollars invested, has a factor equation for its future cash flow of:

$$\tilde{C}_2 = 10 - 5\tilde{F}_{INT} - 1\tilde{F}_{INF}$$

Investment 3 is the stock of DESPERATE, Inc., which, per million dollars invested, has a factor equation for its end-of-period value of:

$$\tilde{C}_3 = 0 + 1\tilde{F}_{INT} + 1\tilde{F}_{INF}$$

Design a proper hedge against inflation and interest rate movements in this environment.

Answer: To design a future cash flow that is insensitive to inflation or interest rate movements, we need to find a costless portfolio of financial investments with an interest rate sensitivity of -2.5 and an inflation sensitivity of -4.5. The three investments are denoted by:

x_1 = the number of contracts in the costless swap investment

x_2 = millions of dollars in the 30-year government bonds

x_3 = millions of dollars in DESPERATE, Inc.

The portfolio of these three investments has a cost of $0x_1 + 1,000,000x_2 + 1,000,000x_3$. Its sensitivity to the interest rate factor is:

$$-5x_1 - 5x_2 + 1x_3$$

Its sensitivity to the inflation factor is:

$$-3x_1 - 1x_2 + 1x_3.$$

Therefore, the hedge portfolio is found by simultaneously solving:

$$0x_1 + 1,000,000x_2 + 1,000,000x_3 = 0$$
$$-5x_1 - 5x_2 + 1x_3 = -2.5$$
$$-3x_1 - 1x_2 + 1x_3 = -4.5$$

Since the first equation says $x_3 = -x_2$, one can substitute for x_3 in the other two equations, implying:

$$-5x_1 - 6x_2 = -2.5$$

and

$$-3x_1 - 2x_2 = -4.5$$

Multiplying the first equation (of the two immediately above) by $-.6$ and adding it to the second equation yields:

$$1.6x_2 = -3$$

or

$$x_2 = -1.875$$

Plugging this back into either of the above equations yields $x_1 = 2.75$. Thus, the solution is:

1. Buy 2.75 swap contracts.
2. Short $1.875 million in 30-year government bonds
3. Buy $1.875 million of DESPERATE, Inc.

21.9 Hedging with Regression

Regression provides a shortcut method for estimating a hedge ratio that minimizes risk exposure. By regressing the cash flow that one is trying to hedge against the value of the financial instrument used in the hedge, one derives a beta coefficient that determines the quantity of the hedging instrument that minimizes variance.[14]

Hedging a Cash Flow with a Single Financial Instrument

Consider a future cash flow $\tilde{C}$, which is random, and a financial instrument with a future value of $\tilde{P}$, also random, per unit bought. If the firm sells β units of the financial instrument in addition to $\tilde{C}$, the variance of the combination of the cash flow and the position in the financial instrument is:

$$\text{var}(\tilde{C}) + \beta^2\text{var}(\tilde{P}) - 2\beta\,\text{cov}(\tilde{C},\tilde{P}) \tag{21.4}$$

Hedge Ratios from Covariance Properties.   Because covariance can be interpreted as the marginal variance, the combination of the cash flow and the hedge instrument that minimizes variance cannot have either a positive marginal variance or a negative marginal variance with the financial instrument. If it has a positive marginal variance, then a small reduction in the holdings of the financial instrument in the combination reduces variance. If it has a negative marginal variance, then a small increase in the holdings of the financial instrument reduces the variance of the combination. Only when the financial instrument has zero covariance with the combination of the financial instrument and the cash flow can we be certain that variance has been minimized.

The covariance of the combination with the financial instrument's payoff is:

$$\text{cov}(\tilde{C} - \beta\tilde{P}, \tilde{P}) = \text{cov}(\tilde{C}, \tilde{P}) - \beta\,\text{cov}(\tilde{P}, \tilde{P}) = \text{cov}(\tilde{C}, \tilde{P}) - \beta\,\text{var}(\tilde{P})$$

This covariance is zero when:

$$\text{cov}(\tilde{C}, \tilde{P}) = \beta\,\text{var}(\tilde{P})$$

or when the number of units of the financial instrument that are sold, β, satisfies:

$$\beta = \frac{\text{cov}(\tilde{C}, \tilde{P})}{\text{var}(\tilde{P})}$$

---

[14]Chapter 4 notes the conditions required for variance minimization and for the portfolio variance formulas used here.

To show the same result with calculus, set the derivative of the variance expression, equation (21.4), to zero and solve for β. The resulting derivative:

$$2\beta \, \text{var}(\tilde{P}) - 2\text{cov}(\tilde{C}, \tilde{P})$$

is zero when:

$$\beta = \frac{\text{cov}(\tilde{C}, \tilde{P})}{\text{var}(\tilde{P})}$$

This is the same result that we achieved more intuitively above.

Note that the β that gives the minimum variance hedge is the regression coefficient (see Chapter 5). This suggests that the minimum variance hedge ratio can be found by using historical data to estimate regression coefficients. Example 21.16 illustrates how to use regression to determine hedge ratios after estimating slope coefficients from historical data.[15]

Example 21.16:   Using Regression to Determine the Hedge Ratio
Consider the problem of hedging a heating-oil contract to deliver 2.5 million barrels of heating oil one year from now with one-month crude oil futures. Historical data suggest that for every $1.00 change in the one-month futures price of crude oil, the "year ahead" heating-oil prices change by $0.75. How many futures contracts should the heating-oil company use to hedge the 2.5 million barrel heating-oil obligation?

   Answer: Since the regression coefficient is .75, and there are 2.5 million barrels for delivery, one should sell contracts to deliver 1.875 million barrels (= 2.5 million × .75 barrels of crude oil.

There are many things that can be learned from regression estimates. For example, commodities tend to have a term structure of volatilities much like the term structure of interest rates in Chapter 9. There are often regular patterns to these volatilities. The ten-year maturity oil forward price for instance, when regressed against the one-year maturity oil forward price has a regression coefficient of about .5, indicating that long-maturing oil forward prices are less volatile than short-maturing forwards. This reflects the fact that when oil prices have historically been high, they tend to decline, and when low, they tend to rise.

Cross Hedging.   Regression techniques also apply to **cross-hedging**, which is hedging across different commodities. Crude oil and heating oil are similar but not identical. Hence, it is possible to find the best hedge of heating oil using crude oil futures, or to hedge the value of a lemon crop with orange juice futures, or whatever commodity one selects as the financial instrument for hedging.

Basis Risk.   In addition, the regression method automatically takes account of basis risk in coming up with the variance-minimizing hedge. Generally, the more basis risk there is in the financial instrument, the smaller the hedge ratio.

Hedging with Multiple Regression

It is also possible to use two or more financial instruments to hedge a risk. For example, Neuberger (1996), studying long-dated oil price obligations from 1986 to 1994, used an

---

[15]Alternatively, managerial forecasts of the cash flows contingent on different values of $\tilde{P}$ could be used to estimate the slope coefficient.

elaboration of the regression technique to suggest that such obligations are best hedged, per barrel, by selling futures contracts to deliver 1.839 barrels of oil seven months ahead and buying contracts to deliver 0.84 barrels of oil six months ahead. He found that using futures contracts of multiple maturities in this way improves the variance reduction of the hedge dramatically.

Example 21.17 illustrates how to use multiple regression to determine hedge ratios for multiple hedging instruments.

Example 21.17:   Using Multiple Regression to Determine the Hedge Ratios

Suppose we have estimated a regression equation for General Motors (GM) in which the left-hand variable is the quarterly change in GM's profits in millions of dollars and the right-hand variables are the quarterly change in the three-month DM/US$ exchange rate futures price (currently 1.5) and the quarterly change in the three-month S&P futures price (currently 700). The coefficient on the first right-hand variable is 70, and the coefficient on the second variable is 2. Interpret these coefficients in terms of risk exposures and discuss their implications for the minimum variance hedge ratio.

Answer: The coefficient of 70 on the exchange rate implies that (holding the S&P 500 fixed) for each DM1 increase in the deutsche mark/dollar exchange rate (e.g., the dollar increases in value from DM1.5 per US$ to DM2.5 per US$, GM's quarterly profits increase by $70 million, on average. The coefficient of 2 on the S&P 500 implies that (holding the DM/US$ exchange rate fixed) for each one-unit increase in the S&P 500 futures (e.g., the three-month S&P 500 futures moves from 700 to 701), GM's quarterly profits are expected to increase by $2 million. To hedge this risk with the two futures instruments, GM should sell contracts on 70 million DM futures and contracts on 2 million units of the S&P 500 index.

21.10 Minimum Variance Portfolios and Mean-Variance Analysis

So far, we have assumed that the real investments of the corporation are fixed and have examined positions in derivative securities that minimize the corporation's risk. There are cases, however, where the corporation can alter the real investments of the corporation as well as its derivatives position. In these cases, the variance-minimizing hedge ratio can differ from the hedge ratio identified with regression analysis. As we discuss below, the regression approach provides the variance minimizing hedge ratio in instances where the hedging instrument is a contract, like a forward or a futures contract, that has zero value. However, when the hedging instrument is costly and the real investment can be scaled up or down in size, the relative weights in the *minimum variance* portfolio differ from the hedge ratio identified with regression analysis.

Hedging to Arrive at the Minimum Variance Portfolio

As Chapter 4 shows, the minimum variance portfolio of a set of stocks is the portfolio with a return that has the same covariance with the returns of each of its component stocks. This idea is easily extended to hedging a real asset with either a costly or a costless financial instrument that is used for hedging. In the case of a costless financial instrument, like a swap or a forward contract, the hedge ratio provided by the minimum variance portfolio from mean-variance analysis is identical to the hedge ratio from regression. That is, *hedging with regression can be viewed as a special case of minimizing variance hedging when the hedging instrument is costless.*

There are situations, however, where the financial instrument is costly and the corporation has flexibility in the size of its real asset. For example, a corporation that wishes to combine the purchase of oil refineries with oil-linked bonds would minimize the variance of that combination by forming a portfolio that has the same covariance with the return of oil refineries and the return of oil-linked bonds. The associated hedge ratio would be appropriate in cases where the size of the oil refinery position in the portfolio is variable. Similarly, an airplane manufacturer of jet airplanes who wishes to hedge the sales price of these airplanes by acquiring stock in an airline company would use the same approach. As we show in Example 21.18 below, these minimum variance combinations will not generally be the same as the hedge positions obtained with regression analysis.

Example 21.18:   Minimum Variance Hedge Ratios from Mean-Variance Analysis
Assume that Boeing is thinking about building a factory to manufacture its new Boeing 777 line. The price at which it will be able to sell the planes is uncertain, but for $1 billion Boeing can purchase a factory that will produce 100 planes for sale five years from now. After analyzing a regression of the historical sales price of 100 Boeing 777s against the return of AMR stock (the parent of American Airlines), Boeing's analysts find the regression coefficient is -2 billion. This means that when AMR's stock price increases by 1 percent, the price of 100 Boeing 777s decline by $20 million on average. Assuming that each plane's price five years from now has a standard deviation of $20 million and the five-year variance of AMR's stock return is .75, identify the minimum variance portfolio combination of AMR stock and the factory, and interpret the result.

Answer: The covariance between AMR's (decimal) stock return and the Boeing 777 plane price per dollar invested is:

$$-1.5 = \frac{-\$2 \text{ billion}}{\$1 \text{ billion}} \times var(AMR \text{ return}) = (-2)(.75)$$

The variance is the sales price per $1 invested in the factory is

$$4 = \left(\frac{\$20 \text{ million} \times 100 \text{ planes}}{1 \text{ billion}}\right)^2$$

The covariance of a minimum variance portfolio with the fraction x invested in the factory and the fraction $1 - x$ in AMR stock has x satisfying the equation that the covariance of the portfolio with the factory return and the AMR return is the same, that is:

$$4x - 1.5(1 - x) = 1.5x + .75(1 - x)$$

This is solved by $x = .29$ and it implies that if Boeing has $1 billion to spend and the factory is shrinkable, the minimum variance portfolio combination is achieved by making a smaller factory that produces 29 planes at a cost of $290 million and buying $710 million of AMR stock.

The hedging solution in Example 21.18 differs from the regression solution. The regression solution has Boeing buy $2 billion of AMR stock and results in a 2-to-1 hedge ratio instead of the 2.45-to-1 hedge ratio (710/290) of Example 21.18. The combination of the $1 billion factory and the $2 billion of AMR stock produces a cash flow that has no correlation with AMR's stock return and makes any further reduction in variance impossible. Note, however, that the regression minimum variance combination requires Boeing to spend $3 billion: $1 billion on the factory and $2 billion on AMR stock. When costless financial instruments for hedging are not available, as in the case of Boeing's factory, managers need to think about downsizing the project as a hedging vehicle rather than using regression blindly.

If the size of the position in the real asset is not alterable, and the hedging instrument is costly, then the hedge ratio provided by the mean-variance method is inappropriate.

Hedging to Arrive at the Tangency Portfolio

Managers implement real investments whenever they have higher mean returns than the financial instruments that track them. In the case of Boeing, $10 million in production costs per plane seems inexpensive compared to the cost of the AMR stock that tracks the future of a 777 series aircraft, which is usually obtained by analyzing a regression like the −2 in Example 21.18. This is not an argument for regression-based hedge ratios as much as it is an argument for bringing mean returns into the picture. As in investment theory (see Chapter 5), managers trade off mean and variance in their project and hedging decisions. In many instances, the proper hedging goal should be the capital market line on the mean-standard deviation diagram instead of some minimum variance criterion.

Example 21.19 illustrates how to achieve a hedged position on the capital market line.

Example 21.19:   Tangency Portfolios from Mean-Variance Analysis

Given the data in Example 21.18: $\sigma_{CC} = 4$, $\sigma_{CP} = -1.5$, and $\sigma_{PP} = .75$, where $\tilde{P}$ represents the AMR investment and C represents the Boeing 777 factory, identify the tangency portfolio mix of factory and AMR stock if the expected selling price of the 100 planes is $5.25 billion, the expected return of AMR stock over five years is 75 percent, and the risk-free rate over five years is 25 percent (or about 5 percent per year).

Answer: Following the analysis in Chapter 5, the equations that solve for the tangency portfolio satisfy the property that the ratio of the covariances of the investment pair are equal to the ratio of the expected excess returns:

$$\frac{4x - 1.5(1 - x)}{-1.5x + .75(1 - x)} = \frac{5.25 - 1 - .25}{.75 - .25}$$

This is solved by $x = .32$. Thus, if Boeing has $1 billion to spend and the factory is scalable, the mean-variance efficient combination of factory and AMR stock is a $320 million factory that produces 32 planes and a purchase of $680 million of AMR stock.

The *tangency portfolio hedge ratio* is based on the idea that capital is fixed, the financial instruments for hedging are given (e.g., AMR stock), and the firm has a trade-off between mean and variance where it wishes to mix the financial instrument and the real investment in proportions that maximize the ratio of the expected excess return of the portfolio to its standard deviation.

The discussion in this section is summarized as follows:

Result 21.8   Regression coefficients represent the hedge ratios that minimize variance given no capital expenditures constraints or constraints on the use of costless financial instruments for hedging. Given flexibility in the scale of a real investment project, a cost to the hedging financial instrument, and a capital expenditure constraint, the techniques of mean-variance analysis for finding the efficient portfolio or the global minimum variance portfolio may be more appropriate for finding a hedge ratio.

21.11 Summary and Conclusions

This chapter addressed the practice of hedging, examining how to use popular financial instruments like forwards, futures, swaps, and options for hedging. In addition, the discussion analyzed a variety of tools to estimate risk exposure and hedge ratios, including factor models, regression, and mean-variance mathematics.

Although the analysis focused on the elimination of risk, risk elimination is not necessarily a desirable goal, because it often comes at a very high price. Rather, the focus of the manager should be on the management of risk. Once a target risk level for a risk exposure is identified, the manager can put the tools developed in this chapter to use. For example, a manager who estimates the firm's exchange rate exposure to be a $12 million decrease in profits for every 1 percent increase in the $/DM exchange rate may target the optimal exchange rate risk exposure at "$7 million." In this case, the manager's hedge is targeted to reduce the firm's exchange rate exposure from $12 million (per 1 percent increase in the $/DM rate) to $7 million (per 1 percent increase in the $/DM rate). This hedging would not be different from that of a manager who found himself with $5 million (=$12 million − $7 million) of exchange rate risk exposure and wanted to eliminate all of this exposure.

Before applying the tools of this chapter, managers need to analyze the firm's asset and liability picture from the broadest perspective possible. Even if they understand how to hedge, many managers may overhedge by failing to recognize the important message of Chapter 11; namely, that options are the key aspects to most projects and most firms. Many firms implement a hedge of their estimated cash flows without recognizing that the option to cancel, expand, downsize, or fundamentally alter their projects may have important implications for hedge ratios. Indeed, these options in the projects often imply that options should be used in the hedging vehicles as well.

In short, straightforward answers and cookbook, albeit complex, formulas for almost any hedging problem can be found in the abundant literature on hedging. They are found in this chapter, too. However, the natural inclination to leave hedging to technicians is a foolish decision, no matter how mathematically skilled or competent such technicians are. Like the running of any major aspect of a business, hedging needs to be guided by artful, creative managers who are fairly skilled in the technical aspects of hedging so as not to be overly impressed by the recommendations of the technicians. Management needs to fully understand not only the motivations for hedging, but also the broader picture of what strategic considerations drive the firm's value and its risk.

Key Concepts

Result 21.1: Futures hedges must be tailed to account for the interest earned on the amount of cash that is exchanged as a consequence of the futures mark-to-market feature. Such tailed hedges require holding less of the futures contract the further one is from the maturity date of the contract. The magnitude of the tail relative to an otherwise identical forward contract hedge depends on the amount of interest earned (on a dollar paid at the date of the hedge) to the maturity date of the futures contract.

Result 21.2: Long-dated obligations hedged with short-term forward agreements need to be tailed if the underlying commodity has a convenience yield. The degree of the tail depends on the convenience yield earned between the maturity date of the forward instrument used to hedge and the date of the long-term obligation. When hedging with futures, a greater degree of tailing is needed (see Result 21.1).

Result 21.3: The greater the sensitivity of the convenience yield to the commodity's spot price, the less risky the long-dated obligation is to buy or sell a commodity.

Result 21.4: The greater the sensitivity of the convenience yield to the price of the underlying commodity, the lower the hedge ratio when hedging long-dated obligations with short-term forward agreements. When hedging with futures, a further tail is needed (see Result 21.1).

Result 21.5: The greater the unhedgeable convenience yield risk, the lower is the hedge ratio for hedging a long-term obligation with a short term forward or futures contract.

Result 21.6: If a firm's exposure to a risk factor is eliminated by acquiring *b* forward contracts, then the firm also can eliminate that risk exposure, if an option's forward delta is Δ, by acquiring b/Δ options.

Result 21.7: Factor risk in cash flows is eliminated by acquiring a portfolio of financial instruments with factor betas exactly the opposite of the factor betas for the firm's cash flows.

Result 21.8: Regression coefficients represent the hedge ratios that minimize variance given no

capital expenditures constraints or constraints on the use of costless financial instruments for hedging. Given flexibility in the scale of a real investment project, a cost to the hedging financial instrument, and a capital expenditure constraint, the techniques of mean-variance analysis for finding the efficient portfolio or the global minimum variance portfolio may be more appropriate for finding a hedge ratio.

Key Terms

basis   764
basis risk   764
basket options   772
basket swaps   765
cash flow at risk (CAR)   748
cash flow hedging   744
convenience yield   756
covered option strategy   769
cross-hedging   778
delta hedging   769
exposures   744
forward delta   773

hedge ratio   744
money market hedge   752
regression method   745
rolling stack   762
simulation method   745
spot delta   773
spot market   749
swap spread   767
tailing the hedge   755
target beta   744
value at risk (VAR)   747
value hedging   744

Exercises

21.1. Consider, again, National Petroleum from Example 20.3 in Chapter 20. In addition to the forward contracts described in Example 20.3, National Petroleum also can buy (put) options that give them the right to sell the oil in one, two, or three years at an exercise price of $20 per barrel. The one-year option costs $2.00, the two-year option $3.00, and the three-year option $3.50 per barrel. What should National Petroleum do to eliminate the possibility of financial distress and still have money to fund new exploration in the event that oil prices increase?

21.2. AB Cable, Wire, and Fiber plans to open up a new factory three years from now, at which point it plans to purchase 1 million pounds of copper. Assume zero-coupon risk-free yields are going to remain at a constant 5 percent (effective annual rate) for all investment horizons, there is no basis risk in forwards or futures, storage of copper is costless, markets are frictionless, and forward spot parity holds. Copper has a 3 percent per year (effective annual rate) convenience yield earned continuously.

a. What should the relative magnitude of the futures and forward prices for copper be, assuming the contracts are of the same maturity? How should futures and forward prices change with contract maturity?

b. Assume that one-year forwards are the only hedging instruments available. How many pounds of copper in forwards should be acquired today to maximally hedge the risk of the copper purchase three years from now? How does the hedge ratio change over time? Provide intuition and describe the rollover strategy at the forward maturity date.

c. Assume that three-month futures are the only hedging instruments available. How many pounds of copper in futures can be acquired today to maximally hedge the risk of the copper purchase three years from now? How does the hedge ratio change over time? Provide intuition and describe the rollover strategy at the futures maturity date.

21.3. Assume a two-factor model for next year's profits of Exxon. The factors are one-year futures prices for oil and one-year futures prices for the

US$/DM exchange rate. The relevant factor equation is:

$$\widetilde{\text{Profit}}_{\text{XON}} = \$1 \text{ billion} + \$10 \text{ million } \tilde{F}_{\text{OIL}} + \$20 \text{ million } \tilde{F}_{\text{\$/DM}} + \tilde{\epsilon}_{\text{XON}}$$

Assume that each one-year oil futures contract purchased has the factor equation:

$$\tilde{C}_{\text{OIL}} = \$10,000 \tilde{F}_{\text{OIL}}$$

Each one-year futures contract on the US$/DM exchange rate has the factor equation:

$$\tilde{C}_{\text{\$/DM}} = \$100,000 \tilde{F}_{\text{\$/DM}}$$

If Exxon wants to reduce its exposure to the two risk factors in half, how can it accomplish this by buying or selling futures contracts?

21.4. Assume that General Motors is planning to acquire an automobile company in Japan. The deal will probably be consummated within a year provided that approval is granted by the proper regulatory authorities in Japan and the United States. The two automakers have agreed upon the terms of the deal. GM will pay ¥100 billion once the deal is consummated. Discuss the advantages and disadvantage of hedging the currency risk in this deal with forwards, options, and swaps.

21.5. Assume that Schering-Plough, a drug manufacturer, has discovered that it is cheaper to manufacture one of its drugs in France than anywhere else. All revenues from the drug will be in the United States. The company estimates that the costs of manufacturing the drug will be FFr 100 million per year and that the factory has a life of 10 years. At the end of the 10 years, a balloon payment on the mortgage from the factory is due. Net of proceeds from salvage value, the company will have to pay FFr 1 billion at the end of 10 years. How can the currency risk of this deal be eliminated with a currency swap?

21.6. Assume that Dell Computer, a worldwide manufacturer and mail-order retailer of personal computers, has estimated the following regression associated with its operations in Europe:

European profits$_t$
= $10 million
+ $8 million
× ($/ECU 1-year forward exchange rate)$_t$
+ $\tilde{\epsilon}_t$

a. How should Dell Computer minimize variance associated with these European operations, using only forward contracts on the $/ECU exchange rate? Is your answer affected by

whether the European operations are fixed or scalable in size?

b. Assuming that European profits are normally distributed, what is Dell's profit at risk at the 5 percent significance level, assuming that the percentage change in the $/ECU exchange rate has a volatility of 10 percent? Ignore $\tilde{\epsilon}$ risk for this calculation.

21.7. Your U.S. based company has an opportunity to break into the British market, but your CEO is concerned about the currency risk of such a venture. You estimate that sales in the United Kingdom will be £2 million (worst-case scenario) or £5 million (best-case scenario) over the next 10 months. The likelihood that each of these scenarios will occur is equal. Your CEO wishes to hedge the expected value of these sales, but is not sure which hedging vehicle to use.

a. You are given the following information and are assigned the task of recommending the best method of hedging (i.e., what is the highest dollar amount you can lock in today).

Current US$/£ spot rate = US$1.55/£

Current forward rate for currency exchanged 10 months from today = US$1.60/£

10-month US$ LIBOR is 6.5 percent per annum

10-month £ LIBOR is 11.7 percent per annum

b. Is there an arbitrage opportunity here? If so, how would you exploit it?

21.8. Suppose you wish to hedge your exposure to oil prices by means of forwards and futures over the next year. You have the following information: the current price of oil is $20 per barrel and the risk-free rate of interest is 10 percent per year compounded annually. Assume that the spot price of oil changes instantaneously from $20 to $21 per barrel.

a. Describe the necessary number of one-year forwards you must hold in order to perfectly hedge a long position in 1 barrel of oil. Then describe any changes in the perfectly hedged position of spot oil and forwards, including any cash that changes hands, when the spot price of oil instantaneously increases by $1.00.

b. Repeat part a for a perfectly hedged position using futures contracts.

c. Repeat parts a and b, assuming that you now want to hedge a short position of 5,000 barrels of oil.

21.9. Assume that TWA has an obligation to deliver

1.5 million barrels of oil in nine months at a fixed price of $24 per barrel. Assume a constant convenience yield of 2 percent per year and a risk-free rate of 9 percent per annum compounded annually.

a. How can TWA hedge all the risk of this obligation in the forward market, using only forwards maturing three months from now and then rolling over new 3-month forwards?

b. How can TWA hedge all the risk of this obligation, using only 3-month futures?

c. Repeat parts a and b, assuming TWA owns 1.5 million barrels of oil.

21.10. General Motors has an obligation to deliver 2 million barrels of oil in six months at a fixed price of $25 per barrel. European options exist to buy oil in six months at $28 per barrel. Assume the six-month annualized (continuously compounded) riskless rate is 5 percent. Due to recent unrest in the Middle East, however, the volatility (i.e., standard deviation) of the annualized percentage change in the price of oil has soared to an incredible 59.44 percent (annualized).

Can General Motors eliminate its exposure to oil price risk generated by the delivery agreement using options, and if so, how many options will it have to buy or sell in order to do this? (*Hint:* The Black-Scholes option pricing equation is valid here.)

21.11. Disney wants to borrow DM 24 million for three years while Metallgesellschaft wants to borrow US$20 million for three years. The spot exchange rate is currently DM1.20/$. Suppose Disney and Metallgesellschaft can borrow deutsche marks and dollars from their domestic banks at the following (annual) fixed interest rates.

	US$	DM
Disney	6.0%	9.7%
Metallgesellschaft	8.4	10.0

Design a currency swap agreement that will benefit both firms and also yield a 0.4 percent profit for the bank acting as an intermediary for the swap.

21.12. Consider a two-factor model, where the factors are interest rate movements and changes in the exchange rate. Your company has a future cash flow with factor betas of 2 on the interest rate factor and 5 on the exchange rate factor. You would like to eliminate your sensitivity to both of

these factors by means of financial securities, but do not wish to use any of the company's cash to do this.

The following investment opportunities are available to you.

- You can purchase 30-year government bonds.
- You can enter into a 2-year interest rate swap agreement.
- You can invest in a foreign index fund.

The following factor equations, with the two factors being changes in interest rates and changes in exchange rates, correspond to the future values of the three investment opportunities, respectively.

$$\tilde{C}_1 = 4 - 4\tilde{F}_{int} \qquad \text{(per \$1 million invested)}$$
$$\tilde{C}_2 = 6 - 2\tilde{F}_{int} + 6\tilde{F}_{ex} \qquad \text{(per \$1 million invested)}$$
$$\tilde{C}_3 = 3 - 3\tilde{F}_{int} - 2\tilde{F}_{ex} \qquad \text{(per \$1 million invested)}$$

Design a proper hedge against interest rate movements and exchange rates in this environment.

21.13. Ford is considering building a factory to produce its new Taurus. The factory will cost $100 million and will produce 10,000 automobiles one year from now. As an analyst at Ford, you run a regression of the historical sales price of 10,000 cars against the return of Ford's stock. You find that the regression coefficient is −$130 million, that the price of a Taurus one year from now has a standard deviation of $1,000, and that the volatility of Ford's stock is 0.5. The risk-free rate over the coming year will be 10 percent.

Your task is the following:

a. To identify the minimum variance portfolio combination of Ford stock and the factory, and to interpret the results.

b. To identify the tangency portfolio mix of factory and stock if the expected selling price of the Taurus is $22,000 and the expected return of Ford stock is 30 percent over the next year.

21.14. The National Basketball Association (NBA) has hired you as a consultant to figure out what the proper mix of Eastern and Western teams should be. An Eastern team has a return variance of .04, a Western team has a return variance of .09, and the correlation between the returns of an Eastern and a Western team is .25. Assume that all Eastern teams are identical and all Western teams are identical. What should the ratio of Eastern to Western teams be if the NBA wants to minimize return variance?

References and Additional Readings

Allen, William. "The Walt Disney Company's Yen Financing." Harvard Case 9-287-058, Harvard Business School Publishing, 1987.

Backus, David; Leora Klapper; and Chris Telmer. "Derivatives at Banc One (1994)." Working paper, New York University, New York, 1995.

Brennan, Michael, and Nicholas Crew. "Hedging Long Maturity Commodity Commitments with Short-Dated Futures Contracts." In *Mathematics of Derivative Securities,* Michael Dempster and Stanley Pliska, eds. Cambridge: Cambridge University Press, 1996.

Culp, Christopher, and Merton Miller. "Metallgesellschaft and the Economics of Synthetic Storage." *Journal of Applied Corporate Finance* 7 (1995), pp. 6–21.

Fama, Eugene, and Kenneth French. "Commodity Futures Prices: Some Evidence on Forecast Power, Premiums, and the Theory of Storage." *Journal of Business* 60, no. 1 (1987), pp. 55–74.

Gibson, Rajna, and Eduardo Schwartz. "Stochastic Convenience Yield and the Pricing of Oil Contingent Claims." *Journal of Finance* 45, no 3 (1990), pp. 959–76.

Grinblatt, Mark, and Narasimhan Jegadeesh. "The Relative Pricing of Eurodollar Futures and Forward Contracts." *Journal of Finance* 51, no. 4 (September 1996), pp. 1499–1522.

Jorion, Philippe. *Value at Risk*. Burr Ridge, IL: Richard D. Irwin, 1997.

Ledoit, Olivier, and Pedro Santa-Clara. "Estimation of Large, Time-Varying Covariance Matrices." UCLA working paper, 1997.

Linsmeier, Thomas J., and Neil D. Pearson. "Risk Measurement: An Introduction to Value at Risk." Working paper, University of Illinois, Urbana-Champaign, 1996.

Margrabe, William. "The Value of an Option to Exchange One Asset for Another." *Journal of Finance* 33, no. 1 (1978), pp. 177–86.

Mello, Antonio, and John Parsons. "Maturity Structure of a Hedge Matters." *Journal of Applied Corporate Finance* 8 (1995), pp. 106–20.

Neuberger, Anthony. "How Well Can You Hedge Long-Term Exposures with Multiple Short-Term Futures Contracts?" Working paper, London Business School, 1996.

Ross, Stephen. "Hedging Long-Run Commitments: Exercises in Incomplete Market Pricing." Working paper, Yale University, New Haven, 1996.

Smithson, Charles; Clifford Smith; and D. Sykes Wilford. *Managing Financial Risk*. Burr Ridge, IL: Richard D. Irwin, 1995.

Interest Rate Risk Management

Learning Objectives

After reading this chapter, you should be able to:

1. Describe the concept of DV01, the dollar value of a one-basis-point decrease (in original and term structure variations) and the concept of duration (in MacAuley, modified, and present value variations).

2. Understand the relation between duration and DV01, and the formulas needed to use either concept for hedging.

3. Implement immunization and contingent immunization strategies, using both duration and DV01.

4. Explain the link between immunization and hedging, and how to use this link to manage the asset base and capital structure of financial institutions.

5. Understand and compute convexity, and know how to use it properly.

In 1995, Orange County, California, declared bankruptcy. This bankruptcy can be attributed to the investments of the county treasurer, Robert Citron. In late 1994, between one-third and one-half of Citron's investments were in "inverse floaters," floating rate bonds with cash flows that decline as interest rates increase and vice versa. The inverse floaters paid 17 percent less twice the short-term interest rate, as long as this number was positive. The sensitivity of these esoteric notes to interest rate movements was about three times the sensitivity to interest rates of fixed-rate debt of comparable maturity. Moreover, Orange County leveraged these positions through repurchase agreements, making the positions three times larger in size than the cash spent on them and therefore about nine times more sensitive to interest rate movements than an unleveraged position in fixed-rate debt of comparable maturity. It did not take a very large increase in interest rates to wipe out Orange County's pool of investable funds.[1]

---

[1]We are grateful to Richard Roll for providing us with some of the details of this bankruptcy.

Chapter 21 described how to hedge many of the sources of risk that corporations face. Here we complete the work in that chapter by analyzing how to change the firm's exposure to an interest rate risk factor. Interest rate risk deserves special treatment because interest rates, in addition to their possible effect on future cash flows, generally affect the present values of cash flows owing to their role in discounting. It is this latter role that makes interest rate risk unique.

In this chapter, you will learn how interest rate risk is managed. The chapter abstracts from the influence of interest rates on future cash flows by assuming that future cash flows are certain. Hence, the risk analysis here focuses only on the role of interest rates in determining present values.

The key to this analysis is understanding the relationship between the price of a financial instrument with riskless future cash flows (i.e., a default-free bond) and its yield to maturity.[2] We introduce two important concepts that describe this relationship, *DV01* and *duration,* compare them to one another, and describe several important applications of each.

In addition to studying the use of these tools for measuring interest rate risk and designing hedges, the chapter examines **immunization**, which is the management of a portfolio of fixed income investments so that they will have a riskless value at some future date, and the concept of **convexity**, which is a measure of the curvature in the price-yield relationship. Convexity is frequently used and misused in bond portfolio analysis and management. We will try to understand the proper use of convexity as well as the pitfalls that lead to its misuse.

Obviously, bond portfolio managers and high-level financial managers in banks and other financial institutions should be familiar with the tools introduced in this chapter. However, it also is important for other individuals, such as corporate treasurers, to acquaint themselves with these tools because they constantly interact with the bond markets. For example, the debt issued by a corporation is priced by the bond market. To properly analyze the firm's debt financing costs, it is essential for corporate treasurers to understand how interest rates affect bond prices. In addition, corporate treasurers often have to fund, manage, or supervise the management of a corporate pension fund. Frequently, the assets in such funds are debt instruments. It would be difficult to meet the obligations of these pension funds without knowledge of the interest rate risk of both the obligations and the debt instruments held by the fund, as well as how to manage this risk. More generally, corporations typically target a maturity structure of their debt, measured as the debt's duration, which is tied to the interest rate sensitivity of the debt.[3] How to achieve that target is one subject of this chapter.

In much of this chapter, we assume that there is a flat term structure of interest rates. Hence, there is only one discount rate for risk-free cash flows of any maturity. Later in the chapter, we relax this simplifying assumption and discuss how to extend the analysis to deal with discount rates that vary with the maturity of the cash flow. The results obtained for hedge ratios and immunization strategies in this chapter work well in most realistic settings, despite being based on assumptions that, while virtuous for the simplicity they add, are not entirely realistic and may even be logically inconsistent.

---

[2]For expositional clarity, we will often use the generic term *bond* to refer to all debt instruments. While we recognize that there are important legal and economic distinctions between bonds, notes, bills, and bank debt such distinctions are not critical for the analysis in this chapter.

[3]Chapters 15 and 20 broadly touched on the reasons why corporations might want short-term instead of long-term debt.

22.1 The Dollar Value of a One Basis Point Decrease (DV01)

Once corporate managers have measured the interest rate risk exposure of a corporation or project, they can reduce its risk exposure by acquiring or issuing bonds, so that the value of the bond position moves in an opposite direction from the value of the corporation or project as interest rates change. To implement a strategy like this, the financial manager needs to acquire familiarity with the tools of interest rate risk management.

One of the most important tools for understanding the relation between interest rates, as measured by a bond's yield-to-maturity, and bond prices is the "dollar value of a one basis point (bp) decrease," or **DV01**,[4] which is a measure of how much a bond's price will increase in response to a one basis point decline in a bond's yield to maturity. If the yield and interest rates are the same—as they would be if there is a flat term structure of interest rates—then DV01s will be useful for estimating interest rate risk. In this case, because high DV01 bonds are more sensitive to interest rate movements than low DV01 bonds, they also are more volatile than low DV01 bonds. In a corporate setting, firms with values that have high DV01s are more exposed to interest rate risk. Hence, if a corporation measures the risk exposure of its stock as having a negative DV01 (e.g., share prices go up when interest rates rise), acquiring a bond position with a positive DV01 will reduce the interest rate exposure of the corporation's equity.

In reality, yields and interest rates differ because the term structure is not flat, making DV01 an inexact hedging tool. DV01, however, works remarkably well as a hedging tool despite this potential problem, as the introduction to this chapter noted.

Methods Used to Compute DV01 for Traded Bonds

There are various ways to compute the DV01 of a bond, outlined below.

Method 1: Price at a Yield One Basis Point below Existing Yield Less Price at Existing Yield.   The method we will generally use to compute a bond's DV01 is the negative of the change in its *full price*[5] for a one basis point *decrease* in its yield-to-maturity. One basis point is 1/100th of 1 percent, implying, for example, that a one basis point decrease in a 10 percent yield to maturity is a decrease from 10.00 percent to 9.99 percent. This is a very small decrease because DV01 is intended to approximate (in absolute magnitude) the derivative of the bond price movement with respect to the bond's *yield to maturity*. This derivative is the negative of the slope of the price-yield curve pictured in Exhibit 22.1.[6] DV01 is determined by a one basis point *decrease* in interest rates, so that the DV01 is positive for most bonds.[7]

Method 2: Use Calculus to Compute the Derivative of the Price-Yield Relationship Directly.   Some bond market participants use calculus to define the DV01 as the absolute magnitude of the slope of the price-yield curve. In this case, the DV01 of a bond with a price of P is computed as:

$$DV01 = -.0001 \frac{dP}{dr} \tag{22.1}$$

---

[4]DV01 is often referred to as the price value of a basis point (PVBP).
[5]See Chapter 2 for a description of full and flat bond prices.
[6]The derivative is negative because of the inverse relationship between price and yield.
[7]This avoids the awkwardness of always having to remember to place a minus sign in front.

EXHIBIT 22.1   Inverse Relation between Price and Yield

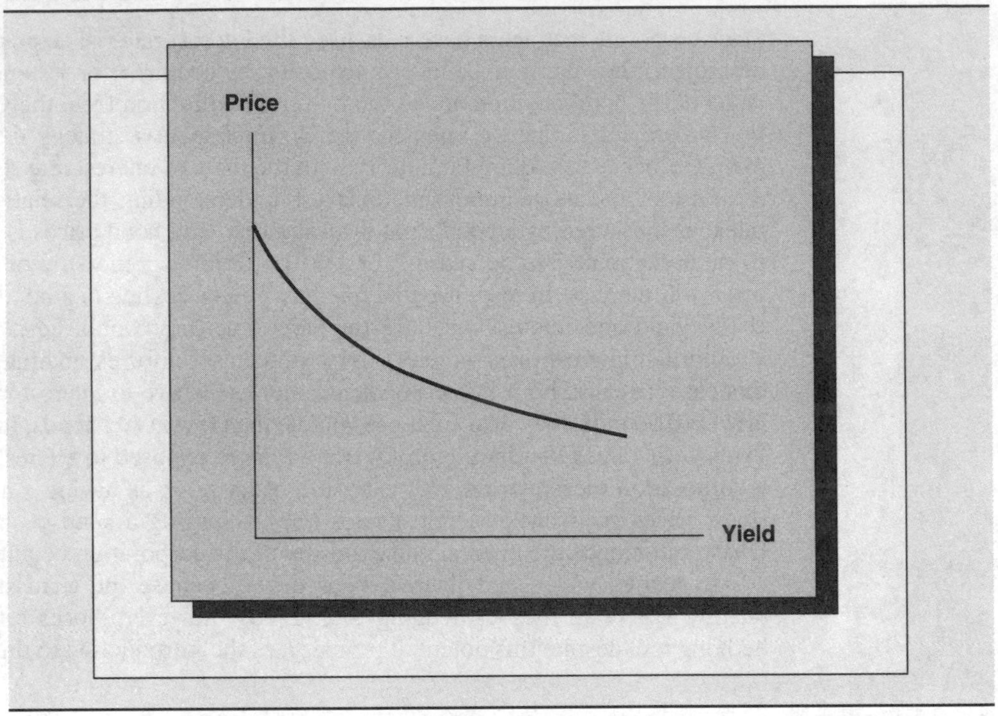

In equation (22.1), *r,* the bond yield, is given in decimal form. This gives a slightly different answer than method 1 because a one basis point decline, although small, is not infinitesimally small, as would be the case with the derivative calculation.

Method 3: Price at a Yield $\frac{1}{2}$ Basis Point below Less Price at $\frac{1}{2}$ Basis Point above Existing Yield.   To approximate the derivative calculation better than that reached with method 1, some practitioners compute DV01 by subtracting the bond's present value at $\frac{1}{2}$ basis point above the current yield to maturity from its present value at $\frac{1}{2}$ basis point below the current yield. As with method 1, this definition of DV01 requires only a calculator for its computation, thus avoiding the use of calculus.

Using a Financial Calculator to Compute DV01 with Method 1.   The differences between these versions of DV01 are negligible. We employ method 1 for most of the examples in this chapter, as in Example 22.1.

Example 22.1:   Computing DV01

Compute the DV01 per $100 face value of a 20-year straight-coupon bond trading at par (see Chapter 2 for a definition) with a semiannual coupon and an 8 percent yield to maturity.

   Answer: Using a financial calculator or computing the present value by hand, we find that at a discount rate of 7.99 percent, the 8 percent coupon bond should trade for approximately $100.10. At a discount rate of 8 percent, it trades at $100. Thus, the DV01 or difference is $0.10 per $100 of face value.

Using DV01 to Estimate Price Changes

One can use DV01 to estimate the price change of a bond or a bond portfolio for small changes in the level of interest rates, as measured by the bond's yield. To obtain the formula for this estimate, rearrange equation (22.1) as follows:

$$dP = -DV01 \times 10,000dr$$

Because $10,000 \, \Delta r$ is the yield change in number of basis points, the noncalculus equivalent of this equation is:

$$\Delta P = -DV01 \times (\Delta \text{ bp}) \tag{22.2}$$

where

ΔP = the change in the bond's price
Δ bp = the interest rate change (in basis points).

Example 22.2 demonstrates how to use this formula to estimate bond price changes.

Example 22.2:   Estimating Bond Price Changes with DV01

A bond position has a DV01 of $300. Its yield is currently 8.0 percent. Estimate the change in the value of the bond position if the yield drops to 7.9 percent.

Answer: Using equation (22.2), a drop of 10 basis points gives a price increase of:

$$\Delta P = -\$300 \times (-10) = \$3,000$$

Note from equation (22.2) that if the DV01 is zero, the change in the price for a small change in yield is zero. We will discuss how to use this insight for interest rate hedging shortly.

DV01s of Various Bond Types and Portfolios

Bonds with long maturities tend to have higher DV01s than short-maturity bonds with similar values. Zero-coupon bonds with long maturities tend to have low DV01s because their prices are low. As a percentage of the price, however, the volatilities of these bonds tend to be high.

DV01s are proportional to the size of a bond position. The DV01 of a $1,000,000 position in a bond (face value or market value) is 10 times the DV01 of a $100,000 position in that same bond. To obtain the DV01 of a bond portfolio, add up the DV01s of all the components in that portfolio.

Practitioners often scale DV01 to be DV01 per $100 of face value or per $1 million of face value. This scaling makes it easy to compare individual bonds, but it is a minor inconvenience when determining the sensitivity of a bond portfolio's total value to yield changes. To overcome this inconvenience, first convert the DV01s per $100 or DV01s per $1 million into the DV01s of the total face values of each bond in the portfolio. Then, add the DV01s of the components of the portfolio to obtain the DV01 of the portfolio itself. Keep in mind two helpful rules when computing the DV01 of a portfolio of bonds:

- To convert a DV01 per $100 face value to a DV01 per actual face value, multiply the actual face value of the portfolio's position in the bond by the DV01 per $100 face value and then divide by $100.

· To convert a DV01 per $1 million face value to a DV01 per actual face value, multiply the actual face value of the portfolio's position in the bond by the DV01 per $1 million face value and then divide by $1 million.

Example 22.3 uses the first of these two rules to compute the DV01 of a portfolio of bonds.

Example 22.3:   The DV01 of a Portfolio of Bonds

Assume that the DV01 of a 30-year U.S. Treasury bond is $0.10 per $100 face amount, the DV01 of a 10-year U.S. Treasury note is $0.06 per $100 face amount, and the DV01 of a 5-year U.S. Treasury note is $0.04 per $100 face amount. Compute the DV01 of a portfolio that has $5 million (face value) of 30-year bonds, $8 million (face value) of 5-year notes, and (a short position) −$16 million (face value) of 10-year notes.

Answer: Sum the products of the face amounts per $100 and the DV01s per $100. The result is:

$$DV01 = \frac{\$5 \text{ million}}{\$100}\left(\$.10\right) + \frac{\$8 \text{ million}}{\$100}\left(\$.04\right) - \frac{\$16 \text{ million}}{100}\left(\$.06\right)$$

$$= \$5,000 + \$3,200 - \$9,600 = -\$1,400$$

The negative DV01 means that the position's value increases when interest rates rise.

Using DV01s to Hedge Interest Rate Risk

DV01s are commonly used for interest rate hedging. This subsection discusses the hedging of interest rate risk in both investment management and corporate settings.

Hedging the Interest Rate Risk of a Bond Portfolio.   A perfectly hedged bond portfolio is a portfolio with no sensitivity to interest rate movements. Result 22.1 characterizes such a portfolio in terms of DV01.

Result 22.1   If the term structure of interest rates is flat, a bond portfolio with a DV01 of zero has no sensitivity to interest rate movements.

Example 22.4 illustrates how to construct a portfolio with a DV01 of zero.

Example 22.4:   Using DV01s to Form Perfect Hedge Portfolios

Assume that changes in the yields of various maturity bonds are identical. How much of a 7-year bond, with a computed DV01 of $0.05 per $100 of face value, should be purchased to perfectly hedge the interest rate risk of the portfolio in Example 22.3, which has a DV01 of −$1400?

Answer: The portfolio to be hedged has a DV01 of −$1400. The DV01 of the portfolio if we buy $x face amount of the 7-year bond is:

$$-\$1400 + \frac{\$0.05x}{100}$$

This equals zero when x is $2.8 million. Thus, a $2.8 million face amount of 7-year bonds hedges the portfolio against interest rate risk.

Equation (22.2) suggests that for the unhedged portfolio constructed in Example 22.3, a 10 basis point decrease in interest rates (e.g., rates decrease from 9.0 percent to 8.9 percent) would (approximately) result in a decline of $14,000 in the portfolio's value. However, after implementing the hedge in Example 22.4, the DV01 of the overall portfolio is zero, so the change in the hedged portfolio's value for a 10 bp decrease in rates is zero (approximately). In this case, the $14,000 decline in the formerly unhedged portfolio is offset by a $14,000 increase in the $2.8 million of 7-year bonds.

Dynamically Updating the Hedge.   The hedge in Example 22.4 needs to be constantly readjusted because as time elapses or bond prices change, the DV01s of bonds change. Thus, it will be necessary to sell or buy additional 7-year bonds as time elapses to maintain a DV01 of zero. In practice, to save on transaction costs, this updating usually involves waiting until a critical threshold of positive or negative DV01 for the "hedged" portfolio is reached before rehedging. The size of the threshold depends on the size of the transaction costs for rehedging and the aversion to interest rate risk.

Managing Corporate Interest Rate Risk Exposure.   Hedging corporate exposure to interest rate risk is virtually identical to hedging the interest rate risk in a bond portfolio. If we estimate a corporation's interest rate risk exposure to be a DV01 of −$1,400, then $2.8 million of the 7-year bonds would perfectly hedge the corporation against interest rate risk.

It is also possible to use the mathematics of Example 22.4 to illustrate how to target an interest rate risk exposure that differs from zero.

Example 22.5:   Using DV01s to Form Imperfect Hedges

The seven-year bond from the last example has a DV01 of $0.05 per $100 face value. Assuming that changes in the yields of bonds of various maturities are identical, how much of the 7-year bond should be bought to change the corporate risk exposure, measured currently as a DV01 of −$1,400, to a risk exposure with a DV01 of −$400?

Answer: Because portfolio DV01s are additive, if we buy x face amount of the 7-year bond, the DV01 of the "portfolio" consisting of the corporation and the 7-year bond is:

$$-\$1,400 + \frac{.05x}{100}$$

The sum of these two terms is −$400 when x equals $2 million. Thus, the $2 million face amount of 7-year bonds generates the target interest rate risk exposure.

How Compounding Frequency Affects the Stated DV01

The stated yield to maturity of a bond depends on the compounding frequency used for the yield.[8] Hence, the meaning of a 1 bp decline in yield and the size of the corresponding DV01 depend on whether annual, semiannual, or monthly compounding is used. The customary frequency for reporting DV01s and yields to maturity depends on the bond's coupon frequency. For example, DV01s for mortgages are typically based on monthly compounded 1 bp declines. DV01s for corporate bonds are reported from semiannually compounded 1 bp declines.

For hedging purposes, the compounding frequency for the 1 bp decline is irrelevant as long as the analyst consistently uses the same compounding frequency when computing DV01s for all the relevant investments. Maintaining this consistency might require

---

[8]See the appendix at the end of the text.

some DV01 conversions. The DV01 conversions between compounding frequencies are given in the following result:

Result 22.2   Let r_n and r_m denote the annualized yield-to-maturity of the bond computed with yields compounded n times a year and m times a year, respectively. The DV01 for a bond or portfolio using compounding of m times a year is $\dfrac{1 + \dfrac{r_n}{n}}{1 + \dfrac{r_m}{m}}$ times the DV01 of a bond using a compounding frequency of n times a year.[9]

---

[9]Here is a calculus proof of Result 22.2. equation (22.1) states that

$$DV01 \text{ (for } r_m) = -.0001 \frac{dP}{dr_m}$$

while

$$DV01 \text{ (for } r_n) = -.0001 \frac{dP}{dr_n}$$

where r_m and r_n are equivalent annualized rates of interest for compounding that occurs m times a year and n times a year, respectively. Dividing each side of the second equation into the corresponding sides of the first equation, we get:

$$\frac{DV01 \text{ (for } r_m)}{DV01 \text{ (for } r_n)} = \frac{dr_n}{dr_m}$$

or

$$DV01 \text{ (for } r_m) = \frac{dr_n}{dr_m} DV01 \text{ (for } r_n)$$

To prove that $\dfrac{dr_n}{dr_m} = \dfrac{1 + \dfrac{r_n}{n}}{1 + \dfrac{r_m}{m}}$, we refer the reader to Appendix A at the end of the text. There, we learn that two equivalent rates that compound m times a year and n times a year satisfy the condition that the future value of a dollar after one year must be the same, that is:

$$\left(1 + \frac{r_n}{n}\right)^n = \left(1 + \frac{r_m}{m}\right)^m$$

After taking the natural logarithm of both sides of this equation, this is:

$$n \ln\left(1 + \frac{r_n}{n}\right) = m \ln\left(1 + \frac{r_m}{m}\right)$$

Taking the derivative of both sides with respect to r_m yields:

$$\left(\frac{1}{1 + \frac{r_n}{n}}\right) \frac{dr_n}{dr_m} = \frac{1}{1 + \frac{r_m}{m}}$$

When rearranged, this says:

$$\frac{dr_n}{dr_m} = \frac{1 + \dfrac{r_n}{n}}{1 + \dfrac{r_m}{m}}$$

22.2 Duration

Duration is a concept that is closely related to DV01. The **duration** of a bond (or a bond portfolio or cash flow stream), denoted *DUR*, is a weighted average of the waiting times (measured in years) for receiving its promised future cash flows. The weight on each time is proportional to the discounted value of the cash flow to be paid at that time; that is, letting *r* denote the yield (or discount rate) for the bond, *P* denote the bond's market price, and C_t denote the cash flow at date *t*, the duration *DUR* of the bond is:

$$DUR = \frac{\left[\dfrac{C_1}{(1+r)}\right]1 + \left[\dfrac{C_2}{(1+r)^2}\right]2 + \ldots + \left[\dfrac{C_T}{(1+r)^T}\right]T}{\dfrac{C_1}{(1+r)} + \dfrac{C_2}{(1+r)^2} + \ldots + \dfrac{C_T}{(1+r)^T}} \tag{22.3}$$

$$= \sum_{t=1}^{T} \left[\frac{PV(C_t)}{P}\right]t$$

Note that the weights, $\dfrac{PV(C_t)}{P}$, always sum to 1.

We now explore some of the properties of duration.

The Duration of Zero-Coupon Bonds

The duration of a zero-coupon bond is the number of years to the maturity date of the bond. Since a zero-coupon bond has only one cash flow, paid at maturity, the weight on its maturity date is one. Hence, a 10-year zero-coupon bond has a duration of 10 years and a 6-year zero-coupon bond has a duration of 6 years. A portfolio of a group of 10-year zero-coupon bonds also would have a duration of 10 years. All cash flows occur at year 10, hence the 10-year timing of these cash flows receives a weight of one.

The Duration of Coupon Bonds

It is useful to view a bond with coupons as a portfolio of zero-coupon bonds. For example, a 10-year bond with a 5 percent coupon paid annually and a $100 face value can be thought of as a 10-year zero-coupon bond with a $105 face value—the principal plus the final coupon—plus nine other zero-coupon bonds, one for each of the first 9 years, each with a face value of $5. A flat term structure of interest rates implies that the discount rate for each of the 10 cash flows is the same, and that duration is simply the (present value) weighted average of the durations of the cash flows that make up the bond, as Example 22.6 shows.

Example 22.6:   Computing the Duration of a Straight Coupon Bond

Compute the duration of a semiannual straight-coupon bond with a 2-year maturity. The bond trades at par and has an 8 percent annualized coupon. Assume the term structure of interest rates is flat.

Answer: Since the bond trades at par and the term structure of interest rates is flat, the semiannually compounded discount rate is 8 percent. (See Result 2.2 in Chapter 2.)

- The first coupon of $4.00 paid six months from now has a present value of $3.846 at 8 percent and thus a weight equal to 3.846 ÷ bond price = .03846.

- The second coupon, one year from now, has a present value of $3.698 and a corresponding weight of .03698.
- The third coupon, 1.5 years from now, has a present value of $3.556 and a corresponding weight of .03556.
- The final cash flow, $104, has a present value of $88.900 and a weight of .889.

Hence, duration, the weighted average of the times the cash flows are paid, is computed as

.03846(.5 years) + .03698(1 year) + .03556(1.5 years) + .88900(2 years) = 1.89 years

Durations of Discount and Premium-Coupon Bonds

Exhibit 22.2 illustrates the duration of a coupon bond, a weighted average of the times at which cash flows are paid, as the fulcrum (the black triangle) on the time scale where the *discounted values* of the cash flows *balance*. As Exhibit 22.3 in comparison with Exhibit 22.2 indicates, the fulcrum in Exhibit 22.2 needs to be shifted to the left to maintain a balance if the coupons increase because such an increase would also increase their discounted values proportionately. Hence, other things being equal, premium bonds have lower durations, and discount bonds, being more like zero-coupon bonds, have higher durations.

How Duration Changes as Time Elapses

Exhibit 22.4 shows the duration of a straight coupon bond with semiannual payments as time elapses, holding the yield to maturity constant. Note that as time elapses, the bond's duration increases at coupon dates. As the coupon is paid, the weights on all the other cash flows are readjusted immediately. Between coupon dates, duration constantly decreases.

Durations of Bond Portfolios

The durations of bond portfolios are computed in the same manner as the durations of coupon bonds. If we were to hold both six-year zero-coupon bonds and eight-year zero-

EXHIBIT 22.2   Duration as a Fulcrum

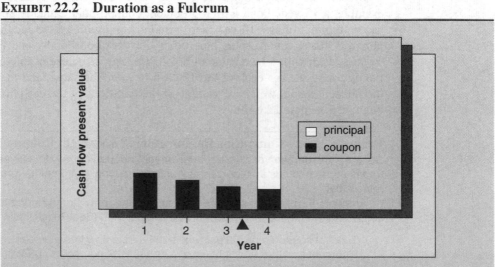

EXHIBIT 22.3   Duration as a Fulcrum (With Larger Coupons)

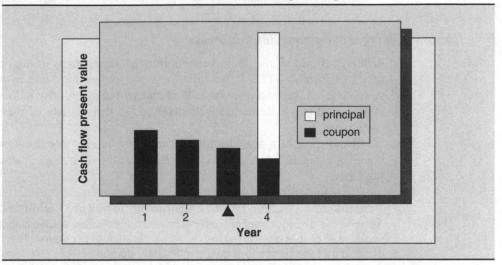

EXHIBIT 22.4   Duration as Time Elapses

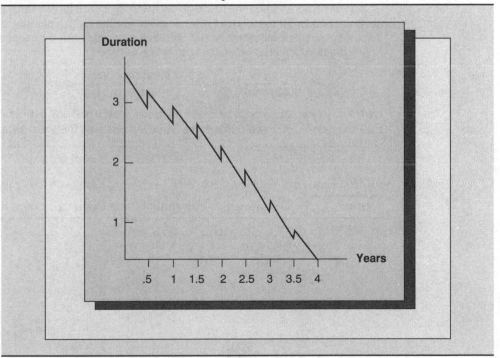

coupon bonds, the duration of the bond portfolio would lie somewhere between six and eight years. Suppose that the discounted value of the six-year and eight-year zero-coupon bonds is $10 million each. Then, since year 6 would have the same weight as year 8 and the weights add to 1, each weight would be .5 and the duration of the $20 million portfolio of the two bonds would be 7 years [= .5(6 years) + .5(8 years)]. This result can be generalized to any portfolio of bonds as indicated below.

Result 22.3   Assuming that the term structure of interest rates is flat, the duration of a portfolio of bonds is the portfolio-weighted average of the durations of the respective bonds in the portfolio.

How Duration Changes as Interest Rates Increase

Result 22.3 implies that an increase in the yield to maturity of the bond decreases duration (see Exhibit 22.5). If we think of a coupon-paying bond as a portfolio of zero-coupon bonds, then an increase in the bond's yield to maturity reduces the weight of the later cash flow payments proportionately more than it reduces the weight of the early cash flows.

Result 22.3 also provides insights into how to alter the duration of a corporation's debt. Example 22.7 demonstrates how this is achieved in a hypothetical situation involving Disney.

Example 22.7:   Changing the Duration of Corporate Liabilities

Assume that Disney's debt obligations have a market value of $2 billion and a duration of five years. Half of this is a 10-year note with a duration of six years. The Disney treasurer has decided that the company should target a debt duration of four years instead of five. Assume that it is possible to issue 4-year par straight-coupon notes, which have a duration of three years. If the proceeds from issuing these notes are used to retire 10-year notes, there will be a reduction in the duration of Disney's liabilities. Assuming a flat yield curve, how many dollars of 4-year notes should Disney issue?

Answer: Disney's existing liabilities consist of $1 billion in 10-year notes with a duration of six years and, by Result 22.3, $1 billion in other liabilities with a duration of four years. If Disney issues $x in notes with three years' duration, and uses the proceeds to retire the 10-year notes, the duration of its new liability structure will be:

$$DUR = \left[\frac{x}{\$2 \text{ billion}}\right] 3 \text{ years} + \left[\frac{\$1 \text{ billion} - x}{\$2 \text{ billion}}\right] 6 \text{ years} + \left[\frac{\$1 \text{ billion}}{\$2 \text{ billion}}\right] 4 \text{ years}$$

$DUR = 4$ years when $x = \$\frac{2}{3}$ billion. Thus, issuing $666,666,667 in three-year notes and using the proceeds to retire two-thirds of the 10-year notes puts Disney at its target liability duration.

EXHIBIT 22.5   Duration as a Fulcrum (With a Higher Discount Rate)

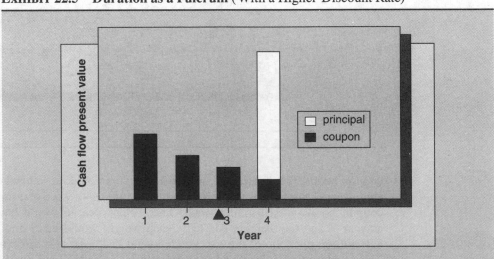

22.3 Linking Duration to DV01

This section develops formulas that link duration to DV01. First, it shows that the duration of a bond is related to the interest rate risk of the bond.

Duration as a Derivative

Duration is a useful tool for managing the interest rate risk of bond portfolios. This suggests that duration is related to the derivative of a bond's price with respect to interest rates. Such a derivative also will enable us to relate duration to DV01. To illustrate the relationship between duration and DV01, consider a 2-year zero-coupon bond with a face value of $100 and a continuously compounded yield to maturity of r. The bond's price is $P = \$100e^{-2r}$ and its duration is two years. Using calculus, the percentage change in the bond's price dP/P for a change in the continuously compounded yield-to-maturity is:

$$\frac{dP/P}{dr} = \frac{dP}{dr}\frac{1}{P} = \$100(-2e^{-2r})\frac{1}{\$100e^{-2r}} = -2 \tag{22.4}$$

Thus, -2, the negative of the bond's duration, is the percentage sensitivity of the bond's price to changes in the bond's continuously compounded yield.

This derivative property can be generalized. When the term structure of interest rates is flat, duration always can be viewed as minus the percentage change in the value of the bond (or portfolio) with respect to changes in its continuously compounded yield to maturity. For example a bond maturing in T years, with cash flows of C_t at date t, $t = 1, \ldots, T$, has a price of:

$$P = \sum_{t=1}^{T} C_t e^{-rt} \tag{22.5}$$

if r is the bond's continuously compounded yield to maturity.

The percentage change in P with respect to the continuously compounded yield is:

$$\frac{dP/P}{dr} = -\frac{1}{P}\left(\sum_{t=1}^{T} tC_t e^{-rt}\right) = -DUR \tag{22.6}$$

This is the negative of duration because the weight assigned to each relevant date (the t's) is the discounted value of the cash flow at that time divided by the discounted value of the entire bond P.

To alter equation (22.6) for different compounding frequencies, note the following formulas:

- If annually compounded yields had been used in place of continuously compounded yields for this analysis, the derivative corresponding to equation (22.6) would be:

$$\frac{dP/P}{dr} = -\frac{1}{1+r}\left[\frac{1}{P}\left(\sum_{t=1}^{T} + \frac{C_t}{(1+r)^t}\right)\right] = -\frac{DUR}{1+r}$$

  indicating that duration is the negative of $(1 + r)$ times the percentage price change for a small change in the yield.

- For semiannually compounded yields, the derivative corresponding to equation (22.6) would be:

$$\frac{dP/P}{dr} = -\frac{1}{1+r/2}\left[\frac{1}{P}\left(\sum_{t=1}^{2T} \frac{t}{2}\frac{C_t}{(1+r/2)^t}\right)\right] = -\frac{DUR}{1+r/2}$$

indicating that duration is the negative of $(1 + r/2)$ times the percentage price change for a small change in the yield.

- For monthly compounded yields, the derivative corresponding to equation (22.6) would be:

$$\frac{dP/P}{dr} = -\frac{1}{1 + r/12}\left[\frac{1}{P}\left(\sum_{t=1}^{12T}\frac{t}{12}\frac{C_t}{(1 + r/12)^t}\right)\right] = -\frac{DUR}{1 + r/12}$$

indicating that duration is the negative of $(1 + r/12)$ times the percentage price change for a small change in the yield.

- As the compounding frequency m becomes infinite, the multiplying factor, $-(1 + r/m)$, converges to -1, which leads to the formula in equation (22.6).

Formulas Relating Duration to DV01

The relation between duration and DV01 is straightforward if the "01" in DV01 is defined as a continuously compounded rate. In this case, DV01 is the product of $-.0001$ and the derivative of the value of the bond with respect to a shift in the bond's continuously compounded yield, that is:

$$DV01 = -.0001\,\frac{dP}{dr}$$

Equation (22.6) implies that duration is the derivative of the percentage change in the value of the bond with respect to the (continuously compounded) yield to maturity, that is:

$$DUR = -\frac{1}{P}\frac{dP}{dr}$$

Solving either of the last two equations for dP/dr and substituting its equivalent value into the other equation gives an equation that relates DV01 to duration:

$$DV01 = DUR \times P \times .0001 \tag{22.7a}$$

Equation (22.7a) suggests the following result:

Result 22.4   Because DV01 can be translated into duration and vice versa, DV01 and duration are equivalent as tools both for measuring interest rate risk and for hedging.

Modified Duration.   If DV01 is based on rates that are compounded m times a year instead of continuously, then the formula relating DV01 to duration is modified as follows:

$$DV01 = \left[\frac{DUR}{1 + \dfrac{r}{m}}\right] \times P \times .0001 \tag{22.7b}$$

The term in brackets is known as **modified duration**.

Effective Duration for Assets and Liabilities with Risky Cash Flow Streams.   Duration is more complicated to implement in a corporate setting without first linking duration to DV01. Because most corporate cash flows are risky, weighting the maturities of uncertain cash flows to come up with a measure of the future timing of cash flows makes little sense. On the other hand, duration, like DV01, is a measure of the interest rate sensitivity of a cash flow, which can alternatively be obtained from a factor model.

Thus, one can compute an **effective duration** of a corporate asset or liability with risk (generated both by the uncertain cash flow stream and by changes in the discount rate(s) for the cash flows in the stream) by first estimating its DV01 as an interest rate sensitivity in a factor model and then inverting equation (22.7) to obtain *DUR*. This effective duration tells us that the corporate asset or liability is of the same sensitivity to interest rate risk per dollar invested as a riskless zero-coupon bond of maturity *DUR*.

Hedging with DV01s or Durations

The last section provided formulas that link DV01 directly to duration. Hence, both duration and DV01 are equally good tools for hedging bond portfolios. Recall that a perfect hedge makes the new portfolio, including the hedge investment, have a DV01 of zero. In order to obtain a DV01 of zero, the ratio of the duration of the unhedged bond portfolio (DUR_B) to the duration of its hedge portfolio (DUR_H) must be inversely proportional to the ratio of the respective market values of the bonds,[10] that is:

$$\frac{DUR_H}{DUR_B} = \frac{P_B}{P_H}$$

When duration is based on noncontinuously compounded yields, this relation is still valid because the durations are both multiplied by the same constant. Of course, our caveat that perfect hedging with DV01s occurs only when the term structure of interest rates is flat applies here as well.

Example 22.8:   Using Duration to Form a Riskless Hedge Position

Giuliana holds $1,000,000 (face value) of 10-year zero-coupon bonds with a yield to maturity of 8 percent compounded semiannually. How can she perfectly hedge this position with a short position in 5-year zero-coupon bonds with a yield to maturity of 8 percent (compounded semiannually)?

Answer: The ratio of the durations of the two bonds is 10/5 = 2. The ratio of their market values should therefore be 1/2. The market value of the 10-year bonds is:

$$\frac{\$1,000,000}{1.04^{20}} = \$456,386.95$$

The market value of the 5-year bonds is:

$$\frac{x}{1.04^{10}}$$

For the market value of the 10-year bond position to be half the value of the 5-year position, *x* must solve:

$$\$456,386.95 = \frac{1}{2}\frac{x}{1.04^{10}}$$

or

$$x = \$1,351,128.34$$

Hence selling short $1,351,128.34 (face value) of the 5-year bonds hedges the 10-year bond position.

---

[10]From equation (22.7a), DV01 is zero when:

$$(DUR_B \times P_B \times .0001) - (DUR_H \times P_H \times .0001) = 0$$

This equation, when rearranged, proves the result.

It is easy to compute what would have happened if the position in the 10-year zero-coupon bonds was left unhedged in the last example. When rearranged, equation (22.6) says:

$$\frac{dP}{P} = -DUR \times dr$$

suggesting that a 10 basis point increase in interest rates (e.g., from 9 percent to 9.1 percent) would decrease the value of the bond portfolio by

$$.001 \times DUR = .001 \times 10 = .01, \text{ or } 1\%$$

Hence, the $1 million bond investment would decline by 1 percent of $1 million, or $10,000, if left unhedged. Under this same interest rate change scenario, the $1.35 million (face value) of five-year zero-coupon bonds also would decline in value by $10,000. Hence, Giuliana constructs a portfolio that has no interest rate sensitivity by selling short $1.35 million of the five-year bonds.

Duration targeting is often used to perfectly hedge pension fund liabilities. A pension that funds its liability for retirement obligations with default-free bonds would want the bonds to have the same interest rate sensitivity as the liabilities. An overfunded pension fund guarantees that there will be no shortage of funding for the pension fund liabilities as a result of interest rate changes. Example 22.9 indicates how to target duration to hedge pension fund assets.

Example 22.9:   Changing the Duration of Pension Fund Assets

As the new manager of the pension fund of the University of California Retirement System, assume that you have analyzed the defined benefits of the plan and computed that the fund's liabilities amount to an $8 billion market value obligation with a duration of 12 years. Unfortunately, while the fund has $9 billion in assets, their duration, largely composed of bonds, is only eight years. This means that a steep decline in interest rates may increase the present value of the obligations by $1 billion more than such a decline increases the value of the fund's assets. While keeping a $1 billion surplus in the pension fund, how can a self-financing investment in 5-year Treasury notes, with a duration of 4 years, and 30-year Treasury bonds, with a duration of 10 years, eliminate this problem?

Answer: If x denotes the amount invested in 30-year bonds and an equivalent dollar amount of 5-year bonds are sold short, the duration of the pension fund assets becomes:

$$DUR = 8 \text{ years} + \left[\frac{x}{\$9 \text{ billion}}\right] 10 \text{ years} - \left[\frac{x}{\$9 \text{ billion}}\right] 4 \text{ years}$$

The ratio of the market values of the assets to the liabilities is 9/8. Hence, the duration of the assets should be 10⅔ years, or 8/9 the 12-year duration of the liabilitles to perfectly hedge interest risk. Solving for x above with DUR = 10⅔ years implies x = $4 billion. Thus, buying $4 billion in 30-year bonds and selling short $4 billion in 5-year bonds will result in the interest rate sensitivity of the pension fund assets matching that of the liabilities.

Example 22.9 points out how to eliminate interest rate sensitivity by matching assets and liabilities in a particular way. The next section examines how to carry this idea forward through time in order to fix an amount available for payment at some horizon date.

22.4 Immunization

Immunization is a technique for locking in the value of a portfolio at the end of a planning horizon. In a sense, immunization turns a portfolio into a zero-coupon bond.

Ordinary Immunization

Immunization was developed by F. M. Redington, an actuary, who showed that if the durations and market values of the assets and liabilities of a financial institution were equal, the equity of the institution would be insensitive to movements in interest rates.[11] We generalize this result here, allowing the ratios of the durations of the assets and liabilities to be inversely proportional to their market value ratios.

Applying Immunization Techniques to Stabilize the Future Value of a Bond Portfolio.   Immunization techniques can be applied to reduce the interest rate sensitivity of the equity of financial institutions or the equity stake of a corporation in a defined benefit pension plan.[12] Today, however, immunization techniques are more often used to stabilize the value of a bond portfolio at the horizon date, which is the date at the end of some planning horizon.

For simplicity, assume that the term structure of interest rates is flat. In this case, the fundamental rule for immunizing a portfolio is to match the duration of the portfolio with the horizon date. For example, a manager with a horizon date of January 1, 2005, should, on January 1, 1999, have a portfolio duration of 6 years; on January 1, 2000, the portfolio duration should be 5 years; on June 30, 2003, it should be 1.5 years.

To implement the immunization strategy, it is important that all coupons, principal payments, and other cash distributions received be reinvested in the portfolio. Maintaining a duration that is matched to the horizon date means that the rate at which these cash distributions are reinvested exactly offsets the gain or loss in the value of the portfolio as interest rates change.

Why Immunization Locks in a Value at the Horizon Date.   To see why this strategy locks in the portfolio value at the horizon date, compare the portfolio with a zero-coupon bond of identical market value which has a maturity, and hence a duration, equal to the duration of the immunized portfolio. A long position in the portfolio and a short position in the zero-coupon bond has both a market value and a duration of zero.

When the duration of the combined long and short position is zero, its sensitivity to interest rate movements and hence its volatility is zero. For a brief instant, it is riskless. As time elapses, keeping it riskless requires adjusting the long position in the portfolio to have the same duration as the maturity of the zero-coupon bond by shortening the duration of the long position over time in order to maintain a duration of zero for the combination of the immunized portfolio (the long position) and the short position in the zero-coupon bond.

Since riskless self-financing investments do not appreciate or depreciate in value, the riskless self-financing combination of the immunized bond portfolio and the short position in the zero-coupon bond—if the former is properly updated over time—will have a value of zero at the maturity date of the zero-coupon bond. At the maturity date, this means that the immunized portfolio has to have a market value equal to the face value (and market value) of the zero-coupon bond.

Result 22.5 summarizes this procedure.

Result 22.5   If the term structure of interest rates is flat, immunization "guarantees" a fixed value for an immunized portfolio at a horizon date. The value obtained is the same as the face value of a zero-coupon bond with (1) the same market value as the original portfolio and (2) a maturity date equal to the horizon date selected as the target date to which the duration of the immunized portfolio is fixed.

---

[11]See Redington (1952).
[12]See Example 22.9.

Viewing the portfolio to be immunized as an asset, and the zero-coupon bond as a liability, we have done exactly what Redington suggested for financial institutions—matching the durations of assets and liabilities with the same market value. Of course, the zero-coupon bond was not actually sold short in order to immunize the portfolio. Rather, we merely pretended to sell short a zero-coupon bond to help clarify what to do to the portfolio to ensure a value at the horizon date.

Example 22.10 shows how to calculate the lock-in value at the horizon date.

Example 22.10:   Computing the Lock-In Amount at Some Horizon Date

The current yield to maturity is 8 percent compounded semiannually for bonds of all maturities. A bond portfolio consists of $10 million (market value) of fixed-income securities. What amount will the portfolio manager be able to lock in three years from now?

Answer: The current market value of the portfolio is $10 million. At 8 percent, the future value of the portfolio in three years is:

$$1.04^6 \times \$10 \text{ million} = \$12.653 \text{ million}$$

Example 22.11 shows how to alter a portfolio to lock in its value.

Example 22.11:   Using Immunization Techniques to Lock In a Payoff

The $10 million portfolio in Example 22.10 is a pension portfolio, which currently has a duration of five years. Half of the portfolio's market value consists of identical maturity zero coupon bonds. The remainder consists of $5 million (market value) of the 2-year straight coupon bonds from Example 22.6. These bonds have a duration of 1.89 years and an 8 percent yield, compounded semiannually.

a. What is the maturity of the zero-coupon bonds in the portfolio?

b. How should the manager rebalance the portfolio between the 2-year straight-coupon bonds and the zero-coupon bonds to immunize it at a 3-year horizon date?

Answer: *a.* The zero-coupon bonds have to have a maturity of 8.11 years because this is the only maturity that makes an equal-weighted average of the 2-year bonds' duration (1.89) and the zero-coupon bonds' duration equal five years.

b. To immunize the portfolio for a horizon of three years, the duration of the portfolio has to be changed to three years. Find weights x and $1 - x$ that make the weighted average of the durations:

$$x(1.89) + (1 - x)8.11 = 3$$

The approximate solution is $x = .82154$. Hence, $8.2154 million of the 2-year straight coupon bonds must be owned, which requires an additional purchase of $3.2154 million (face and market value) of these bonds. To finance the purchase, sell $3.2154 million (market value) of the zero-coupon bonds, which have an aggregate face value of about:

$$\$6.07 \text{ million} = \$3.2154 \text{ million } (1.04)^{16.22}$$

Example 22.11 described what the portfolio manager must do currently to immunize his portfolio for a horizon of three years. However, this manager cannot rest on his laurels. Every day, as time elapses and interest rates change, the immunized portfolio becomes nonimmunized if the manager acts passively. To maintain the immunization, as Example 22.12 illustrates, it is important to constantly update the weighting of the zero-coupon bonds and the 2-year straight-coupon bonds.

Example 22.12: Updating Portfolio Weights in an Immunized Portfolio

What must the portfolio manager do in the future to immunize the portfolio, particularly at the maturity date of the two-year straight-coupon bonds?

Answer: As each day elapses, the portfolio manager must shorten the duration by one day. Some of this shortening will happen even if the manager does nothing, since the duration of both bond types is diminishing as time elapses. However, it is unlikely that this natural shortening of duration will be exactly one day. Hence, the manager must recompute duration periodically for the new interest rate and the time to payment of the cash flows and adjust duration accordingly. This creates a problem after two years has elapsed. At that point, the manager would like the portfolio to have a one-year duration, but would have only zero-coupon bonds maturing in 6.11 years (and a duration of 6.11 years) once the straight-coupon bonds mature. This implies that the manager must begin to use a third security in the portfolio as the maturity date of the straight-coupon bonds nears.

The immunization strategy employed in Examples 22.10–22.12 was equivalent to designing a hypothetical portfolio with a duration of zero. This portfolio consists of the 2-year straight-coupon bonds, 8.11-year zero coupon bonds, and a short position in 3-year zero-coupon bonds that finances the other two positions. If this hypothetical portfolio is managed so that it has a value of zero at the horizon date, the original immunized portfolio is managed so that it has a value equal to that of 3-year zero-coupon bonds with an aggregate face value of $12.653 million.

The same insight can be used to understand Redington's result as it applies to financial institutions. If the assets and liabilities of the financial institution have unequal value, construct fictitious zero-coupon bonds with a market value equal to the market value of the institution's equity (assets minus liabilities) and a maturity equal to the horizon date at which the equity's value needs to be guaranteed. To immunize the equity in this fashion over time, manage a self-financing investment that is long the assets, short the liabilities, and short the zero-coupon bonds, so that it maintains zero duration. This is equivalent to structuring the assets and liabilities of the institution so that they have a duration equal to the maturity of the zero-coupon bonds,[13] as Example 22.13 illustrates for a savings bank.

Example 22.13: Using Immunization to Manage Savings Bank Assets

The assets of a savings bank consist of mortgages with a 4-year duration and a present value of $10 billion. The bank's liabilities consist of customer deposits and CDs with a duration of two years and a present value of $5 billion. Interest rates are 8 percent, compounded annually at all maturities. Assume that the bank's management wants to ensure that the bank has a fixed amount of equity capital at the time the bank's next regulatory examination is scheduled, in two years.

  a. How much equity value can it guarantee at the time of the next regulatory examination?

  b. Given that the savings bank can invest in commercial paper (which can be regarded as a short-term zero-coupon bond with a 3-month maturity) and sell some or all of its mortgage assets, what should the bank do to lock in an equity value two years from now?

Answer: *a.* The current $5 billion in equity can have a "lock-in" value in two years of

$$\$5.832 \text{ billion} \ [= (1.08)^2 \$5 \text{ billion}]$$

---

[13]The self-financing investment will continue to have a value of zero if the immunization procedure is followed, implying that the assets less the liabilities (which equals the equity) will have a value equal to the value of the fictitious zero-coupon bond.

b. To lock in this value, adjust the duration of the equity to two years, and then continually shorten the duration by one day as each day elapses. The current duration of the equity is a weighted average of the durations of the assets and liabilities. Since the assets are twice as large as the liabilities, the asset weight must be 2 and the liability weight must be -1 for the weights to sum to 1. This makes the current equity duration $2 \times (4 \text{ years}) - 1 \times (2 \text{ years}) = 6$ years. To shorten this to two years by changing the asset portfolio, the bank should sell some of the mortgage assets and buy commercial paper. This requires shortening the asset duration to a duration (*DUR*) that satisfies:

$$2 \times DUR - 1(2 \text{ years}) = 2 \text{ years}$$

Thus, *DUR* = 2 years. The market value of mortgage assets *x* and commercial paper assets *y* that have a duration of two years satisfy:

$$\frac{4 + .25y}{x + y} = 2$$

The market values of the mortgage position *x* and of the commercial paper position *y* must sum to \$10 billion, the current value of the bank's assets. Thus, *x* and *y* must also solve:

$$x + y = \$10 \text{ billion}$$

Substituting this into the previous equation yields:

$$\frac{4x + .25(\$10 \text{ billion} - x)}{\$10 \text{ billion}} = 2$$

This is solved by *x* = \$4.67 billion, implying *y* = \$5.33 billion. That is, sell \$5.33 billion of the \$10 billion in mortgage assets and use the proceeds to buy 3-month commercial paper.

Immunization Using DV01

DV01-based techniques are just as appropriate as duration-based techniques for achieving immunization. If the duration of the portfolio matches the duration of an equally valued zero-coupon bond with (1) a maturity equal to the horizon date and (2) a price equal to that of the portfolio, then the DV01 of a long position in the portfolio and a short position in the bond is zero. Maintaining a DV01 of zero for this combined position also guarantees a fixed value portfolio at the horizon date.[14]

Practical Issues to Consider

Although immunization techniques are widely used in bond portfolio and asset-liability management, they cannot perfectly guarantee a value at the horizon date. First, transaction costs make it prohibitively expensive to continually rebalance the portfolio (or the assets and liabilities) to maintain the proper duration, which is constantly declining. For this reason, the necessary rebalancing is done only when the duration match is off by a critical amount. Second, immunization techniques assume that the term structure of interest rates is flat. This is rare even in an approximate sense and, when observed, tends to quickly evolve into upward or (less frequently) downward sloping or oddly shaped yield curves. In spite of these impediments, immunization seems to work well in most instances as a risk-reduction tool. As a consequence, it is popular despite its imperfection.

---

[14]We can easily extend this analysis to asset-liability management.

Contingent Immunization

Contingent immunization is the bond portfolio equivalent of portfolio insurance (which, as illustrated in Chapter 8, is generally used to insure equity portfolios. **Contingent immunization** sets a target value for the bond portfolio at the horizon date that is smaller than the face value of a zero-coupon bond with the same market value as the portfolio. This target value is regarded as a floor below which the future value of the bond portfolio should not fall. The bond portfolio is managed actively without regard for duration until its value falls to a critical level. From that point on, an immunization strategy is followed. In this sense, immunization is contingent on a decline in the bond portfolio to a pre-specified critical point.

We can regard the critical level in contingent immunization as the market value of a zero-coupon bond maturing on the horizon date with a face value equal to the floor value. Hence, this critical value tends to rise over time, although it may fall when interest rates increase.

Immunization and Large Changes in Interest Rates

A $10,000 6-year 8 percent straight-coupon bond with annual coupons trading at par has a duration of approximately five years. If the term structure of interest rates is flat, and the interest rate increases slightly, the reinvested coupons will have an increased value at year 5 that exactly counterbalances the decreased value of the bond in year 5 (i.e., the year 5 value of its cash flows after year 5). The same is true when there is a small decline in interest rates.

It is important, however, to determine how well immunization strategies perform when there are substantial interest rate changes. Interest rates can sometimes jump by large amounts when important economic indicators are announced (e.g., the monthly employment report by the U.S. Department of Labor). Moreover, even a series of small changes in interest rates can amount to a large effective change in interest rates if transaction costs lead investors to undertake a *lax immunization strategy*—failing to maintain the proper duration for the bond at all points in time.

One can be comforted that immunization strategies work "pretty well" for the 8 percent straight-coupon bond described above and even for large interest rate changes such as 25 basis points in one day. A 25 bp decline in interest rates, from 8 percent to 7.75 percent, makes the sum of the year 5 value of the bond and its reinvested coupons equal $14,693.14; in the absence of an interest rate shift, the bond's value is $14,693.28. This is a remarkably insignificant difference! Since a 25 bp shift in the yield of a six-year bond would rarely occur over a single day, we can be fairly confident in stating that immunization in this case would not require exceptionally frequent rebalancing of the portfolio.

The next section discusses how to better quantify this degree of confidence.

22.5 Convexity

Convexity measures how much DV01 changes as the yield of a bond or bond portfolio changes. A portfolio with a DV01 of zero will be insensitive to small interest rate movements and less sensitive to large interest rate movements the smaller the convexity. In other words, the DV01 remains close to zero as interest rates change if convexity is close to zero.

Defining and Interpreting Convexity

Convexity is a measure that determines how secure an investor should feel about a "perfectly hedged" portfolio (e.g., whether a bond pricing screen requires constant monitoring or whether the investor can relax and do other things). If the convexity of a hedged portfolio is zero, even fairly large changes in interest rates over a short time span should not alter the value of the portfolio drastically. If the convexity is large, monitoring the bond pricing screen might be a good idea.

Positive Convexity Is More Typical.   Most bonds have positive convexity, which expresses the type of curvature seen earlier in the price-yield curve (Exhibit 22.1). Exhibit 22.6 portrays price-yield curves for two bonds: one with a large amount of convexity and one with little convexity. In contrast to this picture, bond portfolios, with long and short positions in different bonds, can have positive or "negative convexity."[15]

The Convexity Formula.   At a single point on the price-yield curve for a bond or bond portfolio, the curvature, measured by convexity, is formally defined as follows: The convexity "$CONV(r)$" of a bond or a bond portfolio at a yield to maturity of r is the product of (1) $1,000,000 divided by the bond price and (2) the difference between the current DV01 (of the entire bond position) and the DV01 (of the entire bond position) at a yield of $r + .0001$, that is:

$$CONV(r) = \left(\frac{\$1 \text{ million}}{P}\right)\left[DV01(r) - DV01(r + .0001)\right]$$

DV01 can be viewed as a derivative of the bond price with respect to its yield to maturity. It differs from the derivative primarily in that DV01 multiplies the derivative by a constant. Convexity, *CONV,* is like the second derivative of the portfolio's price with respect to its yield in percent (not its basis point shift). To obtain convexity, multiply the DV01 *difference* by 10,000 (the square of 100) to undo the DV01 convention of multiplying the derivative with respect to the percentage yield by .01 (100 bps is 1 percentage point of interest). In addition, convexity is typically scaled per $100 of market value. Hence, after multiplying the difference between the DV01s at the two yields by 10,000, it is customary to multiply by $100 and divide by the bond price per $100 of face value. Example 22.14 illustrates the calculation.

Example 22.14:   Computing Convexity

Compute the convexity of the 8 percent 2-year par straight-coupon bond analyzed in Example 22.6.

   Answer: The DV01 of this bond is .0181516 per $100 face value at an 8.00 percent yield, since its price at 7.99 percent is $100.0181516. At an 8.01 percent yield, the DV01 is .0181473, the difference between the $100 price at 8.00 percent and the price at 8.01 percent, which is $99.9818527. The difference between the two DV01s is 4.3×10^{-6}. The convexity is .043, which is 1 million divided by 100 times this number.

Implications of Convexity for Immunization Strategies.   The last section indicated that immunizing a portfolio for a T-year horizon requires managing the portfolio, so that when it is combined with a hypothetical short position in a zero-coupon bond of T years

---

[15]Despite its applications in science and mathematics, the word *concavity,* which is probably a better term than *negative convexity,* has yet to find a place in the vocabulary of the bond markets.

Exhibit 22.6   Convexity

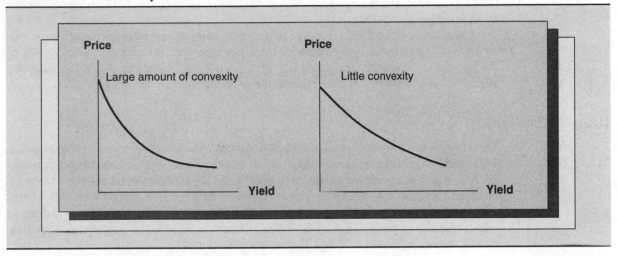

maturity, the duration and value of the combined portfolio is zero. If the convexity of the *actual* portfolio is close to the convexity of the hypothetical *T*-year zero-coupon bond, the investor who is immunizing the portfolio does not have to constantly monitor the bond pricing screen. However, frequent rebalancing is needed to maintain the immunized position of the actual portfolio if its convexity differs substantially from that of the hypothetical portfolio. In the latter case, constant bond price monitoring is required.

Estimating Price Sensitivity to Yield

Investors often use convexity to improve upon the earlier (DV01 or duration-based) estimate of the change in the price of a bond portfolio for a given change in yield. Specifically, letting Δr denote the change in the yield to maturity (in percent form) and P the starting price of the bond or bond portfolio, we can write[16]:

$$\Delta P = -100 DV01 \, \Delta r + .5 \frac{P}{100} CONV(\Delta r)^2 \qquad (22.8)$$

Example 22.15 illustrates how to apply the formula.

Example 22.15:   Using Convexity for Accurate Estimates of Price Change
Compute the change in the price of a bond portfolio with a $200 market value for a 25 basis point increase in yield. At the current yield to maturity, the bond has a DV01 of $0.15 and a convexity of 1.2 (convexity is computed per $100 of market value).

   Answer: Using equation (22.8), the change in price is:

$$-100(\$.15)(.25) + .5 \frac{\$200}{100}(1.2)(.25^2) = -\$3.675$$

Hence, the new price will be $196.325.

---

[16]This equation is derived from the second order Taylor series expansion. See any elementary calculus text for details.

One would estimate the change in price in Example 22.15 as −$3.75 using only DV01 to estimate the change. Using equation (22.8) thus improves the estimate of interest rate sensitivity by $.075.

Convexity (unlike DV01, but like duration) is independent of the scale of the investment. Holding twice as many bonds of the same type does not change the convexity of the portfolio. Moreover, the convexity of a portfolio of bonds is the value-weighted average of the convexity of each bond in the portfolio.

Misuse of Convexity

Throughout this chapter, we have assumed that the term structure of interest rates is flat. This is the traditional approach taken in all but the most sophisticated bond portfolio analysis and it is a good way to begin to understand the issues in bond portfolio management and interest rate hedging. However, we must express caution: Not only is this assumption generally an incorrect portrait of realistic term structures, but it is fraught with a number of pitfalls that are based on inherent flaws in logic. A misguided application of convexity, discussed next, illuminates this point.

Convexity Appears to Be Good.   Equation (22.8) implies that the higher the convexity of a bond portfolio (holding market value and DV01 constant), the larger the value of the portfolio for both an increase and a decline in its yield to maturity. This seems to imply that convexity is a good thing to have in a portfolio and that, other things being equal, investments with a large amount of convexity are in some sense better than investments with little convexity or negative convexity. Exhibit 22.7 illustrates this point by plotting

EXHIBIT 22.7   The Effects of Convexity for Similar Bonds

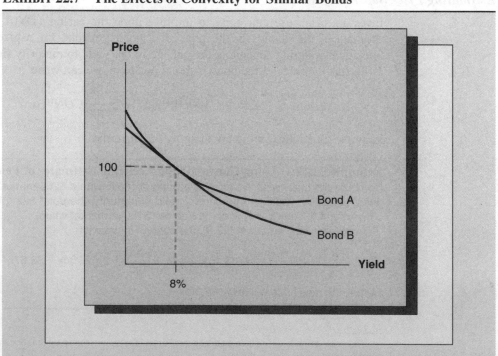

the price-yield curve for two riskless bonds, each with the same market value and DV01 at a yield of 8 percent. Note that as yields change, irrespective of the direction of change, the price of bond A will be higher than that of bond B. Bond A thus appears to be the better bond because it has more convexity.

The flaw in this analysis is that the yields to maturity of the two bonds need not be the same. Unless the term structure of interest rates is flat, nothing suggests that the two bonds should have the same yields at the same time or that when one bond's yield moves up, the other's yield should move up by the same amount. Comparing yields between two bonds is a comparison of apples and oranges.

Arbitrage Exists When the Term Structure of Interest Rates Is Always Flat.   What if the term structure of interest rates is always flat? Is it then possible to construct a pair of bond portfolio investments that look like bond A and bond B? Or is the construction of two such investments impossible? In the flat term structure scenario, it is always possible to create two portfolios with the same market value and the same DV01, but with different convexities. (They already have the same yield to maturity by virtue of the assumption of a flat term structure of interest rates.) However, if one could find two bond portfolios with the characteristics of bonds A and B in Exhibit 22.7 there would be an arbitrage opportunity. By going long in the high-convexity portfolio and short in the low-convexity portfolio, one achieves an investment combination that is self-financing and—for any size move in the interest rate—has a positive value immediately after such move. What this means is that the relationships depicted in Exhibit 22.7 are unlikely to exist in reality.

Changing the Convexity of a Bond Portfolio.   An easy way to increase convexity while holding DV01 and market value constant is to spread payments out around the duration.[17] For example, compare (1) a portfolio consisting of a single 4-year zero-coupon bond worth $2 million, with (2) a $2 million bond portfolio with equal amounts invested in a 3-year zero-coupon bond and a 5-year zero-coupon bond. With a flat term structure curve, the duration of the 2-bond portfolio is the value-weighted average of the durations of the 3- and 5-year bonds, or four years—just like the first zero-coupon bond. The DV01 of the 2-bond portfolio is virtually identical to the DV01 of the 1-bond portfolio[18] because the durations and market values of the two portfolios are the same.

If interest rates decline by 1 bp, the initial effect on the values of the two portfolios will be about the same. However, since the 5-year bond in the 2-bond portfolio now carries relatively more weight, the duration of the 2-bond portfolio will now be closer to five years than to three. For the next basis point decline in interest rates, the price of the 2-bond portfolio, which has a duration exceeding four years, will go up by more than the price of the 1-bond portfolio, which has a duration of exactly four years. This would push the duration even closer to five years. With a higher price and a still higher duration, the DV01 of the 2-bond portfolio would then exceed the DV01 of the 1-bond portfolio by even more, and so on.

Consider the reverse situation. As interest rates increase, the duration of the 3-year bond in the 2-bond portfolio now carries greater weight. Hence, while the first basis point increase has about the same effect on both portfolios, subsequent basis point

---

[17]Note also that bond options, whether put or call options, have more convexity than the underlying bonds themselves. Similarly, floating-rate investments with caps and floors have more convexity than otherwise identical floating-rate investments without caps or floors.

[18]The derivative implementations of the two DV01s are exactly the same.

Exhibit 22.8   Spreading Cash Flow around the Duration of a Coupon Bond

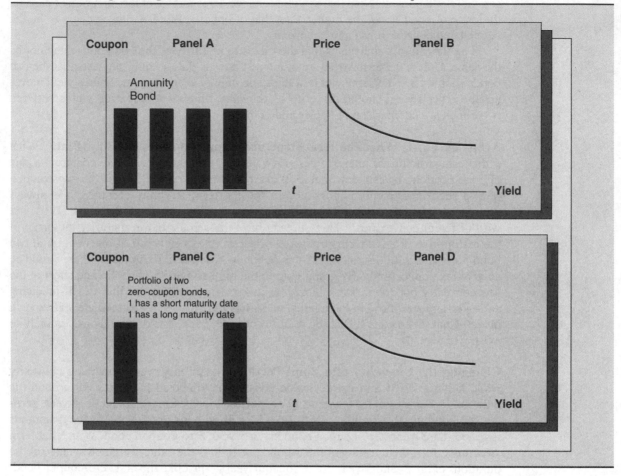

increases result in greater price declines for the 1-bond portfolio because it has a larger duration. In this case, as interest rates move down from the original rate, the DV01 of the 2-bond portfolio exceeds the DV01 of the 1-bond portfolio by increasingly greater amounts. Since DV01s are proportional to the slopes in a price-yield graph, the price-yield graphs of the two portfolios look like those depicted in Exhibit 22.7 where the 1-bond portfolio is bond B and the 2-bond portfolio is bond A.

The previous discussion showed how to increase convexity by spreading payments around the duration of a bond, focusing on zero-coupon bonds. It is possible to generalize this procedure to coupon bonds. Panel A of Exhibit 22.8 plots the cash flows of an annuity bond against time. Below, panel B graphs the annuity bond's price yield curve to illustrate the convexity of the bond. Panel C plots the cash flows of a portfolio of two zero-coupon bonds of different maturities. In panel D, the convexity of the 2-bond portfolio is greater than the convexity of the annuity bond in panel B, seen as greater curvature in the former. Example 22.16 uses numerical computations to demonstrate this difference in convexity between an annuity bond and a portfolio of two zero-coupon bonds.

Example 22.16:   Convexity of an Annuity versus a Portfolio of Zero-Coupon Bonds

Consider a portfolio consisting of an annuity that pays $100 every year for the next 30 years. If 8 percent compounded annually is the market interest rate at all maturities, then the present value of this annuity at 8 percent is:

$$\$100\left(\frac{1}{.08}\right)\left(1 - \frac{1}{1.08^{30}}\right) = \$1,125.7783$$

Its present values at 7.99 percent and 8.01 percent interest rates are, respectively:

$$\$100\left(\frac{1}{.0799}\right)\left(1 - \frac{1}{1.0799^{30}}\right) = \$1,126.8413 \text{ and}$$

$$\$100\left(\frac{1}{.0801}\right)\left(1 - \frac{1}{1.0801^{30}}\right) = \$1,124.7170$$

The DV01s at 8.01 percent and 8.00 percent interest thus equal $1.0613 (= $1,125.7783 − $1,124.7170) and $1.0630 (= $1,126.8413 − $1,125.7783), respectively, implying that the annuity bond's convexity is:

$$\frac{\$1,000,000}{\$1,125.7783}(1.0630 - 1.0613) = 1.510$$

Replacing this annuity with a portfolio consisting of zero-coupon bonds maturing at year 1 and year 30 can increase convexity while maintaining the same DV01 at 8 percent interest. Find such a portfolio.

Answer: The problem requires finding a portfolio with face amounts x and y in the 1-year and 30-year zero-coupon bonds, respectively. For a $1.00 face amount, note that a 1-year zero-coupon bond has a DV01 of $.000085742, while a 30-year zero-coupon bond has a DV01 of $.000276445. Thus, to generate a portfolio with the same present value and DV01 as the annuity, x and y must satisfy the equations:

$$\frac{x}{1.08} + \frac{y}{(1.08)^{30}} = \$1,125.7783 \text{ (present value condition)}$$

$$.000085742x + .000276445y = \$1.0630 \text{ (DV01 condition)}$$

The first equation says $x = \$1,126.7783(1.08) - \dfrac{y}{(1.08)^{29}}$. Substituting this into the second equation gives

$$(.000085742)\left[(\$1125.7783)(1.08) - \frac{y}{(1.08)^{29}}\right] + .000276445y = \$1.0630$$

or

$$y(.000276445 - .000009202476147) = \$0.958747165213$$

Thus, $y = \$3,587.60$ and $x = \$830.80$ (approximately).

The DV01 of the portfolio of zero-coupon bonds is 1.0602 at an 8.01 percent yield and 1.0630 at an 8.00 percent yield. This makes convexity:

$$\frac{\$1,000,000}{\$1,125.7783}(1.0630 - 1.0602), \text{ or } 2.487$$

Example 22.16 illustrates how easy it is to increase convexity at no cost. Using equation (22.8), the difference in convexities for a 25 bp shift upward or downward (to either 7.75 percent or 8.25 percent) implies that the portfolio of two zero-coupon bonds has a larger price than the annuity by the difference in the final terms in equation (22.8):

$$.5\left(\frac{\$1125.778}{100}\right)(2.487 - 1.510)(.25^2) = \$.34$$

Hence, going long in the portfolio of zero-coupon bonds and short in the annuity yields approximately a riskless $.34 for a portfolio of this size.[19] Most portfolios would be much larger, particularly since this is a hedged portfolio. At 10,000 times the size, $3,400 is achieved without risk; at 100,000 times the size, $34,000 is achieved without risk.

It is difficult to believe that such arbitrage profits can be achieved. However, if the term structure of interest rates is always flat, there is no cost to forming a portfolio strategy in this manner. It is easy to prove that arbitrage profits also arise if the yield curve is not flat but shifts in a parallel manner. If convexity is to come at a cost and if there is no arbitrage, term structure shifts must not be parallel.

22.6 Interest Rate Hedging When the Term Structure Is Not Flat

Our analysis of the price-yield relationship of a bond and its implications for interest rate hedging has assumed that the term structure of interest rates is flat. We know that this assumption is unrealistic.

Consider Example 22.3, which computed the DV01 of a portfolio of 5-, 10-, and 30-year bonds. This example points out a potential pitfall in using DV01s for hedging. Example 22.3 adds up the sensitivities of prices to yields to maturity, as if all three of the bonds had simultaneous 1 bp declines in their yields to maturity. However, a 1 bp decrease in the yield to maturity of a 30-year bond does not imply an identical decrease in the yield to maturity of the 10- and 5-year bonds. It does not even imply a decrease in the latter two yields. Therefore, adding these DV01s together is like combining apples and oranges and peaches.

The Yield-Beta Solution

Fortunately, apples and oranges and peaches have something in common—all are fruits. And while the three bonds in Example 22.3 have yields that apply to different maturities, these yields are alike because they are all interest rates. When short-term interest rates go up, long-term rates also tend to go up and vice versa, but not always and certainly not exactly by the same amount. For these reasons, perfect hedging only can be approximated with traditional DV01 methods.

Many practitioners have recognized this limitation of DV01 techniques. As a consequence, they have sought to improve the hedge with a variety of more sophisticated techniques. One of these techniques employs the concept of a **yield beta**, which is the sensitivity of the hedge portfolio's yield to maturity to movements in the yield to maturity of the portfolio one is trying to hedge. The better hedge in this case is the hedge portfolio that makes the sum of:

1. the DV01 of the portfolio that one is trying to hedge and
2. the product of the DV01 of the hedge portfolio and its yield beta

---

[19]This is only an approximation based on the Taylor series expansion. The actual arbitrage difference is closer to $0.37.

equal to zero. If $DV01_H$ denotes the DV01 of the hedge portfolio, $DV01_P$ the DV01 of the original portfolio, and β the yield beta, the hedge solution is represented algebraically by:

$$DV01_P + DV01_H\beta = 0$$

Example 22.17 illustrates how this works.

Example 22.17:   Hedging with the Yield Beta Method

Assume that the DV01 of General Motors' liabilities is $-\$1$ million from GM's perspective. The DV01 of GM's preferred hedging instrument, the Eurodollar futures contract traded on the Chicago Mercantile Exchange, is \$100 per futures contract. For every 1 basis point increase in the yield of GM's liabilities, the Eurodollar futures yield [which is computed as $1 -$ (Eurodollar Futures Price)/100, rises by 1.1 basis points (that is, the futures yield beta is 1.1). How many Eurodollar futures contracts should GM buy or sell if it wants to target a DV01 of \$100,000?]

Answer: To obtain a DV01 of \$100,000 with respect to the yield of its liabilities, GM should buy x Eurodollar futures contracts, where x satisfies:

$$\$100,000 = -\$1,000,000 + \$100(1.1)x$$

Thus, $x = 10,000$.

A limitation of the yield-beta method is that it leaves open the question of how to compute β. The usual approach to beta estimation in other contexts (e.g., stock betas for the CAPM), running a regression of historical yields of the hedge portfolio on the yields of the hedged portfolio is fraught with empirical pitfalls here. For example, the true yield beta tends to change as time elapses, suggesting that the true historical beta differs from the current yield beta. Moreover, slope coefficients estimated in this manner will differ radically, depending on the frequency of data used (e.g., daily versus weekly) and the choice of investment used as the hedging instrument.

More precise hedging requires a sophisticated term structure model. Portfolio managers, corporate executives, and traders who employ such models typically look at the price sensitivity to an interest rate factor in the model and do not use DV01, the sensitivity to the yield to maturity. The relationship between the *price* sensitivity and *yield* sensitivity to a factor is given by the equation:

$$\Delta P = \frac{\Delta r}{\Delta f} \times DV01 \tag{22.9}$$

where

> $P =$ the value of the fixed income security or portfolio
> $r =$ its yield to maturity
> $f =$ the interest rate factor that determines the term structure

This equation states that the change in the value of the security is the product of the change in the yield to maturity with respect to a change in the interest rate factor *and* DV01.[20]

---

[20]The Greek letter Δ implies that we look at the change in the variable to the right of it.

The Parallel Term Structure Shift Solution: Term Structure DV01

It is possible to infer perfect hedge ratios from DV01s alone only if changes in yields to maturity for different maturity bonds are identical. This is an alternative between defining DV01 in terms of (1) the overly simplified 1 bp shift in the yield to maturity of the portfolio or in terms of (2) the highly complicated 1 bp shift in a factor that determines the term structure of interest rates in a sophisticated no-arbitrage model. This "halfway" alternative defines DV01 as the change in value for a 1 bp parallel shift in the entire term structure of interest rates, as Exhibit 22.9 shows. We call this a **term structure DV01**.

Hedging with term structure DV01 is identical to the yield beta method when the yield beta is constrained to be 1. The method also implies that the term $(\Delta r / \Delta f)$ in equation (22.9) is the same for different maturity bonds. Despite its being more realistic than the flat term structure assumption, term structure DV01, like the flat term structure assumption, has an inconsistent logic to it. In particular, as the last section asserted, parallel term structure shifts imply arbitrage. Therefore, be careful about reaching conclusions about profitable strategies using the ordinary DV01 approach or this term structure DV01 approach.

MacAuley Duration and Present Value Duration

When the term structure of interest rates is not flat, the definition of duration is somewhat ambiguous because we do not know how to discount the cash flows to obtain the weights on cash flow maturities that are necessary for a duration computation. One discount rate to consider is the yield to maturity of the bond. Duration computed using the bond's

Exhibit 22.9 Parallel Shift in the Term Structure of Interest Rates by 1 Basis Point

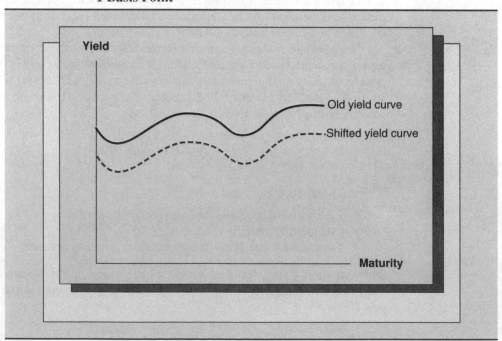

yield to maturity for discounting, known as the **MacAuley duration**, is the more traditional and common method for computing duration.[21] It is implicitly based on the assumption that yields for bonds of all maturities are identical.

An equally viable discounting alternative, however, is to discount cash flows at the yields to maturity of zero-coupon bonds that mature close to the dates the cash flows are to be paid. The discount rates obtained from zero-coupon bonds will differ, depending on the cash flow maturity. For example, if long-term riskless bonds have higher yields to maturity than short-term bonds, the zero-coupon discount rates for riskless cash flows that occur far in the future will be larger than the discount rates for cash flows paid in the near future. Duration using weights on cash flow maturities obtained from discounting cash flows with zero-coupon bond yields is referred to as **present value duration**.

The two durations generally differ unless the bond is riskless and the yields to maturity of riskless cash flows of different maturities are the same. Example 22.18 illustrates the distinction in the way duration is computed, using each of the two duration methods.

Example 22.18:   Computing MacAuley and Present Value Durations

Compute the MacAuley and present value durations for a portfolio of 6- and 8-year zero-coupon bonds, assuming that the 6-year bonds pay $18 million in six years and the 8-year bonds pay $20 million in eight years. Both bonds have market values of $10 million.

Answer: The yield to maturity of the portfolio, which solves:

$$\$20,000,000 = \frac{\$18,000,000}{(1 + r)^6} + \frac{\$20,000,000}{(1 + r)^8}$$

is approximately 9.593 percent per year. This makes the discounted value of the year 6 cash flow (at 9.593 percent) about $10.389 million and the discounted value of the year 8 cash flow (at 9.593 percent) about $9.611 million. The MacAuley duration of the portfolio is:

$$\frac{\$10.389 \text{ million}}{\$20 \text{ million}}(6 \text{ years}) + \frac{\$9.611 \text{ million}}{\$20 \text{ million}}(8 \text{ years}) = 6.9611 \text{ years (approximately)}$$

To find the present value duration, weight six years by the fraction of the bond portfolio's present value contributed by the 6-year bonds (.5 = $10 million/$20 million) and eight years by the fraction contributed by 8-year bonds (.5 = $10 million/$20 million). The present value duration is thus:

$$.5(6 \text{ years}) + .5(8 \text{ years}) = 7 \text{ years}$$

Knowing the cash flows in this example allows us to find the discount rate that makes the present value of the combined cash flows equal $20 million. This single internal rate of return is then used to discount the individual cash flows to obtain the weights on six and eight years for the MacAuley duration. By contrast, present value duration uses different discount rates to obtain the comparable weights on six and eight years.

Example 22.18 also points out that the present value duration of a portfolio is the portfolio-weighted average of the durations of the individual bonds in the portfolio. MacAuley duration does not possess this property unless the term structure of interest rates is flat, in which case MacAuley duration and present value duration are the same.

---

[21]This method was developed by Frederick MacAuley (1938).

Present Value Duration as a Derivative

If the term structure of interest rates is flat, then (as Section 22.3 noted) the negative of a bond's duration is the percentage change in a bond's price with respect to small changes in interest rates. Present value duration does not generally possess this derivative property. With present value duration, there is no single interest rate to take a derivative with respect to. Each cash flow has its own interest rate for discounting! However, it is possible to have a derivative interpretation for present value duration, too, if one makes a minor modification to the derivative; in this case, present value duration can be interpreted as the negative of the percentage change in the bond's value for a small parallel shift in the term structure of continuously compounded interest rates. That is, defining r_t as the appropriate continuously compounded rate for cash flows t years from now and, assuming that for all t's, r_t shifts up by a constant δ, the derivative of the percentage change in the bond's price with respect to δ equals the negative of duration, that is[22,23]:

$$\text{(present value) } DUR = -\frac{1}{P}\frac{dP}{d\delta}$$

This derivative interpretation makes it possible to relate term structure DV01 to present value duration. Specifically, term structure DV01 can be written as a constant times a derivative:

$$\text{(term structure) } DV01 = -.0001\frac{dP}{d\delta}$$

Combining the last two equations implies:

$$\text{(term structure) } DV01 = \text{(present value) } DUR \times P \times .0001$$

22.7 Summary and Conclusions

This chapter described several tools that are important for bond portfolio management and corporate financial management of fixed-income securities and interest rate risk. Managers can use these tools to better understand the relation between yield and market price in order to manage interest rate risk. Among the tools discussed in the chapter were:

1. The concept of DV01, in original and term structure variations, which is a measure of the slope of the price-yield curve.

2. The concept of duration, in MacAuley, modified, and present value variations, which is a weighted average of the time at which a set of cash flows is received.

3. The link between duration and DV01 and the formulas needed to use either of them for hedging.

4. Immunization and contingent immunization, using both duration and DV01, which are methods of converting the cash flows of a bond portfolio into the cash flows of a zero-coupon bond.

5. The link between immunization and hedging and how to use this link for managing the asset base and capital structure of financial institutions and for managing a bond portfolio.

---

[22]Exercise 22.2 at the end of the chapter asks you to prove this.

[23]The adjustment for derivatives with respect to noncontinuously compounded yields with present value duration is not as simple or straightforward. If each gross discount rate $1 + r_t$ for cash flows t years from now is multiplied by $1 + \delta$, then present value duration for a set of discount rates that reflect compounding m times a year is $-1/m$ times the derivative of the percentage change in the price of the bond (or portfolio) with respect to δ.

6. The concept of convexity, which is similar to the slope of the price-yield curve, and how it can be properly used and misused.

The yield curve is not flat and does not shift in a parallel fashion which complicates the use of these tools. Parallel shifts lead to arbitrage, thus making it incumbent upon those who desire a more rigorous analysis of interest rate hedging to develop a sophisticated model of the term structure of interest rates that precludes such arbitrage.

Final Remarks. Wall Street firms have developed a number of sophisticated models that are used to value complicated interest rate derivatives, like the "inverse floater" sold to Orange County (see the opening vignette to this chapter). The basic structure of these interest rate derivatives valuation models is similar to that of the binomial model in Chapter 7. However, here, the risk neutral valuation accounts for interest rate factors that evolve along trees (or grids) with move sizes for these factors determined by the term structure of interest rates and volatility. The level of mathematical sophistication in these models is beyond the scope of any textbook geared toward those seeking a general understanding of corporate finance and financial markets. Indeed, the rocket science associated with these models has given the rocket scientists—often Ph.D.'s in mathematics, statistics, economics, physics, and finance—an unprecedented degree of prestige, compensation, and control over the management and valuation of interest rate derivatives.

The level of technical sophistication in corporate finance has also increased considerably over the last two decades. In some cases, nonfinancial corporations are hiring these same rocket scientists to oversee their hedging operations. However, this is still the exception. After 22 chapters, our message to you is that no matter how sophisticated either investment management or corporate management becomes, there are some fundamental principles in finance that will always be useful.

We believe, for example, that understanding the tools described in this text is all that is necessary to recognize the risk in Orange County's investment in inverse floaters and to skirt the disasters from misguided derivatives trades that have befallen numerous other firms. A serious student of this text, for example, would recognize (perhaps after a bit of thought) that an Orange County inverse floater could be tracked by a portfolio with a weight of 3 on a fixed-rate straight coupon bond and a weight of -2 on par floating rate bonds. Since the floating rate bond's duration is zero, this portfolio has three times the duration of a straight coupon bond (see Result 22.3), and hence, is extremely sensitive to interest rate changes.

In short, one of the basic principles developed in this textbook—the formation of portfolios to track an investment with risks one is familiar with—can be used to understand the risk of a highly complex security, like an inverse floater. The lesson here is that one does not need advanced mathematics or Wall Street's sophisticated models to master finance. One must, however, go beyond a superficial understanding of finance and master its basic principles to succeed as a finance professional in the 21st century. We wrote this text in the hopes of contributing to such an understanding.

Key Concepts

Result 22.1: If the term structure of interest rates is flat, a bond portfolio with a DV01 of zero has no sensitivity to interest rate movements.

Result 22.2: Let r_n and r_m denote the yield to maturity of the bond computed with yields compounded n times a year and m times a year, respectively. The DV01 for a bond or portfolio using compounding of m times a year is $(1 + r_n/n)/(1 + r_m/m)$ times the DV01 of a bond using a compounding frequency of n times a year.

Result 22.3: Assuming that the term structure of interest rates is flat, the duration of a portfolio of bonds is the portfolio-weighted average of the durations of the respective bonds in the portfolio.

Result 22.4: Because DV01 can be translated into duration and vice versa, DV01 and duration are equivalent as tools both for measuring interest rate risk and for hedging.

Result 22.5: If the term structure of interest rates is flat, immunization "guarantees" a fixed value for an immunized portfolio at a horizon date. The value obtained is the same as the face value of a zero-coupon bond with (1) the same market value as the original portfolio and (2) a maturity date equal to the horizon date selected as the target date to which the duration of the immunized portfolio is fixed.

Key Terms

Exercises

22.1. A 3-year coupon bond has payments as follows:

Bond Cash Flow at Year		
1	*2*	*3*
$8	$8	$108

This 8 percent coupon bond is currently trading at par ($100).

a. What is the annually compounded yield of the bond?

b. Compute the MacAuley duration and ordinary DV01 (calculated with respect to the annually compounded bond yield).

c. Using DV01, how much do you expect this bond's price to rise if the yield on the bond declines by 10 basis points compounded annually?

22.2. Prove that if the present value of a cash flow is represented by:

$$PV = (\text{cash flow}) \times exp(-r_t t)$$

and for all t's, r_t shifts up by a constant δ, the derivative of the percentage change in the bond's price with respect to δ equals the negative of present value duration, that is:

$$(\text{present value}) \, DUR = -\frac{1}{P}\frac{dP}{d\delta}$$

22.3. Bond A has a DV01 of $.10 per $100 face value. Bond B has a DV01 of $.05 per $100 face value.

a. If Daniela buys $1 million (face amount) of bond A, what should her position (face amount) in bond B be in order to hedge out all interest rate risk on the portfolio?

b. If bond A and bond B are par bonds (i.e., they have prices equal to their face values and have

equal yields to maturity), what dollar amount needs to be spent on bonds A and B to immunize the bond portfolio to a horizon of seven years if $1 million is spent on the portfolio? (Assume that the DV01s were calculated with respect to a 1 basis point decline in each bond's *continuously compounded* yield to maturity.)

22.4. The DV01 of a Treasury bond maturing on November 15, 2021, with an 8 percent coupon (4 percent paid semiannually) and a $100 face value is $.10. The DV01 of a Treasury note maturing on May 15, 2012, with a 7 percent coupon (3.5 percent paid semiannually) and a $100 face value is $.06.

a. Assume that the next coupon is not the first coupon for either the bond or the note (i.e., there is no long or short first coupon to worry about). What is the accrued interest (per $100 face value) to be paid on both the bond and the note for a purchase with a settlement date of June 11, 2002, for each of these fixed-income securities? *Hint:* See the appendix to Chapter 2.

b. If you held a position of $1 million (face value) in the Treasury bond, what position should you hold in the Treasury note to eliminate all interest rate risk?

22.5. A 2-year default-free straight-coupon bond has annual coupons of $8 per $100 of face value. Assume that a default-free zero-coupon bond with one year to maturity sells for $90 per $100 of face value and that a default-free zero-coupon bond with two years to maturity sells for $80 per $100 of face value.

a. What is the no-arbitrage price of the straight-coupon 8 percent bond?

b. What is the present value duration of the straight-coupon bond given the market value of the bond computed in part *a*?

  c. Assume you hold $1 million face value of the straight-coupon bond. How much in market value of a three-year, zero-coupon bond should you hold (in addition to the straight-coupon bond position) to have an overall position that is perfectly hedged against a parallel shift in the term structure?

22.6. Compute the duration, DV01, and convexity of a semiannual straight-coupon bond with three years to maturity. The bond trades at par with a 6 percent coupon. Assume the term structure of interest rates is flat.

22.7. Compute the duration, DV01, and convexity of a 6 percent 2-year par bond that pays semiannual coupons. Assume the term structure of interest rates is flat.

22.8. Discuss how you might use the 6 percent 2-year bond in exercise 22.7 to hedge a position in the 3-year bond from exercise 22.6?

22.9. How would your answer to exercise 22.8 change if the bond in exercise 22.7 were a 10 percent 2-year premium bond with a yield curve still at a flat 6 percent?

22.10. Discuss qualitatively how your answer to exercise 22.8 would change if the bond in exercise 22.7 was a 10 percent 2-year par bond. (This means that the term structure of interest rates is not flat.)

References and Additional Readings

Fabozzi, Frank. *Bond Markets, Analysis, and Strategies.* 3d ed. Englewood Cliffs, NJ: Prentice-Hall, 1996.

MacAuley, Frederick. *Some Theoretical Problems Suggested by the Movement of Interest Rates, Bond Yields, and Stock Prices in the U.S. since 1856.* New York: National Bureau of Economic Research, 1938.

Kopprasch, Robert. "Understanding Duration and Volatility." New York: Salomon Brothers, 1985; reprinted in *The Handbook of Fixed-Income Securities,* Frank Fabozzi and Irving Pollack, eds. Burr Ridge, IL: Irwin Professional Publishing, 1996.

Redington, F. M. "Review of the Principle of Life-Office Valuations." *Journal of the Institute of Actuaries* 78 (1952), pp. 286–340.

Tuckman, Bruce. *Fixed Income Securities: Tools for Today's Markets.* New York: John Wiley, 1995.

PRACTICAL INSIGHTS FOR PART VI

Allocating Capital for Real Investment

- Managers are likely to make better capital allocation decisions if they hedge their risks because it forces them to use forward and futures prices in their calculations of *NPV* rather than potentially ad hoc estimates of expected value. (Section 20.2)
- Firms sometimes build plants in foreign countries in which they sell their products as a substitute for hedging when it is difficult to effectively hedge real exchange rate risk. (Section 20.8)

Financing the Firm

- The Modigliani-Miller Theorem is very general and implies that, in the absence of market frictions, firms are indifferent about the currencies of their debt obligations and the maturity structure of their debt as well as their debt-equity ratio. (Section 20.1)
- Firms that use derivatives to reduce their probability of financial distress can create value by increasing their debt ratio without increasing their probability of financial distress. (Section 20.2)
- Firms that have high leverage ratios, but also potentially have high financial distress costs, are more likely to use derivatives to hedge. (Section 20.2)
- In general, hedging will benefit debt holders at the expense of equity holders. (Section 20.6)
- Firms can sometimes reduce their funding costs by combining debt instruments with swaps and other derivatives. (Sections 20.7, 21.6)

Knowing Whether and How to Hedge Risk

- Firms can benefit from hedging even when shareholders are not averse to risk. (Section 20.2)
- Firms that are uncertain about whether or not they will have positive tax liabilities have an incentive to hedge since the gains associated with increased income, in the event of bad outcomes in which the firm has excess tax deductions, exceeds the losses associated with an equivalent reduction in income, in the event of a good outcome in which the income is fully taxed. (Section 20.2)
- Firms benefit from hedging if it allows them to avoid the possibility of costly financial distress. (Section 20.2)
- Firms benefit from hedging when external sources of capital are more expensive than internal sources of capital. However, when investment opportunities are positively correlated with the hedgeable risk, firms should only partially hedge. Options may prove to be a particularly good hedging vehicle in this case. (Sections 20.2, 21.7)
- Management performance can be evaluated more accurately if managers are required to hedge extraneous risks. (Section 20.2)
- In most cases, firms benefit from hedging real rather than strictly nominal exchange rate changes. (Section 20.8)
- Factor models are perhaps the best way to think about a firm's risk exposure. (Sections 20.1, 21.1, 21.8)
- Regression slope coefficients give risk-minimizing hedge ratios. (Section 21.9)
- Even though futures and forward prices are often virtually identical, hedge ratios using futures can vastly differ from hedge ratios using forwards. In particular, hedges with futures need to be tailed and thus are generally lower than hedge ratios involving forwards. (Section 21.3)
- The convenience yield of an asset or commodity affects the hedge ratio when hedging long-term commitments with short-term forwards or futures. The larger is the convenience yield, the more correlated it is with the price of the commodity, and the more unpredictable it is, the lower is the risk minimizing hedge ratio. (Section 21.4)
- Firms that set the ratio of the duration of assets and liabilities to the inverse of the ratios of their market values will have equity with a DV01 of 0 which means that their stock price is insensitive to interest rate risk. (Section 22.3)
- It is possible to lock in (that is, immunize) the future value of an interest rate sensitive liability or asset at a horizon date by managing the liability to have a duration that is matched to the horizon date. (Section 22.4)
- Even though DV01 and duration are relatively simple risk estimation and risk management tools in comparison with the techniques on Wall Street, they often provide good approximations of the interest rate risk of an asset or liability and offer useful insights into risk and hedging. (Sections 22.1–22.3, 22.7)

Allocating Funds for Financial Investments

- Bond portfolios that are managed to have DV01s or durations of zero have no interest rate risk. (Section 22.3)

- All else equal, the greater the convexity of an investment, the more valuable it is. However, investors can enhance the convexity of their portfolios at a cost. Investors should be aware that many simple models of interest rate risk do not account for these costs. (Section 22.5)

- Duration and DV01 can be generalized without rocket science term structure models to account for term structures of interest rates that are not flat. (Section 22.6)

EXECUTIVE PERSPECTIVE

David C. Shimko

The failure to account for and control risks has led, fortunately and unfortunately, to several risk management and derivatives disasters since the mid-1980s. Unfortunately, shareholders and taxpayers have unwittingly borne the fallout of these debacles. Fortunately, we now have the opportunity to learn from these mistakes.

These are the lessons taught in Part VI of Grinblatt and Titman's text. Corporate managers who think that risk management is the province of back-office quants[1] should read this material, if not for the value in itself, then for the ability to use the lessons learned to monitor those who take risks. We should learn from the past, as Santayana said, "lest we be condemned to repeat it."

The analysis of Metallgesellschaft AG's poorly conceived hedge, and its implications at the corporate level, is accurate and easy to follow. Clearly, either hedging was not MG's intent, or hedging was entrusted to managers with insufficient judgment or experience to hedge properly. Alarmingly, the same mistakes are repeated constantly in companies around the world. Fortunately for many of these companies, losses have mostly been either small, underscrutinized, or labeled as hedges for accounting purposes and lost in the paperwork. After studying the MG case, no corporate risk manager should undertake a one-for-one hedge of a longer-dated exposure with a shorter-dated one. Ironically, we know this lesson well in the interest rate markets. The presentation in Grinblatt and Titman helps us bridge that intuitive gap and apply financial markets knowledge broadly to the practice of corporate finance.

It's easy to focus on the potential costs of ignoring risk management and thereby miss the hidden opportunity costs. For example, the value-at-risk (VaR) concept helps many managers measure the potential loss associated with an investment activity. Indeed, J.P. Morgan scored a major coup with the RiskMetrics™ product, a relatively simple analytic means to determine VaR transparently. Detractors have rightly argued that the methodology could be improved, but they are missing the main point. The critical importance of VaR is that one can use it to measure risk and, thereby, risk-adjusted performance. VaR is fast becoming a measure of capital that, for many purposes, works better than traditional capital measures. That is, regardless of the cost of a project, its performance should be measured relative to the capital it actually places at risk. A $100 million mine and a zero-cost swap have the same risk if both might lose $40 million. Their performance should be measured relative to the $40 million value-at-risk, not the cash investment.

Since the mid-1970s, managers have mastered the concept of value-added (or EVA, economic value added, or NPV, net present value). In the next 20 years, I hope the same can be said of risk management.

The best managed corporations are starting to evaluate risk and capital management in the same framework. Peter Rugg, the CFO of Triton, funded a greater proportion of his company's Colombian oil production with debt than he otherwise would have been able to do because he had hedged against oil price fluctuations. Essentially, he conserved equity capital by replacing it with contingent capital provided by hedging. (*Translation*: Swaps markets bore the oil price risk instead of equity holders.) The equity capital was released to seek higher returns elsewhere.

The messages for risk management are clear. Defensively, we need risk management to know our potential losses and to facilitate planning to protect ourselves against those losses. Progressively, we need risk management to help us make better investment decisions. Every corporate executive will someday be seen as a risk manager—only some don't know this yet! This book will help those executives be better risk managers.

---

[1]Quants are employees with considerable quantitative background or experience, typically hired by a trading floor or risk management department to build mathematical models for pricing and risk assessment.

Mr. Shimko is vice president, risk management advisory at Bankers Trust. Previously, Mr. Shimko was head of risk management research at J.P. Morgan, Inc.
Note: Opinions expressed by the author do not necessarily reflect the opinion or policies of Bankers Trust or any of its business affiliates.

APPENDIX A
INTEREST RATE MATHEMATICS

Learning Objectives

After reading this appendix, you should be able to:

1. Understand the cash flows generated by long and short positions.
2. Apply the present value and future value formulas for single cash flows, and specially patterned cash flow streams, like annuities and perpetuities, in both level and growing forms.
3. Apply the principle of value additivity to simplify present value calculations of complex cash flow streams.
4. Translate interest rates from one compounding frequency into another.

This appendix reviews some basic tools needed to understand finance such as formulas for accumulating interest and discounting, including the discounting and accumulation of special types of cash flows (e.g., perpetuities and annuities).

A.1 Cash Flows from Long and Short Positions

An ability to understand cash flows is an essential skill for the analysis of an investment or financing decision. Cash coming in results in a cash inflow; cash going out results in a cash outflow.

Cash Flow Sign Conventions. Cash flows are analyzed by representing them as numbers attached to dates in time, with date 0 generally referring to the current date. The sign of the cash flow tells the analyst whether the cash flow is an inflow or an outflow. Inflows have positive signs and outflows have negative signs. For example, the date 0 purchase of 100 shares of IBM stock at $125 per share has a cash flow to the purchaser of −$12,500 at date 0. Assuming that this investor liquidates the 100 shares at date 1 at a sale price of $150 per share, the date 1 cash flow is $15,000.

Obviously, cash inflows are good and cash outflows are bad. As seen above, however, most investments have both cash inflows and outflows. Moreover, most investments have an element of uncertainty to their future cash flows. For some investments, like the purchase of stock, the magnitude of the future cash inflow is uncertain. For other investments, like futures contracts, even the sign of a cash flow at a future date can be uncertain—sometimes this cash flow is an inflow and sometimes it is an outflow.

Short Sales. A short sale of the same IBM stock that is closed out at date 1 creates cash flows that are equal in magnitude but of the opposite sign to those from the purchase of IBM at date 0 and subsequent sale at date 1. In the example described above, the date 0 cash flow would be $12,500, reflecting the cash received on the short sale, and the date 1 cash flow would be −$15,000, reflecting the need to purchase 100 shares of IBM at $150 per share to close the position. In general, a short sale of any investment creates cash flows of equal magnitude but of opposite sign from the investment itself.

Value versus Cash Flow. Note the distinction between an investment's value and its cash flow. The value of IBM stock is always positive; the value is what it costs to purchase IBM. An investor has to pay this cost once and then receives the cost back at some future date. Hence, an investment's cash flow tends to reverse sign, while an investment's value never changes sign.

Arbitrage.   If an investment's cash flow at all dates is sometimes positive but never negative, the investment represents an *arbitrage opportunity*. Such an investment always has good (or, at worst, neutral) cash flow consequences and can never penalize an investor. Arbitrage opportunities are, in essence, money trees. Many of the great insights in finance are based on the assumption that money does not grow on trees.

An investment position that always has negative cash flows is also an arbitrage opportunity, but only for the short seller of the position.

A.2 Interest Rates and Rates of Return in a One-Period Setting

This section and the next develop different ways of looking at rates of return, interest rates, and yields (which, in this appendix, all mean the same thing). We will analyze these concepts in both a single period and multiperiod setting.

Defining a Rate of Return over a Period.   Over a single period (from date 0 to date 1), a rate of return is defined as,

$$r = \frac{P_1 - P_0}{P_0} \tag{A.1a}$$

where

   P_1 = date 1 investment value (plus any cash distributed) like dividends or coupons
   P_0 = date 0 investment value

The Fallacy of Causation.   The numerator in the rate of return formula is the profit or interest earned on the investment over the period and the denominator is the amount paid for the investment. Equation (A.1a) makes it appear as if prices determine rates of return. Rearranging equation (A.1a), however, implies:

$$P_0 = \frac{P_1}{1 + r} \tag{A.1b}$$

or

$$P_1 = P_0(1 + r) \tag{A.1c}$$

Equation (A.1b) makes it seem as if the current or *present value* of the investment is determined by the rate of return. This suggests that a rate of return is a discount rate that translates future values into their date 0 equivalents. Equation (A.1c) makes it seem as if the future value of the investment is determined by the rate of return. This implies that the rate of return is the growth rate of an investment. Of course, all of these equations and interpretations of r are correct and state the same thing. Equations (A.1) thus point out how misleading it can be to think about any type of causation implied by these equations. Any two of the three variables in equations (A.1) determine the third.

Riskless Bonds: Yield versus Price.   Indeed, with riskless bonds, where P_1 is a fixed and known value, knowing the current price P_0 is equivalent to knowing the yield r (which is like a bond's rate of return), and vice versa. Hence, P_0 and r are simply different ways of expressing the same thing. Some investors like to think in terms of yields, others in terms of prices, but neither the current price nor the yield is more fundamental or better than the other.

A.3   Rates of Return in a Multiperiod Setting

Exhibit A.1 illustrates what happens to an investment of P_0 after t periods if it earns a rate of return of r per period and all profit (interest) is reinvested.

EXHIBIT A.1 **The Value of an Investment over Multiple Periods When Interest (Profit) Is Reinvested**

Beginning-of-Period Date	End-of-Period Date	Initial Principal Balance	Interest (profit) Earned over Period	End-of-Period Value
0	1	P_0	$P_0 r$	$P_0 + P_0 r = P_0(1 + r)$
1	2	$P_0(1 + r)$	$P_0(1 + r)r$	$P_0(1 + r) + P_0(1 + r)r = P_0(1 + r)^2$
2	3	$P_0(1 + r)^2$	$P_0(1 + r)^2 r$	$P_0(1 + r)^2 + P_0(1 + r)^2 r = P_0(1 + r)^3$
.	.	.	.	.
.	.	.	.	.
.	.	.	.	.
$t - 1$	t	$P_0(1 + r)^{t-1}$	$P_0(1 + r)^{t-1}r$	$P_0(1 + r)^{t-1} + P_0(1 + r)^{t-1}r = P_0(1 + r)^t$

Exhibit A.1 indicates that when r is the interest rate (or rate of return per period) and all interest (profit) is reinvested, an investment of P_0 dollars at date 0 has a *future value* at date t of:

$$P_t = P_0(1 + r)^t \qquad (A.2)$$

The date 0 value of P_t dollars paid at date t, also known as the *present value* or *discounted value*, comes from rearranging this formula, so that P_0 is on the left-hand side, that is:

$$P_0 = \frac{P_t}{(1 + r)^t} \qquad (A.3)$$

If r is positive, equation (A.3) states that P_0 is smaller the larger t is, other things being equal. Hence, a dollar in the future is worth less than a dollar today. Cash received early is better than cash received late because the earlier one receives money, the greater the interest (profit) that can be earned on it.

Generalizing the Present Value and Future Value Formulas. The present value and future value formulas generalize to any pair of dates t_1 and t_2 that are t periods apart, that is, $t_2 - t_1 = t$. Equation (A.2) represents the value of the date t_1 cash flow at date t_2 and equation (A.3) represents the value of the date t_2 cash flow at t_1 if the two dates are t periods apart. Hence, if $t_1 = 3$ and $t_2 = 8$, equation (A.2), with $t = 5$, would give the value at date 8 of an investment of P_0 dollars at date 3. In addition, t, t_1, or t_2 need not be whole numbers. In other words, t could be .5, 3.8, ⅓, or even some irrational number like π. Thus, if $t_1 = 2.6$ and $t_2 = 7.1$, equation (A.3) with $t = 4.5$ (=7.1 − 2.6) represents the value at date t_1 of P_1 dollars paid at date t_2.

Explicit versus Implicit Interest. Exhibit A.1 and the discussion of the exhibit reads as though we are examining a bank account that earns compound interest. Compound interest rates reflect the interest that is earned on interest. Compound interest arises whenever interest earnings are reinvested in the account to increase the principal balance on which the investor earns future interest. But what about securities that never explicitly pay interest and thus have no interest or profit to reinvest? We also can use the compound interest formulas to refer to the yield or rate of return of these securities.

To see how to apply these formulas when interest (or profit) cannot be reinvested, consider a zero-coupon bond, which is a bond that promises a single payment (known as its face value) at a future date. With a date 0 price of P_0 and a promise to pay a face value of \$100 at date T and nothing prior to date T, the yield (or rate of return) on the bond can still be quoted in compound interest terms. This yield on the bond is the number r that makes:

$$100 = P_0(1 + r)^T$$

implying

$$r = \left(\frac{100}{P_0}\right)^{\frac{1}{T}} - 1 \tag{A.4}$$

Thus, r makes \$100 equal to what the initial principal on the bond would turn into by date T if the bond appreciates at a rate of r per period, and if all profits from appreciation are reinvested in the bond itself.[1] Example A.1 provides a numerical calculation of the yield of a zero-coupon bond.

Example A.1:   Determining the Yield on a Zero-Coupon Bond

Compute the per period yield of a zero-coupon bond with a face value of \$100 at date 20 and a current price of \$45.

Answer: Using the formula presented in equation (A.4):

$$r = \left(\frac{100}{45}\right)^{\frac{1}{20}} - 1 = .040733$$

or about 4.07 percent per period.

Since a zero-coupon bond never pays interest and thus provides nothing to reinvest, the process of quoting a compound interest rate for the bond is merely a convention—a different way of expressing its price. As in the case of the one-period instrument, quoting a bond's price in terms of either its yield or its actual price is a matter of personal preference. Both, in some sense, are different ways of representing the same thing.

A.4   Value Additivity and Present Values of Cash Flow Streams

Present values (or discounted values), henceforth denoted as PV (rather than P_0), and future values obey the principle of *value additivity*; that is, the present (future) value of many cash flows combined is the sum of their individual present (future) values. This implies that the future value at date t of \$14, for example, is the same as the sum of the future values at t of 14 \$1 payments, each made at date 0, or $14(1 + r)^t$. Value additivity also implies that one can generalize equation (A.3) to value a stream of cash payments:

$$C_1 \, C_2 \ldots C_T$$

at dates $1, 2, \ldots, T$, respectively, as:

$$PV = \frac{C_1}{(1 + r)^1} + \frac{C_2}{(1 + r)^2} + \ldots + \frac{C_T}{(1 + r)^T} \tag{A.5}$$

where PV is the present value (or market value) of the cash flow stream, given the discount rate r.

A.5 Annuities and Perpetuities

There are several special cases of the present value formula, equation (A.5), described in the last section. When $C_1 = C_2 = \ldots = C_T = C$, the stream of payments is known as a standard *annuity*.

---

[1]While such profits are implicit if the bond is merely held to maturity, it is possible to make them explicit by selling a portion of the bond to realize the profits and then, redundantly, buying back the sold portion of the bond.

If T is infinite, it is a standard *perpetuity*. Standard annuities and perpetuities have payments that begin at date 1. The present values of standard annuities and perpetuities lend themselves to particularly simple equations. Less standard perpetuities and annuities can have any payment frequency, although it must be regular (e.g. every half period).

Many financial securities have patterns to their cash flows that resemble annuities and perpetuities. For example, mortgages are annuities and straight-coupon bonds are the sum of an annuity and a zero-coupon bond (see Chapter 2). The dividend discount models used to value equity are based on a growing perpetuity formula (see Chapter 10).

Perpetuities. The algebraic representation of the infinite sum that is the present value of a perpetuity is:

$$PV = \frac{C}{(1+r)} + \frac{C}{(1+r)^2} + \frac{C}{(1+r)^3} + \dots \tag{A.6a}$$

A simple and easily memorized formula for PV is found by first multiplying both sides of equation (A.6a) by $1/(1+r)$, implying:

$$\frac{PV}{1+r} = \frac{C}{(1+r)^2} + \frac{C}{(1+r)^3} + \dots \tag{A.6b}$$

Then, subtract the corresponding sides of equation (A.6b) from equation (A.6a) to obtain:

$$PV - \frac{PV}{1+r} = \frac{C}{1+r}$$

which is equivalent to:

$$PV \times \frac{r}{1+r} = \frac{C}{1+r}$$

or

$$PV = \frac{C}{r} \tag{A.7}$$

In sum, *the present value of a perpetuity with payments of* C *each period commencing at date 1 is* C/r *if* r *is the rate of interest per period.*

A perpetuity with payments of C commencing today is the sum of two types of cash flows: (1) A standard perpetuity, paying C every period beginning with a payment at C at date 1, and (2) a payment of C today. The standard perpetuity in item 1 has a present value of C/r. The payment of C today in item 2 has a present value of C. Add them to get the present value of the combined cash flows: $C + C/r$.

Note that the value for the "backward-shifted" perpetuity described in the last paragraph is also equal to $(1+r)C/r$. This can be interpreted as the date 1 value of a payment of C/r at date 0. It should not be surprising that the date 1 value of a perpetuity that begins at date 1 is the same as the date 0 value of a perpetuity that begins at date 0. If we had begun our analysis with this insight, namely that:

$$PV \times (1+r) = PV + C$$

we could have derived the perpetuity formula, $PV = C/r$, by solving this equation for PV.

Deriving the perpetuity formula in this manner illustrates that value additivity, along with the ability to combine, separate, and shift cash flow streams, is often useful for valuation insights. As the previous paragraph demonstrates, to obtain a formula for the present value of a complex cash flow, it is useful to first obtain a present value for a basic type of cash flow stream and then derive the present value of the more complex cash flow stream from it. The ability to manipulate and match various cash flow streams, in whole or in part, is a basic skill that is valuable for financial analysis.

Example A.2 illustrates how to apply this skill in valuing a complex perpetuity.

Example A.2:   Computing the Value of a Complex Perpetuity

What is the value of a perpetuity with payments of $2 every half-year commencing one-half year from now if $r = 10$ percent per year?

Answer: Examine the cash flows of the payoffs, outlined in the following table:

		Cash Flow (in $) at Year			
.5	1	1.5	2	...	
2	2	2	2	...	

This can be viewed as the sum of two perpetuities with annual payments, outlined below:

	Cash Flow (in $) at Year								
	.5	1	1.5	2	2.5	3	3.5	4	...
Perpetuity 1	2	0	2	0	2	0	2	0	...
Perpetuity 2	0	2	0	2	0	2	0	2	...

Perpetuity 2 is worth $2/r or $20. The first perpetuity is like the second perpetuity except that each cash flow occurs one-half period earlier. Let us discount the payoffs of perpetuity 1 to year .5 rather than to year 0. At year .5, the value of perpetuity 1 is $2 + $2/r or $22. Discounting $22 back one-half year earlier, we find that its year 0 value is:

$$\$20.976 = \$22/(1.1)^{.5}$$

Summing the year 0 values of the two perpetuities generates the date 0 value of the original perpetuity with semiannual payments. This is:

$$\$40.976 = \$2/r + \frac{\$2 + \$2/r}{(1 + r)^{.5}} = \$20 + \$20.976$$

The annuity formula derivation in the next subsection also demonstrate how useful it is to be able to manipulate cash flows in creative ways.

Annuities.   A standard annuity with payments of C from date 1 to date T has cash flows outlined in the following table:

	Cash Flow at Date			
1	2	3	...	T
C	C	C	...	C

A standard annuity can thus be viewed as the difference between two perpetuities. The first perpetuity has cash flows outlined in the table below:

	Cash Flow at Date		
1	*2*	*3*	...
C	*C*	*C*	...

The second perpetuity has cash flows that are identical to the first except that they commence at date $T + 1$; that is, they are represented by:

			Cash Flow at Date				
1	*2*	*3*	...	*T*	*T + 1*	*T + 2*	*T + 3*	...
0	0	0	...	0	*C*	*C*	*C*	...

The first perpetuity has a date 0 value of C/r. The second perpetuity has a date T value of C/r, implying a date 0 (i.e., present) value of:

$$\frac{C/r}{(1 + r)^T}$$

The difference in these two perpetual cash flow streams has the same cash flows as the annuity. Hence, the date 0 value of the annuity is the difference in the two date 0 values:

$$PV = C/r - \frac{C/r}{(1 + r)^T} \tag{A.8}$$

Thus, if r *is the rate of interest per period, the present value of an annuity with payments commencing at date 1 and ending at date* T *is:*

$$\frac{C}{r}\left(1 - \frac{1}{(1 + r)^T}\right)$$

Growing Perpetuities. A *growing perpetuity* is a perpetual cash flow stream that grows at a constant rate (denoted here as g) over time, as represented below:

	Cash Flow at Date			
1	*2*	*3*	*4*	...
C	$C(1 + g)$	$C(1 + g)^2$	$C(1 + g)^3$	...

If $g < r$, the present value of this sum is finite and given by the formula:

$$PV = \frac{C}{(1 + r)} + \frac{C(1 + g)}{(1 + r)^2} + \frac{C(1 + g)^2}{(1 + r)^3} + \ldots \tag{A.9a}$$

A simpler formula for this present value is found by first multiplying both sides of equation (A.9a) by $\frac{1+g}{1+r}$, yielding:

$$PV \times \frac{1+g}{1+r} = \frac{C(1+g)}{(1+r)^2} + \frac{C(1+g)^2}{(1+r)^3} + \cdots \qquad (A.9b)$$

Then, subtract the corresponding sides of equation (A.9b) from equation (A.9a) to obtain:

$$PV - PV \times \frac{1+g}{1+r} = \frac{C}{1+r}$$

When rearranged, this implies that *the value of a growing perpetuity with initial payment of* C *dollars one period from now is:*

$$PV = \frac{C}{r-g} \qquad (A.10)$$

Growing Annuities.   A *growing annuity* is identical to a growing perpetuity except that the cash flows terminate at date T. It is possible to derive the present value of this perpetuity from equation (A.10). Applying the reasoning used to derive the annuity formula, we find that a growing annuity is like the difference between two growing perpetuities. One commences at date 1 and has a present value given by equation (A.10). The second perpetuity commences at date $T + 1$ and has a present value equal to:

$$\frac{C(1+g)^T}{(r-g)(1+r)^T}$$

The numerator $C(1+g)^T$ is the initial payment of the growing perpetuity and thus replaces C in the equation. The second product in the denominator $(1+r)^T$ would not appear if we were valuing the perpetuity at date T. However, to find its value at date 0, we discount its date T value an additional T periods. The difference between the date 0 values of the first and second perpetuity is given below. *Thus, the present value of a* T-*period growing annuity, with an initial cash flow of* C, *commencing one period from now and with a growth rate of* g, *is:*

$$PV = \frac{C}{r-g}\left(1 - \frac{(1+g)^T}{(1+r)^T}\right) \qquad (A.11)$$

Unlike perpetuities, growing annuities (with finite horizons) need not assume that $g < r$.

A.6   Simple Interest

The ability to handle compound interest calculations is essential for most of what we do throughout this text. Simple interest calculations are less important, but they are needed to compute accrued interest on bonds and certain financial contracts such as Eurodollar deposits and savings accounts (see Chapter 2). An investment that pays simple interest at a rate of r per period earns interest of rt at the end of t periods for every dollar invested today.

A.7   Time Horizons and Compounding Frequencies

This appendix has developed formulas for present values and future values of cash flows or cash flow streams based on knowing a compound interest rate (or rate of return or yield) per period. Different financial securities, however, define the length of this fundamental period differently. The fundamental time period for mortgages, for example, is one month because mortgage payments are typically made monthly. The fundamental period for government bonds and notes and corporate bonds is six months, which is the length of time between coupon payments.

Annualized Rates.   Finance practitioners long ago recognized that it is difficult to understand the relative profitability of two investments, where one investment states the amount of interest earned in one month while the other states it over six months. To facilitate such comparisons, interest rates on all investments tend to be quoted on an annualized basis. Thus, the rate quoted on a mortgage with monthly payments is 12 times the monthly interest paid per dollar of principal. For the government bond with semiannual coupons, the rate is twice the semiannual coupon (interest) paid.

The annualization adjustment described is imperfect for making comparisons between investments since it does not reflect the interest earned on reinvested interest. As a consequence, annualized interest rates with the same r but different compounding frequencies mean different things. To make use of the formulas developed in the previous sections, where r is the interest earned over a single period per dollar invested at the beginning of the period, one has to translate the rates that are quoted for financial securities back into rates per period and properly compute the number of periods over which the future value or present value is taken. Exhibit A.2 does just this.

Equivalent Rates.   A proper adjustment would convert each rate to the same compounding frequency. If the annualized interest rates for two investments are each translated into an annually compounded rate, the investment with the higher annually compounded rate is the more profitable investment, other things being equal.

Consider, for example, two 16 percent rates—one compounded annually and the other semiannually. A 16 percent annually compounded rate means $1.00 invested at the beginning of the year has a value of $1.16 at the end of the year. However, a 16 percent rate compounded semiannually becomes, according to the translation in Exhibit A.2, an 8 percent rate over a six-month period. At the end of six months, one could reinvest the $1.08 for another six months. With an 8 percent return over the second six months, the $1.08 would have grown to $1.1664 by the end of the year. This 16.64 percent rate, the equivalent annually compounded rate, would be a more appropriate number to use if comparing this investment to one that uses the annually compounded rate. In general, given the investment with the same interest rate r, but different compounding frequencies, the more frequent the compounding frequency, the faster the growth rate of the investment.

If the compounding frequency is m times a year and the annualized rate is r, the amount accumulated from an investment of PV after t years is:

$$P_t = PV \times \left(1 + \frac{r}{m}\right)^{mt} \tag{A.12}$$

Equation (A.12) is another version of equation (A.2), the future value formula, recognizing that the per period interest rate is r/m, and the number of periods in t years is mt.

EXHIBIT A.2   Translating Annualized Interest Rates with Different Compounding Frequencies into Interest Earned per Period

Annualized Interest Rate Quotation Basis	*Interest per Period*	*Length of a Period*
Annually compounded	r	1 year
Semiannually compounded	$r/2$	6 months
Quarterly compounded	$r/4$	3 months
Monthly compounded	$r/12$	1 month
Weekly compounded	$r/52$	1 week
Daily compounded	$r/365$	1 day
Compounded m times a year	r/m	$1/m$ years

If there is continuous compounding, so that m becomes infinite, this formula has the limiting value:

$$P_t = PVe^{rt} \tag{A.13}$$

where e is the base of the natural logarithm, approximately 2.718281828.

Inverting equations (A.12) and (A.13) yields the corresponding present value formulas:

$$PV = \frac{P_t}{\left(1 + \dfrac{r}{m}\right)^{mt}} \tag{A.14}$$

$$PV = P_t e^{-rt} \tag{A.15}$$

To compute the equivalent rate using a different compounding frequency for the same investment, change m, and find the new r that generates the same future value P_t in equation (A.13). Example A.3 illustrates the procedure.

Example A.3:   Finding Equivalent Rates with Different Compounding Frequencies

An investment of \$1.00 that grows to \$1.10 at the end of one year is said to have a return of 10 percent, annually compounded. This is known as the "annually compounded rate of return." What are the equivalent semiannually and continuously compounded rates of growth for this investment?

Answer: Its semiannually compounded rate is approximately 9.76177 percent and its continuously compounded rate is approximately 9.53102 percent. These are found respectively by solving the following equations for r:

$$1.10 = \left(1 + \frac{r}{2}\right)^2$$

and

$$1.10 = e^{rt}$$

A.8 Summary and Conclusions

Interest rate mathematics is at the heart of applications of financial theory. This appendix illustrates interest rate mathematics when cash payoffs are riskless. The valuation and projection of uncertain cash payoffs, discussed in much of the text, depends fundamentally on the mastery of interest rate mathematics for riskless payoffs.

Interest rate mathematics has an element of time travel to it because it involves knowing the amount that a cash payoff at some date will grow to at a future date and, conversely, traveling backward in time, what a cash payoff at some future date is worth at some point in the past.

This ability to go backward and forward in time is not tied to our present place in time. We find the value at year 6 of a cash flow paid at year 10 by placing ourselves at year 10 and going backward in time four years. The cash received at year 10, discounted back four years, gives the value at year 6. Alternatively, the value at year 6 can be obtained by discounting the year 10 cash back to year 0 and then figuring out the future value of this number six years in the future.

In combination with the value additivity principle, this ability to translate cash flows from any point in a time line to any other point in time, in multiple ways, provides a great deal of flexibility in figuring out short and clever ways to value or to project cash flows. In particular, these principles can be applied to value perpetuities and annuities, which are the foundations for many of the types of cash flow streams observed in financial markets.

The principle of value additivity is the foundation of many of the theoretical results developed in modern finance as well as many of the money-making schemes developed by practitioners. It is closely tied to the no-arbitrage principle, which is one of the cornerstones on which modern finance theory is built.

Exercises

A.1. Let *PV* be the present value of a growing perpetuity (the "time 1 perpetuity") with an initial payment of *C* beginning one period from now and a growth rate of *g*. If we move all the cash flows back in time one period, the present value becomes $PV \times (1 + r)$. Note that this is the present value of a growing perpetuity with an initial payment of *C* beginning today (the "time 0 perpetuity").

    a. How do the cash flows of the time 1 perpetuity compare to those of the time 0 perpetuity from time 1 on?

    b. How do the present values of the cash flows discussed in part *a* compare with each other?

    c. How do the cash flows (and present values) for the two perpetuities described in part *a* compare?

    d. Write out a different value for the present value of the time 0 perpetuity in relation to the value of the time 1 perpetuity based on your analysis in parts *b* and *c*.

    e. Solve for *PV* from the equation $PV \times (1 + r) =$ value from part *d*.

A.2. How long will it take your money to double at an annualized interest rate of 8 percent compounded semiannually? How does your answer change if the interest rate is compounded annually?

A.3. A 30-year fixed-rate mortgage has monthly payments of $1,500 per month and a mortgage interest rate of 9 percent per year compounded monthly. If a buyer purchases a home with the cash proceeds of the mortgage loan plus an additional 20 percent down, what is the purchase price of the home?

A.4. What is the annualized interest rate, compounded daily, that is equivalent to 10 percent interest compounded semiannually? What is the daily compounded rate that is equivalent to 10 percent compounded continuously?

A.5. A self-employed investor who has just turned 35 wants to save for his retirement with a Keogh account. He plans to retire on his 65th birthday and wants a monthly income, beginning the month after his 65th birthday, of $2,000 (after taxes) until he dies.

    • He has budgeted conservatively, assuming that he will die at age 95.

    • Assume that until he reaches age 65, the Keogh account earns 8 percent interest, compounded annually, which accumulates tax free.

    • At age 65, assume that the interest accumulated in the Keogh account pays a lump-sum tax at a rate of 30 percent.

    • Thereafter, assume that the investor is in a 0 percent tax bracket and that the interest on his account earns 7 percent interest, compounded monthly.

How much should the investor deposit annually in his Keogh account beginning on his 35th birthday and ending on his 64th birthday to finance his retirement?

A.6. If *r* is the annually compounded interest rate, what is the present value of a deferred perpetuity with annual payments of *C* beginning *t* years from now?

A.7. An investor is comparing a 30-year fixed-rate mortgage with a 15-year fixed-rate mortgage. The 15-year mortgage has a considerably lower interest rate. If the annualized interest rate on the 30-year mortgage in 10 percent, compounded monthly, what rate, compounded monthly on the 15-year mortgage, offers the same monthly payments?

A.8. Graph the relation between the annually compounded interest rate and the present value of a zero-coupon bond paying $100 five years from today. Graph the relation between present value and years to maturity of a zero-coupon bond with an interest rate of 8 percent compounded annually.

A.9. A share of stock can be viewed as a claim to its future dividends. According to one theory, the value of a share of stock is the present value of its future dividends. If the next dividend, occurring one year from now, is $2 per share and dividends, paid annually, are expected to grow at 3 percent per year, what is the value of a share of stock if the discount rate is 7 percent?

A.10. A 35-year-old employee, who expected to work another 30 years, is injured in a plant accident and will never work again. His wages next year will be $40,000. A study of wages across the plant found that every additional year of seniority tends to add 1 percent to the wages of a worker, other things held constant. Assuming a nominal discount rate of 10 percent and an expected rate of inflation of 4 percent per year over the next 40 years, what lump-sum compensation should this worker receive for the lost wages due to the injury?

A.11. Bob invests $1,000 in a simple interest account. Thirty months later, he finds the account has accumulated to $1,212.50.

a. Compute the annualized simple interest rate.

b. Compute the equivalent annualized rate compounded (1) annually, (2) semiannually, (3) quarterly, (4) monthly, and (5) continuously.

c. What rate in part *b* is largest? Why?

A.12. A nine-month T-bill with face value $10,000 currently sells for $9,600. Calculate the annualized simple interest rate.

A.13. Which of the following rates would you prefer: 8.50 percent compounded annually, 8.33 percent compounded semiannually, 8.25 percent compounded quarterly, or 8.16 percent compounded continuously? Why?

A.14. The treasurer of Small Corp. is considering the purchase of a T-bill maturing in seven months. At a rate of 9 percent compounded annually:

a. Calculate the present value of the $10,000 face value T-bill.

b. If you wanted to purchase a seven-month T-bill 30 months from now, what amount must you deposit today?

A.15. Daniela, a junior in high school, is considering a delivery program for a local grocery store to earn extra money for college. Her idea is to buy a used car and deliver groceries after school and on weekends. She estimates the following revenues and expenses.

- Start-up costs of $1,000 for the car and minor repairs.
- Weekly revenue of about $150
- Ongoing maintenance and gasoline costs of about $45 per week.
- After nine months, replacement of the brake pads on the car for about $350.
- Sale of the car at year-end for about $450.

What is the difference between the *PV* of the venture (assuming an annualized rate of 6 percent compounded annually) and its start-up costs?

A.16. Jones Inc. is considering a prospective project with the following future cash inflows: $9,000 at the end of year 1, $9,500 at the end of 15 months, $10,500 at the end of 30 months, and $11,500 at the end of 38 months.

a. What is the *PV* of these cash flows at 7.5 percent compounded annually?

b. How does the *PV* change if the discount rate is 7.5 percent compounded semiannually?

A.17. If the future value of $10,000 today is $13,328, and the interest rate is 9 percent compounded annually:

a. What is the holding period *t* (in years)?

b. How does *t* change if the interest rate is 9 percent compounded semiannually?

c. How does *t* change if the interest rate is 11 percent compounded annually?

A.18. You have just won the California state lottery! As the winner, you have a choice of three payoff programs. Assume the interest rate is 9 percent compounded annually: (1) a lump sum today of $350,000 plus a lump sum 10 years from now of $25,000; (2) a 20-year annuity of $42,500 beginning next year; and (3) a $35,000 sum each year beginning next year paid to you and your descendants (assume your family line will never die out).

a. Which choice is the most favorable?

b. How would your answer change if the interest rate assumption changes to 10 percent?

c. How would your answer change if the interest rate assumption changes to 11 percent?

A.19. You need to insure your home over the next 20 years. You can either pay beginning-of-year premiums with today's premium of $5,000 and future premiums growing at 4 percent per year, or prepay a lump sum of $67,500 for the entire 20 years of coverage.

a. With a rate of 9 percent compounded annually, which of the two choices would you prefer?

b. How would your answer change if the rate were 10 percent compounded annually?

c. What is happening to the *PV* of the annuity as *r* increases?

A.20. Your rich uncle has recently passed away and left you an inheritance in the form of a varying perpetuity. You will receive $2,000 per year from year 3 through 14, $5,000 per year from year 15 through 22, and $3,000 per year thereafter. At a rate of 7 percent compounded annually, what is the *PV* at the start of year 1 of your uncle's generosity?

A.21. You have just had a baby boy and you want to ensure the funding of his college education. Tuition today is $15,000, and it is growing at 4 percent per year. In 18 years, your son will enter a four-year undergraduate program with tuition payments at the beginning of each year.

a. At the rate of 7 percent compounded annually, how much must you deposit today just to cover tuition expenses?

b. What amount must you save at the end of each year over the next 18 years to cover these expenses?

A.22. Your financial planner has advised you to initiate

a retirement account while you are still young. Today is your 35th birthday and you are planning to retire at age 65. Actuarial tables show that individuals in your age group have a life expectancy of about 75. If you want a $50,000 annuity beginning on your 66th birthday which will grow at a rate of 4 percent per year for 10 years:

a. What amount must you deposit at the end of each year through age 65 at a rate of 8 percent compounded annually to fund your retirement account?

b. How would your answer change if the rate is 9 percent?

c. After you have paid your last installment on your 65th birthday, you learn that medical advances have shifted actuarial tables so that you are now expected to live to age 85. Determine the base-year annuity payment supportable under the 4 percent growth plan with a 9 percent interest rate.

A.23. You are considering a new business venture and want to determine the present value of seasonal cash flows. Historical data suggest that quarterly flows will be $3,000 in quarter 1, $4,000 in quarter 2, $5,000 in quarter 3, and $6,000 in quarter 4. The annualized rate is 10 percent, compounded annually.

a. What is the *PV* if this quarterly pattern will continue into the future (i.e., forever)?

b. How would your answer change if growth is 1 percent per year in perpetuity?

c. How would your answer change if this 1 percent growth lasts only 10 years?

References and Additional Readings

Ross, Stephen; Randolph Westerfield; and Bradford Jordan. *Fundamentals of Corporate Finance*. 4th ed. Burr Ridge, IL: Irwin/McGraw-Hill, 1998.

TABLE B.1 Future Value of $1 at the End of t Periods $= (1 + r)^t$

	Interest Rate								
Period	1%	2%	3%	4%	5%	6%	7%	8%	9%
1	1.0100	1.0200	1.0300	1.0400	1.0500	1.0600	1.0700	1.0800	1.0900
2	1.0201	1.0404	1.0609	1.0816	1.1025	1.1236	1.1449	1.1664	1.1881
3	1.0303	1.0612	1.0927	1.1249	1.1576	1.1910	1.2250	1.2597	1.2950
4	1.0406	1.0824	1.1255	1.1699	1.2155	1.2625	1.3108	1.3605	1.4116
5	1.0510	1.1041	1.1593	1.2167	1.2763	1.3382	1.4026	1.4693	1.5386
6	1.0615	1.1262	1.1941	1.2653	1.3401	1.4185	1.5007	1.5869	1.6671
7	1.0721	1.1487	1.2299	1.3159	1.4071	1.5036	1.6058	1.7138	1.8280
8	1.0829	1.1717	1.2668	1.3686	1.4775	1.5938	1.7182	1.8509	1.9926
9	1.0937	1.1951	1.3048	1.4233	1.5513	1.6895	1.8385	1.9990	2.1719
10	1.1046	1.2190	1.3439	1.4802	1.6289	1.7908	1.9672	2.1589	2.3674
11	1.1157	1.2434	1.3842	1.5395	1.7103	1.8983	2.1049	2.3316	2.5804
12	1.1268	1.2682	1.4258	1.6010	1.7959	2.0122	2.2522	2.5182	2.8127
13	1.1381	1.2936	1.4685	1.6651	1.8856	2.1329	2.4098	2.7196	3.0658
14	1.1495	1.3195	1.5126	1.7317	1.9799	2.2609	2.5785	2.9372	3.3417
15	1.1610	1.3459	1.5580	1.8009	2.0789	2.3966	2.7590	3.1722	3.6425
16	1.1726	1.3728	1.6047	1.8730	2.1829	2.5404	2.9522	3.4259	3.9703
17	1.1843	1.4002	1.6528	1.9479	2.2920	2.6928	3.1588	3.7000	4.3276
18	1.1961	1.4282	1.7024	2.0258	2.4066	2.8543	3.3799	3.9960	4.7171
19	1.2081	1.4568	1.7535	2.1068	2.5270	3.0256	3.6165	4.3157	5.1417
20	1.2202	1.4859	1.8061	2.1911	2.6533	3.2071	3.8697	4.6610	5.6044
21	1.2324	1.5157	1.8603	2.2788	2.7860	3.3996	4.1406	5.0338	6.1088
22	1.2447	1.5460	1.9161	2.3699	2.9253	3.6035	4.4304	5.4365	6.6586
23	1.2572	1.5769	1.9736	2.4647	3.0715	3.8197	4.7405	5.8715	7.2579
24	1.2697	1.6084	2.0328	2.5633	3.2251	4.0489	5.0724	6.3412	7.9111
25	1.2824	1.6406	2.0938	2.6658	3.3864	4.2919	5.4274	6.8485	8.6231
30	1.3478	1.8114	2.4273	3.2434	4.3219	5.7435	7.6123	10.063	13.268
40	1.4889	2.2080	3.2620	4.8010	7.0400	10.286	14.974	21.725	31.409
50	1.6446	2.6916	4.3839	7.1067	11.467	18.420	29.457	46.902	74.358
60	1.8167	3.2810	5.8916	10.520	18.679	32.988	57.946	101.26	176.03

TABLE B.1 (*concluded*)

					Interest Rate					
10%	*12%*	*14%*	*15%*	*16%*	*18%*	*20%*	*24%*	*28%*	*32%*	*36%*
1.1000	1.1200	1.1400	1.1500	1.1600	1.1800	1.2000	1.2400	1.2800	1.3200	1.3600
1.2100	1.2544	1.2996	1.3225	1.3456	1.3924	1.4400	1.5376	1.6384	1.7424	1.8496
1.3310	1.4049	1.4815	1.5209	1.5609	1.6430	1.7280	1.9066	2.0972	2.3000	2.5155
1.4641	1.5735	1.6890	1.7490	1.8106	1.9388	2.0736	2.3642	2.6844	3.0360	3.4210
1.6105	1.7623	1.9254	2.0114	2.1003	2.2878	2.4883	2.9316	3.4360	4.0075	4.6526
1.7716	1.9738	2.1950	2.3131	2.4364	2.6996	2.9860	3.6352	4.3980	5.2899	6.3275
1.9487	2.2107	2.5023	2.6600	2.8262	3.1855	3.5832	4.5077	5.6295	6.9826	8.6054
2.1436	2.4760	2.8526	3.0590	3.2784	3.7589	4.2998	5.5895	7.2058	9.2170	11.703
2.3579	2.7731	3.2519	3.5179	3.8030	4.4355	5.1598	6.9310	9.2234	12.166	15.917
2.5937	3.1058	3.7072	4.0456	4.4114	5.2338	6.1917	8.5944	11.806	16.060	21.647
2.8531	3.4785	4.2262	4.6524	5.1173	6.1759	7.4301	10.657	15.112	21.199	29.439
3.1384	3.8960	4.8179	5.3503	5.9360	7.2876	8.9161	13.215	19.343	27.983	40.037
3.4523	4.3635	5.4924	6.1528	6.8858	8.5994	10.699	16.386	24.759	36.937	54.451
3.7975	4.8871	6.2613	7.0757	7.9875	10.147	12.839	20.319	31.691	48.757	74.053
4.1772	5.4736	7.1379	8.1371	9.2655	11.974	15.407	25.196	40.565	64.359	10.071
4.5950	6.1304	8.1372	9.3576	10.748	14.129	18.488	31.243	51.923	84.954	136.97
5.0545	6.8660	9.2765	10.761	12.468	16.672	22.186	38.741	66.461	112.14	186.28
5.5599	7.6900	10.575	12.375	14.463	19.673	26.623	48.039	85.071	148.02	253.34
6.1159	8.6128	12.056	14.232	16.777	23.214	31.948	59.568	108.89	195.39	344.54
6.7275	9.6463	13.743	16.367	19.461	27.393	38.338	73.864	139.38	257.92	468.57
7.4002	10.804	15.668	18.822	22.574	32.324	46.005	91.592	178.41	340.45	637.26
8.1403	12.100	17.861	21.645	26.186	38.142	55.206	113.57	228.36	449.39	866.67
8.9543	13.552	20.362	24.891	30.376	45.008	66.247	140.83	292.30	593.20	1178.7
9.8497	15.179	23.212	28.625	35.236	53.109	79.497	174.63	374.14	783.02	1603.0
10.835	17.000	26.462	32.919	40.874	62.669	95.396	216.54	478.90	1033.6	2180.1
17.449	29.960	50.950	66.212	85.850	143.37	237.38	634.82	1645.5	4142.1	10143.
45.259	93.051	188.88	267.86	378.72	750.38	1469.8	5455.9	19427.	66521.	*
117.39	289.00	700.23	1083.7	1670.7	3927.4	9100.4	46890.	*	*	*
304.48	897.60	2595.9	4384.0	7370.2	20555.	56348.	*	*	*	*

*The factor is greater than 99,999.

TABLE B.2 **Present Value of \$1 to Be Received after *t* Periods = $1/(1 + r)^t$**

	Interest Rate								
Period	*1%*	*2%*	*3%*	*4%*	*5%*	*6%*	*7%*	*8%*	*9%*
1	0.9901	0.9804	0.9709	0.9615	0.9524	0.9434	0.9346	0.9259	0.9174
2	0.9803	0.9612	0.9426	0.9246	0.9070	0.8900	0.8734	0.8573	0.8417
3	0.9706	0.9423	0.9151	0.8890	0.8638	0.8396	0.8163	0.7938	0.7722
4	0.9610	0.9238	0.8885	0.8548	0.8227	0.7921	0.7629	0.7350	0.7084
5	0.9515	0.9057	0.8626	0.8219	0.7835	0.7473	0.7130	0.6806	0.6499
6	0.9420	0.8880	0.8375	0.7903	0.7462	0.7050	0.6663	0.6302	0.5963
7	0.9327	0.8706	0.8131	0.7599	0.7107	0.6651	0.6227	0.5835	0.5470
8	0.9235	0.8535	0.7894	0.7307	0.6768	0.6274	0.5820	0.5403	0.5019
9	0.9143	0.8368	0.7664	0.7026	0.6446	0.5919	0.5439	0.5002	0.4604
10	0.9053	0.8203	0.7441	0.6756	0.6139	0.5584	0.5083	0.4632	0.4224
11	0.8963	0.8043	0.7224	0.6496	0.5847	0.5268	0.4751	0.4289	0.3875
12	0.8874	0.7885	0.7014	0.6246	0.5568	0.4970	0.4440	0.3971	0.3555
13	0.8787	0.7730	0.6810	0.6006	0.5303	0.4688	0.4150	0.3677	0.3262
14	0.8700	0.7579	0.6611	0.5775	0.5051	0.4423	0.3878	0.3405	0.2992
15	0.8613	0.7430	0.6419	0.5553	0.4810	0.4173	0.3624	0.3152	0.2745
16	0.8528	0.7284	0.6232	0.5339	0.4581	0.3936	0.3387	0.2919	0.2519
17	0.8444	0.7142	0.6050	0.5134	0.4363	0.3714	0.3166	0.2703	0.2311
18	0.8360	0.7002	0.5874	0.4936	0.4155	0.3503	0.2959	0.2502	0.2120
19	0.8277	0.6864	0.5703	0.4746	0.3957	0.3305	0.2765	0.2317	0.1945
20	0.8195	0.6730	0.5537	0.4564	0.3769	0.3118	0.2584	0.2145	0.1784
21	0.8114	0.6598	0.5375	0.4388	0.3589	0.2942	0.2415	0.1987	0.1637
22	0.8034	0.6468	0.5219	0.4220	0.3418	0.2775	0.2257	0.1839	0.1502
23	0.7954	0.6342	0.5067	0.4057	0.3256	0.2618	0.2109	0.1703	0.1378
24	0.7876	0.6217	0.4919	0.3901	0.3101	0.2470	0.1971	0.1577	0.1264
25	0.7798	0.6095	0.4776	0.3751	0.2953	0.2330	0.1842	0.1460	0.1160
30	0.7419	0.5521	0.4120	0.3083	0.2314	0.1741	0.1314	0.0994	0.0754
40	0.6717	0.4529	0.3066	0.2083	0.1420	0.0972	0.0668	0.0460	0.0318
50	0.6080	0.3715	0.2281	0.1407	0.0872	0.0543	0.0339	0.0213	0.0134

TABLE B.2   (*concluded*)

					Interest Rate					
10%	*12%*	*14%*	*15%*	*16%*	*18%*	*20%*	*24%*	*28%*	*32%*	*36%*
0.9091	0.8929	0.8772	0.8696	0.8621	0.8475	0.8333	0.8065	0.7813	0.7576	0.7353
0.8264	0.7972	0.7695	0.7561	0.7432	0.7182	0.6944	0.6504	0.6104	0.5739	0.5407
0.7513	0.7118	0.6750	0.6575	0.6407	0.6086	0.5787	0.5245	0.4768	0.4348	0.3975
0.6830	0.6355	0.5921	0.5718	0.5523	0.5158	0.4823	0.4230	0.3725	0.3294	0.2923
0.6209	0.5674	0.5194	0.4972	0.4761	0.4371	0.4019	0.3411	0.2910	0.2495	0.2149
0.5645	0.5066	0.4556	0.4232	0.4104	0.3704	0.3349	0.2751	0.2274	0.1890	0.1580
0.5132	0.4523	0.3996	0.3759	0.3538	0.3139	0.2791	0.2218	0.1776	0.1432	0.1162
0.4665	0.4039	0.3506	0.3269	0.3050	0.2660	0.2326	0.1789	0.1388	0.1085	0.0854
0.4241	0.3606	0.3075	0.2843	0.2630	0.2255	0.1938	0.1443	0.1084	0.0822	0.0628
0.3855	0.3220	0.2697	0.2472	0.2267	0.1911	0.1615	0.1164	0.0847	0.0623	0.0462
0.3505	0.2875	0.2366	0.2149	0.1954	0.1619	0.1346	0.0938	0.0662	0.0472	0.0340
0.3186	0.2567	0.2076	0.1869	0.1685	0.1372	0.1122	0.0757	0.0517	0.0357	0.0250
0.2897	0.2292	0.1821	0.1625	0.1452	0.1163	0.0935	0.0610	0.0404	0.0271	0.0184
0.2633	0.2046	0.1597	0.1413	0.1252	0.0985	0.0779	0.0492	0.0316	0.0205	0.0135
0.2394	0.1827	0.1401	0.1229	0.1079	0.0835	0.0649	0.0397	0.0247	0.0155	0.0099
0.2176	0.1631	0.1229	0.1069	0.0930	0.0708	0.0541	0.0320	0.0193	0.0118	0.0073
0.1978	0.1456	0.1078	0.0929	0.0802	0.0600	0.0451	0.0258	0.0150	0.0089	0.0054
0.1799	0.1300	0.0946	0.0808	0.0691	0.0508	0.0376	0.0208	0.0118	0.0068	0.0039
0.1635	0.1161	0.0829	0.0703	0.0596	0.0431	0.0313	0.0168	0.0092	0.0051	0.0029
0.1486	0.1037	0.0728	0.0611	0.0514	0.0365	0.0261	0.0135	0.0072	0.0039	0.0021
0.1351	0.0926	0.0638	0.0531	0.0443	0.0309	0.0217	0.0109	0.0056	0.0029	0.0016
0.1228	0.0826	0.0560	0.0462	0.0382	0.0262	0.0181	0.0088	0.0044	0.0022	0.0012
0.1117	0.0738	0.0491	0.0402	0.0329	0.0222	0.0151	0.0071	0.0034	0.0017	0.0008
0.1015	0.0659	0.0431	0.0349	0.0284	0.0188	0.0126	0.0057	0.0027	0.0013	0.0006
0.0923	0.0588	0.0378	0.0304	0.0245	0.0160	0.0105	0.0046	0.0021	0.0010	0.0005
0.0573	0.0334	0.0196	0.0151	0.0116	0.0070	0.0042	0.0016	0.0006	0.0002	0.0001
0.0221	0.0107	0.0053	0.0037	0.0026	0.0013	0.0007	0.0002	0.0001	*	*
0.0085	0.0035	0.0014	0.0009	0.0006	0.0003	0.0001	*	*	*	*

*The factor is zero to four decimal places.

TABLE B.3   Present Value of an Annuity of $1 per Period for t Periods = $[1 - 1/(1 + r)^t]/r$

Number of Periods	Interest Rate								
	1%	*2%*	*3%*	*4%*	*5%*	*6%*	*7%*	*8%*	*9%*
1	0.9901	0.9804	0.9709	0.9615	0.9524	0.9434	0.9346	0.9259	0.9174
2	1.9704	1.9416	1.9135	1.8861	1.8594	1.8334	1.8080	1.7833	1.7591
3	2.9410	2.8839	2.8286	2.7751	2.7232	2.6730	2.6243	2.5771	2.5313
4	3.9020	3.8077	3.7171	3.6299	3.5460	3.4651	3.3872	3.3121	3.2397
5	4.8534	4.7135	4.5797	4.4518	4.3295	4.2124	4.1002	3.9927	3.8897
6	5.7955	5.6014	5.4172	5.2421	5.0757	4.9173	4.7665	4.6229	4.4859
7	6.7282	6.4720	6.2303	6.0021	5.7864	5.5824	5.3893	5.2064	5.0330
8	7.6517	7.3255	7.0197	6.7327	6.4632	6.2098	5.9713	5.7466	5.5348
9	8.5660	8.1622	7.7861	7.4353	7.1078	6.8017	6.5152	6.2469	5.9952
10	9.4713	8.9826	8.5302	8.1109	7.7217	7.3601	7.0236	6.7101	6.4177
11	10.3676	9.7868	9.2526	8.7605	8.3064	7.8869	7.4987	7.1390	6.8052
12	11.2551	10.5753	9.9540	9.3851	8.8633	8.3838	7.9427	7.5361	7.1607
13	12.1337	11.3484	10.6350	9.9856	9.3936	8.8527	8.3577	7.9038	7.4869
14	13.0037	12.1062	11.2961	10.5631	9.8986	9.2950	8.7455	8.2442	7.7862
15	13.8651	12.8493	11.9379	11.1184	10.3797	9.7122	9.1079	8.5595	8.0607
16	14.7179	13.5777	12.5611	11.6523	10.8378	10.1059	9.4466	8.8514	8.3126
17	15.5623	14.2919	13.1661	12.1657	11.2741	10.4773	9.7632	9.1216	8.5436
18	16.3983	14.9920	13.7535	12.6593	11.6896	10.8276	10.0591	9.3719	8.7556
19	17.2260	15.6785	14.3238	13.1339	12.0853	11.1581	10.3356	9.6036	8.9501
20	18.0456	16.3514	14.8775	13.5903	12.4622	11.4699	10.5940	9.8181	9.1285
21	18.8570	17.0112	15.4150	14.0292	12.8212	11.7641	10.8355	10.0168	9.2922
22	19.6604	17.6580	15.9369	14.4511	13.1630	12.0416	11.0612	10.2007	9.4424
23	20.4558	18.2922	16.4436	14.8568	13.4886	12.3034	11.2722	10.3741	9.5802
24	21.2434	18.9139	16.9355	15.2470	13.7986	12.5504	11.4693	10.5288	9.7066
25	22.0232	19.5235	17.4131	15.6221	14.0939	12.7834	11.6536	10.6748	9.8226
30	25.8077	22.3965	19.6004	17.2920	15.3725	13.7648	12.4090	11.2578	10.2737
40	32.8347	27.3555	23.1148	19.7928	17.1591	15.0463	13.3317	11.9246	10.7574
50	39.1961	31.4236	25.7298	21.4822	18.2559	15.7619	13.8007	12.2335	10.9617

TABLE B.3 (*concluded*)

					Interest Rate				
10%	*12%*	*14%*	*15%*	*16%*	*18%*	*20%*	*24%*	*28%*	*32%*
0.9091	0.8929	0.8772	0.8696	0.8621	0.8475	0.8333	0.8065	0.7813	0.7576
1.7355	1.6901	1.6467	1.6257	1.6052	1.5656	1.5278	1.4568	1.3916	1.3315
2.4869	2.4018	2.3216	2.2832	2.2459	2.1743	2.1065	1.9813	1.8684	1.7663
3.1699	3.0373	2.9137	2.8550	2.7982	2.6901	2.5887	2.4043	2.2410	2.0957
3.7908	3.6048	3.4331	3.3522	3.2743	3.1272	2.9906	2.7454	2.5320	2.3452
4.3553	4.1114	3.8887	3.7845	3.6847	3.4976	3.3225	3.0205	2.7594	2.5342
4.8684	4.5638	4.2883	4.1604	4.0386	3.8115	3.6046	3.2423	2.9370	2.6775
5.3349	4.9676	4.6389	4.4873	4.3436	4.0776	3.8372	3.4212	3.0758	2.7860
5.7590	5.3282	4.9464	4.7716	4.6065	4.3030	4.0310	3.5655	3.1842	2.8681
6.1446	5.6502	5.2161	5.0188	4.8332	4.4941	4.1925	3.6819	3.2689	2.9304
6.4951	5.9377	5.4527	5.2337	5.0286	4.6560	4.3271	3.7757	3.3351	2.9776
6.8137	6.1944	5.6603	5.4206	5.1971	4.7932	4.4392	3.8514	3.3868	3.0133
7.1034	6.4235	5.8424	5.5831	5.3423	4.9095	4.5327	3.9124	3.4272	3.0404
7.3667	6.6282	6.0021	5.7245	5.4675	5.0081	4.6106	3.9616	3.4587	3.0609
7.6061	6.8109	6.1422	5.8474	5.5755	5.0916	4.6755	4.0013	3.4834	3.0764
7.8237	6.9740	6.2651	5.9542	5.6685	5.1624	4.7296	4.0333	3.5026	3.0882
8.0216	7.1196	6.3729	6.0472	5.7487	5.2223	4.7746	4.0591	3.5177	3.0971
8.2014	7.2497	6.4674	6.1280	5.8178	5.2732	4.8122	4.0799	3.5294	3.1039
8.3649	7.3658	6.5504	6.1982	5.8775	5.3162	4.8435	4.0967	3.5386	3.1090
8.5136	7.4694	6.6231	6.2593	5.9288	5.3527	4.8696	4.1103	3.5458	3.1129
8.6487	7.5620	6.6870	6.3125	5.9731	5.3837	4.8913	4.1212	3.5514	3.1158
8.7715	7.6446	6.7429	6.3587	6.0113	5.4099	4.9094	4.1300	3.5558	3.1180
8.8832	7.7184	6.7921	6.3933	6.0442	5.4321	4.9245	4.1371	3.5592	3.1197
8.9847	7.7843	6.8351	6.4338	6.0726	5.4509	4.9371	4.1428	3.5619	3.1210
9.0770	7.8431	6.8729	6.4641	6.0971	5.4669	4.9476	4.1474	3.5640	3.1220
9.4269	8.0552	7.0027	6.5660	6.1772	5.5168	4.9789	4.1601	3.5693	3.1242
9.7791	8.2438	7.1050	6.6418	6.2335	5.5482	4.9966	4.1659	3.5712	3.1250
9.9148	8.3045	7.1327	6.6605	6.2463	5.5541	4.9995	4.1666	3.5714	3.1250

TABLE B.4   **Future Value of an Annuity of $1 per Period for t Periods $= [(1 + r)^t - 1]/r$**

Number of Periods	1%	2%	3%	4%	5%	6%	7%	8%	9%
				Interest Rate					
1	1.0000	1.0000	1.0000	1.0000	1.0000	1.0000	1.0000	1.0000	1.0000
2	2.0100	2.0200	2.0300	2.0400	2.0500	2.0600	2.0700	2.0800	2.0900
3	3.0301	3.0604	3.0909	3.1216	3.1525	3.1836	3.2149	3.2464	3.2781
4	4.0604	4.1216	4.1836	4.2465	4.3101	4.3746	4.4399	4.5061	4.5731
5	5.1010	5.2040	5.3091	5.4165	5.5256	5.6371	5.7507	5.8666	5.9847
6	6.1520	6.3081	6.4684	6.6330	6.8019	6.9753	7.1533	7.3359	7.5233
7	7.2135	7.4343	7.6625	7.8983	8.1420	8.3938	8.6540	8.9228	9.2004
8	8.2857	8.5830	8.8932	9.2142	9.5491	9.8975	10.260	10.637	11.028
9	9.3685	9.7546	10.159	10.583	11.027	11.491	11.978	12.488	13.021
10	10.462	10.950	11.464	12.006	12.578	13.181	13.816	14.487	15.193
11	11.567	12.169	12.808	13.486	14.207	14.972	15.784	16.645	17.560
12	12.683	13.412	14.192	15.026	15.917	16.870	17.888	18.977	20.141
13	13.809	14.680	15.618	16.627	17.713	18.882	20.141	21.495	22.953
14	14.947	15.974	17.086	18.292	19.599	21.015	22.550	24.215	26.019
15	16.097	17.293	18.599	20.024	21.579	23.276	25.129	27.152	29.361
16	17.258	18.639	20.157	21.825	23.657	25.673	27.888	30.324	33.003
17	18.430	20.012	21.762	23.698	25.840	28.213	30.840	33.750	36.974
18	19.615	21.412	23.414	25.645	28.132	30.906	33.999	37.450	41.301
19	20.811	22.841	25.117	27.671	30.539	33.760	37.379	41.446	46.018
20	22.019	24.297	26.870	29.778	33.066	36.786	40.955	45.762	51.160
21	23.239	25.783	28.676	31.969	35.719	39.993	44.865	50.423	56.765
22	24.472	27.299	30.537	34.248	38.505	43.392	49.006	55.457	62.873
23	25.716	28.845	32.453	36.618	41.430	46.996	53.436	60.893	69.532
24	26.973	30.422	34.426	39.083	44.502	50.816	58.177	66.765	76.790
25	28.243	32.030	36.459	41.646	47.727	54.865	63.249	73.106	84.701
30	34.785	40.568	47.575	56.085	66.439	79.058	94.461	113.28	136.31
40	48.886	60.402	75.401	95.026	120.80	154.76	199.64	259.06	337.88
50	64.463	84.579	112.80	152.67	209.35	290.34	406.53	573.77	815.08
60	81.670	114.05	163.05	237.99	353.58	533.13	813.52	1253.2	1944.8

TABLE B.4   (*concluded*)

					Interest Rate					
10%	*12%*	*14%*	*15%*	*16%*	*18%*	*20%*	*24%*	*28%*	*32%*	*36%*
1.0000	1.0000	1.0000	1.0000	1.0000	1.0000	1.0000	1.0000	1.0000	1.0000	1.0000
2.1000	2.1200	2.1400	2.1500	2.1600	2.1800	2.2000	2.2400	2.2800	2.3200	2.3600
3.3100	3.3744	3.4396	3.4725	3.5056	3.5724	3.6400	3.7776	3.9184	4.0624	4.2096
4.6410	4.7793	4.9211	4.9934	5.0665	5.2154	5.3680	5.6842	6.0156	6.3624	6.7251
6.1051	6.3528	6.6101	6.7424	6.8771	7.1542	7.4416	8.0484	8.6999	9.3983	10.146
7.7156	8.1152	8.5355	8.7537	8.9775	9.4420	9.9299	10.980	12.136	13.406	14.799
9.4872	10.089	10.730	11.067	11.414	12.142	12.916	14.615	16.534	18.696	21.126
11.436	12.300	13.233	13.727	14.240	15.327	16.499	19.123	22.163	25.678	29.732
13.579	14.776	16.085	16.786	17.519	19.086	20.799	24.712	29.369	34.895	41.435
15.937	17.549	19.337	20.304	21.321	23.521	25.959	31.643	38.593	47.062	57.352
18.531	20.655	23.045	24.349	25.733	28.755	32.150	40.238	50.398	63.122	78.998
21.384	24.133	27.271	29.002	30.850	34.931	39.581	50.895	65.510	84.320	108.44
24.523	28.029	32.089	34.352	36.786	42.219	48.497	64.110	84.853	112.30	148.47
27.975	32.393	37.581	40.505	43.672	50.818	59.196	80.496	109.61	149.24	202.93
31.772	37.280	43.842	47.580	51.660	60.965	72.035	100.82	141.30	198.00	276.98
35.950	42.753	50.980	55.717	60.925	72.939	87.442	126.01	181.87	262.36	377.69
40.545	48.884	59.118	65.075	71.673	87.068	105.93	157.25	233.79	347.31	514.66
45.599	55.750	68.394	75.836	84.141	103.74	128.12	195.99	300.25	459.45	700.94
51.159	63.440	78.969	88.212	98.603	123.41	154.74	244.03	385.32	607.47	954.28
57.275	72.052	91.025	102.44	115.38	146.63	186.69	303.60	494.21	802.86	1298.8
64.002	81.699	104.77	118.81	134.84	174.02	225.03	377.46	633.59	1060.8	1767.4
71.403	92.503	120.44	137.63	157.41	206.34	271.03	469.06	812.00	1401.2	2404.7
79.543	104.60	138.30	159.28	183.60	244.49	326.24	582.63	1040.4	1850.6	3271.3
88.497	118.16	158.66	184.17	213.98	289.49	392.48	723.46	1332.7	2443.8	4450.0
98.347	133.33	181.87	212.79	249.21	342.60	471.98	898.09	1706.8	3226.8	6053.0
164.49	241.33	356.79	434.75	530.31	790.95	1181.9	2640.9	5873.2	12941.	28172.3
442.59	767.09	1342.0	1779.1	2360.8	4163.2	7343.9	22729.	69377.	*	*
1163.9	2400.0	4994.5	7217.7	10436.	21813.	45497.	*	*	*	*
3034.8	7471.6	18535.	29220.	46058.	*	*	*	*	*	*

*The factor is greater than 99,999.

TABLE B.5   Cumulative Normal Distribution

d	N(d)	d	N(d)	d	N(d)	d	N(d)	d	N(d)	d	N(d)
−3.00	.0013	−1.58	.0571	−0.76	.2236	0.06	.5239	0.86	.8051	1.66	.9515
−2.95	.0016	−1.56	.0594	−0.74	.2297	0.08	.5319	0.88	.8106	1.68	.9535
−2.90	.0019	−1.54	.0618	−0.72	.2358	0.10	.5398	0.90	.8159	1.70	.9554
−2.85	.0022	−1.52	.0643	−0.70	.2420	0.12	.5478	0.92	.8212	1.72	.9573
−2.80	.0026	−1.50	.0668	−0.68	.2483	0.14	.5557	0.94	.8264	1.74	.9591
−2.75	.0030	−1.48	.0694	−0.66	.2546	0.16	.5636	0.96	.8315	1.76	.9608
−2.70	.0035	−1.46	.0721	−0.64	.2611	0.18	.5714	0.98	.8365	1.78	.9625
−2.65	.0040	−1.44	.0749	−0.62	.2676	0.20	.5793	1.00	.8414	1.80	.9641
−2.60	.0047	−1.42	.0778	−0.60	.2743	0.22	.5871	1.02	.8461	1.82	.9656
−2.55	.0054	−1.40	.0808	−0.58	.2810	0.24	.5948	1.04	.8508	1.84	.9671
−2.50	.0062	−1.38	.0838	−0.56	.2877	0.26	.6026	1.06	.8554	1.86	.9686
−2.45	.0071	−1.36	.0869	−0.54	.2946	0.28	.6103	1.08	.8599	1.88	.9699
−2.40	.0082	−1.34	.0901	−0.52	.3015	0.30	.6179	1.10	.8643	1.90	.9713
−2.35	.0094	−1.32	.0934	−0.50	.3085	0.32	.6255	1.12	.8686	1.92	.9726
−2.30	.0107	−1.30	.0968	−0.48	.3156	0.34	.6331	1.14	.8729	1.94	.9738
−2.25	.0122	−1.28	.1003	−0.46	.3228	0.36	.6406	1.16	.8770	1.96	.9750
−2.20	.0139	−1.26	.1038	−0.44	.3300	0.38	.6480	1.18	.8810	1.98	.9761
−2.15	0.158	−1.24	.1075	−0.42	.3373	0.40	.6554	1.20	.8849	2.00	.9772
−2.10	0.179	−1.22	.1112	−0.40	.3446	0.42	.6628	1.22	.8888	2.05	.9798
−2.05	.0202	−1.20	.1151	−0.38	.3520	0.44	.6700	1.24	.8925	2.10	.9821
−2.00	.0228	−1.18	.1190	−0.36	.3594	0.46	.6773	1.26	.8962	2.15	.9842
−1.98	.0239	−1.16	.1230	−0.34	.3669	0.48	.6844	1.28	.8997	2.20	.9861
−1.96	0.250	−1.14	.1271	−0.32	.3745	0.50	.6915	1.30	.9032	2.25	.9878
−1.94	.0262	−1.12	.1314	−0.30	.3821	0.52	.6985	1.32	.9066	2.30	.9893
−1.92	.0274	−1.10	.1357	−0.28	.3897	0.54	.7054	1.34	.9099	2.35	.9906
−1.90	.0287	−1.08	.1401	−0.26	.3974	0.56	.7123	1.36	.9131	2.40	.9918
−1.88	.0301	−1.06	.1446	−0.24	.4052	0.58	.7191	1.38	.9162	2.45	.9929
−1.86	.0314	−1.04	.1492	−0.22	.4129	0.60	.7258	1.40	.9192	2.50	.9938
−1.84	.0329	−1.02	.1539	−0.20	.4207	0.62	.7324	1.42	.9222	2.55	.9946
−1.82	.0344	−1.00	.1587	−0.18	.4286	0.64	.7389	1.44	.9251	2.60	.9953
−1.80	.0359	−0.98	.1635	−0.16	.4365	0.66	.7454	1.46	.9279	2.65	.9960
−1.78	.0375	−0.96	.1685	−0.14	.4443	0.68	.7518	1.48	.9306	2.70	.9965
−1.76	.0392	−0.94	.1736	−0.12	.4523	0.70	.7580	1.50	.9332	2.75	.9970
−1.74	.0409	−0.92	.1788	−0.10	.4602	0.72	.7642	1.52	.9357	2.80	.9974
−1.72	.0427	−0.90	.1841	−0.08	.4681	0.74	.7704	1.54	.9382	2.85	.9978
−1.70	.0446	−0.88	.1894	−0.06	.4761	0.76	.7764	1.56	.9406	2.90	.9981
−1.68	.0465	−0.86	.1949	−0.04	.4841	0.78	.7823	1.58	.9429	2.95	.9984
−1.66	.0485	−0.84	.2005	−0.02	.4920	0.80	.7882	1.60	.9452	3.00	.9986
−1.64	.0505	−0.82	.2061	0.00	.5000	0.82	.7939	1.62	.9474	3.05	.9989
−1.62	.0526	−0.80	.2119	0.02	.5080	0.84	.7996	1.64	.9495		
−1.60	0.548	−0.78	.2177	0.04	.5160						

This table shows the probability [N(d)] of observing a value less than or equal to d. For example, as illustrated if d is −.24, then N(d) is .4052.

Name Index

Subject Index